C
m
tl

GW00889835

Chambers

CHAMBERS
An imprint of Chambers Harrap Publishers Ltd
7 Hopetoun Crescent, Edinburgh, EH7 4AY

Chambers Harrap is an Hachette UK company
Chambers® is a registered trademark of Chambers Harrap Publishers Ltd

© Chambers Harrap Publishers Ltd 2009

This paperback edition published by Chambers Harrap Publishers
Ltd 2009
First published 2002
Second edition published 2006

Database right Chambers Harrap Publishers Ltd (makers)

A CIP catalogue record for this book is available from the British
Library.

ISBN 978 0550 10636 0

10 9 8 7 6 5 4 3 2 1

www.chambers.co.uk

Designed by Chambers Harrap Publishers Ltd, Edinburgh
Typeset in Souvenir and Frutiger by Chambers Harrap Publishers Ltd,
Edinburgh
Printed and bound in Italy by Legoprint

Contents

Contributors

Editors
Ian Brookes
Lorna Gilmour
Alice Grandison

Publishing Manager
Patrick White

Prepress Manager
Clair Simpson

Prepress
Isla MacLean
Sharon McTeir

Preface

A thesaurus is a book that contains lists of synonyms – that is, words that have a similar meaning to another word. A thesaurus allows you to look up a common word and find a range of words that have the same or nearly the same meaning. This can help you to find a more exact word when the one that comes to mind is not quite right for the occasion, or it can help you to find an alternative word when you don't want to repeat a word you have already used. It is also an extremely helpful resource for solving crosswords and similar puzzles.

Chambers Mini Thesaurus fulfils this basic function, but it also contains two other useful features. Many entries contain opposites (antonyms) of the word, and lists of these are clearly indicated by the symbol ⊟. In addition, there are more than 200 panels scattered through the book containing lists of related words (hyponyms) – words that answer the question, 'What kinds of … are there?'. These panels cover both technical subjects (phobias, parts of the brain, architectural terms) and more general themes (breeds of dog, currencies of the world, types of cake). A complete index of these hyponym panels is given on pages viii and ix.

For this new edition of the thesaurus, we have also included a supplement containing useful reference information about countries of the world.

These features combine to make this book a mine of information. We hope that you enjoy using it.

How to use the thesaurus

Headwords appear in bold at the beginning of each entry.

marine *adj* sea, maritime, naval, nautical, seafaring, sea-going, ocean-going, salt-water.

mariner *n* sailor, seaman, seafarer, deckhand, navigator, tar (*infml*), sea-dog (*infml*), salt (*infml*).

Synonyms are listed after the headword, according to frequency and relevance.

marital *adj* conjugal, matrimonial, married, wedded, nuptial (*fml*), connubial (*fml*).

maritime *adj* marine, nautical, naval, seafaring, sea, seaside, oceanic, coastal.

Parts of speech or word classes (eg *noun* and *verb*) are indicated by abbreviations. A new part of speech within an entry appears on a new line.

mark *n* **1** SPOT, stain, blemish, blot, blotch, smudge, dent, impression, scar, scratch, bruise, line. **2** SYMBOL, sign, indication, emblem, brand, stamp, token, characteristic, feature, proof, evidence, badge. **3** TARGET, goal, aim, objective, purpose.

v **1** STAIN, blemish, blot, smudge, dent, scar, scratch, bruise. **2** BRAND, label, stamp, characterize, identify, distinguish. **3** EVALUATE, assess, correct, grade. **4** HEED, listen, mind, note, observe, regard, notice, take to heart.

marked *adj* **1** NOTICEABLE, obvious, conspicuous, evident, pronounced, distinct, decided, emphatic, considerable, remarkable, apparent, glaring. **2** SUSPECTED, watched, doomed.

E3 1 unnoticeable, slight.

suggestive adj **1** EVOCATIVE, reminiscent, expressive, meaning, indicative. **2** *a suggestive remark*: indecent, immodest, improper, indelicate, off-colour, risqué, bawdy, dirty, smutty, provocative.
F3 1 inexpressive. **2** decent, clean.

suit v **1** SATISFY, gratify, please, answer, match, tally, agree, correspond, harmonize. **2** FIT, befit, become, tailor, adapt, adjust, accommodate, modify.
F3 1 displease, clash.
n outfit, costume, dress, clothing.

Types of suit include:
dress suit, evening suit, tuxedo, business suit, lounge suit, trouser suit, catsuit, jump suit, safari suit, track suit, shell suit, zoot suit.

suitable adj appropriate, fitting, convenient, opportune, suited, due, apt, apposite, relevant, applicable, fit, adequate, satisfactory, acceptable, befitting, becoming, seemly, proper, right.
F3 unsuitable, inappropriate.

sulk v mope, brood, pout.

sulky adj brooding, moody, morose, resentful, grudging, disgruntled, put out, cross, bad-tempered, sullen, aloof, unsociable.

Different meanings are shown in numbered sections, introduced either by a key synonym in capitals or by a phrase in italics showing the word in use.

The sign **F3** indicates antonyms – words that mean the opposite of the headword.

Lists of related words are shown in panels after some entries.

Index of hyponym panels

Lists of related words (hyponyms) appear in the thesaurus after the following entries:

Abbreviations and symbols

adj	adjective
adv	adverb
Aust	Australian
conj	conjunction
fml	formal
infml	informal
interj	interjection
n	noun
N Am	North American
prep	preposition
®	trademark
sl	slang
US	United States
v	verb
⇄	antonym(s)

A

abandon v **1** DESERT, leave, forsake, jilt, ditch (sl), leave in the lurch (infml), maroon, strand, leave behind, scrap. **2** abandon ship: vacate, evacuate, withdraw from, quit. **3** RENOUNCE, resign, give up, forgo, relinquish, surrender, yield, waive, drop.
F3 1 support, maintain, keep. **3** continue.

abandoned adj **1** DESERTED, unoccupied, derelict, neglected, forsaken, forlorn, desolate. **2** DISSOLUTE, wild, uninhibited, wanton, wicked.
F3 1 kept, occupied. **2** restrained.

abandonment n **1** DESERTION, leaving, forsaking, jilting, neglect, scrapping. **2** RENUNCIATION, resignation, giving up, relinquishment, surrender, sacrifice, waiver, dropping, discontinuation.

abashed adj **1** ASHAMED, shamefaced, embarrassed, mortified, humiliated, humbled. **2** CONFUSED, bewildered, nonplussed, confounded, perturbed, discomposed, disconcerted, taken aback, dumbfounded, floored (infml), dismayed.
F3 2 composed, at ease.

abate v **1** DECREASE, reduce, lessen, diminish, decline, sink, dwindle, taper off, fall off. **2** MODERATE, ease, relieve, alleviate, mitigate, remit, pacify, quell, subside, let up (infml), weaken, wane, slacken, slow, fade.
F3 1 increase. **2** strengthen.

abbey n monastery, priory, friary, seminary, convent, nunnery, cloister.

abbreviate v shorten, cut, trim, clip, truncate, curtail, abridge, summarize, précis, abstract, digest, condense, compress, reduce, lessen, shrink, contract.
F3 extend, lengthen, expand, amplify.

abbreviation n shortening, clipping, curtailment, abridgement, summarization, summary, synopsis, résumé, précis, abstract, digest, compression, reduction, contraction.
F3 extension, expansion, amplification.

abdicate v renounce, give up, relinquish, surrender, cede, yield, forgo, abandon, quit, vacate, retire, resign, step down (infml).

abdomen n belly, guts, stomach, tummy (infml), paunch, midriff.

abdominal adj ventral, intestinal, visceral, gastric.

abduct v carry off, run away with, run off with (infml), make off with, spirit away, seduce, kidnap, snatch, seize, appropriate.

aberration n deviation, straying, wandering, divergence, irregularity,

nonconformity, anomaly, oddity, peculiarity, eccentricity, quirk, freak, lapse, defect.
🔁 conformity.

abhor *v* hate, detest, loathe, abominate, shudder at, recoil from, shrink from, spurn, despise.
🔁 love, adore.

abhorrence *n* hate, hatred, aversion, loathing, abomination, horror, repugnance, revulsion, disgust, distaste.
🔁 love, adoration.

abhorrent *adj* detestable, loathsome, abominable, execrable, heinous, obnoxious, odious, hated, hateful, horrible, horrid, offensive, repugnant, repellent, repulsive, revolting, nauseating, disgusting, distasteful.
🔁 delightful, attractive.

abide *v* **1** BEAR, stand, endure, tolerate, put up with, stomach, accept. **2** REMAIN, last, endure, continue, persist.

abide by 1 *abide by the rules*: obey, observe, follow, comply with, adhere to, conform to, submit to, go along with, agree to. **2** FULFIL, discharge, carry out, stand by, hold to, keep to.

ability *n* **1** CAPABILITY, capacity, faculty, facility, potentiality, power. **2** SKILL, dexterity, deftness, adeptness, competence, proficiency, qualification, aptitude, talent, gift, endowment, knack, flair, touch, expertise, know-how (*infml*), genius, forte, strength.
🔁 **1** inability. **2** incompetence, weakness.

abject *adj* **1** CONTEMPTIBLE, worthless, low, mean, ignoble, dishonourable, deplorable,

despicable, vile, sordid, debased, degenerate, submissive, servile, grovelling, slavish. **2** MISERABLE, wretched, forlorn, hopeless, pitiable, pathetic, outcast, degraded.
🔁 **1** proud, exalted.

ablaze *adj* **1** BLAZING, flaming, burning, on fire, ignited, lighted, alight, illuminated, luminous, glowing, aglow, radiant, flashing, gleaming, sparkling, brilliant. **2** IMPASSIONED, passionate, fervent, ardent, fiery, enthusiastic, excited, exhilarated, stimulated, aroused, angry, furious, raging, incensed, frenzied.

able *adj* capable, fit, fitted, dexterous, adroit, deft, adept, competent, proficient, qualified, practised, experienced, skilled, accomplished, clever, expert, masterly, skilful, ingenious, talented, gifted, strong, powerful, effective, efficient, adequate.
🔁 unable, incapable, incompetent, ineffective.

able-bodied *adj* fit, healthy, sound, strong, robust, hardy, tough, vigorous, powerful, hale, hearty, lusty, sturdy, strapping, stout, stalwart, staunch.
🔁 infirm, delicate.

abnormal *adj* odd, strange, singular, peculiar, curious, queer, weird, eccentric, paranormal, unnatural, uncanny, extraordinary, exceptional, unusual, uncommon, unexpected, irregular, anomalous, aberrant, erratic, wayward, deviant, divergent, different.
🔁 normal, regular, typical.

abnormality *n* oddity, peculiarity, singularity, eccentricity, strangeness, bizarreness, unnaturalness,

unusualness, irregularity, exception, anomaly, deformity, flaw, aberration, deviation, divergence, difference.
F3 normality, regularity.

abolish v do away with, annul, nullify, invalidate, quash, repeal, rescind, revoke, cancel, obliterate, blot out, suppress, destroy, eliminate, eradicate, get rid of (*infml*), stamp out, end, put an end to, terminate, subvert, overthrow, overturn.
F3 create, retain, authorize, continue.

abolition n annulment, nullification, invalidation, quashing, repeal, abrogation, cancellation, obliteration, suppression, eradication, extinction, end, ending, termination, subversion, overturning, dissolution.
F3 creation, retention, continuance.

abominable adj loathsome, detestable, hateful, horrid, horrible, abhorrent, execrable, odious, repugnant, repulsive, repellent, disgusting, revolting, obnoxious, nauseating, foul, vile, heinous, atrocious, appalling, terrible, reprehensible, contemptible, despicable, wretched.
F3 delightful, pleasant, desirable.

abominate v hate, loathe, detest, abhor, execrate, despise, condemn.
F3 love, adore.

abomination n hate, hatred, aversion, loathing, abhorrence, repugnance, revulsion, disgust, distaste, hostility, offence, outrage, disgrace, anathema, horror, evil, curse, plague, torment, bête noire.
F3 adoration, delight.

abort v miscarry, terminate, end, stop, arrest, halt, check, frustrate, thwart, nullify, call off, fail.
F3 continue.

abortion n miscarriage, termination, frustration, failure, misadventure.
F3 continuation, success.

abortive adj failed, unsuccessful, fruitless, unproductive, barren, sterile, vain, idle, futile, useless, ineffective, unavailing.
F3 successful, fruitful.

abound v be plentiful, proliferate, flourish, thrive, swell, increase, superabound, swarm, teem, run riot, overflow.

about prep **1** REGARDING, concerning, relating to, referring to, connected with, concerned with, as regards, with regard to, with respect to, with reference to. **2** CLOSE TO, near, nearby, beside, adjacent to. **3** ROUND, around, surrounding, encircling, encompassing, throughout, all over.
adv **1** about twenty: around, approximately, roughly, in the region of, more or less, almost, nearly, approaching, nearing. **2** run about: to and fro, here and there, from place to place.
about to on the point of, on the verge of, all but, ready to, intending to, preparing to.

above prep over, higher than, on top of, superior to, in excess of, exceeding, surpassing, beyond, before, prior to.
F3 below, under.
adv overhead, aloft, on high, earlier.
F3 below, underneath.
adj above-mentioned, above-stated, foregoing, preceding, previous, earlier, prior.

above-board adj honest, legitimate, straight, on the level, fair, fair and square, square, true, open, frank, candid, guileless, straightforward, forthright, truthful,

veracious, trustworthy, honourable, reputable, upright.
F3 dishonest, shady (*infml*), underhand.

abrasion *n* graze, scratch, scratching, scraping, scrape, scouring, grating, grinding, abrading, chafing, chafe, friction, rubbing, erosion, wearing away, wearing down.

abrasive *adj* scratching, scraping, grating, rough, harsh, chafing, frictional, galling, irritating, annoying, sharp, biting, caustic, hurtful, nasty, unpleasant.
F3 smooth, pleasant.

abreast *adj* acquainted, informed, knowledgeable, in the picture, up to speed (*infml*), au courant, up to date, in touch, au fait, conversant, familiar.
F3 unaware, out of touch.

abridge *v* shorten, cut (down), prune, curtail, abbreviate, contract, reduce, decrease, lessen, summarize, précis, abstract, digest, condense, compress, concentrate.
F3 expand, amplify, pad out.

abridgement *n* 1 SHORTENING, cutting, reduction, decrease, diminishing, concentration, contraction, restriction, limitation. 2 SUMMARY, synopsis, résumé, outline, précis, abstract, digest, epitome.
F3 1 expansion, padding.

abroad *adv* 1 OVERSEAS, in foreign parts, out of the country, far and wide, widely, extensively. 2 AT LARGE, around, about, circulating, current.
F3 1 at home.

abrupt *adj* 1 *abrupt departure*: sudden, unexpected, unforeseen, surprising, quick, rapid, swift, hasty, hurried, precipitate. 2 SHEER,

precipitous, steep, sharp. 3 BRUSQUE, curt, terse, short, brisk, snappy, gruff, rude, uncivil, impolite, blunt, direct.
F3 1 gradual, slow, leisurely. 3 expansive, ceremonious, polite.

abscond *v* run away, run off, make off, decamp, flee, fly, escape, bolt, quit, clear out (*infml*), disappear, take French leave.

absence *n* 1 NON-ATTENDANCE, non-appearance, truancy, absenteeism, non-existence. 2 LACK, need, want, deficiency, dearth, scarcity, unavailability, default, omission, vacancy.
F3 1 presence, attendance, appearance. 2 existence.

absent *adj* 1 MISSING, not present, away, out, unavailable, gone, lacking, truant. 2 INATTENTIVE, daydreaming, dreamy, faraway, elsewhere, absent-minded, vacant, vague, distracted, preoccupied, unaware, oblivious, unheeding.
F3 1 present. 2 alert, aware.

absent-minded *adj* forgetful, scatterbrained, absent, abstracted, withdrawn, faraway, distracted, preoccupied, absorbed, engrossed, pensive, musing, dreaming, dreamy, inattentive, unaware, oblivious, unconscious, heedless, unheeding, unthinking, impractical.
F3 attentive, practical, matter-of-fact.

absolute *adj* 1 UTTER, total, complete, entire, full, thorough, exhaustive, supreme, consummate, definitive, conclusive, final, categorical, definite, unequivocal, unquestionable, decided, decisive, positive, sure, certain, genuine, pure, perfect, sheer, unmixed, unqualified, downright, out-and-out, outright.

2 OMNIPOTENT, totalitarian, despotic, autocratic, tyrannical, dictatorial, sovereign, unlimited, unrestricted.

absolutely *adv* utterly, totally, dead, completely, entirely, fully, wholly, thoroughly, exhaustively, perfectly, supremely, unconditionally, conclusively, finally, categorically, definitely, positively, unequivocally, unambiguously, unquestionably, decidedly, decisively, surely, certainly, infallibly, genuinely, truly, purely, exactly, precisely.

absorb *v* **1** TAKE IN, ingest, drink in, imbibe, suck up, soak up, consume, devour, engulf, digest, assimilate, understand, receive, hold, retain. **2** ENGROSS, involve, fascinate, enthral, monopolize, preoccupy, occupy, fill (up).
F3 1 exude.

absorbing *adj* interesting, amusing, entertaining, diverting, engrossing, preoccupying, intriguing, fascinating, captivating, enthralling, spellbinding, gripping, riveting, compulsive, unputdownable (*infml*).
F3 boring, off-putting.

abstain *v* refrain, decline, refuse, reject, resist, forbear, shun, avoid, keep from, stop, cease, desist, give up, renounce, forgo, go without, deny oneself.
F3 indulge.

abstemious *adj* abstinent, self-denying, self-disciplined, disciplined, sober, temperate, moderate, sparing, frugal, austere, ascetic, restrained.
F3 intemperate, gluttonous, luxurious.

abstinence *n* abstaining, abstention, abstemiousness, self-denial, non-indulgence, avoidance, forbearance, refraining, refusal, restraint, self-restraint, self-control, self-discipline, sobriety, teetotalism, temperance, moderation, frugality, asceticism.
F3 indulgence, self-indulgence.

abstract *adj* non-concrete, conceptual, intellectual, hypothetical, theoretical, unpractical, unrealistic, general, generalized, indefinite, metaphysical, philosophical, academic, complex, abstruse, deep, profound, subtle.
F3 concrete, real, actual.
n synopsis, outline, summary, recapitulation, résumé, précis, epitome, digest, abridgement, compression.
v **1** SUMMARIZE, outline, précis, digest, condense, compress, abridge, abbreviate, shorten. **2** EXTRACT, remove, withdraw, isolate, detach, dissociate, separate.
F3 1 expand. **2** insert.

abstraction *n* **1** IDEA, notion, concept, thought, conception, theory, hypothesis, theorem, formula, generalization, generality. **2** INATTENTION, dream, dreaminess, absent-mindedness, distraction, pensiveness, preoccupation, absorption. **3** EXTRACTION, withdrawal, isolation, separation.

absurd *adj* ridiculous, ludicrous, preposterous, fantastic, incongruous, illogical, paradoxical, implausible, untenable, unreasonable, irrational, nonsensical, meaningless, senseless, foolish, silly, stupid, idiotic, crazy, daft (*infml*), farcical, comical, funny, humorous, laughable, risible, derisory.
F3 logical, rational, sensible.

abundant *adj* plentiful, in plenty, full, filled, well-supplied, ample,

generous, bountiful, rich, copious, profuse, lavish, exuberant, teeming, overflowing.
F3 scarce, sparse.

abuse v 1 MISUSE, misapply, exploit, take advantage of, oppress, wrong, ill-treat, maltreat, hurt, injure, molest, damage, spoil, harm. 2 INSULT, swear at, defame, libel, slander, smear, disparage, malign, revile, scold, upbraid.
F3 1 cherish, care for. 2 compliment, praise.
n 1 MISUSE, misapplication, exploitation, imposition, oppression, wrong, ill-treatment, maltreatment, hurt, injury, molestation, damage, spoiling, harm. 2 INSULTS, swearing, cursing, offence, defamation, libel, slander, disparagement, reproach, scolding, upbraiding, tirade.
F3 1 care, attention. 2 compliment, praise.

abusive adj insulting, offensive, rude, scathing, hurtful, injurious, cruel, destructive, defamatory, libellous, slanderous, derogatory, disparaging, pejorative, vilifying, maligning, reviling, censorious, reproachful, scolding, upbraiding.
F3 complimentary, polite.

abyss n gulf, chasm, crevasse, fissure, gorge, canyon, crater, pit, depth, void.

academic adj 1 SCHOLARLY, erudite, learned, well-read, studious, bookish, scholastic, pedagogical, educational, instructional, literary, highbrow. 2 THEORETICAL, hypothetical, conjectural, speculative, notional, abstract, impractical.
n professor, don, master, fellow, lecturer, tutor, student, scholar, man of letters, woman of letters, pedant.

accelerate v quicken, speed, speed up, pick up speed, step up, expedite, hurry, hasten, precipitate, stimulate, facilitate, advance, further, promote, forward.
F3 decelerate, slow down, delay.

accent n pronunciation, enunciation, articulation, brogue, twang (infml), tone, pitch, intonation, inflection, accentuation, stress, emphasis, intensity, force, cadence, rhythm, beat, pulse, pulsation.

accentuate v accent, stress, emphasize, underline, highlight, intensify, strengthen, deepen.
F3 play down, weaken.

accept v 1 accept a gift: take, receive, obtain, acquire, gain, secure. 2 ACKNOWLEDGE, recognize, admit, allow, approve, agree to, consent to, take on, adopt. 3 TOLERATE, put up with, stand, bear, abide, face up to, yield to.
F3 1 refuse, turn down. 2 reject.

acceptable adj satisfactory, tolerable, moderate, passable, adequate, all right, OK (infml), so-so (infml), unexceptionable, admissible, suitable, conventional, correct, desirable, pleasant, gratifying, welcome.
F3 unacceptable, unsatisfactory, unwelcome.

acceptance n 1 TAKING, receipt, obtaining, getting, acquiring, gaining, securing. 2 ACKNOWLEDGEMENT, recognition, admission, concession, affirmation, concurrence, agreement, assent, consent, permission, ratification, approval, stamp of approval, OK (infml), adoption, undertaking, belief, credence.
F3 1 refusal. 2 rejection, dissent.

accepted adj authorized, approved, ratified, sanctioned, agreed, acknowledged, recognized, admitted, confirmed, acceptable, correct, conventional, unorthodox, traditional, customary, time-honoured, established, received, universal, regular, standard, normal, usual, common.
F3 unconventional, unorthodox, controversial.

access n admission, admittance, entry, entering, entrance, gateway, door, key, approach, passage, road, path, course.
F3 exit, outlet.

accessible adj **1** REACHABLE, get-at-able (infml), attainable, achievable, possible, obtainable, available, on hand, ready, handy, convenient, near, nearby. **2** FRIENDLY, affable, approachable, sociable, informal.
F3 1 inaccessible, remote.
2 unapproachable.

accessory n **1** EXTRA, supplement, addition, appendage, attachment, extension, component, fitting, accompaniment, decoration, adornment, frill, trimming.
2 ACCOMPLICE, partner, associate, colleague, confederate, assistant, helper, help, aid.

accident n **1** CHANCE, hazard, fortuity, luck, fortune, fate, serendipity, contingency, fluke.
2 MISFORTUNE, mischance, misadventure, mishap, casualty, blow, calamity, disaster. **3** road accident: collision, crash, shunt (sl), prang (sl), pile-up.

accidental adj unintentional, unintended, inadvertent, unplanned, uncalculated, unexpected, unforeseen, unlooked-for, chance, fortuitous, flukey, uncertain, haphazard, random, casual, incidental.
F3 intentional, deliberate, calculated, premeditated.

acclaim v praise, commend, extol, exalt, honour, hail, salute, welcome, applaud, clap, cheer, celebrate.
n acclamation, praise, commendation, homage, tribute, eulogy, exaltation, honour, welcome, approbation, approval, applause, ovation, clapping, cheers, cheering, shouting, celebration.
F3 criticism, disapproval.

accommodate v **1** LODGE, board, put up, house, shelter. **2** OBLIGE, help, assist, aid, serve, provide, supply, comply, conform. **3** ADAPT, accustom, acclimatize, adjust, modify, fit, harmonize, reconcile, settle, compose.

accommodating adj obliging, indulgent, helpful, co-operative, willing, kind, considerate, unselfish, sympathetic, friendly, hospitable.
F3 disobliging, selfish.

accommodation

> Types of accommodation include:
> flat, apartment, bed-sit, bed-sitter,
> digs (infml), lodgings, hostel, halls
> of residence, dorm (US), rooms,
> residence, dwelling, shelter, pad
> (infml), squat (infml); bed and break-
> fast, board, guest-house, hotel,
> youth hostel, villa, time-share, self-
> catering, motel, inn, pension,
> boarding-house; barracks, billet,
> married quarters. see also **house**;
> **room**.

accompany v **1** ESCORT, attend, convoy, chaperone, usher, conduct, follow. **2** COEXIST, coincide, belong to, go with, complement, supplement.

accomplice n assistant, helper, abettor, mate, henchman, conspirator, collaborator, ally, confederate, partner, associate, colleague, participator, accessory.

accomplish v achieve, attain, do, perform, carry out, execute, fulfil, discharge, finish, complete, conclude, consummate, realize, effect, bring about, engineer, produce, obtain.

accomplished adj skilled, professional, practised, proficient, gifted, talented, skilful, adroit, adept, expert, masterly, consummate, polished, cultivated.
E3 unskilled, inexpert, incapable.

accomplishment n **1** the accomplishment of a task: achievement, attainment, doing, performance, carrying out, execution, fulfilment, discharge, finishing, completion, conclusion, consummation, perfection, realization, fruition, production. **2** SKILL, art, aptitude, faculty, ability, capability, proficiency, gift, talent, forte. **3** EXPLOIT, feat, deed, stroke, triumph.

accord v **1** AGREE, concur, harmonize, match, conform, correspond, suit. **2** GIVE, tender, grant, allow, bestow, endow, confer.
E3 1 disagree. **2** deny.
n accordance, agreement, assent, unanimity, concert, unity, correspondence, conformity, harmony, sympathy.
E3 conflict, discord, disharmony.

accordingly adv in accordance, in accord with, correspondingly, so, as a result, consequently, in consequence,

therefore, thus, hence, properly, suitably.

according to in accordance with, in keeping with, obedient to, in conformity with, in line with, consistent with, commensurate with, in proportion to, in relation to, after, in the light of, in the manner of, after the manner of.

accost v approach, confront, buttonhole, waylay, stop, halt, detain, importune, solicit.

account n **1** an account of what happened: narrative, story, tale, chronicle, history, memoir, record, statement, report, communiqué, write-up, version, portrayal, sketch, description, presentation, explanation. **2** LEDGER, book, books, register, inventory, statement, invoice, bill, tab, charge, reckoning, computation, tally, score, balance.
account for explain, elucidate, illuminate, clear up, rationalize, justify, vindicate, answer for.

accountable adj answerable, responsible, liable, amenable, obliged, bound.

accumulate v gather, assemble, collect, amass, aggregate, cumulate, accrue, grow, increase, multiply, build up, pile up, hoard, stockpile, stash (infml), store.
E3 disseminate.

accumulation n gathering, assembly, collection, growth, increase, build-up, conglomeration, mass, heap, pile, stack, stock, store, reserve, hoard, stockpile.

accuracy n correctness, precision, exactness, authenticity, truth, veracity, closeness, faithfulness, fidelity, carefulness.
E3 inaccuracy.

accurate *adj* correct, right, unerring, precise, exact, well-directed, spot-on (*infml*), faultless, perfect, word-perfect, sound, authentic, factual, nice, true, truthful, veracious, just, proper, close, faithful, well-judged, careful, rigorous, scrupulous, meticulous, strict, minute.
F3 inaccurate, wrong, imprecise, inexact.

accusation *n* charge, allegation, imputation, indictment, denunciation, impeachment, recrimination, complaint, incrimination.

accuse *v* charge, indict, impugn, denounce, arraign, impeach, cite, allege, attribute, impute, blame, censure, recriminate, incriminate, inform against.

accustomed *adj* used, in the habit of, given to, confirmed, seasoned, hardened, inured, disciplined, trained, adapted, acclimatized, acquainted, familiar, wonted, habitual, routine, regular, normal, usual, ordinary, everyday, conventional, customary, traditional, established, fixed, prevailing, general.
F3 unaccustomed, unusual.

ache *v* **1** HURT, be sore, pain, suffer, agonize, throb, pound, twinge, smart, sting. **2** YEARN, long, pine, hanker, desire, crave, hunger, thirst, itch.
n **1** PAIN, hurt, soreness, suffering, anguish, agony, throb, throbbing, pounding, pang, twinge, smarting, stinging. **2** YEARNING, longing, craving, itch.

achieve *v* accomplish, attain, reach, get, obtain, acquire, procure, gain, earn, win, succeed, manage, do, perform, carry out, execute, fulfil,

finish, complete, consummate, effect, bring about, realize, produce.
F3 underachieve, miss, fail.

achievement *n* **1** *the achievement of our aims*: accomplishment, attainment, acquirement, performance, execution, fulfilment, completion, success, realization, fruition. **2** ACT, deed, exploit, feat, effort.

acid *adj* sour, bitter, tart, vinegary, sharp, pungent, acerbic, caustic, corrosive, stinging, biting, mordant, cutting, incisive, trenchant, harsh, hurtful.

acknowledge *v* **1** *acknowledge an error*: admit, confess, own up to, declare, recognize, accept, grant, allow, concede. **2** GREET, address, notice, recognize. **3** *acknowledge a letter*: answer, reply to, respond to, confirm.
F3 **1** deny. **2** ignore.

acknowledged *adj* recognized, accepted, approved, accredited, declared, professed, attested, avowed, confirmed.

acknowledgement *n* **1** ADMISSION, confession, declaration, profession, recognition, acceptance. **2** GREETING, salutation, notice, recognition. **3** ANSWER, reply, response, reaction, affirmation. **4** GRATITUDE, thanks, appreciation, tribute.

acquaint *v* accustom, familiarize, tell, notify, advise, inform, brief, enlighten, divulge, disclose, reveal, announce.

acquaintance *n* **1** AWARENESS, knowledge, understanding, experience, familiarity, intimacy, relationship, association, fellowship, companionship. **2** FRIEND, companion, colleague, associate, contact.

acquire v buy, purchase, procure, appropriate, obtain, get, cop (sl), receive, collect, pick up, gather, net, gain, secure, earn, win, achieve, attain, realize.
F3 relinquish, forfeit.

acquisition n purchase, buy (infml), procurement, appropriation, gain, securing, achievement, attainment, accession, takeover, property, possession.

acquit v absolve, clear, reprieve, let off, exonerate, exculpate, excuse, vindicate, free, liberate, deliver, relieve, release, dismiss, discharge, settle, satisfy, repay.
F3 convict.

acquittal n absolution, clearance, reprieve, exoneration, exculpation, excusing, vindication, freeing, liberation, deliverance, relief, release, dismissal, discharge.
F3 conviction.

acrid adj pungent, sharp, stinging, acid, burning, caustic, acerbic, biting, cutting, incisive, trenchant, sarcastic, sardonic, bitter, acrimonious, virulent, harsh, vitriolic, nasty, malicious, venomous.

acrimonious adj bitter, biting, cutting, trenchant, sharp, virulent, severe, spiteful, censorious, abusive, ill-tempered.
F3 peaceable, kindly.

acrimony n bitterness, rancour, resentment, ill-will, petulance, gall, ill temper, irascibility, trenchancy, sarcasm, astringency, acerbity, harshness, virulence.

act n **1** DEED, action, undertaking, enterprise, operation, manoeuvre,

move, step, doing, execution, accomplishment, achievement, exploit, feat, stroke. **2** put on an act: pretence, make-believe, sham, fake, feigning, dissimulation, affectation, show, front. **3** LAW, statute, ordinance, edict, decree, resolution, measure, bill. **4** TURN, item, routine, sketch, performance, gig (sl).
v **1** BEHAVE, conduct, exert, make, work, function, operate, do, execute, carry out. **2** PRETEND, feign, put on, assume, simulate, mimic, imitate, impersonate, portray, represent, mime, play, perform, enact.
act on 1 act on orders: carry out, fulfil, comply with, conform to, obey, follow, heed, take. **2** AFFECT, influence, alter, modify, change, transform.

acting adj temporary, provisional, interim, stopgap, supply, stand-by, substitute, reserve.
n theatre, stagecraft, artistry, performing, performance, play-acting, melodrama, dramatics, theatricals, portrayal, characterization, impersonation, imitating.

action n **1** ACT, move, deed, exploit, feat, accomplishment, achievement, performance, effort, endeavour, enterprise, undertaking, proceeding, process, activity, liveliness, spirit, energy, vigour, power, force, exercise, exertion, work, functioning, operation, mechanism, movement, motion. **2** killed in action: warfare, battle, conflict, combat, fight, fray, engagement, skirmish, clash. **3** LITIGATION, lawsuit, suit, case, prosecution.

activate v start, initiate, trigger, set off, fire, kick-start (infml), switch on, set in motion, mobilize, propel, move, stir, rouse, arouse, stimulate, motivate, prompt, animate, energize, impel, excite, galvanize.

F3 deactivate, stop, arrest.

active adj **1** BUSY, occupied, on the go (infml), industrious, diligent, hard-working, forceful, spirited, vital, forward, enterprising, enthusiastic, devoted, engaged, involved, committed, militant, activist. **2** AGILE, nimble, sprightly, light-footed, quick, alert, animated, lively, energetic, vigorous. **3** IN OPERATION, functioning, working, running.

F3 1 passive. **2** inert, dormant. **3** inactive.

activity n **1** LIVELINESS, life, activeness, action, motion, movement, commotion, bustle, hustle, industry, labour, exertion, exercise. **2** OCCUPATION, job, work, act, deed, project, scheme, task, venture, enterprise, endeavour, undertaking, pursuit, hobby, pastime, interest.

actor n actress, play-actor, film-actor, movie-actor (US), comedian, tragedian, ham, player, performer, artist, impersonator, mime.

actual adj **1** REAL, existent, substantial, tangible, material, physical, concrete, positive, definite, absolute, certain, unquestionable, indisputable, confirmed, verified, factual, truthful, true, genuine, legitimate, bona fide, authentic, realistic. **2** CURRENT, present, present-day, prevailing, live, living.

F3 1 theoretical, apparent, imaginary.

actually adv in fact, as a matter of fact, as it happens, in truth, in reality, really, truly, indeed, absolutely.

acumen n astuteness, shrewdness, sharpness, keenness, quickness, penetration, insight, intuition, discrimination, discernment, judgement, perception, sense, wit, wisdom, intelligence, cleverness, ingenuity.

acute adj **1** SEVERE, intense, extreme, violent, dangerous, serious, grave, urgent, crucial, vital, decisive, sharp, cutting, poignant, distressing. **2** an acute mind: sharp, keen, incisive, penetrating, astute, shrewd, judicious, discerning, observant, perceptive.

F3 1 mild, slight.

adamant adj hard, resolute, determined, set, firm, insistent, rigid, stiff, inflexible, unbending, unrelenting, intransigent, unyielding, stubborn, uncompromising, tough, fixed, immovable, unshakable.

F3 hesitant, flexible, yielding.

adapt v alter, change, qualify, modify, adjust, convert, remodel, customize, fit, tailor, fashion, shape, harmonize, match, suit, conform, comply, prepare, familiarize, acclimatize.

adaptable adj alterable, changeable, variable, modifiable, adjustable, convertible, conformable, versatile, plastic, malleable, flexible, compliant, amenable, easy-going.

F3 inflexible, refractory.

adaptation n alteration, change, shift, transformation, modification, adjustment, accommodation, conversion, remodelling, reworking, reshaping, refitting, revision, variation, version.

add v append, annex, affix, attach, tack on, join, combine, supplement, augment.

F3 take away, remove.

add up 1 ADD, sum up, tot up, total, tally, count (up), reckon, compute. **2** AMOUNT, come to, constitute, include. **3** *it doesn't add up*: be consistent, hang together, fit, be plausible, be reasonable, make sense, mean, signify, indicate.
F∃ 1 subtract.

addict *n* **1** ENTHUSIAST, fan, buff (*infml*), fiend, freak, devotee, follower, adherent. **2** DRUG-ADDICT, user (*infml*), dope-fiend, druggie (*infml*), junkie (*infml*), tripper (*sl*), mainliner (*sl*).

addicted *adj* dependent, hooked, obsessed, absorbed, devoted, dedicated, fond, inclined, disposed, accustomed.

addiction *n* dependence, craving, habit, monkey (*sl*), obsession.

addition *n* **1** ADDING, annexation, accession, extension, enlargement, increasing, increase, gain. **2** ADJUNCT, supplement, additive, addendum, appendix, appendage, accessory, attachment, extra, increment. **3** SUMMING-UP, totting-up, totalling, counting, reckoning, inclusion.
F∃ 1 removal. **3** subtraction.
in addition additionally, too, also, as well, besides, moreover, further, furthermore, over and above.

additional *adj* added, extra, supplementary, spare, more, further, increased, other, new, fresh.

address *n* **1** RESIDENCE, dwelling, abode, house, home, lodging, direction, inscription, whereabouts, location, situation, place. **2** SPEECH, talk, lecture, sermon, discourse, dissertation.
v lecture, speak to, talk to, greet, salute, hail, invoke, accost, approach, buttonhole.

adept *adj* skilled, accomplished, expert, masterly, experienced, versed, practised, polished, proficient, able, adroit, deft, nimble.

adequate *adj* enough, sufficient, commensurate, requisite, suitable, fit, able, competent, capable, serviceable, acceptable, satisfactory, passable, tolerable, fair, respectable, presentable.
F∃ inadequate, insufficient.

adhere *v* **1** STICK, glue, paste, cement, fix, fasten, attach, join, link, combine, coalesce, cohere, hold, cling, cleave to. **2** *adhere to the agreement*: observe, follow, abide by, comply with, fulfil, obey, keep, heed, respect, stand by.

adherent *n* supporter, upholder, advocate, partisan, follower, disciple, satellite, henchman, hanger-on, votary, devotee, admirer, fan, enthusiast, freak, nut.

adhesion *n* adherence, adhesiveness, bond, attachment, grip, cohesion.

adhesive *adj* sticky, tacky, self-adhesive, gummed, gummy, gluey, adherent, adhering, sticking, clinging, holding, attaching, cohesive.
n glue, gum, paste, cement.

adjacent *adj* adjoining, abutting, touching, contiguous, bordering, alongside, beside, juxtaposed, next-door, neighbouring, next, closest, nearest, close, near.
F∃ remote, distant.

adjoin *v* abut, touch, meet, border, verge, neighbour, interconnect, link, connect, join, combine, unite, couple, attach, annex, add.

adjourn *v* interrupt, suspend, discontinue, break off, delay, stay, defer, postpone, put off, recess, retire.
F3 assemble, convene.

adjournment *n* interruption, suspension, discontinuation, break, pause, recess, delay, stay, deferment, deferral, postponement, putting off, dissolution.

adjudicate *v* judge, arbitrate, umpire, referee, settle, determine, decide, pronounce.

adjust *v* **1** MODIFY, change, adapt, alter, convert, dispose, shape, remodel, fit, accommodate, suit, measure, rectify, regulate, balance, temper, tune, fine-tune, fix, set, arrange, compose, settle, square. **2** ACCUSTOM, habituate, acclimatize, reconcile, harmonize, conform.
F3 1 disarrange, upset.

adjustment *n* **1** MODIFICATION, change, adaptation, alteration, conversion, remodelling, shaping, fitting, accommodation, rectification, regulation, tuning, fixing, setting, arranging, arrangement, ordering, settlement. **2** HABITUATION, orientation, acclimatization, naturalization, reconciliation, harmonization, conforming.

ad-lib *v* improvise, extemporize, make up, invent.
adj impromptu, improvised, extempore, extemporaneous, off-the-cuff, unprepared, unpremeditated, unrehearsed, spontaneous, made up.
F3 prepared.
adv impromptu, extempore, extemporaneously, off the cuff, off the top of one's head, spontaneously, impulsively.

administer *v* **1** *administer an organization*: govern, rule, lead, head, preside over, officiate, manage, run, organize, direct, conduct, control, regulate, superintend, supervise, oversee. **2** GIVE, provide, supply, distribute, dole out, dispense, measure out, mete out, execute, impose, apply.

administration *n* **1** ADMINISTERING, governing, ruling, leadership, management, execution, running, organization, direction, control, superintendence, supervision, overseeing. **2** GOVERNING BODY, regime, government, ministry, leadership, directorship, management, executive, term of office.

administrative *adj* governmental, legislative, authoritative, directorial, managerial, management, executive, organizational, regulatory, supervisory.

admirable *adj* praiseworthy, commendable, laudable, creditable, deserving, worthy, respected, fine, excellent, superior, wonderful, exquisite, choice, rare, valuable.
F3 contemptible, despicable, deplorable.

admiration *n* esteem, regard, respect, reverence, veneration, worship, adoration, affection, approval, praise, appreciation, pleasure, delight, wonder, astonishment, amazement, surprise.
F3 contempt.

admire *v* esteem, respect, revere, venerate, worship, idolize, adore, approve, praise, laud, applaud, appreciate, value.
F3 despise, censure.

admirer n follower, disciple, adherent, supporter, fan, groupie (infml), enthusiast, devotee, worshipper, idolizer, suitor, boyfriend, girlfriend, sweetheart, lover.
F3 critic, opponent.

admissible adj acceptable, tolerable, tolerated, passable, allowable, permissible, allowed, permitted, lawful, legitimate, justifiable.
F3 inadmissible, illegitimate.

admission n confession, granting, acknowledgement, recognition, acceptance, allowance, concession, affirmation, declaration, profession, disclosure, divulgence, revelation, exposé.
F3 denial.

admit v 1 CONFESS, own (up) grant, acknowledge, recognize, accept, allow, concede, agree, affirm, declare, profess, disclose, divulge, reveal. 2 LET IN, allow to enter, give access, accept, receive, take in, introduce, initiate.
F3 1 deny. 2 shut out, exclude.

admittance n admitting, admission, letting in, access, entrance, entry, acceptance, reception, introduction, initiation.
F3 exclusion.

adolescence n teens, puberty, youth, minority, boyhood, girlhood, development, immaturity, youthfulness, boyishness, girlishness.

adolescent adj teenage, young, youthful, juvenile, puerile, boyish, girlish, immature, growing, developing.
n teenager, youth, juvenile, minor.

adopt v take on, accept, assume, take up, appropriate, embrace, follow, choose, select, take in, foster, support, maintain, back, endorse, ratify, approve.
F3 repudiate, disown.

adorable adj lovable, dear, darling, precious, appealing, sweet, winsome, charming, enchanting, captivating, winning, delightful, pleasing, attractive, fetching.
F3 hateful, abominable.

adore v love, cherish, dote on, admire, esteem, honour, revere, venerate, worship, idolize, exalt, glorify.
F3 hate, abhor.

adorn v decorate, deck, bedeck, ornament, crown, trim, garnish, gild, enhance, embellish, doll up, sex up (sl), enrich, grace.

adult adj grown-up, of age, full-grown, fully grown, developed, mature, ripe, ripened.
F3 immature.

adulterate v contaminate, pollute, taint, corrupt, defile, debase, dilute, water down, weaken, devalue, deteriorate.
F3 purify.

advance v 1 PROCEED, go forward, move on, go ahead, progress, prosper, flourish, thrive, improve, push the envelope (infml). 2 ACCELERATE, speed, hasten, send forward. 3 FURTHER, promote, upgrade, foster, support, assist, benefit, facilitate, increase, grow. 4 advance an idea: present, submit, suggest, allege, cite, bring forward, offer, provide, supply, furnish. 5 advance a sum of money: lend, loan, pay beforehand, pay, give.
F3 1 retreat. 2 retard. 3 impede.
n 1 PROGRESS, forward movement, onward movement, headway, step,

advancement, furtherance, breakthrough, development, growth, increase, improvement, amelioration. **2** DEPOSIT, down payment, prepayment, credit, loan.

F3 1 retreat, recession.

in advance beforehand, previously, early, earlier, sooner, ahead, in front, in the lead, in the forefront.

F3 later, behind.

advanced adj leading, foremost, cutting-edge, state-of-the-art, ahead, forward, precocious, progressive, forward-looking, avant-garde, ultra-modern, sophisticated, complex, higher.

F3 backward, retarded, elementary.

advancement n furtherance, promotion, preferment, betterment, improvement, development, growth, rise, gain, advance, progress, headway.

F3 demotion, retardation.

advantage n **1** ASSET, blessing, benefit, good, welfare, interest, service, help, aid, assistance, use, avail, convenience, usefulness, utility, profit, gain, start. **2** LEAD, edge, upper hand, superiority, precedence, pre-eminence, sway.

F3 1 disadvantage, drawback, hindrance.

advantageous adj beneficial, favourable, opportune, convenient, helpful, useful, worthwhile, valuable, profitable, gainful, remunerative, rewarding.

F3 disadvantageous, adverse, damaging.

adventure n exploit, venture, undertaking, enterprise, risk, hazard, chance, speculation, experience, incident, occurrence.

adventurous adj daring, intrepid, bold, audacious, headstrong, impetuous, reckless, rash, risky, venturesome, enterprising.

F3 cautious, chary, prudent.

adverse adj hostile, antagonistic, opposing, opposite, counter, contrary, conflicting, counter-productive, negative, disadvantageous, unfavourable, inauspicious, unfortunate, unlucky, inopportune, detrimental, harmful, noxious, injurious, hurtful, unfriendly, uncongenial.

F3 advantageous, favourable.

adversity n misfortune, ill fortune, bad luck, ill luck, reverse, hardship, hard times, misery, wretchedness, affliction, suffering, distress, sorrow, woe, trouble, trial, tribulation, calamity, disaster, catastrophe.

F3 prosperity.

advertise v publicize, promote, push, plug (infml), praise, hype (sl), trumpet, blazon, herald, announce, declare, proclaim, broadcast, publish, display, make known, inform, notify.

advertisement n advert (infml), ad (infml), commercial, publicity, promotion, promo (infml), plug (infml), hype (sl), display, blurb, announcement, notice, poster, bill, placard, leaflet, handbill, circular, handout, flyer, propaganda.

advice n **1** WARNING, caution, do's and don'ts, injunction, instruction, counsel, help, guidance, direction, suggestion, recommendation, opinion, view. **2** NOTIFICATION, notice, memorandum, communication, information, intelligence.

advisable adj suggested, recommended, sensible, wise,

prudent, judicious, sound, profitable, beneficial, desirable, suitable, appropriate, apt, fitting, fit, proper, correct.

F3 inadvisable, foolish.

advise v **1** COUNSEL, guide, warn, forewarn, caution, instruct, teach, tutor, suggest, recommend, commend, urge. **2** NOTIFY, inform, tell, acquaint, make known, report.

adviser n counsellor, consultant, authority, guide, teacher, tutor, instructor, coach, helper, aide, right-hand man, mentor, confidant(e), counsel, lawyer.

advocate v defend, champion, campaign for, press for, argue for, plead for, justify, urge, encourage, advise, recommend, propose, promote, endorse, support, uphold, patronize, adopt, subscribe to, favour, countenance.

F3 impugn, disparage, deprecate. n defender, supporter, upholder, champion, campaigner, pleader, vindicator, proponent, promoter, speaker, spokesperson.

F3 opponent, critic.

affable adj friendly, amiable, approachable, open, expansive, genial, good-humoured, good-natured, mild, benevolent, kindly, gracious, obliging, courteous, amicable, congenial, cordial, warm, sociable, pleasant, agreeable.

F3 unfriendly, reserved, reticent, cool.

affair n **1** BUSINESS, transaction, operation, proceeding, undertaking, activity, project, responsibility, interest, concern, matter, question, issue, subject, topic, circumstance, happening, occurrence, incident,

episode, event. **2** have an affair: relationship, liaison, intrigue, love affair, romance, amour.

affect v **1** CONCERN, regard, involve, relate to, apply to, bear upon, impinge upon, act on, change, transform, alter, modify, influence, sway, prevail over, attack, strike, impress, interest, stir, move, touch, upset, disturb, perturb, trouble, overcome. **2** ADOPT, assume, put on, feign, simulate, imitate, fake, counterfeit, sham, pretend, profess, aspire to.

affectation n airs, pretentiousness, mannerism, pose, act, show, appearance, façade, pretence, sham, simulation, imitation, artificiality, insincerity.

F3 artlessness, ingenuousness.

affected adj assumed, put-on, feigned, simulated, artificial, fake, counterfeit, sham, phoney (infml), contrived, studied, precious, mannered, pretentious, pompous, stiff, unnatural, insincere.

F3 genuine, natural.

affection n fondness, attachment, devotion, love, tenderness, care, warmth, feeling, kindness, friendliness, goodwill, favour, liking, partiality, inclination, penchant, passion, desire.

F3 dislike, antipathy.

affectionate adj fond, attached, devoted, doting, loving, tender, caring, warm, warm-hearted, kind, friendly, amiable, cordial.

F3 cold, undemonstrative.

affirm v confirm, corroborate, endorse, ratify, certify, witness, testify, swear, maintain, state, assert, declare, pronounce.

F3 refute, deny.

affirmative adj agreeing, concurring, approving, assenting, positive, confirming, corroborative, emphatic.
F3 negative, dissenting.

afflict v strike, visit, trouble, burden, oppress, distress, grieve, pain, hurt, wound, harm, try, harass, beset, plague, torment, torture.
F3 comfort, solace.

affliction n distress, grief, sorrow, misery, depression, suffering, pain, torment, disease, illness, sickness, plague, curse, cross, ordeal, trial, tribulation, trouble, hardship, adversity, misfortune, calamity, disaster.
F3 comfort, consolation, solace, blessing.

affluence n wealthiness, wealth, riches, fortune, substance, property, prosperity, opulence, abundance, profusion, plenty.
F3 poverty.

affluent adj wealthy, rich, moneyed, loaded (sl), flush (infml), well-off, prosperous, well-to-do, opulent, comfortable.
F3 poor, impoverished.

afford v **1** HAVE ENOUGH FOR, spare, allow, manage, sustain, bear. **2** PROVIDE, supply, furnish, give, grant, offer, impart, produce, yield, generate.

affront v offend, insult, abuse, snub, slight, provoke, displease, irritate, annoy, anger, vex, incense, outrage.
F3 compliment, appease.
n offence, insult, slur, rudeness, discourtesy, disrespect, indignity, snub, slight, wrong, injury, abuse, provocation, vexation, outrage.
F3 compliment.

afraid adj frightened, scared, alarmed, terrified, fearful, timorous, daunted, intimidated, faint-hearted, cowardly, reluctant, apprehensive, anxious, nervous, timid, distrustful, suspicious.
F3 unafraid, brave, bold, confident.

after prep following, subsequent to, in consequence of, as a result of, behind, below.
F3 before.

again adv once more, once again, another time, over again, afresh, anew, encore.

against prep **1** against the wall: abutting, adjacent to, close up to, touching, in contact with, on. **2** OPPOSITE TO, facing, fronting, in the face of, confronting, opposing, versus, opposed to, anti (infml), in opposition to, hostile to, resisting, in defiance of, in contrast to.
F32 for, pro.

age n **1** ERA, epoch, day, days, generation, date, time, period, duration, span, years, aeon. **2** OLD AGE, maturity, elderliness, seniority, dotage, senility, decline.
F32 youth.
v grow old, mature, ripen, mellow, season, decline, deteriorate, degenerate.

agency n **1** recruitment agency: bureau, office, department, organization, business, work. **2** MEANS, medium, instrumentality, power, force, influence, effect, intervention, action, activity, operation, mechanism, workings.

agent n **1** SUBSTITUTE, deputy, delegate, envoy, emissary, representative, rep (infml), broker, middleman, go-between, intermediary, negotiator, mover, doer, performer, operator, operative, functionary, worker. **2** INSTRUMENT, vehicle, channel, means, agency, cause, force.

aggravate *v* **1** *aggravate a problem*: exacerbate, worsen, inflame, increase, intensify, heighten, magnify, exaggerate. **2** (*infml*) ANNOY, irritate, vex, irk, exasperate, incense, provoke, tease, pester, harass, bug (*infml*).
F3 1 improve, alleviate. **2** appease, mollify.

aggregate *n* total, sum, amount, whole, totality, entirety, generality, combination, collection, accumulation.
adj cumulative, accumulated, collected, combined, united, added, total, complete, composite, mixed, collective.
F3 individual, particular.

aggression *n* **1** ANTAGONISM, provocation, offence, injury, attack, offensive, assault, onslaught, raid, incursion, invasion, intrusion.
2 AGGRESSIVENESS, militancy, belligerence, combativeness, hostility.
F3 1 peace, resistance. **2** passivity, gentleness.

aggressive *adj* argumentative, quarrelsome, contentious, belligerent, hostile, offensive, provocative, intrusive, invasive, bold, assertive, pushy, go-ahead, forceful, vigorous, zealous, ruthless, destructive.
F3 peaceable, friendly, submissive, timid.

aggrieved *adj* wronged, offended, hurt, injured, insulted, maltreated, ill-used, resentful, pained, distressed, saddened, unhappy, upset, annoyed.
F3 pleased.

aghast *adj* shocked, appalled, horrified, horror-struck, thunderstruck, stunned, stupefied, amazed, astonished, astounded, startled, confounded, dismayed.

agile *adj* active, lively, nimble, spry, sprightly, mobile, flexible, limber, lithe, fleet, quick, swift, brisk, prompt, sharp, acute, alert, quick-witted, clever, adroit, deft.
F3 clumsy, stiff.

agitate *v* **1** ROUSE, arouse, stir up, excite, stimulate, incite, inflame, ferment, work up, worry, trouble, upset, alarm, disturb, unsettle, disquiet, discompose, fluster, ruffle, flurry, unnerve, confuse, distract, disconcert. **2** SHAKE, rattle, rock, stir, beat, churn, toss, convulse.
F3 1 calm, tranquillize.

agitator *n* troublemaker, rabble-rouser, revolutionary, stirrer (*sl*), inciter, instigator.

agony *n* anguish, torment, torture, pain, spasm, throes, suffering, affliction, tribulation, distress, woe, misery, wretchedness.

agree *v* **1** CONCUR, see eye to eye, get on, settle, accord, match, suit, fit, tally, correspond, conform. **2** CONSENT, allow, permit, assent, accede, grant, admit, concede, yield, comply.
F3 1 disagree, differ, conflict. **2** refuse.

agreeable *adj* pleasant, congenial, likable, attractive, delightful, enjoyable, gratifying, satisfying, palatable, acceptable, proper, appropriate, suitable, fitting, in accord, consistent.
F3 disagreeable, nasty, distasteful.

agreement *n* **1** SETTLEMENT, compact, covenant, treaty, pact, contract, deal, bargain, arrangement,

understanding. **2** *be in agreement*: concurrence, accord, concord, unanimity, union, harmony, sympathy, affinity, compatibility, similarity, correspondence, consistency, conformity, compliance, adherence, acceptance.
F3 2 disagreement.

agricultural *adj* agronomic, agrarian, farming, farmed, cultivated, rural, pastoral, bucolic.

agriculture *n* agronomics, farming, husbandry, cultivation, tillage.

ahead *adv* forward, onward, leading, at the head, in front, in the lead, winning, at an advantage, advanced, superior, to the fore, in the forefront, in advance, before, earlier on.

aid *v* help, assist, succour, rally round, relieve, support, subsidize, sustain, second, serve, oblige, accommodate, favour, promote, boost, encourage, expedite, facilitate, ease.
F3 hinder, impede, obstruct.
n help, assistance, prop, support, relief, benefit, subsidy, donation, contribution, funding, grant, sponsorship, patronage, favour, encouragement, service.
F3 hindrance, impediment, obstruction.

ailing *adj* unwell, ill, sick, poorly, indisposed, out of sorts (*infml*), under the weather (*infml*), off-colour, suffering, languishing, sickly, diseased, invalid, infirm, unsound, frail, weak, feeble, failing.
F3 healthy, thriving, flourishing.

ailment *n* illness, sickness, complaint, malady, disease, infection, disorder, affliction, infirmity, disability, weakness.

aim *v* **1** POINT, direct, take aim, level, train, sight, zero in on (*infml*), target.

2 *aim to achieve*: aspire, want, wish, seek, resolve, purpose, intend, propose, mean, plan, design, strive, try, attempt, endeavour.
n aspiration, ambition, hope, dream, desire, wish, plan, design, scheme, purpose, motive, end, intention, object, objective, target, mark, goal, direction, course.

aimless *adj* pointless, purposeless, unmotivated, irresolute, directionless, rambling, undirected, unguided, stray, chance, random, haphazard, erratic, unpredictable, wayward.
F3 purposeful, positive, determined.

air *n* **1** ATMOSPHERE, oxygen, sky, heavens, breath, puff, waft, draught, breeze, wind, blast. **2** APPEARANCE, look, aspect, aura, bearing, demeanour, manner, character, effect, impression, feeling.
v **1** *air a room*: ventilate, aerate, freshen. **2** *air an opinion*: utter, voice, express, give vent to, make known, communicate, tell, declare, reveal, disclose, divulge, expose, make public, broadcast, publish, circulate, disseminate, exhibit, display, parade, publicize.

aircraft

> Types of aircraft include:
> aeroplane, plane, jet, jumbo, Concorde, Airbus®, helicopter, monoplane, two-seater, air-ambulance, freighter, seaplane, glider, hangglider, microlight, hot-air balloon; fighter, Spitfire, bomber, jump-jet, dive-bomber, chopper (*sl*), spyplane, delta-wing, swing-wing, troop-carrier, airship, turbojet, VTOL (vertical take-off and landing), warplane, zeppelin.

airless *adj* unventilated, stuffy, musty, stale, suffocating, stifling, sultry, muggy, close, heavy, oppressive. **F3** airy, fresh.

airy *adj* **1** ROOMY, spacious, open, well-ventilated, draughty, breezy, blowy, windy, gusty. **2** CHEERFUL, happy, light-hearted, high-spirited, lively, nonchalant, offhand. **F3 1** airless, stuffy, close, heavy, oppressive.

aisle *n* gangway, corridor, passage, passageway, alleyway, walkway, path, lane.

alarm *v* frighten, scare, startle, put the wind up (*infml*), terrify, panic, unnerve, daunt, dismay, distress, agitate. **F3** reassure, calm, soothe. *n* **1** FRIGHT, scare, fear, terror, panic, horror, shock, consternation, dismay, distress, anxiety, nervousness, apprehension, trepidation, uneasiness. **2** DANGER SIGNAL, alert, warning, distress signal, siren, bell, alarm-bell. **F3 1** calmness, composure.

alarming *adj* frightening, scary, startling, terrifying, unnerving, daunting, ominous, threatening, dismaying, disturbing, distressing, shocking, dreadful. **F3** reassuring.

alcohol *n* drink, booze (*sl*), liquor, spirits, hard stuff (*sl*), intoxicant.

Alcoholic drinks include: ale, beer, cider, lager, shandy, stout, Guinness®; aquavit, Armagnac, bourbon, brandy, Calvados, Cognac, gin, pink gin, sloe gin, rum, grog, rye, vodka, whisky, hot toddy; wine, mead, perry; absinthe, advocaat, Benedictine, Chartreuse, black velvet, bloody Mary, Buck's fizz, Campari®, cherry brandy, cocktail, Cointreau, crème de menthe, daiquiri, eggnog, ginger wine, kirsch, Marsala, Martini®, ouzo, Pernod®, piña colada, port, punch, retsina, sake, sambuca, sangria, schnapps, sherry, snowball, tequila, Tom Collins, vermouth. *see also* **wine**.

alcoholic *adj* intoxicating, brewed, fermented, distilled, strong, hard. *n* drunk, drunkard, inebriate, hard drinker, dipsomaniac, wino (*sl*), alkie (*sl*).

alcove *n* niche, nook, recess, bay, corner, cubby-hole, compartment, cubicle, booth, carrel.

alert *adj* attentive, wide awake, watchful, vigilant, on the lookout, sharp-eyed, observant, perceptive, sharp-witted, on the ball (*infml*), active, lively, spirited, quick, brisk, agile, nimble, ready, prepared, careful, heedful, circumspect, wary. **F3** slow, listless, unprepared. *v* warn, forewarn, notify, inform, tip off, signal, alarm.

alias *n* pseudonym, false name, assumed name, nom de guerre, nom de plume, pen name, stage name, nickname, sobriquet. *prep* also known as, also called, otherwise, formerly.

alibi *n* defence, justification, story, explanation, excuse, pretext, reason.

alien *adj* strange, unfamiliar, outlandish, incongruous, foreign, exotic, extraterrestrial, extraneous, remote, estranged, separated, opposed, contrary, conflicting, antagonistic, incompatible. **F3** akin.

n foreigner, immigrant, newcomer, stranger, outsider.

E3 native.

alight[1] *v* descend, get down, dismount, get off, disembark, land, touch down, come down, come to rest, settle, light, perch.

E3 ascend, board.

alight[2] *adj* lighted, lit, ignited, on fire, burning, blazing, ablaze, flaming, fiery, lit up, illuminated, bright, radiant, shining, brilliant.

E3 dark.

align *v* **1** STRAIGHTEN, range, line up, make parallel, even (up), adjust, regulate, regularize, order, co-ordinate. **2** ALLY, side, sympathize, associate, affiliate, join, co-operate, agree.

alike *adj* similar, resembling, comparable, akin, analogous, corresponding, equivalent, equal, the same, identical, duplicate, parallel, even, uniform.

E3 dissimilar, unlike, different. *adv* similarly, analogously, correspondingly, equally, in common.

alive *adj* **1** LIVING, having life, live, animate, breathing, existent, in existence, real. **2** LIVELY, animated, spirited, awake, alert, active, brisk, energetic, vigorous, zestful, vivacious, vibrant, vital.

E3 **1** dead, extinct. **2** lifeless, apathetic.

all *adj* **1** EACH, every, each and every, every single, every one of, the whole of, every bit of. **2** COMPLETE, entire, full, total, utter, outright, perfect, greatest.

E3 **1** no, none. *n* everything, sum, total, aggregate, total amount, whole amount, whole,

entirety, utmost, comprehensiveness, universality.

E3 nothing, none. *adv* completely, entirely, wholly, fully, totally, utterly, altogether, wholesale. **all right** *adj* **1** SATISFACTORY, passable, unobjectionable, acceptable, allowable, adequate, fair, average, OK (*infml*). **2** *are you all right?*: well, healthy, unhurt, uninjured, unharmed, unimpaired, whole, sound, safe, secure.

E3 **1** unacceptable, inadequate. *adv* satisfactorily, well enough, passably, unobjectionably, acceptably, suitably, appropriately, adequately, reasonably, OK (*infml*).

E3 unsatisfactorily, unacceptably.

allay *v* alleviate, relieve, soothe, ease, smooth, calm, tranquillize, quiet, quell, pacify, mollify, soften, blunt, lessen, reduce, diminish, check, moderate.

E3 exacerbate, intensify.

allegation *n* accusation, charge, claim, profession, assertion, affirmation, declaration, statement, testimony, plea.

allege *v* assert, affirm, declare, state, attest, maintain, insist, hold, contend, claim, profess, plead.

alleged *adj* supposed, reputed, putative, inferred, so-called, professed, declared, stated, claimed, described, designated, doubtful, dubious, suspect, suspicious.

allegiance *n* loyalty, fidelity, faithfulness, constancy, duty, obligation, obedience, devotion, support, adherence, friendship.

E3 disloyalty, enmity.

allergic *adj* sensitive, hypersensitive, susceptible, affected, incompatible, averse, disinclined, opposed, hostile, antagonistic.

F3 tolerant.

alleviate v relieve, soothe, ease, palliate, mitigate, soften, cushion, dull, deaden, allay, abate, lessen, reduce, diminish, check, moderate, temper, subdue.

F3 aggravate.

alliance n confederation, federation, association, affiliation, coalition, league, bloc, cartel, conglomerate, consortium, syndicate, guild, union, partnership, marriage, agreement, compact, bond, pact, treaty, combination, connection.

F3 separation, divorce, estrangement, enmity, hostility.

allocate v assign, designate, budget, allow, earmark, set aside, allot, apportion, share out, distribute, dispense, mete.

allocation n allotment, lot, apportionment, measure, share, portion, stint, ration, quota, budget, allowance, grant.

allot v divide, ration, apportion, share out, distribute, dispense, mete, dole out, allocate, assign, designate, budget, allow, grant, earmark, set aside.

allotment n division, partition, allocation, apportionment, measure, percentage, lot, portion, share, stint, ration, quota, allowance, grant.

all-out adj complete, full, total, undivided, comprehensive, exhaustive, thorough, intensive, thoroughgoing, wholesale, vigorous, powerful, full-scale, no-holds-barred, maximum, utmost, unlimited, unrestrained, resolute, determined.

F3 perfunctory, half-hearted.

allow v 1 PERMIT, let, enable, authorize, sanction, approve, tolerate, put up with, endure, suffer. 2 ADMIT, confess, own, acknowledge, concede, grant. 3 *allow two hours for the journey*: allot, allocate, assign, apportion, afford, give, provide.

F3 1 forbid, prevent. 2 deny.

allow for take into account, make provision for, make allowances for, provide for, foresee, plan for, arrange for, bear in mind, keep in mind, consider, include.

F3 discount.

allowance n 1 ALLOTMENT, lot, amount, allocation, portion, share, ration, quota. 2 REBATE, reduction, deduction, discount, concession, subsidy, weighting. 3 PAYMENT, remittance, pocket money, grant, maintenance, stipend, pension, annuity.

alloy n blend, compound, composite, amalgam, combination, mixture, fusion, coalescence.

allure v lure, entice, seduce, lead on, tempt, coax, cajole, persuade, win over, disarm, charm, enchant, attract, interest, fascinate, captivate, entrance, beguile.

F3 repel.

n lure, enticement, seduction, temptation, appeal, attraction, magnetism, fascination, glamour, captivation, charm, enchantment.

allusion n mention, reference, citation, quotation, remark, observation, suggestion, hint, intimation, implication, insinuation.

ally n confederate, associate, leaguer, consort, partner, sidekick, colleague, co-worker, collaborator, helper,

helpmate, accomplice, accessory, friend.
E3 antagonist, enemy.
v confederate, affiliate, league, associate, collaborate, join forces, band together, team up, fraternize, side, join, connect, link, marry, unite, unify, amalgamate, combine.
E3 estrange, separate.

almighty *adj* **1** OMNIPOTENT, all-powerful, supreme, absolute, great, invincible. **2** ENORMOUS, severe, intense, overwhelming, overpowering, terrible, awful, desperate.
E3 impotent, weak.

almost *adv* nearly, well-nigh, practically, virtually, just about, as good as, all but, close to, not far from, approaching, nearing, not quite, about, approximately.

alone *adj* only, sole, single, unique, solitary, separate, detached, unconnected, isolated, apart, by oneself, by itself, on one's own, lonely, lonesome, deserted, abandoned, forsaken, forlorn, desolate, unaccompanied, unescorted, unattended, solo, single-handed, unaided, unassisted, mere.
E3 together, accompanied, escorted.

aloof *adj* distant, remote, offish, standoffish, haughty, supercilious, unapproachable, inaccessible, detached, forbidding, cool, chilly, cold, sympathetic, unresponsive, indifferent, uninterested, reserved, unforthcoming, unfriendly, unsociable, formal.
E3 sociable, friendly, concerned.

aloud *adv* out loud, audibly, intelligibly, clearly, plainly, distinctly, loudly, resoundingly,

sonorously, noisily, vociferously.
E3 silently.

alphabet

> Alphabets and writing systems include:
> Braille, Byzantine, cuneiform, Cyrillic, devanagari, finger-alphabet, futhork (or futhark), Greek, Gurmukhi, hieroglyphs, hiragana, ideograph, initial teaching alphabet (i.t.a.), International Phonetic Alphabet (IPA), kana, kanji, katakana, Kufic, Latin, linear A, linear B, logograph, nagari, Neskhi (or Naskhi), ogam (or ogham), pictograph, Roman, runic, syllabary.

also *adv* too, as well, and, plus, along with, including, as well as, additionally, in addition, besides, further, furthermore, moreover.

alter *v* change, vary, diversify, modify, qualify, shift, transpose, adjust, adapt, convert, turn, transmute, transform, reform, reshape, remodel, recast, revise, amend, emend.
E3 fix.

alteration *n* change, variation, variance, difference, diversification, shift, transposition, modification, adjustment, adaptation, conversion, transformation, transfiguration, metamorphosis, reformation, reshaping, remodelling, revision, amendment.
E3 fixity.

alternate *v* interchange, reciprocate, rotate, take turns, follow one another, replace each other, substitute, change, alter, vary, oscillate, fluctuate, intersperse.
adj alternating, every other, every second, interchanging, reciprocal, rotating, alternative.

alternative n option, choice, selection, preference, other, recourse, substitute, back-up.
adj substitute, second, another, other, different, unorthodox, unconventional, fringe, alternate.

altitude n height, elevation, loftiness, tallness, stature.
F3 depth.

altogether adv totally, completely, entirely, wholly, fully, utterly, absolutely, quite, perfectly, thoroughly, in all, all told, in toto, all in all, as a whole, on the whole, generally, in general.

altruistic adj unselfish, self-sacrificing, disinterested, public-spirited, philanthropic, charitable, humanitarian, benevolent, generous, considerate, humane.
F3 selfish.

always adv every time, consistently, invariably, without exception, unfailingly, regularly, repeatedly, continually, constantly, 24-7 (infml), perpetually, unceasingly, eternally, endlessly, evermore, forever, ever.
F3 never.

amalgamate v merge, blend, mingle, commingle, intermix, homogenize, incorporate, alloy, integrate, compound, fuse, coalesce, synthesize, combine, unite, unify, ally.
F3 separate.

amateur n non-professional, layman, ham (infml), dilettante, dabbler, enthusiast, fancier, buff (infml).
F3 professional.
adj non-professional, lay, unpaid, unqualified, untrained, amateurish, inexpert, unprofessional.
F3 professional.

amaze v surprise, startle, astonish, astound, stun, stupefy, daze, stagger, floor (infml), dumbfound, flabbergast (infml), shock, dismay, disconcert, confound, bewilder.

amazement n surprise, astonishment, shock, dismay, confusion, perplexity, bewilderment, admiration, wonderment, wonder, marvel.

ambassador n emissary, envoy, legate, diplomat, consul, plenipotentiary, deputy, representative, agent, minister, apostle.

ambiguity n double meaning, double entendre, equivocality, equivocation, enigma, puzzle, confusion, obscurity, unclearness, vagueness, woolliness, dubiousness, doubt, doubtfulness, uncertainty.
F3 clarity.

ambiguous adj double-meaning, equivocal, double-edged, back-handed, cryptic, enigmatic, puzzling, confusing, obscure, unclear, vague, indefinite, woolly, confused, dubious, doubtful, uncertain, inconclusive, indeterminate.
F3 clear, definite.

ambition n 1 ASPIRATION, aim, goal, target, objective, intent, purpose, design, object, ideal, dream, hope, wish, desire, yearning, longing, hankering, craving, hunger. 2 a woman of ambition: enterprise, drive, push, thrust, striving, eagerness, commitment, zeal.
F3 2 apathy, diffidence.

ambitious adj 1 ASPIRING, hopeful, desirous, intent, purposeful, pushy, bold, assertive, go-ahead, enterprising, driving, energetic,

enthusiastic, eager, keen, striving, industrious, zealous. **2** FORMIDABLE, hard, difficult, arduous, strenuous, demanding, challenging, grandiose, impressive, grandiose, elaborate.
F3 1 lazy, unassuming. **2** modest, uninspiring.

ambivalent adj contradictory, conflicting, clashing, warring, opposed, inconsistent, mixed, confused, fluctuating, vacillating, wavering, hesitant, irresolute, undecided, unresolved, unsettled, uncertain, unsure, doubtful, debatable, inconclusive.

amble v walk, saunter, toddle (infml), stroll, promenade, wander, drift, meander, ramble.
F3 stride, march.

ambush n waylaying, surprise attack, trap, snare, cover, hiding-place.
v lie in wait, waylay, surprise, trap, ensnare.

amenable adj accommodating, flexible, open, agreeable, persuadable, compliant, tractable, submissive, responsive, susceptible, liable, responsible.
F3 intractable.

amend v revise, correct, rectify, emend, fix, repair, mend, remedy, redress, reform, change, alter, adjust, modify, qualify, enhance, improve, ameliorate, better.
F3 impair, worsen.

amendment n revision, correction, corrigendum, rectification, emendation, repair, remedy, reform, change, alteration, adjustment, modification, qualification, clarification, addendum, addition, adjunct, improvement.
F3 impairment, deterioration.

amends n atonement, expiation, requital, satisfaction, recompense, compensation, indemnification, indemnity, reparation, redress, restoration, restitution.

amiable adj affable, friendly, approachable, genial, cheerful, good-tempered, good-natured, kind, obliging, charming, engaging, likable, pleasant, agreeable, congenial, companionable, sociable.
F3 unfriendly, curt, hostile.

amid prep amidst, midst, in the midst of, in the thick of, among, amongst, in the middle of, surrounded by.

amnesty n pardon, forgiveness, absolution, mercy, lenience, indulgence, reprieve, remission, dispensation, immunity, oblivion.

among prep amongst, between, in the middle of, surrounded by, amid, amidst, midst, in the midst of, in the thick of, with, together with.

amount n quantity, number, sum, total, sum total, whole, entirety, aggregate, lot, quota, supply, volume, mass, bulk, measure, magnitude, extent, expanse.
amount to add up to, total, aggregate, come to, make, equal, mean, be tantamount to, be equivalent to, approximate to, become, grow.

amphibian

Amphibians include:
frog, bullfrog, tree frog, toad, horned toad, midwife toad, natterjack, newt, eft, salamander, conger eel, axolotl.

ample adj large, big, extensive, expansive, broad, wide, full, voluminous, roomy, spacious, commodious, great, considerable, substantial, handsome, generous,

bountiful, munificent, liberal, lavish, copious, abundant, plentiful, plenty, unrestricted, profuse, rich.
F3 insufficient, inadequate, meagre.

amplify v enlarge, magnify, expand, dilate, fill out, bulk out, add to, supplement, augment, increase, extend, lengthen, widen, broaden, develop, elaborate, enhance, boost, intensify, strengthen, deepen, heighten, raise.
F3 reduce, decrease, abridge.

amputate v cut off, remove, sever, dissever, separate, dock, lop, curtail, truncate.

amuse v entertain, divert, regale, make laugh, tickle (infml), crease (infml), slay (infml), cheer (up), gladden, enliven, please, charm, delight, enthral, engross, absorb, interest, occupy, recreate, relax.
F3 bore, displease.

amusement n entertainment, diversion, distraction, fun, enjoyment, pleasure, delight, merriment, mirth, hilarity, laughter, joke, prank, game, sport, recreation, hobby, pastime, interest.
F3 boredom, monotony.

amusing adj funny, humorous, hilarious, comical, laughable, ludicrous, droll, witty, facetious, jocular, jolly, enjoyable, pleasant, charming, delightful, entertaining, interesting.
F3 dull, boring.

anaemic adj bloodless, ashen, chalky, livid, pasty, pallid, sallow, whey-faced, pale, wan, colourless, insipid, weak, feeble, ineffectual, enervated, frail, infirm, sickly.
F3 ruddy, sanguine, full-blooded.

anaesthetize v desensitize, numb, deaden, dull, drug, dope, stupefy.

analogy n comparison, simile, metaphor, likeness, resemblance, similarity, parallel, correspondence, equivalence, relation, correlation, agreement.

analyse v break down, separate, divide, take apart, dissect, anatomize, reduce, resolve, sift, investigate, study, examine, scrutinize, review, interpret, test, judge, evaluate, estimate, consider.

analysis n breakdown, separation, division, dissection, reduction, resolution, sifting, investigation, enquiry, study, examination, scrutiny, review, exposition, explication, explanation, interpretation, test, judgement, opinion, evaluation, estimation, reasoning.
F3 synthesis.

analytic adj analytical, dissecting, detailed, in-depth, searching, critical, questioning, enquiring, inquisitive, investigative, diagnostic, systematic, methodical, logical, rational, interpretative, explanatory, expository, studious.

anarchic adj lawless, ungoverned, anarchistic, libertarian, nihilist, revolutionary, rebellious, mutinous, riotous, chaotic, disordered, confused, disorganized.
F3 submissive, orderly.

anarchist n revolutionary, rebel, insurgent, libertarian, nihilist, terrorist.

anarchy n lawlessness, unrule, misrule, anarchism, revolution, rebellion, insurrection, mutiny, riot, pandemonium, chaos, disorder, confusion.
F3 rule, control, order.

anathema n aversion, abhorrence, abomination, object of loathing, bête noire, bugbear, bane, curse, proscription, taboo.

anatomy

Anatomy terms include:
aural, cardiac, cerebral, dental, dorsal, duodenal, gastric, gingival, hepatic, intercostal, jugular, lachrymal, lumbar, membral, nasal, neural, ocular, optical, pectoral, pedal, pulmonary, renal. see also **body; bone; brain; ear; eye; heart**.

ancestor n forebear, forefather, progenitor, predecessor, forerunner, precursor, antecedent.
Ⓔ descendant.

ancestral adj familial, parental, genealogical, lineal, hereditary, genetic.

ancestry n ancestors, forebears, forefathers, progenitors, parentage, family, lineage, line, descent, blood, race, stock, roots, pedigree, genealogy, extraction, derivation, origin, heritage, heredity.

anchor v moor, berth, tie up, make fast, fasten, attach, affix, fix.

ancient adj **1** OLD, aged, time-worn, age-old, antique, antediluvian, prehistoric, fossilized, primeval, immemorial. **2** OLD-FASHIONED, out-of-date, antiquated, archaic, obsolete, bygone, early, original.
Ⓔ 1 recent, contemporary. **2** modern, up-to-date.

anecdote n story, tale, yarn, sketch, reminiscence.

angel n **1** angel of God: archangel, cherub, seraph, divine messenger, principality. **2** DARLING, treasure, saint, paragon, ideal.
Ⓔ 1 devil, fiend.

The nine orders of angels are:
seraph, cherub, throne, domination/dominion, virtue, power, principality, archangel, angel.

angelic adj cherubic, seraphic, celestial, heavenly, divine, holy, pious, saintly, pure, innocent, unworldly, virtuous, lovely, beautiful, adorable.
Ⓔ devilish, fiendish.

anger n annoyance, irritation, antagonism, displeasure, irritability, temper, pique, vexation, ire, rage, fury, wrath, exasperation, outrage, indignation, gall, bitterness, rancour, resentment.
Ⓔ forgiveness, forbearance.
v annoy, irritate, aggravate (infml), wind up (infml), piss off (sl), vex, irk, rile, miff (infml), needle, nettle, bother, ruffle, provoke, antagonize, offend, affront, gall, madden, enrage, incense, infuriate, exasperate, outrage.
Ⓔ please, appease, calm.

angle n **1** CORNER, nook, bend, flexure, hook, crook, elbow, knee, crotch, edge, point. **2** ASPECT, outlook, facet, side, approach, direction, position, standpoint, viewpoint, point of view, slant, perspective.

angry adj annoyed, cross, irritated, aggravated (infml), displeased, uptight (infml), irate, mad (infml), enraged, incensed, infuriated, furious, raging, passionate, heated, hot, exasperated, outraged, indignant, bitter, resentful.
Ⓔ content, happy, calm.

animal n creature, mammal, beast, brute, barbarian, savage, monster, cur, pig, swine.

animate

Animals include:
cat, dog, mouse, rat, rabbit, fox, horse, pig, cow, bull, goat, sheep, monkey, whale, lion, tiger, wolf, deer, camel, bear, giraffe, hippopotamus, rhinoceros, elephant. *see also* **amphibian; bird; cat; cattle; dog; fish; insect; mammal; reptile.**

adj bestial, brutish, inhuman, savage, wild, instinctive, bodily, physical, carnal, fleshly, sensual.

animate *adj* alive, living, live, breathing, conscious.

E3 inanimate.

animated *adj* lively, spirited, buoyant, vibrant, ebullient, vivacious, alive, vital, quick, brisk, vigorous, energetic, active, passionate, impassioned, vehement, ardent, fervent, glowing, radiant, excited, enthusiastic, eager.

E3 lethargic, sluggish, inert.

animosity *n* ill feeling, ill-will, acrimony, bitterness, rancour, resentment, spite, malice, malignity, malevolence, hate, hatred, loathing, antagonism, hostility, enmity, feud.

E3 goodwill.

annex *v* **1** ADD, append, affix, attach, fasten, adjoin, join, connect, unite, incorporate. **2** ACQUIRE, appropriate, seize, usurp, occupy, conquer, take over.

annexe *n* wing, extension, attachment, addition, supplement, expansion.

annihilate *v* eliminate, eradicate, obliterate, erase, wipe out, liquidate (*infml*), murder, assassinate, exterminate, extinguish, raze, destroy, abolish.

anniversary

Names of wedding anniversaries include:
1st paper, 2nd cotton, 3rd leather, 4th flowers/fruit, 5th wood, 6th iron/sugar, 7th copper/wool, 8th bronze/pottery, 9th pottery/willow, 10th tin/aluminium, 11th steel, 12th silk/linen, 13th lace, 14th ivory, 15th crystal, 20th china, 25th silver, 30th pearl, 35th coral, 40th ruby, 45th sapphire, 50th gold, 55th emerald, 60th diamond, 70th platinum.

annotation *n* note, footnote, gloss, comment, commentary, exegesis, explanation, elucidation.

announce *v* declare, proclaim, report, state, reveal, disclose, divulge, make known, notify, intimate, promulgate, propound, publish, broadcast, advertise, publicize, blazon.

E3 suppress.

announcement *n* declaration, proclamation, report, statement, communiqué, dispatch, bulletin, notification, intimation, revelation, disclosure, divulgence, publication, broadcast, advertisement.

announcer *n* broadcaster, newscaster, newsreader, commentator, compère, master of ceremonies, MC, town crier, herald, messenger.

annoy *v* irritate, rile, aggravate (*infml*), displease, anger, vex, irk, madden, exasperate, tease, provoke, ruffle, trouble, disturb, bother, pester, plague, harass, molest.

E3 please, gratify, comfort.

annoyance *n* **1** NUISANCE, pest, disturbance, bother, trouble, bore, bind (*sl*), pain (*infml*), headache (*infml*), tease, provocation. **2** *express one's annoyance*: irritation, aggravation (*infml*), displeasure, anger, vexation, exasperation, harassment.

F3 2 pleasure.

annoyed *adj* irritated, cross, displeased, angry, vexed, piqued, exasperated, provoked, harassed.

F3 pleased.

annoying *adj* irritating, aggravating (*infml*), vexatious, irksome, troublesome, bothersome, tiresome, trying, maddening, exasperating, galling, offensive, teasing, provoking, harassing.

F3 pleasing, welcome.

annul *v* nullify, invalidate, void, rescind, abrogate, suspend, cancel, abolish, quash, repeal, revoke, countermand, negate, retract, recall, reverse.

F3 enact, restore.

anoint *v* **1** OIL, grease, lubricate, embrocate, rub, smear, daub. **2** BLESS, consecrate, sanctify, dedicate.

anomalous *adj* abnormal, atypical, exceptional, irregular, inconsistent, incongruous, deviant, freakish, eccentric, peculiar, odd, unusual, singular, rare.

F3 normal, regular, ordinary.

anomaly *n* abnormality, exception, irregularity, inconsistency, incongruity, aberration, deviation, divergence, departure, freak, misfit, eccentricity, peculiarity, oddity, rarity.

anonymous *adj* unnamed, nameless, unsigned, unacknowledged, unspecified, unidentified, unknown, incognito, faceless, impersonal, nondescript, unexceptional.

F3 named, signed, identifiable, distinctive.

answer *n* **1** REPLY, acknowledgement, response, reaction, rejoinder, retort, riposte, comeback, retaliation, rebuttal, vindication, defence, plea. **2** SOLUTION, explanation.
v **1** REPLY, acknowledge, respond, react, retort, retaliate, refute, solve. **2** *answer one's needs*: fulfil, fill, meet, satisfy, match up to, correspond, correlate, conform, agree, fit, suit, serve, pass.
answer back talk back, retort, riposte, retaliate, contradict, disagree, argue, dispute, rebut.

answerable *adj* liable, responsible, accountable, chargeable, blameworthy, to blame.

antagonism *n* hostility, opposition, rivalry, antipathy, ill feeling, ill-will, animosity, friction, discord, dissension, contention, conflict.

F3 rapport, sympathy, agreement.

antagonist *n* opponent, adversary, enemy, foe, rival, competitor, contestant, contender.

F3 ally, supporter.

antagonistic *adj* conflicting, opposed, adverse, at variance, incompatible, hostile, belligerent, contentious, unfriendly, ill-disposed, averse.

F3 sympathetic, friendly.

antagonize *v* alienate, estrange, disaffect, repel, embitter, offend, insult, provoke, annoy, irritate, anger, incense.

F3 disarm.

anthem *n* hymn, song, chorale, psalm, canticle, chant.

anthology n selection, collection, compilation, compendium, digest, treasury, miscellany.

anticipate v 1 FORESTALL, pre-empt, intercept, prevent, obviate, preclude. 2 EXPECT, foresee, predict, forecast, look for, await, look forward to, hope for, bank on, count upon.

anticlimax n bathos, comedown, let-down, disappointment, fiasco.

antics n foolery, tomfoolery, silliness, buffoonery, clowning, frolics, capers, skylarking, playfulness, mischief, tricks, monkey-tricks, pranks, stunts, doings.

antidote n remedy, cure, counter-agent, antitoxin, neutralizer, countermeasure, corrective.

antipathy n aversion, dislike, hate, hatred, loathing, abhorrence, distaste, disgust, repulsion, antagonism, animosity, ill-will, bad blood, enmity, hostility, opposition, incompatibility. ☒ sympathy, affection, rapport.

antique adj antiquarian, ancient, old, veteran, vintage, quaint, antiquated, old-fashioned, outdated, archaic, obsolete.
n antiquity, relic, bygone, period piece, heirloom, curio, museum piece, curiosity, rarity.

antiquity n ancient times, time immemorial, distant past, olden days, age, old age, oldness, agedness. ☒ modernity, novelty.

antiseptic adj disinfectant, medicated, aseptic, germ-free, clean, pure, unpolluted, uncontaminated, sterile, sterilized, sanitized, sanitary, hygienic.
n disinfectant, germicide, bactericide, purifier, cleanser.

antisocial adj asocial, unacceptable, disruptive, disorderly, rebellious, belligerent, antagonistic, hostile, unfriendly, unsociable, uncommunicative, reserved, retiring, withdrawn, alienated, unapproachable. ☒ sociable, gregarious.

anxiety n worry, concern, care, distress, nervousness, apprehension, dread, foreboding, misgiving, uneasiness, restlessness, fretfulness, impatience, suspense, tension, stress. ☒ calm, composure, serenity.

anxious adj worried, concerned, nervous, apprehensive, afraid, fearful, uneasy, restless, fretful, impatient, in suspense, on tenterhooks, tense, taut, distressed, disturbed, troubled, tormented, tortured. ☒ calm, composed.

apart adv 1 SEPARATELY, independently, individually, singly, alone, on one's own, by oneself, privately, aside, to one side, away, afar, distant, aloof, excluded, isolated, cut off, separated, divorced, separate, distinct. 2 tear apart: to pieces, to bits, into parts, in pieces, in bits, piecemeal. ☒ 1 connected. 2 together.

apathetic adj uninterested, uninvolved, indifferent, cool, unemotional, emotionless, impassive, unmoved, unconcerned, cold, unfeeling, numb, unresponsive, passive, listless, unambitious. ☒ enthusiastic, involved, concerned, feeling, responsive.

apathy n uninterestedness, indifference, coolness, impassivity, unconcern, coldness, insensibility, passivity, listlessness, lethargy, sluggishness, torpor, inertia. ☒ enthusiasm, interest, concern.

ape v copy, imitate, echo, mirror, parrot, mimic, take off, caricature, parody, mock, counterfeit, affect. n monkey.

aplomb n composure, calmness, equanimity, poise, balance, coolness, confidence, assurance, self-assurance, audacity. ☒ discomposure.

apocryphal adj unauthenticated, unverified, unsubstantiated, unsupported, questionable, spurious, equivocal, doubtful, dubious, fabricated, concocted, fictitious, imaginary, legendary, mythical. ☒ authentic, true.

apologetic adj sorry, repentant, penitent, contrite, remorseful, conscience-stricken, regretful, rueful. ☒ unrepentant, impenitent, defiant.

apology n acknowledgement, confession, excuse, explanation, justification, vindication, defence, plea. ☒ defiance.

appal v horrify, shock, outrage, disgust, dismay, disconcert, daunt, intimidate, unnerve, alarm, scare, frighten, terrify. ☒ reassure, encourage.

appalling adj horrifying, horrific, harrowing, shocking, outrageous, atrocious, disgusting, awful, dreadful, frightful, terrible, dire, grim, hideous, ghastly, horrible, horrid, loathsome, daunting, intimidating, unnerving, alarming, frightening, terrifying. ☒ reassuring, encouraging.

apparatus n machine, appliance, gadget, device, contraption, equipment, gear, tackle, outfit, tools, implements, utensils, materials, machinery, system, mechanism, means.

apparent adj seeming, outward, visible, evident, noticeable, perceptible, plain, clear, distinct, marked, unmistakable, obvious, manifest, patent, open, declared. ☒ hidden, obscure.

apparently adv seemingly, ostensibly, outwardly, superficially, plainly, clearly, obviously, manifestly, patently.

apparition n ghost, spectre, phantom, spirit, chimera, vision, manifestation, materialization, presence.

appeal n **1** REQUEST, application, petition, suit, solicitation, plea, entreaty, supplication, prayer, invocation. **2** ATTRACTION, allure, interest, fascination, enchantment, charm, attractiveness, winsomeness, beauty, charisma, magnetism. v **1** appeal for help: ask, request, call, apply, address, petition, sue, solicit, plead, beg, beseech, implore, entreat, supplicate, pray, invoke, call upon. **2** ATTRACT, draw, allure, lure, tempt, entice, invite, interest, engage, fascinate, charm, please.

appear v **1** ARRIVE, enter, turn up, attend, materialize, develop, show (up), come into sight, come into view, loom, rise, surface, arise, occur, crop up, come to light, come out, emerge, issue, be published. **2** SEEM, look, turn out. **3** appear in a show: act, perform, play, take part. ☒ **1** disappear, vanish.

appearance n **1** APPEARING, arrival, advent, coming, rise, emergence, début, introduction. **2** LOOK, expression, face, aspect, air, bearing, demeanour, manner, looks, figure,

form, semblance, show, front, guise, illusion, impression, image.
F3 1 disappearance.

appendix n addition, appendage, adjunct, addendum, supplement, epilogue, codicil, postscript, rider.

appetite n hunger, stomach, relish, zest, taste, propensity, inclination, liking, desire, longing, yearning, craving, eagerness, passion, zeal.
F3 distaste.

appetizing adj mouthwatering, tempting, inviting, appealing, palatable, tasty, delicious, scrumptious (infml), succulent, piquant, savoury.
F3 disgusting, distasteful.

applaud v clap, cheer, acclaim, compliment, congratulate, approve, commend, praise, laud, eulogize, extol.
F3 criticize, censure.

applause n ovation, clapping, cheering, cheers, acclaim, acclamation, accolade, congratulation, approval, commendation, praise.
F3 criticism, censure.

appliance n machine, device, contrivance, contraption, gadget, tool, implement, instrument, apparatus, mechanism.

applicable adj relevant, pertinent, apposite, apt, appropriate, fitting, suited, useful, suitable, fit, proper, valid, legitimate.
F3 inapplicable, inappropriate.

applicant n candidate, interviewee, contestant, competitor, aspirant, suitor, petitioner, inquirer.

application n 1 REQUEST, appeal, petition, suit, claim, inquiry.
2 RELEVANCE, pertinence, function,

purpose, use, value. 3 DILIGENCE, industry, assiduity, effort, commitment, dedication, perseverance, keenness, attentiveness.

apply v 1 REQUEST, ask for, requisition, put in for, appeal, petition, solicit, sue, claim, inquire. 2 apply oneself to a task: address, buckle down, settle down, commit, devote, dedicate, give, direct, concentrate, study, persevere. 3 USE, exercise, utilize, employ, bring into play, engage, harness, ply, wield, administer, execute, implement, assign, direct, bring to bear, practise, resort to. 4 REFER, relate, be relevant, pertain, fit, suit. 5 apply ointment: put on, spread on, lay on, cover with, paint, anoint, smear, rub.

appoint v 1 NAME, nominate, elect, install, choose, select, engage, employ, take on, commission, delegate, assign, allot, designate, command, direct, charge, detail. 2 DECIDE, determine, arrange, settle, fix, set, establish, ordain, decree, destine.
F3 1 reject, dismiss, discharge.

appointment n 1 ARRANGEMENT, engagement, date, meeting, rendezvous, interview, consultation. 2 JOB, position, situation, post, office, place. 3 NAMING, nomination, election, choosing, choice, selection, commissioning, delegation.

appraisal n valuation, rating, survey, inspection, review, examination, once-over (infml), evaluation, assessment, estimate, estimation, judgement, reckoning, opinion, appreciation.

appreciate v 1 ENJOY, relish, savour, prize, treasure, value, cherish, admire, respect, regard, esteem, like, welcome, take kindly to. **2** *appreciate in value*: grow, increase, rise, mount, inflate, gain, strengthen, improve, enhance. **3** UNDERSTAND, comprehend, perceive, realize, recognize, acknowledge, sympathize with, know.

F3 1 despise. **2** depreciate. **3** overlook.

appreciation *n* **1** ENJOYMENT, relish, admiration, respect, regard, esteem, gratitude, gratefulness, thankfulness, indebtedness, obligation, liking, sensitivity, responsiveness, valuation, assessment, estimation, judgement. **2** GROWTH, increase, rise, inflation, gain, improvement, enhancement. **3** UNDERSTANDING, comprehension, perception, awareness, realization, recognition, acknowledgement, sympathy, knowledge.

F3 1 ingratitude. **2** depreciation.

appreciative *adj* **1** GRATEFUL, thankful, obliged, indebted, pleased. **2** ADMIRING, encouraging, enthusiastic, respectful, sensitive, responsive, perceptive, knowledgeable, conscious, mindful.

F3 1 ungrateful.

apprehension *n* dread, foreboding, misgiving, qualm, uneasiness, anxiety, worry, concern, disquiet, alarm, fear, doubt, suspicion, mistrust.

apprehensive *adj* nervous, anxious, worried, concerned, uneasy, doubtful, suspicious, mistrustful, distrustful, alarmed, afraid.

F3 assured, confident.

apprentice *n* trainee, probationer, student, pupil, learner, novice, beginner, starter, recruit, newcomer.

F3 expert.

approach *v* **1** ADVANCE, move towards, draw near, near, gain on, catch up, reach, meet. **2** APPLY TO, appeal to, sound out. **3** BEGIN, commence, set about, undertake, introduce, mention. **4** RESEMBLE, be like, compare with, approximate, come close.

n **1** *the approach of winter*: advance, coming, advent, arrival. **2** ACCESS, road, avenue, way, passage, entrance, doorway, threshold. **3** APPLICATION, appeal, overture, proposition, proposal. **4** ATTITUDE, manner, style, technique, procedure, method, means.

appropriate *adj* applicable, relevant, pertinent, to the point, well-chosen, apt, fitting, meet (*fml*), suitable, fit, befitting, becoming, proper, right, correct, spot-on (*infml*), well-timed, timely, seasonable, opportune.

F3 inappropriate, irrelevant, unsuitable.

v **1** SEIZE, take, expropriate, commandeer, requisition, confiscate, impound, assume, usurp. **2** STEAL, pocket, filch, pilfer, purloin, embezzle, misappropriate.

approval *n* **1** ADMIRATION, esteem, regard, respect, good opinion, liking, appreciation, approbation, favour, recommendation, praise, commendation, acclaim, acclamation, honour, applause. **2** AGREEMENT, concurrence, assent, consent, permission, leave, sanction, authorization, licence, mandate, go-ahead, green light (*infml*), blessing, OK (*infml*), certification, ratification, validation, confirmation, support.

F3 1 disapproval, condemnation.

approve *v* 1 ADMIRE, esteem, regard, like, appreciate, favour, recommend, praise, commend, acclaim, applaud. 2 *approve a proposal*: agree to, assent to, consent to, accede to, allow, permit, pass, sanction, authorize, mandate, bless, countenance, OK (*infml*), ratify, rubber-stamp (*infml*), validate, endorse, support, uphold, second, back, accept, adopt, confirm. **F3** 1 disapprove, condemn.

approximate *adj* estimated, guessed, rough, inexact, loose, close, near, like, similar, relative. **F3** exact. *v* approach, border on, verge on, be tantamount to, resemble.

approximately *adv* roughly, around, about, circa, more or less, loosely, approaching, close to, nearly, just about.

apt *adj* 1 RELEVANT, applicable, apposite, appropriate, fitting, suitable, fit, seemly, proper, correct, accurate, spot-on (*infml*), timely, seasonable. 2 CLEVER, gifted, talented, skilful, expert, intelligent, quick, sharp. 3 LIABLE, prone, given, disposed, likely, ready. **F3** 1 inapt. 2 stupid.

aptitude *n* ability, capability, capacity, faculty, gift, talent, flair, facility, proficiency, cleverness, intelligence, quickness, bent, inclination, leaning, disposition, tendency. **F3** inaptitude.

arbitrary *adj* 1 RANDOM, chance, capricious, inconsistent, discretionary, subjective, instinctive, unreasoned, illogical, irrational, unreasonable. 2 DESPOTIC, tyrannical, dictatorial, autocratic, absolute,

imperious, magisterial, domineering, overbearing, high-handed, dogmatic. **F3** 1 reasoned, rational, circumspect.

arbitrate *v* judge, adjudicate, referee, umpire, mediate, settle, decide, determine.

arbitration *n* judgement, adjudication, intervention, mediation, negotiation, settlement, decision, determination.

arbitrator *n* judge, adjudicator, arbiter, referee, umpire, moderator, mediator, negotiator, intermediary, go-between.

arch *n* archway, bridge, span, dome, vault, concave, bend, curve, curvature, bow, arc, semicircle. *v* bend, curve, bow, arc, vault, camber.

archaic *adj* antiquated, old-fashioned, outmoded, old hat (*infml*), passé, outdated, out-of-date, obsolete, old, ancient, antique, quaint, primitive. **F3** modern, recent.

archetype *n* pattern, model, standard, form, type, prototype, original, precursor, classic, paradigm, ideal.

architect *n* designer, planner, master builder, prime mover, originator, founder, instigator, creator, author, inventor, engineer, maker, constructor, shaper.

architecture

Architectural and building terms include:
alcove, annexe, architrave, baluster, barge-board, baroque, bas-relief, capstone, casement window, classical, copestone (or coping-stone), Corinthian, cornerstone, cornice, coving, dado, dogtooth, dome, Doric, dormer, double-glazing, dry-

stone, duplex, Early English, eaves, Edwardian, elevation, Elizabethan, façade, fanlight, fascia, festoon, fillet, finial, Flemish bond, fluting, French window, frieze, frontispiece, gable, gargoyle, Georgian, Gothic, groin, ground plan, half-timbered, Ionic, jamb, lintel, mullion, Norman, pagoda, pantile, parapet, pinnacle, plinth, Queen Anne, rafters, Regency, reveal, ridge, rococo, Romanesque, roof, rotunda, roughcast, scroll, soffit, stucco, terrazzo, Tudor, Tuscan, wainscot.

archives *n* records, annals, chronicles, memorials, papers, documents, deeds, ledgers, registers, roll.

ardent *adj* fervent, fiery, warm, passionate, impassioned, fierce, vehement, intense, spirited, enthusiastic, eager, keen, dedicated, devoted, zealous.
F3 apathetic, unenthusiastic.

arduous *adj* hard, difficult, tough, rigorous, severe, harsh, formidable, strenuous, tiring, taxing, fatiguing, exhausting, backbreaking, punishing, gruelling, uphill, laborious, onerous.
F3 easy.

area *n* locality, neighbourhood, environment, environs, patch, terrain, district, region, zone, sector, department, province, domain, realm, territory, sphere, field, range, scope, compass, size, extent, expanse, width, breadth, stretch, tract, part, portion, section.

argue *v* 1 QUARREL, squabble, bicker, row, wrangle, haggle, remonstrate, join issue, fight, feud, fall out, disagree, dispute, question, debate, discuss. 2 REASON, assert, contend,

hold, maintain, claim, plead, exhibit, display, show, manifest, demonstrate, indicate, denote, prove, evidence, suggest, imply.

argument *n* 1 QUARREL, squabble, row, wrangle, controversy, debate, discussion, dispute, disagreement, clash, conflict, fight, feud. 2 REASONING, reason, logic, assertion, contention, claim, demonstration, defence, case, synopsis, summary, theme.

argumentative *adj* quarrelsome, contentious, polemical, opinionated, belligerent, perverse, contrary.
F3 complaisant.

arid *adj* 1 *arid landscape*: dry, parched, waterless, desiccated, torrid, barren, infertile, unproductive, desert, waste. 2 DULL, uninteresting, boring, monotonous, tedious, dry, sterile, dreary, colourless, lifeless, spiritless, uninspired.
F3 1 fertile. 2 lively.

arise *v* 1 ORIGINATE, begin, start, commence, derive, stem, spring, proceed, flow, emerge, issue, appear, come to light, crop up, occur, happen, result, ensue, follow. 2 RISE, get up, stand up, go up, ascend, climb, mount, lift, soar, tower.

aristocracy *n* upper class, gentry, nobility, peerage, ruling class, gentility, élite.
F3 common people.

aristocrat *n* noble, patrician, nobleman, noblewoman, peer, peeress, lord, lady.
F3 commoner.

aristocratic *adj* upper-class, highborn, well-born, noble, patrician, blue-blooded, titled, lordly, courtly, gentle, thoroughbred, élite.
F3 plebeian, vulgar.

arm[1] n **1** with arms folded: limb, upper limb, appendage. **2** BRANCH, projection, extension, offshoot, section, division, detachment, department.

arm[2] v provide, supply, furnish, issue, equip, rig, outfit, ammunition, prime, prepare, forearm, gird, steel, brace, reinforce, strengthen, fortify, protect.

armed services

Units in the armed services include:
task-force, militia, garrison; *air force*: wing, squadron, flight; *army*: patrol, troop, corps, platoon, squad, battery, company, brigade, battalion, regiment; *marines*: Royal Marines, commandos; *navy*: fleet, flotilla, squadron, convoy.

Ranks in the armed services include:
air force: aircraftman, aircraftwoman, corporal, sergeant, warrant officer, pilot officer, flying officer, flight lieutenant, squadron-leader, wing commander, group-captain, air-commodore, air-vice-marshal, air-marshal, air-chief-marshal, marshal of the Royal Air Force; *army*: private, lance-corporal, corporal, sergeant, warrant officer, lieutenant, captain, major, lieutenant-colonel, colonel, brigadier, major-general, lieutenant-general, general, field marshal; *navy*: able seaman, rating, petty officer, chief petty officer, sublieutenant, lieutenant, lieutenant-commander, commander, captain, commodore, rear admiral, vice-admiral, admiral, admiral of the fleet. see also **soldier**.

armoured adj armour-plated, steel-plated, iron-clad, reinforced, protected, bullet-proof, bomb-proof.

armoury n arsenal, ordnance depot, ammunition dump, magazine, depot, repository, stock, stockpile.

arms n **1** WEAPONS, weaponry, firearms, guns, artillery, instruments of war, armaments, ordnance, munitions, ammunition. **2** COAT-OF-ARMS, armorial bearings, insignia, heraldic device, escutcheon, shield, crest, heraldry, blazonry.

army n armed force, military, militia, land forces, soldiers, troops, legions, cohorts, multitude, throng, host, horde.

aroma n smell, odour, scent, perfume, fragrance, bouquet, savour.

aromatic adj perfumed, fragrant, sweet-smelling, balmy, redolent, savoury, spicy, pungent.

around prep **1** SURROUNDING, round, encircling, encompassing, enclosing, on all sides of, on every side of. **2** around a dozen: approximate, roughly, about, circa, more or less. adv **1** EVERYWHERE, all over, in all directions, on all sides, about, here and there, to and fro. **2** CLOSE, close by, near, nearby, at hand.

arouse v rouse, startle, wake up, waken, awaken, instigate, summon up, call forth, spark, kindle, inflame, whet, sharpen, quicken, animate, excite, prompt, provoke, stimulate, turn on (sl), galvanize, goad, spur, incite, agitate, stir up, whip up.
F3 calm, lull, quieten.

arrange v **1** ORDER, tidy, range, array, marshal, dispose, distribute, position, set out, lay out, align, group, class,

classify, categorize, sort (out), sift, file, systematize, methodize, regulate, adjust. **2** ORGANIZE, co-ordinate, prepare, fix, plan, project, design, devise, contrive, determine, settle. **3** *arrange music*: adapt, set, score, orchestrate, instrument, harmonize.
F3 1 untidy, disorganize, muddle.

arrangement n **1** ORDER, array, display, disposition, layout, line-up, grouping, classification, structure, system, method, set-up, organization, preparation, planning, plan, scheme, design, schedule. **2** AGREEMENT, settlement, contract, terms, compromise. **3** ADAPTATION, version, interpretation, setting, score, orchestration, instrumentation, harmonization.

array n arrangement, display, show, exhibition, exposition, assortment, collection, assemblage, muster, order, formation, line-up, parade.
v **1** ARRANGE, order, range, dispose, group, line up, align, draw up, marshal, assemble, muster, parade, display, show, exhibit. **2** CLOTHE, dress, robe, deck, adorn, decorate.

arrest v **1** *arrest a criminal*: capture, catch, seize, nick (*infml*), run in, apprehend, detain. **2** STOP, stem, check, restrain, inhibit, halt, interrupt, stall, delay, slow, retard, block, obstruct, impede, hinder.

arrival n appearance, entrance, advent, coming, approach, occurrence.
F3 departure.

arrive v reach, get to, appear, materialize, turn up, show up (*infml*), roll up (*infml*), enter, come, occur, happen.
F3 depart, leave.

arrogant adj haughty, supercilious, disdainful, scornful, contemptuous, superior, condescending, patronizing, high and mighty, lordly, overbearing, high-handed, imperious, self-important, presumptuous, assuming, insolent, proud, conceited, boastful.
F3 humble, unassuming, bashful.

art n **1** FINE ART, painting, sculpture, drawing, artwork, craft, artistry, draughtsmanship, craftsmanship. **2** SKILL, knack, technique, method, aptitude, facility, dexterity, finesse, ingenuity, mastery, expertise, profession, trade. **3** ARTFULNESS, cunning, craftiness, slyness, guile, deceit, trickery, astuteness, shrewdness.

Schools of art include:
abstract, action painting, aestheticism, art deco, art nouveau, Barbizon, baroque, classicism, conceptual art, constructivism, cubism, Dadaism, expressionism, Fauvism, Florentine, folk-art, futurism, Gothic, impressionism, Mannerism, minimal art, Modernism, the Nabis, naturalism, neoclassicism, neoexpressionism, Neo-Impressionism, Neo-Plasticism, op art, plastic art, pop art, Post-Impressionism, post-modernism, Pre-Raphaelitism, realism, Renaissance, rococo, Romanesque, romanticism, Suprematism, surrealism, symbolism, Venetian, vorticism.

Arts and crafts include:
painting, oil painting, watercolour, fresco, portraiture; architecture, drawing, sketching, caricature, animation, illustration; graphics, film, video, digital design; sculpture,

modelling, woodcarving, wood-craft, marquetry, metalwork, enamelling, cloisonné, engraving, etching, pottery, ceramics, mosaic, jewellery, stained glass, photography, lithography, calligraphy, collage, origami, spinning, weaving, batik, silk-screen printing, needlework, tapestry, embroidery, patchwork, crochet, knitting.

artful adj cunning, crafty, sly, foxy, wily, tricky, scheming, designing, deceitful, devious, subtle, sharp, shrewd, smart, clever, masterly, ingenious, resourceful, skilful, dexterous.

E3 artless, naive, ingenuous.

article n 1 *article in a magazine*: feature, report, story, account, piece, review, commentary, composition, essay, paper. 2 ITEM, thing, object, commodity, unit, part, constituent, piece, portion, division.

articulate adj distinct, well-spoken, clear, lucid, intelligible, comprehensible, understandable, coherent, fluent, vocal, expressive, meaningful.

E3 inarticulate, incoherent.

v say, utter, speak, talk, express, voice, vocalize, verbalize, state, pronounce, enunciate, breathe.

articulation n saying, utterance, speaking, talking, expression, voicing, vocalization, verbalization, pronunciation, enunciation, diction, delivery.

artificial adj false, fake, bogus, counterfeit, spurious, phoney (*infml*), pseudo, specious, sham, insincere, assumed, affected, mannered, forced, contrived, made-up, feigned, pretended, simulated, imitation,

mock, synthetic, plastic, man-made, manufactured, non-natural, unnatural.

E3 genuine, true, real, natural.

artisan n craftsman, craftswoman, artificer, journeyman, expert, skilled worker, mechanic, technician.

artist

Types of artist include:
architect, graphic designer, designer, draughtsman, draughtswoman, illustrator, cartoonist, animator, photographer, printer, engraver, goldsmith, silversmith, blacksmith, carpenter, potter, weaver, sculptor, painter.

artiste n performer, entertainer, variety artist, vaudevillian, comic, comedian, comedienne, player, trouper, actor, actress.

artistic adj aesthetic, ornamental, decorative, beautiful, exquisite, elegant, stylish, graceful, harmonious, sensitive, tasteful, refined, cultured, cultivated, skilled, talented, creative, imaginative.

E3 inelegant, tasteless.

artistry n craftsmanship, workmanship, skill, craft, talent, flair, brilliance, genius, finesse, style, mastery, expertise, proficiency, accomplishment, deftness, touch, sensitivity, creativity.

E3 ineptitude.

as conj, prep 1 WHILE, when. 2 SUCH AS, for example, for instance, like, in the manner of. 3 BECAUSE, since, seeing that, considering that, inasmuch as, being.

as for with reference to, as regards, with regard to, on the subject of, in connection with, in relation to, with relation to, with respect to.

ascend v rise, take off, lift off, go up, move up, slope upwards, climb, scale, mount, tower, float up, fly up, soar. **F3** descend.

ascent n **1** ASCENDING, ascension, climb, climbing, scaling, escalation, rise, rising, mounting. **2** SLOPE, gradient, incline, ramp, hill, elevation. **F3 1** descent.

ascertain v find out, learn, discover, determine, fix, establish, settle, locate, detect, identify, verify, confirm, make certain.

ascribe v attribute, credit, accredit, put down, assign, impute, charge, chalk up to.

ashamed adj sorry, apologetic, remorseful, contrite, guilty, conscience-stricken, sheepish, embarrassed, blushing, red-faced, mortified, humiliated, abashed, humbled, crestfallen, distressed, discomposed, confused, reluctant, hesitant, shy, self-conscious, bashful, modest, prudish.
F3 shameless, proud, defiant.

aside adv apart, on one side, in reserve, away, out of the way, separately, in isolation, alone, privately, secretly.
n digression, parenthesis, departure, soliloquy, stage whisper, whisper.

ask v **1** REQUEST, appeal, petition, sue, plead, beg, entreat, implore, clamour, beseech, pray, supplicate, crave, demand, order, bid, require, seek, solicit, invite, summon.
2 INQUIRE, query, question, interrogate, quiz, press.

asleep adj sleeping, napping, snoozing, fast asleep, sound asleep, dormant, resting, inactive, inert, unconscious, numb, dozing.

aspect n angle, direction, elevation, side, facet, feature, face, expression, countenance, appearance, look, air, manner, bearing, attitude, condition, situation, position, standpoint, point of view, view, outlook, prospect, scene.

aspiration n aim, intent, purpose, endeavour, object, objective, goal, ambition, hope, dream, ideal, wish, desire, yearning, longing, craving, hankering.

aspire v aim, intend, purpose, seek, pursue, hope, dream, wish, desire, yearn, long, crave, hanker.

aspiring adj would-be, aspirant, striving, endeavouring, ambitious, enterprising, keen, eager, hopeful, optimistic, wishful, longing.

assassin n murderer, killer, slayer, cut-throat, executioner, hatchet man (infml), gunman, hit-man (sl), liquidator (infml).

assassinate v murder, kill, slay, dispatch, hit (sl), eliminate (infml), liquidate (infml).

assault n **1** ATTACK, offensive, onslaught, blitz, strike, raid, invasion, incursion, storm, storming, charge. **2** charged with assault: battery, grievous bodily harm, GBH (infml), mugging (sl), rape, abuse.
v attack, charge, invade, strike, hit, set upon, fall on, beat up (infml), mug (sl), rape, molest, abuse.

assemble v **1** GATHER, congregate, muster, rally, convene, meet, join up, flock, group, collect, accumulate, amass, bring together, round up, marshal, mobilize. **2** CONSTRUCT, build, put together, piece together, compose, make, fabricate, manufacture.
F3 1 scatter, disperse. **2** dismantle.

assembly n 1 GATHERING, rally, meeting, convention, conference, convocation, congress, council, group, body, company, congregation, flock, crowd, multitude, throng, collection, assemblage.
2 CONSTRUCTION, building, fabrication, manufacture.

assert v affirm, attest, swear, testify to, allege, claim, contend, maintain, insist, stress, protest, defend, vindicate, uphold, promote, declare, profess, state, pronounce, lay down, advance.
F∃ deny, refute.

assertion n affirmation, attestation, word, allegation, claim, contention, insistence, vindication, declaration, profession, statement, pronouncement.
F∃ denial.

assertive adj bold, confident, self-assured, forward, pushy, insistent, emphatic, forceful, firm, decided, strong-willed, dogmatic, opinionated, presumptuous, assuming, overbearing, domineering, aggressive.
F∃ timid, diffident.

assess v gauge, estimate, evaluate, appraise, review, judge, consider, weigh, size up, compute, determine, fix, value, rate, tax, levy, impose, demand.

assessment n gauging, estimation, estimate, evaluation, appraisal, review, judgement, opinion, consideration, calculation, determination, valuation, rating, taxation.

asset n strength, resource, virtue, plus (infml), benefit, advantage, blessing, boon, help, aid.
F∃ liability.

assets n estate, property, possessions, goods, holdings, securities, money, wealth, capital, funds, reserves, resources, means.

assign v 1 ALLOCATE, apportion, grant, give, dispense, distribute, allot, consign, delegate, name, nominate, designate, appoint, choose, select, determine, set, fix, specify, stipulate.
2 ATTRIBUTE, accredit, ascribe, put down.

assignment n commission, errand, task, project, job, position, post, duty, responsibility, charge, appointment, delegation, designation, nomination, selection, allocation, consignment, grant, distribution.

assist v help, aid, abet, rally round, co-operate, collaborate, back, second, support, reinforce, sustain, relieve, benefit, serve, enable, facilitate, expedite, boost, further, advance.
F∃ hinder, thwart.

assistance n help, aid, succour, co-operation, collaboration, backing, support, reinforcement, relief, benefit, service, boost, furtherance.
F∃ hindrance, resistance.

assistant n helper, helpmate, aide, right-hand man, auxiliary, ancillary, subordinate, backer, second, supporter, accomplice, accessory, abettor, collaborator, colleague, partner, ally, confederate, associate.

associate v 1 AFFILIATE, confederate, ally, league, join, amalgamate, combine, unite, link, connect, correlate, relate, couple, pair, yoke.
2 associate with bad company: socialize, mingle, mix, fraternize, consort, hang around (infml).
n partner, ally, confederate, affiliate, collaborator, co-worker, mate,

colleague, peer, compeer, fellow, comrade, companion, friend, sidekick (*infml*), assistant, follower.

association n 1 ORGANIZATION, corporation, company, partnership, league, alliance, coalition, confederation, confederacy, federation, affiliation, consortium, cartel, syndicate, union, society, club, user group, fraternity, fellowship, clique, group, band. 2 BOND, tie, connection, correlation, relation, relationship, involvement, intimacy, friendship, companionship, familiarity.

assorted adj miscellaneous, mixed, varied, different, differing, heterogeneous, diverse, sundry, various, several, manifold.

assortment n miscellany, medley, pot-pourri, jumble, mixture, variety, diversity, collection, selection, choice, arrangement, grouping.

assume v 1 PRESUME, surmise, accept, take for granted, expect, understand, deduce, infer, guess, postulate, suppose, think, believe, imagine, fancy. 2 AFFECT, take on, feign, counterfeit, simulate, put on, pretend. 3 *assume command*: undertake, adopt, embrace, seize, arrogate, commandeer, appropriate, usurp, take over.

assumed adj false, bogus, counterfeit, fake, phoney (*infml*), sham, affected, feigned, simulated, pretended, made-up, fictitious, hypothetical.

F3 true, real, actual.

assumption n presumption, surmise, inference, supposition, guess, conjecture, theory, hypothesis, premise, postulate, idea, notion, belief, fancy.

assurance n 1 ASSERTION, declaration, affirmation, guarantee, pledge, promise, vow, word, oath. 2 CONFIDENCE, self-confidence, aplomb, boldness, audacity, courage, nerve, conviction, sureness, certainty.

F3 2 shyness, doubt, uncertainty.

assure v affirm, guarantee, warrant, pledge, promise, vow, swear, tell, convince, persuade, encourage, hearten, reassure, soothe, comfort, boost, strengthen, secure, ensure, confirm.

assured adj 1 SURE, certain, indisputable, irrefutable, confirmed, positive, definite, settled, fixed, guaranteed, secure. 2 SELF-ASSURED, confident, self-confident, self-possessed, bold, audacious, assertive.

F3 1 uncertain. 2 shy.

astonish v surprise, startle, amaze, astound, stun, stupefy, daze, stagger, floor (*infml*), dumbfound, flabbergast (*infml*), shock, confound, bewilder.

astonishment n surprise, amazement, shock, dismay, consternation, confusion, bewilderment, wonder.

astounding adj surprising, startling, amazing, astonishing, stunning, breathtaking, jaw-dropping (*infml*), stupefying, overwhelming, staggering, shocking, bewildering.

astray adv adrift, off course, lost, amiss, wrong, off the rails (*infml*), awry, off the mark.

astute adj shrewd, prudent, sagacious, wise, canny, knowing, intelligent, sharp, penetrating, keen, perceptive, discerning, subtle, clever, crafty, cunning, sly, wily.

F3 stupid, slow.

asylum n haven, sanctuary, refuge, shelter, retreat, safety.

asymmetric adj unsymmetrical, unbalanced, uneven, crooked, awry, unequal, disproportionate, irregular. **E3** symmetrical.

atheism n unbelief, non-belief, disbelief, scepticism, irreligion, ungodliness, godlessness, impiety, infidelity, paganism, heathenism, free-thinking, rationalism.

atheist n unbeliever, non-believer, disbeliever, sceptic, infidel, pagan, heathen, free-thinker.

athlete n sportsman, sportswoman, runner, gymnast, competitor, contestant, contender.

athletic adj fit, energetic, vigorous, active, sporty, muscular, sinewy, brawny, strapping, robust, sturdy, strong, powerful, well-knit, well-proportioned, wiry. **E3** puny, wimpy (infml).

athletics n sports, games, races, track events, field events, exercises, gymnastics.

atmosphere n 1 AIR, sky, aerospace, heavens, ether. 2 AMBIENCE, environment, surroundings, aura, feel, feeling, mood, spirit, tone, tenor, character, quality, flavour.

atom n molecule, particle, bit, morsel, crumb, grain, spot, speck, mite, shred, scrap, hint, trace, scintilla, jot, iota, whit.

atrocious adj shocking, appalling, abominable, dreadful, terrible, horrible, hideous, ghastly, heinous, grievous, savage, vicious, monstrous, fiendish, ruthless. **E3** admirable, fine.

atrocity n outrage, abomination, enormity, horror, monstrosity,

savagery, barbarity, brutality, cruelty, viciousness, evil, villainy, wickedness, vileness, heinousness, hideousness, atrociousness.

attach v attach a label: affix, stick, adhere, fasten, fix, secure, tie, bind, weld, join, unite, connect, link, couple, add, annex. 2 ASCRIBE, attribute, impute, assign, put, place, associate, relate to, belong. **E3 1** detach, unfasten.

attachment n 1 ACCESSORY, fitting, fixture, extension, appendage, extra, supplement, addition, adjunct, codicil. 2 FONDNESS, affection, tenderness, love, liking, partiality, loyalty, devotion, friendship, affinity, attraction, bond, tie, link.

attack n 1 OFFENSIVE, blitz, bombardment, invasion, incursion, foray, raid, strike, charge, rush, onslaught, assault, battery, aggression, criticism, censure, abuse. 2 SEIZURE, fit, convulsion, paroxysm, spasm, stroke.
v 1 INVADE, raid, strike, storm, charge, assail, assault, set about, set upon, fall on, lay into, do over (sl). 2 CRITICIZE, censure, blame, denounce, revile, malign, abuse. **E3 1** defend, protect.

attacker n assailant, mugger (sl), aggressor, invader, raider, critic, detractor, reviler, abuser, persecutor. **E3** defender, supporter.

attain v accomplish, achieve, fulfil, complete, effect, realize, earn, reach, touch, arrive at, grasp, get, acquire, obtain, procure, secure, gain, win, net.

attainment n accomplishment, achievement, feat, fulfilment, completion, consummation, realization, success, ability, capability, competence, proficiency, skill, art, talent, gift, aptitude, facility, mastery.

attempt n try, endeavour, shot (*infml*), go (*infml*), stab (*infml*), bash (*infml*), push, effort, struggle, bid, undertaking, venture, trial, experiment.
v try, endeavour, have a go (*infml*), aspire, seek, strive, undertake, tackle, venture, experiment.

attend v 1 *attend a meeting*: be present, go to, frequent, visit. 2 ESCORT, chaperone, accompany, usher, follow, guard, look after, take care of, nurse, tend, minister to, help, serve, wait on. 3 PAY ATTENTION, listen, hear, heed, mind, mark, note, notice, observe.
attend to deal with, see to, take care of, look after, manage, direct, control, oversee, supervise.

attendance n presence, appearance, turnout, audience, house, crowd, gate.

attendant n aide, helper, assistant, auxiliary, steward, waiter, servant, page, retainer, guide, marshal, usher, escort, companion, follower, guard, custodian.
adj accompanying, attached, associated, related, incidental, resultant, consequent, subsequent.

attention n alertness, vigilance, concentration, heed, notice, observation, regard, mindfulness, awareness, recognition, thought, contemplation, consideration, concern, care, treatment, service.
F3 inattention, disregard, carelessness.

attentive adj 1 ALERT, awake, vigilant, watchful, observant,

concentrating, heedful, mindful, careful, conscientious. 2 CONSIDERATE, thoughtful, kind, obliging, accommodating, polite, courteous, devoted.
F3 1 inattentive, heedless. 2 inconsiderate.

attitude n feeling, disposition, mood, aspect, manner, bearing, pose, posture, stance, position, point of view, opinion, view, outlook, perspective, approach.

attract v pull, draw, lure, allure, entice, seduce, tempt, invite, induce, incline, appeal to, interest, engage, fascinate, enchant, charm, bewitch, captivate, excite.
F3 repel, disgust.

attraction n pull, draw, magnetism, lure, allure, bait, enticement, inducement, seduction, temptation, invitation, appeal, interest, fascination, enchantment, charm, captivation.
F3 repulsion.

attractive adj pretty, fair, fetching, good-looking, handsome, beautiful, gorgeous, stunning, glamorous, lovely, pleasant, pleasing, agreeable, appealing, winsome, winning, enticing, seductive, tempting, inviting, interesting, sexy (*infml*), engaging, fascinating, charming, captivating, magnetic.
F3 unattractive, repellent.

attribute v ascribe, accredit, credit, impute, assign, put down, blame, charge, refer, apply.
n property, quality, virtue, point, aspect, facet, feature, trait, characteristic, idiosyncrasy, peculiarity, quirk, note, mark, sign, symbol.

auburn adj red, chestnut, tawny, russet, copper, Titian.

audible adj clear, distinct, recognizable, perceptible, discernible, detectable, appreciable.
F3 inaudible, silent, unclear.

audience n spectators, onlookers, house, auditorium, listeners, viewers, crowd, turnout, bums-on-seats (infml), gathering, assembly, congregation, fans, devotees, regulars, following, public.

audit n examination, inspection, check, verification, investigation, scrutiny, analysis, review, statement, balancing.

augur v bode, forebode, herald, presage, portend, prophesy, predict, promise, signify.

auspices n aegis, authority, patronage, sponsorship, backing, support, protection, charge, care, supervision, control, influence, guidance.

auspicious adj favourable, propitious, encouraging, cheerful, bright, rosy, promising, hopeful, optimistic, fortunate, lucky, opportune, happy, prosperous.
F3 inauspicious, ominous.

austere adj **1** STARK, bleak, plain, simple, unadorned, grim, forbidding. **2** SEVERE, stern, strict, cold, formal, rigid, rigorous, exacting, hard, harsh, spartan, grave, serious, solemn, sober, abstemious, self-denying, restrained, economical, frugal, ascetic, self-disciplined, puritanical, chaste.
F3 1 ornate, elaborate. **2** genial.

austerity n plainness, simplicity, severity, coldness, formality, hardness, harshness, solemnity, abstemiousness, abstinence, economy, asceticism, puritanism.
F3 elaborateness, materialism.

authentic adj genuine, true, real, actual, certain, bona fide, legitimate, honest, valid, original, pure, factual, accurate, true-to-life, faithful, reliable, trustworthy.
F3 false, fake, counterfeit, spurious.

authenticate v guarantee, warrant, vouch for, attest, authorize, accredit, validate, certify, endorse, confirm, verify, corroborate.

authenticity n genuineness, certainty, authoritativeness, validity, truth, veracity, truthfulness, honesty, accuracy, correctness, faithfulness, fidelity, reliability, dependability, trustworthiness.
F3 spuriousness, invalidity.

author n **1** WRITER, novelist, dramatist, playwright, composer, pen, penman, penwoman. **2** CREATOR, founder, originator, initiator, parent, prime mover, mover, inventor, designer, architect, planner, maker, producer.

authoritarian adj strict, disciplinarian, severe, harsh, rigid, inflexible, unyielding, dogmatic, doctrinaire, absolute, autocratic, dictatorial, despotic, tyrannical, oppressive, domineering, imperious.
F3 liberal.

authoritative adj scholarly, learned, official, authorized, legitimate, valid, approved, sanctioned, accepted, definitive, decisive, authentic, factual, true, truthful, accurate, faithful, convincing, sound, reliable, dependable, trustworthy.
F3 unofficial, unreliable.

authority n **1** SOVEREIGNTY, supremacy, rule, sway, control, dominion, influence, power, force, government, administration, officialdom. **2** AUTHORIZATION, permission, sanction, permit, warrant, licence, credentials, right, prerogative. **3** *an authority on antiques*: expert, pundit, connoisseur, specialist, professional, master, scholar.

authorize v legalize, validate, ratify, confirm, license, entitle, accredit, empower, enable, commission, warrant, permit, allow, consent to, sanction, approve, give the go-ahead.

autocracy n absolutism, totalitarianism, dictatorship, despotism, tyranny, authoritarianism, fascism. **F3** democracy.

autocrat n absolutist, totalitarian, dictator, despot, tyrant, authoritarian, (little) Hitler (*infml*), fascist.

autocratic adj absolute, all-powerful, totalitarian, despotic, tyrannical, authoritarian, dictatorial, domineering, overbearing, imperious. **F3** democratic, liberal.

automatic adj **1** AUTOMATED, self-activating, mechanical, mechanized, programmed, self-regulating, computerized, push-button, robotic, self-propelling, unmanned. **2** SPONTANEOUS, reflex, knee-jerk (*infml*), involuntary, unwilled, unconscious, unthinking, natural, instinctive, routine, necessary, certain, inevitable, unavoidable, inescapable.

autonomy n self-government, self-rule, home rule, sovereignty, independence, self-determination, freedom, free will. **F3** subjection, compulsion.

auxiliary adj ancillary, assistant, subsidiary, accessory, secondary, supporting, supportive, helping, assisting, aiding, extra, supplementary, spare, reserve, back-up, emergency, substitute.

available adj free, vacant, to hand, within reach, at hand, accessible, handy, convenient, on hand, ready, on tap, obtainable, off-the-shelf (*infml*). **F3** unavailable.

avalanche n landslide, landslip, cascade, torrent, deluge, flood, inundation, barrage.

avant-garde adj innovative, innovatory, pioneering, experimental, unconventional, far-out (*sl*), way-out (*sl*), progressive, advanced, forward-looking, enterprising, inventive. **F3** conservative.

avarice n covetousness, rapacity, acquisitiveness, greed, greediness, meanness. **F3** generosity, liberality.

avaricious adj covetous, grasping, rapacious, acquisitive, greedy, mercenary, mean, miserly. **F3** generous.

avenge v take revenge for, take vengeance for, punish, requite, repay, retaliate.

average n mean, mid-point, norm, standard, rule, par, medium, run. **F3** extreme, exception.
adj mean, medial, median, middle, intermediate, medium, moderate, satisfactory, fair, mediocre, middling, indifferent, so-so (*infml*), passable, tolerable, undistinguished, run-of-the-mill, ordinary, everyday, common, usual, normal, regular, standard, vanilla (*infml*), typical, unexceptional. **F3** extreme, exceptional, remarkable.

averse *adj* reluctant, unwilling, loth, disinclined, ill-disposed, hostile, opposed, antagonistic, unfavourable. ☒ willing, keen, sympathetic.

aversion *n* dislike, hate, hatred, loathing, detestation, abhorrence, abomination, horror, phobia, reluctance, unwillingness, disinclination, distaste, disgust, revulsion, repugnance, repulsion, hostility, opposition, antagonism. ☒ liking, sympathy, desire.

avert *v* turn away, deflect, turn aside, parry, fend off, ward off, stave off, forestall, frustrate, prevent, obviate, avoid, evade.

aviation *n* aeronautics, flying, flight, aircraft industry.

avid *adj* eager, earnest, keen, enthusiastic, fanatical, devoted, dedicated, zealous, ardent, fervent, intense, passionate, insatiable, ravenous, hungry, thirsty, greedy, grasping, covetous. ☒ indifferent.

avoid *v* evade, elude, sidestep, dodge, shirk, duck (*infml*), escape, get out of, bypass, circumvent, balk, prevent, avert, shun, abstain from, refrain from, steer clear of.

avoidable *adj* escapable, preventable. ☒ inevitable.

avowed *adj* sworn, declared, professed, self-proclaimed, self-confessed, confessed, admitted, acknowledged, open, overt.

awake *v* awaken, waken, wake, wake up, rouse, arouse.
adj wakeful, wide awake, aroused, alert, vigilant, watchful, observant, attentive, conscious, aware, sensitive, alive.

awakening *n* awaking, wakening, waking, rousing, arousal, stimulation, animating, enlivening, activation, revival, birth.

award *v* give, present, distribute, dispense, bestow, confer, accord, endow, gift, grant, allot, apportion, assign, allow, determine.
n prize, trophy, decoration, medal, presentation, dispensation, bestowal, conferral, endowment, gift, grant, allotment, allowance, adjudication, judgement, decision, order.

aware *adj* conscious, alive to, sensitive, appreciative, sentient, familiar, conversant, acquainted, informed, up-to-speed (*infml*), enlightened, au courant, knowing, knowledgeable, cognizant, mindful, heedful, attentive, observant, sharp, alert, on the ball (*infml*), clued-up (*infml*), shrewd, sensible. ☒ unaware, oblivious, insensitive.

awe *n* wonder, veneration, reverence, respect, admiration, amazement, astonishment, fear, terror, dread, apprehension. ☒ contempt.

awe-inspiring *adj* wonderful, sublime, magnificent, stupendous, overwhelming, breathtaking, stupefying, stunning, astonishing, amazing, impressive, imposing, majestic, solemn, moving, awesome, formidable, daunting, intimidating, fearsome. ☒ contemptible, tame.

awful *adj* terrible, dreadful, fearful, frightful, ghastly, unpleasant, nasty, horrible, hideous, ugly, gruesome, dire, abysmal, atrocious, horrific, shocking, appalling, alarming, spine-chilling. ☒ wonderful, excellent.

awkward *adj* **1** CLUMSY, gauche, inept, inexpert, unskilful, bungling, ham-fisted, unco-ordinated, ungainly, graceless, ungraceful, inelegant, cumbersome, clunky (*infml*), unwieldy, inconvenient, difficult, fiddly, delicate, troublesome, perplexing. **2** *feeling awkward in their presence*: uncomfortable, ill at ease, embarrassed. **3** OBSTINATE, stubborn, unco-operative, irritable, touchy, prickly, rude, unpleasant.
F3 1 graceful, elegant, convenient, handy. **2** comfortable, relaxed. **3** amenable, pleasant.

axe *n* hatchet, chopper, cleaver, tomahawk, battle-axe.
v **1** CUT (DOWN), fell, hew, chop, cleave, split. **2** CANCEL, terminate, discontinue, remove, withdraw, eliminate, get rid of, throw out, dismiss, discharge, sack (*infml*), fire (*infml*).

axiom *n* principle, fundamental, truth, truism, precept, dictum, byword, maxim, adage, aphorism.

axis *n* centre-line, vertical, horizontal, pivot, hinge.

axle *n* shaft, spindle, rod, pin, pivot.

B

babble *v* **1** CHATTER, gabble, jabber, cackle, prate, mutter, mumble, murmur. **2** *the stream babbled*: burble, gurgle.
n chatter, gabble, clamour, hubbub, gibberish, burble, murmur.

babe *n* baby, infant, suckling, child, tiny, toddler, rugrat (*sl*).

baby *n* babe, infant, suckling, child, tiny, toddler, rugrat (*sl*).
adj miniature, small-scale, mini (*infml*), midget, small, little, tiny, minute, diminutive.

babyish *adj* childish, juvenile, puerile, infantile, silly, foolish, soft (*infml*), sissy (*infml*), baby, young, immature, naive.
F∃ mature, precocious.

back *n* rear, stern, end, tail, tail end, hind part, hindquarters, posterior, backside, reverse.
F∃ front, face.
v **1** GO BACKWARDS, reverse, recede, regress, backtrack, retire, withdraw, back away, recoil.
2 SUPPORT, sustain, assist, side with, champion, advocate, encourage, promote, boost, favour, sanction, countenance, endorse, second, countersign, sponsor, finance, subsidize, underwrite.
F∃ 1 advance, approach.
2 discourage, weaken.

adj rear, end, tail, posterior, hind, hindmost, reverse.
F∃ front.

back down concede, yield, give in, surrender, submit, retreat, withdraw, back-pedal, do a U-turn (*infml*).

back out abandon, give up, chicken out (*infml*), withdraw, pull out (*infml*), resign, recant, go back on, cancel.

back up confirm, corroborate, substantiate, endorse, second, champion, support, reinforce, bolster, assist, aid.
F∃ let down.

backbone *n* **1** SPINE, spinal column, vertebrae, vertebral column, mainstay, support, core, foundation.
2 COURAGE, mettle, pluck, nerve, grit, determination, resolve, tenacity, steadfastness, toughness, stamina, strength, power.
F∃ 2 spinelessness, weakness.

backfire *v* recoil, rebound, ricochet, boomerang, miscarry, fail, flop.

background *n* **1** SETTING, surroundings, environment, context, circumstances. **2** HISTORY, record, credentials, experience, grounding, preparation, education, upbringing, breeding, culture, tradition.

backing *n* support, accompaniment, aid, assistance, helpers, championing, advocacy, encouragement, moral support, favour, sanction, promotion, endorsement, seconding, patronage, sponsorship, finance, funds, grant, subsidy.

backlash n reaction, response, repercussion, reprisal, retaliation, recoil, kickback, backfire, boomerang.

backlog n accumulation, stock, supply, resources, reserve, reserves, excess.

backsliding n lapse, relapse, apostasy, defection, desertion, defaulting.

backward adj 1 a backward step: retrograde, retrogressive, regressive. 2 SHY, bashful, reluctant, unwilling, hesitant, hesitating, wavering, slow, behind, behindhand, late, immature, underdeveloped, retarded, subnormal, stupid.

F3 1 forward. 2 precocious.

bacteria n germs, bugs (infml), viruses, microbes, micro-organisms, bacilli.

bad adj 1 UNPLEASANT, disagreeable, nasty, undesirable, unfortunate, distressing, adverse, detrimental, harmful, damaging, injurious, serious, grave, severe, harsh. 2 EVIL, wicked, sinful, criminal, corrupt, immoral, vile. 3 bad workmanship: poor, inferior, substandard, shoddy (infml), imperfect, faulty, defective, deficient, unsatisfactory, useless. 4 ROTTEN, mouldy, decayed, spoilt, putrid, rancid, sour, off, tainted, contaminated. 5 a bad child: naughty, mischievous, ill-behaved, disobedient.

F3 1 good, pleasant, mild, slight. 2 virtuous. 3 skilled. 4 fresh. 5 well-behaved.

badge n identification, emblem, device, insignia, sign, mark, token, stamp, brand, trademark, logo.

badly adv 1 GREATLY, extremely, exceedingly, intensely, deeply, acutely, bitterly, painfully, seriously, desperately, severely, critically, crucially. 2 WICKEDLY, criminally, immorally, shamefully, unfairly. 3 WRONG, wrongly, incorrectly, improperly, defectively, faultily, imperfectly, inadequately, unsatisfactorily, poorly, incompetently, negligently, carelessly. 4 UNFAVOURABLY, adversely, unfortunately, unsuccessfully.

F3 3 well.

bad-tempered adj irritable, cross, crotchety, crabbed, crabby, snappy, grumpy, querulous, petulant, fractious, stroppy (infml), arsey (sl).

F3 good-tempered, genial, equable.

baffle v puzzle, perplex, mystify, bemuse, bewilder, confuse, confound, bamboozle (infml), flummox (infml), daze, upset, disconcert, foil, thwart, frustrate, hinder, check, defeat, stump (infml).

F3 enlighten, help.

bag n 1 CATCH, capture, trap, land, kill, shoot. 2 OBTAIN, acquire, get, gain, corner, take, grab, appropriate, commandeer, reserve.
n container, sack, case, suitcase, grip, carrier, hold-all, handbag, shoulder-bag, satchel, rucksack, haversack, pack.

baggage n luggage, suitcases, bags, belongings, things, equipment, gear, paraphernalia, impedimenta (fml).

baggy adj loose, slack, roomy, ill-fitting, billowing, bulging, floppy, sagging, droopy.

F3 tight, firm.

bail *n* security, surety, pledge, bond, guarantee, warranty.

bait *n* lure, incentive, inducement, bribe, temptation, enticement, allurement, attraction.

F∃ disincentive.

v tease, provoke, goad, irritate, annoy, irk, needle (*infml*), harass, persecute, torment.

balance *v* 1 STEADY, poise, stabilize, level, square, equalize, equate, match, counterbalance, counteract, neutralize, offset, adjust. 2 COMPARE, consider, weigh, estimate.

F∃ 1 unbalance, overbalance.

n 1 EQUILIBRIUM, steadiness, stability, evenness, symmetry, equality, parity, equity, equivalence, correspondence. 2 COMPOSURE, self-possession, poise, equanimity. 3 REMAINDER, rest, residue, surplus, difference.

F∃ 1 imbalance, instability.

balcony *n* terrace, veranda, porch (*US*), gallery, upper circle, gods.

bald *adj* 1 BALD-HEADED, hairless, smooth, uncovered. 2 BARE, naked, unadorned, plain, simple, severe, stark, barren, treeless.
3 *a bald statement*: forthright, direct, straight, outright, downright, straightforward.

F∃ 1 hairy, hirsute. 2 adorned.

bale *n* bundle, truss, pack, package, parcel.

balk, baulk *v* 1 FLINCH, recoil, shrink, jib, boggle, hesitate, refuse, resist, dodge, evade, shirk. 2 THWART, frustrate, foil, forestall, disconcert, baffle, hinder, obstruct, check, stall, bar, prevent, defeat, counteract.

ball [1] *n* sphere, globe, orb, globule, drop, conglomeration, pellet, pill, shot, bullet, slug (*infml*).

ball [2] *n* dance, dinner-dance, party, soirée, masquerade, carnival, assembly.

ballad *n* poem, song, folk-song, shanty, carol, ditty.

ballet

> Terms used in ballet include:
> à pointe, arabesque, attitude, ballerina, prima ballerina, ballon, barre, battement, batterie, capriole, chassé, choreography, company, corps de ballet, coryphée, divertissement, écarté, élévation, entrechat, five positions, fouetté, fouetté en tournant, glissade, jeté, grand jeté, leotard, pas de deux, pas seul, pirouette, plié, pointes, sur les pointes, port de bras, régisseur, point shoe, tutu.

ballot *n* poll, polling, vote, voting, election, referendum, plebiscite.

ban *v* forbid, prohibit, disallow, proscribe, bar, exclude, ostracize, outlaw, banish, suppress, restrict.

F∃ allow, permit, authorize.

n prohibition, embargo, veto, boycott, stoppage, restriction, suppression, censorship, outlawry, proscription, condemnation, denunciation, curse, taboo.

F∃ permission, dispensation.

banal *adj* trite, commonplace, ordinary, everyday, humdrum, boring, unimaginative, hackneyed, clichéd, stock, stereotyped, corny (*infml*), stale, threadbare, tired, empty.

F∃ original, fresh, imaginative.

band [1] *n* strip, belt, ribbon, tape, bandage, binding, tie, ligature, bond, strap, cord, chain.

band [2] *n* 1 TROOP, gang, crew, group, herd, flock, party, body, association,

company, society, club, clique. **2** *the band played on*: group, orchestra, ensemble.
v group, gather, join, unite, ally, collaborate, consolidate, amalgamate, merge, affiliate, federate.
F3 disband, disperse.

bandage *n* dressing, plaster, compress, ligature, tourniquet, swathe, swaddle.
v bind, dress, cover, swathe, swaddle.

bandit *n* robber, thief, brigand, marauder, outlaw, highwayman, pirate, buccaneer, hijacker, cowboy, gunman, desperado, gangster.

bandy[1] *v* exchange, swap, trade, barter, interchange, reciprocate, pass, toss, throw.

bandy[2] *adj* bandy-legged, bow-legged, curved, bowed, bent, crooked.

bang *n* **1** BLOW, hit, knock, bump, crash, collision, smack, punch, thump, wallop (*infml*), stroke, whack (*infml*). **2** *a loud bang*: explosion, detonation, pop, boom, clap, peal, clang, clash, thud, thump, slam, noise, report, shot.
v **1** STRIKE, hit, bash, knock, bump, rap, drum, hammer, pound, thump, stamp. **2** EXPLODE, burst, detonate, boom, echo, resound, crash, slam, clatter, clang, peal, thunder.
adv straight, directly, headlong, right, precisely, slap, smack, hard, noisily, suddenly, abruptly.

banish *v* expel, eject, evict, deport, transport, exile, outlaw, ban, bar, debar, exclude, shut out, ostracize, excommunicate, dismiss, oust, dislodge, remove, get rid of, discard, dispel, eliminate, eradicate.
F3 recall, welcome.

banishment *n* expulsion, eviction, deportation, expatriation,

transportation, exile, outlawry, ostracism, excommunication.
F3 return, recall, welcome.

bank[1] *n* accumulation, fund, pool, reservoir, depository, repository, treasury, savings, reserve, store, stock, stockpile, hoard, cache.
v deposit, save, keep, store, accumulate, stockpile.
F3 spend.

bank[2] *n* heap, pile, mass, mound, earthwork, ridge, rampart, embankment, side, slope, tilt, edge, shore.
v **1** HEAP, pile, stack, mass, amass, accumulate, mound, drift. **2** SLOPE, incline, pitch, slant, tilt, tip.

bank[3] *n* array, panel, bench, group, tier, rank, line, row, series, succession, sequence, train.

bankrupt *adj* insolvent, in liquidation, ruined, failed, beggared, destitute, impoverished, broke (*infml*), spent, exhausted, depleted, lacking.
F3 solvent, wealthy.
n insolvent, debtor, pauper.

banner *n* flag, standard, colours, ensign, pennant, streamer.

banquet *n* feast, dinner, meal, repast (*fml*), treat.

banter *n* joking, jesting, pleasantry, badinage, repartee, word play, chaff, chaffing, kidding (*infml*), ribbing (*sl*), derision, mockery, ridicule.

baptism *n* christening, dedication, beginning, initiation, introduction, debut, launch, launching, immersion, sprinkling, purification.

baptize *v* christen, name, call, term, style, title, introduce, initiate, enrol, recruit, immerse, sprinkle, purify, cleanse.

bar n **1** PUBLIC HOUSE, pub (infml), inn, tavern, saloon, lounge, counter. **2** SLAB, block, lump, chunk, wedge, ingot, nugget. **3** ROD, stick, shaft, pole, stake, stanchion, batten, cross-piece, rail, railing, paling, barricade. **4** OBSTACLE, impediment, hindrance, obstruction, barrier, stop, check, deterrent. v **1** EXCLUDE, debar, ban, forbid, prohibit, prevent, preclude, hinder, obstruct, restrain. **2** bar the door: barricade, lock, bolt, latch, fasten, secure.

barbarian n savage, brute, ruffian, hooligan, vandal, lout, oaf, boor, philistine, ignoramus, illiterate.

barbaric adj barbarous, primitive, wild, savage, fierce, ferocious, cruel, inhuman, brutal, brutish, uncivilized, uncouth, vulgar, coarse, crude, rude.
F3 humane, civilized, gracious.

barbarity n barbarousness, wildness, savagery, ferocity, viciousness, cruelty, inhumanity, brutality, brutishness, rudeness.
F3 civilization, humanity, civility.

barbed adj **1** PRICKLY, spiny, thorny, spiked, pronged, hooked, jagged, toothed, pointed. **2** a barbed remark: cutting, caustic, acid, hurtful, unkind, nasty, snide, hostile, critical.

bare adj **1** NAKED, nude, unclothed, undressed, stripped, denuded, uncovered, exposed. **2** PLAIN, simple, unadorned, unfurnished, empty, barren, bald, stark, basic, essential.
F3 1 clothed. **2** decorated, detailed.

barely adv hardly, scarcely, only just, just, almost.

bargain n **1** DEAL, transaction, contract, treaty, pact, pledge, promise, agreement, understanding, arrangement, negotiation. **2** DISCOUNT, reduction, snip, giveaway, special offer. v negotiate, haggle, deal, trade, traffic, barter, buy, sell, transact, contract, covenant, promise, agree.

bargain for expect, anticipate, plan for, include, reckon on, look for, foresee, imagine, contemplate, consider.

barge v bump, hit, collide, impinge, shove, elbow, push (in), muscle in, butt in, interrupt, gatecrash, intrude, interfere.
n canal-boat, flatboat, narrow-boat, houseboat, lighter.

bark n yap, woof, yelp, snap, snarl, growl, bay, howl.
v yap, woof, yelp, snap, snarl, growl, bay, howl.

baroque adj elaborate, ornate, rococo, florid, flamboyant, OTT (infml), exuberant, vigorous, bold, convoluted, overdecorated, overwrought, extravagant, fanciful, fantastic, grotesque.
F3 plain, simple.

barracks n garrison, camp, encampment, guardhouse, quarters, billet, lodging, accommodation.

barrage n bombardment, shelling, gunfire, cannonade, broadside, volley, salvo, burst, assault, attack, onset, onslaught, deluge, torrent, stream, storm, hail, rain, shower, mass, profusion.

barrel n cask, keg, tun, butt, water-butt.

barren adj **1** ARID, dry, desert, desolate, waste, empty, flat, dull, uninteresting, uninspiring, uninformative, unrewarding, unproductive, profitless, unfruitful, fruitless, pointless, useless, boring. **2** INFERTILE, sterile, childless, unprolific, unbearing.

F3 1 productive, fruitful, useful. **2** fertile.

barricade n blockade, obstruction, barrier, fence, stockade, bulwark, rampart, protection.
v block, obstruct, bar, fortify, defend, protect.

barrier n **1** WALL, fence, railing, barricade, blockade, boom, rampart, fortification, ditch, frontier, boundary, bar, check. **2** a barrier to success: obstacle, hurdle, stumbling-block, impediment, obstruction, hindrance, handicap, limitation, restriction, drawback, difficulty.

bartender n barman, barmaid, barkeeper, publican.

barter v exchange, swap, trade, traffic, deal, negotiate, bargain, haggle.

base n **1** the base of the statue: bottom, foot, pedestal, plinth, stand, rest, support, foundation, bed, groundwork. **2** BASIS, fundamental, essential, principal, key, heart, core, essence, root, origin, source. **3** HEADQUARTERS, centre, post, station, camp, settlement, home, starting point.
v establish, found, ground, locate, station, build, construct, derive, depend, hinge.

baseless adj groundless, unfounded, unsupported, unsubstantiated, unauthenticated, unconfirmed, unjustified, uncalled-for, gratuitous.

F3 justifiable.

bashful adj shy, retiring, backward, reticent, reserved, unforthcoming, hesitant, shrinking, nervous, timid, coy, diffident, modest, inhibited, self-conscious, embarrassed, blushing, abashed, shamefaced, sheepish.

F3 bold, confident, aggressive, in-your-face (infml).

basic adj fundamental, elementary, primary, root, underlying, key, central, inherent, intrinsic, essential, indispensable, mission-critical (infml), vital, necessary, important.

F3 inessential, minor, peripheral.

basically adv fundamentally, at bottom, at heart, inherently, intrinsically, essentially, principally, primarily.

basics n fundamentals, rudiments, principles, essentials, necessaries, practicalities, brass tacks (infml), grass roots, bedrock, rock bottom, core, facts.

basin n bowl, dish, sink, crater, cavity, hollow, depression, dip.

basis n base, bottom, footing, support, foundation, ground, groundwork, fundamental, premise, principle, essential, heart, core, thrust.

bask v sunbathe, lie, lounge, relax, laze, wallow, revel, delight in, enjoy, relish, savour.

basket n hamper, creel, pannier, punnet, bassinet.

bass adj deep, low, low-toned, grave, resonant.

bastion n stronghold, citadel, fortress, defence, bulwark, mainstay, support, prop, pillar, rock.

batch n lot, consignment, parcel, pack, bunch, set, assortment, collection, assemblage, group, contingent, amount, quantity.

bath n wash, scrub, soak, shower, douche, tub (US), Jacuzzi®.
v bathe, wash, clean, soak, shower.

bathe v swim, wet, moisten, immerse, wash, cleanse, rinse, soak, steep, flood, cover, suffuse.
n swim, dip, paddle, wash, rinse, soak.

battalion n army, force, brigade, regiment, squadron, company, platoon, division, contingent, legion, horde, multitude, throng, host, mass, herd.

batter v beat, pound, pummel, buffet, smash, dash, pelt, lash, thrash, wallop (infml), abuse, maltreat, ill-treat, manhandle, maul, assault, hurt, injure, bruise, disfigure, mangle, distress, crush, demolish, destroy, ruin, shatter.

battered adj beaten, abused, ill-treated, injured, bruised, weather-beaten, dilapidated, tumbledown, ramshackle, crumbling, damaged, crushed.

battle n war, warfare, hostilities, action, conflict, strife, combat, fight, engagement, encounter, attack, fray, skirmish, clash, struggle, contest, campaign, crusade, row, disagreement, dispute, debate, controversy.
v fight, combat, war, feud, contend, struggle, strive, campaign, crusade, agitate, clamour, contest, argue, dispute.

battle-cry n war cry, war song, slogan, motto, watchword, catchword.

baulk see balk.

bay¹ n gulf, bight, arm, inlet, cove.

bay² n recess, alcove, niche, nook, opening, compartment, cubicle, booth, stall, carrel.

bay³ v howl, roar, bellow, bell, bawl, cry, holler (infml), bark.

bazaar n market, marketplace, mart, exchange, sale, fair, fête, bring-and-buy.

be v 1 EXIST, breathe, live, inhabit, reside, dwell. 2 STAY, remain, abide, last, endure, persist, continue, survive, stand, prevail, obtain. 3 HAPPEN, occur, arise, come about, take place, come to pass, befall, develop.

beach n sand, sands, shingle, shore, strand, seashore, seaside, water's edge, coast, seaboard.

beacon n signal, fire, watch fire, bonfire, light, beam, lighthouse, flare, rocket, sign.

bead n drop, droplet, drip, globule, glob (infml), blob, dot, bubble, pearl, jewel, pellet.

beaker n glass, tumbler, jar, cup, mug, tankard.

beam n 1 a beam of light: ray, shaft, gleam, glint, glimmer, glow. 2 PLANK, board, timber, rafter, joist, girder, spar, boom, bar, support.
v 1 EMIT, broadcast, transmit, radiate, shine, glare, glitter, glow, glimmer. 2 SMILE, grin.

bear v 1 CARRY, convey, transport, move, bring. 2 HOLD, support, shoulder, uphold, sustain, maintain, harbour, cherish. 3 bear children: give birth to, breed, propagate, beget, engender, produce, generate, develop, yield, bring forth, give up. 4 TOLERATE, stand, put up with, endure, abide, suffer, permit, allow, admit.

bear on refer to, relate to, affect, concern, involve.

bear out confirm, endorse, support, uphold, prove, demonstrate, corroborate, substantiate, vindicate, justify.

bear up persevere, soldier on, carry on, suffer, endure, survive, withstand.

bear with tolerate, put up with, endure, suffer, forbear, be patient with, make allowances for.

bearable adj tolerable, endurable, sufferable, supportable, sustainable, acceptable, manageable.
F3 unbearable, intolerable.

bearded adj unshaven, bristly, whiskered, tufted, hairy, hirsute, shaggy, bushy.
F3 beardless, clean-shaven, smooth.

bearer n carrier, conveyor, porter, courier, messenger, runner, holder, possessor.

bearing n *have no bearing on the matter*: relevance, significance, connection, relation, reference. **2** DEMEANOUR, manner, mien, air, aspect, attitude, behaviour, comportment, poise, deportment, carriage, posture.

bearings n orientation, position, situation, location, whereabouts, course, track, way, direction, aim.

beast n animal, creature, brute, monster, savage, barbarian, pig, swine, devil, fiend.

beat v **1** WHIP, flog, lash, tan (*infml*), cane, strap, thrash, lay into, hit, punch, strike, swipe, knock, bang, wham, bash, pound, hammer, batter, buffet, pelt, bruise. **2** PULSATE, pulse, throb, thump, race, palpitate, flutter, vibrate, quiver, tremble, shake, quake. **3** DEFEAT, trounce, best, worst, hammer (*infml*), slaughter (*sl*), conquer, overcome, overwhelm, vanquish, subdue, surpass, excel, outdo, outstrip, outrun.
n **1** PULSATION, pulse, stroke, throb, thump, palpitation, flutter. **2** RHYTHM,

time, tempo, metre, measure, rhyme, stress, accent. **3** *a police officer's beat*: round, rounds, territory, circuit, course, journey, way, path, route.

beat up (*infml*) attack, assault, knock about, knock around, batter, do over (*infml*).

beaten adj **1** HAMMERED, stamped, forged, wrought, worked, formed, shaped, fashioned. **2** WHISKED, whipped, mixed, blended, frothy, foamy.

beating n **1** CORPORAL PUNISHMENT, chastisement, whipping, flogging, caning, thrashing. **2** DEFEAT, conquest, rout, ruin, downfall.

beautiful adj attractive, fair, pretty, lovely, good-looking, handsome, gorgeous, radiant, ravishing, stunning (*infml*), pleasing, appealing, alluring, charming, delightful, fine, exquisite.
F3 ugly, plain, hideous.

beautify v embellish, enhance, improve, grace, gild, garnish, decorate, ornament, deck, bedeck, adorn, array, glamorize, titivate (*infml*), tart up (*sl*).
F3 disfigure, spoil.

beauty n attractiveness, fairness, prettiness, loveliness, (good) looks, handsomeness, glamour, appeal, allure, charm, grace, elegance, symmetry, excellence.
F3 ugliness, repulsiveness.

because conj as, for, since, owing to, on account of, by reason of, due to.

beckon v summon, motion, gesture, signal, nod, wave, gesticulate, call, invite, attract, pull, draw, lure, allure, entice, tempt, coax.

become v **1** *become old-fashioned*: turn, grow, get, change into, develop into. **2** SUIT, befit, flatter, enhance, grace, embellish, ornament, set off, harmonize.

bed n **1** lie down on the bed: divan, couch, bunk, berth, cot, mattress, pallet, sack (sl). **2** LAYER, stratum, substratum, matrix, base, bottom, foundation, groundwork, watercourse, channel. **3** bed of flowers: garden, border, patch, plot.

Types of bed include:
four-poster, chaise-longue, day-bed, bed-settee, divan, camp-bed, bunk, water-bed, cot, cradle.

bedclothes n bedding, bed-linen, sheets, pillowcases, pillowslips, covers, blankets, bedspreads, coverlets, quilts, eiderdowns, pillows.
bedraggled adj untidy, unkempt, dishevelled, disordered, scruffy, slovenly, messy, dirty, muddy, muddied, soiled, wet, sodden, drenched.
E3 neat, tidy, clean.
before adv ahead, in front, in advance, sooner, earlier, formerly, previously.
E3 after, later.
beforehand adv in advance, preliminarily, already, before, previously, earlier, sooner.
befriend v help, aid, assist, succour, back, support, stand by, uphold, sustain, comfort, encourage, welcome, favour, benefit, take under one's wing, make friends with, get to know.
E3 neglect, oppose.
beg v request, require, desire, crave, beseech, plead, entreat, implore, pray, supplicate, petition, solicit, cadge, scrounge, sponge.
beggar n mendicant, supplicant, pauper, down-and-out, tramp, vagrant, cadger, scrounger, sponger.

begin v start, commence, set about, embark on, set in motion, kick in (infml), activate, originate, initiate, introduce, found, institute, instigate, arise, spring, emerge, appear.
E3 end, finish, cease.
beginner n novice, tiro, starter, learner, trainee, apprentice, student, freshman, fresher, recruit, cub, tenderfoot, fledgling.
E3 veteran, old hand, expert.
beginning n start, commencement, onset, outset, opening, preface, prelude, introduction, initiation, establishment, inauguration, inception, starting point, birth, dawn, origin, source, fountainhead, root, seed, emergence, rise.
E3 end, finish.
begrudge v resent, grudge, mind, object to, envy, covet, stint.
E3 allow.
beguile v **1** CHARM, enchant, bewitch, captivate, amuse, entertain, divert, distract, occupy, engross. **2** DECEIVE, fool, hoodwink, dupe, trick, cheat, delude, mislead.
behalf n sake, account, good, interest, benefit, advantage, profit, name, authority, side, support.
behave v act, react, respond, work, function, run, operate, perform, conduct oneself, acquit oneself, comport oneself (fml).
behaviour n conduct, comportment (fml), manner, manners, actions, doings, dealings, ways, habits, action, reaction, response, functioning, operation, performance.
behead v decapitate, execute, guillotine.

behind prep 1 FOLLOWING, after, later than, causing, responsible for, instigating, initiating. 2 SUPPORTING, backing, for.
adv after, following, next, subsequently, behindhand, late, overdue, in arrears, in debt.
n rump, rear, posterior (infml), buttocks, seat, bottom, backside (infml), bum (sl), butt (US infml), arse (sl), ass (US sl), tail (infml).

beige adj buff, fawn, mushroom, camel, sandy, khaki, coffee, neutral.

being n 1 EXISTENCE, actuality, reality, life, animation, essence, substance, nature, soul, spirit. 2 CREATURE, animal, beast, human being, mortal, person, individual, thing, entity.

belated adj late, tardy, overdue, delayed, behindhand, unpunctual.
E3 punctual, timely.

belch v burp (infml), hiccup, emit, discharge, disgorge, spew.
n burp (infml), hiccup.

beleaguered adj harassed, pestered, badgered, bothered, worried, vexed, plagued, persecuted, surrounded, beset, besieged.

belief n 1 CONVICTION, persuasion, credit, trust, reliance, confidence, assurance, certainty, sureness, presumption, expectation, feeling, intuition, impression, notion, theory, view, opinion, judgement. 2 IDEOLOGY, faith, creed, doctrine, dogma, tenet, principle.
E3 1 disbelief.

believable adj credible, imaginable, conceivable, acceptable, plausible, possible, likely, probable, authoritative, reliable, trustworthy.
E3 unbelievable, incredible, unconvincing.

believe v accept, wear (infml), swallow (infml), credit, trust, count on, depend on, rely on, swear by, hold, maintain, postulate, assume, presume, gather, speculate, conjecture, guess, imagine, think, consider, reckon, suppose, deem, judge.
E3 disbelieve, doubt.

believer n convert, proselyte, disciple, follower, adherent, devotee, zealot, supporter, upholder.
E3 unbeliever, sceptic.

belittle v minimize, play down, dismiss, underrate, undervalue, underestimate, lessen, diminish, detract from, deprecate, decry, disparage, run down, deride, scorn, ridicule.
E3 exaggerate, praise.

belligerent adj aggressive, militant, argumentative, quarrelsome, contentious, combative, pugnacious, violent, bullying, antagonistic, warring, warlike, bellicose.
E3 peaceable.

bellow v roar, yell, shout, bawl, cry, scream, shriek, howl, clamour.

belong v fit, go with, be part of, attach to, link up with, tie up with, be connected with, relate to.

belongings n possessions, property, chattels, goods, effects, things, stuff (infml), gear (infml), paraphernalia.

beloved adj loved, adored, cherished, treasured, prized, precious, pet, favourite, dearest, dear, darling, admired, revered.

below adv beneath, under, underneath, down, lower, lower down. **F3** above.

prep **1** UNDER, underneath, beneath. **2** INFERIOR TO, lesser than, subordinate to, subject to.
F3 above.

belt n **1** SASH, girdle, waistband, girth, strap. **2** STRIP, band, swathe, stretch, tract, area, region, district, zone, layer.

bemused adj confused, muddled, bewildered, puzzled, perplexed, dazed, befuddled, stupefied.
F3 clear-headed, clear, lucid.

bench n **1** SEAT, form, settle, pew, ledge, counter, table, stall, workbench, worktable. **2** COURT, courtroom, tribunal, judiciary, judicature, judge, magistrate.

bend v curve, turn, deflect, swerve, veer, diverge, twist, contort, flex, shape, mould, buckle, bow, incline, lean, stoop, crouch.
F3 straighten.
n curvature, curve, arc, bow, loop, hook, crook, elbow, angle, corner, turn, twist, zigzag.

beneath adv below, under, underneath, lower, lower down.
prep **1** UNDER, underneath, below, lower than. **2** UNWORTHY OF, unbefitting.

benefactor n philanthropist, patron, sponsor, angel (infml), backer, supporter, promoter, donor, contributor, subscriber, provider, helper, friend, well-wisher.
F3 opponent, persecutor.

beneficial adj advantageous, favourable, useful, helpful, profitable, rewarding, valuable, improving, edifying, wholesome.
F3 harmful, detrimental, useless.

beneficiary n payee, receiver, recipient, inheritor, legatee, heir, heiress, successor.

benefit n advantage, good, welfare, interest, favour, help, aid, assistance, service, use, avail, gain, profit, asset, blessing.
F3 disadvantage, harm, damage.
v help, aid, assist, serve, avail, advantage, profit, improve, enhance, better, further, advance, promote.
F3 hinder, harm, undermine.

benevolent adj philanthropic, humanitarian, charitable, generous, liberal, munificent, altruistic, benign, humane, kind, kindly, well-disposed, compassionate, caring, considerate.
F3 mean, selfish, malevolent.

benign adj **1** BENEVOLENT, good, gracious, gentle, kind, obliging, friendly, amiable, genial, sympathetic. **2** a benign tumour: curable, harmless. **3** FAVOURABLE, propitious, beneficial, temperate, mild, warm, refreshing, restorative, wholesome.
F3 1 hostile. **2** malignant. **3** harmful, unpleasant.

bent adj **1** ANGLED, curved, bowed, arched, folded, doubled, twisted, hunched, stooped. **2** (infml) DISHONEST, crooked (infml), illegal, criminal, corrupt, untrustworthy.
F3 1 straight, upright. **2** honest.
n tendency, inclination, leaning, preference, ability, capacity, faculty, aptitude, facility, gift, talent, knack, flair, forte.

bent on determined, resolved, set, fixed, inclined, disposed.

bequeath v will, leave, bestow, gift, endow, grant, settle, hand down, pass on, impart, transmit, assign, entrust, commit.

bequest n legacy, inheritance, heritage, trust, bestowal, endowment, gift, donation, estate, devisal, settlement.

bereavement n loss, deprivation, dispossession, death.

bereft adj deprived, robbed, stripped, destitute, devoid, lacking, wanting, minus.

berserk adj mad, crazy, demented, insane, deranged, frantic, frenzied, wild, raging, furious, violent, rabid, raving. **F3** sane, calm.

berth n **1** BED, bunk, hammock, billet. **2** MOORING, anchorage, quay, wharf, dock, harbour, port.

beside prep alongside, abreast of, next to, adjacent, abutting, bordering, neighbouring, next door to, close to, near, overlooking.

besides adv also, as well, too, in addition, additionally, further, furthermore, moreover.
prep apart from, other than, in addition to, over and above.

besiege v **1** LAY SIEGE TO, blockade, surround, encircle, confine. **2** TROUBLE, bother, importune, assail, beset, beleaguer, harass, pester, badger, nag, hound, plague.

besotted adj infatuated, doting, obsessed, smitten, hypnotized, spellbound, intoxicated. **F3** indifferent, disenchanted.

best adj optimum, optimal, premium, first, foremost, leading, unequalled, unsurpassed, matchless, incomparable, supreme, greatest, highest, largest, finest, excellent, outstanding, superlative, first-rate, first-class, top-drawer (infml), blue-chip (infml), perfect. **F3** worst.

adv greatly, extremely, exceptionally, excellently, superlatively. **F3** worst.
n finest, cream, prime, élite, top, first, pick, choice, favourite. **F3** worst.

bestow v award, present, grant, confer, endow, bequeath, commit, entrust, impart, transmit, allot, apportion, accord, give, donate, lavish. **F3** withhold, deprive.

bet n wager, flutter (infml), gamble, speculation, risk, venture, stake, ante, bid, pledge.
v wager, gamble, punt, speculate, risk, hazard, chance, venture, lay, stake, bid, pledge.

betray v **1** betray a friend: inform on, shop (sl), sell (out), double-cross, stab in the back, desert, abandon, forsake. **2** DISCLOSE, give away, tell, divulge, expose, reveal, show, manifest. **F3 1** defend, protect. **2** conceal, hide.

betrayal n treachery, treason, sell-out, disloyalty, backstabbing, unfaithfulness, double-dealing, duplicity, deception, trickery, falseness. **F3** loyalty, protection.

betrayer n traitor, Judas, informer, grass (sl), supergrass (sl), double-crosser, backstabber, deceiver, conspirator, renegade, apostate. **F3** protector, supporter.

better adj **1** SUPERIOR, bigger, larger, longer, greater, worthier, finer, surpassing, preferable. **2** IMPROVING, progressing, on the mend, recovering, fitter, healthier, stronger, recovered, restored. **F3 1** inferior. **2** worse.
v **1** IMPROVE, ameliorate, enhance, raise, further, promote, forward,

reform, mend, correct. **2** SURPASS, top, beat, outdo, outstrip, overtake.
E3 1 worsen, deteriorate.

between prep mid, amid, amidst, among, amongst.

beverage n drink, draught, liquor, liquid refreshment.

bevy n gathering, band, company, troupe, group, flock, gaggle, pack, bunch, crowd, throng.

beware v watch out, look out, mind, take heed, steer clear of, avoid, shun, guard against.

bewilder v confuse, muddle, disconcert, confound, bamboozle (infml), baffle, puzzle, perplex, mystify, daze, stupefy, disorient.

bewildered adj confused, muddled, uncertain, disoriented, nonplussed, bamboozled (infml), baffled, puzzled, perplexed, mystified, bemused, surprised, stunned.
E3 unperturbed, collected.

bewitch v charm, enchant, allure, beguile, spellbind, possess, captivate, enrapture, obsess, fascinate, entrance, hypnotize.

beyond prep past, further than, apart from, away from, remote from, out of range of, out of reach of, above, over, superior to.

bias n slant, angle, distortion, bent, leaning, inclination, tendency, propensity, partiality, favouritism, prejudice, one-sidedness, unfairness, bigotry, intolerance.
E3 impartiality, fairness.

biased adj slanted, angled, distorted, warped, twisted, loaded, weighted, influenced, swayed, partial, predisposed, prejudiced, one-sided, unfair, bigoted, blinkered, jaundiced.
E3 impartial, fair.

bicker v squabble, row, quarrel, wrangle, argue, scrap, spar, fight, clash, disagree, dispute.
E3 agree.

bicycle n cycle, bike (infml), two-wheeler, push-bike, racer, mountain-bike, tandem, penny-farthing.

bid v **1** ASK, request, desire, instruct, direct, command, enjoin, require, charge, call, summon, invite, solicit. **2** he bid more than the painting was worth: offer, proffer, tender, submit, propose.
n **1** OFFER, tender, sum, amount, price, advance, submission, proposal. **2** ATTEMPT, effort, try, go (infml), endeavour, venture.

big adj **1** LARGE, great, sizable, considerable, substantial, huge, enormous, immense, massive, colossal, gigantic, mammoth, burly, bulky, extensive, spacious, vast, voluminous. **2** IMPORTANT, significant, momentous, serious, main, principal, eminent, prominent, influential. **3** that's big of you: generous, magnanimous, gracious, unselfish.
E3 1 small, little. **2** insignificant, unknown.

bigot n chauvinist, sectarian, racist, sexist, dogmatist, fanatic, zealot.
E3 liberal, humanitarian.

bigoted adj prejudiced, biased, intolerant, illiberal, narrow-minded, narrow, blinkered, closed, dogmatic, opinionated, obstinate.
E3 tolerant, liberal, broad-minded, enlightened.

bigotry n prejudice, discrimination, bias, injustice, unfairness, intolerance, narrow-mindedness, chauvinism, jingoism, sectarianism, racism, racialism, sexism, dogmatism, fanaticism.

⊞ tolerance.

bilious *adj* **1** IRRITABLE, choleric, cross, grumpy, crotchety, testy, grouchy, peevish. **2** SICK, queasy, nauseated, sickly, out of sorts (*infml*).

bill *n* **1** INVOICE, statement, account, charges, reckoning, tally, score. **2** CIRCULAR, leaflet, handout, bulletin, handbill, broadsheet, advertisement, notice, poster, placard, playbill, programme. **3** *parliamentary bill*: proposal, measure, legislation.

v invoice, charge, debit.

billet *n* **1** ACCOMMODATION, quarters, barracks, lodging, housing, berth. **2** EMPLOYMENT, post, occupation.

billow *v* swell, expand, bulge, puff out, fill out, balloon, rise, heave, surge, roll, undulate.

bind *v* **1** ATTACH, fasten, secure, clamp, stick, tie, lash, truss, strap, bandage, cover, dress, wrap. **2** OBLIGE, force, compel, constrain, necessitate, restrict, confine, restrain, hamper.

binding *adj* obligatory, compulsory, mandatory, necessary, requisite, permanent, conclusive, irrevocable, unalterable, indissoluble, unbreakable, strict.

n border, edging, trimming, tape, bandage, covering, wrapping.

biography *n* life story, life, history, autobiography, memoirs, recollections, curriculum vitae, account, record.

biology

> Biology terms include:
> clone, evolution, animal kingdom, bacillus, bacteria, cell, chromosome, class, coccus, corpuscle, cytoplasm, deoxyribonucleic acid (DNA), diffusion, ecosystem, embryo, enzyme, evolution, excretion, flora and fauna, food chain, fossil, gene, genetic engineering, genetically modified, germ, hereditary, meiosis, membrane, metabolism, micro-organism, microbe, mitosis, molecule, mutation, natural selection, nucleus, nutrition, order, organism, osmosis, parasitism, photosynthesis, pollution, protein, protoplasm, reproduction, respiration, ribonucleic acid (RNA), ribosome, secretion, species, symbiosis, virus.

bird

> Birds include:
> sparrow, thrush, starling, blackbird, blue tit, chaffinch, greenfinch, bullfinch, dunnock, robin, wagtail, swallow, tit, wren, martin, swift, crow, magpie, dove, pigeon, skylark, nightingale, linnet, warbler, jay, jackdaw, rook, raven, cuckoo, woodpecker, yellowhammer; duck, mallard, eider, teal, swan, goose, heron, stork, flamingo, pelican, kingfisher, moorhen, coot, lapwing, peewit, plover, curlew, snipe, avocet, seagull, guillemot, tern, petrel, crane, bittern, albatross, gannet, cormorant, auk, puffin, dipper; eagle, owl, hawk, sparrow-hawk, falcon, kestrel, osprey, buzzard, vulture, condor; emu, ostrich, kiwi, peacock, penguin; chicken, grouse, partridge, pheasant, quail, turkey; canary, budgerigar, budgie (*infml*), cockatiel, cockatoo, lovebird, parakeet, parrot, macaw, toucan, myna bird, mockingbird, kookaburra, bird of paradise.

birth n 1 CHILDBIRTH, parturition, confinement, delivery, nativity. **2** *of noble birth*: ancestry, family, parentage, descent, line, lineage, genealogy, pedigree, blood, stock, race, extraction, background, breeding. **3** BEGINNING, rise, emergence, origin, source, derivation.

birthplace n place of origin, native town, native country, fatherland, mother country, roots, provenance, source, fount.

bisect v halve, divide, separate, split, intersect, cross, fork, bifurcate.

bit n fragment, part, segment, piece, slice, crumb, morsel, scrap, atom, mite, whit, jot, iota, grain, speck. **bit by bit** gradually, little by little, step by step, piecemeal.
F3 wholesale.

bitchy adj catty, snide, nasty, mean, spiteful, malicious, vindictive, backbiting, venomous, cruel, vicious.
F3 kind.

bite v 1 CHEW, masticate, munch, gnaw, nibble, champ, crunch, crush. **2** *the dog bit her hand*: nip, pierce, wound, tear, rend. **3** SMART, sting, tingle. **4** GRIP, hold, seize, pinch, take effect.
n **1** NIP, wound, sting, smarting, pinch. **2** *a bite to eat*: snack, refreshment, mouthful, morsel, taste. **3** PUNGENCY, piquancy, kick (*infml*), punch.

biting adj **1** COLD, freezing, bitter, harsh, severe. **2** CUTTING, incisive, piercing, penetrating, raw, stinging, sharp, tart, caustic, scathing, cynical, hurtful.
F3 1 mild. **2** bland.

bitter adj **1** SOUR, tart, sharp, acrid, acid, vinegary, unsweetened. **2** RESENTFUL, embittered, jaundiced,

cynical, rancorous, acrimonious, acerbic, hostile. **3** INTENSE, severe, harsh, fierce, cruel, savage, merciless, painful, stinging, biting, freezing, raw.
F3 1 sweet. **2** contented. **3** mild.

bizarre adj strange, odd, queer, curious, weird, peculiar, eccentric, way-out (*infml*), off-the-wall (*infml*), left-field (*US infml*), outlandish, ludicrous, ridiculous, fantastic, extravagant, grotesque, freakish, abnormal, deviant, unusual, extraordinary.
F3 normal, ordinary.

black adj **1** JET-BLACK, coal-black, jet, ebony, sable, inky, sooty, dusky, swarthy. **2** DARK, unlit, moonless, starless, overcast, dingy, gloomy, sombre, funereal. **3** FILTHY, dirty, soiled, grimy, grubby.
F3 1 white. **2** bright. **3** clean.
v boycott, blacklist, ban, bar, taboo.

black out v **1** FAINT, pass out, collapse, flake out (*infml*). **2** DARKEN, eclipse, cover up, conceal, suppress, withhold, censor, gag.

blacken v **1** DARKEN, dirty, soil, smudge, cloud. **2** DEFAME, malign, slander, libel, vilify, revile, denigrate, detract, smear, besmirch, sully, stain, tarnish, taint, defile, discredit, dishonour.
F3 2 praise, enhance.

blackmail n extortion, chantage, hush money (*infml*), intimidation, protection, pay-off, ransom.
v extort, bleed, milk, squeeze, hold to ransom, threaten, lean on (*infml*), force, compel, coerce, demand.

blackout n **1** *a news blackout*: suppression, censorship, cover-up (*infml*), concealment, secrecy. **2** FAINT,

coma, unconsciousness, oblivion.
3 POWER CUT, power failure.

blade n edge, knife, dagger, sword, scalpel, razor, vane.

blame n censure, criticism, stick (*sl*), reprimand, reproof, reproach, recrimination, condemnation, accusation, charge, rap (*sl*), incrimination, guilt, culpability, fault, responsibility, accountability, liability, onus.
υ accuse, charge, tax, reprimand, chide, reprove, upbraid, reprehend, admonish, rebuke, reproach, censure, criticize, find fault with, disapprove, condemn.
E3 exonerate, vindicate.

blameless adj innocent, guiltless, clear, faultless, perfect, unblemished, stainless, virtuous, sinless, upright, above reproach, irreproachable, unblamable, unimpeachable, squeaky clean (*infml*).
E3 guilty, blameworthy.

blanch υ blench, whiten, pale, fade, bleach.
E3 colour, blush, redden.

bland adj boring, monotonous, humdrum, tedious, dull, uninspiring, uninteresting, unexciting, nondescript, characterless, flat, insipid, tasteless, weak, mild, smooth, soft, gentle, non-irritant.
E3 lively, stimulating, sharp.

blank adj **1** *a blank page*: empty, unfilled, void, clear, bare, unmarked, pristine, plain, clean, white.
2 EXPRESSIONLESS, deadpan, poker-faced, impassive, apathetic, glazed, vacant, uncomprehending.
n space, gap, break, void, emptiness, vacancy, vacuity, nothingness, vacuum.

blanket n covering, coating, coat, layer, film, carpet, rug, cloak, mantle, cover, sheet, envelope, wrapper, wrapping.
υ cover, coat, eclipse, hide, conceal, mask, cloak, surround, muffle, deaden, obscure, cloud.

blare υ trumpet, clamour, roar, blast, boom, resound, ring, peal, clang, hoot, toot, honk.

blasé adj nonchalant, offhand, unimpressed, unmoved, unexcited, jaded, weary, bored, uninterested, uninspired, apathetic, indifferent, cool, unconcerned.
E3 excited, enthusiastic.

blaspheme υ profane, desecrate, swear, curse, imprecate, damn, execrate, revile, abuse.

blasphemous adj profane, impious, sacrilegious, imprecatory, godless, ungodly, irreligious, irreverent.

blasphemy n profanity, curse, expletive, imprecation, cursing, swearing, execration, impiety, irreverence, sacrilege, desecration, violation, outrage.

blast n **1** EXPLOSION, detonation, bang, crash, clap, crack, volley, burst, outburst, discharge. **2** *a blast of cold air*: draught, gust, gale, squall, storm, tempest. **3** SOUND, blow, blare, roar, boom, peal, hoot, wail, scream, shriek.
υ **1** EXPLODE, blow up, burst, shatter, destroy, demolish, ruin, assail, attack.
2 SOUND, blare, roar, boom, peal, hoot, wail, scream, shriek.

blatant adj flagrant, brazen, barefaced, arrant, open, overt, undisguised, ostentatious, glaring, conspicuous, obtrusive, prominent, pronounced, obvious, sheer, outright, unmitigated.

blaze n fire, flames, conflagration, bonfire, flare-up, explosion, blast, burst, outburst, radiance, brilliance, glare, flash, gleam, glitter, glow, light, flame.
v burn, flame, flare (up), erupt, explode, burst, fire, flash, gleam, glare, beam, shine, glow.

bleach v whiten, blanch, decolorize, fade, pale, lighten.

bleak adj **1** GLOOMY, sombre, leaden, grim, dreary, dismal, depressing, joyless, cheerless, comfortless, hopeless, discouraging, disheartening. **2** COLD, chilly, raw, weather-beaten, unsheltered, windy, windswept, exposed, open, barren, bare, empty, desolate, gaunt.
F∃ 1 bright, cheerful.

bleed v **1** HAEMORRHAGE, gush, spurt, flow, run, exude, weep, ooze, seep, trickle. **2** DRAIN, suck dry, exhaust, squeeze, milk, sap, reduce, deplete.

blemish n flaw, imperfection, defect, fault, deformity, disfigurement, birthmark, naevus, spot, mark, speck, smudge, blotch, blot, stain, taint.
v flaw, deface, disfigure, spoil, mar, damage, impair, spot, mark, blot, blotch, stain, sully, taint, tarnish.

blend v **1** MERGE, amalgamate, coalesce, compound, synthesize, fuse, unite, combine, mix, mingle. **2** HARMONIZE, complement, fit, match.
F∃ 1 separate.
n compound, composite, alloy, amalgam, amalgamation, synthesis, fusion, combination, union, mix, mixture, concoction.

bless v **1** ANOINT, sanctify, consecrate, hallow, dedicate, ordain. **2** PRAISE, extol, magnify, glorify, exalt, thank. **3** APPROVE, countenance, favour, grace, bestow, endow, provide.
F∃ 1 curse. **2** condemn.

blessed adj **1** HOLY, sacred, hallowed, sanctified, revered, adored, divine. **2** HAPPY, contented, glad, joyful, joyous, lucky, fortunate, prosperous, favoured, endowed.
F∃ 1 cursed.

blessing n **1** CONSECRATION, dedication, benediction, grace, thanksgiving, invocation. **2** BENEFIT, advantage, favour, godsend, windfall, gift, gain, profit, help, service. **3** give a proposal one's blessing: approval, concurrence, backing, support, authority, sanction, consent, permission, leave.
F∃ 2 curse, blight. **3** condemnation.

blight n curse, bane, evil, scourge, affliction, disease, cancer, canker, fungus, mildew, rot, decay, pollution, contamination, corruption, infestation.
F∃ blessing, boon.
v spoil, mar, injure, undermine, ruin, wreck, crush, shatter, destroy, annihilate, blast, wither, shrivel, frustrate, disappoint.
F∃ bless.

blind adj **1** SIGHTLESS, unsighted, unseeing, eyeless, purblind, partially sighted. **2** IMPETUOUS, impulsive, hasty, rash, reckless, wild, mad, indiscriminate, careless, heedless, mindless, unthinking, unreasoning, irrational. **3** blind to their needs: ignorant, oblivious, unaware, unconscious, unobservant,

inattentive, neglectful, indifferent, insensitive, thoughtless, inconsiderate. **4** CLOSED, obstructed, hidden, concealed, obscured.
F3 1 sighted. **2** careful, cautious. **3** aware, sensitive.
n screen, cover, cloak, mask, camouflage, masquerade, front, façade, distraction, smokescreen, cover-up (*infml*).

bliss *n* blissfulness, ecstasy, euphoria, rapture, joy, happiness, gladness, blessedness, paradise, heaven.
F3 misery, hell, damnation.

blissful *adj* ecstatic, euphoric, elated, enraptured, rapturous, delighted, enchanted, joyful, joyous, happy.
F3 miserable, wretched.

blister *n* sore, swelling, cyst, boil, abscess, ulcer, pustule, pimple, carbuncle.

blizzard *n* snowstorm, squall, storm, tempest.

bloated *adj* swollen, puffy, blown up, inflated, distended, dilated, expanded, enlarged, turgid, bombastic.
F3 thin, shrunken, shrivelled.

blob *n* drop, droplet, globule, glob (*infml*), bead, pearl, bubble, dab, spot, gob, lump, mass, ball, pellet, pill.

block *n* **1** *a block of stone:* piece, lump, mass, chunk, hunk, square, cube, brick, bar. **2** OBSTACLE, barrier, bar, jam, blockage, stoppage, resistance, obstruction, impediment, hindrance, let, delay.
v choke, clog, plug, stop up, dam up, close, bar, obstruct, impede, hinder, stonewall, stop, check, arrest, halt, thwart, scotch, deter.

blockade *n* barrier, barricade, siege, obstruction, occlusion, block, restriction, stoppage, closure.

blockage *n* blocking, obstruction, stoppage, occlusion, block, clot, jam, log-jam, gridlock, congestion, hindrance, impediment.

blond, blonde *adj* fair, flaxen, golden, fair-haired, golden-haired, light-coloured, bleached.

blood *n* extraction, birth, descent, lineage, family, kindred, relations, ancestry, descendants, kinship, relationship.

bloodcurdling *adj* horrifying, chilling, spine-chilling, hair-raising, white-knuckle (*infml*), terrifying, frightening, scary, dreadful, fearful, horrible, horrid, horrendous.

bloodshed *n* killing, murder, slaughter, massacre, blood-bath, butchery, carnage, gore, bloodletting.

bloodthirsty *adj* murderous, homicidal, warlike, savage, barbaric, barbarous, brutal, ferocious, vicious, cruel, inhuman, ruthless.

bloody *adj* bleeding, bloodstained, gory, sanguinary, murderous, savage, brutal, ferocious, fierce, cruel.

bloom *n* **1** BLOSSOM, flower, bud. **2** PRIME, heyday, perfection, blush, flush, glow, rosiness, beauty, radiance, lustre, health, vigour, freshness.
v bud, sprout, grow, wax, develop, mature, blossom, flower, blow, open.
F3 fade, wither.

blossom *n* in bloom, flower, bud.
v develop, mature, bloom, flower, blow, flourish, thrive, prosper, succeed.
F3 fade, wither.

blot n spot, stain, smudge, blotch, smear, mark, speck, blemish, flaw, fault, defect, taint, disgrace.
v spot, mark, stain, smudge, blur, sully, taint, tarnish, spoil, mar, disfigure, disgrace.

blot out obliterate, cancel, delete, erase, expunge, darken, obscure, shadow, eclipse.

blotch n patch, splodge, splotch, splash, smudge, blot, spot, mark, stain, blemish.

blotchy adj spotty, spotted, patchy, uneven, smeary, blemished, reddened, inflamed.

blow¹ v **1** BREATHE, exhale, pant, puff, waft, fan, flutter, float, flow, stream, rush, whirl, whisk, sweep, fling, buffet, drive, blast. **2** blow a horn: play, sound, pipe, trumpet, toot, blare.
n puff, draught, flurry, gust, blast, wind, gale, squall, tempest.

blow over die down, subside, end, finish, cease, pass, vanish, disappear, dissipate, fizzle out, peter out.

blow up 1 EXPLODE, go off, detonate, burst, blast, bomb. **2** LOSE ONE'S TEMPER, blow one's top (infml), erupt, hit the roof (infml), rage, go mad (infml). **3** INFLATE, pump up, swell, fill (out), puff up, distend, dilate, expand, enlarge, magnify, exaggerate, overstate.

blow² n **1** a blow on the head: concussion, box, cuff, clip, clout, swipe, biff (infml), bash, slap, smack, whack (infml), wallop (infml), belt (infml), buffet, bang, clap, knock, rap, stroke, thump, punch. **2** MISFORTUNE, affliction, reverse, setback, comedown, disappointment, upset, jolt, shock, bombshell, calamity, catastrophe, disaster.

blowy adj breezy, windy, fresh, blustery, gusty, squally, stormy.

bludgeon v **1** BEAT, strike, club, batter, cosh (sl), cudgel. **2** FORCE, coerce, bulldoze, badger, hector, harass, browbeat, bully, terrorize, intimidate.

blue adj **1** AZURE, sapphire, cobalt, ultramarine, navy, indigo, aquamarine, turquoise, cyan.
2 DEPRESSED, low, down in the dumps (infml), dejected, downcast, dispirited, down-hearted, despondent, gloomy, glum, dismal, sad, unhappy, miserable, melancholy, morose, fed up (infml). **3** a blue joke: obscene, offensive, indecent, improper, coarse, vulgar, lewd, dirty, pornographic, bawdy, smutty, near the bone, near the knuckle, risqué.
E3 2 cheerful, happy. **3** decent, clean.

blueprint n archetype, prototype, model, pattern, design, outline, draft, sketch, pilot, guide, plan, scheme, project.

bluff v lie, pretend, feign, sham, fake, deceive, delude, mislead, hoodwink, blind, bamboozle (infml), fool.
n lie, idle boast, bravado, humbug, pretence, show, sham, fake, fraud, trick, scam (infml), subterfuge, deceit, deception.

blunder n mistake, error, solecism, howler (infml), bloomer (infml), clanger (infml), inaccuracy, slip, boob (infml), indiscretion, gaffe, faux pas, slip-up (infml), oversight, fault, cock-up (sl).
v stumble, flounder, bumble, err, slip up (infml), miscalculate, misjudge, bungle, botch, fluff (infml), mismanage, cock up (sl).

blunt adj 1 UNSHARPENED, dull, worn, pointless, rounded, stubbed. 2 FRANK, candid, direct, forthright, unceremonious, explicit, plain-spoken, honest, downright, outspoken, tactless, insensitive, rude, impolite, uncivil, brusque, curt, abrupt.

F3 1 sharp, pointed. 2 subtle, tactful.

v dull, take the edge off, dampen, soften, deaden, numb, anaesthetize, alleviate, allay, abate, weaken.

F3 sharpen, intensify.

blur v smear, smudge, mist, fog, befog, cloud, becloud, blear, dim, darken, obscure, mask, conceal, soften.

n smear, smudge, blotch, haze, mist, fog, cloudiness, fuzziness, indistinctness, muddle, confusion, dimness, obscurity.

blurred adj out of focus, fuzzy, unclear, indistinct, vague, ill-defined, faint, hazy, misty, foggy, cloudy, bleary, dim, obscure, confused.

F3 clear, distinct.

blurt out exclaim, cry, gush, spout, utter, tell, reveal, disclose, divulge, blab (infml), let out, leak, let slip, spill the beans (infml).

F3 bottle up, hush up.

blush v flush, redden, colour, glow.

F3 blanch.

n flush, reddening, rosiness, ruddiness, colour, glow.

blushing adj flushed, red, rosy, glowing, confused, embarrassed, ashamed, modest.

F3 pale, white, composed.

bluster v boast, brag, crow, talk big (infml), swagger, strut, vaunt, show off, rant, roar, storm, bully, hector.

n boasting, crowing, bravado, bluff, swagger.

blustery adj windy, gusty, squally, stormy, tempestuous, violent, wild, boisterous.

F3 calm.

board n 1 a wooden board: sheet, panel, slab, plank, beam, timber, slat. 2 COMMITTEE, council, panel, jury, commission, directorate, directors, trustees, advisers. 3 MEALS, food, provisions, rations.

v get on, embark, mount, enter, catch.

boast v brag, crow, swank (infml), claim, exaggerate, talk big (infml), bluster, trumpet, vaunt, strut, swagger, show off, exhibit, possess.

F3 belittle, deprecate.

n brag, swank (infml), claim, vaunt, pride, joy, gem, treasure.

boastful adj proud, conceited, vain, swollen-headed, big-headed (infml), puffed up, bragging, crowing, swanky (infml), cocky, showy.

F3 modest, self-effacing, humble.

boat

Types of boat or ship include:
canoe, dinghy, lifeboat, rowing-boat, kayak, coracle, skiff, punt, sampan, dhow, gondola, pedalo, catamaran, trimaran, yacht; cabin cruiser, motorboat, speedboat, trawler, barge, narrow-boat, house-boat, dredger, junk, smack, lugger; hovercraft, hydrofoil; clipper, cut-ter, ketch, packet, brig, schooner, square-rigger, galleon, tug, ferry, paddle-steamer, freighter, liner, container ship, tanker; warship, battleship, destroyer, submarine, U-boat, frigate, aircraft-carrier, cruiser, dreadnought, corvette, minesweeper, man-of-war.

bob *v* bounce, hop, skip, spring, jump, leap, twitch, jerk, jolt, shake, quiver, wobble, oscillate, nod, bow, curtsy.

bob up appear, emerge, arrive, show up (*infml*), materialize, rise, surface, pop up, spring up, crop up, arise.

bodily *adj* physical, corporeal, carnal, fleshly, real, actual, tangible, substantial, concrete, material.
E3 spiritual.
adv altogether, en masse, collectively, as a whole, completely, fully, wholly, entirely, totally, in toto.
E3 piecemeal.

body *n* **1** ANATOMY, physique, build, figure, trunk, torso. **2** CORPSE, cadaver, carcase, stiff (*sl*). **3** COMPANY, association, society, corporation, confederation, bloc, cartel, syndicate, congress, collection, group, band, crowd, throng, multitude, mob, mass. **4** CONSISTENCY, density, solidity, firmness, mass, substance, essence, fullness, richness.

> Body parts include:
> biceps, bone, cartilage, diaphragm, elbow, epidermis, epiglottis, Fallopian tubes, foreskin, funny bone, genitalia, gristle, groin, gullet, hamstring, hock, ligament, mammary, muscle, oesophagus, spine, tendon, triceps, umbilicus, uterus, uvula, voice-box, vulva, windpipe, wisdom tooth, womb. *see also* **anatomy**; **bone**; **brain**; **ear**; **eye**; **heart**.

bodyguard *n* guard, protector, minder (*infml*).

bog *n* marsh, swamp, fen, mire, quagmire, quag, slough, morass, quicksands, marshland, swampland, wetlands.

bog down encumber, hinder, impede, overwhelm, deluge, sink, stick, slow down, slow up, delay, retard, halt, stall.

bogus *adj* false, fake, counterfeit, forged, fraudulent, phoney (*infml*), spurious, sham, pseudo, artificial, imitation, dummy.
E3 genuine, true, real, valid.

bohemian *adj* artistic, arty (*infml*), unconventional, unorthodox, nonconformist, alternative, eccentric, offbeat, way-out (*sl*), bizarre, exotic.
E3 bourgeois, conventional, orthodox.
n beatnik, hippie, drop-out, new-ager, nonconformist.
E3 bourgeois, conformist.

boil¹ *v* **1** SIMMER, stew, seethe, brew, gurgle, bubble, fizz, effervesce, froth, foam, steam. **2** *boil with anger*: erupt, explode, rage, rave, storm, fulminate, fume.

boil down reduce, concentrate, distil, condense, digest, abstract, summarize, abridge.

boil² *n* pustule, abscess, gumboil, ulcer, tumour, pimple, carbuncle, blister, inflammation.

boiling *adj* **1** *boiling water*: turbulent, gurgling, bubbling, steaming. **2** HOT, baking, roasting, scorching, blistering. **3** ANGRY, indignant, incensed, infuriated, enraged, furious, fuming, flaming.

boisterous *adj* exuberant, rumbustious (*infml*), rollicking, bouncy, turbulent, tumultuous, loud, noisy, clamorous, rowdy, rough, disorderly, riotous, wild, unrestrained, unruly, obstreperous.
E3 quiet, calm, restrained.

bold *adj* **1** FEARLESS, dauntless, daring, audacious, brave, courageous, valiant, heroic, gallant, intrepid, adventurous, venturesome, enterprising, plucky, spirited, confident, outgoing. **2** EYE-CATCHING, striking, conspicuous, prominent, strong, pronounced, bright, vivid, colourful, loud, flashy, showy, flamboyant. **3** BRAZEN, brash, forward, shameless, unabashed, cheeky (*infml*), impudent, insolent. **F3** cautious, timid, shy. **2** faint, restrained.

bolt *n* bar, rod, shaft, pin, peg, rivet, fastener, latch, catch, lock. *v* **1** FASTEN, secure, bar, latch, lock. **2** ABSCOND, escape, flee, fly, run, sprint, rush, dash, hurtle. **3** *bolt one's food:* gulp, wolf, gobble, gorge, devour, cram, stuff.

bomb *n* atom bomb, petrol bomb, shell, bombshell, explosive, charge, grenade, mine, torpedo, rocket, missile, projectile. *v* bombard, shell, torpedo, attack, blow up, destroy.

bombard *v* attack, assault, assail, pelt, pound, strafe, blast, bomb, shell, blitz, besiege, hound, harass, pester.

bombardment *n* attack, assault, air-raid, bombing, shelling, blitz, barrage, cannonade, fusillade, salvo, fire, flak.

bombastic *adj* grandiloquent, magniloquent, grandiose, pompous, high-flown, inflated, bloated, windy, wordy, verbose.

bond *n* **1** CONNECTION, relation, link, tie, union, affiliation, attachment, affinity. **2** CONTRACT, covenant, agreement, pledge, promise, word, obligation. **3** FETTER, shackle, manacle, chain, cord, band, binding. *v* connect, fasten, bind, unite, fuse, glue, gum, paste, stick, seal.

bondage *n* imprisonment, incarceration, captivity, confinement, restraint, slavery, enslavement, serfdom, servitude, subservience, subjection, subjugation, yoke. **F3** freedom, independence.

bone

Human bones include:
clavicle, coccyx, collar bone, femur, fibula, hip-bone, humerus, ilium, ischium, mandible, maxilla, meta-carpal, metatarsal, patella, pelvis, pubis, radius, rib, scapula, shoulder blade, skull, sternum, stirrup bone, temporal, thigh-bone, tibia, ulna, vertebra.

bonus *n* advantage, benefit, plus (*infml*), extra, perk (*infml*), perquisite, commission, dividend, premium, prize, reward, honorarium, tip, gratuity, gift, handout. **F3** disadvantage, disincentive.

bony *adj* thin, lean, angular, lanky, gawky, gangling, skinny, scrawny, emaciated, rawboned, gaunt, drawn. **F3** fat, plump.

book *n* volume, tome, publication, work, booklet, tract.

Types of book include:
hardback, paperback, softback; bestseller; fiction, novel, story, thriller, romantic novel; children's book, primer, picture-book, annual; reference book, encyclopedia, dictionary, lexicon, thesaurus, concordance, anthology, compendium, omnibus, atlas, guidebook, gazetteer, directory, handbook, manual, cookbook, yearbook, almanac, catalogue; notebook, exercise-book, textbook, scrapbook, album, sketchbook, diary, Filofax®, jotter,

pad, ledger; libretto, manuscript, hymn-book, hymnal, prayer book, psalter, missal, lectionary. *see also* **literature**.

v reserve, bag (*infml*), engage, charter, procure, order, arrange, organize, schedule, programme.
F3 cancel.

boom *v* 1 BANG, crash, roar, thunder, roll, rumble, resound, reverberate, blast, explode. 2 FLOURISH, thrive, prosper, succeed, develop, grow, increase, gain, expand, swell, escalate, intensify, strengthen, explode.
F3 2 fail, collapse, slump.
n 1 BANG, clap, crash, roar, thunder, rumble, reverberation, blast, explosion, burst. 2 INCREASE, growth, expansion, gain, upsurge, jump, spurt, boost, upturn, improvement, advance, escalation, explosion.
F3 2 failure, collapse, slump, recession, depression.

boon *n* blessing, advantage, benefit, godsend, windfall, favour, kindness, gift, present, grant, gratuity.
F3 disadvantage, blight.

boorish *adj* uncouth, oafish, loutish, ill-mannered, rude, coarse, crude, vulgar, unrefined, uncivilized, uneducated, ignorant.
F3 polite, refined, cultured.

boost *n* improvement, enhancement, expansion, increase, rise, jump, increment, addition, supplement, booster, lift, hoist, heave, push, thrust, help, advancement, promotion, praise, encouragement, fillip, ego-trip (*sl*).
F3 setback, blow.
v raise, elevate, improve, enhance, develop, enlarge, expand, amplify, increase, augment, heighten, lift, hoist, jack up, heave, push, thrust, help, aid, assist, advance, further, promote, advertise, plug (*infml*), praise, talk up (*infml*), inspire, encourage, foster, support, sustain, bolster, supplement.
F3 hinder, undermine, talk down (*infml*).

boot *n* gumboot, wellington, welly (*infml*), galosh, overshoe, walking-boot, riding-boot, top-boot.

booth *n* kiosk, stall, stand, hut, box, compartment, cubicle, carrel.

booty *n* loot, plunder, pillage, spoils, swag (*sl*), haul, gains, takings, pickings, winnings.

border *n* 1 BOUNDARY, frontier, bound, bounds, confine, confines, limit, demarcation, borderline, margin, fringe, periphery, surround, perimeter, circumference, edge, rim, brim, verge, brink. 2 TRIMMING, frill, valance, skirt, hem, frieze.
border on 1 ADJOIN, abut, touch, impinge, join, connect, communicate with. 2 RESEMBLE, approximate, approach, verge on.

bore¹ *v* drill, mine, pierce, perforate, penetrate, sink, burrow, tunnel, undermine, sap.

bore² *v* tire, weary, fatigue, jade, trouble, bother, worry, irritate, annoy, vex, irk.
F3 interest, excite.
n (*infml*) nuisance, bother, bind (*infml*), drag (*infml*), bummer (*sl*), pain (*infml*), headache (*infml*).
F3 pleasure, delight.

boredom *n* tedium, tediousness, monotony, dullness, apathy, listlessness, weariness, world-weariness.
F3 interest, excitement.

boring *adj* tedious, monotonous, routine, repetitious, uninteresting, unexciting, uneventful, dull, dreary, humdrum, commonplace, trite, unimaginative, uninspired, dry, stale, flat, insipid.
F3 interesting, exciting, stimulating, original.

borrow *v* steal, pilfer, filch, lift, plagiarize, crib, copy, imitate, mimic, echo, take, draw, derive, obtain, adopt, use, scrounge, cadge, sponge, appropriate, usurp.
F3 lend.

bosom *n* **1** BUST, breasts, chest, breast. **2** HEART, core, centre, midst, protection, shelter, sanctuary.

boss *n* employer, governor, master, owner, manager, head, chief, leader, supremo, administrator, executive, director, manager, foreman, gaffer, superintendent, overseer, supervisor.
boss around order around, order about, domineer, tyrannize, bully, bulldoze, browbeat, push around, dominate.

bossy *adj* authoritarian, autocratic, tyrannical, despotic, dictatorial, domineering, overbearing, oppressive, lordly, high-handed, imperious, insistent, assertive, demanding, exacting.
F3 unassertive.

bother *v* disturb, inconvenience, harass, hassle (*infml*), pester, plague, nag, annoy, irritate, irk, molest, trouble, worry, concern, alarm, dismay, distress, upset, vex.
n inconvenience, trouble, problem, difficulty, hassle (*infml*), fuss, bustle, flurry, nuisance, pest, annoyance, irritation, aggravation (*infml*), vexation, worry, strain.

bottle *n* phial, flask, carafe, decanter, flagon, demijohn.
bottle up hide, conceal, restrain, curb, hold back, suppress, inhibit, restrict, enclose, contain.
F3 unbosom, unburden.

bottleneck *n* hold-up, traffic jam, gridlock, snarl-up, congestion, clogging, blockage, obstruction, block, obstacle.

bottom *n* **1** UNDERSIDE, underneath, sole, base, foot, plinth, pedestal, support, foundation, substructure, ground, floor, bed, depths, nadir. **2** RUMP, rear, behind, posterior (*infml*), buttocks, seat, backside (*infml*), bum (*sl*), butt (*US infml*), arse (*sl*), ass (*US sl*), tail (*infml*).
F3 1 top.

bottomless *adj* deep, profound, fathomless, unfathomed, unplumbed, immeasurable, measureless, infinite, boundless, limitless, unlimited, inexhaustible.
F3 shallow, limited.

bounce *v* spring, jump, leap, bound, bob, ricochet, rebound, recoil.
n **1** SPRING, bound, springiness, elasticity, give, resilience, rebound, recoil. **2** EBULLIENCE, exuberance, vitality, vivacity, energy, vigour, go (*infml*), zip (*infml*), animation, liveliness.

bound[1] *adj* **1** FASTENED, secured, fixed, tied (up), chained, held, restricted, bandaged. **2** LIABLE, committed, duty-bound, obliged, required, forced, compelled, constrained, destined, fated, doomed, sure, certain.

bound[2] *v* jump, leap, vault, hurdle, spring, bounce, bob, hop, skip, frisk, gambol, frolic, caper, prance.
n jump, leap, vault, spring, bounce,

bob, hop, skip, gambol, frolic, caper, dance, prance.

boundary n border, frontier, barrier, line, borderline, demarcation, bounds, confines, limits, margin, fringe, verge, brink, edge, perimeter, extremity, termination.

boundless adj unbounded, limitless, unlimited, unconfined, countless, untold, incalculable, vast, immense, measureless, immeasurable, infinite, endless, unending, interminable, inexhaustible, unflagging, indefatigable.
E3 limited, restricted.

bounds n confines, limits, borders, marches, margins, fringes, periphery, circumference, edges, extremities.

bounty n 1 GENEROSITY, liberality, munificence, largesse, almsgiving, charity, philanthropy, beneficence, kindness. 2 REWARD, recompense, premium, bonus, gratuity, gift, present, donation, grant, allowance.

bouquet n 1 bouquet of flowers: bunch, posy, nosegay, spray, corsage, buttonhole, wreath, garland. 2 AROMA, smell, odour, scent, perfume, fragrance.

bourgeois adj middle-class, materialistic, conservative, traditional, conformist, conventional, hide-bound, unadventurous, dull, humdrum, banal, commonplace, trite, unoriginal, unimaginative.
E3 bohemian, unconventional, original.

bout n 1 FIGHT, battle, engagement, encounter, struggle, set-to, match, contest, competition, round, heat. 2 PERIOD, spell, time, stint, turn, go (infml), term, stretch, run, course, session, spree, attack, fit.

bow v 1 bow one's head: incline, bend, nod, bob, curtsy, genuflect (fml), kowtow, salaam, stoop. 2 YIELD, give in, consent, surrender, capitulate, submit, acquiesce, concede, accept, comply, defer. 3 SUBDUE, overpower, conquer, vanquish, crush, subjugate. n inclination, bending, nod, bob, curtsy, genuflexion (fml), kowtow, salaam, obeisance (fml), salutation, acknowledgement.

bow out withdraw, pull out, desert, abandon, defect, back out, chicken out (infml), retire, resign, quit, stand down, step down, give up.

bowels n 1 INTESTINES, viscera, entrails, guts, insides, innards (infml). 2 DEPTHS, interior, inside, middle, centre, core, heart.

bowl [1] n receptacle, container, vessel, dish, basin, sink.

bowl [2] v throw, hurl, fling, pitch, roll, spin, whirl, rotate, revolve.

bowl over surprise, amaze, astound, astonish, stagger, stun, dumbfound, flabbergast (infml), floor (infml).

box [1] n container, receptacle, case, crate, carton, packet, pack, package, present, chest, coffer, trunk, coffin. v case, encase, package, pack, wrap.

box in enclose, surround, circumscribe, cordon off, hem in, corner, trap, confine, restrict, imprison, cage, coop up, contain.

box [2] v fight, spar, punch, hit, strike, slap, buffet, cuff, clout, sock (sl), wallop (infml), whack (infml).

boxer n pugilist, fighter, prizefighter, sparring partner, featherweight, lightweight, welterweight, middleweight, heavyweight.

boxing n pugilism, prizefighting, fisticuffs, sparring.

boy n son, lad, youngster, kid (*infml*), nipper (*infml*), stripling, youth, fellow.

boycott v refuse, reject, embargo, black, ban, prohibit, disallow, bar, exclude, blacklist, outlaw, ostracize, cold-shoulder, ignore, spurn. **F3** encourage, support.

boyfriend n young man, man, fellow (*infml*), bloke (*infml*), admirer, date, sweetheart, lover, fiancé, partner.

brace n pair, couple, twosome, duo. v strengthen, reinforce, fortify, bolster, buttress, prop, shore (up), support, steady, tighten, fasten, tie, strap, bind, bandage.

bracing adj fresh, crisp, refreshing, reviving, strengthening, fortifying, tonic, rousing, stimulating, exhilarating, invigorating, enlivening, energizing, brisk, energetic, vigorous. **F3** weakening, debilitating.

braid v plait, interweave, interlace, intertwine, weave, lace, twine, entwine, ravel, twist, wind. **F3** undo, unravel.

brain n 1 CEREBRUM, grey matter, head, mind, intellect, nous, brains (*infml*), intelligence, wit, reason, sense, common sense, shrewdness, understanding. 2 MASTERMIND, intellectual, highbrow, egghead (*infml*), scholar, expert, boffin, genius, prodigy. **F3 2** simpleton.

Parts of the brain include:
brain stem, cerebellum, cerebral cortex (grey matter), cerebrum, corpus callosum, frontal lobe, hypothalamus, medulla oblongata, mesencephalon, occipital lobe, parietal lobe, pineal body, pituitary gland, pons Varolii, temporal lobe, thalamus.

brainy adj intellectual, intelligent, clever, smart, bright, brilliant. **F3** dull.

brake n check, curb, rein, restraint, control, restriction, constraint, drag. v slow, decelerate, retard, drag, slacken, moderate, check, halt, stop, pull up. **F3** accelerate.

branch n 1 BOUGH, limb, sprig, shoot, offshoot, arm, wing, prong. 2 *a different branch of the company*: department, office, part, section, division, subsection, subdivision. **branch out** diversify, vary, develop, expand, enlarge, extend, broaden out, increase, multiply, proliferate, ramify.

brand n make, brand-name, tradename, trademark, logo, mark, symbol, sign, emblem, label, stamp, hallmark, grade, quality, class, kind, type, sort, line, variety, species. v mark, stamp, label, type, stigmatize, burn, scar, stain, taint, disgrace, discredit, denounce, censure.

brandish v wave, flourish, shake, raise, swing, wield, flash, flaunt, exhibit, display, parade.

brash adj 1 BRAZEN, forward, impertinent, impudent, insolent, rude, cocky, assured, bold, audacious. 2 RECKLESS, rash, impetuous, impulsive, hasty, precipitate, foolhardy, incautious, indiscreet. **F3 1** reserved. **2** cautious.

bravado n swagger, boasting, bragging, bluster, bombast, talk, boast, vaunting, showing off, parade, show, pretence. **F3** modesty, restraint.

brave adj courageous, plucky, unafraid, fearless, dauntless, undaunted, bold, audacious, daring,

intrepid, stalwart, hardy, stoical, resolute, stout-hearted, valiant, gallant, heroic, indomitable.
F3 cowardly, afraid, timid.
v face, confront, defy, challenge, dare, stand up to, face up to, suffer, endure, bear, withstand.
F3 capitulate.

bravery *n* courage, pluck, guts (*infml*), fearlessness, dauntlessness, boldness, audacity, daring, intrepidity, stalwartness, hardiness, fortitude, resolution, stout-heartedness, valiance, valour, gallantry, heroism, indomitability, grit, mettle, spirit.
F3 cowardice, faint-heartedness, timidity.

brawl *n* fight, punch-up (*infml*), scrap, scuffle, dust-up (*infml*), mêlée, free-for-all, fray, affray, broil, fracas, rumpus, disorder, row, argument, quarrel, squabble, altercation, dispute, clash.
v fight, scrap, scuffle, wrestle, tussle, row, argue, quarrel, squabble, wrangle, dispute.

brawny *adj* muscular, sinewy, athletic, well-built, burly, beefy, hunky (*infml*), hefty, solid, bulky, hulking, massive, strapping, strong, powerful, vigorous, sturdy, robust, hardy, stalwart.
F3 slight, frail.

brazen *adj* blatant, flagrant, brash, brassy, bold, forward, in-your-face (*infml*), saucy, pert, barefaced, impudent, insolent, defiant, shameless, unashamed, unabashed, immodest.
F3 shamefaced, modest.

breach *n* **1** *a breach of the rules*: violation, contravention, infringement, trespass, disobedience, offence, transgression, lapse,

disruption. **2** QUARREL, disagreement, dissension, difference, variance, schism, rift, rupture, split, division, separation, parting, estrangement, alienation, disaffection, dissociation. **3** BREAK, crack, rift, rupture, fissure, cleft, crevice, opening, aperture, gap, space, hole, chasm.

bread *n* loaf, roll, food, provisions, diet, fare, nourishment, nutriment, sustenance, subsistence, necessities.

> Types of bread and rolls include:
> bagel, baguette, brioche, challah, chapati, ciabatta, cottage loaf, croissant, flatbread, focaccia, French bread, Granary®, milk bread, nan (or naan), pitta, puri (or poori), pumpernickel, roti, ryebread, soda bread, sourdough, wholemeal, wholewheat.

breadth *n* width, broadness, wideness, latitude, thickness, size, magnitude, measure, scale, range, reach, scope, compass, span, sweep, extent, expanse, spread, comprehensiveness, extensiveness, vastness.

break *v* **1** FRACTURE, crack, snap, split, sever, separate, divide, rend, smash, disintegrate, splinter, shiver, shatter, ruin, destroy, demolish. **2** *break the law*: violate, contravene, infringe, breach, disobey, flout. **3** PAUSE, halt, stop, discontinue, interrupt, suspend, rest. **4** SUBDUE, tame, weaken, enfeeble, impair, undermine, demoralize. **5** *break the news*: tell, inform, impart, divulge, disclose, reveal, announce. **6** *break a record*: exceed, beat, better, excel, surpass, outdo, outstrip.
F3 **1** mend. **2** keep, observe, abide by. **4** strengthen.

n **1** FRACTURE, crack, split, rift, rupture, schism, separation, tear, gash, fissure, cleft, crevice, opening, gap, hole, breach. **2** INTERVAL, intermission, interlude, interruption, pause, halt, lull, let-up (*infml*), respite, rest, breather (*infml*), time out, holiday. **3** OPPORTUNITY, chance, advantage, fortune, luck.

break away separate, split, part company, detach, secede, leave, depart, quit, run away, escape, flee, fly.

break down *the van broke down*: fail, stop, pack up (*infml*), conk out (*sl*), seize up, give way, collapse, crack up (*infml*). **2** ANALYSE, dissect, separate, itemize, detail.

break in 1 INTERRUPT, butt in, interpose, interject, intervene, intrude, encroach, impinge. **2** BURGLE, rob, raid, invade.

break off 1 DETACH, snap off, sever, separate, part, divide, disconnect. **2** PAUSE, interrupt, suspend, discontinue, halt, stop, cease, end, finish, terminate.

break out 1 START, begin, commence, arise, emerge, happen, occur, erupt, flare up, burst out. **2** ESCAPE, abscond, bolt, flee.

break up 1 DISMANTLE, take apart, demolish, destroy, disintegrate, splinter, sever, divide, split, part, separate, divorce. **2** DISBAND, disperse, dissolve, adjourn, suspend, stop, finish, terminate.

breakable adj brittle, fragile, delicate, flimsy, insubstantial, frail. **E3** unbreakable, durable, sturdy.

breakdown n **1** FAILURE, collapse, disintegration, malfunction, interruption, stoppage. **2** ANALYSIS,
dissection, itemization, classification, categorization.

break-in n burglary, house-breaking, robbery, raid, invasion, intrusion, trespass.

breakthrough n discovery, find, finding, invention, innovation, advance, progress, headway, step, leap, development, improvement.

break-up n divorce, separation, parting, split, rift, finish, termination, dissolution, dispersal, disintegration, crumbling.

breakwater n groyne, mole, jetty, pier, quay, wharf, dock.

breath n **1** AIR, breathing, respiration, inhalation, exhalation, sigh, gasp, pant, gulp. **2** BREEZE, puff, waft, gust. **3** AROMA, smell, odour, whiff. **4** HINT, suggestion, suspicion, undertone, whisper, murmur.

breathe v **1** RESPIRE, inhale, exhale, expire, sigh, gasp, pant, puff. **2** SAY, utter, express, voice, articulate, murmur, whisper, impart, tell. **3** INSTIL, imbue, infuse, inject, inspire.

breathless adj **1** SHORT-WINDED, out of breath, panting, puffing, puffed (out), exhausted, winded, gasping, wheezing, choking. **2** *breathless anticipation*: expectant, impatient, eager, agog, excited, feverish, anxious.

breathtaking adj awe-inspiring, impressive, magnificent, overwhelming, amazing, astonishing, jaw-dropping (*infml*), stunning, exciting, thrilling, stirring, moving.

breed v **1** REPRODUCE, procreate, multiply, propagate, hatch, bear, bring forth, rear, raise, bring up, educate, train, instruct. **2** PRODUCE, create, originate, arouse, cause, occasion, engender, generate, make, foster, nurture, nourish, cultivate, develop. *n* species, strain, variety, family, ilk, sort, kind, type, stamp, stock, race, progeny, line, lineage, pedigree.

breeding *n* **1** REPRODUCTION, procreation, nurture, development, rearing, raising, upbringing, education, training, background, ancestry, lineage, stock. **2** MANNERS, politeness, civility, gentility, urbanity, refinement, culture, polish.
F3 2 vulgarity.

breeze *n* wind, gust, flurry, waft, puff, breath, draught, air.

breezy *adj* **1** WINDY, blowing, fresh, airy, gusty, blustery, squally. **2** ANIMATED, lively, vivacious, jaunty, buoyant, blithe, debonair, carefree, cheerful, easy-going (*infml*), casual, informal, light, bright, exhilarating.
F3 1 still. **2** staid, serious.

brevity *n* briefness, shortness, terseness, conciseness, succinctness, pithiness, crispness, incisiveness, abruptness, curtness, impermanence, ephemerality, transience, transitoriness.
F3 verbosity, permanence, longevity.

brew *v* **1** INFUSE, stew, boil, seethe, ferment, prepare, soak, steep, mix, cook. **2** PLOT, scheme, plan, project, devise, contrive, concoct, hatch, excite, foment, build up, gather, develop.
n infusion, drink, beverage, liquor, potion, broth, gruel, stew, mixture, blend, concoction, preparation, fermentation, distillation.

bribe *n* incentive, inducement, allurement, enticement, back-hander (*infml*), kickback, payola, refresher (*infml*), sweetener (*infml*), hush money

(*infml*), protection money.
v corrupt, suborn, buy off, reward.

bribery *n* corruption, graft (*sl*), palm-greasing, inducement, lubrication.

bric-à-brac *n* knick-knacks, ornaments, curios, antiques, trinkets, baubles.

bridal *adj* wedding, nuptial, marriage, matrimonial, marital, conjugal.

bridge *n* arch, span, causeway, link, connection, bond, tie.

Types of bridge include: suspension bridge, arch bridge, cantilever bridge, flying bridge, fly-over, overpass, footbridge, railway bridge, viaduct, aqueduct, hump-back bridge, toll bridge, pontoon bridge, Bailey bridge, rope bridge, drawbridge, swing bridge.

v span, cross, traverse, fill, link, connect, couple, join, unite, bind.

bridle *v* check, curb, restrain, control, govern, master, subdue, moderate, repress, contain.

brief *adj* **1** SHORT, terse, succinct, concise, pithy, crisp, compressed, thumbnail, laconic, abrupt, sharp, brusque, blunt, curt, surly. **2** SHORT-LIVED, momentary, ephemeral, transient, fleeting, passing, transitory, temporary, limited, cursory, hasty, quick, swift, fast.
F3 1 long. **2** lengthy.
n **1** ORDERS, instructions, directions, remit, mandate, directive, advice, briefing, data, information. **2** OUTLINE, summary, précis, dossier, case, defence, argument. *v* instruct, direct, explain, guide, advise, prepare, prime, inform, fill in (*infml*), gen up (*sl*), get up to speed (*infml*).

briefing n meeting, conference, preparation, priming, filling-in (infml), gen (sl), low-down (sl), information, advice, guidance, directions, instructions, orders.

bright adj 1 LUMINOUS, illuminated, radiant, shining, beaming, flashing, gleaming, glistening, glittering, sparkling, twinkling, shimmering, glowing, brilliant, resplendent, glorious, splendid, dazzling, glaring, blazing, intense, vivid. 2 HAPPY, cheerful, glad, joyful, merry, jolly, lively, vivacious, upbeat (infml). 3 the future looks bright: promising, propitious, auspicious, favourable, rosy, optimistic, hopeful, encouraging. 4 CLEVER, brainy (infml), smart, intelligent, quick-witted, quick, sharp, acute, keen, astute, perceptive. 5 CLEAR, transparent, translucent, lucid. 6 a bright day: fine, sunny, cloudless, unclouded.
F3 1 dull. 3 sad. 3 depressing. 4 stupid. 5 muddy. 6 dark.

brighten v 1 LIGHT UP, illuminate, lighten, clear up. 2 POLISH, burnish, rub up, shine, gleam, glow. 3 CHEER UP, gladden, hearten, encourage, enliven, perk up.
F3 1 darken. 2 dull, tarnish.

brilliance n 1 TALENT, virtuosity, genius, greatness, distinction, excellence, aptitude, cleverness. 2 RADIANCE, brightness, sparkle, dazzle, intensity, vividness, gloss, lustre, sheen, glamour, glory, magnificence, splendour.

brilliant adj 1 a brilliant pianist: gifted, talented, accomplished, expert, skilful, masterly, exceptional, outstanding, superb, illustrious,

famous, celebrated. 2 SPARKLING, glittering, scintillating, dazzling, glaring, blazing, intense, vivid, bright, shining, glossy, showy, glorious, magnificent, splendid. 3 CLEVER, brainy (infml), intelligent, quick, astute.
F3 1 undistinguished. 2 dull. 3 stupid.

brim n rim, perimeter, circumference, lip, edge, margin, border, brink, verge, top, limit.

bring v 1 CARRY, bear, convey, transport, fetch, take, deliver, escort, accompany, usher, guide, conduct, lead. 2 CAUSE, produce, engender, create, prompt, provoke, force, attract, draw.
bring about cause, occasion, create, produce, generate, effect, accomplish, achieve, fulfil, realize, manage, engineer, manoeuvre, manipulate.
bring in earn, net, gross, produce, yield, fetch, return, accrue, realize.
bring off achieve, accomplish, fulfil, execute, discharge, perform, succeed, win.
bring on cause, occasion, induce, lead to, give rise to, generate, inspire, prompt, provoke, precipitate, expedite, accelerate, advance.
F3 inhibit.
bring out 1 EMPHASIZE, stress, highlight, enhance, draw out. 2 PUBLISH, print, issue, launch, introduce.
bring up 1 REAR, raise, foster, nurture, educate, teach, train, form. 2 bring up a subject: introduce, broach, mention, submit, propose. 3 VOMIT, regurgitate, throw up (infml).

brink n verge, threshold, edge, margin, fringe, border, boundary, limit, extremity, lip, rim, brim, bank.

brisk *adj* 1 ENERGETIC, vigorous, quick, snappy, lively, spirited, active, busy, bustling, agile, nimble, alert. 2 INVIGORATING, exhilarating, stimulating, bracing, refreshing, fresh, crisp.
F3 lazy, sluggish.

bristle *n* hair, whisker, stubble, spine, prickle, barb, thorn.

bristly *adj* hairy, whiskered, bearded, unshaven, stubbly, rough, spiny, prickly, spiky, thorny.
F3 clean-shaven, smooth.

brittle *adj* breakable, fragile, delicate, frail, crisp, crumbly, crumbling, friable, shattery, shivery.
F3 durable, resilient.

broad *adj* 1 WIDE, large, vast, roomy, spacious, capacious, ample, extensive, widespread. 2 WIDE-RANGING, far-reaching, encyclopedic, catholic, eclectic, all-embracing, inclusive, comprehensive, general, sweeping, universal, unlimited.
F3 1 narrow. 2 restricted.

broadcast *v* air, show, transmit, beam, relay, televise, report, announce, publicize, advertise, publish, circulate, promulgate, disseminate, spread.
n transmission, programme, show.

broaden *v* widen, thicken, swell, spread, enlarge, expand, extend, stretch, increase, augment, develop, open up, branch out, diversify.

broad-minded *adj* liberal, tolerant, permissive, enlightened, free-thinking, open-minded, receptive, unbiased, unprejudiced.
F3 narrow-minded, intolerant, biased.

brochure *n* leaflet, booklet, pamphlet, prospectus, broadsheet, handbill, circular, handout, flyer, folder.

broke *adj* insolvent, penniless, bankrupt, bust, ruined, impoverished, destitute.
F3 solvent, rich, affluent.

broken *adj* 1 FRACTURED, burst, ruptured, severed, separated, faulty, defective, out of order, shattered, destroyed, demolished. 2 DISJOINTED, disconnected, fragmentary, discontinuous, interrupted, intermittent, spasmodic, erratic, hesitating, stammering, halting, imperfect. 3 *a broken man*: beaten, defeated, crushed, demoralized, down, weak, feeble, exhausted, tamed, subdued, oppressed.
F3 1 fluent.

broken-down *adj* dilapidated, worn-out, ruined, collapsed, decayed, inoperative, out of order.

broken-hearted *adj* heartbroken, inconsolable, devastated, grief-stricken, desolate, despairing, miserable, wretched, mournful, sorrowful, sad, unhappy, dejected, despondent, crestfallen, disappointed.

brooch *n* badge, pin, clip, clasp.

brood *v* ponder, ruminate, meditate, muse, mull over, go over, rehearse, dwell on, agonize, fret, mope.
n clutch, chicks, hatch, litter, young, offspring, issue, progeny, children, family.

brook *n* stream, rivulet, beck, burn, watercourse, channel.

brother *n* sibling, relation, relative, comrade, friend, mate, partner, colleague, associate, fellow, companion, monk, friar.

brotherhood n fraternity, association, society, league, confederation, confederacy, alliance, union, guild, fellowship, community, clique.

browbeat v bully, coerce, dragoon, bulldoze, awe, cow, intimidate, threaten, tyrannize, domineer, overbear, oppress, hound.
F∃ coax.

brown adj mahogany, chocolate, coffee, hazel, bay, chestnut, umber, sepia, tan, tawny, russet, rust, rusty, brunette, dark, dusky, sunburnt, tanned, bronzed, browned, toasted.

browse v **1** LEAF THROUGH, flick through, dip into, skim, survey, scan, peruse. **2** GRAZE, pasture, feed, eat, nibble.

bruise v discolour, blacken, mark, blemish, pound, pulverize, crush, hurt, injure, insult, offend, grieve. n contusion, discoloration, black eye, shiner (sl), mark, blemish, injury.

brush¹ n broom, sweeper, besom.
v **1** CLEAN, sweep, flick, burnish, polish, shine. **2** TOUCH, contact, graze, kiss, stroke, rub, scrape.
brush aside dismiss, pooh-pooh, belittle, disregard, ignore, flout, override.
brush off disregard, ignore, slight, snub, cold-shoulder, rebuff, dismiss, spurn, reject, repulse, disown, repudiate.
brush up REVISE, relearn, improve, polish up, study, read up, swot (infml). **2** REFRESH, freshen up, clean, tidy.

brush² n scrub, thicket, bushes, shrubs, brushwood, undergrowth, ground cover.

brush³ n confrontation, encounter, clash, conflict, fight, scrap, skirmish, set-to, tussle, dust-up (infml), fracas.

brusque adj abrupt, sharp, short, terse, curt, gruff, surly, discourteous, impolite, uncivil, blunt, tactless, undiplomatic.
F∃ courteous, polite, tactful.

brutal adj animal, bestial, beastly, brutish, inhuman, savage, bloodthirsty, vicious, ferocious, cruel, inhumane, remorseless, pitiless, merciless, ruthless, callous, insensitive, unfeeling, heartless, harsh, gruff, rough, coarse, crude, rude, uncivilized, barbarous.
F∃ kindly, humane, civilized.

brutality n savagery, bloodthirstiness, viciousness, ferocity, cruelty, inhumanity, violence, atrocity, ruthlessness, callousness, roughness, coarseness, barbarism, barbarity.
F∃ gentleness, kindness.

brute n animal, beast, swine, creature, monster, ogre, devil, fiend, savage, sadist, bully, lout.

bubble n blister, vesicle, globule, ball, drop, droplet, bead.
v effervesce, fizz, sparkle, froth, foam, seethe, boil, burble, gurgle.

bubbly adj **1** EFFERVESCENT, fizzy, sparkling, carbonated, frothy, foaming, sudsy. **2** LIVELY, bouncy, happy, merry, elated, excited, hyper (infml).
F∃ 1 flat, still. **2** lethargic.

bucket n pail, can, bail, scuttle, vessel.

buckle n clasp, clip, catch, fastener.
v **1** buckle one's belt: fasten, clasp, catch, hook, hitch, connect, close, secure. **2** BEND, warp, twist, distort,

bulge, cave in, fold, wrinkle, crumple, collapse.

bud n shoot, sprout, germ, embryo.
v shoot, sprout, burgeon, develop, grow.
E3 wither, waste away.

budding adj potential, promising, embryonic, burgeoning, developing, growing, flowering.

budge v move, stir, shift, remove, dislodge, push, roll, slide, propel, sway, influence, persuade, convince, change, bend, yield, give (way).

budget n finances, funds, resources, means, allowance, allotment, allocation, estimate.
v plan, estimate, allow, allot, allocate, apportion, ration.

buff[1] adj yellowish-brown, straw, sandy, fawn, khaki.
v polish, burnish, shine, smooth, rub, brush.

buff[2] n expert, connoisseur, enthusiast, fan, admirer, devotee, addict, fiend, freak.

buffer n shock-absorber, bumper, fender, pad, cushion, pillow, intermediary, screen, shield.

buffet[1] n snack-bar, counter, café, cafeteria.

buffet[2] v batter, hit, strike, knock, bang, bump, push, shove, pound, pummel, beat, thump, box, cuff, clout, slap.
n blow, knock, bang, bump, jar, jolt, push, shove, thump, box, cuff, clout, slap, smack.

bug n **1** VIRUS, bacterium, germ, microbe, micro-organism, infection, disease. **2** FAULT, defect, flaw, blemish, imperfection, failing, error, gremlin (infml).
v (infml) annoy, irritate, vex, irk,

needle (infml), bother, disturb, harass, badger.

build v **1** ERECT, raise, construct, fabricate, make, form, constitute, assemble, knock together, develop, enlarge, extend, increase, augment, escalate, intensify. **2** BASE, found, establish, institute, inaugurate, initiate, begin.
E3 1 destroy, demolish, knock down, lessen.
n physique, figure, body, form, shape, size, frame, structure.

build up strengthen, reinforce, fortify, extend, expand, develop, amplify, increase, escalate, intensify, heighten, boost, improve, enhance, publicize, advertise, promote, plug (infml), hype (sl), talk up (infml).
E3 weaken, lessen.

building n edifice, dwelling, erection, construction, fabrication, structure, architecture.

Types of building include:
house, bungalow, cottage, block of flats, cabin, farmhouse, villa, mansion, château, castle, palace; church, chapel, cathedral, abbey, monastery, temple, synagogue, pagoda, mosque; shop, store, garage, factory, warehouse, silo, office block, tower block, skyscraper, high-rise, theatre, cinema, multiplex, gymnasium, restaurant, café, hotel, pub (infml), public house, inn, school, college, museum, library, hospital, prison, power station, observatory; barracks, fort, fortress, monument, mausoleum; shed, barn, outhouse, stable, mill, lighthouse, pier, pavilion, boathouse, summerhouse, gazebo, windmill. see also **house**; **shop**.

build-up n **1** ENLARGEMENT, expansion, development, increase, gain, growth, escalation. **2** ACCUMULATION, mass, load, heap, stack, store, stockpile.
F3 1 reduction, decrease.

bulge n **1** SWELLING, bump, lump, hump, distension, protuberance, projection. **2** RISE, increase, surge, upsurge, intensification.
v swell, puff out, bulb, hump, dilate, expand, enlarge, distend, protrude, project.

bulk n size, magnitude, dimensions, extent, amplitude, bigness, largeness, immensity, volume, mass, weight, substance, body, preponderance, majority, most.

bulky adj substantial, big, large, huge, enormous, immense, mammoth, massive, colossal, hulking, hefty, heavy, weighty, unmanageable, unwieldy, awkward, cumbersome.
F3 insubstantial, small, handy.

bullet n shot, pellet, ball, slug (infml), missile, projectile.

bulletin n report, newsflash, dispatch, communiqué, statement, announcement, notification, communication, message.

bully n persecutor, tormentor, browbeater, intimidator, bully-boy, heavy (sl), ruffian, tough.
v persecute, torment, terrorize, bulldoze, coerce, browbeat, bullyrag, intimidate, cow, tyrannize, domineer, overbear, oppress, push around.

bump v **1** HIT, strike, knock, bang, crash, collide (with). **2** JOLT, jerk, jar, jostle, rattle, shake, bounce.
n **1** BLOW, hit, knock, bang, thump,

thud, smash, crash, collision, impact, jolt, jar, shock. **2** LUMP, swelling, bulge, hump, protuberance.

bump into meet, encounter, run into, chance upon, come across.

bump off (infml) kill, murder, assassinate, eliminate (sl), liquidate (sl), do in (sl), top (sl).

bumper adj plentiful, abundant, large, great, enormous, massive, excellent, exceptional.
F3 small.

bumptious adj self-important, pompous, officious, overbearing, pushy, assertive, over-confident, presumptuous, forward, impudent, arrogant, cocky, conceited, swaggering, boastful, full of oneself, egotistical.
F3 humble, modest.

bumpy adj jerky, jolting, bouncy, choppy, rough, lumpy, knobbly, knobby, uneven, irregular.
F3 smooth, even.

bunch n **1** BUNDLE, sheaf, tuft, clump, cluster, batch, lot, heap, pile, stack, mass, number, quantity, collection, assortment. **2** bunch of flowers: bouquet, posy, spray. **3** GANG, band, troop, team, party, gathering, flock, swarm, crowd, mob, multitude.
v group, bundle, cluster, collect, assemble, congregate, gather, flock, herd, crowd, mass, pack, huddle.
F3 disperse, scatter, spread out.

bundle n bunch, sheaf, roll, bale, truss, parcel, package, packet, carton, box, bag, pack, batch, consignment, group, set, collection, assortment, quantity, mass, accumulation, pile, stack, heap.
v pack, wrap, bale, truss, bind, tie, fasten.

bungle *v* mismanage, cock up (*sl*), screw up (*sl*), foul up (*infml*), mess up (*infml*), ruin, spoil, mar, botch, fudge, blunder.

buoy *n* float, marker, signal, beacon. **buoy up** support, sustain, raise, lift, boost, encourage, cheer, hearten. **Ⓕ₃** depress, discourage.

buoyant *adj* **1** *in buoyant mood*: light-hearted, carefree, bright, cheerful, happy, joyful, lively, animated, bouncy. **2** FLOATABLE, floating, afloat, light, weightless. **Ⓕ₃ 1** depressed, despairing. **2** heavy.

burden *n* cargo, load, weight, deadweight, encumbrance, millstone, onus, responsibility, obligation, duty, strain, stress, worry, anxiety, care, trouble, trial, affliction, sorrow. *v* load, weigh down, encumber, handicap, bother, worry, tax, strain, overload, lie heavy on, oppress, overwhelm. **Ⓕ₃** unburden, relieve.

bureau *n* service, agency, office, branch, department, division, counter, desk.

bureaucracy *n* administration, government, ministry, civil service, the authorities, the system, officialdom, red tape, regulations.

burglar *n* housebreaker, robber, thief, pilferer, trespasser.

burglary *n* housebreaking, break-in, robbery, theft, stealing, trespass.

burial *n* burying, interment, entombment, funeral, obsequies.

burly *adj* big, well-built, hulking, hunky (*infml*), hefty, heavy, stocky, sturdy, brawny, beefy, muscular, athletic, strapping, strong, powerful. **Ⓕ₃** small, puny, wimpy (*infml*), thin, slim.

burn *v* **1** FLAME, blaze, flare, flash, glow, flicker, smoulder, smoke, fume, simmer, seethe. **2** IGNITE, light, kindle, incinerate, cremate, consume, corrode. **3** SCALD, scorch, parch, shrivel, singe, char, toast, brand, sear, smart, sting, bite, hurt, tingle.

burning *adj* **1** ABLAZE, aflame, afire, fiery, flaming, blazing, flashing, gleaming, glowing, smouldering, alight, lit, illuminated. **2** HOT, scalding, scorching, searing, piercing, acute, smarting, stinging, prickling, tingling, biting, caustic, pungent. **3** *burning desire*: ardent, fervent, eager, earnest, intense, vehement, passionate, impassioned, frantic, frenzied, consuming. **4** *burning issue*: urgent, pressing, important, significant, crucial, essential, vital. **Ⓕ₃ 2** cold. **3** apathetic. **4** unimportant.

burrow *n* warren, hole, earth, set, den, lair, retreat, shelter, tunnel. *v* tunnel, dig, delve, excavate, mine, undermine.

burst *v* puncture, rupture, tear, split, crack, break, fragment, shatter, shiver, disintegrate, explode, blow up, erupt, gush, spout, rush, run. *n* **1** PUNCTURE, blow-out (*infml*), rupture, split, crack, break, breach, explosion, blast, bang, eruption. **2** DISCHARGE, gush, spurt, surge, rush, spate, torrent, outpouring, outburst, outbreak, fit.

bury *v* **1** *bury the dead*: inter, entomb, lay to rest, shroud. **2** SINK, submerge, immerse, plant, implant, embed, conceal, hide, cover, enshroud, engulf, enclose, engross, occupy, engage, absorb. **Ⓕ₃ 1** disinter, exhume. **2** uncover.

bush n 1 SHRUB, hedge, thicket.
2 SCRUB, brush, scrubland,
backwoods, wilds.

business n 1 TRADE, commerce,
industry, manufacturing, dealings,
transactions, bargaining, trading,
buying, selling. 2 COMPANY, firm,
corporation, establishment,
organization, concern, enterprise,
venture. 3 JOB, occupation, work,
employment, trade, profession, line,
calling, career, vocation, duty, task,
responsibility. 4 AFFAIR, matter, issue,
subject, topic, question, problem,
point.

businesslike adj professional,
efficient, thorough, systematic,
methodical, organized, orderly,
well-ordered, practical, matter-of-
fact, precise, correct, formal,
impersonal.
F3 inefficient, disorganized.

businessman, businesswoman
n entrepreneur, industrialist, trader,
merchant, tycoon, magnate,
capitalist, financier, employer,
executive.

bust n 1 SCULPTURE, head, torso,
statue. 2 BOSOM, breasts, chest,
breast.

bustle v dash, rush, scamper, scurry,
hurry, hasten, scramble, fuss.
n activity, stir, commotion, tumult,
agitation, excitement, fuss, ado, flurry,
hurry, haste.

busy adj occupied, engaged, tied up
(infml), employed, working, slaving,
stirring, restless, tireless, diligent,
industrious, active, lively, energetic,
strenuous, tiring, full, crowded,
swarming, teeming, bustling, hectic,
eventful.
F3 idle, lazy, quiet.

v occupy, engage, employ, engross,
absorb, immerse, interest, concern,
bother.

busybody n meddler, nosey parker
(infml), intruder, pry, gossip,
eavesdropper, snoop, snooper,
troublemaker.

butt[1] n stub, end, tip, tail, base, foot,
shaft, stock, handle, haft.

butt[2] n target, mark, object, subject,
victim, laughing-stock, dupe.

butt[3] v, n hit, bump, knock, buffet,
push, shove, ram, thrust, punch, jab,
prod, poke.

butt in interrupt, cut in, interpose,
intrude, meddle, interfere.

butterfly

> **Types of butterfly include:**
> red admiral, white admiral, apollo,
> cabbage-white, brimstone, mea-
> dow-brown, Camberwell beauty,
> comma, copper, fritillary, gate-
> keeper, grayling, hairstreak, mon-
> arch, orange-tip, painted lady,
> peacock, purple emperor, ringlet,
> skipper, swallow-tail, tortoiseshell.
> see also **moth**.

buttocks n rump, hindquarters, rear,
posterior (infml), seat, bottom, behind,
backside (infml), arse (sl), ass (US sl).

buttonhole v accost, waylay, catch,
grab, nab, detain, importune.

buttress n support, prop, stay,
brace, pier, strut, stanchion, mainstay,
reinforcement.
v support, prop up, shore up, hold up,
brace, strengthen, reinforce, bolster
up, sustain.
F3 undermine, weaken.

buy v purchase, invest in (infml), pay
for, procure, acquire, obtain, get.
F3 sell.
n purchase, acquisition, bargain, deal.

buyer *n* purchaser, shopper, consumer, customer, vendee, emptor. **E3** seller, vendor.

by *prep* near, next to, beside, along, over, through, via, past.
adv near, close, handy, at hand, past, beyond, away, aside.

bypass *v* avoid, dodge, sidestep, skirt, circumvent, ignore, neglect, omit.
n ring road, detour, diversion.

by-product *n* consequence, result, side-effect, fallout (*infml*), repercussion, after-effect.

bystander *n* spectator, onlooker, looker-on, watcher, observer, witness, eye-witness, passer-by.

C

cabin *n* **1** BERTH, quarters, compartment, room. **2** HUT, shack, shanty, lodge, chalet, cottage, shed, shelter.

cabinet *n* cupboard, closet, dresser, case, locker.

cable *n* line, rope, cord, chain, wire, flex, lead.

cadge *v* scrounge, sponge, beg, hitch.

café *n* coffee shop, tea shop, tea room, coffee bar, cafeteria, snack bar, buffet, bistro, brasserie, restaurant.

cage *v* encage, coop up, shut up, confine, restrain, fence in, imprison, impound, incarcerate, lock up.

F3 release, let out, free, spring (*sl*).
n aviary, coop, hutch, enclosure, pen, pound, corral.

cajole *v* coax, persuade, get round, wheedle, flatter, sweet-talk (*infml*), butter up (*infml*), tempt, lure, seduce, entice, beguile, mislead, dupe.

F3 bully, force, compel.

cake *v* coat, cover, encrust, dry, harden, solidify, consolidate, coagulate, congeal, thicken.
n **1** *tea and cakes*: gâteau, fancy, bun, pie, flan. **2** LUMP, mass, bar, slab, block, loaf.

> **Types of cake include:**
> angel-food cake, banana cake, Battenberg cake, birthday cake, Black Forest gâteau, brownie, carrot cake, Chelsea bun, chocolate cake, cream-cake, Christmas cake, Danish pastry, doughnut, Dundee cake, Eccles cake, éclair, flapjack, fruitcake, gateau, Genoa cake, gingerbread, hot cross bun, lardy-cake, Madeira cake, poppyseed cake, Sachertorte, sponge cake, sultana cake, Victoria sponge, yeast cake; French cake, madeleine, muffin, queen-cake.

calamitous *adj* disastrous, catastrophic, ruinous, devastating, deadly, fatal, dire, ghastly, dreadful, tragic, woeful, grievous.

F3 good, fortunate, happy.

calamity *n* disaster, catastrophe, mishap, misadventure, mischance, misfortune, adversity, reverse, trial, tribulation, affliction, distress, tragedy, ruin, downfall.

F3 blessing, godsend.

calculate *v* compute, work out, count, enumerate, reckon, figure, determine, weigh, rate, value, estimate, gauge, judge, consider, plan, intend, aim.

calculating adj crafty, cunning, sly, devious, scheming, designing, contriving, sharp, shrewd.
E3 artless, naive.

calculation n sum, computation, answer, result, reckoning, figuring, estimate, forecast, judgement, planning, deliberation.

calibre n **1** DIAMETER, bore, gauge, size, measure. **2** candidates of the right calibre: talent, gifts, strength, worth, merit, quality, character, ability, capacity, faculty, stature, distinction.

call v **1** NAME, christen, baptize, title, entitle, dub, style, term, label, designate. **2** SHOUT, yell, exclaim, cry. **3** SUMMON, invite, bid, convene, assemble. **4** TELEPHONE, phone, ring (up), contact.
n **1** CRY, exclamation, shout, yell, scream. **2** VISIT, ring, summons, invitation. **3** there's no call for it: demand, need, occasion, cause, excuse, justification, reason, grounds, right. **4** APPEAL, request, plea, order, command, claim, announcement, signal.

call for 1 DEMAND, require, need, necessitate, involve, entail, occasion, suggest. **2** FETCH, collect, pick up.

call off cancel, drop, abandon, discontinue, break off, withdraw.

calling n mission, vocation, career, profession, occupation, job, trade, business, line, work, employment, field, province, pursuit.

callous adj heartless, hard-hearted, cold, indifferent, uncaring, unsympathetic, unfeeling, insensitive, hardened, thick-skinned.
E3 kind, caring, sympathetic, sensitive.

calm adj **1** COMPOSED, self-possessed, collected, cool, dispassionate, unemotional, impassive, unmoved, placid, sedate, imperturbable, unflappable, unexcitable, laid back (sl), relaxed, unexcited, unruffled, unflustered, unperturbed, undisturbed, untroubled, unapprehensive. **2** calm waters: smooth, still, windless, unclouded, mild, tranquil, serene, peaceful, quiet, uneventful, restful.
E3 1 excitable, worried, anxious. **2** rough, wild, stormy.
v compose, soothe, relax, sedate, tranquillize, hush, quieten, placate, pacify.
E3 excite, worry.
n calmness, stillness, tranquillity, serenity, peacefulness, peace, quiet, hush, repose.
E3 storminess, restlessness.

camera

> Types of camera include:
> automatic, bellows, binocular, box Brownie®, camera obscura, cine, compact, daguerreotype, digital, disc, disposable, Instamatic®, miniature, subminiature, panoramic, pinhole, plate, Polaroid®, reflex, single-lens reflex (SLR), twin-lens reflex (TLR), security, sound, Steadicam®, stereo, Super 8®, TV, video, camcorder, webcam.

> Camera parts include:
> eye-cup, eye-piece magnifier; flash-bulb, flashcube, flashgun, hot shoe; lens, afocal lens, close-up lens, fish-eye lens, macro lens, telephoto lens, teleconverter, wide-angle lens, zoom lens, lens cap, lens hood, lens shield, viewfinder, right-angle finder. see also **photograph**.

camouflage n disguise, guise, masquerade, mask, cloak, screen, blind, front, cover, concealment, deception.
v disguise, mask, cloak, veil, screen, cover, conceal, hide, obscure.
F3 uncover, reveal.

campaign n crusade, movement, promotion, drive, push, offensive, attack, battle, expedition, operation.
v crusade, promote, push, advocate, fight, battle.

cancel v call off, abort, abandon, drop, abolish, annul, quash, rescind, revoke, repeal, countermand, delete, erase, obliterate, eliminate, offset, compensate, redeem, neutralize, nullify.

cancer n **1** EVIL, blight, canker, pestilence, sickness, corruption, rot. **2** TUMOUR, growth, malignancy, carcinoma.

candid adj frank, open, truthful, honest, sincere, forthright, straightforward, ingenuous, guileless, simple, plain, clear, unequivocal, blunt, outspoken.
F3 guarded, evasive, devious.

candidate n applicant, aspirant, contender, contestant, competitor, entrant, runner, possibility, nominee, claimant, pretender, suitor.

candour n frankness, openness, truthfulness, honesty, plain-dealing, sincerity, straightforwardness, directness, ingenuousness, guilelessness, naiveté, artlessness, simplicity, plainness, bluntness, unequivocalness, outspokenness.
F3 evasiveness, deviousness.

canopy n awning, covering, shade, shelter, sunshade, umbrella.

cantankerous adj irritable, irascible, grumpy, grouchy, crusty, crotchety, crabbed, crabby, testy, bad-tempered, ill-humoured, cross, peevish, difficult, perverse, contrary, quarrelsome.
F3 good-natured, easy-going (infml).

canvass v **1** ELECTIONEER, agitate, campaign, solicit, ask for, seek, poll. **2** EXAMINE, inspect, scrutinize, study, scan, investigate, analyse, sift, discuss, debate.
n poll, survey, examination, scrutiny, investigation, inquiry.

canyon n gorge, ravine, gully, valley.

cap v exceed, surpass, transcend, better, beat, outdo, outstrip, eclipse, complete, finish, crown, top, cover.
n **1** HAT, skullcap, beret, tam-o'-shanter, baseball cap. **2** LID, top, cover.

capability n ability, capacity, faculty, power, potential, means, facility, competence, qualification, skill, proficiency, talent.
F3 inability, incompetence.

capable adj able, competent, efficient, qualified, experienced, accomplished, skilful, proficient, gifted, talented, masterly, clever, intelligent, fitted, suited, apt, liable, disposed.
F3 incapable, incompetent, useless.

capacity n **1** VOLUME, space, room, size, dimensions, magnitude, extent, compass, range, scope. **2** CAPABILITY, ability, faculty, power, potential, competence, efficiency, skill, gift, talent, genius, cleverness, intelligence, aptitude, readiness. **3** in her capacity as president: role, function, position, office, post, appointment, job.

cape[1] *n* headland, head, promontory, point, ness, peninsula.

cape[2] *n* cloak, shawl, wrap, robe, poncho, coat.

capital *n* funds, finance, principal, money, cash, savings, investment(s), wealth, means, wherewithal, resources, assets, property, stock.

capitalize on profit from, take advantage of, exploit, cash in on.

capitulate *v* surrender, throw in the towel, yield, give in, relent, submit, succumb.
F3 fight on.

capsize *v* overturn, turn over, turn turtle, invert, keel over, upset.

capsule *n* **1** TABLET, pill, lozenge. **2** SHELL, sheath, pod.

captain *n* commander, master, skipper, pilot, head, chief, leader, boss, officer.

captivate *v* charm, enchant, bewitch, beguile, fascinate, enthral, hypnotize, mesmerize, lure, allure, seduce, win, attract, enamour, infatuate, enrapture, dazzle.
F3 repel, disgust, appal.

captive *n* prisoner, hostage, slave, detainee, internee, convict.
adj imprisoned, caged, confined, restricted, secure, locked up, enchained, enslaved, ensnared.
F3 free.

captivity *n* custody, detention, imprisonment, incarceration, internment, confinement, restraint, bondage, duress, slavery, servitude.
F3 freedom.

capture *v* catch, trap, snare, take, seize, arrest, apprehend, imprison, secure.
n catching, trapping, taking, seizure, arrest, imprisonment.

car *n* automobile, motor car, motor, vehicle.

Types of car include:
saloon, hatchback, fastback, estate, sports car, cabriolet, convertible, limousine, limo (*infml*), Mini®, bubble-car, coupé, station wagon, people carrier (*infml*), shooting brake, veteran car, vintage car, four-wheel drive, Jeep®, buggy, Land Rover®, Range Rover®, panda car, patrol car, taxi, cab.

---

carcase *n* body, corpse, cadaver, remains, relics, skeleton, shell, structure, framework, hulk.

care *n* **1** WORRY, anxiety, stress, strain, pressure, concern, trouble, distress, affliction, tribulation, vexation. **2** CAREFULNESS, caution, prudence, forethought, vigilance, watchfulness, pains, meticulousness, attention, heed, regard, consideration, interest. **3** *in their care*: keeping, custody, guardianship, protection, ward, charge, responsibility, control, supervision.
F3 2 carelessness, thoughtlessness, inattention, neglect.
v worry, mind, bother.

care for 1 LOOK AFTER, nurse, tend, mind, watch over, protect, minister to, attend. **2** LIKE, be fond of, love, be keen on, enjoy, delight in, want, desire.

career *n* vocation, calling, life-work, occupation, pursuit, profession, trade, job, employment, livelihood.
v rush, dash, tear, hurtle, race, run, gallop, speed, shoot, bolt.

carefree *adj* unworried, untroubled, unconcerned, blithe, happy-go-lucky, cheery, light-hearted, cheerful, happy, easy-going (*infml*), laid back (*infml*).
F3 worried, anxious, despondent.

careful adj **1** CAUTIOUS, prudent, circumspect, judicious, wary, chary, vigilant, watchful, alert, attentive, mindful. **2** METICULOUS, painstaking, conscientious, scrupulous, thorough, detailed, punctilious, particular, accurate, precise, thoughtful.
F3 1 careless, inattentive, thoughtless, reckless. **2** careless.

careless adj **1** UNTHINKING, thoughtless, inconsiderate, uncaring, unconcerned, heedless, unmindful, forgetful, remiss, negligent, irresponsible, unguarded. **2** careless work: inaccurate, messy, untidy, disorderly, sloppy, neglectful, slipshod, slap-dash, hasty, cursory, offhand, casual.
F3 1 thoughtful, prudent. **2** careful, accurate, meticulous.

caress v stroke, pet, fondle, cuddle, hug, embrace, kiss, touch, rub.
n stroke, pat, fondle, cuddle, hug, embrace, kiss.

caretaker n janitor, porter, watchman, keeper, custodian, curator, warden, superintendent.

cargo n freight, load, pay-load, lading, tonnage, shipment, consignment, contents, goods, merchandise, baggage.

caricature n cartoon, parody, lampoon, burlesque, satire, send-up, take-off, imitation, representation, distortion, travesty.
v parody, mock, ridicule, satirize, send up, take off, mimic, distort, exaggerate.

carnage n bloodshed, blood-bath, butchery, slaughter, killing, murder, massacre, holocaust.

carnival n festival, fiesta, gala, jamboree, fête, fair, holiday, jubilee, celebration, merrymaking, revelry.

carriage n **1** COACH, wagon, car, vehicle. **2** DEPORTMENT, posture, bearing, air, manner, mien, demeanour, behaviour, conduct. **3** CARRYING, conveyance, transport, transportation, delivery, postage.

carry v **1** BRING, convey, transport, haul, move, transfer, relay, release, conduct, take, fetch. **2** BEAR, shoulder, support, underpin, maintain, uphold, sustain, suffer, stand.

carry on CONTINUE, proceed, last, endure, maintain, keep on, persist, persevere. **2** carry on a business: operate, run, manage, administer.
F3 1 stop, finish.

carry out do, perform, undertake, discharge, conduct, execute, implement, fulfil, accomplish, achieve, realize, bring off.

cart n barrow, handcart, wheelbarrow, wagon, truck.
v move, convey, transport, haul, lug (infml), hump (infml), bear, carry.

carton n box, packet, pack, case, container, package, parcel.

cartoon n comic strip, animation, sketch, drawing, caricature, parody.

cartridge n cassette, canister, cylinder, tube, container, case, capsule, shell, magazine, round, charge.

carve v cut, slice, hack, hew, chisel, chip, sculpt, sculpture, shape, form, fashion, mould, etch, engrave, incise, indent.

cascade n rush, gush, outpouring, flood, deluge, torrent, avalanche, cataract, waterfall, falls, fountain, shower.
F3 trickle.

v rush, gush, surge, flood, overflow, spill, tumble, fall, descend, shower, pour, plunge, pitch.

case[1] *n* container, receptacle, holder, suitcase, trunk, crate, box, carton, casket, chest, cabinet, showcase, casing, cartridge, shell, capsule, sheath, cover, jacket, wrapper.

case[2] *n* **1** CIRCUMSTANCES, context, state, condition, position, situation, contingency, occurrence, occasion, event, specimen, example, instance, illustration, point. **2** LAWSUIT, suit, trial, proceedings, action, process, cause, argument, dispute.

cash *n* money, hard money, ready money, banknotes, notes, coins, change, legal tender, currency, hard currency, bullion, funds, resources, wherewithal.

v encash, exchange, realize, liquidate.

cashier *n* clerk, teller, treasurer, bursar, purser, banker, accountant.

cask *n* barrel, tun, hogshead, firkin, vat, tub, butt.

cast *v* **1** THROW, hurl, lob, pitch, fling, toss, sling, shy, launch, impel, drive, direct, project, shed, emit, diffuse, spread, scatter. **2** MOULD, shape, form, model, found.

n **1** COMPANY, troupe, actors, players, performers, entertainers, characters, dramatis personae. **2** CASTING, mould, shape, form.

cast down depress, discourage, dishearten, deject, sadden, crush, desolate.

F3 cheer up, encourage.

castle *n* stronghold, fortress, citadel, keep, tower, château, palace, mansion, stately home, country house.

Parts of a castle include:
approach, bailey, barbican, bartizan, bastion, battlements, brattice, buttress, corbel, courtyard, crenel, crenellation, donjon, drawbridge, dungeon, embrasure, foss (or fosse), gatehouse, inner wall, keep, merlon, moat, motte, mound, outer bailey, parapet, portcullis, postern, rampart, scarp, stockade, tower, lookout tower, turret, ward, watchtower.

---

casual *adj* **1** *a casual meeting*: chance, fortuitous, accidental, unintentional, unpremeditated, unexpected, unforeseen, irregular, random, occasional, incidental, superficial, cursory. **2** NONCHALANT, blasé, lackadaisical, negligent, couldn't-care-less (*infml*), apathetic, indifferent, unconcerned, informal, offhand, relaxed, laid back (*infml*).

F3 **1** deliberate, planned. **2** formal.

casualty *n* injury, loss, death, fatality, victim, sufferer, injured, injured person, wounded, dead person.

cat

Breeds of cat include:
Abyssinian, American shorthair, Balinese, Birman, Bombay, British shorthair, Burmese, Chinchilla, Cornish Rex, Devon Rex, domestic tabby, Egyptian Mau, Exotic, Havana, Himalayan, Japanese Bobtail, Korat, Maine Coon, Manx, Norwegian Forest, Persian, Rag-doll, Russian Blue, Scottish Fold, Siamese, Singapura, Somali, Tiffanie, Tonkinese, tortoiseshell, Turkish Angora, Turkish Van.

catalogue n list, inventory, roll, register, roster, schedule, record, table, index, directory, gazetteer, brochure, prospectus.
v list, register, record, index, classify, alphabetize, file.

catapult v hurl, fling, throw, pitch, toss, sling, launch, propel, shoot, fire.

cataract n waterfall, falls, rapids, force, cascade, downpour, torrent, deluge.

catastrophe n disaster, calamity, cataclysm, debacle, fiasco, failure, ruin, devastation, tragedy, blow, reverse, mischance, misfortune, adversity, affliction, trouble, upheaval.

catch v 1 SEIZE, grab, take, hold, grasp, grip, clutch, capture, trap, entrap, snare, ensnare, hook, net, arrest, apprehend. 2 HEAR, understand, perceive, recognize. 3 SURPRISE, expose, unmask, find (out), discover, detect, discern. 4 *catch a cold*: contract, get, develop, go down with.
E3 1 drop, release, free. 2 miss.
n 1 FASTENER, clip, hook, clasp, hasp, latch, bolt. 2 DISADVANTAGE, drawback, snag, hitch, obstacle, problem.

catch up gain on, draw level with, overtake.

catching adj infectious, contagious, communicable, transmittable.

catchword n catch-phrase, slogan, motto, watchword, byword, password.

catchy adj memorable, haunting, popular, melodic, tuneful, attractive, captivating.
E3 dull, boring.

categorical adj absolute, total, utter, unqualified, unreserved, unconditional, downright, positive,
definite, emphatic, unequivocal, clear, explicit, express, direct.
E3 tentative, qualified, vague.

categorize v class, classify, group, sort, grade, rank, order, list.

category n class, classification, group, grouping, sort, type, section, division, department, chapter, head, heading, grade, rank, order, list.

cater v provision, victual, provide, supply, furnish, serve, indulge, pander.

catholic adj broad, wide, wide-ranging, universal, global, general, comprehensive, inclusive, all-inclusive, all-embracing, liberal, tolerant, broad-minded.
E3 narrow, limited, narrow-minded.

cattle n cows, bulls, oxen, livestock, stock, beasts.

Breeds of cattle include:
Aberdeen Angus, Africander, Alderney, Ankole, Ayrshire, Blonde d'Aquitaine, brahmin, Brown Swiss, cattabu, cattalo, Charolais, Devon, dexter, Durham, Friesian, Galloway, Guernsey, Hereford, Highland, Holstein, Jersey, Limousin, longhorn, Luing, redpoll, Santa Gertrudis, Shetland, shorthorn, Simmental.

---

cause n 1 SOURCE, origin, beginning, root, basis, spring, originator, creator, producer, maker, agent, agency. 2 REASON, motive, grounds, motivation, stimulus, incentive, inducement, impulse. 3 *a worthy cause*: object, purpose, end, ideal, belief, conviction, movement, undertaking, enterprise.
E3 1 effect, result, consequence.
v begin, give rise to, lead to, result in, occasion, bring about, effect, produce,

generate, create, precipitate, motivate, stimulate, provoke, incite, induce, force, compel.
F3 stop, prevent.

caustic *adj* corrosive, acid, burning, stinging, biting, cutting, mordant, trenchant, keen, pungent, bitter, acrimonious, sarcastic, scathing, virulent, severe.
F3 soothing, mild.

caution *n* **1** CARE, carefulness, prudence, vigilance, watchfulness, alertness, heed, discretion, forethought, deliberation, wariness. **2** WARNING, caveat, injunction, admonition, advice, counsel.
F3 1 carelessness, recklessness. *v* warn, admonish, advise, urge.

cautious *adj* careful, prudent, circumspect, judicious, vigilant, watchful, alert, heedful, discreet, tactful, chary, wary, cagey (*infml*), guarded, tentative, softly-softly, unadventurous.
F3 incautious, imprudent, heedless, reckless.

cavalcade *n* procession, parade, march-past, troop, array, retinue, train.

cavalier *n* horseman, equestrian, knight, gentleman, gallant, escort, partner.
adj supercilious, condescending, lordly, haughty, lofty, arrogant, swaggering, insolent, scornful, disdainful, curt, offhand, free-and-easy.

cave *n* cavern, grotto, hole, pothole, hollow, cavity.

cave in collapse, subside, give way, yield, fall, slip.

cavernous *adj* hollow, concave, gaping, yawning, echoing, resonant, deep, sunken.

cavity *n* hole, gap, dent, hollow, crater, pit, well, sinus, ventricle.

cavort *v* caper, frolic, gambol, prance, skip, dance, frisk, sport, romp.

cease *v* stop, desist, refrain, pack in (*sl*), halt, call a halt, break off, discontinue, finish, end, conclude, terminate, fail, die.
F3 begin, start, commence.

ceaseless *adj* endless, unending, never-ending, eternal, everlasting, continuous, non-stop, incessant, interminable, constant, perpetual, continual, persistent, untiring, unremitting.
F3 occasional, irregular.

cede *v* surrender, give up, resign, abdicate, renounce, abandon, yield, relinquish, convey, transfer, hand over, grant, allow, concede.

celebrate *v* commemorate, remember, observe, keep, rejoice, toast, drink to, honour, exalt, glorify, praise, extol, eulogize, commend, bless, solemnize.

celebrated *adj* famous, well-known, famed, renowned, illustrious, glorious, eminent, distinguished, notable, prominent, outstanding, popular, acclaimed, exalted, revered.
F3 unknown, obscure, forgotten.

celebration *n* commemoration, remembrance, observance, anniversary, jubilee, festival, gala, merrymaking, jollification, revelry, festivity, party, rave-up (*infml*).

Celebrations include: anniversary, banquet, baptism, bar mitzvah, bat mitzvah, birthday, centenary, christening, coming-of-age, confirmation, feast, festival, fête, gala, graduation, harvest-festival, homecoming, Independence Day, jubilee, marriage, Mayday, name-day, party, reception, retirement, reunion, saint's day, thanksgiving, wedding. *see also* **anniversary**; **party**.

celebrity n celeb (*infml*), personage, dignitary, VIP (*infml*), luminary, worthy, personality, name, big name, star, superstar, megastar.
F3 nobody, nonentity.

celibacy n singleness, bachelorhood, spinsterhood, virginity, chastity, purity, abstinence, continence.

cell n dungeon, prison, room, cubicle, chamber, compartment, cavity, unit.

cellar n basement, crypt, vault, storeroom, wine cellar.

cement v stick, bond, weld, solder, join, unite, bind, combine.
n plaster, mortar, concrete.

cemetery n burial-ground, graveyard, churchyard.

censor v cut, edit, blue-pencil, bowdlerize, expurgate.

censorious adj condemnatory, disapproving, disparaging, fault-finding, carping, cavilling, critical, hypercritical, severe.
F3 complimentary, approving.

censure n condemnation, blame, disapproval, criticism, admonishment, admonition, reprehension, reproof, reproach, rebuke, reprimand, telling-off (*infml*).
F3 praise, compliments, approval, brownie points (*infml*).
v condemn, denounce, blame, criticize, castigate, admonish, reprehend, reprove, upbraid, reproach, rebuke, reprimand, scold, tell off (*infml*).
F3 praise, compliment, approve.

central adj middle, mid, inner, interior, focal, main, chief, key, principal, primary, fundamental, vital, essential, important.
F3 peripheral, minor, secondary.

centre n middle, mid-point, bull's-eye, heart, core, nucleus, pivot, hub, focus, crux.
F3 edge, periphery, outskirts.
v focus, concentrate, converge, gravitate, revolve, pivot, hinge.

ceremonial adj formal, official, stately, solemn, ritual, ritualistic.
F3 informal, casual.
n ceremony, formality, protocol, solemnity, ritual, rite.

ceremonious adj stately, dignified, grand, solemn, ritual, civil, polite, courteous, deferential, courtly, formal, stiff, starchy, exact, precise, punctilious.
F3 unceremonious, informal, relaxed.

ceremony n **1** *wedding ceremony*: service, rite, commemoration, observance, celebration, function, parade. **2** ETIQUETTE, protocol, decorum, propriety, formality, form, niceties, ceremonial, ritual, pomp, show.

certain adj **1** SURE, positive, assured, confident, convinced, undoubted, indubitable, unquestionable, incontrovertible, undeniable, irrefutable, plain, conclusive, absolute, convincing, true.
2 INEVITABLE, unavoidable, bound, destined, fated. **3** SPECIFIC, special, particular, individual, precise, express, fixed, established, settled, decided, definite. **4** DEPENDABLE, reliable, trustworthy, constant, steady, stable.
F3 1 uncertain, unsure, hesitant, doubtful. **2** unlikely. **4** unreliable.

certainly adv of course, naturally, definitely, for sure, undoubtedly, doubtlessly.

certainty n sureness, positiveness, assurance, confidence, conviction, faith, trust, truth, validity, fact, reality, inevitability.

F3 uncertainty, doubt, hesitation.

certificate n document, award, diploma, qualification, credentials, testimonial, guarantee, endorsement, warrant, licence, authorization, pass, voucher.

certify v declare, attest, aver, assure, guarantee, endorse, corroborate, confirm, vouch, testify, witness, verify, authenticate, validate, authorize, license.

chain n 1 FETTER, manacle, restraint, bond, link, coupling, union. 2 chain of events: sequence, succession, progression, string, train, series, set.
v tether, fasten, secure, bind, restrain, confine, fetter, shackle, manacle, handcuff, enslave.

F3 release, free.

chair

Types of chair include:
easy-chair, armchair, rocking-chair, recliner, dining-chair, carver, kitchen chair, stool, swivel-chair, high-chair.

chairman, chairwoman n chairperson, chair, president, convenor, organizer, director, master of ceremonies, MC, toastmaster, speaker.

challenge v 1 DARE, defy, throw down the gauntlet, confront, brave, accost, provoke, test, tax, try.
2 DISPUTE, question, query, protest, object to.

n dare, defiance, confrontation, provocation, test, trial, hurdle, obstacle, problem, question, ultimatum.

champion n winner, victor, conqueror, hero, guardian, protector, defender, vindicator, patron, backer, supporter, upholder, advocate.
v defend, stand up for, back, support, maintain, uphold, espouse, advocate, promote.

chance n 1 ACCIDENT, fortuity, coincidence, fluke (infml), luck, fortune, providence, fate, destiny, risk, gamble, speculation, possibility, prospect, probability, likelihood, odds. 2 a second chance: opportunity, opening, occasion, time.

F3 1 certainty.

v 1 RISK, hazard, gamble, wager, stake, try, venture. 2 HAPPEN, occur.
adj fortuitous, casual, accidental, inadvertent, unintentional, unintended, unforeseen, unlooked-for, random, haphazard, incidental.

F3 deliberate, intentional, foreseen, certain.

change v alter, modify, convert, reorganize, reform, remodel, restyle, transform, transfigure, metamorphose, mutate, vary, fluctuate, vacillate, shift, displace, swap, exchange, trade, switch, transpose, substitute, replace, alternate, interchange.
n alteration, modification, conversion, transformation, metamorphosis, mutation, variation, fluctuation, shift, exchange, transposition, substitution, interchange, difference, diversion, novelty, innovation, variety, transition, revolution, upheaval.

changeable adj variable, mutable, fluid, kaleidoscopic, shifting, mobile, unsettled, uncertain, unpredictable, unreliable, erratic, irregular, inconstant, fickle, capricious, volatile, unstable, unsteady, wavering, vacillating.
F3 constant, reliable.

channel n 1 DUCT, conduit, main, groove, furrow, trough, gutter, canal, flume, watercourse, waterway, strait, sound. 2 *channel of communication*: route, course, path, avenue, way, means, medium, approach, passage.
v direct, guide, conduct, convey, send, transmit, force.

chant n plainsong, psalm, song, melody, chorus, refrain, slogan, war cry.
v recite, intone, sing, chorus.

chaos n disorder, confusion, disorganization, anarchy, lawlessness, tumult, pandemonium, bedlam.
F3 order.

chaotic adj disordered, confused, disorganized, topsy-turvy, deranged, anarchic, lawless, riotous, tumultuous, unruly, uncontrolled.
F3 ordered, organized.

chap n fellow, bloke (*infml*), guy (*infml*), man, boy, person, individual, character, sort, type.

chapter n part, section, division, clause, topic, episode, period, phase, stage.

character n 1 PERSONALITY, nature, disposition, temperament, temper, constitution, make-up, individuality, peculiarity, feature, attributes, quality, type, stamp, calibre, reputation, status, position, trait. 2 LETTER, figure, symbol, sign, mark, type, cipher, rune, hieroglyph, ideograph.
3 INDIVIDUAL, person, sort, type, role, part.

characteristic adj distinctive, distinguishing, individual, idiosyncratic, peculiar, specific, special, typical, representative, symbolic, symptomatic.
F3 uncharacteristic, untypical.
n peculiarity, idiosyncrasy, mannerism, feature, trait, attribute, property, quality, hallmark, mark, symptom.

characterize v typify, mark, stamp, brand, identify, distinguish, indicate, represent, portray.

charge v 1 *charge a high price*: ask, demand, levy, exact, debit. 2 ACCUSE, indict, impeach, incriminate, blame. 3 ATTACK, assail, storm, rush.
n 1 PRICE, cost, fee, rate, amount, expense, expenditure, outlay, payment. 2 ACCUSATION, indictment, allegation, imputation. 3 ATTACK, assault, onslaught, sortie, rush. 4 *in your charge*: custody, keeping, care, safekeeping, guardianship, ward, trust, responsibility, duty.

charitable adj philanthropic, humanitarian, benevolent, benign, kind, compassionate, sympathetic, understanding, considerate, generous, magnanimous, liberal, tolerant, broad-minded, lenient, forgiving, indulgent, gracious.
F3 uncharitable, inconsiderate, unforgiving.

charity n 1 GENEROSITY, bountifulness, alms-giving, beneficence, philanthropy, unselfishness, altruism, benevolence, benignity, kindness, goodness, humanity, compassion, tender-heartedness, love, affection,

clemency, indulgence. **2** ALMS, gift, handout, aid, relief, assistance.
E∃1 selfishness, malice.

charm *v* please, delight, enrapture, captivate, fascinate, beguile, enchant, bewitch, mesmerize, attract, allure, cajole, win, enamour.
E∃ repel.
n **1** ATTRACTION, allure, magnetism, appeal, desirability, fascination, enchantment, spell, sorcery, magic. **2** *lucky charm*: trinket, talisman, amulet, fetish, idol.

charming *adj* pleasing, delightful, pleasant, lovely, captivating, enchanting, attractive, fetching, appealing, sweet, winsome, seductive, winning, irresistible.
E∃ ugly, unattractive, repulsive.

chart *n* diagram, table, graph, map, plan, blueprint.
v map, map out, sketch, draw, draft, outline, delineate, mark, plot, place.

charter *n* right, privilege, prerogative, authorization, permit, licence, franchise, concession, contract, indenture, deed, bond, document.
v hire, rent, lease, commission, engage, employ, authorize, sanction, license.

chase *v* pursue, follow, hunt, track, drive, expel, rush, hurry.

chasm *n* gap, opening, gulf, abyss, void, hollow, cavity, crater, breach, rift, split, cleft, fissure, crevasse, canyon, gorge, ravine.

chaste *adj* pure, virginal, unsullied, undefiled, immaculate, abstinent, continent, celibate, virtuous, moral, innocent, wholesome, modest, decent, plain, simple, austere.
E∃ corrupt, lewd, vulgar, indecorous.

chasten *v* humble, humiliate, tame, subdue, repress, curb, moderate, soften, discipline, punish, correct, chastise, castigate, reprove.

chastise *v* punish, discipline, correct, beat, flog, whip, lash, scourge, smack, spank, castigate, reprove, admonish, scold, upbraid, berate, censure.

chat *n* talk, conversation, natter (*infml*), gossip, chinwag (*infml*), tête-à-tête, heart-to-heart.
v talk, crack, natter (*infml*), gossip, chatter, rabbit (on) (*infml*).

chatter *v, n* prattle, babble, chat, natter (*infml*), gossip, tattle.

chatty *adj* talkative, gossipy, newsy, friendly, informal, colloquial, familiar.
E∃ quiet.

cheap *adj* **1** INEXPENSIVE, reasonable, dirt-cheap, bargain, reduced, cut-price, knock-down, budget, economy, economical. **2** TAWDRY, tatty, cheapo (*sl*), shoddy, inferior, second-rate, worthless, vulgar, common, poor, paltry, mean, contemptible, despicable, low.
E∃1 expensive, costly. **2** superior, noble, admirable.

cheapen *v* devalue, degrade, lower, demean, depreciate, belittle, disparage, denigrate, downgrade.

cheat *v* defraud, swindle, diddle, short-change, do (*infml*), rip off (*sl*), fleece, con (*infml*), double-cross, mislead, deceive, dupe, fool, trick, hoodwink, bamboozle (*infml*), beguile.
n cheater, dodger, fraud, swindler, shark (*infml*), con man (*infml*), extortioner, double-crosser, impostor, charlatan, deceiver, trickster, rogue.

check *v* **1** EXAMINE, inspect, scrutinize, give the once-over (*infml*), investigate, probe, test, monitor, study, research, compare, cross-check, confirm, verify. **2** *check an impulse*: curb, bridle, restrain, control, limit, repress, inhibit, damp, thwart, hinder, impede, obstruct, bar, retard, delay, stop, arrest, halt.
n **1** EXAMINATION, inspection, scrutiny, once-over (*infml*), check-up, investigation, audit, test, research. **2** CURB, restraint, control, limitation, constraint, inhibition, damper, blow, disappointment, reverse, setback, frustration, hindrance, impediment, obstruction, stoppage.

cheek *n* impertinence, impudence, insolence, disrespect, effrontery, brazenness, temerity, audacity, nerve (*infml*), gall.

cheeky *adj* impertinent, impudent, insolent, disrespectful, forward, brazen, pert, saucy (*infml*), audacious. **F3** respectful, polite.

cheer *v* **1** ACCLAIM, hail, clap, applaud. **2** COMFORT, console, brighten, gladden, warm, uplift, elate, exhilarate, encourage, hearten. **F3 1** boo, jeer. **2** dishearten.
n acclamation, hurrah, bravo, applause, ovation.
cheer up encourage, hearten, take heart, rally, buck up (*infml*), perk up (*infml*).

cheerful *adj* happy, glad, contented, joyful, joyous, blithe, carefree, light-hearted, cheery, good-humoured, sunny, optimistic, enthusiastic, hearty, genial, jovial, jolly, merry, lively, animated, bright, chirpy, breezy, jaunty, buoyant, sparkling. **F3** sad, dejected, depressed.

cheese

Varieties of cheese include:
bel paese, Bleu d'Auvergne, Blue Vinny, Boursin®, Brie, caboc, Caerphilly, Cambozola®, Camembert, Cheddar, Cheshire, cottage cheese, cream cheese, crowdie, curd cheese, Danish blue, Derby, dolcelatte, double Gloucester, Dunlop, Edam, Emmental, ewe-cheese, feta, fromage frais, Gloucester, goat's cheese, Gorgonzola, Gouda, Gruyère, Jarlsberg®, Lancashire, Leicester, Limburger, mascarpone, Monterey Jack, mozzarella, Neufchâtel, Orkney, Parmesan, Pont-L'Évêque, Port Salut, processed cheese, provolone, quark, Red Leicester, Red Windsor, ricotta, Roquefort, sage Derby, Stilton®, stracchino, Vacherin, Wensleydale.

chemical element

The chemical elements (with their symbols) are:
actinium (Ac), aluminium (Al), americium (Am), antimony (Sb), argon (Ar), arsenic (As), astatine (At), barium (Ba), berkelium (Bk), beryllium (Be), bismuth (Bi), bohrium (Bh), boron (B), bromine (Br), cadmium (Cd), caesium (Cs), calcium (Ca), californium (Cf), carbon (C), cerium (Ce), chlorine (Cl), chromium (Cr), cobalt (Co), copper (Cu), curium (Cm), darmstadtium (Ds), dubnium (Db), dysprosium (Dy), einsteinium (Es), erbium (Er), europium (Eu), fermium (Fm), fluorine (F), francium (Fr), gadolinium (Gd), gallium (Ga), germanium (Ge), gold (Au), hafnium (Hf), hassium (Hs), helium (He), holmium

(Ho), hydrogen (H), indium (In), iodine (I), iridium (Ir), iron (Fe), krypton (Kr), lanthanum (La), lawrencium (Lr), lead (Pb), lithium (Li), lutetium (Lu), magnesium (Mg), manganese (Mn), meitnerium (Mt), mendelevium (Md), mercury (Hg), molybdenum (Mo), neodymium (Nd), neon (Ne), neptunium (Np), nickel (Ni), niobium (Nb), nitrogen (N), nobelium (No), osmium (Os), oxygen (O), palladium (Pd), phosphorus (P), platinum (Pt), plutonium (Pu), polonium (Po), potassium (K), praseodymium (Pr), promethium (Pm), protactinium (Pa), radium (Ra), radon (Rn), rhenium (Re), rhodium (Rh), roentgenium (Rg), rubidium (Rb), ruthenium (Ru), rutherfordium (Rf), samarium (Sm), scandium (Sc), seaborgium (Sg), selenium (Se), silicon (Si), silver (Ag), sodium (Na), strontium (Sr), sulphur (S), tantalum (Ta), technetium (Tc), tellurium (Te), terbium (Tb), thallium (Tl), thorium (Th), thulium (Tm), tin (Sn), titanium (Ti), tungsten (W), uranium (U), vanadium (V), xenon (Xe), ytterbium (Yb), yttrium (Y), zinc (Zn), zirconium (Zr).

chemistry

Terms used in chemistry include: acid, alkali, analysis, atom, atomic number, atomic structure, base, bond, buffer, catalyst, chain reaction, combustion, compound, corrosion, covalent bond, crystal, diffusion, distillation, electrode, electrolysis, electron, element, emulsion, equation, formula, free radical, gas, halogen, hydrolysis, indicator, inert, ion, isomer, isotope, liquid, litmus paper, litmus test, mass, mixture, mole, molecule, neutron, noble gas, nucleus, oxidation, periodic table, pH, polymer, proton, radioactivity, reaction, reduction, salt, solid, solution, solvent, subatomic particle, substance, suspension, symbol, synthesis, valency.

cherish v foster, care for, look after, nurse, nurture, nourish, sustain, support, harbour, shelter, entertain, hold dear, value, prize, treasure.

chest n trunk, crate, box, case, casket, coffer, strongbox.

chew v masticate, gnaw, munch, champ, crunch, grind.

chief adj leading, foremost, uppermost, highest, supreme, grand, arch, premier, principal, main, key, central, prime, prevailing, predominant, pre-eminent, outstanding, vital, essential, primary, major.

Ea minor, unimportant.

n ruler, chieftain, lord, master, supremo, head, principal, leader, commander, captain, governor, boss, director, manager, superintendent, superior, ringleader.

chiefly adv mainly, mostly, for the most part, predominantly, principally, primarily, essentially, especially, generally, usually.

child n youngster, kid (infml), nipper (infml), brat (infml), baby, infant, toddler, tot (infml), rugrat (US infml), minor, juvenile, offspring, issue, progeny, descendant.

childhood n babyhood, infancy, boyhood, girlhood, schooldays, youth, adolescence, minority, immaturity.

childish adj babyish, boyish, girlish, infantile, puerile, juvenile, immature, silly, foolish, frivolous.
F3 mature, sensible.

childlike adj innocent, naive, ingenuous, artless, guileless, credulous, trusting, trustful, simple, natural.

chill v **1** COOL, refrigerate, freeze, ice. **2** FRIGHTEN, terrify, dismay, dishearten, discourage, depress, dampen.
F3 1 warm, heat.
n coolness, cold, coldness, frigidity, rawness, bite, nip, crispness.
F3 warmth.

chilly adj **1** chilly weather: cold, fresh, brisk, crisp, nippy (infml), wintry. **2** a chilly response: cool, frigid, unsympathetic, unwelcoming, aloof, stony, unfriendly, hostile.
F3 1 warm. **2** friendly.

chime v sound, strike, toll, ring, peal, clang, dong, jingle, tinkle.

china adj porcelain, ceramic, pottery, earthenware, terracotta.

Chinese calendar

The animals representing the years in which people are born: rat, buffalo, tiger, rabbit (or hare), dragon, snake, horse, goat (or sheep), monkey, rooster, dog, pig.

chink n crack, rift, cleft, fissure, crevice, slot, opening, aperture, gap, space.

chip n **1** NOTCH, nick, scratch, dent, flaw. **2** FRAGMENT, scrap, wafer, sliver, flake, shaving, paring.
v chisel, whittle, nick, notch, gash, damage.

chirp v, n chirrup, tweet, cheep, peep, twitter, warble, sing, pipe, whistle.

chivalrous adj gentlemanly, polite, courteous, gallant, heroic, valiant, brave, courageous, bold, noble, honourable.
F3 ungallant, cowardly.

chivalry n gentlemanliness, politeness, courtesy, gallantry, bravery, courage, boldness.

choice n option, alternative, selection, variety, pick, preference, say, decision, dilemma, election, discrimination, choosing, opting.
adj best, superior, prime, plum, excellent, fine, exquisite, exclusive, select, hand-picked, special, prize, valuable, precious.
F3 inferior, poor.

choke v **1** THROTTLE, strangle, asphyxiate, suffocate, stifle, smother, suppress. **2** OBSTRUCT, constrict, congest, clog, block, dam, bar, close, stop. **3** COUGH, gag, retch.

choose v pick, select, single out, designate, predestine, opt for, plump for, vote for, settle on, fix on, adopt, elect, prefer, wish, desire, see fit.

choosy adj selective, discriminating, picky (infml), fussy, particular, finicky, fastidious, exacting.
F3 undemanding.

chop v cut, hack, hew, lop, sever, truncate, cleave, divide, split, slash.
chop up cut (up), slice (up), divide, cube, dice, mince.

choppy adj rough, turbulent, tempestuous, stormy, squally, ruffled, wavy, uneven, broken.
F3 calm, still.

chore n task, job, errand, duty, burden.

chorus n **1** REFRAIN, burden, response, call, shout. **2** CHOIR, choristers, singers, vocalists, ensemble.

christen v baptize, name, call, dub, title, style, term, designate, inaugurate, use.

Christmas n Xmas, Noel, Yule, Yuletide.

chronic adj **1** INCURABLE, deep-seated, recurring, incessant, persistent, inveterate, confirmed, habitual, ingrained, deep-rooted. **2** (infml) a chronic film: awful, terrible, dreadful, appalling, atrocious. **F3 1** acute, temporary.

chronological adj historical, consecutive, sequential, progressive, ordered.

chubby adj plump, podgy, fleshy, flabby, stout, portly, rotund, round, tubby, paunchy. **F3** slim, skinny.

chuckle v laugh, giggle, titter, snigger, chortle, snort, crow.

chunk n lump, hunk, mass, wodge (infml), wedge, block, slab, piece, portion.

church n chapel, house of God, cathedral, minster, abbey, temple.

cinema n **1** an admirer of German cinema: films, pictures, movies (infml), flicks (sl), the big screen, the silver screen. **2** working in a cinema: movie theatre, multiplex, picture-house, picture-palace, fleapit (infml).

circle n **1** RING, loop, disc, cycle, turn, revolution, circuit, orbit, circumference, perimeter. **2** circle of friends: group, band, company, crowd, set, clique, coterie, club, society, fellowship, fraternity. v **1** RING, loop, encircle, surround, gird, encompass, enclose, hem in, circumscribe, circumnavigate. **2** ROTATE, revolve, pivot, gyrate, whirl, turn, coil, wind.

circuit n lap, orbit, revolution, tour, journey, course, route, track, round, beat, district, area, region, circumference, boundary, bounds, limit, range, compass, ambit.

circuitous adj roundabout, periphrastic, indirect, oblique, devious, tortuous, winding, meandering, rambling, labyrinthine. **F3** direct, straight.

circular adj round, annular, ring-shaped, hoop-shaped, disc-shaped. n handbill, leaflet, pamphlet, notice, announcement, advertisement, letter.

Circular things include:
ball, coronet, crown, disc, discus, halo, hoop, saucer, sphere, tyre, wheel, wreath.

circulate v **1** circulate information: spread, diffuse, broadcast, publicize, publish, issue, propagate, pass round, distribute. **2** GO ROUND, rotate, revolve, gyrate, whirl, swirl, flow.

circulation n **1** BLOOD-FLOW, flow, motion, rotation, circling. **2** SPREAD, transmission, dissemination, distribution.

circumference n circuit, perimeter, rim, edge, outline, boundary, border, bounds, limits, extremity, margin, verge, fringe, periphery.

circumstances n details, particulars, facts, items, elements, factors, conditions, state, state of affairs, situation, position, status, lifestyle, means, resources.

cistern n tank, reservoir, sink, basin.

citadel n fortress, stronghold, bastion, castle, keep, tower, fortification, acropolis.

cite v quote, adduce, name, specify, enumerate, mention, refer to, advance, bring up.

citizen n city-dweller, townsman, townswoman, inhabitant, denizen, resident, householder, taxpayer, subject.

city n metropolis, town, municipality, conurbation.

civic adj city, urban, municipal, borough, community, local, public, communal.

civil adj **1** POLITE, courteous, well-mannered, well-bred, courtly, refined, civilized, polished, urbane, affable, complaisant, obliging, accommodating. **2** civil affairs: domestic, home, national, internal, interior, state, municipal, civic. **E3 1** uncivil, discourteous, rude. **2** international, military.

civility n politeness, courteousness, courtesy, breeding, refinement, urbanity, graciousness, affability, amenity. **E3** discourtesy, rudeness.

civilization n progress, advancement, development, education, enlightenment, cultivation, culture, refinement, sophistication, urbanity. **E3** barbarity, primitiveness.

civilize v tame, humanize, educate, enlighten, cultivate, refine, polish, sophisticate, improve, perfect.

civilized adj advanced, developed, educated, enlightened, cultured, refined, sophisticated, urbane, polite, sociable. **E3** uncivilized, barbarous, primitive.

claim v **1** ALLEGE, pretend, profess, state, affirm, assert, maintain, contend, hold, insist. **2** claim a refund: ask, request, require, need, demand, exact, take, collect.
n **1** ALLEGATION, pretension,

affirmation, assertion, contention, insistence. **2** APPLICATION, petition, request, requirement, demand, call, right, privilege.

clairvoyant adj psychic, prophetic, visionary, telepathic, extra-sensory. n psychic, fortune-teller, prophet, prophetess, visionary, seer, soothsayer, augur, oracle, diviner, telepath.

clammy adj damp, moist, sweaty, sweating, sticky, slimy, dank, muggy, heavy, close.

clamp n vice, grip, press, brace, bracket, fastener.
v fasten, secure, fix, clinch, grip, brace.

clan n tribe, family, house, race, society, brotherhood, fraternity, confraternity, sect, faction, group, band, set, clique, coterie.

clap v **1** APPLAUD, acclaim, cheer. **2** SLAP, smack, pat, wallop (infml), whack (infml), bang.

clarify v **1** EXPLAIN, throw light on, illuminate, elucidate, gloss, define, simplify, resolve, clear up. **2** REFINE, purify, filter, clear. **E3 1** obscure, confuse. **2** cloud.

clarity n clearness, transparency, lucidity, simplicity, intelligibility, comprehensibility, explicitness, unambiguousness, obviousness, definition, precision. **E3** obscurity, vagueness, imprecision.

clash v **1** CRASH, bang, clank, clang, jangle, clatter, rattle, jar. **2** CONFLICT, disagree, quarrel, wrangle, grapple, fight, feud, war.
n **1** CRASH, bang, jangle, clatter, noise. **2** a clash with the police: confrontation, showdown, conflict, disagreement, fight, brush.

clasp n 1 FASTENER, buckle, clip, pin, hasp, hook, catch. 2 HOLD, grip, grasp, embrace, hug.
v 1 HOLD, grip, grasp, clutch, embrace, enfold, hug, squeeze, press. 2 FASTEN, connect, attach, grapple, hook, clip, pin.

class n 1 CATEGORY, classification, group, set, section, division, department, sphere, grouping, order, league, rank, status, caste, quality, grade, type, genre, sort, kind, species, genus, style. 2 *a French class*: lesson, lecture, seminar, tutorial, course.
v categorize, classify, group, sort, rank, grade, rate, designate, brand.

classic adj typical, characteristic, standard, regular, usual, traditional, time-honoured, established, archetypal, model, exemplary, ideal, best, finest, first-rate, consummate, definitive, masterly, excellent, ageless, immortal, undying, lasting, enduring, abiding.
F3 unrepresentative, second-rate.
n standard, model, prototype, exemplar, masterwork, masterpiece, pièce de résistance.

classical adj elegant, refined, pure, traditional, excellent, well-proportioned, symmetrical, harmonious, restrained.
F3 modern, inferior.

classification n categorization, taxonomy, sorting, grading, arrangement, systematization, codification, tabulation, cataloguing.

classify v categorize, class, group, pigeonhole, sort, grade, rank, arrange, dispose, distribute, systematize, codify, tabulate, file, catalogue.

clause n article, item, part, section, subsection, paragraph, heading, chapter, passage, condition, proviso, provision, specification, point.

claw n talon, nail, pincer, nipper, gripper.
v scratch, scrabble, scrape, graze, tear, rip, lacerate, maul, mangle.

clean adj 1 WASHED, laundered, sterile, aseptic, antiseptic, hygienic, sanitary, sterilized, decontaminated, purified, pure, unadulterated, fresh, unpolluted, uncontaminated, immaculate, spotless, unspotted, unstained, unsoiled, unsullied, perfect, faultless, flawless, unblemished. 2 *a clean life*: innocent, guiltless, virtuous, upright, moral, honest, honourable, respectable, decent, chaste. 3 SMOOTH, regular, straight, neat, tidy.
F3 1 dirty, polluted. 2 dishonourable, indecent. 3 rough.
v wash, bath, launder, rinse, wipe, sponge, scrub, scour, mop, swab, sweep, vacuum, dust, freshen, deodorize, cleanse, purge, purify, decontaminate, disinfect, sanitize, sterilize, clear, filter.
F3 dirty, defile.

cleanser n soap, soap powder, detergent, cleaner, solvent, scourer, scouring powder, purifier, disinfectant.

clear adj 1 PLAIN, distinct, comprehensible, intelligible, coherent, lucid, explicit, precise, unambiguous, well-defined, apparent, evident, patent, obvious, manifest, conspicuous, unmistakable, unquestionable. 2 SURE, certain, positive, definite, convinced. 3 *clear water*: transparent, limpid, crystalline, glassy, see-through, clean, unclouded, colourless. **4** *a clear day*: cloudless, unclouded, fine, bright, sunny, light, luminous, undimmed. **5** UNOBSTRUCTED, unblocked, open, free, empty, unhindered, unimpeded. **6** AUDIBLE, perceptible, pronounced, distinct, recognizable.

E₃ 1 unclear, vague, ambiguous, confusing. **2** unsure, muddled. **3** opaque, cloudy. **4** dull. **5** blocked. **6** inaudible, indistinct.

v **1** UNBLOCK, unclog, decongest, free, rid, extricate, disentangle, loosen. **2** CLEAN, wipe, erase, cleanse, refine, filter, tidy, empty, unload. **3** ACQUIT, exculpate, exonerate, absolve, vindicate, excuse, justify, free, liberate, release, let go.

E₃ 1 block. **2** dirty, defile. **3** condemn.

clear up 1 EXPLAIN, clarify, elucidate, unravel, solve, resolve, answer. **2** TIDY, order, sort, rearrange, remove.

clearance *n* **1** AUTHORIZATION, sanction, endorsement, permission, consent, leave, OK (*infml*), go-ahead, green light (*infml*). **2** SPACE, gap, headroom, margin, allowance.

clearing *n* space, gap, opening, glade, dell.

clergy *n* clergymen, churchmen, clerics, the church, the cloth, ministry, priesthood.

clergyman *n* churchman, cleric, ecclesiastic, divine, man of God, minister, priest, reverend, father, vicar, pastor, padre, parson, rector, canon, dean, deacon, chaplain, curate, presbyter, rabbi.

clerical *adj* **1** OFFICE, secretarial, white-collar, official, administrative. **2** ECCLESIASTIC(AL), pastoral,

ministerial, priestly, episcopal, canonical, sacerdotal.

clever *adj* intelligent, brainy (*infml*), bright, smart, witty, gifted, expert, knowledgeable, adroit, apt, able, capable, quick, quick-witted, sharp, keen, shrewd, knowing, discerning, cunning, ingenious, inventive, resourceful, sensible, rational.

E₃ foolish, stupid, senseless, ignorant.

cliché *n* platitude, commonplace, banality, truism, bromide, chestnut, stereotype.

client *n* customer, patron, regular, buyer, shopper, consumer, user, patient, applicant.

cliff *n* bluff, face, rock-face, scar, scarp, escarpment, crag, overhang, precipice.

climate *n* weather, temperature, setting, milieu, environment, ambience, atmosphere, feeling, mood, temper, disposition, tendency, trend.

climax *n* culmination, height, high point, highlight, acme, zenith, peak, summit, top, head.

E₃ nadir.

climb *v* ascend, scale, shin up, clamber, mount, rise, soar, top.

climb down retract, eat one's words, back down, retreat, do a U-turn.

cling *v* clasp, clutch, grasp, grip, stick, adhere, cleave, fasten, embrace, hug.

clip¹ *v* trim, snip, cut, prune, pare, shear, crop, dock, poll, truncate, curtail, shorten, abbreviate.

clip² *v* pin, staple, fasten, attach, fix, hold.

clipping *n* cutting, snippet, quotation, citation, passage, section, excerpt, extract, clip.

clique n circle, set, coterie, group, bunch, pack, gang, crowd, faction, clan.

cloak n cape, mantle, robe, wrap, coat, cover, shield, mask, front, pretext.

v cover, veil, mask, screen, hide, conceal, obscure, disguise, camouflage.

clock

> Types of clock or watch include:
> alarm-clock, digital clock, mantel clock, bracket clock, carriage clock, cuckoo clock, longcase clock, grandfather clock, grandmother clock, speaking clock, Tim (*infml*); wristwatch, fob-watch, chronograph, stopwatch; chronometer; sundial.

clog v block, choke, stop up, bung up, dam, congest, jam, obstruct, impede, hinder, hamper, burden.
F3 unblock.

close¹ v **1** SHUT, fasten, secure, lock, bar, obstruct, block, clog, plug, cork, stop up, fill, seal, fuse, join, unite. **2** END, finish, complete, conclude, terminate, wind up, stop, cease.
F3 1 open, separate. **2** start.
n end, finish, completion, conclusion, culmination, ending, finale, dénouement, termination, cessation, stop, pause.

close² adj **1** NEAR, nearby, at hand, neighbouring, adjacent, adjoining, impending, imminent. **2** INTIMATE, dear, familiar, attached, devoted, loving. **3** OPPRESSIVE, heavy, muggy, humid, sultry, sweltering, airless, stifling, suffocating, stuffy, unventilated. **4** MISERLY, mean, parsimonious, tight (*infml*), stingy, niggardly. **5** SECRETIVE,

uncommunicative, taciturn, private, secret, confidential. **6** *a close translation*: exact, precise, accurate, strict, literal, faithful. **7** *pay close attention*: fixed, concentrated, intense, keen. **8** DENSE, solid, packed, cramped.
F3 1 far, distant. **2** cool, unfriendly. **3** fresh, airy. **4** generous. **5** open. **6** rough.

clot n lump, mass, thrombus, thrombosis, clotting, coagulation.
v coalesce, curdle, coagulate, congeal, thicken, solidify, set, gel.

cloth n **1** FABRIC, material, stuff, textile. **2** RAG, face-cloth, flannel, dish-cloth, floorcloth, duster, towel.

clothe v dress, put on, robe, attire, deck, outfit, rig, vest, invest, drape, cover.
F3 undress, strip, disrobe.

clothes n clothing, garments, wear, attire, garb, gear (*infml*), togs (*infml*), outfit, get-up (*infml*), dress, costume, wardrobe.

> Clothes include:
> suit, coat, dress, skirt, top, trousers, shorts; leotard, salopette; hat, scarf, glove, mitten, muffler, earmuffs, leg warmers, sock, tie, bow tie, cravat, stole, shawl, belt, braces, cummerbund, veil, yashmak. *see also* **coat**; **dress**; **hat**; **nightwear**; **shoe**; **skirt**; **suit**; **top**; **trousers**; **underwear**.

cloud n vapour, haze, mist, fog, gloom, darkness, obscurity.
v mist, fog, blur, dull, dim, darken, shade, shadow, overshadow, eclipse, veil, shroud, obscure, muddle, confuse, obfuscate.
F3 clear.

Types of cloud include:
cirrus, cirrostratus, cirrocumulus, altocumulus, altostratus, cumulus, stratocumulus, nimbostratus, fractostratus, fractocumulus, cumulonimbus, stratus.

cloudy *adj* nebulous, hazy, misty, foggy, blurred, blurry, opaque, milky, muddy, dim, indistinct, obscure, dark, murky, sombre, leaden, lowering, overcast, dull, sunless.
Ea clear, bright, sunny, cloudless.

clown *n* buffoon, comic, comedian, joker, jester, fool, harlequin, pierrot.

club *n* **1** ASSOCIATION, society, company, league, guild, order, union, fraternity, group, set, circle, clique. **2** BAT, stick, mace, bludgeon, truncheon, cosh (*sl*), cudgel. *v* hit, strike, beat, bash, clout, clobber (*sl*), bludgeon, cosh (*sl*), batter, pummel.

clue *n* hint, tip, suggestion, idea, notion, lead, tip-off, pointer, sign, indication, evidence, trace, suspicion, inkling, intimation.

clump *n* cluster, bundle, bunch, mass, tuft, thicket.
v tramp, clomp, stamp, stomp, plod, lumber, thump, thud.

clumsy *adj* bungling, ham-fisted, unhandy, unskilful, inept, bumbling, blundering, lumbering, gauche, ungainly, gawky (*infml*), unco-ordinated, awkward, ungraceful, uncouth, rough, crude, ill-made, shapeless, unwieldy, heavy, bulky, cumbersome.
Ea careful, graceful, elegant.

cluster *n* bunch, clump, batch, group, knot, mass, crowd, gathering, collection, assembly.
v bunch, group, gather, collect, assemble, flock.

clutch *v* hold, clasp, grip, hang on to, grasp, seize, snatch, grab, catch, grapple, embrace.

clutter *n* litter, mess, jumble, untidiness, disorder, disarray, muddle, confusion.
v litter, encumber, fill, cover, strew, scatter.

coach *n* trainer, instructor, tutor, teacher.
v train, drill, instruct, teach, tutor, cram, prepare.

coagulate *v* clot, curdle, congeal, thicken, solidify, gel.
Ea melt.

coalition *n* merger, amalgamation, combination, integration, fusion, alliance, league, bloc, compact, federation, confederation, confederacy, association, affiliation, union.

coarse *adj* **1** ROUGH, unpolished, unfinished, uneven, lumpy, unpurified, unrefined, unprocessed. **2** *coarse humour*: bawdy, ribald, earthy, smutty, vulgar, crude, offensive, foul-mouthed, boorish, loutish, rude, impolite, indelicate, improper, indecent, immodest.
Ea 1 smooth, fine. **2** refined, sophisticated, polite.

coast *n* coastline, seaboard, shore, beach, seaside.
v free-wheel, glide, slide, sail, cruise, drift.

coat *n* **1** FUR, hair, fleece, pelt, hide, skin. **2** LAYER, coating, covering.

Types of coat, cloak and jacket include:
overcoat, greatcoat, car-coat, duffel coat, Afghan, frock-coat, tail-coat, bomber jacket, dinner jacket, donkey jacket, hacking-jacket, reefer,

pea-jacket, shooting jacket, safari jacket, Eton jacket, matinee jacket, tuxedo, blazer, raincoat, trench coat, mackintosh, mac (*infml*), Burberry®, parka, anorak, cagoul, windcheater, jerkin, blouson, cape, cloak, poncho.

v cover, paint, spread, smear, plaster.

coating *n* covering, layer, dusting, wash, coat, blanket, sheet, membrane, film, glaze, varnish, finish, veneer, lamination, overlay.

coax *v* persuade, cajole, wheedle, sweet-talk (*infml*), soft-soap, flatter, beguile, allure, entice, tempt.

cocky *adj* arrogant, bumptious, self-important, conceited, vain, swollen-headed, egotistical, swaggering, brash, cocksure, self-assured, self-confident, overconfident.
E3 humble, modest, shy.

code *n* **1** ETHICS, rules, regulations, principles, system, custom, convention, etiquette, manners. **2** *written in code*: cipher, secret language.

coerce *v* force, drive, compel, constrain, pressurize, bully, intimidate, browbeat, bludgeon, bulldoze, dragoon, press-gang.

coercion *n* force, duress, compulsion, constraint, pressure, bullying, intimidation, threats, browbeating.

coffee

Types of coffee include:
black coffee, white coffee, cappuccino, espresso, latte; arabica, Blue Mountain, Colombian, Costa Rican, Java, Mocha, Kenyan; light roast, dark roast, French roast; filter, ground, instant, percolated; decaffeinated, decaf (*infml*).

coffer *n* casket, case, box, chest, trunk, strongbox, treasury, repository.

cognition *n* perception, awareness, knowledge, apprehension, discernment, insight, comprehension, understanding, intelligence, reasoning.

cohere *v* **1** STICK, adhere, cling, fuse, unite, bind, combine, coalesce, consolidate. **2** *the argument does not cohere*: agree, square, correspond, harmonize, hold, hang together.
E3 1 separate.

coherent *adj* articulate, intelligible, comprehensible, meaningful, lucid, consistent, logical, reasoned, rational, sensible, orderly, systematic, organized.
E3 incoherent, unintelligible, meaningless.

coil *v* wind, spiral, convolute, curl, loop, twist, writhe, snake, wreathe, twine, entwine.
n roll, curl, loop, ring, convolution, spiral, corkscrew, helix, twist.

coin *v* invent, make up, think up, conceive, devise, formulate, originate, create, fabricate, produce, mint, forge.
n piece, bit, money, cash, change, small change, loose change, silver, copper.

coincide *v* coexist, synchronize, agree, concur, correspond, square, tally, accord, harmonize, match.

coincidence *n* **1** CHANCE, accident, eventuality, fluke (*infml*), luck, fortuity, synchronicity. **2** COEXISTENCE, conjunction, concurrence, correspondence, correlation.

coincidental *adj* **1** CHANCE, accidental, casual, unintentional, unplanned, flukey (*infml*), lucky, fortuitous. **2** COINCIDENT, coincident, concurrent, simultaneous, synchronous.

F3 1 deliberate, planned.

cold *adj* **1** UNHEATED, cool, chilled, chilly, chill, shivery, nippy, parky (*infml*), raw, biting, bitter, wintry, frosty, icy, glacial, freezing, frozen, arctic, polar. **2** UNSYMPATHETIC, unmoved, unfeeling, stony, frigid, unfriendly, distant, aloof, standoffish, reserved, undemonstrative, unresponsive, indifferent, lukewarm.

F3 1 hot, warm. **2** friendly, responsive.

n coldness, chill, chilliness, coolness, frigidity, iciness.

F3 warmth.

cold-blooded *adj* cruel, inhuman, brutal, savage, barbaric, barbarous, merciless, pitiless, callous, unfeeling, heartless.

F3 compassionate, merciful.

collaborate *v* conspire, collude, work together, co-operate, join forces, team up, participate.

collaboration *n* conspiring, collusion, association, alliance, partnership, teamwork, co-operation.

collaborator *n* co-worker, associate, partner, team-mate, colleague, assistant, accomplice, traitor, turncoat.

collapse *v* **1** collapse with exhaustion: faint, pass out, crumple. **2** FALL, sink, founder, fail, fold (*infml*), fall apart, disintegrate, crumble, subside, cave in.

n failure, breakdown, flop, debacle, downfall, ruin, disintegration, subsidence, cave-in, faint, exhaustion.

colleague *n* workmate, co-worker, team-mate, partner, collaborator, ally, associate, confederate, confrère, comrade, companion, aide, helper, assistant, auxiliary.

collect *v* gather, assemble, congregate, convene, muster, rally, converge, cluster, aggregate, accumulate, amass, heap, hoard, stockpile, save, acquire, obtain, secure.

F3 disperse, scatter.

collected *adj* composed, self-possessed, placid, serene, calm, unruffled, unperturbed, imperturbable, cool.

F3 anxious, worried, agitated.

collection *n* **1** GATHERING, assembly, convocation, congregation, crowd, group, cluster, accumulation, conglomeration, mass, heap, pile, hoard, stockpile, store. **2** SET, assemblage, assortment, job-lot, anthology, compilation.

collective *adj* united, combined, concerted, co-operative, joint, common, shared, corporate, democratic, composite, aggregate, cumulative.

F3 individual.

Collective nouns (by animal) include:

shrewdness of *apes*, cete of *badgers*, sloth of *bears*, swarm of *bees*, herd of *buffaloes*, clowder of *cats*, drove or herd of *cattle*, murder of *crows*, herd of *deer*, pack of *dogs*, school of *dolphins*, dole of *doves*, team or paddling of *ducks*, charm of *finches*, shoal of *fish*, skulk of *foxes*, gaggle or skein of *geese*, herd or tribe of *goats*, down or husk of *hares*, cast of *hawks*, brood of *hens*, string of horses, pack of *hounds*, troop of *kangaroos*, kindle of *kittens*, exaltation of *larks*, leap of *leopards*, pride of *lions*, swarm of *locusts*, troop of *monkeys*, watch of *nightingales*, parliament of *owls*, covey of *partridges*, muster of *peacocks*, rookery of *penguins*, nye of *pheasants*, litter of *pigs*, school of *porpoises*, bury of *rabbits*, unkindness of *ravens*, building of *rooks*, pod of *seals*, flock of *sheep*, murmuration of *starlings*, school or gam of *whales*, pack or rout of *wolves*.

collector

Names of collectors and enthusiasts include:
zoophile (*animals*), antiquary (*antiques*), campanologist (*bell-ringing*), ornithologist (*birds*), bibliophile (*books*), audiophile (*broadcast and recorded sound*), lepidopterist (*butterflies*), cartophilist (*cigarette cards*), numismatist (*coins/medals*), gourmet (*good food*), gastronome (*good-living*), discophile (*gramophone records*), hippophile (*horses*), entomologist (*insects*), phillumenist (*matches/matchboxes*), deltiologist (*postcards*), arachnologist (*spiders/arachnids*), philatelist (*stamps*), arctophile (*teddy bears*).

collide *v* crash, bump, smash, clash, conflict, confront, meet.

collision *n* impact, crash, bump, smash, accident, pile-up, clash, conflict, confrontation, opposition.

colloquial *adj* conversational, informal, familiar, everyday, vernacular, idiomatic.
Ｆ₃ formal.

collude *v* conspire, plot, connive, collaborate, scheme, machinate, intrigue.

colonist *n* colonial, settler, immigrant, emigrant, pioneer.

colonize *v* settle, occupy, people, populate.

colony *n* settlement, outpost, dependency, dominion, possession, territory, province.

colossal *adj* huge, enormous, immense, vast, massive, gigantic, mega (*infml*), mammoth, monstrous, monumental.
Ｆ₃ tiny, minute.

colour *n* **1** HUE, shade, tinge, tone, tincture, tint, dye, paint, wash, pigment, pigmentation, coloration, complexion. **2** VIVIDNESS, brilliance, rosiness, ruddiness, glow, liveliness, animation.

The range of colours includes:
red, crimson, scarlet, vermilion, cherry, cerise, magenta, maroon, burgundy, ruby; orange, tangerine, apricot, coral, salmon, peach, amber; brown, chestnut, mahogany, bronze, auburn, rust, copper, cinnamon, chocolate, tan, sepia, taupe, beige, fawn; yellow, lemon, canary, ochre, saffron, topaz, gold; green, chartreuse, eau de nil, emerald, jade, lime, avocado, sage, khaki; blue, turquoise, aquamarine, cobalt, sapphire, indigo, navy; purple, violet, mauve, plum, lavender, lilac; pink, rose; white, magnolia, cream, ecru; grey, silver, charcoal; black, ebony, jet.

v **1** PAINT, crayon, dye, tint, stain, tinge. **2** BLUSH, flush, redden. **3** *colour one's judgement*: affect, bias, prejudice, distort, pervert, exaggerate, falsify.

colourful *adj* **1** MULTICOLOURED, kaleidoscopic, variegated, parti-coloured, vivid, bright, brilliant, rich, intense. **2** *a colourful description*: vivid, graphic, picturesque, lively, stimulating, exciting, interesting.
F3 1 colourless, drab.

colourless *adj* **1** TRANSPARENT, neutral, bleached, washed out, faded, pale, ashen, sickly, anaemic. **2** INSIPID, lacklustre, dull, dreary, drab, plain, characterless, unmemorable, uninteresting, tame.
F3 1 colourful. **2** bright, exciting.

column *n* **1** PILLAR, post, shaft, upright, support, obelisk. **2** LIST, line, row, rank, file, procession, queue, string.

comb *v* **1** *comb one's hair*: groom, neaten, tidy, untangle. **2** SEARCH, hunt, scour, sweep, sift, screen, rake, rummage, ransack.

combat *n* war, warfare, hostilities, action, battle, fight, skirmish, struggle, conflict, clash, encounter, engagement, contest, bout, duel. *v* fight, battle, strive, struggle, contend, contest, oppose, resist, withstand, defy.

combination *n* **1** BLEND, mix, mixture, composite, amalgam, synthesis, compound. **2** MERGER, amalgamation, unification, alliance, coalition, association, federation, confederation, confederacy, combine, consortium, syndicate, union, integration, fusion, coalescence, connection.

combine *v* merge, amalgamate, unify, blend, mix, integrate, incorporate, synthesize, compound, fuse, bond, bind, join, connect, link, marry, unite, pool, associate, co-operate.
F3 divide, separate, detach.

come *v* advance, move towards, approach, near, draw near, reach, attain, arrive, enter, appear, materialize, happen, occur.
F3 go, depart, leave.

come about happen, occur, come to pass, transpire, result, arise.

come across find, discover, chance upon, happen upon, bump into, meet, encounter, notice.

come along develop, improve, progress.

come apart disintegrate, fall to bits, break, separate, split, tear.

come between separate, part, divide, split up, disunite, estrange, alienate.

come down descend, fall, reduce, decline, deteriorate, worsen, degenerate.

come in enter, appear, show up (*infml*), arrive, finish.

come off happen, occur, take place, succeed.

come on begin, appear, advance, proceed, progress, develop, improve, thrive, succeed.

come out result, end, conclude, terminate.

come out with say, state, affirm, declare, exclaim, disclose, divulge.

come round 1 *come round from the anaesthetic*: recover, wake, awake. **2** YIELD, relent, concede, allow, grant, accede.

come through endure, withstand, survive, prevail, triumph, succeed, accomplish, achieve.

come up rise, arise, happen, occur, crop up.

comeback n return, reappearance, resurgence, revival, recovery.

comedian n comic, clown, humorist, wit, joker, wag.

comedown n anticlimax, let-down, disappointment, deflation, blow, reverse, decline, descent, demotion, humiliation, degradation.

comedy n farce, slapstick, clowning, hilarity, drollery, humour, wit, joking, jesting, facetiousness.

comfort v ease, soothe, relieve, alleviate, assuage, console, cheer, gladden, reassure, hearten, encourage, invigorate, strengthen, enliven, refresh.
n 1 CONSOLATION, compensation, cheer, reassurance, encouragement, alleviation, relief, help, aid, support. 2 EASE, relaxation, luxury, snugness, cosiness, wellbeing, satisfaction, contentment, enjoyment.
E3 1 distress. 2 discomfort.

comfortable adj 1 SNUG, cosy, comfy (infml), relaxing, restful, easy, convenient, pleasant, agreeable, enjoyable, delightful. 2 AT EASE, relaxed, contented, happy.
3 AFFLUENT, well-off, well-to-do, prosperous.
E3 1 uncomfortable, unpleasant. 2 uneasy, nervous. 3 poor.

comic adj funny, hilarious, side-splitting, comical, droll, humorous, witty, amusing, entertaining, diverting, joking, facetious, light, farcical, ridiculous, ludicrous, absurd, laughable, priceless (infml), rich (infml).
E3 tragic, serious.
n comedian, comedienne, gagster (infml), joker, jester, clown, buffoon, humorist, wit, wag.

coming adj next, forthcoming, impending, imminent, due, approaching, near, future, aspiring, rising, up-and-coming.
n advent, approach, arrival, accession.

command v 1 ORDER, bid, charge, enjoin, direct, instruct, require, demand, compel. 2 LEAD, head, rule, reign, govern, control, dominate, manage, supervise.
n 1 COMMANDMENT, decree, edict, precept, mandate, order, bidding, charge, injunction, directive, direction, instruction, requirement. 2 be in command: power, authority, leadership, control, domination, dominion, rule, sway, government, management.

commander n leader, head, chief, boss, commander-in-chief, general, admiral, captain, commanding officer, officer.

commemorate v celebrate, solemnize, remember, memorialize, mark, honour, salute, immortalize, observe, keep.

commemoration n celebration, observance, remembrance, tribute, honouring, ceremony.

commence v begin, start, embark on, originate, initiate, inaugurate, open, launch.
E3 finish, end, cease.

commend v 1 PRAISE, compliment, acclaim, extol, applaud, approve, recommend. 2 COMMIT, entrust, confide, consign, deliver, yield.
E3 criticize, censure.

comment v say, mention, interpose, interject, remark, observe, note, annotate, interpret, explain, elucidate, criticize.

n statement, remark, observation, note, annotation, footnote, marginal note, explanation, elucidation, illustration, exposition, commentary, criticism.

commentary *n* narration, voice-over, analysis, description, review, critique, explanation, notes, treatise.

commentator *n* sportscaster, broadcaster, reporter, narrator, commenter, critic, annotator, interpreter.

commerce *n* trade, traffic, business, dealings, relations, dealing, trafficking, exchange, marketing, merchandising.

commercial *adj* trade, trading, business, sales, profit-making, profitable, sellable, saleable, popular, monetary, financial, mercenary, venal.

commission *n* 1 ASSIGNMENT, mission, errand, task, job, duty, function, appointment, employment, mandate, warrant, authority, charge, trust. 2 COMMITTEE, board, delegation, deputation, representative. 3 *commission on a sale*: percentage, cut (*infml*), rake-off (*infml*), allowance, fee.
v nominate, select, appoint, engage, employ, authorize, empower, delegate, depute, send, order, request, ask for.

commit *v* 1 *commit a crime*: do, perform, execute, enact, perpetrate. 2 ENTRUST, confide, commend, consign, deliver, hand over, give, deposit. 3 BIND, obligate, pledge, engage, involve.
commit oneself decide, undertake, promise, pledge, bind oneself.

commitment *n* undertaking, guarantee, assurance, promise, word, pledge, vow, engagement, involvement, dedication, devotion, adherence, loyalty, tie, obligation, duty, responsibility, liability.
F3 vacillation, wavering.

committee *n* council, board, panel, jury, commission, advisory group, think-tank, working party, task force.

common *adj* 1 FAMILIAR, customary, habitual, usual, daily, everyday, routine, regular, frequent, widespread, prevalent, general, universal, standard, average, ordinary, plain, simple, workaday, run-of-the-mill, undistinguished, unexceptional, conventional, accepted, popular, commonplace. 2 VULGAR, coarse, unrefined, crude, inferior, low, ill-bred, loutish, plebeian, proletarian. 3 COMMUNAL, public, shared, mutual, joint, collective.
F3 1 uncommon, unusual, rare, noteworthy. 2 tasteful, refined.

commonplace *adj* ordinary, everyday, common, humdrum, pedestrian, banal, trite, widespread, frequent, hackneyed, stock, stale, obvious, worn out, boring, uninteresting, threadbare.
F3 memorable, exceptional.

commonsense *adj* commonsensical, matter-of-fact, sensible, level-headed, sane, sound, reasonable, practical, down-to-earth, pragmatic, hard-headed, realistic, shrewd, astute, prudent, judicious.
F3 foolish, unreasonable, unrealistic.

commotion *n* agitation, hurly-burly, turmoil, tumult, excitement, ferment, fuss, bustle, ado, to-do (*infml*), uproar, furore, ballyhoo (*infml*), hullabaloo (*infml*), racket, hubbub, rumpus, fracas, disturbance, bust-up (*infml*), disorder, riot.

communal *adj* public, community, shared, joint, collective, general, common.
F3 private, personal.

commune *n* collective, co-operative, kibbutz, community, fellowship, colony, settlement.
v converse, discourse, communicate, make contact.

communicate *v* **1** ANNOUNCE, declare, proclaim, report, reveal, disclose, divulge, impart, inform, acquaint, intimate, notify, publish, disseminate, spread, diffuse, transmit, convey. **2** TALK, converse, commune, correspond, write, phone, telephone, e-mail, contact.

communication *n* information, intelligence, intimation, disclosure, contact, connection, transmission, dissemination.

Forms of communication include: broadcasting, radio, wireless, television, TV, cable TV, digital TV, satellite, video, teletext; newspaper, press, news, magazine, journal, website, blog (*infml*), advertising, publicity, poster, leaflet, pamphlet, brochure, catalogue; post, dispatch, correspondence, letter, e-mail, snail mail (*infml*), postcard, aerogram, telegram, cable, wire (*infml*), chain letter, junk mail, junk fax, mailshot; conversation, word, message, dialogue, speech, gossip, grapevine (*infml*); conference call, videoconference; notice, announcement, bulletin, communiqué, circular, memo, note, report, broadcast, webcast; telephone, mobile phone, cellphone, text message, SMS (short message service), intercom, answering machine, voice mail, walkie-talkie, pager, bleeper, Tannoy®, telex, teleprinter, facsimile, fax, computer, Dictaphone®, PDA (personal digital assistant), BlackBerry®; megaphone, loudhailer; radar, Morse code, semaphore, Braille, sign language.

communicative *adj* talkative, voluble, expansive, informative, chatty, sociable, friendly, forthcoming, outgoing, extrovert, unreserved, free, open, frank, candid.
F3 quiet, reserved, reticent, secretive.

community *n* district, locality, population, people, populace, public, residents, nation, state, colony, commune, kibbutz, society, association, fellowship, brotherhood, fraternity.

commute *v* **1** REDUCE, decrease, shorten, curtail, lighten, soften, mitigate, remit, adjust, modify, alter, change, exchange, alternate.
2 *commute by train*: travel, journey.

compact *adj* small, short, brief, terse, succinct, concise, condensed, compressed, close, dense, impenetrable, solid, firm.
F3 large, rambling, diffuse.

companion *n* fellow, comrade, friend, buddy (*infml*), crony (*infml*), intimate, confidant(e), ally, confederate, colleague, associate, partner, mate, consort, escort, chaperone, attendant, aide, assistant, accomplice, follower.

companionship *n* fellowship, comradeship, camaraderie, esprit de corps, support, friendship, company, togetherness, conviviality, sympathy, rapport.

company n **1** a manufacturing company: firm, business, concern, association, corporation, establishment, house, partnership, syndicate, cartel, consortium. **2** TROUPE, group, band, ensemble, set, circle, crowd, throng, body, troop, crew, party, assembly, gathering, community, society. **3** GUESTS, visitors, callers, society, companionship, fellowship, support, attendance, presence.

comparable adj similar, alike, related, akin, cognate, corresponding, analogous, equivalent, tantamount, proportionate, commensurate, parallel, equal.
E3 dissimilar, unlike, unequal.

compare v liken, equate, contrast, juxtapose, balance, weigh, correlate, resemble, match, equal, parallel.

comparison n juxtaposition, analogy, parallel, correlation, relationship, likeness, resemblance, similarity, comparability, contrast, distinction.

compartment n section, division, subdivision, category, pigeonhole, cubbyhole, niche, alcove, bay, area, stall, booth, cubicle, locker, carrel, cell, chamber, berth, carriage.

compassion n kindness, tenderness, fellow-feeling, humanity, mercy, pity, sympathy, commiseration, condolence, sorrow, concern, care.
E3 cruelty, indifference.

compassionate adj kind-hearted, kindly, tender-hearted, tender, caring, warm-hearted, benevolent, humanitarian, humane, merciful, clement, lenient, pitying.

sympathetic, understanding, supportive.
E3 cruel, indifferent.

compatible adj harmonious, consistent, congruous, matching, consonant, accordant, suitable, reconcilable, adaptable, conformable, sympathetic, like-minded, well-matched, similar.
E3 incompatible, antagonistic, contradictory.

compel v force, make, constrain, oblige, necessitate, drive, urge, impel, coerce, pressurize, hustle, browbeat, bully, strongarm, bulldoze, press-gang, dragoon.

compelling adj forceful, coercive, imperative, urgent, pressing, irresistible, overriding, powerful, cogent, persuasive, convincing, conclusive, incontrovertible, irrefutable, gripping, enthralling, spellbinding, mesmeric, compulsive.
E3 weak, unconvincing, boring.

compensate v balance, counterbalance, cancel, neutralize, counteract, offset, redress, satisfy, requite, repay, refund, reimburse, indemnify, recompense, reward, remunerate, atone, redeem, make good, restore.

compensation n amends, redress, satisfaction, requital, repayment, refund, reimbursement, indemnification, indemnity, damages, reparation, recompense, reward, payment, remuneration, return, restoration, restitution, consolation, comfort.

compete v vie, contest, fight, battle, struggle, strive, oppose, challenge, rival, emulate, contend, participate, take part.

competent adj capable, able, adept, efficient, trained, qualified, well-qualified, skilled, experienced, proficient, expert, masterly, equal, fit, suitable, appropriate, satisfactory, adequate, sufficient.
F3 incompetent, incapable, unable, inefficient.

competition n **1** CONTEST, championship, tournament, cup, event, race, match, game, quiz. **2** RIVALRY, opposition, challenge, contention, conflict, struggle, strife, competitiveness, combativeness. **3** COMPETITORS, rivals, opponents, challengers, field.

competitive adj combative, contentious, antagonistic, aggressive, pushy, ambitious, keen, cut-throat.

competitor n contestant, contender, entrant, candidate, challenger, opponent, adversary, antagonist, rival, emulator, competition, opposition.

compile v compose, put together, collect, gather, garner, cull, accumulate, amass, assemble, marshal, organize, arrange.

complacent adj smug, self-satisfied, gloating, triumphant, proud, self-righteous, unconcerned, serene, self-assured, pleased, gratified, contented, satisfied.
F3 diffident, concerned, discontented.

complain v protest, grumble, grouse, gripe, beef, carp, fuss, lament, bemoan, bewail, moan, whine, whinge (infml), groan, growl.

complaint n **1** PROTEST, objection, grumble, grouse, gripe, beef, moan, grievance, dissatisfaction, annoyance, fault-finding, criticism, censure, accusation, charge. **2** a chest complaint: ailment, illness, sickness, disease, malady, malaise, indisposition, affliction, disorder, trouble, upset.

complementary adj reciprocal, interdependent, correlative, interrelated, corresponding, matching, twin, fellow, companion.
F3 contradictory, incompatible.

complete adj **1** UTTER, total, absolute, downright, out-and-out, thorough, perfect. **2** FINISHED, ended, concluded, over, done, accomplished, achieved. **3** UNABRIDGED, unabbreviated, unedited, unexpurgated, integral, whole, entire, full, undivided, intact.
F3 1 partial. **2** incomplete. **3** abridged.
v finish, end, close, conclude, wind up, terminate, finalize, settle, clinch, perform, discharge, execute, fulfil, realize, accomplish, achieve, consummate, crown, perfect.

completion n finish, end, close, conclusion, termination, finalization, settlement, discharge, closure, fulfilment, realization, accomplishment, achievement, attainment, fruition, culmination, consummation, perfection.

complex adj complicated, intricate, elaborate, involved, convoluted, circuitous, tortuous, devious, mixed, varied, diverse, multiple, composite, compound, ramified.
F3 simple, easy.
n **1** NETWORK, structure, system, scheme, organization, establishment, institute, development. **2** FIXATION, obsession, preoccupation, hang-up (infml), phobia.

complexion n **1** SKIN, colour, colouring, pigmentation. **2** LOOK, appearance, aspect, light, character, nature, type, kind.

complicate v compound, elaborate, involve, muddle, mix up, confuse, tangle, entangle.
F3 simplify.

complicated adj complex, intricate, elaborate, involved, convoluted, tortuous, difficult, problematic, puzzling, perplexing.
F3 simple, easy.

complication n difficulty, drawback, snag, obstacle, problem, ramification, repercussion, complexity, intricacy, elaboration, convolution, tangle, web, confusion, mixture.

compliment n flattery, admiration, favour, approval, congratulations, tribute, honour, accolade, bouquet, commendation, praise, eulogy.
F3 insult, criticism.
v flatter, admire, commend, praise, extol, congratulate, applaud, salute.
F3 insult, condemn.

complimentary adj **1** FLATTERING, admiring, favourable, approving, appreciative, congratulatory, commendatory, eulogistic.
2 complimentary ticket: free, gratis, honorary, courtesy.
F3 1 insulting, unflattering, critical.

comply v agree, consent, assent, accede, yield, submit, defer, respect, observe, obey, fall in, conform, follow, perform, discharge, fulfil, satisfy, meet, oblige, accommodate.
F3 defy, disobey.

component n part, constituent, ingredient, element, factor, item, unit, piece, bit, spare part.

compose v **1** CONSTITUTE, make up, form. **2** CREATE, invent, devise, write, arrange, produce, make, form, fashion, build, construct, frame. **3** CALM, soothe, quiet, still, settle, tranquillize, quell, pacify, control, regulate.

composed adj calm, tranquil, serene, relaxed, unworried, unruffled, level-headed, cool, collected, self-possessed, confident, imperturbable, unflappable, placid.
F3 agitated, hyper (infml), worried, troubled.

composition n **1** MAKING, production, formation, creation, invention, design, formulation, writing, compilation, proportion. **2** CONSTITUTION, make-up, combination, mixture, form, structure, configuration, layout, arrangement, organization, harmony, consonance, balance, symmetry. **3** a musical composition: work, opus, piece, study, exercise.

composure n calm, tranquillity, serenity, ease, coolness, self-possession, confidence, assurance, self-assurance, aplomb, poise, dignity, imperturbability, placidity, equanimity, dispassion, impassivity.
F3 agitation, nervousness, discomposure.

compound v **1** COMBINE, amalgamate, unite, fuse, coalesce, synthesize, alloy, blend, mix, mingle, intermingle. **2** WORSEN, exacerbate, aggravate, complicate, intensify, heighten, magnify, increase, augment.
n alloy, blend, mixture, medley, composite, amalgam, synthesis,

fusion, composition, amalgamation, combination.

adj composite, mixed, multiple, complex, complicated, intricate.

comprehend *v* 1 UNDERSTAND, conceive, see, grasp, get it (*infml*), fathom, penetrate, tumble to (*infml*), realize, appreciate, know, apprehend, perceive, discern, take in, assimilate. **2** INCLUDE, comprise, encompass, embrace, cover.

E3 1 misunderstand.

comprehensible *adj* understandable, intelligible, coherent, explicit, clear, lucid, plain, simple, straightforward.

E3 incomprehensible, obscure.

comprehension *n* understanding, conception, grasp, realization, appreciation, knowledge, apprehension, perception, discernment, judgement, sense, intelligence.

E3 incomprehension, unawareness.

comprehensive *adj* thorough, exhaustive, full, complete, encyclopedic, compendious, broad, wide, extensive, sweeping, general, blanket, inclusive, all-inclusive, all-embracing, across-the-board.

E3 partial, incomplete, selective.

compress *v* press, squeeze, crush, squash, flatten, jam, wedge, cram, stuff, compact, concentrate, condense, contract, telescope, shorten, abbreviate, summarize.

E3 expand, diffuse.

comprise *v* consist of, include, contain, incorporate, embody, involve, encompass, embrace, cover.

compromise *v* 1 NEGOTIATE, bargain, arbitrate, settle, agree, concede, make concessions, meet halfway, adapt, adjust. **2** *compromise one's principles*: weaken, undermine, expose, endanger, imperil, jeopardize, risk, prejudice. **3** DISHONOUR, discredit, embarrass, involve, implicate.

n bargain, trade-off, settlement, agreement, concession, give and take, co-operation, accommodation, adjustment.

E3 disagreement, intransigence.

compulsive *adj* 1 IRRESISTIBLE, overwhelming, overpowering, uncontrollable, compelling, driving, urgent. **2** *a compulsive gambler*: obsessive, hardened, incorrigible, irredeemable, incurable, hopeless.

compulsory *adj* obligatory, mandatory, imperative, forced, required, requisite, set, stipulated, binding, contractual.

E3 optional, voluntary, discretionary.

computer *n* personal computer, PC, mainframe, processor, word-processor, data processor, calculator, adding machine.

Computing terms include:
mainframe, microcomputer, mini-computer, PC (personal computer), AppleMac®, Mac (*infml*), iMac®; hardware, CPU (central processing unit), disk drive, joy-stick, keyboard, laptop, light pen, microprocessor, modem, monitor, motherboard, mouse, mouse mat, notebook, palmtop, peripheral, port, printer, screen, sound card, graphics card, VDU (visual display unit); software, program, shell program, freeware, shareware; disk, magnetic disk, floppy disk, hard disk, optical disk, magnetic tape; programming lan-

guage, AWK, BASIC, C, COBOL, FORTRAN, Java®, Pascal, Perl, Python; memory, backing storage, RAM (Random Access Memory), ROM (Read Only Memory), CD-ROM (Compact Disc Read Only Memory), CD-R (Compact Disc Recordable), DVD (Digital Versatile Disk); access, ASCII (American Standard Code for Information Interchange), back-up, bit, boot, buffer, byte, kilobyte, megabyte, gigabyte, character, chip, silicon chip, computer game, computer graphics, terminal, cursor, data, databank, database, default, desktop publishing (DTP), digitizer, directory, DOS (disk operating system), e-mail, broadband, dial-up, file, firewall, format, FTP (File Transfer Protocol), function, graphics, hacking, icon, interface, intranet, Linux, Mac OS®, macro, menu, MSDOS (Microsoft® disk operating system), network, peripheral, pixel, scrolling, spellchecker, spreadsheet, template, toggle, toolbar, Unicode, Unix®, user-friendly, user interface, virtual reality, virus, virus-checker, window, Windows®, word-processing, workstation, worm. *see also* **Internet**.

con *v* trick, hoax, dupe, deceive, mislead, inveigle, hoodwink, bamboozle (*infml*), cheat, double-cross, swindle, defraud, rip off (*sl*), rook.
n confidence trick, trick, bluff, deception, swindle, fraud.

concave *adj* hollow, hollowed, cupped, scooped, excavated, sunken, depressed.
F3 convex.

conceal *v* hide, obscure, disguise, camouflage, mask, screen, veil, cloak, cover, bury, submerge, smother, suppress, keep dark, keep quiet, hush up (*infml*).
F3 reveal, disclose, uncover.

concede *v* **1** ADMIT, confess, acknowledge, recognize, own, grant, allow, accept. **2** YIELD, give up, surrender, relinquish, forfeit, sacrifice.
F3 1 deny.

conceit *n* conceitedness, vanity, boastfulness, swagger, egotism, self-love, self-importance, cockiness, self-satisfaction, complacency, pride, arrogance.
F3 modesty, diffidence.

conceited *adj* vain, boastful, swollen-headed, bigheaded (*infml*), egotistical, self-important, cocky, self-satisfied, complacent, smug, proud, arrogant, stuck-up (*infml*), toffee-nosed (*infml*).
F3 modest, self-effacing, diffident, humble.

conceivable *adj* imaginable, credible, believable, thinkable, tenable, possible, likely, probable.
F3 inconceivable, unimaginable.

conceive *v* **1** IMAGINE, envisage, visualize, see, grasp, understand, comprehend, realize, appreciate, believe, think, suppose. **2** INVENT, design, devise, formulate, create, originate, form, produce, develop.

concentrate *v* **1** FOCUS, converge, centre, cluster, crowd, congregate, gather, collect, accumulate. **2** APPLY ONESELF, think, pay attention, attend. **3** CONDENSE, evaporate, reduce, thicken, intensify.
F3 1 disperse. **3** dilute.

concentrated adj **1** concentrated liquid: condensed, evaporated, reduced, thickened, dense, rich, strong, undiluted. **2** INTENSE, intensive, all-out, concerted, hard, deep.

F3 1 diluted. **2** half-hearted.

concentration n **1** CONVERGENCE, centralization, cluster, crowd, grouping, collection, accumulation, agglomeration, conglomeration. **2** ATTENTION, heed, absorption, application, single-mindedness, intensity. **3** COMPRESSION, reduction, consolidation, denseness, thickness.

F3 1 dispersal. **2** distraction. **3** dilution.

concept n idea, notion, plan, theory, hypothesis, thought, abstraction, conception, conceptualization, visualization, image, picture, impression.

conception n **1** CONCEPT, idea, notion, thought. **2** KNOWLEDGE, understanding, appreciation, perception, visualization, image, picture, impression, inkling, clue. **3** INVENTION, design, birth, beginning, origin, outset, initiation, inauguration, formation. **4** from conception to birth: impregnation, insemination, fertilization.

concern v **1** UPSET, distress, trouble, disturb, bother, worry. **2** RELATE TO, refer to, regard, involve, interest, affect, touch.
n **1** a cause for concern: anxiety, worry, unease, disquiet, care, sorrow, distress. **2** REGARD, consideration, attention, heed, thought. **3** it's not my concern: duty, responsibility, charge, job, task, field,

business, affair, matter, problem, interest, involvement. **4** COMPANY, firm, business, corporation, establishment, enterprise, organization.

F3 1 joy. **2** indifference.

concerned adj **1** ANXIOUS, worried, uneasy, apprehensive, upset, unhappy, distressed, troubled, disturbed, bothered, attentive, caring. **2** CONNECTED, related, involved, implicated, complicit, interested, affected.

F3 1 unconcerned, indifferent, apathetic.

concerning prep about, regarding, with regard to, as regards, respecting, with reference to, relating to, in the matter of.

concerted adj combined, united, joint, collective, shared, collaborative, co-ordinated, organized, prearranged, planned.

F3 separate, unco-ordinated, disorganized.

concession n compromise, adjustment, grant, allowance, exception, privilege, favour, indulgence, permit, admission, acknowledgement.

concise adj short, brief, terse, succinct, pithy, compendious, compact, compressed, condensed, abridged, abbreviated, summary, synoptic.

F3 diffuse, wordy.

conclude v **1** INFER, deduce, assume, surmise, suppose, reckon, judge. **2** END, close, finish, complete, consummate, cease, terminate, culminate. **3** SETTLE, resolve, decide, establish, determine, clinch.

F3 2 start, commence.

conclusion n **1** INFERENCE, deduction, assumption, opinion, conviction, judgement, verdict, decision, resolution, settlement, result, consequence, outcome, upshot, answer, solution. **2** END, close, finish, completion, consummation, termination, culmination, finale.

conclusive adj final, ultimate, definitive, decisive, clear, convincing, definite, undeniable, irrefutable, indisputable, incontrovertible, unarguable, unanswerable, clinching. ⊟ inconclusive, questionable.

concoct v fabricate, invent, devise, contrive, formulate, plan, plot, hatch, brew, prepare, develop.

concoction n brew, potion, preparation, mixture, blend, compound, creation, contrivance.

concrete adj real, actual, factual, solid, physical, material, substantial, tangible, touchable, perceptible, visible, firm, definite, specific, explicit. ⊟ abstract, vague.

concurrent adj simultaneous, synchronous, contemporaneous, coinciding, coincident, concomitant, coexisting, coexistent.

condemn v disapprove, reprehend, reprove, upbraid, reproach, castigate, blame, disparage, revile, denounce, censure, slam (infml), slate (infml), damn, doom, convict. ⊟ praise, approve.

condemnation n disapproval, reproof, reproach, castigation, blame, disparagement, denunciation, censure, thumbs-down (infml), damnation, conviction, sentence, judgement. ⊟ praise, approval.

condensation n **1** condensation of liquid: distillation, liquefaction, precipitation, concentration, evaporation, reduction, consolidation. **2** ABRIDGEMENT, précis, synopsis, digest, contraction, compression, curtailment.

condense v condense a book: shorten, curtail, abbreviate, abridge, précis, summarize, encapsulate, contract, compress, compact. **2** DISTIL, precipitate, concentrate, evaporate, reduce, thicken, solidify, coagulate. ⊟ **1** expand. **2** dilute.

condescend v deign, see fit, stoop, bend, lower oneself, patronize, talk down.

condescending adj patronizing, disdainful, supercilious, snooty, snobbish, haughty, lofty, superior, lordly, imperious. ⊟ gracious, humble.

condition n **1** CASE, state, circumstances, position, situation, predicament, plight. **2** REQUIREMENT, obligation, prerequisite, terms, stipulation, proviso, qualification, limitation, restriction, rule. **3** a heart condition: disorder, defect, weakness, infirmity, problem, complaint, disease. **4** out of condition: fitness, health, state, shape, form, fettle, nick (sl). v indoctrinate, brainwash, influence, mould, educate, train, groom, equip, prepare, prime, accustom, season, temper, adapt, adjust, tune.

conditional adj provisional, qualified, limited, restricted, tied, relative, dependent, contingent. ⊟ unconditional, absolute.

conditions n surroundings, environment, milieu, setting, atmosphere, background, context, circumstances, situation, state.

condom n sheath, French letter (sl), johnnie (sl), rubber (sl), protective.

condone v forgive, pardon, excuse, overlook, ignore, disregard, tolerate, brook, allow.
F3 condemn, censure.

conducive adj leading, tending, contributory, productive, advantageous, beneficial, favourable, helpful, encouraging.
F3 detrimental, adverse, unfavourable.

conduct n 1 good conduct: behaviour, comportment, actions, ways, manners, bearing, attitude. 2 ADMINISTRATION, management, direction, running, organization, operation, control, supervision, leadership, guidance.
v 1 ADMINISTER, manage, run, organize, orchestrate, chair, control, handle, regulate. 2 ACCOMPANY, escort, usher, lead, guide, direct, pilot, steer. 3 conduct heat: convey, carry, bear, transmit. 4 conduct oneself: behave, acquit, comport, act.

confer v 1 DISCUSS, debate, deliberate, consult, talk, converse. 2 BESTOW, award, present, give, grant, accord, impart, lend.

conference n meeting, convention, congress, convocation, symposium, forum, discussion, debate, consultation.

confess v admit, confide, own (up), come clean (infml), grant, concede, acknowledge, recognize, affirm, assert, profess, declare, disclose, divulge, expose.
F3 deny, conceal.

confession n admission, acknowledgement, affirmation, assertion, profession, declaration, disclosure, divulgence, revelation, unburdening.
F3 denial, concealment.

confide v confess, admit, reveal, disclose, divulge, whisper, breathe, tell, impart, unburden.
F3 hide, suppress.

confidence n certainty, faith, credence, trust, reliance, dependence, assurance, composure, calmness, self-possession, self-confidence, self-reliance, self-assurance, boldness, courage.
F3 distrust, diffidence.

confident adj sure, certain, positive, convinced, assured, composed, self-possessed, cool, self-confident, self-reliant, self-assured, unselfconscious, bold, fearless, dauntless, unabashed.
F3 doubtful, diffident.

confidential adj secret, top secret, classified, restricted, hush-hush (infml), off-the-record, private, personal, intimate, privy.

confine v enclose, circumscribe, bound, limit, restrict, cramp, constrain, imprison, incarcerate, intern, cage, shut up, immure, bind, shackle, trammel, restrain, repress, inhibit.
F3 free.

confinement n 1 IMPRISONMENT, incarceration, internment, custody, detention, house arrest. 2 CHILDBIRTH, birth, labour, delivery.
F3 1 freedom, liberty.

confines n limits, bounds, border, boundary, frontier, circumference, perimeter, edge.

confirm v **1** ENDORSE, back, support, reinforce, strengthen, fortify, validate, authenticate, corroborate, substantiate, verify, prove, evidence. **2** ESTABLISH, fix, settle, clinch, ratify, sanction, approve.
F3 1 refute, deny.

confirmation n ratification, sanction, approval, assent, acceptance, agreement, endorsement, backing, support, validation, authentication, corroboration, substantiation, verification, proof, evidence, testimony, smoking gun (*infml*).
F3 denial.

confirmed adj inveterate, entrenched, dyed-in-the-wool, rooted, established, long-established, long-standing, habitual, chronic, seasoned, hardened, incorrigible, incurable.

confiscate v seize, appropriate, expropriate, remove, take away, impound, sequester, commandeer.
F3 return, restore.

conflict n **1** DIFFERENCE, variance, discord, contention, disagreement, dissension, dispute, opposition, antagonism, hostility, friction, strife, unrest, confrontation. **2** BATTLE, war, warfare, combat, fight, contest, engagement, skirmish, set-to, fracas, brawl, quarrel, feud, encounter, clash.
F3 1 agreement, harmony, concord.
v differ, clash, collide, disagree, contradict, oppose, contest, fight, combat, battle, war, strive, struggle, contend.
F3 agree, harmonize.

conform v agree, accord, harmonize, match, correspond, tally, square,
adapt, adjust, accommodate, comply, obey, follow.
F3 differ, conflict, rebel.

conformity n conventionality, orthodoxy, traditionalism, compliance, observance, allegiance, affinity, agreement, consonance, harmony, correspondence, congruity, likeness, similarity, resemblance.
F3 nonconformity, rebellion, difference.

confound v **1** CONFUSE, bewilder, baffle, perplex, mystify, bamboozle (*infml*), nonplus, surprise, amaze, astonish, astound, flabbergast (*infml*), dumbfound, stupefy. **2** *confound their plans*: thwart, upset, defeat, overwhelm, overthrow, destroy, demolish, ruin.

confront v face, meet, encounter, accost, address, oppose, challenge, defy, brave, beard.
F3 evade.

confrontation n encounter, clash, collision, showdown, conflict, disagreement, fight, battle, quarrel, set-to, engagement, contest.

confuse v **1** PUZZLE, baffle, perplex, mystify, confound, bewilder, disorient, disconcert, fluster, discompose, upset, embarrass, mortify. **2** MUDDLE, mix up, mistake, jumble, disarrange, disorder, tangle, entangle, involve, mingle.
F3 1 enlighten, clarify.

confused adj **1** MUDDLED, jumbled, disarranged, disordered, untidy, disorderly, higgledy-piggledy (*infml*), chaotic, disorganized. **2** PUZZLED, baffled, perplexed, flummoxed (*infml*), nonplussed, bewildered, disorientated.
F3 1 orderly.

confusion n 1 DISORDER, disarray, untidiness, mess, clutter, jumble, muddle, mix-up, disorganization, chaos, turmoil, commotion, upheaval. 2 MISUNDERSTANDING, puzzlement, perplexity, mystification, bewilderment.
F3 1 order. 2 clarity.

congeal v clot, curdle, coalesce, coagulate, thicken, stiffen, harden, solidify, set, gel, freeze.
F3 dissolve, melt.

congested adj clogged, blocked, jammed, packed, stuffed, crammed, full, crowded, overcrowded, overflowing, teeming.
F3 clear.

congestion n clogging, blockage, overcrowding, jam, traffic jam, snarl-up (infml), gridlock, bottleneck.

conglomeration n mass, agglomeration, aggregation, accumulation, collection, assemblage, composite, medley, hotchpotch.

congratulate v praise, felicitate, compliment, wish well.
F3 commiserate.

congregate v gather, assemble, collect, muster, rally, rendezvous, meet, convene, converge, flock, crowd, throng, mass, accumulate, cluster, clump, conglomerate.
F3 disperse.

congregation n assembly, crowd, throng, multitude, host, flock, parishioners, parish, laity, fellowship.

conical adj cone-shaped, pyramidal, tapering, tapered, pointed.

conjecture v speculate, theorize, hypothesize, guess, estimate, reckon, suppose, surmise, assume, infer, imagine, suspect.
n speculation, theory, hypothesis, notion, guesswork, guess, estimate,

supposition, surmise, assumption, presumption, conclusion, inference, extrapolation, projection.

conjure v summon, invoke, rouse, raise, bewitch, charm, fascinate, compel.

conjure up evoke, create, produce, excite, awaken, recollect, recall.

connect v join, link, unite, couple, combine, fasten, affix, attach, relate, associate, ally.
F3 disconnect, cut off, detach.

connected adj joined, linked, united, coupled, combined, related, akin, associated, affiliated, allied.
F3 disconnected, unconnected.

connection n junction, coupling, fastening, attachment, bond, tie, link, association, alliance, relation, relationship, interrelation, contact, communication, correlation, correspondence, relevance.
F3 disconnection.

connoisseur n authority, specialist, expert, judge, devotee, buff (infml), gourmet, epicure.

connotation n implication, suggestion, hint, nuance, undertone, overtone, colouring, association.

conquer v 1 DEFEAT, beat, overthrow, vanquish, rout, overrun, best, worst, get the better of, overcome, surmount, win, succeed, triumph, prevail, overpower, master, crush, subdue, quell, subjugate, humble. 2 SEIZE, take, annex, occupy, possess, acquire, obtain.
F3 1 surrender, yield, give in.

conqueror n victor, winner, champion, champ (infml), hero, vanquisher, master, lord.

conquest n victory, triumph, defeat, overthrow, coup, rout, mastery, subjugation, subjection, invasion, occupation, capture, appropriation, annexation, acquisition.

conscience n principles, standards, morals, ethics, scruples, qualms.

conscientious adj diligent, hard-working, scrupulous, painstaking, thorough, meticulous, punctilious, particular, careful, attentive, responsible, upright, honest, faithful, dutiful.

E3 careless, irresponsible, unreliable.

conscious adj 1 AWAKE, alive, responsive, sentient, sensible, rational, reasoning, alert. 2 AWARE, self-conscious, heedful, mindful, knowing, deliberate, intentional, calculated, premeditated, studied, wilful, voluntary.

E3 1 unconscious. 2 unaware.

consciousness n awareness, sentience, sensibility, knowledge, intuition, realization, recognition.

E3 unconsciousness.

consecrate v sanctify, hallow, bless, dedicate, devote, ordain, venerate, revere, exalt.

consecutive adj sequential, successive, continuous, unbroken, uninterrupted, following, succeeding, running.

E3 discontinuous.

consent v agree, concur, accede, assent, approve, permit, allow, grant, admit, concede, acquiesce, yield, comply.

E3 refuse, decline, oppose.
n agreement, concurrence, assent, approval, permission, go-ahead, green light (infml), sanction, concession, acquiescence, compliance.

E3 disagreement, refusal, opposition.

consequence n 1 RESULT, outcome, issue, end, upshot, effect, side effect, repercussion. 2 of no consequence: importance, significance, concern, value, weight, note, eminence, distinction.

E3 1 cause. 2 unimportance, insignificance.

consequent adj resultant, resulting, ensuing, subsequent, following, successive, sequential.

conservation n keeping, safe-keeping, custody, saving, economy, husbandry, maintenance, upkeep, preservation, protection, safeguarding, ecology, environmentalism.

E3 destruction.

conservative adj Tory, right-wing, hidebound, die-hard, reactionary, establishmentarian, unprogressive, conventional, traditional, moderate, middle-of-the-road, cautious, guarded, sober.

E3 left-wing, liberal, radical, innovative.
n Tory, right-winger, die-hard, stick-in-the-mud, reactionary, traditionalist, moderate.

E3 left-winger, liberal, radical.

conservatory n greenhouse, glasshouse, hothouse.

conserve v keep, save, store up, hoard, maintain, preserve, protect, guard, safeguard.

E3 use, waste, squander.

consider v 1 PONDER, deliberate, reflect, contemplate, meditate, muse, mull over, chew over, examine, study, weigh, respect, remember, take into account. 2 consider it an honour: regard, deem, think, believe, judge, rate, count.

considerable adj great, large, big, sizable, substantial, tidy (infml), ample, plentiful, abundant, lavish, marked, noticeable, perceptible, appreciable, reasonable, tolerable, respectable, important, significant, noteworthy, distinguished, influential. **E3** small, slight, insignificant, unremarkable.

considerate adj kind, thoughtful, caring, attentive, obliging, helpful, charitable, unselfish, altruistic, gracious, sensitive, tactful, discreet. **E3** inconsiderate, thoughtless, selfish.

consideration n 1 THOUGHT, deliberation, reflection, contemplation, meditation, examination, analysis, scrutiny, review, attention, notice, regard. 2 KINDNESS, thoughtfulness, care, attention, regard, respect. **E3** 1 disregard. 2 thoughtlessness.

consign v entrust, commit, devote, hand over, transfer, deliver, convey, ship, banish, relegate.

consignment n cargo, shipment, load, batch, delivery, goods.

consistency n 1 of the consistency of porridge: viscosity, thickness, density, firmness. 2 STEADINESS, regularity, evenness, uniformity, sameness, identity, constancy, steadfastness. 3 AGREEMENT, accordance, correspondence, congruity, compatibility, harmony. **E3** 3 inconsistency.

consistent adj 1 STEADY, stable, regular, uniform, unchanging, undeviating, constant, persistent, unfailing, dependable. 2 AGREEING, accordant, consonant, congruous, compatible, harmonious, logical. **E3** 1 irregular, erratic. 2 inconsistent.

consist of comprise, be composed of, contain, include, incorporate, embody, embrace, involve, amount to.

console v comfort, cheer, hearten, encourage, relieve, soothe, calm. **E3** upset, agitate.

consolidate v reinforce, strengthen, secure, stabilize, unify, unite, join, combine, amalgamate, fuse, cement, compact, condense, thicken, harden, solidify.

conspicuous adj apparent, visible, noticeable, marked, clear, obvious, evident, patent, manifest, prominent, striking, blatant, flagrant, glaring, ostentatious, showy, flashy, garish. **E3** inconspicuous, concealed, hidden.

conspiracy n plot, scheme, intrigue, machination, fix (infml), frame-up (infml), collusion, league, treason.

conspirator n conspirer, plotter, schemer, intriguer, traitor.

conspire v plot, scheme, intrigue, manoeuvre, connive, collude, hatch, devise.

constancy n 1 STABILITY, steadiness, permanence, firmness, regularity, uniformity, resolution, perseverance, tenacity. 2 LOYALTY, faithfulness, fidelity, devotion. **E3** 1 change, irregularity. 2 fickleness.

constant adj 1 CONTINUOUS, unbroken, never-ending, non-stop, endless, interminable, ceaseless, incessant, eternal, everlasting, perpetual, continual, unremitting, relentless, persistent, resolute, persevering, unflagging, unwavering, stable, steady, unchanging, unvarying, changeless, immutable, invariable, unalterable, fixed, permanent, firm, even, regular, uniform. **2** *a constant friend*: loyal, faithful, staunch, steadfast, dependable, trustworthy, true, devoted.

F3 1 variable, irregular, fitful, occasional. **2** disloyal, fickle.

constituent *adj* component, integral, essential, basic, intrinsic, inherent.
n ingredient, element, factor, principle, component, part, bit, section, unit.

F3 whole.

constitute *v* represent, make up, compose, comprise, form, create, establish, set up, found.

constrain *v* **1** FORCE, compel, oblige, necessitate, drive, impel, urge. **2** LIMIT, confine, constrict, restrain, check, curb, bind.

constrained *adj* uneasy, embarrassed, inhibited, reticent, reserved, guarded, stiff, forced, unnatural.

F3 relaxed, free.

constraint *n* **1** FORCE, duress, compulsion, coercion, pressure, necessity, deterrent. **2** RESTRICTION, limitation, hindrance, restraint, check, curb, damper.

constrict *v* squeeze, compress, pinch, cramp, narrow, tighten, contract, shrink, choke, strangle, inhibit, limit, restrict.

F3 expand.

construct *v* build, erect, raise, elevate, make, manufacture, fabricate, assemble, put together, compose, form, shape, fashion, model, design, engineer, create, found, establish, formulate.

F3 demolish, destroy.

construction *n* building, edifice, erection, structure, fabric, form, shape, figure, model, manufacture, fabrication, assembly, composition, constitution, formation, creation.

F3 destruction.

constructive *adj* practical, productive, positive, helpful, useful, valuable, beneficial, advantageous.

F3 destructive, negative, unhelpful.

consult *v* refer to, ask, question, interrogate, confer, discuss, debate, deliberate.

consultant *n* adviser, expert, authority, specialist.

consultation *n* discussion, deliberation, dialogue, conference, meeting, hearing, interview, examination, appointment, session.

consume *v* **1** EAT, drink, swallow, devour, gobble. **2** USE, absorb, spend, expend, deplete, drain, exhaust, use up, dissipate, squander, waste. **3** DESTROY, demolish, annihilate, devastate, ravage.

consumer *n* user, end-user, customer, buyer, purchaser, shopper.

consumption *n* use, utilization, spending, expenditure, depletion, exhaustion, waste.

contact *n* touch, impact, juxtaposition, contiguity, communication, meeting, junction, union, connection, association.
v approach, apply to, reach, get hold of, get in touch with, telephone, phone, ring, call, notify.

contagious *adj* infectious, catching, communicable, transmissible, spreading, epidemic.

contain *v* **1** INCLUDE, comprise, incorporate, embody, involve, embrace, enclose, hold,

accommodate, seat. **2** *contain one's feelings*: repress, stifle, restrain, control, check, curb, limit.
F3 **1** exclude.

container *n* receptacle, vessel, holder.

contaminate *v* infect, pollute, adulterate, taint, soil, sully, defile, corrupt, deprave, debase, stain, tarnish.
F3 purify.

contemplate *v* **1** MEDITATE, reflect on, ponder, mull over, deliberate, consider, regard, view, survey, observe, study, examine, inspect, scrutinize. **2** EXPECT, foresee, envisage, plan, design, propose, intend, mean.

contemporary *adj* **1** MODERN, current, present, present-day, recent, latest, up-to-date, fashionable, up-to-the-minute, ultra-modern.
2 CONTEMPORANEOUS, coexistent, concurrent, synchronous, simultaneous.
F3 **1** out-of-date, old-fashioned.

contempt *n* scorn, disdain, condescension, derision, ridicule, mockery, disrespect, dishonour, disregard, neglect, dislike, loathing, detestation.
F3 admiration, regard.

contemptible *adj* despicable, shameful, ignominious, low, mean, vile, detestable, loathsome, abject, wretched, pitiful, paltry, worthless.
F3 admirable, honourable.

contemptuous *adj* scornful, disdainful, sneering, supercilious, condescending, arrogant, haughty, high and mighty, cynical, derisive, insulting, disrespectful, insolent.
F3 humble, respectful.

contend *v* **1** MAINTAIN, hold, argue, allege, assert, declare, affirm.
2 COMPETE, vie, contest, dispute, clash, wrestle, grapple, struggle, strive, cope.

content *v* satisfy, humour, indulge, gratify, please, delight, appease, pacify, placate.
F3 displease.
n **1** SUBSTANCE, matter, essence, gist, meaning, significance, text, subject matter, ideas, contents, load, burden. **2** CAPACITY, volume, size, measure.
adj satisfied, fulfilled, contented, untroubled, pleased, happy, willing.
F3 dissatisfied, troubled.

contented *adj* happy, glad, pleased, cheerful, comfortable, relaxed, content, satisfied.
F3 discontented, unhappy, annoyed.

contentment *n* contentedness, happiness, gladness, pleasure, gratification, comfort, ease, complacency, peace, peacefulness, serenity, equanimity, content, satisfaction, fulfilment.
F3 unhappiness, discontent, dissatisfaction.

contents *n* **1** *the contents of the package*: constituents, parts, elements, ingredients, content, load, items. **2** CHAPTERS, divisions, subjects, topics, themes.

contest *n* competition, game, match, tournament, encounter, fight, battle, set-to, combat, conflict, struggle, dispute, debate, controversy.
v **1** DISPUTE, debate, question, doubt, challenge, oppose, argue against, litigate, deny, refute. **2** COMPETE, vie, contend, strive, fight.
F3 **1** accept.

contestant n competitor, contender, player, participant, entrant, candidate, aspirant, rival, opponent.

context n background, setting, surroundings, framework, frame of reference, situation, position, circumstances, conditions.

contingent n body, company, deputation, delegation, detachment, section, group, set, batch, quota, complement.

continual adj constant, perpetual, incessant, interminable, eternal, everlasting, regular, frequent, recurrent, repeated.
F3 occasional, intermittent, temporary.

continuation n resumption, maintenance, prolongation, extension, development, furtherance, addition, supplement.
F3 cessation, termination.

continue v resume, recommence, carry on, go on, proceed, persevere, stick at, persist, last, endure, survive, remain, abide, stay, rest, pursue, sustain, maintain, lengthen, prolong, extend, project.
F3 discontinue, stop.

continuity n flow, progression, succession, sequence, linkage, interrelationship, connection, cohesion.
F3 discontinuity.

continuous adj unbroken, uninterrupted, consecutive, non-stop, endless, ceaseless, unending, unceasing, constant, unremitting, prolonged, extended, continued, lasting.
F3 discontinuous, broken, sporadic.

contort v twist, distort, warp, wrench, disfigure, deform, misshape, convolute, gnarl, knot, writhe, squirm, wriggle.

contour n outline, silhouette, shape, form, figure, curve, relief, profile, character, aspect.

contraception n birth control, family planning.

contract v 1 SHRINK, lessen, diminish, reduce, shorten, curtail, abbreviate, abridge, condense, compress, constrict, narrow, tighten, tense, shrivel, wrinkle. 2 contract pneumonia: catch, get, go down with, develop. 3 PLEDGE, promise, undertake, agree, stipulate, arrange, negotiate, bargain.
F3 1 expand, enlarge, lengthen.
n bond, commitment, engagement, covenant, treaty, convention, pact, compact, agreement, transaction, deal, bargain, settlement, arrangement, understanding.

contradict v deny, disaffirm, confute, challenge, oppose, impugn, dispute, counter, negate, gainsay.
F3 agree, confirm, corroborate.

contradictory adj contrary, opposite, paradoxical, conflicting, discrepant, inconsistent, incompatible, antagonistic, irreconcilable, opposed, repugnant.
F3 consistent.

contraption n contrivance, device, gadget, apparatus, rig, machine, mechanism.

contrary adj 1 OPPOSITE, counter, reverse, conflicting, antagonistic, opposed, adverse, hostile.
2 PERVERSE, awkward, disobliging, difficult, wayward, obstinate, intractable, cantankerous, stroppy (infml).
F3 1 like. 2 obliging.
n opposite, converse, reverse.

contrast n difference, dissimilarity, disparity, divergence, distinction, differentiation, comparison, foil, antithesis, opposition.
F3 similarity.
v compare, differentiate, distinguish, discriminate, differ, oppose, clash, conflict.

contravene v infringe, violate, break, breach, disobey, defy, flout, transgress.
F3 uphold, observe, obey.

contribute v donate, subscribe, chip in (infml), add, give, bestow, provide, supply, furnish, help, lead, conduce.
F3 withhold.

contribution n donation, subscription, gift, gratuity, handout, grant, offering, input, addition.

contributor n **1** DONOR, subscriber, giver, patron, benefactor, sponsor, backer, supporter. **2** WRITER, journalist, reporter, correspondent, freelance.

contrite adj sorry, regretful, remorseful, repentant, penitent, conscience-stricken, chastened, humble, ashamed.

contrivance n **1** INVENTION, device, contraption, gadget, implement, appliance, machine, mechanism, apparatus, equipment, gear.
2 STRATAGEM, ploy, trick, dodge, ruse, expedient, plan, design, project, scheme, plot, intrigue, machination.

contrived adj unnatural, artificial, false, forced, strained, laboured, mannered, elaborate, overdone.
F3 natural, genuine.

control v **1** LEAD, govern, rule, command, direct, manage, oversee, supervise, superintend, run, operate.
2 control the temperature: regulate, adjust, monitor, verify. **3** control one's temper: restrain, check, curb, subdue, repress, hold back, contain.
n **1** POWER, charge, authority, command, mastery, government, rule, direction, management, oversight, supervision, superintendence, discipline, guidance. **2** RESTRAINT, check, curb, repression. **3** INSTRUMENT, dial, switch, button, knob, lever.

controversial adj contentious, polemical, disputed, doubtful, questionable, debatable, disputable.

controversy n debate, discussion, war of words, polemic, dispute, disagreement, argument, quarrel, squabble, wrangle, strife, contention, dissension.
F3 accord, agreement.

convenience n **1** ACCESSIBILITY, availability, handiness, usefulness, use, utility, serviceability, service, benefit, advantage, help, suitability, fitness. **2** all modern conveniences: facility, amenity, appliance.
F3 1 inconvenience.

convenient adj nearby, at hand, accessible, available, handy, useful, commodious, beneficial, helpful, labour-saving, adapted, fitted, suited, suitable, fit, appropriate, opportune, timely, well-timed.
F3 inconvenient, awkward.

convention n **1** CUSTOM, tradition, practice, usage, protocol, etiquette, formality, matter of form, code.
2 ASSEMBLY, congress, conference, meeting, council, delegates, representatives.

conventional adj traditional, orthodox, formal, correct, proper, prevalent, prevailing, accepted,

received, expected, unoriginal, ritual, routine, usual, customary, regular, standard, normal, ordinary, straight, stereotyped, hidebound, pedestrian, commonplace, common, run-of-the-mill.
F3 unconventional, unusual, exotic.

converge v focus, concentrate, approach, merge, coincide, meet, join, combine, gather.
F3 diverge, disperse.

convergence n concentration, approach, merging, confluence, blending, meeting, coincidence, junction, intersection, union.
F3 divergence, separation.

conversation n talk, chat, gossip, discussion, discourse, dialogue, exchange, communication.

converse n opposite, reverse, contrary, antithesis, obverse.
adj opposite, reverse, counter, contrary, reversed, transposed.

conversion n alteration, change, transformation, adaptation, modification, remodelling, reconstruction, reorganization, reformation, regeneration, rebirth.

convert v **1** ALTER, change, turn, transform, adapt, modify, remodel, restyle, revise, reorganize. **2** WIN OVER, convince, reform, proselytize.

convex adj rounded, bulging, protuberant.
F3 concave.

convey v carry, bear, bring, fetch, move, transport, send, forward, deliver, transfer, conduct, guide, transmit, communicate, impart, tell, relate, reveal.

convict v condemn, sentence, imprison.
n criminal, felon, culprit, prisoner.

conviction n assurance, confidence, fervour, earnestness, certainty, firmness, persuasion, view, opinion, belief, faith, creed, tenet, principle.

convince v assure, persuade, sway, win over, bring round, reassure, satisfy.

convincing adj persuasive, cogent, powerful, telling, impressive, credible, plausible, likely, probable, conclusive, incontrovertible.
F3 unconvincing, improbable.

convoluted adj twisting, winding, meandering, tortuous, involved, complicated, complex, tangled.
F3 straight, straightforward.

convoy n fleet, escort, guard, protection, attendance, train.

convulsion n **1** FIT, seizure, paroxysm, spasm, cramp, contraction, tic, tremor. **2** ERUPTION, outburst, furore, disturbance, commotion, tumult, agitation, turbulence, upheaval.

convulsive adj jerky, spasmodic, fitful, sporadic, uncontrolled, violent.

cook

Ways of cooking include:
bake, barbecue, boil, braise, broil, casserole, chargrill, coddle, deep-fry, fry, grill, microwave, poach, pot-roast, roast, sauté, scramble, sear, simmer, spit-roast, steam, stew, stir-fry, toast, heat.

cook up concoct, prepare, brew, invent, fabricate, contrive, devise, plan, plot, scheme.

cool adj **1** CHILLY, fresh, breezy, nippy, cold, chilled, iced, refreshing. **2** CALM, unruffled, unexcited, composed, self-possessed, level-headed, unemotional, quiet, relaxed,

laid-back (*infml*). **3** *a cool reception*: unfriendly, unwelcoming, cold, frigid, lukewarm, half-hearted, unenthusiastic, apathetic, uninterested, unresponsive, uncommunicative, reserved, distant, aloof, standoffish.
F3 1 warm, hot. **2** excited, angry. **3** friendly, welcoming.
v **1** CHILL, refrigerate, ice, freeze, fan. **2** MODERATE, lessen, temper, dampen, quiet, abate, calm, allay, assuage.
F3 1 warm, heat. **2** excite.
n coolness, calmness, collectedness, composure, poise, self-possession, self-discipline, self-control, control, temper.

co-operate *v* collaborate, work together, play ball (*infml*), help, assist, aid, contribute, participate, combine, unite, conspire.

co-operation *n* helpfulness, assistance, participation, collaboration, teamwork, unity, co-ordination, give-and-take.
F3 opposition, rivalry, competition.

co-operative *adj* **1** HELPFUL, supportive, obliging, accommodating, willing. **2** COLLECTIVE, joint, shared, combined, united, concerted, co-ordinated.
F3 1 unco-operative, rebellious.

co-ordinate *v* organize, arrange, systematize, tabulate, integrate, mesh, synchronize, harmonize, match, correlate, regulate.

cope *v* manage, carry on, survive, get by, make do.
cope with deal with, encounter, contend with, struggle with, grapple with, wrestle with, handle, manage, weather.

copious *adj* abundant, plentiful, inexhaustible, overflowing, profuse, rich, lavish, bountiful, liberal, full, ample, generous, extensive, great, huge.
F3 scarce, meagre.

copy *n* duplicate, carbon copy, photocopy, Photostat®, Xerox®, facsimile, reproduction, print, tracing, transcript, transcription, replica, clone, model, pattern, archetype, representation, image, likeness, counterfeit, forgery, fake, imitation, borrowing, plagiarism, crib.
F3 original.
v duplicate, photocopy, reproduce, print, trace, transcribe, forge, counterfeit, simulate, imitate, impersonate, mimic, ape, parrot, repeat, echo, mirror, follow, emulate, borrow, plagiarize, crib.

cord *n* string, twine, rope, line, cable, flex, connection, link, bond, tie.

core *n* kernel, nucleus, heart, centre, middle, nub, crux, essence, gist, nitty-gritty (*infml*).
F3 surface, exterior.

corner *n* **1** *round the corner*: angle, joint, crook, bend, turning. **2** NOOK, cranny, niche, recess, cavity, hole, hideout, hide-away, retreat.

corporation *n* council, authorities, association, society, organization, company, firm, combine, conglomerate.

corpse *n* body, stiff (*sl*), carcase, skeleton, remains.

correct *v* **1** *correct an error*: rectify, put right, right, emend, remedy, cure, debug, redness, adjust, regulate, improve, amend. **2** PUNISH, discipline, reprimand, reprove, reform.

adj **1** *the correct answer*: right,
accurate, precise, exact, strict, true,
truthful, word-perfect, faultless,
flawless. **2** PROPER, acceptable, OK
(*infml*), standard, regular, just,
appropriate, fitting.
F3 **1** incorrect, wrong, inaccurate.

correction *n* rectification,
emendation, adjustment, alteration,
modification, amendment,
improvement.

correspond *v* **1** MATCH, fit, answer,
conform, tally, square, agree, concur,
coincide, correlate, accord,
harmonize, dovetail, complement.
2 COMMUNICATE, write.

correspondence *n* **1**
COMMUNICATION, writing, letters,
post, mail. **2** CONFORMITY,
agreement, concurrence,
coincidence, correlation, relation,
analogy, comparison,
comparability, similarity,
resemblance, congruity, equivalence,
harmony, match.
F3 **2** divergence, incongruity.

correspondent *n* journalist,
reporter, contributor, writer.

corresponding *adj* matching,
complementary, reciprocal,
interrelated, analogous, equivalent,
similar, identical.

corridor *n* aisle, passageway,
passage, hallway, hall, lobby.

corroborate *v* confirm, prove, bear
out, support, endorse, ratify,
substantiate, validate, authenticate,
document, underpin, sustain.
F3 contradict.

corrode *v* erode, wear away, eat
away, consume, waste, rust, oxidize,
tarnish, impair, deteriorate, crumble,
disintegrate.

corrosive *adj* corroding, acid,
caustic, cutting, abrasive, erosive,
wearing, consuming, wasting.

corrugated *adj* ridged, fluted,
grooved, channelled, furrowed,
wrinkled, crinkled, rumpled, creased.

corrupt *adj* rotten, unscrupulous,
unprincipled, unethical, immoral,
fraudulent, shady (*infml*), dishonest,
bent (*infml*), crooked (*infml*),
untrustworthy, depraved, degenerate,
dissolute.
F3 ethical, virtuous, upright, honest,
trustworthy.
v contaminate, pollute, adulterate,
taint, defile, debase, pervert, deprave,
lead astray, lure, bribe, suborn.
F3 purify.

corruption *n* unscrupulousness,
immorality, impurity, depravity,
degeneration, degradation,
perversion, distortion, dishonesty,
crookedness (*infml*), fraud, shadiness
(*infml*), bribery, extortion, vice,
wickedness, iniquity, evil.
F3 honesty, virtue.

cosmetic *adj* superficial, surface.
F3 essential.

cosmetics *n* make-up, grease paint.

Types of cosmetics include:
blusher, cleanser, concealer, exfoli-
ant, eyebrow pencil, eyelash dye,
eyeliner, eyeshadow, face-cream,
face-mask, face pack, face-powder,
facial scrub, false eyelashes, foundation, kohl pencil, lip-gloss, lip
liner, lipstick, mascara, moisturizer,
nail polish, nail varnish, rouge,
toner.

cosmopolitan *adj* worldly, worldly-
wise, well-travelled, sophisticated,
urbane, international, universal.
F3 insular, parochial, rustic.

cosset v coddle, mollycoddle, baby, pamper, indulge, spoil, pet, fondle, cuddle, cherish.

cost n 1 EXPENSE, outlay, payment, disbursement, expenditure, charge, price, rate, amount, figure, worth. 2 DETRIMENT, harm, injury, hurt, loss, deprivation, sacrifice, penalty, price.

costly adj 1 EXPENSIVE, dear, pricey (infml), exorbitant, excessive, lavish, rich, splendid, valuable, precious, priceless. 2 HARMFUL, damaging, disastrous, catastrophic, loss-making.
F∃ 1 cheap, inexpensive.

costume n outfit, uniform, livery, robes, vestments, dress, clothing, get-up (infml), fancy dress.

cosy adj snug, comfortable, comfy (infml), warm, sheltered, secure, homely, intimate.
F∃ uncomfortable, cold.

cottage n lodge, chalet, bungalow, hut, cabin, shack.

couch

Types of couch include:
settee, sofa, chaise-longue, ottoman, studio couch, chesterfield.

council n committee, panel, board, cabinet, ministry, parliament, congress, assembly, convention, conference.

counsel n 1 ADVICE, suggestion, recommendation, direction, information, guidance, deliberation, consideration, forethought. 2 counsel for the defence: lawyer, advocate, solicitor, attorney, barrister.
v advise, warn, caution, suggest, recommend, advocate, urge, exhort, guide, direct, instruct.

count v 1 NUMBER, enumerate, list, include, reckon, calculate, compute, tell, check, add, total, tot up, score. 2 MATTER, signify, qualify. 3 count yourself lucky: consider, regard, deem, judge, think, reckon, hold.
n numbering, enumeration, poll, reckoning, calculation, computation, sum, total, tally.

count on depend on, rely on, bank on, reckon on, expect, believe, trust.

counter adv against, in opposition, conversely.
adj contrary, opposite, opposing, conflicting, contradictory, contrasting, opposed, against, adverse.
v parry, resist, offset, answer, respond, retaliate, retort, return, meet.

counteract v neutralize, counterbalance, offset, countervail, act against, oppose, resist, hinder, check, thwart, frustrate, foil, defeat, undo, negate, annul, invalidate.
F∃ support, assist.

counterfeit v fake, forge, fabricate, copy, imitate, impersonate, pretend, feign, simulate, sham.
adj fake, false, phoney (infml), forged, copied, fraudulent, bogus, pseudo, sham, spurious, imitation, artificial, simulated, feigned, pretended.
F∃ genuine, authentic, real.
n fake, forgery, copy, reproduction, imitation, fraud, sham.

counterpart n equivalent, opposite number, complement, supplement, match, fellow, mate, twin, duplicate, copy.

countless adj innumerable, myriad, numberless, unnumbered, untold, incalculable, infinite, endless, immeasurable, measureless, limitless.
F∃ finite, limited.

country n **1** STATE, nation, people, kingdom, realm, principality. **2** COUNTRYSIDE, green belt, farmland, provinces, sticks (*infml*), boondocks (*US infml*), backwoods, wilds. **3** TERRAIN, land, territory, region, area, district.
F3 2 town, city.
adj rural, provincial, agrarian, agricultural, pastoral, rustic, bucolic, landed.
F3 urban.

countryside n landscape, scenery, country, green belt, farmland, outdoors.

county n shire, province, region, area, district.

couple n pair, brace, twosome, duo.
v pair, match, marry, wed, unite, join, link, connect, fasten, hitch, clasp, buckle, yoke.

coupon n voucher, token, slip, check, ticket, certificate.

courage n bravery, pluck, guts (*infml*), fearlessness, dauntlessness, heroism, gallantry, valour, boldness, audacity, nerve, daring, resolution, fortitude, spirit, mettle.
F3 cowardice, fear.

courageous adj brave, plucky, fearless, dauntless, indomitable, heroic, gallant, valiant, lion-hearted, hardy, bold, audacious, daring, intrepid, resolute.
F3 cowardly, afraid.

course n **1** CURRICULUM, syllabus, classes, lessons, lectures, studies. **2** FLOW, movement, advance, progress, development, furtherance, order, sequence, series, succession, progression. **3** DURATION, time, period, term, passage. **4** DIRECTION, way, path, track, road, route, channel, trail, line, circuit, orbit, trajectory,

flight path. **5** *course of action*: plan, schedule, programme, policy, procedure, method, mode.

court n **1** LAW-COURT, bench, bar, tribunal, trial, session. **2** COURTYARD, yard, quadrangle, square, cloister, forecourt, enclosure. **3** ENTOURAGE, attendants, retinue, suite, train, cortège.

courteous adj polite, civil, respectful, well-mannered, well-bred, ladylike, gentlemanly, gracious, obliging, considerate, attentive, gallant, courtly, urbane, debonair, refined, polished.
F3 discourteous, impolite, rude.

courtesy n politeness, civility, respect, manners, breeding, graciousness, consideration, attention, gallantry, urbanity.
F3 discourtesy, rudeness.

courtier n noble, nobleman, lord, lady, steward, page, attendant, follower, flatterer, sycophant, toady.

courtyard n yard, quadrangle, quad (*infml*), area, enclosure, court.

cove n bay, bight, inlet, estuary, firth, fiord, creek.

cover v **1** HIDE, conceal, obscure, shroud, veil, screen, mask, disguise, camouflage. **2** *covered with mud*: coat, spread, daub, plaster, encase, wrap, envelop, clothe, dress. **3** SHELTER, protect, shield, guard, defend. **4** *cover a topic*: deal with, treat, consider, examine, investigate, encompass, embrace, incorporate, embody, involve, include, contain, comprise.
F3 1 uncover. **2** strip. **3** expose. **4** exclude.
n **1** COATING, covering, top, lid, cup, veil, screen, mask, front, façade, jacket, wrapper, case, envelope, clothing, dress, bedspread, canopy.

2 SHELTER, refuge, protection, shield, guard, defence, concealment, disguise, camouflage.

cover up (*infml*) conceal, hide, whitewash, dissemble, suppress, hush up, keep dark, repress.
⊟ disclose, reveal.

covering *n* layer, coat, coating, blanket, film, veneer, skin, crust, shell, casing, housing, wrapping, clothing, protection, mask, overlay, cover, top, shelter, roof.

cover-up *n* concealment, whitewash, smokescreen, front, façade, pretence, conspiracy, complicity.

covet *v* envy, begrudge, crave, long for, yearn for, hanker for, want, desire, fancy (*infml*), lust after.

coward *n* craven, faint-heart, chicken (*infml*), scaredy-cat, yellow-belly (*sl*), wimp (*infml*), renegade, deserter.
⊟ hero.

cowardice *n* cowardliness, faint-heartedness, timorousness, spinelessness.
⊟ courage, valour.

cowardly *adj* faint-hearted, craven, fearful, timorous, scared, unheroic, chicken-hearted, chicken-livered, chicken (*infml*), yellow-bellied (*sl*), yellow (*sl*), spineless, weak, weak-kneed, soft.
⊟ brave, courageous, bold.

cower *v* crouch, grovel, skulk, shrink, flinch, cringe, quail, tremble, shake, shiver.

coy *adj* modest, demure, prudish, diffident, shy, bashful, timid, shrinking, backward, retiring, self-effacing, reserved, evasive, arch, flirtatious, coquettish, skittish, kittenish.
⊟ bold, forward.

crack *v* SPLIT, burst, fracture, break, snap, shatter, splinter, chip.
2 EXPLODE, burst, pop, crackle, snap, crash, clap, smack, slap, whack (*infml*).
3 *crack a code*: decipher, work out, solve.

n **1** BREAK, fracture, split, rift, gap, crevice, chink, line, flaw, chip.
2 EXPLOSION, burst, pop, snap, crash, clap, blow, smack, slap, whack (*infml*).
3 JOKE, quip, witticism, gag (*infml*), wisecrack, gibe, dig.
adj (*infml*) first-class, first-rate, top-notch (*infml*), excellent, superior, choice, hand-picked.

crack down on clamp down on, end, stop, put a stop to, crush, suppress, check, repress, act against.

crack up go mad, go to pieces, break down, collapse.

cradle *n* **1** COT, crib, bed. **2** SOURCE, origin, spring, wellspring, fount, fountainhead, birthplace, beginning.
v hold, support, rock, lull, nurse, nurture, tend.

craft *n* **1** SKILL, expertise, mastery, talent, knack, ability, aptitude, dexterity, cleverness, art, handicraft, handiwork. **2** TRADE, business, calling, vocation, job, occupation, work, employment. **3** VESSEL, boat, ship, aircraft, spacecraft, spaceship.

craftsman, craftswoman *n* artisan, technician, master, maker, wright, smith.

craftsmanship *n* artistry, workmanship, technique, dexterity, expertise, mastery.

crafty *adj* sly, cunning, artful, wily, devious, subtle, scheming, calculating, designing, deceitful, fraudulent, sharp, shrewd, astute, canny.
⊟ artless, naive.

cram v stuff, jam, ram, force, press, squeeze, crush, compress, pack, crowd, overfill, glut, gorge.

cramp[1] v hinder, hamper, obstruct, impede, inhibit, handicap, thwart, frustrate, check, restrict, confine, shackle, tie.

cramp[2] n pain, ache, twinge, pang, contraction, convulsion, spasm, crick, stitch, pins and needles, stiffness.

cramped adj narrow, tight, uncomfortable, restricted, confined, crowded, packed, squashed, squeezed, overcrowded, jam-packed, congested. **E3** spacious.

crash n **1** car crash: accident, collision, bump, smash, pile-up, smash-up (infml), wreck. **2** BANG, clash, clatter, clang, thud, thump, boom, thunder, racket, din. **3** stock-market crash: collapse, failure, ruin, downfall, bankruptcy, depression. v **1** COLLIDE, hit, knock, bump, bang. **2** BREAK, fracture, smash, dash, shatter, splinter, shiver, fragment, disintegrate. **3** FALL, topple, pitch, plunge, collapse, fail, fold (up), go under, go bust (infml).

crate n container, box, case, tea-chest, packing-box, packing-case.

crave v hunger for, thirst for, long for, yearn for, pine for, hanker after, fancy (infml), desire, want, need, require. **E3** dislike.

craving n appetite, hunger, thirst, longing, yearning, hankering, lust, desire, urge. **E3** dislike, distaste.

crawl v **1** CREEP, inch, edge, slither, wriggle. **2** GROVEL, cringe, toady, fawn, flatter, suck up (sl).

craze n fad, novelty, fashion, vogue, mode, trend, rage (infml), thing

(infml), obsession, preoccupation, mania, frenzy, passion, infatuation, enthusiasm.

crazy adj **1** MAD, insane, lunatic, unbalanced, deranged, demented, crazed, potty (infml), barmy (infml), daft (infml), silly, foolish, idiotic, senseless, unwise, imprudent, nonsensical, absurd, ludicrous, ridiculous, preposterous, outrageous, half-baked, impracticable, irresponsible, wild, berserk. **2** (infml) crazy about golf: enthusiastic, fanatical, zealous, ardent, passionate, infatuated, enamoured, smitten, mad, wild. **E3 1** sane, sensible. **2** indifferent.

creak v squeak, groan, grate, scrape, rasp, scratch, grind, squeal, screech.

cream n **1** PASTE, emulsion, oil, lotion, ointment, salve, cosmetic. **2** BEST, pick, élite, prime.

creamy adj **1** CREAM-COLOURED, off-white, yellowish-white. **2** MILKY, buttery, oily, smooth, velvety, rich, thick.

crease v fold, pleat, wrinkle, pucker, crumple, rumple, crinkle, crimp, corrugate, ridge. n fold, line, pleat, tuck, wrinkle, pucker, ruck, crinkle, corrugation, ridge, groove.

create v invent, coin, formulate, compose, design, devise, concoct, hatch, originate, initiate, found, establish, set up, institute, cause, occasion, produce, generate, engender, make, form, appoint, install, invest, ordain. **E3** destroy.

creation n **1** MAKING, formation, constitution, invention, concoction, origination, foundation, establishment, institution, production, generation, procreation, conception, birth. **2** INVENTION, brainchild, concept, product, handiwork, chef d'oeuvre, achievement.

F3 1 destruction.

creative adj artistic, inventive, original, imaginative, inspired, visionary, talented, gifted, clever, ingenious, resourceful, fertile, productive.

F3 unimaginative.

creator n maker, inventor, designer, architect, author, originator, initiator.

creature n animal, beast, bird, fish, organism, being, mortal, individual, person, man, woman, body, soul.

credentials n diploma, certificate, reference, testimonial, recommendation, accreditation, authorization, warrant, licence, permit, passport, identity card, papers, documents, deed, title.

credibility n integrity, reliability, trustworthiness, plausibility, probability.

F3 implausibility.

credible adj believable, imaginable, conceivable, thinkable, tenable, plausible, likely, probable, possible, reasonable, persuasive, convincing, sincere, honest, trustworthy, reliable, dependable.

F3 incredible, unbelievable, implausible, unreliable.

credit n acknowledgement, recognition, thanks, approval, commendation, praise, acclaim, tribute, glory, fame, prestige, distinction, honour, reputation, esteem, estimation.

F3 discredit, shame.

v believe, swallow (infml), subscribe to, trust, rely on. accept,

F3 disbelieve.

creditable adj honourable, reputable, respectable, estimable, admirable, commendable, praiseworthy, good, excellent, exemplary, worthy, deserving.

F3 shameful, blameworthy.

credulous adj naive, gullible, wide-eyed, trusting, unsuspecting, uncritical.

F3 sceptical, suspicious.

creed n belief, faith, persuasion, credo, catechism, doctrine, principles, tenets, articles, canon, dogma.

creek n inlet, estuary, cove, bay, bight.

creep v inch, edge, tiptoe, steal, sneak, slink, crawl, slither, worm, wriggle, squirm, grovel, writhe.

creepy adj eerie, spooky, sinister, threatening, frightening, scary, terrifying, hair-raising, nightmarish, macabre, gruesome, horrible, unpleasant, disturbing.

crest n **1** the crest of the hill: crown, top, peak, summit, pinnacle, apex, head. **2** TUFT, tassel, plume, comb, mane. **3** INSIGNIA, device, symbol, emblem, badge.

crevice n crack, fissure, split, rift, cleft, slit, chink, cranny, gap, hole, opening, break.

crew n team, party, squad, troop, corps, company, gang, band, bunch, crowd, mob, set, lot.

crime n law-breaking, lawlessness, delinquency, offence, felony, misdemeanour, misdeed, wrongdoing, misconduct, transgression, violation, sin, iniquity, vice, villainy, wickedness, atrocity, outrage.

Crimes include:
theft, robbery, burglary, larceny, pilfering, mugging, poaching; assault, rape, grievous bodily harm, GBH (*infml*), battery, manslaughter, homicide, murder, assassination; fraud, bribery, corruption, embezzlement, extortion, blackmail; arson, treason, terrorism, hijack, piracy, kidnapping, sabotage, vandalism, hooliganism, drug-smuggling, forgery, counterfeiting, perjury, joy-riding, drink-driving.

criminal *n* law-breaker, crook, felon, delinquent, offender, wrongdoer, miscreant, culprit, perpetrator, convict, prisoner.
adj illegal, unlawful, illicit, lawless, wrong, culpable, indictable, crooked (*infml*), bent (*infml*), dishonest, corrupt, wicked, scandalous, deplorable.
E3 legal, lawful, honest, upright.
cringe *v* shrink, recoil, shy, start, flinch, wince, quail, tremble, quiver, cower, crouch, bend, bow, stoop, grovel, crawl, creep.
cripple *v* lame, paralyse, disable, handicap, injure, maim, mutilate, damage, impair, spoil, ruin, destroy, sabotage, incapacitate, weaken, debilitate.
crippled *adj* lame, paralysed, disabled, handicapped, incapacitated.
crisis *n* emergency, extremity, crunch (*infml*), catastrophe, disaster, calamity, dilemma, quandary, predicament, difficulty, trouble, problem.
crisp *adj* **1** *a crisp biscuit*: crispy, crunchy, brittle, crumbly, firm, hard.

2 BRACING, invigorating, refreshing, fresh, brisk. **3** TERSE, pithy, snappy, brief, short, clear, incisive.
E3 1 soggy, limp, flabby. **2** muggy. **3** wordy, vague.
criterion *n* standard, norm, touchstone, benchmark, yardstick, measure, gauge, rule, principle, canon, test.
critic *n* reviewer, commentator, analyst, pundit, authority, expert, judge, censor, carper, fault-finder, attacker, knocker (*infml*).
critical *adj* **1** *at the critical moment*: crucial, vital, essential, all-important, momentous, decisive, urgent, pressing, serious, grave, dangerous, perilous. **2** ANALYTICAL, diagnostic, penetrating, probing, discerning, perceptive. **3** UNCOMPLIMENTARY, derogatory, disparaging, disapproving, censorious, carping, fault-finding, cavilling, nit-picking (*infml*).
E3 1 unimportant. **3** complimentary, appreciative.
criticism *n* **1** CONDEMNATION, disapproval, disparagement, fault-finding, censure, blame, brickbat, flak (*infml*). **2** REVIEW, critique, assessment, evaluation, appraisal, judgement, analysis, commentary, appreciation.
E3 1 praise, commendation.
criticize *v* **1** CONDEMN, slate (*infml*), slam (*infml*), knock (*infml*), disparage, carp, find fault, censure, blame.
2 REVIEW, assess, evaluate, appraise, judge, analyse.
E3 1 praise, commend.
crockery *n* dishes, tableware, china, porcelain, earthenware, stoneware, pottery.

Items of crockery include:
cup, saucer, coffee cup, mug,
beaker, plate, side plate, dinner
plate, bowl, cereal bowl, soup bowl,
salad bowl, sugar bowl, jug, milk-
jug, basin, pot, teapot, coffee pot,
meat dish, butter-dish, tureen, gravy
boat, cruet, tea set, dinner service.

crook n criminal, thief, robber,
swindler, cheat, shark (infml), rogue,
villain.

crooked adj 1 ASKEW, skew-whiff
(infml), awry, lopsided, asymmetric,
irregular, uneven, off-centre, tilted,
slanting, bent, angled, hooked,
curved, bowed, warped, distorted,
misshapen, deformed, twisted,
tortuous, winding, zigzag. 2 (infml)
ILLEGAL, unlawful, illicit, criminal,
nefarious, dishonest, deceitful, bent
(infml), corrupt, fraudulent, shady
(infml), shifty, underhand,
treacherous, unscrupulous,
unprincipled, unethical.
F3 1 straight. 2 honest.

crop n growth, yield, produce, fruits,
harvest, vintage, gathering.
v cut, snip, clip, shear, trim, pare,
prune, lop, shorten, curtail.

crop up arise, emerge, appear, arrive,
occur, happen.

cross adj 1 IRRITABLE, annoyed,
angry, vexed, shirty (infml), bad-
tempered, ill-tempered, crotchety,
grumpy, grouchy, irascible, crabby,
short, snappy, snappish, surly, sullen,
fractious, fretful, impatient.
2 TRANSVERSE, crosswise, oblique,
diagonal, intersecting, opposite,
reciprocal.
F3 1 placid, pleasant.
v 1 cross the river: go across, traverse,
ford, bridge, span. 2 INTERSECT, meet,

criss-cross, lace, intertwine.
3 CROSSBREED, interbreed,
mongrelize, hybridize, cross-fertilize,
cross-pollinate, blend, mix.
4 THWART, frustrate, foil, hinder,
impede, obstruct, block, oppose.
n 1 BURDEN, load, affliction,
misfortune, trouble, worry, trial,
tribulation, grief, misery, woe.
2 CROSSBREED, hybrid, mongrel,
blend, mixture, amalgam,
combination.

crouch v squat, kneel, stoop, bend,
bow, hunch, duck, cower, cringe.

crowd n 1 THRONG, multitude, host,
mob, masses, populace, people,
public, riff-raff, rabble, horde, swarm,
flock, herd, pack, press, crush,
squash, assembly, company, group,
bunch, lot, set, circle, clique.
2 SPECTATORS, gate, attendance,
audience.
v gather, congregate, muster, huddle,
mass, throng, swarm, flock, surge,
stream, push, shove, elbow, jostle,
press, squeeze, bundle, pile, pack,
congest, cram, compress.

crowded adj full, filled, packed,
jammed, jam-packed, congested,
cramped, overcrowded,
overpopulated, busy, teeming,
swarming, overflowing.
F3 empty.

crown n 1 CORONET, diadem, tiara,
circlet, wreath, garland. 2 PRIZE,
trophy, reward, honour, laurels.
3 SOVEREIGN, monarch, king, queen,
ruler, sovereignty, monarchy, royalty.
4 TOP, tip, apex, crest, summit,
pinnacle, peak, acme.
v 1 ENTHRONE, anoint, adorn, festoon,
honour, dignify, reward. 2 TOP, cap,
complete, fulfil, consummate, perfect.

crucial *adj* urgent, pressing, vital, essential, key, pivotal, central, important, momentous, decisive, critical, trying, testing, searching.
F3 unimportant, trivial.

crude *adj* **1** RAW, unprocessed, unrefined, rough, unfinished, unpolished, natural, primitive. **2** VULGAR, coarse, rude, indecent, obscene, gross, dirty, lewd.
F3 1 refined, finished. **2** polite, decent.

cruel *adj* fierce, ferocious, vicious, savage, barbarous, bloodthirsty, murderous, cold-blooded, sadistic, brutal, inhuman, inhumane, unkind, malevolent, spiteful, callous, heartless, unfeeling, merciless, pitiless, flinty, hard-hearted, stony-hearted, implacable, ruthless, remorseless, relentless, unrelenting, inexorable, grim, hellish, atrocious, bitter, harsh, severe, cutting, painful, excruciating.
F3 kind, compassionate, merciful.

cruelty *n* ferocity, viciousness, savagery, barbarity, bloodthirstiness, murderousness, violence, sadism, brutality, bestiality, inhumanity, spite, venom, callousness, heartlessness, hard-heartedness, mercilessness, ruthlessness, tyranny, harshness, severity.
F3 kindness, compassion, mercy.

crumble *v* fragment, break up, decompose, disintegrate, decay, degenerate, deteriorate, collapse, crush, pound, grind, powder, pulverize.

crumple *v* crush, wrinkle, pucker, crinkle, rumple, crease, fold, collapse.

crunch *v* munch, chomp, champ, masticate, grind, crush.

crusade *n* campaign, drive, push, movement, cause, undertaking, expedition, holy war, jihad.

crush *v* **1** SQUASH, compress, squeeze, press, pulp, break, smash, pound, pulverize, grind, crumble, crumple, wrinkle. **2** *the rebels were crushed*: conquer, vanquish, demolish, devastate, overpower, overwhelm, overcome, quash, quell, subdue, put down, humiliate, shame, abash.

crust *n* surface, exterior, outside, covering, coat, coating, layer, film, skin, rind, shell, scab, incrustation, caking, concretion.

crux *n* nub, heart, core, essence.

cry *v* **1** WEEP, sob, blubber, wail, bawl, whimper, snivel. **2** SHOUT, call, exclaim, roar, bellow, yell, scream, shriek, screech.
n **1** WEEP, sob, blubber, wail, bawl, whimper, snivel. **2** SHOUT, call, plea, exclamation, roar, bellow, yell, scream, shriek.

cryptic *adj* enigmatic, ambiguous, equivocal, puzzling, perplexing, mysterious, strange, bizarre, secret, hidden, veiled, obscure, abstruse, esoteric, dark, occult.
F3 straightforward, clear, obvious.

cuddle *v* hug, embrace, clasp, hold, nurse, nestle, snuggle, pet, fondle, caress.

cuddly *adj* cuddlesome, lovable, huggable, plump, soft, warm, cosy.

cue *n* signal, sign, nod, hint, suggestion, reminder, prompt, incentive, stimulus.

cuff *v* hit, thump, box, clip, knock, biff (*infml*), buffet, slap, smack, strike, clout, clobber (*sl*), belt (*infml*), beat, whack (*infml*).

culminate v climax, end (up), terminate, close, conclude, finish, consummate.
F3 start, begin.

culmination n climax, height, peak, pinnacle, summit, top, crown, perfection, consummation, finale, conclusion, completion.
F3 start, beginning.

culprit n guilty party, offender, perpetrator, wrongdoer, miscreant, law-breaker, criminal, felon, delinquent.

cult n **1** SECT, denomination, school, movement, party, faction. **2** CRAZE, fad, fashion, vogue, trend.

cultivate v **1** FARM, till, work, plough, grow, sow, plant, tend, harvest. **2** FOSTER, nurture, cherish, help, aid, support, encourage, promote, further, work on, develop, train, prepare, polish, refine, improve, enrich.
F3 2 neglect.

cultural adj artistic, aesthetic, liberal, civilizing, humanizing, enlightening, educational, edifying, improving, enriching, elevating.

culture n **1** CIVILIZATION, society, lifestyle, way of life, customs, mores, the arts. **2** CULTIVATION, taste, education, enlightenment, breeding, gentility, refinement, politeness, urbanity.

cultured adj cultivated, civilized, advanced, enlightened, educated, well-read, well-informed, scholarly, highbrow, well-bred, refined, polished, genteel, urbane.
F3 uncultured, uneducated, ignorant.

cumbersome adj awkward, inconvenient, bulky, unwieldy, unmanageable, burdensome, clunky (infml), onerous, heavy, weighty.
F3 convenient, manageable.

cunning adj crafty, sly, artful, wily, tricky, devious, subtle, deceitful, guileful, sharp, shrewd, astute, canny, knowing, deep, imaginative, ingenious, skilful, deft, dexterous.
F3 naive, ingenuous, gullible.
n craftiness, slyness, artfulness, trickery, deviousness, subtlety, deceitfulness, guile, sharpness, shrewdness, astuteness, ingenuity, cleverness, adroitness.

cup n mug, tankard, beaker, goblet, chalice, trophy.

cupboard n cabinet, locker, closet, wardrobe.

Types of cupboard, cabinet and chest include:

china cabinet, Welsh dresser, sideboard, buffet, chest of drawers, tallboy, chiffonier, commode, ottoman, chest, coffer, blanket box.

---

curb v restrain, constrain, restrict, contain, control, check, moderate, bridle, muzzle, suppress, subdue, repress, inhibit, hinder, impede, hamper, retard.
F3 encourage, foster.

curdle v coagulate, congeal, clot, thicken, turn, sour, ferment.

cure v **1** HEAL, remedy, correct, restore, repair, mend, relieve, ease, alleviate, help. **2** PRESERVE, dry, smoke, salt, pickle, kipper.
n remedy, antidote, panacea, medicine, specific, corrective, restorative, healing, treatment, therapy, alleviation, recovery.

curiosity n **1** INQUISITIVENESS, nosiness, prying, snooping, interest. **2** CURIO, objet d'art, antique, bygone, novelty, trinket, knick-knack. **3** ODDITY, rarity, freak, phenomenon, spectacle.

curious adj **1** INQUISITIVE, nosey, prying, meddlesome, questioning, inquiring, interested. **2** a curious sight: odd, queer, funny (infml), strange, peculiar, bizarre, mysterious, puzzling, extraordinary, unusual, rare, unique, novel, exotic, unconventional, unorthodox, quaint.

F3 1 uninterested, indifferent.
2 ordinary, usual, normal.

curl v crimp, frizz, wave, ripple, bend, curve, meander, loop, turn, twist, wind, wreathe, twine, coil, spiral, corkscrew, scroll.

F3 uncurl.

n wave, kink, swirl, twist, ringlet, coil, spiral, whorl.

curly adj wavy, kinky, curling, spiralled, corkscrew, curled, crimped, permed, frizzy, fuzzy.

F3 straight.

currency n **1** MONEY, legal tender, coinage, coins, notes, bills.
2 ACCEPTANCE, publicity, popularity, vogue, circulation, prevalence, exposure.

Currencies of the world include:
baht (Thailand), bolivar (Venezuela), dinar (Iraq, Jordan, etc), dirham (Morocco, UAE), dollar (US, Canada, Australia, NZ, etc), dong (Vietnam), euro (most EU countries), forint (Hungary), franc (Switzerland, Liechtenstein, etc), hryvnia (Ukraine), koruna (Czech Republic, Slovakia), krona (Sweden), króna (Iceland), krone (Denmark, Norway), kuna (Croatia), kyat (Myanmar), lari (Georgia), lek (Albania), leu (Romania, Moldova), lev (Bulgaria), lira (Turkey, Malta), naira (Nigeria), peso (Mexico, Cuba, Argentina, Chile, etc), pound (UK, Egypt, etc), rand

(S Africa), real (Brazil), rial (Iran, Oman), ringgit (Malaysia), riyal (Saudi Arabia, Yemen, Qatar), rouble (Russia, Belarus), rupee (India, Pakistan, etc), rupiah (Indonesia), shekel (Israel), shilling (Kenya, Uganda, etc), som (Uzbekistan, Kyrgyzstan), tolar (Slovenia), won (N Korea, S Korea), yen (Japan), yuan (China), zloty (Poland).

current adj present, on-going, existing, contemporary, present-day, modern, fashionable, up-to-date, up-to-the-minute, trendy (infml), popular, widespread, prevalent, common, general, prevailing, reigning, accepted.

F3 obsolete, old-fashioned.

n draught, stream, jet, flow, drift, tide, course, trend, tendency, undercurrent, mood, feeling.

curse n **1** SWEAR-WORD, oath, expletive, obscenity, profanity, blasphemy. **2** JINX, anathema, bane, evil, plague, scourge, affliction, trouble, torment, ordeal, calamity, disaster.

F3 2 blessing, advantage.

v **1** SWEAR, blaspheme, damn, condemn, denounce, fulminate.
2 BLIGHT, plague, scourge, afflict, trouble, torment.

F3 2 bless.

curtail v shorten, truncate, cut, trim, abridge, abbreviate, lessen, decrease, reduce, restrict.

F3 lengthen, extend, prolong.

curtain n blind, screen, backdrop, hanging, drapery, tapestry.

curve v bend, arch, arc, bow, bulge, hook, crook, turn, wind, twist, spiral, coil.

n bend, turn, arc, trajectory, loop, camber, curvature.

curved *adj* bent, arched, bowed, rounded, humped, convex, concave, crooked, twisted, sweeping, sinuous, serpentine.
F3 straight.

cushion *n* pad, buffer, shock absorber, bolster, pillow, headrest, hassock.
v soften, deaden, dampen, absorb, muffle, stifle, suppress, lessen, mitigate, protect, bolster, buttress, support.

custody *n* **1** KEEPING, possession, charge, care, safe-keeping, protection, preservation, custodianship, trusteeship, guardianship, supervision. **2** DETENTION, confinement, imprisonment, incarceration.

custom *n* tradition, usage, use, habit, routine, procedure, practice, policy, way, manner, style, form, convention, etiquette, formality, observance, ritual.

customary *adj* traditional, conventional, accepted, established, habitual, routine, regular, usual, normal, ordinary, everyday, familiar, common, general, popular, fashionable, prevailing.
F3 unusual, rare.

customer *n* client, patron, regular, punter (*infml*), consumer, shopper, buyer, purchaser, prospect.

cut *v* **1** CLIP, trim, crop, shear, mow, shave, pare, chop, hack, hew, slice, carve, divide, part, split, bisect, dock, lop, sever, prune, excise, incise, penetrate, pierce, stab, wound, nick, gash, slit, slash, lacerate, score, engrave, chisel, sculpt. **2** REDUCE, decrease, lower, shorten, curtail, abbreviate, abridge, condense, précis, edit, delete. **3** IGNORE, cold-shoulder, spurn, avoid, snub, slight, rebuff, insult.
n **1** INCISION, wound, nick, gash, slit, slash, rip, laceration. **2** *spending cuts*: reduction, decrease, lowering, cutback, saving, economy.

cut down 1 *cut down a tree*: fell, hew, lop, level, raze. **2** REDUCE, decrease, lower, lessen, diminish.

cut in interrupt, butt in, interject, interpose, intervene, intrude.

cut off 1 SEVER, amputate, separate, isolate, disconnect, block, obstruct, intercept. **2** STOP, end, halt, suspend, discontinue, disown, disinherit.

cut out excise, extract, remove, delete, eliminate, exclude, debar, stop, cease.

cut up chop, dice, mince, dissect, divide, carve, slice, slash.

Types of cutting tools and implements include:
axe, billhook, blade, chisel, chopper, clippers, guillotine, hedge trimmer, knife, flick-knife, penknife, pocket knife, Stanley knife®, Swiss army knife, lopper, machete, mower, lawnmower, plane, razor, saw, chainsaw, fretsaw, hack-saw, jigsaw, scalpel, scissors, scythe, secateurs, shears, pinking-shears, sickle, Strimmer®, sword.

---

cutback *n* cut, saving, economy, retrenchment, reduction, downsizing, decrease, lowering, lessening.

cutlery

Items of cutlery include:
knife, butter-knife, carving-knife, fish-knife, steak knife, cheese knife, bread knife, fork, carving-fork, corn holders, spoon, dessertspoon, tablespoon, teaspoon, soupspoon, caddy spoon, apostle spoon, ladle, salad servers, fish-slice, cake server, sugar tongs, chopsticks, canteen of cutlery.

cut-price *adj* reduced, sale, discount, bargain, cheap, low-priced.

cutting *adj* sharp, keen, pointed, trenchant, incisive, penetrating, piercing, wounding, stinging, biting, mordant, caustic, acid, scathing, sarcastic, malicious, bitter, raw, chill.
n clipping, extract, piece.

cycle *n* circle, round, rotation, revolution, series, sequence, phase, period, era, age, epoch, aeon.

cylinder *n* column, barrel, drum, reel, bobbin, spool, spindle.

cynic *n* sceptic, doubter, pessimist, killjoy, spoilsport (*infml*), scoffer, knocker (*infml*).

cynical *adj* sceptical, doubtful, distrustful, pessimistic, negative, scornful, derisive, contemptuous, sneering, scoffing, mocking, sarcastic, sardonic, ironic.

cynicism *n* scepticism, doubt, disbelief, distrust, pessimism, scorn, sarcasm, irony.

D

dab v pat, tap, daub, swab, wipe.
n **1** BIT, dollop (*infml*), drop, speck,
spot, trace, smear, smudge, fleck.
2 TOUCH, pat, stroke, tap.

dabble v **1** TRIFLE, tinker, toy, dally,
potter. **2** PADDLE, moisten, wet,
sprinkle, splash.

dabbler n amateur, dilettante, trifler.
F3 professional, expert.

daft adj **1** FOOLISH, crazy, silly, stupid,
absurd, dotty (*infml*), idiotic, inane.
2 INSANE, mad, lunatic, simple, crazy,
mental. **3** (*infml*) INFATUATED.
F3 1 sensible. **2** sane.

daily adj **1** REGULAR, routine, everyday,
customary, common, commonplace,
ordinary. **2** EVERYDAY, diurnal (*fml*).

dainty adj **1** DELICATE, elegant,
exquisite, refined, fine, graceful, neat,
charming, delectable. **2** FASTIDIOUS,
fussy, particular, scrupulous, nice (*fml*).
F3 1 gross, clumsy.

dam n barrier, barrage, embankment,
blockage, obstruction, hindrance.
v block, confine, restrict, check,
barricade, staunch, stem, obstruct.

damage n harm, injury, hurt,
destruction, devastation, loss,
suffering, mischief, mutilation,
impairment, detriment.
F3 repair.
v harm, injure, hurt, spoil, ruin,
impair, mar, wreck, deface, mutilate,

weaken, tamper with, play havoc with,
incapacitate.
F3 mend, repair, fix.

damn v **1** CURSE, swear, blast,
imprecate, blaspheme. **2** ABUSE,
revile, denounce, criticize, censure,
slate (*infml*), denunciate, execrate,
castigate, slam (*infml*). **3** CONDEMN,
doom, sentence.
F3 1 bless.

damnation n condemnation, doom,
denunciation, perdition,
excommunication, anathema.

damp n dampness, moisture,
clamminess, dankness, humidity, wet,
dew, drizzle, fog, mist, vapour.
F3 dryness.
adj moist, wet, clammy, dank, humid,
dewy, muggy, drizzly, misty, soggy.

dampen v **1** MOISTEN, wet, spray.
2 DISCOURAGE, dishearten, deter,
dash, dull, deaden, restrain, check,
depress, dismay, reduce, lessen,
moderate, decrease, diminish, muffle,
stifle, smother.
F3 1 dry. **2** encourage.

dance n ball, hop (*infml*), knees-up
(*infml*), social, shindig (*infml*).

Dances include:
waltz, quickstep, foxtrot, tango,
polka, one-step, military two-step,
veleta, lancers, rumba, merengue,

samba, salsa, macarena, mambo, bossa nova, beguine, fandango, flamenco, mazurka, bolero, paso doble, cancan; rock 'n' roll, jive, twist, stomp, bop, jitterbug; black bottom, Charleston, cha-cha, turkey-trot; Paul Jones, jig, reel, quadrille, Highland fling, morris dance, clogdance, hoedown, hokey cokey, Lambeth Walk, conga, belly-dance; galliard, gavotte, minuet.

Types of dancing include:
ballet, tap, ballroom, old-time, disco, folk, country, Irish, Highland, Latin-American, flamenco, clog dancing, stepdancing, line-dancing, morris dancing, limbo-dancing, breakdancing, robotics.

Dance functions include:
disco, dance, social, tea dance, barn dance, ball, fancy dress ball, charity ball, hunt ball, hop (infml), knees-up (sl), shindig (infml), rave (infml), prom (US), ceilidh.

danger n **1** in danger of falling: insecurity, endangerment, jeopardy, precariousness, liability, vulnerability. **2** the dangers of smoking: risk, threat, peril, hazard, menace.
E3 1 safety, security. **2** safety.

dangerous adj unsafe, insecure, risky, threatening, breakneck, hairy (infml), hazardous, perilous, precarious, reckless, treacherous, vulnerable, menacing, exposed, alarming, critical, severe, serious, grave, daring, nasty.
E3 safe, secure, harmless.

dangle v **1** HANG, droop, swing, sway, flap, trail. **2** TEMPT, entice, flaunt, flourish, lure, tantalize.

dank adj damp, moist, clammy, dewy, slimy, soggy.
E3 dry.

dappled adj speckled, mottled, spotted, stippled, dotted, flecked, freckled, variegated, bespeckled, piebald, checkered.

dare v **1** RISK, venture, brave, hazard, adventure, endanger, stake, gamble. **2** CHALLENGE, goad, provoke, taunt. **3** DEFY, presume.
n challenge, provocation, taunt, gauntlet.

daredevil n adventurer, desperado, madcap.
E3 coward.

daring adj bold, adventurous, intrepid, fearless, brave, plucky, audacious, dauntless, reckless, rash, impulsive, valiant.
E3 cautious, timid, afraid.
n boldness, fearlessness, courage, bravery, nerve, audacity, guts (infml), intrepidity, defiance, pluck, rashness, spirit, grit, gall, prowess.
E3 caution, timidity, cowardice.

dark adj **1** a dark room: unlit, overcast, black, dim, unilluminated, shadowy, murky, cloudy, dusky, dingy. **2** a dark manner: gloomy, grim, cheerless, dismal, bleak, forbidding, sombre, sinister, mournful, ominous, menacing, drab. **3** dark secrets: hidden, mysterious, obscure, secret, unintelligible, enigmatic, cryptic, abstruse.
E3 1 light. **2** bright, cheerful. **3** comprehensible.
n **1** DARKNESS, dimness, night, night-time, nightfall, gloom, dusk, twilight, murkiness. **2** CONCEALMENT, secrecy, obscurity.
E3 1 light. **2** openness.

darken v 1 DIM, obscure, blacken, cloud (over), shadow, overshadow, eclipse. 2 DEPRESS, sadden.
F3 1 lighten. 2 brighten.

darling n beloved, dear, dearest, favourite, sweetheart, love, pet, angel, treasure.
adj dear, beloved, adored, cherished, precious, treasured.

dart v 1 DASH, bound, sprint, flit, flash, fly, rush, run, race, spring, tear. 2 THROW, hurl, fling, shoot, sling, launch, propel, send.
n bolt, arrow, barb, shaft.

dash v 1 RUSH, dart, hurry, race, sprint, run, bolt, tear. 2 FLING, throw, crash, hurl. 3 DISCOURAGE, disappoint, dampen, confound, blight, ruin, destroy, spoil, frustrate, smash, shatter.
n 1 DROP, pinch, touch, flavour, soupçon, suggestion, hint, bit, little. 2 SPRINT, dart, bolt, rush, spurt, race, run.

dashing adj 1 LIVELY, vigorous, spirited, gallant, daring, bold, plucky, exuberant. 2 SMART, stylish, elegant, debonair, showy, flamboyant.
F3 1 lethargic. 2 dowdy.

data n information, documents, facts, input, statistics, figures, details, materials.

date n 1 TIME, age, period, era, stage, epoch. 2 APPOINTMENT, engagement, assignation, meeting, rendezvous. 3 ESCORT, steady (infml), partner, friend.

out-of-date adj old-fashioned, unfashionable, outdated, obsolete, dated, outmoded, antiquated, passé.
F3 fashionable, modern.

up-to-date adj fashionable, modern, current, contemporary.
F3 old-fashioned, dated.

daunt v 1 DISCOURAGE, dishearten, put off, dispirit, deter. 2 INTIMIDATE, overawe, unnerve, alarm, dismay, frighten, scare.
F3 encourage.

dauntless adj fearless, undaunted, resolute, brave, courageous, bold, intrepid, daring, plucky, valiant.
F3 discouraged, disheartened.

dawdle v delay, loiter, lag, hang about, dally, trail, potter, dilly-dally (infml).
F3 hurry.

dawn n 1 SUNRISE, daybreak, morning, daylight. 2 BEGINNING, start, emergence, onset, origin, birth, advent.
F3 1 dusk. 2 end.
v 1 BREAK, brighten, lighten, gleam, glimmer. 2 BEGIN, appear, emerge, open, develop, originate, rise.

day n 1 DAYTIME, daylight. 2 AGE, period, time, date, era, generation, epoch.
F3 night.

day after day regularly, continually, endlessly, persistently, monotonously, perpetually, relentlessly.

day by day gradually, progressively, slowly but surely, steadily.

daydream n fantasy, imagining, reverie, castles in the air, pipe dream, vision, musing, wish, dream, figment.
v fantasize, imagine, muse, fancy, dream.

daze v 1 STUN, stupefy, shock. 2 DAZZLE, bewilder, blind, confuse, baffle, dumbfound, amaze, surprise, startle, perplex, astonish, flabbergast (infml), astound, stagger.
n bewilderment, confusion, stupor, trance, shock, distraction.

dazzle *v* **1** DAZE, blind, confuse, blur. **2** SPARKLE, fascinate, impress, overwhelm, awe, overawe, scintillate, bedazzle, amaze, astonish, bewitch, stupefy.
n sparkle, brilliance, magnificence, splendour, scintillation, glitter, glare.

dead *adj* **1** LIFELESS, deceased, inanimate, defunct, departed, late, gone. **2** UNRESPONSIVE, apathetic, dull, indifferent, insensitive, numb, cold, frigid, lukewarm, torpid. **3** EXHAUSTED, tired, worn out, dead-beat (*infml*). **4** EXACT, absolute, perfect, unqualified, utter, outright, complete, entire, total, downright.
F3 1 alive. **2** lively. **3** refreshed.

deaden *v* reduce, blunt, muffle, lessen, quieten, suppress, weaken, numb, diminish, stifle, alleviate, anaesthetize, desensitize, smother, check, abate, allay, dampen, hush, mute, paralyse.
F3 heighten.

deadlock *n* standstill, stalemate, impasse, halt.

deadly *adj* **1** *deadly poison*: lethal, fatal, dangerous, venomous, destructive, pernicious, malignant, murderous, mortal. **2** *a deadly lecture*: dull, boring, uninteresting, tedious, monotonous. **3** *deadly aim*: unerring, effective, true.
F3 1 harmless. **2** exciting.

deaf *adj* **1** HARD OF HEARING, stone-deaf. **2** UNCONCERNED, indifferent, unmoved, oblivious, heedless, unmindful.
F3 2 aware, conscious.

deafening *adj* piercing, ear-splitting, booming, resounding, thunderous, ringing, roaring.
F3 quiet.

deal *v* **1** APPORTION, distribute, share, dole out, divide, allot, dispense, assign, mete out, give, bestow. **2** TRADE, negotiate, traffic, bargain, treat.
n **1** QUANTITY, amount, extent, degree, portion, share. **2** AGREEMENT, contract, understanding, pact, transaction, bargain, buy. **3** ROUND, hand, distribution.
deal with attend to, concern, see to, manage, handle, cope with, treat, consider, oversee.

dealer *n* trader, merchant, wholesaler, marketer, merchandizer.

dear *adj* **1** LOVED, beloved, treasured, valued, cherished, precious, favourite, esteemed, intimate, close, darling, familiar. **2** EXPENSIVE, high-priced, costly, overpriced, pric(e)y (*infml*).
F3 1 disliked, hated. **2** cheap.
n beloved, loved one, precious, darling, treasure.

dearly *adv* **1** *he loves her dearly*: fondly, affectionately, lovingly, devotedly, tenderly. **2** *I wish it dearly*: greatly, extremely, profoundly.

dearth *n* scarcity, shortage, insufficiency, inadequacy, deficiency, lack, want, absence, scantiness, sparsity, need, paucity, poverty, famine.
F3 excess, abundance.

death *n* **1** DECEASE, end, finish, loss, demise, departure, fatality, cessation, passing, expiration, dissolution. **2** DESTRUCTION, ruin, undoing, annihilation, downfall, extermination, extinction, obliteration, eradication.
F3 1 life, birth.

deathly *adj* **1** ASHEN, grim, haggard, pale, pallid, ghastly, wan. **2** FATAL, deadly, mortal, intense.

debase v 1 DEGRADE, demean, devalue, disgrace, dishonour, shame, humble, humiliate, lower, reduce, abase, defile. 2 CONTAMINATE, pollute, corrupt, adulterate, taint.
F3 1 elevate. 2 purify.

debatable adj questionable, uncertain, disputable, contestable, controversial, arguable, open to question, doubtful, contentious, undecided, unsettled, problematical, dubious, moot.
F3 unquestionable, certain, incontrovertible.

debate v 1 DISPUTE, argue, discuss, contend, wrangle. 2 CONSIDER, deliberate, ponder, reflect, meditate on, mull over, weigh.
n discussion, argument, controversy, disputation, deliberation, consideration, contention, dispute, reflection, polemic.

debauchery n depravity, intemperance, overindulgence, dissipation, licentiousness, dissoluteness, excess, decadence, wantonness, lewdness, carousal, orgy, revel, lust, riot.
F3 restraint, temperance.

debilitate v weaken, enervate, undermine, sap, incapacitate, wear out, exhaust, impair.
F3 strengthen, invigorate, energize.

debris n remains, ruins, rubbish, waste, wreck, wreckage, litter, fragments, rubble, trash, pieces, bits, sweepings, drift.

debt n indebtedness, obligation, debit, arrears, due, liability, duty, bill, commitment, claim, score.
F3 credit, asset.

debtor n borrower, bankrupt, insolvent, defaulter, mortgagor.
F3 creditor.

debunk v expose, deflate, show up, ridicule, mock, explode, lampoon.

debut n introduction, launching, beginning, entrance, presentation, inauguration, première, appearance, initiation.

decadent adj 1 CORRUPT, debased, debauched, depraved, dissolute, immoral, degenerate, degraded, self-indulgent. 2 DECAYING, declining.
F3 1 moral.

decay v 1 ROT, go bad, putrefy, decompose, spoil, perish, mortify. 2 DECLINE, deteriorate, disintegrate, corrode, crumble, waste away, degenerate, dwindle, shrivel, wither, sink.
F3 2 flourish, grow.
n 1 ROT, decomposition, rotting, perishing. 2 DECLINE, deterioration, disintegration, degeneration, collapse, decadence, wasting, failing, withering, fading.

decease n death, dying, demise, departure, passing, dissolution.

deceased adj dead, departed, former, late, lost, defunct, expired, gone, finished, extinct.
n dead, departed.

deceit n deception, pretence, cheating, misrepresentation, fraud, duplicity, trickery, fraudulence, double-dealing, underhandedness, fake, guile, sham, subterfuge, swindle, treachery, hypocrisy, artifice, ruse, cunning, slyness, craftiness, stratagem, wile, imposition, feint, shift, abuse.
F3 honesty, openness, frankness.

deceitful adj dishonest, deceptive, deceiving, false, insincere, untrustworthy, double-dealing, fraudulent, two-faced (infml),

deceive v mislead, delude, cheat, betray, fool, take in (infml), trick, dissemble, hoax, con (infml), have on (infml), take for a ride (infml), double-cross (infml), dupe, kid (infml), swindle, impose upon, bamboozle (infml), two-time (infml), lead on, outwit, hoodwink, beguile, ensnare, camouflage, abuse, befool, gull.

decency n propriety, courtesy, modesty, decorum, respectability, civility, correctness, fitness, etiquette, helpfulness.

F3 impropriety, discourtesy.

decent adj **1** RESPECTABLE, proper, fitting, decorous, chaste, seemly, suitable, modest, appropriate, presentable, pure, fit, becoming, befitting, nice. **2** KIND, obliging, courteous, helpful, generous, polite, gracious. **3** ADEQUATE, acceptable, satisfactory, reasonable, sufficient, tolerable, competent.

F3 1 indecent. **2** disobliging.

deception n deceit, pretence, trick, cheat, fraud, imposture, lie, dissembling, deceptiveness, insincerity, con (infml), sham, subterfuge, artifice, hypocrisy, bluff, treachery, hoax, fraudulence, duplicity, ruse, snare, stratagem, leg-pull (infml), illusion, wile, guile, craftiness, cunning.

F3 openness, honesty.

deceptive adj dishonest, false, fraudulent, misleading, unreliable, illusive, fake, illusory, spurious, mock, fallacious, ambiguous, specious.

F3 genuine, artless, open.

decide v choose, determine, resolve, reach a decision, settle, elect, opt, judge, adjudicate, conclude, fix, purpose, decree.

decided adj **1** DEFINITE, certain, undeniable, indisputable, absolute, clear-cut, undisputed, unmistakable, unquestionable, positive, unambiguous, categorical, distinct, emphatic. **2** RESOLUTE, decisive, determined, firm, unhesitating, deliberate, forthright.

F3 1 inconclusive. **2** irresolute.

decipher v decode, unscramble, crack, construe, interpret, make out (infml), figure out (infml), understand, transliterate.

F3 encode.

decision n **1** RESULT, conclusion, outcome, verdict, finding, settlement, judgement, arbitration, ruling. **2** DETERMINATION, decisiveness, firmness, resolve, purpose.

decisive adj **1** CONCLUSIVE, definite, definitive, absolute, final. **2** DETERMINED, resolute, decided, positive, firm, forceful, forthright, strong-minded. **3** SIGNIFICANT, critical, crucial, influential, momentous, fateful.

F3 1 inconclusive. **2** indecisive. **3** insignificant.

declaration n **1** AFFIRMATION, acknowledgement, assertion, statement, testimony, attestation, disclosure, profession, revelation. **2** ANNOUNCEMENT, notification, pronouncement, proclamation, edict, manifesto, promulgation.

declare v 1 AFFIRM, assert, claim, profess, maintain, state, attest, certify, confess, confirm, disclose, reveal, show, aver, swear, testify, witness, validate. 2 ANNOUNCE, proclaim, pronounce, decree, broadcast.

decline v 1 REFUSE, reject, deny, forgo, avoid, balk. 2 DIMINISH, decrease, dwindle, lessen, fall, sink, wane. 3 DECAY, deteriorate, worsen, degenerate. 4 DESCEND, sink, slope, dip, slant.
F3 3 improve. 4 rise.
n 1 DETERIORATION, dwindling, lessening, decay, degeneration, weakening, worsening, failing, downturn, diminution, falling-off, recession, diminution, abatement. 2 DESCENT, dip, declivity, declination, hill, slope, incline, divergence, deviation.
F3 1 improvement. 2 rise.

decode v decipher, interpret, unscramble, translate, transliterate, uncipher.
F3 encode.

decompose v disintegrate, rot, decay, putrefy, break down, break up, crumble, spoil, dissolve, separate, fester.

décor n decoration, furnishings, colour scheme, ornamentation, scenery.

decorate v 1 ORNAMENT, adorn, beautify, embellish, trim, deck, tart up (sl), grace, enrich, prettify, trick out. 2 RENOVATE, do up (infml), paint, paper, colour, refurbish. 3 HONOUR, crown, cite, garland, bemedal.

decoration n 1 ORNAMENT, adornment, ornamentation, trimming, embellishment, beautification, garnish, flourish,

enrichment, elaboration, frill, scroll, bauble. 2 AWARD, medal, order, badge, garland, crown, colours, ribbon, laurel, star, emblem.

decorative adj ornamental, fancy, adorning, beautifying, embellishing, non-functional, pretty, ornate, enhancing.
F3 plain.

decorum n propriety, seemliness, etiquette, good manners, respectability, protocol, behaviour, decency, dignity, deportment, restraint, politeness, modesty, grace, breeding.
F3 impropriety, indecorum, bad manners.

decoy n lure, trap, enticement, inducement, ensnarement, pretence, attraction, bait.
v bait, lure, entrap, entice, ensnare, allure, tempt, deceive, attract, seduce, lead, draw.

decrease v lessen, lower, diminish, dwindle, decline, fall off, reduce, subside, abate, cut down, contract, drop, ease, shrink, taper, wane, slim, slacken, peter out, curtail.
F3 increase.
n lessening, reduction, decline, falling-off, dwindling, loss, diminution, abatement, cutback, contraction, downturn, ebb, shrinkage, subsidence, step-down.
F3 increase.

decree n order, command, law, ordinance, regulation, ruling, statute, act, enactment, edict, proclamation, mandate, precept, interlocution.
v order, command, rule, lay down, dictate, decide, determine, ordain, prescribe, proclaim, pronounce, enact.

decrepit adj dilapidated, run-down, rickety, broken-down, worn-out, tumble-down.

dedicate v 1 DEVOTE, commit, assign, give over to, pledge, present, offer, sacrifice, surrender. 2 CONSECRATE, bless, sanctify, set apart, hallow. 3 dedicate a book: inscribe, address.

dedicated adj devoted, committed, enthusiastic, single-minded, whole-hearted, single-hearted, zealous, given over to, purposeful.
F3 uncommitted, apathetic.

dedication n 1 COMMITMENT, devotion, single-mindedness, whole-heartedness, allegiance, attachment, adherence, faithfulness, loyalty, self-sacrifice. 2 CONSECRATION, hallowing, presentation. 3 INSCRIPTION, address.
F3 1 apathy.

deduce v derive, infer, gather, conclude, reason, surmise, understand, draw, glean.

deduct v subtract, take away, remove, reduce by, decrease by, knock off (infml), withdraw.
F3 add.

deduction n 1 INFERENCE, reasoning, finding, conclusion, corollary, assumption, result. 2 SUBTRACTION, reduction, decrease, diminution, abatement, withdrawal, discount, allowance.
F3 2 addition, increase.

deed n 1 ACTION, act, achievement, performance, exploit, feat, fact, truth, reality. 2 DOCUMENT, contract, record, title, transaction, indenture (fml).

deep adj 1 PROFOUND, bottomless, unplumbed, fathomless, yawning, immersed. 2 OBSCURE, mysterious,

difficult, recondite, abstruse, esoteric. 3 WISE, perceptive, discerning, profound, learned, astute. 4 INTENSE, serious, earnest, extreme. 5 LOW, bass, resonant, booming.
F3 1 shallow, open. 2 clear, plain, open. 3 superficial. 4 light. 5 high.

deepen v 1 INTENSIFY, grow, increase, strengthen, reinforce, magnify. 2 HOLLOW, scoop out.

deep-seated adj ingrained, entrenched, deep-rooted, fixed, confirmed, deep, settled.
F3 eradicable, temporary.

deface v damage, spoil, disfigure, blemish, impair, mutilate, mar, sully, tarnish, vandalize, deform, obliterate, injure, destroy.
F3 repair.

defamation n vilification, aspersion (fml), slander, libel, disparagement, slur, smear, innuendo, scandal.
F3 commendation, praise.

defamatory adj vilifying, slanderous, libellous, denigrating, disparaging, pejorative, insulting, injurious, derogatory.
F3 complimentary, appreciative.

default n failure, absence, neglect, non-payment, omission, deficiency, lapse, fault, want, lack, defect.
v fail, evade, defraud, neglect, dodge, swindle, backslide.

defaulter n non-payer, offender.

defeat v 1 CONQUER, beat, overpower, subdue, overthrow, worst, repel, subjugate, overwhelm, rout, ruin, thump (infml), quell, vanquish (fml). 2 FRUSTRATE, confound, balk, get the better of, disappoint, foil, thwart, baffle, checkmate.
n 1 CONQUEST, beating, overthrow, rout, subjugation, vanquishment

defeatist

off152

deficiency

(fml). **2** FRUSTRATION, failure, setback, reverse, disappointment, checkmate.

defeatist n pessimist, quitter, prophet of doom.
F3 optimist.
adj pessimistic, resigned, fatalistic, despondent, helpless, hopeless, despairing, gloomy.
F3 optimistic.

defect n imperfection, fault, flaw, deficiency, failing, mistake, inadequacy, blemish, error, bug (infml), shortcoming, want, weakness, frailty, lack, spot, absence, taint.
v desert, break faith, rebel, apostatize (fml), revolt, renege.

defective adj faulty, imperfect, out of order, flawed, deficient, broken, abnormal.
F3 in order, operative.

defence n **1** PROTECTION, resistance, security, fortification, cover, safeguard, shelter, guard, shield, deterrence, barricade, bastion, immunity, bulwark, rampart, buttress. **2** JUSTIFICATION, explanation, excuse, argument, exoneration, plea, vindication, apologia (fml), pleading, alibi, case.
F3 1 attack, assault. **2** accusation.

defenceless adj unprotected, undefended, unarmed, unguarded, vulnerable, exposed, helpless, powerless.
F3 protected, guarded.

defend v **1** PROTECT, guard, safeguard, shelter, fortify, secure, shield, screen, cover, contest. **2** SUPPORT, stand up for, stand by, uphold, endorse, vindicate, champion, argue for, speak up for, justify, plead.
F3 1 attack. **2** accuse.

defendant n accused, offender, prisoner, respondent.

defender n **1** PROTECTOR, guard, bodyguard. **2** SUPPORTER, advocate, vindicator, champion, patron, sponsor, counsel.
F3 1 attacker. **2** accuser.

defensive adj **1** PROTECTIVE, defending, safeguarding, wary, opposing, cautious, watchful. **2** SELF-JUSTIFYING, apologetic.

defer¹ v delay, postpone, put off, adjourn, hold over, shelve, suspend, procrastinate, prorogue (fml), protract, waive.

defer² v yield, give way, comply, submit, accede, capitulate, respect, bow.

deference n **1** SUBMISSION, submissiveness, compliance, acquiescence, obedience, yielding. **2** RESPECT, regard, honour, esteem, reverence, courtesy, civility, politeness, consideration.
F3 1 resistance. **2** contempt.

defiance n opposition, confrontation, resistance, challenge, disobedience, rebelliousness, contempt, insubordination, disregard, insolence.
F3 compliance, acquiescence, submissiveness.

defiant adj challenging, resistant, antagonistic, aggressive, rebellious, insubordinate, disobedient, intransigent, bold, contumacious (fml), insolent, obstinate, unco-operative, provocative.
F3 compliant, acquiescent, submissive.

deficiency n **1** SHORTAGE, lack, inadequacy, scarcity, insufficiency, dearth, want, scantiness, absence,

deficit. **2** IMPERFECTION, shortcoming, weakness, fault, defect, flaw, failing, frailty.
F3 1 excess, surfeit. **2** perfection.

deficient adj **1** INADEQUATE, insufficient, scarce, short, lacking, wanting, meagre, scanty, skimpy, incomplete. **2** IMPERFECT, impaired, flawed, faulty, defective, unsatisfactory, inferior, weak.
F3 1 excessive. **2** perfect.

deficit n shortage, shortfall, deficiency, loss, arrears, lack, default.
F3 excess.

defile v pollute, violate, contaminate, degrade, dishonour, desecrate, debase, soil, stain, sully, tarnish, taint, profane, corrupt, disgrace.

define v **1** define the boundaries: bound, limit, delimit, demarcate, mark out. **2** define the meaning: explain, characterize, describe, interpret, expound, determine, designate, specify, spell out, detail.

definite adj **1** CERTAIN, settled, sure, positive, fixed, decided, determined, assured, guaranteed. **2** CLEAR, clear-cut, exact, precise, specific, explicit, particular, obvious, marked.
F3 1 indefinite. **2** vague.

definitely adv positively, surely, unquestionably, absolutely, certainly, categorically, undeniably, clearly, doubtless, unmistakably, plainly, obviously, indeed, easily.

definition n **1** DELINEATION, demarcation, delimitation. **2** EXPLANATION, description, interpretation, exposition, clarification, elucidation, determination. **3** DISTINCTNESS, clarity, precision, clearness, focus, contrast, sharpness.

definitive adj decisive, conclusive, final, authoritative, standard, correct, ultimate, reliable, exhaustive, perfect, exact, absolute, complete.
F3 interim.

deflate v **1** FLATTEN, puncture, collapse, exhaust, squash, empty, contract, void, shrink, squeeze. **2** DEBUNK, humiliate, put down (infml), dash, dispirit, humble, mortify, disconcert. **3** DECREASE, devalue, reduce, lessen, lower, diminish, depreciate, depress.
F3 1 inflate. **2** boost. **3** increase.

deflect v deviate, diverge, turn (aside), swerve, veer, sidetrack, twist, avert, wind, glance off, bend, ricochet.

deform v distort, contort, disfigure, warp, mar, pervert, ruin, spoil, twist.

deformed adj distorted, misshapen, contorted, disfigured, crippled, crooked, bent, twisted, warped, buckled, defaced, mangled, maimed, marred, ruined, mutilated, perverted, corrupted.

deformity n distortion, misshapenness, malformation, disfigurement, abnormality, irregularity, misproportion, defect, ugliness, monstrosity, corruption.

defraud v cheat, swindle, dupe, fleece, sting (infml), rip off (infml), do (infml), diddle (infml), rob, trick, con (infml), rook, deceive, delude, embezzle, beguile.

deft adj adept, handy, dexterous, nimble, skilful, adroit, agile, expert, nifty, proficient, able, neat, clever.
F3 clumsy, awkward.

defunct adj **1** DEAD, deceased, departed, gone, expired, extinct. **2** OBSOLETE, invalid, inoperative, expired.
F3 1 alive, live. **2** operative.

defy v 1 *defy the authorities*:
challenge, confront, resist, dare,
brave, face, repel, spurn, beard, flout,
withstand, disregard, scorn, despise,
defeat, provoke, thwart. **2** *her writings
defy categorization*: elude, frustrate,
baffle, foil.
** F3 1** obey. **2** permit.

degenerate *adj* dissolute,
debauched, depraved, degraded,
debased, base, low, decadent, corrupt,
fallen, immoral, mean, degenerated,
perverted, deteriorated.
F3 moral, upright.
v decline, deteriorate, sink, decay, rot,
slip, worsen, regress, fall off, lapse.
F3 improve.

degradation *n* **1** DETERIORATION,
degeneration, decline, downgrading,
demotion. **2** ABASEMENT, humiliation,
mortification, dishonour, disgrace,
shame, ignominy, decadence.
F3 1 virtue. **2** enhancement.

degrade v **1** DISHONOUR, disgrace,
debase, abase, shame, humiliate,
humble, discredit, demean, lower,
weaken, impair, deteriorate, cheapen,
adulterate, corrupt. **2** DEMOTE,
depose, downgrade, deprive, cashier.
F3 1 exalt. **2** promote.

degree *n* **1** GRADE, class, rank, order,
position, standing, status. **2** EXTENT,
measure, range, stage, step, level,
intensity, standard. **3** LEVEL, limit,
unit, mark.

deify v exalt, elevate, worship, glorify,
idolize, extol, venerate, immortalize,
ennoble, glorify.

deign v condescend, stoop, lower
oneself, consent, demean oneself.

deity *n* god, goddess, divinity,
godhead, idol, demigod,
demigoddess, power, immortal.

dejected *adj* downcast, despondent,
depressed, downhearted,
disheartened, down, low, melancholy,
disconsolate, sad, miserable, cast
down, gloomy, glum, crestfallen,
dismal, wretched, doleful, morose,
spiritless.
F3 cheerful, high-spirited, happy.

delay v **1** OBSTRUCT, hinder, impede,
hold up, check, hold back, set back,
stop, halt, detain. **2** DEFER, put off,
postpone, procrastinate, suspend,
shelve, hold over, stall. **3** DAWDLE,
linger, lag, loiter, dilly-dally (*infml*),
tarry.
F3 1 accelerate. **2** bring forward.
3 hurry.
n **1** OBSTRUCTION, hindrance,
impediment, hold-up, check, setback,
stay, stoppage. **2** DEFERMENT,
postponement, procrastination,
suspension. **3** DAWDLING, lingering,
tarrying. **4** INTERRUPTION, lull,
interval, wait.
F3 1 hastening. **3** hurry.
4 continuation.

delegate *n* representative, agent,
envoy, messenger, deputy,
ambassador, commissioner.
v authorize, appoint, depute,
charge, commission, assign,
empower, entrust, devolve, consign,
designate, nominate, name, hand
over.

delegation *n* **1** DEPUTATION,
commission, legation, mission,
contingent, embassy.
2 AUTHORIZATION, commissioning,
assignment.

delete v erase, remove, cross out,
cancel, rub out, strike (out), obliterate,
edit (out), blot out, efface.
F3 add, insert.

deliberate v consider, ponder, reflect, think, cogitate, meditate, mull over, debate, discuss, weigh, consult. adj 1 INTENTIONAL, planned, calculated, prearranged, premeditated, willed, conscious, designed, considered, advised. 2 CAREFUL, unhurried, thoughtful, methodical, cautious, circumspect, studied, prudent, slow, ponderous, measured, heedful.
E3 1 unintentional, accidental. 2 hasty.

deliberation n 1 CONSIDERATION, reflection, thought, calculation, forethought, meditation, rumination, study, debate, discussion, consultation, speculation. 2 CARE, carefulness, caution, circumspection, prudence.

delicacy n 1 DAINTINESS, fineness, elegance, exquisiteness, lightness, precision. 2 REFINEMENT, sensitivity, subtlety, finesse, discrimination, tact, niceness. 3 TITBIT, dainty, taste, sweetmeat, savoury, relish.
E3 1 coarseness, roughness. 2 tactlessness.

delicate adj 1 FINE, fragile, dainty, exquisite, flimsy, elegant, graceful. 2 FRAIL, weak, ailing, faint. 3 SENSITIVE, scrupulous, discriminating, careful, accurate, precise. 4 SUBTLE, muted, pastel, soft.
E3 1 coarse, clumsy. 2 healthy.

delicious adj 1 ENJOYABLE, pleasant, agreeable, delightful. 2 APPETIZING, palatable, tasty, delectable, scrumptious (infml), yummy (infml), mouth-watering, succulent, savoury.
E3 1 unpleasant. 2 unpalatable, yucky (infml).

delight n bliss, happiness, joy, pleasure, ecstasy, enjoyment, gladness, rapture, transport, gratification, jubilation.
E3 disgust, displeasure.
v please, charm, gratify, enchant, tickle, thrill, ravish.
E3 displease, dismay.
delight in enjoy, relish, like, love, appreciate, revel in, take pride in, glory in, savour.
E3 dislike, hate.

delighted adj charmed, elated, happy, pleased, enchanted, captivated, ecstatic, thrilled, overjoyed, jubilant, joyous.
E3 disappointed, dismayed.

delightful adj charming, enchanting, captivating, enjoyable, pleasant, thrilling, agreeable, pleasurable, engaging, attractive, pleasing, gratifying, entertaining, fascinating.
E3 nasty, unpleasant.

delinquency n crime, offence, wrong-doing, misbehaviour, misconduct, law-breaking, misdemeanour, criminality.

delinquent n offender, criminal, wrong-doer, law-breaker, hooligan, culprit, miscreant (fml).

delirious adj demented, raving, incoherent, beside oneself, deranged, frenzied, light-headed, wild, mad, frantic, insane, crazy, ecstatic.
E3 sane.

deliver v 1 deliver a parcel: convey, bring, send, give, carry, supply. 2 SURRENDER, hand over, relinquish, yield, transfer, grant, entrust, commit. 3 UTTER, speak, proclaim, pronounce. 4 ADMINISTER, inflict, direct. 5 SET FREE, liberate, release, emancipate.

delivery n 1 CONVEYANCE, consignment, dispatch, transmission, transfer, surrender. 2 ARTICULATION, enunciation, speech, utterance, intonation, elocution. 3 CHILDBIRTH, labour, confinement.

delude v deceive, mislead, beguile, dupe, take in, trick, hoodwink, hoax, cheat, misinform.

deluge n flood, inundation, downpour, torrent, spate, rush. v flood, inundate, drench, drown, overwhelm, soak, swamp, engulf, submerge.

delusion n illusion, hallucination, fancy, misconception, misapprehension, deception, misbelief, fallacy.

demand v ASK, request, call for, insist on, solicit, claim, exact, inquire, question, interrogate. 2 NECESSITATE, need, require, involve.
n 1 REQUEST, question, claim, order, inquiry, desire, interrogation. 2 NEED, necessity, call.

demanding adj hard, difficult, challenging, exacting, taxing, tough, exhausting, wearing, back-breaking, insistent, pressing, urgent, trying.
Fꜟ easy, undemanding, easy-going.

demean v lower, humble, degrade, humiliate, debase, abase, descend, stoop, condescend.
Fꜟ exalt, enhance.

demeanour n bearing, manner, deportment, conduct, behaviour, air.

demented adj mad, insane, lunatic, out of one's mind, crazy, loony (sl), deranged, unbalanced, frenzied.
Fꜟ sane.

demise n 1 DEATH, decease, end, passing, departure, termination, expiration. 2 DOWNFALL, fall,

collapse, failure, ruin. 3 TRANSFER, conveyance, inheritance, transmission, alienation.

democracy n self-government, commonwealth, autonomy, republic.

democratic adj self-governing, representative, egalitarian, autonomous, popular, populist, republican.

demolish v 1 DESTROY, dismantle, knock down, pull down, flatten, bulldoze, raze, tear down, level. 2 RUIN, defeat, destroy, annihilate, wreck, overturn, overthrow.
Fꜟ 1 build up.

demolition n destruction, dismantling, levelling, razing.

demon n 1 DEVIL, fiend, evil spirit, fallen angel, imp. 2 VILLAIN, devil, rogue, monster.

demonstrable adj verifiable, provable, arguable, attestable, self-evident, obvious, evident, certain, clear, positive.
Fꜟ unverifiable.

demonstrate v 1 SHOW, display, prove, establish, exhibit, substantiate, manifest, testify to, indicate. 2 EXPLAIN, illustrate, describe, teach. 3 PROTEST, march, parade, rally, picket, sit in.

demonstration n 1 DISPLAY, exhibition, manifestation, proof, confirmation, affirmation, substantiation, validation, evidence, testimony, expression. 2 EXPLANATION, illustration, description, exposition, presentation, test, trial. 3 PROTEST, march, demo (infml), rally, picket, sit-in, parade.

demonstrative adj affectionate, expressive, expansive, emotional, open, loving.
Fꜟ reserved, cold, restrained.

demoralize v 1 DISCOURAGE, dishearten, dispirit, undermine, depress, deject, crush, lower, disconcert. 2 CORRUPT, deprave, debase.

E3 1 encourage. 2 improve.

demote v downgrade, degrade, relegate, reduce, cashier.

E3 promote, upgrade.

demur v disagree, dissent, object, take exception, refuse, protest, dispute, balk, scruple, doubt, hesitate.

demure adj modest, reserved, reticent, prim, coy, shy, retiring, prissy, grave, prudish, sober, strait-laced, staid.

E3 wanton, forward.

den n lair, hide-out, hole, retreat, study, hide-away, shelter, sanctuary, haunt.

denial n 1 CONTRADICTION, negation, dissent, repudiation, disavowal, disclaimer, dismissal, renunciation. 2 REFUSAL, rebuff, rejection, prohibition, veto.

denigrate v disparage, run down, slander, revile, defame, malign, vilify, decry, besmirch, impugn, belittle, abuse, assail, criticize.

E3 praise, acclaim.

denomination n 1 CLASSIFICATION, category, class, kind, sort. 2 RELIGION, persuasion, sect, belief, faith, creed, communion, school.

denote v indicate, stand for, signify, represent, symbolize, mean, express, designate, typify, mark, show, imply.

dénouement n climax, culmination, conclusion, outcome, upshot, pay-off (infml), finale, resolution, finish, solution, close.

denounce v condemn, censure, accuse, revile, decry, attack, inform against, betray, impugn, vilify, fulminate.

E3 acclaim, praise.

dense adj 1 COMPACT, thick, compressed, condensed, close, close-knit, heavy, solid, opaque, impenetrable, packed, crowded. 2 STUPID, thick (infml), crass, dull, slow, slow-witted.

E3 1 thin, sparse. 2 quick-witted, clever.

dent n hollow, depression, dip, concavity, indentation, crater, dimple, dint, pit.

v depress, gouge, push in, indent.

denude v strip, divest, expose, uncover, bare, deforest.

E3 cover, clothe.

denunciation n condemnation, denouncement, censure, accusation, incrimination, invective, criticism.

E3 praise.

deny v 1 deny God's existence: contradict, oppose, refute, disagree with, disaffirm, disprove. 2 deny one's parentage: disown, disclaim, renounce, repudiate, recant. 3 deny their human rights: refuse, turn down, forbid, reject, withhold, rebuff, veto.

E3 1 admit. 3 allow.

depart v 1 GO, leave, withdraw, exit, make off, quit, decamp, take one's leave, absent oneself, set off, remove, retreat, migrate, escape, disappear, retire, vanish. 2 DEVIATE, digress, differ, diverge, swerve, veer.

E3 1 arrive, return. 2 keep to.

departed adj dead, deceased, gone, late, expired.

department n 1 DIVISION, branch, subdivision, section, sector, office,

station, unit, region, district.
2 SPHERE, realm, province, domain, field, area, concern, responsibility, speciality, line.

departure n 1 EXIT, going, leave-taking, removal, withdrawal, retirement, exodus. 2 DEVIATION, digression, divergence, variation, innovation, branching (out), difference, change, shift, veering.
F3 1 arrival, return.

dependable adj reliable, trustworthy, steady, trusty, responsible, faithful, unfailing, sure, honest, conscientious, certain.
F3 unreliable, fickle.

dependence n 1 RELIANCE, confidence, faith, trust, need, expectation. 2 SUBORDINATION, attachment, subservience, helplessness, addiction.
F3 2 independence.

dependent adj 1 RELIANT, helpless, weak, immature, subject, subordinate, vulnerable. 2 CONTINGENT, conditional, determined by, relative.
F3 1 independent.

depend on 1 RELY UPON, count on, bank on (infml), calculate on, reckon on (infml), build upon, trust in, lean on, expect. 2 HINGE ON, rest on, revolve around, be contingent upon, hang on.

depict v portray, illustrate, delineate, sketch, outline, draw, picture, paint, trace, describe, characterize, detail.

deplete v empty, drain, exhaust, evacuate, use up, expend, run down, reduce, lessen, decrease.

deplorable adj 1 GRIEVOUS, lamentable, pitiable, regrettable, unfortunate, wretched, distressing, sad, miserable, heartbreaking, melancholy, disastrous, dire, appalling. 2 REPREHENSIBLE, disgraceful, scandalous, shameful, dishonourable, disreputable.
F3 1 excellent. 2 commendable.

deplore v 1 GRIEVE FOR, lament, mourn, regret, bemoan, rue.
2 CENSURE, condemn, denounce, deprecate.
F3 2 extol.

deploy v dispose, arrange, position, station, use, utilize, distribute.

deport v expel, banish, exile, extradite, transport, expatriate, oust, ostracize.

depose v demote, dethrone, downgrade, dismiss, unseat, topple, disestablish, displace, oust.

deposit v 1 LAY, drop, place, put, settle, dump (infml), park, precipitate, sit, locate. 2 SAVE, store, hoard, bank, amass, consign, entrust, lodge, file.
n 1 SEDIMENT, accumulation, dregs, precipitate, lees, silt. 2 SECURITY, stake, down payment, pledge, retainer, instalment, part payment, money.

depot n 1 military depot: storehouse, store, warehouse, depository, repository, arsenal. 2 bus depot: station, garage, terminus.

deprave v corrupt, debauch, debase, degrade, pervert, subvert, infect, demoralize, seduce.
F3 improve, reform.

depraved adj corrupt, debauched, degenerate, perverted, debased, dissolute, immoral, base, shameless, licentious, wicked, sinful, vile, evil.
F3 moral, upright.

depreciate v 1 DEVALUE, deflate, downgrade, decrease, reduce, lower, drop, fall, lessen, decline, slump.

2 DISPARAGE, belittle, undervalue, underestimate, underrate, slight.
🔁 **1** appreciate. **2** overrate.

depreciation *n* **1** DEVALUATION, deflation, depression, slump, fall.
2 DISPARAGEMENT, belittlement, understimation.

depress *v* **1** DEJECT, sadden, dishearten, discourage, oppress, upset, daunt, burden, overburden.
2 WEAKEN, undermine, sap, tire, drain, exhaust, weary, impair, reduce, lessen, press, lower, level. **3** DEVALUE, bring down, lower.
🔁 **1** cheer. **2** fortify. **3** increase, raise.

depressed *adj* **1** DEJECTED, low-spirited, melancholy, dispirited, sad, unhappy, low, down, downcast, disheartened, fed up (*infml*), miserable, moody, cast down, discouraged, glum, downhearted, distressed, despondent, morose, crestfallen, pessimistic. **2** POOR, disadvantaged, deprived, destitute. **3** SUNKEN, recessed, concave, hollow, indented, dented.
🔁 **1** cheerful. **2** affluent. **3** convex, protuberant.

depressing *adj* dejecting, dismal, bleak, gloomy, saddening, cheerless, dreary, disheartening, sad, melancholy, sombre, grey, black, daunting, discouraging, heartbreaking, distressing, hopeless.
🔁 cheerful, encouraging.

depression *n* **1** DEJECTION, despair, despondency, melancholy, low spirits, sadness, gloominess, doldrums, blues (*infml*), glumness, dumps (*infml*), hopelessness. **2** RECESSION, slump, stagnation, hard times, decline, inactivity. **3** INDENTATION, hollow, dip, concavity, dent, dimple, valley, pit,

sink, dint, bowl, cavity, basin, impression, dish, excavation.
🔁 **1** cheerfulness. **2** prosperity, boom. **3** convexity, protuberance.

deprive *v* **1** DISPOSSESS, strip, divest, denude, bereave, expropriate, rob.
2 DENY, withhold, refuse.
🔁 **1** endow. **2** provide.

deprived *adj* poor, needy, underprivileged, disadvantaged, impoverished, destitute, lacking, bereft.
🔁 prosperous.

depth *n* **1** DEEPNESS, profoundness, extent, measure, drop. **2** MIDDLE, midst, abyss, deep, gulf. **3** WISDOM, insight, discernment, penetration.
4 INTENSITY, strength.
🔁 **1** shallowness. **2** surface.

deputation *n* commission, delegation, embassy, mission, representatives, legation.

deputize *v* **1** REPRESENT, stand in for, substitute, replace, understudy, double. **2** DELEGATE, commission.

deputy *n* representative, agent, delegate, proxy, substitute, second-in-command, ambassador, commissioner, lieutenant, surrogate, subordinate, assistant, locum.

deranged *adj* disordered, demented, crazy, mad, lunatic, insane, unbalanced, disturbed, confused, frantic, delirious, distraught, berserk.
🔁 sane, calm.

derelict *adj* abandoned, neglected, deserted, forsaken, desolate, discarded, dilapidated, ruined.

deride *v* ridicule, mock, scoff, scorn, jeer, sneer, satirize, knock (*infml*), gibe, disparage, insult, belittle, disdain, taunt.
🔁 respect, praise.

derision n ridicule, mockery, scorn, contempt, scoffing, satire, sneering, disrespect, insult, disparagement, disdain.

F3 respect, praise.

derisive adj mocking, scornful, contemptuous, disrespectful, irreverent, jeering, disdainful, taunting.

F3 respectful, flattering.

derivation n source, origin, root, beginning, etymology, extraction, foundation, genealogy, ancestry, basis, descent, deduction, inference.

derivative adj unoriginal, acquired, copied, borrowed, derived, imitative, obtained, second-hand, secondary, plagiarized, cribbed (infml), hackneyed, trite.
n derivation, offshoot, by-product, development, branch, outgrowth, spin-off, product, descendant.

derive v **1** GAIN, obtain, get, draw, extract, receive, procure, acquire, borrow. **2** ORIGINATE, arise, spring, flow, emanate, descend, proceed, stem, issue, follow, develop. **3** INFER, deduce, trace, gather, glean.

derogatory adj insulting, pejorative, offensive, disparaging, depreciative, critical, defamatory, injurious.

F3 flattering.

descend v **1** DROP, go down, fall, plummet, plunge, tumble, swoop, sink, arrive, alight, dismount, dip, slope, subside. **2** DEGENERATE, deteriorate. **3** CONDESCEND, deign, stoop. **4** ORIGINATE, proceed, spring, stem.

F3 1 ascend, rise.

descendants n offspring, children, issue, progeny, successors, lineage, line, seed (fml).

descent n **1** FALL, drop, plunge, dip, decline, incline, slope. **2** COMEDOWN, debasement, degradation. **3** ANCESTRY, parentage, heredity, family tree, genealogy, lineage, extraction, origin.

F3 1 ascent, rise.

describe v portray, depict, delineate, illustrate, characterize, specify, draw, define, detail, explain, express, tell, narrate, outline, relate, recount, present, report, sketch, mark out, trace.

description n **1** PORTRAYAL, representation, characterization, account, delineation, depiction, sketch, presentation, report, outline, explanation, exposition, narration. **2** SORT, type, kind, variety, specification, order.

descriptive adj illustrative, explanatory, expressive, detailed, graphic, colourful, pictorial, vivid.

desert [1] n wasteland, wilderness, wilds, void.
adj bare, barren, waste, wild, uninhabited, uncultivated, dry, arid, infertile, desolate, sterile, solitary.

desert [2] v abandon, forsake, leave, maroon, strand, decamp, defect, give up, renounce, relinquish, jilt, abscond, quit.

F3 stand by, support.

desert [3] n **1** DUE, right, reward, deserts, return, retribution, come-uppance (infml), payment, recompense, remuneration. **2** WORTH, merit, virtue.

deserted adj abandoned, forsaken, empty, derelict, desolate, godforsaken, neglected, underpopulated, stranded, isolated, bereft, vacant, betrayed,

lonely, solitary, unoccupied.
F3 populous.
deserter n runaway, absconder,
escapee, truant, renegade, defector,
rat (infml), traitor, fugitive, betrayer,
apostate, backslider, delinquent.
deserve v earn, be worthy of, merit,
be entitled to, warrant, justify, win,
rate, incur.
deserved adj due, earned, merited,
justifiable, warranted, right, rightful,
well-earned, suitable, proper, fitting,
fair, just, appropriate, apt, legitimate,
apposite, meet (fml).
F3 gratuitous, undeserved.
deserving adj worthy, estimable,
exemplary, praiseworthy, admirable,
commendable, laudable, righteous.
F3 undeserving, unworthy.
design n **1** BLUEPRINT, draft, pattern,
plan, prototype, sketch, drawing,
outline, model, guide. **2** STYLE,
shape, form, figure, structure,
organization, arrangement,
composition, construction, motif.
3 AIM, intention, goal, purpose, plan,
end, object, objective, scheme, plot,
project, meaning, target, undertaking.
v **1** PLAN, plot, intend, devise,
purpose, aim, scheme, shape, project,
propose, tailor, mean. **2** SKETCH,
draft, outline, draw (up). **3** INVENT,
originate, conceive, create, think up,
develop, construct, fashion, form,
model, fabricate, make.
designation n **1** NAME, title, label,
epithet, nickname. **2** INDICATION,
specification, description, definition,
classification, category. **3**
NOMINATION, appointment, selection.
designer n deviser, originator,
maker, stylist, inventor, creator,
contriver, fashioner, architect, author.

designing adj artful, crafty,
scheming, conspiring, devious,
intriguing, plotting, tricky, wily, sly,
deceitful, cunning, guileful,
underhand, sharp, shrewd.
F3 artless, naive.
desirable adj **1** ADVANTAGEOUS,
profitable, worthwhile, advisable,
appropriate, expedient, beneficial,
preferable, sensible, eligible, good,
pleasing. **2** ATTRACTIVE, alluring, sexy
(infml), seductive, fetching, tempting.
F3 1 undesirable. **2** unattractive.
desire v **1** ASK, request, petition,
solicit. **2** WANT, wish for, covet, long
for, need, crave, hunger for, yearn for,
fancy (infml), hanker after.
n **1** WANT, longing, wish, need,
yearning, craving, hankering,
appetite, aspiration. **2** LUST, passion,
concupiscence (fml), ardour. **3** REQUEST,
petition, appeal, supplication.
desist v stop, cease, leave off, refrain,
discontinue, end, break off, give up,
halt, abstain, suspend, pause, peter
out, remit, forbear (fml).
F3 continue, resume.
desolate adj **1** DESERTED,
uninhabited, abandoned,
unfrequented, barren, bare, arid,
bleak, gloomy, dismal, dreary, lonely,
god-forsaken, forsaken, waste,
depressing. **2** FORLORN, bereft,
depressed, dejected, forsaken,
despondent, distressed, melancholy,
miserable, lonely, gloomy,
disheartened, dismal, downcast,
solitary, wretched.
F3 1 populous. **2** cheerful.
v devastate, lay waste, destroy,
despoil, spoil, wreck, denude,
depopulate, ruin, waste, ravage,
plunder, pillage.

desolation n 1 DESTRUCTION, ruin, devastation, ravages. 2 DEJECTION, despair, despondency, gloom, misery, sadness, melancholy, sorrow, unhappiness, anguish, grief, distress, wretchedness. 3 BARRENNESS, bleakness, emptiness, forlornness, loneliness, isolation, solitude, wildness.

despair v lose heart, lose hope, give up, give in, collapse, surrender.
Ea hope.
n despondency, gloom, hopelessness, desperation, anguish, inconsolableness, melancholy, misery, wretchedness.
Ea cheerfulness, resilience.

despairing adj despondent, distraught, inconsolable, desolate, desperate, heart-broken, suicidal, grief-stricken, hopeless, disheartened, dejected, miserable, wretched, sorrowful, dismayed, downcast.
Ea cheerful, hopeful.

despatch see **dispatch**.

desperado n bandit, criminal, brigand, gangster, hoodlum (infml), outlaw, ruffian, thug, cut-throat, law-breaker.

desperate adj 1 HOPELESS, inconsolable, wretched, despondent, abandoned. 2 RECKLESS, rash, impetuous, audacious, daring, dangerous, do-or-die, foolhardy, risky, hazardous, hasty, precipitate, wild, violent, frantic, frenzied, determined. 3 CRITICAL, acute, serious, severe, extreme, urgent.
Ea 1 hopeful. 2 cautious.

desperately adv dangerously, critically, gravely, hopelessly, seriously, severely, badly, dreadfully, fearfully, frightfully.

desperation n 1 DESPAIR, despondency, anguish, hopelessness, misery, agony, distress, pain, sorrow, trouble, worry, anxiety. 2 RECKLESSNESS, rashness, frenzy, madness, hastiness.

despicable adj contemptible, vile, worthless, detestable, disgusting, mean, wretched, disgraceful, disreputable, shameful, reprobate.
Ea admirable, noble.

despise v scorn, deride, look down on, disdain, condemn, spurn, undervalue, slight, revile, deplore, dislike, detest, loathe.
Ea admire.

despite prep in spite of, notwithstanding, regardless of, in the face of, undeterred by, against, defying.

despondent adj depressed, dejected, disheartened, downcast, down, low, gloomy, glum, discouraged, miserable, melancholy, sad, sorrowful, doleful, despairing, heart-broken, inconsolable, mournful, wretched.
Ea cheerful, heartened, hopeful.

despot n autocrat, tyrant, dictator, oppressor, absolutist, boss.

despotic adj autocratic, tyrannical, imperious, oppressive, dictatorial, authoritarian, domineering, absolute, overbearing, arbitrary, arrogant.
Ea democratic, egalitarian, liberal, tolerant.

despotism n autocracy, totalitarianism, tyranny, dictatorship, absolutism, oppression, repression.
Ea democracy, egalitarianism, liberalism, tolerance.

dessert

Types of dessert include:
ice cream, charlotte russe, cheese-cake, crème caramel, egg custard, fruit salad, fruit cocktail, gateau, millefeuille, pavlova, profiterole, Sachertorte, soufflé, summer pudding, Bakewell tart, banoffee pie, trifle, yogurt, sundae, syllabub, queen of puddings, Christmas pudding, tapioca, rice pudding, spotted dick, roly-poly pudding, tiramisu, zabaglione.

destination n 1 GOAL, aim, objective, object, purpose, target, end, intention, aspiration, design, ambition. 2 JOURNEY'S END, terminus, station, stop.

destined adj 1 FATED, doomed, inevitable, predetermined, ordained, certain, foreordained, meant, unavoidable, inescapable, intended, designed, appointed. 2 BOUND, directed, en route, headed, heading, scheduled, assigned, booked.

destiny n fate, doom, fortune, karma, lot (fml), portion (fml), predestination, kismet.

destitute adj 1 LACKING, needy, wanting, devoid of, bereft, innocent of, deprived, deficient, depleted. 2 POOR, penniless, poverty-stricken, impoverished, down and out (infml), distressed, bankrupt.
F∃ 2 prosperous, rich.

destroy v 1 DEMOLISH, ruin, shatter, wreck, devastate, smash, break, crush, overthrow, sabotage, undo, dismantle, thwart, undermine, waste, gut, level, ravage, raze, torpedo, unshape. 2 KILL, annihilate, eliminate, extinguish, eradicate, dispatch, slay (fml), nullify.
F∃ 1 build up. 2 create.

destruction n 1 RUIN, devastation, shattering, crushing, wreckage, demolition, defeat, downfall, overthrow, ruination, desolation, undoing, wastage, havoc, ravagement. 2 ANNIHILATION, extermination, eradication, elimination, extinction, slaughter, massacre, end, liquidation, nullification.
F∃ 2 creation.

destructive adj 1 destructive storms: devastating, damaging, catastrophic, disastrous, deadly, harmful, fatal, disruptive, lethal, ruinous, detrimental, hurtful, malignant, mischievous, nullifying, slaughterous. 2 destructive criticism: adverse, hostile, negative, discouraging, disparaging, contrary, undermining, subversive, vicious.
F∃ 1 creative. 2 constructive.

desultory adj random, erratic, aimless, disorderly, haphazard, irregular, spasmodic, inconsistent, undirected, unco-ordinated, unsystematic, unmethodical, fitful, disconnected, loose, capricious.
F∃ systematic, methodical.

detach v separate, disconnect, unfasten, disjoin, cut off, disengage, remove, undo, uncouple, sever, dissociate, isolate, loosen, free, unfix, unhitch, segregate, divide, disentangle, estrange.
F∃ attach.

detached adj 1 SEPARATE, disconnected, dissociated, severed, free, loose, divided, discrete. 2 ALOOF, dispassionate, impersonal, neutral, impartial, independent, disinterested, objective.
F∃ 1 connected. 2 involved.

detachment n **1** ALOOFNESS, remoteness, coolness, unconcern, indifference, impassivity, disinterestedness, neutrality, impartiality, objectivity, fairness. **2** SEPARATION, disconnection, disunion, disengagement. **3** SQUAD, unit, force, corps, brigade, patrol, task force.

detail n particular, item, factor, element, aspect, component, feature, point, specific, ingredient, attribute, count, respect, technicality, complication, intricacy, triviality, fact, thoroughness, elaboration, meticulousness, refinement, nicety. v **1** LIST, enumerate, itemize, specify, catalogue, recount, relate. **2** ASSIGN, appoint, charge, delegate, commission.

detailed adj comprehensive, exhaustive, full, blow-by-blow (infml), thorough, minute, exact, specific, particular, itemized, intricate, elaborate, complex, complicated, meticulous, descriptive.
E3 cursory, general.

detain v **1** DELAY, hold (up), hinder, impede, check, retard, slow, stay, stop. **2** CONFINE, arrest, intern, hold, restrain, keep.
E3 2 release.

detect v **1** NOTICE, ascertain, note, observe, perceive, recognize, discern, distinguish, identify, sight, spot, spy. **2** UNCOVER, catch, discover, disclose, expose, find, track down, unmask, reveal.

detective n investigator, private eye (infml), gumshoe (US sl), sleuth (infml), sleuth-hound (infml).

detention n **1** DETAINMENT, custody, confinement, imprisonment,

restraint, incarceration, constraint, quarantine. **2** DELAY, hindrance, holding back.
E3 1 release.

deter v discourage, put off, inhibit, intimidate, dissuade, daunt, turn off (infml), check, caution, warn, restrain, hinder, frighten, disincline, prevent, prohibit, stop.
E3 encourage.

deteriorate v **1** WORSEN, decline, degenerate, depreciate, go downhill (infml), fail, fall off, lapse, slide, relapse, slip. **2** DECAY, disintegrate, decompose, weaken, fade.
E3 1 improve. **2** progress.

determination n **1** RESOLUTENESS, tenacity, firmness, will-power, perseverance, persistence, purpose, backbone, guts (infml), grit (infml), steadfastness, single-mindedness, will, insistence, conviction, dedication, drive, fortitude. **2** DECISION, judgement, settlement, resolution, conclusion.
E3 1 irresolution.

determine v **1** DECIDE, settle, resolve, make up one's mind, choose, conclude, fix on, elect, clinch, finish. **2** DISCOVER, establish, find out, ascertain, identify, check, detect, verify. **3** AFFECT, influence, govern, control, dictate, direct, guide, regulate, ordain.

determined adj resolute, firm, purposeful, strong-willed, single-minded, persevering, persistent, strong-minded, steadfast, tenacious, dogged, insistent, intent, fixed, convinced, decided, unflinching.
E3 irresolute, wavering.

deterrent n hindrance, impediment, obstacle, repellent,

check, bar, discouragement, obstruction, curb, restraint, difficulty.
F3 incentive, encouragement.

detest v hate, abhor, loathe, abominate, execrate (fml), dislike, recoil from, deplore, despise.
F3 adore, love.

detestable adj hateful, loathsome, abhorrent, abominable, repellent, obnoxious, execrable (fml), despicable, revolting, repulsive, repugnant, offensive, vile, disgusting, accursed (fml), heinous, shocking, sordid.
F3 adorable, admirable.

detour n deviation, diversion, indirect route, circuitous route, roundabout route, digression, byroad, byway, bypath, bypass.

detract (from) v diminish, subtract from, take away from, reduce, lessen, lower, devaluate, depreciate, belittle, disparage.
F3 add to, enhance, praise.

detriment n damage, harm, hurt, disadvantage, loss, ill, injury, disservice, evil, mischief, prejudice.
F3 advantage, benefit.

detrimental adj damaging, harmful, hurtful, adverse, disadvantageous, injurious, prejudicial, mischievous, destructive.
F3 advantageous, favourable, beneficial.

devastate v **1** DESTROY, desolate, lay waste, demolish, spoil, despoil, wreck, ruin, ravage, waste, ransack, plunder, level, raze, pillage, sack. **2** DISCONCERT, overwhelm, take aback, confound, shatter (infml), floor (infml), nonplus, discomfit.

devastating adj **1** devastating storms: destructive, disastrous.

2 a devastating argument: effective, incisive, overwhelming, stunning.

devastation n destruction, desolation, havoc, ruin, wreckage, ravages, demolition, annihilation, pillage, plunder, spoliation.

develop v **1** ADVANCE, evolve, expand, progress, foster, flourish, mature, prosper, branch out. **2** ELABORATE, amplify, argument, enhance, unfold. **3** ACQUIRE, contract, begin, generate, create, invent. **4** RESULT, come about, grow, ensue, arise, follow, happen.

development n **1** GROWTH, evolution, advance, blossoming, elaboration, furtherance, progress, unfolding, expansion, extension, spread, increase, improvement, maturity, promotion, refinement, issue. **2** OCCURRENCE, happening, event, change, outcome, situation, result, phenomenon.

deviate v diverge, veer, turn (aside), digress, swerve, vary, differ, depart, stray, yaw, wander, err, go astray, go off the rails (infml), drift, part.

deviation n divergence, aberration, departure, abnormality, irregularity, variance, variation, digression, eccentricity, anomaly, deflection, alteration, disparity, discrepancy, detour, fluctuation, change, quirk, shift, freak.
F3 conformity, regularity.

device n **1** TOOL, implement, appliance, gadget, contrivance, contraption (infml), apparatus, utensil, instrument, machine. **2** SCHEME, ruse, strategy, plan, plot, gambit, manoeuvre, wile, trick, dodge (infml), machination. **3** EMBLEM, symbol, motif, logo (*infml*), design, insignia, crest, badge, shield.

devil n **1** DEMON, Satan, fiend, evil spirit, arch-fiend, Lucifer, imp, Evil One, Prince of Darkness, Adversary, Beelzebub, Mephistopheles, Old Nick (*infml*), Old Harry (*infml*). **2** BRUTE, rogue, monster, ogre.

devious adj **1** UNDERHAND, deceitful, dishonest, disingenuous, double-dealing, scheming, tricky (*infml*), insidious, insincere, calculating, cunning, evasive, wily, sly, slippery (*infml*), surreptitious, treacherous, misleading. **2** INDIRECT, circuitous, rambling, roundabout, wandering, winding, tortuous, erratic.
F3 straightforward.

devise v invent, contrive, plan, plot, design, conceive, arrange, formulate, imagine, scheme, construct, concoct, forge, frame, project, shape, form.

devoid adj lacking, wanting, without, free, bereft, destitute, deficient, deprived, barren, empty, vacant, void.
F3 endowed.

devote v dedicate, consecrate, commit, give oneself, set apart, set aside, reserve, apply, allocate, allot, sacrifice, enshrine, assign, appropriate, surrender, pledge.

devoted adj dedicated, ardent, committed, loyal, faithful, devout, loving, staunch, steadfast, true, constant, fond, unswerving, tireless, concerned, attentive, caring.
F3 indifferent, disloyal.

devotee n enthusiast, fan (*infml*), fanatic, addict, aficionado, follower, supporter, zealot, adherent, admirer, disciple, buff (*infml*), freak (*infml*), merchant (*infml*), fiend (*infml*), hound.

devotion n **1** DEDICATION, commitment, consecration, ardour, loyalty, allegiance, adherence, zeal, support, love, passion, fervour, fondness, attachment, adoration, affection, faithfulness, reverence, steadfastness, regard, earnestness. **2** DEVOUTNESS, piety, godliness, faith, holiness, spirituality. **3** PRAYER, worship.
F3 1 inconstancy. **2** irreverence.

devour v **1** EAT, consume, guzzle, gulp, gorge, gobble, bolt, wolf down, swallow, stuff (*infml*), cram, polish off (*infml*), gormandize, feast on, relish, revel in. **2** DESTROY, consume, absorb, engulf, ravage, dispatch.

devout adj **1** SINCERE, earnest, devoted, fervent, genuine, staunch, steadfast, ardent, passionate, serious, whole-hearted, constant, faithful, intense, heartfelt, zealous, unswerving, deep, profound. **2** PIOUS, godly, religious, reverent, prayerful, saintly, holy, orthodox.
F3 1 insincere. **2** irreligious.

dexterous adj deft, adroit, agile, able, nimble, proficient, skilful, clever, expert, nifty, nippy, handy, facile, nimble-fingered, neat-handed.
F3 clumsy, inept, awkward.

diabolical adj devilish, fiendish, demonic, hellish, damnable, evil, infernal, wicked, vile, dreadful, outrageous, shocking, disastrous, excruciating, atrocious.

diagnose v identify, determine, recognize, pinpoint, distinguish, analyse, explain, isolate, interpret, investigate.

diagnosis n identification, verdict, explanation, conclusion, answer, interpretation, analysis, opinion, investigation, examination, scrutiny.

diagonal adj oblique, slanting, cross, crosswise, sloping, crooked, angled, cornerways.

diagram n plan, sketch, chart, drawing, figure, representation, schema, illustration, outline, graph, picture, layout, table.

dial n circle, disc, face, clock, control. v phone, ring, call (up).

dialect n idiom, language, regionalism, patois, provincialism, vernacular, argot, jargon, accent, lingo (infml), speech, diction.

dialectic adj dialectical, logical, rational, argumentative, analytical, rationalistic, logistic, polemical, inductive, deductive.
n dialectics, logic, reasoning, rationale, disputation, analysis, debate, argumentation, contention, discussion, polemics, induction, deduction.

dialogue n **1** CONVERSATION, interchange, discourse, communication, talk, exchange, discussion, converse, debate, conference. **2** LINES, script.

diametric adj diametrical, opposed, opposite, contrary, counter, contrasting, antithetical.

diary n journal, day-book, logbook, chronicle, year-book, appointment book, engagement book.

diatribe n tirade, invective, abuse, harangue, attack, onslaught, denunciation, criticism, insult, reviling, upbraiding.
E3 praise, eulogy.

dictate v **1** SAY, speak, utter, announce, pronounce, transmit. **2** COMMAND, order, direct, decree, instruct, rule.
n command, decree, precept, principle, rule, direction, injunction,

edict, order, ruling, statute, requirement, ordinance, law, bidding, mandate, ultimatum, word.

dictator n despot, autocrat, tyrant, supremo (infml), Big Brother (infml).

dictatorial adj tyrannical, despotic, totalitarian, authoritarian, autocratic, oppressive, imperious, domineering, bossy (infml), absolute, repressive, overbearing, arbitrary, dogmatic.
E3 democratic, egalitarian, liberal.

diction n speech, articulation, language, elocution, enunciation, intonation, pronunciation, inflection, fluency, delivery, expression, phrasing.

dictionary n lexicon, glossary, thesaurus, vocabulary, wordbook, encyclopedia, concordance.

dictum n pronouncement, ruling, maxim, decree, dictate, edict, fiat (fml), precept, axiom, command, order, utterance.

didactic adj instructive, educational, educative, pedagogic, prescriptive, pedantic, moralizing, moral.

die v **1** DECEASE, perish, pass away, expire, depart, breathe one's last, peg out (infml), snuff it (sl), bite the dust (infml), kick the bucket (sl). **2** DWINDLE, fade, ebb, sink, wane, wilt, wither, peter out, decline, decay, finish, lapse, end, disappear, vanish, subside. **3** LONG FOR, pine for, yearn, desire.
E3 1 live.

die-hard n reactionary, intransigent, hardliner, blimp (infml), ultra-conservative, old fogey (infml), stick-in-the-mud (infml), rightist, fanatic.

diet n **1** FOOD, nutrition, provisions, sustenance, rations, foodstuffs, subsistence. **2** FAST, abstinence, regimen.

v lose weight, slim, fast, reduce, abstain, weight-watch (*infml*).

differ *v* **1** VARY, diverge, deviate, depart from, contradict, contrast. **2** DISAGREE, argue, conflict, oppose, dispute, dissent, be at odds with, clash, quarrel, fall out, debate, contend, take issue.

F3 **1** conform. **2** agree.

difference *n* **1** DISSIMILARITY, unlikeness, discrepancy, divergence, diversity, variation, variety, distinctness, distinction, deviation, differentiation, contrast, disparity, singularity, exception. **2** DISAGREEMENT, clash, dispute, conflict, contention, controversy. **3** REMAINDER, rest.

F3 **1** conformity. **2** agreement.

different *adj* **1** DISSIMILAR, unlike, contrasting, divergent, inconsistent, deviating, at odds, clashing, opposed. **2** VARIED, various, diverse, miscellaneous, assorted, disparate, many, numerous, several, sundry, other. **3** UNUSUAL, unconventional, unique, distinct, distinctive, extraordinary, individual, original, special, strange, separate, peculiar, rare, bizarre, anomalous.

F3 **1** similar. **2** same. **3** conventional.

differentiate *v* distinguish, tell apart, discriminate, contrast, separate, mark off, individualize, particularize.

difficult *adj* **1** HARD, laborious, demanding, arduous, strenuous, tough, wearisome, uphill, formidable. **2** COMPLEX, complicated, intricate, involved, abstruse, obscure, dark, knotty, thorny, problematical, perplexing, abstract, baffling, intractable. **3** UNMANAGEABLE, perverse, troublesome, trying, unco-operative, tiresome, stubborn, obstinate, intractable.

F3 **1** easy. **2** straightforward. **3** manageable.

difficulty *n* **1** HARDSHIP, trouble, labour, arduousness, painfulness, trial, tribulation, awkwardness. **2** PROBLEM, predicament, dilemma, quandary, perplexity, embarrassment, plight, distress, fix (*infml*), mess (*infml*), jam (*infml*), spot (*infml*), hiccup (*infml*), hang-up. **3** OBSTACLE, hindrance, hurdle, impediment, objection, opposition, block, complication, pitfall, protest, stumbling-block.

F3 **1** ease.

diffidence *n* unassertiveness, modesty, shyness, self-consciousness, self-effacement, timidity, insecurity, reserve, bashfulness, humility, inhibition, meekness, self-distrust, self-doubt, hesitancy, reluctance, backwardness. **F3** confidence.

diffident *adj* unassertive, modest, shy, timid, self-conscious, self-effacing, insecure, bashful, abashed, meek, reserved, withdrawn, tentative, shrinking, inhibited, hesitant, reluctant, unsure, shamefaced. **F3** assertive, confident.

diffuse *adj* **1** *diffuse outbreaks of rain:* scattered, unconcentrated, diffused, dispersed, disconnected. **2** *a diffuse prose style:* verbose, imprecise, wordy, rambling, long-winded, waffling (*infml*), vague, discursive. **F3** **1** concentrated. **2** succinct. *v* spread, scatter, disperse, distribute, propagate, dispense, disseminate, circulate, dissipate. **F3** concentrate.

dig *v* **1** EXCAVATE, penetrate, burrow, mine, quarry, scoop, tunnel, till, gouge, delve, pierce. **2** POKE, prod. **3** INVESTIGATE, probe, go into, research, search.
n gibe, jeer, sneer, taunt, crack, insinuation, insult, wisecrack.
F3 compliment.

dig up discover, unearth, uncover, disinter, expose, extricate, exhume, find, retrieve, track down.
F3 bury, obscure.

digest *v* **1** ABSORB, assimilate, incorporate, process, dissolve. **2** TAKE IN, absorb, assimilate, grasp, study, consider, contemplate, meditate, ponder. **3** SHORTEN, summarize, condense, compress, reduce.
n summary, abridgement, abstract, précis, synopsis, résumé, reduction, abbreviation, compression, compendium.

dignified *adj* stately, solemn, imposing, majestic, noble, august, lordly, lofty, exalted, formal, distinguished, grave, impressive, reserved, honourable.
F3 undignified, lowly.

dignitary *n* worthy, notable, VIP (*infml*), high-up, personage, bigwig (*infml*).

dignity *n* stateliness, propriety, solemnity, decorum, courtliness, grandeur, loftiness, majesty, honour, eminence, importance, nobility, self-respect, self-esteem, standing, poise, respectability, greatness, status, pride.

digress *v* diverge, deviate, stray, wander, go off at a tangent, drift, depart, ramble.

dilapidated *adj* ramshackle, shabby, broken-down, neglected, tumble-down, uncared-for, rickety, decrepit, crumbling, run-down, worn-out, ruined, decayed, decaying.

dilate *v* distend, enlarge, expand, spread, broaden, widen, increase, extend, stretch, swell.
F3 contract.

dilatory *adj* delaying, procrastinating, slow, tardy, tarrying, sluggish, lingering, lackadaisical, slack.
F3 prompt.

dilemma *n* quandary, conflict, predicament, problem, catch-22 (*infml*), difficulty, puzzle, embarrassment, perplexity, plight.

diligent *adj* assiduous, industrious, hard-working, conscientious, painstaking, busy, attentive, tireless, careful, meticulous, persevering, persistent, studious.
F3 negligent, lazy.

dilute *v* adulterate, water down, thin (out), attenuate, weaken, diffuse, diminish, decrease, lessen, reduce, temper, mitigate.
F3 concentrate.

dim *adj* **1** DARK, dull, dusky, cloudy, shadowy, gloomy, sombre, dingy, lacklustre, feeble, imperfect. **2** INDISTINCT, blurred, hazy, ill-defined, obscure, misty, unclear, foggy, fuzzy, vague, faint, weak. **3** STUPID, dense, obtuse, thick (*infml*), doltish.
F3 1 bright. **2** distinct. **3** bright, intelligent.
v darken, dull, obscure, cloud, blur, fade, tarnish, shade.
F3 brighten, illuminate.

dimension(s) *n* extent, measurement, measure, size, scope, magnitude, largeness, capacity, mass, scale, range, bulk, importance, greatness.

diminish v **1** DECREASE, lessen, reduce, lower, contract, decline, dwindle, shrink, recede, taper off, wane, weaken, abate, fade, sink, subside, ebb, slacken, cut. **2** BELITTLE, disparage, deprecate, devalue.
F3 increase. **2** exaggerate.

diminutive adj undersized, small, tiny, little, miniature, minute, infinitesimal, wee, petite, midget, mini (infml), teeny (infml), teeny-weeny (infml), Lilliputian, dinky (infml), pint-size(d) (infml), pocket (-sized), pygmy.
F3 big, large, oversized.

din n noise, row, racket, clash, clatter, clamour, pandemonium, uproar, commotion, crash, hullabaloo (infml), hubbub, outcry, shout, babble.
F3 quiet, calm.

dine v eat, feast, sup, lunch, banquet, feed.

dingy adj dark, drab, grimy, murky, faded, dull, dim, shabby, soiled, discoloured, dirty, dreary, gloomy, seedy, sombre, obscure, run-down, colourless, dusky, worn.
F3 bright, clean.

dinner n meal, supper, tea (infml), banquet, feast, spread, repast (fml).

dinosaur n

Dinosaurs include:
allosaurus, ankylosaurus, apato-saurus, brachiosaurus, brontosaur-us, camptosaurus, compsognathus, corythosaurus, diplodocus, hetero-dontosaurus, iguanodon, ornitho-mimus, pachycephalosaurus, para-saurolophus, plateosaurus, stego-saurus, styracosaurus, triceratops, tyrannosaurus, velociraptor.

dip v **1** PLUNGE, immerse, submerge, duck, dunk, bathe, douse, sink. **2** DESCEND, decline, drop, fall, subside, slump, sink, lower.
n **1** HOLLOW, basin, decline, hole, concavity, incline, depression, fall, slope, slump, lowering. **2** BATHE, immersion, plunge, soaking, ducking, swim, drenching, infusion, dive.

diplomacy n **1** TACT, tactfulness, finesse, delicacy, discretion, savoir-faire, subtlety, skill, craft. **2** STATECRAFT, statesmanship, politics, negotiation, manoeuvring.

diplomat n go-between, mediator, negotiator, ambassador, envoy, conciliator, peacemaker, moderator, politician.

diplomatic adj tactful, politic, discreet, judicious, subtle, sensitive, prudent, discreet.
F3 tactless.

dire adj **1** DISASTROUS, dreadful, awful, appalling, calamitous, catastrophic. **2** DESPERATE, urgent, grave, drastic, crucial, extreme, alarming, ominous.

direct v **1** CONTROL, manage, run, administer, organize, lead, govern, regulate, superintend, supervise. **2** INSTRUCT, command, order, charge. **3** GUIDE, lead, conduct, point. **4** AIM, point, focus, turn.
adj **1** STRAIGHT, undeviating, through, uninterrupted. **2** STRAIGHTFORWARD, outspoken, blunt, frank, unequivocal, sincere, candid, honest, explicit. **3** IMMEDIATE, first-hand, face-to-face, personal.
F3 1 circuitous. **2** equivocal. **3** indirect.

direction n **1** CONTROL, administration, management,

government, supervision, guidance, leadership. **2** ROUTE, way, line, road.

directions n instructions, guidelines, orders, briefing, guidance, recommendations, indication, plan.

directive n command, instruction, order, regulation, ruling, imperative, dictate, decree, charge, mandate, injunction, ordinance, edict, fiat, notice.

directly adv **1** IMMEDIATELY, instantly, promptly, right away, speedily, forthwith, instantaneously, quickly, soon, presently, straightaway, straight. **2** FRANKLY, bluntly, candidly, honestly.

director n manager, head, boss, chief, controller, executive, principal, governor, leader, organizer, supervisor, administrator, producer, conductor.

dirt n **1** EARTH, soil, clay, dust, mud. **2** FILTH, grime, muck, mire, excrement, stain, smudge, slime, tarnish. **3** INDECENCY, impurity, obscenity, pornography.

dirty adj **1** FILTHY, grimy, grubby, mucky, soiled, unwashed, foul, messy, muddy, polluted, squalid, dull, miry, scruffy, shabby, sullied, clouded, dark. **2** INDECENT, obscene, filthy, smutty, sordid, salacious, vulgar, pornographic, corrupt.
F₃ **1** clean. **2** decent.
v pollute, soil, stain, foul, mess up, defile, smear, smirch, spoil, smudge, sully, muddy, blacken.
F₃ clean, cleanse.

disability n handicap, impairment, disablement, disorder, inability, incapacity, infirmity, defect, unfitness, disqualification, affliction, ailment, complaint, weakness.

disable v cripple, lame, incapacitate, damage, handicap, impair, debilitate, disqualify, weaken, immobilize, invalidate, paralyse, prostrate.

disabled adj handicapped, incapacitated, impaired, infirm, crippled, lame, immobilized, maimed, weak, weakened, paralysed, wrecked.
F₃ able, able-bodied.

disadvantage n **1** HARM, damage, detriment, hurt, injury, loss, prejudice. **2** DRAWBACK, snag, hindrance, handicap, impediment, inconvenience, flaw, nuisance, weakness, trouble.
F₃ **2** advantage, benefit.

disadvantaged adj deprived, underprivileged, poor, handicapped, impoverished, struggling.
F₃ privileged.

disadvantageous adj harmful, detrimental, inopportune, unfavourable, prejudicial, adverse, damaging, hurtful, injurious, inconvenient, ill-timed.
F₃ advantageous, auspicious.

disaffected adj disloyal, hostile, estranged, alienated, antagonistic, rebellious, dissatisfied, disgruntled, discontented.
F₃ loyal.

disaffection n disloyalty, hostility, alienation, discontentment, resentment, ill-will, dissatisfaction, animosity, coolness, unfriendliness, antagonism, disharmony, discord, disagreement, aversion, dislike.
F₃ loyalty, contentment.

disagree v **1** DISSENT, oppose, quarrel, argue, bicker, fall out (infml), wrangle, fight, squabble, contend, dispute, contest, object. **2** CONFLICT, clash, diverge, contradict, counter,

differ, deviate, depart, run counter to, vary.
F3 1 agree. **2** correspond.

disagreeable adj **1** a disagreeable old man: bad-tempered, ill-humoured, difficult, peevish, rude, surly, churlish, irritable, contrary, cross, brusque. **2** a disagreeable taste: disgusting, offensive, repulsive, repellent, obnoxious, unsavoury, objectionable, nasty.
F3 1 amiable, pleasant. **2** agreeable.

disagreement n **1** DISPUTE, argument, conflict, altercation (fml), quarrel, clash, dissent, falling-out, contention, strife, misunderstanding, squabble, tiff (infml), wrangle.
2 DIFFERENCE, variance, unlikeness, disparity, discrepancy, deviation, discord, dissimilarity, incompatibility, divergence, diversity, incongruity.
F3 1 agreement, harmony.
2 similarity.

disappear v **1** VANISH, wane, recede, fade, evaporate, dissolve, ebb.
2 GO, depart, withdraw, retire, flee, fly, escape, scarper (infml), hide.
3 END, expire, perish, pass.
F3 1 appear. **3** emerge.

disappearance n vanishing, fading, evaporation, departure, loss, going, passing, melting, desertion, flight.
F3 appearance, manifestation.

disappoint v fail, dissatisfy, let down, disillusion, dash, dismay, disenchant, sadden, thwart, vex, frustrate, foil, dishearten, disgruntle, disconcert, hamper, hinder, deceive, defeat, delude.
F3 satisfy, please, delight.

disappointed adj let down, frustrated, thwarted, disillusioned, dissatisfied, miffed (infml), upset,

discouraged, disgruntled, disheartened, distressed, down-hearted, saddened, despondent, depressed.
F3 pleased, satisfied.

disappointment n **1** FRUSTRATION, dissatisfaction, failure, disenchantment, disillusionment, displeasure, discouragement, distress, regret. **2** FAILURE, let-down, setback, comedown, blow, misfortune, fiasco, disaster, calamity, washout (infml), damp squib (infml), swiz (infml), swizzle (infml).
F3 1 pleasure, satisfaction, delight.
2 success.

disapproval n censure, disapprobation (fml), condemnation, criticism, displeasure, reproach, objection, dissatisfaction, denunciation, dislike.
F3 approbation (fml), approval.

disapprove of censure, condemn, blame, take exception to, object to, deplore, denounce, disparage, dislike, reject, spurn.
F3 approve of.

disarm v **1** DISABLE, unarm, demilitarize, demobilize, deactivate, disband. **2** APPEASE, conciliate, win, mollify, persuade.
F3 1 arm.

disarray n disorder, confusion, chaos, mess, muddle, shambles (infml), disorganization, clutter, untidiness, unruliness, jumble, indiscipline, tangle, upset.
F3 order.

disaster n calamity, catastrophe, misfortune, reverse, tragedy, blow, accident, act of God, cataclysm, debacle, mishap, failure, flop (infml), fiasco, ruin, stroke, trouble,

mischance, ruination.
F3 success, triumph.

disastrous adj calamitous, catastrophic, cataclysmic, devastating, ruinous, tragic, unfortunate, dreadful, dire, terrible, destructive, ill-fated, fatal, miserable.
F3 successful, auspicious.

disband v disperse, break up, scatter, dismiss, demobilize, part company, separate, dissolve.
F3 assemble, muster.

disbelief n unbelief, incredulity, doubt, scepticism, suspicion, distrust, mistrust, rejection.
F3 belief.

disbelieve v discount, discredit, repudiate, reject, mistrust, suspect.
F3 believe, trust.

disc n **1** CIRCLE, face, plate, ring. **2** RECORD, album, LP, CD, MiniDisc®. **3** DISK, diskette, hard disk, floppy disk, CD-ROM, DVD.

discard v reject, abandon, dispose of, get rid of, jettison, dispense with, cast aside, ditch (*infml*), dump (*infml*), drop, scrap, shed, remove, relinquish.
F3 retain, adopt.

discern v **1** PERCEIVE, make out, observe, detect, recognize, see, ascertain, notice, determine, discover, descry. **2** DISCRIMINATE, distinguish, differentiate, judge.

discernible adj perceptible, noticeable, detectable, appreciable, distinct, observable, recognizable, visible, apparent, clear, obvious, plain, patent, manifest, discoverable.
F3 imperceptible.

discerning adj discriminating, perceptive, astute, clear-sighted, sensitive, shrewd, wise, sharp, subtle, sagacious, penetrating, acute,

piercing, critical, eagle-eyed.
F3 dull, obtuse.

discharge v **1** LIBERATE, free, pardon, release, clear, absolve, exonerate, acquit, relieve, dismiss. **2** EXECUTE, carry out, perform, fulfil, dispense. **3** FIRE, shoot, let off, detonate, explode. **4** EMIT, sack (*infml*), remove, fire (*infml*), expel, oust, eject.
F3 1 detain. **2** neglect. **4** appoint.
n **1** LIBERATION, release, acquittal, exoneration. **2** EMISSION, secretion, ejection. **3** EXECUTION, accomplishment, fulfilment.
F3 1 confinement, detention.
2 absorption. **3** neglect.

disciple n follower, convert, proselyte, adherent, believer, devotee, supporter, learner, pupil, student.

disciplinarian n authoritarian, taskmaster, autocrat, stickler, despot, tyrant.

discipline n **1** TRAINING, exercise, drill, practice. **2** PUNISHMENT, chastisement, correction.
3 STRICTNESS, restraint, regulation, self-control, orderliness.
F3 3 indiscipline.
v **1** TRAIN, instruct, drill, educate, exercise, break in. **2** CHECK, control, correct, restrain, govern. **3** PUNISH, chastise, chasten, penalize, reprimand, castigate.

disclaim v deny, disown, repudiate, abandon, renounce, reject, abjure (*fml*).
F3 accept, confess.

disclose v **1** DIVULGE, make known, reveal, tell, confess, let slip, relate, publish, communicate, impart, leak (*infml*). **2** EXPOSE, reveal, uncover, lay bare, unveil, discover.
F3 conceal.

disclosure n divulgence, exposure, exposé, revelation, publication, leak (*infml*), discovery, admission, acknowledgement, announcement, declaration.

discomfort n ache, pain, uneasiness, malaise, trouble, distress, disquiet, hardship, vexation, irritation, annoyance.
F3 comfort, ease.

disconcerting adj disturbing, confusing, upsetting, unnerving, alarming, bewildering, off-putting (*infml*), distracting, embarrassing, awkward, baffling, perplexing, dismaying, bothersome.

disconnect v cut off, disengage, uncouple, sever, separate, detach, unplug, unhook, part, divide.
F3 attach, connect.

disconnected adj confused, incoherent, rambling, unco-ordinated, unintelligible, loose, irrational, disjointed, illogical, jumbled.
F3 coherent, connected.

disconsolate adj desolate, dejected, dispirited, sad, melancholy, unhappy, wretched, miserable, gloomy, forlorn, inconsolable, crushed, heavy-hearted, hopeless.
F3 cheerful, joyful.

discontent n uneasiness, dissatisfaction, disquiet, restlessness, fretfulness, unrest, impatience, vexation, regret.
F3 content.

discontented adj dissatisfied, fed up (*infml*), disgruntled, unhappy, browned off (*infml*), cheesed off (*infml*), disaffected, miserable, exasperated, complaining.
F3 contented, satisfied.

discontinue v stop, end, finish, cease, break off, terminate, halt, drop, suspend, abandon, cancel, interrupt.
F3 continue.

discord n 1 DISSENSION, disagreement, discordance, clashing, disunity, incompatibility, conflict, difference, dispute, contention, friction, division, opposition, strife, split, wrangling. 2 DISSONANCE, disharmony, cacophony (*fml*), jangle, jarring, harshness.
F3 1 concord, agreement.
2 harmony.

discordant adj 1 DISAGREEING, conflicting, at odds, clashing, contradictory, incongruous, incompatible, inconsistent.
2 DISSONANT, cacophonous (*fml*), grating, jangling, jarring, harsh.
F3 1 harmonious.

discount[1] v 1 DISREGARD, ignore, overlook, disbelieve, gloss over.
2 REDUCE, deduct, mark down, knock off (*infml*).

discount[2] n reduction, rebate, allowance, cut, concession, deduction, mark-down.

discourage v 1 DISHEARTEN, dampen, dispirit, depress, demoralize, dismay, unnerve, deject, disappoint.
2 DETER, dissuade, hinder, put off, restrain, prevent.
F3 1 hearten. 2 encourage.

discouragement n 1 DOWNHEARTEDNESS, despondency, pessimism, dismay, depression, dejection, despair, disappointment.
2 DETERRENT, damper, setback, impediment, obstacle, opposition, hindrance, restraint, rebuff.
F3 1 encouragement. 2 incentive.

discourse n 1 CONVERSATION, dialogue, chat, communication, talk, converse, discussion. 2 SPEECH, address, oration (fml), lecture, sermon, essay, treatise, dissertation, homily. v converse, talk, discuss, debate, confer, lecture.

discourteous adj rude, bad-mannered, ill-mannered, impolite, boorish, disrespectful, ill-bred, uncivil, unceremonious, insolent, offhand, curt, brusque, abrupt.
E3 courteous, polite.

discover v 1 FIND, uncover, unearth, dig up, disclose, reveal, light on, locate. 2 ASCERTAIN, determine, realize, notice, recognize, perceive, see, find out, spot, discern, learn, detect. 3 ORIGINATE, invent, pioneer.
E3 1 miss. 2 conceal, cover (up).

discovery n 1 BREAKTHROUGH, find, origination, introduction, innovation, invention, exploration. 2 DISCLOSURE, detection, revelation, location.

discredit v 1 DISBELIEVE, distrust, doubt, question, mistrust, challenge. 2 DISPARAGE, dishonour, degrade, defame, disgrace, slander, slur, smear, reproach, vilify.
E3 1 believe. 2 honour.
n 1 DISBELIEF, distrust, doubt, mistrust, scepticism, suspicion. 2 DISHONOUR, disrepute, censure, aspersion, disgrace, blame, shame, reproach, slur, smear, scandal.
E3 1 belief. 2 credit.

discreditable adj dishonourable, disreputable, disgraceful, reprehensible, scandalous, blameworthy, shameful, infamous, degrading, improper.
E3 creditable.

discreet adj tactful, careful, diplomatic, politic, prudent, cautious, delicate, judicious, reserved, wary, sensible.
E3 tactless, indiscreet.

discrepancy n difference, disparity, variance, variation, inconsistency, dissimilarity, discordance, divergence, disagreement, conflict, inequality.

discretion n 1 TACT, diplomacy, judiciousness, caution, prudence, wisdom, circumspection, discernment, judgement, care, carefulness, consideration, wariness. 2 CHOICE, freedom, preference, will, wish.
E3 1 indiscretion.

discriminate v distinguish, differentiate, discern, tell apart, make a distinction, segregate, separate.
E3 confuse, confound.
discriminate (against) be prejudiced, be biased, victimize.

discriminating adj discerning, fastidious, selective, critical, perceptive, particular, tasteful, astute, sensitive, cultivated.

discrimination n 1 BIAS, prejudice, intolerance, unfairness, bigotry, favouritism, inequity, racism, sexism. 2 DISCERNMENT, judgement, acumen, perception, acuteness, insight, penetration, subtlety, keenness, refinement, taste.

discursive adj rambling, digressing, wandering, long-winded, meandering, wide-ranging, circuitous.
E3 terse.

discuss v debate, talk about, confer, argue, consider, deliberate, converse, consult, examine.

discussion n debate, conference, argument, conversation, dialogue, exchange, consultation, discourse, deliberation, consideration, analysis, review, examination, scrutiny, seminar, symposium.

disdain n scorn, contempt, arrogance, haughtiness, derision, sneering, dislike, snobbishness.
F₃ admiration, respect.

disdainful adj scornful, contemptuous, derisive, haughty, aloof, arrogant, supercilious, sneering, superior, proud, insolent.
F₃ respectful.

disease n illness, sickness, ill-health, infirmity, complaint, disorder, ailment, indisposition, malady, condition, affliction, infection, epidemic.
F₃ health.

diseased adj sick, ill, unhealthy, ailing, unsound, contaminated, infected.
F₃ healthy.

disembark v land, arrive, alight, debark.
F₃ embark.

disembodied adj bodiless, incorporeal (fml), ghostly, phantom, spiritual, immaterial, intangible.

disengage v disconnect, detach, loosen, free, extricate, undo, release, liberate, separate, disentangle, untie, withdraw.
F₃ connect, engage.

disentangle v **1** LOOSE, free, extricate, disconnect, untangle, disengage, detach, unravel, separate, unfold. **2** RESOLVE, clarify, simplify.
F₃ 1 entangle.

disfigure v deface, blemish, mutilate, scar, mar, deform, distort, damage, spoil.
F₃ adorn, embellish.

disgrace n shame, ignominy, disrepute, dishonour, disfavour, humiliation, defamation, discredit, scandal, reproach, slur, stain.
F₃ honour, esteem.
v shame, dishonour, abase, defame, humiliate, disfavour, stain, discredit, reproach, slur, sully, taint, stigmatize.
F₃ honour, respect.

disgraceful adj shameful, dishonourable, disreputable, ignominious, scandalous, shocking, unworthy, dreadful, appalling.
F₃ honourable, respectable.

disguise v **1** CONCEAL, cover, camouflage, mask, hide, dress up, cloak, screen, veil, shroud. **2** FALSIFY, deceive, dissemble, misrepresent, fake, fudge.
F₃ reveal, expose.
n concealment, camouflage, cloak, cover, costume, mask, front, façade, masquerade, deception, pretence, travesty, screen, veil.

disgust v offend, displease, nauseate, revolt, sicken, repel, outrage, put off.
F₃ delight, please.
n revulsion, repulsion, repugnance, distaste, aversion, abhorrence, nausea, loathing, detestation, hatred.

disgusted adj repelled, repulsed, revolted, offended, appalled, outraged.
F₃ attracted, delighted.

disgusting adj repugnant, repellent, revolting, offensive, sickening, nauseating, odious, foul, unappetizing, unpleasant, vile, obscene, abominable, detestable, objectionable, nasty.
F₃ delightful, pleasant.

dish n plate, bowl, platter, food, recipe.

dish out distribute, give out, hand out, hand round, dole out, allocate, mete out, inflict.

dish up serve, present, ladle, spoon, dispense, scoop.

dishearten v discourage, dispirit, dampen, cast down, depress, dismay, dash, disappoint, deject, daunt, crush, deter.
F3 encourage, hearten.

dishevelled adj tousled, unkempt, uncombed, untidy, bedraggled, messy, ruffled, slovenly, disordered.
F3 neat, tidy.

dishonest adj untruthful, fraudulent, deceitful, false, lying, deceptive, double-dealing, cheating, crooked (infml), treacherous, unprincipled, swindling, shady (infml), corrupt, disreputable.
F3 honest, trustworthy, scrupulous.

dishonesty n deceit, falsehood, falsity, fraudulence, fraud, criminality, insincerity, treachery, cheating, crookedness (infml), corruption, unscrupulousness, trickery.
F3 honesty, truthfulness.

dishonour v disgrace, shame, humiliate, debase, defile, degrade, defame, discredit, demean, debauch.
F3 honour.
n disgrace, abasement, humiliation, shame, degradation, discredit, disrepute, indignity, ignominy, reproach, slight, slur, scandal, insult, disfavour, outrage, aspersion, abuse, discourtesy.
F3 honour.

disillusioned adj disenchanted, disabused, undeceived, disappointed.

disinclined adj averse, reluctant, resistant, indisposed, loath, opposed, hesitant.
F3 inclined, willing.

disinfect v sterilize, fumigate, sanitize, decontaminate, cleanse, purify, purge, clean.
F3 contaminate, infect.

disinfectant n sterilizer, antiseptic, sanitizer.

disintegrate v break up, decompose, fall apart, crumble, rot, moulder, separate, splinter.

disinterest n disinterestedness, impartiality, neutrality, detachment, unbiasedness, dispassionateness, fairness.

disinterested adj unbiased, neutral, impartial, unprejudiced, dispassionate, detached, uninvolved, open-minded, equitable, even-handed, unselfish.
F3 biased, concerned.

disjointed adj 1 DISCONNECTED, dislocated, divided, separated, disunited, displaced, broken, fitful, split, disarticulated. 2 INCOHERENT, aimless, confused, disordered, loose, unconnected, bitty, rambling, spasmodic.
F3 2 coherent.

dislike n aversion, hatred, repugnance, hostility, distaste, disinclination, disapproval, disapprobation, displeasure, animosity, antagonism, enmity, detestation, disgust, loathing.
F3 liking, predilection.
v hate, detest, object to, loathe, abhor, abominate, disapprove, shun, despise, scorn.
F3 like, favour.

dislocate v disjoint, displace, misplace, disengage, put out (infml), disorder, shift, disconnect, disrupt, disunite.

dislodge v displace, eject, remove, oust, extricate, shift, move, uproot.

disloyal adj treacherous, faithless, false, traitorous, two-faced (infml), backstabbing, unfaithful, apostate, unpatriotic.
E3 loyal, trustworthy.

dismal adj dreary, gloomy, depressing, bleak, cheerless, dull, drab, low-spirited, melancholy, sad, sombre, lugubrious, forlorn, despondent, dark, sorrowful, long-faced (infml), hopeless, discouraging.
E3 cheerful, bright.

dismantle v demolish, take apart, disassemble, strip.
E3 assemble, put together.

dismay v alarm, daunt, frighten, unnerve, unsettle, scare, put off, dispirit, distress, disconcert, dishearten, discourage, disillusion, depress, horrify, disappoint.
E3 encourage, hearten.
n consternation, alarm, distress, apprehension, agitation, dread, fear, trepidation, fright, horror, terror, discouragement, disappointment.
E3 boldness, encouragement.

dismember v disjoint, amputate, dissect, dislocate, divide, mutilate, sever.
E3 assemble, join.

dismiss v 1 the class was dismissed: discharge, free, let go, release, send away, remove, drop, discord, banish. 2 dismiss employees: sack (infml), make redundant, lay off, fire (infml), relegate. 3 dismiss it from your mind: discount, disregard, reject, repudiate, set aside, shelve, spurn.
E3 1 retain. 2 appoint. 3 accept.

disobey v contravene, infringe, violate, transgress, flout, disregard, defy, ignore, resist, rebel.
E3 obey.

disorder n 1 CONFUSION, chaos, muddle, disarray, mess, untidiness, shambles (infml), clutter, disorganization, jumble. 2 DISTURBANCE, tumult, riot, confusion, commotion, uproar, fracas, brawl, fight, clamour, quarrel. 3 ILLNESS, complaint, disease, sickness, disability, ailment, malady, affliction.
E3 1 neatness, order. 2 law and order, peace.
v disturb, mess up, disarrange, mix up, muddle, upset, disorganize, confuse, confound, clutter, jumble, discompose, scatter, unsettle.
E3 arrange, organize.

disorderly adj 1 DISORGANIZED, confused, chaotic, irregular, messy, untidy. 2 UNRULY, undisciplined, unmanageable, obstreperous, rowdy, turbulent, rebellious, lawless.
E3 1 neat, tidy. 2 well-behaved.

disorganize v disorder, disrupt, disturb, disarrange, muddle, upset, confuse, discompose, jumble, play havoc with, unsettle, break up, destroy.
E3 organize.

disown v repudiate, renounce, disclaim, deny, cast off, disallow, reject, abandon.
E3 accept, acknowledge.

disparaging adj derisive, derogatory, mocking, scornful, critical, insulting, snide (infml).
E3 flattering, praising.

dispassionate adj detached, objective, impartial, neutral, disinterested, impersonal, fair,

cool, calm, composed.
F3 biased, emotional.

dispatch, despatch v **1** SEND, express, transmit, forward, consign, expedite, accelerate. **2** DISPOSE OF, finish, perform, discharge, conclude. **3** KILL, murder, execute.
F3 1 receive.
n **1** COMMUNICATION, message, report, bulletin, communiqué, news, letter, account. **2** PROMPTNESS, speed, alacrity, expedition, celerity, haste, rapidity, swiftness.
F3 2 slowness.

dispense v **1** DISTRIBUTE, give out, apportion, allot, allocate, assign, share, mete out. **2** ADMINISTER, apply, implement, enforce, discharge, execute, operate.
dispense with dispose of, get rid of, abolish, discard, omit, disregard, cancel, forgo, ignore, waive.

disperse v scatter, dispel, spread, distribute, diffuse, dissolve, break up, dismiss, separate.
F3 gather.

displace v **1** DISLODGE, move, shift, misplace, disturb, dislocate. **2** DEPOSE, oust, remove, replace, dismiss, discharge, supplant, eject, evict, succeed, supersede.

display v **1** SHOW, present, demonstrate, exhibit. **2** BETRAY, disclose, reveal, show, expose. **3** SHOW OFF, flourish, parade, flaunt.
F3 1 conceal. **2** disguise.
n show, exhibition, demonstration, presentation, parade, spectacle, revelation.

displease v offend, annoy, irritate, anger, upset, put out (infml), infuriate, exasperate, incense.
F3 please.

displeasure n offence, annoyance, disapproval, irritation, resentment, disfavour, anger, indignation, wrath.
F3 pleasure.

disposal n **1** ARRANGEMENT, grouping, order. **2** CONTROL, direction, command. **3** REMOVAL, riddance, discarding, jettisoning.

disposed adj liable, inclined, predisposed, prone, likely, apt, minded, subject, ready, willing.
F3 disinclined.

dispose of 1 DEAL WITH, decide, settle. **2** GET RID OF, discard, scrap, destroy, dump (infml), ditch (infml), jettison.
F3 2 keep.

disposition n character, nature, temperament, inclination, make-up, bent, leaning, predisposition, constitution, habit, spirit, tendency, proneness.

disproportionate adj unequal, uneven, incommensurate, excessive, unreasonable.
F3 balanced.

disprove v refute, rebut, confute, discredit, invalidate, contradict, expose.
F3 confirm, prove.

dispute v argue, debate, question, contend, challenge, discuss, doubt, contest, contradict, deny, quarrel, clash, wrangle, squabble.
F3 agree.
n argument, debate, disagreement, controversy, conflict, contention, quarrel, wrangle, feud, strife, squabble.
F3 agreement, settlement.

disqualify v **1** INCAPACITATE, disable, invalidate. **2** DEBAR, preclude, rule out, disentitle, eliminate, prohibit.
F3 2 qualify, accept.

disquiet n anxiety, worry, concern, nervousness, uneasiness, restlessness, alarm, distress, fretfulness, fear, disturbance, trouble. **Ea** calm, reassurance.

disregard v **1** IGNORE, overlook, discount, neglect, pass over, disobey, make light of, turn a blind eye to (*infml*), brush aside. **2** SLIGHT, snub, despise, disdain, disparage. **Ea 1** heed, pay attention to. **2** respect. n neglect, negligence, inattention, oversight, indifference, disrespect, contempt, disdain, brush-off (*infml*). **Ea** attention, heed.

disrepair n dilapidation, deterioration, decay, collapse, ruin, shabbiness. **Ea** good repair.

disreputable adj **1** DISGRACEFUL, discreditable, dishonourable, unrespectable, notorious, scandalous, shameful, shady, louche, base, contemptible, low, mean, shocking. **2** SCRUFFY, shabby, seedy, unkempt. **Ea 1** respectable. **2** smart.

disrespectful adj rude, discourteous, impertinent, impolite, impudent, insolent, uncivil, unmannerly, cheeky, insulting, irreverent, contemptuous. **Ea** polite, respectful.

disrupt v disturb, disorganize, confuse, interrupt, break up, unsettle, intrude, upset.

dissatisfaction n discontent, displeasure, dislike, discomfort, disappointment, frustration, annoyance, irritation, exasperation, regret, resentment. **Ea** satisfaction.

dissect v **1** DISMEMBER, anatomize. **2** ANALYSE, investigate, scrutinize, examine, inspect, pore over.

dissension n disagreement, discord, dissent, dispute, contention, conflict, strife, friction, quarrel. **Ea** agreement.

dissent v disagree, differ, protest, object, refuse, quibble. **Ea** assent. n disagreement, difference, dissension, discord, resistance, opposition, objection. **Ea** agreement, conformity.

disservice n disfavour, injury, wrong, bad turn, harm, unkindness, injustice. **Ea** favour.

dissident adj disagreeing, differing, dissenting, discordant, nonconformist, heterodox (*fml*). **Ea** acquiescent, orthodox. n dissenter, protester, nonconformist, rebel, agitator, revolutionary, schismatic, recusant. **Ea** assenter.

dissimilar adj unlike, different, divergent, disparate, unrelated, incompatible, mismatched, diverse, various, heterogeneous. **Ea** similar, like.

dissipate v **1** he dissipated his inheritance: spend, waste, squander, expend, consume, deplete, fritter away, burn up. **2** the clouds dissipated: disperse, vanish, disappear, dispel, diffuse, evaporate, dissolve. **Ea 1** accumulate. **2** appear.

dissociate v separate, detach, break off, disunite, disengage, disconnect, cut off, disband, divorce, disrupt, isolate, segregate. **Ea** associate, join.

dissolute adj dissipated, debauched, degenerate, depraved, wanton, abandoned, corrupt, immoral,

licentious, lewd, wild.
F3 restrained, virtuous.

dissolution n 1 DISINTEGRATION,
decomposition, separation,
resolution, division. 2 ENDING,
termination, conclusion, finish,
discontinuation, divorce, dismissal,
dispersal, destruction, overthrow.
3 EVAPORATION, disappearance.

dissolve v 1 EVAPORATE,
disintegrate, liquefy, melt.
2 DECOMPOSE, disintegrate, disperse,
break up, disappear, crumble. 3 END,
terminate, separate, sever, divorce.

dissuade v deter, discourage, put off,
disincline.
F3 persuade.

distance n 1 SPACE, interval, gap,
extent, range, reach, length, width.
2 ALOOFNESS, reserve, coolness,
coldness, remoteness.
F3 1 closeness. 2 approachability.

distant adj 1 FAR, faraway, far-flung,
out-of-the-way, remote, outlying,
abroad, dispersed. 2 ALOOF, cool,
reserved, standoffish (infml), formal,
cold, restrained, stiff.
F3 1 close. 2 approachable.

distaste n dislike, aversion,
repugnance, disgust, revulsion,
loathing, abhorrence.
F3 liking.

distasteful adj disagreeable,
offensive, unpleasant, objectionable,
repulsive, obnoxious, repugnant,
unsavoury, loathsome, abhorrent.
F3 pleasing.

distinct adj 1 SEPARATE, different,
detached, individual, dissimilar.
2 CLEAR, plain, evident, obvious,
apparent, marked, definite,
noticeable, recognizable.
F3 2 indistinct, vague.

distinction n 1 DIFFERENTIATION,
discrimination, discernment,
separation, difference, dissimilarity,
contrast. 2 CHARACTERISTIC,
peculiarity, individuality, feature,
quality, mark. 3 RENOWN, fame,
celebrity, prominence, eminence,
importance, reputation, greatness,
honour, prestige, repute, superiority,
worth, merit, excellence, quality.
F3 3 unimportance, obscurity.

distinctive adj characteristic,
distinguishing, individual, peculiar,
different, unique, singular, special,
original, extraordinary, idiosyncratic.
F3 ordinary, common.

distinguish v 1 DIFFERENTIATE, tell
apart, discriminate, determine,
categorize, characterize, classify.
2 DISCERN, perceive, identify, ascertain,
make out, recognize, see, discriminate.

distinguished adj famous, eminent,
celebrated, well-known, acclaimed,
illustrious, notable, noted, renowned,
famed, honoured, outstanding,
striking, marked, extraordinary,
conspicuous.
F3 insignificant, obscure,
unimpressive.

distort v 1 DEFORM, contort, bend,
misshape, disfigure, twist, warp.
2 FALSIFY, misrepresent, pervert,
slant, colour, garble.

distract v 1 DIVERT, sidetrack, deflect.
2 CONFUSE, disconcert, bewilder,
confound, disturb, perplex, puzzle.
3 AMUSE, occupy, divert, engross.

distraught adj agitated, anxious,
overwrought, upset, distressed,
distracted, beside oneself, worked up,
frantic, hysterical, raving, mad, wild,
crazy.
F3 calm, untroubled.

distress n **1** ANGUISH, grief, misery, sorrow, heartache, affliction, suffering, torment, wretchedness, sadness, worry, anxiety, desolation, pain, agony. **2** ADVERSITY, hardship, poverty, need, privation, destitution, misfortune, trouble, difficulties, trial.
F3 **1** content. **2** comfort, ease.
v upset, afflict, grieve, disturb, trouble, sadden, worry, torment, harass, harrow, pain, agonize, bother.
F3 comfort.

distribute v **1** DISPENSE, allocate, dole out, dish out, share, deal, divide, apportion. **2** DELIVER, hand out, spread, issue, circulate, diffuse, disperse, scatter.
F3 **2** collect.

distribution n **1** ALLOCATION, apportionment, division, sharing. **2** CIRCULATION, spreading, scattering, delivery, dissemination, supply, dealing, handling. **3** ARRANGEMENT, grouping, classification, organization.
F3 **2** collection.

district n region, area, quarter, neighbourhood, locality, sector, precinct, parish, locale, community, vicinity, ward.

distrust v mistrust, doubt, disbelieve, suspect, question.
F3 trust.
n mistrust, doubt, disbelief, suspicion, misgiving, wariness, scepticism, question, qualm.
F3 trust.

disturb v **1** DISRUPT, interrupt, distract. **2** AGITATE, unsettle, upset, distress, worry, fluster, annoy, bother. **3** DISARRANGE, disorder, confuse, upset.
F3 **2** reassure. **3** order.

disturbance n **1** DISRUPTION, agitation, interruption, intrusion, upheaval, upset, confusion, annoyance, bother, trouble, hindrance. **2** DISORDER, uproar, commotion, tumult, turmoil, fracas, fray, brawl, riot.
F3 **1** peace. **2** order.

disuse n neglect, desuetude (fml), abandonment, discontinuance, decay.
F3 use.

ditch n trench, dyke, channel, gully, furrow, moat, drain, level, watercourse.

dither v hesitate, shilly-shally (infml), waver, vacillate.

dive v plunge, plummet, dip, submerge, jump, leap, nose-dive, fall, drop, swoop, descend, pitch.
n **1** PLUNGE, lunge, header, jump, leap, nose-dive, swoop, dash, spring. **2** (infml) BAR, club, saloon.

diverge v **1** DIVIDE, branch, fork, separate, spread, split. **2** DEVIATE, digress, stray, wander. **3** DIFFER, vary, disagree, dissent, conflict.
F3 **1** converge. **3** agree.

diverse adj various, varied, varying, sundry, different, differing, assorted, dissimilar, miscellaneous, discrete, separate, several, distinct.
F3 similar, identical.

diversify v vary, change, expand, branch out, spread out, alter, mix, assort.

diversion n **1** DEVIATION, detour. **2** AMUSEMENT, entertainment, distraction, pastime, recreation, relaxation, play, game. **3** ALTERATION, change.

diversity n variety, dissimilarity, difference, variance, assortment, range, medley.
F3 similarity, likeness.

divert v **1** DEFLECT, redirect, reroute, side-track, avert, distract, switch. **2** AMUSE, entertain, occupy, distract, interest.

divide v **1** SPLIT, separate, part, cut, break up, detach, bisect, disconnect. **2** DISTRIBUTE, share, allocate, deal out, allot, apportion. **3** DISUNITE, separate, estrange, alienate. **4** CLASSIFY, group, sort, grade, segregate.
F3 1 join. **2** collect. **3** unite.

divine adj **1** GODLIKE, superhuman, supernatural, celestial, heavenly, angelic, spiritual. **2** HOLY, sacred, sanctified, consecrated, transcendent, exalted, glorious, religious, supreme.
F3 1 human. **2** mundane.

divinity n god, goddess, deity, godliness, holiness, sanctity, godhead, spirit.

division n **1** SEPARATION, detaching, parting, cutting, disunion. **2** BREACH, rupture, split, schism, disunion, estrangement, disagreement, feud. **3** DISTRIBUTION, sharing, allotment, apportionment. **4** SECTION, sector, segment, part, department, category, class, compartment, branch.
F3 1 union. **2** unity. **3** collection. **4** whole.

divorce n dissolution, annulment, break-up, split-up, rupture, separation, breach, disunion.
v separate, part, annul, split up, sever, dissolve, divide, dissociate.
F3 marry, unite.

divulge v disclose, reveal, communicate, tell, leak (infml), impart, confess, betray, uncover, let slip, expose, publish, proclaim.

dizzy adj **1** GIDDY, faint, light-headed, woozy (infml), shaky, reeling.

2 CONFUSED, bewildered, dazed, muddled.

do v **1** PERFORM, carry out, execute, accomplish, achieve, fulfil, implement, complete, undertake, work, put on, present, conclude, end, finish. **2** BEHAVE, act, conduct oneself. **3** FIX, prepare, organize, arrange, deal with, look after, manage, produce, make, create, cause, proceed. **4** SUFFICE, satisfy, serve.
n (infml) function, affair, event, gathering, party, occasion.

do away with get rid of, dispose of, exterminate, eliminate, abolish, discontinue, remove, destroy, discard, kill, murder.

do up 1 FASTEN, tie, lace, pack. **2** RENOVATE, restore, decorate, redecorate, modernize, repair.

do without dispense with, abstain from, forgo, give up, relinquish.

docile adj tractable, co-operative, manageable, submissive, obedient, amenable, controlled, obliging.
F3 truculent, unco-operative.

dock[1] n harbour, wharf, quay, boat-yard, pier, waterfront, marina.
v anchor, moor, drop anchor, land, berth, put in, tie up.

dock[2] v crop, clip, cut, shorten, curtail, deduct, reduce, lessen, withhold, decrease, subtract, diminish.

doctor n physician, medic (infml), doc (infml), quack (infml), clinician.

Types of medical doctor include: general practitioner, GP, family doctor, family practitioner, locum, hospital doctor, houseman, intern, resident, registrar, consultant, medical officer (MO), dentist, veterinary surgeon, vet (infml).

v **1** ALTER, tamper with, falsify, misrepresent, pervert, adulterate, change, disguise, dilute. **2** REPAIR, fix, patch up.

doctrine *n* dogma, creed, belief, tenet, principle, teaching, precept, conviction, opinion, canon.

document *n* paper, certificate, deed, record, report, form, instrument (*fml*). *v* **1** RECORD, report, chronicle, list, detail, cite. **2** SUPPORT, prove, corroborate, verify.

dodge *v* avoid, elude, evade, swerve, side-step, shirk, shift.
n trick, ruse, ploy, wile, scheme, stratagem, machination, manoeuvre.

dog *n* hound, cur, mongrel, canine, puppy, pup, bitch, mutt (*infml*), pooch (*infml*).

Breeds of dog include:
Afghan hound, Alsatian, basset-hound, beagle, Border collie, borzoi, bulldog, bull-mastiff, bull-terrier, cairn terrier, chihuahua, chow, cocker spaniel, collie, corgi, dachshund, Dalmatian, Doberman pinscher, fox-hound, fox-terrier, German shepherd, golden retriever, Great Dane, greyhound, husky, Irish wolfhound, Jack Russell, King Charles spaniel, Labrador, lhasa apso, lurcher, Maltese, Old English sheepdog, Pekingese, pit bull terrier, pointer, poodle, pug, Rottweiler, saluki, sausage-dog (*infml*), schnauzer, Scottie (*infml*), Scottish terrier, Sealyham, setter, sheltie, shih tzu, springer spaniel, St Bernard, terrier, whippet, West Highland terrier, Westie (*infml*), wolf-hound, Yorkshire terrier.

v pursue, follow, trail, track, tail, hound, shadow, plague, harry, haunt, trouble, worry.

dogged *adj* determined, resolute, persistent, persevering, intent, tenacious, firm, steadfast, staunch, single-minded, indefatigable, steady, unshakable, stubborn, obstinate, relentless, unyielding.
F∃ irresolute, apathetic.

dogma *n* doctrine, creed, belief, precept, principle, article (of faith), credo, tenet, conviction, teaching, opinion.

dogmatic *adj* opinionated, assertive, authoritative, positive, doctrinaire, dictatorial, doctrinal, categorical, emphatic, overbearing, arbitrary.

dole out distribute, allocate, hand out, dish out, apportion, allot, mete out, share, divide, deal, issue, ration, dispense, administer, assign.

domain *n* **1** DOMINION, kingdom, realm, territory, region, empire, lands, province. **2** FIELD, area, speciality, concern, department, sphere, discipline, jurisdiction.

domestic *adj* **1** HOME, family, household, home-loving, stay-at-home, homely, house-trained, tame, pet, private. **2** INTERNAL, indigenous, native.
n servant, maid, charwoman, char, daily help, daily, au pair.

domesticate *v* tame, house-train, break, train, accustom, familiarize.

dominant *adj* **1** AUTHORITATIVE, controlling, governing, ruling, powerful, assertive, influential. **2** PRINCIPAL, main, outstanding, chief, important, predominant, primary, prominent, leading, pre-eminent, prevailing, prevalent, commanding.
F∃ 1 submissive. **2** subordinate.

dominate v **1** CONTROL, domineer, govern, rule, direct, monopolize, master, lead, overrule, prevail, overbear, tyrannize. **2** OVERSHADOW, eclipse, dwarf.

domineering adj overbearing, authoritarian, imperious, autocratic, bossy (infml), dictatorial, despotic, masterful, high-handed, oppressive, tyrannical, arrogant.
F3 meek, servile.

dominion n **1** POWER, authority, domination, command, control, rule, sway, jurisdiction, government, lordship, mastery, supremacy, sovereignty. **2** DOMAIN, country, territory, province, colony, realm, kingdom, empire.

donate v give, contribute, present, bequeath, cough up (infml), fork out (infml), bestow (fml), confer (fml), subscribe.
F3 receive.

donation n gift, present, offering, grant, gratuity, largess(e), contribution, presentation, subscription, alms, benefaction (fml), bequest.

done adj **1** FINISHED, over, accomplished, completed, ended, concluded, settled, realized, executed. **2** CONVENTIONAL, acceptable, proper. **3** COOKED, ready.

donor n giver, donator, benefactor, contributor, philanthropist, provider, fairy godmother (infml).
F3 beneficiary.

doom n **1** FATE, fortune, destiny, portion, lot. **2** DESTRUCTION, catastrophe, downfall, ruin, death, death-knell. **3** CONDEMNATION, judgement, sentence, verdict.
v condemn, damn, consign, judge, sentence, destine.

doomed adj condemned, damned, fated, ill-fated, ill-omened, cursed, destined, hopeless, luckless, ill-starred.

door n opening, entrance, entry, exit, doorway, portal, hatch.

dope n **1** NARCOTIC, drugs, marijuana, cannabis, opiate, hallucinogen. **2** FOOL, dolt, idiot, half-wit (infml), dimwit (infml), dunce, simpleton, clot (infml), blockhead. **3** INFORMATION, facts, low-down (infml), details.
v drug, sedate, anaesthetize, stupefy, medicate, narcotize, inject, doctor.

dormant adj **1** INACTIVE, asleep, sleeping, inert, resting, slumbering, sluggish, torpid, hibernating, fallow, comatose. **2** LATENT, unrealized, potential, undeveloped, undisclosed.
F3 1 active, awake. **2** realized, developed.

dose n measure, dosage, amount, portion, quantity, draught, potion, prescription, shot.
v medicate, administer, prescribe, dispense, treat.

dot n point, spot, speck, mark, fleck, circle, pin-point, atom, decimal point, full stop, iota, jot.
v spot, sprinkle, stud, dab, punctuate.

dote on adore, idolize, treasure, admire, indulge.

double adj dual, twofold, twice, duplicate, twin, paired, doubled, coupled.
F3 single, half.
v duplicate, enlarge, increase, repeat, multiply, fold, magnify.
n twin, duplicate, copy, clone, replica, doppelgänger, lookalike, spitting image (infml), ringer (infml), image, counterpart, impersonator.

at the double immediately, at once, quickly, without delay.

double-cross v cheat, swindle, defraud, trick, con (infml), hoodwink, betray, two-time (infml), mislead.

doubt v 1 DISTRUST, mistrust, query, question, suspect, fear. 2 BE UNCERTAIN, be dubious, hesitate, vacillate, waver.
F3 believe, trust.
n 1 DISTRUST, suspicion, mistrust, scepticism, reservation, misgiving, incredulity, apprehension, hesitation. 2 UNCERTAINTY, difficulty, confusion, ambiguity, problem, indecision, perplexity, dilemma, quandary.
F3 1 trust, faith. 2 certainty, belief.

doubtful adj 1 doubtful about his future: uncertain, unsure, undecided, suspicious, irresolute, wavering, hesitant, vacillating, tentative, sceptical. 2 writing of doubtful origin: dubious, questionable, unclear, ambiguous, vague, obscure, debatable.
F3 1 certain, decided. 2 definite, settled.

doubtless adv 1 CERTAINLY, without doubt, undoubtedly, unquestionably, indisputably, no doubt, clearly, surely, of course, truly, precisely. 2 PROBABLY, presumably, most likely, seemingly, supposedly.

dour adj 1 GLOOMY, dismal, forbidding, grim, morose, unfriendly, dreary, austere, sour, sullen. 2 HARD, inflexible, unyielding, rigid, severe, rigorous, strict, obstinate.
F3 1 cheerful, bright. 2 easy-going.

douse, dowse v 1 SOAK, saturate, steep, submerge, immerse, dip, duck, drench, dunk, plunge. 2 EXTINGUISH, put out, blow out, smother, snuff.

dowdy adj unfashionable, ill-dressed, frumpish, drab, shabby, tatty (infml), frowsy, tacky (infml), dingy, old-fashioned, slovenly.
F3 fashionable, smart.

down v 1 KNOCK DOWN, fell, floor, prostrate, throw, topple. 2 SWALLOW, drink, gulp, swig (infml), knock back (infml).

down and out destitute, impoverished, penniless, derelict, ruined.

downcast adj dejected, depressed, despondent, sad, unhappy, miserable, down, low, disheartened, dispirited, blue (infml), fed up (infml), discouraged, disappointed, crestfallen, dismayed.
F3 cheerful, happy, elated.

downfall n fall, ruin, failure, collapse, destruction, disgrace, debacle, undoing, overthrow.

downgrade v 1 DEGRADE, demote, lower, humble. 2 DISPARAGE, denigrate, belittle, run down, decry.
F3 1 upgrade, improve. 2 praise.

downhearted adj depressed, dejected, despondent, sad, downcast, discouraged, disheartened, low-spirited, unhappy, gloomy, glum, dismayed.
F3 cheerful, enthusiastic.

downpour n cloudburst, deluge, rainstorm, flood, inundation, torrent.

downright adj, adv absolute(ly), outright, plain(ly), utter(ly), clear(ly), complete(ly), out-and-out, frank(ly), explicit(ly).

down-trodden adj oppressed, subjugated, subservient, exploited, trampled on, abused, tyrannized, victimized, helpless.

downward adj descending, declining, downhill, sliding, slipping.
F₃ upward.

dowse see **douse**.

doze v sleep, nod off, drop off, snooze (infml), kip (infml), zizz (sl).
n nap, catnap, siesta, snooze (infml), forty winks (infml), kip (infml), shut-eye (infml), zizz (sl).

drab adj dull, dingy, dreary, dismal, gloomy, flat, grey, lacklustre, cheerless, sombre, shabby.
F₃ bright, cheerful.

draft¹ v draw (up), outline, sketch, plan, design, formulate, compose.
n outline, sketch, plan, delineation, abstract, rough, blueprint, protocol (fml).

draft² n bill of exchange, cheque, money order, letter of credit, postal order.

drag v 1 DRAW, pull, haul, lug, tug, trail, tow. 2 GO SLOWLY, creep, crawl, lag.
n (infml) bore, annoyance, nuisance, pain (infml), bother.

drain v 1 EMPTY, remove, evacuate, draw off, strain, dry, milk, bleed.
2 DISCHARGE, trickle, flow out, leak, ooze. 3 EXHAUST, consume, sap, use up, deplete, drink up, swallow.
F₃ 1 fill.
n 1 CHANNEL, conduit, culvert, duct, outlet, trench, ditch, pipe, sewer.
2 DEPLETION, exhaustion, sap, strain.

drama n 1 PLAY, acting, theatre, show, spectacle, stagecraft, scene, melodrama. 2 EXCITEMENT, crisis, turmoil.

Forms of drama include:
comedy, black comedy, comedy of manners, commedia dell'arte, duo-logue, farce, fringe theatre, Grand Guignol, kabuki, kitchen-sink, legit-imate drama, masque, melodrama, mime, miracle play, monologue, morality play, mummers' play, mys-tery play, Noh, pantomime, play, theatre-in-the-round, theatre of the absurd, theatre of cruelty, tragedy.

dramatic adj 1 EXCITING, striking, stirring, thrilling, marked, significant, expressive, impressive. 2 HISTRIONIC, exaggerated, melodramatic, flamboyant.

dramatize v 1 STAGE, put on, adapt.
2 ACT, play-act, exaggerate, overdo, overstate.

drape v cover, wrap, hang, fold, drop, suspend.

drastic adj extreme, radical, strong, forceful, severe, harsh, far-reaching, desperate, dire.
F₃ moderate, cautious.

draught n PUFF, current, influx, flow. 2 DRINK, potion, quantity.
3 PULLING, traction.

draw v 1 ATTRACT, allure, entice, bring in, influence, persuade, elicit.
2 PULL, drag, haul, tow, tug.
3 DELINEATE, map out, sketch, portray, trace, pencil, depict, design.
4 TIE, be equal, be even.
F₃ 1 repel. 2 push.
n 1 ATTRACTION, enticement, lure, appeal, bait, interest. 2 TIE, stalemate, dead-heat.

draw out protract, extend, prolong, drag out, spin out, elongate, stretch, lengthen, string out.
F₃ shorten.

draw up 1 DRAFT, compose, formulate, prepare, frame, write out. 2 PULL UP, stop, halt, run in.

drawback n disadvantage, snag, hitch, obstacle, impediment, hindrance, difficulty, flaw, fault, fly in the ointment (*infml*), catch, stumbling block, nuisance, trouble, defect, handicap, deficiency, imperfection. **F3** advantage, benefit.

drawing *n* sketch, picture, outline, representation, delineation, portrayal, illustration, cartoon, graphic, portrait.

dread *v* fear, shrink from, quail, cringe at, flinch, shy, shudder, tremble.
n fear, apprehension, misgiving, trepidation, dismay, alarm, horror, terror, fright, disquiet, worry, qualm. **F3** confidence, security.

dreadful *adj* awful, terrible, frightful, horrible, appalling, dire, shocking, ghastly, horrendous, tragic, grievous, hideous, tremendous. **F3** wonderful, comforting.

dream *n* **1** VISION, illusion, reverie, trance, fantasy, daydream, nightmare, hallucination, delusion, imagination. **2** ASPIRATION, wish, hope, ambition, desire, pipe-dream, ideal, goal, design, speculation.
v imagine, envisage, fancy, fantasize, daydream, hallucinate, conceive, visualize, conjure up, muse.
dream up invent, devise, conceive, think up, imagine, concoct, hatch, create, spin, contrive.

dreamer *n* idealist, visionary, fantasizer, romancer, daydreamer, star-gazer, theorizer. **F3** realist, pragmatist.

dreamy *adj* **1** FANTASTIC, unreal, imaginary, shadowy, vague, misty. **2** IMPRACTICAL, fanciful, daydreaming, romantic, visionary, faraway, absent, musing, pensive. **F3 1** real. **2** practical, down-to-earth.

dreary *adj* **1** *a dreary job*: boring, tedious, uneventful, dull, humdrum, routine, monotonous, wearisome, commonplace, colourless, lifeless. **2** *a dreary landscape*: gloomy, depressing, drab, dismal, bleak, sombre, sad, mournful. **F3 1** interesting. **2** cheerful.

dregs *n* **1** SEDIMENT, deposit, residue, lees, grounds, scum, dross, trash, waste. **2** OUTCASTS, rabble, riff-raff, scum, down-and-outs.

drench *v* soak, saturate, steep, wet, douse, souse, immerse, inundate, duck, flood, imbue, drown.

dress *n* **1** FROCK, gown, robe. **2** CLOTHES, clothing, garment(s), outfit, costume, garb, get-up (*infml*), gear (*infml*), togs (*infml*).

> Types of dress include:
> evening dress, cocktail dress, pinafore dress, wedding dress, shirt-waister, caftan, kimono, sari.

v **1** CLOTHE, put on, garb, rig, robe, wear, don, decorate, deck, garnish, trim, adorn, fit, drape. **2** ARRANGE, adjust, dispose, prepare, groom, straighten. **3** BANDAGE, tend, treat. **F3 1** strip, undress.
dress up beautify, adorn, embellish, improve, deck, doll up, tart up (*infml*), sex up (*sl*), gild, disguise.

dribble *v* **1** TRICKLE, drip, leak, run, seep, drop, ooze. **2** DROOL, slaver, slobber, drivel.

drift *v* **1** WANDER, waft, stray, float, freewheel, coast. **2** GATHER, accumulate, pile up, drive.
n **1** ACCUMULATION, mound, pile, bank, mass, heap. **2** TREND, tendency, course, direction, flow, movement, current, rush, sweep. **3** MEANING, intention, implication, gist, tenor,

thrust, significance, aim, design, scope.

drill v **1** TEACH, train, instruct, coach, practise, school, rehearse, exercise, discipline. **2** BORE, pierce, penetrate, puncture, perforate.
n **1** INSTRUCTION, training, practice, coaching, exercise, repetition, tuition, preparation, discipline. **2** BORER, awl, bit, gimlet.

drink v **1** IMBIBE, swallow, sip, drain, down, gulp, swig (infml), knock back (infml), sup, quaff, absorb, guzzle, partake of (fml), swill. **2** GET DRUNK, booze (infml), tipple (infml), indulge, carouse, revel, tank up (infml).
n **1** BEVERAGE, liquid refreshment, draught, sip, swallow, swig (infml), gulp. **2** ALCOHOL, spirits, booze (infml), liquor, tipple (infml), tot, the bottle (infml), stiffener (infml).

drip v drop, dribble, trickle, plop, drizzle, splash, sprinkle, weep.
n **1** DROP, trickle, dribble, leak, bead, tear. **2** (infml) WEAKLING, wimp (infml), softy (infml), bore, wet (infml), ninny (infml).

drive v **1** DIRECT, control, manage, operate, run, handle, motivate. **2** FORCE, compel, impel, coerce, constrain, press, push, urge, dragoon, goad, guide, oblige. **3** STEER, motor, propel, ride, travel.
n **1** ENERGY, enterprise, ambition, initiative, get-up-and-go (infml), vigour, motivation, determination. **2** CAMPAIGN, crusade, appeal, effort, action. **3** EXCURSION, outing, journey, ride, spin, trip, jaunt. **4** URGE, instinct, impulse, need, desire.

drive at imply, allude to, intimate, mean, suggest, hint, get at, intend, refer to, signify, insinuate, indicate.

driving adj compelling, forceful, vigorous, dynamic, energetic, forthright, heavy, violent, sweeping.

drizzle n mist, mizzle, rain, spray, shower.
v spit, spray, sprinkle, rain, spot, shower.

droop v **1** HANG (DOWN), dangle, sag, bend. **2** LANGUISH, decline, flag, falter, slump, lose heart, wilt, wither, drop, faint, fall down, fade, slouch. **F3 1** straighten. **2** flourish, rise.

drop n **1** DROPLET, bead, tear, drip, bubble, globule, trickle. **2** DASH, pinch, spot, sip, trace, dab. **3** FALL, decline, falling-off, lowering, downturn, decrease, reduction, slump, plunge, deterioration. **4** DESCENT, precipice, slope, chasm, abyss.
v **1** FALL, sink, decline, plunge, plummet, tumble, dive, descend, lower, droop, depress, diminish.
2 ABANDON, forsake, desert, give up, relinquish, reject, jilt, leave, renounce, throw over, repudiate, cease, discontinue, quit.
F3 rise.

drop off 1 NOD OFF, doze, snooze (infml), have forty winks (infml).
2 DECLINE, fall off, decrease, dwindle, lessen, diminish, slacken.
3 DELIVER, set down, leave.
F3 1 wake up. **2** increase. **3** pick up.

drop out back out, abandon, cry off, withdraw, forsake, leave, quit.

drought n dryness, aridity, parchedness, dehydration, desiccation, shortage, want.

drove n herd, horde, gathering, crowd, multitude, swarm, throng, flock, company, mob, press.

drown v **1** SUBMERGE, immerse, inundate, go under, flood, sink, deluge, engulf, drench. **2** OVERWHELM, overpower, overcome, swamp, wipe out, extinguish.

drowsy *adj* sleepy, tired, lethargic, nodding, dreamy, dozy, somnolent (*fml*).
F3 alert, awake.

drudge *n* toiler, menial, dogsbody (*infml*), hack, servant, slave, factotum, worker, skivvy (*infml*), galley-slave, lackey.
v plod, toil, work, slave, plug away (*infml*), grind (*infml*), labour, beaver (*infml*).
F3 idle, laze.

drudgery *n* labour, donkey-work (*infml*), hack-work, slog (*infml*), grind (*infml*), slavery, sweat, sweated labour, toil, skivvying, chore.

drug *n* medication, medicine, remedy, potion.

Types of drug include:
anaesthetic, analgesic, antibiotic, antidepressant, antihistamine, barbiturate, hallucinogenic, narcotic, opiate, sedative, steroid, stimulant, tranquillizer; aspirin, codeine, paracetamol, morphine, penicillin, diazepam, temazepam, Valium®, Prozac®, Viagra®, cortisone, insulin, digitalis, laudanum, quinine, cannabis, marijuana, LSD, acid, ecstasy, E (*sl*), heroin, smack (*sl*), opium, cocaine, crack, dope (*infml*).
see also **medicine**.

v medicate, sedate, tranquillize, dope (*infml*), anaesthetize, dose, knock out (*infml*), stupefy, deaden, numb.

drum *v* beat, pulsate, tap, throb, thrum, tattoo, reverberate, rap.
drum up obtain, round up, collect, gather, solicit, canvass, petition, attract.

drunk *adj* inebriated, intoxicated, under the influence, drunken, stoned (*sl*), legless (*sl*), paralytic (*infml*), sloshed (*infml*), merry (*infml*), tight (*infml*), tipsy (*infml*), tanked up (*infml*), tiddly (*infml*), plastered (*infml*), loaded (*infml*), lit up (*infml*), sozzled (*infml*), well-oiled (*infml*), canned (*sl*), blotto (*sl*).
F3 sober, temperate, abstinent, teetotal.

drunkard *n* drunk, inebriate, alcoholic, dipsomaniac, boozer (*infml*), wino (*infml*), tippler (*infml*), soak (*infml*), lush (*infml*), sot (*infml*).

dry *adj* **1** ARID, parched, thirsty, dehydrated, desiccated, barren. **2** BORING, dull, dreary, tedious, monotonous. **3** *dry humour:* ironic, cynical, droll, deadpan, sarcastic, cutting.
F3 1 wet. **2** interesting.
v dehydrate, parch, desiccate, drain, shrivel, wither.
F3 soak.

dual *adj* double, twofold, duplicate, duplex, binary, combined, paired, twin, matched.

dubious *adj* **1** DOUBTFUL, uncertain, undecided, unsure, wavering, unsettled, suspicious, sceptical, hesitant. **2** QUESTIONABLE, debatable, unreliable, ambiguous, suspect, obscure, fishy (*infml*), shady (*infml*).
F3 1 certain. **2** trustworthy.

duck *v* **1** CROUCH, stoop, bob, bend. **2** AVOID, dodge, evade, shirk, sidestep. **3** DIP, immerse, plunge, dunk, dive, submerge, douse, souse, wet, lower.

due *adj* **1** OWED, owing, payable, unpaid, outstanding, in arrears. **2** RIGHTFUL, fitting, appropriate, proper, merited, deserved, justified,

suitable. **3** ADEQUATE, enough, sufficient, ample, plenty of.
4 EXPECTED, scheduled.
F3 1 paid. **3** inadequate.
adv exactly, direct(ly), precisely, straight, dead (*infml*).

duel *n* affair of honour, combat, contest, fight, clash, competition, rivalry, encounter.

dull *adj* **1** BORING, uninteresting, unexciting, flat, dreary, monotonous, tedious, uneventful, humdrum, unimaginative, dismal, lifeless, plain, insipid, heavy. **2** DARK, gloomy, drab, murky, indistinct, grey, cloudy, lacklustre, opaque, dim, overcast. **3** UNINTELLIGENT, dense, dim, dimwitted (*infml*), thick (*infml*), stupid, slow.
F3 1 interesting, exciting. **2** bright. **3** intelligent, clever.
v **1** BLUNT, alleviate, mitigate, moderate, lessen, relieve, soften. **2** DEADEN, numb, paralyse. **3** DISCOURAGE, dampen, subdue, sadden. **4** DIM, obscure, fade.

dumb *adj* silent, mute, soundless, speechless, tongue-tied, inarticulate, mum (*infml*).

dumbfounded *adj* astonished, amazed, astounded, overwhelmed, speechless, taken aback, thrown (*infml*), startled, overcome, confounded, flabbergasted (*infml*), staggered, confused, bowled over, dumb, floored (*infml*), paralysed.

dummy *n* **1** COPY, duplicate, imitation, counterfeit, substitute. **2** MODEL, lay-figure, mannequin, figure, form. **3** TEAT, pacifier.
adj **1** ARTIFICIAL, fake, imitation, false, bogus, mock, sham, phoney. **2** SIMULATED, practice, trial.

dump *v* **1** DEPOSIT, drop, offload, throw down, let fall, unload, empty out, discharge, park. **2** GET RID OF, scrap, throw away, dispose of, ditch, tip, jettison.
n **1** RUBBISH-TIP, junk-yard, rubbish-heap, tip. **2** HOVEL, slum, shack, shanty, hole (*infml*), joint (*infml*), pigsty, mess.

dungeon *n* cell, prison, jail, gaol, cage, lock-up, keep, oubliette, vault.

dupe *n* victim, sucker (*infml*), fool, gull, mug (*infml*), push-over (*infml*), fall guy (*infml*), pawn, puppet, instrument, stooge (*infml*), simpleton.
v deceive, delude, fool, trick, outwit, con (*infml*), cheat, hoax, swindle, rip off (*infml*), take in, hoodwink, defraud, bamboozle (*infml*).

duplicate *adj* identical, matching, twin, twofold, corresponding, matched.
n copy, replica, clone, reproduction, photocopy, carbon (copy), match, facsimile.
v copy, reproduce, repeat, photocopy, double, clone, echo.

durable *adj* lasting, enduring, long-lasting, abiding, hard-wearing, strong, sturdy, tough, unfading, substantial, sound, reliable, dependable, stable, resistant, persistent, constant, permanent, firm, fixed, fast.
F3 perishable, weak, fragile.

duress *n* constraint, coercion, compulsion, pressure, restraint, threat, force.

dusk *n* twilight, sunset, nightfall, evening, sundown, gloaming, darkness, dark, gloom, shadows, shade.
F3 dawn, brightness.

dust n powder, particles, dirt, earth, soil, ground, grit, grime.

dusty adj **1** DIRTY, grubby, filthy. **2** POWDERY, granular, crumbly, chalky, sandy.

F3 1 clean. **2** solid, hard.

dutiful adj obedient, respectful, conscientious, devoted, filial, reverential, submissive.

duty n **1** OBLIGATION, responsibility, assignment, calling, charge, role, task, job, business, function, work, office, service. **2** OBEDIENCE, respect, loyalty. **3** TAX, toll, tariff, levy, customs, excise. **on duty** at work, engaged, busy.

dwarf n **1** PERSON OF RESTRICTED GROWTH, midget, pygmy, Tom Thumb, Lilliputian. **2** GNOME, goblin.
adj miniature, small, tiny, pocket, mini (infml), diminutive, petite, Lilliputian, baby.

F3 large.

v **1** STUNT, retard, check. **2** OVERSHADOW, tower over, dominate.

dwell v live, inhabit, reside, stay, settle, populate, people, lodge, rest, abide (fml).

dwindle v diminish, decrease, decline, lessen, subside, ebb, fade, weaken, taper off, tail off, shrink, peter out, fall, wane, waste away, die out, wither, shrivel, disappear.

F3 increase, grow.

dye n colour, colouring, stain, pigment, tint, tinge.
v colour, tint, stain, pigment, tinge, imbue.

dying adj moribund, passing, final, going, mortal, not long for this world, perishing, failing, fading, vanishing.

F3 reviving.

dynamic adj forceful, powerful, energetic, vigorous, go-ahead, high-powered, driving, self-starting, spirited, vital, lively, active.

F3 inactive, apathetic.

dynasty n house, line, succession, dominion, regime, government, rule, empire, sovereignty.

E

eager *adj* **1** KEEN, enthusiastic, fervent, intent, earnest, zealous. **2** LONGING, yearning.
F3 1 unenthusiastic, indifferent.

ear *n* **1** ATTENTION, heed, notice, regard. **2** *an ear for language*: perception, sensitivity, discrimination, appreciation, hearing, skill, ability.

> **Parts of the ear include:**
> anvil (incus), auditory canal, auditory nerve, auricle, cochlea, concha, eardrum, eustachian tube, hammer (malleus), helix, labyrinth, lobe, pinna, semicircular canal, stirrup (stapes), tragus, tympanum, vestibule.

early *adj* **1** *early symptoms*: forward, advanced, premature, untimely, undeveloped. **2** *early theatre*: primitive, ancient, primeval. *adv* ahead of time, in good time, beforehand, in advance, prematurely.
F3 late.

earn *v* **1** *earn a good salary*: receive, obtain, make, get, draw, bring in (*infml*), gain, realize, gross, reap. **2** *earn one's reputation*: deserve, merit, warrant, win, rate.
F3 1 spend, lose.

earnest *adj* **1** RESOLUTE, devoted, ardent, conscientious, intent, keen, fervent, firm, fixed, eager,

enthusiastic, steady. **2** SERIOUS, sincere, solemn, grave, heartfelt.
F3 1 apathetic. **2** frivolous, flippant.

earnings *n* pay, income, salary, wages, profits, gain, proceeds, reward, receipts, return, revenue, remuneration, stipend.
F3 expenditure, outgoings.

earth *n* **1** WORLD, planet, globe, sphere. **2** LAND, ground, soil, clay, loam, sod, humus.

earthenware *n* pottery, ceramics, crockery, pots.

earthly *adj* **1** *our earthly life*: material, physical, human, worldly, mortal, mundane, fleshly, secular, sensual, profane, temporal. **2** *no earthly explanation*: possible, likely, conceivable, slightest.
F3 1 spiritual, heavenly.

earthy *adj* crude, coarse, vulgar, bawdy, rough, raunchy (*infml*), down-to-earth, ribald, robust.
F3 refined, modest.

ease *n* **1** FACILITY, effortlessness, skilfulness, deftness, dexterity, naturalness, cleverness. **2** COMFORT, contentment, peace, affluence, repose, leisure, relaxation, rest, quiet, happiness.
F3 1 difficulty. **2** discomfort.
v **1** *ease the pain*: alleviate, moderate, lessen, lighten, relieve, mitigate,

abate, relent, allay, assuage, relax, comfort, calm, soothe, facilitate, smooth. **2** ease it into position: inch, steer, slide, still.

E3 1 aggravate, intensify, worsen.

easily adv **1** EFFORTLESSLY, comfortably, readily, simply. **2** BY FAR, undoubtedly, indisputably, definitely, certainly, doubtlessly, clearly, far and away, undeniably, simply, surely, probably, well.

E3 1 laboriously.

easy adj **1** EFFORTLESS, simple, uncomplicated, undemanding, straightforward, manageable, cushy (infml). **2** RELAXED, carefree, easy-going, comfortable, informal, calm, natural, leisurely.

E3 1 difficult, demanding, exacting. **2** tense, uneasy.

easy-going adj relaxed, tolerant, laid-back (infml), amenable, happy-go-lucky (infml), carefree, calm, even-tempered, serene.

E3 strict, intolerant, critical.

eat v **1** CONSUME, feed, swallow, devour, chew, scoff (infml), munch, dine. **2** CORRODE, erode, wear away, decay, rot, crumble, dissolve.

eatable adj edible, palatable, good, wholesome, digestible, comestible (fml), harmless.

E3 inedible, unpalatable.

eavesdrop v listen in, spy, overhear, snoop (infml), tap (infml), bug (infml), monitor.

eccentric adj odd, peculiar, abnormal, unconventional, strange, quirky, weird, way-out (infml), queer, outlandish, idiosyncratic, bizarre, freakish, erratic, singular, dotty.

E3 conventional, orthodox, normal.

n nonconformist, oddball (infml),

oddity, crank (infml), freak (infml), character (infml).

eccentricity n unconventionality, strangeness, peculiarity, nonconformity, abnormality, oddity, weirdness, idiosyncrasy, singularity, quirk, freakishness, aberration, anomaly, capriciousness.

E3 conventionality, ordinariness.

ecclesiastical adj church, churchly, religious, clerical, priestly, divine, spiritual.

echo v **1** REVERBERATE, resound, repeat, reflect, reiterate, ring. **2** IMITATE, copy, reproduce, mirror, resemble, mimic.

n **1** REVERBERATION, reiteration, repetition, reflection. **2** IMITATION, copy, reproduction, mirror image, image, parallel.

eclipse v **1** BLOT OUT, obscure, cloud, veil, darken, dim. **2** OUTDO, overshadow, outshine, surpass, transcend.

n **1** OBSCURATION, overshadowing, darkening, shading, dimming. **2** DECLINE, failure, fall, loss.

economic adj **1** COMMERCIAL, business, industrial. **2** FINANCIAL, budgetary, fiscal, monetary. **3** PROFITABLE, profit-making, money-making, productive, cost-effective, viable.

economical adj **1** THRIFTY, careful, prudent, saving, sparing, frugal. **2** CHEAP, inexpensive, low-priced, reasonable, cost-effective, modest, efficient.

E3 1 wasteful. **2** expensive, uneconomical.

economize v save, cut back, tighten one's belt (infml), cut costs.

E3 waste, squander.

economy *n* thrift, saving, restraint, prudence, frugality, parsimony, providence, husbandry.
F3 extravagance.

ecstasy *n* delight, rapture, bliss, elation, joy, euphoria, frenzy, exaltation, fervour.
F3 misery, torment.

ecstatic *adj* elated, blissful, joyful, rapturous, overjoyed, euphoric, delirious, frenzied, fervent.
F3 downcast.

eddy *n* whirlpool, swirl, vortex, twist. *v* swirl, whirl.

edge *n* 1 BORDER, rim, boundary, limit, brim, threshold, brink, fringe, margin, outline, side, verge, line, perimeter, periphery, lip.
2 ADVANTAGE, superiority, force.
3 SHARPNESS, acuteness, keenness, incisiveness, pungency, zest.
v creep, inch, ease, sidle.

edgy *adj* on edge, nervous, tense, anxious, ill at ease, keyed-up, touchy, irritable.
F3 calm.

edible *adj* eatable, palatable, digestible, wholesome, good, harmless.
F3 inedible.

edict *n* command, order, proclamation, law, decree, regulation, pronouncement, ruling, mandate, statute, injunction, manifesto.

edifice *n* building, construction, structure, erection.

edify *v* instruct, improve, enlighten, inform, guide, educate, nurture, teach.

edit *v* correct, emend, revise, rewrite, reorder, rearrange, adapt, check, compile, rephrase, select, polish, annotate, censor.

edition *n* copy, volume, impression, printing, issue, version, number.

educate *v* teach, train, instruct, tutor, coach, school, inform, cultivate, edify, drill, improve, discipline, develop.

educated *adj* learned, taught, schooled, trained, knowledgeable, informed, instructed, lettered, cultured, civilized, tutored, refined, well-bred.
F3 uneducated, uncultured.

education *n* teaching, training, schooling, tuition, tutoring, coaching, guidance, instruction, cultivation, culture, scholarship, improvement, enlightenment, knowledge, nurture, development.

Educational terms include:
A-level, A/S-level, assisted place, baccalaureate, bursar, campus, catchment area, classroom, co-education, Common Entrance, course, curriculum, degree, diploma, eleven-plus, examination, exercise-book, final exam, finals, further education, GCSE (General Certificate of Secondary Education), graduation, half-term, head boy, head girl, head teacher, Higher, Advanced Higher, higher education, homework, intake, invigilator, lecture, literacy, matriculation, mixed-ability, modular course, National Curriculum, NVQ (national vocational qualification), numeracy, O-level, PTA (parent teacher association), playground, playtime, prefect, primary education, proctor, professor, pupil, qualification, refresher course, register, report, SAT (Student Aptitude Test, Standard Assessment Task), SCE (Scottish Certificate of Education), scholarship, term, secondary education,

statemented, streaming, student, student grant, student loan, study, subject, syllabus, teacher, teacher training, tertiary education, test paper, textbook, thesis, timetable, truancy, university entrance, work experience, YTS (Youth Training Scheme). see also **school**.

eerie adj weird, strange, uncanny, spooky (infml), creepy, frightening, scary, spine-chilling.

effect n **1** OUTCOME, result, conclusion, consequence, upshot, aftermath, issue. **2** POWER, force, impact, efficacy, impression, strength. **3** MEANING, significance, import. v cause, execute, create, achieve, accomplish, perform, produce, make, initiate, fulfil, complete.
in effect in fact, actually, really, in reality, to all intents and purposes, for all practical purposes, essentially, effectively, virtually.
take effect be effective, become operative, come into force, come into operation, kick in (infml), be implemented, begin, work.

effective adj **1** EFFICIENT, efficacious, productive, adequate, capable, useful. **2** OPERATIVE, in force, functioning, current, active. **3** STRIKING, impressive, forceful, cogent, powerful, persuasive, convincing, telling.
F3 1 ineffective, powerless.

effects n belongings, possessions, property, goods, gear (infml), movables, chattels (fml), things, trappings.

effeminate adj unmanly, womanly, womanish, feminine, sissy (infml), delicate.
F3 manly.

effervescent adj **1** BUBBLY, sparkling, fizzy, frothy, carbonated, foaming. **2** LIVELY, ebullient, vivacious, animated, buoyant, exhilarated, enthusiastic, exuberant, excited, vital.
F3 1 flat. **2** dull.

efficiency n effectiveness, competence, proficiency, skill, expertise, skilfulness, capability, ability, productivity.
F3 inefficiency, incompetence.

efficient adj effective, competent, proficient, skilful, capable, able, productive, well-organized, businesslike, powerful, well-conducted.
F3 inefficient, incompetent.

effort n **1** EXERTION, strain, application, struggle, trouble, energy, toil, striving, pains, travail (fml). **2** ATTEMPT, try, go (infml), endeavour, shot, stab. **3** ACHIEVEMENT, accomplishment, feat, exploit, production, creation, deed, product, work.

effortless adj easy, simple, undemanding, facile, painless, smooth.
F3 difficult.

effrontery n audacity, impertinence, insolence, cheek (infml), impudence, temerity, boldness, brazenness, cheekiness, gall, nerve, presumption, disrespect, arrogance, brashness.
F3 respect, timidity.

effusive adj fulsome, gushing, unrestrained, expansive, ebullient, demonstrative, profuse, overflowing, enthusiastic, exuberant, extravagant, lavish, talkative, voluble.
F3 reserved, restrained.

egotism n egoism, egomania, self-centredness, self-importance, conceitedness, self-regard, self-love, self-conceit, narcissism, self-admiration, vanity, bigheadedness (*infml*).
F3 humility.

egotistic adj egoistic, egocentric, self-centred, self-important, conceited, vain, swollen-headed (*infml*), bigheaded (*infml*), boasting, bragging.
F3 humble.

ejaculate v **1** DISCHARGE, eject, spurt, emit. **2** EXCLAIM, call, blurt (out), cry, shout, yell, utter, scream.

eject v **1** EMIT, expel, discharge, spout, spew, evacuate, vomit. **2** OUST, evict, throw out, drive out, turn out, expel, remove, banish, deport, dismiss, exile, kick out, fire (*infml*), sack (*infml*).

elaborate adj **1** *elaborate plans*: detailed, careful, thorough, exact, extensive, painstaking, precise, perfected, minute, laboured, studied. **2** *elaborate design*: intricate, complex, complicated, involved, ornamental, ornate, fancy, decorated, ostentatious, showy, fussy.
F3 2 simple, plain.
v amplify, develop, enlarge, expand, flesh out, polish, improve, refine, devise, explain.
F3 précis, simplify.

elapse v pass, lapse, go by, slip away.

elastic adj **1** PLIABLE, flexible, stretchable, supple, resilient, yielding, springy, rubbery, pliant, plastic, bouncy, buoyant. **2** ADAPTABLE, accommodating, flexible, tolerant, adjustable.
F3 1 rigid. **2** inflexible.

elasticity n **1** PLIABILITY, flexibility,

resilience, stretch, springiness, suppleness, give, plasticity, bounce, buoyancy. **2** ADAPTABILITY, flexibility, tolerance, adjustability.
F3 1 rigidity. **2** inflexibility.

elated adj exhilarated, excited, euphoric, ecstatic, exultant, jubilant, overjoyed, joyful.
F3 despondent, downcast.

elbow v jostle, nudge, push, shove, bump, crowd, knock, shoulder.

elder adj older, senior, first-born, ancient.
F3 younger.

elderly adj aging, aged, old, hoary, senile.
F3 young, youthful.

elect v choose, pick, opt for, select, vote for, prefer, adopt, designate, appoint, determine.
adj choice, élite, chosen, designated, designate, picked, prospective, selected, to be, preferred, hand-picked.

election n choice, selection, voting, ballot, poll, appointment, determination, decision, preference.

elector n selector, voter, constituent.

electric adj electrifying, exciting, stimulating, thrilling, charged, dynamic, stirring, tense, rousing.
F3 unexciting, flat.

electrify v thrill, excite, shock, invigorate, animate, stimulate, stir, rouse, fire, jolt, galvanize, amaze, astonish, astound, stagger.
F3 bore.

elegant adj stylish, chic, fashionable, modish, smart, refined, polished, genteel, smooth, tasteful, fine, exquisite, beautiful, graceful, handsome, delicate, neat, artistic.
F3 inelegant, unrefined, unfashionable.

elegy n dirge, lament, requiem, plaint.

element n factor, component, constituent, ingredient, member, part, piece, fragment, feature, trace.
E3 whole.

elementary adj basic, fundamental, rudimentary, principal, primary, clear, easy, introductory, straightforward, uncomplicated, simple.
E3 advanced.

elements n basics, fundamentals, foundations, principles, rudiments, essentials.

elevate v **1** LIFT, raise, hoist, heighten, intensify, magnify. **2** EXALT, advance, promote, aggrandize, upgrade. **3** UPLIFT, rouse, boost, brighten.
E3 1 lower. **2** downgrade.

elevated adj raised, lofty, exalted, high, grand, noble, dignified, sublime.
E3 base.

elevation n **1** RISE, promotion, advancement, preferment, aggrandizement. **2** EXALTATION, loftiness, grandeur, eminence, nobility. **3** HEIGHT, altitude, hill, rise.
E3 1 demotion. **2** dip.

elicit v evoke, draw out, derive, extract, obtain, exact, extort, cause.

eligible adj qualified, fit, appropriate, suitable, acceptable, worthy, proper, desirable.
E3 ineligible.

eliminate v remove, get rid of, cut out, take out, exclude, delete, dispense with, rub out, omit, reject, disregard, dispose of, drop, do away with, eradicate, expel, extinguish, stamp out, exterminate, knock out, kill, murder.
E3 include, accept.

élite n best, elect, aristocracy, upper classes, nobility, gentry, crème de la crème, top drawer, establishment, high society.
adj choice, best, exclusive, selected, first-class, top-notch, aristocratic, noble, upper-class.

elocution n delivery, articulation, diction, enunciation, pronunciation, oratory, rhetoric, speech, utterance.

elongated adj lengthened, extended, prolonged, protracted, stretched, long.

elope v run off, run away, decamp, bolt, abscond, do a bunk (infml), escape, steal away, leave, disappear.

eloquent adj articulate, fluent, well-expressed, glib, expressive, vocal, voluble, persuasive, moving, forceful, graceful, plausible, stirring, vivid.
E3 inarticulate, tongue-tied.

elucidate v explain, clarify, clear up, interpret, spell out, illustrate, unfold.
E3 confuse.

elude v **1** AVOID, escape, evade, dodge, shirk, duck (infml), flee. **2** PUZZLE, frustrate, baffle, confound, thwart, stump, foil.

elusive adj **1** INDEFINABLE, intangible, unanalysable, subtle, puzzling, baffling, transient, transitory. **2** EVASIVE, shifty, slippery, tricky.

emaciated adj thin, gaunt, lean, haggard, wasted, scrawny, skeletal, pinched, attenuated, meagre, lank.
E3 plump, well-fed.

emanate v **1** ORIGINATE, proceed, arise, derive, issue, spring, stem, flow, come, emerge. **2** DISCHARGE, send out, emit, give out, give off, radiate.

emancipate v free, liberate, release, set free, enfranchise, deliver, discharge,

loose, unchain, unshackle, unfetter.
F3 enslave.

embankment n causeway, dam, rampart, levee, earthwork.

embargo n restriction, ban, prohibition, restraint, proscription, bar, barrier, interdiction (*fml*), impediment, check, hindrance, blockage, stoppage, seizure.

embark v board (ship), go aboard, take ship.
F3 disembark.

embark on begin, start, commence, set about, launch, undertake, enter, initiate, engage.
F3 complete, finish.

embarrass v disconcert, mortify, show up, discompose, fluster, humiliate, shame, distress.

embarrassment n **1** SELF-CONSCIOUSNESS, discomposure, chagrin, mortification, humiliation, shame, awkwardness, confusion, bashfulness. **2** DIFFICULTY, constraint, predicament, distress, discomfort.

embellish v adorn, ornament, decorate, deck, dress up, sex up (*sl*), beautify, gild, garnish, festoon, elaborate, embroider, enrich, exaggerate, enhance, varnish, grace.
F3 simplify, denude.

embellishment n adornment, ornament, ornamentation, decoration, elaboration, garnish, trimming, gilding, enrichment, enhancement, embroidery, exaggeration.

embezzle v appropriate, misappropriate, steal, pilfer, filch, pinch (*infml*).

embezzlement n appropriation, misappropriation, pilfering, fraud, stealing, theft, filching.

embittered adj bitter, disaffected, sour, disillusioned.

emblem n symbol, sign, token, representation, logo, insignia, device, crest, mark, badge, figure.

embodiment n incarnation, personification, exemplification, expression, epitome, example, incorporation, realization, representation, manifestation, concentration.

embody v **1** PERSONIFY, exemplify, represent, stand for, symbolize, incorporate, express, manifest. **2** INCLUDE, contain, integrate.

embrace v **1** HUG, clasp, cuddle, hold, grasp, squeeze. **2** INCLUDE, encompass, incorporate, contain, comprise, cover, involve. **3** ACCEPT, take up, welcome.
n hug, cuddle, clasp, clinch (*infml*).

embroil v involve, implicate, entangle, enmesh, mix up, incriminate.

embryo n nucleus, germ, beginning, root.

embryonic adj undeveloped, rudimentary, immature, early, germinal, primary.
F3 developed.

emerge v **1** ARISE, rise, surface, appear, develop, crop up (*infml*), transpire, turn up, materialize. **2** EMANATE, issue, proceed.
F3 1 disappear.

emergence n appearance, rise, advent, coming, dawn, development, arrival, disclosure, issue.
F3 disappearance.

emergency n crisis, danger, difficulty, exigency (*fml*), predicament, plight, pinch, strait, quandary.

emigrate *v* migrate, relocate, move, depart.

eminence *n* distinction, fame, pre-eminence, prominence, renown, reputation, greatness, importance, esteem, note, prestige, rank.

eminent *adj* distinguished, famous, prominent, illustrious, outstanding, notable, pre-eminent, prestigious, celebrated, renowned, noteworthy, conspicuous, esteemed, important, well-known, elevated, respected, great, high-ranking, grand, superior.
F3 unknown, obscure, unimportant.

emissary *n* ambassador, agent, envoy, messenger, delegate, herald, courier, representative, scout, deputy, spy.

emission *n* discharge, issue, ejection, emanation, ejaculation, diffusion, transmission, exhalation, radiation, release, exudation, vent.

emit *v* discharge, issue, eject, emanate, exude, give out, give off, diffuse, radiate, release, shed, vent.
F3 absorb.

emotion *n* feeling, passion, sensation, sentiment, ardour, fervour, warmth, reaction, vehemence, excitement.

emotional *adj* **1** FEELING, passionate, sensitive, responsive, ardent, tender, warm, roused, demonstrative, excitable, enthusiastic, fervent, impassioned, moved, sentimental, zealous, hot-blooded, heated, tempestuous, overcharged, temperamental, fiery. **2** EMOTIVE, moving, poignant, thrilling, touching, stirring, heart-warming, exciting, pathetic.
F3 1 unemotional, cold, detached, calm.

emphasis *n* stress, weight, significance, importance, priority, underscoring, accent, force, power, prominence, pre-eminence, attention, intensity, strength, urgency, positiveness, insistence, mark, moment.

emphasize *v* stress, accentuate, underline, highlight, accent, feature, dwell on, weight, point up, spotlight, play up, insist on, press home, intensify, strengthen, punctuate.
F3 play down, understate.

emphatic *adj* forceful, positive, insistent, certain, definite, decided, unequivocal, absolute, categorical, earnest, marked, pronounced, significant, strong, striking, vigorous, distinct, energetic, forcible, important, impressive, momentous, powerful, punctuated, telling, vivid, graphic, direct.
F3 tentative, hesitant, understated.

empire *n* **1** SUPREMACY, sovereignty, rule, authority, command, government, jurisdiction, control, power, sway. **2** DOMAIN, dominion, kingdom, realm, commonwealth, territory.

employ *v* **1** ENGAGE, hire, take on, recruit, enlist, commission, retain, fill, occupy, take up. **2** USE, utilize, make use of, apply, bring to bear, ply, exercise.

employee *n* worker, member of staff, job-holder, hand, wage-earner.

employer *n* boss, proprietor, owner, manager, gaffer (*infml*), management, company, firm, business, establishment.

employment *n* **1** JOB, work, occupation, situation, business, calling, profession, line (*infml*), vocation, trade, pursuit, craft. **2** ENLISTMENT, employ, engagement, hire.

F3 1 unemployment.

empower *v* authorize, warrant, enable, license, sanction, permit, entitle, commission, delegate, qualify.

emptiness *n* **1** VACUUM, vacantness, void, hollowness, hunger, bareness, barrenness, desolation. **2** FUTILITY, meaninglessness, worthlessness, aimlessness, ineffectiveness, unreality.

F3 1 fullness.

empty *adj* **1** VACANT, void, unoccupied, uninhabited, unfilled, deserted, bare, hollow, desolate, blank, clear. **2** FUTILE, aimless, meaningless, senseless, trivial, vain, worthless, useless, insubstantial, ineffective, insincere. **3** VACUOUS, inane, expressionless, blank, vacant.

F3 1 full. **2** meaningful.

v drain, exhaust, discharge, clear, evacuate, vacate, pour out, unload, void, gut.

F3 fill.

empty-headed *adj* inane, silly, frivolous, scatter-brained (*infml*), feather-brained (*infml*), ditzy (*infml*).

emulate *v* match, copy, mimic, follow, imitate, echo, compete with, contend with, rival, vie with.

enable *v* equip, qualify, empower, authorize, sanction, warrant, allow, permit, prepare, fit, facilitate, license, commission, endue.

F3 prevent, inhibit, forbid.

enact *v* **1** DECREE, ordain, order, authorize, command, legislate, sanction, ratify, pass, establish.

2 ACT (OUT), perform, play, portray, represent, depict.

F3 1 repeal, rescind.

enamoured *adj* charmed, infatuated, in love with, enchanted, captivated, entranced, smitten, keen, taken, fascinated, fond.

enchant *v* **1** CAPTIVATE, charm, fascinate, enrapture, attract, allure, appeal, delight, thrill. **2** ENTRANCE, enthral, bewitch, spellbind, hypnotize, mesmerize.

F3 1 repel.

enclose *v* encircle, encompass, surround, fence, hedge, hem in, bound, encase, embrace, envelop, confine, hold, shut in, wrap, pen, cover, circumscribe, incorporate, include, insert, contain, comprehend.

enclosure *n* pen, pound, compound, paddock, fold, stockade, sty, arena, corral, court, ring, cloister.

encompass *v* **1** ENCIRCLE, circle, ring, surround, gird, envelop, circumscribe, hem in, enclose, hold. **2** INCLUDE, cover, embrace, contain, comprise, admit, incorporate, involve, embody, comprehend.

encounter *v* **1** MEET, come across, run into (*infml*), happen on, chance upon, run across, confront, face, experience. **2** FIGHT, clash with, combat, cross swords with (*infml*), engage, grapple with, struggle, strive, contend.

n **1** MEETING, brush, confrontation. **2** CLASH, fight, combat, conflict, contest, battle, set-to (*infml*), dispute, engagement, action, skirmish, run-in, collision.

encourage *v* **1** HEARTEN, exhort, stimulate, spur, reassure, rally, inspire, incite, egg on (*infml*), buoy up,

cheer, urge, rouse, comfort, console.
2 PROMOTE, advance, aid, boost,
forward, further, foster, support, help,
strengthen.
F3 1 discourage, depress.
2 discourage.

encouragement *n* **1** REASSURANCE,
inspiration, cheer, exhortation,
incitement, pep talk (*infml*), urging,
stimulation, consolation, succour
(*fml*). **2** PROMOTION, help, aid, boost,
shot in the arm (*infml*), incentive,
support, stimulus.
F3 1 discouragement, disapproval.

encouraging *adj* heartening,
promising, hopeful, reassuring,
stimulating, uplifting, auspicious,
cheering, comforting, bright, rosy,
cheerful, satisfactory.
F3 discouraging.

encroach *v* intrude, invade, impinge,
trespass, infringe, usurp, overstep,
make inroads, muscle in (*infml*).

encumber *v* burden, overload, weigh
down, saddle, oppress, handicap,
hamper, hinder, impede, slow down,
obstruct, inconvenience, prevent,
retard, cramp.

encumbrance *n* burden,
cumbrance, load, cross, millstone,
albatross, difficulty, handicap,
impediment, obstruction, obstacle,
inconvenience, hindrance, liability.

end *n* **1** FINISH, conclusion,
termination, close, completion,
cessation, culmination, dénouement.
2 EXTREMITY, boundary, edge, limit,
tip. **3** REMAINDER, tip, butt, left-over,
remnant, stub, scrap, fragment. **4** AIM,
object, objective, purpose, intention,
goal, point, reason, design. **5** RESULT,
outcome, consequence, upshot.
6 DEATH, demise, destruction,

extermination, downfall, doom, ruin,
dissolution.
F3 1 beginning, start. **6** birth.
v **1** FINISH, close, cease, conclude,
stop, terminate, complete, culminate,
wind up. **2** DESTROY, annihilate,
exterminate, extinguish, ruin, abolish,
dissolve.
F3 1 begin, start.

endanger *v* imperil, hazard,
jeopardize, risk, expose, threaten,
compromise.
F3 protect.

endearing *adj* lovable, charming,
appealing, attractive, winsome,
delightful, enchanting.

endeavour *n* attempt, effort, go
(*infml*), try, shot (*infml*), stab (*infml*),
undertaking, enterprise, aim, venture.
v attempt, try, strive, aim, aspire,
undertake, venture, struggle, labour,
take pains.

ending *n* end, close, finish,
completion, termination, conclusion,
culmination, climax, resolution,
consummation, dénouement, finale,
epilogue.
F3 beginning, start.

endless *adj* **1** INFINITE, boundless,
unlimited, measureless.
2 EVERLASTING, ceaseless,
perpetual, constant, continual,
continuous, undying, eternal,
interminable, monotonous.
F3 1 finite, limited. **2** temporary.

endorse *v* **1** APPROVE, sanction,
authorize, support, back, affirm,
ratify, confirm, vouch for, advocate,
warrant, recommend, subscribe to,
sustain, adopt. **2** SIGN, countersign.

endorsement *n* **1** APPROVAL,
sanction, authorization, support,
backing, affirmation, ratification,

confirmation, advocacy, warrant, recommendation, commendation, seal of approval, testimonial, OK (*infml*). **2** SIGNATURE, countersignature.

endow *v* bestow, bequeath, leave, will, give, donate, endue (*fml*), confer, grant, present, award, finance, fund, support, make over, furnish, provide, supply.

endowment *n* **1** BEQUEST, legacy, award, grant, fund, gift, provision, settlement, donation, bestowal, benefaction, dowry, income, revenue. **2** TALENT, attribute, faculty, gift, ability, quality, flair, genius, qualification.

endurance *n* fortitude, patience, staying power, stamina, resignation, stoicism, tenacity, perseverance, resolution, stability, persistence, strength, toleration.

endure *v* **1** *endure hardship*: bear, stand, put up with, tolerate, weather, brave, cope with, face, go through, experience, submit to, suffer, sustain, swallow, undergo, withstand, stick, stomach, allow, permit, support. **2** *a peace that will endure for ever*: last, abide (*fml*), remain, live, survive, stay, persist, hold, prevail.

enemy *n* adversary, opponent, foe (*fml*), rival, antagonist, the opposition, competitor, opposer, other side. Fꓱ friend, ally.

energetic *adj* lively, vigorous, active, animated, dynamic, forceful, potent, powerful, strenuous, high-powered. Fꓱ lethargic, sluggish, inactive, idle.

energy *n* liveliness, vigour, activity, animation, drive, dynamism, get-up-and-go (*infml*), life, spirit, verve, vivacity, vitality, zest, zeal, ardour, fire,

efficiency, force, forcefulness, zip (*infml*), strength, power, intensity, exertion, stamina. Fꓱ lethargy, inertia, weakness.

enforce *v* impose, administer, implement, apply, execute, discharge, insist on, compel, oblige, urge, carry out, constrain, require, coerce, prosecute, reinforce.

engage *v* **1** PARTICIPATE, take part, embark on, take up, practise, involve. **2** ATTRACT, allure, draw, captivate, charm, catch. **3** OCCUPY, engross, absorb, busy, tie up, grip. **4** EMPLOY, hire, appoint, take on, enlist, enrol, commission, recruit, contract. **5** INTERLOCK, mesh, interconnect, join, interact, attach. **6** FIGHT, battle with, attack, take on, encounter, assail, combat. Fꓱ **2** repel. **4** dismiss, discharge. **5** disengage.

engaged *adj* **1** *engaged in his work*: occupied, busy, engrossed, immersed, absorbed, preoccupied, involved, employed. **2** *engaged to be married*: promised, betrothed (*fml*), pledged, spoken for, committed. **3** *the phone is engaged*: busy, tied up, unavailable.

engagement *n* **1** APPOINTMENT, meeting, date, arrangement, assignation, fixture, rendezvous. **2** PROMISE, pledge, betrothal (*fml*), commitment, obligation, assurance, vow, troth (*fml*). **3** FIGHT, battle, combat, conflict, action, encounter, confrontation, contest.

engaging *adj* charming, attractive, appealing, captivating, pleasing, delightful, winsome, lovable, likable, pleasant, fetching, fascinating, agreeable. Fꓱ repulsive, repellent.

engine n motor, machine, mechanism, appliance, contraption, apparatus, device, instrument, tool, locomotive, dynamo.

Types of engine include:
diesel, donkey, dynamo, fuel-injection, internal-combustion, jet, petrol, steam, turbine, turbojet, turboprop, twin-cam, V-engine.

engineer n **1** MECHANIC, technician, engine driver. **2** DESIGNER, originator, planner, inventor, deviser, mastermind, architect.
v plan, contrive, devise, manoeuvre, cause, manipulate, control, bring about, mastermind, originate, orchestrate, effect, plot, scheme, manage, create, rig.

engrave v **1** INSCRIBE, cut, carve, chisel, etch, chase. **2** *engraved on her mind*: imprint, impress, fix, stamp, lodge, ingrain.

engraving n print, impression, inscription, carving, etching, woodcut, plate, block, cutting, chiselling, mark.

engross v absorb, occupy, engage, grip, hold, preoccupy, rivet, fascinate, captivate, enthral, arrest, involve, intrigue.
Fa bore.

enhance v heighten, intensify, increase, improve, elevate, magnify, swell, exalt, raise, lift, boost, strengthen, reinforce, embellish.
Fa reduce, minimize.

enigma n mystery, riddle, puzzle, conundrum, problem, poser (*infml*), brain-teaser.

enigmatic adj mysterious, puzzling, cryptic, obscure, strange, perplexing.
Fa simple, straightforward.

enjoy v take pleasure in, delight in, appreciate, like, relish, revel in, be fond of, rejoice in, savour.
Fa dislike, hate.

enjoy oneself have a good time, have fun, make merry.

enjoyable adj pleasant, agreeable, delightful, pleasing, gratifying, entertaining, amusing, fun, delicious, good, satisfying.
Fa disagreeable.

enjoyment n **1** PLEASURE, delight, amusement, gratification, entertainment, relish, joy, fun, happiness, diversion, indulgence, recreation, zest, satisfaction. **2** POSSESSION, use, advantage, benefit.
Fa **1** displeasure.

enlarge v increase, expand, augment, add to, grow, extend, magnify, inflate, swell, wax, stretch, multiply, develop, amplify, blow up, widen, broaden, lengthen, heighten, elaborate.
Fa diminish, shrink.

enlighten v instruct, edify, educate, inform, illuminate, teach, counsel, apprise, advise.
Fa confuse.

enlightened adj informed, aware, knowledgeable, educated, civilized, cultivated, refined, sophisticated, conversant, wise, reasonable, liberal, open-minded, literate.
Fa ignorant, confused.

enlist v engage, enrol, register, sign up, recruit, conscript, employ, volunteer, join (up), gather, muster, secure, obtain, procure, enter.

enmity n animosity, hostility, antagonism, discord, strife, feud, antipathy, acrimony, bitterness, hatred, aversion, ill-will, bad blood, rancour, malevolence, malice, venom.
Fa friendship.

enormity n atrocity, outrage, iniquity, horror, evil, crime, abomination, monstrosity, wickedness, vileness, depravity, atrociousness, viciousness.

enormous adj huge, immense, vast, gigantic, massive, colossal, gross, gargantuan, monstrous, mammoth, jumbo (infml), tremendous, prodigious.
F3 small, tiny.

enough adj sufficient, adequate, ample, plenty, abundant.
n sufficiency, adequacy, plenty, abundance.
adv sufficiently, adequately, reasonably, tolerably, passably, moderately, fairly, satisfactorily, amply.

enquire see **inquire**.

enquiry see **inquiry**.

enrage v incense, infuriate, anger, madden, provoke, incite, inflame, exasperate, irritate, rile.
F3 calm, placate.

enrich v 1 ENDOW, enhance, improve, refine, develop, cultivate, augment. 2 ADORN, ornament, beautify, embellish, decorate, grace.
F3 1 impoverish.

enrol v 1 REGISTER, enlist, sign on, sign up, join up, recruit, engage, admit. 2 RECORD, list, note, inscribe.

enrolment n registration, recruitment, enlistment, admission, acceptance.

ensemble n 1 WHOLE, total, entirety, sum, aggregate, set, collection. 2 OUTFIT, costume, get-up (infml), rig-out (infml). 3 GROUP, band, company, troupe, chorus.

ensign n banner, standard, flag, colours, pennant, jack, badge.

enslave v subjugate, subject, dominate, bind, enchain, yoke.
F3 free, emancipate.

ensue v follow, issue, proceed, succeed, result, arise, happen, turn out, befall, flow, derive, stem.
F3 precede.

ensure v 1 CERTIFY, guarantee, warrant. 2 PROTECT, guard, safeguard, secure.

entail v involve, necessitate, occasion, require, demand, cause, give rise to, lead to, result in.

entangle v enmesh, ensnare, embroil, involve, implicate, snare, tangle, entrap, trap, catch, mix up, knot, ravel, muddle.
F3 disentangle.

enter v 1 COME IN, go in, arrive, insert, introduce, board, penetrate. 2 RECORD, log, note, register, take down, inscribe. 3 JOIN, embark upon, enrol, enlist, set about, sign up, participate, commence, start, begin.
F3 1 depart. 3 delete.

enterprise n 1 UNDERTAKING, venture, project, plan, effort, operation, programme, endeavour. 2 INITIATIVE, resourcefulness, drive, adventurousness, boldness, get-up-and-go (infml), push, energy, enthusiasm, spirit. 3 BUSINESS, company, firm, establishment, concern.
F3 2 apathy.

enterprising adj venturesome, adventurous, bold, daring, go-ahead, imaginative, resourceful, self-reliant, enthusiastic, energetic, keen, ambitious, aspiring, spirited, active.
F3 unenterprising, lethargic.

entertain v 1 AMUSE, divert, please, delight, cheer. 2 RECEIVE, have guests,

accommodate, put up, treat.
3 HARBOUR, countenance, contemplate, consider, imagine, conceive.

F3 1 bore. **3** reject.

entertainer *n*

Entertainers include:
acrobat, actor, actress, busker, chat-show host, clown, comedian, comic, conjuror, dancer, disc jockey, DJ (*infml*), escapologist, game-show host, hypnotist, ice-skater, impressionist, jester, juggler, magician, mimic, mind-reader, minstrel, musician, presenter, singer, song-and-dance act, stand-up comedian, stripper (*infml*), striptease-artist, trapeze-artist, tight-rope walker, ventriloquist; performer, artiste. *see also* **musician; singer**.

entertaining *adj* amusing, diverting, fun, delightful, interesting, pleasant, pleasing, humorous, witty.
F3 boring.

entertainment *n* **1** AMUSEMENT, diversion, recreation, enjoyment, play, pastime, fun, sport, distraction, pleasure. **2** SHOW, spectacle, performance, extravaganza.

Forms of entertainment include:
cinema, cartoon, video, DVD, radio, television, theatre, pantomime; game show, documentary, docu-soap, sitcom, soap opera; dance, disco, discothèque, concert, recital, musical, opera, variety show, music hall, revue, karaoke, cabaret, night-club, casino; magic-show, puppet-show, Punch-and-Judy show, circus, gymkhana, waxworks, zoo, rodeo, carnival, pageant, fête, festival, fireworks.

enthral *v* captivate, entrance, enchant, fascinate, charm, beguile, thrill, intrigue, hypnotize, mesmerize, engross.

F3 bore.

enthusiasm *n* zeal, ardour, fervour, passion, keenness, eagerness, vehemence, warmth, frenzy, excitement, earnestness, relish, spirit, devotion, craze, mania, rage.
F3 apathy.

enthusiast *n* devotee, zealot, admirer, fan (*infml*), supporter, follower, buff (*infml*), freak (*infml*), fanatic, fiend (*infml*), lover.

enthusiastic *adj* keen, ardent, eager, fervent, vehement, passionate, warm, whole-hearted, zealous, vigorous, spirited, earnest, devoted, avid, excited, exuberant.

F3 unenthusiastic, apathetic.

entice *v* tempt, lure, attract, seduce, lead on, draw, coax, persuade, induce, sweet-talk (*infml*).

entire *adj* complete, whole, total, full, intact, perfect.

F3 incomplete, partial.

entirely *adv* completely, wholly, totally, fully, utterly, unreservedly, absolutely, in toto, thoroughly, altogether, perfectly, solely, exclusively, every inch.

F3 partially.

entitle *v* **1** AUTHORIZE, qualify, empower, enable, allow, permit, license, warrant. **2** NAME, call, term, title, style, christen, dub, label, designate.

entity *n* being, existence, thing, body, creature, individual, organism, substance.

entrance[1] *n* **1** ACCESS, admission, admittance, entry, entrée. **2** ARRIVAL,

appearance, debut, initiation, introduction, start. **3** OPENING, way in, door, doorway, gate.
F3 departure. **3** OPENING.

entrance² *v* charm, enchant, enrapture, captivate, bewitch, spellbind, fascinate, delight, ravish, transport, hypnotize, mesmerize.
F3 repel.

entrant *n* **1** NOVICE, beginner, newcomer, initiate, convert, probationer. **2** COMPETITOR, candidate, contestant, contender, entry, participant, player.

entreat *v* beg, implore, plead with, beseech, crave, supplicate, pray, invoke, ask, petition, request, appeal to.

entreaty *n* appeal, plea, prayer, petition, supplication, suit, invocation, cry, solicitation, request.

entrench *v* establish, fix, embed, dig in, ensconce, install, lodge, root, ingrain, settle, seat, plant, anchor, set.
F3 dislodge.

entrust *v* trust, commit, confide, consign, authorize, charge, assign, turn over, commend, depute, invest, delegate, deliver.

entry *n* **1** ENTRANCE, appearance, admittance, admission, access, entrée, introduction. **2** OPENING, entrance, door, doorway, access, threshold, way in, passage, gate. **3** RECORD, item, minute, note, memorandum, statement, account. **4** ENTRANT, competitor, contestant, candidate, participant, player.
F3 **2** exit.

enumerate *v* list, name, itemize, cite, detail, specify, count, number, relate, recount, spell out, tell,

mention, calculate, quote, recite, reckon.

enunciate *v* **1** ARTICULATE, pronounce, vocalize, voice, express, say, speak, utter, sound. **2** STATE, declare, proclaim, announce, propound.

envelop *v* wrap, enfold, enwrap, encase, cover, swathe, shroud, engulf, enclose, encircle, encompass, surround, cloak, veil, blanket, conceal, obscure, hide.

envelope *n* wrapper, wrapping, cover, case, casing, sheath, covering, shell, skin, jacket, coating.

enviable *adj* desirable, privileged, favoured, blessed, fortunate, lucky, advantageous, sought-after, excellent, fine.
F3 unenviable.

envious *adj* covetous, jealous, resentful, green (with envy), dissatisfied, grudging, jaundiced, green-eyed (*infml*).

environment *n* surroundings, conditions, circumstances, milieu, atmosphere, habitat, situation, element, medium, background, ambience, setting, context, territory, domain.

envisage *v* visualize, imagine, picture, envision, conceive of, preconceive, predict, anticipate, foresee, image, see, contemplate.

envoy *n* agent, representative, ambassador, diplomat, messenger, legate, emissary, minister, delegate, deputy, courier, intermediary.

envy *n* covetousness, jealousy, resentfulness, resentment, dissatisfaction, grudge, ill-will, malice, spite.
v covet, resent, begrudge, grudge, crave.

epidemic adj widespread, prevalent, rife, rampant, pandemic, sweeping, wide-ranging, prevailing.
n plague, outbreak, spread, rash, upsurge, wave.

epilogue n afterword, postscript, coda, conclusion.
F3 foreword, prologue, preface.

episode n **1** INCIDENT, event, occurrence, happening, occasion, circumstance, experience, adventure, matter, business. **2** INSTALMENT, part, chapter, passage, section, scene.

epitome n **1** PERSONIFICATION, embodiment, representation, model, archetype, type, essence. **2** SUMMARY, abstract, abridgement, digest.

epoch n age, era, period, time, date.

equable adj **1** an equable person: even-tempered, placid, calm, serene, unexcitable, tranquil, unflappable, composed, level-headed, easy-going. **2** an equable climate: uniform, even, consistent, constant, regular, temperate, unvarying, steady, stable, smooth.
F3 **1** excitable. **2** variable.

equal adj **1** IDENTICAL, the same, alike, like, equivalent, corresponding, commensurate, comparable. **2** EVEN, uniform, regular, unvarying, balanced, matched. **3** COMPETENT, able, adequate, fit, capable, suitable.
F3 **1** different. **2** unequal. **3** unsuitable.
n peer, counterpart, equivalent, coequal, match, parallel, twin, fellow.
v match, parallel, correspond to, balance, square with, tally with, equalize, equate, rival, level, even.

equality n **1** UNIFORMITY, evenness, equivalence, correspondence, balance, parity, par, symmetry, proportion, identity, sameness, likeness. **2** IMPARTIALITY, fairness, justice, egalitarianism.
F3 **2** inequality.

equalize v level, even up, match, equal, equate, draw level, balance, square, standardize, compensate, smooth.

equate v compare, liken, match, pair, correspond to, correspond with, balance, parallel, equalize, offset, square, agree, tally, juxtapose.

equation n equality, correspondence, equivalence, balancing, agreement, parallel, pairing, comparison, match, likeness, juxtaposition.

equilibrium n **1** BALANCE, poise, symmetry, evenness, stability. **2** EQUANIMITY, self-possession, composure, calmness, coolness, serenity.
F3 **1** imbalance.

equip v provide, fit out, supply, furnish, prepare, arm, fit up, kit out, stock, endow, rig, dress, array, deck out.

equipment n apparatus, gear, supplies, tackle, rig-out (infml), tools, material, furnishings, baggage, outfit, paraphernalia, stuff, things, accessories, furniture.

equivalence n identity, parity, correspondence, agreement, likeness, interchangeability, similarity, substitutability, correlation, parallel, conformity, sameness.
F3 unlikeness, dissimilarity.

equivalent adj equal, same, similar, substitutable, corresponding, alike, comparable, interchangeable, even, tantamount, twin.
F3 unlike, different.

equivocal *adj* ambiguous, uncertain, obscure, vague, evasive, oblique, misleading, dubious, confusing, indefinite.
F3 unequivocal, clear.

equivocate *v* prevaricate, evade, dodge, fence, beat about the bush (*infml*), hedge, mislead.

era *n* age, epoch, period, date, day, days, time, aeon, stage, century.

eradicate *v* eliminate, annihilate, get rid of, remove, root out, suppress, destroy, exterminate, extinguish, weed out, stamp out, abolish, erase, obliterate.

erase *v* obliterate, rub out, expunge (*fml*), delete, blot out, cancel, efface, get rid of, remove, eradicate.

erect *adj* upright, straight, vertical, upstanding, standing, raised, rigid, stiff.
v build, construct, put up, establish, set up, elevate, assemble, found, form, institute, initiate, raise, rear, lift, mount, pitch, create.

erode *v* wear away, eat away, wear down, corrode, abrade, consume, grind down, disintegrate, deteriorate, spoil.

erosion *n* wear, corrosion, abrasion, attrition, denudation, disintegration, deterioration, destruction, undermining.

erotic *adj* aphrodisiac, seductive, sexy, sensual, titillating, pornographic, lascivious, stimulating, suggestive, amorous, amatory, venereal, carnal, lustful, voluptuous.

err *v* 1 MAKE A MISTAKE, be wrong, miscalculate, mistake, misjudge, slip up, blunder, misunderstand. 2 DO WRONG, sin, misbehave, go astray, offend, transgress, deviate.

errand *n* commission, charge, mission, assignment, message, task, job, duty.

erratic *adj* changeable, variable, fitful, fluctuating, inconsistent, irregular, unstable, shifting, inconstant, unpredictable, unreliable, aberrant, abnormal, eccentric, desultory, meandering.
F3 steady, consistent, stable.

erroneous *adj* incorrect, wrong, mistaken, false, untrue, inaccurate, inexact, invalid, illogical, unfounded, faulty, flawed.
F3 correct, right.

error *n* mistake, inaccuracy, slip, slip-up, blunder, howler (*infml*), gaffe, faux pas, solecism, lapse, miscalculation, misunderstanding, misconception, misapprehension, misprint, oversight, omission, fallacy, flaw, fault, wrong.

erudite *adj* learned, scholarly, well-educated, knowledgeable, lettered, educated, well-read, literate, academic, cultured, wise, highbrow, profound.
F3 illiterate, ignorant.

erupt *v* break out, explode, belch, discharge, burst, gush, spew, spout, eject, expel, emit, flare up, vomit, break.

eruption *n* 1 OUTBURST, discharge, ejection, emission, explosion, flare-up. 2 RASH, outbreak, inflammation.

escalate *v* increase, intensify, grow, accelerate, rise, step up, heighten, raise, spiral, magnify, enlarge, expand, extend, mount, ascend, climb, amplify.
F3 decrease, diminish.

escapade *n* adventure, exploit, fling, prank, caper, romp, spree, lark (*infml*), antic, stunt, trick.

escape v **1** GET AWAY, break free, run away, bolt, abscond, flee, fly, decamp, break loose, break out, do a bunk (infml), flit, slip away, shake off, slip. **2** AVOID, evade, elude, dodge, skip, shun. **3** LEAK, seep, flow, drain, gush, issue, discharge, ooze, trickle, pour forth, pass.

n **1** GETAWAY, flight, bolt, flit, break-out, decampment, jail-break. **2** AVOIDANCE, evasion. **3** LEAK, seepage, leakage, outflow, gush, drain, discharge, emission, spurt, outpour, emanation. **4** ESCAPISM, diversion, distraction, recreation, relaxation, pastime, safety-valve.

escapist n dreamer, daydreamer, fantasizer, wishful thinker, non-realist, ostrich (infml).
Ｆ⃝ realist.

escort n **1** COMPANION, chaperone, partner, attendant, aide, squire, guide, bodyguard, protector. **2** ENTOURAGE, company, retinue, suite, train, guard, convoy, cortège.
v accompany, partner, chaperone, guide, lead, usher, conduct, guard, protect.

esoteric adj recondite, obscure, abstruse, cryptic, inscrutable, mysterious, mystic, mystical, occult, hidden, secret, confidential, private, inside.
Ｆ⃝ well-known, familiar.

especially adv **1** CHIEFLY, mainly, principally, primarily, pre-eminently, above all. **2** PARTICULARLY, specially, markedly, notably, exceptionally, outstandingly, expressly, supremely, uniquely, unusually, strikingly, very.

essay n composition, dissertation, paper, article, assignment, thesis, piece, commentary, critique, discourse, treatise, review, leader, tract.

essence n **1** NATURE, being, quintessence, substance, soul, spirit, core, centre, heart, meaning, quality, significance, life, entity, crux, kernel, marrow, pith, character, characteristics, attributes, principle. **2** CONCENTRATE, extract, distillation, spirits.

essential adj **1** FUNDAMENTAL, basic, intrinsic, inherent, principal, main, key, characteristic, definitive, typical, constituent. **2** CRUCIAL, indispensable, necessary, vital, requisite, required, needed, important.
Ｆ⃝ **1** incidental. **2** dispensable, inessential.
n necessity, prerequisite, must, requisite, sine qua non (fml), requirement, basic, fundamental, necessary, principle.
Ｆ⃝ inessential.

establish v **1** SET UP, found, start, form, institute, create, organize, inaugurate, introduce, install, plant, settle, secure, lodge, base. **2** PROVE, substantiate, demonstrate, authenticate, ratify, verify, validate, certify, confirm, affirm.
Ｆ⃝ **1** uproot. **2** refute.

establishment n **1** FORMATION, setting up, founding, creation, foundation, installation, institution, inauguration. **2** BUSINESS, company, firm, institute, organization, concern, institution, enterprise. **3** RULING CLASS, the system, the authorities, the powers that be.

estate n **1** POSSESSIONS, effects, assets, belongings, holdings, property, goods, lands. **2** AREA, development, land, manor. **3** (fml) STATUS, standing, situation, position, class, place, condition, state, rank.

estimate v assess, reckon, evaluate, calculate, gauge, guess, value, conjecture, consider, judge, think, number, count, compute, believe. n reckoning, valuation, judgement, guess, approximation, assessment, estimation, evaluation, computation, opinion.

estimation n **1** JUDGEMENT, opinion, belief, consideration, estimate, view, evaluation, assessment, reckoning, conception, calculation, computation. **2** RESPECT, regard, appreciation, esteem, credit.

estranged adj divided, separate, alienated, disaffected, antagonized. **E3** reconciled, united.

estuary n inlet, mouth, firth, fjord, creek, arm, sea-loch.

eternal adj **1** eternal bliss: unending, endless, ceaseless, everlasting, never-ending, infinite, limitless, immortal, undying, imperishable. **2** eternal truths: unchanging, timeless, enduring, lasting, perennial, abiding. **3** (infml) eternal quarrelling: constant, continuous, perpetual, incessant, interminable. **E3 1** ephemeral, temporary. **2** changeable.

eternity n **1** EVERLASTINGNESS, endlessness, everlasting, imperishability, infinity, timelessness, perpetuity, immutability, ages, age, aeon. **2** AFTER-LIFE, hereafter, immortality, heaven, paradise, next world, world to come.

ethical adj moral, principled, just, right, proper, virtuous, honourable,

fair, upright, righteous, seemly, honest, good, correct, commendable, fitting, noble, meet (fml). **E3** unethical.

ethics n moral values, morality, principles, standards, code, moral philosophy, rules, beliefs, propriety, conscience, equity.

ethnic adj racial, native, indigenous, traditional, tribal, folk, cultural, national, aboriginal.

ethos n attitude, beliefs, standards, manners, ethics, morality, code, principles, spirit, tenor, rationale, character, disposition.

etiquette n code, formalities, standards, correctness, conventions, customs, protocol (fml), rules, manners, politeness, courtesy, civility, decorum, ceremony, decency.

euphemism n evasion, polite term, substitution, politeness, understatement.

euphoria n elation, ecstasy, bliss, rapture, high spirits, well-being, high (infml), exhilaration, exultation, joy, intoxication, jubilation, transport, glee, exaltation, enthusiasm, cheerfulness. **E3** depression, despondency.

evacuate v **1** LEAVE, depart, withdraw, quit, remove, retire from, clear (out) (infml), abandon, desert, forsake, vacate, decamp, relinquish. **2** EMPTY, eject, void, expel, discharge, eliminate, defecate, purge.

evacuation n **1** DEPARTURE, withdrawal, retreat, exodus, removal, quitting, desertion, abandonment, clearance, relinquishment, retirement, vacation. **2** EMPTYING, expulsion, ejection, discharge, elimination, defecation, urination.

evade v **1** *evade one's duties*: elude, avoid, escape, dodge, shirk, steer clear of, shun, sidestep, duck (*infml*), balk, skive (*infml*), fend off, chicken out (*infml*), cop out (*infml*). **2** *evade a question*: prevaricate, equivocate, fence, fudge, parry, quibble, hedge. **F3 1** confront, face.

evaluate v value, assess, appraise, estimate, reckon, calculate, gauge, judge, rate, size up, weigh, compute, rank.

evaluation n valuation, appraisal, assessment, estimation, estimate, judgement, reckoning, calculation, opinion, computation.

evaporate v **1** DISAPPEAR, dematerialize, vanish, melt (away), dissolve, disperse, dispel, dissipate, fade. **2** VAPORIZE, dry, dehydrate, exhale.

evasion n avoidance, escape, dodge, equivocation, excuse, prevarication, put-off, trickery, subterfuge, shirking.

F3 frankness, directness.

evasive adj equivocating, indirect, prevaricating, devious, shifty (*infml*), unforthcoming, slippery (*infml*), misleading, deceitful, deceptive, cagey (*infml*), oblique, secretive, tricky, cunning.

F3 direct, frank.

eve n day before, verge, brink, edge, threshold.

even adj **1** LEVEL, flat, smooth, horizontal, flush, parallel, plane. **2** STEADY, unvarying, constant, regular, uniform. **3** EQUAL, balanced, matching, same, similar, like, symmetrical, fifty-fifty, level, side by side, neck and neck (*infml*), even-stevens (*infml*). **4** EVEN-TEMPERED,

calm, placid, serene, tranquil, composed, unruffled. **5** EVEN-HANDED, balanced, equitable, fair, impartial.

F3 1 uneven. **3** unequal.

v smooth, flatten, level, match, regularize, balance, equalize, align, square, stabilize, steady, straighten.

evening n nightfall, dusk, eve, eventide, twilight, sunset, sundown.

event n **1** HAPPENING, occurrence, incident, occasion, affair, circumstance, episode, eventuality, experience, matter, case, adventure, business, fact, possibility, milestone. **2** CONSEQUENCE, result, outcome, conclusion, end, effect, issue, termination. **3** GAME, match, competition, contest, tournament, engagement.

even-tempered adj calm, level-headed, placid, stable, tranquil, serene, composed, cool, steady, peaceful, peaceable.

F3 excitable, erratic.

eventful adj busy, exciting, lively, active, full, interesting, remarkable, significant, memorable, momentous, notable, noteworthy, unforgettable.

F3 dull, ordinary.

eventual adj final, ultimate, resulting, concluding, ensuing, future, later, subsequent, prospective, projected, planned, impending.

eventually adv finally, ultimately, at last, in the end, at length, subsequently, after all, sooner or later.

ever adv **1** ALWAYS, evermore, for ever, perpetually, constantly, at all times, continually, endlessly. **2** AT ANY TIME, in any case, in any circumstances, at all, on any account.

F3 1 never.

everlasting *adj* eternal, undying, never-ending, endless, immortal, infinite, imperishable, constant, permanent, perpetual, indestructible, timeless.

F3 temporary, transient.

everyday *adj* ordinary, common, commonplace, day-to-day, familiar, run-of-the-mill, regular, plain, routine, usual, workaday, common-or-garden (*infml*), normal, customary, stock, accustomed, conventional, daily, habitual, monotonous, frequent, simple, informal.

F3 unusual, exceptional, special.

everyone *n* everybody, one and all, each one, all and sundry, the whole world.

everywhere *adv* all around, all over, throughout, far and near, far and wide, high and low, ubiquitous, left, right and centre (*infml*).

evict *v* expel, eject, dispossess, put out, turn out, turf out (*infml*), kick out (*infml*), force out, remove, cast out, chuck out (*infml*), oust, dislodge, expropriate.

evidence *n* **1** PROOF, verification, confirmation, affirmation, grounds, substantiation, documentation, data. **2** TESTIMONY, declaration. **3** INDICATION, manifestation, suggestion, sign, mark, hint, demonstration, token.

evident *adj* clear, obvious, manifest, apparent, plain, patent, visible, conspicuous, noticeable, clear-cut, unmistakable, perceptible, distinct, discernible, tangible, incontestable, indisputable, incontrovertible.

evidently *adv* clearly, apparently, plainly, patently, manifestly, obviously, seemingly, undoubtedly, doubtless(ly), indisputably.

evil *adj* **1** WICKED, wrong, sinful, bad, immoral, vicious, vile, malevolent, iniquitous, cruel, base, corrupt, heinous, malicious, malignant, devilish, depraved, mischievous. **2** HARMFUL, pernicious, destructive, deadly, detrimental, hurtful, poisonous. **3** DISASTROUS, ruinous, calamitous, catastrophic, adverse, dire, inauspicious. **4** OFFENSIVE, noxious, foul.
n **1** WICKEDNESS, wrong-doing, wrong, immorality, badness, sin, sinfulness, vice, viciousness, iniquity, depravity, baseness, corruption, malignity, mischief, heinousness. **2** ADVERSITY, affliction, calamity, disaster, misfortune, suffering, sorrow, ruin, catastrophe, blow, curse, distress, hurt, harm, ill, injury, misery, woe.

evoke *v* summon (up), call, elicit, invoke, arouse, stir, raise, stimulate, call forth, call up, conjure up, awaken, provoke, excite, recall.

F3 suppress.

evolution *n* development, growth, progression, progress, expansion, increase, ripening, derivation, descent.

evolve *v* develop, grow, increase, mature, progress, unravel, expand, enlarge, emerge, descend, derive, result, elaborate.

exact *adj* **1** PRECISE, accurate, correct, faithful, literal, flawless, faultless, right, true, veracious, definite, explicit, detailed, specific, strict, unerring, close, factual, identical, express, word-perfect, blow-by-blow (*infml*). **2** CAREFUL, scrupulous, particular, rigorous, methodical, meticulous, orderly, painstaking.

F3 **1** inexact, imprecise.
v extort, extract, claim, insist on, wrest,

wring, compel, demand, command, force, impose, require, squeeze, milk (infml).

exacting adj demanding, difficult, hard, laborious, arduous, rigorous, taxing, tough, harsh, painstaking, severe, strict, unsparing.
F3 easy.

exactly adv 1 PRECISELY, accurately, literally, faithfully, correctly, specifically, rigorously, scrupulously, veraciously, verbatim, carefully, faultlessly, unerringly, strictly, to the letter, particularly, methodically, explicitly, expressly, dead (infml).
2 ABSOLUTELY, definitely, precisely, indeed, certainly, truly, quite, just, unequivocally.
F3 1 inaccurately, roughly.

exaggerate v overstate, overdo, magnify, overemphasize, emphasize, embellish, embroider, enlarge, amplify, oversell, pile it on (infml).
F3 understate.

examination n 1 INSPECTION, enquiry, scrutiny, study, survey, search, analysis, exploration, investigation, probe, appraisal, observation, research, review, scan, once-over (infml), perusal, check, check-up, audit, critique. 2 TEST, exam, quiz, questioning, cross-examination, cross-questioning, trial, inquisition, interrogation, viva.

examine v 1 INSPECT, investigate, scrutinize, study, survey, analyse, explore, enquire, consider, probe, review, scan, check (out), ponder, pore over, sift, vet, weigh up, appraise, assay, audit, peruse, case (sl). 2 TEST, quiz, question, cross-examine, cross-question, interrogate, grill (infml), catechize (fml).

example n instance, case, case in point, illustration, exemplification, sample, specimen, model, pattern, ideal, archetype, prototype, standard, type, lesson, citation.

exasperate v infuriate, annoy, anger, incense, irritate, madden, provoke, get on someone's nerves, enrage, irk, rile, rankle, rouse, get to (infml), goad, vex.
F3 appease, pacify.

excavate v dig (out), dig up, hollow, burrow, tunnel, delve, unearth, mine, quarry, disinter, gouge, scoop, exhume, uncover.

excavation n hole, hollow, pit, quarry, mine, dugout, dig, diggings, burrow, cavity, crater, trench, trough, shaft, ditch, cutting.

exceed v surpass, outdo, outstrip, beat, better, pass, overtake, top, outshine, eclipse, outreach, outrun, transcend, cap, overdo, overstep.

excel v 1 SURPASS, outdo, beat, outclass, outperform, outrank, eclipse, better. 2 BE EXCELLENT, succeed, shine, stand out, predominate.

excellence n superiority, pre-eminence, distinction, merit, supremacy, quality, worth, fineness, eminence, goodness, greatness, virtue, perfection, purity.

excellent adj superior, first-class, first-rate, prime, superlative, unequalled, outstanding, surpassing, remarkable, distinguished, great, good, exemplary, select, superb, admirable, commendable, top-notch (infml), splendid, noteworthy, notable, fine, wonderful, worthy.
F3 inferior, second-rate.

except prep excepting, but, apart from, other than, save, omitting, not counting, leaving out, excluding, except for, besides, bar, minus, less. v leave out, omit, bar, exclude, reject, rule out.

exception n oddity, anomaly, deviation, abnormality, irregularity, peculiarity, inconsistency, rarity, special case, quirk.

exceptional adj 1 ABNORMAL, unusual, anomalous, strange, odd, irregular, extraordinary, peculiar, special, rare, uncommon. 2 OUTSTANDING, remarkable, phenomenal, prodigious, notable, noteworthy, superior, unequalled, marvellous.
F3 1 normal. 2 mediocre.

excerpt n extract, passage, portion, section, selection, quote, quotation, part, citation, scrap, fragment.

excess n 1 SURFEIT, overabundance, glut, plethora, superfluity, superabundance, surplus, overflow, overkill, remainder, left-over. 2 OVERINDULGENCE, dissipation, immoderateness, intemperance, extravagance, unrestraint, debauchery.
F3 1 deficiency. 2 restraint.
adj extra, surplus, spare, redundant, remaining, residual, left-over, additional, superfluous, supernumerary.
F3 inadequate.

excessive adj immoderate, inordinate, extreme, undue, uncalled-for, disproportionate, unnecessary, unneeded, superfluous, unreasonable, exorbitant, extravagant, steep (infml).
F3 insufficient.

exchange v barter, change, trade, swap, switch, replace, interchange, convert, commute, substitute, reciprocate, bargain, bandy. n 1 CONVERSATION, discussion, chat. 2 TRADE, commerce, dealing, market, traffic, barter, bargain. 3 INTERCHANGE, swap, switch, replacement, substitution, reciprocity.

excitable adj temperamental, volatile, passionate, emotional, highly-strung, fiery, hot-headed, hasty, nervous, hot-tempered, irascible, quick-tempered, sensitive, susceptible.
F3 calm, stable.

excite v 1 MOVE, agitate, disturb, upset, touch, stir up, thrill, elate, turn on (infml), impress. 2 AROUSE, rouse, animate, awaken, fire, inflame, kindle, motivate, stimulate, engender, inspire, instigate, incite, induce, ignite, galvanize, generate, provoke, sway, quicken, evoke.
F3 1 calm.

excited adj aroused, roused, stimulated, stirred, thrilled, elated, enthusiastic, eager, moved, high (infml), worked up, wrought-up, overwrought, restless, frantic, frenzied, wild.
F3 calm, apathetic.

excitement n 1 UNREST, ado, action, activity, commotion, fuss, tumult, flurry, furore, adventure. 2 DISCOMPOSURE, agitation, passion, thrill, animation, elation, enthusiasm, restlessness, kicks (infml), ferment, fever, eagerness, stimulation.
F3 1 calm. 2 apathy.

exciting adj stimulating, stirring, intoxicating, exhilarating, thrilling, rousing, moving, enthralling,

electrifying, nail-biting (*infml*), white-knuckle (*infml*), cliff-hanging (*infml*), striking, sensational, provocative, inspiring, interesting.
F3 dull, unexciting.

exclaim *v* cry (out), declare, blurt (out), call, yell, shout, proclaim, utter.

exclamation *n* cry, call, yell, shout, expletive, interjection, ejaculation, outcry, utterance.

exclude *v* **1** BAN, bar, prohibit, disallow, veto, proscribe, forbid, blacklist. **2** OMIT, leave out, keep out, refuse, reject, ignore, shut out, rule out, ostracize, eliminate. **3** EXPEL, eject, evict, excommunicate.
F3 1 admit. **2** include.

exclusive *adj* **1** SOLE, single, unique, only, undivided, unshared, whole, total, peculiar. **2** RESTRICTED, limited, closed, private, narrow, restrictive, choice, select, discriminative, cliquey, chic, classy (*infml*), elegant, fashionable, posh (*infml*), snobbish.

excruciating *adj* agonizing, painful, severe, tormenting, unbearable, insufferable, acute, intolerable, intense, sharp, piercing, extreme, atrocious, racking, harrowing, savage, burning, bitter.

excursion *n* outing, trip, jaunt, expedition, day trip, awayday, journey, tour, airing, breather, junket (*infml*), ride, drive, walk, ramble.

excuse *v* **1** FORGIVE, pardon, overlook, absolve, acquit, exonerate, tolerate, ignore, indulge. **2** RELEASE, free, discharge, liberate, let off, relieve, spare, exempt. **3** CONDONE, explain, mitigate, justify, vindicate, defend, apologize for.
F3 1 criticize. **2** punish.
n justification, explanation, grounds,

defence, plea, alibi, reason, apology, pretext, pretence, exoneration, evasion, cop-out (*infml*), shift, substitute.

execute *v* **1** PUT TO DEATH, kill, liquidate, hang, electrocute, shoot, guillotine, decapitate, behead. **2** CARRY OUT, perform, do, accomplish, achieve, fulfil, complete, discharge, effect, enact, deliver, enforce, finish, implement, administer, consummate, realize, dispatch, expedite, validate, serve, render, sign.

execution *n* **1** DEATH PENALTY, capital punishment, killing, hanging, electrocution, firing squad, shooting, guillotining, decapitation, beheading. **2** ACCOMPLISHMENT, operation, performance, completion, achievement, administration, effect, enactment, implementation, realization, discharge, dispatch, consummation, enforcement. **3** STYLE, technique, rendition, delivery, performance, manner, mode.

executive *n* **1** ADMINISTRATION, management, government, leadership, hierarchy. **2** ADMINISTRATOR, manager, organizer, leader, controller, director, governor, official.
adj administrative, managerial, controlling, supervisory, regulating, decision-making, governing, organizing, directing, directorial, organizational, leading, guiding.

exemplary *adj* **1** MODEL, ideal, perfect, admirable, excellent, faultless, flawless, correct, good, commendable, praiseworthy, worthy, laudable, estimable, honourable. **2** CAUTIONARY, warning.
F3 1 imperfect, unworthy.

exemplify v illustrate, demonstrate, show, instance, represent, typify, manifest, embody, epitomize, exhibit, depict, display.

exempt v excuse, release, relieve, let off, free, absolve, discharge, dismiss, liberate, spare.
adj excused, not liable, immune, released, spared, absolved, discharged, excluded, free, liberated, clear.
E₃ liable.

exercise v **1** USE, utilize, employ, apply, exert, practise, wield, try, discharge. **2** TRAIN, drill, practise, work out (infml), keep fit. **3** WORRY, disturb, trouble, upset, burden, distress, vex, annoy, agitate, afflict.
n **1** TRAINING, drill, practice, effort, exertion, task, lesson, work, discipline, activity, physical jerks (infml), work-out (infml), aerobics, labour. **2** USE, utilization, employment, application, implementation, practice, operation, discharge, assignment, fulfilment, accomplishment.

exert v use, utilize, employ, apply, exercise, bring to bear, wield, expend.
exert oneself strive, struggle, strain, make every effort, take pains, toil, labour, work, sweat (infml), endeavour, apply oneself.

exertion n **1** EFFORT, industry, labour, toil, work, struggle, diligence, assiduousness, perseverance, pains, endeavour, attempt, strain, travail (fml), trial. **2** USE, utilization, employment, application, exercise, operation, action.
E₃ 1 idleness, rest.

exhaust v **1** CONSUME, empty, deplete, drain, sap, spend, waste, squander, dissipate, impoverish, use up, finish, dry, bankrupt. **2** TIRE (OUT), weary, fatigue, tax, strain, weaken, overwork, wear out.
E₃ 1 renew. **2** refresh.
n emission, exhalation, discharge, fumes.

exhausted adj **1** EMPTY, finished, depleted, spent, used up, drained, dry, worn out, void. **2** TIRED (OUT), dead tired, dead-beat (infml), all in (infml), done (in) (infml), fatigued, weak, washed-out, whacked (infml), knackered (infml), jaded.
E₃ 1 fresh. **2** vigorous.

exhausting adj tiring, strenuous, taxing, gruelling, arduous, hard, laborious, backbreaking, draining, severe, testing, punishing, formidable, debilitating.
E₃ refreshing.

exhaustion n fatigue, tiredness, weariness, debility, feebleness, jet-lag.
E₃ freshness, liveliness.

exhaustive adj comprehensive, all-embracing, all-inclusive, far-reaching, complete, extensive, encyclopedic, full-scale, thorough, full, in-depth, intensive, detailed, definitive, all-out, sweeping.
E₃ incomplete, restricted.

exhibit v display, show, present, demonstrate, manifest, expose, parade, reveal, express, disclose, indicate, air, flaunt, offer.
E₃ conceal.
n display, exhibition, show, illustration, model.

exhibition n display, show, demonstration, demo (infml), exhibit, presentation, manifestation, spectacle, exposition, expo (infml), showing, fair, performance, airing, representation, showcase.

exhilarate *v* thrill, excite, elate, animate, enliven, invigorate, vitalize, stimulate.
F3 bore.

exile *n* **1** BANISHMENT, deportation, expatriation, expulsion, ostracism, transportation. **2** EXPATRIATE, refugee, émigré, deportee, outcast. *v* banish, expel, deport, expatriate, drive out, ostracize, oust.

exist *v* **1** BE, live, abide, continue, endure, have one's being, breathe, prevail. **2** SUBSIST, survive. **3** BE PRESENT, occur, happen, be available, remain.

existence *n* **1** BEING, life, reality, actuality, continuance, continuation, endurance, survival, breath, subsistence. **2** CREATION, the world. **3** (*fml*) ENTITY, creature, thing.
F3 death, non-existence.

exit *n* **1** DEPARTURE, going, retreat, withdrawal, leave-taking, retirement, farewell, exodus. **2** DOOR, way out, doorway, gate, vent.
F3 entrance, arrival. **2** entrance.
v depart, leave, go, retire, withdraw, take one's leave, retreat, issue.
F3 arrive, enter.

exonerate *v* **1** ABSOLVE, acquit, clear, vindicate, exculpate (*fml*), justify, pardon, discharge. **2** EXEMPT, excuse, spare, let off, release, relieve.
F3 incriminate.

exorbitant *adj* excessive, unreasonable, unwarranted, undue, inordinate, immoderate, extravagant, extortionate, enormous, preposterous.
F3 reasonable, moderate.

exotic *adj* **1** FOREIGN, alien, imported, introduced. **2** UNUSUAL, striking, different, unfamiliar, extraordinary, bizarre, curious,

strange, fascinating, colourful, peculiar, outlandish.
F3 1 native. **2** ordinary.

expand *v* **1** STRETCH, swell, widen, lengthen, thicken, magnify, multiply, inflate, broaden, blow up, open out, fill out, fatten. **2** INCREASE, grow, extend, enlarge, develop, amplify, spread, branch out, diversify, elaborate.
F3 1 contract.

expanse *n* extent, space, area, breadth, range, stretch, sweep, field, plain, tract.

expansive *adj* **1** FRIENDLY, genial, outgoing, open, affable, sociable, talkative, warm, communicative, effusive. **2** EXTENSIVE, broad, comprehensive, wide-ranging, all-embracing, thorough.
F3 1 reserved, cold. **2** restricted, narrow.

expect *v* **1** *expect the money soon*: anticipate, await, look forward to, hope for, look for, bank on, bargain for, envisage, predict, forecast, contemplate, project, foresee.
2 *expect you to comply*: require, want, wish, insist on, demand, rely on, count on. **3** *expect you're right*: suppose, surmise, assume, believe, think, presume, imagine, reckon, guess (*infml*), trust.

expectant *adj* **1** AWAITING, anticipating, hopeful, in suspense, ready, apprehensive, anxious, watchful, eager, curious. **2** PREGNANT, expecting (*infml*), with child (*fml*).

expedition *n* **1** JOURNEY, excursion, trip, voyage, tour, exploration, trek, safari, hike, sail, ramble, raid, quest, pilgrimage, mission, crusade.
2 (*fml*) PROMPTNESS, speed, alacrity, haste.

expel v **1** DRIVE OUT, eject, evict, banish, throw out, ban, bar, oust, exile, expatriate. **2** DISCHARGE, evacuate, void, cast out.
F3 1 welcome.

expend v **1** SPEND, pay, disburse (*fml*), fork out (*infml*). **2** CONSUME, use (up), dissipate, exhaust, employ.
F3 1 save. 2 conserve.

expenditure n spending, expense, outlay, outgoings, disbursement (*fml*), payment, output.
F3 income.

expense n spending, expenditure, disbursement (*fml*), outlay, payment, loss, cost, charge.

expensive adj dear, high-priced, costly, exorbitant, extortionate, steep (*infml*), extravagant, lavish.
F3 cheap, inexpensive.

experience n **1** KNOWLEDGE, familiarity, know-how, involvement, participation, practice, understanding. **2** INCIDENT, event, episode, happening, encounter, occurrence, adventure.
F3 1 inexperience.
v undergo, go through, live through, suffer, feel, endure, encounter, face, meet, know, try, perceive, sustain.

experienced adj **1** PRACTISED, knowledgeable, familiar, capable, competent, well-versed, expert, accomplished, qualified, skilled, tried, trained, professional. **2** MATURE, seasoned, wise, veteran.
F3 1 inexperienced, unskilled.

experiment n trial, test, investigation, experimentation, research, examination, trial run, venture, trial and error, attempt, procedure, proof.
v try, test, investigate, examine, research, sample, verify.

experimental adj trial, test, exploratory, empirical (*fml*), tentative, provisional, speculative, pilot, preliminary, trial-and-error.

expert n specialist, connoisseur, authority, professional, pro (*infml*), dab hand (*infml*), maestro, virtuoso. adj proficient, adept, skilled, skilful, knowledgeable, experienced, able, practised, professional, masterly, specialist, qualified, virtuoso.
F3 amateurish, novice.

expertise n expertness, proficiency, skill, skilfulness, know-how, knack (*infml*), knowledge, mastery, dexterity, virtuosity.
F3 inexperience.

expire v end, cease, finish, stop, terminate, close, conclude, discontinue, run out, lapse, die, depart, decease, perish.
F3 begin.

explain v **1** INTERPRET, clarify, describe, define, make clear, elucidate, simplify, resolve, solve, spell out, translate, unfold, unravel, untangle, illustrate, demonstrate, disclose, expound, teach. **2** JUSTIFY, excuse, account for, rationalize.
F3 1 obscure, confound.

explanation n **1** INTERPRETATION, clarification, definition, elucidation, illustration, demonstration, account, description, exegesis (*fml*).
2 JUSTIFICATION, excuse, warrant, rationalization. **3** ANSWER, meaning, motive, reason, key, sense, significance.

explanatory adj descriptive, interpretive, explicative, demonstrative, expository (*fml*), justifying.

explicit adj **1** CLEAR, distinct, exact, categorical, absolute, certain, positive, precise, specific, unambiguous, express, definite, declared, detailed, stated. **2** OPEN, direct, frank, outspoken, straightforward, unreserved, plain.

E3 1 implicit, unspoken, vague.

explode v **1** BLOW UP, burst, go off, set off, detonate, discharge, blast, erupt. **2** DISCREDIT, disprove, give the lie to, debunk, invalidate, refute, rebut, repudiate.

E3 2 prove, confirm.

exploit n deed, feat, adventure, achievement, accomplishment, attainment, stunt.
v USE, utilize, capitalize on, profit by, turn to account, take advantage of, cash in on, make capital out of.
2 MISUSE, abuse, oppress, ill-treat, impose on, manipulate, rip off (infml), fleece (infml).

exploration n **1** INVESTIGATION, examination, enquiry, research, scrutiny, study, inspection, analysis, probe. **2** EXPEDITION, survey, reconnaissance, search, trip, tour, voyage, travel, safari.

explore v **1** INVESTIGATE, examine, inspect, research, scrutinize, probe, analyse. **2** TRAVEL, tour, search, reconnoitre, prospect, scout, survey.

explosion n detonation, blast, burst, outburst, discharge, eruption, bang, outbreak, clap, crack, fit, report.

explosive adj unstable, volatile, sensitive, tense, fraught, charged, touchy, overwrought, dangerous, hazardous, perilous, stormy.

E3 stable, calm.

expose v **1** REVEAL, show, exhibit, display, disclose, uncover, bring to light, present, manifest, detect, divulge, unveil, unmask, denounce. **2** ENDANGER, jeopardize, imperil, risk, hazard.

E3 1 conceal. **2** cover up.

exposed adj bare, open, revealed, laid bare, unprotected, vulnerable, exhibited, on display, on show, on view, shown, susceptible.

E3 covered, sheltered.

exposure n **1** REVELATION, uncovering, disclosure, exposé, showing, unmasking, unveiling, display, airing, exhibition, presentation, publicity, manifestation, discovery, divulgence. **2** FAMILIARITY, experience, knowledge, contact. **3** JEOPARDY, danger, hazard, risk, vulnerability.

express v **1** ARTICULATE, verbalize, utter, voice, say, speak, state, communicate, pronounce, tell, assert, declare, put across, formulate, intimate, testify, convey. **2** SHOW, manifest, exhibit, disclose, divulge, reveal, indicate, denote, depict, embody. **3** SYMBOLIZE, stand for, represent, signify, designate.
adj **1** SPECIFIC, explicit, exact, definite, clear, categorical, precise, distinct, clear-cut, certain, plain, manifest, particular, stated, unambiguous. **2** FAST, speedy, rapid, quick, high-speed, non-stop.

E3 1 vague.

expression n **1** LOOK, air, aspect, countenance, appearance, mien (fml). **2** REPRESENTATION, manifestation, demonstration, indication, exhibition, embodiment, show, sign, symbol, style. **3** UTTERANCE, verbalization, communication, articulation, statement, assertion, announcement, declaration, pronouncement, speech. **4** TONE, intonation, delivery, diction, enunciation, modulation, wording. **5** PHRASE, term, turn of phrase, saying, set phrase, idiom.

expressionless adj dull, blank, dead-pan, impassive, straight-faced, poker-faced (infml), inscrutable, empty, vacuous, glassy.

E3 expressive.

expressive adj eloquent, meaningful, forceful, telling, revealing, informative, indicative, communicative, demonstrative, emphatic, moving, poignant, lively, striking, suggestive, significant, thoughtful, vivid, sympathetic.

expulsion n ejection, eviction, exile, banishment, removal, discharge, exclusion, dismissal.

exquisite adj **1** BEAUTIFUL, attractive, dainty, delicate, charming, elegant, delightful, lovely, pleasing. **2** PERFECT, flawless, fine, excellent, choice, precious, rare, outstanding. **3** REFINED, discriminating, meticulous, sensitive, impeccable. **4** INTENSE, keen, sharp, poignant. **E3 1** ugly. **2** flawed. **3** unrefined.

extend v **1** SPREAD, stretch, reach, continue. **2** ENLARGE, increase, expand, develop, amplify, lengthen, widen, elongate, draw out, protract, prolong, spin out, unwind. **3** OFFER, give, grant, hold out, impart, present, bestow, confer.

E3 2 contract, shorten. **3** withhold.

extension n **1** ENLARGEMENT, increase, stretching, broadening, widening, lengthening, expansion, elongation, development, enhancement, protraction, continuation. **2** ADDITION,

supplement, appendix, annexe, addendum (fml). **3** DELAY, postponement.

extensive adj **1** BROAD, comprehensive, far-reaching, large-scale, thorough, widespread, universal, extended, all-inclusive, general, pervasive, prevalent. **2** LARGE, huge, roomy, spacious, vast, voluminous, long, lengthy, wide. **E3 1** restricted, narrow. **2** small.

extent n **1** DIMENSION(S), amount, magnitude, expanse, size, area, bulk, degree, breadth, quantity, spread, stretch, volume, width, measure, duration, term, time. **2** LIMIT, bounds, lengths, range, reach, scope, compass, sphere, play, sweep.

exterior n outside, surface, covering, coating, face, façade, shell, skin, finish, externals, appearance.
E3 inside, interior.
adj outer, outside, outermost, surface, external, superficial, surrounding, outward, peripheral, extrinsic.
E3 inside, interior.

exterminate v annihilate, eradicate, destroy, eliminate, massacre, abolish, wipe out.

external adj outer, surface, outside, exterior, superficial, outward, outermost, apparent, visible, extraneous, extrinsic, extramural, independent.
E3 internal.

extinct adj **1** DEFUNCT, dead, gone, obsolete, ended, exterminated, terminated, vanished, lost, abolished. **2** EXTINGUISHED, quenched, inactive, out.
E3 1 living.

extinction n annihilation, extermination, death, eradication, obliteration, destruction, abolition, excision.

extinguish v 1 PUT OUT, blow out, snuff out, stifle, smother, douse, quench. 2 ANNIHILATE, exterminate, eliminate, destroy, kill, eradicate, erase, expunge, abolish, remove, end, suppress.

extort v extract, wring, exact, coerce, force, milk (infml), blackmail, squeeze, bleed (infml), bully.

extortionate adj exorbitant, excessive, grasping, exacting, immoderate, rapacious, unreasonable, oppressive, blood-sucking (infml), rigorous, severe, hard, harsh, inordinate.

extra adj 1 ADDITIONAL, added, auxiliary, supplementary, new, more, further, ancillary, fresh, other. 2 EXCESS, spare, superfluous, supernumerary, surplus, unused, unneeded, leftover, reserve, redundant.
F3 1 integral. 2 essential.
n addition, supplement, extension, accessory, appendage, bonus, complement, adjunct, addendum (fml), attachment.
adv especially, exceptionally, extraordinarily, particularly, unusually, remarkably, extremely.

extract v 1 REMOVE, take out, draw out, exact, uproot, withdraw.
2 DERIVE, draw, distil, obtain, get, gather, glean, wrest, wring, elicit.
3 CHOOSE, select, cull, abstract, cite, quote.
F3 1 insert.
n 1 DISTILLATION, essence, juice.
2 EXCERPT, passage, selection, clip, cutting, quotation, abstract, citation.

extraordinary adj remarkable, unusual, exceptional, notable, noteworthy, outstanding, unique, special, strange, peculiar, rare, surprising, amazing, wonderful, unprecedented, marvellous, fantastic, significant, particular.
F3 commonplace, ordinary.

extravagance n 1 OVERSPENDING, profligacy, squandering, waste.
2 EXCESS, immoderation, recklessness, profusion, outrageousness, folly.
F3 thrift. 2 moderation.

extravagant adj 1 PROFLIGATE, prodigal, spendthrift, thriftless, wasteful, reckless. 2 IMMODERATE, flamboyant, preposterous, outrageous, ostentatious, pretentious, lavish, ornate, flashy (infml), fanciful, fantastic, wild. 3 OVERPRICED, exorbitant, expensive, excessive, costly.
F3 1 thrifty. 2 moderate.
3 reasonable.

extreme adj 1 INTENSE, great, immoderate, inordinate, utmost, utter, out-and-out, maximum, acute, downright, extraordinary, exceptional, greatest, highest, unreasonable, remarkable.
2 FARTHEST, far-off, faraway, distant, endmost, outermost, remotest, uttermost, final, last, terminal, ultimate. 3 RADICAL, zealous, extremist, fanatical. 4 DRASTIC, dire, uncompromising, stern, strict, rigid, severe, harsh.
F3 1 mild. 3 moderate.
n extremity, limit, maximum, ultimate, utmost, excess, top, pinnacle, peak, height, end, climax, depth, edge, termination.

extremity n 1 EXTREME, limit, boundary, brink, verge, bound, border, apex, height, tip, top, edge, excess, end, acme, termination, peak, pinnacle, margin, terminal, terminus, ultimate, pole, maximum, minimum, frontier, depth. **2** CRISIS, danger, emergency, plight, hardship.

extricate *v* disentangle, clear, disengage, free, deliver, liberate, release, rescue, relieve, remove, withdraw.

F3 involve.

extroverted *adj* outgoing, friendly, sociable, amicable, amiable, exuberant.

F3 introverted.

exuberant *adj* **1** LIVELY, vivacious, spirited, zestful, high-spirited, effervescent, ebullient, enthusiastic, sparkling, excited, exhilarated, effusive, cheerful, fulsome. **2** PLENTIFUL, lavish, overflowing, plenteous.

F3 1 apathetic. **2** scarce.

exult *v* rejoice, revel, delight, glory, celebrate, relish, crow, gloat, triumph.

eye *n* **1** APPRECIATION, discrimination, discernment,

perception, recognition. **2** VIEWPOINT, opinion, judgement, mind. **3** WATCH, observation, lookout.

Parts of the eye include:
aqueous humour, blind spot, choroid, ciliary body, cone, conjunctiva, cornea, eyelash, eyelid, fovea, iris, lachrymal duct, lens, ocular muscle, optic nerve, pupil, retina, rod, sclera, suspensory ligament, vitreous humour.

---

v look at, watch, regard, observe, stare at, gaze at, glance at, view, scrutinize, scan, examine, peruse, study, survey, inspect, contemplate.

eyesight *n* vision, sight, perception, observation, view.

eyesore *n* ugliness, blemish, monstrosity, blot on the landscape, carbuncle (*infml*), disfigurement, horror, blight, atrocity, mess.

eye-witness *n* witness, observer, spectator, looker-on, onlooker, bystander, viewer, passer-by.

F

fable *n* allegory, parable, story, tale, yarn, myth, legend, fiction, fabrication, invention, lie, untruth, falsehood, tall story, old wives' tale.

fabric *n* **1** CLOTH, material, textile, stuff, web, texture. **2** STRUCTURE, framework, construction, make-up, constitution, organization, infrastructure, foundations.

Fabrics include:
alpaca, angora, astrakhan, barathea, bouclé, cashmere, chenille, duffel, felt, flannel, fleece, Harris tweed®, mohair, paisley, pashmina, serge, Shetland wool, tweed, vicuña, wool, worsted; brocade, buckram, calico, cambric, candlewick, canvas, chambray, cheesecloth, chino, chintz, cord, corduroy, cotton, crêpe, denim, drill, jean, flannelette, fleece, gaberdine, gingham, jersey, lawn, linen, lisle, madras, moleskin, muslin, needlecord, piqué, poplin, sateen, seersucker, terry, ticking, Viyella®, webbing, winceyette; grosgrain, damask, lace, chiffon, georgette, gossamer, voile, organza, organdie, tulle, net, crêpe de Chine, silk, taffeta, shantung, velvet, velour; polycotton, polyester, rayon, nylon, Crimplene®, Terylene®, Lurex®, Lycra®, lamé; hessian, horsehair, sharkskin.

fabricate *v* **1** FAKE, falsify, forge, invent, make up, trump up, concoct. **2** MAKE, manufacture, construct, assemble, build, erect, form, shape, fashion, create, devise.
E∃ 2 demolish, destroy.

fabulous *adj* **1** WONDERFUL, marvellous, fantastic, superb, breathtaking, spectacular, phenomenal, amazing, astounding, unbelievable, incredible, inconceivable. **2** *a fabulous beast*: mythical, legendary, fabled, fantastic, fictitious, invented, imaginary.
E∃ 2 real.

face *n* **1** FEATURES, countenance, visage, physiognomy. **2** EXPRESSION, look, appearance, air. **3** *pull a face*: grimace, frown, scowl, pout.
4 EXTERIOR, outside, surface, cover, front, façade, aspect, side.
v **1** BE OPPOSITE, give on to, front, overlook. **2** CONFRONT, face up to, deal with, cope with, tackle, brave, defy, oppose, encounter, meet, experience. **3** COVER, coat, dress, clad, overlay, veneer.
face to face opposite, eye to eye, eyeball to eyeball, in confrontation.
face up to accept, come to terms with, acknowledge, recognize, cope with, deal with, confront, meet head-on, stand up to.

facet n surface, plane, side, face, aspect, angle, point, feature, characteristic.

facetious adj flippant, frivolous, playful, jocular, jesting, tongue-in-cheek, funny, amusing, humorous, comical, witty.
⊟ serious.

facile adj easy, simple, simplistic, ready, quick, hasty, glib, fluent, smooth, slick, plausible, shallow, superficial.
⊟ complicated, profound.

facilitate v ease, help, assist, further, promote, forward, expedite, speed up.

facilities n amenities, services, conveniences, resources, prerequisites, equipment, mod cons (infml), means, opportunities.

facility n ease, effortlessness, readiness, quickness, fluency, proficiency, skill, skilfulness, talent, gift, knack, ability.

fact n **1** facts and figures: information, datum, detail, particular, specific, point, item, circumstance, event, incident, occurrence, happening, act, deed, fait accompli. **2** REALITY, actuality, truth.
⊟ 2 fiction.
in fact actually, in actual fact, in point of fact, as a matter of fact, in reality, really, indeed.

faction n splinter group, ginger group, minority, division, section, contingent, party, camp, set, clique, coterie, cabal, junta, lobby, pressure group.

factor n cause, influence, circumstance, contingency, consideration, element, ingredient, component, part, point, aspect, fact, item, detail.

factory n works, plant, mill, shop floor, assembly line, manufactory.

factual adj true, historical, actual, real, genuine, authentic, correct, accurate, precise, exact, literal, faithful, close, detailed, unbiased, objective.
⊟ false, fictitious, imaginary, fictional.

faculties n wits, senses, intelligence, reason, powers, capabilities.

faculty n ability, capability, capacity, power, facility, knack, gift, talent, skill, aptitude, bent.

fad n craze, rage (infml), mania, fashion, mode, vogue, trend, whim, fancy, affectation.

fade v **1** DISCOLOUR, bleach, blanch, blench, pale, whiten, dim, dull.
2 DECLINE, fall, diminish, dwindle, ebb, wane, disappear, vanish, flag, weaken, droop, wilt, wither, shrivel, perish, die.

fail v **1** GO WRONG, miscarry, misfire, flop, miss, flunk (sl), fall through, come to grief, collapse, fold (infml), go bankrupt, go bust, go under, founder, sink, decline, fall, weaken, dwindle, fade, wane, peter out, cease, die. **2** fail to pay a bill: omit, neglect, forget.
3 LET DOWN, disappoint, leave, desert, abandon, forsake.
⊟ 1 succeed, prosper.

failing n weakness, foible, fault, defect, imperfection, flaw, blemish, drawback, deficiency, shortcoming, failure, lapse, error.
⊟ strength, advantage.

failure n **1** MISCARRIAGE, flop, wash-out (infml), fiasco, disappointment, loss, defeat, downfall, decline, decay, deterioration, ruin, bankruptcy, crash, collapse, breakdown, stoppage.

2 OMISSION, slip-up (*infml*), neglect, negligence, failing, shortcoming, deficiency.

F3 1 success, prosperity.

faint *adj* **1** SLIGHT, weak, feeble, soft, low, hushed, muffled, subdued, faded, bleached, light, pale, dull, dim, hazy, indistinct, vague. **2** *I feel faint*: dizzy, giddy, woozy (*infml*), light-headed, weak, feeble, exhausted.

F3 1 strong, clear.

v black out, pass out, swoon, collapse, flake out (*infml*), keel over (*infml*), drop.

n blackout, swoon, collapse, unconsciousness.

fair[1] *adj* **1** JUST, equitable, square, even-handed, dispassionate, impartial, objective, disinterested, unbiased, unprejudiced, right, proper, lawful, legitimate, honest, trustworthy, upright, honourable.
2 FAIR-HAIRED, fair-headed, blond(e), light. **3** *fair weather*: fine, dry, sunny, bright, clear, cloudless, unclouded. **4** AVERAGE, moderate, middling, not bad, all right, OK (*infml*), satisfactory, adequate, acceptable, tolerable, reasonable, passable, mediocre, so-so (*infml*).

F3 1 unfair. **2** dark. **3** inclement, cloudy. **4** excellent, poor.

fair[2] *n* show, exhibition, exposition, expo (*infml*), market, bazaar, fête, festival, carnival, gala.

faith *n* **1** BELIEF, credit, trust, reliance, dependence, conviction, confidence, assurance. **2** RELIGION, denomination, persuasion, church, creed, dogma. **3** FAITHFULNESS, fidelity, loyalty, allegiance, honour, sincerity, honesty, truthfulness.

F3 1 mistrust. **3** unfaithfulness, treachery.

faithful *adj* **1** LOYAL, devoted, staunch, steadfast, constant, trusty, reliable, dependable, true. **2** *a faithful description*: accurate, precise, exact, strict, close, true, truthful.

F3 1 disloyal, treacherous.
2 inaccurate, vague.

fake *v* forge, fabricate, counterfeit, copy, imitate, simulate, feign, sham, pretend, put on, affect, assume.

n forgery, copy, reproduction, replica, imitation, simulation, sham, hoax, fraud, phoney (*infml*), impostor, charlatan.

adj forged, counterfeit, false, spurious, phoney (*infml*), pseudo, bogus, assumed, affected, sham, artificial, simulated, mock, imitation, reproduction.

F3 genuine.

fall *v* **1** TUMBLE, stumble, trip, topple, keel over, collapse, slump, crash.
2 DESCEND, go down, drop, slope, incline, slide, sink, dive, plunge, plummet, nose-dive, pitch.
3 DECREASE, lessen, decline, diminish, dwindle, fall off, subside.

F3 2 rise. **3** increase.

n **1** TUMBLE, descent, slope, incline, dive, plunge, decrease, reduction, lessening, drop, decline, dwindling, slump, crash. **2** *the fall of Rome*: defeat, conquest, overthrow, downfall, collapse, surrender, capitulation.

fall apart break, go to pieces, shatter, disintegrate, crumble, decompose, decay, rot.

fall asleep drop off, doze off, nod off (*infml*).

fall back on resort to, have recourse to, use, turn to, look to.

fall behind lag, trail, drop back.

fall in cave in, come down, collapse, give way, subside, sink.

fall in with agree with, assent to, go along with, accept, comply with, co-operate with.

fall off decrease, lessen, drop, slump, decline, deteriorate, worsen, slow, slacken.

fall out quarrel, argue, squabble, bicker, fight, clash, disagree, differ. **F3** agree.

fall through come to nothing, fail, miscarry, founder, collapse. **F3** come off, succeed.

fallacy n misconception, delusion, mistake, error, flaw, inconsistency, falsehood. **F3** truth.

fallow adj uncultivated, unplanted, unsown, undeveloped, unused, idle, inactive, dormant, resting.

false adj 1 INCORRECT, wrong, mistaken, erroneous, inaccurate, inexact, misleading, faulty, fallacious, invalid. 2 UNREAL, artificial, synthetic, imitation, simulated, mock, fake, counterfeit, forged, feigned, pretended, sham, bogus, assumed, fictitious. 3 *false friends*: disloyal, unfaithful, faithless, lying, deceitful, insincere, hypocritical, two-faced (*infml*), double-dealing, treacherous, unreliable. **F3** 1 true, correct, right. 2 real, genuine. 3 faithful, reliable.

falsehood n untruth, lie, fib, story, fiction, fabrication, perjury, untruthfulness, deceit, deception, dishonesty. **F3** truth, truthfulness.

falsify v alter, cook (*infml*), tamper with, doctor, distort, pervert, misrepresent, misstate, forge, counterfeit, fake.

falter v totter, stumble, stammer, stutter, hesitate, waver, vacillate, flinch, quail, shake, tremble, flag, fail.

fame n renown, celebrity, stardom, prominence, eminence, illustriousness, glory, honour, esteem, reputation, name.

familiar adj 1 EVERYDAY, routine, household, common, ordinary, well-known, recognizable. 2 INTIMATE, close, confidential, friendly, informal, free, free-and-easy, relaxed. 3 *familiar with the procedure*: aware, acquainted, abreast, knowledgeable, versed, conversant. **F3** 1 unfamiliar, strange. 2 formal, reserved. 3 unfamiliar, ignorant.

familiarity n 1 INTIMACY, liberty, closeness, friendliness, sociability, openness, naturalness, informality. 2 AWARENESS, acquaintance, experience, knowledge, understanding, grasp.

familiarize v accustom, acclimatize, school, train, coach, instruct, prime, brief.

family n 1 RELATIVES, relations, kin, kindred, kinsmen, people, folk (*infml*), ancestors, forebears, children, offspring, issue, progeny, descendants. 2 CLAN, tribe, race, dynasty, house, pedigree, ancestry, parentage, descent, line, lineage, extraction, blood, stock, birth. 3 CLASS, group, classification.

Members of a family include: ancestor, forebear, forefather, descendant, offspring, heir; husband, wife, spouse, parent, mother, grandparent, grandfather, grandmother, grandchild, grandson, granddaughter, child, son, daughter, brother, half-brother, sister, half-sister, sibling, uncle, aunt, nephew, niece, cousin, godparent, godchild, stepfather, stepmother, stepchild, foster-parent, foster-child.

family tree ancestry, pedigree, genealogy, line, lineage, extraction.

famine n starvation, hunger, destitution, want, scarcity, dearth.
F≠ plenty.

famous adj well-known, famed, renowned, celebrated, noted, great, distinguished, illustrious, eminent, honoured, acclaimed, glorious, legendary, remarkable, notable, prominent, signal.
F≠ unheard-of, unknown, obscure.

fan[1] v **1** COOL, ventilate, air, air-condition, air-cool, blow, refresh. **2** INCREASE, provoke, stimulate, rouse, arouse, excite, agitate, stir up, work up, whip up.
n extractor fan, ventilator, air-conditioner, blower, propeller, vane.

fan[2] n enthusiast, admirer, supporter, follower, adherent, devotee, lover, buff (infml), fiend, freak.

fanatic n zealot, devotee, enthusiast, addict, fiend, freak, maniac, visionary, bigot, extremist, militant, activist.

fanatical adj overenthusiastic, extreme, passionate, zealous, fervent, burning, mad, wild, frenzied, rabid, obsessive, single-minded, bigoted, visionary.
F≠ moderate, unenthusiastic.

fanaticism n extremism, monomania, single-mindedness, obsessiveness, madness, infatuation, bigotry, zeal, fervour, enthusiasm, dedication.
F≠ moderation.

fanciful adj imaginary, mythical, fabulous, fantastic, visionary, romantic, fairytale, airy-fairy, vaporous, whimsical, wild, extravagant, curious.
F≠ real, ordinary.

fancy v **1** LIKE, be attracted to, take a liking to, take to, go for, prefer, favour, desire, wish for, long for, yearn for. **2** THINK, conceive, imagine, dream of, picture, conjecture, believe, suppose, reckon, guess.
F≠ dislike.
n **1** DESIRE, craving, hankering, urge, liking, fondness, inclination, preference. **2** NOTION, thought, impression, imagination, dream, fantasy.
F≠ dislike, aversion. **2** fact, reality.
adj elaborate, ornate, decorated, ornamented, rococo, baroque, elegant, extravagant, fantastic, fanciful, far-fetched.
F≠ plain.

fantastic adj **1** WONDERFUL, marvellous, sensational, superb, excellent, first-rate, tremendous, terrific, great, incredible, unbelievable, overwhelming, enormous, extreme. **2** STRANGE, weird, odd, exotic, outlandish, fanciful, fabulous, imaginative, visionary.
F≠ **1** ordinary. **2** real.

fantasy n dream, daydream, reverie, pipe-dream, nightmare, vision, hallucination, illusion, mirage, apparition, invention, fancy, flight of fancy, delusion, misconception, imagination, unreality.
F≠ reality.

far adv a long way, a good way, miles (infml), much, greatly, considerably,

extremely, decidedly, incomparably.
F3 near, close.

adj distant, far-off, faraway, far-flung, outlying, remote, out-of-the-way, god-forsaken, removed, far-removed, further, opposite, other.
F3 nearby, close.

farce n **1** COMEDY, slapstick, buffoonery, satire, burlesque. **2** TRAVESTY, sham, parody, joke, mockery, ridiculousness, absurdity, nonsense.

fare n **1** *pay one's fare*: charge, cost, price, fee, passage. **2** FOOD, eatables (*infml*), provisions, rations, sustenance, meals, diet, menu, board, table.

far-fetched *adj* implausible, improbable, unlikely, dubious, incredible, unbelievable, fantastic, preposterous, crazy, unrealistic.
F3 plausible.

farm n ranch, farmstead, grange, homestead, station, land, holding, acreage, acres.

Types of farm include:
arable farm, cattle ranch, dairy farm, free-range farm, mixed farm, organic farm, sheep station, croft, smallholding, estate, plantation, wind farm.

v cultivate, till, work the land, plant, operate.

farmer n agriculturist, crofter, smallholder, husbandman, yeoman.

farming n agriculture, cultivation, husbandry, crofting.

far-reaching *adj* broad, extensive, widespread, sweeping, important, significant, momentous.
F3 insignificant.

fascinate *v* absorb, engross, intrigue, delight, charm, captivate, spellbind, enthral, rivet, transfix, hypnotize, mesmerize.
F3 bore, repel.

fascination n interest, attraction, lure, magnetism, pull, charm, enchantment, spell, sorcery, magic.
F3 boredom, repulsion.

fashion n **1** MANNER, way, method, mode, style, shape, form, pattern, line, cut, look, appearance, type, sort, kind. **2** VOGUE, trend, mode, style, fad, craze, rage (*infml*), latest (*infml*), custom, convention.
v create, form, shape, mould, model, design, fit, tailor, alter, adjust, adapt, suit.

fashionable *adj* chic, smart, elegant, stylish, modish, à la mode, in vogue, trendy (*infml*), in all the rage (*infml*), popular, prevailing, current, latest, up-to-the-minute, contemporary, modern, up-to-date.
F3 unfashionable.

fast¹ *adj* **1** QUICK, swift, rapid, brisk, accelerated, speedy, nippy (*infml*), hasty, hurried, flying. **2** FASTENED, secure, fixed, immovable, immobile, firm, tight.
F3 1 slow, unhurried. **2** loose.
adv quickly, swiftly, rapidly, speedily, like a flash, like a shot, hastily, hurriedly, apace, presto.
F3 slowly, gradually.

fast² *v* go hungry, diet, starve, abstain.
n fasting, diet, starvation, abstinence.
F3 gluttony, self-indulgence.

fasten *v* fix, attach, clamp, grip, anchor, rivet, nail, seal, close, shut, lock, bolt, secure, tie, bind, chain, link, interlock, connect, join, unite, do up, button, lace, buckle.
F3 unfasten, untie.

fat *adj* plump, obese, tubby, stout, corpulent, portly, round, rotund, paunchy, pot-bellied, overweight, heavy, beefy, solid, chubby, podgy, fleshy, flabby, gross.
F3 thin, slim, poor.
n fatness, obesity, overweight, corpulence, paunch, pot (belly), blubber, flab (*infml*).

fatal *adj* deadly, lethal, mortal, killing, incurable, malignant, terminal, final, destructive, calamitous, catastrophic, disastrous.
F3 harmless.

fatality *n* death, mortality, loss, casualty, deadliness, lethality, disaster.

fate *n* destiny, providence, chance, future, fortune, horoscope, stars, lot, doom, end, outcome, ruin, destruction, death.

fated *adj* destined, predestined, preordained, foreordained, doomed, unavoidable, inevitable, inescapable, certain, sure.
F3 avoidable.

fateful *adj* crucial, critical, decisive, important, momentous, significant, fatal, lethal, disastrous.
F3 unimportant.

father *n* **1** PARENT, begetter, procreator, progenitor, sire (*fml*), papa, dad (*infml*), daddy (*infml*), old man (*infml*), patriarch, elder, forefather, ancestor, forebear, predecessor. **2** FOUNDER, creator, originator, inventor, maker, architect, author, patron, leader, prime mover. **3** PRIEST, padre, abbé, curé.
v beget, procreate, sire, produce.

fathom *v* **1** MEASURE, gauge, plumb, sound, probe, penetrate.
2 UNDERSTAND, comprehend, grasp, see, work out, get to the bottom of, interpret.

fatigue *n* tiredness, weariness, exhaustion, lethargy, listlessness, lassitude, weakness, debility.
F3 energy.
v tire, wear out, weary, exhaust, drain, weaken, debilitate.

fatten *v* feed, nourish, build up, overfeed, cram, stuff, bloat, swell, fill out, spread, expand, thicken.

fatty *adj* fat, greasy, oily.

fault *n* **1** DEFECT, flaw, blemish, imperfection, deficiency, shortcoming, weakness, failing, foible, negligence, omission, oversight. **2** ERROR, mistake, blunder, slip-up (*infml*), slip, lapse, misdeed, offence, wrong, sin. **3** *it's your fault*: responsibility, accountability, liability, culpability.
v find fault with, pick holes in, criticize, knock (*infml*), impugn, censure, blame, call to account.
F3 praise.
at fault (in the) wrong, blameworthy, to blame, responsible, guilty, culpable.

faultless *adj* perfect, flawless, unblemished, spotless, immaculate, unsullied, pure, blameless, exemplary, model, correct, accurate.
F3 faulty, imperfect, flawed.

faulty *adj* imperfect, defective, flawed, blemished, damaged, impaired, out of order, broken, wrong.
F3 faultless.

favour *n* **1** APPROVAL, esteem, support, backing, sympathy, goodwill, patronage, favouritism, preference, partiality. **2** *he did me a favour*: kindness, service, good turn, courtesy.
F3 disapproval.
v **1** PREFER, choose, opt for, like,

favourable

approve, support, back, advocate, champion. **2** HELP, assist, aid, benefit, promote, encourage, pamper, spoil.
F3 1 dislike. **2** mistreat.
in favour of for, supporting, on the side of.
F3 against.

favourable *adj* beneficial, advantageous, helpful, fit, suitable, convenient, timely, opportune, good, fair, promising, auspicious, hopeful, positive, encouraging, complimentary, enthusiastic, friendly, amicable, well-disposed, kind, sympathetic, understanding, reassuring.
F3 unfavourable, unhelpful, negative.

favourite *adj* preferred, favoured, pet, best-loved, dearest, beloved, esteemed, chosen.
F3 hated.
n preference, choice, pick, pet, blue-eyed boy, teacher's pet, the apple of one's eye, darling, idol.
F3 bête noire, pet hate.

favouritism *n* nepotism, preferential treatment, preference, partiality, one-sidedness, partisanship, bias, injustice.
F3 impartiality.

fear *n* alarm, fright, terror, horror, panic, agitation, worry, anxiety, consternation, concern, dismay, distress, uneasiness, qualms, misgivings, apprehension, trepidation, dread, foreboding, awe, phobia, nightmare.
F3 courage, bravery, confidence.
v take fright, shrink from, dread, shudder at, tremble, worry, suspect, anticipate, expect, foresee, respect, venerate.

fearful *adj* **1** FRIGHTENED, afraid, scared, alarmed, nervous, anxious, tense, uneasy, apprehensive, hesitant, nervy, panicky. **2** TERRIBLE, fearsome (*fml*), dreadful, awful, frightful, atrocious, shocking, appalling, monstrous, gruesome, hideous, ghastly, horrible.
F3 1 brave, courageous, fearless.
2 wonderful, delightful.

feasible *adj* practicable, practical, workable, achievable, attainable, realizable, viable, reasonable, possible, likely.
F3 impossible.

feast *n* **1** BANQUET, dinner, spread, blow-out (*sl*), binge (*infml*), beano (*infml*), junket. **2** FESTIVAL, holiday, gala, fête, celebration, revels.
v gorge, binge (*infml*), pig out (*sl*), eat one's fill, wine and dine, treat, entertain.

feat *n* exploit, deed, act, accomplishment, achievement, attainment, performance, undertaking.

feature *n* **1** ASPECT, facet, point, factor, attribute, quality, property, trait, lineament, characteristic, peculiarity, mark, hallmark, speciality, highlight. **2** *a magazine feature*: column, article, report, story, piece, item, comment.
v **1** EMPHASIZE, highlight, spotlight, play up, promote, show, present.
2 APPEAR, figure, participate, act, perform, star.

fee *n* charge, terms, bill, account, pay, remuneration, payment, retainer, subscription, reward, recompense, hire, toll.

feeble *adj* **1** WEAK, faint, exhausted, frail, delicate, puny, sickly, infirm, powerless, helpless. **2** INADEQUATE, lame, poor, thin, flimsy, ineffective, incompetent, indecisive.

F3 1 strong, effective.

feed v nourish, cater for, provide for, supply, sustain, suckle, nurture, foster, strengthen, fuel, graze, pasture, eat, dine.

n food, fodder, forage, pasture, silage.

feed on eat, consume, devour, live on, exist on.

feel v **1** EXPERIENCE, go through, undergo, suffer, endure, enjoy. **2** TOUCH, finger, handle, manipulate, hold, stroke, caress, fondle, paw, fumble, grope. **3** feel soft: seem, appear. **4** THINK, believe, consider, reckon, judge. **5** SENSE, perceive, notice, observe, know.

n texture, surface, finish, touch, knack, sense, impression, feeling, quality.

feel for pity, sympathize (with), empathize (with), commiserate (with), be sorry for.

feel like fancy, want, desire.

feeling n **1** SENSATION, perception, sense, instinct, hunch, suspicion, inkling, impression, idea, notion, opinion, view, point of view. **2** EMOTION, passion, intensity, warmth, compassion, sympathy, understanding, pity, concern, affection, fondness, sentiment, sentimentality, susceptibility, sensibility, sensitivity, appreciation. **3** AIR, aura, atmosphere, mood, quality.

fell v cut down, hew, knock down, strike down, floor, level, flatten, raze, demolish.

fellow n **1** PERSON, man, boy, chap (infml), bloke (infml), guy (infml),

individual, character. **2** PEER, compeer, equal, partner, associate, colleague, co-worker, companion, comrade, friend, counterpart, match, mate, twin, double.

adj co-, associate, associated, related, like, similar.

fellowship n **1** COMPANIONSHIP, camaraderie, communion, familiarity, intimacy. **2** ASSOCIATION, league, guild, society, club, fraternity, brotherhood, sisterhood, order.

female adj feminine, she-, girlish, womanly.

F3 male.

feminine adj **1** FEMALE, womanly, ladylike, graceful, gentle, tender. **2** EFFEMINATE, unmanly, womanish, girlish, girly, sissy.

F3 1 masculine. **2** manly.

feminism n women's movement, women's lib(eration), female emancipation, women's rights.

fence n barrier, railing, paling, wall, hedge, windbreak, guard, defence, barricade, stockade, rampart. v **1** SURROUND, encircle, bound, hedge, wall, enclose, pen, coop, confine, restrict, separate, protect, guard, defend, fortify. **2** PARRY, dodge, evade, hedge, equivocate, quibble, pussyfoot, stonewall.

fencing

Fencing terms include: appel, coquille, en garde, épée, feint, foible, foil, forte, lunge, parry, counter-parry, pink, piste, plastron, remise, riposte, counter-riposte, sabre, tac-au-tac, thrust, touché, volt.

fend for look after, take care of, shift for, support, maintain, sustain, provide for.

fend off ward off, beat off, parry, deflect, avert, resist, repel, repulse, hold at bay, keep off, shut out.

ferment v 1 BUBBLE, effervesce, froth, foam, boil, seethe, smoulder, fester, brew, rise. 2 ROUSE, stir up, excite, work up, agitate, foment, incite, provoke, inflame, heat.
n unrest, agitation, turbulence, stir, excitement, turmoil, disruption, commotion, tumult, hubbub, uproar, furore, frenzy, fever, glow.
Fa calm.

ferocious adj vicious, savage, fierce, wild, barbarous, barbaric, brutal, inhuman, cruel, sadistic, murderous, bloodthirsty, violent, merciless, pitiless, ruthless.
Fa gentle, mild, tame.

ferocity n viciousness, savagery, fierceness, wildness, barbarity, brutality, inhumanity, cruelty, sadism, bloodthirstiness, violence, ruthlessness.
Fa gentleness, mildness.

ferry n ferry-boat, car ferry, ship, boat, vessel.
v transport, ship, convey, carry, take, shuttle, taxi, drive, run, move, shift.

fertile adj fruitful, productive, generative, yielding, prolific, teeming, abundant, plentiful, rich, lush, luxuriant, fat.
Fa infertile, barren, sterile, unproductive.

fertilize v 1 IMPREGNATE, inseminate, pollinate. 2 fertilize land: enrich, feed, dress, compost, manure, dung.

fertilizer n dressing, compost, manure, dung.

fervent adj ardent, earnest, eager, enthusiastic, whole-hearted, excited, energetic, vigorous, fiery, spirited, intense, vehement, passionate, full-blooded, zealous, devout, heartfelt, impassioned, emotional, warm.
Fa cool, indifferent, apathetic.

fervour n ardour, eagerness, enthusiasm, excitement, animation, energy, vigour, spirit, verve, intensity, vehemence, passion, zeal, warmth.
Fa apathy.

fester v ulcerate, gather, suppurate, discharge, putrefy, rot, decay, rankle, smoulder.

festival n celebration, commemoration, anniversary, jubilee, holiday, feast, gala, fête, carnival, fiesta, party, merrymaking, entertainment, festivities.

festive adj celebratory, festal, holiday, gala, carnival, happy, joyful, merry, hearty, cheery, jolly, jovial, cordial, convivial.
Fa gloomy, sombre, sober.

festivity n celebration, jubilation, feasting, banqueting, fun, enjoyment, pleasure, entertainment, sport, amusement, merriment, merrymaking, revelry, jollity, joviality, conviviality.

festoon v adorn, deck, bedeck, garland, wreathe, drape, hang, swathe, decorate, garnish.

fetch v 1 fetch a bucket: get, collect, bring, carry, transport, deliver, escort. 2 SELL FOR, go for, bring in, yield, realize, make, earn.

fetching adj attractive, pretty, sweet, cute, charming, enchanting, fascinating, captivating.
Fa repellent.

fête n fair, bazaar, sale of work, garden party, gala, carnival, festival.
v entertain, treat, regale, welcome, honour, lionize.

feud n vendetta, quarrel, row, argument, disagreement, dispute, conflict, strife, discord, animosity, ill will, bitterness, enmity, hostility, antagonism, rivalry.
F3 agreement, peace.

fever n 1 FEVERISHNESS, (high) temperature, delirium. 2 EXCITEMENT, agitation, turmoil, unrest, restlessness, heat, passion, ecstasy.

feverish adj 1 DELIRIOUS, hot, burning, flushed. 2 EXCITED, impatient, agitated, restless, nervous, overwrought, frenzied, frantic, hectic, hasty, hurried.
F3 1 cool. 2 calm.

few adj scarce, rare, uncommon, sporadic, infrequent, sparse, thin, scant, scanty, meagre, inconsiderable, inadequate, insufficient, in short supply.
F3 many.
pron not many, hardly any, one or two, a couple, scattering, sprinkling, handful, some.
F3 many.

fibre n 1 FILAMENT, strand, thread, nerve, sinew, pile, texture.
2 moral fibre: character, calibre, backbone, strength, stamina, toughness, courage, resolution, determination.

fickle adj inconstant, disloyal, unfaithful, faithless, treacherous, unreliable, unpredictable, changeable, capricious, mercurial, irresolute, vacillating.
F3 constant, steady, stable.

fiction n 1 FANTASY, fancy, imagination, figment, invention, fabrication, concoction, improvisation, story-telling. 2 NOVEL, romance, story, tale, yarn, fable,

parable, legend, myth, lie.
F3 2 non-fiction, fact, truth.

fictional adj literary, invented, made-up, imaginary, make-believe, legendary, mythical, mythological, fabulous, non-existent, unreal.
F3 factual, real.

fictitious adj false, untrue, invented, made-up, fabricated, apocryphal, imaginary, non-existent, bogus, counterfeit, spurious, assumed, supposed.
F3 true, genuine.

fiddle v 1 fiddling with her necklace: play, tinker, toy, trifle, tamper, mess around, meddle, interfere, fidget.
2 CHEAT, swindle, diddle, cook the books (infml), juggle, manoeuvre, racketeer, graft (sl).
n swindle, con (infml), scam (infml), rip-off (sl), fraud, racket, sharp practice, graft (sl).

fiddling adj trifling, petty, trivial, insignificant, negligible, paltry.
F3 important, significant.

fidelity n 1 FAITHFULNESS, loyalty, allegiance, devotion, constancy, reliability. 2 ACCURACY, exactness, precision, closeness, adherence.
F3 1 infidelity, inconstancy, treachery. 2 inaccuracy.

fidget v squirm, wriggle, shuffle, twitch, jerk, jump, fret, fuss, bustle, fiddle, mess about, play around.

fidgety adj restless, impatient, uneasy, nervous, agitated, jittery, jumpy, twitchy, on edge.
F3 still.

field n 1 GRASSLAND, meadow, pasture, paddock, playing-field, ground, pitch, green, lawn. 2 RANGE, scope, bounds, limits, confines, territory, area, province, domain.

sphere, environment, department, discipline, speciality, line, forte. **3** PARTICIPANTS, entrants, contestants, competitors, contenders, runners, candidates, applicants, opponents, opposition, competition.

fiend n **1** EVIL SPIRIT, demon, devil, monster. **2** a health fiend: enthusiast, fanatic, addict, devotee, freak (infml), nut (infml).

fiendish adj devilish, diabolical, infernal, wicked, malevolent, cunning, cruel, inhuman, savage, monstrous, unspeakable.

fierce adj ferocious, vicious, savage, cruel, brutal, merciless, aggressive, dangerous, murderous, frightening, menacing, threatening, stern, grim, relentless, raging, wild, passionate, intense, strong, powerful.
F3 gentle, kind, calm.

fiery adj **1** BURNING, afire, flaming, aflame, blazing, ablaze, red-hot, glowing, aglow, flushed, hot, torrid, sultry. **2** PASSIONATE, inflamed, ardent, fervent, impatient, excitable, impetuous, impulsive, hot-headed, fierce, violent, heated.
F3 1 cold. **2** impassive.

fight v **1** WRESTLE, box, fence, joust, brawl, scrap, scuffle, tussle, skirmish, combat, battle, do battle, war, wage war, clash, cross swords, engage, grapple, struggle, strive, contend. **2** QUARREL, argue, dispute, squabble, bicker, wrangle. **3** OPPOSE, contest, campaign against, resist, withstand, defy, stand up to.
n **1** BOUT, contest, duel, combat, action, battle, war, hostilities, brawl, scrap, scuffle, tussle, struggle, skirmish, set-to, clash, engagement,

brush, encounter, conflict, fray, free-for-all, fracas, riot. **2** QUARREL, row, argument, dispute, dissension.

fight back 1 RETALIATE, defend oneself, resist, put up a fight, retort, reply. **2** fight back the tears: hold back, restrain, curb, control, repress, bottle up, contain, suppress.

fight off hold off, keep at bay, ward off, stave off, resist, repel, rebuff, beat off, rout, put to flight.

fighter n combatant, contestant, contender, disputant, boxer, wrestler, pugilist, prizefighter, soldier, trouper, mercenary, warrior, man-at-arms, swordsman, gladiator.

figurative adj metaphorical, symbolic, emblematic, representative, allegorical, parabolic, descriptive, pictorial.
F3 literal.

figure n **1** NUMBER, numeral, digit, integer, sum, amount. **2** SHAPE, form, outline, silhouette, body, frame, build, physique. **3** public figure: dignitary, celebrity, personality, character, person. **4** DIAGRAM, illustration, picture, drawing, sketch, image, representation, symbol.
v RECKON, guess, estimate, judge, think, believe. **2** FEATURE, appear, crop up.

figure out work out, calculate, compute, reckon, puzzle out, resolve, fathom, understand, see, make out, decipher.

figurehead n mouthpiece, front man, name, dummy, puppet.

filament n fibre, strand, thread, hair, whisker, wire, string, pile.

file¹ v rub (down), sand, abrade, scour, scrape, grate, rasp, hone, whet, shave, plane, smooth, polish.

file² *n* folder, dossier, portfolio, binder, case, record, documents, data, information.

v record, register, note, enter, process, store, classify, categorize, pigeonhole, catalogue.

file³ *n* line, queue, column, row, procession, cortège, train, string, stream, trail.

v march, troop, parade, stream, trail.

fill *v* **1** REPLENISH, stock, supply, furnish, satisfy, pack, crowd, cram, stuff, congest, block, clog, plug, bung, cork, stop, close, seal. **2** PERVADE, imbue, permeate, soak, impregnate. **3** *fill a post:* take up, hold, occupy, discharge, fulfil.

F3 1 empty, drain.

fill in 1 *fill in a form:* complete, fill out, answer. **2** (*infml*) STAND IN, deputize, understudy, substitute, replace, represent, act for. **3** (*infml*) BRIEF, inform, advise, acquaint, bring up to date, bring up to speed (*infml*).

filling *n* contents, inside, stuffing, padding, wadding, filler.

adj satisfying, nutritious, square, solid, substantial, heavy, large, big, generous, ample.

F3 insubstantial.

film *n* **1** MOTION PICTURE, picture, movie (*infml*), video, feature film, short, documentary. **2** LAYER, covering, dusting, coat, coating, glaze, skin, membrane, tissue, sheet, veil, screen, cloud, mist, haze.

v photograph, shoot, video, videotape.

filter *v* strain, sieve, sift, screen, refine, purify, clarify, percolate, ooze, seep, leak, trickle, dribble.

n strainer, sieve, sifter, colander, mesh, gauze, membrane.

filth *n* **1** DIRT, grime, muck, dung, excrement, faeces, sewage, refuse, rubbish, garbage, trash, slime, sludge, effluent, pollution, contamination, corruption, impurity, uncleanness, foulness, sordidness, squalor. **2** OBSCENITY, pornography, smut, indecency, vulgarity, coarseness.

F3 1 cleanness, cleanliness, purity.

filthy *adj* **1** DIRTY, soiled, unwashed, grimy, grubby, mucky, muddy, slimy, sooty, unclean, impure, foul, gross, sordid, squalid, vile, low, mean, base, contemptible, despicable. **2** OBSCENE, pornographic, smutty, bawdy, suggestive, indecent, offensive, foul-mouthed, vulgar, coarse, corrupt, depraved.

F3 1 clean, pure. **2** decent.

final *adj* last, latest, closing, concluding, finishing, end, ultimate, terminal, dying, last-minute, eventual, conclusive, definitive, decisive, definite, incontrovertible.

F3 first, initial.

finale *n* climax, dénouement, culmination, crowning glory, end, conclusion, close, curtain, epilogue.

finalize *v* conclude, finish, complete, round off, resolve, settle, agree, decide, close, clinch, sew up (*infml*), wrap up (*infml*).

finally *adv* lastly, in conclusion, ultimately, eventually, at last, at length, in the end, conclusively, once and for all, for ever, irreversibly, irrevocably, definitely.

finance *n* economics, money management, accounting, banking, investment, stock market, business, commerce, trade, money, funding, sponsorship, subsidy.

v pay for, fund, sponsor, back,

support, underwrite, guarantee, subsidize, capitalize, float, set up.

finances n accounts, affairs, budget, bank account, income, revenue, liquidity, resources, assets, capital, wealth, money, cash, funds, wherewithal.

financial adj monetary, money, pecuniary, economic, fiscal, budgetary, commercial.

financier n financialist, banker, stockbroker, money-maker, investor, speculator, venture capitalist.

find v 1 DISCOVER, locate, track down, trace, retrieve, recover, unearth, uncover, expose, reveal, come across, chance on, stumble on, meet, encounter, detect, recognize, notice, observe, perceive, realize, learn. **2** ATTAIN, achieve, win, reach, gain, obtain, get. **3** *find it difficult*: consider, think, judge, declare.
F∃ 1 lose.

find out 1 LEARN, ascertain, discover, detect, note, observe, perceive, realize. **2** UNMASK, expose, show up, uncover, reveal, disclose, catch, suss out (*sl*), rumble (*sl*), tumble to (*infml*).

finding n FIND, discovery, breakthrough. **2** DECISION, conclusion, judgement, verdict, pronouncement, decree, recommendation, award.

fine [1] adj 1 EXCELLENT, outstanding, exceptional, superior, exquisite, splendid, magnificent, brilliant, beautiful, handsome, attractive, elegant, lovely, nice, good. **2** THIN, slender, fine, gauzy, powdery, flimsy, fragile, delicate, dainty. **3** SATISFACTORY, acceptable, all right, OK (*infml*). **4** *fine weather*: bright, sunny, clear, cloudless, dry, fair.

F∃ 1 mediocre. **2** thick, coarse. **4** cloudy.

fine [2] n penalty, punishment, forfeit, forfeiture, damages.

finger v touch, handle, manipulate, feel, stroke, caress, fondle, paw, fiddle with, toy with, play about with, meddle with.

finicky adj 1 PARTICULAR, finickety, pernickety, fussy, choosy (*infml*), fastidious, meticulous, scrupulous, critical, hypercritical, nit-picking. **2** FIDDLY, intricate, tricky, difficult, delicate.
F∃ 1 easy-going. **2** easy.

finish v 1 END, terminate, stop, cease, complete, accomplish, achieve, fulfil, discharge, deal with, do, conclude, close, wind up, settle, round off, culminate, perfect. **2** DESTROY, ruin, exterminate, get rid of, annihilate, defeat, overcome, rout, overthrow. **3** USE (UP), consume, devour, eat, drink, exhaust, drain, empty.
F∃ 1 begin, start.
n 1 END, termination, completion, conclusion, close, ending, finale, culmination. **2** SURFACE, appearance, texture, grain, polish, shine, gloss, lustre, smoothness.
F∃ 1 beginning, start, commencement.

finite adj limited, restricted, bounded, demarcated, terminable, definable, fixed, measurable, calculable, countable, numbered.
F∃ infinite.

fire n 1 FLAMES, blaze, bonfire, conflagration, inferno, burning, combustion. **2** PASSION, feeling, excitement, enthusiasm, spirit, intensity, heat, radiance, sparkle.
v 1 IGNITE, light, kindle, set fire to, set

on fire, set alight. **2** *fire a missile*:
shoot, launch, set off, let off, detonate,
explode. **3** DISMISS, discharge, sack
(*infml*), eject. **4** EXCITE, whet, enliven,
galvanize, electrify, stir, arouse, rouse,
stimulate, inspire, incite, spark off,
trigger off.

on fire burning, alight, ignited, flaming,
in flames, aflame, blazing, ablaze, fiery.

firm [1] *adj* **1** *firm ground*: dense,
compressed, compact, concentrated,
set, solid, hard, unyielding, stiff, rigid,
inflexible. **2** FIXED, embedded, fast,
tight, secure, fastened, anchored,
immovable, motionless, stationary,
steady, stable, sturdy, strong.
3 ADAMANT, unshakable, resolute,
determined, dogged, unwavering,
strict, constant, steadfast, staunch,
dependable, true, sure, convinced,
definite, settled, committed.
F3 1 soft, flabby. **2** unsteady.
3 hesitant.

firm [2] *n* company, corporation,
business, enterprise, concern, house,
establishment, institution,
organization, association,
partnership, syndicate,
conglomerate.

first *adj* **1** INITIAL, opening,
introductory, preliminary, elementary,
primary, basic, fundamental.
2 ORIGINAL, earliest, earlier, prior,
primitive, primeval, oldest, eldest,
senior. **3** CHIEF, main, key, cardinal,
principal, head, leading, ruling,
sovereign, highest, uppermost,
paramount, prime, predominant,
pre-eminent.
F3 1 last, final.
adv initially, to begin with, to start
with, at the outset, beforehand,
originally, in preference, rather,
sooner.

first name forename, Christian name,
baptismal name, given name.

first-rate *adj* first-class, A1, second-
to-none, matchless, peerless, top, top-
notch (*infml*), top-flight, leading,
supreme, superior, prime, excellent,
outstanding, superlative, exceptional,
splendid, superb, fine, admirable.
F3 inferior.

fish

> **Types of fish include:**
> brisling, cod, coley, Dover sole,
> haddock, hake, halibut, herring,
> mackerel, pilchard, plaice, rainbow
> trout, salmon, sardine, sole, sprat,
> trout, tuna, turbot, whitebait; bass,
> bream, brill, carp, catfish, chub, con-
> ger eel, dab, dace, dogfish, dory, eel,
> goldfish, guppy, marlin, minnow,
> monkfish, mullet, perch, pike, pi-
> ranha, roach, shark, skate, snapper,
> stickleback, stingray, sturgeon,
> swordfish, tench, whiting.

v angle, trawl, delve, hunt, seek, invite,
solicit.

fish out produce, take out, extract, find,
come up with, dredge up, haul up.

fishing *n* angling, trawling.

fit [1] *adj* **1** SUITABLE, appropriate, apt,
fitting, correct, right, proper, ready,
prepared, able, capable, competent,
qualified, eligible, worthy. **2** HEALTHY,
well, able-bodied, in good form, in
good shape, sound, sturdy, strong,
robust, hale and hearty.
F3 1 unsuitable, unworthy. **2** unfit.
v **1** MATCH, correspond, conform,
follow, agree, concur, tally, suit,
harmonize, go, belong, dovetail,
interlock, join, meet, arrange, place,
position, accommodate. **2** ALTER,
modify, change, adjust, adapt, tailor,
shape, fashion.

fit out equip, rig out, kit out, outfit, provide, supply, furnish, prepare, arm.

**fit² ** n seizure, convulsion, spasm, paroxysm, attack, outbreak, bout, spell, burst, surge, outburst, eruption, explosion.

fitful adj sporadic, intermittent, occasional, spasmodic, erratic, irregular, uneven, broken, disturbed.
F3 steady, regular.

fitted adj 1 fitted wardrobe: built-in, permanent. 2 EQUIPPED, rigged out, provided, furnished, appointed, prepared, armed. 3 SUITED, right, suitable, fit, qualified.

fitting adj apt, appropriate, suitable, fit, correct, right, proper, seemly, meet (fml), desirable, deserved.
F3 unsuitable, improper.
n connection, attachment, accessory, part, component, piece, unit, fitment.

fittings n equipment, furnishings, furniture, fixtures, installations, fitments, accessories, extras.

fix v 1 FASTEN, secure, tie, bind, attach, join, link, couple, anchor, pin, nail, rivet, stick, glue, cement, set, harden, solidify, stiffen, stabilize, plant, root, implant, embed, establish, install, place, locate, position. 2 fix a date: arrange, set, specify, define, agree on, decide, determine, settle, resolve, finalize. 3 MEND, repair, correct, rectify, adjust, restore.
F3 1 move, shift. 3 damage.
n (infml) dilemma, quandary, predicament, plight, difficulty, hole (infml), corner, spot (infml), mess, muddle.

fix up arrange, organize, plan, lay on, provide, supply, furnish, equip, settle, sort out, produce, bring about.

fixation n preoccupation, obsession, mania, fetish, thing (infml), infatuation, compulsion, hang-up (infml), complex.

fixed adj decided, settled, established, definite, arranged, planned, set, firm, rigid, inflexible, steady, secure, fast, rooted, permanent.
F3 variable.

fizz v effervesce, sparkle, bubble, froth, foam, fizzle, hiss, sizzle, sputter, spit.

fizzy adj effervescent, sparkling, aerated, carbonated, gassy, bubbly, bubbling, frothy, foaming.

flabbergasted adj amazed, confounded, astonished, astounded, staggered, dumbfounded, speechless, stunned, dazed, overcome, overwhelmed, bowled over.

flabby adj fleshy, soft, yielding, flaccid, limp, floppy, drooping, hanging, sagging, slack, loose, lax, weak, feeble.
F3 firm, strong.

**flag¹ ** v lessen, diminish, decline, fall (off), abate, subside, sink, slump, dwindle, peter out, fade, fail, weaken, slow, falter, tire, weary, wilt, droop, sag, flop, faint, die.
F3 revive.

**flag² ** n ensign, jack, pennant, colours, standard, banner, streamer.
v 1 SIGNAL, wave, salute, motion.
2 MARK, indicate, label, tag, note.

flail v thresh, thrash, beat, whip.

flair n skill, ability, aptitude, faculty, gift, talent, facility, knack, mastery, genius, feel, taste, discernment, acumen, style, elegance, stylishness, panache.
F3 inability, ineptitude.

flake n scale, peeling, paring, shaving, sliver, wafer, chip, splinter.
v scale, peel, chip, splinter.

flamboyant adj showy, ostentatious, flashy, gaudy, colourful, brilliant, dazzling, striking, extravagant, rich, elaborate, ornate, florid.

E3 modest, restrained.

flame v burn, flare, blaze, glare, flash, beam, shine, glow, radiate.
n **1** FIRE, blaze, light, brightness, heat, warmth. **2** PASSION, ardour, fervour, enthusiasm, zeal, intensity, radiance.

flaming adj **1** a flaming torch: burning, alight, aflame, blazing, fiery, brilliant, scintillating, red-hot, glowing, smouldering. **2** INTENSE, vivid, aroused, impassioned, hot, raging, frenzied.

flammable adj inflammable, ignitable, combustible.

E3 non-flammable, incombustible, flameproof, fire-resistant.

flank n side, edge, quarter, wing, loin, hip, thigh.
v edge, fringe, skirt, line, border, bound, confine, wall, screen.

flap v flutter, vibrate, wave, agitate, shake, wag, swing, swish, thrash, beat.
n **1** FOLD, fly, lapel, tab, lug, tail, skirt, aileron. **2** (infml) PANIC, state (infml), fuss, commotion, fluster, agitation, flutter, dither, tizzy (infml).

flare v **1** FLAME, burn, blaze, glare, flash, flicker, burst, explode, erupt. **2** BROADEN, widen, flare out, spread out, splay.
n **1** FLAME, blaze, glare, flash, flicker, burst. **2** BROADENING, widening, splay.

flare up erupt, break out, explode, blow up.

flash v **1** BEAM, shine, light up, flare, blaze, glare, gleam, glint, flicker, twinkle, sparkle, glitter, shimmer. **2** the train flashed past: streak, fly, dart, race, dash.
n beam, ray, shaft, spark, blaze, flare, burst, streak, gleam, glint, flicker, twinkle, sparkle, shimmer.

flashy adj showy, ostentatious, flamboyant, glamorous, bold, loud, garish, gaudy, jazzy, flash, tawdry, cheap, vulgar, tasteless.

E3 plain, tasteful.

flat[1] adj **1** LEVEL, plane, even, smooth, uniform, unbroken, horizontal, outstretched, prostrate, prone, recumbent, reclining, low. **2** DULL, boring, monotonous, tedious, uninteresting, unexciting, stale, lifeless, dead, spiritless, lacklustre, vapid, insipid, weak, watery, empty, pointless. **3** a flat refusal: absolute, utter, total, unequivocal, categorical, positive, unconditional, unqualified, point-blank, direct, straight, explicit, plain, final. **4** a flat tyre: punctured, burst, deflated, collapsed.

E3 1 bumpy, vertical. **2** exciting, full. **3** equivocal.

flat out at top speed, at full speed, all out, for all one is worth.

flat[2] n an apartment, penthouse, maisonette, tenement, flatlet, rooms, suite, bed-sit(ter).

flatten v **1** SMOOTH, iron, press, roll, crush, squash, compress, level, even out. **2** KNOCK DOWN, prostrate, floor, fell, demolish, raze, overwhelm, subdue.

flatter v praise, compliment, sweet-talk (infml), adulate, fawn, butter up (infml), wheedle, humour, play up to, court, curry favour with.

E3 criticize.

flattery n adulation, eulogy, sweet talk (*infml*), soft soap (*infml*), flannel (*infml*), blarney, cajolery, fawning, toadyism, sycophancy, ingratiation, servility.
F3 criticism.

flavour n **1** TASTE, tang, smack, savour, relish, zest, zing (*infml*), aroma, odour. **2** QUALITY, property, character, style, aspect, feeling, feel, atmosphere. **3** HINT, suggestion, touch, tinge, tone.
v season, spice, ginger up, infuse, imbue.

flavouring n seasoning, zest, essence, extract, additive.

flaw n defect, imperfection, fault, blemish, spot, mark, speck, crack, crevice, fissure, cleft, split, rift, break, fracture, weakness, shortcoming, failing, fallacy, lapse, slip, error, mistake.

flawed adj imperfect, defective, faulty, blemished, marked, damaged, spoilt, marred, cracked, chipped, broken, unsound, fallacious, erroneous.
F3 flawless, perfect.

flawless adj perfect, faultless, unblemished, spotless, immaculate, stainless, sound, intact, whole, unbroken, undamaged.
F3 flawed, imperfect.

fleck v dot, spot, mark, speckle, dapple, mottle, streak, sprinkle, dust.
n dot, point, spot, mark, speck, speckle, streak.

flee v run away, bolt, fly, take flight, take off, make off, cut and run, escape, get away, decamp, abscond, leave, depart, withdraw, retreat, vanish, disappear.
F3 stay.

fleet n flotilla, armada, navy, task force, squadron.

fleeting adj short, brief, flying, short-lived, momentary, ephemeral, transient, transitory, passing, temporary.
F3 lasting, permanent.

flesh n body, tissue, fat, muscle, brawn, skin, meat, pulp, substance, matter, physicality.

flex v bend, bow, curve, angle, ply, double up, tighten, contract.
F3 straighten, extend.
n cable, wire, lead, cord.

flexible adj **1** BENDABLE, bendy (*infml*), pliable, pliant, plastic, malleable, mouldable, elastic, stretchy, springy, yielding, supple, lithe, limber, double-jointed, mobile. **2** ADAPTABLE, adjustable, amenable, accommodating, variable, open.
F3 1 inflexible, rigid.

flick v hit, strike, rap, tap, touch, dab, flip, jerk, whip, lash.
n rap, tap, touch, dab, flip, jerk, click.
flick through flip through, thumb through, leaf through, glance at, skim, scan.

flicker v flash, blink, wink, twinkle, sparkle, glimmer, shimmer, gutter, flutter, vibrate, quiver, waver.
n flash, gleam, glint, twinkle, glimmer, spark, trace, drop, iota, atom, indication.

flight[1] n **1** FLYING, aviation, aeronautics, air transport, air travel. **2** JOURNEY, trip, voyage.

flight[2] n fleeing, escape, getaway, breakaway, exit, departure, exodus, retreat.

flimsy adj thin, fine, light, slight, insubstantial, ethereal, fragile, delicate, shaky, rickety, makeshift,

weak, feeble, meagre, inadequate, shallow, superficial, trivial, poor, unconvincing, implausible.
F3 sturdy.

flinch v wince, start, cringe, cower, quail, tremble, shake, quake, shudder, shiver, shrink, recoil, draw back, balk, shy away, duck, shirk, withdraw, retreat, flee.

fling v throw, hurl, pitch, lob, toss, chuck (*infml*), cast, sling, catapult, launch, propel, send, let fly, heave, jerk.

flip v flick, spin, twirl, twist, turn, toss, throw, cast, pitch, jerk, flap.
n flick, spin, twirl, twist, turn, toss, jerk, flap.

flippant adj facetious, light-hearted, frivolous, superficial, offhand, flip, glib, pert, saucy (*infml*), cheeky (*infml*), impudent, impertinent, rude, disrespectful, irreverent.
F3 serious, respectful.

flirt v chat up, make up to, lead on, philander, dally.
flirt with consider, entertain, toy with, play with, trifle with, dabble in, try.

flit v dart, speed, flash, fly, wing, flutter, whisk, skim, slip, pass, bob, dance.

float v 1 GLIDE, sail, swim, bob, drift, waft, hover, hang. 2 LAUNCH, initiate, set up, promote.
F3 1 sink.

floating adj 1 AFLOAT, buoyant, unsinkable, sailing, swimming, bobbing, drifting. 2 VARIABLE, fluctuating, movable, migratory, transitory, wandering, unattached, free, uncommitted.
F3 1 sinking. 2 fixed.

flock v herd, swarm, troop, converge, mass, bunch, cluster, huddle, crowd,

throng, group, gather, collect, congregate.
n herd, pack, crowd, throng, multitude, mass, bunch, cluster, group, gathering, assembly, congregation.

flog v beat, whip, lash, flagellate, scourge, birch, cane, flay, drub, thrash, whack (*infml*), chastise, punish.

flogging n beating, whipping, lashing, flagellation, scourging, birching, caning, flaying, thrashing, hiding.

flood v 1 DELUGE, inundate, soak, drench, saturate, fill, overflow, immerse, submerge, engulf, swamp, overwhelm, drown. 2 FLOW, pour, stream, rush, surge, gush.
n deluge, inundation, downpour, torrent, flow, tide, stream, rush, spate, outpouring, overflow, glut, excess, abundance, profusion.
F3 drought, trickle, dearth.

floor n 1 FLOORING, ground, base, basis. 2 *on the third floor*: storey, level, stage, landing, deck, tier.
v (*infml*) defeat, overwhelm, beat, stump (*infml*), frustrate, confound, perplex, baffle, puzzle, bewilder, disconcert, throw.

flop v 1 DROOP, hang, dangle, sag, drop, fall, topple, tumble, slump, collapse. 2 FAIL, misfire, fall flat, founder, fold.
n failure, non-starter, fiasco, debacle, wash-out (*infml*), disaster.

floppy adj droopy, hanging, dangling, sagging, limp, loose, baggy, soft, flabby.
F3 firm.

florid adj 1 FLOWERY, ornate, elaborate, fussy, overelaborate, baroque, rococo, flamboyant,

flotsam n jetsam, wreckage, debris, rubbish, junk, oddments.

flounder v wallow, struggle, grope, fumble, blunder, stagger, stumble, falter.

flourish v 1 THRIVE, grow, wax, increase, flower, blossom, bloom, develop, progress, get on, do well, prosper, succeed, boom. 2 BRANDISH, wave, shake, twirl, swing, display, wield, flaunt, parade, vaunt.

F3 1 decline, languish, fail.

n display, parade, show, gesture, wave, sweep, fanfare, ornament, decoration, panache, pizzazz (infml).

flourishing adj thriving, blooming, prosperous, successful, booming.

flout v defy, disobey, violate, break, disregard, spurn, reject, scorn, jeer at, scoff at, mock, ridicule.

F3 obey, respect, regard.

flow v 1 CIRCULATE, ooze, trickle, ripple, bubble, well, spurt, squirt, gush, spill, run, pour, cascade, rush, stream, teem, flood, overflow, surge, sweep, move, drift, slip, slide, glide, roll, swirl. 2 ORIGINATE, derive, arise, spring, emerge, issue, result, proceed, emanate.

n course, flux, tide, current, drift, outpouring, stream, deluge, cascade, spurt, gush, flood, spate, abundance, plenty.

flower n 1 BLOOM, blossom, bud, floret. 2 BEST, cream, pick, choice, élite.

Flowers include:
African violet, alyssum, anemone, aster, aubrieta, azalea, begonia, bluebell, busy Lizzie (impatiens), calendula, candytuft, carnation, chrysanthemum, cornflower, cowslip, crocus, cyclamen, daffodil, dahlia, daisy, delphinium, forget-me-not, foxglove (digitalis), freesia, fuchsia, gardenia, geranium, gladiolus, hollyhock, hyacinth, iris (flag), lily of the valley, lobelia, lupin, marigold, narcissus, nasturtium, orchid, pansy, petunia, pink (dianthus), phlox, poinsettia, polyanthus, poppy, primrose, primula, rose, salvia, snapdragon (antirrhinum), snowdrop, stock, sunflower, sweetpea, sweet william, tulip, verbena, violet, wallflower, zinnia. see also plant; shrub.

Parts of a flower include:
anther, calyx, capitulum, carpel, corolla, corymb, dichasium, filament, gynoecium, monochasium, nectary, ovary, ovule, panicle, pedicel, petal, pistil, raceme, receptacle, sepal, spadix, spike, stalk, stamen, stigma, style, thalamus, torus, umbel.

v bud, burgeon, bloom, blossom, open, come out.

flowery adj florid, ornate, elaborate, fancy, baroque, rhetorical.

F3 plain, simple.

fluctuate v vary, change, alter, shift, rise and fall, seesaw, ebb and flow, alternate, swing, sway, oscillate, vacillate, waver.

fluent adj flowing, smooth, easy, effortless, articulate, eloquent, voluble, glib, ready.

F3 broken, inarticulate, tongue-tied.

fluff n down, nap, pile, fuzz, floss, lint, dust.

fluffy adj furry, fuzzy, downy, feathery, fleecy, woolly, hairy, shaggy, velvety, silky, soft.

grandiloquent. 2 a florid complexion: ruddy, red, purple.

F3 1 plain, simple. 2 pale.

fluid adj **1** LIQUID, liquefied, aqueous, watery, running, runny, melted, molten. **2** a fluid situation: variable, changeable, unstable, inconstant, shifting, mobile, adjustable, adaptable, flexible, open. **3** fluid movements: flowing, smooth, graceful.
E3 1 solid. **2** stable.
n liquid, solution, liquor, juice, gas, vapour.

flurry n **1** BURST, outbreak, spell, spurt, gust, blast, squall. **2** BUSTLE, hurry, fluster, fuss, to-do, commotion, tumult, whirl, disturbance, stir, flap (infml).

flush[1] v BLUSH, go red, redden, crimson, colour, burn, glow, suffuse. **2** CLEANSE, wash, rinse, hose, swab, clear, empty, evacuate.
adj **1** ABUNDANT, lavish, generous, full, overflowing, rich, wealthy, moneyed, prosperous, well-off, well-heeled, well-to-do. **2** LEVEL, even, smooth, flat, plane, square, true.

flush[2] v start, rouse, disturb, drive out, force out, expel, eject, run to earth, discover, uncover.

fluster v bother, upset, embarrass, disturb, perturb, agitate, ruffle, discompose, confuse, confound, unnerve, disconcert, rattle (infml), put off, distract.
E3 calm.
n flurry, bustle, commotion, disturbance, turmoil, state (infml), agitation, embarrassment, flap (infml), dither, tizzy (infml).
E3 calm.

fluted adj grooved, furrowed, channelled, corrugated, ribbed, ridged.

flutter v flap, wave, beat, bat, flicker, vibrate, palpitate, agitate, shake, tremble, quiver, shiver, ruffle, ripple, twitch, toss, waver, fluctuate.
n flapping, beat, flicker, vibration, palpitation, tremble, tremor, quiver, shiver, shudder, twitch.

flux n fluctuation, instability, change, alteration, modification, fluidity, flow, movement, motion, transition, development.
E3 stability, rest.

fly v **1** TAKE OFF, rise, ascend, mount, soar, glide, float, hover, flit, wing. **2** RACE, sprint, dash, tear, rush, hurry, speed, zoom, shoot, dart, career.
fly at attack, go for, fall upon.

foam n froth, lather, suds, head, bubbles, effervescence.
v froth, lather, bubble, effervesce, fizz, boil, seethe.

fob off foist, pass off, palm off (infml), get rid of, dump, unload, inflict, dispense, deceive, put off.

focus n focal point, target, centre, heart, core, nucleus, kernel, crux, hub, axis, linchpin, pivot, hinge.
v converge, meet, join, centre, concentrate, aim, direct, fix, spotlight, home in, zoom in, zero in (infml).

fog n **1** MIST, haze, cloud, gloom, murkiness, smog, pea-souper. **2** PERPLEXITY, puzzlement, confusion, bewilderment, daze, trance, vagueness, obscurity.
v mist, steam up, cloud, dull, dim, darken, obscure, blur, confuse, muddle.

foggy adj misty, hazy, smoggy, cloudy, murky, dark, shadowy, dim, indistinct, obscure.
E3 clear.

foil[1] v defeat, outwit, frustrate, thwart, baffle, counter, nullify, stop, check, obstruct, block, circumvent, elude.
E3 abet.

foil[2] *n* setting, background, relief, contrast, complement, balance.

fold *v* **1** BEND, ply, double, overlap, tuck, pleat, crease, crumple, crimp, crinkle. **2** *the business folded*: fail, go bust, shut down, collapse, crash. **3** ENFOLD, embrace, hug, clasp, envelop, wrap (up), enclose, entwine, intertwine.
n bend, turn, layer, ply, overlap, tuck, pleat, crease, knife-edge, line, wrinkle, furrow, corrugation.

folder *n* file, binder, folio, portfolio, envelope, holder.

folk *n* people, society, nation, race, tribe, clan, family, kin, kindred.
adj ethnic, national, traditional, native, indigenous, tribal, ancestral.

follow *v* **1** *night follows day*: come after, succeed, come next, replace, supersede, supplant. **2** CHASE, pursue, go after, hunt, track, trail, shadow, tail, hound, catch.
3 ACCOMPANY, (go along) with, escort, attend. **4** RESULT, ensue, develop, emanate, arise. **5** OBEY, comply with, adhere to, heed, mind, observe, conform to, carry out, practise. **6** GRASP, understand, comprehend, fathom.
F3 1 precede. **3** abandon, desert. **5** disobey.

follow through continue, pursue, see through, finish, complete, conclude, fulfil, implement.

follow up investigate, check out, continue, pursue, reinforce, consolidate.

follower *n* attendant, retainer, helper, companion, sidekick (*infml*), apostle, disciple, pupil, imitator, emulator, adherent, hanger-on,

believer, convert, backer, supporter, admirer, fan, devotee, freak (*infml*), buff (*infml*).
F3 leader, opponent.

following *adj* subsequent, next, succeeding, successive, resulting, ensuing, consequent, later.
F3 previous.
n followers, suite, retinue, entourage, circle, fans, admirers, supporters, support, backing, patronage, clientèle, audience, public.

folly *n* foolishness, stupidity, senselessness, rashness, recklessness, irresponsibility, indiscretion, craziness, madness, lunacy, insanity, idiocy, imbecility, silliness, absurdity, nonsense.
F3 wisdom, prudence, sanity.

fond *adj* affectionate, warm, tender, caring, loving, adoring, devoted, doting, indulgent.

fond of partial to, attached to, enamoured of, keen on, addicted to, hooked on.

fondle *v* caress, stroke, pat, pet, cuddle.

food *n* foodstuffs, comestibles, eatables (*infml*), provisions, stores, rations, eats (*infml*), grub (*sl*), nosh (*sl*), scran (*infml*), refreshment, sustenance, nourishment, nutrition, nutriment, subsistence, feed, fodder, diet, fare, cooking, cuisine, menu, board, table, larder.

Types of food include:

biscuit, bread, cake, cheese, fish, fruit, meat, nut, soup, vegetable; chips, French fries; pasta, cannelloni, fettuccine, ravioli, spaghetti bolognese, tortellini, lasagne; fish and chips, fish cake, fish-finger, kedgeree, gefilte fish, kipper, pickled herring, scampi, prawn cocktail, caviar; meat, casserole, cassoulet, hotpot, shepherd's pie, cottage pie, chilli con carne, balti, biriyani, chop suey, enchilada, moussaka, paella, pakora, samosa, pizza, ragout, risotto, tandoori, vindaloo, Wiener schnitzel, smorgasbord, stovies, stroganoff, French toast, welsh rarebit, brawn, faggot, rissole, haggis, black pudding, pâté, sausage, salami, frankfurter, hot dog, fritter, beefburger, hamburger, Big Mac®, egg, omelette, quiche, tofu, Quorn®, Yorkshire pudding, toad-in-the-hole, taco; gingerbread, shortbread, macaroon; sauce, dip, dressing, gravy. see also **bread; cake; cheese; dessert; fish; fruit; meat; nut; pasta; pastry; sauce; soup; sweet; vegetable**.

fool n blockhead, fat-head, butthead (sl), nincompoop (infml), ass (infml), chump (infml), ninny (infml), clot (infml), dope (infml), twit (infml), nitwit (infml), nit (infml), dunce, dimwit, simpleton, halfwit, idiot, imbecile, moron, dupe, sucker (infml), mug (infml), stooge, clown, jester. v deceive, take in, delude, mislead, dupe, gull, hoodwink, put one over on, trick, hoax, con (infml), cheat, swindle, diddle (infml), string along (infml), have on (infml), kid (infml), tease, joke, jest.

fool about lark about, horse around (sl), play about, mess about (infml), mess around (infml).

foolhardy adj rash, reckless, imprudent, ill-advised, irresponsible.
F3 cautious, prudent.

foolish adj stupid, senseless, unwise, ill-advised, ill-considered, short-sighted, half-baked, daft (infml), crazy, mad, insane, idiotic, moronic, hare-brained, half-witted, simple-minded, simple, unintelligent, inept, inane, silly, absurd, ridiculous, ludicrous, nonsensical.
F3 wise, prudent.

foolproof adj idiot-proof, infallible, fail-safe, sure, certain, sure-fire (infml), guaranteed.
F3 unreliable.

footing n base, foundation, basis, ground, relations, relationship, terms, conditions, state, standing, status, grade, rank, position, balance, foothold, purchase.

footprint n footmark, track, trail, trace, vestige.

forage n fodder, pasturage, feed, food, foodstuffs.
v rummage, search, cast about, scour, hunt, scavenge, ransack, plunder, raid.

forbid v prohibit, disallow, ban, proscribe, interdict, veto, refuse, deny, outlaw, debar, exclude, rule out, preclude, prevent, block, hinder, inhibit.
F3 allow, permit, approve.

forbidden adj prohibited, banned, proscribed, taboo, vetoed, outlawed, out of bounds.

forbidding adj stern, formidable, awesome, daunting, off-putting, uninviting, menacing, threatening, ominous, sinister, frightening.
F3 approachable, congenial.

force n 1 COMPULSION, impulse, influence, coercion, constraint, pressure, duress, violence, aggression. 2 POWER, might, strength, intensity, effort, energy, vigour, drive, dynamism, stress, emphasis. **3** ARMY, troop, body, corps, regiment, squadron, battalion, division, unit, detachment, patrol.

F∃ 2 weakness.

v **1** COMPEL, make, oblige, necessitate, urge, coerce, constrain, press, pressurize, lean on (*infml*), press-gang, bulldoze, drive, propel, push, thrust. **2** PRISE, wrench, wrest, extort, exact, wring.

forced *adj* unnatural, stiff, wooden, stilted, laboured, strained, false, artificial, contrived, feigned, affected, insincere.

F∃ spontaneous, sincere.

forceful *adj* strong, mighty, powerful, potent, effective, compelling, convincing, persuasive, cogent, telling, weighty, urgent, emphatic, vehement, forcible, dynamic, energetic, vigorous.

F∃ weak, feeble.

forebear *n* ancestor, forefather, father, predecessor, forerunner, antecedent.

F∃ descendant.

foreboding *n* misgiving, anxiety, worry, apprehension, dread, fear, omen, sign, token, premonition, warning, prediction, prognostication, intuition, feeling.

forecast *v* predict, prophesy, foretell, foresee, anticipate, expect, estimate, calculate.

n prediction, prophecy, expectation, prognosis, outlook, projection, guess, guesstimate (*infml*).

forefront *n* front, front line, firing line, van, vanguard, lead, fore, avant-garde.

F∃ rear.

foregoing *adj* preceding, antecedent, above, previous, earlier, former, prior.

F∃ following.

foreign *adj* alien, immigrant, imported, international, external, outside, overseas, exotic, faraway, distant, remote, strange, unfamiliar, unknown, uncharacteristic, incongruous, extraneous, borrowed.

F∃ native, indigenous.

foreigner *n* alien, immigrant, incomer, stranger, newcomer, visitor.

F∃ native.

foremost *adj* first, leading, front, chief, main, principal, primary, cardinal, paramount, central, highest, uppermost, supreme, prime, pre-eminent.

forerunner *n* predecessor, ancestor, antecedent, precursor, harbinger, herald, envoy, sign, token.

F∃ successor, follower.

foresee *v* envisage, anticipate, expect, forecast, predict, prophesy, prognosticate, foretell, forebode, divine.

foreshadow *v* prefigure, presage, augur, predict, prophesy, signal, indicate, promise.

foresight *n* anticipation, planning, forethought, far-sightedness, vision, caution, prudence, circumspection, care, readiness, preparedness, provision, precaution.

F∃ improvidence.

forestall *v* pre-empt, anticipate, preclude, obviate, avert, head off, ward off, parry, balk, frustrate, thwart, hinder, prevent.

foretaste *n* preview, trailer, sample, specimen, example, whiff, indication, warning, premonition.

foretell v prophesy, forecast, predict, prognosticate, augur, presage, signify, foreshadow, forewarn.

forethought n preparation, planning, forward planning, provision, precaution, anticipation, foresight, far-sightedness, circumspection, prudence, caution. **E3** improvidence, carelessness.

forever adv continually, constantly, 24-7 (infml), persistently, incessantly, perpetually, endlessly, eternally, always, evermore, for all time, permanently.

foreword n preface, introduction, prologue. **E3** appendix, postscript, epilogue.

forfeit n loss, surrender, confiscation, sequestration, penalty, fine, damages. v lose, give up, surrender, relinquish, sacrifice, forgo, renounce, abandon.

forge v **1** MAKE, mould, cast, shape, form, fashion, beat out, hammer out, work, create, invent. **2** forge a document: fake, counterfeit, falsify, copy, imitate, simulate, feign.

forgery n fake, counterfeit, copy, replica, reproduction, imitation, dud (infml), phoney (infml), sham, fraud. **E3** original.

forget v omit, fail, neglect, let slip, overlook, disregard, ignore, lose sight of, dismiss, think no more of, unlearn. **E3** remember, recall, recollect.

forgetful adj absent-minded, dreamy, inattentive, oblivious, negligent, lax, heedless. **E3** attentive, heedful.

forgive v pardon, absolve, excuse, exonerate, exculpate, acquit, remit, let off, overlook, condone. **E3** punish, censure.

forgiveness n pardon, absolution, exoneration, acquittal, remission, amnesty, mercy, clemency, leniency. **E3** punishment, censure, blame.

forgiving adj merciful, clement, lenient, tolerant, forbearing, indulgent, kind, humane, compassionate, soft-hearted, mild. **E3** merciless, censorious, harsh.

forgo v give up, yield, surrender, relinquish, sacrifice, forfeit, waive, renounce, abandon, resign, pass up, do without, abstain from, refrain from. **E3** claim, indulge in.

fork v split, divide, part, separate, diverge, branch (off).

forlorn adj deserted, abandoned, forsaken, forgotten, bereft, friendless, lonely, lost, homeless, destitute, desolate, hopeless, unhappy, miserable, wretched, helpless, pathetic, pitiable. **E3** cheerful.

form v **1** SHAPE, mould, model, fashion, make, manufacture, produce, create, found, establish, build, construct, assemble, put together, arrange, organize. **2** COMPRISE, constitute, make up, compose. **3** APPEAR, take shape, materialize, crystallize, grow, develop. n **1** APPEARANCE, shape, mould, cast, cut, outline, silhouette, figure, build, frame, structure, format, model, pattern, design, arrangement, organization, system. **2** a form of punishment: type, kind, sort, order, species, variety, genre, style, manner, nature, character, description. **3** CLASS, year, grade, stream. **4** on top form: health, fitness, fettle, condition, spirits. **5** ETIQUETTE, protocol, custom, convention, ritual, behaviour, manners. 6 QUESTIONNAIRE, document, paper, sheet.

formal adj 1 OFFICIAL, ceremonial, stately, solemn, conventional, orthodox, correct, fixed, set, regular. 2 PRIM, starchy, stiff, strict, rigid, precise, exact, punctilious, ceremonious, stilted, reserved.
F3 2 informal, casual.

formality n custom, convention, ceremony, ritual, procedure, matter of form, bureaucracy, red tape, protocol, etiquette, form, correctness, propriety, decorum, politeness.
F3 informality.

formation n 1 STRUCTURE, construction, composition, constitution, configuration, format, organization, arrangement, grouping, pattern, design, figure. 2 CREATION, generation, production, manufacture, appearance, development, establishment.

former adj past, ex-, one-time, sometime, late, departed, old, old-time, ancient, bygone, earlier, prior, previous, preceding, antecedent, foregoing, above.
F3 current, present, future, following.

formerly adv once, previously, earlier, before, at one time, lately.
F3 currently, now, later.

formidable adj daunting, challenging, intimidating, threatening, frightening, terrifying, terrific, frightful, fearful, great, huge, tremendous, prodigious, impressive, awesome, overwhelming, staggering.

formula n recipe, prescription, proposal, blueprint, code, wording, rubric, rule, principle, form, procedure, technique, method, way.

formulate v create, invent, originate, found, form, devise, work out, plan, design, draw up, frame, define, express, state, specify, detail, develop, evolve.

forsake v desert, abandon, jilt, throw over, discard, jettison, reject, disown, leave, quit, give up, surrender, relinquish, renounce, forgo.

fort n fortress, castle, tower, citadel, stronghold, fortification, garrison, station, camp.

forthcoming adj 1 their forthcoming wedding: impending, imminent, approaching, coming, future, prospective, projected, expected. 2 COMMUNICATIVE, talkative, chatty, conversational, sociable, informative, expansive, open, frank, direct.
F3 2 reticent, reserved.

forthright adj direct, straightforward, blunt, frank, candid, plain, open, bold, outspoken, in-your-face (infml).
F3 devious, secretive.

fortify v 1 STRENGTHEN, reinforce, brace, shore up, buttress, garrison, defend, protect, secure. 2 INVIGORATE, sustain, support, boost, encourage, hearten, cheer, reassure.
F3 1 weaken.

fortitude n courage, bravery, valour, grit, pluck, resolution, determination, perseverance, firmness, strength of mind, willpower, hardihood, endurance, stoicism.
F3 cowardice, fear.

fortuitous adj accidental, chance, random, arbitrary, casual, incidental, unforeseen, lucky, fortunate, providential.
F3 intentional, planned.

fortunate adj lucky, providential, happy, felicitous, prosperous, successful, well-off, timely, well-timed, opportune, convenient, propitious, advantageous, favourable, auspicious. **E3** unlucky, unfortunate, unhappy.

fortune n **1** WEALTH, riches, treasure, mint (infml), pile (infml), income, means, assets, estate, property, possessions, affluence, prosperity, success. **2** LUCK, chance, accident, providence, fate, destiny, doom, lot, portion, life, history, future.

forward adj **1** FIRST, head, front, fore, foremost, leading, onward, progressive, go-ahead, forward-looking, enterprising. **2** CONFIDENT, assertive, pushy, bold, audacious, brazen, brash, barefaced, cheeky (infml), impudent, impertinent, fresh (sl), familiar, presumptuous. **3** EARLY, advance, precocious, premature, advanced, well-advanced, well-developed.

E3 1 backward, retrograde. **2** shy, modest. **3** late, retarded.
adv forwards, ahead, on, onward, out, into view.
v advance, promote, further, foster, encourage, support, back, favour, help, assist, aid, facilitate, accelerate, speed, hurry, hasten, expedite, dispatch, send (on), post, transport, ship.
E3 impede, obstruct, hinder, slow.

foster v raise, rear, bring up, nurse, care for, take care of, nourish, feed, sustain, support, promote, advance, encourage, stimulate, cultivate, nurture, cherish, entertain, harbour.
E3 neglect, discourage.

foul adj **1** DIRTY, filthy, unclean, tainted, polluted, contaminated, rank, fetid, stinking, smelly, putrid, rotten, nauseating, offensive, repulsive, revolting, disgusting, squalid. **2** foul

language: obscene, lewd, smutty, indecent, coarse, vulgar, gross, blasphemous, abusive. **3** NASTY, disagreeable, wicked, vicious, vile, base, abhorrent, disgraceful, shameful. **4** foul weather: bad, unpleasant, rainy, wet, stormy, rough.
E3 1 clean. **4** fine.
v **1** DIRTY, soil, stain, sully, defile, taint, pollute, contaminate. **2** BLOCK, obstruct, clog, choke, foul up.
3 ENTANGLE, catch, snarl, twist, ensnare.
E3 1 clean. **2** clear. **3** disentangle.

found v **1** START, originate, create, initiate, institute, inaugurate, set up, establish, endow, organize. **2** BASE, ground, bottom, rest, settle, fix, plant, raise, build, erect, construct.

foundation n **1** BASE, foot, bottom, ground, bedrock, substance, basis, footing. **2** SETTING UP, establishment, institution, inauguration, endowment, organization, groundwork.

founder[1] n originator, initiator, father, mother, benefactor, creator, author, architect, designer, inventor, maker, builder, constructor, organizer.

founder[2] v sink, go down, submerge, subside, collapse, break down, fall, come to grief, fail, misfire, miscarry, abort, fall through, come to nothing.

fountain n **1** SPRAY, jet, spout, spring, well, wellspring, reservoir, waterworks. **2** SOURCE, origin, fount, font, fountainhead, wellhead.

fracture n break, crack, fissure, cleft, rupture, split, rift, rent, schism, breach, gap, opening.
v break, crack, rupture, split, splinter, chip.
E3 join.

fragile *adj* brittle, breakable, frail, delicate, flimsy, dainty, fine, slight, insubstantial, weak, feeble, infirm. **F3** robust, tough, durable.

fragment *n* piece, bit, part, portion, fraction, particle, crumb, morsel, scrap, remnant, shred, chip, splinter, shiver, sliver, shard.
v break, shatter, splinter, shiver, crumble, disintegrate, come to pieces, come apart, break up, divide, split (up), disunite.
F3 hold together, join.

fragmentary *adj* bitty, piecemeal, scrappy, broken, disjointed, disconnected, separate, scattered, sketchy, partial, incomplete.
F3 whole, complete.

fragrance *n* perfume, scent, smell, odour, aroma, bouquet.

fragrant *adj* perfumed, scented, sweet-smelling, sweet, balmy, aromatic, odorous.
F3 unscented.

frail *adj* delicate, brittle, breakable, fragile, flimsy, insubstantial, slight, puny, weak, feeble, infirm, vulnerable.
F3 robust, tough, strong.

frailty *n* weakness, foible, failing, deficiency, shortcoming, fault, defect, flaw, blemish, imperfection, fallibility, susceptibility.
F3 strength, robustness, toughness.

frame *v* **1** COMPOSE, formulate, conceive, devise, contrive, concoct, cook up, plan, map out, sketch, draw up, draft, shape, form, model, fashion, mould, forge, assemble, put together, build, construct, fabricate, make. **2** SURROUND, enclose, box in, case, mount. **3** *I've been framed*: set up, fit up (*sl*), trap.
n **1** STRUCTURE, fabric, framework,

skeleton, carcase, shell, casing, chassis, construction, bodywork, body, build, form. **2** MOUNT, mounting, setting, surround, border, edge.

frame of mind state of mind, mindset, mood, humour, temper, disposition, spirit, outlook, attitude.

framework *n* structure, fabric, bare bones, skeleton, shell, frame, outline, plan, foundation, groundwork.

franchise *n* concession, licence, charter, authorization, privilege, right, liberty, freedom, immunity, exemption.

frank *adj* honest, truthful, sincere, candid, blunt, open, free, plain, direct, forthright, straight, straightforward, downright, outspoken.
F3 insincere, evasive.

frankly *adv* to be frank, to be honest, in truth, honestly, candidly, bluntly, openly, freely, plainly, directly, straight.
F3 insincerely, evasively.

frantic *adj* agitated, overwrought, fraught, desperate, beside oneself, furious, raging, mad, wild, raving, frenzied, berserk, hectic.
F3 calm, composed.

fraternize *v* mix, mingle, socialize, consort, associate, affiliate, unite, sympathize.
F3 shun, ignore.

fraud *n* **1** DECEIT, deception, guile, cheating, swindling, double-dealing, sharp practice, fake, counterfeit, forgery, sham, hoax, trick. **2** (*infml*) CHARLATAN, impostor, pretender, phoney (*infml*), bluffer, hoaxer, cheat, swindler, double-dealer, con man (*infml*).

fraudulent adj dishonest, crooked (infml), criminal, deceitful, deceptive, false, bogus, phoney (infml), sham, counterfeit, swindling, double-dealing.

Ⓕ honest, genuine.

fray n brawl, scuffle, dust-up (infml), free-for-all, set-to, clash, conflict, fight, combat, battle, quarrel, row, rumpus, disturbance, riot.

frayed adj ragged, tattered, worn, threadbare, unravelled.

freak n 1 MONSTER, mutant, monstrosity, malformation, deformity, irregularity, anomaly, abnormality, aberration, oddity, curiosity, quirk, caprice, vagary, twist, turn.
2 ENTHUSIAST, fanatic, addict, devotee, fan, buff (infml), fiend (infml), nut (infml).
adj abnormal, atypical, unusual, exceptional, odd, queer, bizarre, aberrant, capricious, erratic, unpredictable, unexpected, surprise, chance, fortuitous, flukey.
Ⓕ normal, common.

free adj 1 AT LIBERTY, at large, loose, unattached, unrestrained, liberated, emancipated, independent, democratic, self-governing. 2 free time: spare, available, idle, unemployed, unoccupied, vacant, empty. 3 free tickets: gratis, without charge, free of charge, complimentary, on the house.
4 CLEAR, unobstructed, unimpeded, open. 5 GENEROUS, liberal, open-handed, lavish, charitable, hospitable.
Ⓕ 1 imprisoned, confined, restricted.
2 busy, occupied.
v release, let go, loose, turn loose, set free, untie, unbind, unchain, unleash, liberate, emancipate, rescue, deliver,

save, ransom, disentangle, disengage, extricate, clear, rid, relieve, unburden, exempt, absolve, acquit.
Ⓕ imprison, confine.

free of lacking, devoid of, without, unaffected by, immune to, exempt from, safe from.

freedom n 1 LIBERTY, emancipation, deliverance, release, exemption, immunity, impunity.
2 INDEPENDENCE, autonomy, self-government, home rule. 3 RANGE, scope, play, leeway, latitude, licence, privilege, power, free rein, free hand, opportunity, informality.
Ⓕ 1 captivity, confinement.
3 restriction.

freely adv 1 READILY, willingly, voluntarily, spontaneously, easily.
2 give freely: generously, liberally, lavishly, extravagantly, amply, abundantly. 3 speak freely: frankly, candidly, unreservedly, openly, plainly.
Ⓕ 2 grudgingly. 3 evasively, cautiously.

freeze v 1 ICE OVER, ice up, glaciate, congeal, solidify, harden, stiffen.
2 DEEP-FREEZE, ice, refrigerate, chill, cool. 3 STOP, suspend, fix, immobilize, hold.
n 1 FROST, freeze-up. 2 STOPPAGE, halt, standstill, shutdown, suspension, interruption, postponement, stay, embargo, moratorium.

freezing adj icy, frosty, glacial, arctic, polar, Siberian, wintry, raw, bitter, biting, cutting, penetrating, numbing, cold, chilly.
Ⓕ hot, warm.

freight n cargo, load, lading, pay-load, contents, goods, merchandise, consignment, shipment, transportation, conveyance, carriage, haulage.

frenzied adj frantic, frenetic, hectic, feverish, desperate, furious, wild, uncontrolled, mad, demented, hysterical.
F3 calm, composed.

frenzy n **1** TURMOIL, agitation, distraction, derangement, madness, lunacy, mania, hysteria, delirium, fever. **2** BURST, fit, spasm, paroxysm, convulsion, seizure, outburst, transport, passion, rage, fury.
F3 1 calm, composure.

frequent adj **1** NUMEROUS, countless, incessant, constant, continual, persistent, repeated, recurring, regular. **2** COMMON, commonplace, everyday, familiar, usual, customary.
F3 infrequent.
v visit, patronize, attend, haunt, hang out (infml), associate with, hang about with (infml), hang out with (infml).

fresh adj **1** ADDITIONAL, supplementary, extra, more, further, other. **2** NEW, novel, innovative, original, different, unconventional, modern, up-to-date, recent, latest. **3** REFRESHING, bracing, invigorating, brisk, crisp, keen, cool, fair, bright, clear, pure. **4** fresh fruit: raw, natural, unprocessed, crude. **5** REFRESHED, revived, restored, renewed, rested, invigorated, energetic, vigorous, lively, alert. **6** PERT, saucy (infml), cheeky (infml), disrespectful, impudent, insolent, bold, brazen, forward, familiar, presumptuous.
F3 2 old, hackneyed. **3** stale. **4** processed. **5** tired.

freshen v **1** AIR, ventilate, purify. **2** REFRESH, restore, revitalize, reinvigorate, liven, enliven, spruce up, tart up (infml).
F3 2 tire.

fret v **1** WORRY, agonize, brood, pine. **2** VEX, irritate, nettle, bother, trouble, torment.

friction n **1** DISAGREEMENT, dissension, dispute, disharmony, conflict, antagonism, hostility, opposition, rivalry, animosity, ill feeling, bad blood, resentment. **2** RUBBING, chafing, irritation, abrasion, scraping, grating, rasping, erosion, wearing away, resistance.

friend n mate (infml), pal (infml), chum (infml), buddy (infml), crony (infml), homeboy (sl), intimate, confidant(e), bosom friend, soul mate, comrade, ally, partner, associate, companion, playmate, pen-friend, acquaintance, well-wisher, supporter.
F3 enemy, opponent.

friendly adj **1** AMIABLE, affable, genial, kind, kindly, neighbourly, helpful, sympathetic, fond, affectionate, familiar, intimate, close, matey (infml), pally (infml), chummy (infml), companionable, sociable, outgoing, approachable, receptive, comradely, amicable, peaceable, well-disposed, favourable. **2** a friendly atmosphere: convivial, congenial, cordial, welcoming, warm.
F3 1 hostile, unsociable. **2** cold.

friendship n closeness, intimacy, familiarity, affinity, rapport, attachment, affection, fondness, love, harmony, concord, goodwill, friendliness, alliance, fellowship, comradeship.
F3 enmity, animosity.

fright n shock, scare, alarm, consternation, dismay, dread, apprehension, trepidation, fear, terror, horror, panic.

frighten v alarm, daunt, unnerve, dismay, intimidate, terrorize, scare, startle, scare stiff, terrify, petrify, horrify, appal, shock.
Ƒ꒾ reassure, calm.

frightening adj alarming, daunting, formidable, fearsome, scary, terrifying, hair-raising, bloodcurdling, spine-chilling, petrifying, traumatic.

frightful adj unpleasant, disagreeable, awful, dreadful, fearful, terrible, appalling, shocking, harrowing, unspeakable, dire, grim, ghastly, hideous, horrible, horrid, grisly, macabre, gruesome.
Ƒ꒾ pleasant, agreeable.

frigid adj 1 UNFEELING, unresponsive, passionless, unloving, cool, aloof, passive, lifeless. 2 FROZEN, icy, frosty, glacial, arctic, cold, chill, chilly, wintry.
Ƒ꒾ 1 responsive. 2 hot.

frilly adj ruffled, crimped, gathered, frilled, trimmed, lacy, fancy, ornate.
Ƒ꒾ plain.

fringe n 1 MARGIN, periphery, outskirts, edge, perimeter, limits, borderline. 2 BORDER, edging, trimming, tassel, frill, valance. adj unconventional, unorthodox, unofficial, alternative, avant-garde.
Ƒ꒾ conventional, mainstream.

frisk v jump, leap, skip, hop, bounce, caper, dance, gambol, frolic, romp, play, sport.

frisky adj lively, spirited, high-spirited, frolicsome, playful, romping, rollicking, bouncy.
Ƒ꒾ quiet.

fritter v waste, squander, dissipate, idle, misspend, blow (sl).

frivolity n fun, gaiety, flippancy, facetiousness, jest, light-heartedness, levity, triviality, superficiality, silliness, folly, nonsense.
Ƒ꒾ seriousness.

frivolous adj trifling, trivial, unimportant, shallow, superficial, light, flippant, jocular, light-hearted, juvenile, puerile, foolish, silly, idle, vain, pointless.
Ƒ꒾ serious, sensible.

frolic v gambol, caper, romp, play, lark around, rollick, make merry, frisk, prance, cavort, dance.
n fun, amusement, sport, gaiety, jollity, merriment, revel, romp, prank, lark, caper, high jinks, antics.

front n 1 at the front: face, aspect, frontage, façade, outside, exterior, facing, cover, obverse, top, head, lead, vanguard, forefront, front line, foreground, forepart, bow.
2 PRETENCE, show, air, appearance, look, expression, manner, façade, cover, mask, disguise, pretext, cover-up.
Ƒ꒾ 1 back, rear.
adj fore, leading, foremost, head, first.
Ƒ꒾ back, rear, last.
in front ahead, leading, first, in advance, before, preceding.
Ƒ꒾ behind.

frontier n border, boundary, borderline, limit, edge, perimeter, confines, marches, bounds, verge.

frosty adj 1 ICY, frozen, freezing, frigid, wintry, cold, chilly.
2 UNFRIENDLY, unwelcoming, cool, aloof, standoffish, stiff, discouraging.
Ƒ꒾ warm.

froth n bubbles, effervescence, foam, lather, suds, head, scum.
v foam, lather, ferment, fizz, effervesce, bubble.

frown v scowl, glower, lour, glare, grimace.
n scowl, glower, dirty look (*infml*), glare, grimace.

frown on disapprove of, object to, dislike, discourage.
F3 approve of.

frozen adj iced, chilled, icy, icebound, ice-covered, arctic, ice-cold, frigid, freezing, numb, solidified, stiff, rigid, fixed.
F3 warm.

frugal adj thrifty, penny-wise, parsimonious, careful, provident, saving, economical, sparing, meagre.
F3 wasteful, generous.

fruit

Varieties of fruit include:

apple, crab-apple, pear, orange, mandarin, minneola, clementine, satsuma, tangerine; apricot, peach, plum, nectarine, cherry, sloe, damson, greengage, grape, gooseberry, rhubarb, tomato; banana, pineapple, olive, lemon, lime, Ugli®, star fruit, lychee, date, fig, grapefruit, kiwi fruit, mango, papaya, guava, passion fruit, avocado; melon, cantaloupe, watermelon; strawberry, raspberry, blackberry, bilberry, loganberry, elderberry, blueberry, boysenberry, cranberry; redcurrant, blackcurrant.

fruitful adj **1** FERTILE, rich, teeming, plentiful, abundant, prolific, productive. **2** REWARDING, profitable, advantageous, beneficial, worthwhile, well-spent, useful, successful.
F3 1 barren. **2** fruitless.

fruition n realization, fulfilment, attainment, achievement, completion, maturity, ripeness, consummation, perfection, success, enjoyment.

fruitless adj unsuccessful, abortive, useless, futile, pointless, vain, idle, hopeless, barren, sterile.
F3 fruitful, successful, profitable.

frustrate v **1** THWART, foil, balk, baffle, block, check, spike, defeat, circumvent, forestall, counter, nullify, neutralize, inhibit. **2** DISAPPOINT, discourage, dishearten, depress.
F3 1 further, promote. **2** encourage.

fuel n **1** *a tax on fuel*: combustible, propellant, motive power.
2 PROVOCATION, incitement, encouragement, ammunition, material.

Fuels include:

gas, Calor Gas®, propane, butane, methane, acetylene, electricity, coal, coke, anthracite, charcoal, oil, petrol, gasoline, diesel, derv, paraffin, kerosene, methylated spirit, wood, logs, peat, nuclear power.

v incite, inflame, fire, encourage, fan, feed, nourish, sustain, stoke up.
F3 discourage, damp down.

fugitive n escapee, runaway, deserter, refugee.
adj fleeting, transient, transitory, passing, short, brief, flying, temporary, ephemeral, elusive.
F3 permanent.

fulfil v complete, finish, conclude, consummate, perfect, realize, achieve, accomplish, perform, execute, discharge, implement, carry out, comply with, observe, keep, obey, conform to, satisfy, fill, answer.
F3 fail, break.

fulfilment *n* completion, perfection, consummation, realization, achievement, accomplishment, success, performance, execution, discharge, implementation, observance, satisfaction.

F3 failure.

full *adj* **1** FILLED, loaded, packed, crowded, crammed, stuffed, jammed. **2** ENTIRE, whole, intact, total, complete, unabridged, unexpurgated. **3** THOROUGH, comprehensive, exhaustive, all-inclusive, broad, vast, extensive, ample, generous, abundant, plentiful, copious, profuse. **4** *a full voice*: rich, resonant, loud, deep, clear, distinct. **5** *at full speed*: maximum, top, highest, greatest, utmost.

F3 1 empty. **2** partial, incomplete. **3** superficial.

full-grown *adj* adult, grown-up, of age, mature, ripe, developed, full-blown, full-scale.

F3 young, undeveloped.

fully *adv* completely, totally, utterly, wholly, entirely, thoroughly, altogether, quite, positively, without reserve, perfectly.

F3 partly.

fumble *v* grope, feel, bungle, botch, mishandle, mismanage.

fume *v* **1** SMOKE, smoulder, boil, steam. **2** RAGE, storm, rant, rave, seethe.

fumes *n* exhaust, smoke, gas, vapour, haze, fog, smog, pollution.

fumigate *v* deodorize, disinfect, sterilize, purify, cleanse.

fun *n* enjoyment, pleasure, amusement, entertainment, diversion, distraction, recreation, play, sport, game, foolery, tomfoolery, horseplay, skylarking, romp, merrymaking, mirth, craic (*Irish*), jollity, jocularity, joking, jesting.

make fun of rag, jeer at, ridicule, laugh at, mock, taunt, tease, rib (*sl*).

function *n* **1** ROLE, part, office, duty, charge, responsibility, concern, job, task, occupation, business, activity, purpose, use. **2** RECEPTION, party, gathering, affair, do (*infml*), dinner, luncheon.

v work, operate, run, go, serve, act, perform, behave.

functional *adj* working, operational, practical, useful, utilitarian, utility, plain, hard-wearing.

F3 useless, decorative.

fund *n* pool, kitty, treasury, repository, storehouse, store, reserve, stock, hoard, cache, stack, mine, well, source, supply.

v finance, capitalize, endow, subsidize, underwrite, sponsor, back, support, promote, float.

fundamental *adj* basic, primary, first, rudimentary, elementary, underlying, integral, central, principal, cardinal, prime, main, key, essential, mission-critical (*infml*), indispensable, vital, necessary, crucial, important.

funds *n* money, finance, backing, capital, resources, savings, wealth, cash.

funeral *n* burial, interment, entombment, cremation, obsequies, wake.

fungus

Types of fungus include:
blight, botrytis, candida, mildew, ergot, mould, mushroom, penicillium, potato blight, rust, scab, smut, toadstool, yeast. *see also* **mushroom**.

funnel *v* channel, direct, convey, move, transfer, pass, pour, siphon, filter.

funny *adj* **1** HUMOROUS, amusing, entertaining, comic, comical, hilarious, witty, facetious, droll, farcical, laughable, ridiculous, absurd, silly. **2** ODD, strange, peculiar, curious, queer, weird, unusual, remarkable, puzzling, perplexing, mysterious, suspicious, dubious.

E3 1 serious, solemn, sad. **2** normal, ordinary, usual.

furious *adj* **1** ANGRY, mad (*infml*), up in arms (*infml*), livid, enraged, infuriated, incensed, raging, fuming, boiling. **2** VIOLENT, wild, fierce, intense, vigorous, frantic, boisterous, stormy, tempestuous.

E3 1 calm, pleased.

furnish *v* equip, fit out, decorate, rig, stock, provide, supply, afford, grant, give, offer, present.

E3 divest.

furniture *n* equipment, appliances, furnishings, fittings, fitments, household goods, movables, possessions, effects, things.

Types of furniture include:
table, chair, suite, couch, pouffe, footstool, beanbag, bed, desk, bureau, secretaire, bookcase, cabinet, cupboard, dumb-waiter, fireplace, overmantel, fender, firescreen, hall-stand, umbrella-stand, mirror, magazine rack, wardrobe, armoire, vanity unit, washstand. *see also* **bed**; **chair**; **couch**; **cupboard**; **table**.

---

furrow *n* groove, channel, trench, hollow, rut, track, line, crease, wrinkle. *v* seam, flute, corrugate, groove, crease, wrinkle, draw together, knit.

further *adj* more, additional, supplementary, extra, fresh, new, other.

v advance, forward, promote, champion, push, encourage, foster, help, aid, assist, ease, facilitate, speed, hasten, accelerate, expedite.

E3 stop, frustrate.

furthermore *adv* moreover, what's more, in addition, further, besides, also, too, as well, additionally.

furthest *adj* farthest, furthermost, remotest, outermost, outmost, extreme, ultimate, utmost, uttermost.

E3 nearest.

furtive *adj* surreptitious, sly, stealthy, secretive, underhand, hidden, covert, secret.

E3 open.

fury *n* anger, rage, wrath, frenzy, madness, passion, vehemence, fierceness, ferocity, violence, wildness, turbulence, power.

E3 calm, peacefulness.

fusion *n* melting, smelting, welding, union, synthesis, blending, coalescence, amalgamation, integration, conflation, merger, federation.

fuss *n* bother, trouble, hassle (*infml*), palaver, to-do (*infml*), hoo-ha (*infml*), furore, squabble, row, commotion, stir, fluster, confusion, upset, worry, agitation, flap (*infml*), excitement, bustle, flurry, hurry.

E3 calm.

v complain, grumble, fret, worry, flap (*infml*), take pains, bother, bustle, fidget.

fussy *adj* **1** PARTICULAR, fastidious, scrupulous, finicky, pernickety, difficult, hard to please, choosy (*infml*), discriminating. **2** FANCY, elaborate, ornate, cluttered.

F∃ 1 casual, uncritical. **2** plain.

futile *adj* pointless, useless, worthless, vain, idle, wasted, fruitless, profitless, unavailing, unsuccessful, abortive, unprofitable, unproductive, ineffective, barren, empty, hollow, forlorn.

F∃ fruitful, profitable.

futility *n* pointlessness, uselessness, worthlessness, vanity, emptiness, hollowness, aimlessness.

F∃ use, purpose.

future *n* hereafter, tomorrow, outlook, prospects, expectations.

F∃ past.

adj prospective, designate, to be, fated, destined, to come, forthcoming, in the offing, impending, coming, approaching, expected, planned, unborn, later, subsequent, eventual.

F∃ past.

fuzzy *adj* **1** FRIZZY, fluffy, furry, woolly, fleecy, downy, velvety, napped. **2** BLURRED, unfocused, ill-defined, unclear, vague, faint, hazy, shadowy, woolly, muffled, distorted.

F∃ 2 clear, distinct.

G

gadget n tool, appliance, device, contrivance, contraption, thing, thingumajig (*infml*), invention, novelty, gimmick.

gag[1] v muffle, muzzle, silence, quiet, stifle, throttle, suppress, curb, check, still.

gag[2] n (*infml*) joke, jest, quip, crack, wisecrack, one-liner, pun, witticism, funny (*infml*).

gaiety n happiness, glee, cheerfulness, joie de vivre, jollity, merriment, mirth, hilarity, fun, merrymaking, revelry, festivity, celebration, joviality, good humour, high spirits, light-heartedness, liveliness, brightness, brilliance, sparkle, colour, colourfulness, show, showiness.

F3 sadness, drabness.

gaily adv happily, joyfully, merrily, blithely, brightly, brilliantly, colourfully, flamboyantly.

F3 sadly, dully.

gain v 1 EARN, make, produce, gross, net, clear, profit, yield, bring in, reap, harvest, win, capture, secure, obtain, acquire, procure. 2 REACH, arrive at, come to, get to, attain, achieve, realize. 3 *gain speed*: increase, pick up, gather, collect, advance, progress, improve.

F3 1 lose. 3 lose.

n earnings, proceeds, income, revenue, winnings, profit, return, yield, dividend, growth, increase, increment, rise, advance, progress, headway, improvement, advantage, benefit, attainment, achievement, acquisition.

F3 loss.

gain on close with, narrow the gap, approach, catch up, level with, overtake, outdistance, leave behind.

gala n festivity, celebration, festival, carnival, jubilee, jamboree, fête, fair, pageant, procession.

gale n 1 WIND, squall, storm, hurricane, tornado, typhoon, cyclone. 2 BURST, outburst, outbreak, fit, eruption, explosion, blast.

gallant adj chivalrous, gentlemanly, courteous, polite, gracious, courtly, noble, dashing, heroic, valiant, brave, courageous, fearless, dauntless, bold, daring.

F3 ungentlemanly, cowardly.

gallery n art gallery, museum, arcade, passage, walk, balcony, circle, gods (*infml*), spectators.

gallop v bolt, run, sprint, race, career, fly, dash, tear, speed, zoom, shoot, dart, rush, hurry, hasten.

F3 amble.

galvanize v electrify, shock, jolt, prod, spur, provoke, stimulate, stir, move, arouse, excite, fire, invigorate, vitalize.

gamble v bet, wager, have a flutter (*infml*), try one's luck, punt, play, game, stake, chance, take a chance, risk, hazard, venture, speculate, back. n bet, wager, flutter (*infml*), punt, lottery, chance, risk, venture, speculation.

gambler n better, punter.

gambol v caper, frolic, frisk, skip, jump, bound, hop, bounce.

game [1] n **1** RECREATION, play, sport, pastime, diversion, distraction, entertainment, amusement, fun, frolic, romp, joke, jest. **2** COMPETITION, contest, match, round, tournament, event, meeting. **3** GAME BIRDS, animals, meat, flesh, prey, quarry, bag, spoils.

> Types of indoor game include:
> board-game, backgammon, chess,
> Chinese checkers, Cluedo®,
> draughts, halma, ludo, mah-jong,
> Monopoly®, nine men's morris,
> Scrabble®, snakes and ladders,
> Trivial Pursuit®; card-game, bac-
> carat, beggar-my-neighbour, bezique,
> blackjack, brag, bridge, canasta,
> chemin de fer, crib (*infml*), cribbage,
> faro, gin rummy, rummy, happy fam-
> ilies, old maid, patience, Pelman-
> ism, piquet, poker, pontoon, vingt-
> et-un, snap, solitaire, twenty-one,
> whist; bagatelle, pinball, billiards,
> pool, snooker, bowling, tenpin
> bowling, bowls, darts, dice, craps,
> dominoes, roulette, shove-halfpen-
> ny, table tennis, Ping-Pong®.

> Types of children's game include:
> battleships, blindman's buff, cha-
> rades, Chinese whispers, conse-

quences, five-stones, forfeits, hang-man, hide-and-seek, I-spy, jacks, jack-straws, musical chairs, noughts and crosses, pass the parcel, piggy-in-the-middle, pin the tail on the donkey, postman's knock, sardines, Simon says, spillikins, spin the bottle, tiddlywinks.

game [2] adj (*infml*) **1** game for anything: willing, inclined, ready, prepared, eager. **2** BOLD, daring, intrepid, brave, courageous, fearless, resolute, spirited.

🖃 **1** unwilling. **2** cowardly.

gamut n scale, series, range, sweep, scope, compass, spectrum, field, area.

gang n group, band, ring, pack, herd, mob, crowd, circle, clique, coterie, set, lot, team, crew, squad, shift, party.

gangster n mobster, desperado, hoodlum, ruffian, rough, tough, thug, heavy (*sl*), racketeer, bandit, brigand, robber, criminal, crook (*infml*).

gaol see **jail**.

gaoler see **jailer**.

gap n **1** SPACE, blank, void, hole, opening, crack, chink, crevice, cleft, breach, rift, divide, divergence, difference. **2** INTERRUPTION, break, recess, pause, lull, interlude, intermission, interval.

gape v **1** STARE, gaze, gawp (*infml*), goggle, gawk (*infml*). **2** OPEN, yawn, part, split, crack.

gaping adj open, yawning, broad, wide, vast, cavernous.

🖃 tiny.

garage n lock-up, petrol station, gas station (*US*), service station.

garble v confuse, muddle, jumble, scramble, mix up, twist, distort, pervert, slant, misrepresent, falsify.

🖃 decipher.

garden n yard, backyard, plot, allotment, orchard, park.

garish adj gaudy, lurid, loud, glaring, flashy, showy, tawdry, vulgar, tasteless.
F3 quiet, tasteful.

garland n wreath, festoon, decoration, flowers, laurels, honours.
υ wreathe, festoon, deck, adorn, crown.

garments n clothes, clothing, wear, attire, gear (infml), togs (infml), outfit, get-up (infml), dress, costume, uniform.

garnish υ decorate, adorn, ornament, trim, embellish, enhance, grace, set off.
F3 divest.
n decoration, ornament, trimming, embellishment, enhancement, relish.

gash υ cut, wound, slash, slit, incise, lacerate, tear, rend, split, score, gouge.
n cut, wound, slash, slit, incision, laceration, tear, rent, split, score, gouge.

gasp υ pant, puff, blow, breathe, wheeze, choke, gulp.
n pant, puff, blow, breath, gulp, exclamation.

gate n barrier, door, doorway, gateway, opening, entrance, exit, access, passage.

gather υ **1** CONGREGATE, convene, muster, rally, round up, assemble, collect, group, amass, accumulate, hoard, stockpile, heap, pile up, build. **2** INFER, deduce, conclude, surmise, assume, understand, learn, hear.
3 FOLD, pleat, tuck, pucker. **4** gather flowers: pick, pluck, cull, select, reap, harvest, glean.
F3 1 scatter, dissipate.

gathering n assembly, convocation, convention, meeting, round-up, rally, get-together, jamboree, party, group, company, congregation, mass, crowd, throng, turnout.

gaudy adj bright, brilliant, glaring, garish, loud, flashy, showy, ostentatious, tinselly, glitzy (infml), tawdry, vulgar, tasteless.
F3 drab, plain.

gauge υ estimate, guess, judge, assess, evaluate, value, rate, reckon, figure, calculate, compute, count, measure, weigh, determine, ascertain.
n **1** STANDARD, norm, criterion, benchmark, yardstick, rule, guideline, indicator, measure, meter, test, sample, example, model, pattern.
2 SIZE, magnitude, measure, capacity, bore, calibre, thickness, width, span, extent, scope, height, depth, degree.

gaunt adj **1** HAGGARD, hollow-eyed, angular, bony, thin, lean, lank, skinny, scraggy, scrawny, skeletal, emaciated, wasted. **2** BLEAK, stark, bare, desolate, forlorn, dismal, dreary, grim, harsh.
F3 1 plump.

gawky adj awkward, clumsy, maladroit, gauche, inept, oafish, ungainly, gangling, unco-ordinated, graceless.
F3 graceful.

gay adj **1** HAPPY, joyful, jolly, merry, cheerful, blithe, sunny, carefree, debonair, fun-loving, pleasure-seeking, vivacious, lively, animated, playful, light-hearted. **2** gay colours: vivid, rich, bright, brilliant, sparkling, festive, colourful, gaudy, garish, flashy, showy, flamboyant.
3 HOMOSEXUAL, lesbian, queer (sl), pink (infml).
F3 1 sad, gloomy. **3** heterosexual, straight (sl).

gaze *n* homosexual, homo (*sl*), queer (*sl*), poof (*sl*), lesbian, dike (*sl*).
F3 heterosexual.

gaze *v* stare, contemplate, regard, watch, view, look, gape, wonder.
n stare, look.

gear *n* 1 EQUIPMENT, kit, outfit, tackle, apparatus, tools, instruments, accessories. 2 GEARWHEEL, cogwheel, cog, gearing, mechanism, machinery, works. 3 (*infml*) BELONGINGS, possessions, things, stuff, baggage, luggage, paraphernalia. 4 (*infml*) CLOTHES, clothing, garments, attire, dress, garb (*infml*), togs (*infml*), get-up (*infml*).

gel, jell *v* set, congeal, coagulate, crystallize, harden, thicken, solidify, materialize, come together, finalize, form, take shape.

gelatinous *adj* jelly-like, jellied, congealed, rubbery, glutinous, gummy, gluey, gooey (*infml*), sticky, viscous.

gem *n* gemstone, precious stone, stone, jewel, treasure, prize, masterpiece, pièce de résistance.

Gems and gemstones include: diamond, zircon, marcasite, rhinestone, pearl, moonstone, onyx, opal, mother-of-pearl, amber, citrine, topaz, agate, tiger's-eye, jasper, morganite, ruby, garnet, rose quartz, beryl, cornelian, coral, amethyst, sapphire, turquoise, lapis lazuli, emerald, aquamarine, bloodstone, jade, peridot, tourmaline, jet.

---

genealogy *n* family tree, pedigree, lineage, ancestry, descent, derivation, extraction, family, line.

general *adj* 1 *a general statement*: broad, sweeping, blanket, all-inclusive, comprehensive, universal, global, total, across-the-board, widespread, prevalent, extensive, overall, panoramic. 2 VAGUE, ill-defined, indefinite, imprecise, inexact, approximate, loose, unspecific. 3 USUAL, regular, normal, typical, ordinary, everyday, customary, conventional, common, public.
F3 1 particular, limited. 2 specific. 3 rare.

generally *adv* usually, normally, as a rule, by and large, on the whole, mostly, mainly, chiefly, broadly, commonly, universally.

generate *v* produce, engender, whip up, arouse, cause, bring about, give rise to, create, originate, initiate, make, form, breed, propagate.
F3 prevent.

generation *n* 1 AGE GROUP, age, era, epoch, period, time. 2 PRODUCTION, creation, origination, formation, genesis, procreation, reproduction, propagation, breeding.

generosity *n* liberality, munificence, open-handedness, bounty, charity, magnanimity, philanthropy, kindness, big-heartedness, benevolence, goodness.
F3 meanness, selfishness.

generous *adj* 1 LIBERAL, free, bountiful, open-handed, unstinting, unsparing, lavish. 2 MAGNANIMOUS, charitable, philanthropic, public-spirited, unselfish, kind, big-hearted, benevolent, good, high-minded, noble. 3 AMPLE, full, plentiful, abundant, copious, overflowing.
F3 1 mean, miserly. 2 selfish. 3 meagre.

genial *adj* affable, amiable, friendly, convivial, cordial, kindly, kind, warm-

hearted, warm, hearty, jovial, jolly, cheerful, happy, good-natured, easy-going (*infml*), agreeable, pleasant.
F3 cold.

genius *n* **1** VIRTUOSO, maestro, master, past master, expert, adept, egghead (*infml*), intellectual, mastermind, brain, intellect.
2 INTELLIGENCE, brightness, brilliance, ability, aptitude, gift, talent, flair, knack, bent, inclination, propensity, capacity, faculty.

gentle *adj* **1** KIND, kindly, amiable, tender, soft-hearted, compassionate, sympathetic, merciful, mild, placid, calm, tranquil. **2** *a gentle slope*: gradual, slow, easy, smooth, moderate, slight, light, imperceptible. **3** SOOTHING, peaceful, serene, quiet, soft, balmy.
F3 **1** unkind, rough, harsh, wild.

genuine *adj* real, actual, natural, pure, original, authentic, veritable, true, bona fide, legitimate, honest, sincere, frank, candid, earnest.
F3 artificial, false, insincere.

germ *n* **1** MICRO-ORGANISM, microbe, bacterium, bacillus, virus, bug (*infml*). **2** BEGINNING, start, origin, source, cause, spark, rudiment, nucleus, root, seed, embryo, bud, sprout.

germinate *v* bud, sprout, shoot, develop, grow, swell.

gesticulate *v* wave, signal, gesture, indicate, sign.

gesture *n* act, action, movement, motion, indication, sign, signal, wave, gesticulation.
v indicate, sign, motion, beckon, point, signal, wave, gesticulate.

get *v* **1** OBTAIN, acquire, procure, come by, receive, earn, gain, win, secure, achieve, realize. **2** *it's getting*

dark: become, turn, go, grow. **3** *get him to help*: persuade, coax, induce, urge, influence, sway. **4** MOVE, go, come, reach, arrive. **5** FETCH, collect, pick up, take, catch, capture, seize, grab. **6** CONTRACT, catch, pick up, develop, come down with.
F3 **1** lose. **4** leave.

get across communicate, transmit, convey, impart, put across, bring home to.

get ahead advance, progress, get on, go places (*infml*), thrive, flourish, prosper, succeed, make good, make it, get there (*infml*).
F3 fall behind, fail.

get along **1** COPE, manage, get by, survive, fare, progress, develop. **2** AGREE, harmonize, get on, hit it off.

get at **1** REACH, attain, find, discover. **2** (*infml*) BRIBE, suborn, corrupt, influence. **3** (*infml*) MEAN, intend, imply, insinuate, hint, suggest. **4** (*infml*) CRITICIZE, find fault with, pick on, attack, make fun of.

get away escape, get out, break out, break away, run away, flee, depart, leave.

get back recover, regain, recoup, repossess, retrieve.

get down **1** DEPRESS, sadden, dishearten, dispirit. **2** DESCEND, dismount, disembark, alight, get off.
F3 **1** encourage. **2** board.

get in enter, penetrate, infiltrate, arrive, come, land, embark.

get off **1** *get off a train*: alight, disembark, dismount, descend. **2** REMOVE, detach, separate, shed, get down.
F3 **1** get on. **2** put on.

get on **1** BOARD, embark, mount, ascend. **2** COPE, manage, fare, get along, make out, prosper, succeed. **3** CONTINUE, proceed, press on, advance, progress.

get off.

get out 1 ESCAPE, flee, break out, extricate oneself, free oneself, leave, quit, vacate, evacuate, clear out, clear off (*infml*). **2** *she got out a pen*: take out, produce.

get over 1 RECOVER FROM, shake off, survive. **2** SURMOUNT, overcome, defeat, deal with. **3** COMMUNICATE, get across, convey, put over, impart, explain.

get round 1 CIRCUMVENT, bypass, evade, avoid. **2** PERSUADE, win over, talk round, coax, prevail upon.

get together assemble, collect, gather, congregate, rally, meet, join, unite, collaborate.

get up stand (up), arise, rise, ascend, climb, mount, scale.

ghastly *adj* awful, dreadful, frightful, terrible, grim, gruesome, hideous, horrible, horrid, loathsome, repellent, shocking, appalling.

delightful, attractive.

ghost *n* spectre, phantom, spook (*infml*), apparition, visitant, spirit, wraith, soul, shade, shadow.

ghostly *adj* eerie, spooky (*infml*), creepy, supernatural, unearthly, ghostlike, spectral, wraith-like, phantom, illusory.

giant *n* monster, titan, colossus, Goliath, Hercules.
adj gigantic, colossal, titanic, mammoth, jumbo (*infml*), king-size, huge, enormous, immense, vast, large.

gibe, jibe *n* jeer, sneer, mockery, ridicule, taunt, derision, scoff, dig (*infml*), crack (*infml*), poke, quip.

giddy *adj* **1** DIZZY, faint, light-headed, unsteady, reeling, vertiginous. **2** SILLY, flighty, wild.

gift *n* **1** PRESENT, offering, donation, contribution, bounty, largess, gratuity, tip, bonus, freebie (*sl*), legacy, bequest, endowment. **2** TALENT, genius, flair, aptitude, bent, knack, power, faculty, attribute, ability, capability, capacity.

gifted *adj* talented, adept, skilful, expert, masterly, skilled, accomplished, able, capable, clever, intelligent, bright, brilliant.

gigantic *adj* huge, enormous, immense, vast, giant, colossal, mega (*infml*), titanic, mammoth, gargantuan, Brobdingnagian.

tiny, Lilliputian, nano-.

giggle *v, n* titter, snigger, chuckle, chortle, laugh.

gilded *adj* gilt, gold, golden, gold-plated.

gimmick *n* attraction, ploy, stratagem, ruse, scheme, trick, stunt, dodge, device, contrivance, gadget.

gingerly *adv* tentatively, hesitantly, warily, cautiously, carefully, delicately.

boldly, carelessly.

gipsy *see* **gypsy**.

girdle *n* belt, sash, band, waistband, corset.

girl *n* lass, young woman, girlfriend, sweetheart, daughter.

girth *n* **1** CIRCUMFERENCE, perimeter, measure, size, bulk. **2** STRAP, band.

gist *n* pith, essence, marrow, substance, matter, meaning, significance, import, sense, idea, drift, direction, point, nub, core, quintessence.

give *v* **1** PRESENT, award, confer, offer, lend, donate, contribute, provide, supply, furnish, grant, bestow, endow, gift, make over, hand over, deliver, entrust, commit, devote. **2** *give news*: communicate, transmit, impart, utter, announce, declare, pronounce, publish, set forth. **3** CONCEDE, allow, admit, yield, give way, surrender. **4** *give trouble*: cause, occasion, make, produce, do, perform. **5** SINK, yield, bend, give way, break, collapse, fall.

F3 1 take, withhold. **5** withstand.

give away betray, inform on, expose, uncover, divulge, let slip, disclose, reveal, leak, let out.

give in surrender, capitulate, submit, yield, give way, concede, give up, quit.

F3 hold out.

give off emit, discharge, release, give out, send out, throw out, pour out, exhale, exude, produce.

give out 1 DISTRIBUTE, hand out, dole out, deal. **2** ANNOUNCE, declare, broadcast, publish, disseminate, communicate, transmit, impart, notify, advertise.

give up 1 STOP, cease, quit, resign, abandon, renounce, relinquish, waive. **2** SURRENDER, capitulate, give in.

F3 1 start. **2** hold out.

given *adj* **1** *a given number*: specified, particular, definite. **2** INCLINED, disposed, likely, liable, prone.

glad *adj* **1** PLEASED, delighted, gratified, contented, happy, joyful, merry, cheerful, cheery, bright. **2** WILLING, eager, keen, ready, inclined, disposed.

F3 1 sad, unhappy. **2** unwilling, reluctant.

glamorous *adj* smart, elegant, attractive, beautiful, gorgeous,

enchanting, captivating, alluring, appealing, fascinating, exciting, dazzling, glossy, colourful.

F3 plain, drab, boring.

glamour *n* attraction, allure, appeal, fascination, charm, magic, beauty, elegance, glitter, prestige.

glance *v* peep, peek, glimpse, view, look, scan, skim, leaf, flip, thumb, dip, browse.

n peep, peek, glimpse, look.

glare *v* **1** GLOWER, look daggers, frown, scowl, stare. **2** DAZZLE, blaze, flame, flare, shine, reflect.

n **1** BLACK LOOK, dirty look (*infml*), frown, scowl, stare.

2 BRIGHTNESS, brilliance, blaze, flame, dazzle, spotlight.

glaring *adj* blatant, flagrant, open, conspicuous, manifest, patent, obvious, outrageous, gross.

F3 hidden, concealed, minor.

glassy *adj* **1** GLASSLIKE, smooth, slippery, icy, shiny, glossy, transparent, clear. **2** *a glassy stare*: expressionless, blank, empty, vacant, dazed, fixed, glazed, cold, lifeless, dull.

glaze *v* coat, enamel, gloss, varnish, lacquer, polish, burnish.

n coat, coating, finish, enamel, varnish, lacquer, polish, shine, lustre, gloss.

gleam *n* glint, flash, beam, ray, flicker, glimmer, shimmer, sparkle, glitter, gloss, glow.

v glint, flash, glance, flare, shine, glisten, glimmer, glitter, sparkle, shimmer, glow.

glib *adj* fluent, easy, facile, quick, ready, talkative, plausible, insincere, smooth, slick, suave, smooth-tongued.

F3 tongue-tied, implausible.

glide v slide, slip, skate, skim, fly, float, drift, sail, coast, roll, run, flow.

glimmer v glow, shimmer, glisten, glitter, sparkle, twinkle, wink, blink, flicker, gleam, shine.
n 1 GLOW, shimmer, sparkle, twinkle, flicker, glint, gleam. 2 TRACE, hint, suggestion, grain.

glimpse n peep, peek, squint, glance, look, sight, sighting, view.
v spy, espy, spot, catch sight of, sight, view.

glint v flash, gleam, shine, reflect, glitter, sparkle, twinkle, glimmer.
n flash, gleam, shine, reflection, glitter, sparkle, twinkle, glimmer.

glisten v shine, gleam, glint, glitter, sparkle, twinkle, glimmer, shimmer.

glitter v sparkle, spangle, scintillate, twinkle, shimmer, glimmer, glisten, glint, gleam, flash, shine.
n sparkle, coruscation, scintillation, twinkle, shimmer, glimmer, glint, gleam, flash, shine, lustre, sheen, brightness, radiance, brilliance, splendour, showiness, glamour, tinsel.

gloat v triumph, glory, exult, rejoice, revel in, relish, crow, boast, vaunt, rub it in (infml).

global adj universal, worldwide, international, general, all-encompassing, total, thorough, exhaustive, comprehensive, all-inclusive, encyclopedic, wide-ranging.
F3 parochial, limited.

globe n world, earth, planet, sphere, ball, orb, round.

gloom n 1 DEPRESSION, low spirits, despondency, dejection, sadness, unhappiness, glumness, melancholy, misery, desolation, despair. 2 DARK,

darkness, shade, shadow, dusk, twilight, dimness, obscurity, cloud, cloudiness, dullness.
F3 1 cheerfulness, happiness.
2 brightness.

gloomy adj 1 DEPRESSED, down, low, despondent, dejected, downcast, dispirited, down-hearted, sad, miserable, glum, morose, pessimistic, cheerless, dismal, depressing. 2 DARK, sombre, shadowy, dim, obscure, overcast, dull, dreary.
F3 1 cheerful. 2 bright.

glorious adj 1 ILLUSTRIOUS, eminent, distinguished, famous, renowned, noted, great, noble, splendid, magnificent, grand, majestic, triumphant. 2 FINE, bright, radiant, shining, brilliant, dazzling, beautiful, gorgeous, superb, excellent, wonderful, marvellous, delightful, heavenly.
F3 1 unknown.

glory n 1 FAME, renown, celebrity, illustriousness, greatness, eminence, distinction, honour, prestige, kudos, triumph. 2 PRAISE, homage, tribute, worship, veneration, adoration, exaltation, blessing, thanksgiving, gratitude. 3 BRIGHTNESS, radiance, brilliance, beauty, splendour, resplendence, magnificence, grandeur, majesty, dignity.

gloss[1] n 1 POLISH, varnish, lustre, sheen, shine, brightness, brilliance.
2 SHOW, appearance, semblance, surface, front, façade, veneer, window-dressing.

gloss over conceal, hide, veil, mask, disguise, camouflage, cover up, whitewash, explain away.

gloss[2] n annotation, note, footnote, explanation, elucidation, interpretation, translation, definition, comment, commentary.

v annotate, define, explain, elucidate, interpret, construe, translate, comment.

glossy *adj* shiny, sheeny, lustrous, sleek, silky, smooth, glassy, polished, burnished, glazed, enamelled, bright, shining, brilliant.

F3 matt.

glow *n* **1** LIGHT, gleam, glimmer, radiance, luminosity, brightness, vividness, brilliance, splendour. **2** ARDOUR, fervour, intensity, warmth, passion, enthusiasm, excitement. **3** FLUSH, blush, rosiness, redness, burning.

v **1** SHINE, radiate, gleam, glimmer, burn, smoulder. **2** *their faces glowed*: flush, blush, colour, redden.

glower *v* glare, look daggers, frown, scowl.

n glare, black look, dirty look (*infml*), frown, scowl, stare, look.

glowing *adj* **1** BRIGHT, luminous, vivid, vibrant, rich, warm, flushed, red, flaming. **2** *a glowing review*: complimentary, enthusiastic, ecstatic, rhapsodic, rave (*infml*).

F3 1 dull, colourless. **2** restrained.

glue *n* adhesive, gum, paste, size, cement.

v stick, affix, gum, paste, seal, bond, cement, fix.

glut *n* surplus, excess, superfluity, surfeit, overabundance, superabundance, saturation, overflow.

F3 scarcity, lack.

glutton *n* gourmand, gormandizer, guzzler, gorger, gobbler, pig.

F3 ascetic.

gluttony *n* gourmandise, gormandism, greed, greediness,

voracity, insatiability, piggishness.

F3 abstinence, asceticism.

gnarled *adj* gnarly, knotted, knotty, twisted, contorted, distorted, rough, rugged, weather-beaten.

gnaw *v* **1** BITE, nibble, munch, chew, eat, devour, consume, erode, wear, haunt. **2** WORRY, niggle, fret, trouble, plague, nag, prey.

go *v* **1** MOVE, pass, advance, progress, proceed, make for, travel, journey, start, begin, depart, leave, take one's leave, retreat, withdraw, disappear, vanish. **2** OPERATE, function, work, run, act, perform. **3** EXTEND, spread, stretch, reach, span, continue, unfold. **4** *time goes quickly*: pass, elapse, lapse, roll on.

F3 break down, fail.

n (*infml*) **1** *have a go*: attempt, try, shot (*infml*), bash (*infml*), stab (*infml*), turn. **2** ENERGY, get-up-and-go (*infml*), vitality, life, spirit, dynamism, effort.

go about approach, begin, set about, address, tackle, attend to, undertake, engage in, perform.

go ahead begin, proceed, carry on, continue, advance, progress, move.

go away depart, leave, clear off (*infml*), withdraw, retreat, disappear, vanish.

go back return, revert, backslide, retreat.

go by 1 PASS, elapse, flow. **2** *go by the rules*: observe, follow, comply with, heed.

go down descend, sink, set, fall, drop, decrease, decline, deteriorate, degenerate, fail, founder, go under, collapse, fold (*infml*).

go for 1 (*infml*) CHOOSE, prefer, favour, like, admire, enjoy. **2** ATTACK, assail, set about, lunge at.

go in for enter, take part in, participate in, engage in, take up, embrace, adopt, undertake, practise, pursue, follow.

go into discuss, consider, review, examine, study, scrutinize, investigate, inquire into, check out, probe, delve into, analyse, dissect.

go off 1 DEPART, leave, quit, abscond, vanish, disappear. **2** EXPLODE, blow up, detonate. **3** *the milk has gone off*: deteriorate, turn, sour, go bad, rot.

go on 1 CONTINUE, carry on, proceed, persist, stay, endure, last. **2** CHATTER, rabbit (*infml*), witter (*infml*), ramble on. **3** HAPPEN, take place.

go out exit, depart, leave.

go over examine, peruse, study, revise, scan, read, inspect, check, review, repeat, rehearse, list.

go through 1 SUFFER, undergo, experience, bear, tolerate, endure, withstand. **2** INVESTIGATE, check, examine, look, search, hunt, explore. **3** USE, consume, exhaust, spend, squander.

go together match, harmonize, accord, fit.

go with 1 MATCH, harmonize, co-ordinate, blend, complement, suit, fit, correspond. **2** ACCOMPANY, escort, take, usher.
F3 1 clash.

go without abstain, forgo, do without, manage without, lack, want.

goad *v* prod, prick, spur, impel, push, drive, provoke, incite, instigate, arouse, stimulate, prompt, urge, nag, hound, harass, annoy, irritate, vex.

go-ahead *n* permission, authorization, clearance, green light (*infml*), sanction, assent, consent, OK (*infml*), agreement.
F3 ban, veto, embargo.

adj enterprising, pioneering, progressive, ambitious, up-and-coming, dynamic, energetic.
F3 unenterprising, sluggish.

goal *n* target, mark, objective, aim, intention, object, purpose, end, ambition, aspiration.

gobble *v* bolt, guzzle, gorge, cram, stuff, devour, consume, put away (*infml*), swallow, gulp.

go-between *n* intermediary, mediator, liaison, contact, middleman, broker, dealer, agent, messenger, medium.

God *n* Supreme Being, Creator, Providence, Lord, Almighty, Holy One, Jehovah, Yahweh, Allah, Brahma, Zeus.

god, goddess *n* deity, divinity, idol, spirit, power.

god-forsaken *adj* remote, isolated, lonely, bleak, desolate, abandoned, deserted, forlorn, dismal, dreary, gloomy, miserable, wretched, depressing.

godless *adj* ungodly, atheistic, heathen, pagan, irreligious, unholy, impious, sacrilegious, profane, irreverent, bad, evil, wicked.
F3 godly, pious.

godly *adj* religious, holy, pious, devout, God-fearing, righteous, good, virtuous, pure, innocent.
F3 godless, impious.

godsend *n* blessing, boon, stroke of luck, windfall, miracle.
F3 blow, setback.

golden *adj* **1** GOLD, gilded, gilt, yellow, blond(e), fair, bright, shining, lustrous, resplendent. **2** PROSPEROUS, successful, glorious, excellent, happy, joyful, favourable, auspicious, promising, rosy.

good adj **1** ACCEPTABLE, satisfactory, pleasant, agreeable, nice, enjoyable, pleasing, commendable, excellent, great (infml), super (infml), first-class, first-rate, superior, advantageous, beneficial, favourable, auspicious, helpful, useful, worthwhile, profitable, appropriate, suitable, fitting. **2** good at her job: competent, proficient, skilled, expert, accomplished, professional, skilful, clever, talented, gifted, fit, able, capable, dependable, reliable. **3** KIND, considerate, gracious, benevolent, charitable, philanthropic. **4** VIRTUOUS, exemplary, moral, upright, honest, trustworthy, worthy, righteous. **5** WELL-BEHAVED, obedient, well-mannered. **6** THOROUGH, complete, whole, substantial, considerable. **Fa** **1** bad, poor. **2** incompetent. **3** unkind, inconsiderate. **4** wicked, immoral. **5** naughty, disobedient. n **1** VIRTUE, morality, goodness, righteousness, right. **2** USE, purpose, avail, advantage, profit, gain, worth, merit, usefulness, service. **3** for your own good: welfare, wellbeing, interest, sake, behalf, benefit, convenience.

good-bye n farewell, adieu, au revoir, valediction, leave-taking, parting.

good-humoured adj cheerful, happy, jovial, genial, affable, amiable, friendly, congenial, pleasant, good-tempered, approachable. **Fa** ill-humoured.

good-looking adj attractive, handsome, beautiful, fair, pretty, personable, presentable. **Fa** ugly, plain.

good-natured adj kind, kindly, kind-hearted, sympathetic, benevolent, helpful, neighbourly, gentle, good-tempered, approachable, friendly, tolerant, patient. **Fa** ill-natured.

goodness n virtue, uprightness, rectitude, honesty, probity, kindness, compassion, graciousness, goodwill, benevolence, unselfishness, generosity, friendliness, helpfulness. **Fa** badness, wickedness.

goods n **1** PROPERTY, chattels, effects, possessions, belongings, paraphernalia, stuff, things, gear (infml). **2** MERCHANDISE, wares, commodities, stock, freight.

goodwill n benevolence, kindness, generosity, favour, friendliness, friendship, zeal. **Fa** ill-will.

gore v pierce, penetrate, stab, spear, stick, impale, wound.

gorge n canyon, ravine, gully, defile, chasm, abyss, cleft, fissure, gap, pass. v feed, guzzle, gobble, devour, bolt, wolf, gulp, swallow, cram, stuff, fill, sate, surfeit, glut, overeat. **Fa** fast.

gorgeous adj magnificent, splendid, grand, glorious, superb, fine, rich, sumptuous, luxurious, brilliant, dazzling, showy, glamorous, attractive, beautiful, handsome, good-looking, delightful, pleasing, lovely, enjoyable, good. **Fa** dull, plain.

gory adj bloody, sanguinary, bloodstained, blood-soaked, grisly, brutal, savage, murderous.

gossip n **1** IDLE TALK, prattle, chitchat, tittle-tattle, rumour, hearsay, report, scandal. **2** GOSSIP-MONGER, scandalmonger, whisperer, prattler,

babbler, chatterbox, nosey parker (*infml*), busybody, talebearer, tell-tale, tattler.

v talk, chat, natter, chatter, gabble, prattle, tattle, tell tales, whisper, rumour.

gouge *v* chisel, cut, hack, incise, score, groove, scratch, claw, gash, slash, dig, scoop, hollow, extract.

gourmet *n* gastronome, epicure, epicurean, connoisseur, bon vivant.

govern *v* **1** RULE, reign, direct, manage, superintend, supervise, oversee, preside, lead, head, command, influence, guide, conduct, steer, pilot. **2** *govern one's temper*: dominate, master, control, regulate, curb, check, restrain, contain, quell, subdue, tame, discipline.

government *n* **1** *blame the government*: administration, executive, ministry, Establishment, authorities, powers that be, state, regime. **2** RULE, sovereignty, sway, direction, management, superintendence, supervision, surveillance, command, charge, authority, guidance, conduct, domination, dominion, control, regulation, restraint.

Government systems include: absolutism, autocracy, commonwealth, communism, democracy, despotism, dictatorship, empire, federation, hierocracy, junta, kingdom, monarchy, plutocracy, republic, theocracy, triumvirate. see also **parliament**.

governor *n* ruler, commissioner, administrator, executive, director, manager, leader, head, chief, commander, superintendent, supervisor, overseer, controller, boss.

gown *n* robe, dress, frock, dressing-gown, habit, costume.

grab *v* seize, snatch, take, nab (*infml*), pluck, snap up, catch hold of, grasp, clutch, grip, catch, bag, capture, collar (*infml*), commandeer, appropriate, usurp, annex.

grace *n* **1** GRACEFULNESS, poise, beauty, attractiveness, loveliness, shapeliness, elegance, tastefulness, refinement, polish, breeding, manners, etiquette, decorum, decency, courtesy, charm. **2** KINDNESS, kindliness, compassion, consideration, goodness, virtue, generosity, charity, benevolence, goodwill, favour, forgiveness, indulgence, mercy, leniency, pardon, reprieve. **3** *say grace*: blessing, benediction, thanksgiving, prayer.

F3 2 cruelty, harshness.

v favour, honour, dignify, distinguish, embellish, enhance, set off, trim, garnish, decorate, ornament, adorn.

F3 spoil, detract from.

graceful *adj* easy, flowing, smooth, supple, agile, deft, natural, slender, fine, tasteful, elegant, beautiful, charming, suave.

F3 graceless, awkward, clumsy, ungainly.

gracious *adj* elegant, refined, polite, courteous, well-mannered, considerate, sweet, obliging, accommodating, kind, compassionate, kindly, benevolent, generous, magnanimous, charitable, hospitable, forgiving, indulgent, lenient, mild, clement, merciful.

F3 ungracious.

grade *n* rank, status, standing, station, place, position, level, stage, degree, step, rung, notch, mark,

brand, quality, standard, condition, size, order, group, class, category.
v sort, arrange, categorize, order, group, class, rate, size, rank, range, classify, evaluate, assess, value, mark, brand, label, pigeonhole, type.

gradient *n* slope, incline, hill, bank, rise, declivity.

gradual *adj* slow, leisurely, unhurried, easy, gentle, moderate, regular, even, measured, steady, continuous, progressive, step-by-step.
≠ sudden, precipitate.

gradually *adv* little by little, bit by bit, imperceptibly, inch by inch, step by step, progressively, by degrees, piecemeal, slowly, gently, cautiously, gingerly, moderately, evenly, steadily.

graduate *v* 1 *graduate from medical school:* pass, qualify. **2** CALIBRATE, mark off, measure out, proportion, grade, arrange, range, order, rank, sort, group, classify.

graft *n* implant, implantation, transplant, splice, bud, sprout, shoot, scion.
v engraft, implant, insert, transplant, join, splice.

grain *n* **1** BIT, piece, fragment, scrap, morsel, crumb, granule, particle, molecule, atom, jot, iota, mite, speck, modicum, trace. **2** SEED, kernel, corn, cereals. **3** TEXTURE, fibre, weave, pattern, marking, surface.

grand *adj* **1** MAJESTIC, regal, stately, splendid, magnificent, glorious, superb, sublime, fine, excellent, outstanding, striking, impressive, imposing, monumental, large, noble, lordly, lofty, pompous, pretentious, grandiose, ambitious. **2** SUPREME, pre-eminent, leading, head, chief, arch, highest, senior,

great, illustrious.
≠ **1** humble, common, poor.

grandeur *n* majesty, stateliness, pomp, state, dignity, splendour, magnificence, nobility, greatness, illustriousness, importance.
≠ humbleness, lowliness, simplicity.

grandiose *adj* pompous, pretentious, high-flown, lofty, ambitious, extravagant, ostentatious, showy, flamboyant, grand, majestic, stately, magnificent, impressive, imposing, monumental.
≠ unpretentious.

grant *v* **1** GIVE, donate, present, award, confer, bestow, impart, transmit, dispense, apportion, assign, allot, allocate, provide, supply. **2** ADMIT, acknowledge, concede, allow, permit, consent to, agree to, accede to.
≠ **1** withhold. **2** deny.
n allowance, subsidy, concession, award, bursary, scholarship, gift, donation, endowment, bequest, annuity, pension, honorarium.

granular *adj* grainy, granulated, gritty, sandy, lumpy, rough, crumbly, friable.

graph *n* diagram, chart, table, grid.

graphic *adj* vivid, descriptive, expressive, striking, telling, lively, realistic, explicit, clear, lucid, specific, detailed, blow-by-blow, visual, pictorial, diagrammatic, illustrative.
≠ vague, impressionistic.

grapple *v* seize, grasp, snatch, grab, grip, clutch, clasp, hold, wrestle, tussle, struggle, contend, fight, combat, clash, engage, encounter, face, confront, tackle, deal with, cope with.
≠ release, avoid, evade.

grasp *v* **1** HOLD, clasp, clutch, grip, grapple, seize, snatch, grab, catch. **2** *grasp a concept*: understand, comprehend, get (*infml*), follow, see, realize.
n **1** GRIP, clasp, hold, embrace, clutches, possession, control, power. **2** UNDERSTANDING, comprehension, apprehension, mastery, familiarity, knowledge.

grasping *adj* avaricious, greedy, rapacious, acquisitive, mercenary, mean, selfish, miserly, close-fisted, tight-fisted, parsimonious.
F3 generous.

grass *n* turf, lawn, green, grassland, field, meadow, pasture, prairie, pampas, savanna, steppe.

Types of grass include:
bamboo, barley, beard-grass, bent, bluegrass, cane, cocksfoot, corn, couch grass, esparto, fescue, kangaroo-grass, knotgrass, maize, marram, meadow foxtail, meadow-grass, millet, oats, paddy, pampas grass, papyrus, rattan, reed, rice, rye, rye grass, sorghum, squirrel-tail grass, sugar cane, twitch grass, wheat, wild oat.

grate *v* **1** GRIND, shred, mince, pulverize, rub, rasp, scrape. **2** JAR, set one's teeth on edge, annoy, irritate, aggravate (*infml*), get on one's nerves, vex, irk, exasperate.

grateful *adj* thankful, appreciative, indebted, obliged, obligated, beholden.
F3 ungrateful.

gratify *v* satisfy, fulfil, indulge, pander to, humour, favour, please, gladden, delight, thrill.
F3 frustrate, thwart.

grating [1] *adj* harsh, rasping, scraping, squeaky, strident, discordant, jarring, annoying, irritating, unpleasant, disagreeable.
F3 harmonious, pleasing.

grating [2] *n* grate, grill, grid, lattice, trellis.

gratitude *n* gratefulness, thankfulness, thanks, appreciation, acknowledgement, recognition, indebtedness, obligation.
F3 ingratitude, ungratefulness.

gratuitous *adj* wanton, unnecessary, needless, superfluous, unwarranted, unjustified, groundless, undeserved, unprovoked, uncalled-for, unasked-for, unsolicited, voluntary, free, gratis, complimentary.
F3 justified, provoked.

gratuity *n* tip, bonus, perk (*infml*), gift, present, donation, reward, recompense.

grave [1] *n* burial-place, tomb, vault, crypt, sepulchre, mausoleum, pit, barrow, tumulus, cairn.

grave [2] *adj* **1** *a grave mistake*: important, significant, weighty, momentous, serious, critical, vital, crucial, urgent, acute, severe, dangerous, hazardous. **2** SOLEMN, dignified, sober, sedate, serious, thoughtful, pensive, grim, long-faced, quiet, reserved, subdued, restrained.
F3 1 trivial, light, slight. **2** cheerful.

graveyard *n* cemetery, burial-ground, churchyard.

gravity *n* **1** IMPORTANCE, significance, seriousness, urgency, acuteness, severity, danger. **2** SOLEMNITY, dignity, sobriety, seriousness, thoughtfulness, sombreness, reserve, restraint. **3** GRAVITATION, attraction, pull, weight, heaviness.
F3 1 triviality. **2** levity.

graze v scratch, scrape, skin, abrade, rub, chafe, shave, brush, skim, touch. n scratch, scrape, abrasion.

grease n oil, lubrication, fat, lard, dripping, tallow.

greasy adj oily, fatty, lardy, buttery, smeary, slimy, slippery, smooth, waxy.

great adj **1** LARGE, big, huge, enormous, massive, colossal, gigantic, mammoth, immense, vast, impressive. **2** with great care: considerable, pronounced, extreme, excessive, inordinate. **3** FAMOUS, renowned, celebrated, illustrious, eminent, distinguished, prominent, noteworthy, notable, remarkable, outstanding, grand, glorious, fine. **4** IMPORTANT, significant, serious, major, principal, primary, main, chief, leading. **5** (infml) EXCELLENT, first-rate, superb, wonderful, marvellous, tremendous, terrific, fantastic, fabulous.
F3 1 small. **2** slight. **3** unknown. **4** unimportant, insignificant.

greed n **1** HUNGER, ravenousness, gluttony, gourmandism, voracity, insatiability. **2** ACQUISITIVENESS, covetousness, desire, craving, longing, eagerness, avarice, selfishness.
F3 1 abstemiousness, self-restraint.

greedy adj **1** HUNGRY, starving, ravenous, gluttonous, gormandizing, voracious, insatiable. **2** ACQUISITIVE, covetous, desirous, craving, eager, impatient, avaricious, grasping, selfish.
F3 1 abstemious.

green adj **1** GRASSY, leafy, verdant, unripe, unseasoned, tender, fresh, budding, blooming, flourishing. **2** green with envy: envious, covetous, jealous, resentful. **3** IMMATURE, naive,

unsophisticated, ignorant, inexperienced, untrained, raw, new, recent, young. **4** ECOLOGICAL, environmental, eco-friendly, environmentally aware.
n common, lawn, grass, turf.

greenhouse n glasshouse, hothouse, conservatory, pavilion, vinery, orangery.

greet v hail, salute, acknowledge, address, accost, meet, receive, welcome.
F3 ignore.

greeting n salutation, acknowledgement, wave, hallo, the time of day, address, reception, welcome.

greetings n regards, respects, compliments, salutations, best wishes, good wishes, love.

gregarious adj sociable, outgoing, extrovert, friendly, affable, social, convivial, cordial, warm.
F3 unsociable.

grey adj **1** NEUTRAL, colourless, pale, ashen, leaden, dull, cloudy, overcast, dim, dark, murky. **2** GLOOMY, dismal, cheerless, depressing, dreary, bleak.

grief n sorrow, sadness, unhappiness, depression, dejection, desolation, distress, misery, woe, heartbreak, mourning, bereavement, heartache, anguish, agony, pain, suffering, affliction, trouble, regret, remorse.
F3 happiness, delight.

grievance n complaint, moan (infml), grumble (infml), resentment, objection, protest, charge, wrong, injustice, injury, damage, trouble, affliction, hardship, trial, tribulation.

grieve v **1** SORROW, mope, lament, mourn, wail, cry, weep. **2** SADDEN, upset, dismay, distress, afflict, pain, hurt, wound.

F3 1 rejoice. 2 please, gladden.

grim adj 1 UNPLEASANT, horrible, horrid, ghastly, gruesome, grisly, sinister, frightening, fearsome, terrible, shocking. 2 STERN, severe, harsh, dour, forbidding, surly, sullen, morose, gloomy, depressing, unattractive.

F3 1 pleasant. 2 attractive.

grimace n frown, scowl, pout, smirk, sneer, face.

v make a face, pull a face, frown, scowl, pout, smirk, sneer.

grime n dirt, muck, filth, soot, dust.

grimy adj dirty, mucky, grubby, soiled, filthy, sooty, smutty, dusty, smudgy.

F3 clean.

grind v crush, pound, pulverize, powder, mill, grate, scrape, gnash, rut, abrade, sand, file, smooth, polish, sharpen, whet.

grip n hold, grasp, clasp, embrace, clutches, control, power.

v 1 HOLD, grasp, clasp, clutch, seize, grab, catch. 2 FASCINATE, thrill, enthral, spellbind, mesmerize, hypnotize, rivet, engross, absorb, involve, engage, compel.

grisly adj gruesome, gory, grim, macabre, horrid, horrible, ghastly, awful, frightful, terrible, dreadful, abominable, appalling, shocking.

F3 delightful.

grit n gravel, pebbles, shingle, sand, dust.

v clench, gnash, grate, grind.

groan n moan, sigh, cry, whine, wail, lament, complaint, objection, protest, outcry.

F3 cheer.

v moan, sigh, cry, whine, wail, lament, complain, object, protest.

F3 cheer.

groom v 1 SMARTEN, neaten, tidy, spruce up, clean, brush, curry, preen, dress. 2 groomed for her new post: prepare, train, school, educate, drill.

groove n furrow, rut, track, slot, channel, gutter, trench, hollow, indentation, score.

F3 ridge.

grope v feel, fumble, scrabble, flounder, cast about, fish, search, probe.

gross adj 1 gross misconduct: serious, grievous, blatant, flagrant, glaring, obvious, plain, sheer, utter, outright, shameful, shocking. 2 OBSCENE, lewd, improper, indecent, offensive, rude, coarse, crude, vulgar, tasteless. 3 FAT, obese, overweight, big, large, huge, colossal, hulking, bulky, heavy. 4 gross earnings: inclusive, all-inclusive, total, aggregate, entire, complete, whole.

F3 3 slight. 4 net.

grotesque adj bizarre, odd, weird, unnatural, freakish, monstrous, hideous, ugly, unsightly, misshapen, deformed, distorted, twisted, fantastic, fanciful, extravagant, absurd, surreal, macabre.

F3 normal, graceful.

ground n 1 BOTTOM, foundation, surface, land, terrain, dry land, terra firma, earth, soil, clay, loam, dirt, dust. 2 football ground: field, pitch, stadium, arena, park.

v 1 BASE, found, establish, set, fix, settle. 2 PREPARE, introduce, initiate, familiarize with, acquaint with, inform, instruct, teach, train, drill, coach, tutor.

groundless *adj* baseless, unfounded, unsubstantiated, unsupported, empty, imaginary, false, unjustified, unwarranted, unprovoked, uncalled-for.
E₃ well-founded, reasonable, justified.

grounds¹ *n* land, terrain, holding, estate, property, territory, domain, gardens, park, campus, surroundings, fields, acres.

grounds² *n* base, foundation, justification, excuse, vindication, reason, motive, inducement, cause, occasion, call, score, account, argument, principle, basis.

group *n* band, gang, pack, team, crew, troop, squad, detachment, party, faction, set, circle, clique, club, society, association, organization, company, gathering, congregation, crowd, collection, bunch, clump, cluster, conglomeration, constellation, batch, lot, combination, formation, grouping, class, classification, category, genus, species.
v **1** GATHER, collect, assemble, congregate, mass, cluster, clump, bunch. **2** *group them according to size*: sort, range, arrange, marshal, organize, order, class, classify, categorize, band, link, associate.

grovel *v* crawl, creep, ingratiate oneself, toady, suck up (*sl*), flatter, fawn, cringe, cower, kowtow, defer, demean oneself.

grow *v* **1** INCREASE, rise, expand, enlarge, swell, spread, extend, stretch, develop, proliferate, mushroom. **2** ORIGINATE, arise, issue, spring, germinate, shoot, sprout, bud, flower, mature, develop, progress, thrive, flourish, prosper. **3** CULTIVATE, farm,

produce, propagate, breed, raise.
4 *grow cold*: become, get, go, turn.
E₃ 1 decrease, shrink.

growl *v* snarl, snap, yap, rumble, roar.

grown-up *adj* adult, mature, of age, full-grown, fully-fledged.
E₃ young, immature.
n adult, man, woman.
E₃ child.

growth *n* **1** INCREASE, rise, extension, enlargement, expansion, spread, proliferation, development, evolution, progress, advance, improvement, success, prosperity.
2 TUMOUR, lump, swelling, protuberance, outgrowth.
E₃ 1 decrease, decline, failure.

grub *v* dig, burrow, delve, probe, root, rummage, forage, ferret, hunt, search, scour, explore.
n maggot, worm, larva, pupa, caterpillar, chrysalis.

grubby *adj* dirty, soiled, unwashed, mucky, grimy, filthy, squalid, seedy, scruffy.
E₃ clean.

grudge *n* resentment, bitterness, envy, jealousy, spite, malice, enmity, antagonism, hate, dislike, animosity, ill-will, hard feelings, grievance.
E₃ favour.
v begrudge, resent, envy, covet, dislike, take exception to, object to, mind.

grudging *adj* reluctant, unwilling, hesitant, half-hearted, unenthusiastic, resentful, envious, jealous.

gruelling *adj* hard, difficult, taxing, demanding, tiring, exhausting, laborious, arduous, strenuous, backbreaking, harsh, severe, tough, punishing.
E₃ easy.

gruesome adj horrible, disgusting, repellent, repugnant, repulsive, hideous, grisly, macabre, grim, ghastly, awful, terrible, horrific, shocking, monstrous, abominable.
F3 pleasant.

gruff adj **1** CURT, brusque, abrupt, blunt, rude, surly, sullen, grumpy, bad-tempered. **2** a gruff voice: rough, harsh, rasping, guttural, throaty, husky, hoarse.
F3 1 friendly, courteous.

grumble v complain, moan, whine, bleat, grouch, gripe, mutter, murmur, carp, find fault.

grumpy adj bad-tempered, ill-tempered, churlish, crotchety, crabbed, cantankerous, cross, irritable, surly, sullen, sulky, grouchy, discontented.
F3 contented.

guarantee n warranty, insurance, assurance, promise, word of honour, pledge, oath, bond, security, collateral, surety, endorsement, testimonial.
v assure, promise, pledge, swear, vouch for, answer for, warrant, certify, underwrite, endorse, secure, protect, insure, ensure, make sure, make certain.

guard v protect, safeguard, save, preserve, shield, screen, shelter, cover, defend, patrol, police, escort, supervise, oversee, watch, look out, mind, beware.
n **1** PROTECTOR, defender, custodian, warder, escort, bodyguard, minder (sl), watchman, lookout, sentry, picket, patrol, security.
2 PROTECTION, safeguard, defence, wall, barrier, screen, shield, bumper, buffer, pad.

guarded adj cautious, wary, careful, watchful, discreet, non-committal, reticent, reserved, secretive, cagey (infml).
F3 communicative, frank.

guardian n trustee, curator, custodian, keeper, warden, protector, preserver, defender, champion, guard, warder, escort, attendant.

guess v speculate, conjecture, predict, estimate, judge, reckon, work out, suppose, assume, surmise, think, believe, imagine, fancy, feel, suspect.
n prediction, estimate, speculation, conjecture, supposition, assumption, belief, fancy, idea, notion, theory, hypothesis, opinion, feeling, suspicion, intuition.

guesswork n speculation, conjecture, estimation, reckoning, supposition, assumption, surmise, intuition.

guest n visitor, caller, boarder, lodger, resident, patron, regular.

guidance n leadership, direction, management, control, teaching, instruction, advice, counsel, counselling, help, instructions, directions, guidelines, indications, pointers, recommendations.

guide v lead, conduct, direct, navigate, point, steer, pilot, manoeuvre, usher, escort, accompany, attend, control, govern, manage, oversee, supervise, superintend, advise, counsel, influence, educate, teach, instruct, train.
n **1** LEADER, courier, navigator, pilot, helmsman, steersman, usher, escort, chaperone, attendant, companion, adviser, counsellor, mentor, guru, teacher, instructor. **2** MANUAL,

handbook, guidebook, user guide, catalogue, directory. **3** GUIDELINE, example, model, standard, criterion, indication, pointer, signpost, sign, marker.

guilt n **1** *he confessed his guilt*: culpability, responsibility, blame, disgrace, dishonour. **2** *a feeling of guilt*: guilty conscience, conscience, shame, self-condemnation, self-reproach, regret, remorse, contrition.
F3 1 innocence, righteousness.
2 shamelessness.

guilty adj **1** CULPABLE, responsible, blamable, blameworthy, offending, wrong, sinful, wicked, criminal, convicted. **2** CONSCIENCE-STRICKEN, ashamed, shamefaced, sheepish, sorry, regretful, remorseful, contrite, penitent, repentant.
F3 1 innocent, guiltless, blameless.
2 shameless.

gulf n bay, basin, gap, opening, separation, rift, split, breach, cleft, chasm, gorge, abyss, void.

gullible adj credulous, suggestible, impressionable, trusting, unsuspecting, foolish, naive, green, unsophisticated, innocent.
F3 astute.

gully n channel, watercourse, gutter, ditch, ravine.

gulp v swallow, swig, swill, knock back (infml), bolt, wolf (infml), gobble, guzzle, devour, stuff.
F3 sip, nibble.
n swallow, swig, draught, mouthful.

gum n adhesive, glue, paste, cement.
v stick, glue, paste, fix, cement, seal, clog.

gun n firearm, handgun, pistol, revolver, shooter (sl), shooting iron (sl), rifle, shotgun, machine gun, sub-machine gun, Uzi, bazooka, howitzer, cannon.

gurgle v bubble, babble, burble, murmur, ripple, lap, splash, crow.
n babble, murmur, ripple.

gush v **1** FLOW, run, pour, stream, cascade, flood, rush, burst, spurt, spout, jet. **2** ENTHUSE, chatter, babble, jabber, go on (infml), drivel.
n flow, outflow, stream, torrent, cascade, flood, tide, rush, burst, outburst, spurt, spout, jet.

gust n blast, burst, rush, flurry, blow, puff, breeze, wind, gale, squall.

gusto n zest, relish, appreciation, enjoyment, pleasure, delight, enthusiasm, exuberance, élan, verve, zeal.
F3 distaste, apathy.

gut v **1** *gut fish*: disembowel, draw, clean (out). **2** STRIP, clear, empty, rifle, ransack, plunder, loot, sack, ravage.

guts n **1** INTESTINES, bowels, viscera, entrails, insides, innards (infml), belly, stomach. **2** (infml) COURAGE, bravery, pluck, grit, nerve, mettle.

gutter n drain, sluice, ditch, trench, trough, channel, duct, conduit, passage, pipe, tube.

guy n fellow, bloke (infml), chap (infml), man, boy, youth, person, individual.

Gypsy n Roma, Romany, Traveller.

gypsy, gipsy n traveller, wanderer, nomad, tinker.

gyrate v turn, revolve, rotate, twirl, pirouette, spin, whirl, wheel, circle, spiral.

H

habit *n* custom, usage, practice, routine, rule, second nature, way, manner, mode, wont, inclination, tendency, bent, mannerism, quirk, addiction, dependence, fixation, obsession, weakness.

habitat *n* home, abode, domain, element, environment, surroundings, locality, territory, terrain.

habitual *adj* **1** CUSTOMARY, traditional, wonted, routine, usual, ordinary, common, natural, normal, standard, regular, recurrent, fixed, established, familiar. **2** *habitual drinker*: confirmed, inveterate, hardened, addicted, dependent, persistent.

E3 1 occasional, infrequent.

hack ¹ *v* cut, chop, hew, notch, gash, slash, lacerate, mutilate, mangle.

hack ² *n* scribbler, journalist, drudge, slave.

hackneyed *adj* stale, overworked, tired, worn-out, time-worn, threadbare, unoriginal, corny (*infml*), clichéd, stereotyped, stock, banal, trite, commonplace, common, pedestrian, uninspired.

E3 original, new, fresh.

hag *n* crone, witch, battle-axe (*infml*), shrew, termagant, vixen.

haggard *adj* drawn, gaunt, careworn, thin, wasted, shrunken,

pinched, pale, wan, ghastly.

E3 hale.

haggle *v* bargain, negotiate, barter, wrangle, squabble, bicker, quarrel, dispute.

hail ¹ *n* barrage, bombardment, volley, torrent, shower, rain, storm. *v* pelt, bombard, shower, rain, batter, attack, assail.

hail ² *v* greet, address, acknowledge, salute, wave, signal to, flag down, shout, call, acclaim, cheer, applaud, honour, welcome.

hair *n* locks, tresses, shock, mop, mane, barnet (*infml*).

hairdresser *n* hairstylist, stylist, barber, coiffeur, coiffeuse.

hairless *adj* bald, bald-headed, shorn, tonsured, shaven, clean-shaven, beardless.

E3 hairy, hirsute.

hair-raising *adj* frightening, scary, terrifying, horrifying, shocking, bloodcurdling, spine-chilling, white-knuckle (*infml*), eerie, alarming, startling, thrilling.

hairstyle *n* style, coiffure, hairdo (*infml*), cut, haircut, set, perm (*infml*).

Hairstyles include:
Afro, bangs, beehive, bob, bouffant, braid, bun, bunches, buzzcut, chignon, combover, cornrows, crew cut, dreadlocks, Eton crop, French

pleat, fringe, Marcel wave, mohican, mullet, page-boy, perm, pigtail, plait, pompadour, ponytail, pouffe, quiff, ringlets, shingle, short back and sides, skinhead, tonsure, topknot.

hairy *adj* hirsute, bearded, shaggy, bushy, fuzzy, furry, woolly.
F3 bald, clean-shaven.

half *n* fifty per cent, bisection, hemisphere, semicircle, section, segment, portion, share, fraction.
adj semi-, halved, divided, fractional, part, partial, incomplete, moderate, limited.
F3 whole.
adv partly, partially, incompletely, moderately, slightly.
F3 completely.

half-hearted *adj* lukewarm, cool, weak, feeble, passive, apathetic, uninterested, indifferent, neutral.
F3 whole-hearted, enthusiastic.

halfway *adv* midway, in the middle, centrally.
adj middle, central, equidistant, mid, midway, intermediate.

hall *n* hallway, corridor, passage, passageway, entrance-hall, foyer, vestibule, lobby, concert-hall, auditorium, chamber, assembly room.

hallmark *n* stamp, mark, trademark, brand-name, sign, indication, symbol, emblem, device, badge.

hallucinate *v* dream, imagine, see things, daydream, fantasize, freak out (*sl*), trip (*sl*).

hallucination *n* illusion, mirage, vision, apparition, dream, daydream, fantasy, figment, delusion, freak-out (*sl*), trip (*sl*).

halt *v* stop, draw up, pull up, pause, wait, rest, break off, discontinue,

cease, desist, quit, end, terminate, check, stem, curb, obstruct, impede.
F3 start, continue.
n stop, stoppage, arrest, interruption, break, pause, rest, standstill, end, close, termination.
F3 start, continuation.

halting *adj* hesitant, stuttering, stammering, faltering, stumbling, broken, imperfect, laboured, awkward.
F3 fluent.

halve *v* bisect, cut in half, split in two, divide, split, share, cut down, reduce, lessen.

hammer *v* hit, strike, beat, drum, bang, bash, pound, batter, knock, drive, shape, form, make.
n mallet, gavel.

hammer out settle, sort out, negotiate, thrash out, produce, bring about, accomplish, complete, finish.

hamper *v* hinder, impede, obstruct, slow down, hold up, frustrate, thwart, prevent, handicap, hamstring, shackle, cramp, restrict, curb, restrain.
F3 aid, facilitate.

hand *n* **1** FIST, palm, paw (*infml*), mitt (*sl*). **2** *give me a hand*: help, aid, assistance, support, participation, part, influence. **3** WORKER, employee, operative, workman, labourer, farm-hand, hireling.
v give, pass, offer, submit, present, yield, deliver, transmit, conduct, convey.

at hand near, close, to hand, handy, accessible, available, ready, imminent.

hand down bequeath, will, pass on, transfer, give, grant.

hand out distribute, deal out, give out, share out, dish out (*infml*), mete out, dispense.

hand over yield, relinquish, surrender, turn over, deliver, release, give, donate, present.
F3 keep, retain.

handbook n manual, instruction book, guide, guidebook, user guide, companion.

handful n few, sprinkling, scattering, smattering.
F3 a lot, many.

handicap n obstacle, block, barrier, impediment, stumbling-block, hindrance, drawback, disadvantage, restriction, limitation, penalty, disability, impairment, defect, shortcoming.
F3 assistance, advantage.
v impede, hinder, disadvantage, hold back, retard, hamper, burden, encumber, restrict, limit, disable.
F3 help, assist.

handicraft n craft, art, craftwork, handwork, handiwork.

handiwork n work, doing, responsibility, achievement, product, result, design, invention, creation, production, skill, workmanship, craftsmanship, artisanship.

handle n grip, handgrip, knob, stock, shaft, hilt.
v 1 TOUCH, finger, feel, fondle, pick up, hold, grasp. **2** handle a situation: tackle, treat, deal with, manage, cope with, control, supervise.

handout n 1 CHARITY, alms, dole, largess(e), share, issue, free sample, freebie (sl). **2** LEAFLET, flyer, circular, bulletin, statement, press release, literature.

hands n care, custody, possession, charge, authority, command, power, control, supervision.

handsome adj **1** GOOD-LOOKING, attractive, fair, personable, elegant. **2** GENEROUS, liberal, large, considerable, ample.
F3 1 ugly, unattractive. **2** mean.

handwriting n writing, script, hand, fist (infml), penmanship, calligraphy.

handy adj **1** AVAILABLE, to hand, ready, at hand, near, accessible, convenient, practical, useful, helpful. **2** SKILFUL, proficient, expert, skilled, clever, practical.
F3 1 inconvenient. **2** clumsy.

hang v **1** SUSPEND, dangle, swing, drape, drop, flop, droop, sag, trail. **2** FASTEN, attach, fix, stick. **3** hang in the air: float, drift, hover, linger, remain, cling.

hang about hang around, linger, loiter, dawdle, waste time, associate with, frequent, haunt.

hang back hold back, demur, hesitate, shy away, recoil.

hang on 1 WAIT, hold on, remain, hold out, endure, continue, carry on, persevere, persist. **2** GRIP, grasp, hold fast. **3** DEPEND ON, hinge on, turn on.
F3 1 give up.

hanger-on n follower, minion, lackey, toady, sycophant, parasite, sponger, dependant.

hang-up n inhibition, difficulty, problem, obsession, preoccupation, thing (infml), bother, mental block.

hanker for hanker after, crave, hunger for, thirst for, want, wish for, desire, covet, yearn for, long for, pine for, itch for.

hankering n craving, hunger, thirst, wish, desire, yearning, longing, itch, urge.

haphazard adj random, chance, casual, arbitrary, hit-or-miss, unsystematic, disorganized, disorderly, careless, slapdash, slipshod.

F3 methodical, orderly.

happen v occur, take place, arise, crop up, develop, materialize (*infml*), come about, result, ensue, follow, turn out, transpire.

happening n occurrence, phenomenon, event, incident, episode, occasion, adventure, experience, accident, chance, circumstance, case, affair.

happiness n joy, joyfulness, gladness, cheerfulness, contentment, pleasure, delight, glee, elation, bliss, ecstasy, euphoria.

F3 unhappiness, sadness.

happy adj 1 JOYFUL, jolly, merry, cheerful, glad, pleased, delighted, thrilled, elated, satisfied, content, contented. 2 *a happy coincidence*: lucky, fortunate, felicitous, favourable, appropriate, apt, fitting.

F3 1 unhappy, sad, discontented. 2 unfortunate, inappropriate.

harangue n diatribe, tirade, lecture, speech, address.

v lecture, preach, hold forth, spout, declaim, address.

harass v pester, badger, harry, plague, torment, persecute, exasperate, vex, annoy, irritate, bother, disturb, hassle (*infml*), trouble, worry, stress, tire, wear out, exhaust, fatigue.

harbour n port, dock, quay, wharf, marina, mooring, anchorage, haven, shelter.

v 1 HIDE, conceal, protect, shelter.

2 *harbour a feeling*: hold, retain, cling to, entertain, foster, nurse, nurture, cherish, believe, imagine.

hard adj 1 SOLID, firm, unyielding, tough, strong, dense, impenetrable, stiff, rigid, inflexible. 2 DIFFICULT, arduous, strenuous, laborious, tiring, exhausting, backbreaking, complex, complicated, involved, knotty, baffling, puzzling, perplexing. 3 HARSH, severe, strict, callous, unfeeling, unsympathetic, cruel, pitiless, merciless, ruthless, unrelenting, distressing, painful, unpleasant.

F3 1 soft, yielding. 2 easy, simple. 3 kind, pleasant.

adv industriously, diligently, assiduously, doggedly, steadily, laboriously, strenuously, earnestly, keenly, intently, strongly, violently, intensely, energetically, vigorously.

hard up poor, broke (*infml*), penniless, impoverished, in the red, bankrupt, bust, short, lacking.

F3 rich.

harden v solidify, set, freeze, bake, stiffen, strengthen, reinforce, fortify, buttress, brace, steel, nerve, toughen, season, accustom, train.

F3 soften, weaken.

hard-headed adj shrewd, astute, businesslike, level-headed, clear-thinking, sensible, realistic, pragmatic, practical, hard-boiled, tough, unsentimental.

F3 unrealistic.

hard-hearted adj callous, unfeeling, cold, hard, stony, heartless, unsympathetic, cruel, inhuman, pitiless, merciless.

F3 soft-hearted, kind, merciful.

hard-hitting adj condemnatory, critical, unsparing, no-holds-barred, vigorous, forceful, tough.

F3 mild.

hardly adv barely, scarcely, just, only just, not quite, not at all, by no means.

hardship n misfortune, adversity, trouble, difficulty, affliction, distress, suffering, trial, tribulation, want, need, privation, austerity, poverty, destitution, misery.
F3 ease, comfort, prosperity.

hard-wearing adj durable, lasting, strong, tough, sturdy, stout, rugged, resilient.
F3 delicate.

hard-working adj industrious, diligent, assiduous, conscientious, zealous, busy, energetic.
F3 idle, lazy.

hardy adj strong, tough, sturdy, robust, vigorous, fit, sound, healthy.
F3 weak, unhealthy.

harm n damage, loss, injury, hurt, detriment, ill, misfortune, wrong, abuse.
F3 benefit.
v damage, impair, blemish, spoil, mar, ruin, hurt, injure, wound, ill-treat, maltreat, abuse, misuse.
F3 benefit, improve.

harmful adj damaging, detrimental, pernicious, noxious, unhealthy, unwholesome, injurious, dangerous, hazardous, poisonous, toxic, destructive.
F3 harmless.

harmless adj safe, innocuous, non-toxic, inoffensive, gentle, innocent.
F3 harmful, dangerous, destructive.

harmonious adj 1 MELODIOUS, tuneful, musical, sweet-sounding.
2 MATCHING, co-ordinated, balanced, compatible, like-minded, agreeable, cordial, amicable, friendly, sympathetic.
F3 1 discordant.

harmonize v match, co-ordinate, balance, fit in, suit, tone, blend, correspond, agree, reconcile, accommodate, adapt, arrange, compose.
F3 clash.

harmony n 1 TUNEFULNESS, tune, melody, euphony. 2 live in harmony: agreement, unanimity, accord, concord, unity, compatibility, like-mindedness, peace, goodwill, rapport, sympathy, understanding, amicability, friendliness, co-operation, co-ordination, balance, symmetry, correspondence, conformity.
F3 1 discord. 2 conflict.

harness n tackle, gear, equipment, reins, straps, tack.
v control, channel, use, utilize, exploit, make use of, employ, mobilize, apply.

harrowing adj distressing, upsetting, heart-rending, disturbing, alarming, frightening, terrifying, nerve-racking, traumatic, agonizing, excruciating.

harry v badger, pester, nag, chivvy, harass, plague, torment, persecute, annoy, vex, worry, trouble, bother, hassle (infml), disturb, molest.

harsh adj 1 SEVERE, strict, Draconian, unfeeling, cruel, hard, pitiless, austere, Spartan, bleak, grim, comfortless.
2 a harsh sound: rough, coarse, rasping, croaking, guttural, grating, jarring, discordant, strident, raucous, sharp, shrill, unpleasant. 3 BRIGHT, dazzling, glaring, gaudy, lurid.
F3 1 lenient. 2 soft.

harvest n 1 HARVEST-TIME, ingathering, reaping, collection.
2 CROP, yield, return, produce, fruits, result, consequence.

v reap, mow, pick, gather, collect, accumulate, amass.

hash *n* mess, botch, muddle, mix-up, jumble, confusion, hotchpotch, mishmash.

haste *n* hurry, rush, hustle, bustle, speed, velocity, rapidity, swiftness, quickness, briskness, urgency, rashness, recklessness, impetuosity. ◆ slowness.

hasten *v* hurry, rush, make haste, run, sprint, dash, tear, race, fly, bolt, accelerate, speed (up), quicken, expedite, dispatch, precipitate, urge, press, advance, step up. ◆ dawdle, delay.

hasty *adj* hurried, rushed, impatient, headlong, rash, reckless, heedless, thoughtless, impetuous, impulsive, hot-headed, fast, quick, rapid, swift, speedy, brisk, prompt, short, brief, cursory. ◆ slow, careful, deliberate.

hat

> Hats include:
> trilby, bowler, fedora, top hat, Homburg, derby (*US*), pork-pie hat, flatcap, beret, bonnet, Tam o' Shanter, tammy, deerstalker, stovepipe hat, Stetson®, ten-gallon hat, boater, sunhat, panama, straw hat, picturehat, pill-box, cloche, beanie (*US*), poke-bonnet, mob-cap, turban, fez, sombrero, sou'wester, glengarry, bearskin, busby, peaked cap, sailor hat, baseball cap, Balaclava, hood, snood, toque, helmet, mortarboard, skullcap, yarmulka, mitre, biretta.

hatch *v* **1** INCUBATE, brood, breed.
2 CONCOCT, formulate, originate, think up, dream up, devise, contrive, plot, scheme, design, plan, project.

hate *v* dislike, despise, detest, loathe, abhor, abominate, execrate. ◆ like, love.
n hatred, aversion, dislike, loathing, abhorrence, abomination. ◆ liking, love.

hatred *n* hate, aversion, dislike, detestation, loathing, repugnance, revulsion, abhorrence, abomination, execration, animosity, ill-will, antagonism, hostility, antipathy. ◆ liking, love.

haughty *adj* lofty, imperious, high and mighty, supercilious, cavalier, snooty (*infml*), contemptuous, disdainful, scornful, superior, snobbish, arrogant, proud, stuck-up (*infml*), conceited. ◆ humble, modest.

haul *v* pull, heave, tug, draw, tow, drag, trail, move, transport, convey, carry, cart, lug, hump (*infml*). ◆ push.
n loot, booty, plunder, swag (*sl*), spoils, takings, gain, yield, find.

haunt *v* **1** FREQUENT, patronize, visit.
2 *memories haunted her:* plague, torment, trouble, disturb, recur, prey on, beset, obsess, possess.
n resort, hangout (*infml*), stamping-ground, den, meeting-place, rendezvous.

haunting *adj* memorable, unforgettable, persistent, recurrent, evocative, nostalgic, poignant. ◆ unmemorable.

have *v* **1** OWN, possess, get, obtain, gain, acquire, procure, secure, receive, accept, keep, hold. **2** FEEL, experience, enjoy, suffer, undergo, endure, put up with. **3** CONTAIN, include, comprise, incorporate, consist of. **4** *have a baby*: give birth to, bear.

F3 1 lack.

have to must, be forced, be compelled, be obliged, be required, ought, should.

haven *n* harbour, port, anchorage, shelter, refuge, sanctuary, asylum, retreat.

havoc *n* chaos, confusion, disorder, disruption, damage, destruction, ruin, wreck, rack and ruin, devastation, waste, desolation.

haywire *adj* wrong, tangled, out of control, crazy, mad, wild, chaotic, confused, disordered, disorganized, topsy-turvy.

hazard *n* risk, danger, peril, jeopardy, threat, death-trap, accident, chance.

F3 safety.

v **1** RISK, endanger, jeopardize, expose. **2** CHANCE, gamble, stake, venture, suggest, speculate.

hazardous *adj* risky, dangerous, unsafe, perilous, precarious, insecure, chancy, difficult, tricky.

F3 safe, secure.

haze *n* mist, fog, cloud, steam, vapour, film, mistiness, smokiness, dimness, obscurity.

hazy *adj* misty, foggy, smoky, clouded, cloudy, milky, fuzzy, blurred, ill-defined, veiled, obscure, dim, faint, unclear, indistinct, vague, indefinite, uncertain.

F3 clear, bright, definite.

head *n* **1** SKULL, cranium, brain, mind, mentality, brains (*infml*), intellect, intelligence, understanding, thought. **2** TOP, peak, summit, crown, tip, apex, height, climax, front, fore, lead. **3** LEADER, chief, captain, commander, boss, director, manager,

superintendent, principal, head teacher, ruler.

F3 1 foot, tail. **2** base, foot. **3** subordinate.

adj leading, front, foremost, first, chief, main, prime, principal, top, highest, supreme, premier, dominant, pre-eminent.

v lead, rule, govern, command, direct, manage, run, superintend, oversee, supervise, control, guide, steer.

head for make for, go towards, direct towards, aim for, point to, turn for, steer for.

head off forestall, intercept, intervene, interpose, deflect, divert, fend off, ward off, avert, prevent, stop.

heading *n* title, name, headline, rubric, caption, section, division, category, class.

headland *n* promontory, cape, head, point, foreland.

headlong *adj* hasty, precipitate, impetuous, impulsive, rash, reckless, dangerous, breakneck, head-first.

adv head first, hurriedly, hastily, precipitately, rashly, recklessly, heedlessly, thoughtlessly, wildly.

headquarters *n* HQ, base (camp), head office, nerve centre.

headstrong *adj* stubborn, obstinate, intractable, pigheaded, wilful, self-willed, perverse, contrary.

F3 tractable, docile.

headway *n* advance, progress, way, improvement.

heady *adj* intoxicating, strong, stimulating, exhilarating, thrilling, exciting.

heal *v* cure, remedy, mend, restore, treat, soothe, salve, settle, reconcile, patch up.

health n fitness, constitution, form, shape, trim, fettle, condition, tone, state, healthiness, good condition, wellbeing, welfare, soundness, robustness, strength, vigour.
F3 illness, infirmity.

healthy adj **1** WELL, fit, good, fine, in condition, in good shape, in fine fettle, sound, sturdy, robust, strong, vigorous, hale and hearty, blooming, flourishing, thriving. **2** healthy food: wholesome, nutritious, nourishing, bracing, invigorating, healthful.
F3 1 ill, sick, infirm.

heap n pile, stack, mound, mountain, lot, mass, accumulation, collection, hoard, stockpile, store.
v pile, stack, mound, bank, build, amass, accumulate, collect, gather, hoard, stockpile, store, load.

hear v **1** LISTEN, catch, pick up, overhear, eavesdrop, heed, pay attention. **2** LEARN, find out, discover, ascertain, understand, gather. **3** JUDGE, try, examine, investigate.

hearing n **1** EARSHOT, sound, range, reach, ear, perception. **2** TRIAL, inquiry, investigation, inquest, audition, interview, audience.

hearsay n rumour, word of mouth, talk, gossip, tittle-tattle, report, buzz (infml).

heart n **1** SOUL, mind, character, disposition, nature, temperament, feeling, emotion, sentiment, love, tenderness, compassion, sympathy, pity. **2** lose heart: courage, bravery, boldness, spirit, resolution, determination. **3** CENTRE, middle, core, kernel, nucleus, nub, crux, essence.
F3 2 cowardice. **3** periphery.

by heart by rote, parrot-fashion, pat, off pat, word for word, verbatim.

> **Parts of the heart include:**
> aortic valve, aorta, bicuspid valve, carotid artery, vena cava, atrium, pulmonary artery, pulmonary veins, ventricle, mitral valve, myocardium, pulmonary valve, tricuspid valve, ventricular septum.

heartbreaking adj distressing, sad, tragic, harrowing, heart-rending, pitiful, agonizing, grievous, bitter, disappointing.
F3 heartwarming, heartening.

heartbroken adj broken-hearted, desolate, sad, miserable, dejected, despondent, downcast, crestfallen, disappointed, dispirited, grieved, crushed.
F3 delighted, elated.

hearten v comfort, console, reassure, cheer (up), buck up (infml), encourage, boost, inspire, stimulate, rouse, pep up (infml).
F3 dishearten, depress, dismay.

heartfelt adj deep, profound, sincere, honest, genuine, earnest, ardent, fervent, whole-hearted, warm.
F3 insincere, false.

heartless adj unfeeling, uncaring, cold, hard, hard-hearted, callous, unkind, cruel, inhuman, brutal, pitiless, merciless.
F3 kind, considerate, sympathetic, merciful.

heart-rending adj harrowing, heartbreaking, agonizing, pitiful, piteous, pathetic, tragic, sad, distressing, moving, affecting, poignant.

heartwarming adj pleasing, gratifying, satisfying, cheering, heartening, encouraging, touching, moving, affecting.
F3 heartbreaking.

hearty adj 1 ENTHUSIASTIC, whole-hearted, unreserved, heartfelt, sincere, genuine, warm, friendly, cordial, jovial, cheerful, ebullient, exuberant, boisterous, energetic, vigorous.
2 *a hearty breakfast*: large, sizable, substantial, filling, ample, generous.
F3 1 half-hearted, cool, cold.

heat n 1 HOTNESS, warmth, sultriness, closeness, high temperature, fever. 2 ARDOUR, fervour, fieriness, passion, intensity, vehemence, fury, excitement, impetuosity, earnestness, zeal.
F3 1 cold(ness). 2 coolness.
v warm, boil, toast, cook, bake, roast, reheat, warm up, inflame, excite, animate, rouse, stimulate, flush, glow.
F3 cool, chill.

heated adj angry, furious, raging, passionate, fiery, stormy, tempestuous, bitter, fierce, intense, vehement, violent, frenzied.
F3 calm.

heave v 1 PULL, haul, drag, tug, raise, lift, hitch, hoist, lever, rise, surge.
2 THROW, fling, hurl, cast, toss, chuck, let fly. 3 RETCH, vomit, throw up (*infml*), spew.

heaven n sky, firmament, next world, hereafter, after-life, paradise, utopia, ecstasy, rapture, bliss, happiness, joy.
F3 hell.

heavenly adj 1 BLISSFUL, wonderful, glorious, beautiful, lovely, delightful, out of this world. 2 CELESTIAL, unearthly, supernatural, spiritual, divine, godlike, angelic, immortal, sublime, blessed.
F3 1 hellish. 2 infernal.

heavy adj 1 WEIGHTY, hefty, ponderous, burdensome, massive, large, bulky, solid, dense, stodgy.

2 *heavy work*: hard, difficult, tough, arduous, laborious, strenuous, demanding, taxing, harsh, severe.
3 OPPRESSIVE, intense, serious, dull, tedious.
F3 1 light. 2 easy.

heavy-handed adj clumsy, awkward, unsubtle, tactless, insensitive, thoughtless, oppressive, overbearing, domineering, autocratic.

hectic adj busy, frantic, frenetic, chaotic, fast, feverish, excited, heated, furious, wild.
F3 leisurely.

hedge n hedgerow, screen, windbreak, barrier, fence, dike, boundary.
v 1 SURROUND, enclose, hem in, confine, restrict, fortify, guard, shield, protect, safeguard, cover. 2 STALL, temporize, equivocate, dodge, sidestep, evade, duck.

heed v listen, pay attention, mind, note, regard, observe, follow, obey.
F3 ignore, disregard.

heedless adj oblivious, unthinking, careless, negligent, rash, reckless, inattentive, unobservant, thoughtless, unconcerned.
F3 heedful, mindful, attentive.

hefty adj heavy, weighty, big, large, burly, hulking, beefy, brawny, strong, powerful, vigorous, robust, strapping, solid, substantial, massive, colossal, bulky, unwieldy.
F3 slight, small.

height n 1 HIGHNESS, altitude, elevation, tallness, loftiness, stature.
2 TOP, summit, peak, pinnacle, apex, crest, crown, zenith, apogee, culmination, climax, extremity, maximum, limit, ceiling.
F3 1 depth.

heighten v raise, elevate, increase, add to, magnify, intensify, strengthen, sharpen, improve, enhance.
F3 lower, decrease, diminish.

hell n **1** heaven and hell: underworld, Hades, inferno, lower regions, nether world, abyss. **2** SUFFERING, anguish, agony, torment, ordeal, nightmare, misery.
F3 1 heaven.

hellish adj infernal, devilish, diabolical, fiendish, accursed, damnable, monstrous, abominable, atrocious, dreadful.
F3 heavenly.

helm n tiller, wheel, driving seat, reins, saddle, command, control, leadership, direction.

help v **1** AID, assist, lend a hand, serve, be of use, collaborate, co-operate, back, stand by, support. **2** IMPROVE, ameliorate, relieve, alleviate, mitigate, ease, facilitate.
F3 1 hinder. **2** worsen.
n aid, assistance, collaboration, co-operation, support, advice, guidance, service, use, utility, avail, benefit.
F3 hindrance.

helper n assistant, deputy, auxiliary, subsidiary, attendant, right-hand man, PA, mate, partner, associate, colleague, collaborator, accomplice, ally, supporter, second.

helpful adj **1** USEFUL, practical, constructive, worthwhile, valuable, beneficial, advantageous. **2** a helpful person: co-operative, obliging, neighbourly, friendly, considerate, caring, kind, sympathetic, supportive.
F3 1 useless, futile.

helping n serving, portion, share, ration, amount, plateful, piece, dollop (infml).

helpless adj weak, feeble, powerless, dependent, vulnerable, exposed, unprotected, defenceless, abandoned, friendless, destitute, forlorn, incapable, incompetent, infirm, disabled, paralysed.
F3 strong, independent, competent.

hem n edge, border, margin, fringe, trimming.
hem in surround, enclose, box in, confine, restrict.

henpecked adj dominated, subjugated, browbeaten, bullied, intimidated, meek, timid.
F3 dominant.

herald n messenger, courier, harbinger, forerunner, precursor, omen, token, signal, sign, indication.
v announce, proclaim, broadcast, advertise, publicize, trumpet, pave the way, precede, usher in, show, indicate, promise.

herb n

Herbs and spices include:
angelica, anise, basil, bay, berga-mot, borage, camomile, chervil, chives, comfrey, cumin, dill, fennel, garlic, hyssop, lemon balm,,lovage, marjoram, mint, oregano, parsley, rosemary, sage, savory, sorrel, tarra-gon, thyme; allspice, caper, caraway seeds, cardamom, cayenne pepper, chilli, cinnamon, cloves, coriander, curry powder, ginger, mace, mus-tard, nutmeg, paprika, pepper, saf-fron, sesame, turmeric, vanilla.

herd n drove, flock, swarm, pack, press, crush, mass, horde, throng, multitude, crowd, mob, the masses, rabble.
v **1** FLOCK, congregate, gather, collect, assemble, rally. **2** LEAD, guide, shepherd, round up, drive, force.

hereditary *adj* inherited, bequeathed, handed down, family, ancestral, inborn, inbred, innate, natural, congenital, genetic.

heresy *n* heterodoxy, unorthodoxy, free-thinking, apostasy, dissidence, schism, blasphemy.
Ⓕ orthodoxy.

heretic *n* free-thinker, nonconformist, apostate, dissident, dissenter, revisionist, separatist, schismatic, sectarian, renegade.
Ⓕ conformist.

heretical *adj* heterodox, unorthodox, free-thinking, rationalistic, schismatic, impious, irreverent, iconoclastic, blasphemous.
Ⓕ orthodox, conventional, conformist.

heritage *n* **1** INHERITANCE, legacy, bequest, endowment, lot, portion, share, birthright, due. **2** HISTORY, past, tradition, culture.

hermit *n* recluse, solitary, monk, ascetic, anchorite.

hero *n* protagonist, lead, celebrity, star, superstar, idol, paragon, goody (*infml*), champion, conqueror.

heroic *adj* brave, courageous, fearless, dauntless, undaunted, lion-hearted, stout-hearted, valiant, bold, daring, intrepid, adventurous, gallant, chivalrous, noble, selfless.
Ⓕ cowardly, timid.

heroism *n* bravery, courage, valour, boldness, daring, intrepidity, gallantry, prowess, selflessness.
Ⓕ cowardice, timidity.

hesitant *adj* hesitating, reluctant, half-hearted, uncertain, unsure, indecisive, irresolute, vacillating, wavering, tentative, wary, shy, timid,

halting, stammering, stuttering.
Ⓕ decisive, resolute, confident, fluent.

hesitate *v* pause, delay, wait, be reluctant, be unwilling, think twice, hold back, shrink from, scruple, boggle, demur, vacillate, waver, be uncertain, dither, shilly-shally, falter, stumble, halt, stammer, stutter.
Ⓕ decide.

hesitation *n* pause, delay, reluctance, unwillingness, hesitance, scruple(s), qualm(s), misgivings, doubt, second thoughts, vacillation, uncertainty, indecision, irresolution, faltering, stumbling, stammering, stuttering.
Ⓕ eagerness, assurance.

hew *v* cut, fell, axe, lop, chop, hack, sever, split, carve, sculpt, sculpture, fashion, model, form, shape, make.

heyday *n* peak, prime, flush, bloom, flowering, golden age, boom time.

hidden *adj* **1** *a hidden door*: concealed, covered, shrouded, veiled, disguised, camouflaged, unseen, secret. **2** OBSCURE, dark, occult, secret, covert, close, cryptic, mysterious, abstruse, mystical, latent, ulterior.
Ⓕ 1 showing, apparent. **2** obvious.

hide¹ *v* **1** CONCEAL, cover, cloak, shroud, veil, screen, mask, disguise, camouflage, obscure, shadow, eclipse, bury, stash (*infml*), secrete, withhold, keep dark, suppress. **2** TAKE COVER, shelter, lie low, go to ground, hole up (*infml*).
Ⓕ 1 reveal, show, display.

hide² *n* skin, pelt, fell, fur, leather.

hidebound *adj* set, rigid, entrenched, narrow-minded, strait-

laced, conventional, ultra-
conservative.
Ea liberal, progressive.

hideous adj ugly, repulsive,
grotesque, monstrous, horrid, ghastly,
awful, dreadful, frightful, terrible,
grim, gruesome, macabre, terrifying,
shocking, appalling, disgusting,
revolting, horrible.
Ea beautiful, attractive.

hiding[1] n beating, flogging,
whipping, caning, spanking,
thrashing, walloping (infml).

hiding[2] n concealment, cover,
veiling, screening, disguise,
camouflage.

hiding-place n hide-away, hideout,
lair, den, hole, hide, cover, refuge,
haven, sanctuary, retreat.

hierarchy n pecking order, ranking,
grading, scale, series, ladder,
echelons, strata.

high adj **1** TALL, lofty, elevated,
soaring, towering. **2** GREAT, strong,
intense, extreme. **3** IMPORTANT,
influential, powerful, eminent,
distinguished, prominent, chief,
leading, senior. **4** HIGH-PITCHED,
soprano, treble, sharp, shrill, piercing.
5 a high price: expensive, dear, costly,
exorbitant, excessive.
Ea 1 low, short. **3** lowly. **4** deep.
5 cheap.

high-born adj noble, aristocratic,
blue-blooded, thoroughbred.
Ea low-born.

highbrow n intellectual, egghead
(infml), scholar, academic.
adj intellectual, sophisticated,
cultured, cultivated, academic,
bookish, brainy (infml), deep, serious,
classical.
Ea low-brow.

high-class adj upper-class, posh
(infml), classy (infml), top-class, top-
flight, high-quality, quality, de luxe,
superior, excellent, first-rate, choice,
select, exclusive.
Ea ordinary, mediocre.

high-flown adj florid, extravagant,
exaggerated, elaborate, flamboyant,
ostentatious, pretentious, high-
standing, grandiose, pompous,
bombastic, turgid, artificial, stilted,
affected, lofty, highfalutin, la-di-da
(infml), supercilious.

high-handed adj overbearing,
domineering, bossy (infml),
imperious, dictatorial, autocratic,
despotic, tyrannical, oppressive,
arbitrary.

highlight n high point, high spot,
peak, climax, best, cream.
v underline, emphasize, stress,
accentuate, play up, point up,
spotlight, illuminate, show up, set off,
focus on, feature.

highly adv very, greatly,
considerably, decidedly, extremely,
immensely, tremendously,
exceptionally, extraordinarily,
enthusiastically, warmly, well.

highly-strung adj sensitive,
neurotic, nervy, jumpy, edgy,
temperamental, excitable, restless,
nervous, tense.
Ea calm.

high-minded adj lofty, noble,
moral, ethical, principled, idealistic,
virtuous, upright, righteous,
honourable, worthy.
Ea immoral, unscrupulous.

high-powered adj powerful,
forceful, driving, aggressive, dynamic,
go-ahead, enterprising, energetic,
vigorous.

high-spirited adj boisterous, bouncy, exuberant, effervescent, frolicsome, ebullient, sparkling, vibrant, vivacious, lively, energetic, spirited, dashing, bold, daring.
F3 quiet, sedate.

hijack v commandeer, expropriate, skyjack, seize, take over.

hike v ramble, walk, trek, tramp, trudge, plod.
n ramble, walk, trek, tramp, march.

hilarious adj funny, amusing, comical, side-splitting, hysterical (infml), uproarious, noisy, rollicking, merry, jolly, jovial.
F3 serious, grave.

hilarity n mirth, laughter, fun, amusement, levity, frivolity, merriment, jollity, conviviality, high spirits, boisterousness, exuberance, exhilaration.
F3 seriousness, gravity.

hill n 1 HILLOCK, knoll, mound, prominence, eminence, elevation, foothill, down, fell, mountain, height. 2 a steep hill: slope, incline, gradient, ramp, rise, ascent, acclivity, drop, descent, declivity.

hinder v hamper, obstruct, impede, encumber, handicap, hamstring, hold up, delay, retard, slow down, hold back, check, curb, stop, prevent, frustrate, thwart, oppose.
F3 help, aid, assist.

hindrance n obstruction, impediment, handicap, encumbrance, obstacle, stumbling-block, barrier, bar, check, restraint, restriction, limitation, difficulty, drag, snag, hitch, drawback, disadvantage, inconvenience, deterrent.
F3 help, aid, assistance.

hinge v centre, turn, revolve, pivot, hang, depend, rest.

hint n TIP, advice, suggestion, help, clue, inkling, suspicion, tip-off, reminder, indication, sign, pointer, mention, allusion, intimation, insinuation, implication, innuendo. 2 a hint of garlic: touch, trace, tinge, taste, dash, soupçon, speck.
v suggest, prompt, tip off, indicate, imply, insinuate, intimate, allude, mention.

hire v rent, let, lease, charter, commission, book, reserve, employ, take on, sign up, engage, appoint, retain.
F3 dismiss, fire.
n rent, rental, fee, charge, cost, price.

hiss v 1 WHISTLE, shrill, whizz, sizzle. 2 JEER, mock, ridicule, deride, boo, hoot.

historic adj momentous, consequential, important, significant, epoch-making, notable, remarkable, outstanding, extraordinary, celebrated, renowned, famed, famous.
F3 unimportant, insignificant, unknown.

historical adj real, actual, authentic, factual, documented, recorded, attested, verifiable.
F3 legendary, fictional.

history n 1 PAST, olden days, days of old, antiquity. 2 CHRONICLE, record, annals, archives, chronology, account, narrative, story, tale, saga, biography, life, autobiography, memoirs.

hit v 1 STRIKE, knock, tap, smack, slap, thrash, whack (infml), bash, thump, clout, punch, belt (infml), wallop (infml), beat, batter. 2 BUMP,

collide with, bang, crash, smash, damage, harm.
n **1** STROKE, shot, blow, knock, tap, slap, smack, bash, bump, collision, impact, crash, smash. **2** SUCCESS, triumph, winner (*sl*).
F∃ 2 failure.

hit back retaliate, reciprocate, counter-attack, strike back.

hit on chance on, stumble on, light on, discover, invent, realize, arrive at, guess.

hit out lash out, assail, attack, rail, denounce, condemn, criticize.

hitch *v* **1** FASTEN, attach, tie, harness, yoke, couple, connect, join. **2** PULL, heave, yank (*infml*), tug, jerk, hoist, hike (up) (*infml*).
F∃ 1 unhitch, unfasten.
n delay, hold-up, trouble, problem, difficulty, mishap, setback, hiccup, drawback, snag, catch, impediment, hindrance.

hoard *n* collection, accumulation, mass, heap, pile, fund, reservoir, supply, reserve, store, stockpile, cache, treasure-trove.
v collect, gather, amass, accumulate, save, put by, lay up, store, stash away (*infml*), stockpile, keep, treasure.
F∃ use, spend, squander.

hoarse *adj* husky, croaky, throaty, guttural, gravelly, gruff, growling, rough, harsh, rasping, grating, raucous, discordant.
F∃ clear, smooth.

hoax *n* trick, prank, practical joke, put-on, joke, leg-pull (*infml*), spoof, fake, fraud, deception, bluff, humbug, cheat, swindle, con (*infml*).
v trick, deceive, take in, fool, dupe, gull, delude, have on (*infml*), pull someone's leg (*infml*), con (*infml*),

swindle, take for a ride (*infml*), cheat, hoodwink, bamboozle (*infml*), bluff.

hobble *v* limp, stumble, falter, stagger, totter, dodder, shuffle.

hobby *n* pastime, diversion, recreation, relaxation, pursuit, sideline.

> **Hobbies include:**
> aerobics, astronomy, ballet, ball-room dancing, beekeeping, bird-watching, bridge, bungee jumping, camping, chess, climbing, collect-ing, computer games, cooking, cro-chet, crosswords, darts, diving, DIY, extreme sports, gardening, hill-walking, horse-riding, jigsaws, kite-flying, knitting, martial arts, model railways, orienteering, origami, paintball, patchwork, photography, pottery, quilting, skateboarding, snooker, sports, wargaming, wine-tasting, woodwork, yoga. *see also* **dance; martial art; sport.**

hoist *v* lift, elevate, raise, erect, jack up, winch up, heave, rear, uplift.
n jack, winch, crane, tackle, lift, elevator.

hold *v* **1** GRIP, grasp, clutch, clasp, embrace, have, own, possess, keep, retain. **2** *hold a meeting*: conduct, carry on, continue, call, summon, convene, assemble. **3** CONSIDER, regard, deem, judge, reckon, think, believe, maintain. **4** BEAR, support, sustain, carry, comprise, contain, accommodate. **5** IMPRISON, detain, stop, arrest, check, curb, restrain. **6** CLING, stick, adhere, stay.
F∃ 1 drop. **5** release, free, liberate.
n **1** GRIP, grasp, clasp, embrace. **2** INFLUENCE, power, sway, mastery, dominance, authority, control, leverage.

hold back 1 CONTROL, curb, check, restrain, suppress, stifle, retain, withhold, repress, inhibit. **2** HESITATE, delay, desist, refrain, shrink, refuse. **F3 1** release.

hold forth speak, talk, lecture, discourse, orate, preach, declaim.

hold off 1 FEND OFF, ward off, stave off, keep off, repel, rebuff. **2** PUT OFF, postpone, defer, delay, wait.

hold out 1 OFFER, give, present, extend. **2** LAST, continue, persist, endure, persevere, stand fast, hang on. **F3 2** give in, yield.

hold up 1 SUPPORT, sustain, brace, shore up, lift, raise. **2** DELAY, detain, retard, slow, hinder, impede.

hold with agree with, go along with, approve of, countenance, support, subscribe to, accept.

holder n **1** holders of British passports: bearer, owner, possessor, proprietor, keeper, custodian, occupant, incumbent. **2** CONTAINER, receptacle, case, housing, cover, sheath, rest, stand.

hold-up n **1** DELAY, wait, hitch, setback, snag, difficulty, trouble, obstruction, stoppage, (traffic) jam, bottleneck. **2** ROBBERY, heist (sl), stick-up (sl).

hole n aperture, opening, orifice, pore, puncture, perforation, eyelet, tear, split, vent, outlet, shaft, slot, gap, breach, break, crack, fissure, fault, defect, flaw, dent, dimple, depression, hollow, cavity, crater, pit, excavation, cavern, cave, chamber, pocket, niche, recess, burrow, nest, lair, retreat.

holiday n vacation, recess, leave, time off, day off, break, rest, half-term, bank-holiday, feast-day, festival, celebration, anniversary.

holiness n sacredness, sanctity, spirituality, divinity, piety, devoutness, godliness, saintliness, virtuousness, righteousness, purity. **F3** impiety.

hollow adj **1** CONCAVE, indented, depressed, sunken, deep, cavernous, empty, vacant, unfilled. **2** FALSE, artificial, deceptive, insincere, meaningless, empty, vain, futile, fruitless, worthless. **F3 1** solid. **2** real.

n hole, pit, well, cavity, crater, excavation, cavern, cave, depression, concavity, basin, bowl, cup, dimple, dent, indentation, groove, channel, trough, valley.

v dig, excavate, burrow, tunnel, scoop, gouge, channel, groove, furrow, pit, dent, indent.

holy adj **1** holy ground: sacred, hallowed, consecrated, sanctified, dedicated, blessed, venerated, revered, spiritual, divine, evangelical. **2** PIOUS, religious, devout, godly, God-fearing, saintly, virtuous, good, righteous, faithful, pure, perfect. **F3 1** unsanctified. **2** impious, irreligious.

homage n recognition, acknowledgement, tribute, honour, praise, adulation, admiration, regard, esteem, respect, deference, reverence, adoration, awe, veneration, worship, devotion.

home n residence, domicile, dwelling-place, abode, base, house, pied-à-terre, hearth, fireside, birthplace, home town, home ground, territory, habitat, element. adj domestic, household, family, internal, local, national, inland. **F3** foreign, international.

at home 1 COMFORTABLE, relaxed, at ease. **2** FAMILIAR, knowledgeable, experienced, skilled.

homeland n native land, native country, fatherland, motherland.

homeless adj itinerant, travelling, nomadic, wandering, vagrant, rootless, unsettled, displaced, dispossessed, evicted, exiled, outcast, abandoned, forsaken, destitute, down-and-out.
n travellers, vagabonds, vagrants, tramps, down-and-outs, dossers (sl), squatters.

homely adj homelike, homey, comfortable, cosy, snug, relaxed, informal, friendly, intimate, familiar, everyday, ordinary, domestic, natural, plain, simple, modest, unassuming, unpretentious, unsophisticated, folksy, homespun.
F∃ grand, formal.

homicide n murder, manslaughter, assassination, killing, bloodshed.

homogeneous adj uniform, consistent, unvarying, identical, similar, alike, akin, kindred, analogous, comparable, harmonious, compatible.
F∃ different.

homosexual n gay, queer (sl), poof (sl), lesbian, dike (sl).
F∃ heterosexual, straight (sl).
adj gay, queer (sl), lesbian.

hone v sharpen, whet, point, edge, grind, file, polish.

honest adj **1** TRUTHFUL, sincere, frank, candid, blunt, outspoken, direct, straight, outright, forthright, straightforward, plain, simple, open, above-board, legitimate, legal, lawful, on the level (infml), fair, just, impartial, objective. **2** LAW-ABIDING, virtuous,

upright, ethical, moral, high-minded, scrupulous, honourable, reputable, respectable, reliable, trustworthy, true, genuine, real.
F∃ 1 dishonest. **2** dishonourable.

honestly adv truly, really, truthfully, sincerely, frankly, directly, outright, plainly, openly, legitimately, legally, lawfully, on the level, fairly, justly, objectively, honourably, in good faith.
F∃ dishonestly, dishonourably.

honesty n **1** TRUTHFULNESS, sincerity, frankness, candour, bluntness, outspokenness, straightforwardness, plain-speaking, explicitness, openness, legitimacy, legality, equity, fairness, justness, objectivity, even-handedness.
2 VIRTUE, uprightness, honour, integrity, morality, scrupulousness, trustworthiness, genuineness, veracity.
F∃ 1 dishonesty.

honorary adj unpaid, unofficial, titular, nominal, in name only, honorific, formal.
F∃ paid.

honour n **1** REPUTATION, good name, repute, renown, distinction, esteem, regard, respect, credit, dignity, self-respect, pride, integrity, morality, decency, rectitude, probity. **2** AWARD, accolade, commendation, acknowledgement, recognition, tribute, privilege. **3** PRAISE, acclaim, homage, admiration, reverence, worship, adoration.
F∃ 1 dishonour, disgrace.
v **1** PRAISE, acclaim, exalt, glorify, pay homage to, decorate, crown, celebrate, commemorate, remember, admire, esteem, respect, revere, worship, prize, value. **2** honour a promise: keep,

observe, respect, fulfil, carry out, discharge, execute, perform.
F∃ 1 dishonour, disgrace.

honourable adj great, eminent, distinguished, renowned, respected, worthy, prestigious, trusty, reputable, respectable, virtuous, upright, upstanding, straight, honest, trustworthy, true, sincere, noble, high-minded, principled, moral, ethical, fair, just, right, proper, decent.
F∃ dishonourable, unworthy, dishonest.

hoodwink v deceive, dupe, fool, take in, delude, bamboozle (infml), have on (infml), mislead, hoax, trick, cheat, con (infml), rook, gull, swindle.

hook n crook, sickle, peg, barb, trap, snare, catch, fastener, clasp, hasp.
v **1** BEND, crook, curve, curl. **2** CATCH, capture, bag, grab, trap, snare, ensnare, entangle. **3** FASTEN, clasp, hitch, fix, secure.

hooligan n ruffian, rowdy, hoodlum, mobster, bovver boy (sl), thug, tough, lout, yob (sl), vandal, delinquent.

hoop n ring, circle, round, loop, wheel, band, girdle, circlet.

hoot n, v call, cry, shout, shriek, whoop, toot, beep, whistle, boo, jeer, laugh, howl.

hop v jump, leap, spring, bound, vault, skip, dance, prance, frisk, limp, hobble.
n jump, leap, spring, bound, vault, bounce, step, skip, dance.

hope n hopefulness, optimism, ambition, aspiration, wish, desire, longing, dream, expectation, anticipation, prospect, promise, belief, confidence, assurance, conviction, faith.
F∃ pessimism, despair.

v aspire, wish, desire, long, expect, await, look forward, anticipate, contemplate, foresee, believe, trust, rely, reckon on, assume.
F∃ despair.

hopeful adj **1** OPTIMISTIC, bullish (infml), confident, assured, expectant, sanguine, cheerful, buoyant.
2 a hopeful sign: encouraging, heartening, reassuring, favourable, auspicious, promising, rosy, bright.
F∃ 1 pessimistic, despairing. **2** discouraging.

hopeless adj **1** PESSIMISTIC, defeatist, negative, despairing, demoralized, downhearted, dejected, despondent, forlorn, wretched.
2 UNATTAINABLE, unachievable, impracticable, impossible, vain, foolish, futile, useless, pointless, worthless, poor, helpless, lost, irremediable, irreparable, incurable.
F∃ 1 hopeful, optimistic. **2** curable.

horde n band, gang, pack, herd, drove, flock, swarm, crowd, mob, throng, multitude, host.

horizon n skyline, vista, prospect, compass, range, scope, perspective.

horrible adj unpleasant, disagreeable, nasty, unkind, horrid, disgusting, revolting, offensive, repulsive, hideous, grim, ghastly, awful, dreadful, frightful, fearful, terrible, abominable, shocking, appalling, horrific.
F∃ pleasant, agreeable, lovely, attractive.

horrific adj horrifying, shocking, appalling, awful, dreadful, ghastly, gruesome, terrifying, frightening, scary, horrendous, bloodcurdling.

horrify v shock, outrage, scandalize, appal, disgust, sicken, dismay, alarm,

startle, scare, frighten, terrify.
F3 please, delight.

horror n **1** recoil in horror: shock, outrage, disgust, revulsion, repugnance, abhorrence, loathing, dismay, consternation, alarm, fright, fear, terror, panic, dread, apprehension. **2** GHASTLINESS, awfulness, frightfulness, hideousness. **F3 1** approval, delight.

horseman, horsewoman n equestrian, rider, jockey, cavalryman, hussar.

horseplay n clowning, buffoonery, foolery, tomfoolery, skylarking, pranks, capers, high jinks, fun and games, rough-and-tumble.

hospitable adj friendly, sociable, welcoming, receptive, cordial, amicable, congenial, convivial, genial, kind, gracious, generous, liberal. **F3** inhospitable, unfriendly, hostile.

hospitality n friendliness, sociability, welcome, accommodation, entertainment, conviviality, warmth, cheer, generosity, open-handedness. **F3** unfriendliness.

host[1] n **1** COMPÈRE, master of ceremonies, presenter, announcer, anchorman, anchorwoman, linkman. **2** PUBLICAN, innkeeper, landlord, proprietor.
v present, introduce, compère.

host[2] n multitude, myriad, array, army, horde, crowd, throng, swarm, pack, band.

hostage n prisoner, captive, pawn, surety, security, pledge.

hostel n youth hostel, residence, dosshouse (sl), boarding-house, guest-house, hotel, inn.

hostile adj belligerent, warlike, ill-disposed, unsympathetic, unfriendly, inhospitable, inimical, antagonistic, opposed, adverse, unfavourable, contrary, opposite.
F3 friendly, welcoming, favourable.

hostilities n war, warfare, battle, fighting, conflict, strife, bloodshed.

hostility n opposition, aggression, belligerence, enmity, estrangement, antagonism, animosity, ill-will, malice, resentment, hate, hatred, dislike, aversion, abhorrence.
F3 friendliness, friendship.

hot adj **1** WARM, heated, fiery, burning, scalding, blistering, scorching, roasting, baking, boiling, steaming, sizzling, sweltering, sultry, torrid, tropical. **2** SPICY, peppery, piquant, sharp, pungent, strong.
F3 1 cold, cool. **2** mild.

hotchpotch n mishmash, medley, miscellany, collection, mix, mixture, jumble, confusion, mess.

hotel n boarding-house, guest-house, pension, motel, inn, public house, pub (infml), hostel.

hotheaded adj headstrong, impetuous, impulsive, hasty, rash, reckless, fiery, volatile, hot-tempered, quick-tempered.
F3 cool, calm.

hothouse n greenhouse, glasshouse, conservatory, orangery, vinery.

hound v chase, pursue, hunt (down), drive, goad, prod, chivvy, nag, pester, badger, harry, harass, persecute.

house n **1** BUILDING, dwelling, residence, home. **2** DYNASTY, family, clan, tribe.

Types of house include:
semi-detached, semi (infml), de-tached, terraced, town house, coun-cil house, cottage, prefab (infml),

pied-à-terre, bungalow; flat, bedsit (or bedsitter), apartment, studio flat, maisonette, penthouse, granny flat, duplex (US), condominium (US); manor, hall, lodge, grange, villa, mansion, rectory, vicarage, parsonage, manse, croft, farmhouse, homestead, ranchhouse, chalet, log cabin, shack, shanty, hut, igloo, hacienda.

v **1** LODGE, quarter, billet, board, accommodate, put up, take in, shelter, harbour. **2** HOLD, contain, protect, cover, sheathe, place, keep, store.

household *n* family, family circle, house, home, ménage, establishment, set-up.

adj domestic, home, family, ordinary, plain, everyday, common, familiar, well-known, established.

householder *n* resident, tenant, occupier, occupant, owner, landlady, freeholder, leaseholder, proprietor, landlord, home-owner, head of the household.

housing *n* **1** ACCOMMODATION, houses, homes, dwellings, habitation, shelter. **2** CASING, case, container, holder, covering, cover, sheath, protection.

hovel *n* shack, shanty, cabin, hut, shed, dump, hole (*infml*).

hover *v* **1** HANG, poise, float, drift, fly, flutter, flap. **2** *he hovered by the door*: pause, linger, hang about, hesitate, waver, fluctuate, seesaw.

however *conj* nevertheless, nonetheless, still, yet, even so, notwithstanding, though, anyhow.

howl *n, v* wail, cry, shriek, scream, shout, yell, roar, bellow, bay, yelp, hoot, moan, groan.

hub *n* centre, middle, focus, focal point, axis, pivot, linchpin, nerve centre, core, heart.

hubbub *n* noise, racket, din, clamour, commotion, disturbance, riot, uproar, hullabaloo, rumpus, confusion, disorder, tumult, hurly-burly, chaos, pandemonium.
F3 peace, quiet.

huddle *n* **1** CLUSTER, clump, knot, mass, crowd, muddle, jumble. **2** CONCLAVE, conference, meeting. *v* cluster, gravitate, converge, meet, gather, congregate, crowd, flock, throng, press, cuddle, snuggle, nestle, curl up, crouch, hunch.
F3 disperse.

hue *n* colour, shade, tint, dye, tinge, nuance, tone, complexion, aspect, light.

huff *n* pique, sulks, mood, bad mood, anger, rage, passion.

hug *v* embrace, cuddle, squeeze, enfold, hold, clasp, clutch, grip, cling to, enclose.
n embrace, cuddle, squeeze, clasp, hold, clinch.

huge *adj* immense, vast, enormous, massive, colossal, titanic, giant, gigantic, mammoth, monumental, tremendous, great, big, large, bulky, unwieldy.
F3 tiny, minute.

hulking *adj* massive, heavy, unwieldy, bulky, awkward, ungainly.
F3 small, delicate.

hull *n* body, frame, framework, structure, casing, covering.

hullabaloo *n* fuss, palaver, to-do (*infml*), outcry, furore, hue and cry, uproar, pandemonium, rumpus, disturbance, commotion, hubbub.
F3 calm, peace.

hum v buzz, whirr, purr, drone, thrum, croon, sing, murmur, mumble, throb, pulse, vibrate.
n buzz, whirr, purring, drone, murmur, mumble, throb, pulsation, vibration.

human adj 1 MORTAL, fallible, susceptible, reasonable, rational.
2 KIND, considerate, understanding, humane, compassionate.
F3 2 inhuman.
n human being, mortal, homo sapiens, man, woman, child, person, individual, body, soul.

humane adj kind, compassionate, sympathetic, understanding, kind-hearted, good-natured, gentle, tender, loving, mild, lenient, merciful, forgiving, forbearing, kindly, benevolent, charitable, humanitarian, good.
F3 inhumane, cruel.

humanitarian adj benevolent, charitable, philanthropic, public-spirited, compassionate, humane, altruistic, unselfish.
F3 selfish, self-seeking.
n philanthropist, benefactor, good Samaritan, do-gooder, altruist.
F3 egoist, self-seeker.

humanity n 1 HUMAN RACE, humankind, mankind, womankind, mortality, people. 2 HUMANENESS, kindness, compassion, fellow-feeling, understanding, tenderness, benevolence, generosity, goodwill.
F3 2 inhumanity.

humanize v domesticate, tame, civilize, cultivate, educate, enlighten, edify, improve, better, polish, refine.

humble adj 1 MEEK, submissive, unassertive, self-effacing, polite, respectful, deferential, servile, subservient, sycophantic,

obsequious. 2 LOWLY, low, mean, insignificant, unimportant, common, commonplace, ordinary, plain, simple, modest, unassuming, unpretentious, unostentatious.
F3 1 proud, assertive. 2 important, pretentious.
v bring down, lower, bring low, abase, demean, sink, discredit, disgrace, shame, humiliate, mortify, chasten, crush, deflate, subdue.
F3 exalt.

humbug n 1 DECEPTION, pretence, sham, fraud, swindle, trick, hoax, deceit, trickery. 2 NONSENSE, rubbish, baloney (sl), bunkum (infml), claptrap (infml), eye-wash (infml), bluff, cant, hypocrisy.

humdrum adj boring, tedious, monotonous, routine, dull, dreary, uninteresting, uneventful, ordinary, mundane, everyday, commonplace.
F3 lively, unusual, exceptional.

humid adj damp, moist, dank, clammy, sticky, muggy, sultry, steamy.
F3 dry.

humiliate v mortify, embarrass, confound, crush, break, deflate, chasten, shame, disgrace, discredit, degrade, demean, humble, bring low.
F3 dignify, exalt.

humiliation n mortification, embarrassment, shame, disgrace, dishonour, ignominy, abasement, deflation, put-down, snub, rebuff, affront.
F3 gratification, triumph.

humility n meekness, submissiveness, deference, self-abasement, servility, humbleness, lowliness, modesty, unpretentiousness.
F3 pride, arrogance, assertiveness.

humorist n wit, satirist, comedian, comic, joker, wag, jester, clown.

humorous adj funny, amusing, comic, entertaining, witty, satirical, jocular, facetious, playful, waggish, droll, whimsical, comical, farcical, zany (infml) ludicrous, absurd, hilarious, side-splitting.
Fa serious, humourless.

humour n **1** WIT, drollery, jokes, jesting, badinage, repartee, facetiousness, satire, comedy, farce, fun, amusement. **2** in a bad humour: mood, temper, frame of mind, spirits, disposition, temperament.
v go along with, comply with, accommodate, gratify, indulge, pamper, spoil, favour, please, mollify, flatter.

humourless adj boring, tedious, dull, dry, solemn, serious, glum, morose.
Fa humorous, witty.

hump n hunch, lump, knob, bump, projection, protuberance, bulge, swelling, mound, prominence.

hunch n premonition, presentiment, intuition, suspicion, feeling, impression, idea, guess.
v hump, bend, curve, arch, stoop, crouch, squat, huddle, draw in, curl up.

hunger n **1** HUNGRINESS, emptiness, starvation, malnutrition, famine, appetite, ravenousness, voracity, greed, greediness. **2** hunger for power: desire, craving, longing, yearning, itch, thirst.
v starve, want, wish, desire, crave, hanker, long, yearn, pine, ache, itch, thirst.

hungry adj **1** STARVING, underfed, undernourished, peckish (infml),

empty, hollow, famished, ravenous, greedy. **2** hungry for knowledge: desirous, craving, longing, aching, thirsty, eager, avid.
Fa 1 satisfied, full.

hunk n chunk, lump, piece, block, slab, wedge, mass, clod.

hunt v **1** CHASE, pursue, hound, dog, stalk, track, trail. **2** SEEK, look for, search, scour, rummage, forage, investigate.
n chase, pursuit, search, quest, investigation.

hurdle n jump, fence, wall, hedge, barrier, barricade, obstacle, obstruction, stumbling-block, hindrance, impediment, handicap, problem, snag, difficulty, complication.

hurl v throw, toss, fling, sling, catapult, project, propel, fire, launch, send.

hurricane n gale, tornado, typhoon, cyclone, whirlwind, squall, storm, tempest.

hurried adj rushed, hectic, hasty, precipitate, speedy, quick, swift, rapid, passing, brief, short, cursory, superficial, shallow, careless, slapdash.
Fa leisurely.

hurry v rush, dash, fly, get a move on (infml), hasten, quicken, speed up, hustle, push.
Fa slow down, delay.
n rush, haste, quickness, speed, urgency, hustle, bustle, flurry, commotion.
Fa leisureliness, calm.

hurt v **1** my leg hurts: ache, pain, throb, sting. **2** INJURE, wound, maltreat, ill-treat, bruise, cut, burn, torture, maim, disable. **3** DAMAGE, impair, harm, mar, spoil. **4** UPSET, sadden, grieve, distress, afflict, offend, annoy.

n pain, soreness, discomfort, suffering, injury, wound, damage, harm, distress, sorrow.

adj **1** INJURED, wounded, bruised, grazed, cut, scarred, maimed.

2 UPSET, sad, saddened, distressed, aggrieved, annoyed, offended, affronted.

hurtful *adj* **1** UPSETTING, wounding, vicious, cruel, mean, unkind, nasty, malicious, spiteful, catty, derogatory, scathing, cutting. **2** HARMFUL, damaging, injurious, pernicious, destructive.

E3 1 kind.

hurtle *v* dash, tear, race, fly, shoot, speed, rush, charge, plunge, dive, crash, rattle.

husband *n* spouse, partner, mate, better half, hubby (*infml*), groom, married man.

hush *v* quieten, silence, shush, still, settle, compose, calm, soothe, subdue.

E3 disturb, rouse.

n quietness, silence, peace, stillness, repose, calm, calmness, tranquillity, serenity.

E3 noise, clamour.

interj quiet, hold your tongue, shut up, not another word.

hush up keep dark, suppress, conceal, cover up, stifle, gag.

E3 publicize.

hush-hush *adj* secret, confidential, classified, restricted, under wraps (*infml*), top-secret.

E3 open, public.

husk *n* covering, case, shell, pod, hull, rind, bran, chaff.

husky *adj* hoarse, croaky, croaking, low, throaty, guttural, gruff, rasping, rough, harsh.

hustle *v* hasten, rush, hurry, bustle, force, push, shove, thrust, bundle, elbow, jostle.

hut *n* cabin, shack, shanty, booth, shed, lean-to, shelter, den.

hybrid *n* cross, crossbreed, half-breed, mongrel, composite, combination, mixture, amalgam, compound.

adj crossbred, mongrel, composite, combined, mixed, heterogeneous, compound.

E3 pure-bred.

hygiene *n* sanitariness, sanitation, sterility, disinfection, cleanliness, purity, wholesomeness.

E3 insanitariness.

hygienic *adj* sanitary, sterile, aseptic, germ-free, disinfected, clean, pure, salubrious, healthy, wholesome.

E3 unhygienic, insanitary.

hyperbole *n* overstatement, exaggeration, magnification, extravagance.

E3 understatement.

hypnotic *adj* mesmerizing, soporific, sleep-inducing, spellbinding, fascinating, compelling, irresistible, magnetic.

hypnotism *n* hypnosis, mesmerism, suggestion.

hypnotize *v* mesmerize, spellbind, bewitch, enchant, entrance, fascinate, captivate, magnetize.

hypocrisy *n* insincerity, double-talk, double-dealing, falsity, deceit, deception, pretence.

E3 sincerity.

hypocritical *adj* insincere, two-faced, self-righteous, double-dealing, false, hollow, deceptive, spurious, deceitful, dissembling, pharisaic(al). �림 sincere, genuine.

hypothesis *n* theory, thesis, premise, postulate, proposition, supposition, conjecture, speculation.

hypothetical *adj* theoretical, imaginary, supposed, assumed, proposed, conjectural, speculative. ✚ real, actual.

hysteria *n* agitation, frenzy, panic, hysterics, neurosis, mania, madness. ✚ calm, composure.

hysterical *adj* **1** FRANTIC, frenzied, berserk, uncontrollable, mad, raving, crazed, demented, overwrought, neurotic, hyper (*infml*). **2** (*infml*) HILARIOUS, uproarious, side-splitting, priceless (*infml*), rich (*infml*). ✚ **1** calm, composed, self-possessed.

I

ice n frost, rime, icicle, glacier, iciness, frostiness, coldness, chill. v freeze, refrigerate, chill, cool, frost.

icon n idol, portrait, image, representation, symbol.

icy adj **1** ICE-COLD, arctic, polar, glacial, freezing, frozen, raw, bitter, biting, cold, chill, chilly. **2** *icy roads*: frosty, slippery, glassy, frozen, icebound, frostbound. **3** HOSTILE, cold, stony, cool, indifferent, aloof, distant, formal.

F3 1 hot. **3** friendly, warm.

idea n **1** THOUGHT, concept, notion, theory, hypothesis, guess, conjecture, belief, opinion, view, viewpoint, judgement, conception, vision, image, impression, perception, interpretation, understanding, inkling, suspicion, clue. **2** *a good idea*: brainwave, suggestion, proposal, proposition, recommendation, plan, scheme, design. **3** AIM, intention, purpose, reason, point, object.

ideal n perfection, epitome, acme, paragon, exemplar, example, model, pattern, archetype, prototype, type, image, criterion, standard. adj **1** PERFECT, dream, utopian, best, optimum, optimal, supreme, highest, model, archetypal. **2** UNREAL, imaginary, theoretical, hypothetical, unattainable, impractical, idealistic.

idealist n perfectionist, romantic, visionary, dreamer, optimist.

F3 realist, pragmatist.

idealistic adj perfectionist, utopian, visionary, romantic, quixotic, starry-eyed, optimistic, unrealistic, impractical, impracticable.

F3 realistic, pragmatic.

idealize v utopianize, romanticize, glamorize, glorify, exalt, worship, idolize.

F3 caricature.

identical adj same, self-same, indistinguishable, interchangeable, twin, duplicate, like, alike, corresponding, matching, equal, equivalent.

F3 different.

identification n **1** RECOGNITION, detection, diagnosis, naming, labelling, classification. **2** EMPATHY, association, involvement, rapport, relationship, sympathy, fellow-feeling. **3** IDENTITY CARD, documents, papers, credentials.

identify v recognize, know, pick out, single out, distinguish, perceive, make out, discern, notice, detect, diagnose, name, label, tag, specify, pinpoint, place, catalogue, classify.

identify with empathize with, relate to, associate with, respond to, sympathize with, feel for.

identity n **1** INDIVIDUALITY, particularity, singularity, uniqueness, self, personality, character, existence. **2** SAMENESS, likeness.

ideology n philosophy, world-view, ideas, principles, tenets, doctrine(s), convictions, belief(s), faith, creed, dogma.

idiocy n folly, stupidity, silliness, senselessness, lunacy.
E3 wisdom, sanity.

idiom n phrase, expression, colloquialism, language, turn of phrase, phraseology, style, usage, jargon, vernacular.

idiosyncrasy n characteristic, peculiarity, singularity, oddity, eccentricity, freak, quirk, habit, mannerism, trait, feature.

idiosyncratic adj personal, individual, characteristic, distinctive, peculiar, strange, odd, eccentric, quirky.
E3 general, common.

idiot n fool, blockhead, ass (infml), nitwit (infml), dimwit, halfwit, imbecile, moron, cretin, simpleton, dunce, ignoramus.

idiotic adj foolish, stupid, silly, absurd, senseless, daft (infml), lunatic, insane, foolhardy, harebrained, halfwitted, moronic, cretinous, crazy.
E3 sensible, sane.

idle adj **1** INACTIVE, inoperative, unused, unoccupied, unemployed, jobless, redundant. **2** LAZY, work-shy, indolent. **3** idle talk: empty, trivial, casual, futile, vain, pointless, unproductive.
E3 1 active. **2** busy.
v do nothing, laze, lounge, take it easy, kill time, potter, loiter, dawdle, fritter, waste, loaf, slack, skive (infml).
E3 work.

idol n icon, effigy, image, graven image, god, deity, fetish, favourite, darling, hero, heroine, pin-up.

idolize v hero-worship, lionize, exalt, glorify, worship, venerate, revere, admire, adore, love, dote on.
E3 despise.

idyllic adj perfect, idealized, heavenly, delightful, charming, picturesque, pastoral, rustic, unspoiled, peaceful, happy.
E3 unpleasant.

ignite v set fire to, set alight, catch fire, flare up, burn, conflagrate, fire, kindle, touch off, spark off.
E3 quench.

ignoble adj low, mean, petty, base, vulgar, wretched, contemptible, despicable, vile, heinous, infamous, disgraceful, dishonourable, shameless.
E3 noble, worthy, honourable.

ignominious adj humiliating, mortifying, degrading, undignified, shameful, dishonourable, disreputable, disgraceful, despicable, scandalous.
E3 triumphant, honourable.

ignorance n unintelligence, illiteracy, unawareness, unconsciousness, oblivion, unfamiliarity, inexperience, innocence, naiveté.
E3 knowledge, wisdom.

ignorant adj uneducated, illiterate, unread, untaught, untrained, inexperienced, stupid, clueless (infml), uninitiated, unenlightened, uninformed, ill-informed, unwitting, unaware, unconscious, oblivious.
E3 educated, knowledgeable, clever, wise.

ignore *v* disregard, take no notice of, shut one's eyes to, overlook, pass over, neglect, omit, reject, snub, cold-shoulder.
₣₃ notice, observe.

ill *adj* **1** SICK, poorly, unwell, indisposed, laid up, ailing, off-colour, out of sorts (*infml*), under the weather (*infml*), seedy, queasy, diseased, unhealthy, infirm, frail. **2** *an ill omen*: bad, evil, damaging, harmful, injurious, detrimental, adverse, unfavourable, inauspicious, unpromising, sinister, ominous, threatening, unlucky, unfortunate, difficult, harsh, severe, unkind, unfriendly, antagonistic.
₣₃ 1 well. **2** good, favourable, fortunate.

ill-advised *adj* imprudent, injudicious, unwise, foolish, ill-considered, thoughtless, hasty, rash, short-sighted, misguided, inappropriate.
₣₃ wise, sensible, well-advised.

ill-bred *adj* bad-mannered, ill-mannered, discourteous, impolite, rude, coarse, indelicate.
₣₃ well-bred, polite.

illegal *adj* unlawful, illicit, criminal, wrong, forbidden, prohibited, banned, outlawed, unauthorized, under-the-counter, black-market, unconstitutional, wrongful.
₣₃ legal, lawful.

illegible *adj* unreadable, indecipherable, scrawled, obscure, faint, indistinct.
₣₃ legible.

illegitimate *adj* **1** *an illegitimate child*: natural, bastard, born out of wedlock (*fml*). **2** ILLEGAL, unlawful, illicit, unauthorized, unwarranted,

improper, incorrect, inadmissible, spurious, invalid, unsound.
₣₃ 1 legitimate. **2** legal.

ill-fated *adj* doomed, ill-starred, ill-omened, unfortunate, unlucky, luckless, unhappy.
₣₃ lucky.

illicit *adj* illegal, unlawful, criminal, wrong, illegitimate, improper, forbidden, prohibited, unauthorized, unlicensed, black-market, contraband, ill-gotten, under-the-counter, furtive, clandestine.
₣₃ legal, permissible.

illness *n* disease, disorder, complaint, ailment, sickness, ill health, ill-being, indisposition, infirmity, disability, affliction.

illogical *adj* irrational, unreasonable, unscientific, invalid, unsound, faulty, fallacious, specious, sophistical, inconsistent, senseless, meaningless, absurd.
₣₃ logical.

ill-treat *v* maltreat, abuse, injure, harm, damage, neglect, mistreat, mishandle, misuse, wrong, oppress.

illuminate *v* **1** LIGHT, light up, brighten, decorate. **2** ENLIGHTEN, edify, instruct, elucidate, illustrate, explain, clarify, clear up.
₣₃ 1 darken. **2** mystify.

illumination *n* light, lights, lighting, beam, ray, brightness, radiance, decoration, ornamentation.
₣₃ darkness.

illusion *n* apparition, mirage, hallucination, figment, fantasy, fancy, delusion, misapprehension, misconception, error, fallacy.
₣₃ reality, truth.

illusory *adj* illusive, deceptive, misleading, apparent, seeming,

deluding, delusive, unreal, unsubstantial, sham, false, fallacious, untrue, mistaken.
F3 real.

illustrate *v* draw, sketch, depict, picture, show, exhibit, demonstrate, exemplify, explain, interpret, clarify, elucidate, illuminate, decorate, ornament, adorn.

illustration *n* **1** PICTURE, plate, half-tone, photograph, drawing, sketch, figure, representation, decoration. **2** EXAMPLE, specimen, instance, case, analogy, demonstration, explanation, interpretation.

illustrious *adj* great, noble, eminent, distinguished, celebrated, famous, famed, renowned, noted, prominent, outstanding, remarkable, notable, brilliant, excellent, splendid, magnificent, glorious, exalted.
F3 ignoble, inglorious.

ill-will *n* hostility, antagonism, bad blood, enmity, unfriendliness, malevolence, malice, spite, animosity, ill-feeling, resentment, hard feelings, grudge, dislike, aversion, hatred.
F3 goodwill, friendship.

image *n* **1** IDEA, notion, concept, impression, perception. **2** REPRESENTATION, likeness, picture, portrait, icon, effigy, figure, statue, idol, replica, reflection.

imaginable *adj* conceivable, thinkable, believable, credible, plausible, likely, possible.
F3 unimaginable.

imaginary *adj* imagined, fanciful, illusory, hallucinatory, visionary, pretend, make-believe, unreal, non-existent, fictional, fabulous, legendary, mythological, made-up, invented, fictitious,

assumed, supposed, hypothetical.
F3 real.

imagination *n* imaginativeness, creativity, inventiveness, originality, inspiration, insight, ingenuity, resourcefulness, enterprise, wit, vision, mind's eye, fancy, illusion.
F3 unimaginativeness, reality.

imaginative *adj* creative, inventive, innovative, original, inspired, visionary, ingenious, clever, resourceful, enterprising, fanciful, fantastic, vivid.
F3 unimaginative.

imagine *v* **1** PICTURE, visualize, envisage, conceive, fancy, fantasize, pretend, make believe, conjure up, dream up, think up, invent, devise, create, plan, project. **2** *I imagine so:* think, believe, judge, suppose, guess, conjecture, assume, take it, gather.

imbalance *n* unevenness, inequality, disparity, disproportion, unfairness, partiality, bias.
F3 balance, parity.

imbecile *n* idiot, halfwit, simpleton, moron, cretin, fool, blockhead, bungler.

imbue *v* permeate, impregnate, pervade, suffuse, fill, saturate, steep, inculcate, instil, tinge, tint.

imitate *v* copy, emulate, follow, ape, mimic, impersonate, take off, caricature, parody, send up, spoof, mock, parrot, repeat, echo, mirror, duplicate, reproduce, simulate, counterfeit, forge.

imitation *n* **1** MIMICRY, impersonation, impression, take-off, caricature, parody, send-up, spoof, mockery, travesty. **2** COPY, duplicate, reproduction, replica, simulation, counterfeit, fake, forgery, sham,

likeness, resemblance, reflection, dummy.
adj artificial, synthetic, man-made, ersatz, fake, phoney (*infml*), mock, pseudo, reproduction, simulated, sham, dummy.
F3 genuine.

imitative adj copying, mimicking, parrot-like, unoriginal, derivative, plagiarized, second-hand, simulated, mock.

imitator n mimic, impersonator, impressionist, parrot, copycat (*infml*), copier, emulator, follower.

immaculate adj perfect, unblemished, flawless, faultless, impeccable, spotless, clean, spick and span, pure, unsullied, undefiled, untainted, stainless, blameless, innocent.
F3 blemished, stained, contaminated.

immaterial adj irrelevant, insignificant, unimportant, minor, trivial, trifling, inconsequential.
F3 relevant, important.

immature adj young, under-age, adolescent, juvenile, childish, puerile, infantile, babyish, raw, crude, callow, inexperienced, green, unripe, undeveloped.
F3 mature.

immeasurable adj vast, immense, infinite, limitless, unlimited, boundless, unbounded, endless, bottomless, inexhaustible, incalculable, inestimable.
F3 limited.

immediate adj **1** INSTANT, instantaneous, direct, prompt, swift, current, present, existing, urgent, pressing. **2** NEAREST, next, adjacent, near, close, recent.
F3 **1** delayed. **2** distant.

immediately adv now, straight away, right away, at once, instantly, directly, forthwith, without delay, promptly, unhesitatingly.
F3 eventually, never.

immense adj vast, great, huge, enormous, massive, giant, gigantic, tremendous, monumental.
F3 tiny, minute.

immensity n magnitude, bulk, expanse, vastness, greatness, hugeness, enormousness, massiveness.
F3 minuteness.

immerse v plunge, submerge, submerse, sink, duck, dip, douse, bathe.

immigrant n incomer, settler, newcomer, alien.
F3 emigrant.

imminent adj impending, forthcoming, in the offing, approaching, coming, near, close, looming, menacing, threatening, brewing, in the air.
F3 remote, far-off.

immobile adj stationary, motionless, unmoving, still, stock-still, static, immovable, rooted, fixed, frozen, rigid, stiff.
F3 mobile, moving.

immobilize v stop, halt, fix, freeze, transfix, paralyse, cripple, disable.
F3 mobilize.

immodest adj indecent, revealing, shameless, forward, improper, immoral, obscene, lewd, coarse, risqué.

immoral adj unethical, wrong, bad, sinful, evil, wicked, unscrupulous, unprincipled, dishonest, corrupt, depraved, degenerate, dissolute, lewd, indecent, pornographic, obscene, impure.

FI moral, right, good.

immortal adj undying, imperishable, eternal, everlasting, perpetual, endless, ceaseless, lasting, enduring, abiding, timeless, ageless.

FI mortal.

immortalize v celebrate, commemorate, memorialize, perpetuate, enshrine.

immovable adj fixed, rooted, immobile, stuck, fast, secure, stable, constant, firm, set, determined, resolute, adamant, unshakable, obstinate, unyielding.

FI movable.

immune adj invulnerable, insusceptible, resistant, proof, protected, safe, exempt, free, clear.

FI susceptible.

immunity n resistance, protection, exemption, indemnity, impunity, exoneration, freedom, liberty, licence, franchise, privilege, right.

FI susceptibility.

immunize v vaccinate, inoculate, inject, protect, safeguard.

impact n 1 the impact of the reforms: effect, consequences, repercussions, impression, power, influence, significance, meaning. 2 COLLISION, crash, smash, bang, bump, blow, knock, contact, jolt, shock, brunt.

impair v damage, harm, injure, hinder, mar, spoil, worsen, undermine, weaken, reduce, lessen, diminish, blunt.

FI improve, enhance.

impale v pierce, puncture, perforate, run through, spear, lance, spike, skewer, spit, stick, transfix.

impart v tell, relate, communicate, make known, disclose, divulge, reveal, convey, pass on, give, grant, confer, offer, contribute, lend.

FI withhold.

impartial adj objective, dispassionate, detached, disinterested, neutral, non-partisan, unbiased, unprejudiced, open-minded, fair, just, equitable, even-handed, equal.

FI biased, prejudiced.

impasse n deadlock, stalemate, dead end, cul-de-sac, blind alley, halt, standstill.

impassive adj expressionless, calm, composed, unruffled, unconcerned, cool, unfeeling, unemotional, unmoved, imperturbable, unexcitable, stoical, indifferent, dispassionate.

FI responsive, moved.

impatience n eagerness, keenness, restlessness, agitation, anxiety, nervousness, irritability, intolerance, shortness, brusqueness, haste, rashness.

FI patience.

impatient adj eager, keen, restless, fidgety, fretful, edgy, irritable, snappy, hot-tempered, quick-tempered, intolerant, brusque, abrupt, impetuous, hasty, precipitate, headlong.

FI patient.

impeach v accuse, charge, indict, arraign, denounce, impugn, disparage, criticize, censure, blame.

impeccable adj perfect, faultless, precise, exact, flawless, unblemished, stainless, immaculate, pure, irreproachable, blameless, innocent.

FI faulty, flawed, corrupt.

impede v hinder, hamper, obstruct, block, clog, slow, retard, hold up,

delay, check, curb, restrain, thwart, disrupt, stop, bar.
≠ aid, promote, further.

impediment *n* hindrance, obstacle, obstruction, barrier, bar, block, stumbling-block, snag, difficulty, handicap, check, curb, restraint, restriction.
≠ aid.

impel *v* urge, force, oblige, compel, constrain, drive, propel, push, spur, goad, prompt, motivate, stimulate, excite, instigate, motivate, inspire, move.
≠ deter, dissuade.

impending *adj* imminent, forthcoming, approaching, coming, close, near, looming, menacing, threatening.
≠ remote.

impenetrable *adj* **1** *impenetrable jungle*: solid, thick, dense, impassable. **2** UNINTELLIGIBLE, incomprehensible, unfathomable, baffling, mysterious, cryptic, enigmatic, obscure, dark, inscrutable.
≠ 2 accessible, understandable.

imperative *adj* compulsory, obligatory, essential, vital, crucial, pressing, urgent.
≠ optional, unimportant.

imperceptible *adj* inappreciable, indiscernible, inaudible, faint, slight, negligible, infinitesimal, microscopic, minute, tiny, small, fine, subtle, gradual.
≠ perceptible.

imperfect *adj* faulty, flawed, defective, damaged, broken, chipped, deficient, incomplete.
≠ perfect.

imperfection *n* fault, flaw, defect, blemish, deficiency, shortcoming, weakness, failing.
≠ perfection.

imperial *adj* sovereign, supreme, royal, regal, majestic, grand, magnificent, great, noble.

imperil *v* endanger, jeopardize, risk, hazard, expose, compromise, threaten.

imperious *adj* overbearing, domineering, autocratic, despotic, tyrannical, dictatorial, high-handed, commanding, arrogant, haughty.
≠ humble.

impersonal *adj* formal, official, businesslike, bureaucratic, faceless, aloof, remote, distant, detached, neutral, objective, dispassionate, cold, frosty, glassy.
≠ informal, friendly.

impersonate *v* imitate, mimic, take off, parody, caricature, mock, masquerade as, pose as, act, portray.

impertinence *n* rudeness, impoliteness, disrespect, insolence, impudence, cheek (*infml*), brass (*sl*), effrontery, nerve (*infml*), audacity, boldness, brazenness, forwardness, presumption.
≠ politeness, respect.

impertinent *adj* rude, impolite, ill-mannered, discourteous, disrespectful, insolent, impudent, cheeky (*infml*), saucy (*infml*), pert, bold, brazen, forward, presumptuous, fresh.
≠ polite, respectful.

imperturbable *adj* unexcitable, unflappable (*infml*), calm, tranquil, composed, collected, self-possessed, cool, unmoved, unruffled.

impervious *adj* **1** IMPERMEABLE, waterproof, damp-proof, watertight, hermetic, closed, sealed, impenetrable. **2** *impervious to criticism*: immune, invulnerable, untouched, unaffected, unmoved, resistant.

F3 1 porous, pervious. **2** responsive, vulnerable.

impetuous adj impulsive, spontaneous, unplanned, unpremeditated, hasty, precipitate, rash, reckless, thoughtless, unthinking.

F3 cautious, wary, circumspect.

impetus n impulse, momentum, force, energy, power, drive, boost, push, spur, stimulus, incentive, motivation.

impinge v hit, touch (on), affect, influence, encroach, infringe, intrude, trespass, invade.

implacable adj inexorable, relentless, remorseless, merciless, pitiless, cruel, ruthless, intransigent, inflexible.

F3 compassionate.

implant v graft, engraft, embed, sow, plant, fix, root, insert, instil, inculcate.

implausible adj improbable, unlikely, far-fetched, dubious, suspect, unconvincing, weak, flimsy, thin, transparent.

F3 plausible, likely, reasonable.

implement n tool, instrument, utensil, gadget, device, apparatus, appliance.

v enforce, effect, bring about, carry out, execute, discharge, perform, do, fulfil, complete, accomplish, realize.

implicate v involve, embroil, entangle, incriminate, compromise, include, concern, connect, associate.

F3 exonerate.

implication n **1** INFERENCE, insinuation, suggestion, meaning, significance, ramification, repercussion. **2** INVOLVEMENT,

entanglement, incrimination, connection, association.

implicit adj **1** IMPLIED, inferred, insinuated, indirect, unsaid, unspoken, tacit, understood. **2** implicit belief: unquestioning, utter, total, full, complete, absolute, unqualified, unreserved, wholehearted.

F3 1 explicit. **2** half-hearted.

imply v suggest, insinuate, hint, intimate, mean, signify, point to, indicate, involve, require.

F3 state.

impolite adj rude, discourteous, bad-mannered, ill-mannered, ill-bred, disrespectful, insolent, rough, coarse, vulgar, abrupt.

F3 polite, courteous.

importance n momentousness, significance, consequence, substance, matter, concern, interest, usefulness, value, worth, weight, influence, mark, prominence, eminence, distinction, esteem, prestige, status, standing.

F3 unimportance.

important adj **1** MOMENTOUS, noteworthy, significant, meaningful, relevant, material, salient, urgent, vital, essential, key, primary, major, substantial, valuable, seminal, weighty, serious, grave, far-reaching. **2** LEADING, foremost, high-level, high-ranking, influential, powerful, pre-eminent, prominent, outstanding, eminent, noted.

F3 1 unimportant, insignificant, trivial.

impose v **1** INTRODUCE, institute, enforce, promulgate, exact, levy, set, fix, put, place, lay, inflict, burden, encumber, saddle. **2** INTRUDE, butt in,

encroach, trespass, obtrude, force oneself, presume, take liberties.

imposing *adj* impressive, striking, grand, stately, majestic, dignified.
F∃ unimposing, modest.

imposition *n* **1** INTRODUCTION, infliction, exaction, levying.
2 INTRUSION, encroachment, liberty, burden, constraint, charge, duty, task, punishment.

impossible *adj* hopeless, impracticable, unworkable, unattainable, unachievable, unobtainable, insoluble, unreasonable, unacceptable, inconceivable, unthinkable, preposterous, absurd, ludicrous, ridiculous.
F∃ possible.

impostor *n* fraud, fake, phoney (*infml*), quack, charlatan, impersonator, pretender, con man (*infml*), swindler, cheat, rogue.

impotent *adj* powerless, helpless, unable, incapable, ineffective, incompetent, inadequate, weak, feeble, frail, infirm, disabled, incapacitated, paralysed.
F∃ potent, strong.

impoverished *adj* poor, needy, impecunious, poverty-stricken, destitute, bankrupt, ruined.
F∃ rich.

impracticable *adj* unworkable, unfeasible, unattainable, unachievable, impossible, non-viable, useless, unserviceable, inoperable.
F∃ practicable.

impractical *adj* unrealistic, idealistic, romantic, starry-eyed, impracticable, unworkable, impossible, awkward, inconvenient.
F∃ practical, realistic, sensible.

imprecise *adj* inexact, inaccurate, approximate, estimated, rough, loose, indefinite, vague, woolly, hazy, ill-defined, sloppy, ambiguous, equivocal.
F∃ precise, exact.

impregnable *adj* impenetrable, unconquerable, invincible, unbeatable, unassailable, indestructible, fortified, strong, solid, secure, safe, invulnerable.
F∃ vulnerable.

impregnate *v* **1** SOAK, steep, saturate, fill, permeate, pervade, suffuse, imbue. **2** INSEMINATE, fertilize.

impress *v* **1** *I'm not impressed*: strike, move, touch, affect, influence, stir, inspire, excite, grab (*sl*). **2** STAMP, imprint, mark, indent, instil, inculcate.

impression *n* **1** FEELING, awareness, consciousness, sense, illusion, idea, notion, opinion, belief, conviction, suspicion, hunch, memory, recollection. **2** STAMP, mark, print, dent, outline. **3** IMPERSONATION, imitation, take-off, parody, send-up. **4** *make a good impression*: effect, impact, influence.

impressionable *adj* naive, gullible, susceptible, vulnerable, sensitive, responsive, open, receptive.

impressive *adj* striking, imposing, grand, powerful, effective, stirring, exciting, moving, touching.
F∃ unimpressive, uninspiring.

imprint *n* print, mark, stamp, impression, sign, logo.
v print, mark, brand, stamp, impress, engrave, etch.

imprison *v* jail, incarcerate, intern, detain, send down (*infml*), put away

(*infml*), lock up, cage, confine, shut in.
F3 release, free.

imprisonment *n* incarceration, internment, detention, custody, confinement.

F3 freedom, liberty.

improbable *adj* uncertain, questionable, doubtful, unlikely, dubious, implausible, unconvincing, far-fetched, preposterous, unbelievable, incredible.

F3 probable, likely, convincing.

impromptu *adj* improvised, extempore, ad-lib, off the cuff, unscripted, unrehearsed, unprepared, spontaneous.

F3 rehearsed.

adv extempore, ad lib, off the cuff, off the top of one's head, spontaneously, on the spur of the moment.

improper *adj* wrong, incorrect, irregular, unsuitable, inappropriate, inopportune, incongruous, out of place, indecent, rude, vulgar, unseemly, unbecoming, shocking.

F3 proper, appropriate, decent.

improve *v* better, ameliorate, enhance, polish, touch up, mend, rectify, correct, amend, reform, upgrade, increase, pick up, develop, look up, advance, progress, get better, recover, recuperate, rally, perk up, mend one's ways, turn over a new leaf.

F3 worsen, deteriorate, decline.

improvement *n* betterment, amelioration, enhancement, rectification, correction, amendment, reformation, increase, rise, upswing, gain, development, advance, progress, furtherance, recovery, rally.

F3 deterioration, decline.

improvise *v* 1 CONTRIVE, devise, concoct, invent, throw together, make do. 2 EXTEMPORIZE, ad-lib, play by ear, vamp.

imprudent *adj* unwise, ill-advised, foolish, short-sighted, rash, reckless, hasty, irresponsible, careless, heedless, impolitic, indiscreet.

F3 prudent, wise, cautious.

impudence *n* impertinence, cheek (*infml*), effrontery, nerve (*infml*), face (*infml*), boldness, insolence, rudeness, presumption.

F3 politeness.

impudent *adj* impertinent, cheeky (*infml*), saucy (*infml*), bold, forward, shameless, cocky, insolent, rude, presumptuous, fresh.

F3 polite.

impulse *n* 1 URGE, wish, desire, inclination, whim, notion, instinct, feeling, passion. 2 IMPETUS, momentum, force, pressure, drive, thrust, push, incitement, stimulus, motive.

impulsive *adj* impetuous, rash, reckless, hasty, quick, spontaneous, automatic, instinctive, intuitive.

F3 cautious, premeditated.

impure *adj* 1 UNREFINED, adulterated, diluted, contaminated, polluted, tainted, infected, corrupt, debased, unclean, dirty, foul. 2 OBSCENE, indecent, immodest.

F3 1 pure. 2 chaste, decent.

impurity *n* adulteration, contamination, pollution, infection, corruption, dirtiness, contaminant, dirt, filth, foreign body, mark, spot.

F3 purity.

inability *n* incapability, incapacity, powerlessness, impotence, inadequacy, weakness, handicap, disability.

F3 ability.

inaccessible *adj* isolated, remote, unfrequented, unapproachable, unreachable, unget-at-able (*infml*), unattainable.

F3 accessible.

inaccuracy *n* mistake, error, miscalculation, slip, blunder, fault, defect, imprecision, inexactness, unreliability.

F3 accuracy, precision.

inaccurate *adj* incorrect, wrong, erroneous, mistaken, faulty, flawed, defective, imprecise, inexact, loose, unreliable, unfaithful, untrue.

F3 accurate, correct.

inaction *n* inactivity, immobility, inertia, rest, idleness, lethargy, torpor, stagnation.

F3 action.

inactive *adj* immobile, inert, idle, unused, inoperative, dormant, passive, sedentary, lazy, lethargic, sluggish, torpid, sleepy.

F3 active, working, busy.

inadequacy *n* **1** INSUFFICIENCY, lack, shortage, dearth, want, deficiency, scantiness, meagreness, defectiveness, ineffectiveness, inability, incompetence. **2** *the inadequacies of the system*: fault, defect, imperfection, weakness, failing, shortcoming.

F3 1 adequacy.

inadequate *adj* **1** INSUFFICIENT, short, wanting, deficient, scanty, sparse, meagre, niggardly. **2** INCOMPETENT, incapable, unequal, unqualified, ineffective, faulty, defective, imperfect, unsatisfactory.

F3 1 adequate. **2** satisfactory.

inadmissible *adj* unacceptable, irrelevant, immaterial, inappropriate, disallowed, prohibited.

F3 admissible.

inadvertent *adj* accidental, chance, unintentional, unintended, unplanned, unpremeditated, careless.

F3 deliberate, conscious, careful.

inadvisable *adj* unwise, imprudent, injudicious, foolish, silly, ill-advised, misguided, indiscreet.

F3 advisable, wise.

inane *adj* senseless, foolish, stupid, unintelligent, silly, idiotic, fatuous, frivolous, trifling, puerile, mindless, vapid, empty, vacuous, vain, worthless, futile.

F3 sensible.

inanimate *adj* lifeless, dead, defunct, extinct, unconscious, inactive, inert, dormant, immobile, stagnant, spiritless, dull.

F3 animate, living, alive.

inappropriate *adj* unsuitable, inapt, ill-suited, ill-fitted, irrelevant, incongruous, out of place, untimely, ill-timed, tactless, improper, unseemly, unbecoming, unfitting.

F3 appropriate, suitable.

inarticulate *adj* incoherent, unintelligible, incomprehensible, unclear, indistinct, hesitant, faltering, halting, tongue-tied, speechless, dumb.

F3 articulate.

inattention *n* carelessness, negligence, disregard, absent-mindedness, forgetfulness, daydreaming, preoccupation.

inattentive *adj* distracted, dreamy, daydreaming, preoccupied, absent-minded, unmindful, heedless, regardless, careless, negligent.

F3 attentive.

inaudible *adj* silent, noiseless, imperceptible, faint, indistinct, muffled, muted, low, mumbled. ⊟ audible, loud.

inaugural *adj* opening, introductory, first, initial.

inaugurate *v* institute, originate, begin, commence, start, set up, open, launch, introduce, usher in, initiate, induct, ordain, invest, install, commission, dedicate, consecrate.

inauspicious *adj* unfavourable, bad, unlucky, unfortunate, unpromising, discouraging, threatening, ominous, black. ⊟ auspicious, promising.

inborn *adj* innate, inherent, natural, native, congenital, inbred, hereditary, inherited, ingrained, instinctive, intuitive. ⊟ learned.

incalculable *adj* countless, untold, inestimable, limitless, unlimited, immense, vast. ⊟ limited, restricted.

incapable *adj* unable, powerless, impotent, helpless, weak, feeble, unfit, unsuited, unqualified, incompetent, inept, inadequate, ineffective. ⊟ capable.

incapacitate *v* disable, cripple, paralyse, immobilize, disqualify, put out of action, lay up, scupper (*infml*).

incapacity *n* incapability, inability, disability, powerlessness, impotence, ineffectiveness, weakness, feebleness, inadequacy, incompetency. ⊟ capability.

incarnation *n* personification, embodiment, manifestation, impersonation.

incautious *adj* careless, imprudent, injudicious, ill-judged, unthinking, thoughtless, inconsiderate, rash, reckless, hasty, impulsive. ⊟ cautious, careful.

incense *v* anger, enrage, infuriate, madden, exasperate, irritate, rile, provoke, excite. ⊟ calm.

incentive *n* bait, lure, enticement, carrot (*infml*), sweetener (*sl*), reward, encouragement, inducement, reason, motive, impetus, spur, stimulus, motivation. ⊟ disincentive, discouragement, deterrent.

incessant *adj* ceaseless, unceasing, endless, never-ending, interminable, continual, persistent, constant, perpetual, eternal, everlasting, continuous, unbroken, unremitting, non-stop. ⊟ intermittent, sporadic, periodic, temporary.

incidence *n* frequency, commonness, prevalence, extent, range, amount, degree, rate, occurrence.

incident *n* **1** OCCURRENCE, happening, event, episode, adventure, affair, occasion, instance.
2 CONFRONTATION, clash, fight, skirmish, commotion, disturbance, scene, upset, mishap.

incidental *adj* accidental, chance, random, minor, non-essential, secondary, subordinate, subsidiary, ancillary, supplementary, accompanying, attendant, related, contributory. ⊟ important, essential.

incinerate *v* burn, cremate, reduce to ashes, torch (*infml*).

incision n cut, opening, slit, gash, notch.

incisive adj cutting, keen, sharp, acute, trenchant, piercing, penetrating, biting, caustic, acid, astute, perceptive.
F3 vague.

incite v prompt, instigate, rouse, foment, stir up, whip up, work up, excite, animate, provoke, stimulate, spur, goad, impel, drive, urge, encourage, egg on (infml).
F3 restrain.

incitement n prompting, instigation, agitation, provocation, spur, goad, impetus, stimulus, motivation, encouragement, inducement, incentive.
F3 discouragement.

inclement adj intemperate, harsh, severe, stormy, tempestuous, rough.
F3 fine.

inclination n **1** LIKING, fondness, taste, predilection, preference, partiality, bias, tendency, trend, disposition, propensity, leaning. **2** an inclination of 45 degrees: angle, slope, gradient, incline, pitch, slant, tilt, bend, bow, nod.
F3 1 disinclination, dislike.

incline v **1** DISPOSE, influence, persuade, affect, bias, prejudice. **2** LEAN, slope, slant, tilt, tip, bend, bow, tend, veer.
n slope, gradient, ramp, hill, rise, ascent, acclivity, dip, descent, declivity.

inclined adj liable, likely, given, apt, disposed of, a mind, willing.

include v comprise, incorporate, embody, comprehend, contain, enclose, embrace, encompass, cover, subsume, take in, add, allow for, take

into account, involve, rope in.
F3 exclude, omit, eliminate.

inclusion n incorporation, involvement, addition, insertion.
F3 exclusion.

inclusive adj comprehensive, full, all-in, all-inclusive, all-embracing, blanket, across-the-board, general, catch-all, overall, sweeping.
F3 exclusive, narrow.

incognito adj in disguise, disguised, masked, veiled, unmarked, unidentified, unrecognizable, unknown.
F3 undisguised.

incoherent adj unintelligible, incomprehensible, inarticulate, rambling, stammering, stuttering, unconnected, disconnected, broken, garbled, scrambled, confused, muddled, jumbled, disordered.
F3 coherent, intelligible.

income n revenue, returns, proceeds, gains, profits, interest, takings, receipts, earnings, pay, salary, wages, means.
F3 expenditure, expenses.

incoming adj arriving, entering, approaching, coming, homeward, returning, ensuing, succeeding, next, new.
F3 outgoing.

incomparable adj matchless, unmatched, unequalled, unparalleled, unrivalled, peerless, supreme, superlative, superb, brilliant.
F3 ordinary, run-of-the-mill, poor.

incompatible adj irreconcilable, contradictory, conflicting, at variance, inconsistent, clashing, mismatched, unsuited.
F3 compatible.

incompetent *adj* incapable, unable, unfit, inefficient, inexpert, unskilful, bungling, stupid, useless, ineffective. **E‡** competent, able.

incomplete *adj* deficient, lacking, short, unfinished, abridged, partial, part, fragmentary, broken, imperfect, defective.
E‡ complete, exhaustive.

incomprehensible *adj* unintelligible, impenetrable, unfathomable, above one's head, puzzling, perplexing, baffling, mysterious, inscrutable, obscure, opaque.
E‡ comprehensible, intelligible.

inconceivable *adj* unthinkable, unimaginable, mind-boggling (*infml*), staggering, unheard-of, unbelievable, incredible, implausible.
E‡ conceivable.

inconclusive *adj* unsettled, undecided, open, uncertain, indecisive, ambiguous, vague, unconvincing, unsatisfying.
E‡ conclusive.

incongruous *adj* inappropriate, unsuitable, out of place, out of keeping, inconsistent, conflicting, incompatible, irreconcilable, contradictory, contrary.
E‡ consistent, compatible.

inconsequential *adj* minor, trivial, trifling, unimportant, insignificant, immaterial.
E‡ important.

inconsiderable *adj* small, slight, negligible, trivial, petty, minor, unimportant, insignificant.
E‡ considerable, large.

inconsiderate *adj* unkind, uncaring, unconcerned, selfish, self-centred, intolerant, insensitive, tactless, rude,

thoughtless, unthinking, careless, heedless.
E‡ considerate.

inconsistent *adj* **1** CONFLICTING, at variance, at odds, incompatible, contradictory, contrary, incongruous, discordant. **2** CHANGEABLE, variable, irregular, unpredictable, varying, unstable, unsteady, inconstant, fickle.
E‡2 constant.

inconsolable *adj* heartbroken, brokenhearted, devastated, desolate, despairing, wretched.

inconspicuous *adj* hidden, concealed, camouflaged, plain, ordinary, unobtrusive, discreet, low-key, modest, unassuming, quiet, retiring, insignificant.
E‡ conspicuous, noticeable, obtrusive.

incontrovertible *adj* indisputable, unquestionable, irrefutable, undeniable, certain, clear, self-evident.
E‡ questionable, uncertain.

inconvenience *n* awkwardness, difficulty, annoyance, nuisance, hindrance, drawback, bother, trouble, fuss, upset, disturbance, disruption.
E‡ convenience.
v bother, disturb, disrupt, put out, trouble, upset, irk.

inconvenient *adj* awkward, ill-timed, untimely, inopportune, unsuitable, difficult, embarrassing, annoying, troublesome, unwieldy, unmanageable.
E‡ convenient.

incorporate *v* include, embody, contain, subsume, take in, absorb, assimilate, integrate, combine, unite, merge, blend, mix, fuse, coalesce, consolidate.
E‡ separate.

incorrect adj wrong, mistaken, erroneous, inaccurate, imprecise, inexact, false, untrue, faulty, ungrammatical, improper, illegitimate, inappropriate, unsuitable.
F∃ correct.

incorrigible adj irredeemable, incurable, inveterate, hardened, hopeless.

incorruptible adj honest, straight, upright, moral, honourable, trustworthy, unbribable, just.
F∃ corruptible.

increase v raise, boost, add to, improve, enhance, advance, step up, intensify, strengthen, heighten, grow, develop, build up, wax, enlarge, extend, prolong, expand, spread, swell, magnify, multiply, proliferate, rise, mount, soar, escalate.
F∃ decrease, reduce, decline.
n rise, surge, upsurge, upturn, gain, boost, addition, increment, advance, step-up, intensification, growth, development, enlargement, extension, expansion, spread, proliferation, escalation.
F∃ decrease, reduction, decline.

incredible adj unbelievable, improbable, implausible, far-fetched, preposterous, absurd, impossible, inconceivable, unthinkable, unimaginable, extraordinary, amazing, astonishing, astounding.
F∃ credible, believable.

incredulity n unbelief, disbelief, scepticism, doubt, distrust, mistrust.
F∃ credulity.

incredulous adj unbelieving, disbelieving, unconvinced, sceptical, doubting, distrustful, suspicious, dubious, doubtful, uncertain.
F∃ credulous.

incriminate v inculpate, implicate, involve, accuse, charge, impeach, indict, point the finger at, blame.
F∃ exonerate.

incur v suffer, sustain, provoke, arouse, bring upon oneself, expose oneself to, meet with, run up, earn.

incurable adj 1 an incurable disease: terminal, fatal, untreatable, inoperable, hopeless.
2 INCORRIGIBLE, inveterate, hardened, dyed-in-the-wool.
F∃ 1 curable.

indebted adj obliged, grateful, thankful.

indecency n immodesty, indecorum, impurity, obscenity, pornography, lewdness, vulgarity, coarseness, crudity, foulness, grossness.
F∃ decency, modesty.

indecent adj improper, immodest, impure, indelicate, offensive, obscene, pornographic, lewd, licentious, vulgar, coarse, crude, dirty, filthy, foul, gross, outrageous, shocking.
F∃ decent, modest.

indecision n indecisiveness, irresolution, vacillation, wavering, hesitation, hesitancy, ambivalence, uncertainty, doubt.
F∃ decisiveness, resolution.

indecisive adj undecided, irresolute, undetermined, vacillating, wavering, in two minds, hesitating, faltering, tentative, uncertain, unsure, doubtful, inconclusive, indefinite, indeterminate, unclear.
F∃ decisive.

indeed adv really, actually, in fact, certainly, positively, truly, undeniably, undoubtedly, to be sure.

indefensible adj unjustifiable, inexcusable, unforgivable, unpardonable, insupportable, untenable, wrong, faulty.
F3 defensible, excusable.

indefinite adj unknown, uncertain, unsettled, unresolved, undecided, undetermined, undefined, unspecified, unlimited, ill-defined, vague, indistinct, unclear, obscure, ambiguous, imprecise, inexact, loose, general.
F3 definite, limited, clear.

indefinitely adv for ever, eternally, endlessly, continually, ad infinitum.

indelible adj lasting, enduring, permanent, fast, ineffaceable, ingrained, indestructible.
F3 erasable.

indemnity n compensation, reimbursement, remuneration, reparation, insurance, guarantee, security, protection, immunity, amnesty.

indentation n notch, nick, cut, serration, dent, groove, furrow, depression, dip, hollow, pit, dimple.

independence n autonomy, self-government, self-determination, self-rule, home rule, sovereignty, freedom, liberty, individualism, separation.
F3 dependence.

independent adj 1 AUTONOMOUS, self-governing, self-determining, sovereign, absolute, non-aligned, neutral, impartial, unbiased. 2 FREE, liberated, unconstrained, individualistic, unconventional, self-sufficient, self-supporting, self-reliant, unaided. 3 INDIVIDUAL, self-contained, separate, unconnected, unrelated.
F3 1 dependent.

indescribable adj indefinable, inexpressible, unutterable, unspeakable.
F3 describable.

indestructible adj unbreakable, durable, tough, strong, lasting, enduring, abiding, permanent, eternal, everlasting, immortal, imperishable.
F3 breakable, mortal.

indeterminate adj unspecified, unstated, undefined, unfixed, imprecise, inexact, indefinite, vague, open-ended, undecided, undetermined, uncertain.
F3 known, specified, fixed.

index n 1 *index of names:* table, key, list, catalogue, directory, guide. 2 INDICATOR, pointer, needle, hand, sign, token, mark, indication, clue.

indicate v register, record, show, reveal, display, manifest, point to, designate, specify, point out, mark, signify, mean, denote, express, suggest, imply.

indication n mark, sign, manifestation, evidence, symptom, signal, warning, omen, intimation, suggestion, hint, clue, note, explanation.

indicator n pointer, needle, marker, sign, symbol, token, signal, display, dial, gauge, meter, index, guide, signpost.

indict v charge, accuse, arraign, impeach, summon, summons, prosecute, incriminate.
F3 exonerate.

indifference n apathy, unconcern, coldness, coolness, inattention, disregard, negligence, neutrality, disinterestedness.
F3 interest, concern.

indifferent adj 1 UNINTERESTED, unenthusiastic, unexcited, apathetic, unconcerned, unmoved, uncaring, unsympathetic, cold, cool, distant, aloof, detached, uninvolved, neutral, disinterested. 2 MEDIOCRE, average, middling, passable, moderate, fair, ordinary.
F3 1 interested, caring. 2 excellent.

indigenous adj native, aboriginal, original, local, home-grown.
F3 non-indigenous, foreign.

indignant adj annoyed, angry, irate, heated, fuming, livid, furious, incensed, infuriated, exasperated, outraged.
F3 pleased, delighted.

indignation n annoyance, anger, ire, wrath, rage, fury, exasperation, outrage, scorn, contempt.
F3 pleasure, delight.

indirect adj 1 ROUNDABOUT, circuitous, rambling, winding, meandering, zigzag, tortuous. 2 an indirect effect: secondary, incidental, unintended, subsidiary, ancillary.
F3 1 direct. 2 primary.

indiscreet adj tactless, undiplomatic, impolitic, injudicious, imprudent, unwise, foolish, rash, reckless, hasty, careless, heedless, unthinking.
F3 discreet, cautious.

indiscretion n mistake, error, slip, boob (infml), faux pas, gaffe, tactlessness, rashness, recklessness, foolishness, folly.

indiscriminate adj general, sweeping, wholesale, random, haphazard, hit or miss, aimless, unsystematic, unmethodical, mixed, motley, miscellaneous.
F3 selective, specific, precise.

indispensable adj vital, essential, basic, key, crucial, imperative, required, requisite, needed, necessary.
F3 dispensable, unnecessary.

indisposed adj ill, sick, unwell, poorly, ailing, laid up.
F3 well.

indisputable adj incontrovertible, unquestionable, irrefutable, undeniable, absolute, undisputed, definite, positive, certain, sure.
F3 doubtful.

indistinct adj unclear, ill-defined, blurred, fuzzy, misty, hazy, shadowy, obscure, dim, faint, muffled, confused, unintelligible, vague, woolly, ambiguous, indefinite.
F3 distinct, clear.

individual n person, being, creature, party, body, soul, character, fellow.
adj distinctive, characteristic, idiosyncratic, peculiar, singular, unique, exclusive, special, personal, own, proper, respective, several, separate, distinct, specific, personalized, particular, single.
F3 collective, shared, general.

individuality n character, personality, distinctiveness, peculiarity, singularity, uniqueness, separateness, distinction.
F3 sameness.

indoctrinate v brainwash, teach, instruct, school, ground, train, drill.

induce v 1 CAUSE, effect, bring about, occasion, give rise to, lead to, incite, instigate, prompt, provoke, produce, generate. 2 COAX, prevail upon, encourage, press, persuade, talk into, move, influence, draw, tempt.
F3 2 discourage, deter.

inducement n lure, bait, attraction, enticement, encouragement, incentive, reward, spur, stimulus, motive, reason.
F3 disincentive.

indulge v gratify, satisfy, humour, pander to, go along with, give in to, yield to, favour, pet, cosset, pamper, mollycoddle, spoil, treat, regale.

indulgence n extravagance, luxury, excess, immoderation, intemperance, favour, tolerance.

indulgent adj tolerant, easy-going (infml), lenient, permissive, generous, liberal, kind, fond, tender, understanding, patient.
F3 strict, harsh.

industrialist n manufacturer, producer, magnate, tycoon, baron, captain of industry, capitalist, financier.

industrious adj busy, productive, hard-working, diligent, assiduous, conscientious, zealous, active, energetic, tireless, persistent, persevering.
F3 lazy, idle.

industry n 1 the steel industry: business, trade, commerce, manufacturing, production.
2 INDUSTRIOUSNESS, diligence, application, effort, labour, toil, persistence, perseverance, determination.

inebriated adj drunk, intoxicated, tipsy, merry.
F3 sober.

inedible adj uneatable, unpalatable, indigestible, harmful, noxious, poisonous, deadly.
F3 edible.

ineffective adj useless, worthless, vain, idle, futile, unavailing, fruitless,
unproductive, unsuccessful, powerless, impotent, ineffectual, inadequate, weak, feeble, inept, incompetent.
F3 effective, effectual.

inefficient adj uneconomic, wasteful, money-wasting, time-wasting, incompetent, inexpert, unworkmanlike, slipshod, sloppy, careless, negligent.
F3 efficient.

inelegant adj graceless, ungraceful, clumsy, awkward, laboured, ugly, unrefined, crude, unpolished, rough, unsophisticated, uncultivated, uncouth.
F3 elegant.

ineligible adj disqualified, ruled out, unacceptable, undesirable, unworthy, unsuitable, unfit, unqualified, unequipped.
F3 eligible.

inept adj awkward, clumsy, bungling, incompetent, unskilful, inexpert, foolish, stupid.
F3 competent, skilful.

inequality n unequalness, difference, diversity, dissimilarity, disparity, unevenness, disproportion, bias, prejudice.
F3 equality.

inert adj immobile, motionless, unmoving, still, inactive, inanimate, lifeless, dead, passive, unresponsive, apathetic, dormant, idle, lazy, lethargic, sluggish, torpid, sleepy.
F3 lively, animated.

inertia n immobility, stillness, inactivity, passivity, unresponsiveness, apathy, idleness, laziness, lethargy, torpor.
F3 activity, liveliness.

inescapable adj inevitable, unavoidable, destined, fated, certain, sure, irrevocable, unalterable.
F3 escapable.

inevitable adj unavoidable, inescapable, necessary, definite, certain, sure, decreed, ordained, destined, fated, automatic, assured, fixed, unalterable, irrevocable, inexorable.
F3 avoidable, uncertain, alterable.

inexcusable adj indefensible, unforgivable, unpardonable, intolerable, unacceptable, outrageous, shameful, blameworthy, reprehensible.
F3 excusable, justifiable.

inexhaustible adj **1** an inexhaustible supply: unlimited, limitless, boundless, unbounded, infinite, endless, never-ending, abundant. **2** INDEFATIGABLE, tireless, untiring, unflagging, unwearied, unwearying.
F3 1 limited.

inexpensive adj cheap, low-priced, reasonable, modest, bargain, budget, low-cost, economical.
F3 expensive, dear.

inexperience n inexpertness, ignorance, unfamiliarity, strangeness, newness, rawness, naiveté, innocence.
F3 experience.

inexperienced adj inexpert, untrained, unskilled, amateur, probationary, apprentice, unacquainted, unfamiliar, unaccustomed, new, fresh, raw, callow, immature, naive, unsophisticated, innocent.
F3 experienced, mature.

inexplicable adj unexplainable, unaccountable, strange, mystifying,

puzzling, baffling, mysterious, enigmatic, unfathomable, incomprehensible, incredible, unbelievable, miraculous.
F3 explicable.

inexpressive adj unexpressive, expressionless, deadpan, inscrutable, blank, vacant, empty, emotionless, impassive.
F3 expressive.

infallible adj accurate, unerring, unfailing, foolproof, fail-safe, sure-fire (infml), certain, sure, reliable, dependable, trustworthy, sound, perfect, faultless, impeccable.
F3 fallible.

infamous adj notorious, ill-famed, disreputable, disgraceful, shameful, shocking, outrageous, scandalous, wicked, iniquitous.
F3 illustrious, glorious.

infamy n notoriety, disrepute, disgrace, shame, dishonour, discredit, ignominy, wickedness.
F3 glory.

infancy n **1** BABYHOOD, childhood, youth. **2** BEGINNING, start, commencement, inception, outset, birth, dawn, genesis, emergence, origins, early stages.
F3 1 adulthood.

infant n baby, toddler, tot (infml), rugrat (infml), child, babe (fml), babe in arms (fml).
F3 adult.
adj newborn, baby, young, youthful, juvenile, immature, growing, developing, rudimentary, early, initial, new.
F3 adult, mature.

infantile adj babyish, childish, puerile, juvenile, young, youthful, adolescent, immature.
F3 adult, mature.

infatuated adj besotted, obsessed, enamoured, smitten (infml), crazy (infml), spellbound, mesmerized, captivated, fascinated, enraptured, ravished.

F∃ indifferent, disenchanted.

infatuation n besottedness, obsession, fixation, passion, crush (sl), love, fondness, fascination.

F∃ indifference, disenchantment.

infect v contaminate, pollute, defile, taint, blight, poison, corrupt, pervert, influence, affect, touch, inspire.

infection n illness, disease, virus, epidemic, contagion, pestilence, contamination, pollution, defilement, taint, blight, poison, corruption, influence.

infectious adj contagious, communicable, transmissible, infective, catching, spreading, epidemic, virulent, deadly, contaminating, polluting, defiling, corrupting.

infer v derive, extrapolate, deduce, conclude, assume, presume, surmise, gather, understand.

inference n deduction, conclusion, corollary, consequence, assumption, presumption, surmise, conjecture, extrapolation, construction, interpretation, reading.

inferior adj 1 LOWER, lesser, minor, secondary, junior, subordinate, subsidiary, second-class, low, humble, menial. 2 inferior work: substandard, second-rate, mediocre, bad, poor, unsatisfactory, slipshod, shoddy.

F∃ 1 superior. 2 excellent.

n subordinate, junior, underling (infml), minion, vassal, menial.

F∃ superior.

inferiority n 1 SUBORDINATION, subservience, humbleness, lowliness, meanness, insignificance. 2 MEDIOCRITY, imperfection, inadequacy, slovenliness, shoddiness.

F∃ 1 superiority. 2 excellence.

infernal adj hellish, satanic, devilish, diabolical, fiendish, accursed, damned.

F∃ heavenly.

infertile adj barren, sterile, childless, unproductive, unfruitful, arid, parched, dried-up.

F∃ fertile, fruitful.

infest v swarm, teem, throng, flood, overrun, invade, infiltrate, penetrate, permeate, pervade, ravage.

infidelity n adultery, unfaithfulness, faithlessness, disloyalty, duplicity, treachery, betrayal, cheating, falseness.

F∃ fidelity, faithfulness.

infiltrate v penetrate, enter, creep into, insinuate, intrude, pervade, permeate, filter, percolate.

infinite adj limitless, unlimited, boundless, unbounded, endless, never-ending, inexhaustible, bottomless, innumerable, numberless, uncountable, countless, untold, incalculable, inestimable, immeasurable, unfathomable, vast, immense, enormous, huge, absolute, total.

F∃ finite, limited.

infinitesimal adj tiny, minute, microscopic, minuscule, inconsiderable, insignificant, negligible, inappreciable, imperceptible.

F∃ great, large, enormous.

infinity n eternity, perpetuity, limitlessness, boundlessness, endlessness, inexhaustibility, countlessness, immeasurableness, vastness, immensity.
E3 finiteness, limitation.

infirm adj weak, feeble, frail, ill, unwell, poorly, sickly, failing, faltering, unsteady, shaky, wobbly, doddery, lame.
E3 healthy, strong.

inflame v anger, enrage, infuriate, incense, exasperate, madden, provoke, stimulate, excite, rouse, arouse, agitate, foment, kindle, ignite, fire, heat, fan, fuel, increase, intensify, worsen, aggravate.
E3 cool, quench.

inflamed adj sore, swollen, septic, infected, poisoned, red, hot, heated, fevered, feverish.

inflammable adj flammable, combustible, burnable.
E3 non-flammable, incombustible, flameproof.

inflammation n soreness, painfulness, tenderness, swelling, abscess, infection, redness, heat, rash, sore, irritation.

inflate v blow up, pump up, blow out, puff out, swell, distend, bloat, expand, enlarge, increase, boost, exaggerate.
E3 deflate.

inflation n expansion, increase, rise, escalation, hyperinflation.
E3 deflation.

inflexible adj rigid, stiff, hard, solid, set, fixed, fast, immovable, firm, strict, stringent, unbending, unyielding, adamant, resolute, relentless, implacable, uncompromising, stubborn, obstinate, intransigent, entrenched, dyed-in-the-wool.
E3 flexible, yielding, adaptable.

inflict v impose, enforce, perpetrate, wreak, administer, apply, deliver, deal, mete out, lay, burden, exact, levy.

influence n power, sway, rule, authority, domination, mastery, hold, control, direction, guidance, bias, prejudice, pull, pressure, effect, impact, weight, importance, prestige, standing.
v dominate, control, manipulate, direct, guide, manoeuvre, change, alter, modify, affect, impress, move, stir, arouse, rouse, sway, persuade, induce, incite, instigate, prompt, motivate, dispose, incline, bias, prejudice, predispose.

influential adj dominant, controlling, leading, authoritative, charismatic, persuasive, convincing, compelling, inspiring, moving, powerful, potent, effective, telling, strong, weighty, momentous, important, significant, instrumental, guiding.
E3 ineffective, unimportant.

influx n inflow, inrush, invasion, arrival, stream, flow, rush, flood, inundation.

inform v tell, advise, notify, communicate, impart, leak, tip off, acquaint, fill in (infml), brief, instruct, enlighten, illuminate.
inform on betray, incriminate, shop (sl), tell on (infml), squeal (sl), blab, grass (sl), denounce.

informal adj unofficial, unceremonious, casual, relaxed, easy, free, natural, simple, unpretentious, familiar, colloquial.
E3 formal, solemn.

information n facts, data, input, gen (infml), bumf (sl), intelligence, news, report, bulletin, communiqué, message, word, advice, notice, briefing, instruction, knowledge, dossier, database, databank, clues, evidence.

informative adj educational, instructive, edifying, enlightening, illuminating, revealing, forthcoming, communicative, chatty, gossipy, newsy, helpful, useful, constructive. **F3** uninformative.

informed adj 1 *we'll keep you informed*: familiar, conversant, acquainted, enlightened, briefed, primed, posted, up to date, abreast, au fait, in the know (*infml*). 2 *an informed opinion*: well-informed, authoritative, expert, versed, well-read, erudite, learned, knowledgeable, well-researched. **F3** 1 ignorant, unaware.

informer n informant, grass (*sl*), supergrass (*sl*), betrayer, traitor, Judas, tell-tale, sneak, spy, mole (*infml*).

infringe v 1 BREAK, violate, contravene, transgress, overstep, disobey, defy, flout, ignore. 2 INTRUDE, encroach, trespass, invade.

infuriate v anger, vex, enrage, incense, exasperate, madden, provoke, rouse, annoy, irritate, rile, antagonize. **F3** calm, pacify.

ingenious adj clever, shrewd, cunning, crafty, skilful, masterly, imaginative, creative, inventive, resourceful, original, innovative. **F3** unimaginative.

ingenuous adj artless, guileless, innocent, honest, sincere, frank, open, plain, simple, unsophisticated, naive, trusting. **F3** artful, sly.

ingrained adj fixed, rooted, deep-rooted, deep-seated, entrenched, immovable, ineradicable, permanent, inbuilt, inborn, inbred.

ingratiate v curry favour, flatter, creep, crawl, grovel, fawn, get in with.

ingratitude n ungratefulness, thanklessness, unappreciativeness, ungraciousness. **F3** gratitude, thankfulness.

ingredient n constituent, element, factor, component, part.

inhabit v live, dwell, reside, occupy, possess, colonize, settle, people, populate, stay.

inhabitant n resident, dweller, citizen, native, occupier, occupant, inmate, tenant, lodger.

inherent adj inborn, inbred, innate, inherited, hereditary, native, natural, inbuilt, built-in, intrinsic, ingrained, essential, fundamental, basic.

inherit v succeed to, accede to, assume, come into, be left, receive.

inheritance n legacy, bequest, heritage, birthright, heredity, descent, succession.

inheritor n heir, heiress, successor, beneficiary, recipient.

inhibit v discourage, repress, hold back, suppress, curb, check, restrain, hinder, impede, obstruct, interfere with, frustrate, thwart, prevent, stop, stanch, stem. **F3** encourage, assist.

inhibited adj repressed, self-conscious, shy, reticent, withdrawn, reserved, guarded, subdued. **F3** uninhibited, open, relaxed.

inhibition n repression, hang-up (*sl*), self-consciousness, shyness, reticence, reserve, restraint, curb, check, hindrance, impediment, obstruction, bar.

F3 freedom.

inhuman adj barbaric, barbarous, animal, bestial, vicious, savage, sadistic, cold-blooded, brutal, cruel, inhumane.

F3 human.

inhumane adj unkind, insensitive, callous, unfeeling, heartless, cold-hearted, hard-hearted, pitiless, ruthless, cruel, brutal, inhuman.

F3 humane, kind, compassionate.

initial adj first, beginning, opening, introductory, inaugural, original, primary, early, formative.

F3 final, last.

initially adv at first, at the beginning, to begin with, to start with, originally, first, firstly, first of all.

F3 finally, in the end.

initiate v begin, start, commence, originate, pioneer, institute, set up, introduce, launch, open, inaugurate, instigate, activate, trigger, prompt, stimulate, cause.

initiation n admission, reception, entrance, entry, debut, introduction, enrolment, induction, investiture, installation, inauguration, inception.

initiative n 1 ENERGY, drive, dynamism, get-up-and-go (infml), ambition, enterprise, resourcefulness, inventiveness, originality, innovativeness. 2 SUGGESTION, recommendation, action, lead, first move, first step.

inject v 1 inject drugs: inoculate, vaccinate, shoot (sl). 2 INTRODUCE, insert, add, bring, infuse, instil.

injection n inoculation, vaccination, jab (infml), shot (infml), fix (sl), dose, insertion, introduction.

injunction n command, order, directive, ruling, mandate, direction, instruction, precept.

injure v hurt, harm, damage, impair, spoil, mar, ruin, disfigure, deface, mutilate, wound, cut, break, fracture, maim, disable, cripple, lame, ill-treat, maltreat, abuse, offend, wrong, upset, put out.

injury n wound, cut, lesion, fracture, trauma, hurt, mischief, ill, harm, damage, impairment, ruin, disfigurement, mutilation, ill-treatment, abuse, insult, offence, wrong, injustice.

injustice n unfairness, inequality, disparity, discrimination, oppression, bias, prejudice, one-sidedness, partisanship, partiality, favouritism, wrong, iniquity.

F3 justice, fairness.

inkling n suspicion, idea, notion, faintest (infml), glimmering, clue, hint, intimation, suggestion, allusion, indication, sign, pointer.

inlet n bay, cove, creek, fiord, opening, entrance, passage.

inn n public house, pub (infml), local (infml), tavern, hostelry, hotel.

innate adj inborn, inbred, inherent, intrinsic, native, natural, instinctive, intuitive.

F3 acquired, learnt.

inner adj internal, interior, inside, inward, innermost, central, middle, concealed, hidden, secret, private, personal, intimate, mental, psychological, spiritual, emotional.

F3 outer, outward.

innocence n 1 GUILTLESSNESS, blamelessness, honesty, virtue, righteousness, purity, chastity, virginity, incorruptibility,

harmlessness, innocuousness.
2 ARTLESSNESS, guilelessness,
naiveté, inexperience, ignorance,
naturalness, simplicity,
unsophistication, unworldliness,
credulity, gullibility, trustfulness.
F3 1 guilt. **2** experience.

innocent *adj* **1** *innocent of the crime*:
guiltless, blameless, irreproachable,
unimpeachable, honest, upright,
virtuous, righteous, sinless, faultless,
impeccable, stainless, spotless,
immaculate, unsullied, untainted,
uncontaminated, pure, chaste,
virginal, incorrupt, inoffensive,
harmless, innocuous. **2** ARTLESS,
guileless, ingenuous, naive, green,
inexperienced, fresh, natural,
simple, unsophisticated, unworldly,
childlike, credulous, gullible,
trusting.
F3 1 guilty. **2** experienced.

innocuous *adj* harmless, safe,
inoffensive, unobjectionable,
innocent.
F3 harmful.

innovation *n* newness, novelty,
neologism, modernization, progress,
reform, change, alteration, variation,
departure.

innovative *adj* new, fresh, original,
creative, imaginative, inventive,
resourceful, enterprising, go-ahead,
progressive, reforming, bold, daring,
adventurous.
F3 conservative, unimaginative.

innuendo *n* insinuation, aspersion,
slur, whisper, hint, intimation,
suggestion, implication.

innumerable *adj* numberless,
unnumbered, countless, uncountable,
untold, incalculable, infinite,
numerous, many.

inoculation *n* vaccination,
immunization, protection, injection,
shot (*infml*), jab (*infml*).

inoffensive *adj* harmless,
innocuous, innocent, peaceable,
mild, unobtrusive, unassertive, quiet,
retiring.
F3 offensive, harmful, provocative.

inordinate *adj* excessive,
immoderate, unwarranted, undue,
unreasonable, disproportionate, great.
F3 moderate, reasonable.

inquire, enquire *v* ask, question,
quiz, query, investigate, look into,
probe, examine, inspect, scrutinize,
search, explore.

inquiry, enquiry *n* question, query,
investigation, inquest, hearing,
inquisition, examination, inspection,
scrutiny, study, survey, poll, search,
probe, exploration.

inquisitive *adj* curious, questioning,
probing, searching, prying, peeping,
snooping, nosey, interfering,
meddlesome, intrusive.

insane *adj* **1** MAD, crazy, mentally ill,
lunatic, mental (*sl*), demented,
deranged, unhinged, disturbed.
2 FOOLISH, stupid, senseless,
impractical.
F3 1 sane. **2** sensible.

insanity *n* madness, craziness,
lunacy, mental illness, neurosis,
psychosis, mania, dementia,
derangement, folly, stupidity,
senselessness, irresponsibility.
F3 sanity.

insatiable *adj* unquenchable,
unsatisfiable, ravenous, voracious,
immoderate, inordinate.

inscribe *v* engrave, etch, carve, cut,
incise, imprint, impress, stamp, print,
write, sign, autograph, dedicate.

inscription *n* engraving, epitaph, caption, legend, lettering, words, writing, signature, autograph, dedication.

inscrutable *adj* incomprehensible, unfathomable, impenetrable, deep, inexplicable, unexplainable, baffling, mysterious, enigmatic, cryptic, hidden.
E3 comprehensible, expressive.

insect

> Insects include:
>
> fly, gnat, midge, mosquito, tsetse-fly, locust, dragonfly, cranefly, daddy long-legs (*infml*), horsefly, mayfly, butterfly, moth, bee, bumblebee, wasp, hornet, aphid, black fly, greenfly, whitefly, ladybird, ladybug (*US*), water boatman, lacewing; beetle, cockroach, roach (*US*), earwig, stick insect, grasshopper, cricket, cicada, flea, louse, nit, termite, glow-worm, woodworm, weevil, woodlouse.

> Parts of an insect include:
>
> abdomen, antenna, cercus, compound eye, forewing, head, hindwing, mandible, mouthpart, ocellus, ovipositor, spiracle, thorax.

insecure *adj* **1** ANXIOUS, worried, nervous, uncertain, unsure, afraid. **2** UNSAFE, dangerous, hazardous, perilous, precarious, unsteady, shaky, loose, unprotected, defenceless, exposed, vulnerable.
E3 1 confident, self-assured. **2** secure, safe.

insensible *adj* numb, anaesthetized, dead, cold, insensitive, unresponsive, blind, deaf, unconscious, unaware, oblivious, unmindful.
E3 conscious.

insensitive *adj* hardened, tough, resistant, impenetrable, impervious, immune, unsusceptible, thick-skinned, unfeeling, impassive, indifferent, unaffected, unmoved, untouched, uncaring, unconcerned, callous, thoughtless, tactless, crass.
E3 sensitive.

inseparable *adj* indivisible, indissoluble, inextricable, close, intimate, bosom, devoted.
E3 separable.

insert *v* put, place, put in, stick in, push in, introduce, implant, embed, engraft, set, inset, let in, interleave, intercalate, interpolate, interpose. *n* insertion, enclosure, inset, notice, advertisement, supplement, addition.

inside *n* interior, content, contents, middle, centre, heart, core.
E3 outside.
adv within, indoors, internally, inwardly, secretly, privately.
E3 outside.
adj interior, internal, inner, innermost, inward, secret, classified, confidential, private.

insides *n* entrails, guts, intestines, bowels, innards (*infml*), organs, viscera, belly, stomach.

insidious *adj* subtle, sly, crafty, cunning, wily, deceptive, devious, stealthy, surreptitious, furtive, sneaking, treacherous.
E3 direct, straightforward.

insight *n* awareness, knowledge, comprehension, understanding, grasp, apprehension, perception, intuition, sensitivity, discernment, judgement, acumen, penetration, observation, vision, wisdom, intelligence.

insignificant *adj* unimportant, irrelevant, meaningless,

inconsequential, minor, trivial, trifling, petty, paltry, small, tiny, insubstantial, inconsiderable, negligible, non-essential.
F3 significant, important.

insincere adj hypocritical, two-faced, double-dealing, lying, untruthful, dishonest, deceitful, devious, unfaithful, faithless, untrue, false, feigned, pretended, phoney (infml), hollow.
F3 sincere.

insinuate v imply, suggest, allude, hint, intimate, get at (infml), indicate.

insipid adj tasteless, flavourless, unsavoury, unappetizing, watery, weak, bland, wishy-washy (infml), colourless, drab, dull, monotonous, boring, uninteresting, tame, flat, lifeless, spiritless, characterless, trite, unimaginative, dry.
F3 tasty, spicy, piquant, appetizing.

insist v demand, require, urge, stress, emphasize, repeat, reiterate, dwell on, harp on, assert, maintain, claim, contend, hold, vow, swear, persist, stand firm.

insistence n demand, entreaty, exhortation, urging, stress, emphasis, repetition, reiteration, assertion, claim, contention, persistence, determination, resolution, firmness.

insistent adj demanding, importunate, emphatic, forceful, pressing, urgent, dogged, tenacious, persistent, persevering, relentless, unrelenting, unremitting, incessant.

insolent adj rude, abusive, insulting, disrespectful, cheeky (infml), impertinent, impudent, saucy (infml), bold, forward, fresh, presumptuous, arrogant, defiant, insubordinate.
F3 polite, respectful.

insoluble adj unsolvable, unexplainable, inexplicable, incomprehensible, unfathomable, impenetrable, obscure, mystifying, puzzling, perplexing, baffling.
F3 explicable.

insolvent adj bankrupt, bust, failed, ruined, broke (infml), penniless, destitute.
F3 solvent.

inspect v check, vet, look over, examine, search, investigate, scrutinize, study, scan, survey, superintend, supervise, oversee, visit.

inspection n check, check-up, examination, scrutiny, scan, study, survey, review, search, investigation, supervision, visit.

inspector n supervisor, superintendent, overseer, surveyor, controller, scrutineer, checker, tester, examiner, investigator, reviewer, critic.

inspiration n 1 CREATIVITY, imagination, genius, muse, influence, encouragement, stimulation, motivation, spur, stimulus. 2 IDEA, brainwave, insight, illumination, revelation, awakening.

inspire v encourage, hearten, influence, impress, animate, enliven, quicken, galvanize, fire, kindle, stir, arouse, trigger, spark off, prompt, spur, motivate, provoke, stimulate, excite, exhilarate, thrill, enthral, enthuse, imbue, infuse.

inspiring adj encouraging, heartening, uplifting, invigorating, stirring, rousing, stimulating, exciting, exhilarating, thrilling, enthralling, moving, affecting, memorable, impressive.
F3 uninspiring, dull.

instability n unsteadiness, shakiness, vacillation, wavering, irresolution, uncertainty, unpredictability, changeableness, variability, fluctuation, volatility, capriciousness, fickleness, inconstancy, unreliability, insecurity, unsafeness, unsoundness.
F3 stability.

install v fix, fit, lay, put, place, position, locate, site, situate, station, plant, settle, establish, set up, introduce, institute, inaugurate, invest, induct, ordain.

instalment n **1** pay in instalments: payment, repayment, portion. **2** EPISODE, chapter, part, section, division.

instant n flash, twinkling, trice, moment, tick (infml), split second, second, minute, time, occasion. adj instantaneous, immediate, on-the-spot, direct, prompt, urgent, unhesitating, quick, fast, rapid, swift.
F3 slow.

instead adv alternatively, preferably, rather.
instead of in place of, in lieu of, on behalf of, in preference to, rather than.

instigate v initiate, set on, start, begin, cause, generate, inspire, move, influence, encourage, urge, spur, prompt, provoke, stimulate, incite, stir up, whip up, foment, rouse, excite.

instil v infuse, imbue, insinuate, introduce, inject, implant, inculcate, impress, din into (infml).

instinct n intuition, sixth sense, gut reaction (infml), impulse, urge, feeling, hunch, flair, knack, gift, talent, feel, faculty, ability, aptitude, predisposition, tendency.

instinctive adj natural, native, inborn, innate, inherent, intuitive, impulsive, involuntary, automatic, mechanical, reflex, spontaneous, immediate, unthinking, unpremeditated, gut (infml), visceral.
F3 conscious, voluntary, deliberate.

institute v originate, initiate, introduce, enact, begin, start, commence, create, establish, set up, organize, found, inaugurate, open, launch, appoint, install, invest, induct, ordain.
F3 cancel, discontinue, abolish. n school, college, academy, conservatory, foundation, institution.

institution n **1** CUSTOM, tradition, usage, practice, ritual, convention, rule, law. **2** ORGANIZATION, association, society, guild, concern, corporation, foundation, establishment, institute, hospital, home. **3** INITIATION, introduction, enactment, inception, creation, establishment, formation, founding, foundation, installation.

instruct v **1** TEACH, educate, tutor, coach, train, drill, ground, school, discipline. **2** ORDER, command, direct, mandate, tell, inform, notify, advise, counsel, guide.

instruction n **1** follow the instructions: direction, recommendation, advice, guidance, information, order, command, injunction, mandate, directive, ruling. **2** EDUCATION, schooling, lesson(s), tuition, teaching, training, coaching, drilling, grounding, preparation.

instructive adj informative, educational, edifying, enlightening, illuminating, helpful, useful.
F3 unenlightening.

instructor n teacher, master, mistress, tutor, coach, trainer, demonstrator, exponent, adviser, mentor, guide, guru.

instrument n 1 TOOL, implement, utensil, appliance, gadget, contraption, device, contrivance, apparatus, mechanism. 2 AGENT, agency, vehicle, organ, medium, factor, channel, way, means.

instrumental adj active, involved, complicit, contributory, conducive, influential, useful, helpful, auxiliary, subsidiary.

F3 obstructive, unhelpful.

insufferable adj intolerable, unbearable, detestable, loathsome, dreadful, impossible.

F3 pleasant, tolerable.

insufficiency n inadequacy, shortage, deficiency, lack, scarcity, dearth, want, need, poverty.

F3 sufficiency, excess.

insufficient adj inadequate, short, deficient, lacking, sparse, scanty, scarce.

F3 sufficient, excessive.

insular adj parochial, provincial, cut off, detached, isolated, remote, withdrawn, inward-looking, blinkered, closed, narrow-minded, narrow, limited, petty.

insulate v cushion, pad, lag, cocoon, protect, shield, shelter, isolate, separate, cut off.

insult v abuse, call names, disparage, revile, libel, slander, slight, snub, injure, affront, offend, outrage.

F3 compliment, praise.

n abuse, rudeness, insolence, defamation, libel, slander, slight, snub, affront, indignity, offence, outrage.

F3 compliment, praise.

insurance n cover, protection, safeguard, security, provision, assurance, indemnity, guarantee, warranty, policy, premium.

insure v cover, protect, assure, underwrite, indemnify, guarantee, warrant.

insurmountable adj insuperable, unconquerable, invincible, overwhelming, hopeless, impossible.

F3 surmountable.

insurrection n rising, uprising, insurgence, riot, rebellion, mutiny, revolt, revolution, coup, putsch.

intact adj unbroken, all in one piece, whole, complete, integral, entire, perfect, sound, undamaged, unhurt, uninjured.

F3 broken, incomplete, damaged.

intangible adj insubstantial, imponderable, elusive, fleeting, airy, shadowy, vague, indefinite, abstract, unreal, invisible.

F3 tangible, real.

integral adj 1 an integral part: intrinsic, constituent, elemental, basic, fundamental, necessary, essential, indispensable. 2 COMPLETE, entire, full, whole, undivided.

F3 1 extra, additional, unnecessary.

integrate v assimilate, merge, join, unite, combine, amalgamate, incorporate, coalesce, fuse, knit, mesh, mix, blend, harmonize.

F3 divide, separate.

integrity n 1 HONESTY, uprightness, probity, incorruptibility, purity, morality, principle, honour, virtue, goodness, righteousness. 2 COMPLETENESS, wholeness, unity, coherence, cohesion.

F3 1 dishonesty. 2 incompleteness.

intellect n mind, brain(s), brainpower, intelligence, genius, reason, understanding, sense, wisdom, judgement.
E3 stupidity.

intellectual adj academic, scholarly, intelligent, studious, thoughtful, cerebral, mental, highbrow, cultural.
E3 low-brow.
n thinker, academic, highbrow, egghead, mastermind, genius.
E3 low-brow.

intelligence n 1 INTELLECT, reason, wit(s), brain(s) (infml), brainpower, cleverness, brightness, aptitude, quickness, alertness, discernment, perception, understanding, comprehension. 2 INFORMATION, facts, data, low-down (sl), knowledge, findings, news, report, warning, tip-off.
E3 1 stupidity, foolishness.

intelligent adj clever, bright, smart, brainy (infml), quick, alert, quick-witted, sharp, acute, knowing, knowledgeable, well-informed, thinking, rational, sensible.
E3 unintelligent, stupid, foolish.

intend v aim, have a mind, contemplate, mean, propose, plan, project, scheme, plot, design, purpose, resolve, determine, destine, mark out, earmark, set apart.

intense adj great, deep, profound, strong, powerful, forceful, fierce, harsh, severe, acute, sharp, keen, eager, earnest, ardent, fervent, fervid, passionate, vehement, energetic, violent, intensive, concentrated, heightened.
E3 moderate, mild, weak.

intensify v increase, step up, escalate, heighten, hot up (infml), fire, boost, fuel, aggravate, add to, strengthen, reinforce, sharpen, whet, quicken, deepen, concentrate, emphasize, enhance.
E3 reduce, weaken.

intensive adj concentrated, thorough, exhaustive, comprehensive, detailed, in-depth, thoroughgoing, all-out, intense.
E3 superficial.

intent adj determined, resolved, resolute, set, bent, concentrated, eager, earnest, committed, steadfast, fixed, alert, attentive, concentrating, preoccupied, engrossed, wrapped up, absorbed, occupied.
E3 absent-minded, distracted.

intention n aim, purpose, object, end, point, target, goal, objective, idea, plan, design, view, intent, meaning.

intentional adj designed, wilful, conscious, planned, deliberate, prearranged, premeditated, calculated, studied, intended, meant.
E3 unintentional, accidental.

intercede v mediate, arbitrate, intervene, plead, entreat, beseech, speak.

intercept v head off, ambush, interrupt, cut off, stop, arrest, catch, take, seize, check, block, obstruct, delay, frustrate, thwart.

interchangeable adj reciprocal, equivalent, similar, identical, the same, synonymous, standard.
E3 different.

interest n 1 IMPORTANCE, significance, note, concern, care, attention, notice, curiosity, involvement, participation. 2 leisure interests: activity, pursuit, pastime, hobby, diversion, amusement.

3 ADVANTAGE, benefit, profit, gain.
F3 1 boredom.
v concern, involve, touch, move, attract, appeal to, divert, amuse, occupy, engage, absorb, engross, fascinate, intrigue.
F3 bore.

interested *adj* **1** ATTENTIVE, curious, absorbed, engrossed, fascinated, enthusiastic, keen, attracted.
2 CONCERNED, involved, affected.
F3 1 uninterested, indifferent, apathetic. **2** disinterested, unaffected.

interesting *adj* attractive, appealing, entertaining, engaging, absorbing, engrossing, fascinating, intriguing, compelling, gripping, stimulating, thought-provoking, curious, unusual.
F3 uninteresting, boring, monotonous, tedious.

interfere *v* **1** INTRUDE, poke one's nose in, pry, butt in, interrupt, intervene, meddle, tamper. **2** HINDER, hamper, obstruct, block, impede, handicap, cramp, inhibit, conflict, clash.
F3 2 assist.

interference *n* **1** INTRUSION, prying, interruption, intervention, meddling.
2 OBSTRUCTION, opposition, conflict, clashing.
F3 2 assistance.

interim *adj* temporary, provisional, stopgap, makeshift, improvised, stand-in, acting, caretaker.
n meantime, meanwhile, interval.

interior *adj* **1** INTERNAL, inside, inner, central, inward, mental, spiritual, private, secret, hidden.
2 HOME, domestic, inland, up-country, remote.
F3 1 exterior, external.

n inside, centre, middle, core, heart, depths.
F3 exterior, outside.

interjection *n* exclamation, ejaculation, cry, shout, call, interpolation.

intermediary *n* mediator, go-between, middleman, broker, agent.

intermediate *adj* midway, halfway, in-between, middle, mid, median, mean, intermediary, intervening, transitional.
F3 extreme.

interminable *adj* endless, never-ending, ceaseless, perpetual, limitless, unlimited, long, long-winded, long-drawn-out, dragging, wearisome.
F3 limited, brief.

intermission *n* interval, entr'acte, interlude, break, recess, rest, respite, breather (*infml*), breathing-space, pause, lull, let-up (*infml*), remission, suspension, interruption, halt, stop, stoppage, cessation.

intermittent *adj* occasional, periodic, sporadic, spasmodic, fitful, erratic, irregular, broken.
F3 continuous, constant.

internal *adj* **1** INSIDE, inner, interior, inward. **2** INTIMATE, private, personal.
3 DOMESTIC, in-house.
F3 1 external, outside, outer.

international *adj* global, worldwide, intercontinental, cosmopolitan, universal, general.
F3 national, local, parochial.

Internet

Internet terms include:
the Internet, the Net (*infml*), the World Wide Web, the Information Superhighway; HTML (Hypertext Markup Language), XML (Extensible

Markup Language), XSL (Extensible Style Language), CSS (Cascading Style Sheet), javascript; applet, browser, cache, CGI (Common Gateway Interface), cookie, broadband account, dial-up account, domain hosting, domain name, dotcom, download, e-commerce, e-mail, frame, FTP (File Transfer Protocol), gateway, GIF (Graphics Interchange Format), home page, http (Hypertext Transfer Protocol), ISP (Internet Service Provider), JPEG (Joint Photographic Experts Group), MP3, navigation bar, online, plug-in, PNG (Portable Network Graphics), portal, search engine, stylesheet, surfing, up-time, W3C (World Wide Web Consortium), web authoring, webcam, webcast, webmaster, webpage, web server, website.

interplay n exchange, interchange, interaction, reciprocation, give-and-take.

interpose v insert, introduce, interject, interpolate, put in, thrust in, interrupt, intrude, interfere, come between, intervene, step in, mediate.

interpret v explain, expound, elucidate, clarify, throw light on, define, paraphrase, translate, render, decode, decipher, solve, make sense of, understand, construe, read, take.

interpretation n explanation, clarification, analysis, translation, rendering, version, performance, reading, understanding, sense, meaning.

interrogate v question, quiz, examine, cross-examine, grill, give the third degree, pump, debrief.

interrogation n questioning, cross-questioning, examination, cross-examination, grilling, third degree, inquisition, inquiry, inquest.

interrupt v intrude, barge in (infml), butt in, interject, break in, heckle, disturb, disrupt, interfere, obstruct, check, hinder, hold up, stop, halt, suspend, discontinue, cut off, disconnect, punctuate, separate, divide, cut, break.

interruption n intrusion, interjection, disturbance, disruption, obstruction, impediment, obstacle, hitch, pause, break, halt, stop, stoppage, suspension, discontinuance, disconnection, separation, division.

intersect v cross, criss-cross, cut across, bisect, divide, meet, converge.

intersection n junction, interchange, crossroads, crossing.

intertwine v entwine, interweave, interlace, interlink, twist, twine, cross, weave.

interval n interlude, intermission, break, rest, pause, delay, wait, interim, meantime, meanwhile, gap, opening, space, distance, period, spell, time, season.

intervene v 1 STEP IN, mediate, arbitrate, interfere, interrupt, intrude. 2 OCCUR, happen, elapse, pass.

intervention n involvement, interference, intrusion, mediation, agency, intercession.

interview n audience, consultation, talk, dialogue, meeting, conference, press conference, oral examination, viva.
v question, interrogate, examine, vet.

intestines n bowels, guts, entrails, insides, innards (infml), offal, viscera, vitals.

intimacy n friendship, closeness, familiarity, confidence, confidentiality, privacy.
F3 distance.

intimate [1] v hint, insinuate, imply, suggest, indicate, communicate, impart, tell, state, declare, announce.

intimate [2] adj friendly, informal, familiar, cosy, warm, affectionate, dear, bosom, close, near, confidential, secret, private, personal, internal, innermost, deep, penetrating, detailed, exhaustive.
F3 unfriendly, cold, distant.
n friend, bosom friend, confidant(e), associate.
F3 stranger.

intimidate v daunt, cow, overawe, appal, dismay, alarm, scare, frighten, terrify, threaten, menace, terrorize, bully, browbeat, bludgeon, coerce, pressure, pressurize, lean on (sl).

intolerable adj unbearable, unendurable, insupportable, unacceptable, insufferable, impossible.
F3 tolerable.

intolerant adj impatient, prejudiced, bigoted, narrow-minded, small-minded, opinionated, dogmatic, illiberal, uncharitable.
F3 tolerant, liberal.

intonation n modulation, tone, accentuation, inflection.

intoxicated adj 1 DRUNK, drunken, inebriated, tipsy. 2 EXCITED, elated, exhilarated, thrilled.
F3 1 sober.

intoxicating adj 1 intoxicating liquor: alcoholic, strong. 2 EXCITING, stimulating, heady, exhilarating, thrilling.
F3 2 sobering.

intoxication n 1 DRUNKENNESS, inebriation, tipsiness. 2 EXCITEMENT, elation, exhilaration, euphoria.
F3 1 sobriety.

intrepid adj bold, daring, brave, courageous, plucky, valiant, lion-hearted, fearless, dauntless, undaunted, stout-hearted, stalwart, gallant, heroic.
F3 cowardly, timid.

intricate adj elaborate, fancy, ornate, rococo, complicated, complex, sophisticated, involved, convoluted, tortuous, tangled, entangled, knotty, perplexing, difficult.
F3 simple, plain, straightforward.

intrigue n 1 PLOT, scheme, conspiracy, collusion, machination, manoeuvre, stratagem, ruse, wile, trickery, double-dealing, sharp practice. 2 ROMANCE, liaison, affair, amour, intimacy.
v 1 FASCINATE, rivet, puzzle, tantalize, attract, charm, captivate. 2 PLOT, scheme, conspire, connive, machinate, manoeuvre.
F3 1 bore.

introduce v 1 INSTITUTE, begin, start, commence, establish, found, inaugurate, launch, open, bring in, announce, present, acquaint, familiarize, initiate. 2 PUT FORWARD, advance, submit, offer, propose, suggest.
F3 1 end, conclude. 2 remove, take away.

introduction n 1 INSTITUTION, beginning, start, commencement, establishment, inauguration, launch, presentation, debut, initiation. 2 FOREWORD, preface, preamble, prologue, preliminaries, overture,

prelude, lead-in, opening.
F∃ 1 removal, withdrawal.
2 appendix, conclusion.

introductory adj preliminary, preparatory, opening, inaugural, first, initial, early, elementary, basic.

introspective adj inward-looking, contemplative, meditative, pensive, thoughtful, brooding, introverted, self-centred, reserved, withdrawn.
F∃ outward-looking.

introverted adj introspective, inward-looking, self-centred, withdrawn, shy, reserved, quiet.
F∃ extroverted.

intrude v interrupt, butt in, meddle, interfere, violate, infringe, encroach, trespass.
F∃ withdraw, stand back.

intruder n trespasser, prowler, burglar, raider, invader, infiltrator, interloper, gatecrasher.

intrusion n interruption, interference, violation, infringement, encroachment, trespass, invasion, incursion.
F∃ withdrawal.

intuition n instinct, sixth sense, perception, discernment, insight, hunch, feeling, gut feeling (infml).
F∃ reasoning.

intuitive adj instinctive, spontaneous, involuntary, innate, untaught.
F∃ reasoned.

inundate v flood, deluge, swamp, engulf, submerge, immerse, drown, bury, overwhelm, overrun.

invade v enter, penetrate, infiltrate, burst in, descend on, attack, raid, seize, occupy, overrun, swarm over, infest, pervade, encroach, infringe, violate.
F∃ withdraw, evacuate.

invalid[1] adj sick, ill, poorly, ailing, sickly, weak, feeble, frail, infirm, disabled, bedridden.
F∃ healthy.
n patient, convalescent.

invalid[2] adj **1** FALSE, fallacious, unsound, ill-founded, unfounded, baseless, illogical, irrational, unscientific, wrong, incorrect.
2 ILLEGAL, null, void, worthless.
F∃ 1 valid. **2** legal.

invaluable adj priceless, inestimable, incalculable, precious, valuable, useful.
F∃ worthless, cheap.

invariable adj fixed, set, unvarying, unchanging, unchangeable, permanent, constant, steady, unwavering, uniform, rigid, inflexible, habitual, regular.
F∃ variable.

invariably adv always, without exception, without fail, unfailingly, consistently, regularly, habitually.
F∃ never.

invasion n attack, offensive, onslaught, raid, incursion, foray, breach, penetration, infiltration, intrusion, encroachment, infringement, violation.
F∃ withdrawal, evacuation.

invent v conceive, think up, design, discover, create, originate, formulate, frame, devise, contrive, improvise, fabricate, make up, concoct, cook up, trump up, imagine, dream up.

invention n **1** her latest invention: design, creation, brainchild, discovery, development, device, gadget. **2** LIE, falsehood, deceit, fabrication, fiction, tall story, fantasy, figment.
3 INVENTIVENESS, imagination, creativity, innovation, originality,

ingenuity, inspiration, genius.

F3 2 truth.

inventive *adj* imaginative, creative, innovative, original, ingenious, resourceful, fertile, inspired, gifted, clever.

inventor *n* designer, discoverer, creator, originator, author, architect, maker, scientist, engineer.

inverse *adj* inverted, upside down, transposed, reversed, opposite, contrary, reverse, converse.

invert *v* upturn, turn upside down, overturn, capsize, upset, transpose, reverse.

F3 right.

invertebrate

> Invertebrates include:
> *sponges:* calcareous, glass, horny; *jellyfish, corals and sea anemones:* Portuguese man-of-war, box jellyfish, dead men's fingers, sea gooseberry, Venus's girdle; *echinoderms:* sea lily, feather-star, starfish, crown-of-thorns starfish, brittlestar, sea urchin, sand dollar, sea cucumber; *worms:* annelid, arrow worm, bristle-worm, earthworm, eelworm, flatworm, fluke, hookworm, leech, liver fluke, lugworm, ragworm, ribbon-worm, roundworm, sea mouse, tapeworm, threadworm; *crustaceans:* acornbarnacle, barnacle, brine-shrimp, crab, crayfish, daphnia, fiddler crab, fish-louse, goose-barnacle, hermitcrab, king prawn, krill, lobster, mantis shrimp, pill-bug, prawn, sand hopper, shrimp, spider crab, spiny lobster, water flea, woodlouse; *centipede, millipede; arachnids:* spider, black widow, tarantula, scorpion, mite, tick.

invest *v* SPEND, lay out, put in, sink. 2 PROVIDE, supply, endow, vest, empower, authorize, sanction.

investigate *v* inquire into, look into, consider, examine, study, inspect, scrutinize, analyse, go into, probe, explore, search, sift.

investigation *n* inquiry, inquest, hearing, examination, study, research, survey, review, inspection, scrutiny, analysis, probe, exploration, search.

investigator *n* examiner, researcher, detective, sleuth (*infml*), private detective, private eye (*infml*).

investment *n* asset, speculation, venture, stake, contribution, outlay, expenditure, transaction.

invigorate *v* vitalize, energize, animate, enliven, liven up, quicken, strengthen, fortify, brace, stimulate, inspire, exhilarate, perk up, refresh, freshen, revitalize, rejuvenate.

F3 tire, weary, dishearten.

invincible *adj* unbeatable, unconquerable, insuperable, insurmountable, indomitable, unassailable, impregnable, impenetrable, invulnerable, indestructible.

F3 beatable.

invisible *adj* unseen, out of sight, hidden, concealed, disguised, inconspicuous, indiscernible, imperceptible, infinitesimal, microscopic, imaginary, non-existent.

F3 visible.

invitation *n* request, solicitation, call, summons, temptation, enticement, allurement, come-on (*infml*), encouragement, inducement, provocation, incitement, challenge.

invite v ask, call, summon, welcome, encourage, lead, draw, attract, tempt, entice, allure, bring on, provoke, ask for, request, solicit, seek.

inviting adj welcoming, appealing, attractive, tempting, seductive, enticing, alluring, pleasing, delightful, captivating, fascinating, intriguing, tantalizing.
F3 uninviting, unappealing.

invoke v call upon, conjure, appeal to, petition, solicit, implore, entreat, beg, beseech, supplicate, pray.

involuntary adj spontaneous, unconscious, automatic, mechanical, reflex, instinctive, conditioned, impulsive, unthinking, blind, uncontrolled, unintentional.
F3 deliberate, intentional.

involve v **1** REQUIRE, necessitate, mean, imply, entail, include, incorporate, embrace, cover, take in, affect, concern. **2** IMPLICATE, incriminate, inculpate, draw in, mix up, embroil, associate. **3** ENGAGE, occupy, absorb, engross, preoccupy, hold, grip, rivet.
F3 1 exclude.

involved adj **1** CONCERNED, implicated, complicit, mixed up, caught up, in on (sl), participating. **2** an involved explanation: complicated, complex, intricate, elaborate, tangled, knotty, tortuous, confusing.
F3 1 uninvolved. **2** simple.

involvement n concern, interest, responsibility, association, connection, participation, implication, entanglement.

invulnerable adj safe, secure, unassailable, impenetrable, invincible, indestructible.
F3 vulnerable.

inward adj incoming, entering, inside, interior, internal, inner, innermost, inmost, personal, private, secret, confidential.
F3 outward, external.

iota n scrap, bit, mite, jot, speck, trace, hint, grain, particle, atom.

irate adj annoyed, irritated, indignant, up in arms, angry, enraged, mad (infml), furious, infuriated, incensed, worked up, fuming, livid, exasperated.
F3 calm, composed.

iron adj rigid, inflexible, adamant, determined, hard, steely, tough, strong.
F3 pliable, weak.
v press, smooth, flatten.

iron out resolve, settle, sort out, straighten out, clear up, put right, reconcile, deal with, get rid of, eradicate, eliminate.

ironic adj ironical, sarcastic, sardonic, scornful, contemptuous, derisive, sneering, scoffing, mocking, satirical, wry, paradoxical.

irony n sarcasm, mockery, satire, paradox, contrariness, incongruity.

irrational adj unreasonable, unsound, illogical, absurd, crazy, wild, foolish, silly, senseless, unwise.
F3 rational.

irreconcilable adj incompatible, opposed, conflicting, clashing, contradictory, inconsistent.
F3 reconcilable.

irrefutable adj undeniable, incontrovertible, indisputable, incontestable, unquestionable, unanswerable, certain, sure.

irregular adj **1** ROUGH, bumpy, uneven, crooked. **2** VARIABLE, fluctuating, wavering, erratic, fitful, intermittent, sporadic, spasmodic,

occasional, random, haphazard, disorderly, unsystematic.
3 ABNORMAL, unconventional, unorthodox, improper, unusual, exceptional, anomalous.
F3 1 smooth, level. **2** regular.
3 conventional.

irrelevant *adj* immaterial, beside the point, inapplicable, inappropriate, unrelated, unconnected, inconsequent, peripheral, tangential.
F3 relevant.

irreplaceable *adj* indispensable, essential, vital, unique, priceless, peerless, matchless, unmatched.
F3 replaceable.

irrepressible *adj* ebullient, bubbly, uninhibited, buoyant, resilient, boisterous, uncontrollable, ungovernable, unstoppable.

irreproachable *adj* irreprehensible, blameless, unimpeachable, faultless, impeccable, perfect, unblemished, immaculate, stainless, spotless, pure.
F3 blameworthy, culpable.

irresistible *adj* overwhelming, overpowering, unavoidable, inevitable, inescapable, uncontrollable, potent, compelling, imperative, pressing, urgent, tempting, seductive, ravishing, enchanting, charming, fascinating.
F3 resistible, avoidable.

irresponsible *adj* unreliable, untrustworthy, careless, negligent, thoughtless, heedless, ill-considered, rash, reckless, wild, carefree, light-hearted, immature.
F3 responsible, cautious.

irreverent *adj* **1** IMPIOUS, godless, irreligious, profane, sacrilegious, blasphemous. **2** DISRESPECTFUL, discourteous, rude, impudent,

impertinent, mocking, flippant.
F3 1 reverent. **2** respectful.

irreversible *adj* irrevocable, unalterable, final, permanent, lasting, irreparable, irremediable, irretrievable, incurable, hopeless.
F3 reversible, remediable, curable.

irrevocable *adj* unalterable, unchangeable, changeless, invariable, immutable, final, fixed, settled, predetermined, irreversible, irretrievable.
F3 alterable, flexible, reversible.

irrigate *v* water, flood, inundate, wet, moisten, dampen.

irritable *adj* cross, bad-tempered, ill-tempered, crotchety, crusty, cantankerous, crabby, testy, short-tempered, snappish, snappy, short, impatient, touchy, edgy, thin-skinned, hypersensitive, prickly, peevish, fretful, fractious.
F3 good-tempered, cheerful.

irritate *v* **1** ANNOY, get on one's nerves, aggravate (*infml*), bug (*infml*), bother, harass, rouse, provoke, rile, anger, enrage, infuriate, incense, exasperate, peeve, put out.
2 INFLAME, chafe, rub, tickle, itch.
F3 please, gratify.

irritation *n* displeasure, dissatisfaction, annoyance, aggravation, provocation, anger, vexation, indignation, fury, exasperation, irritability, crossness, testiness, snappiness, impatience.
F3 pleasure, satisfaction, delight.

isolate *v* set apart, sequester, seclude, keep apart, segregate, quarantine, insulate, cut off, detach, remove, disconnect, separate, divorce, alienate, shut out, ostracize, exclude.
F3 assimilate, incorporate.

isolated *adj* **1** REMOTE, out-of-the-way, outlying, god-forsaken, deserted, unfrequented, secluded, detached, cut off, lonely, solitary, single. **2** *an isolated occurrence*: unique, special, exceptional, atypical, unusual, freak, abnormal, anomalous.

F∃ 1 populous. **2** typical.

isolation *n* quarantine, solitude, solitariness, loneliness, remoteness, seclusion, retirement, withdrawal, exile, segregation, insulation, separation, detachment, disconnection, dissociation, alienation.

issue *n* **1** MATTER, affair, concern, problem, point, subject, topic, question, debate, argument, dispute, controversy. **2** PUBLICATION, release, distribution, supply, delivery, circulation, promulgation, broadcast, announcement. **3** *last week's issue*: copy, number, instalment, edition, impression, printing.

v **1** PUBLISH, release, distribute, supply, deliver, give out, deal out, circulate, promulgate, broadcast, announce, put out, emit, produce. **2** ORIGINATE, stem, spring, rise, emerge, burst forth, gush, flow, proceed, emanate, arise.

itch *v* tickle, irritate, tingle, prickle, crawl.

n **1** ITCHINESS, tickle, irritation, prickling. **2** EAGERNESS, keenness, desire, longing, yearning, hankering, craving.

item *n* **1** OBJECT, article, thing, piece, component, ingredient, element, factor, point, detail, particular, aspect, feature, consideration, matter. **2** *an item in the local paper*: article, piece, report, account, notice, entry, paragraph.

itinerant *adj* travelling, peripatetic, roving, roaming, wandering, rambling, nomadic, migratory, rootless, unsettled.

F∃ stationary, settled.

itinerary *n* route, course, journey, tour, circuit, plan, programme, schedule.

J

jab v poke, prod, dig, nudge, stab, push, elbow, lunge, punch, tap, thrust.

jackpot n prize, winnings, kitty, pool, pot, reward, award, big time (infml), bonanza, stakes.

jaded adj fatigued, exhausted, dulled, played-out, tired, tired out, weary, spent, bored, fagged (infml).
F3 fresh, refreshed.

jagged adj uneven, irregular, notched, indented, rough, serrated, saw-edged, toothed, ragged, pointed, ridged, craggy, barbed, broken.
F3 even, smooth.

jail, gaol n prison, jailhouse, custody, lock-up, penitentiary, pen (US sl), guardhouse, inside (infml), nick (sl), clink (sl).
v imprison, incarcerate, lock up, put away, send down, confine, detain, intern, impound, immure.

jailer, gaoler n prison officer, warden, warder, guard, screw (sl), keeper, captor.

jam¹ v 1 CRAM, pack, wedge, squash, squeeze, press, crush, crowd, congest, ram, stuff, confine, force. 2 BLOCK, clog, obstruct, stall, stick.
n 1 CRUSH, crowd, press, congestion, pack, mob, throng, bottleneck, traffic jam. 2 PREDICAMENT, trouble, quandary, plight, fix (infml).

jam² n conserve, preserve, jelly, spread, marmalade.

jangle v clank, clash, jar, clatter, jingle, chime, rattle, vibrate.
n clang, clash, rattle, jar, cacophony, dissonance, din, discord, racket, reverberation.
F3 euphony.

jar¹ n pot, container, vessel, receptacle, crock, pitcher, urn, vase, flagon, jug, mug.

jar² v 1 JOLT, agitate, rattle, shake, vibrate, jangle, rock, disturb, discompose. 2 ANNOY, irritate, grate, nettle (infml), offend, upset, irk. 3 BICKER, quarrel, clash, disagree.

jargon n 1 PARLANCE, cant, argot, vernacular, idiom. 2 NONSENSE, gobbledegook (infml), mumbo-jumbo (infml), gibberish.

jarring adj discordant, jangling, harsh, grating, irritating, cacophonous, rasping, strident, upsetting, disturbing, jolting.

jaundiced adj 1 BITTER, cynical, pessimistic, sceptical, distrustful, disbelieving, envious, jealous, hostile, jaded, suspicious, resentful.
2 DISTORTED, biased, prejudiced, preconceived.

jaunty adj sprightly, lively, perky, breezy, buoyant, high-spirited, self-confident, carefree, airy, cheeky,

debonair, dapper, smart, showy, spruce.
F3 depressed, dowdy.

jealous adj **1** ENVIOUS, covetous, grudging, resentful, green (infml), green-eyed (infml). **2** SUSPICIOUS, wary, distrustful, anxious, possessive, protective.
F3 1 contented, satisfied.

jealousy n **1** ENVY, covetousness, grudge, resentment, spite, ill-will.
2 SUSPICION, distrust, mistrust, possessiveness.

jeer v mock, scoff, taunt, jibe, ridicule, sneer, deride, make fun of, chaff, barrack, twit, knock (infml), heckle, banter.
n mockery, derision, ridicule, taunt, jibe, sneer, scoff, abuse, catcall, dig (infml), hiss, hoot.

jell see gel.

jeopardize v endanger, imperil, risk, hazard, venture, gamble, chance, threaten, menace, expose, stake.
F3 protect, safeguard.

jeopardy n danger, peril, risk, hazard, endangerment, venture, vulnerability, precariousness, insecurity, exposure, liability.
F3 safety, security.

jerk n jolt, tug, twitch, jar, jog, yank, wrench, pull, pluck, lurch, throw, thrust, shrug.
v jolt, tug, twitch, jog, yank, wrench, pull, jiggle, lurch, pluck, thrust, shrug, throw, bounce.

jerky adj fitful, twitchy, spasmodic, jumpy, jolting, convulsive, disconnected, bumpy, bouncy, shaky, rough, unco-ordinated, uncontrolled, incoherent.
F3 smooth.

jest n joke, quip, wisecrack (infml), witticism, crack (infml), banter,

fooling, gag (infml), prank, kidding (infml), leg-pull (infml), trick, hoax, practical joke.
v joke, quip, fool, kid (infml), tease, mock, jeer.

jet [1] n gush, spurt, spout, spray, spring, sprinkler, sprayer, fountain, flow, stream, squirt.

jet [2] adj black, pitch-black, ebony, sable, sooty.

jetty n breakwater, pier, dock, groyne, quay, wharf.

jewel n **1** GEM, precious stone, gemstone, ornament, rock (sl).
2 TREASURE, find, prize, rarity, paragon, pearl.

jewellery

Types of jewellery include:
bangle, bracelet, charm bracelet, anklet, cuff link, tiepin, lapel pin, brooch, cameo, earring, nose-ring, toe-ring, ring, signet ring, necklace, necklet, choker, pendant, locket, chain, beads, amulet, torque, tiara, coronet, diadem.

Jewish calendar

The Jewish calendar and its Gregorian equivalents:
Tishri (September-October), Heshvan (October-November), Kislev (November-December), Tevet (December-January), Shebat or Shevat (January-February), Adar (February-March), Adar Sheni (leap years only), Nisan (March-April), Iyyar or Iyar (April-May), Sivan (May-June), Tammuz (June-July), Ab or Av (July-August), Elul (August-September).

jibe see gibe.

jig v jerk, prance, caper, hop, jump, twitch, skip, bounce, bob, wiggle, shake, wobble.

jilt v abandon, reject, desert, discard, ditch (infml), drop, spurn, betray.

jingle v clink, tinkle, ring, chime, chink, jangle, clatter, rattle.
n **1** CLINK, tinkle, ringing, clang, rattle, clangour. **2** RHYME, verse, song, tune, ditty, doggerel, melody, poem, chant, chorus.

jingoism n chauvinism, flag-waving, patriotism, nationalism, imperialism, warmongering, insularity.

jinx n spell, curse, evil eye, hex, voodoo, hoodoo, black magic, gremlin (infml), charm, plague.
v curse, bewitch, bedevil, doom, plague.

job n **1** she has a good job: work, employment, occupation, position, post, situation, profession, career, calling, vocation, trade, métier, capacity, business, livelihood.
2 it's a difficult job: task, chore, duty, responsibility, charge, commission, mission, activity, affair, concern, proceeding, project, enterprise, office, pursuit, role, undertaking, venture, province, part, place, share, errand, function, contribution, stint, assignment, consignment.

jobless adj unemployed, out of work, laid off, on the dole, inactive, redundant.
E3 employed.

jocular adj joking, jesting, funny, jocose (fml), humorous, jovial, amusing, comical, entertaining, facetious, droll, whimsical, teasing, witty.
E3 serious.

jog v **1** JOLT, jar, bump, jostle, jerk, joggle, nudge, poke, shake, prod, bounce, push, rock. **2** PROMPT, remind, stir, arouse, activate, stimulate. **3** RUN, trot.
n **1** JOLT, bump, jerk, nudge, shove, push, poke, prod, shake. **2** RUN, trot.

join v **1** UNITE, connect, combine, conjoin, attach, link, amalgamate, fasten, merge, marry, couple, yoke, tie, splice, knit, cement, add, adhere, annex. **2** ABUT, adjoin, border (on), verge on, touch, meet, coincide, march with. **3** ASSOCIATE, affiliate, accompany, ally, enlist, enrol, enter, sign up, team.
E3 1 divide, separate. **3** leave.

joint n junction, connection, union, juncture, intersection, hinge, knot, articulation, seam.
adj combined, common, communal, joined, shared, united, collective, amalgamated, mutual, co-operative, co-ordinated, consolidated, concerted.

joke n **1** JEST, quip, crack (infml), gag (infml), witticism, wisecrack (infml), one-liner (infml), pun, hoot, whimsy, yarn. **2** TRICK, jape, lark, prank, spoof, fun.
v jest, quip, clown, fool, pun, wisecrack (infml), kid (infml), tease, banter, mock, laugh, frolic, gambol.

joker n comedian, comedienne, comic, wit, humorist, jester, trickster, wag, clown, buffoon, kidder, droll, card (infml), character, sport.

jolly adj jovial, merry, cheerful, playful, hearty, happy, exuberant.
E3 sad.

jolt v **1** JAR, jerk, jog, bump, jostle, knock, bounce, shake, push. **2** UPSET, startle, shock, surprise, stun, discompose, disconcert, disturb.
n **1** JAR, jerk, jog, bump, blow, impact, lurch, shake. **2** SHOCK, surprise, reversal, setback, start.

jostle v push, shove, jog, bump, elbow, hustle, jolt, crowd, shoulder, joggle, shake, squeeze, throng.

jot down write down, take down, note, list, record, scribble, register, enter.

journal n newspaper, periodical, magazine, fanzine, e-zine, paper, publication, review, weekly, monthly, register, chronicle, diary, weblog, blog (infml), gazette, daybook, log, record.

journalist n reporter, news-writer, hack, correspondent, editor, columnist, feature-writer, commentator, broadcaster, contributor.

journey n voyage, trip, travel, expedition, passage, trek, tour, ramble, outing, wanderings, safari, progress.
v travel, voyage, go, trek, tour, roam, rove, proceed, wander, tramp, ramble, range, gallivant.

jovial adj jolly, cheery, merry, affable, cordial, genial.
F3 gloomy.

joy n happiness, gladness, delight, pleasure, bliss, ecstasy, elation, joyfulness, exultation, gratification, rapture.
F3 despair, grief.

joyful adj happy, pleased, delighted, glad, elated, ecstatic, triumphant.
F3 sorrowful.

jubilant adj joyful, rejoicing, overjoyed, delighted, elated, triumphant, exuberant, excited, euphoric, thrilled.

jubilee n celebration, commemoration, anniversary, festival, festivity, gala, fête, carnival.

judge n 1 JUSTICE, Law Lord, magistrate, arbiter, adjudicator, arbitrator, mediator, moderator, referee, umpire, beak (sl).
2 CONNOISSEUR, authority, expert, evaluator, assessor, critic.
v 1 ADJUDICATE, arbitrate, try, referee, umpire, decree, mediate, examine, sentence, review, rule, find.
2 ASCERTAIN, determine, decide, assess, appraise, evaluate, estimate, value, distinguish, discern, reckon, believe, think, consider, conclude, rate. 3 CONDEMN, criticize, doom.

judgement n 1 VERDICT, sentence, ruling, decree, conclusion, decision, arbitration, finding, result, mediation, order. 2 DISCERNMENT, discrimination, understanding, wisdom, prudence, common sense, sense, intelligence, taste, shrewdness, penetration, enlightenment.
3 ASSESSMENT, evaluation, appraisal, estimate, opinion, view, belief, diagnosis. 4 CONVICTION, damnation, punishment, retribution, doom, fate, misfortune.

judicial adj legal, forensic, official, discriminating, critical, impartial.

judicious adj wise, prudent, careful, cautious, astute, discerning, informed, shrewd, thoughtful, reasonable, sensible, sound, well-judged, well-advised, considered.
F3 injudicious.

jug n pitcher, carafe, ewer, flagon, urn, jar, vessel, container.

juggle v alter, change, manipulate, falsify, rearrange, rig, doctor (infml), cook (infml), disguise.

juice n liquid, fluid, extract, essence, sap, secretion, nectar, liquor.

juicy adj 1 SUCCULENT, moist, lush, watery. 2 (infml) INTERESTING, colourful, sensational, racy, risqué, suggestive, lurid.

F3 1 dry.

jumble *v* disarrange, confuse, disorganize, mix (up), muddle, shuffle, tangle.

F3 order.

n disorder, disarray, confusion, mess, chaos, mix-up, muddle, clutter, mixture, hotchpotch, mishmash (*infml*), medley.

jump *v* **1** LEAP, spring, bound, vault, clear, bounce, skip, hop, prance, frolic, gambol. **2** START, flinch, jerk, recoil, jump out of one's skin (*infml*), wince, quail. **3** OMIT, leave out, miss, skip, pass over, bypass, disregard, ignore, avoid, digress. **4** RISE, increase, gain, appreciate, ascend, escalate, mount, advance, surge, spiral.

n **1** LEAP, spring, bound, vault, hop, skip, bounce, prance, frisk, frolic, pounce. **2** START, jerk, jolt, jar, lurch, shock, spasm, quiver, shiver, twitch. **3** BREAK, gap, interruption, lapse, omission, interval, breach, switch. **4** RISE, increase, escalation, boost, advance, increment, upsurge, upturn, mounting. **5** HURDLE, fence, gate, hedge, barricade, obstacle.

jumpy *adj* nervous, anxious, agitated, apprehensive, jittery, tense, edgy, fidgety, shaky.

F3 calm, composed.

junction *n* joint, join, joining, connection, juncture, union, intersection, linking, coupling, meeting-point, confluence.

junior *adj* younger, minor, lesser, lower, subordinate, secondary, subsidiary, inferior.

F3 senior.

junk *n* rubbish, refuse, trash, debris, garbage, waste, scrap, litter, clutter, oddments, rummage, dregs, wreckage.

jurisdiction *n* power, authority, control, influence, dominion, province, sovereignty, command, domination, rule, prerogative (*fml*), sway, orbit, bounds, area, field, scope, range, reach, sphere, zone.

just *adj* **1** *a just ruler*: fair, equitable, impartial, unbiased, unprejudiced, fair-minded, even-handed, objective, righteous, upright, virtuous, honourable, good, honest, irreproachable. **2** *a just punishment*: deserved, merited, fitting, well-deserved, appropriate, suitable, due, proper, reasonable, rightful, lawful, legitimate.

F3 1 unjust. **2** undeserved.

justice *n* **1** FAIRNESS, equity, impartiality, objectivity, equitableness, justness, legitimacy, honesty, right, rightfulness, rightness, justifiableness, reasonableness, rectitude. **2** LEGALITY, law, penalty, recompense, reparation, satisfaction. **3** JUDGE, Justice of the Peace, JP, magistrate.

F3 1 injustice, unfairness.

justifiable *adj* defensible, excusable, warranted, reasonable, justified, lawful, legitimate, acceptable, explainable, forgivable, pardonable, understandable, valid, well-founded, right, proper, explicable, fit, tenable.

F3 unjustifiable.

justification *n* defence, plea, mitigation, apology, explanation, excuse, vindication, warrant, rationalization, reason, grounds.

justify *v* vindicate, exonerate, warrant, substantiate, defend, acquit, absolve, excuse, forgive, explain, pardon, validate, uphold, sustain, support, maintain, establish.

jut out project, protrude, stick out, overhang, extend.

F∃ recede.

juvenile n child, youth, minor, young person, youngster, adolescent, teenager, boy, girl, kid (*infml*), infant. *adj* young, youthful, immature, childish, puerile, infantile, adolescent, babyish, unsophisticated.

F∃ mature.

juxtaposition n contiguity, proximity, nearness, closeness, contact, vicinity, immediacy.

K

keel over 1 OVERTURN, capsize, founder, collapse, upset. **2** FAINT, pass out, swoon, fall, drop, stagger, topple over.

keen *adj* **1** EAGER, avid, fervent, enthusiastic, earnest, devoted, diligent, industrious. **2** ASTUTE, shrewd, clever, perceptive, wise, discerning, quick, deep, sensitive. **3** SHARP, piercing, penetrating, incisive, acute, pointed, intense, pungent, trenchant.

F3 1 apathetic. **2** superficial. **3** dull.

keep *v* **1** RETAIN, hold, preserve, hold on to, hang on to, store, stock, possess, amass, accumulate, collect, stack, conserve, deposit, heap, pile, place, maintain, furnish. **2** CARRY ON, keep on, continue, persist, remain. **3** LOOK AFTER, tend, care for, have charge of, have custody of, maintain, provide for, subsidize, support, sustain, be responsible for, foster, mind, protect, shelter, guard, defend, watch (over), shield, safeguard, feed, nurture, manage. **4** DETAIN, delay, retard, check, hinder, hold (up), impede, obstruct, prevent, block, curb, interfere with, restrain, limit, inhibit, deter, hamper, keep back, control, constrain, arrest, withhold. **5** OBSERVE, comply with, respect, obey, fulfil, adhere to, recognize, keep up, keep faith with, commemorate, celebrate, hold, maintain, perform, perpetuate, mark, honour.
n **1** SUBSISTENCE, board, livelihood, living, maintenance, support, upkeep, means, food, nourishment, nurture. **2** FORT, fortress, tower, castle, citadel, stronghold, dungeon.

keep back 1 RESTRAIN, check, constrain, curb, impede, limit, prohibit, retard, stop, control, delay. **2** HOLD BACK, restrict, suppress, withhold, conceal, censor, hide, hush up, stifle, reserve, retain.

keep in 1 REPRESS, keep back, inhibit, bottle up, conceal, stifle, suppress, hide, control, restrain, quell, stop up. **2** CONFINE, detain, shut in, coop up.

F3 1 declare. **2** release.

keep on continue, carry on, endure, persevere, persist, keep at it, last, remain, stay, stay the course, soldier on (*infml*), hold on, retain, maintain.

keep up 1 KEEP PACE, equal, contend, compete, vie, rival, match, emulate. **2** CONTINUE, maintain, persevere, support, sustain, preserve.

keeper *n* guard, custodian, curator, caretaker, attendant, guardian, overseer, steward, warder, jailer, gaoler, warden, supervisor, minder (*infml*), inspector, conservator (*fml*), defender, governor, superintendent, surveyor.

keepsake n memento, souvenir, remembrance, relic, reminder, token, pledge, emblem.

kernel n core, grain, seed, nucleus, heart, nub, essence, germ, marrow, substance, nitty-gritty (infml), gist.

key n **1** CLUE, cue, indicator, pointer, explanation, sign, answer, solution, interpretation, means, secret. **2** GUIDE, glossary, translation, legend, code, table, index. adj important, essential, vital, crucial, necessary, principal, decisive, central, chief, main, major, leading, basic, fundamental.

keynote n core, centre, heart, substance, theme, gist, essence, emphasis, accent, stress.

keystone n cornerstone, core, crux, base, basis, foundation, ground, linchpin, principle, root, mainspring, source, spring, motive.

kick v **1** BOOT, hit, strike, jolt. **2** (infml) GIVE UP, quit, stop, leave off, abandon, desist from, break. n **1** BLOW, recoil, jolt, striking. **2** (infml) STIMULATION, thrill, excitement.

kick off begin, commence, start, open, get under way, open the proceedings, set the ball rolling, introduce, inaugurate, initiate.

kick out eject, evict, expel, oust, remove, chuck out (infml), discharge, dismiss, get rid of, sack (infml), throw out, reject.

kid [1] n child, youngster, youth, juvenile, infant, girl, boy, teenager, lad, nipper (infml), tot (infml).

kid [2] v tease, joke, have on (infml), hoax, fool, pull someone's leg (infml), pretend, trick, delude, dupe, con (infml), jest, hoodwink, humbug, bamboozle.

kidnap v abduct, capture, seize, hold to ransom, snatch, hijack, steal.

kill v **1** SLAUGHTER, murder, slay, put to death, exterminate, assassinate, do to death, do in (infml), bump off (infml), finish off, massacre, smite (fml), execute, eliminate (sl), destroy, dispatch (infml), do away with, butcher, annihilate, liquidate (sl), knock off (infml), rub out (sl). **2** STIFLE, deaden, smother, quash, quell, suppress.

killer n murderer, assassin, executioner, destroyer, slaughterer, exterminator, butcher (infml), cut-throat, gunman, hatchet man (sl), hit-man (sl).

killing n **1** SLAUGHTER, murder, massacre, homicide, assassination, execution, slaying, manslaughter, extermination, carnage, bloodshed, elimination, fatality, liquidation. **2** (infml) GAIN, fortune, windfall, profit, lucky break, coup, clean-up (infml), success, stroke of luck, bonanza (infml), hit, big hit. adj (infml) **1** FUNNY, hilarious, comical, amusing, side-splitting (infml), ludicrous. **2** EXHAUSTING, hard, taxing, arduous.

kind n sort, type, class, category, set, variety, character, genus, genre, style, brand, family, breed, race, nature, persuasion, description, species, stamp, temperament, manner. adj benevolent, kind-hearted, kindly, good-hearted, good-natured, helpful, obliging, humane, generous, compassionate, charitable, amiable, friendly, congenial, soft-hearted, thoughtful, warm, warm-hearted, considerate, courteous, sympathetic, tender-hearted, understanding, lenient, mild, hospitable, gentle, indulgent, neighbourly, tactful, giving, good, loving, gracious.

E3 cruel, inconsiderate, unhelpful.

kindle v 1 IGNITE, light, set alight, set on fire. **2** INFLAME, fire, stir, thrill, stimulate, rouse, arouse, awaken, excite, fan, incite, inspire, induce, provoke.

kindly adj benevolent, kind, compassionate, charitable, good-natured, helpful, warm, generous, cordial, favourable, giving, indulgent, pleasant, sympathetic, tender, gentle, mild, patient, polite.

E3 cruel, uncharitable.

kindness n 1 BENEVOLENCE, kindliness, charity, magnanimity, compassion, generosity, hospitality, humanity, loving-kindness (fml), courtesy, friendliness, good will, goodness, grace, indulgence, tolerance, understanding, gentleness. **2** FAVOUR, good turn, assistance, help, service.

E3 1 cruelty, inhumanity. **2** disservice.

king n monarch, ruler, sovereign, majesty, emperor, chief, chieftain, prince, supremo, leading light (infml).

kingdom n monarchy, sovereignty, reign, realm, empire, dominion, commonwealth, nation, principality, state, country, domain, dynasty, province, sphere, territory, land, division.

kink n 1 CURL, twist, bend, dent, indentation, knot, loop, crimp, coil, tangle, wrinkle. **2** QUIRK, eccentricity, idiosyncrasy, foible, perversion.

kinship n 1 KIN, blood, relation. **2** AFFINITY, similarity, association, alliance, connection, correspondence, relationship, tie, community, conformity.

kiosk n booth, stall, stand, news-stand, bookstall, cabin, box, counter.

kiss v 1 CARESS, peck (infml), smooch (infml), neck (infml), snog (sl).
2 TOUCH, graze, glance, brush, lick, scrape, fan.
n peck (infml), smack (infml), smacker (sl).

kit n equipment, gear, apparatus, supplies, tackle, provisions, outfit, implements, set, tools, trappings, rig, instruments, paraphernalia, utensils, effects, luggage, baggage.

kit out equip, fit out, outfit, supply, fix up, furnish, prepare, arm, deck out, dress.

knack n flair, faculty, facility, hang (infml), bent, skill, talent, genius, gift, trick, propensity, ability, expertise, skilfulness, forte, capacity, handiness, dexterity, quickness, turn.

knapsack n bag, pack, haversack, rucksack, backpack.

knead v manipulate, press, massage, work, ply, squeeze, shape, rub, form, mould, knuckle.

knell n toll, ringing, chime, peel, knoll.

knick-knack n trinket, trifle, bauble, gewgaw, gimcrack, bric-à-brac, plaything.

knife n blade, cutter, carver, dagger, pen-knife, pocket-knife, switchblade, jack-knife, flick-knife, machete.
v cut, rip, slash, stab, pierce, wound.

knit v 1 JOIN, unite, secure, connect, tie, fasten, link, mend, interlace, intertwine. **2** KNOT, loop, crochet, weave. **3** WRINKLE, furrow.

knock v hit, strike, rap, thump, pound, slap, smack.
n blow, box, rap, thump, cuff, clip, pounding, hammering, slap, smack.

knock about 1 WANDER, travel, roam, rove, saunter, traipse, ramble, range. **2** ASSOCIATE, go around. **3** BEAT UP, batter, abuse, mistreat, hurt, hit, bash, damage, maltreat, manhandle, bruise, buffet.

knock down demolish, destroy, fell, floor, level, wreck, raze, pound, batter, clout, smash, wallop.

knock off 1 (infml) FINISH, cease, stop, pack (it) in, clock off, clock out, terminate. **2** (infml) STEAL, rob, pilfer, pinch (infml), nick (infml), filch. **3** DEDUCT, take away. **4** (sl) KILL, murder, slay, assassinate, do away with, bump off (infml), do in (infml), waste (sl).

knockout n success, triumph, sensation, hit, smash (infml), smash-hit (infml), winner, stunner (infml).
F3 flop, loser.

knot v tie, secure, bind, entangle, tangle, knit, entwine, ravel, weave.
n **1** TIE, bond, joint, fastening, loop, splice, hitch. **2** BUNCH, cluster, clump, group.

> Types of knot include:
> bend, Blackwall hitch, bow, bow-line, running bowline, carrick bend, clove-hitch, Englishman's tie (or knot), figure of eight, fisherman's bend, fisherman's knot, granny knot, half-hitch, hangman's knot, hitch, loop knot, overhand knot (or thumb knot), reef-knot (or square knot), rolling hitch, sheepshank, sheet bend, slipknot, surgeon's knot, swab hitch, timber-hitch, Turk's head, wall knot, weaver's knot, Windsor knot.

know v **1** she knows French: understand, comprehend, apprehend, perceive, notice, be aware, fathom, experience, realize, see, undergo. **2** I know George: be acquainted with, be familiar with, recognize, identify. **3** know a good wine: distinguish, discriminate, discern, differentiate, make out, tell.

knowledge n **1** LEARNING, scholarship, erudition, education, schooling, instruction, tuition, information, enlightenment, know-how. **2** ACQUAINTANCE, familiarity, awareness, cognizance, intimacy, consciousness. **3** UNDERSTANDING, comprehension, cognition, apprehension, recognition, judgement, discernment, ability, grasp, wisdom, intelligence.
F3 1 ignorance. **2** unawareness.

knowledgeable adj **1** EDUCATED, scholarly, learned, well-informed, lettered, intelligent. **2** AWARE, acquainted, conscious, familiar, au fait, in the know (infml), conversant, experienced.
F3 1 ignorant.

known adj acknowledged, recognized, well-known, noted, obvious, patent, plain, admitted, familiar, avowed, commonplace, published, confessed, celebrated, famous.

kowtow v defer, cringe, fawn, grovel, pander, suck up (infml), brown-nose (US sl), toady (infml), flatter, kneel.

L

label n **1** TAG, ticket, docket, mark, marker, sticker, trademark. **2** DESCRIPTION, categorization, identification, characterization, classification, badge, brand. v **1** TAG, mark, stamp. **2** DEFINE, describe, classify, categorize, characterize, identify, class, designate, brand, call, dub, name.

laborious adj **1** HARD, arduous, difficult, strenuous, tough, backbreaking, wearisome, tiresome, uphill, onerous, heavy, toilsome. **2** HARD-WORKING, industrious, painstaking, indefatigable, diligent. **F3 1** easy, effortless. **2** lazy.

labour n **1** WORK, task, job, chore, toil, effort, exertion, drudgery, grind (infml), slog (infml), sweat (infml). **2** WORKERS, employees, workforce, labourers. **3** CHILDBIRTH, birth, delivery, labour pains, contractions. **F3 1** ease, leisure. **2** management. v **1** WORK, toil, drudge, slave, strive, endeavour, struggle, grind (infml), sweat (infml), plod, travail (fml). **2** TOSS, pitch, roll. **3** OVERDO, overemphasize, dwell on, elaborate, overstress, strain. **F3 1** laze, idle, lounge.

labourer n manual worker, blue-collar worker, navvy, hand, worker, drudge, hireling.

labyrinth n maze, complexity, intricacy, complication, puzzle, riddle, windings, tangle, jungle.

lace n **1** NETTING, mesh-work, open-work, tatting, crochet. **2** STRING, cord, thong, tie, shoelace, bootlace. v **1** TIE, do up, fasten, thread, close, bind, attach, string, intertwine, interweave. **2** ADD TO, mix in, spike (infml), fortify.

lacerate v tear, rip, rend, cut, gash, slash, wound, claw, mangle, maim, torture, torment, distress, afflict.

lack n need, want, scarcity, shortage, insufficiency, dearth, deficiency, absence, scantiness, vacancy, void, privation, deprivation, destitution, emptiness. **F3** abundance, profusion. v need, want, require, miss.

lacking adj needing, wanting, without, short of, missing, minus, inadequate, deficient, defective, flawed.

lacklustre adj drab, dull, flat, boring, leaden, lifeless, unimaginative, dim. **F3** brilliant, inspired.

laconic adj terse, succinct, pithy, concise, crisp, taciturn, short, curt, brief. **F3** verbose, wordy.

lad n boy, youth, youngster, kid (infml), schoolboy, chap, guy (infml), fellow.

lag v dawdle, loiter, hang back, linger, straggle, trail, saunter, delay, shuffle, tarry, idle.
F3 hurry, lead.

lair n den, burrow, hole, nest, earth, form, roost, retreat, hideout, refuge, sanctuary, stronghold.

lake n lagoon, reservoir, loch, mere, tarn.

lame adj **1** DISABLED, handicapped, crippled, limping, hobbling. **2** WEAK, feeble, flimsy, inadequate, unsatisfactory.
F3 1 able-bodied. **2** convincing.

lament v mourn, bewail, bemoan, grieve, sorrow, weep, wail, complain, deplore, regret.
F3 rejoice, celebrate.
n lamentation, dirge, elegy, requiem, threnody (fml), complaint, moan, wail.

lamentable adj **1** DEPLORABLE, regrettable, mournful, distressing, tragic, unfortunate, sorrowful.
2 MEAGRE, low, inadequate, insufficient, mean, unsatisfactory, pitiful, miserable, poor, disappointing.

lampoon n satire, skit, caricature, parody, send-up (infml), spoof, take-off (infml), burlesque.
v satirize, caricature, parody, send up, take off (infml), spoof, make fun of, ridicule, mock, burlesque.

land n **1** EARTH, ground, soil, terra firma. **2** PROPERTY, grounds, estate, real estate, country, countryside, farmland, tract. **3** COUNTRY, nation, region, territory, province.
v **1** ALIGHT, disembark, dock, berth, touch down, come to rest, arrive, deposit, wind up, end up, drop, settle, turn up. **2** OBTAIN, secure, gain, get, acquire, net, capture, achieve, win.

landlord n owner, proprietor, host, publican, innkeeper, hotelier, restaurateur, hotel-keeper, freeholder.
F3 tenant.

landmark n feature, monument, signpost, turning-point, watershed, milestone, beacon, cairn.

landscape n scene, scenery, view, panorama, outlook, vista, prospect, countryside, aspect.

landslide n landslip, rock-fall, avalanche.
adj overwhelming, decisive, emphatic, runaway.

language n **1** SPEECH, vocabulary, terminology, parlance. **2** TALK, conversation, discourse. **3** WORDING, style, phraseology, phrasing, expression, utterance, diction.

Language terms include:
brogue, dialect, idiom, patois, tongue, pidgin, creole, lingua franca, vernacular, argot, cant, jargon, double-speak, gobbledegook, buzzword, journalese, lingo (infml), patter, slang, rhyming slang; etymology, lexicography, linguistics, phonetics, semantics, syntax, usage, grammar, orthography, sociolinguistics.

Languages of the world include:
Afrikaans, Amharic, Arabic, Armenian, Bantu, Basque, Belorussian, Bengali, Burmese, Catalan, Chinese, Cornish, Czech, Danish, Dari, Dutch, English, Esperanto, Estonian, Farsi, Finnish, Flemish, French, Gaelic, German, Greek, Hawaiian, Hebrew, Hindi, Hungarian, Icelandic, Indonesian, Inuit, Irish, Italian, Japanese, Korean, Kurdish, Lapp, Latin, Latvian,

Lithuanian, Magyar, Malay, Maltese, Mandarin, Manx, Maori, Nahuatl, Norwegian, Pashto, Persian, Polish, Portuguese, Punjabi, Quechua, Romanian, Romany, Russian, Sanskrit, Serbo-Croat, Sinhalese, Slovak, Slovene, Somali, Spanish, Swahili, Swedish, Tamil, Thai, Tibetan, Tupí, Turkish, Ukrainian, Urdu, Vietnamese, Volapük, Welsh, Yiddish, Zulu.

languish v **1** WILT, droop, fade, fail, flag, wither, waste away, weaken, sink, faint, decline, mope, waste, grieve, sorrow, sigh, sicken. **2** PINE, yearn, want, long, desire, hanker, hunger.
F3 1 flourish.

lanky adj gaunt, gangling, scrawny, tall, thin, scraggy, weedy.
F3 short, squat.

lap¹ v drink, sip, sup, lick.

lap² n circuit, round, orbit, tour, loop, course, circle, distance.
v wrap, fold, envelop, enfold, swathe, surround, cover, swaddle, overlap.

lapse n **1** ERROR, slip, mistake, negligence, omission, oversight, fault, failing, indiscretion, aberration, backsliding, relapse. **2** FALL, descent, decline, drop, deterioration. **3** BREAK, gap, interval, lull, interruption, intermission, pause.
v **1** DECLINE, fall, sink, drop, deteriorate, slide, slip, fail, worsen, degenerate, backslide. **2** EXPIRE, run out, end, stop, terminate.

large adj **1** BIG, huge, immense, massive, vast, sizable, great, giant, gigantic, bulky, enormous, king-sized, broad, considerable, monumental, substantial. **2** FULL, extensive, generous, liberal, roomy, plentiful,

spacious, grand, sweeping, grandiose.
F3 1 small, tiny.
at large free, at liberty, on the loose, on the run, independent.

largely adv mainly, principally, chiefly, generally, primarily, predominantly, mostly, considerably, by and large, widely, extensively, greatly.

lark n escapade, antic, fling, prank, romp, skylark (infml), revel, mischief, frolic, caper, game.

lash¹ n blow, whip, stroke, swipe, hit. v **1** WHIP, flog, beat, hit, thrash, strike, scourge. **2** ATTACK, criticize, lay into, scold.

lash² v tie, bind, fasten, secure, make fast, join, affix, rope, tether, strap.

last¹ adj final, ultimate, closing, latest, rearmost, terminal, furthest, concluding, remotest, utmost, extreme, conclusive, definitive.
F3 first, initial.
adv finally, ultimately, behind, after.
F3 first, firstly.
at last eventually, finally, in the end, in due course, at length.

last² v continue, endure, remain, persist, keep (on), survive, hold out, carry on, wear, stay, hold on, stand up, abide (fml).
F3 cease, stop, fade.

lasting adj enduring, unchanging, unceasing, unending, continuing, permanent, perpetual, lifelong, long-standing, long-term.
F3 brief, fleeting, short-lived.

latch n fastening, catch, bar, bolt, lock, hook, hasp.

late adj **1** OVERDUE, behind, behind-hand, slow, unpunctual, delayed, last-minute. **2** FORMER, previous, departed, dead, deceased, past, preceding, old. **3** RECENT, up-to-date, current, fresh, new.

F3 1 early, punctual.

lately *adv* recently, of late, latterly.

latent *adj* potential, dormant, undeveloped, unrealized, lurking, unexpressed, unseen, secret, concealed, hidden, invisible, underlying, veiled.

F3 active, conspicuous.

later *adv* next, afterwards, subsequently, after, successively.

F3 earlier.

lateral *adj* sideways, side, oblique, sideward, edgeways, marginal, flanking.

lather *n* **1** FOAM, suds, soap-suds, froth, bubbles, soap, shampoo. **2** AGITATION, fluster, fuss, dither, state (*infml*), flutter, flap (*infml*), fever. *v* foam, froth, soap, shampoo, whip up.

latitude *n* **1** SCOPE, range, room, space, play, clearance, breadth, width, spread, sweep, reach, span, field, extent. **2** FREEDOM, liberty, licence, leeway, indulgence.

latter *adj* last-mentioned, last, later, closing, concluding, ensuing, succeeding, successive, second.

F3 former.

laugh *v* chuckle, giggle, guffaw, snigger, titter, chortle, split one's sides, fall about (*infml*), crease up (*infml*). *n* giggle, chuckle, snigger, titter, guffaw, chortle, lark, scream (*infml*), hoot (*infml*), joke.

laugh at mock, ridicule, deride, jeer, make fun of, scoff at, scorn, taunt.

laughable *adj* **1** FUNNY, amusing, comical, humorous, hilarious, droll, farcical, diverting. **2** RIDICULOUS, absurd, ludicrous, preposterous,

nonsensical, derisory, derisive.

F3 1 serious.

laughing-stock *n* figure of fun, butt, victim, target, fair game.

laughter *n* laughing, giggling, chuckling, chortling, guffawing, tittering, hilarity, amusement, merriment, mirth, glee, convulsions.

launch *v* **1** PROPEL, dispatch, discharge, send off, project, float, set in motion, throw, fire. **2** BEGIN, commence, start, embark on, establish, found, open, initiate, inaugurate, introduce, instigate.

lavatory *n* toilet, loo (*infml*), WC, bathroom, cloakroom, washroom, rest room (*N Am*), water-closet, public convenience, Ladies (*infml*), Gents (*infml*), bog (*sl*), john (*US sl*), urinal, powder-room.

lavish *adj* **1** ABUNDANT, lush, luxuriant, plentiful, profuse, unlimited, prolific. **2** GENEROUS, liberal, open-handed, extravagant, thriftless, prodigal, immoderate, intemperate, unstinting.

F3 1 scant. **2** frugal, thrifty.

law *n* **1** RULE, act, decree, edict, order, statute, regulation, command, ordinance, charter, constitution, enactment. **2** PRINCIPLE, axiom, criterion, standard, precept, formula, code, canon. **3** JURISPRUDENCE, legislation, litigation.

law-abiding *adj* obedient, upright, orderly, lawful, honest, honourable, decent, good.

F3 lawless.

lawful *adj* legal, legitimate, permissible, legalized, authorized, allowable, warranted, valid, proper, rightful.

F3 illegal, unlawful, illicit.

lawless adj disorderly, rebellious, anarchic(al), unruly, riotous, mutinous, unrestrained, chaotic, wild, reckless.

F3 law-abiding.

lawsuit n litigation, suit, action, proceedings, case, prosecution, dispute, process, trial, argument, contest, cause.

lawyer n solicitor, barrister, advocate, attorney, counsel, QC.

lax adj 1 CASUAL, careless, easy-going, slack, lenient, negligent, remiss. 2 IMPRECISE, inexact, indefinite, loose.

F3 1 strict. 2 exact.

lay[1] v 1 PUT, place, deposit, set down, settle, lodge, plant, set, establish, leave. 2 ARRANGE, position, set out, locate, work out, devise, prepare, present, submit. 3 ATTRIBUTE, ascribe, assign, charge.

lay in store (up), stock up, amass, accumulate, hoard, stockpile, gather, collect, build up, glean.

lay into (infml) attack, assail, pitch into, set about, tear into, let fly at, hit out at.

lay off 1 DISMISS, discharge, make redundant, sack (infml), pay off, let go. 2 (infml) GIVE UP, drop, stop, quit, cease, desist, leave off, leave alone, let up.

lay on provide, supply, cater, furnish, give, set up.

lay out 1 DISPLAY, set out, spread out, exhibit, arrange, plan, design. 2 (infml) KNOCK OUT, fell, flatten, demolish. 3 (infml) SPEND, pay, shell out (infml), fork out (infml), give, invest.

lay up store up, hoard, accumulate, amass, keep, save, put away.

lay[2] adj 1 LAIC, secular. 2 AMATEUR, non-professional, non-specialist.

F3 1 clergy. 2 expert.

layer n 1 COVER, coating, coat, covering, film, blanket, mantle, sheet, lamina. 2 STRATUM, seam, thickness, tier, bed, plate, row, ply.

layman n 1 LAYPERSON, parishioner. 2 AMATEUR, outsider.

F3 1 clergyman. 2 expert.

layout n arrangement, design, outline, plan, sketch, draft, map.

laze v idle, loaf (infml), lounge, sit around, lie around, loll.

lazy adj idle, slothful, slack, work-shy, inactive, lethargic.

F3 industrious.

lead v 1 GUIDE, conduct, escort, steer, pilot, usher. 2 RULE, govern, head, preside over, direct, supervise. 3 INFLUENCE, persuade, incline. 4 SURPASS, outdo, excel, outstrip, transcend. 5 PASS, spend, live, undergo.

F3 follow.

n 1 PRIORITY, precedence, first place, start, van, vanguard, advantage, edge, margin. 2 LEADERSHIP, guidance, direction, example, model. 3 CLUE, hint, indication, guide, tip, suggestion. 4 TITLE ROLE, starring part, principal.

lead off begin, commence, open, get going, start (off), inaugurate, initiate, kick off (infml), start the ball rolling.

lead on entice, lure, seduce, tempt, draw on, beguile, persuade, string along, deceive, trick.

lead to cause, result in, produce, bring about, bring on, contribute to, tend towards.

lead up to prepare (the way) for, approach, introduce, make overtures, pave the way.

leader n head, chief, director, ruler, principal, commander, captain, boss (*infml*), superior, chieftain, ringleader, guide, conductor.
F3 follower.

leadership n direction, control, command, management, authority, guidance, domination, pre-eminence, premiership, administration, sway, directorship.

leading adj main, principal, chief, primary, first, supreme, outstanding, foremost, dominant, ruling, superior, greatest, highest, governing, pre-eminent, number one.
F3 subordinate.

leaflet n pamphlet, booklet, brochure, circular, handout.

league n 1 ASSOCIATION, confederation, alliance, union, federation, confederacy, coalition, combination, band, syndicate, guild, consortium, cartel, combine, partnership, fellowship, compact.
2 CATEGORY, class, level, group.
in league allied, collaborating, conspiring.

leak n 1 CRACK, hole, opening, puncture, crevice, chink. **2** LEAKAGE, leaking, seepage, drip, oozing, percolation. **3** DISCLOSURE, divulgence.
v **1** SEEP, drip, ooze, escape, spill, trickle, percolate, exude, discharge.
2 DIVULGE, disclose, reveal, let slip, make known, make public, tell, give away, pass on.

leaky adj leaking, holey, perforated, punctured, split, cracked, porous, permeable.

lean[1] v **1** SLANT, slope, bend, tilt, list, tend. **2** RECLINE, prop, rest. **3** INCLINE, favour, prefer.

lean[2] adj **1** THIN, skinny, bony, gaunt, lank, angular, slim, scraggy, scrawny, emaciated. **2** SCANTY, inadequate, bare, barren.
F3 fat.

leaning n tendency, inclination, propensity, partiality, liking, bent, bias, disposition, aptitude.

leap v **1** JUMP (OVER), bound, spring, vault, clear, skip, hop, bounce, caper, gambol. **2** SOAR, surge, increase, rocket, escalate, rise.
F3 2 drop, fall.
n **1** JUMP, bound, spring, vault, hop, skip, caper. **2** INCREASE, upsurge, upswing, surge, rise, escalation.

learn v **1** GRASP, comprehend, understand, master, acquire, pick up, gather, assimilate, discern.
2 MEMORIZE, learn by heart.
3 DISCOVER, find out, ascertain, hear, detect, determine.

learned adj scholarly, erudite, well-informed, well-read, cultured, academic, lettered, literate, intellectual, versed.
F3 uneducated, illiterate.

learner n novice, beginner, student, trainee, pupil, scholar, apprentice.

learning n scholarship, erudition, education, schooling, knowledge, information, letters, study, wisdom, tuition, culture, edification, research.

lease v let, loan, rent, hire, sublet, charter.

least adj smallest, lowest, minimum, fewest, slightest, poorest.
F3 most.

leave v **1** DEPART, go, go away, set out, take off, decamp, exit, move, quit, retire, withdraw, disappear, do a bunk (*infml*). **2** ABANDON, desert, forsake, give up, drop, relinquish, renounce,

pull out, surrender, desist, cease.
3 ASSIGN, commit, entrust, consign, bequeath, will, hand down, leave behind, leave over, transmit.
F3 1 arrive. **3** receive.

leave off stop, cease, discontinue, desist, abstain, refrain, lay off, quit, terminate, break off, end, halt, give over.

leave out omit, exclude, overlook, ignore, except, disregard, pass over, count out, cut (out), eliminate, neglect, reject, cast aside, bar.

leave[2] n **1** PERMISSION, authorization, consent, allowance, sanction, concession, dispensation, indulgence, liberty, freedom.
2 HOLIDAY, time off, vacation, sabbatical, furlough.
F3 1 refusal, rejection.

lecture n **1** DISCOURSE, address, lesson, speech, talk, instruction.
2 REPRIMAND, rebuke, reproof, scolding, harangue, censure, chiding, telling-off (infml), talking-to (infml), dressing-down (infml).
v **1** TALK, teach, hold forth, speak, expound, address. **2** REPRIMAND, reprove, scold, admonish, harangue, chide, censure, tell off (infml).

ledge n shelf, sill, mantle, ridge, projection, step.

leeway n space, room, latitude, elbow-room, play, scope.

left adj **1** LEFT-HAND, port, sinistral.
2 LEFT-WING, socialist, radical, progressive, revolutionary, liberal, communist, red (infml).
F3 1 right. **2** right-wing.

left-overs n leavings, remainder, remains, remnants, residue, surplus, scraps, sweepings, refuse, dregs, excess.

leg n **1** LIMB, member, shank, pin (infml), stump (infml). **2** SUPPORT, prop, upright, brace. **3** STAGE, part, section, portion, stretch, segment, lap.

legacy n bequest, endowment, gift, heritage, inheritance, birthright, estate, heirloom.

legal adj **1** LAWFUL, legitimate, permissible, sanctioned, allowed, authorized, allowable, legalized, constitutional, valid, warranted, above-board, proper, rightful.
2 JUDICIAL, forensic.
F3 1 illegal.

Legal terms include:
courts: county court, courthouse, courtroom, Court of Appeal, Court of Protection, Court of Session, Crown Court, European Court of Human Rights, European Court of Justice, High Court of Justice, House of Lords, International Court of Justice, juvenile court, magistrates' court, Old Bailey, sheriff court, small claims court, Supreme Court (N Am); *criminal law:* acquittal, age of consent, alibi, arrest, bail, caution, charge, confession, contempt of court, dock, fine, guilty, indictment, innocent, malice aforethought, pardon, parole, plead guilty, plead not guilty, prisoner, probation, remand, reprieve, sentence; *marriage and divorce:* adultery, alimony, annulment, bigamy, decree absolute, decree nisi, divorce, maintenance, settlement; *people:* accessory, accomplice, accused, advocate, Attorney-General, barrister, brief (infml), clerk of the court, client, commissioner of oaths, convict, coroner, criminal, defendant, Director of Public Prose-

cutions, DPP, executor, felon, judge, jury, Justice of the Peace, JP, juvenile, Law Lord, lawyer, Lord Advocate, Lord Chancellor, Lord Chief Justice, liquidator, magistrate, notary public, offender, plaintiff, procurator fiscal, receiver, Queen's Counsel, QC, sheriff, solicitor, witness, young offender; *property or ownership*: asset, conveyance, copyright, deed, easement, endowment, estate, exchange of contracts, fee simple, foreclosure, freehold, inheritance, intestacy, lease, leasehold, legacy, mortgage, patent, tenancy, title, trademark, will; *miscellaneous*: act of God, act of parliament, adjournment, affidavit, agreement, allegation, amnesty, appeal, arbitration, bar, bill of rights, bench, brief, bylaw, charter, civil law, claim, codicil, common law, constitution, court case, court martial, cross-examine, custody, damages, defence, equity, eviction, evidence, extradition, hearing, hung jury, indemnity, injunction, inquest, inquiry, judgement, judiciary, lawsuit, legal aid, liability, mandate, misadventure, miscarriage of justice, oath, party, penalty, power of attorney, precedent, probate, proceedings, proof, proxy, public inquiry, repeal, sanction, settlement, statute, subpoena, sue, summons, testimony, trial, tribunal, verdict, waiver, ward of court, warrant, will, writ. *see also* **crime**.

legalize *v* legitimize, license, permit, sanction, allow, authorize, warrant, validate, approve.

legend *n* **1** MYTH, story, tale, folktale, fable, fiction, narrative. **2** INSCRIPTION, caption, key, motto.

legendary *adj* **1** MYTHICAL, fabulous, story-book, fictitious, traditional. **2** FAMOUS, celebrated, renowned, well-known, illustrious.

legible *adj* readable, intelligible, decipherable, clear, distinct, neat.
F3 illegible.

legislate *v* enact, ordain, authorize, codify, constitutionalize, prescribe, establish.

legislation *n* **1** LAW, statute, regulation, bill, act, charter, authorization, ruling, measure. **2** LAW-MAKING, enactment, codification.

legislative *adj* law-making, law-giving, judicial, parliamentary, congressional, senatorial.

legislator *n* law-maker, law-giver, member of parliament, parliamentarian.

legislature *n* assembly, chamber, house, parliament, congress, senate.

legitimate *adj* **1** LEGAL, lawful, authorized, statutory, rightful, proper, correct, real, acknowledged.
2 REASONABLE, sensible, admissible, acceptable, justifiable, warranted, well-founded, valid, true.
F3 **1** illegal. **2** invalid.

leisure *n* relaxation, rest, spare time, time off, ease, freedom, liberty, recreation, retirement, holiday, vacation.
F3 work.

leisurely *adj* unhurried, slow, relaxed, comfortable, easy, unhasty, tranquil, restful, gentle, carefree, laid-back (*infml*), lazy, loose.
F3 rushed, hectic.

lend *v* **1** LOAN, advance. **2** GIVE, grant, bestow, provide, furnish,

confer, supply, impart, contribute.
F3 1 borrow.

length n 1 EXTENT, distance, measure, reach, piece, portion, section, segment. 2 DURATION, period, term, stretch, space, span.

lengthen v stretch, extend, elongate, draw out, prolong, protract, spin out, eke (out), pad out, increase, expand, continue.
F3 reduce, shorten.

lengthy adj long, prolonged, protracted, extended, lengthened, overlong, long-drawn-out, long-winded, rambling, diffuse, verbose, drawn-out, interminable.
F3 brief, concise.

lenient adj tolerant, forbearing, sparing, indulgent, merciful, forgiving, soft-hearted, kind, mild, gentle, compassionate.
F3 strict, severe.

lessen v decrease, reduce, diminish, lower, ease, abate, contract, die down, dwindle, lighten, slow down, weaken, shrink, abridge, de-escalate, erode, minimize, narrow, moderate, slack, flag, fail, deaden, impair.
F3 grow, increase.

lesser adj lower, secondary, inferior, smaller, subordinate, slighter, minor.
F3 greater.

lesson n 1 CLASS, period, instruction, lecture, tutorial, teaching, coaching. 2 ASSIGNMENT, exercise, homework, practice, task, drill. 3 EXAMPLE, model, warning, deterrent.

let v 1 PERMIT, allow, give leave, give permission, authorize, consent to, agree to, sanction, grant, OK, enable, tolerate. 2 LEASE, hire, rent.
F3 1 prohibit, forbid.

let in admit, accept, receive, take in, include, incorporate, welcome.
F3 prohibit, bar, forbid.

let off 1 EXCUSE, absolve, pardon, exempt, forgive, acquit, exonerate, spare, ignore, liberate, release. 2 DISCHARGE, detonate, fire, explode, emit.
F3 1 punish.

let out 1 FREE, release, let go, discharge, leak (infml). 2 REVEAL, disclose, make known, utter, betray, let slip.
F3 1 keep in.

let up abate, subside, ease (up), moderate, slacken, diminish, decrease, stop, end, cease, halt.
F3 continue.

let-down n anticlimax, disappointment, disillusionment, set-back, betrayal, desertion, wash-out (infml).

lethal adj fatal, deadly, deathly, mortal, dangerous, poisonous, noxious, destructive, devastating.
F3 harmless, safe.

lethargy n lassitude, listlessness, sluggishness, torpor, dullness, inertia, slowness, apathy, inaction, indifference, sleepiness, drowsiness, stupor.
F3 liveliness.

letter n 1 NOTE, message, line, missive, epistle (fml), dispatch, communication, chit, acknowledgement. 2 CHARACTER, symbol, sign, grapheme.

level adj 1 FLAT, smooth, even, flush, horizontal, aligned, plane. 2 EQUAL, balanced, even, on a par, neck and neck (infml), even-stevens (infml), matching, uniform.
F3 1 uneven. 2 unequal.

v **1** DEMOLISH, destroy, devastate, flatten, knock down, raze, pull down, bulldoze, tear down, lay low. **2** EVEN OUT, flush, plane, smooth, equalize. **3** DIRECT, point.

n **1** HEIGHT, elevation, altitude. **2** POSITION, rank, status, class, degree, grade, standard, standing, plane, echelon, layer, stratum, storey, stage, zone.

level-headed *adj* calm, balanced, even-tempered, sensible, steady, reasonable, composed, cool, unflappable, sane, self-possessed, dependable.

lever *n* bar, crowbar, jemmy, joy-stick, handle.

v force, prise, pry, raise, dislodge, jemmy, shift, move, heave.

levity *n* light-heartedness, frivolity, facetiousness, flippancy, irreverence, triviality, silliness.

F3 seriousness.

levy *v* tax, impose, exact, demand, charge.

n tax, toll, subscription, contribution, duty, fee, tariff, collection.

lewd *adj* obscene, smutty, indecent, bawdy, pornographic, salacious, licentious, lascivious, impure, vulgar, unchaste, lustful.

F3 decent, chaste.

liability *n* **1** ACCOUNTABILITY, duty, obligation, responsibility, onus. **2** DEBT, arrears, indebtedness. **3** DRAWBACK, disadvantage, hindrance, impediment, drag (*infml*).

liable *adj* **1** INCLINED, likely, apt, disposed, prone, tending, susceptible. **2** RESPONSIBLE, answerable, accountable, amenable.

liaison *n* **1** CONTACT, connection, go-between, link. **2** LOVE AFFAIR, affair,

romance, intrigue, amour, entanglement.

liar *n* falsifier, perjurer, deceiver, fibber (*infml*).

libel *n* defamation, slur, smear, slander, vilification, aspersion, calumny.

v defame, slur, smear, slander, vilify, malign.

libellous *adj* defamatory, vilifying, slanderous, derogatory, maligning, injurious, scurrilous, untrue.

liberal *adj* **1** BROAD-MINDED, open-minded, tolerant, lenient. **2** PROGRESSIVE, reformist, moderate. **3** GENEROUS, ample, bountiful, lavish, plentiful, handsome.

F3 **1** narrow-minded. **2** conservative. **3** mean, miserly.

liberate *v* free, emancipate, release, let loose, let go, let out, set free, deliver, unchain, discharge, rescue, ransom.

F3 imprison, enslave.

liberty *n* **1** FREEDOM, emancipation, release, independence, autonomy. **2** LICENCE, permission, sanction, right, authorization, dispensation, franchise. **3** FAMILIARITY, disrespect, overfamiliarity, presumption, impertinence, impudence.

F3 **1** imprisonment. **3** respect.

at liberty free, unconstrained, unrestricted, not confined.

licence *n* **1** PERMISSION, permit, leave, warrant, authorization, authority, certificate, charter, right, imprimatur, entitlement, privilege, dispensation, carte blanche, freedom, liberty, exemption, independence. **2** ABANDON, dissipation, excess, immoderation, indulgence, lawlessness, unruliness, anarchy,

disorder, debauchery, dissoluteness, impropriety, irresponsibility.
F3 1 prohibition, restriction.
2 decorum, moderation.

license *v* permit, allow, authorize, certify, warrant, entitle, empower, sanction, commission, accredit.
F3 ban, prohibit.

licentious *adj* debauched, dissolute, profligate, lascivious, immoral, abandoned, lewd, promiscuous, libertine, impure, lax, lustful, disorderly, wanton, unchaste.
F3 modest, chaste.

lick *v* touch, lap, dart, flick, flicker, play over.

lie [1] *v* perjure, misrepresent, fabricate, falsify, fib (*infml*), invent, equivocate, prevaricate, forswear oneself (*fml*). *n* falsehood, untruth, falsification, fabrication, invention, fiction, deceit, fib (*infml*), falsity, white lie, prevarication, whopper (*infml*), porkie (*infml*).
F3 truth.

lie [2] *v* be, exist, dwell, belong, extend, remain.

lie down repose, rest, recline, stretch out, lounge, couch, laze.

life *n* 1 BEING, existence, animation, breath, viability, entity, soul.
2 DURATION, course, span, career.
3 LIVELINESS, vigour, vitality, vivacity, verve, zest, energy, élan, spirit, sparkle, activity.

lifeless *adj* 1 DEAD, deceased, defunct, cold, unconscious, inanimate, insensible, stiff.
2 LETHARGIC, listless, sluggish, dull, apathetic, passive, insipid, colourless, slow. 3 BARREN, bare, empty, desolate, arid.
F3 1 alive. 2 lively.

lifelike *adj* realistic, true-to-life, real, true, vivid, natural, authentic, faithful, exact, graphic.
F3 unrealistic, unnatural.

lifelong *adj* lifetime, long-lasting, long-standing, persistent, lasting, enduring, abiding, permanent, constant.
F3 impermanent, temporary.

lift *v* 1 *she lifted the chair*: raise, elevate, hoist, upraise. 2 *he lifted their spirits*: uplift, exalt, buoy up, boost.
3 *the ban has been lifted*: revoke, cancel, relax.
F3 1 drop. 2 lower.

light [1] *n* 1 ILLUMINATION, brightness, brilliance, luminescence, radiance, glow, ray, shine, glare, gleam, glint, lustre, flash, blaze. 2 LAMP, lantern, lighter, match, torch, candle, bulb, beacon. 3 DAY, daybreak, daylight, daytime, dawn, sunrise.
4 ENLIGHTENMENT, explanation, elucidation, understanding.
F3 1 darkness. 3 night.
v 1 IGNITE, fire, set alight, set fire to, kindle. 2 ILLUMINATE, light up, lighten, brighten, flash, cheer, switch on, turn on, put on.
F3 1 extinguish. 2 darken.
adj 1 ILLUMINATED, bright, brilliant, luminous, glowing, shining, well-lit, sunny. 2 PALE, pastel, fair, blond(e), bleached, faded, faint.
F3 1 dark. 2 black.

light [2] *adj* 1 WEIGHTLESS, insubstantial, delicate, airy, buoyant, flimsy, feathery, slight. 2 TRIVIAL, inconsiderable, trifling, inconsequential, worthless.
3 CHEERFUL, cheery, carefree, lively, merry, blithe. 4 ENTERTAINING, amusing, funny, humorous,

frivolous, witty, pleasing.
F3 1 heavy, weighty. **2** important, serious. **3** solemn. **4** serious.

lighten[1] v illuminate, illumine, brighten, light up, shine.
F3 darken.

lighten[2] v **1** EASE, lessen, unload, lift, relieve, reduce, mitigate, alleviate. **2** BRIGHTEN, cheer, encourage, hearten, inspirit, uplift, gladden, revive, elate, buoy up, inspire.
F3 1 burden. **2** depress.

light-headed adj **1** FAINT, giddy, dizzy, woozy (infml), delirious. **2** FLIGHTY, scatter-brained (infml), ditzy (infml), foolish, frivolous, silly, superficial, shallow, feather-brained (infml), flippant, vacuous, trifling.
F3 2 level-headed, solemn.

light-hearted adj cheerful, joyful, jolly, happy-go-lucky, bright, carefree, untroubled, merry, sunny, glad, elated, jovial, playful.
F3 sad, unhappy, serious.

likable adj loveable, pleasing, appealing, agreeable, charming, engaging, winsome, pleasant, amiable, congenial, attractive, sympathetic.
F3 unpleasant, disagreeable.

like[1] adj similar, resembling, alike, same, identical, equivalent, akin, corresponding, related, relating, parallel, allied, analogous, approximating.
F3 unlike, dissimilar.

like[2] v **1** ENJOY, delight in, care for, admire, appreciate, love, adore, hold dear, esteem, cherish, prize, relish, revel in, approve, take (kindly) to. **2** PREFER, choose, select, feel inclined, go for (infml), desire, want, wish.
F3 1 dislike. **2** reject.

likelihood n likeliness, probability, possibility, chance, prospect, liability.
F3 improbability, unlikeliness.

likely adj **1** PROBABLE, possible, anticipated, expected, liable, prone, tending, predictable, odds-on (infml), inclined, foreseeable. **2** CREDIBLE, believable, plausible, feasible, reasonable. **3** PROMISING, hopeful, pleasing, appropriate, proper, suitable.
F3 1 unlikely. **3** unsuitable.
adv probably, presumably, like as not, in all probability, no doubt, doubtlessly.

liken v compare, equate, match, parallel, relate, juxtapose, associate, set beside.

likeness n **1** SIMILARITY, resemblance, affinity, correspondence. **2** REPRESENTATION, image, copy, reproduction, replica, facsimile, effigy, picture, portrait, photograph, counterpart. **3** SEMBLANCE, guise, appearance, form.
F3 1 dissimilarity, unlikeness.

likewise adv moreover, furthermore, in addition, similarly, also, further, besides, by the same token, too.

liking n fondness, love, affection, preference, partiality, affinity, predilection, penchant, taste, attraction, appreciation, proneness, propensity, inclination, tendency, bias, desire, weakness, fancy, soft spot.
F3 dislike, aversion, hatred.

limb n **1** ARM, leg, member, appendage. **2** BRANCH, projection, offshoot, wing, fork, extension, part, spur, extremity, bough.

limber up loosen up, warm up, work out, exercise, prepare.

limelight n fame, celebrity, spotlight, stardom, recognition, renown, attention, prominence, publicity, public eye.

limit n 1 BOUNDARY, bound, border, frontier, confines, edge, brink, threshold, verge, brim, end, perimeter, rim, compass, termination, ultimate, utmost, terminus, extent. 2 CHECK, curb, restraint, restriction, limitation, ceiling, maximum, cut-off point, saturation point, deadline.
v check, curb, restrict, limit, constrain, confine, demarcate, delimit, bound, hem in, ration, specify, hinder.

limitation n 1 CHECK, restriction, curb, control, constraint, restraint, delimitation, demarcation, block. 2 INADEQUACY, shortcoming, disadvantage, drawback, condition, qualification, reservation.
E3 1 extension.

limited adj restricted, circumscribed, constrained, controlled, confined, checked, defined, finite, fixed, minimal, narrow, inadequate, insufficient.
E3 limitless.

limitless adj unlimited, unbounded, boundless, undefined, immeasurable, incalculable, infinite, countless, endless, never-ending, unending, inexhaustible, untold, vast.
E3 limited.

limp¹ v hobble, falter, stumble, hop, shuffle, shamble.

limp² adj 1 FLABBY, drooping, flaccid, floppy, loose, slack, relaxed, lax, soft, flexible, pliable, limber. 2 TIRED, weary, exhausted, spent, weak, worn out, lethargic, debilitated, enervated.
E3 1 stiff. 2 vigorous.

line¹ n 1 STROKE, band, bar, stripe, mark, strip, rule, dash, strand, streak, underline, score, scratch. 2 ROW, rank, queue, file, column, sequence, series, procession, chain, trail. 3 LIMIT, boundary, border, borderline, edge, frontier, demarcation. 4 STRING, rope, cord, cable, thread, filament, wire. 5 PROFILE, contour, outline, silhouette, figure, formation, configuration. 6 CREASE, wrinkle, furrow, groove, corrugation. 7 COURSE, path, direction, track, route, axis. 8 APPROACH, avenue, course (of action), belief, ideology, policy, system, position, practice, procedure, method, scheme. 9 OCCUPATION, business, trade, profession, vocation, job, activity, interest, employment, department, calling, field, province, forte, area, pursuit, specialization, specialism, speciality. 10 ANCESTRY, family, descent, extraction, lineage, pedigree, stock, race, breed.

line up 1 ALIGN, range, straighten, marshal, order, regiment, queue up, form ranks, fall in, array, assemble. 2 ORGANIZE, lay on, arrange, prepare, produce, procure, secure, obtain.

line² v encase, cover, fill, pad, stuff, reinforce.

lineage n (fml) ancestry, descent, extraction, genealogy, family, line, pedigree, race, stock, birth, breed, house, heredity, ancestors, forebears, descendants, offspring, succession.

lined adj 1 RULED, feint. 2 WRINKLED, furrowed, wizened, worn.
E3 1 unlined. 2 smooth.

line-up n array, arrangement, queue, row, selection, cast, team, bill.

linger v loiter, delay, dally, tarry, wait, remain, stay, hang on, lag,

procrastinate, dawdle, dilly-dally (*infml*), idle, stop, endure, hold out, last, persist, survive.
E3 leave, rush.

lining *n* inlay, interfacing, padding, backing, encasement, stiffening.

link *n* **1** CONNECTION, bond, tie, association, joint, relationship, tie-up, union, knot, liaison, attachment, communication. **2** PART, piece, element, member, constituent, component, division.
v connect, join, couple, tie, fasten, unite, bind, amalgamate, merge, associate, ally, bracket, identify, relate, yoke, attach, hook up, join forces, team up.
E3 separate, unfasten.

lip *n* edge, brim, border, brink, rim, margin, verge.

liquid *n* liquor, fluid, juice, drink, sap, solution, lotion.
adj fluid, flowing, liquefied, watery, wet, runny, melted, molten, thawed, clear, smooth.
E3 solid.

liquidate *v* **1** ANNIHILATE, terminate, do away with, dissolve, kill, murder, massacre, assassinate, destroy, dispatch, abolish, eliminate, exterminate, remove, finish off, rub out (*infml*). **2** PAY (OFF), close down, clear, discharge, wind up, sell.

liquor *n* alcohol, intoxicant, strong drink, spirits, drink, hard stuff (*infml*), booze (*infml*).

list [1] *n* catalogue, roll, inventory, register, enumeration, schedule, index, listing, record, file, directory, table, tabulation, tally, series, syllabus, invoice.
v enumerate, register, itemize, catalogue, index, tabulate, record, file,

enrol, enter, note, bill, book, set down, write down.

list [2] *v* lean, incline, tilt, slope, heel (over), tip.

listen *v* hark, attend, pay attention, hear, heed, hearken, hang on (someone's) words, prick up one's ears, take notice, lend an ear, eavesdrop, overhear, give ear.

listless *adj* sluggish, lethargic, languid, torpid, enervated, spiritless, limp, lifeless, inert, inactive, impassive, indifferent, uninterested, vacant, apathetic, indolent, depressed, bored, heavy.
E3 energetic, enthusiastic.

literal *adj* **1** VERBATIM, word-for-word, strict, close, actual, precise, faithful, exact, accurate, factual, true, genuine, unexaggerated. **2** PROSAIC, unimaginative, uninspired, matter-of-fact, down-to-earth, humdrum.
E3 1 imprecise, loose. **2** imaginative.

literary *adj* educated, well-read, bookish, learned, erudite, scholarly, lettered, literate, cultured, cultivated, refined, formal.
E3 ignorant, illiterate.

literature *n* **1** WRITINGS, letters, paper(s). **2** INFORMATION, leaflet(s), pamphlet(s), circular(s), brochure(s), hand-out(s), bumf (*infml*).

Types of literature include:
allegory, anti-novel, autobiography, belles-lettres (*fml*), biography, classic novel, crime fiction, criticism, drama, epic, epistle, essay, fiction, Gothic novel, lampoon, libretto, magnum opus, non-fiction, novel, novella, parody, pastiche, penny dreadful (*infml*), picaresque novel, poetry, polemic, prose, pulp fiction, roman novel, saga, satire, science

fiction, thesis, tragedy, treatise, triad, trilogy, verse. *see also* **poem**; **story**.

litigation *n* lawsuit, action, suit, case, prosecution, process, contention.

litter *n* **1** RUBBISH, debris, refuse, waste, mess, disorder, clutter, confusion, disarray, untidiness, junk (*infml*), muck, jumble, fragments, shreds. **2** OFFSPRING, young, progeny (*fml*), brood, family.
v strew, scatter, mess up, disorder, clutter.
E3 tidy.

little *adj* **1** SMALL, short, tiny, wee (*infml*), minute, teeny (*infml*), diminutive, miniature, infinitesimal, mini, microscopic, petite, pint-size(d) (*infml*), slender. **2** SHORT-LIVED, brief, fleeting, passing, transient. **3** INSUFFICIENT, sparse, scant, meagre, paltry, skimpy. **4** INSIGNIFICANT, inconsiderable, negligible, trivial, petty, trifling, unimportant.
E3 **1** big. **2** lengthy. **3** ample. **4** considerable.
adv barely, hardly, scarcely, rarely, seldom, infrequently, not much.
E3 frequently.
n bit, dash, pinch, spot, trace, drop, dab, speck, touch, taste, particle, hint, fragment, modicum, trifle.
E3 lot.

live[1] *v* **1** BE, exist, breathe, draw breath. **2** LAST, endure, continue, remain, persist, survive. **3** DWELL, inhabit, reside, lodge, abide. **4** PASS, spend, lead.
E3 **1** die. **2** cease.

live[2] *adj* **1** ALIVE, living, existent. **2** LIVELY, vital, active, energetic, dynamic, alert, vigorous. **3** BURNING, glowing, blazing, ignited. **4** RELEVANT, current, topical, pertinent, controversial.
E3 **1** dead. **2** apathetic.

livelihood *n* occupation, employment, job, living, means, income, maintenance, work, support, subsistence, sustenance.

lively *adj* **1** ANIMATED, alert, active, energetic, spirited, vivacious, vigorous, sprightly, spry, agile, nimble, quick, keen. **2** CHEERFUL, blithe, merry, frisky, perky, breezy, chirpy (*infml*), frolicsome. **3** BUSY, bustling, brisk, crowded, eventful, exciting, buzzing. **4** VIVID, bright, colourful, stimulating, stirring, invigorating, racy, refreshing, sparkling.
E3 **1** moribund, apathetic. **3** inactive.

liven up enliven, vitalize, put life into, rouse, invigorate, animate, energize, brighten, stir (up), buck up (*infml*), pep up (*infml*), perk up (*infml*), hot up (*infml*).
E3 dishearten.

livery *n* uniform, costume, regalia, dress, clothes, clothing, apparel (*fml*), attire, vestments, suit, garb, habit.

livid *adj* **1** LEADEN, black-and-blue, bruised, discoloured, greyish, purple. **2** PALE, pallid, ashen, blanched, bloodless, wan, waxy, pasty. **3** (*infml*) ANGRY, furious, infuriated, irate, outraged, enraged, raging, fuming, indignant, incensed, exasperated, mad (*infml*).
E3 **3** calm.

living *adj* alive, breathing, existing, live, current, extant, operative, strong, vigorous, active, lively, vital, animated.
E3 dead, sluggish.
n **1** BEING, life, animation, existence.

2 LIVELIHOOD, maintenance, support, income, subsistence, sustenance, work, job, occupation, profession, benefice, way of life.

load n **1** BURDEN, onus, encumbrance, weight, pressure, oppression, millstone. **2** CARGO, consignment, shipment, goods, lading, freight.
v **1** BURDEN, weigh down, encumber, overburden, oppress, trouble, weight, saddle with. **2** PACK, pile, heap, freight, fill, stack.

loaded adj burdened, charged, laden, full, weighted.

loafer n (infml) idler, layabout (infml), shirker, skiver (infml), sluggard, wastrel, lounger, ne'er-do-well, lazybones (infml), couch potato (infml).

loan n advance, credit, mortgage, allowance.
v lend, advance, credit, allow.

loathe v hate, detest, abominate, abhor, despise, dislike.
E3 adore, love.

loathing n hatred, detestation, abhorrence, abomination, repugnance, revulsion, repulsion, dislike, disgust, aversion, horror.
E3 affection, love.

loathsome adj detestable, abhorrent, odious, repulsive, abominable, hateful, repugnant, repellent, offensive, horrible, disgusting, vile, revolting, nasty.

lobby v campaign for, press for, demand, persuade, call for, urge, push for, influence, solicit, pressure, promote.
n **1** VESTIBULE, foyer, porch, anteroom, hall, hallway, waiting-room, entrance hall, corridor,

passage. **2** PRESSURE GROUP, campaign, ginger group.

local adj regional, provincial, community, district, neighbourhood, parochial, vernacular, small-town, limited, narrow, restricted, parish(-pump).
E3 national.
n **1** INHABITANT, citizen, resident, native. **2** (infml) PUB.

locality n neighbourhood, vicinity, district, area, locale, region, position, place, site, spot, scene, setting.

locate v **1** FIND, discover, unearth, run to earth (infml), track down, detect, lay one's hands on (infml), pin-point, identify. **2** SITUATE, settle, fix, establish, place, put, set, seat.

location n position, situation, place, locus, whereabouts, venue, site, locale, bearings, spot, point.

lock n fastening, bolt, clasp, padlock.
v **1** FASTEN, secure, bolt, latch, seal, shut. **2** JOIN, unite, engage, link, mesh, entangle, entwine, clench. **3** CLASP, hug, embrace, grasp, encircle, enclose, clutch, grapple.
E3 unlock.

lock out shut out, refuse admittance to, keep out, exclude, bar, debar.

lock up imprison, jail, confine, shut in, shut up, incarcerate, secure, cage, pen, detain, close up.
E3 free.

lodge n hut, cabin, cottage, chalet, shelter, retreat, den, gatehouse, house, hunting-lodge, meeting-place, club, haunt.
v **1** ACCOMMODATE, put up (infml), quarter, board, billet, shelter. **2** LIVE, stay, reside. **3** FIX, imbed, implant, get stuck. **4** DEPOSIT, place, put, submit, register.

lodger n boarder, paying guest, resident, tenant, roomer, inmate, guest.

lodgings n accommodation, digs (*infml*), dwelling, quarters, billet, abode, boarding-house, rooms, pad (*infml*), residence.

log n 1 TIMBER, trunk, block, chunk.
2 RECORD, diary, journal, weblog, blog (*infml*), logbook, daybook, account, tally.
v record, register, write up, note, book, chart, tally.

logic n reasoning, reason, sense, deduction, rationale, argumentation.

logical adj reasonable, rational, reasoned, coherent, consistent, valid, sound, well-founded, clear, sensible, deducible, methodical, well-organized.
F3 illogical, irrational.

loiter v dawdle, hang about, idle, linger, dally, dilly-dally (*infml*), delay, mooch (*infml*), lag, saunter.

lone adj single, sole, one, only, isolated, solitary, separate, separated, unattached, unaccompanied, unattended.
F3 accompanied.

loneliness n aloneness, isolation, lonesomeness, solitariness, solitude, seclusion, desolation.

lonely adj 1 ALONE, friendless, lonesome, solitary, abandoned, forsaken, companionless, unaccompanied, destitute.
2 ISOLATED, uninhabited, remote, out-of-the-way, unfrequented, secluded, deserted, deserted, forsaken, desolate.
F3 1 popular. 2 crowded, populous.

long adj lengthy, extensive, extended, expanded, prolonged,

protracted, stretched, spread out, sustained, expansive, far-reaching, long-drawn-out, interminable, slow.
F3 brief, short, fleeting, abbreviated.

long for yearn for, crave, want, wish, desire, dream of, hanker for, pine, thirst for, lust after, covet, itch for, yen for (*infml*).

longing n craving, desire, yearning, hungering, hankering, yen, thirst, wish, urge, coveting, aspiration, ambition.

long-lasting adj permanent, imperishable, enduring, unchanging, unfading, continuing, abiding, long-standing, prolonged, protracted.
F3 short-lived, ephemeral, transient.

long-standing adj established, long-established, long-lived, long-lasting, enduring, abiding, time-honoured, traditional.

long-suffering adj uncomplaining, forbearing, forgiving, tolerant, easy-going, patient, stoical.

long-winded adj lengthy, overlong, prolonged, diffuse, verbose, wordy, voluble, long-drawn-out, discursive, repetitious, rambling, tedious.
F3 brief, terse.

look v 1 WATCH, see, observe, view, survey, regard, gaze, study, stare, examine, inspect, scrutinize, glance, contemplate, scan, peep, gawp (*infml*).
2 SEEM, appear, show, exhibit, display.
n 1 VIEW, survey, inspection, examination, observation, sight, review, once-over (*infml*), glance, glimpse, gaze, peek. 2 APPEARANCE, aspect, manner, semblance, mien, expression, bearing, face, complexion.

look after take care of, mind, care for, attend to, take charge of, tend, keep an eye on, watch over, protect, supervise, guard.

Ea neglect.

look down on despise, scorn, sneer at, hold in contempt, disdain, look down one's nose at (*infml*), turn one's nose up at (*infml*).

Ea esteem, approve.

look forward to anticipate, await, expect, hope for, long for, envisage, envision, count on, wait for, look for.

look into investigate, probe, research, study, go into, examine, enquire about, explore, check out, inspect, scrutinise, look over, plumb, fathom.

look out pay attention, watch out, beware, be careful, keep an eye out.

look over inspect, examine, check, give a once-over (*infml*), cast an eye over, look through, scan, view.

look up 1 SEARCH FOR, research, hunt for, find, track down. **2** VISIT, call on, drop in on, look in on, pay a visit to, stop by, drop by. **3** IMPROVE, get better, pick up, progress, come on.

look up to admire, esteem, respect, revere, honour, have a high opinion of.

look-alike *n* double, replica, twin, spitting image (*infml*), living image, clone, spit (*infml*), ringer (*infml*), doppelgänger.

look-out *n* **1** GUARD, sentry, watch, watch-tower, watchman, sentinel, tower, post. **2** (*infml*) CONCERN, responsibility, worry, affair, business, problem.

loom *v* appear, emerge, take shape, menace, threaten, impend, hang over, dominate, tower, overhang, rise, soar, overshadow, overtop.

loop *n* hoop, ring, circle, noose, coil, eyelet, loophole, spiral, curve, curl, kink, twist, whorl, twirl, turn, bend.

v coil, encircle, roll, bend, circle, curve round, turn, twist, spiral, connect, join, knot, fold, braid.

loophole *n* let-out, escape, evasion, excuse, pretext, plea, pretence.

loose *adj* **1** FREE, unfastened, untied, movable, unattached, insecure, wobbly. **2** SLACK, lax, baggy, hanging. **3** IMPRECISE, vague, inexact, ill-defined, indefinite, inaccurate, indistinct.

Ea 1 firm, secure. **2** tight. **3** precise.

loosen *v* **1** EASE, relax, loose, slacken, undo, unbind, untie, unfasten. **2** FREE, set free, release, let go, let out, deliver.

Ea 1 tighten.

loot *n* spoils, booty, plunder, haul, swag (*infml*).

v plunder, pillage, rob, sack, rifle, raid, maraud, ransack, ravage.

lop-sided *adj* asymmetrical, unbalanced, askew, off balance, uneven.

Ea balanced, symmetrical.

lord *n* **1** PEER, noble, earl, duke, count, baron. **2** MASTER, ruler, superior, overlord, leader, commander, governor, king.

lordly *adj* **1** NOBLE, dignified, aristocratic. **2** PROUD, arrogant, disdainful, haughty, imperious, condescending, high-handed, domineering, overbearing.

Ea 1 low(ly). **2** humble.

lore *n* knowledge, wisdom, learning, erudition, scholarship, traditions, teaching, beliefs, sayings.

lose *v* **1** MISLAY, misplace, forget, miss, forfeit. **2** WASTE, squander, dissipate, use up, exhaust, expend, drain. **3** FAIL, fall short, suffer defeat.

Ea 1 gain. **2** make. **3** win.

loser n failure, also-ran, runner-up, flop (infml), no-hoper.
E3 winner.

loss n 1 DEPRIVATION, disadvantage, defeat, failure, losing, bereavement, damage, destruction, ruin, hurt.
2 WASTE, depletion, disappearance, deficiency, deficit.
E3 1 gain.

lost adj 1 MISLAID, missing, vanished, disappeared, misplaced, astray.
2 CONFUSED, disoriented, bewildered, puzzled, baffled, perplexed, preoccupied. 3 WASTED, squandered, ruined, destroyed.
E3 1 found.

lot n 1 COLLECTION, batch, assortment, quantity, group, set, crowd. 2 SHARE, portion, allowance, ration, quota, part, piece, parcel.

lotion n ointment, balm, cream, salve.

lottery n 1 DRAW, raffle, sweepstake.
2 SPECULATION, venture, risk, gamble, crapshoot (N Am).

loud adj 1 NOISY, deafening, booming, resounding, ear-piercing, ear-splitting, piercing, thundering, blaring, clamorous, vociferous.
2 GARISH, gaudy, glaring, flashy, brash, showy, ostentatious, tasteless.
E3 1 quiet. 2 subdued.

lounge v relax, loll, idle, laze, waste time, kill time, lie about, take it easy, sprawl, recline, lie back, slump.
n sitting-room, living-room, drawing-room, day-room, parlour.

lovable adj adorable, endearing, winsome, captivating, charming, engaging, attractive, fetching, sweet, lovely, pleasing, delightful.
E3 detestable, hateful.

love v 1 he loves his wife: adore, cherish, dote on, treasure, hold dear, idolize, worship. 2 I love macaroons: like, take pleasure in, enjoy, delight in, appreciate, desire, fancy.
E3 detest, hate.
n adoration, affection, fondness, attachment, regard, liking, amorousness, ardour, devotion, adulation, passion, rapture, tenderness, warmth, inclination, infatuation, delight, enjoyment, soft spot (infml), weakness, taste, friendship.
E3 detestation, hate, loathing.

lovely adj beautiful, charming, delightful, attractive, enchanting, pleasing, pleasant, pretty, adorable, agreeable, enjoyable, sweet, winning, exquisite.
E3 ugly, hideous.

lover n beloved, admirer, boyfriend, girlfriend, sweetheart, suitor, mistress, fiancé(e), flame (infml).

loving adj amorous, affectionate, devoted, doting, fond, ardent, passionate, warm, warm-hearted, tender.

low adj 1 SHORT, small, squat, stunted, little, shallow, deep, depressed, sunken. 2 INADEQUATE, deficient, poor, sparse, meagre, paltry, scant, insignificant.
3 UNHAPPY, depressed, downcast, gloomy. 4 BASE, coarse, vulgar, mean, contemptible. 5 CHEAP, inexpensive, reasonable. 6 SUBDUED, muted, soft.
E3 1 high. 2 high. 3 cheerful.
4 honourable. 5 exorbitant. 6 loud.

lower adj inferior, lesser, subordinate, secondary, minor, second-class, low-level, lowly, junior.
E3 higher.

v **1** DROP, depress, sink, descend, let down. **2** REDUCE, decrease, cut, lessen, diminish.

F3 **1** raise. **2** increase.

lowly *adj* humble, low-born, obscure, poor, plebeian, plain, simple, modest, ordinary, inferior, meek, mild, mean, submissive, subordinate.

F3 lofty, noble.

low-spirited *adj* depressed, gloomy, heavy-hearted, low, down, down-hearted, despondent, fed up (*infml*), sad, unhappy, miserable, moody.

F3 high-spirited, cheerful.

loyal *adj* true, faithful, steadfast, staunch, devoted, trustworthy, sincere, patriotic.

F3 disloyal, treacherous.

loyalty *n* allegiance, faithfulness, fidelity, devotion, steadfastness, constancy, trustworthiness, reliability, patriotism.

F3 disloyalty, treachery.

lubricate *v* oil, grease, smear, wax, lard.

luck *n* **1** CHANCE, fortune, accident, fate, fortuity (*fml*), fluke (*infml*), destiny. **2** GOOD FORTUNE, success, break (*infml*), godsend.

F3 **1** design. **2** misfortune.

luckily *adv* fortunately, happily, providentially.

F3 unfortunately.

lucky *adj* fortunate, favoured, auspicious, successful, prosperous, timely.

F3 unlucky.

lucrative *adj* profitable, well-paid, remunerative, advantageous.

F3 unprofitable.

ludicrous *adj* absurd, ridiculous, preposterous, nonsensical, laughable, farcical, silly, comical, funny, outlandish, crazy (*infml*).

F3 serious.

lug *v* pull, drag, haul, carry, tow, heave, hump.

luggage

> Types of luggage include:
> case, suitcase, vanity case, bag, hold-all, portmanteau, valise, overnight bag, kit-bag, flight bag, hand-luggage, tote bag, travel bag, Gladstone bag, grip, rucksack, bergen, knapsack, haversack, backpack, bum bag, fanny pack (*US*), money belt, briefcase, attaché-case, portfolio, satchel, basket, hamper, trunk, chest, box, pet carrier.

lukewarm *adj* cool, half-hearted, apathetic, tepid, indifferent, unenthusiastic, uninterested, unresponsive, unconcerned.

lull *v* soothe, subdue, calm, hush, pacify, quieten down, quiet, quell, compose.

F3 agitate.

n calm, peace, quiet, tranquillity, stillness, let-up, pause, hush, silence.

F3 agitation.

lumber [1] *n* clutter, jumble, rubbish, bits and pieces, odds and ends, junk.

lumber [2] *v* clump, shamble, plod, shuffle, stump, trundle.

luminous *adj* glowing, illuminated, lit, lighted, radiant, shining, fluorescent, brilliant, lustrous, bright.

lump *n* **1** MASS, cluster, clump, clod, ball, bunch, piece, chunk, cake, hunk, nugget, wedge. **2** SWELLING, growth, bulge, bump, protuberance, protrusion, tumour.

v collect, mass, gather, cluster, combine, coalesce, group, consolidate, unite.

lunacy n madness, insanity, aberration, derangement, mania, craziness (infml), idiocy, imbecility, folly, absurdity, stupidity.
F3 sanity.

lunatic n psychotic, psychopath, madman, maniac, loony (infml), nutcase (infml), nutter (infml), fruitcake (infml).
adj mad, insane, deranged, psychotic, irrational, crazy (infml), bonkers (infml).
F3 sane.

lunge v thrust, jab, stab, pounce, plunge, pitch into, charge, dart, dash, dive, poke, strike (at), fall upon, grab (at), hit (at), leap.
n thrust, stab, pounce, charge, jab, pass, cut, spring.

lurch v roll, rock, pitch, sway, stagger, reel, list.

lure v tempt, entice, draw, attract, allure, seduce, ensnare, lead on.
n temptation, enticement, attraction, bait, inducement.

lurid adj **1** SENSATIONAL, shocking, startling, graphic, exaggerated. **2** MACABRE, gruesome, gory, ghastly, grisly. **3** BRIGHTLY COLOURED, garish, glaring, loud, vivid.

lurk v skulk, prowl, lie in wait, crouch, lie low, hide, snoop.

luscious adj delicious, juicy, succulent, appetizing, mouth-watering, sweet, tasty, savoury, desirable.

lush adj **1** FLOURISHING, luxuriant, abundant, prolific, overgrown, green, verdant. **2** SUMPTUOUS, opulent, ornate, plush, rich.

lust n **1** SENSUALITY, libido, lechery, licentiousness, lewdness. **2** CRAVING, desire, appetite, longing, passion, greed, covetousness.
lust after desire, crave, yearn for, want, need, hunger for, thirst for.

lustre n **1** SHINE, gloss, sheen, gleam, glow, brilliance, brightness, radiance, sparkle, resplendence, burnish, glitter, glint. **2** GLORY, honour, prestige, illustriousness.

lusty adj robust, strong, sturdy, vigorous, hale, hearty, healthy, gutsy (infml), energetic, strapping, rugged, powerful.

luxurious adj sumptuous, opulent, lavish, de luxe, plush, magnificent, splendid, expensive, costly, self-indulgent, pampered.
F3 austere, spartan.

luxury n sumptuousness, opulence, hedonism, splendour, affluence, richness, magnificence, pleasure, indulgence, gratification, comfort, extravagance, satisfaction.
F3 austerity.

lying adj deceitful, dishonest, false, untruthful, double-dealing, two-faced (infml).
F3 honest, truthful.
n dishonesty, untruthfulness, deceit, falsity, fibbing (infml), perjury, duplicity, fabrication, double-dealing.
F3 honesty, truthfulness.

M

macabre *adj* gruesome, grisly, grim, horrible, frightful, dreadful, ghostly, eerie.

machine *n* **1** INSTRUMENT, device, contrivance, tool, mechanism, engine, apparatus, appliance. **2** AGENCY, organization, structure, system.

machinery *n* **1** INSTRUMENTS, mechanism, tools, apparatus, equipment, tackle, gear.
2 ORGANIZATION, channels, structure, system, procedure.

mad *adj* **1** INSANE, lunatic, unbalanced, psychotic, deranged, demented, out of one's mind, crazy (*infml*), nuts (*infml*), barmy (*infml*), bonkers (*infml*). **2** (*infml*) ANGRY, furious, enraged, infuriated, incensed. **3** IRRATIONAL, illogical, unreasonable, absurd, preposterous, foolish.
4 FANATICAL, enthusiastic, infatuated, ardent.
F∃ 1 sane. **2** calm. **3** sensible.
4 apathetic.

madden *v* anger, enrage, infuriate, incense, exasperate, provoke, annoy, irritate.
F∃ calm, pacify.

madly *adv* **1** *he rolled his eyes madly*: insanely, dementedly, hysterically, wildly. **2** *madly cleaning up*: excitedly, frantically, furiously, recklessly, violently, energetically, rapidly,

hastily, hurriedly. **3** *madly in love*: intensely, extremely, exceedingly, fervently, devotedly.

madman, madwoman *n* lunatic, psychotic, psychopath, maniac, loony (*infml*), nutcase (*infml*), fruitcake (*infml*).

magazine *n* **1** JOURNAL, periodical, paper, weekly, monthly, quarterly.
2 ARSENAL, storehouse, ammunition dump, depot, ordnance.

magic *n* **1** SORCERY, enchantment, occultism, black art, witchcraft, wicca, spell. **2** CONJURING, illusion, sleight of hand, trickery. **3** CHARM, fascination, glamour, allure.
adj charming, enchanting, bewitching, fascinating, spellbinding.

magician *n* sorcerer, miracle-worker, conjuror, enchanter, wizard, witch, warlock, spellbinder, wonder-worker.

magnanimous *adj* generous, liberal, open-handed, benevolent, selfless, charitable, big-hearted, kind, noble, unselfish, ungrudging.
F∃ mean.

magnate *n* tycoon, captain of industry, industrialist, mogul, entrepreneur, plutocrat, baron, personage, notable.

magnetic *adj* attractive, alluring, fascinating, charming, mesmerizing, seductive, irresistible, entrancing, captivating, gripping, absorbing, charismatic.

E3 repellent, repulsive.

magnetism n attraction, allure, fascination, charm, lure, appeal, drawing power, draw, pull, hypnotism, mesmerism, charisma, grip, magic, power, spell.

magnificent adj splendid, grand, imposing, impressive, glorious, gorgeous, brilliant, excellent, majestic, superb, sumptuous, noble, elegant, fine, rich.

E3 modest, humble, poor.

magnify v enlarge, amplify, increase, expand, intensify, boost, enhance, greaten, heighten, deepen, build up, talk up, exaggerate, dramatize, overemphasize, overplay, overstate, overdo, blow up (infml).

E3 belittle, play down.

magnitude n 1 SIZE, extent, measure, amount, expanse, dimensions, mass, proportions, quantity, volume, bulk, largeness, space, strength, amplitude. 2 IMPORTANCE, consequence, significance, weight, greatness, moment, intensity.

maiden n girl, virgin, lass, lassie, damsel (fml), miss.

mail n post, letters, correspondence, packages, parcels, delivery. v post, send, dispatch, forward.

maim v mutilate, wound, incapacitate, injure, disable, hurt, impair, cripple, lame.

main adj principal, chief, leading, first, foremost, predominant, pre-eminent, primary, prime, supreme, paramount, central, cardinal,

outstanding, essential, critical, crucial, necessary, vital.

E3 minor, unimportant, insignificant. n pipe, duct, conduit, channel, cable, line.

mainly adv primarily, principally, chiefly, in the main, mostly, on the whole, for the most part, generally, in general, especially, as a rule, above all, largely, overall.

mainstay n support, buttress, bulwark, linchpin, prop, pillar, backbone, foundation.

maintain v 1 CARRY ON, continue, keep (up), sustain, retain. 2 CARE FOR, conserve, look after, take care of, preserve, support, finance, supply. 3 ASSERT, affirm, claim, contend, declare, hold, state, insist, believe, fight for.

E3 2 neglect. 3 deny.

maintenance n 1 CONTINUATION, continuance, perpetuation. 2 CARE, conservation, preservation, support, repairs, protection, upkeep, running. 3 KEEP, subsistence, living, livelihood, allowance, alimony.

E3 2 neglect.

majestic adj magnificent, grand, dignified, noble, royal, stately, splendid, imperial, impressive, exalted, imposing, regal, sublime, superb, lofty, monumental, pompous.

E3 lowly, unimpressive, uninposing.

majesty n grandeur, glory, dignity, magnificence, nobility, royalty, resplendence, splendour, stateliness, pomp, exaltedness, impressiveness, loftiness.

major adj greater, chief, main, larger, bigger, higher, leading, outstanding, notable, supreme, uppermost, significant, crucial, important, key,

keynote, great, senior, older, superior, pre-eminent, vital, weighty.
F3 minor, unimportant, trivial.

majority n 1 BULK, mass, preponderance, most, greater part. 2 ADULTHOOD, maturity, manhood, womanhood, years of discretion.
F3 1 minority.

make v 1 CREATE, manufacture, fabricate, construct, build, produce, put together, originate, compose, form, shape. 2 CAUSE, bring about, effect, accomplish, occasion, give rise to, generate, render, perform. 3 COERCE, force, oblige, constrain, compel, prevail upon, pressurize, press, require. 4 APPOINT, elect, designate, nominate, ordain, install. 5 EARN, gain, net, obtain, acquire. 6 CONSTITUTE, compose, comprise, add up to, amount to.
F3 1 dismantle. 5 spend.
n brand, sort, type, style, variety, manufacture, model, mark, kind, form, structure.

make off run off, run away, depart, bolt, leave, fly, cut and run (infml), beat a hasty retreat (infml), clear off (infml).

make out 1 DISCERN, perceive, decipher, distinguish, recognize, see, detect, discover, understand, work out, grasp, follow, fathom. 2 DRAW UP, complete, fill in, write out. 3 MAINTAIN, imply, claim, assert, describe, demonstrate, prove. 4 MANAGE, get on, progress, succeed, fare (fml).

make up 1 CREATE, invent, devise, fabricate, construct, originate, formulate, dream up, compose. 2 COMPLETE, fill, supply, meet, supplement. 3 COMPRISE, constitute, compose, form. 4 BE RECONCILED,

make peace, settle differences, bury the hatchet (infml), forgive and forget, call it quits (infml).

make up for compensate for, make good, make amends for, redress, recompense, redeem, atone for.

make-believe n pretence, imagination, fantasy, unreality, playacting, role-play, dream, charade.
F3 reality.

maker n creator, manufacturer, constructor, builder, producer, director, architect, author.

makeshift adj temporary, improvised, rough and ready, provisional, substitute, stop-gap, expedient, make-do.
F3 permanent.

make-up n 1 COSMETICS, paint, powder, maquillage, war paint (infml). 2 CONSTITUTION, nature, composition, character, construction, form, format, formation, arrangement, organization, style, structure, assembly.

maladjusted adj disturbed, unstable, confused, alienated, neurotic, estranged.
F3 well-adjusted.

male adj masculine, manly, virile, boyish, laddish (infml), he-.
F3 female.

malevolent adj malicious, malign, spiteful, vindictive, ill-natured, hostile, vicious, venomous, evil-minded.
F3 benevolent, kind.

malformation n irregularity, deformity, distortion, warp.

malformed adj misshapen, irregular, deformed, distorted, twisted, warped, crooked, bent.
F3 perfect.

malfunction n fault, defect, failure, breakdown.
v break down, go wrong, fail.

malice n malevolence, enmity, animosity, ill-will, hatred, hate, spite, vindictiveness, bitterness.
E3 love.

malicious adj malevolent, ill-natured, malign, spiteful, venomous, vicious, vengeful, evil-minded, bitter, resentful.
E3 kind, friendly.

malign adj malignant, malevolent, bad, evil, harmful, hurtful, injurious, destructive, hostile.
E3 benign.
v defame, slander, libel, disparage, abuse, run down (infml), harm, injure.
E3 praise.

malignant adj **1** MALEVOLENT, malicious, spiteful, evil, hostile, vicious, venomous, destructive, harmful, hurtful, pernicious. **2** FATAL, deadly, incurable, dangerous, cancerous, uncontrollable, virulent.
E3 1 kind. **2** benign.

malpractice n misconduct, mismanagement, negligence, impropriety, dereliction of duty (fml), abuse, misdeed.

maltreat v ill-treat, mistreat, misuse, abuse, injure, harm, damage, hurt.
E3 care for.

mammal

Mammals include:
aardvark, anteater, antelope, armadillo, baboon, badger, bat, bear, bush-baby, camel, cat, chimpanzee, cow, deer, dog, dolphin, duck-billed platypus, dugong, echidna, elephant, ferret, flying lemur, fox, gibbon, giraffe, goat, gorilla, hedgehog, hippopotamus, horse, human being, hyena, leopard, lion, manatee, meerkat, mole, monkey, orang utan, otter, pig, porpoise, raccoon, rhinoceros, sea cow, seal, sea lion, sheep, shrew, sloth, tapir, tiger, walrus, weasel, whale, wolf, zebra. see also **cat**; **cattle**; **dog**; **marsupial**; **monkey**; **rodent**.

mammoth adj enormous, huge, vast, colossal, gigantic, giant, massive, immense, monumental, mighty.
E3 tiny, minute.

man n **1** MALE, gentleman, gent (infml), fellow, bloke (infml), chap (infml), guy (infml). **2** HUMAN BEING, person, individual, adult, human. **3** HUMANITY, humankind, mankind, human race, people, Homo sapiens, mortals. **4** MANSERVANT, servant, worker, employee, hand, soldier, valet, houseman, houseboy.
v staff, crew, take charge of, operate, occupy.

manacle v handcuff, shackle, restrain, fetter, chain, put in chains, bind, curb, check, hamper, inhibit.
E3 free, unshackle.

manage v **1** ACCOMPLISH, succeed, bring about, bring off, effect. **2** ADMINISTER, direct, run, command, govern, preside over, rule, superintend, supervise, oversee, conduct. **3** CONTROL, influence, deal with, handle, operate, manipulate, guide. **4** COPE, fare, survive, get by, get along, get on, make do.
E3 1 fail. **2** mismanage.

manageable adj tractable, governable, controllable, amenable, submissive, docile.
E3 unmanageable.

management n **1** ADMINISTRATION, direction, control, government,

command, running, superintendence, supervision, charge, care, handling. **2** MANAGERS, directors, directorate, executive, executives, governors, board, bosses (*infml*), supervisors.
F3 1 mismanagement. **2** workers.

manager *n* director, executive, administrator, controller, superintendent, supervisor, overseer, governor, organizer, head, boss (*infml*).

mandate *n* order, command, decree, edict, injunction, charge, directive, warrant, authorization, authority, instruction, commission, sanction.

mandatory *adj* obligatory, compulsory, binding, required, necessary, requisite, essential.
F3 optional.

mangle *v* mutilate, disfigure, mar, maim, spoil, butcher, destroy, deform, wreck, twist, maul, distort, crush, cut, hack, tear, rend.

mangy *adj* seedy, shabby, scruffy, scabby, tatty (*infml*), shoddy, moth-eaten, dirty, mean.

manhandle *v* **1** *the porters manhandled the baggage*: haul, heave, hump, pull, push, shove, tug. **2** *the police manhandled the demonstrators*: maul, mistreat, maltreat, misuse, abuse, knock about (*infml*), rough up (*infml*).

manhood *n* **1** ADULTHOOD, maturity. **2** MASCULINITY, virility, manliness, manfulness, machismo (*infml*).

mania *n* **1** MADNESS, insanity, lunacy, psychosis, derangement, disorder, aberration, craziness (*infml*), frenzy. **2** PASSION, craze, rage, obsession, compulsion, enthusiasm, fad (*infml*), infatuation, fixation, craving.

> Manias (by name of disorder) include:
>
> dipsomania (*alcohol*), bibliomania (*books*), ailuromania (*cats*), necromania (*dead bodies*), thanatomania (*death*), cynomania (*dogs*), pyromania (*fire-raising*), anthomania (*flowers*), hippomania (*horses*), mythomania (*lying and exaggerating*), egomania (*oneself*), ablutomania (*personal cleanliness*), hedonomania (*pleasure*), megalomania (*power*), theomania (*religion*), nymphomania (*sex*), monomania (*single idea or thing*), kleptomania (*stealing*), logomania (*talking*), ergomania (*work*). see also **phobia**.

---

maniac *n* **1** LUNATIC, madman, madwoman, psychotic, psychopath, loony (*infml*). **2** ENTHUSIAST, fan (*infml*), fanatic, fiend (*infml*), freak (*infml*).

manifest *adj* obvious, evident, clear, apparent, plain, open, patent, noticeable, conspicuous, unmistakable, visible, unconcealed.
F3 unclear.
v show, exhibit, display, demonstrate, reveal, set forth, expose, prove, illustrate, establish.
F3 conceal.

manifestation *n* display, exhibition, demonstration, show, revelation, exposure, disclosure, appearance, expression, sign, indication.

manifesto *n* statement, declaration, policies, platform.

manifold *adj* (*fml*) many, numerous, varied, various, diverse, multiple, kaleidoscopic, abundant, copious.

manipulate *v* **1** HANDLE, control, wield, operate, use, manoeuvre, influence, engineer, guide, direct, steer, negotiate, work. **2** FALSIFY, rig, juggle with, doctor (*infml*), cook (*infml*), fiddle (*infml*).

mankind *n* humankind, humanity, human race, man, Homo sapiens, people.

manly *adj* masculine, male, virile, manful, macho (*infml*), robust.

man-made *adj* synthetic, manufactured, simulated, imitation, artificial.
F3 natural.

manner *n* **1** WAY, method, means, fashion, style, procedure, process, form. **2** BEHAVIOUR, conduct, bearing, demeanour, air, appearance, look, character.

mannerism *n* idiosyncrasy, peculiarity, characteristic, quirk, trait, feature, foible, habit.

manners *n* behaviour, conduct, demeanour, etiquette, politeness, bearing, courtesy, formalities, social graces, p's and q's.

manoeuvre *n* move, movement, operation, action, exercise, plan, ploy, plot, ruse, stratagem, machination, gambit, tactic, trick, scheme, dodge (*infml*).
v **1** MOVE, manipulate, handle, guide, pilot, steer, navigate, jockey, direct, drive, exercise. **2** CONTRIVE, engineer, plot, scheme, wangle (*infml*), pull strings (*infml*), manipulate, manage, plan, devise, negotiate.

mantle *n* cloak, cover, covering, cape, hood, blanket, shawl, veil, wrap, shroud, screen.

manual *n* handbook, guide, guidebook, instructions, Bible, vade mecum, directions.
adj hand-operated, by hand, physical, human.

manufacture *v* **1** MAKE, produce, construct, build, fabricate, create, assemble, mass-produce, turn out, process, forge, form. **2** INVENT, make up, concoct, fabricate, think up.
n production, making, construction, fabrication, mass-production, assembly, creation, formation.

manufacturer *n* maker, producer, industrialist, constructor, factory-owner, builder, creator.

manure *n* fertilizer, compost, muck, dung.

many *adj* numerous, countless, lots of (*infml*), manifold (*fml*), various, varied, sundry, diverse, umpteen (*infml*).
F3 few.

map *n* chart, plan, street plan, atlas, graph, plot.

mar *v* spoil, impair, harm, hurt, damage, deface, disfigure, mutilate, injure, maim, scar, detract from, mangle, ruin, wreck, tarnish.
F3 enhance.

marauder *n* bandit, brigand, robber, raider, plunderer, pillager, pirate, buccaneer, outlaw, ravager, predator.

march *v* walk, stride, parade, pace, file, tread, stalk.
n **1** STEP, pace, stride. **2** WALK, trek, hike, footslog (*infml*). **3** PROCESSION, parade, demonstration, demo (*infml*). **4** ADVANCE, development, progress, evolution, passage.

margin *n* **1** BORDER, edge, boundary, bound, periphery, perimeter, rim, brink, limit, confine, verge, side, skirt. **2** ALLOWANCE, play, leeway, latitude, scope, room, space, surplus, extra.

marginal *adj* borderline, peripheral, negligible, minimal, insignificant,

minor, slight, doubtful, low, small.
F3 central, core.

marine *adj* sea, maritime, naval, nautical, seafaring, sea-going, ocean-going, salt-water.

mariner *n* sailor, seaman, seafarer, deckhand, navigator, tar (*infml*), sea-dog (*infml*), salt (*infml*).

marital *adj* conjugal, matrimonial, married, wedded, nuptial (*fml*), connubial (*fml*).

maritime *adj* marine, nautical, naval, seafaring, sea, seaside, oceanic, coastal.

mark *n* **1** SPOT, stain, blemish, blot, blotch, smudge, dent, impression, scar, scratch, bruise, line. **2** SYMBOL, sign, indication, emblem, brand, stamp, characteristic, feature, proof, evidence, badge. **3** TARGET, goal, aim, objective, purpose.
v STAIN, blemish, blot, smudge, dent, scar, scratch, bruise. **2** BRAND, label, stamp, characterize, identify, distinguish. **3** EVALUATE, assess, correct, grade. **4** HEED, listen, mind, note, observe, regard, notice, take to heart.

marked *adj* **1** NOTICEABLE, obvious, conspicuous, evident, pronounced, distinct, decided, emphatic, considerable, remarkable, apparent, glaring. **2** SUSPECTED, watched, doomed.
F3 **1** unnoticeable, slight.

market *n* mart, marketplace, bazaar, fair, exchange, outlet.
v sell, retail, hawk, peddle.
F3 buy.

maroon *v* abandon, cast away, desert, put ashore, strand, leave, isolate.

marriage *n* **1** MATRIMONY, wedlock, wedding, nuptials (*fml*). **2** UNION,

alliance, merger, coupling, amalgamation, link, association, confederation.
F3 **1** divorce. **2** separation.

marrow *n* essence, heart, nub, kernel, core, soul, spirit, substance, quick, stuff, gist.

marry *v* **1** WED, join in matrimony, tie the knot (*infml*), get hitched (*infml*), get spliced (*infml*). **2** UNITE, ally, join, merge, match, link, knit.
F3 **1** divorce. **2** separate.

marsh *n* marshland, bog, swamp, fen, morass, quagmire, slough.

marshal *v* **1** ARRANGE, dispose, order, line up, align, array, rank, organize, assemble, gather, muster, group, collect, draw up, deploy.
2 GUIDE, lead, escort, conduct, usher.

marsupial

> Marsupials include:
>
> bandicoot, cuscus, kangaroo, rat-kangaroo, tree kangaroo, wallaroo, koala, marsupial mole, marsupial mouse, opossum, pademelon, phalanger, Tasmanian devil, Tasmanian wolf, wallaby, wombat.

martial *adj* warlike, military, belligerent, soldierly, militant, heroic, brave.

martial art

> Martial arts include:
>
> *unarmed:* aikido, capoeira, judo, ju-jitsu, karate, kempo, kick boxing, kung fu, tae kwon do, t'ai chi, wushu; *weapons:* bojutsu, kendo, kenjutsu, kumdo, kyodo.

marvel *n* wonder, miracle, phenomenon, prodigy, spectacle, sensation, genius.
v wonder, gape, gaze, be amazed at.

marvellous adj **1** WONDERFUL, excellent, splendid, superb, magnificent, terrific (infml), super, fantastic (infml). **2** EXTRAORDINARY, amazing, astonishing, astounding, miraculous, remarkable, surprising, unbelievable, incredible, glorious.
F3 1 terrible, awful. **2** ordinary, run-of-the-mill.

masculine adj **1** MALE, manlike, manly, mannish, virile, macho, laddish (infml). **2** VIGOROUS, strong, strapping, robust, powerful, muscular, red-blooded, bold, brave, gallant, resolute, stout-hearted.
F3 feminine.

mash v crush, pulp, beat, pound, pulverize, pummel, grind, smash.

mask n disguise, camouflage, façade, front, concealment, cover-up, cover, guise, pretence, semblance, cloak, veil, blind, show, veneer, visor.
v disguise, camouflage, cover, conceal, cloak, veil, hide, obscure, screen, shield.
F3 expose, uncover.

masquerade n **1** MASQUE, masked ball, costume ball, fancy dress party. **2** DISGUISE, counterfeit, cover-up, cover, deception, front, pose, pretence, guise, cloak.
v disguise, impersonate, pose, pass oneself off, mask, play, pretend, profess, dissimulate.

mass n **1** HEAP, pile, load, accumulation, aggregate, collection, conglomeration, combination, entirety, whole, totality, sum, lot, group, batch, bunch. **2** QUANTITY, multitude, throng, troop, crowd, band, horde, mob. **3** MAJORITY, body, bulk. **4** SIZE, dimension, magnitude, immensity. **5** LUMP, piece, chunk, block, hunk.

adj widespread, large-scale, extensive, comprehensive, general, indiscriminate, popular, across-the-board, sweeping, wholesale, blanket.
F3 limited, small-scale.
v collect, gather, assemble, congregate, crowd, rally, cluster, muster, swarm, throng.
F3 separate.

massacre n slaughter, murder, extermination, carnage, butchery, holocaust, blood bath, annihilation, killing.
v slaughter, butcher, murder, mow down, wipe out, exterminate, annihilate, kill, decimate.

massage n manipulation, kneading, rubbing, rub-down.
v manipulate, knead, rub (down).

massive adj huge, immense, enormous, vast, colossal, gigantic, mega (infml), big, bulky, monumental, solid, substantial, heavy, large-scale, extensive.
F3 tiny, small.

master n **1** RULER, chief, governor, head, lord, captain, boss (infml), employer, commander, controller, director, manager, superintendent, overseer, principal, overlord, owner. **2** EXPERT, genius, virtuoso, past master, maestro, dab hand (infml), ace (infml), pro (infml). **3** TEACHER, tutor, instructor, schoolmaster, guide, guru, preceptor (fml).
F3 1 servant, underling. **2** amateur. **3** learner, pupil.
adj **1** CHIEF, principal, main, leading, foremost, prime, predominant, controlling, great, grand. **2** EXPERT, masterly, skilled, skilful, proficient.
F3 1 subordinate. **2** inept.
v **1** CONQUER, defeat, subdue,

subjugate, vanquish, triumph over, overcome, quell, rule, control. **2** LEARN, grasp, acquire, get the hang of (infml), manage.

masterful adj **1** ARROGANT, authoritative, domineering, overbearing, high-handed, despotic, dictatorial, autocratic, bossy (infml), tyrannical, powerful. **2** EXPERT, masterly, skilful, skilled, dexterous, first-rate, professional.

E3 1 humble. **2** inept, unskilful.

masterly adj expert, skilled, skilful, dexterous, adept, adroit, first-rate, ace (infml), excellent, superb, superior, supreme.

E3 inept, clumsy.

masterpiece n master-work, magnum opus, pièce de résistance, chef d'oeuvre, jewel.

mastery n **1** PROFICIENCY, skill, ability, command, expertise, virtuosity, knowledge, know-how, dexterity, familiarity, grasp. **2** CONTROL, command, domination, supremacy, upper hand, dominion, authority.

E3 1 incompetence. **2** subjugation.

match n **1** CONTEST, competition, bout, game, test, trial. **2** EQUAL, equivalent, peer, counterpart, fellow, mate, rival, copy, double, replica, look-alike, twin, duplicate. **3** MARRIAGE, alliance, union, partnership, affiliation.
v **1** EQUAL, compare, measure up to, rival, compete, oppose, contend, vie, pit against. **2** FIT, go with, accord, agree, suit, correspond, harmonize, tally, co-ordinate, blend, adapt, go together, relate, tone with, accompany. **3** JOIN, marry, unite, mate, link, couple, combine,

ally, pair, yoke, team.

E3 2 clash. **3** separate.

matching adj corresponding, comparable, equivalent, like, identical, co-ordinating, similar, duplicate, same, twin.

E3 clashing.

matchless adj unequalled, peerless, incomparable, unmatched, unparalleled, unsurpassed, unrivalled, inimitable, unique.

mate n **1** FRIEND, companion, comrade, pal (infml), colleague, partner, fellow-worker, co-worker, associate. **2** SPOUSE, husband, wife. **3** ASSISTANT, helper, subordinate. **4** MATCH, fellow, twin.
v **1** COUPLE, pair, breed, copulate. **2** JOIN, match, marry, wed.

material n **1** STUFF, substance, body, matter. **2** FABRIC, textile, cloth. **3** INFORMATION, facts, data, evidence, constituents, work, notes.
adj **1** PHYSICAL, concrete, tangible, substantial. **2** RELEVANT, significant, important, meaningful, pertinent, essential, vital, indispensable, serious.

E3 1 abstract. **2** irrelevant.

materialize v appear, arise, take shape, turn up, happen, occur.

E3 disappear.

mathematics

Mathematical terms include:
acute angle, addition, algebra, angle, area, average, axis, Cartesian co-ordinates, coefficient, concentric, constant, co-ordinate, cosine, cube, cube root, decimal, degree, denominator, diameter, division, equation, exponential, factor, formula, fraction, function, geometry, gradient, integer, irrational number, locus, mean, me-

dian, minus, mode, multiplication, natural number, negative, number, numerator, origin, parallel, percentage, perimeter, perpendicular, pi, plane, plus, positive, prime number, probability, product, Pythagoras's theorem, quadrant, quadratic, quadrilateral, quotient, radius, ratio, rational number, real number, reciprocal, recurring decimal, reflex angle, remainder, right-angle, scalar, set, sine, square, square root, symmetry, tangent, total, trigonometry, vector, volume, zero.

matrimonial adj marital, nuptial, marriage, wedding, married, wedded, conjugal.

matter n 1 SUBJECT, issue, topic, question, affair, business, concern, event, episode, incident.
2 IMPORTANCE, significance, consequence, note. 3 TROUBLE, problem, difficulty, worry.
4 SUBSTANCE, stuff, material, body, content.
v count, be important, make a difference, mean something.

matter-of-fact adj unemotional, prosaic, emotionless, straightforward, sober, unimaginative, flat, deadpan (infml).
F3 emotional.

mature adj 1 ADULT, grown-up, grown, full-grown, fully fledged, complete, perfect, perfected, well-thought-out. 2 RIPE, ripened, seasoned, mellow, ready.
F3 1 childish. 2 immature.
v grow up, come of age, develop, mellow, ripen, perfect, age, bloom, fall due.

maturity n 1 ADULTHOOD, majority, womanhood, manhood, wisdom,

experience. 2 RIPENESS, readiness, mellowness, perfection.
F3 1 childishness. 2 immaturity.

maul v abuse, ill-treat, manhandle, maltreat, molest, paw, beat (up), knock about, rough up, claw, lacerate, batter.

maxim n saying, proverb, adage, axiom, aphorism, epigram, motto, byword, precept, rule.

maximum adj greatest, highest, largest, biggest, most, utmost, supreme.
F3 minimum.
n most, top (point), utmost, upper limit, peak, pinnacle, summit, height, ceiling, extremity, zenith (fml).
F3 minimum.

maybe adv perhaps, possibly, perchance (fml).
F3 definitely.

maze n labyrinth, network, tangle, web, complex, confusion, puzzle, intricacy.

meadow n field, grassland, pasture, lea.

meagre adj 1 SCANTY, sparse, inadequate, deficient, skimpy, paltry, negligible, poor. 2 THIN, puny, insubstantial, bony, emaciated, scrawny, slight.
F3 1 ample. 2 fat.

meal

Meals include:
breakfast, wedding breakfast, elevenses (infml), brunch, lunch, luncheon, tea, tea party, tiffin, afternoon tea, cream tea, high tea, evening meal, dinner, TV dinner, supper, harvest supper, fork supper, banquet, feast, barbecue, barbie (infml), buffet, picnic, snack, take-away.

mean¹ *adj* **1** MISERLY, niggardly, parsimonious, selfish, tight (*infml*), tight-fisted, stingy (*infml*), penny-pinching (*infml*). **2** UNKIND, unpleasant, nasty, bad-tempered, cruel. **3** LOWLY, base, poor, humble, wretched.
F3 1 generous. **2** kind. **3** splendid.

mean² *v* **1** SIGNIFY, represent, denote, stand for, symbolize, suggest, indicate, imply. **2** INTEND, aim, propose, design. **3** CAUSE, give rise to, involve, entail.

mean³ *adj* average, intermediate, middle, halfway, median, normal.
F3 extreme.
n average, middle, mid-point, norm, median, compromise, middle course, middle way, happy medium, golden mean.
F3 extreme.

meander *v* **1** WIND, zigzag, turn, twist, snake, curve. **2** WANDER, stray, amble, ramble, stroll.

meaning *n* **1** SIGNIFICANCE, sense, import, implication, gist, trend, explanation, interpretation. **2** AIM, intention, purpose, object, idea. **3** VALUE, worth, point.

meaningful *adj* **1** IMPORTANT, significant, relevant, valid, useful, worthwhile, material, purposeful, serious. **2** EXPRESSIVE, speaking, suggestive, warning, pointed.
F3 1 unimportant, worthless.

meaningless *adj* **1** SENSELESS, pointless, purposeless, useless, insignificant, aimless, futile, insubstantial, trifling, trivial. **2** EMPTY, hollow, vacuous, vain, worthless, nonsensical, absurd.
F3 1 important, meaningful.
2 worthwhile.

means *n* **1** METHOD, mode, way, medium, course, agency, process, instrument, channel, vehicle.
2 RESOURCES, funds, money, income, wealth, riches, substance, wherewithal, fortune, affluence.

measure *n* **1** PORTION, ration, share, allocation, quota. **2** SIZE, quantity, magnitude, amount, degree, extent, range, scope, proportion. **3** RULE, gauge, scale, standard, criterion, norm, touchstone, yardstick, test, meter. **4** STEP, course, action, deed, procedure, method, act, bill, statute.
v quantify, evaluate, assess, weigh, value, gauge, judge, sound, fathom, determine, calculate, estimate, plumb, survey, compute, measure out, measure off.
measure up to equal, meet, match, compare with, touch, rival, make the grade.

measured *adj* deliberate, planned, reasoned, slow, unhurried, steady, studied, well-thought-out, calculated, careful, considered, precise.

measurement *n* **1** DIMENSION, size, extent, amount, magnitude, area, capacity, height, depth, length, width, weight, volume. **2** ASSESSMENT, evaluation, estimation, computation, calculation, calibration, gauging, judgement, appraisal, appreciation, survey.

> SI base units include:
> ampere, candela, kelvin, kilogram, metre, mole, second.

> SI derivatives and other measurements include:
> acre, angstrom, atmosphere, bar, barrel, becquerel, bushel, cable, calorie, centimetre, century, chain,

coulomb, cubic centimetre, cubic foot, cubic inch, cubic metre, cubic yard, day, decade, decibel, degree, dyne, erg, farad, fathom, fluid ounce, fresnel, foot, foot-pound, furlong, gallon, gill, gram, hand, hectare, hertz, horsepower, hour, hundredweight, inch, joule, kilometre, knot, league, litre, lumen, micrometre, mile, millennium, millibar, millilitre, minute, month, nautical mile, newton, ohm, ounce, pascal, peck, pint, pound, radian, rod, siemens, span, square centimetre, square foot, square inch, square kilometre, square metre, square mile, square yard, steradian, stone, therm, ton, tonne, volt, watt, week, yard, year.

meat n **1** FLESH. **2** (*infml*) FOOD, rations, provisions, nourishment, subsistence, eats (*infml*).

Kinds of meat include:
bacon, beef, pork, lamb, mutton, ham, gammon, chicken, turkey, goose, duck, rabbit, hare, venison, pheasant, grouse, partridge, pigeon, quail; offal, liver, heart, tongue, kidney, brains, pig's knuckle, trotters, oxtail, sweetbread, tripe; steak, mince.

Cuts of meat include:
shoulder, collar, loin, hock, leg, chop, shin, knuckle, rib, spare rib, breast, brisket, chine, cutlet, fillet, rump, scrag, silverside, topside, sirloin, flank, escalope, neck, saddle.

mechanical adj automatic, involuntary, instinctive, routine, habitual, impersonal, emotionless, cold, matter-of-fact, unfeeling, perfunctory, lifeless, dead, dull. **E3** conscious.

mechanism n **1** MACHINE, machinery, engine, appliance, instrument, tool, motor, works, workings, gadget, device, apparatus, contrivance, gears, components. **2** MEANS, method, agency, process, procedure, system, technique, medium, structure, operation, functioning, performance.

meddle v interfere, intervene, pry, snoop (*infml*), intrude, butt in, tamper.

meddlesome adj interfering, meddling, prying, intrusive, intruding, mischievous.

mediate v arbitrate, conciliate, intervene, referee, umpire, intercede, moderate, reconcile, negotiate, resolve, settle, step in.

mediator n arbitrator, referee, umpire, intermediary, negotiator, go-between, interceder, judge, moderator, intercessor, conciliator, peacemaker, Ombudsman.

medical

Medical terms include:
abortion, allergy, amniocentesis, amputation, analgesic, antibiotic, antiseptic, bandage, barium meal, biopsy, blood bank, blood count, blood donor, blood-group, blood pressure, blood test, caesarean, cardiopulmonary resuscitation (CPR), case history, casualty, cauterization, cervical smear, check-up, childbirth, circulation, circumcision, clinic, complication, compress, consultant, consultation, contraception, convulsion, cure, diagnosis, dialysis, dislocate, dissection, doctor, donor, dressing, enema, exam-

ination, gene, hormone replacement therapy (HRT), hospice, hospital, immunization, implantation, incubation, infection, inflammation, injection, injury, inoculation, intensive care, keyhole surgery, in vitro fertilization (IVF), labour, laser treatment, miscarriage, mouth-to-mouth, nurse, ointment, operation, paraplegia, post-mortem, pregnancy, prescription, prognosis, prosthesis, psychosomatic, quarantine, radiotherapy, recovery, rehabilitation, relapse, remission, respiration, resuscitation, scan, side effect, sling, smear test, specimen, splint, sterilization, steroid, surgery, suture, symptom, syndrome, therapy, tourniquet, tranquillizer, transfusion, transplant, trauma, treatment, tumour, ultrasound scanning, vaccination, vaccine, virus, X-ray.

medicinal adj therapeutic, healing, remedial, curative, restorative, medical.
medicine n medication, drug, cure, remedy, medicament, prescription, pharmaceutical, panacea.

> Types of medicine include:
> tablet, capsule, pill, pain-killer, lozenge, pastille, gargle, linctus, tonic, laxative, suppository, antacid, ointment, eye-drops, ear-drops, nasal spray, inhaler, antibiotic, penicillin, emetic, gripe-water. see also **drug**.

> Forms of alternative medicine include:
> acupressure, acupuncture, aromatherapy, ayurveda, Chinese medicine, chiropractic, craniosacral therapy, herbalism, homeopathy, hypnotherapy, iridology, naturopathy, osteopathy, reflexology, reiki, Rolfing, shiatsu.

mediocre adj ordinary, average, middling, medium, indifferent, unexceptional, undistinguished, so-so (infml), run-of-the-mill, bog-standard (infml), commonplace, insignificant, second-rate, inferior, uninspired.
F₃ exceptional, extraordinary, distinctive.
mediocrity n **1** ORDINARINESS, unimportance, insignificance, poorness, inferiority, indifference. **2** NONENTITY, nobody.
meditate v **1** REFLECT, ponder, ruminate, contemplate, muse, brood, think. **2** THINK OVER, consider, deliberate, mull over, study, speculate, scheme, plan, devise, intend.
medium adj average, middle, median, mean, medial, intermediate, middling, midway, standard, fair.
n **1** AVERAGE, middle, mid-point, middle ground, compromise, centre, happy medium, golden mean.
2 MEANS, agency, channel, vehicle, instrument, way, mode, form, avenue, organ. **3** PSYCHIC, spiritualist, spiritist, clairvoyant.
medley n assortment, mixture, miscellany, pot-pourri, hotchpotch, hodge-podge, collection, jumble.
meek adj modest, long-suffering, forbearing, humble, docile, patient, unassuming, unpretentious, resigned, gentle, peaceful, tame, timid, submissive, spiritless.
F₃ arrogant, assertive, rebellious.
meet v **1** ENCOUNTER, come across, run across, run into, chance on, bump

into (*infml*). **2** EXPERIENCE, encounter, face, go through, undergo, endure. **3** GATHER, collect, assemble, congregate, convene. **4** FULFIL, satisfy, match, answer, measure up to, equal, discharge, perform. **5** JOIN, converge, come together, connect, cross, intersect, touch, abut, unite.
E3 **3** scatter. **5** diverge.

meeting *n* **1** ENCOUNTER, confrontation, rendezvous, engagement, assignation, introduction, tryst (*fml*). **2** ASSEMBLY, gathering, congregation, conference, convention, rally, get-together, forum, conclave, session. **3** CONVERGENCE, confluence, junction, intersection, union.

melancholy *adj* depressed, dejected, downcast, down, down-hearted, gloomy, low, low-spirited, heavy-hearted, sad, unhappy, despondent, dispirited, miserable, mournful, dismal, sorrowful, moody.
E3 cheerful, elated, joyful.
n depression, dejection, gloom, despondency, low spirits, blues (*infml*), sadness, unhappiness, sorrow.
E3 elation, joy.

mellow *adj* **1** MATURE, ripe, juicy, full-flavoured, sweet, tender, mild. **2** GENIAL, cordial, affable, pleasant, relaxed, placid, serene, tranquil, cheerful, happy, jolly. **3** SMOOTH, melodious, rich, rounded, soft.
E3 **1** unripe. **2** cold. **3** harsh.
v mature, ripen, improve, sweeten, soften, temper, season, perfect.

melodious *adj* tuneful, musical, melodic, harmonious, dulcet, sweet-sounding, euphonious (*fml*), silvery.
E3 discordant, grating, harsh.

melodramatic *adj* histrionic, theatrical, overdramatic, exaggerated, overemotional, sensational, hammy (*infml*).

melody *n* tune, music, song, refrain, harmony, theme, air, strain.

melt *v* liquefy, dissolve, thaw, fuse, deliquesce (*fml*).
E3 freeze, solidify.

melt away disappear, vanish, fade, evaporate, dissolve, disperse.

member *n* adherent, associate, subscriber, representative, comrade, fellow.

memento *n* souvenir, keepsake, remembrance, reminder, token, memorial, record, relic.

memoirs *n* reminiscences, recollections, autobiography, life story, diary, chronicles, annals, journals, records, confessions, experiences.

memorable *adj* unforgettable, remarkable, significant, impressive, notable, noteworthy, extraordinary, important, outstanding, momentous.
E3 forgettable, trivial, unimportant.

memorial *n* remembrance, monument, souvenir, memento, record, stone, plaque, mausoleum.
adj commemorative, celebratory.

memorize *v* learn, learn by heart, commit to memory, remember.
E3 forget.

memory *n* recall, retention, recollection, remembrance, reminiscence, commemoration.
E3 forgetfulness.

menace *v* threaten, frighten, alarm, intimidate, terrorize, loom.
n **1** INTIMIDATION, threat, terrorism, warning. **2** DANGER, peril, hazard, jeopardy, risk. **3** NUISANCE, annoyance, pest.

mend v 1 REPAIR, renovate, restore, refit, fix, patch, cobble, darn, heal.
2 RECOVER, get better, improve.
3 REMEDY, correct, rectify, reform, revise.
E3 1 break. 2 deteriorate. 3 destroy.

menial adj low, lowly, humble, base, dull, humdrum, routine, degrading, demeaning, ignominious, unskilled, subservient, servile, slavish.
n servant, domestic, labourer, minion, attendant, drudge, slave, underling, skivvy (infml), dog's-body (infml).

mental adj 1 INTELLECTUAL, abstract, conceptual, cognitive, cerebral, theoretical, rational.
2 (infml) MAD, insane, lunatic, crazy, unbalanced, deranged, psychotic, disturbed, loony (infml).
E3 1 physical. 2 sane.

mentality n 1 INTELLECT, brains, understanding, faculty, rationality.
2 FRAME OF MIND, character, disposition, personality, psychology, outlook.

mention v refer to, speak of, allude to, touch on, name, cite, namecheck, acknowledge, bring up, report, make known, impart, declare, communicate, broach, divulge, disclose, intimate, point out, reveal, state, hint at, quote.
n reference, allusion, citation, observation, recognition, remark, acknowledgement, announcement, notification, tribute, indication.

mercenary adj 1 GREEDY, avaricious, covetous, grasping, acquisitive, materialistic. 2 HIRED, paid, venal.

merchandise n goods, commodities, stock, produce, products, wares, cargo, freight, shipment.

merchant n trader, dealer, broker, trafficker, wholesaler, retailer, seller, shopkeeper, vendor.

merciful adj compassionate, forgiving, forbearing, humane, lenient, sparing, tender-hearted, pitying, gracious, humanitarian, kind, liberal, sympathetic, generous, mild.
E3 hard-hearted, merciless.

merciless adj pitiless, relentless, unmerciful, ruthless, hard-hearted, hard, heartless, implacable, inhumane, unforgiving, remorseless, unpitying, unsparing, severe, cruel, callous, inhuman.
E3 compassionate, merciful.

mercy n 1 COMPASSION, clemency, forgiveness, forbearance, leniency, pity, humanitarianism, kindness, grace. 2 BLESSING, godsend, good luck, relief.
E3 1 cruelty, harshness.

mere adj sheer, plain, simple, bare, utter, pure, absolute, complete, stark, unadulterated, common, paltry, petty.

merge v join, unite, combine, converge, amalgamate, blend, coalesce, mix, intermix, mingle, melt into, fuse, meet, meld, incorporate, consolidate.

merger n amalgamation, union, fusion, combination, coalition, consolidation, confederation, incorporation.

merit n worth, excellence, value, quality, good, goodness, virtue, asset, credit, advantage, strong point, talent, justification, due, claim.
E3 fault.
v deserve, be worthy of, earn, justify, warrant.

merriment n fun, jollity, mirth, hilarity, laughter, conviviality, craic

(*Irish*), festivity, amusement, revelry, frolic, liveliness, joviality.
F∃ gloom, seriousness.

merry *adj* jolly, light-hearted, mirthful, joyful, happy, convivial, festive, cheerful, glad.
F∃ gloomy, melancholy, sober.

mesh *n* net, network, netting, lattice, web, tangle, entanglement, snare, trap.
v engage, interlock, dovetail, fit, connect, harmonize, co-ordinate, combine, come together.

mess *n* **1** CHAOS, untidiness, disorder, disarray, confusion, muddle, jumble, clutter, disorganization, mix-up, shambles (*infml*). **2** DIFFICULTY, trouble, predicament, fix (*infml*).
F∃ 1 order, tidiness.

mess about mess around, fool around, play, play around, play about, muck about (*infml*), interfere, tamper, trifle.

mess up 1 DISARRANGE, jumble, muddle, tangle, dishevel, disrupt. **2** BOTCH, bungle, spoil, muck up (*infml*).

message *n* **1** COMMUNICATION, bulletin, dispatch, communiqué, report, missive (*fml*), errand, letter, memorandum, note, notice, cable, e-mail, text. **2** MEANING, idea, point, theme, moral.

messenger *n* courier, emissary (*fml*), envoy, go-between, herald, runner, carrier, bearer, harbinger, agent, ambassador.

messy *adj* untidy, unkempt, dishevelled, disorganized, chaotic, sloppy, slovenly, confused, dirty, grubby, muddled, cluttered.
F∃ neat, ordered, tidy.

metamorphosis *n* change, alteration, transformation, rebirth, regeneration, transfiguration, conversion, modification, change-over.

metaphor *n* figure of speech, allegory, analogy, symbol, picture, image.

metaphorical *adj* figurative, allegorical, symbolic.

meteoric *adj* rapid, speedy, swift, sudden, overnight, instantaneous, momentary, brief, spectacular, brilliant, dazzling.

mete out allot, apportion, deal out, dole out, hand out, measure out, share out, ration out, portion, distribute, dispense, divide out, assign, administer.

method *n* **1** WAY, approach, means, course, manner, mode, fashion, process, procedure, route, technique, style, plan, scheme, programme. **2** ORGANIZATION, order, structure, system, pattern, form, planning, regularity, routine.

methodical *adj* systematic, structured, organized, ordered, orderly, tidy, regular, planned, efficient, disciplined, businesslike, deliberate, neat, scrupulous, precise, meticulous, strict.
F∃ chaotic, irregular, confused.

meticulous *adj* precise, scrupulous, exact, punctilious, fussy, detailed, accurate, thorough, fastidious, painstaking, strict.
F∃ careless, slapdash.

metropolis *n* capital, city, municipality, megalopolis.

mettle *n* **1** CHARACTER, temperament, disposition. **2** SPIRIT, courage, vigour, nerve, boldness, daring, indomitability, pluck, resolve, valour, bravery, fortitude.

microbe n micro-organism, bacterium, bacillus, germ, virus, pathogen, bug (infml).

microscopic adj minute, tiny, minuscule, infinitesimal, indiscernible, imperceptible, negligible.
E3 huge, enormous.

middle adj central, halfway, mean, median, intermediate, inner, inside, intervening.
n centre, halfway point, midpoint, mean, heart, core, midst, inside, bull's eye.
E3 extreme, end, edge, beginning, border.

middling adj mediocre, medium, ordinary, moderate, average, unexceptional, unremarkable, run-of-the-mill, indifferent, modest, passable, tolerable, so-so (infml), OK (infml).

midget n person of restricted growth, pygmy, dwarf, Tom Thumb, gnome.
E3 giant.
adj tiny, small, miniature, little, pocket, pocket-sized.
E3 giant.

midst n middle, centre, mid-point, heart, hub, interior.

migrant n traveller, wanderer, itinerant, emigrant, immigrant, rover, nomad, globe-trotter, drifter, gypsy, tinker, vagrant.

migrate v move, resettle, relocate, wander, roam, move, journey, emigrate, travel, voyage, trek, drift.

mild adj **1** mild manners: gentle, calm, peaceable, placid, tender, soft, good-natured, kind, amiable, lenient, compassionate. **2** mild weather: calm, temperate, warm, balmy, clement, fair, pleasant. **3** mild coffee: bland, mellow, smooth, subtle, soothing.
E3 1 harsh, fierce. **2** stormy. **3** strong.

militant adj aggressive, belligerent, vigorous, fighting, warring.
E3 pacifist, peaceful.
n activist, combatant, fighter, struggler, warrior, aggressor, belligerent.

military adj martial, armed, soldierly, warlike, service.
n army, armed forces, soldiers, forces, services.

militate against oppose, counter, counteract, count against, tell against, weigh against, contend, resist.

milk v drain, bleed, tap, extract, draw off, exploit, use, express, press, pump, siphon, squeeze, wring.

milky adj white, milk-white, chalky, opaque, clouded, cloudy.

mill n **1** FACTORY, plant, works, workshop, foundry. **2** GRINDER, crusher, quern, roller.
v grind, pulverize, powder, pound, crush, roll, press, grate.

mime n dumb show, pantomime, gesture, mimicry.
v gesture, signal, act out, represent, simulate, impersonate, mimic.

mimic v imitate, parody, caricature, take off (infml), ape, parrot, impersonate, echo, mirror, simulate, look like.
n imitator, impersonator, impressionist, caricaturist, copy-cat (infml), copy.

mimicry n imitation, imitating, impersonation, copying, parody, impression, caricature, take-off (infml), burlesque.

mince v **1** CHOP, cut, hash, dice, grind, crumble. **2** DIMINISH, suppress, play down, tone down, hold back, moderate, weaken, soften, spare.

mind *n* **1** INTELLIGENCE, intellect, brains, reason, sense, understanding, wits, mentality, thinking, thoughts, grey matter (*infml*), head, genius, concentration, attention, spirit, psyche. **2** MEMORY, remembrance, recollection. **3** OPINION, view, point of view, belief, attitude, judgement, feeling, sentiment. **4** INCLINATION, disposition, tendency, will, wish, intention, desire.
v **1** CARE, object, take offence, resent, disapprove, dislike. **2** REGARD, heed, pay attention, pay heed to, note, obey, listen to, comply with, follow, observe, be careful, watch. **3** LOOK AFTER, take care of, attend to, guard, have charge of, keep an eye on (*infml*).
bear in mind consider, remember, note.
make up one's mind decide, choose, determine, settle, resolve.
mindful *adj* aware, conscious, alive (to), alert, attentive, careful, watchful, wary.
E3 heedless, inattentive.
mindless *adj* **1** THOUGHTLESS, senseless, illogical, irrational, stupid, foolish, gratuitous, negligent.
2 MECHANICAL, automatic, tedious.
E3 1 thoughtful, intelligent.
mine *n* **1** PIT, colliery, coalfield, excavation, vein, seam, shaft, trench, deposit. **2** SUPPLY, source, stock, store, reserve, fund, hoard, treasury, wealth.
v excavate, dig for, dig up, delve, quarry, extract, unearth, tunnel, remove, undermine.
mineral

Minerals include:
alabaster, albite, anhydrite, asbestos, aventurine, azurite, bentonite, bloodstone, blue john, borax, cairn-gorm, calamine, calcite, calcspar, cassiterite, chalcedony, chlorite, chrysoberyl, cinnabar, corundum, dolomite, emery, feldspar, fluorite, fluorspar, fool's gold, galena, graphite, gypsum, haematite, halite, hornblende, hyacinth, idocrase, jacinth, jargoon, kaolinite, lapis lazuli, lazurite, magnetite, malachite, mica, microcline, montmorillonite, orthoclase, plumbago, pyrites, quartz, rock salt, rutile, sanidine, silica, smithsonite, sodalite, sphalerite, spinel, talc, uralite, uranite, vesuvianite, wurtzite, zircon.

mingle *v* **1** MIX, intermingle, intermix, combine, blend, merge, unite, alloy, coalesce, join, compound.
2 ASSOCIATE, socialize, circulate, hobnob (*infml*), rub shoulders (*infml*).
miniature *adj* tiny, small, scaled-down, minute, diminutive, baby, pocket-sized, pint-size(d) (*infml*), little, mini (*infml*).
E3 giant.
minimal *adj* least, smallest, minimum, slightest, littlest, negligible, minute, token.
minimize *v* **1** REDUCE, decrease, diminish. **2** BELITTLE, make light of, make little of, disparage, deprecate, discount, play down, underestimate, underrate.
E3 1 maximize.
minimum *n* least, lowest point, slightest, bottom.
E3 maximum.
adj minimal, least, lowest, slightest, smallest, littlest, tiniest.
E3 maximum.
minion *n* **1** ATTENDANT, follower, underling, lackey, hireling.
2 DEPENDANT, hanger-on, favourite,

darling, sycophant, yes-man (*infml*), bootlicker (*infml*).

minister *n* **1** OFFICIAL, office-holder, politician, dignitary, diplomat, ambassador, delegate, envoy, consul, cabinet minister, agent, aide, administrator, executive. **2** MEMBER OF THE CLERGY, churchman, churchwoman, cleric, parson, priest, pastor, vicar, preacher, ecclesiastic (*fml*), divine.

v attend, serve, tend, take care of, wait on, cater to, accommodate, nurse.

ministry *n* **1** GOVERNMENT, cabinet, department, office, bureau, administration. **2** THE CHURCH, holy orders, the priesthood.

minor *adj* lesser, secondary, smaller, inferior, subordinate, subsidiary, junior, younger, insignificant, inconsiderable, negligible, petty, trivial, trifling, second-class, unclassified, slight, light.

F∃ major, significant, important.

mint *v* coin, stamp, strike, cast, forge, punch, make, manufacture, produce, construct, devise, fashion, invent, make up.

adj perfect, brand-new, fresh, immaculate, unblemished, excellent, first-class.

minute¹ *n* moment, second, instant, flash, jiffy (*infml*), tick (*infml*).

minute² *adj* **1** TINY, infinitesimal, minuscule, microscopic, miniature, inconsiderable, negligible, small. **2** DETAILED, precise, meticulous, painstaking, close, critical, exhaustive.

F∃ **1** gigantic, huge. **2** cursory, superficial.

minutes *n* proceedings, record(s), notes, memorandum, transcript, transactions, details, tapes.

miracle *n* wonder, marvel, prodigy, phenomenon.

miraculous *adj* wonderful, marvellous, phenomenal, extraordinary, amazing, astounding, astonishing, unbelievable, supernatural, incredible, inexplicable, unaccountable, superhuman.

F∃ natural, normal.

mirage *n* illusion, optical illusion, hallucination, fantasy, phantasm.

mirror *n* **1** GLASS, looking-glass, reflector. **2** REFLECTION, likeness, image, double, copy.

v reflect, echo, imitate, copy, represent, show, depict, mimic.

mirth *n* merriment, hilarity, gaiety, fun, laughter, jollity, jocularity, amusement, revelry, glee, cheerfulness.

F∃ gloom, melancholy.

misapprehension *n* misunderstanding, misconception, misinterpretation, misreading, error, mistake, fallacy, delusion.

misappropriate *v* steal, embezzle, peculate, pocket, swindle (*infml*), misspend, misuse, misapply, abuse, pervert.

misbehave *v* offend, transgress, trespass, get up to mischief, mess about, muck about (*infml*), play up, act up (*infml*).

misbehaviour *n* misconduct, misdemeanour, impropriety, disobedience, naughtiness, insubordination.

miscalculate *v* misjudge, get wrong, slip up, blunder, boob (*infml*), miscount, overestimate, underestimate.

miscarriage *n* failure, breakdown, abortion, mishap, mismanagement,

error, ruination, disappointment.
E3 success.

miscarry *v* fail, abort, come to
nothing, fall through, misfire, founder,
come to grief.
E3 succeed.

miscellaneous *adj* mixed, varied,
various, assorted, diverse, diversified,
sundry, motley, jumbled,
indiscriminate.

miscellany *n* mixture, variety,
assortment, collection, anthology,
medley, mixed bag, pot-pourri,
hotchpotch, jumble, diversity.

mischief *n* **1** TROUBLE, harm, evil,
damage, injury, disruption.
2 MISBEHAVIOUR, naughtiness,
impishness, pranks.

mischievous *adj* **1** MALICIOUS, evil,
spiteful, vicious, wicked, pernicious,
destructive, injurious. **2** NAUGHTY,
impish, rascally, roguish, playful,
teasing.
E3 **1** kind. **2** well-behaved, good.

misconception *n*
misapprehension, misunderstanding,
misreading, error, fallacy, delusion,
the wrong end of the stick (*infml*).

misconduct *n* misbehaviour,
impropriety, misdemeanour,
malpractice, mismanagement,
wrong-doing.

miser *n* niggard, skinflint, penny-
pincher (*infml*), Scrooge.
E3 spendthrift.

miserable *adj* **1** UNHAPPY, sad,
dejected, despondent, downcast,
heartbroken, wretched, distressed,
crushed. **2** CHEERLESS, depressing,
dreary, impoverished, shabby,
gloomy, dismal, forlorn, joyless,
squalid. **3** CONTEMPTIBLE, despicable,
ignominious, detestable, disgraceful,

deplorable, shameful. **4** MEAGRE,
paltry, niggardly, worthless, pathetic,
pitiful.
E3 **1** cheerful, happy. **2** pleasant.
4 generous.

miserly *adj* mean, niggardly, tight,
stingy (*infml*), sparing, parsimonious,
cheese-paring, beggarly, penny-
pinching (*infml*), mingy (*infml*).
E3 generous, spendthrift.

misery *n* **1** UNHAPPINESS, sadness,
suffering, distress, depression,
despair, gloom, grief, wretchedness,
affliction. **2** PRIVATION, hardship,
deprivation, poverty, want,
oppression, destitution. **3** (*infml*)
SPOILSPORT, pessimist, killjoy,
wet blanket (*infml*), party pooper
(*infml*).
E3 **1** contentment. **2** comfort.

misfire *v* miscarry, go wrong, abort,
fail, fall through, flop (*infml*), founder,
fizzle out, come to grief.
E3 succeed.

misfit *n* individualist,
nonconformist, eccentric, maverick,
drop-out, loner, lone wolf.
E3 conformist.

misfortune *n* bad luck, mischance,
mishap, ill-luck, setback, reverse,
calamity, catastrophe, disaster, blow,
accident, tragedy, trouble, hardship,
trial, tribulation.
E3 luck, success.

misgiving *n* doubt, uncertainty,
hesitation, qualm, reservation,
apprehension, scruple, suspicion,
second thoughts, niggle, anxiety,
worry, fear.
E3 confidence.

misguided *adj* misled,
misconceived, ill-considered, ill-
advised, ill-judged, imprudent, rash,

misplaced, deluded, foolish, erroneous.

F3 sensible, wise.

mishap n misfortune, ill-fortune, misadventure, accident, setback, calamity, disaster, adversity.

misinterpret v misconstrue, misread, misunderstand, mistake, distort, garble.

misjudge v miscalculate, mistake, misinterpret, misconstrue, misunderstand, overestimate, underestimate.

mislay v lose, misplace, miss, lose sight of.

mislead v misinform, misdirect, deceive, delude, lead astray, fool.

misleading adj deceptive, confusing, unreliable, ambiguous, biased, loaded, evasive, tricky (infml).

F3 unequivocal, authoritative, informative.

mismanage v mishandle, botch, bungle, make a mess of, mess up, misrule, misspend, misjudge, foul up, mar, waste.

misprint n mistake, error, erratum, literal, typo (infml).

misrepresent v distort, falsify, slant, pervert, twist, garble, misquote, exaggerate, minimize, misconstrue, misinterpret.

miss v **1** FAIL, miscarry, lose, let slip, let go, omit, overlook, pass over, slip, leave out, mistake, trip, misunderstand, err. **2** AVOID, escape, evade, dodge, forego, skip, bypass, circumvent. **3** PINE FOR, long for, yearn for, regret, grieve for, mourn, sorrow for, want, wish, need, lament.
n failure, error, blunder, mistake, omission, oversight, fault, flop (infml), fiasco.

misshapen adj deformed, distorted, twisted, malformed, warped, contorted, crooked, crippled, grotesque, ugly, monstrous.

F3 regular, shapely.

missile n projectile, shot, guided missile, arrow, shaft, dart, rocket, bomb, shell, flying bomb, grenade, torpedo, weapon.

missing adj absent, lost, lacking, gone, mislaid, unaccounted-for, wanting, disappeared, astray, strayed, misplaced.

F3 found, present.

mission n **1** TASK, undertaking, assignment, operation, campaign, crusade, business, errand. **2** CALLING, duty, purpose, vocation, raison d'être, aim, charge, office, job, work.
3 COMMISSION, ministry, delegation, deputation, legation, embassy.

missionary n evangelist, campaigner, preacher, proselytizer, apostle, crusader, propagandist, champion, promoter, emissary, envoy, ambassador.

mist n haze, fog, vapour, smog, cloud, condensation, film, spray, drizzle, dew, steam, veil, dimness.
mist over cloud over, fog, dim, blur, steam up, obscure, veil.

F3 clear.

mistake n error, inaccuracy, slip, slip-up, oversight, lapse, blunder, clanger (infml), boob (infml), gaffe, fault, faux pas, solecism (fml), indiscretion, misjudgement, miscalculation, misunderstanding, misprint, misspelling, misreading, mispronunciation, howler (infml).
v misunderstand, misapprehend, misconstrue, misjudge, misread, miscalculate, confound, confuse,

slip up, blunder, err, boob (*infml*).

mistaken *adj* wrong, incorrect, erroneous, inaccurate, inexact, untrue, inappropriate, ill-judged, inauthentic, false, deceived, deluded, misinformed, misled, faulty.
F3 correct, right.

mistreat *v* abuse, ill-treat, ill-use, maltreat, harm, hurt, batter, injure, knock about, molest.

mistress *n* **1** LOVER, live-in lover, kept woman, concubine, courtesan, girlfriend, paramour, woman, lady-love. **2** TEACHER, governess, tutor.

mistrust *n* distrust, doubt, suspicion, wariness, misgiving, reservations, qualm, hesitancy, chariness, caution, uncertainty, scepticism, apprehension.
F3 trust.
v distrust, doubt, suspect, be wary of, beware, have reservations, fear.
F3 trust.

misty *adj* hazy, foggy, cloudy, blurred, fuzzy, murky, smoky, unclear, dim, indistinct, obscure, opaque, vague, veiled.
F3 clear.

misunderstand *v* misapprehend, misconstrue, misinterpret, misjudge, mistake, get wrong, miss the point, mishear, get hold of the wrong end of the stick (*infml*).
F3 understand.

misunderstanding *n* **1** MISTAKE, error, misapprehension, misconception, misjudgement, misinterpretation, misreading, mix-up. **2** DISAGREEMENT, argument, dispute, conflict, clash, difference, breach, quarrel, discord, rift.
F3 1 understanding. **2** agreement.

misuse *n* mistreatment, maltreatment, abuse, harm, ill-treatment, misapplication, misappropriation, waste, perversion, corruption, exploitation.
v abuse, misapply, misemploy, ill-use, ill-treat, harm, mistreat, wrong, distort, injure, corrupt, pervert, waste, squander, misappropriate, exploit, dissipate.

mitigating *adj* extenuating, justifying, vindicating, modifying, qualifying.

mix *v* **1** COMBINE, blend, mingle, intermingle, intermix, amalgamate, compound, homogenize, synthesize, merge, join, unite, coalesce, fuse, incorporate, fold in. **2** ASSOCIATE, consort, fraternize, socialize, mingle, join, hobnob (*infml*).
F3 1 divide, separate.
n mixture, blend, amalgam, assortment, combination, conglomerate, compound, fusion, synthesis, medley, composite, mishmash (*infml*).

mix up confuse, bewilder, muddle, perplex, puzzle, confound, mix, jumble, complicate, garble, involve, implicate, disturb, upset, snarl up.

mixed *adj* **1** *mixed race*: combined, hybrid, mingled, crossbred, mongrel, blended, composite, compound, incorporated, united, amalgamated, fused. **2** *mixed biscuits*: assorted, varied, miscellaneous, diverse, diversified, motley. **3** *mixed feelings*: ambivalent, equivocal, conflicting, contradicting, uncertain.

mixture *n* mix, blend, combination, amalgamation, amalgam, compound, conglomeration, composite, coalescence, alloy, brew, synthesis, union, fusion, concoction, cross, hybrid, assortment, variety, miscellany, medley, mélange, mixed bag, pot-pourri, jumble, hotchpotch.

moan n lament, lamentation, sob, wail, howl, whimper, whine, grumble, complaint, grievance, groan.
v **1** LAMENT, wail, sob, weep, howl, groan, whimper, mourn, grieve. **2** (infml) COMPLAIN, grumble, whine, whinge (infml), gripe (infml), carp.
F∃ 1 rejoice.

mob n **1** CROWD, mass, throng, multitude, horde, host, swarm, gathering, group, collection, flock, herd, pack, set, tribe, troop, company, crew, gang. **2** POPULACE, rabble, masses, hoi polloi, plebs (infml), riff-raff (infml).
v crowd, crowd round, surround, swarm round, jostle, overrun, set upon, besiege, descend on, throng, pack, pester, charge.

mobile adj **1** MOVING, movable, portable, peripatetic, travelling, roaming, roving, itinerant, wandering, migrant. **2** FLEXIBLE, agile, active, energetic, nimble. **3** CHANGING, changeable, ever-changing, expressive, lively.
F∃ 1 immobile.

mobilize v assemble, marshal, rally, conscript, muster, call up, enlist, activate, galvanize, organize, prepare, ready, summon, animate.

mock v **1** RIDICULE, jeer, make fun of, laugh at, disparage, deride, scoff, sneer, taunt, scorn, tease. **2** IMITATE, simulate, mimic, ape, caricature, satirize.
adj imitation, counterfeit, artificial, sham, simulated, synthetic, false, fake, forged, fraudulent, bogus, phoney (infml), pseudo, spurious, feigned, faked, pretended, dummy.

mockery n **1** RIDICULE, jeering, scoffing, scorn, derision, contempt, disdain, disrespect, sarcasm. **2** PARODY, satire, sham, travesty.

mocking adj scornful, derisive, contemptuous, sarcastic, satirical, taunting, scoffing, sardonic, snide (infml), insulting, irreverent, impudent, disrespectful, disdainful, cynical.

model n **1** COPY, replica, representation, facsimile, imitation, mock-up. **2** EXAMPLE, exemplar, pattern, standard, ideal, mould, prototype, template. **3** DESIGN, style, type, version, mark. **4** MANNEQUIN, dummy, sitter, subject, poser.
adj exemplary, perfect, typical, ideal.
v **1** MAKE, form, fashion, mould, sculpt, carve, cast, shape, work, create, design, plan. **2** DISPLAY, wear, show off.

moderate adj **1** MEDIOCRE, medium, ordinary, fair, indifferent, average, middle-of-the-road. **2** REASONABLE, restrained, sensible, calm, controlled, cool, mild, well-regulated.
F∃ 1 exceptional. **2** immoderate.
v control, regulate, decrease, lessen, soften, restrain, tone down, play down, diminish, ease, curb, calm, check, modulate, repress, subdue, soft-pedal, tame, subside, pacify, mitigate, allay, alleviate, abate, dwindle.

moderately adv somewhat, quite, rather, fairly, slightly, reasonably, passably, to some extent.
F∃ extremely.

moderation n **1** DECREASE, reduction. **2** RESTRAINT, self-control, caution, control, composure, sobriety, abstemiousness, temperance, reasonableness.

modern *adj* current, contemporary, up-to-date, new, fresh, latest, late, novel, present, present-day, recent, up-to-the-minute, newfangled (*infml*), advanced, avant-garde, progressive, modernistic, innovative, inventive, state-of-the-art, go-ahead, fashionable, stylish, in vogue, in style, modish, trendy (*infml*).
F3 old-fashioned, old, out-of-date, antiquated.

modernize *v* renovate, refurbish, rejuvenate, regenerate, streamline, revamp, renew, update, improve, do up, redesign, reform, remake, remodel, refresh, transform, modify, progress.
F3 regress.

modest *adj* **1** UNASSUMING, humble, self-effacing, quiet, reserved, retiring, unpretentious, discreet, bashful, shy. **2** MODERATE, ordinary, unexceptional, fair, reasonable, limited, small.
F3 1 immodest, conceited.
2 exceptional, excessive.

modesty *n* humility, humbleness, self-effacement, reticence, reserve, quietness, decency, propriety, demureness, shyness, bashfulness, coyness.
F3 immodesty, vanity, conceit.

modify *v* **1** CHANGE, alter, redesign, revise, vary, adapt, adjust, transform, reform, convert, improve, reorganize. **2** MODERATE, reduce, temper, tone down, limit, soften, qualify.

modulate *v* modify, adjust, balance, alter, soften, lower, regulate, vary, harmonize, inflect, tune.

moist *adj* damp, clammy, humid,

wet, dewy, rainy, muggy, marshy, drizzly, watery, soggy.
F3 dry, arid.

moisten *v* moisturize, dampen, damp, wet, water, lick, irrigate.
F3 dry.

moisture *n* water, liquid, wetness, wateriness, damp, dampness, dankness, humidity, vapour, dew, mugginess, condensation, steam, spray.
F3 dryness.

molest *v* **1** ANNOY, disturb, bother, harass, irritate, persecute, pester, plague, tease, torment, hound, upset, worry, trouble, badger. **2** ATTACK, accost, assail, hurt, ill-treat, maltreat, mistreat, abuse, harm, injure.

mollusc

> Molluscs include:
> abalone, clam, cockle, cowrie,
> cuttlefish, limpet, mussel, nautilus,
> nudibranch, octopus, oyster, peri-
> winkle, scallop, slug, snail, squid,
> tusk-shell, whelk.

moment *n* second, instant, minute, split second, trice, jiffy (*infml*), tick (*infml*).

momentary *adj* brief, short, short-lived, temporary, transient, transitory, fleeting, ephemeral, hasty, quick, passing.
F3 lasting, permanent.

momentous *adj* significant, important, critical, crucial, decisive, weighty, grave, serious, vital, fateful, historic, earth-shaking, epoch-making, eventful, major.
F3 insignificant, unimportant, trivial.

momentum *n* impetus, force, energy, impulse, drive, power, thrust, speed, velocity, impact, incentive, stimulus, urge, strength, push.

monarch n sovereign, crowned head, ruler, king, queen, emperor, empress, prince, princess, tsar, potentate.

monarchy n **1** KINGDOM, empire, principality, realm, domain, dominion. **2** ROYALISM, sovereignty, autocracy, monocracy, absolutism, despotism, tyranny.

monastery n friary, priory, abbey, cloister, charterhouse.

monastic adj reclusive, withdrawn, secluded, cloistered, austere, ascetic, celibate, contemplative.
F3 secular, worldly.

monetary adj financial, fiscal, pecuniary (fml), budgetary, economic, capital, cash.

money n currency, cash, legal tender, banknotes, coin, funds, capital, dough (infml), dosh (infml), riches, wealth.

mongrel n cross, crossbreed, hybrid, half-breed.
adj crossbred, hybrid, half-breed, bastard, mixed, ill-defined.
F3 pure-bred, pedigree.

monitor n **1** SCREEN, display, VDU, recorder, scanner. **2** SUPERVISOR, watchdog, overseer, invigilator, adviser, prefect.
v check, watch, keep track of, keep under surveillance, keep an eye on, follow, track, supervise, observe, note, survey, trace, scan, record, plot, detect.

monkey n **1** PRIMATE, simian, ape. **2** (infml) SCAMP, imp, urchin, brat, rogue, scallywag (infml), rascal.

Monkeys include:
baboon, capuchin, colobus monkey, drill, mandrill, guenon, guereza, howler monkey, langur, macaque, mangabey, marmoset, douroucouli, proboscis monkey, rhesus monkey, saki, spider monkey, squirrel monkey, tamarin, titi, toque, uakari, woolly monkey.

monopolize v dominate, take over, appropriate, corner, control, hog (infml), engross, occupy, preoccupy, take up, tie up.
F3 share.

monotonous adj boring, dull, tedious, uninteresting, tiresome, wearisome, unchanging, uneventful, unvaried, uniform, toneless, flat, colourless, repetitive, routine, plodding, humdrum, soul-destroying.
F3 lively, varied, colourful.

monotony n tedium, dullness, boredom, sameness, tiresomeness, uneventfulness, flatness, wearisomeness, uniformity, routine, repetitiousness.
F3 liveliness, colour.

monster n **1** BEAST, fiend, brute, barbarian, savage, villain, giant, ogre, ogress, troll, mammoth. **2** FREAK, monstrosity, mutant.
adj huge, gigantic, giant, colossal, enormous, immense, massive, monstrous, jumbo, mammoth, vast, tremendous.
F3 tiny, minute.

monstrous adj **1** WICKED, evil, vicious, cruel, criminal, heinous, outrageous, scandalous, disgraceful, atrocious, abhorrent, dreadful, frightful, horrible, horrifying, terrible. **2** UNNATURAL, inhuman, freakish, grotesque, hideous, deformed, malformed, misshapen. **3** HUGE, enormous, colossal, gigantic, vast, immense, massive, mammoth.

monument n memorial, cenotaph, headstone, gravestone, tombstone, shrine, mausoleum, cairn, barrow, cross, marker, obelisk, pillar, statue, relic, remembrance, commemoration, testament, reminder, record, memento, evidence, token.

monumental adj **1** IMPRESSIVE, imposing, awe-inspiring, awesome, overwhelming, significant, important, epoch-making, historic, magnificent, majestic, memorable, notable, outstanding, abiding, immortal, lasting, classic. **2** HUGE, immense, enormous, colossal, vast, tremendous, massive, great. **3** COMMEMORATIVE, memorial.
F3 1 insignificant, unimportant.

mood n **1** DISPOSITION, frame of mind, state of mind, temper, humour, spirit, tenor, whim. **2** BAD TEMPER, sulk, the sulks, pique, melancholy, depression, blues (infml), doldrums, dumps (infml).

moody adj changeable, temperamental, unpredictable, capricious, irritable, short-tempered, crabby (infml), crotchety, crusty (infml), testy, touchy, morose, angry, broody, mopy, sulky, sullen, gloomy, melancholy, miserable, downcast, doleful, glum, impulsive, fickle, flighty.
F3 equable, cheerful.

moon v idle, loaf, mooch, languish, pine, mope, brood, daydream, dream, fantasize.

moor[1] v fasten, secure, tie up, drop anchor, anchor, berth, dock, make fast, fix, hitch, bind.
F3 loose.

moor[2] n moorland, heath, fell, upland.

mop n head of hair, shock, mane, tangle, thatch, mass.

v swab, sponge, wipe, clean, wash, absorb, soak.

mope v brood, fret, sulk, pine, languish, droop, despair, grieve, idle.

moral adj ethical, virtuous, good, right, principled, honourable, decent, upright, upstanding, straight, righteous, high-minded, honest, incorruptible, proper, blameless, chaste, clean-living, pure, just, noble.
F3 immoral.

n lesson, message, teaching, dictum, meaning, maxim, adage, precept, saying, proverb, aphorism, epigram.

morale n confidence, spirits, esprit de corps, self-esteem, state of mind, heart, mood.

morality n ethics, morals, ideals, principles, standards, virtue, rectitude, righteousness, decency, goodness, honesty, integrity, justice, uprightness, propriety, conduct, manners.
F3 immorality.

morals n morality, ethics, principles, standards, ideals, integrity, scruples, behaviour, conduct, habits, manners.

morbid adj **1** GHOULISH, ghastly, gruesome, macabre, hideous, horrid, grim. **2** GLOOMY, pessimistic, melancholy, sombre. **3** SICK, unhealthy, unwholesome, insalubrious.

more adj further, extra, additional, added, new, fresh, increased, other, supplementary, repeated, alternative, spare.
F3 less.

adv further, longer, again, besides, moreover, better.
F3 less.

moreover adv furthermore, further, besides, in addition, as well as, also, additionally, what is more.

morning n daybreak, daylight, dawn, sunrise, break of day, before noon.

morose adj ill-tempered, bad-tempered, moody, sullen, sulky, surly, gloomy, grim, gruff, sour, taciturn, glum, grouchy (infml), crabby (infml), saturnine.
F3 cheerful, communicative.

morsel n bit, scrap, piece, fragment, crumb, bite, mouthful, nibble, taste, soupçon, titbit, slice, fraction, modicum, grain, atom, part.

mortal adj **1** WORLDLY, earthly, bodily, human, perishable, temporal. **2** FATAL, lethal, deadly. **3** EXTREME, great, severe, intense, grave, awful.
F3 1 immortal.
n human being, human, individual, person, being, body, creature.
F3 immortal, god.

mortality n **1** HUMANITY, death, impermanence, perishability. **2** FATALITY, death rate.
F3 1 immortality.

mortified adj humiliated, shamed, ashamed, humbled, embarrassed, crushed.

mostly adv mainly, on the whole, principally, chiefly, generally, usually, largely, for the most part, as a rule.

moth

Types of moth include:
brown-tail, buff-tip, burnet, carpet, cinnabar, clothes, death's-head, emperor, gypsy, hawk-moth, Kentish glory, lackey, lappet, leopard, lobster, magpie, oak-egger, peach-blossom, peppered, puss, red underwing, silkworm, silver-Y, swallow-tail, tiger, turnip, tussock, wax, winter. see also **butterfly**.

mother n **1** PARENT, procreator (fml), progenitress (fml), birth mother, dam, mamma, mum (infml), mummy (infml), mom (US infml), matriarch, ancestor, matron, old woman (infml). **2** ORIGIN, source.
v **1** BEAR, produce, nurture, raise, rear, nurse, care for, cherish. **2** PAMPER, spoil, baby, indulge, overprotect, fuss over.

motherly adj maternal, caring, comforting, affectionate, kind, loving, protective, warm, tender, gentle, fond.
F3 neglectful, uncaring.

motif n theme, idea, topic, concept, pattern, design, figure, form, logo, shape, device, ornament, decoration.

motion n **1** MOVEMENT, action, mobility, moving, activity, locomotion, moving, travel, transit, passage, passing, progress, change, flow, inclination. **2** GESTURE, gesticulation, signal, sign, wave, nod. **3** PROPOSAL, suggestion, recommendation, proposition.
v signal, gesture, gesticulate, sign, wave, nod, beckon, direct, usher.

motionless adj unmoving, still, stationary, static, immobile, at a standstill, fixed, halted, at rest, resting, standing, paralysed, inanimate, lifeless, frozen, rigid, stagnant.
F3 active, moving.

motivate v prompt, incite, impel, spur, provoke, stimulate, drive, lead, stir, urge, push, propel, persuade, move, inspire, encourage, cause, trigger, induce, kindle, draw, arouse, bring.
F3 deter, discourage.

motive n ground(s), cause, reason, purpose, motivation, object, intention, influence, rationale, thinking, incentive, impulse, stimulus, inspiration, incitement, urge, encouragement, design, desire, consideration.

F3 deterrent, disincentive.

mottled adj speckled, dappled, blotchy, flecked, piebald, stippled, streaked, tabby, spotted, freckled, variegated.

F3 monochrome, uniform.

motto n saying, slogan, maxim, watchword, catchword, byword, precept, proverb, adage, formula, rule, golden rule, dictum.

mould[1] n **1** CAST, form, die, template, pattern, matrix. **2** SHAPE, form, format, pattern, structure, style, type, build, construction, cut, design, kind, model, sort, stamp, arrangement, brand, frame, character, nature, quality, line, make.
v **1** FORGE, cast, shape, stamp, make, form, create, design, construct, sculpt, model, work. **2** INFLUENCE, direct, control.

mould[2] n mildew, fungus, mouldiness, mustiness, blight.

mouldy adj mildewed, blighted, musty, decaying, corrupt, rotten, fusty, putrid, bad, spoiled, stale.

F3 fresh, wholesome.

mound n **1** HILL, hillock, hummock, rise, knoll, bank, dune, elevation, ridge, embankment, earthwork. **2** HEAP, pile, stack.

mount v **1** PRODUCE, put on, set up, prepare, stage, exhibit, display, launch. **2** INCREASE, grow, accumulate, multiply, rise, intensify, soar, swell. **3** CLIMB, ascend, get up, go up, get on, clamber up, scale, get astride.

F3 **2** decrease, diminish, subside.

3 descend, dismount, go down.
n horse, steed, support, mounting.

mountain n **1** HEIGHT, elevation, mount, peak, mound, alp, tor, massif. **2** HEAP, pile, stack, mass, abundance, backlog.

mountainous adj **1** CRAGGY, rocky, hilly, high, highland, upland, alpine, soaring, steep. **2** HUGE, towering, enormous, immense.

F3 **1** flat. **2** tiny.

mourn v grieve, lament, sorrow, bemoan, miss, regret, deplore, weep, wail.

F3 rejoice.

mournful adj sorrowful, sad, unhappy, desolate, grief-stricken, heavy-hearted, heartbroken, broken-hearted, cast-down, downcast, miserable, tragic, woeful, melancholy, sombre, depressed, dejected, gloomy, dismal.

F3 joyful.

mourning n bereavement, grief, grieving, lamentation, sadness, sorrow, desolation, weeping.

F3 rejoicing.

mouth n **1** LIPS, jaws, trap (infml), gob (sl). **2** OPENING, aperture, orifice, cavity, entrance, gateway, inlet, estuary.
v enunciate, articulate, utter, pronounce, whisper, form.

movable adj mobile, portable, transportable, changeable, alterable, adjustable, flexible, transferable.

F3 fixed, immovable.

move v **1** STIR, go, advance, budge, change, proceed, progress, make strides. **2** TRANSPORT, carry, transfer. **3** DEPART, go away, leave, decamp, migrate, remove, move house, relocate. **4** PROMPT, stimulate, urge,

impel, drive, propel, motivate, incite, persuade, induce, inspire. **5** AFFECT, touch, agitate, stir, impress, excite.
n **1** MOVEMENT, motion, step, manoeuvre, action, device, stratagem. **2** REMOVAL, relocation, migration, transfer.

movement n **1** REPOSITIONING, move, moving, relocation, activity, act, action, agitation, stirring, transfer, passage. **2** CHANGE, development, advance, evolution, current, drift, flow, shift, progress, progression, trend, tendency. **3** CAMPAIGN, crusade, drive, group, organization, party, faction.

moving adj **1** MOBILE, active, in motion. **2** TOUCHING, affecting, poignant, impressive, emotive, arousing, stirring, inspiring, inspirational, exciting, thrilling, persuasive, stimulating.
E3 1 immobile. **2** unemotional.

mow v cut, trim, crop, clip, shear, scythe.

much adv greatly, considerably, a lot, frequently, often.
adj copious, plentiful, ample, considerable, a lot, abundant, great, substantial.
n plenty, a lot, lots (infml), loads (infml), heaps (infml), lashings (infml).
E3 little.

muck n dirt, dung, manure, mire, filth, mud, sewage, slime, gunge (infml), ordure, scum, sludge.
muck up ruin, wreck, spoil, mess up, make a mess of, botch, bungle, screw up (infml), cock up (sl).

mud n clay, mire, ooze, dirt, sludge, silt.

muddle v **1** DISORGANIZE, disorder, mix up, mess up, jumble, scramble,

tangle. **2** CONFUSE, bewilder, bemuse, perplex.
n chaos, confusion, disorder, mess, mix-up, jumble, clutter, tangle.

muddy adj **1** DIRTY, foul, miry, mucky, marshy, boggy, swampy, quaggy, grimy. **2** CLOUDY, indistinct, obscure, opaque, murky, hazy, blurred, fuzzy, dull.
E3 1 clean. **2** clear.

muffle v **1** WRAP, envelop, cloak, swathe, cover. **2** DEADEN, dull, quieten, silence, stifle, dampen, muzzle, suppress.
E3 2 amplify.

mug^1 n cup, beaker, pot, tankard.

mug^2 v set upon, attack, assault, waylay, steal from, rob, beat up, jump (on).

muggy adj humid, sticky, stuffy, sultry, close, clammy, oppressive, sweltering, moist, damp.
E3 dry.

mull over reflect on, ponder, contemplate, think over, think about, ruminate, consider, weigh up, chew over, meditate, study, examine, deliberate.

multiple adj many, numerous, manifold, various, several, sundry, collective.

multiply v increase, proliferate, expand, spread, reproduce, propagate, breed, accumulate, intensify, extend, build up, augment, boost.
E3 decrease, lessen.

multitude n crowd, throng, horde, swarm, mob, mass, herd, congregation, host, lot, lots, legion, public, people, populace.
E3 few, scattering.

munch v eat, chew, crunch, masticate (fml).

mundane *adj* banal, ordinary, everyday, commonplace, prosaic, humdrum, workaday, routine.
F3 extraordinary.

municipal *adj* civic, city, town, urban, borough, community, public.

murder *n* homicide, killing, manslaughter, slaying, assassination, massacre, bloodshed.
v kill, slaughter, slay, assassinate, butcher, massacre.

murderer *n* killer, homicide, slayer, slaughterer, assassin, butcher, cut-throat.

murderous *adj* **1** HOMICIDAL, brutal, barbarous, bloodthirsty, bloody, cut-throat, killing, lethal, cruel, savage, ferocious, deadly. **2** (*infml*) DIFFICULT, exhausting, strenuous, unpleasant, dangerous.

murky *adj* dark, dismal, gloomy, dull, overcast, misty, foggy, dim, cloudy, obscure, veiled, grey.
F3 bright, clear.

murmur *n* mumble, muttering, whisper, undertone, humming, rumble, drone, grumble.
v mutter, mumble, whisper, buzz, hum, rumble, purr, burble.

muscular *adj* brawny, beefy (*infml*), sinewy, athletic, powerfully built, strapping, hefty, powerful, husky, robust, stalwart, vigorous, strong.
F3 puny, flabby, weak.

mushroom

Types of mushroom and toadstool include:
edible: beefsteak fungus, blewits, boletus, chestnut mushroom, button mushroom, cep, champignon, chanterelle, fairy-ring, honey fungus, horn of plenty, horse mushroom, lawyer's wig, morel, oyster mushroom, parasol mushroom, penny-bun, porcini, saffron milk cap, shaggy ink-cap, shiitake, truffle; *inedible/poisonous:* amanita, death-cap, destroying angel, false morel, fly agaric, ink-cap, milk cap, sulphur tuft.

music

Types of music include:
acid house, adult-oriented rock (AOR), ambient, ballet, bluegrass, blues, boogie-woogie, Cajun, calypso, chamber, choral, classical, country-and-western, dance, disco, Dixieland, doo-wop, drum and bass, electronic, folk, folk rock, funk, fusion, gangsta, garage, glam rock, gospel, grunge, hard-core, heavy metal, hip-hop, honky-tonk, house, incidental, instrumental, jazz, jazz-funk, jazz-rock, jive, jungle, middle-of-the-road (MOR), operatic, orchestral, pop, punk rock, ragtime, rap, reggae, rhythm and blues (R & B), rock, rock and roll, salsa, samba, ska, skiffle, soul, swing, techno, thrash metal, trance, trip hop.

musical *adj* tuneful, melodious, melodic, harmonious, dulcet, sweet-sounding, lyrical.
F3 discordant, unmusical.

Musical instruments include:
stringed: balalaika, banjo, cello, clarsach, double-bass, guitar, harp, hurdy-gurdy, lute, lyre, mandolin, sitar, spinet, ukulele, viola, violin, fiddle (*infml*), zither; *keyboard:* accordion, concertina, clavichord, harmonium, harpsichord, keyboard, melodeon, organ, Wurlitzer®, piano, grand piano, Pianola®,

player-piano, synthesizer, virginals; *wind:* bagpipes, bassoon, bugle, clarinet, cor anglais, cornet, didgeridoo, euphonium, fife, flugelhorn, flute, French horn, harmonica, horn, kazoo, mouth-organ, oboe, Pan-pipes, piccolo, recorder, saxophone, sousaphone, trombone, trumpet, tuba, uillean pipes; *percussion:* castanets, cymbal, glockenspiel, maracas, marimba, tambourine, triangle, tubular bells, xylophone; *drums:* bass drum, bodhran, bongo, kettledrum, snaredrum, tabla, tenor drum, timpani, tom-tom.

Musical terms include:
accompaniment, alto, arpeggio, arrangement, bar, baritone, bass, beat, cadence, chord, clef, bass clef, treble clef, coda, contralto, counterpoint, crotchet, descant, downbeat, encore, ensemble, finale, flat, harmony, key, medley, melody, middle C, minim, natural, note, octave, orchestra, pitch, quaver, rest, rhythm, scale, score, semibreve, semiquaver, semitone, sharp, solo, soprano, stave, syncopation, tempo, tenor, timbre, time signature, tone, tonic sol-fa, treble, tremolo, tuning, unison, up-beat, vibrato, virtuoso.

Musical directions include:
a cappella, accelerando, adagio, ad lib, affettuoso, agitato, alla breve, allargando, allegretto, allegro, amoroso, andante, animato, arco, a tempo, cantabile, con brio, con fuoco, con moto, crescendo, da capo, decrescendo, diminuendo, dolce, doloroso, fine, forte, fortissimo, glissando, grave, larghetto, largo, legato, lento,

maestoso, marcato, mezza voce, mezzo-forte, moderato, molto, non troppo, obbligato, pianissimo, piano, pizzicato, presto, rallentando, ritenuto, semplice, sempre, senza, sforzando, smorzando, sostenuto, sotto voce, spiritoso, staccato, subito, tacet, tanto, tenuto, tutti, vigoroso, vivace.

musician

Musicians include:
instrumentalist, accompanist, player; bugler, busker, cellist, clarinettist, drummer, fiddler, flautist, guitarist, harpist, lutenist, oboist, organist, percussionist, pianist, piper, soloist, trombonist, trumpeter, violinist; singer, vocalist, balladeer, diva, prima donna; conductor; band, orchestra, group, backing group, ensemble, chamber orchestra, choir, duo, duet, trio, quartet, quintet, sextet, septet, octet, nonet.

muster *v* assemble, convene, gather, call together, mobilize, round up, marshal, come together, congregate, collect, group, meet, rally, mass, throng, call up, summon, enrol.

musty *adj* mouldy, mildewy, stale, stuffy, fusty, dank, airless, decayed, smelly.

mutation *n* change, alteration, variation, modification, transformation, deviation, anomaly, evolution.

mute *adj* silent, dumb, voiceless, wordless, speechless, mum (*infml*), unspoken, noiseless, unexpressed, unpronounced.
F3 vocal, talkative.
v tone down, subdue, muffle, lower,

moderate, dampen, deaden, soften, silence.

mutilate *v* **1** MAIM, injure, dismember, disable, disfigure, lame, mangle, cut to pieces, cut up, butcher. **2** SPOIL, mar, damage, cut, censor.

mutinous *adj* rebellious, insurgent, insubordinate, disobedient, seditious, revolutionary, riotous, subversive, bolshie (*infml*), unruly.

F3 obedient, compliant.

mutiny *n* rebellion, insurrection, revolt, revolution, rising, uprising, insubordination, disobedience, defiance, resistance, riot, strike. *v* rebel, revolt, rise up, resist, protest, disobey, strike.

mutter *v* **1** MUMBLE, murmur, rumble. **2** COMPLAIN, grumble, grouse (*infml*).

mutual *adj* reciprocal, shared, common, joint, interchangeable, interchanged, exchanged, complementary.

muzzle *v* restrain, stifle, suppress, gag, mute, silence, censor, choke.

mysterious *adj* enigmatic, cryptic, mystifying, inexplicable, incomprehensible, puzzling, perplexing, obscure, strange, unfathomable, mystical, baffling, curious, hidden, insoluble, secret, weird, secretive, veiled, dark, furtive.

F3 straightforward, comprehensible.

mystery *n* **1** ENIGMA, puzzle, secret, riddle, conundrum, question. **2** OBSCURITY, secrecy, ambiguity.

mystical *adj* occult, arcane, mystic, esoteric, supernatural, paranormal, transcendental, metaphysical, hidden, mysterious.

mystify *v* puzzle, bewilder, baffle, perplex, confound, confuse.

myth *n* legend, fable, fairy tale, allegory, parable, saga, story, fiction, tradition, fancy, fantasy, superstition.

mythical *adj* **1** MYTHOLOGICAL, legendary, fabled, fairytale. **2** FICTITIOUS, imaginary, made-up, invented, make-believe, non-existent, unreal, pretended, fanciful.

F3 1 historical. **2** actual, real.

mythology *n* legend, myths, lore, tradition(s), folklore, folk-tales, tales.

Mythological creatures and spirits include:

abominable snowman (or yeti), afrit, basilisk, bigfoot, brownie, bunyip, centaur, Cerberus, chimera, cockatrice, Cyclops, dragon, dryad, elf, Erinyes (or Furies), fairy, faun, genie, gnome, goblin, golem, Gorgon, griffin, harpy, hippocampus, hippogriff, hobgoblin, imp, kelpie, kraken, lamia, leprechaun, Loch Ness monster, mermaid, merman, Minotaur, naiad, nereid, nymph, ogre, ogress, orc, oread, Pegasus, phoenix, pixie, roc, salamander, sasquatch, satyr, sea serpent, silkie, siren, Sphinx, sylph, troll, unicorn, vampire, werewolf, wyvern.

N

nag v scold, berate, irritate, annoy, pester, badger, plague, torment, harass, henpeck (*infml*), harry, vex, upbraid, goad.

nail v fasten, attach, secure, pin, tack, fix, join.
n **1** FASTENER, pin, tack, spike, skewer. **2** TALON, claw.

naive adj unsophisticated, ingenuous, innocent, unaffected, artless, guileless, simple, natural, childlike, open, trusting, unsuspecting, gullible, credulous, wide-eyed.
F3 experienced, sophisticated.

naiveté n ingenuousness, innocence, inexperience, naturalness, simplicity, openness, frankness, gullibility, credulity.
F3 experience, sophistication.

naked adj **1** NUDE, bare, undressed, unclothed, uncovered, stripped, stark-naked, disrobed, denuded, in the altogether (*infml*). **2** OPEN, unadorned, undisguised, unqualified, plain, stark, overt, blatant, exposed.
F3 1 clothed, covered. **2** concealed.

name n **1** TITLE, appellation (*fml*), designation, label, term, epithet, handle (*infml*). **2** REPUTATION, character, repute, renown, esteem, eminence, fame, honour, distinction, note.

v **1** CALL, christen, baptize, term, title, entitle, dub, label, style. **2** DESIGNATE, nominate, cite, choose, select, specify, classify, commission, appoint.

nameless adj **1** UNNAMED, anonymous, unidentified, unknown, obscure. **2** INEXPRESSIBLE, indescribable, unutterable, unspeakable, unmentionable, unheard-of.
F3 1 named.

namely adv that is, ie, specifically, viz, that is to say.

nap v doze, sleep, snooze (*infml*), nod (off), drop off, rest, kip (*infml*).
n rest, sleep, siesta, catnap, forty winks (*infml*), kip (*infml*).

narcotic n drug, opiate, sedative, tranquillizer, pain-killer.
adj soporific, hypnotic, sedative, analgesic, pain-killing, numbing, dulling, calming, stupefying.

narrate v tell, relate, report, recount, describe, unfold, recite, state, detail.

narrative n story, tale, chronicle, account, history, report, detail, statement.

narrator n storyteller, chronicler, reporter, raconteur, commentator, writer.

narrow adj **1** TIGHT, confined, constricted, cramped, slim, slender, thin, fine, tapering, close. **2** LIMITED, restricted, circumscribed. **3** NARROW-MINDED, biased, bigoted, exclusive, dogmatic.

E3 1 wide. **2** broad. **3** broad-minded, tolerant.

v constrict, limit, tighten, reduce, diminish, simplify.

E3 broaden, widen, increase.

narrow-minded *adj* illiberal, biased, bigoted, prejudiced, reactionary, small-minded, conservative, intolerant, insular, petty.

E3 broad-minded.

nasty *adj* **1** UNPLEASANT, repellent, repugnant, repulsive, objectionable, offensive, disgusting, sickening, horrible, filthy, foul, polluted, obscene. **2** MALICIOUS, mean, spiteful, vicious, malevolent.

E3 1 agreeable, pleasant, decent. **2** benevolent, kind.

nation *n* country, people, race, state, realm, population, community, society.

national *adj* countrywide, civil, domestic, nationwide, state, internal, general, governmental, public, widespread, social.

n citizen, native, subject, inhabitant, resident.

nationalism *n* patriotism, allegiance, loyalty, chauvinism, xenophobia, jingoism.

nationality *n* race, nation, ethnic group, birth, tribe, clan.

native *adj* **1** LOCAL, indigenous, domestic, vernacular, home, aboriginal, autochthonous (*fml*), mother, original. **2** INBORN, inherent, innate, inbred, hereditary, inherited, congenital, instinctive, natural, intrinsic, natal.

n inhabitant, resident, national, citizen, dweller, aborigine, autochthon (*fml*).

E3 foreigner, outsider, stranger.

natural *adj* **1** ORDINARY, normal, common, regular, standard, usual, typical. **2** INNATE, inborn, instinctive, intuitive, inherent, congenital, native, indigenous. **3** GENUINE, pure, authentic, unrefined, unprocessed, unmixed, real. **4** SINCERE, unaffected, genuine, artless, ingenuous, guileless, simple, unsophisticated, open, candid, spontaneous.

E3 1 unnatural. **2** acquired. **3** artificial. **4** affected, disingenuous.

naturalistic *adj* natural, realistic, true-to-life, representational, lifelike, graphic, real-life, photographic.

naturally *adv* **1** OF COURSE, as a matter of course, simply, obviously, logically, typically, certainly, absolutely. **2** NORMALLY, genuinely, instinctively, spontaneously.

nature *n* **1** ESSENCE, quality, character, features, disposition, attributes, personality, make-up, constitution, temperament, mood, outlook, temper. **2** KIND, sort, type, description, category, variety, style, species. **3** UNIVERSE, world, creation, earth, environment. **4** COUNTRYSIDE, country, landscape, scenery, natural history.

naughty *adj* **1** BAD, badly behaved, mischievous, disobedient, wayward, exasperating, playful, roguish. **2** INDECENT, obscene, bawdy, risqué, smutty.

E3 1 good, well-behaved. **2** decent.

nausea *n* **1** VOMITING, sickness, retching, queasiness, biliousness. **2** DISGUST, revulsion, loathing, repugnance.

nauseate v sicken, disgust, revolt, repel, offend, turn one's stomach (*infml*).

nautical adj naval, marine, maritime, sea-going, seafaring, sailing, oceanic, boating.

navigate v steer, drive, direct, pilot, guide, handle, manoeuvre, cruise, sail, skipper, voyage, journey, cross, helm, plot, plan.

navigation n sailing, steering, cruising, voyaging, seamanship, helmsmanship.

navy n fleet, ships, flotilla, armada, warships.

near adj **1** NEARBY, close, bordering, adjacent, adjoining, alongside, neighbouring. **2** IMMINENT, impending, forthcoming, coming, approaching. **3** DEAR, familiar, close, related, intimate, akin.
E3 1 far. **2** distant. **3** remote.

nearby adj near, neighbouring, adjoining, adjacent, accessible, convenient, handy.
E3 faraway.
adv near, within reach, at close quarters, close at hand, not far away.

nearly adv almost, practically, virtually, closely, approximately, more or less, as good as, just about, roughly, well-nigh.
E3 completely, totally.

neat adj **1** TIDY, orderly, smart, spruce, trim, clean, spick-and-span (*infml*), shipshape. **2** DEFT, clever, adroit, skilful, expert. **3** UNDILUTED, unmixed, unadulterated, straight, pure.
E3 1 untidy. **2** clumsy. **3** diluted.

nebulous adj vague, hazy, imprecise, indefinite, indistinct, cloudy, misty, obscure, uncertain, unclear, dim, ambiguous, confused, fuzzy, shapeless, amorphous.
E3 clear.

necessary adj needed, required, essential, compulsory, indispensable, vital, mission-critical, imperative, mandatory, obligatory, needful, unavoidable, inevitable, inescapable, inexorable, certain.
E3 unnecessary, inessential, unimportant.

necessitate v require, involve, entail, call for, demand, oblige, force, constrain, compel.

necessity n **1** REQUIREMENT, obligation, prerequisite, essential, fundamental, need, want, compulsion, demand.
2 INDISPENSABILITY, inevitability, needfulness. **3** POVERTY, destitution, hardship.

need v miss, lack, want, require, demand, call for, necessitate, have need of, have to, crave.
n **1** a need for caution: call, demand, obligation, requirement. **2** the country's needs: essential, necessity, requisite, prerequisite, desideratum. **3** a need for equipment: want, lack, insufficiency, inadequacy, neediness, shortage.

needless adj unnecessary, gratuitous, uncalled-for, unwanted, redundant, superfluous, useless, pointless, purposeless.
E3 necessary, essential.

needy adj poor, destitute, impoverished, penniless, disadvantaged, deprived, poverty-stricken, underprivileged.
E3 affluent, wealthy, well-off.

negate v **1** NULLIFY, annul, cancel, invalidate, undo, countermand, abrogate (*fml*), neutralize, quash, retract, reverse, revoke, rescind, wipe out, void, repeal. **2** DENY, contradict, oppose, disprove, refute, repudiate.

F3 2 affirm.

negative *adj* **1** CONTRADICTORY, contrary, denying, opposing, invalidating, neutralizing, nullifying, annulling. **2** UNCO-OPERATIVE, cynical, pessimistic, unenthusiastic, uninterested, unwilling.

F3 1 affirmative, positive.
2 constructive, positive.
n contradiction, denial, opposite, refusal.

neglect *v* **1** DISREGARD, ignore, leave alone, abandon, pass by, rebuff, scorn, disdain, slight, spurn. **2** FORGET, fail (in), omit, overlook, let slide, shirk, skimp.

F3 1 cherish, appreciate. **2** remember.
n negligence, disregard, carelessness, failure, inattention, indifference, slackness, dereliction of duty, forgetfulness, heedlessness, oversight, slight, disrespect.

F3 care, attention, concern.

negligence *n* inattentiveness, carelessness, laxity, neglect, slackness, thoughtlessness, forgetfulness, indifference, omission, oversight, disregard, failure, default.

F3 attentiveness, care, regard.

negligent *adj* neglectful, inattentive, remiss, thoughtless, casual, lax, careless, indifferent, offhand, nonchalant, slack, uncaring, forgetful.

F3 attentive, careful, scrupulous.

negligible *adj* unimportant, insignificant, small, imperceptible, trifling, trivial, minor, minute.

F3 significant.

negotiate *v* **1** CONFER, deal, mediate, arbitrate, bargain, arrange, transact, work out, manage, settle, consult, contract. **2** GET ROUND, cross, surmount, traverse, pass.

negotiation *n* mediation, arbitration, debate, discussion, diplomacy, bargaining, transaction.

negotiator *n* arbitrator, go-between, mediator, intermediary, moderator, intercessor, adjudicator, broker, ambassador, diplomat.

neighbourhood *n* district, locality, vicinity, community, locale, environs, confines, surroundings, region, proximity.

neighbouring *adj* adjacent, bordering, near, nearby, adjoining, connecting, next, surrounding.

F3 distant, remote.

neighbourly *adj* sociable, friendly, amiable, kind, helpful, genial, hospitable, obliging, considerate, companionable.

nerve *n* **1** COURAGE, bravery, mettle, pluck, guts (*infml*), spunk (*infml*), spirit, vigour, intrepidity, daring, fearlessness, firmness, resolution, fortitude, steadfastness, will, determination, endurance, force.
2 (*infml*) AUDACITY, impudence, cheek (*infml*), effrontery, brazenness, boldness, chutzpah (*infml*), impertinence, insolence.

F3 1 weakness. **2** timidity.

nerve-racking *adj* harrowing, distressing, trying, stressful, tense, maddening, worrying, difficult, frightening.

nerves *n* nervousness, tension, stress, anxiety, worry, strain, fretfulness.

nervous *adj* highly-strung, excitable, anxious, agitated, nervy (*infml*), on

edge, edgy, jumpy (*infml*), jittery
(*infml*), tense, fidgety, apprehensive,
neurotic, shaky, uneasy, worried,
flustered, fearful.
F3 calm, relaxed.

nest *n* **1** BREEDING-GROUND, den,
roost, eyrie, lair. **2** RETREAT, refuge,
haunt, hideaway.

nestle *v* snuggle, huddle, cuddle, curl
up.

net¹ *n* mesh, web, network, netting,
open-work, lattice, lace.
v catch, trap, snare, ensnare,
entangle, nab (*infml*).

net² *adj* nett, clear, after tax, final,
lowest.
v bring in, clear, earn, make, realize,
receive, gain, obtain, accumulate.

network *n* system, organization,
arrangement, structure,
interconnections, complex, grid, net,
maze, mesh, labyrinth, channels,
circuitry, convolution, grill, tracks.

neurosis *n* disorder, affliction,
abnormality, disturbance,
derangement, deviation, obsession,
phobia.

neurotic *adj* disturbed,
maladjusted, anxious, nervous,
overwrought, unstable, unhealthy,
deviant, abnormal, compulsive,
obsessive.

neuter *v* castrate, emasculate,
doctor, geld, spay.

neutral *adj* **1** IMPARTIAL,
uncommitted, unbiased, non-aligned,
disinterested, unprejudiced,
undecided, non-partisan, non-
committal, objective, indifferent,
dispassionate, even-handed. **2** DULL,
nondescript, colourless, drab,
expressionless, indistinct.
F3 **1** biased, partisan. **2** colourful.

neutralize *v* counteract,
counterbalance, offset, negate,
cancel, nullify, invalidate, undo,
frustrate.

never-ending *adj* everlasting,
eternal, non-stop, perpetual,
unceasing, uninterrupted,
unremitting, interminable, incessant,
unbroken, permanent, persistent,
unchanging, relentless.
F3 fleeting, transitory.

nevertheless *adv* nonetheless,
notwithstanding, still, anyway, even
so, yet, however, anyhow, but,
regardless.

new *adj* **1** NOVEL, original, fresh,
different, unfamiliar, unusual, brand-
new, mint, unknown, unused, virgin,
newborn. **2** MODERN, contemporary,
current, latest, recent, up-to-date, up-
to-the-minute, topical, trendy (*infml*),
ultra-modern, advanced, newfangled
(*infml*). **3** CHANGED, altered,
modernized, improved, renewed,
restored, redesigned. **4** ADDED,
additional, extra, more,
supplementary.
F3 **1** usual. **2** outdated, out-of-date.
3 old.

newcomer *n* immigrant, alien,
foreigner, incomer, colonist, settler,
arrival, outsider, stranger, novice,
beginner.

news *n* report, account, information,
intelligence, dispatch, communiqué,
bulletin, gossip, hearsay, rumour,
statement, story, word, tidings, latest,
release, scandal, revelation, lowdown
(*infml*), exposé, disclosure, gen (*infml*),
advice.

next *adj* **1** ADJACENT, adjoining,
neighbouring, nearest, closest.
2 FOLLOWING, subsequent,

succeeding, ensuing, later.

E3 2 previous, preceding.

adv afterwards, subsequently, later, then.

nibble *n* bite, morsel, taste, titbit, bit, crumb, snack, piece.

v bite, eat, peck, pick at, gnaw.

nice *adj* 1 PLEASANT, agreeable, delightful, charming, likable, attractive, good, kind, friendly, well-mannered, polite, respectable.

2 SUBTLE, delicate, fine, fastidious, discriminating, scrupulous, precise, exact, accurate, careful, strict.

E3 1 nasty, disagreeable, unpleasant. 2 careless.

nicety *n* 1 DELICACY, refinement, subtlety, distinction, nuance.

2 PRECISION, accuracy, meticulousness, scrupulousness, minuteness, finesse.

niche *n* 1 RECESS, alcove, hollow, nook, cubby-hole, corner, opening.

2 POSITION, place, vocation, calling, métier, slot.

nick *n* 1 NOTCH, indentation, chip, cut, groove, dent, scar, scratch, mark.

2 (*sl*) PRISON, jail, police station.

v 1 NOTCH, cut, dent, indent, chip, score, scratch, scar, mark, damage, snick. 2 (*sl*) STEAL, pilfer, knock off (*infml*), pinch (*infml*).

nickname *n* pet name, sobriquet, epithet, diminutive.

night *n* night-time, darkness, dark, dead of night.

E3 day, daytime.

nightfall *n* sunset, dusk, twilight, evening, gloaming.

E3 dawn, sunrise.

nightmare *n* 1 BAD DREAM, hallucination. 2 ORDEAL, horror, torment, trial.

nightwear

Types of nightwear include: nightdress, nightie (*infml*), pyjamas, bed-jacket, bedsocks, dressing-gown, housecoat, negligee.

nil *n* nothing, zero, none, nought, naught, love, duck, zilch (*sl*).

nimble *adj* agile, active, lively, sprightly, spry, smart, quick, brisk, nippy (*infml*), deft, alert, light-footed, prompt, ready, swift, quick-witted.

E3 clumsy, slow.

nip [1] *v* bite, pinch, squeeze, snip, clip, tweak, catch, grip, nibble.

nip [2] *n* dram, draught, shot, swallow, mouthful, drop, sip, taste, portion.

nobility *n* 1 NOBLENESS, dignity, grandeur, illustriousness, stateliness, majesty, magnificence, eminence, excellence, superiority, uprightness, honour, virtue, worthiness.

2 ARISTOCRACY, peerage, nobles, gentry, élite, lords, high society.

E3 1 baseness. 2 proletariat.

Titles of the nobility include: baron, baroness, baronet, count, countess, dame, dowager, duchess, duke, earl, grand duke, knight, lady, laird, life peer, lord, marchioness, marquess, marquis, peer, peeress, seigneur, squire, thane, viscount, viscountess.

noble *n* aristocrat, peer, lord, lady, nobleman, noblewoman.

E3 commoner.

adj 1 ARISTOCRATIC, high-born, titled, high-ranking, patrician, blue-blooded (*infml*). 2 MAGNIFICENT, magnanimous, splendid, stately, generous, dignified, distinguished, eminent, grand, great, honoured, honourable, imposing, impressive,

majestic, virtuous, worthy, excellent, elevated, fine, gentle.
F3 **1** low-born. **2** ignoble, base, contemptible.

nobody n no-one, nothing, nonentity, menial, cipher.
F3 somebody.

nod v **1** GESTURE, indicate, sign, signal, salute, acknowledge. **2** AGREE, assent. **3** SLEEP, doze, drowse, nap. n gesture, indication, sign, signal, salute, greeting, beck, acknowledgement.

noise n sound, din, racket, row, clamour, clash, clatter, commotion, outcry, hubbub, uproar, cry, blare, talk, pandemonium, tumult, babble.
F3 quiet, silence.
v report, rumour, publicize, announce, circulate.

noiseless adj silent, inaudible, soundless, quiet, mute, still, hushed.
F3 loud, noisy.

noisy adj loud, deafening, ear-splitting, clamorous, piercing, vocal, vociferous, tumultuous, boisterous, obstreperous.
F3 quiet, silent, peaceful.

nomad n traveller, wanderer, itinerant, rambler, roamer, rover, migrant.

nominal adj **1** TITULAR, supposed, purported, professed, ostensible, so-called, theoretical, self-styled, puppet, symbolic. **2** TOKEN, minimal, trifling, trivial, insignificant, small.
F3 **1** actual, genuine, real.

nominate v propose, choose, select, name, designate, submit, suggest, recommend, put up, present, elect, appoint, assign, commission, elevate, term.

nomination n proposal, choice, selection, submission, suggestion, recommendation, designation, election, appointment.

nominee n candidate, entrant, contestant, appointee, runner, assignee.

nonchalant adj unconcerned, detached, dispassionate, offhand, blasé, indifferent, casual, cool, collected, apathetic, careless, insouciant.
F3 concerned, careful.

non-committal adj guarded, unrevealing, cautious, wary, reserved, ambiguous, discreet, equivocal, evasive, circumspect, careful, neutral, indefinite, politic, tactful, tentative, vague.

nonconformist n dissenter, rebel, individualist, dissident, radical, protester, heretic, iconoclast, eccentric, maverick, secessionist.
F3 conformist.

nondescript adj featureless, indeterminate, undistinguished, unexceptional, ordinary, commonplace, plain, dull, uninspiring, uninteresting, unclassified.
F3 distinctive, remarkable.

none pron no-one, not any, not one, nobody, nil, zero.

nonplussed adj disconcerted, confounded, taken aback, stunned, bewildered, astonished, astounded, dumbfounded, perplexed, stumped, flabbergasted, flummoxed, puzzled, baffled, dismayed, embarrassed.

nonsense n rubbish, trash, drivel, balderdash, gibberish, gobbledygook, senselessness, stupidity, silliness, foolishness, folly, rot (infml), blather,

twaddle, ridiculousness, claptrap (infml), cobblers (sl).
F3 sense, wisdom.

nonsensical adj ridiculous, meaningless, senseless, foolish, inane, irrational, silly, incomprehensible, ludicrous, absurd, fatuous, crazy (infml).
F3 reasonable, sensible, logical.

non-stop adj never-ending, uninterrupted, continuous, incessant, constant, endless, interminable, unending, unbroken, round-the-clock, on-going.
F3 intermittent, occasional.

nook n recess, alcove, corner, cranny, niche, cubby-hole, hide-out, retreat, shelter, cavity.

norm n average, mean, standard, rule, pattern, criterion, model, yardstick, benchmark, measure, reference.

normal adj usual, standard, general, common, ordinary, conventional, average, regular, routine, typical, mainstream, natural, accustomed, well-adjusted, straight, rational, reasonable.
F3 abnormal, irregular, peculiar.

normality n usualness, commonness, ordinariness, regularity, routine, conventionality, balance, adjustment, typicality, naturalness, reason, rationality.
F3 abnormality, irregularity, peculiarity.

normally adv ordinarily, usually, as a rule, typically, commonly, characteristically.
F3 abnormally, exceptionally.

nosegay n bouquet, posy, spray, bunch.

nosey adj inquisitive, meddlesome, prying, interfering, snooping, curious, eavesdropping.

nostalgia n yearning, longing, regretfulness, remembrance, reminiscence, homesickness, pining.

nostalgic adj yearning, longing, wistful, emotional, regretful, sentimental, homesick.

notable adj noteworthy, remarkable, noticeable, striking, extraordinary, impressive, outstanding, marked, unusual, celebrated, distinguished, famous, eminent, well-known, notorious, renowned, rare.
F3 ordinary, commonplace, usual.
n celebrity, notability, VIP, personage, somebody, dignitary, luminary, worthy.
F3 nobody, nonentity.

notably adv markedly, noticeably, particularly, remarkably, strikingly, conspicuously, distinctly, especially, impressively, outstandingly, eminently.

notation n symbols, characters, code, signs, alphabet, system, script, noting, record, shorthand.

notch n cut, nick, indentation, incision, score, groove, cleft, mark, snip, degree, grade, step.
υ cut, nick, score, scratch, indent, mark.

note n 1 COMMUNICATION, letter, message, memorandum, reminder, memo (infml), line, jotting, record. 2 ANNOTATION, comment, gloss, remark. 3 INDICATION, signal, token, mark, symbol. 4 EMINENCE, distinction, consequence, fame, renown, reputation. 5 HEED, attention, regard, notice, observation.
υ 1 NOTICE, observe, perceive, heed, detect, mark, remark, mention, see, witness. 2 RECORD, register, write down, enter.

noted adj famous, well-known, renowned, notable, celebrated, eminent, prominent, great, acclaimed, illustrious, distinguished, respected, recognized.
F3 obscure, unknown.

notes n jottings, record, impressions, report, sketch, outline, synopsis, draft.

noteworthy adj remarkable, significant, important, notable, memorable, exceptional, extraordinary, unusual, outstanding.
F3 commonplace, unexceptional, ordinary.

nothing n nought, zero, nothingness, zilch (sl), nullity, non-existence, emptiness, void, nobody, nonentity.
F3 something.

notice v note, remark, perceive, observe, mind, see, discern, distinguish, mark, detect, heed, spot.
F3 ignore, overlook.
n **1** NOTIFICATION, announcement, information, declaration, communication, intelligence, news, warning, instruction.
2 ADVERTISEMENT, poster, sign, bill.
3 REVIEW, comment, criticism.
4 ATTENTION, observation, awareness, note, regard, consideration, heed.

noticeable adj perceptible, observable, appreciable, unmistakable, conspicuous, evident, manifest, clear, distinct, significant, striking, plain, obvious, measurable.
F3 inconspicuous, unnoticeable.

notification n announcement, information, notice, declaration, advice, warning, intelligence, message, publication, statement, communication.

notify v inform, tell, advise, announce, declare, warn, acquaint, alert, publish, disclose, reveal.

notion n **1** IDEA, thought, concept, conception, belief, impression, view, opinion, understanding, apprehension. **2** INCLINATION, wish, whim, fancy, caprice.

notoriety n infamy, disrepute, dishonour, disgrace, scandal.

notorious adj infamous, disreputable, scandalous, dishonourable, disgraceful, ignominious, flagrant, well-known.

nought n zero, nil, zilch, naught, nothing, nothingness.

nourish v **1** NURTURE, feed, foster, care for, provide for, sustain, support, tend, nurse, maintain, cherish.
2 STRENGTHEN, encourage, promote, cultivate, stimulate.

nourishment n nutrition, food, sustenance, diet.

novel adj new, original, fresh, innovative, unfamiliar, unusual, uncommon, different, imaginative, unconventional, strange.
F3 hackneyed, familiar, ordinary.
n fiction, story, tale, narrative, romance.

novelty n **1** NEWNESS, originality, freshness, innovation, unfamiliarity, uniqueness, difference, strangeness.
2 GIMMICK, gadget, trifle, memento, knick-knack, curiosity, souvenir, trinket, bauble, gimcrack.

novice n beginner, tiro, learner, pupil, trainee, probationer, apprentice, neophyte (fml), amateur, newcomer.
F3 expert.

now adv **1** IMMEDIATELY, at once, directly, instantly, straight away, promptly, next. **2** AT PRESENT, nowadays, these days.

noxious adj harmful, poisonous, pernicious, toxic, injurious, unhealthy, deadly, destructive, noisome, foul.
F3 innocuous, wholesome.

nuance n subtlety, suggestion, shade, hint, suspicion, gradation, distinction, overtone, refinement, touch, trace, tinge, degree, nicety.

nub n centre, heart, core, nucleus, kernel, crux, gist, pith, point, essence.

nucleus n centre, heart, nub, core, focus, kernel, pivot, basis, crux.

nude adj naked, bare, undressed, unclothed, stripped, stark-naked, uncovered, starkers (infml), in one's birthday suit (infml).
F3 clothed, dressed.

nudge v, n poke, prod, shove, dig, jog, prompt, push, elbow, bump.

nuisance n annoyance, inconvenience, bother, irritation, pest, pain (infml), drag (infml), bore, problem, trial, trouble, drawback.

null adj void, invalid, ineffectual, useless, vain, worthless, powerless, inoperative.
F3 valid.

nullify v annul, revoke, cancel, invalidate, abrogate, abolish, negate, rescind, quash, repeal, counteract.
F3 validate.

numb adj benumbed, insensible, unfeeling, deadened, insensitive, frozen, immobilized.
F3 sensitive.
v deaden, anaesthetize, freeze, immobilize, paralyse, dull, stun.
F3 sensitize.

number n **1** FIGURE, numeral, digit, integer, unit. **2** TOTAL, sum, aggregate, collection, amount, quantity, several, many, company, crowd, multitude, throng, horde. **3** COPY, issue, edition, impression, volume, printing.
v count, calculate, enumerate, reckon, total, add, compute, include.

numerous adj many, abundant, several, plentiful, copious, profuse, sundry.
F3 few.

nurse v **1** TEND, care for, look after, treat. **2** BREAST-FEED, feed, suckle, nurture, nourish. **3** PRESERVE, sustain, support, cherish, encourage, keep, foster, promote.
n sister, matron, nursemaid, nanny.

nurture n **1** FOOD, nourishment. **2** REARING, upbringing, training, care, cultivation, development, education, discipline.
v **1** FEED, nourish, nurse, tend, care for, foster, support, sustain. **2** BRING UP, rear, cultivate, develop, educate, instruct, train, school, discipline.

nut

Varieties of nut include:
almond, beech nut, Brazil nut, cashew, chestnut, cobnut, coconut, filbert, hazelnut, macadamia, monkey-nut, peanut, pecan, pine nut, pistachio, walnut.

nutrition n food, nourishment, sustenance.

nutritious adj nourishing, nutritive, wholesome, healthful, health-giving, good, beneficial, strengthening, substantial, invigorating.
F3 bad, unwholesome.

O

oasis n **1** SPRING, watering-hole.
2 REFUGE, haven, island, sanctuary, retreat.

oath n **1** VOW, pledge, promise, word, affirmation, assurance, word of honour. **2** CURSE, imprecation, swearword, profanity, expletive, blasphemy.

obedient adj compliant, docile, acquiescent, submissive, tractable, yielding, dutiful, law-abiding, deferential, respectful, subservient, observant.
F3 disobedient, rebellious, wilful.

obesity n fatness, overweight, corpulence, stoutness, grossness, plumpness, portliness, bulk.
F3 thinness, slenderness, skinniness.

obey v **1** COMPLY, submit, surrender, yield, be ruled by, bow to, take orders from, defer (to), give way, follow, observe, abide by, adhere to, conform, heed, keep, mind, respond. **2** CARRY OUT, discharge, execute, act upon, fulfil, perform.
F3 1 disobey.

object[1] n **1** THING, entity, article, body. **2** AIM, objective, purpose, goal, target, intention, motive, end, reason, point, design. **3** TARGET, recipient, butt, victim.

object[2] v protest, oppose, demur, take exception, disapprove, refuse, complain, rebut, repudiate.
F3 agree, acquiesce.

objection n protest, dissent, disapproval, opposition, demur, complaint, challenge, scruple.
F3 agreement, assent.

objectionable adj unacceptable, unpleasant, offensive, obnoxious, repugnant, disagreeable, abhorrent, detestable, deplorable, despicable.
F3 acceptable.

objective adj impartial, unbiased, detached, unprejudiced, open-minded, equitable, dispassionate, even-handed, neutral, disinterested, just, fair.
F3 subjective.
n object, aim, goal, end, purpose, ambition, mark, target, intention, design.

obligation n duty, responsibility, onus, charge, commitment, liability, requirement, bond, contract, debt, burden, trust.

obligatory adj compulsory, mandatory, statutory, required, binding, essential, necessary, enforced.
F3 optional.

oblige v **1** COMPEL, constrain, coerce, require, make, necessitate, force, bind. **2** HELP, assist, accommodate, do a favour, serve, gratify, please.

obliging adj accommodating,

co-operative, helpful, considerate, agreeable, friendly, kind, civil.
F3 unhelpful.

oblique *adj* slanting, sloping, inclined, angled, tilted.

obliterate *v* eradicate, destroy, annihilate, delete, blot out, wipe out, erase.

oblivion *n* obscurity, nothingness, unconsciousness, void, limbo.
F3 awareness.

oblivious *adj* unaware, unconscious, inattentive, careless, heedless, blind, insensible, negligent.
F3 aware.

obnoxious *adj* unpleasant, disagreeable, disgusting, loathsome, nasty, horrid, odious, repulsive, revolting, repugnant, sickening, nauseating.
F3 pleasant.

obscene *adj* indecent, improper, immoral, impure, filthy, dirty, bawdy, lewd, licentious, pornographic, scurrilous, suggestive, disgusting, foul, shocking, shameless, offensive.
F3 decent, wholesome.

obscenity *n* **1** INDECENCY, immodesty, impurity, impropriety, lewdness, licentiousness, suggestiveness, pornography, dirtiness, filthiness, foulness, grossness, indelicacy, coarseness.
2 ATROCITY, evil, outrage, offence.
3 PROFANITY, expletive, swear-word, four-letter word.

obscure *adj* **1** UNKNOWN, unimportant, little-known, unheard-of, undistinguished, nameless, inconspicuous, humble, minor.
2 INCOMPREHENSIBLE, enigmatic, cryptic, recondite, esoteric, arcane, mysterious, deep, abstruse, confusing.

3 INDISTINCT, unclear, indefinite, shadowy, blurred, cloudy, faint, hazy, dim, misty, shady, vague, murky, gloomy, dusky.
F3 1 famous, renowned. **2** intelligible, straightforward. **3** clear, definite.
v conceal, cloud, obfuscate, hide, cover, blur, disguise, mask, overshadow, shadow, shade, cloak, veil, shroud, darken, dim, eclipse, screen, block out.
F3 clarify, illuminate.

obsequious *adj* servile, ingratiating, grovelling, fawning, sycophantic, cringing, deferential, flattering, smarmy (*infml*), unctuous, oily, submissive, subservient, slavish.

observance *n* **1** ADHERENCE, compliance, observation, performance, obedience, fulfilment, honouring, notice, attention.
2 RITUAL, custom, ceremony, practice, celebration.

observant *adj* attentive, alert, vigilant, watchful, perceptive, eagle-eyed, wide awake, heedful.
F3 unobservant.

observation *n* **1** ATTENTION, notice, examination, inspection, scrutiny, monitoring, study, watching, consideration, discernment.
2 REMARK, comment, utterance, thought, statement, pronouncement, reflection, opinion, finding, note.

observe *v* **1** WATCH, see, study, notice, contemplate, keep an eye on, perceive. **2** REMARK, comment, say, mention. **3** ABIDE BY, comply with, honour, keep, fulfil, celebrate, perform.
F3 1 miss. **3** break, violate.

observer *n* watcher, spectator, viewer, witness, looker-on, onlooker, eyewitness, commentator, bystander, beholder.

obsess v preoccupy, dominate, rule, monopolize, haunt, grip, plague, prey on, possess.

obsession n preoccupation, fixation, idée fixe, ruling passion, compulsion, fetish, hang-up (*infml*), infatuation, mania, enthusiasm.

obsessive adj consuming, compulsive, gripping, fixed, haunting, tormenting, maddening.

obsolete adj outmoded, disused, out of date, old-fashioned, passé, dated, outworn, old, antiquated, antique, dead, extinct.
F3 modern, current, up-to-date.

obstacle n barrier, bar, obstruction, impediment, hurdle, hindrance, check, snag, stumbling-block, drawback, difficulty, hitch, catch, stop, interference, interruption.
F3 advantage, help.

obstinate adj stubborn, inflexible, immovable, intractable, pig-headed (*infml*), unyielding, intransigent, persistent, dogged, headstrong, bloody-minded (*sl*), strong-minded, self-willed, steadfast, firm, determined, wilful.
F3 flexible, tractable.

obstruct v block, impede, hinder, prevent, check, frustrate, hamper, clog, choke, bar, barricade, stop, stall, retard, restrict, thwart, inhibit, hold up, curb, arrest, slow down, interrupt, interfere with, shut off, cut off, obscure.
F3 assist, further.

obstruction n barrier, blockage, bar, barricade, hindrance, impediment, check, stop, stoppage, difficulty.
F3 help.

obstructive adj hindering, delaying, blocking, stalling, unhelpful, awkward, difficult, restrictive, inhibiting.
F3 co-operative, helpful.

obtain v **1** ACQUIRE, get, gain, come by, attain, procure, secure, earn, achieve. **2** PREVAIL, exist, hold, be in force, be the case, stand, reign, rule, be prevalent.

obtrusive adj **1** PROMINENT, protruding, noticeable, obvious, blatant, forward. **2** INTRUSIVE, interfering, prying, meddling, nosey (*infml*), pushy (*infml*).
F3 unobtrusive.

obtuse adj slow, stupid, thick (*infml*), dull, dense, crass, dumb (*infml*), stolid, dull-witted, thick-skinned.
F3 bright, sharp.

obvious adj evident, self-evident, manifest, patent, clear, plain, distinct, transparent, undeniable, unmistakable, conspicuous, glaring, apparent, open, unconcealed, visible, noticeable, perceptible, pronounced, recognizable, self-explanatory, straightforward, prominent.
F3 unclear, indistinct, obscure.

obviously adv plainly, clearly, evidently, manifestly, undeniably, unmistakably, without doubt, certainly, distinctly, of course.

occasion n **1** EVENT, occurrence, incident, time, instance, chance, case, opportunity. **2** REASON, cause, excuse, justification, ground(s). **3** CELEBRATION, function, affair, party.

occasional adj periodic, intermittent, irregular, sporadic, infrequent, uncommon, incidental, odd, rare, casual.
F3 frequent, regular, constant.

occasionally *adv* sometimes, on occasion, from time to time, at times, at intervals, now and then, now and again, irregularly, periodically, every so often, once in a while, off and on, infrequently.

F3 frequently, often, always.

occult *adj* mystical, supernatural, magical, esoteric, mysterious, concealed, arcane, recondite, obscure, secret, hidden, veiled.

occupant *n* occupier, holder, inhabitant, resident, householder, tenant, user, lessee, squatter, inmate.

occupation *n* 1 JOB, profession, work, vocation, employment, trade, post, calling, business, line, pursuit, craft, walk of life, activity. 2 INVASION, seizure, conquest, control, takeover. 3 OCCUPANCY, possession, holding, tenancy, tenure, residence, habitation, use.

occupy *v* 1 INHABIT, live in, possess, reside in, stay in, take possession of, own. 2 ABSORB, take up, engross, engage, hold, involve, preoccupy, amuse, busy, interest. 3 INVADE, seize, capture, overrun, take over. 4 FILL, take up, use.

occur *v* happen, come about, take place, transpire, chance, come to pass, materialize, befall, develop, crop up, arise, appear, turn up, obtain, result, exist, be present, be found.

occurrence *n* 1 INCIDENT, event, happening, affair, circumstance, episode, instance, case, development, action. 2 INCIDENCE, existence, appearance, manifestation.

odd *adj* 1 UNUSUAL, strange, uncommon, peculiar, abnormal, exceptional, curious, atypical, different, queer, bizarre, eccentric,

remarkable, unconventional, weird, irregular, extraordinary, outlandish, rare. 2 OCCASIONAL, incidental, irregular, random, casual. 3 UNMATCHED, unpaired, single, spare, surplus, left-over, remaining, sundry, various, miscellaneous.

F3 1 normal, usual. 2 regular.

oddity *n* 1 ABNORMALITY, peculiarity, rarity, eccentricity, idiosyncrasy, phenomenon, quirk. 2 CURIOSITY, character, freak, misfit.

oddment *n* bit, scrap, left-over, fragment, offcut, end, remnant, shred, snippet, patch.

odds *n* 1 LIKELIHOOD, probability, chances. 2 ADVANTAGE, edge, lead, superiority.

odious *adj* offensive, loathsome, unpleasant, obnoxious, disgusting, hateful, repulsive, revolting, repugnant, foul, execrable, detestable, abhorrent, horrible, horrid, abominable.

F3 pleasant.

odour *n* smell, scent, fragrance, aroma, perfume, redolence, stench, stink (*infml*).

off *adj* 1 ROTTEN, bad, sour, turned, rancid, mouldy, decomposed. 2 CANCELLED, postponed. 3 AWAY, absent, gone. 4 SUBSTANDARD, below par, disappointing, unsatisfactory, slack.

adv away, elsewhere, out, at a distance, apart, aside.

off-colour *adj* indisposed, off form, under the weather, unwell, sick, out of sorts, ill, poorly.

offence *n* 1 MISDEMEANOUR, transgression, violation, wrong, wrong-doing, infringement, crime, misdeed, sin, trespass. 2 AFFRONT, insult, injury. **3** RESENTMENT, indignation, pique, umbrage, outrage, hurt, hard feelings.

offend v **1** HURT, insult, injure, affront, wrong, wound, displease, snub, upset, annoy, outrage. **2** DISGUST, repel, sicken. **3** TRANSGRESS, sin, violate, err. **F3 1** please.

offender n transgressor, wrong-doer, culprit, perpetrator, criminal, miscreant, guilty party, law-breaker, delinquent.

offensive adj **1** DISAGREEABLE, unpleasant, objectionable, displeasing, disgusting, odious, obnoxious, repellent, repugnant, revolting, loathsome, vile, nauseating, nasty, detestable, abominable. **2** INSOLENT, abusive, rude, insulting, impertinent. **F3 1** pleasant. **2** polite. n attack, assault, onslaught, invasion, raid, sortie.

offer v **1** PRESENT, make available, advance, extend, put forward, submit, suggest, hold out, provide, sell. **2** PROFFER, propose, bid, tender. **3** VOLUNTEER, come forward, show willing (infml). n proposal, bid, submission, tender, suggestion, proposition, overture, approach, attempt, presentation.

offering n present, gift, donation, contribution, subscription.

offhand adj casual, unconcerned, uninterested, take-it-or-leave-it (infml), brusque, abrupt, perfunctory, informal, cavalier, careless. **F3** calculated, planned. adv impromptu, off the cuff, extempore (fml), off the top of one's head.

office n **1** RESPONSIBILITY, duty, obligation, charge, commission, occupation, situation, post, employment, function, appointment, business, role, service. **2** WORKPLACE, workroom, bureau.

officer n official, office-holder, public servant, functionary, dignitary, bureaucrat, administrator, representative, executive, agent, appointee.

official adj authorized, authoritative, legitimate, formal, licensed, accredited, certified, approved, authenticated, authentic, bona fide, proper. **F3** unofficial. n office-bearer, officer, functionary, bureaucrat, executive, representative, agent.

officiate v preside, superintend, conduct, chair, manage, oversee, run.

officious adj obtrusive, dictatorial, intrusive, bossy (infml), interfering, meddlesome, over-zealous, self-important, pushy (infml), forward, bustling, importunate (fml).

offload v unburden, unload, jettison, dump, drop, deposit, get rid of, discharge.

off-putting adj intimidating, daunting, disconcerting, discouraging, disheartening, formidable, unnerving, unsettling, demoralizing, disturbing.

offset v counterbalance, compensate for, cancel out, counteract, make up for, balance out, neutralize.

offshoot n branch, outgrowth, limb, arm, development, spin-off, by-product, appendage.

offspring n child, children, young, issue, progeny (fml), brood, heirs,

successors, descendants.
E∃ parent(s).

often adv frequently, repeatedly, regularly, generally, again and again, time after time, time and again, much. **E∃** rarely, seldom, never.

ogre n giant, monster, fiend, bogeyman, demon, devil, troll.

oil v grease, lubricate, anoint.

oily adj 1 GREASY, fatty. 2 UNCTUOUS, smooth, obsequious, ingratiating, smarmy (infml), glib, flattering.

ointment n salve, balm, cream, lotion, liniment, embrocation.

OK adj acceptable, all right, fine, permitted, in order, fair, satisfactory, cushty (sl), reasonable, tolerable, passable, not bad, good, adequate, convenient, correct, accurate. n authorization, approval, endorsement, go-ahead, permission, green light, consent, agreement. v approve, authorize, pass, give the go-ahead to, give the green light to (infml), rubber-stamp, agree to. interj all right, fine, very well, agreed, right, yes.

old adj 1 AGED, elderly, advanced in years, grey, senile. 2 ANCIENT, original, primitive, antiquated, mature. 3 LONG-STANDING, long-established, time-honoured, traditional. 4 OBSOLETE, old-fashioned, out of date, worn-out, decayed, decrepit. 5 FORMER, previous, earlier, one-time, ex-. **E∃** 1 young. 2 new. 4 modern. 5 current.

old-fashioned adj outmoded, out of date, outdated, dated, unfashionable, obsolete, behind the times, antiquated, archaic, passé, obsolescent. **E∃** modern, up-to-date.

omen n portent, sign, warning, premonition, foreboding, augury, indication.

ominous adj portentous, inauspicious, foreboding, menacing, sinister, fateful, unpromising, threatening. **E∃** auspicious, favourable.

omission n exclusion, gap, oversight, failure, lack, neglect, default, avoidance.

omit v leave out, exclude, miss out, pass over, overlook, drop, skip, eliminate, forget, neglect, leave undone, fail, disregard, edit out. **E∃** include.

once adv formerly, previously, in the past, at one time, long ago, in times past, once upon a time, in the old days. **at once 1** IMMEDIATELY, instantly, directly, right away, straightaway, without delay, now, promptly, forthwith. **2** SIMULTANEOUSLY, together, at the same time.

oncoming adj approaching, advancing, upcoming, looming, onrushing, gathering.

one adj 1 SINGLE, solitary, lone, individual, only. 2 UNITED, harmonious, like-minded, whole, entire, complete, equal, identical, alike.

onerous adj oppressive, burdensome, demanding, laborious, hard, taxing, difficult, troublesome, exacting, exhausting, heavy, weighty. **E∃** easy, light.

one-sided adj 1 UNBALANCED, unequal, lopsided. 2 UNFAIR, unjust, prejudiced, biased, partial, partisan. 3 UNILATERAL, independent. **E∃** 1 balanced. 2 impartial. 3 bilateral, multilateral.

ongoing adj **1** CONTINUING, continuous, unbroken, uninterrupted, constant. **2** DEVELOPING, evolving, progressing, growing, in progress, unfinished, unfolding.

onlooker n bystander, observer, spectator, looker-on, eye-witness, witness, watcher, viewer.

only adv just, at most, merely, simply, purely, barely, exclusively, solely.
adj sole, single, solitary, lone, unique, exclusive, individual.

onset n **1** BEGINNING, start, commencement, inception, outset, outbreak. **2** ASSAULT, attack, onslaught, onrush.
F3 1 end, finish.

onslaught n attack, assault, offensive, charge, bombardment, blitz.

onus n burden, responsibility, load, obligation, duty, liability, task.

onward(s) adv forward, on, ahead, in front, beyond, forth.
F3 backward(s).

ooze v seep, exude, leak, percolate, escape, dribble, drip, drop, discharge, bleed, secrete, emit, overflow with, filter, drain.

opaque adj **1** CLOUDY, clouded, murky, dull, dim, hazy, muddied, muddy, turbid. **2** OBSCURE, unclear, impenetrable, incomprehensible, unintelligible, enigmatic, difficult.
F3 1 transparent. **2** clear, obvious.

open adj **1** UNCLOSED, ajar, gaping, uncovered, unfastened, unlocked, unsealed, yawning, lidless.
2 UNRESTRICTED, free, unobstructed, clear, accessible, exposed, unprotected, unsheltered, vacant, wide, available. **3** OVERT, obvious, plain, evident, manifest, noticeable,

flagrant, conspicuous. **4** UNDECIDED, unresolved, unsettled, debatable, problematic, moot. **5** FRANK, candid, honest, guileless, natural, ingenuous, unreserved.
F3 1 shut. **2** restricted. **3** hidden.
4 decided. **5** reserved.
v **1** UNFASTEN, undo, unlock, uncover, unseal, unblock, uncork, clear, expose. **2** EXPLAIN, divulge, disclose, lay bare. **3** EXTEND, spread (out), unfold, separate, split. **4** BEGIN, start, commence, inaugurate, initiate, set in motion, launch.
F3 1 close, shut. **3** hide. **4** end, finish.

open-air adj outdoor, alfresco.
F3 indoor.

opening n **1** APERTURE, breach, gap, orifice, break, chink, crack, fissure, cleft, chasm, hole, split, vent, rupture. **2** START, onset, beginning, inauguration, inception, birth, dawn, launch. **3** OPPORTUNITY, chance, occasion, break (infml), place, vacancy.
F3 2 close, end.
adj beginning, commencing, starting, first, inaugural, introductory, initial, early, primary.
F3 closing.

openly adv overtly, frankly, candidly, blatantly, flagrantly, plainly, unashamedly, unreservedly, glaringly, in public, in full view, shamelessly.
F3 secretly, slyly.

operate v it operates on batteries: function, act, perform, run, work, go. **2** she can operate that machine: control, handle, manage, use, utilize, manoeuvre.

operation n **1** FUNCTIONING, action, running, motion, movement, performance, working. **2** INFLUENCE, manipulation, handling, management, use, utilization. **3** UNDERTAKING, enterprise, affair, procedure, proceeding, process, business, deal, transaction, effort. **4** CAMPAIGN, action, task, manoeuvre, exercise.

operational *adj* working, in working order, usable, functional, going, viable, workable, ready, prepared, in service.

F3 out of order.

operative *adj* **1** OPERATIONAL, in operation, in force, functioning, active, effective, efficient, in action, workable, viable, serviceable, functional. **2** KEY, crucial, important, relevant, significant.

F3 1 inoperative, out of service.

opinion *n* belief, judgement, view, point of view, idea, perception, stance, theory, impression, feeling, sentiment, estimation, assessment, conception, mind, notion, way of thinking, persuasion, attitude.

opinionated *adj* dogmatic, doctrinaire, dictatorial, arrogant, inflexible, obstinate, stubborn, uncompromising, single-minded, prejudiced, biased, bigoted.

F3 open-minded.

opponent *n* adversary, enemy, antagonist, foe, competitor, contestant, challenger, opposer, opposition, rival, objector, dissident.

F3 ally.

opportunity *n* chance, opening, break (*infml*), occasion, possibility, hour, moment.

oppose *v* **1** RESIST, withstand, counter, attack, combat, contest, stand up to, take a stand against, take issue with, confront, defy, face, fight, fly in the face of, hinder, obstruct, bar, check, prevent, thwart. **2** COMPARE, contrast, match, offset, counterbalance, play off.

F3 1 defend, support.

opposed *adj* in opposition, against, hostile, conflicting, opposing, opposite, antagonistic, clashing, contrary, incompatible, anti.

F3 in favour.

opposite *adj* **1** FACING, fronting, corresponding. **2** OPPOSED, antagonistic, conflicting, contrary, hostile, adverse, contradictory, antithetical, irreconcilable, unlike, reverse, inconsistent, different, contrasted, differing.

F3 same.

n reverse, converse, contrary, antithesis, contradiction, inverse.

F3 same.

opposition *n* **1** ANTAGONISM, hostility, resistance, obstructiveness, unfriendliness, disapproval. **2** OPPONENT, antagonist, rival, foe, other side.

F3 1 co-operation, support. **2** ally, supporter.

oppress *v* **1** BURDEN, afflict, lie heavy on, harass, depress, sadden, torment, vex. **2** SUBJUGATE, suppress, subdue, overpower, overwhelm, crush, trample, tyrannize, persecute, maltreat, abuse.

oppression *n* tyranny, subjugation, subjection, repression, despotism, suppression, injustice, cruelty, brutality, abuse, persecution, maltreatment, harshness, hardship.

oppressive *adj* **1** AIRLESS, stuffy, close, stifling, suffocating, sultry, muggy, heavy. **2** TYRANNICAL, despotic, overbearing, overwhelming, repressive, harsh, unjust, inhuman, cruel, brutal, burdensome, onerous, intolerable.

E3 1 airy. **2** just, gentle.

oppressor n tyrant, bully, taskmaster, slave-driver, despot, dictator, persecutor, tormentor, intimidator, autocrat.

optimistic adj confident, assured, sanguine, hopeful, positive, cheerful, buoyant, bright, idealistic, expectant.

E3 pessimistic.

optimum adj best, ideal, perfect, optimal, superlative, top, choice.

E3 worst.

option n choice, alternative, preference, possibility, selection.

optional adj voluntary, discretionary, elective, free, unforced.

E3 compulsory.

oral adj verbal, spoken, unwritten, vocal.

E3 written.

orbit n **1** CIRCUIT, cycle, circle, course, path, trajectory, track, revolution, rotation. **2** RANGE, scope, domain, influence, sphere of influence, compass.

v revolve, circle, encircle, circumnavigate.

ordeal n trial, test, tribulation(s), affliction, trouble(s), suffering, anguish, agony, pain, persecution, torture, nightmare.

order n **1** COMMAND, directive, decree, injunction, instruction, direction, edict, ordinance, mandate, regulation, rule, precept, law. **2** REQUISITION, request, booking, commission, reservation, application, demand. **3** ARRANGEMENT, organization, grouping, disposition,

sequence, categorization, classification, method, pattern, plan, system, array, layout, line-up, structure. **4** PEACE, quiet, calm, tranquillity, harmony, law and order, discipline. **5** ASSOCIATION, society, community, fraternity, brotherhood, sisterhood, lodge, guild, company, organization, denomination, sect, union. **6** CLASS, kind, sort, type, rank, species, hierarchy, family.

E3 3 confusion, disorder. **4** anarchy.

v **1** COMMAND, instruct, direct, bid, decree, require, authorize. **2** REQUEST, reserve, book, apply for, requisition. **3** ARRANGE, organize, dispose, classify, group, marshal, sort out, lay out, manage, control, catalogue.

out of order 1 BROKEN, broken down, not working, inoperative. **2** DISORDERED, disorganized, out of sequence. **3** UNSEEMLY, improper, uncalled-for, incorrect, wrong.

orderly adj **1** ORDERED, systematic, neat, tidy, regular, methodical, in order, well-organized, well-regulated. **2** WELL-BEHAVED, controlled, disciplined, law-abiding.

E3 1 chaotic. **2** disorderly.

ordinary adj common, commonplace, regular, routine, standard, average, everyday, run-of-the-mill, bog-standard (infml), usual, unexceptional, unremarkable, typical, normal, customary, common-or-garden, plain, familiar, habitual, simple, conventional, modest, mediocre, indifferent, pedestrian, prosaic, undistinguished.

E3 extraordinary, unusual.

organ n **1** DEVICE, instrument, implement, tool, element, process, structure, unit, member. **2** MEDIUM, agency, forum, vehicle, voice, mouthpiece, publication, newspaper, periodical, journal.

organic *adj* natural, biological, living, animate.

organization *n* **1** ASSOCIATION, institution, society, company, firm, corporation, federation, group, league, club, confederation, consortium. **2** ARRANGEMENT, system, classification, methodology, order, formation, grouping, method, plan, structure, pattern, composition, configuration, design.

organize *v* **1** STRUCTURE, co-ordinate, arrange, order, group, marshal, classify, systematize, tabulate, catalogue. **2** ESTABLISH, found, set up, develop, form, frame, construct, shape, run.
F∃ 1 disorganize.

orgy *n* debauch, carousal, revelry, bout, bacchanalia, indulgence, excess, spree.

orientation *n* **1** SITUATION, bearings, location, direction, position, alignment, placement, attitude.
2 INITIATION, training, acclimatization, familiarization, adaptation, adjustment, settling in.

origin *n* **1** SOURCE, spring, fount, foundation, base, cause, derivation, provenance, roots, well-spring.
2 BEGINNING, commencement, start, inauguration, launch, dawning, creation, emergence. **3** ANCESTRY, descent, extraction, heritage, family, lineage, parentage, pedigree, birth, paternity, stock.
F∃ 2 end, termination.

original *adj* **1** FIRST, early, earliest, initial, primary, archetypal, rudimentary, embryonic, starting,

opening, commencing, first-hand.
2 NOVEL, innovative, new, creative, fresh, imaginative, inventive, unconventional, unusual, unique.
F∃ 1 latest. **2** hackneyed, unoriginal.
n prototype, master, paradigm, model, pattern, archetype, standard, type.

originate *v* **1** RISE, arise, spring, stem, issue, flow, proceed, derive, come, evolve, emerge, be born.
2 CREATE, invent, inaugurate, introduce, give birth to, develop, discover, establish, begin, commence, start, set up, launch, pioneer, conceive, form, produce, generate.
F∃ 1 end, terminate.

ornament *n* decoration, adornment, embellishment, garnish, trimming, accessory, frill, trinket, bauble, jewel.
v decorate, adorn, embellish, garnish, trim, beautify, brighten, dress up, deck, gild.

ornamental *adj* decorative, embellishing, adorning, attractive, showy.

ornate *adj* elaborate, ornamented, fancy, decorated, baroque, rococo, florid, flowery, fussy, busy, sumptuous.
F∃ plain.

orthodox *adj* conformist, conventional, accepted, official, traditional, usual, well-established, established, received, customary, conservative, recognized, authoritative.
F∃ nonconformist, unorthodox.

ostensible *adj* alleged, apparent, presumed, seeming, supposed, so-called, professed, outward, pretended, superficial.
F∃ real.

ostentatious adj showy, flashy, pretentious, vulgar, loud, garish, gaudy, flamboyant, conspicuous, extravagant.

E3 restrained.

ostracize v exclude, banish, exile, expel, excommunicate, reject, segregate, send to Coventry, shun, snub, boycott, blacklist, blackball, avoid, cold-shoulder (infml), cut.

E3 accept, welcome.

other adj **1** DIFFERENT, dissimilar, unlike, separate, distinct, contrasting. **2** MORE, further, extra, additional, supplementary, spare, alternative.

oust v expel, eject, depose, displace, turn out, throw out, overthrow, evict, drive out, unseat, dispossess, disinherit, replace, topple.

E3 install, settle.

out adj **1** AWAY, absent, elsewhere, not at home, gone, outside, abroad. **2** REVEALED, exposed, disclosed, public, evident, manifest. **3** FORBIDDEN, unacceptable, impossible, disallowed, excluded. **4** OUT OF DATE, passé, unfashionable, old-fashioned, dated, passé, antiquated. **5** EXTINGUISHED, finished, expired, dead, used up.

E3 1 in. **2** concealed. **3** allowed. **4** up to date.

outbreak n eruption, outburst, explosion, flare-up, upsurge, flash, rash, epidemic.

outburst n outbreak, eruption, explosion, flare-up, outpouring, burst, fit, gush, surge, storm, spasm, seizure, gale, attack, fit of temper.

outcast n castaway, exile, pariah, outsider, untouchable, refugee, reject, persona non grata.

outcome n result, consequence,

upshot, conclusion, effect, end result.

outcry n protest, complaint, protestation, objection, dissent, indignation, uproar, cry, exclamation, clamour, row, commotion, noise, hue and cry, hullabaloo (infml), outburst.

outdated adj out of date, old-fashioned, dated, unfashionable, outmoded, behind the times, obsolete, obsolescent, antiquated, archaic.

E3 fashionable, modern.

outdo v surpass, exceed, beat, excel, outstrip, outshine, get the better of, overcome, outclass, outdistance.

outdoor adj out-of-door(s), outside, open-air.

E3 indoor.

outer adj **1** EXTERNAL, exterior, outside, outward, surface, superficial, peripheral. **2** OUTLYING, distant, remote, further.

E3 1 internal. **2** inner.

outfit n **1** CLOTHES, costume, ensemble, get-up (infml), togs (infml), garb. **2** EQUIPMENT, gear (infml), kit, rig, trappings, paraphernalia. **3** (infml) ORGANIZATION, firm, business, corporation, company, group, team, unit, set, set-up, crew, gang, squad.

outgoing adj **1** SOCIABLE, friendly, unreserved, amiable, warm, approachable, expansive, open, extrovert, cordial, easy-going, communicative, demonstrative, sympathetic. **2** DEPARTING, retiring, former, last, past, ex-.

E3 1 reserved. **2** incoming.

outing n excursion, expedition, jaunt, pleasure trip, awayday, trip, spin, picnic.

outlandish adj unconventional, unfamiliar, bizarre, strange, odd,

weird, eccentric, alien, exotic, barbarous, foreign, extraordinary.
F3 familiar, ordinary.

outlaw n bandit, brigand, robber, desperado, highwayman, criminal, marauder, pirate, fugitive.
v ban, disallow, forbid, prohibit, exclude, embargo, bar, debar, banish, condemn.
F3 allow, legalize.

outlay n expenditure, expenses, outgoings, disbursement (fml), cost, spending.
F3 income.

outlet n 1 EXIT, way out, vent, egress, escape, opening, release, safety valve, channel. **2** RETAILER, shop, store, market.
F3 1 entry, inlet.

outline n 1 SUMMARY, synopsis, précis, bare facts, sketch, thumbnail sketch, abstract. **2** PROFILE, form, contour, silhouette, shape.
v sketch, summarize, draft, trace, rough out.

outlook n 1 VIEW, viewpoint, point of view, attitude, perspective, frame of mind, angle, slant, standpoint, opinion. **2** EXPECTATIONS, future, forecast, prospect, prognosis.

outlying adj distant, remote, far-off, far-away, far-flung, outer, provincial.
F3 inner.

out-of-the-way adj remote, isolated, far-flung, far-off, far-away, distant, inaccessible, little-known, obscure, unfrequented.

output n production, productivity, product, yield, manufacture, achievement.

outrage n 1 ANGER, fury, rage, indignation, shock, affront, horror.
2 ATROCITY, offence, injury, enormity, barbarism, crime, violation, evil, scandal.
v anger, infuriate, affront, incense, enrage, madden, disgust, injure, offend, shock, scandalize.

outrageous adj 1 ATROCIOUS, abominable, shocking, scandalous, offensive, disgraceful, monstrous, heinous, unspeakable, horrible.
2 EXCESSIVE, exorbitant, immoderate, unreasonable, extortionate, inordinate, preposterous.
F3 2 acceptable, reasonable.

outright adj total, utter, absolute, complete, downright, out-and-out, unqualified, unconditional, perfect, pure, thorough, direct, definite, categorical, straightforward.
F3 ambiguous, indefinite.
adv 1 TOTALLY, absolutely, completely, utterly, thoroughly, openly, without restraint, straightforwardly, positively, directly, explicitly. **2** killed outright: instantaneously, at once, there and then, instantly, immediately.

outset n start, beginning, opening, inception, commencement, inauguration, kick-off (infml).
F3 end, conclusion.

outside adj 1 EXTERNAL, exterior, outer, surface, superficial, outward, extraneous, outdoor, outermost, extreme. **2** an outside chance: remote, marginal, distant, faint, slight, slim, negligible.
F3 1 inside.
n exterior, façade, front, surface, face, appearance, cover.
F3 inside.

outsider n stranger, intruder, alien, non-member, non-resident, foreigner, newcomer, visitor, interloper, misfit, odd man out.

outskirts n suburbs, vicinity, periphery, fringes, borders, boundary, edge, margin.
F3 centre.

outspoken adj candid, frank, forthright, blunt, unreserved, plain-spoken, direct, explicit.
F3 diplomatic, reserved.

outstanding adj **1** EXCELLENT, distinguished, eminent, pre-eminent, celebrated, exceptional, superior, remarkable, prominent, superb, great, notable, impressive, striking, superlative, important, noteworthy, memorable, special, extraordinary. **2** OWING, unpaid, due, unsettled, unresolved, uncollected, pending, payable, remaining, ongoing, leftover.
F3 1 ordinary, unexceptional. **2** paid, settled.

outstrip v surpass, exceed, better, outdo, beat, top, transcend, outshine, pass, gain on, leave behind, leave standing, outrun, outdistance, overtake, eclipse.

outward adj external, exterior, outer, outside, surface, superficial, visible, apparent, observable, evident, supposed, professed, public, obvious, ostensible.
F3 inner, private.

outwardly adv apparently, externally, to all appearances, visibly, superficially, supposedly, seemingly, on the surface, at first sight.

outweigh v override, prevail over, overcome, take precedence over, cancel out, make up for, compensate for, predominate.

outwit v outsmart, outthink, get the better of, trick, better, beat, dupe, cheat, deceive, defraud, swindle.

outworn adj outdated, out of date, outmoded, stale, discredited, defunct, old-fashioned, hackneyed, rejected, obsolete, disused, exhausted.
F3 fresh, new.

oval adj egg-shaped, elliptical, ovoid, ovate.

ovation n applause, acclaim, acclamation, praises, plaudits (fml), tribute, clapping, cheering, bravos.
F3 abuse, catcalls.

over adj finished, ended, done with, concluded, past, gone, completed, closed, in the past, settled, up, forgotten, accomplished.
adv **1** ABOVE, beyond, overhead, on high. **2** EXTRA, remaining, surplus, superfluous, left, unclaimed, unused, unwanted, in excess, in addition.
prep **1** ABOVE, on, on top of, upon, in charge of, in command of.
2 EXCEEDING, more than, in excess of.

overact v overplay, exaggerate, overdo, ham (infml).
F3 underact, underplay.

overall adj total, all-inclusive, all-embracing, comprehensive, inclusive, general, universal, global, broad, blanket, complete, all-over.
F3 narrow, specific.
adv in general, on the whole, by and large, broadly, generally speaking.

overbearing adj imperious, domineering, arrogant, dictatorial, tyrannical, high-handed, haughty, bossy (infml), cavalier, autocratic, oppressive.
F3 meek, unassertive.

overcast adj cloudy, grey, dull, dark, sombre, sunless, hazy, lowering.
F3 bright, clear.

overcharge v surcharge, short-change, cheat, extort, rip off (infml),

sting (*infml*), do (*infml*), diddle (*infml*).
Fæ undercharge.

overcome *v* conquer, defeat, beat, surmount, triumph over, vanquish, rise above, master, overpower, overwhelm, overthrow, subdue.

overcrowded *adj* congested, packed (out), jam-packed, crammed full, chock-full, overpopulated, overloaded, swarming.
Fæ deserted, empty.

overdo *v* exaggerate, go too far, carry to excess, go overboard (*infml*), lay it on thick (*infml*), overindulge, overstate, overact, overplay, overwork.

overdue *adj* late, behindhand, behind schedule, delayed, owing, unpunctual, slow.
Fæ early.

overeat *v* gorge, binge, overindulge, guzzle, stuff oneself, make a pig of oneself, pig out (*infml*), gormandize.
Fæ abstain, starve.

overflow *v* spill, overrun, run over, pour over, well over, brim over, bubble over, surge, flood, inundate, deluge, shower, submerge, soak, swamp, teem.
n overspill, spill, inundation, flood, overabundance, surplus.

overhang *v* jut, project, bulge, protrude, stick out, extend.

overhaul *v* **1** RENOVATE, repair, service, recondition, mend, examine, inspect, check, survey, re-examine, fix. **2** OVERTAKE, pull ahead of, outpace, outstrip, gain on, pass.
n reconditioning, repair, renovation, check, service, examination, inspection, going-over (*infml*).

overhead *adv* above, up above, on high, upward.
Fæ below, underfoot.

adj elevated, aerial, overhanging, raised.

overjoyed *adj* delighted, elated, euphoric, ecstatic, in raptures, enraptured, thrilled, jubilant, over the moon (*infml*).
Fæ sad, disappointed.

overload *v* burden, oppress, strain, tax, weigh down, overcharge, encumber.

overlook *v* **1** FRONT ON TO, face, look on to, look over, command a view of. **2** MISS, disregard, ignore, omit, neglect, pass over, let pass, let ride, slight. **3** EXCUSE, forgive, pardon, condone, wink at, turn a blind eye to.
Fæ 2 notice. **3** penalize.

overpower *v* overcome, conquer, overwhelm, vanquish, defeat, beat, subdue, overthrow, quell, master, crush, immobilize, floor.

overpowering *adj* overwhelming, powerful, strong, forceful, irresistible, uncontrollable, compelling, extreme, oppressive, suffocating, unbearable, nauseating, sickening.

overrate *v* overestimate, overvalue, overpraise, magnify, blow up, make too much of.
Fæ underrate.

overrule *v* overturn, override, countermand, revoke, reject, rescind, reverse, invalidate, cancel, vote down.

overrun *v* **1** INVADE, occupy, infest, overwhelm, inundate, run riot, spread over, swamp, surge over, ravage, overgrow. **2** EXCEED, overshoot, overstep, overreach.

overseer *n* supervisor, boss (*infml*), chief, foreman, forewoman, manager, superintendent.

overshadow *v* **1** OBSCURE, cloud, darken, dim, spoil, veil. **2** OUTSHINE, eclipse, excel, surpass, dominate, dwarf, put in the shade, rise above, tower above.

oversight n **1** LAPSE, omission, fault, error, slip-up, mistake, blunder, carelessness, neglect. **2** SUPERVISION, responsibility, care, charge, control, custody, keeping, administration, management, direction.

overt adj open, manifest, plain, evident, observable, obvious, apparent, public, professed, unconcealed.
F3 covert, secret.

overtake v **1** PASS, catch up with, outdistance, outstrip, draw level with, pull ahead of, overhaul. **2** COME UPON, befall, happen, strike, engulf.

overthrow v depose, oust, bring down, topple, unseat, displace, dethrone, conquer, vanquish, beat, defeat, crush, overcome, overpower, overturn, overwhelm, subdue, master, abolish, upset.
F3 install, protect, reinstate, restore. n ousting, unseating, defeat, deposition, dethronement, fall, rout, undoing, suppression, downfall, end, humiliation, destruction, ruin.

overtone n suggestion, intimation, nuance, hint, undercurrent, insinuation, connotation, association, feeling, implication, sense, flavour.

overture n **1** APPROACH, advance, offer, invitation, proposal, proposition, suggestion, signal, move, motion. **2** PRELUDE, opening,

introduction, opening move, (opening) gambit.

overturn v **1** CAPSIZE, upset, upturn, tip over, topple, overbalance, keel over, knock over, spill. **2** OVERTHROW, repeal, rescind, reverse, annul, abolish, destroy, quash, set aside.

overwhelm v **1** OVERCOME, overpower, destroy, defeat, crush, rout, devastate. **2** OVERRUN, inundate, snow under, submerge, swamp, engulf. **3** CONFUSE, bowl over, stagger, floor.

overwork v overstrain, overload, exploit, exhaust, overuse, overtax, strain, wear out, oppress, burden, weary.

overwrought adj tense, agitated, keyed up, on edge, worked up, wound up, frantic, overcharged, overexcited, excited, beside oneself, uptight (infml), hyper (infml).
F3 calm.

owing adj unpaid, due, owed, in arrears, outstanding, payable, overdue.

owing to because of, as a result of, on account of, thanks to.

own adj personal, individual, private, particular, idiosyncratic.
v possess, have, hold, retain, keep, enjoy.

own up admit, confess, come clean (infml), tell the truth, acknowledge.

owner n possessor, holder, landlord, landlady, proprietor, proprietress, master, mistress, freeholder.

P

pace n **1** STEP, stride, walk, gait, tread. **2** SPEED, rate, velocity, celerity, quickness, rapidity, tempo.
υ step, stride, walk, march, tramp, pound, patrol, mark out, measure.

pacifist n peace-lover, conscientious objector, peacemaker, peace-monger, dove.

E3 warmonger, hawk.

pacify υ appease, conciliate, placate, mollify, calm, compose, soothe, assuage, allay, moderate, soften, lull, still, quiet, silence, quell, crush, put down, tame, subdue.

E3 anger.

pack n **1** PACKET, box, carton, parcel, package, bundle, burden, load, backpack, rucksack, haversack, knapsack, kitbag. **2** GROUP, company, troop, herd, flock, band, crowd, gang, mob.
υ **1** WRAP, parcel, package, bundle, stow, store. **2** FILL, load, charge, cram, stuff, crowd, throng, press, ram, wedge, compact, compress.

package n parcel, pack, packet, box, carton, bale, consignment.
υ parcel (up), wrap (up), pack (up), box, batch.

packed adj filled, full, jam-packed, chock-a-block, crammed, crowded, congested.

E3 empty, deserted.

packet n pack, carton, box, bag, package, parcel, case, container, wrapper, wrapping, packing.

pact n treaty, convention, covenant, bond, alliance, cartel, contract, deal, bargain, compact, agreement, arrangement, understanding.

E3 disagreement, quarrel.

pad n **1** CUSHION, pillow, wad, buffer, padding, protection. **2** WRITING-PAD, note-pad, jotter, block.
υ fill, stuff, wad, pack, wrap, line, cushion, protect.

pad out expand, inflate, fill out, augment, amplify, elaborate, flesh out, lengthen, stretch, protract, spin out.

padding n **1** FILLING, stuffing, wadding, packing, protection. **2** VERBIAGE, verbosity, wordiness, waffle (*infml*), bombast, hot air.

paddle[1] n oar, scull.
υ row, oar, scull, propel, steer.

paddle[2] υ wade, splash, slop, dabble.

pagan n heathen, atheist, unbeliever, infidel, idolater.

E3 believer.
adj heathen, irreligious, atheistic, godless, infidel, idolatrous.

page[1] n leaf, sheet, folio, side.

page[2] n page-boy, attendant, messenger, bell-boy, footman, servant.

v call, send for, summon, bid, announce.

pageant *n* procession, parade, show, display, tableau, scene, play, spectacle, extravaganza.

pageantry *n* pomp, ceremony, grandeur, magnificence, splendour, glamour, glitter, spectacle, parade, display, show, extravagance, theatricality, drama, melodrama.

pain *n* **1** HURT, ache, throb, cramp, spasm, twinge, pang, stab, sting, smart, soreness, tenderness, discomfort, distress, suffering, affliction, trouble, anguish, agony, torment, torture. **2** (*infml*) NUISANCE, bother, bore (*infml*), annoyance, vexation, burden, headache (*infml*).
v hurt, afflict, torment, torture, agonize, distress, upset, sadden, grieve.
F3 please, delight, gratify.

pained *adj* hurt, injured, wounded, stung, offended, aggrieved, distressed, upset, saddened, grieved.
F3 pleased, gratified.

painful *adj* **1** SORE, tender, aching, throbbing, smarting, stabbing, agonizing, excruciating. **2** *a painful experience*: unpleasant, disagreeable, distressing, upsetting, saddening, harrowing, traumatic. **3** HARD, difficult, laborious, tedious.
F3 1 painless, soothing. **2** pleasant, agreeable. **3** easy.

pain-killer *n* analgesic, anodyne, anaesthetic, palliative, sedative, drug, remedy.

painless *adj* pain-free, trouble-free, effortless, easy, simple, undemanding.
F3 painful, difficult.

pains *n* trouble, bother, effort, labour, care, diligence.

painstaking *adj* careful, meticulous, scrupulous, thorough, conscientious, diligent, assiduous, industrious, hardworking, dedicated, devoted, persevering.
F3 careless, negligent.

paint *n* colour, colouring, pigment, dye, tint, stain.

> **Points include:**
> acrylic, colourwash, distemper, eggshell, emulsion, enamel, gloss, gouache, matt, oil paint, oils, pastel, poster paint, primer, undercoat, watercolour, whitewash.

v **1** COLOUR, dye, tint, stain, lacquer, varnish, glaze, apply, daub, coat, cover, decorate. **2** PORTRAY, depict, describe, recount, picture, represent.

painting *n* oil painting, oil, watercolour, picture, portrait, landscape, still life, miniature, illustration, fresco, mural.

pair *n* couple, brace, twosome, duo, twins, two of a kind.
v match (up), twin, team, mate, marry, wed, splice, join, couple, link, bracket, put together.
F3 separate, part.

palace *n* castle, château, mansion, stately home, basilica, dome.

palatable *adj* tasty, appetizing, eatable, edible, acceptable, satisfactory, pleasant, enjoyable, attractive.
F3 unpalatable, unacceptable, unpleasant, disagreeable.

palate *n* taste, appreciation, liking, relish, enjoyment, appetite, stomach, heart.

palatial *adj* grand, magnificent, splendid, majestic, regal, stately, grandiose, imposing, luxurious, de luxe, sumptuous, opulent, plush, spacious.

pale *adj* **1** PALLID, livid, ashen, ashy, white, chalky, pasty, pasty-faced, waxen, waxy, wan, sallow, anaemic. **2** *pale blue*: light, pastel, faded, washed-out, bleached, colourless, insipid, vapid, weak, feeble, faint, dim. **Fª 1** ruddy. **2** dark.
v whiten, blanch, bleach, fade, dim. **Fª** colour, blush.

pall[1] *n* shroud, veil, mantle, cloak, cloud, shadow, gloom, damper.

pall[2] *v* tire, weary, jade, sate, satiate, cloy, sicken.

palm *n* hand, paw (*infml*), mitt (*sl*).
v take, grab, snatch, appropriate.
palm off foist, impose, fob off, offload, unload, pass off.

palpable *adj* solid, substantial, material, real, touchable, tangible, visible, apparent, clear, plain, obvious, evident, manifest, conspicuous, blatant, unmistakable.
Fª impalpable, imperceptible, intangible, elusive.

palpitate *v* flutter, quiver, tremble, shiver, vibrate, beat, pulsate, pound, thump, throb.

paltry *adj* meagre, derisory, contemptible, mean, low, miserable, wretched, poor, sorry, small, slight, trifling, inconsiderable, negligible, trivial, minor, petty, unimportant, insignificant, worthless.
Fª substantial, significant, valuable.

pamper *v* cosset, coddle, mollycoddle, humour, gratify, indulge, overindulge, spoil, pet, fondle.
Fª neglect, ill-treat.

pamphlet *n* leaflet, brochure, booklet, folder, circular, handout, notice.

pan *n* saucepan, frying-pan, pot, casserole, container, vessel.

panache *n* flourish, flamboyance, ostentation, style, flair, élan, dash, spirit, enthusiasm, zest, energy, vigour, verve.

pandemonium *n* chaos, disorder, confusion, commotion, rumpus, turmoil, turbulence, tumult, uproar, din, bedlam, hubbub, hullabaloo, hue and cry, to-do (*infml*).
Fª order, calm, peace.

pander to humour, indulge, pamper, please, gratify, satisfy, fulfil, provide, cater to.

panel *n* board, committee, jury, team.

pang *n* pain, ache, twinge, stab, sting, prick, stitch, gripe, spasm, throe, agony, anguish, discomfort, distress.

panic *n* agitation, flap (*infml*), dismay, consternation, fright, fear, horror, terror, frenzy, hysteria.
Fª calmness, confidence.
v order, lose one's nerve, lose one's head, go to pieces, flap (*infml*), overreact.
Fª relax.

panic-stricken *adj* alarmed, frightened, horrified, terrified, petrified, scared stiff, in a cold sweat, panicky, frantic, frenzied, hysterical.
Fª relaxed, confident.

panorama *n* view, vista, prospect, scenery, landscape, scene, spectacle, perspective, overview, survey.

panoramic *adj* scenic, wide, sweeping, extensive, far-reaching, widespread, overall, general, universal.
Fª narrow, restricted, limited.

pant *v* puff, blow, gasp, wheeze, breathe, sigh, heave, throb, palpitate.

pants *n* **1** UNDERPANTS, drawers, panties, briefs, knickers (*infml*), Y-fronts, boxer shorts, boxers (*infml*), trunks, shorts. **2** TROUSERS, slacks, jeans.

paper *n* **1** NEWSPAPER, daily, broadsheet, tabloid, rag (*sl*), journal, organ. **2** DOCUMENT, credential, authorization, identification, certificate, deed. **3** *a paper on alternative medicine*: essay, composition, dissertation, thesis, treatise, article, report.

> Types of paper include:
> art paper, bank paper, blotting-paper, bond, carbon paper, cartridge-paper, crêpe paper, greaseproof paper, graph paper, manila, note-paper, parchment paper, rag-paper, recycled paper, rice paper, silver paper, tissue paper, toilet paper, tracing paper, vellum, wallpaper, wrapping-paper, writing-paper; A4, A3, foolscap, legal (*US*), letter (*US*), quarto, atlas, crown.

parable *n* fable, allegory, lesson, moral tale, story.

parade *n* procession, cavalcade, motorcade, march, column, file, train, review, ceremony, spectacle, pageant, show, display, exhibition.
v **1** MARCH, process, file past. **2** SHOW, display, exhibit, show off, vaunt, flaunt, brandish.

paradise *n* heaven, Utopia, Shangri-La, Elysium, Eden, bliss, delight.
F3 hell, Hades.

paradox *n* contradiction, inconsistency, incongruity, absurdity, oddity, anomaly, mystery, enigma, riddle, puzzle.

paradoxical *adj* self-contradictory, contradictory, conflicting, inconsistent, incongruous, absurd, illogical, improbable, impossible,

mysterious, enigmatic, puzzling, baffling.

paragon *n* ideal, exemplar, epitome, quintessence, model, pattern, archetype, prototype, standard, criterion.

paragraph *n* passage, section, part, portion, subsection, subdivision, clause, item.

parallel *adj* equidistant, aligned, coextensive, alongside, analogous, equivalent, corresponding, matching, like, similar, resembling.
F3 divergent, different.
n **1** MATCH, equal, twin, duplicate, analogue, equivalent, counterpart. **2** SIMILARITY, resemblance, likeness, correspondence, correlation, equivalence, analogy, comparison.
v match, echo, conform, agree, correspond, correlate, compare, liken.
F3 diverge, differ.

paralyse *v* cripple, lame, disable, incapacitate, immobilize, anaesthetize, numb, deaden, freeze, transfix, halt, stop.

paralysed *adj* paralytic, paraplegic, quadriplegic, crippled, lame, disabled, incapacitated, immobilized, numb.
F3 able-bodied.

paralysis *n* paraplegia, quadriplegia, palsy, numbness, deadness, immobility, halt, standstill, stoppage, shutdown.

parameter *n* variable, guideline, indication, criterion, specification, limitation, restriction, limit, boundary.

paramount *adj* supreme, highest, topmost, predominant, pre-eminent, prime, principal, main, chief, cardinal, primary, first, foremost.
F3 lowest, last.

paraphernalia n equipment, gear, tackle, apparatus, accessories, trappings, bits and pieces, odds and ends, belongings, effects, stuff, things, baggage.

paraphrase n rewording, rephrasing, restatement, version, interpretation, rendering, translation.
υ reword, rephrase, restate, interpret, render, translate.

parasite n sponger, scrounger, cadger, hanger-on, leech, bloodsucker.

parcel n package, packet, pack, box, carton, bundle.
υ package, pack, wrap, bundle, tie up.
parcel out divide, carve up, apportion, allocate, allot, share out, dispense, dole out, deal out, mete out.

parch υ dry (up), desiccate, dehydrate, bake, burn, scorch, sear, blister, wither, shrivel.

parched adj **1** ARID, waterless, dry, dried up, dehydrated, scorched, withered, shrivelled. **2** (infml) THIRSTY, gasping (infml).

pardon υ forgive, condone, overlook, excuse, vindicate, acquit, absolve, remit, let off, reprieve, free, liberate, release.
F3 punish, discipline.
n forgiveness, mercy, clemency, indulgence, amnesty, excuse, acquittal, absolution, reprieve, release, discharge.
F3 punishment, condemnation.

pardonable adj forgivable, excusable, justifiable, warrantable, understandable, allowable, permissible, minor, venial.
F3 inexcusable.

pare υ peel, skin, shear, clip, trim, crop, cut, dock, lop, prune, cut back, reduce, decrease.

parent n father, mother, dam, sire, progenitor, begetter, procreator, guardian.

parish n district, community, parishioners, church, churchgoers, congregation, flock, fold.

park n grounds, estate, parkland, gardens, woodland, reserve, pleasure-ground.
υ put, position, deposit, leave.

parliament n legislature, senate, congress, house, assembly, convocation, council, diet.

Names of parliaments and political assemblies include:
House of Representatives, Senate (Australia); Nationalrat, Bundesrat (Austria); Narodno Sobraniye (Bulgaria); House of Commons, Senate (Canada); National People's Congress (China); Folketing (Denmark); People's Assembly (Egypt); Eduskunta (Finland); National Assembly, Senate (France); Bundesrat, Bundestag, Landtag (Germany); Althing (Iceland); Lok Sabha, Rajya Sabha (India); Majlis (Iran); Dáil Eireann, Seanad (Republic of Ireland); Knesset (Israel); Camera dei Deputati, Senato (Italy); House of Representatives, House of Councillors (Japan); Tweede Kamer, Eerste Kamer (Netherlands); House of Representatives (New Zealand); Northern Ireland Assembly (Northern Ireland); Odelsting, Lagting (Norway); Sejm, Senate (Poland); Cortes (Portugal); State Duma, Federation Council (Russia); Scottish Parliament (Scotland); National Council of Provinces, National Assembly (South

Africa); Congress of Deputies, Senate (*Spain*); Riksdag (*Sweden*); Nationalrat, Ständerat (*Switzerland*); Porte (*Turkey*); House of Commons, House of Lords (*UK*); House of Representatives, Senate (*US*); National Assembly (*Vietnam*), Welsh Assembly (*Wales*).

parliamentary *adj* governmental, senatorial, congressional, legislative, law-making.

parochial *adj* insular, provincial, parish-pump, petty, small-minded, narrow-minded, inward-looking, blinkered, limited, restricted, confined.

F∃ national, international.

parody *n* caricature, lampoon, burlesque, satire, send-up, spoof, skit, mimicry, imitation, take-off, travesty, distortion.

v caricature, lampoon, burlesque, satirize, send up, spoof, mimic, imitate, ape, take off.

paroxysm *n* fit, seizure, spasm, convulsion, attack, outbreak, outburst, explosion.

parry *v* ward off, fend off, repel, repulse, field, deflect, block, avert, avoid, evade, duck, dodge, sidestep, shun.

parson *n* vicar, rector, priest, minister, pastor, preacher, clergyman, reverend, cleric, churchman.

part *n* **1** COMPONENT, constituent, element, factor, piece, bit, particle, fragment, scrap, segment, fraction, portion, share, section, division, department, branch, sector, district, region, territory. **2** ROLE, character, duty, task, responsibility, office, function, capacity.

F∃ 1 whole, totality.

v separate, detach, disconnect, sever, split, tear, break, break up, take apart, dismantle, come apart, split up, divide, disunite, part company, disband, disperse, scatter, leave, depart, withdraw, go away.

part with relinquish, let go of, give up, yield, surrender, renounce, forgo, abandon, discard, jettison.

partial *adj* **1** *a partial victory*: incomplete, limited, restricted, imperfect, fragmentary, unfinished. **2** BIASED, prejudiced, partisan, one-sided, discriminatory, unfair, unjust, predisposed, coloured, affected.

F∃ 1 complete, total. **2** impartial, disinterested, unbiased, fair.

partial to fond of, keen on, crazy about (*infml*), mad about (*infml*).

partiality *n* liking, fondness, predilection (*fml*), proclivity, inclination, preference, predisposition.

participant *n* entrant, contributor, participator, member, party, co-operator, helper, worker.

participate *v* take part, join in, contribute, engage, be involved, enter, share, partake.

participation *n* involvement, sharing, partnership, co-operation, contribution, assistance.

particle *n* bit, piece, fragment, scrap, shred, sliver, speck, morsel, crumb, iota, whit, jot, tittle, atom, grain, drop.

particular *adj* **1** *on that particular day*: specific, precise, exact, distinct, special, peculiar. **2** EXCEPTIONAL, remarkable, notable, marked, thorough, unusual, uncommon. **3** FUSSY, discriminating, choosy (*infml*), finicky, fastidious.

F∃ 1 general.

n detail, specific, point, feature, item, fact, circumstance.

particularly *adv* **1** EXCEPTIONALLY, remarkably, notably, extraordinarily, unusually, uncommonly, surprisingly. **2** IN PARTICULAR, especially, specifically, explicitly, distinctly.

parting *n* **1** DEPARTURE, going, leave-taking, farewell, goodbye, adieu. **2** DIVERGENCE, separation, division, partition, rift, split, rupture, breaking. **F3 1** meeting. **2** convergence. *adj* departing, farewell, last, dying, final, closing, concluding. **F3** first.

partisan *n* devotee, adherent, follower, disciple, backer, supporter, champion, stalwart, guerrilla, irregular. *adj* biased, prejudiced, partial, predisposed, discriminatory, one-sided, factional, sectarian. **F3** impartial.

partition *n* **1** DIVIDER, barrier, wall, panel, screen, room-divider. **2** DIVISION, break-up, splitting, separation, parting, severance. *v* **1** SEPARATE, divide, subdivide, wall off, fence off, screen. **2** SHARE, divide, split up, parcel out.

partly *adv* somewhat, to some extent, to a certain extent, up to a point, slightly, fractionally, moderately, relatively, in part, partially, incompletely. **F3** completely, totally.

partner *n* associate, ally, confederate, colleague, team-mate, collaborator, accomplice, helper, mate, sidekick (*infml*), opposite number (*infml*), companion, comrade, consort, spouse, husband, wife.

partnership *n* **1** ALLIANCE, confederation, affiliation, combination, union, syndicate, co-operative, association, society, corporation, company, firm, fellowship, fraternity, brotherhood. **2** COLLABORATION, co-operation, participation, sharing.

party *n* **1** CELEBRATION, festivity, social, do (*infml*), knees-up (*sl*), rave-up (*sl*), get-together, gathering, reunion, function, reception, at-home, housewarming. **2** *a search party*: team, squad, crew, gang, band, group, company, detachment. **3** *a political party*: faction, side, league, cabal, alliance, association, grouping, combination. **4** PERSON, individual, litigant, plaintiff, defendant.

Types of party include:
acid-house party, baby shower (*N Am*), barbecue, beanfeast (*infml*), beano (*infml*), birthday party, bridal shower (*N Am*), bun-fight (*infml*), ceilidh, dinner party, disco, disco-theque, garden party, Hallowe'en party, hen party, hooley, hootenanny (*N Am infml*), house-warming, orgy, picnic, pyjama party, rave, slumber party (*US infml*), social, soirée, stag night, stag party, tea party, welcoming party, wrap party.

---

pass¹ *v* **1** SURPASS, exceed, go beyond, outdo, outstrip, overtake, leave behind. **2** *pass time*: spend, while away, fill, occupy. **3** GO PAST, go by, elapse, lapse, proceed, roll, flow, run, move, go, disappear, vanish. **4** GIVE, hand, transfer, transmit. **5** ENACT, ratify, validate, adopt, authorize, sanction, approve. **6** *pass an exam*: succeed, get through, qualify, graduate.

n **1** THROW, kick, move, lunge, swing. **2** PERMIT, passport, identification, ticket, licence, authorization, warrant, permission.

pass away die, pass on, expire, decease, give up the ghost.

pass off 1 FEIGN, counterfeit, fake, palm off. **2** HAPPEN, occur, take place, go off.

pass out 1 FAINT, lose consciousness, black out, collapse, flake out, keel over (*infml*), drop. **2** GIVE OUT, hand out, dole out, distribute, deal out, share out.

pass over disregard, ignore, overlook, miss, omit, leave, neglect.

pass² *n* col, defile, gorge, ravine, canyon, gap, passage.

passable *adj* **1** SATISFACTORY, acceptable, allowable, tolerable, average, ordinary, unexceptional, moderate, fair, adequate, all right, OK (*infml*), mediocre. **2** CLEAR, unobstructed, unblocked, open, navigable.

F3 1 unacceptable, excellent. **2** obstructed, blocked, impassable.

passage *n* **1** PASSAGEWAY, aisle, corridor, hall, hallway, lobby, vestibule, doorway, opening, entrance, exit. **2** THOROUGHFARE, way, route, road, avenue, path, lane, alley. **3** EXTRACT, excerpt, quotation, text, paragraph, section, piece, clause, verse. **4** JOURNEY, voyage, trip, crossing.

passenger *n* traveller, voyager, commuter, rider, fare, hitch-hiker.

passer-by *n* bystander, witness, looker-on, onlooker, spectator.

passing *adj* ephemeral, transient, short-lived, temporary, momentary, fleeting, brief, short, cursory, hasty, quick, slight, superficial, shallow, casual, incidental.

F3 lasting, permanent.

passion *n* feeling, emotion, love, adoration, infatuation, fondness, affection, lust, itch, desire, craving, fancy, mania, obsession, craze, eagerness, keenness, avidity, zest, enthusiasm, fanaticism, zeal, ardour, fervour, warmth, heat, fire, spirit, intensity, vehemence, anger, indignation, fury, rage, outburst.

F3 coolness, indifference, self-possession.

passionate *adj* **1** ARDENT, fervent, eager, keen, avid, enthusiastic, fanatical, zealous, warm, hot, fiery, inflamed, aroused, excited, impassioned, intense, strong, fierce, vehement, violent, stormy, tempestuous, wild, frenzied. **2** EMOTIONAL, excitable, hot-headed, impetuous, impulsive, quick-tempered, irritable. **3** LOVING, affectionate, lustful, erotic, sexy, sensual, sultry.

F3 1 phlegmatic, laid back (*infml*). **3** frigid.

passive *adj* receptive, unassertive, submissive, docile, unresisting, non-violent, patient, resigned, long-suffering, indifferent, apathetic, lifeless, inert, inactive, non-participating.

F3 active, lively, responsive, involved.

past *adj* **1** OVER, ended, finished, completed, done, over and done with. **2** FORMER, previous, preceding, foregoing, late, recent. **3** ANCIENT, bygone, olden, early, gone, no more, extinct, defunct, forgotten.

F3 2 future.

n **1** *in the past*: history, former times,

olden days, antiquity. **2** LIFE, background, experience, track record.
F3 1 future.

pasta

Forms and shapes of pasta include:

agnolotti, anelli, bucatini, cannelloni, capelletti, conchiglie, ditali, elbow macaroni, farfalle, fedelini, fettuccine, fusilli, lasagne, linguini, lumache, macaroni, mezzani, noodles, penne, ravioli, rigatoni, spaghetti, tagliarini, tagliatelle, tortellini, vermicelli, ziti.

paste n adhesive, glue, gum, mastic, putty, cement.
v stick, glue, gum, cement, fix.

pastel adj delicate, soft, soft-hued, light, pale, subdued, faint.

pastime n hobby, activity, game, sport, recreation, play, fun, amusement, entertainment, diversion, distraction, relaxation.
F3 work, employment.

pastoral adj **1** RURAL, country, rustic, bucolic, agricultural, agrarian, idyllic. **2** ECCLESIASTICAL, clerical, priestly, ministerial.
F3 1 urban.

pastry

Types of pastry include:

biscuit-crumb pastry, choux, filo pastry, flaky pastry, flan pastry, hot-water crust pastry, pâte à savarin, pâte brisée, pâte sablée, pâte sucrée, puff pastry, rough puff-pastry, shortcrust pastry, short pastry, suet-crust pastry, sweet pastry, wholemeal pastry.

pasture n grass, grassland, meadow, field, paddock, pasturage, grazing.

pasty adj pale, pallid, wan, anaemic, pasty-faced, sickly, unhealthy.
F3 ruddy, healthy.

pat v tap, dab, slap, touch, stroke, caress, fondle, pet.
n tap, dab, slap, touch, stroke, caress.
adv precisely, exactly, perfectly, flawlessly, faultlessly, fluently.
F3 imprecisely, inaccurately, wrongly.
adj glib, fluent, smooth, slick, ready, easy, facile, simplistic.

patch n piece, bit, scrap, spot, area, stretch, tract, plot, lot, parcel.
v mend, repair, fix, cover, reinforce.

patchy adj uneven, irregular, inconsistent, variable, random, fitful, erratic, sketchy, bitty, spotty, blotchy.
F3 even, uniform, regular, consistent.

patent adj obvious, evident, conspicuous, manifest, clear, transparent, apparent, visible, palpable, unequivocal, open, overt, blatant, flagrant, glaring.
F3 hidden, opaque.

path n route, course, direction, way, passage, road, avenue, lane, footpath, bridleway, trail, track, walk.

pathetic adj **1** PITIABLE, poor, sorry, lamentable, miserable, sad, distressing, moving, touching, poignant, plaintive, heart-rending, heartbreaking. **2** (infml) CONTEMPTIBLE, derisory, deplorable, useless, worthless, inadequate, meagre, feeble.
F3 1 cheerful. **2** admirable, excellent, valuable.

patience n calmness, composure, self-control, restraint, tolerance, forbearance, endurance, fortitude, long-suffering, submission, resignation, stoicism, persistence, perseverance, diligence.
F3 impatience, intolerance, exasperation.

patient adj calm, composed, self-possessed, self-controlled, restrained, even-tempered, mild, lenient, indulgent, understanding, forgiving, tolerant, accommodating, forbearing, long-suffering, uncomplaining, submissive, resigned, philosophical, stoical, persistent, persevering.
F3 impatient, restless, intolerant, exasperated.
n invalid, sufferer, case, client.

patriotic adj nationalistic, chauvinistic, jingoistic, loyal, flag-waving.

patrol n 1 GUARD, sentry, sentinel, watchman. **2** on patrol: watch, surveillance, policing, protection, defence.
v police, guard, protect, defend, go the rounds, tour, inspect.

patron n 1 BENEFACTOR, philanthropist, sponsor, backer, supporter, sympathizer, advocate, champion, defender, protector, guardian, helper. **2** CUSTOMER, client, frequenter, regular, shopper, buyer, purchaser, subscriber.

patronage n custom, business, trade, sponsorship, backing, support.

patronize v 1 SPONSOR, fund, back, support, maintain, help, assist, promote, foster, encourage.
2 FREQUENT, shop at, buy from, deal with.

patronizing adj condescending, stooping, overbearing, high-handed, haughty, superior, snobbish, supercilious, disdainful.
F3 humble, lowly.

patter v tap, pat, pitter-patter, beat, pelt, scuttle, scurry.
n 1 PATTERING, tapping, pitter-patter, beating. **2** a salesman's patter: chatter,

gabble, jabber, line, pitch, spiel (sl), jargon, lingo (infml).

pattern n 1 SYSTEM, method, order, plan. **2** DECORATION, ornamentation, ornament, figure, motif, design, style. **3** MODEL, template, stencil, guide, original, prototype, standard, norm.

patterned adj decorated, ornamented, figured, printed.
F3 plain.

paunch n abdomen, belly, pot-belly, beer-belly, corporation (infml).

pause v halt, stop, cease, discontinue, break off, interrupt, take a break, rest, wait, delay, hesitate.
n halt, stoppage, interruption, break, rest, breather (infml), lull, let-up (infml), respite, gap, interval, interlude, intermission, wait, delay, hesitation.

pave v flag, tile, floor, surface, cover, asphalt, tarmac, concrete.

paw v maul, manhandle, mishandle, molest.
n foot, pad, forefoot, hand.

pawn¹ n dupe, puppet, tool, instrument, toy, plaything.

pawn² v deposit, pledge, stake, mortgage, hock (sl), pop (sl).

pay v 1 REMIT, settle, discharge, reward, remunerate, recompense, reimburse, repay, refund, spend, pay out. **2** BENEFIT, profit, pay off, bring in, yield, return. **3** ATONE, make amends, compensate, answer, suffer.
n remuneration, wages, salary, earnings, income, fee, stipend, honorarium, emoluments, payment, reward, recompense, compensation, reimbursement.

pay back 1 REPAY, refund, reimburse, recompense, settle, square.
2 RETALIATE, get one's own back,

take revenge, get even with, reciprocate, counter-attack.

pay off 1 DISCHARGE, settle, square, clear. **2** DISMISS, fire, sack (*infml*). **3** *the preparations paid off*: succeed, work.

pay out spend, disburse, hand over, fork out (*infml*), shell out (*infml*), lay out.

payable *adj* owed, owing, unpaid, outstanding, in arrears, due, mature.

payment *n* remittance, settlement, discharge, premium, outlay, advance, deposit, instalment, contribution, donation, allowance, reward, remuneration, pay, fee, hire, fare, toll.

peace *n* **1** SILENCE, quiet, hush, stillness, rest, relaxation, tranquillity, calm, calmness, composure, contentment. **2** ARMISTICE, truce, ceasefire, conciliation, concord, harmony, agreement, treaty.
F∃ 1 noise, disturbance. **2** war, disagreement.

peaceable *adj* pacific, peace-loving, unwarlike, non-violent, conciliatory, friendly, amicable, inoffensive, gentle, placid, easy-going (*infml*), mild.
F∃ belligerent, aggressive.

peaceful *adj* quiet, still, restful, relaxing, tranquil, serene, calm, placid, unruffled, undisturbed, untroubled, friendly, amicable, peaceable, pacific, gentle.
F∃ noisy, disturbed, troubled, violent.

peacemaker *n* appeaser, conciliator, mediator, arbitrator, intercessor, peace-monger, pacifist.

peak *n* top, summit, pinnacle, crest, crown, zenith, height, maximum, climax, culmination, apex, tip, point.
F∃ nadir, trough.
v climax, culminate, come to a head.

peal *n* chime, carillon, toll, knell, ring, clang, ringing, reverberation, rumble, roar, crash, clap.
v chime, toll, ring, clang, resonate, reverberate, resound, rumble, roll, roar, crash.

peasant *n* rustic, provincial, yokel, bumpkin, oaf, boor, lout.

peculiar *adj* **1** *a peculiar sound*: strange, odd, curious, funny, weird, bizarre, extraordinary, unusual, abnormal, exceptional, unconventional, offbeat, eccentric, way-out (*sl*), outlandish, exotic. **2** CHARACTERISTIC, distinctive, specific, particular, special, individual, personal, idiosyncratic, unique, singular.
F∃ 1 ordinary, normal. **2** general.

peculiarity *n* oddity, bizarreness, abnormality, exception, eccentricity, quirk, mannerism, feature, trait, mark, quality, attribute, characteristic, distinctiveness, particularity, idiosyncrasy.

pedantic *adj* stilted, fussy, particular, precise, exact, punctilious, hair-splitting, nit-picking, finical, academic, bookish, erudite.
F∃ imprecise, informal, casual.

peddle *v* sell, vend, flog (*infml*), hawk, tout, push, trade, traffic, market.

pedestal *n* plinth, stand, support, mounting, foot, base, foundation, platform, podium.

pedestrian *n* walker, foot-traveller.
adj dull, boring, flat, uninspired, banal, mundane, run-of-the-mill, commonplace, ordinary, mediocre, indifferent, prosaic, stodgy, plodding.
F∃ exciting, imaginative.

pedigree n genealogy, family tree, lineage, ancestry, descent, line, family, parentage, derivation, extraction, race, breed, stock, blood.

peel v pare, skin, strip, scale, flake (off).
n skin, rind, zest, peeling.

peep v look, peek, glimpse, spy, squint, peer, emerge, issue, appear.
n look, peek, glimpse, glance, squint.

peephole n spyhole, keyhole, pinhole, hole, opening, aperture, slit, chink, crack, fissure, cleft, crevice.

peer¹ v look, gaze, scan, scrutinize, examine, inspect, spy, snoop, peep, squint.

peer² n **1** ARISTOCRAT, noble, nobleman, lord, duke, marquess, marquis, earl, count, viscount, baron. **2** EQUAL, counterpart, equivalent, match, fellow.

peerage n aristocracy, nobility, upper crust.

peeress n aristocrat, noble, noblewoman, lady, dame, duchess, marchioness, countess, viscountess, baroness.

peevish adj petulant, querulous, fractious, fretful, touchy, irritable, cross, grumpy, ratty (infml), crotchety, ill-tempered, crabbed, cantankerous, crusty, snappy, short-tempered, surly, sullen, sulky.
F3 good-tempered.

peg v **1** FASTEN, secure, fix, attach, join, mark. **2** peg prices: control, stabilize, limit, freeze, fix, set.
n pin, dowel, hook, knob, marker, post, stake.

pejorative adj derogatory, disparaging, belittling, slighting, unflattering, uncomplimentary,
unpleasant, bad, negative.
F3 complimentary.

pelt v **1** THROW, hurl, bombard, shower, assail, batter, beat, hit, strike. **2** POUR, teem, rain cats and dogs (infml). **3** RUSH, hurry, charge, belt (infml), tear, dash, speed, career.

pen¹ n fountain-pen, ballpoint, rollerball, Biro®, felt-tip pen, light pen, mouse pen.
v write, compose, draft, scribble, jot down.

pen² n enclosure, fold, stall, sty, coop, cage, hutch.
v enclose, fence, hedge, hem in, confine, coop, coop, shut up.

penalize v punish, discipline, correct, fine, handicap.
F3 reward.

penalty n punishment, retribution, fine, forfeit, handicap, disadvantage.
F3 reward.

penance n atonement, reparation, punishment, penalty, mortification.

pendant n medallion, locket, necklace.

pending adj impending, in the offing, forthcoming, imminent, undecided, in the balance.
F3 finished, settled.

penetrate v pierce, stab, prick, puncture, probe, sink, bore, enter, infiltrate, permeate, seep, pervade, suffuse.

penetrating adj piercing, stinging, biting, incisive, sharp, keen, acute, shrewd, discerning, perceptive, observant, profound, deep, searching, probing.
F3 blunt.

penitence n repentance, contrition, remorse, regret, shame, self-reproach.

penitent adj repentant, contrite, sorry, apologetic, remorseful, regretful, conscience-stricken, shamefaced, humble.
F3 unrepentant, hard-hearted, callous.

penniless adj poor, poverty-stricken, impoverished, destitute, bankrupt, ruined, bust, broke (*infml*), stony-broke (*sl*).
F3 rich, wealthy, affluent.

pension n annuity, superannuation, allowance, benefit.

pensive adj thoughtful, reflective, contemplative, meditative, ruminative, absorbed, preoccupied, absent-minded, wistful, solemn, serious, sober.
F3 carefree.

pent-up adj repressed, inhibited, restrained, bottled-up, suppressed, stifled.

people n persons, individuals, humans, human beings, mankind, humanity, folk, public, general public, populace, rank and file, population, inhabitants, citizens, community, society, race, nation.
v populate, inhabit, occupy, settle, colonize.

pep n energy, vigour, verve, spirit, vitality, liveliness, get-up-and-go (*infml*), exuberance, high spirits.
pep up (*infml*) invigorate, vitalize, liven up, quicken, stimulate, excite, exhilarate, inspire.
F3 tone down.

perceive v **1** SEE, discern, make out, detect, discover, spot, catch sight of, notice, observe, view, remark, note, distinguish, recognize. **2** SENSE, feel, apprehend, learn, realize, appreciate, be aware of, know, grasp, understand, gather, deduce, conclude.

perceptible adj perceivable, discernible, detectable, appreciable, distinguishable, observable, noticeable, obvious, evident, conspicuous, clear, plain, apparent, visible.
F3 imperceptible, inconspicuous.

perception n sense, feeling, impression, idea, conception, apprehension, awareness, consciousness, observation, recognition, grasp, understanding, insight, discernment, taste.

perceptive adj discerning, observant, sensitive, responsive, aware, alert, quick, sharp, astute, shrewd.
F3 unobservant.

perch v land, alight, settle, sit, roost, balance, rest.

percolate v filter, strain, seep, ooze, leak, drip, penetrate, permeate, pervade.

peremptory adj imperious, commanding, dictatorial, autocratic, authoritative, assertive, high-handed, overbearing, domineering, bossy (*infml*), abrupt, curt, summary, arbitrary.

perennial adj lasting, enduring, everlasting, eternal, immortal, undying, imperishable, unceasing, incessant, never-ending, constant, continual, uninterrupted, perpetual, persistent, unfailing.

perfect adj **1** FAULTLESS, impeccable, flawless, immaculate, spotless, blameless, pure, superb, excellent, matchless, incomparable. **2** EXACT, precise, accurate, right, correct, true. **3** IDEAL, model, exemplary, ultimate, consummate, expert, accomplished, experienced, skilful. **4** *perfect strangers*: utter, absolute, sheer, complete, entire, total.

F3 1 imperfect, flawed, blemished. **2** inaccurate, wrong. **3** inexperienced, unskilled.

v fulfil, consummate, complete, finish, polish, refine, elaborate.

F3 spoil, mar.

perfection *n* faultlessness, flawlessness, excellence, superiority, ideal, model, paragon, crown, pinnacle, acme, consummation, completion.

F3 imperfection, flaw.

perfectionist *n* idealist, purist, pedant, stickler.

perfectly *adv* **1** UTTERLY, absolutely, quite, thoroughly, completely, entirely, wholly, totally, fully. **2** FAULTLESSLY, flawlessly, impeccably, ideally, exactly, correctly.

F3 1 partially. **2** imperfectly, badly.

perforate *v* hole, punch, drill, bore, pierce, prick, stab, puncture, penetrate.

perforation *n* hole, bore, prick, puncture, dotted line.

perform *v* **1** DO, carry out, execute, discharge, fulfil, satisfy, complete, achieve, accomplish, bring off, pull off, effect, bring about. **2** *perform a play*: stage, put on, present, enact, represent, act, play, appear as. **3** FUNCTION, work, operate, behave, produce.

performance *n* **1** SHOW, act, play, appearance, gig (*sl*), presentation, production, interpretation, rendition, representation, portrayal, acting. **2** ACTION, deed, doing, carrying out, execution, implementation, discharge, fulfilment, completion,

achievement, accomplishment. **3** FUNCTIONING, operation, behaviour, conduct.

performer *n* actor, actress, player, artiste, entertainer.

perfume *n* scent, fragrance, smell, odour, aroma, bouquet, sweetness, balm, essence, cologne, toilet water, incense.

perhaps *adv* maybe, possibly, conceivably, feasibly.

peril *n* danger, hazard, risk, jeopardy, uncertainty, insecurity, threat, menace.

F3 safety, security.

perilous *adj* dangerous, unsafe, hazardous, risky, chancy, precarious, insecure, unsure, vulnerable, exposed, menacing, threatening, dire.

F3 safe, secure.

perimeter *n* circumference, edge, border, boundary, frontier, limit, bounds, confines, fringe, margin, periphery.

F3 middle, centre, heart.

period *n* era, epoch, age, generation, date, years, time, term, season, stage, phase, stretch, turn, session, interval, space, span, spell, cycle.

periodic *adj* occasional, infrequent, sporadic, intermittent, recurrent, repeated, regular, periodical, seasonal.

periodical *n* magazine, journal, publication, weekly, monthly, quarterly.

peripheral *adj* **1** MINOR, secondary, incidental, unimportant, irrelevant, unnecessary, marginal, borderline, surface, superficial. **2** OUTLYING, outer, outermost.

F3 1 major, crucial. **2** central.

perish *v* rot, decay, decompose,

disintegrate, crumble, collapse, fall, die, expire, pass away.

perishable adj destructible, biodegradable, decomposable, short-lived.

E3 imperishable, durable.

perk n perquisite, fringe benefit, benefit, bonus, dividend, gratuity, tip, extra, plus (infml).

perk up (infml) brighten, cheer up, buck up (infml), revive, liven up, pep up (infml), rally, recover, improve, look up.

permanence n fixedness, stability, imperishability, perpetuity, constancy, endurance, durability.

E3 impermanence, transience.

permanent adj fixed, stable, unchanging, imperishable, indestructible, unfading, eternal, everlasting, lifelong, perpetual, constant, steadfast, perennial, long-lasting, lasting, enduring, durable.

E3 temporary, ephemeral, fleeting.

permeable adj porous, absorbent, absorptive, penetrable.

E3 impermeable, watertight.

permeate v pass through, soak through, filter through, seep through, penetrate, infiltrate, pervade, imbue, saturate, impregnate, fill.

permissible adj permitted, allowable, allowed, admissible, all right, acceptable, proper, authorized, sanctioned, lawful, legal, legitimate.

E3 prohibited, banned, forbidden.

permission n consent, assent, agreement, approval, go-ahead, green light (infml), authorization, sanction, leave, warrant, permit, licence, dispensation, freedom, liberty.

E3 prohibition.

permissive adj liberal, broad-minded, tolerant, forbearing, lenient, easy-going (infml), indulgent, overindulgent, lax, free.

E3 strict, rigid.

permit v allow, let, consent, agree, admit, grant, authorize, sanction, warrant, license.

E3 prohibit, forbid.

n pass, passport, visa, licence, warrant, authorization, sanction, permission.

E3 prohibition.

perpendicular adj vertical, upright, erect, straight, sheer, plumb.

E3 horizontal.

perpetrate v commit, carry out, execute, do, perform, inflict, wreak.

perpetual adj eternal, everlasting, infinite, endless, unending, never-ending, interminable, ceaseless, unceasing, incessant, continuous, uninterrupted, constant, persistent, continual, repeated, recurrent, perennial, permanent, lasting, enduring, abiding, unchanging.

E3 intermittent, temporary, ephemeral, transient.

perpetuate v continue, keep up, maintain, preserve, keep alive, immortalize, commemorate.

perplex v puzzle, baffle, mystify, stump, confuse, muddle, confound, bewilder, dumbfound.

persecute v hound, pursue, hunt, bother, worry, annoy, pester, harass, molest, abuse, ill-treat, maltreat, oppress, tyrannize, victimize, martyr, distress, afflict, torment, torture, crucify.

E3 pamper, spoil.

persecution n harassment, molestation, abuse, maltreatment, discrimination, oppression, subjugation, suppression, tyranny, punishment, torture, martyrdom.

perseverance n persistence, determination, resolution, doggedness, tenacity, diligence, assiduity, dedication, commitment, constancy, steadfastness, stamina, endurance, indefatigability.

persevere v continue, carry on, stick at it (infml), keep going, soldier on, persist, plug away (infml), remain, stand firm, stand fast, hold on, hang on.

E3 give up, quit, stop, discontinue.

persist v remain, linger, last, endure, abide, carry on, keep at it, persevere, insist.

E3 desist, stop.

persistent adj 1 INCESSANT, endless, never-ending, interminable, continuous, unrelenting, relentless, unremitting, constant, steady, continual, repeated, perpetual, lasting, enduring. 2 persistent effort: persevering, determined, resolute, dogged, tenacious, stubborn, obstinate, steadfast, zealous, tireless, unflagging, indefatigable.

person n individual, being, human being, human, man, woman, body, soul, character, type.

personal adj own, private, confidential, intimate, special, particular, individual, exclusive, idiosyncratic, distinctive.

E3 public, general, universal.

personality n 1 CHARACTER, nature, disposition, temperament, individuality, psyche, traits, make-up. 2 CELEBRITY, celeb (infml), notable, personage, public figure, VIP (infml), star.

personify v embody, epitomize, typify, exemplify, symbolize, represent, mirror.

personnel n staff, workforce, workers, employees, crew, human resources, manpower, people, members.

perspective n aspect, angle, slant, attitude, standpoint, viewpoint, point of view, vista, scene, prospect, outlook, proportion, relation.

perspiration n sweat, secretion, moisture, wetness.

perspire v sweat, exude, secrete, swelter, drip.

persuade v coax, prevail upon, lean on, cajole, wheedle, inveigle, talk into, induce, bring round, win over, convince, convert, sway, influence, lead on, incite, prompt, urge.

E3 dissuade, deter, discourage.

persuasion n 1 COAXING, cajolery, wheedling, inducement, enticement, pull, power, influence, conviction, conversion. 2 OPINION, school (of thought), party, faction, side, conviction, faith, belief, denomination, sect.

persuasive adj convincing, plausible, cogent, sound, valid, influential, forceful, weighty, effective, telling, potent, compelling, moving, touching.

E3 unconvincing.

pertinent adj appropriate, suitable, fitting, apt, apposite, relevant, to the point, material, applicable.

E3 inappropriate, unsuitable, irrelevant.

perturb v disturb, bother, trouble, upset, worry, alarm, disconcert, unsettle, discompose, ruffle,

fluster, agitate, vex, rattle (*infml*).
F3 reassure, compose.

peruse *v* study, pore over, read, browse, look through, scan, scrutinize, examine, inspect, check.

pervade *v* affect, penetrate, permeate, percolate, charge, fill, imbue, infuse, suffuse, saturate, impregnate.

pervasive *adj* prevalent, common, extensive, widespread, general, universal, inescapable, omnipresent, ubiquitous.

perverse *adj* contrary, wayward, wrong-headed, wilful, headstrong, stubborn, obstinate, unyielding, intransigent, disobedient, rebellious, troublesome, unmanageable, ill-tempered, cantankerous, unreasonable, incorrect, improper.
F3 obliging, co-operative, reasonable.

perversion *n* **1** CORRUPTION, depravity, debauchery, immorality, vice, wickedness, deviance, kinkiness (*infml*), abnormality. **2** TWISTING, distortion, misrepresentation, travesty, misinterpretation, aberration, deviation, misuse, misapplication.

pervert *v* **1** *pervert the truth*: twist, warp, distort, misrepresent, falsify, garble, misinterpret. **2** CORRUPT, lead astray, deprave, debauch, debase, degrade, abuse, misuse, misapply.
n deviant, debauchee, degenerate, weirdo (*infml*), perv (*infml*).

perverted *adj* twisted, warped, distorted, deviant, kinky (*infml*), pervy (*infml*), unnatural, abnormal, unhealthy, corrupt, depraved, debauched, debased, immoral, evil, wicked.
F3 natural, normal.

pessimistic *adj* negative, cynical, fatalistic, defeatist, resigned, hopeless, despairing, despondent, dejected, downhearted, glum, morose, melancholy, depressed, dismal, gloomy, bleak.
F3 optimistic.

pest *n* nuisance, bother, annoyance, irritation, vexation, trial, curse, scourge, bane, blight, bug.

pester *v* nag, badger, hound, hassle (*infml*), harass, plague, torment, provoke, worry, bother, disturb, annoy, irritate, pick on, get at (*infml*).

pet *n* favourite, darling, idol, treasure, jewel.
adj favourite, favoured, preferred, dearest, cherished, special, particular, personal.
v stroke, caress, fondle, cuddle, kiss, neck (*sl*), snog (*sl*).

peter out dwindle, taper off, fade, wane, ebb, fail, cease, stop.

petition *n* appeal, round robin, application, request, solicitation, plea, entreaty, prayer, supplication, invocation.
v appeal, call upon, ask, crave, solicit, bid, urge, press, implore, beg, plead, entreat, beseech, supplicate, pray.

petrify *v* terrify, horrify, appal, paralyse, numb, stun, dumbfound.

petty *adj* **1** MINOR, unimportant, insignificant, trivial, secondary, lesser, small, little, slight, trifling, paltry, inconsiderable, negligible. **2** SMALL-MINDED, mean, ungenerous, grudging, spiteful.
F3 1 important, significant. **2** generous.

petulant *adj* fretful, peevish, cross, irritable, snappish, bad-tempered, ill-humoured, moody, sullen, sulky, sour, ungracious.

phantom n ghost, spectre, spirit, apparition, vision, hallucination, illusion, figment.

phase n stage, step, time, period, spell, season, chapter, position, point, aspect, state, condition.

phase out wind down, run down, ease off, taper off, eliminate, dispose of, get rid of, remove, withdraw, close, terminate.

phenomenal adj marvellous, sensational, stupendous, amazing, remarkable, extraordinary, exceptional, unusual, unbelievable, incredible.

phenomenon n **1** OCCURRENCE, happening, event, incident, episode, fact, appearance, sight. **2** WONDER, marvel, miracle, prodigy, rarity, curiosity, spectacle, sensation.

philanthropic adj humanitarian, public-spirited, altruistic, unselfish, benevolent, kind, charitable, alms-giving, generous, liberal, open-handed.
E3 misanthropic.

philanthropist n humanitarian, benefactor, patron, sponsor, giver, donor, contributor, altruist.
E3 misanthrope.

philanthropy n humanitarianism, public-spiritedness, altruism, unselfishness, benevolence, kind-heartedness, charity, alms-giving, patronage, generosity, liberality, open-handedness.
E3 misanthropy.

philosophical adj **1** a philosophical discussion: metaphysical, abstract, theoretical, analytical, rational, logical, erudite, learned, wise, thoughtful. **2** RESIGNED, patient, stoical, unruffled, calm, composed.

philosophy n reason, thought, thinking, wisdom, knowledge, ideology, world-view, doctrine, beliefs, convictions, values, principles, attitude, viewpoint.

Philosophical terms include: absolutism, a posteriori, a priori, atomism, deduction, deontology, determinism, dialectical material- ism, dualism, egoism, empiricism, Epicureanism, epistemology, eth- ics, existentialism, fatalism, he- donism, humanism, idealism, iden- tity, induction, instrumentalism, interactionism, intuition, libertar- ianism, logic, logical positivism, materialism, metaphysics, monism, naturalism, nihilism, nominalism, objectivism, ontology, phenomen- alism, phenomenology, positivism, pragmatism, prescriptivism, ration- alism, realism, reductionism, relat- ivism, scepticism, scholasticism, sensationalism, solipsism, stoicism, structuralism, subjectivism, syllo- gism, teleology, utilitarianism.

phlegmatic adj placid, stolid, impassive, unemotional, unconcerned, indifferent, matter-of-fact, stoical.
E3 emotional, passionate.

phobia n fear, terror, dread, anxiety, neurosis, obsession, hang-up (infml), thing (infml), aversion, dislike, hatred, horror, loathing, revulsion, repulsion.
E3 love, liking.

Phobias (by name of object feared) include: zoophobia (animals), apiphobia (bees), ailurophobia (cats), necro- phobia (corpses), scotophobia (darkness), cynophobia (dogs), claustrophobia (*enclosed places*), pantophobia (*everything*), pyrophobia (*fire*), xenophobia (*foreigners*), phasmophobia (*ghosts*), acrophobia (*high places*), hippophobia (*horses*), entomophobia (*insects*), astraphobia (*lightning*), autophobia (*loneliness*), agoraphobia (*open spaces*), toxiphobia (*poison*), herpetophobia (*reptiles*), ophidiophobia (*snakes*), tachophobia (*speed*), arachnophobia (*spiders*), triskaidekaphobia (*thirteen*), brontophobia (*thunder*), hydrophobia (*water*).

phone *v* telephone, ring (up), call (up), dial, contact, get in touch, give a buzz (*infml*), give a tinkle (*infml*).
phoney *adj* fake, counterfeit, forged, bogus, trick, false, spurious, assumed, affected, put-on, sham, pseudo, imitation.
F3 real, genuine.
photocopy *v* copy, duplicate, Photostat®, Xerox®, print, run off.
n copy, duplicate, Photostat®, Xerox®.
photograph *n* photo, snap, snapshot, print, shot, slide, transparency, picture, image, likeness.
v snap, take, film, shoot, video, record.

Photographic equipment includes:
camera, camcorder; cable release, remote control; battery, stand, tripod, flash umbrella, boom arm; film, cartridge film, cassette film, disc film; filter, colour filter, heat filter, polarizing filter; memory card, memory reader; light meter, exposure meter, spot meter; diffuser, barn-doors, parabolic reflector, snoot; developing bath, developing tank, dry mounting press, enlarger,

fixing bath, focus magnifier, lightbox, negative carrier, print washer, contact printer, safelight, stop bath, Vertoscope®, viewer; slide mount, slide viewer, slide projector, film projector, screen; cassette adaptor, tele-cine converter. *see also* **camera**.

phrase *n* construction, clause, idiom, expression, saying, utterance, remark.
v word, formulate, frame, couch, present, put, express, say, utter, pronounce.

physical *adj* bodily, corporeal, fleshy, incarnate, mortal, earthly, material, concrete, solid, substantial, tangible, visible, real, actual.
F3 mental, spiritual.

physician *n* doctor, medical practitioner, medic (*infml*), general practitioner, GP, houseman, intern, registrar, consultant, specialist, healer.

physics

Terms used in physics include:
absolute zero, acceleration, atom, Big Bang theory, boiling point, centre of gravity, centrifugal force, charge, circuit, critical mass, current, density, diffraction, discharge, dynamics, electricity, electromagnetic, electron, energy, equilibrium, evaporation, field, force, freezing point, frequency, friction, gamma ray, grand unified theory (GUT), gravity, half-life, inertia, infrared, interference, ion, kinetic energy, laser, latent heat, lens, longitudinal wave, magnetic field, magnetism, mass, microwave, molecule, moment, momentum, motion, neutron, nuclear fission, nuclear fusion, nucleus, oscillation, parti-

cle, photon, polarity, potential energy, pressure, proton, quantum, radiation, radioactivity, radio wave, reflection, refraction, relativity, resistance, semiconductor, SI unit, sound wave, spectrum, superstring theory, surface tension, transverse wave, ultrasound, ultraviolet, velocity, viscosity, volume, wave, X-ray.

physique n body, figure, shape, form, build, frame, structure, constitution, make-up.

pick v 1 SELECT, choose, opt for, decide on, settle on, single out. 2 GATHER, collect, pluck, harvest, cull. n 1 CHOICE, selection, option, decision, preference. 2 BEST, cream, flower, élite, elect.

pick on bully, torment, persecute, nag, get at (infml), needle (infml), bait.

pick out spot, notice, perceive, recognize, distinguish, tell apart, separate, single out, hand-pick, choose, select.

pick up 1 LIFT, raise, hoist. 2 I'll pick you up at eight: call for, fetch, collect. 3 LEARN, master, grasp, gather. 4 IMPROVE, rally, recover, perk up (infml). 5 BUY, purchase. 6 OBTAIN, acquire, gain. 7 pick up an infection: catch, contract, get.

picket n picketer, protester, demonstrator, striker. v protest, demonstrate, boycott, blockade, enclose, surround.

pickle v preserve, conserve, souse, marinade, steep, cure, salt.

pictorial adj graphic, diagrammatic, schematic, representational, vivid, striking, expressive, illustrated, picturesque, scenic.

picture n 1 PAINTING, portrait, landscape, drawing, sketch, illustration, engraving, photograph, print, representation, likeness, image, effigy. 2 DEPICTION, portrayal, description, account, report, impression. 3 the picture of health: embodiment, personification, epitome, archetype, essence. 4 FILM, movie (infml), motion picture. v 1 IMAGINE, envisage, envision, conceive, visualize, see. 2 DEPICT, describe, represent, show, portray, draw, sketch, paint, photograph, illustrate.

picturesque adj 1 ATTRACTIVE, beautiful, pretty, charming, quaint, idyllic, scenic. 2 DESCRIPTIVE, graphic, vivid, colourful, striking. **F3** 1 unattractive. 2 dull.

piece n 1 FRAGMENT, bit, scrap, morsel, mouthful, bite, lump, chunk, slice, sliver, shred, offcut, sample, component, constituent, element, part, segment, section, division, fraction, share, portion, quantity. 2 ARTICLE, item, study, work, composition, creation, specimen, example.

pier n 1 JETTY, breakwater, landing-stage, quay, wharf. 2 SUPPORT, upright, pillar, post.

pierce v penetrate, enter, stick into, puncture, drill, bore, probe, perforate, punch, prick, stab, lance, bayonet, run through, spear, skewer, spike, impale, transfix.

piercing adj 1 a piercing cry: shrill, high-pitched, loud, ear-splitting, sharp. 2 PENETRATING, probing, searching. 3 COLD, bitter, raw, biting, keen, fierce, severe, wintry, frosty, freezing. 4 PAINFUL, agonizing, excruciating, stabbing, lacerating.

piety n piousness, devoutness,

godliness, saintliness, holiness, sanctity, religion, faith, devotion, reverence.

F3 impiety, irreligion.

pig n **1** SWINE, hog, sow, boar, animal, beast, brute. **2** GLUTTON, gourmand.

pigeonhole n compartment, niche, slot, cubby-hole, cubicle, locker, box, place, section.

v compartmentalize, label, classify, sort, file, catalogue.

pigment n colour, hue, tint, dye, stain, paint, colouring, tincture.

pile¹ n stack, heap, mound, mountain, mass, accumulation, collection, assortment, hoard, stockpile.

v stack, heap, mass, amass, accumulate, build up, gather, assemble, collect, hoard, stockpile, store, load, pack, jam, crush, crowd, flock, flood, stream, rush, charge.

pile² n post, column, upright, support, bar, beam, foundation.

pile³ n nap, shag, plush, fur, hair, fuzz, down.

pilfer v steal, pinch (*infml*), nick (*infml*), knock off (*sl*), filch, lift, shoplift, rob, thieve.

pilgrim n crusader, traveller, wanderer.

pilgrimage n crusade, mission, expedition, journey, trip, tour.

pill n tablet, capsule, pellet.

pillar n **1** COLUMN, shaft, post, mast, pier, upright, pile, support, prop. **2** MAINSTAY, bastion, tower of strength.

pilot n **1** FLYER, aviator, airman. **2** NAVIGATOR, steersman, helmsman, coxswain, captain, leader, director, guide.

v fly, drive, steer, direct, control, handle, manage, operate, run, conduct, lead, guide, navigate.

adj experimental, trial, test, model.

pimple n spot, zit (*sl*), blackhead, boil, swelling.

pin v tack, nail, fix, affix, attach, join, staple, clip, fasten, secure, hold down, restrain, immobilize.

n tack, nail, screw, spike, rivet, bolt, peg, fastener, clip, staple, brooch.

pin down 1 PINPOINT, identify, determine, specify. **2** FORCE, make, press, pressurize.

pinch v **1** SQUEEZE, compress, crush, press, tweak, nip, hurt, grip, grasp. **2** (*infml*) STEAL, nick, pilfer, filch, snatch.

n **1** SQUEEZE, tweak, nip. **2** DASH, soupçon, taste, bit, speck, jot, mite. **3** EMERGENCY, crisis, predicament, difficulty, hardship, pressure, stress.

pine v long, yearn, ache, sigh, grieve, mourn, wish, desire, crave, hanker, hunger, thirst.

pinnacle n **1** PEAK, summit, top, cap, crown, crest, apex, vertex, acme, zenith, height, eminence. **2** SPIRE, steeple, turret, pyramid, cone, obelisk, needle.

pinpoint v identify, spot, distinguish, locate, place, home in on, zero in on (*infml*), pin down, determine, specify, define.

pioneer n colonist, settler, frontiersman, frontierswoman, explorer, developer, pathfinder, trail-blazer, leader, innovator, inventor, discoverer, founder.

v invent, discover, originate, create, initiate, instigate, begin, start, launch, institute, found, establish, set up, develop, open up.

pious adj **1** DEVOUT, godly, saintly,

holy, spiritual, religious, reverent, good, virtuous, righteous, moral. **2** SANCTIMONIOUS, holier-than-thou, self-righteous, goody-goody (*infml*), hypocritical.

F3 1 impious, irreligious, irreverent.

pipe *n* tube, hose, piping, tubing, pipeline, line, main, flue, duct, conduit, channel, passage, conveyor. *v* **1** CHANNEL, funnel, siphon, carry, convey, conduct, transmit, supply, deliver. **2** WHISTLE, chirp, tweet, cheep, peep, twitter, sing, warble, trill, play, sound.

piquant *adj* **1** *piquant sauce*: spicy, tangy, savoury, salty, peppery, pungent, sharp, biting, stinging. **2** LIVELY, spirited, stimulating, provocative, interesting, sparkling.

F3 1 bland, insipid. **2** dull, banal.

pique *n* annoyance, irritation, vexation, displeasure, offence, huff (*infml*), resentment, grudge.

piqued *adj* annoyed, irritated, vexed, riled, angry, displeased, offended, miffed (*infml*), peeved (*infml*), put out, resentful.

pit *n* mine, coalmine, excavation, trench, ditch, hollow, depression, indentation, dent, hole, cavity, crater, pothole, gulf, chasm, abyss.

pitch *v* **1** THROW, fling, toss, chuck (*infml*), lob, bowl, hurl, heave, sling, fire, launch, aim, direct. **2** PLUNGE, dive, plummet, drop, fall headlong, tumble, lurch, roll, wallow. **3** *pitch camp*: erect, put up, set up, place, station, settle, plant, fix.
n **1** *cricket pitch*: ground, field, playing-field, arena, stadium. **2** SOUND, tone, timbre, modulation, frequency, level. **3** GRADIENT, incline, slope, tilt, angle, degree, steepness.

piteous *adj* poignant, moving, touching, distressing, heart-rending, plaintive, mournful, sad, sorrowful, woeful, wretched, pitiful, pitiable, pathetic.

pitfall *n* danger, peril, hazard, trap, snare, stumbling-block, catch, snag, drawback, difficulty.

pith *n* importance, significance, moment, weight, value, consequence, substance, matter, marrow, meat, gist, essence, crux, nub, heart, core, kernel.

pithy *adj* succinct, concise, compact, terse, short, brief, pointed, trenchant, forceful, cogent, telling.

F3 wordy, verbose.

pitiful *adj* **1** CONTEMPTIBLE, despicable, low, mean, vile, shabby, deplorable, lamentable, woeful, inadequate, hopeless, pathetic (*infml*), insignificant, paltry, worthless. **2** PITEOUS, doleful, mournful, distressing, heart-rending, pathetic, pitiable, sad, miserable, wretched, poor, sorry.

pitiless *adj* merciless, cold-hearted, unsympathetic, unfeeling, uncaring, hard-hearted, callous, cruel, inhuman, brutal, cold-blooded, ruthless, relentless, unremitting, inexorable, harsh.

F3 merciful, compassionate, kind, gentle.

pittance *n* modicum, crumb, drop (in the ocean), chicken-feed (*infml*), peanuts (*sl*), trifle.

pitted *adj* dented, holey, potholed, pockmarked, blemished, scarred, marked, notched, indented, rough.

pity *n* **1** SYMPATHY, commiseration, regret, understanding, fellow-feeling, compassion, kindness, tenderness, mercy, forbearance. **2** *what a pity!*:

shame, misfortune, bad luck.

F3 1 cruelty, anger, scorn.

v feel sorry for, feel for, sympathize with, commiserate with, grieve for, weep for.

pivot *n* axis, hinge, axle, spindle, kingpin, linchpin, swivel, hub, focal point, centre, heart.

v **1** SWIVEL, turn, spin, revolve, rotate, swing. **2** DEPEND, rely, hinge, hang, lie.

placard *n* poster, bill, notice, sign, advertisement.

placate *v* appease, pacify, conciliate, mollify, calm, assuage, soothe, lull, quiet.

F3 anger, enrage, incense, infuriate.

place *n* **1** SITE, locale, venue, location, situation, spot, point, position, seat, space, room. **2** CITY, town, village, locality, neighbourhood, district, area, region. **3** BUILDING, property, dwelling, residence, house, flat, apartment, home.

v put, set, plant, fix, position, locate, situate, rest, settle, lay, stand, deposit, leave.

in place of instead of, in lieu of, as a replacement for, as a substitute for, as an alternative to.

out of place inappropriate, unsuitable, unfitting, unbecoming, unseemly.

take place happen, occur, come about.

placid *adj* calm, composed, unruffled, untroubled, cool, self-possessed, level-headed, imperturbable, mild, gentle, equable, even-tempered, serene, tranquil, still, quiet, peaceful, restful.

F3 excitable, agitated, disturbed.

plagiarize *v* crib, copy, reproduce, imitate, counterfeit, pirate, infringe copyright, poach, steal, lift, appropriate, borrow.

plague *n* **1** PESTILENCE, epidemic, disease, infection, contagion, infestation. **2** NUISANCE, annoyance, curse, scourge, trial, affliction, torment, calamity.

v annoy, vex, bother, disturb, trouble, distress, upset, pester, harass, hound, haunt, bedevil, afflict, torment, torture, persecute.

plain *adj* **1** *plain cookery:* ordinary, basic, simple, vanilla (*infml*), unpretentious, modest, unadorned, unelaborate, restrained. **2** OBVIOUS, evident, patent, clear, understandable, apparent, visible, unmistakable. **3** FRANK, candid, blunt, outspoken, direct, forthright, straightforward, unambiguous, plain-spoken, open, honest, truthful. **4** UNATTRACTIVE, ugly, unprepossessing, unlovely. **5** *plain fabric:* unpatterned, unvariegated, uncoloured, self-coloured.

F3 1 fancy, elaborate. **2** unclear, obscure. **3** devious, deceitful. **4** attractive, good-looking. **5** patterned.

n grassland, prairie, steppe, lowland, flat, plateau, tableland.

plaintive *adj* doleful, mournful, melancholy, wistful, sad, sorrowful, grief-stricken, piteous, heart-rending, high-pitched.

plan *n* **1** BLUEPRINT, layout, diagram, chart, map, drawing, sketch, representation, design. **2** IDEA, suggestion, proposal, proposition, project, scheme, plot, system, method, procedure, strategy, programme, schedule, scenario.

v **1** PLOT, scheme, design, invent, devise, contrive, formulate, frame, draft, outline, prepare, organize, arrange. **2** AIM, intend, propose, contemplate, envisage, foresee.

planet

> Planets within the Earth's solar system (nearest the sun shown first) are:
>
> Mercury, Venus, Earth, Mars, Jupiter, Saturn, Uranus, Neptune, Pluto.

plant n factory, works, foundry, mill, shop, yard, workshop, machinery, apparatus, equipment, gear.
v **1** SOW, seed, bury, transplant.
2 INSERT, put, place, set, fix, lodge, root, settle, found, establish.

> Plants include:
> annual, biennial, perennial, herbaceous plant, evergreen, succulent, cultivar, hybrid, house plant, pot plant; flower, herb, shrub, bush, tree, vegetable, grass, vine, weed, cereal, wild flower, air-plant, water plant, cactus, fern, moss, algae, lichen, fungus; bulb, corm, seedling, sapling, bush, climber. **see also flower; fungus; grass; shrub; tree.**

plaster n sticking-plaster, dressing, bandage, plaster of Paris, mortar, stucco.
v daub, smear, coat, cover, spread.

plastic adj soft, pliable, flexible, supple, malleable, mouldable, ductile, receptive, impressionable, manageable.
F3 rigid, inflexible.

plate n **1** DISH, platter, salver, helping, serving, portion.
2 ILLUSTRATION, picture, print, lithograph.
v coat, cover, overlay, veneer, laminate, electroplate, anodize, galvanize.

platform n **1** STAGE, podium, dais, rostrum, stand. **2** POLICY, party line, principles, tenets, manifesto, programme, objectives.

platitude n banality, commonplace, truism, cliché, chestnut.

plausible adj credible, believable, reasonable, logical, likely, possible, probable, convincing, persuasive, smooth-talking, glib.
F3 implausible, unlikely, improbable.

play v **1** AMUSE ONESELF, have fun, enjoy oneself, revel, sport, romp, frolic, caper. **2** PARTICIPATE, take part, join in, compete. **3** *France played Italy*: oppose, vie with, challenge, take on. **4** ACT, perform, portray, represent, impersonate.
F3 1 work.
n **1** FUN, amusement, entertainment, diversion, recreation, sport, game, hobby, pastime. **2** DRAMA, tragedy, comedy, farce, show, performance. **3** MOVEMENT, action, flexibility, give, leeway, latitude, margin, scope, range, room, space.
F3 1 work.

play down minimize, make light of, gloss over, underplay, understate, undervalue, underestimate.
F3 exaggerate.

play on exploit, take advantage of, turn to account, profit by, trade on, capitalize on.

play up 1 EXAGGERATE, highlight, spotlight, accentuate, emphasize, stress. **2** MISBEHAVE, malfunction, trouble, bother, annoy, hurt.

playboy n philanderer, womanizer, ladies' man, rake, libertine.

player n **1** CONTESTANT, competitor, participant, sportsman, sportswoman. **2** PERFORMER, entertainer, artiste, actor, actress, musician, instrumentalist.

playful adj sportive, frolicsome, lively, spirited, mischievous, roguish, impish, puckish, kittenish, good-natured, jesting, teasing, humorous, tongue-in-cheek.

F3 serious.

playwright n dramatist, scriptwriter, screenwriter.

plea n **1** APPEAL, petition, request, entreaty, supplication, prayer, invocation. **2** DEFENCE, justification, excuse, explanation, claim.

plead v **1** BEG, implore, beseech, entreat, appeal, petition, ask, request. **2** plead ignorance: assert, maintain, claim, allege.

pleasant adj agreeable, nice, fine, lovely, delightful, charming, likable, amiable, friendly, affable, good-humoured, cheerful, congenial, enjoyable, amusing, pleasing, gratifying, satisfying, acceptable, welcome, refreshing.

F3 unpleasant, nasty, unfriendly.

please v **1** DELIGHT, charm, captivate, entertain, amuse, cheer, gladden, humour, indulge, gratify, satisfy, content, suit. **2** WANT, wish, desire, like, prefer, choose, think fit.

F3 1 displease, annoy, anger, sadden.

pleased adj contented, satisfied, gratified, glad, happy, delighted, thrilled, euphoric.

F3 displeased, annoyed.

pleasing adj gratifying, satisfying, acceptable, good, pleasant, agreeable, nice, delightful, charming, attractive, engaging, winning.

F3 unpleasant, disagreeable.

pleasure n amusement, entertainment, recreation, fun,

enjoyment, gratification, satisfaction, contentment, happiness, joy, delight, comfort, solace.

F3 sorrow, pain, trouble, displeasure.

pleat v tuck, fold, crease, flute, crimp, gather, pucker.

pledge n **1** PROMISE, vow, word of honour, oath, bond, covenant, guarantee, warrant, assurance, undertaking. **2** DEPOSIT, security, surety, bail.

v promise, vow, swear, contract, engage, undertake, vouch, guarantee, secure.

plentiful adj ample, abundant, profuse, copious, overflowing, lavish, generous, liberal, bountiful, fruitful, productive.

F3 scarce, scanty, rare.

plenty n abundance, profusion, plethora, lots (infml), loads (infml), masses (infml), heaps (infml), piles (infml), stacks (infml), enough, sufficiency, quantity, mass, volume, fund, mine, store.

F3 scarcity, lack, want, need.

pliable adj **1** FLEXIBLE, pliant, bendable, bendy (infml), supple, lithe, malleable, plastic, yielding. **2** ADAPTABLE, accommodating, manageable, tractable, docile, compliant, biddable, persuadable, responsive, receptive, impressionable, susceptible.

F3 2 rigid, inflexible, headstrong.

plight n predicament, quandary, dilemma, extremity, trouble, difficulty, straits, state, condition, situation, circumstances, case.

plod v **1** TRUDGE, tramp, stump, lumber, plough through. **2** DRUDGE, labour, toil, grind, slog, persevere, soldier on.

plot n **1** CONSPIRACY, intrigue, machination, scheme, plan, stratagem. **2** STORY, narrative, subject, theme, storyline, thread, outline, scenario. **3** plot of land: patch, tract, area, allotment, lot, parcel.
v **1** CONSPIRE, intrigue, machinate, scheme, hatch, lay, cook up, devise, contrive, plan, project, design, draft. **2** CHART, map, mark, locate, draw, calculate.

plotter n conspirator, intriguer, machinator, schemer.

ploy n manoeuvre, stratagem, tactic, move, device, contrivance, scheme, game, trick, artifice, dodge, wile, ruse, subterfuge.

pluck n courage, bravery, spirit, mettle, nerve (infml), guts (infml), grit, backbone, fortitude, resolution, determination.
E3 cowardice.
v **1** PULL, draw, tug, snatch, pull off, remove, pick, collect, gather, harvest. **2** pluck a guitar: pick, twang, strum.

plucky adj brave, courageous, bold, daring, intrepid, heroic, valiant, spirited.
E3 cowardly, weak, feeble.

plug n **1** STOPPER, bung, cork, spigot. **2** (infml) ADVERTISEMENT, publicity, mention, puff.
v **1** STOP (UP), bung, cork, block, choke, close, seal, fill, pack, stuff. **2** (infml) ADVERTISE, publicize, promote, push, mention.

plumb adv **1** VERTICALLY, perpendicularly. **2** PRECISELY, exactly, dead, slap (infml), bang (infml).
v sound, fathom, measure, gauge, penetrate, probe, search, explore.

plummet v plunge, dive, nose-dive, descend, drop, fall, tumble.
E3 soar.

plump adj fat, obese, dumpy, tubby, stout, round, rotund, portly, chubby, podgy, fleshy, full, ample, buxom.
E3 thin, skinny.

plump for opt for, choose, select, favour, back, support.

plunder v loot, pillage, ravage, devastate, sack, raid, ransack, rifle, steal, rob, strip.
n loot, pillage, booty, swag (sl), spoils, pickings, ill-gotten gains, prize.

plunge v **1** DIVE, jump, nose-dive, swoop, dive-bomb, plummet, descend, go down, sink, drop, fall, pitch, tumble, hurtle, career, charge, dash, rush, tear. **2** IMMERSE, submerge, dip.
n dive, jump, swoop, descent, drop, fall, tumble, immersion, submersion.

ply n layer, fold, thickness, strand, sheet, leaf.

poach v steal, pilfer, appropriate, trespass, encroach, infringe.

pocket n pouch, bag, envelope, receptacle, compartment, hollow, cavity.
adj small, little, mini (infml), concise, compact, portable, miniature.
v take, appropriate, help oneself to, lift, pilfer, filch, steal, nick (infml), pinch (infml).

pod n shell, husk, case, hull.

poem

Types of poem include:
ballad, elegy, epic, haiku, idyll, lay, limerick, lyric, madrigal, nursery rhyme, ode, pastoral, roundelay, sonnet, tanka.

poet n versifier, rhymer, rhymester, lyricist, bard, minstrel.

poetic adj poetical, lyrical, moving, artistic, graceful, flowing, metrical,

rhythmical, versified, rhyming.
E3 prosaic.

poignant adj moving, touching, affecting, tender, distressing, upsetting, heartbreaking, heart-rending, piteous, pathetic, sad, painful, agonizing.

point n 1 FEATURE, attribute, aspect, facet, detail, particular, item, subject, topic. 2 what's the point?: use, purpose, motive, reason, object, intention, aim, end, goal, objective. 3 ESSENCE, crux, core, pith, gist, thrust, meaning, drift, burden. 4 PLACE, position, situation, location, site, spot. 5 MOMENT, instant, juncture, stage, time, period. 6 DOT, spot, mark, speck, full stop.
v 1 point a gun: aim, direct, train, level. 2 INDICATE, signal, show, signify, denote, designate.

point out show, indicate, draw attention to, point to, reveal, identify, specify, mention, bring up, allude to, remind.

point-blank adj direct, forthright, straightforward, plain, explicit, open, unreserved, blunt, frank, candid.
adv directly, forthrightly, straightforwardly, plainly, explicitly, openly, bluntly, frankly, candidly.

pointed adj sharp, keen, edged, barbed, cutting, incisive, trenchant, biting, penetrating, telling.

pointer n 1 ARROW, indicator, needle, hand. 2 TIP, recommendation, suggestion, hint, guide, indication, advice, warning, caution.

pointless adj useless, futile, vain, fruitless, unproductive, unprofitable, worthless, senseless, absurd, meaningless, aimless.
E3 useful, profitable, meaningful.

poise n calmness, composure, self-possession, presence of mind, coolness, equanimity, aplomb, assurance, dignity, elegance, grace, balance, equilibrium.
v balance, position, hover, hang, suspend.

poised adj 1 DIGNIFIED, graceful, calm, composed, unruffled, collected, self-possessed, cool, self-confident, assured. 2 poised for action: prepared, ready, set, waiting, expectant.

poison n toxin, venom, bane, blight, cancer, malignancy, contagion, contamination, corruption.
v infect, contaminate, pollute, taint, adulterate, corrupt, deprave, pervert, warp.

poisonous adj toxic, venomous, lethal, deadly, fatal, mortal, noxious, pernicious, malicious.

poke v prod, stab, jab, stick, thrust, push, shove, nudge, elbow, dig, butt, hit, punch.
n prod, jab, thrust, shove, nudge, dig, butt, punch.

pole [1] n bar, rod, stick, shaft, spar, upright, post, stake, mast, staff.

pole [2] n antipode, extremity, extreme, limit.

poles apart irreconcilable, worlds apart, incompatible, like chalk and cheese.

police n police force, constabulary, the Law (infml), the Bill (sl), the fuzz (sl).
v check, control, regulate, monitor, watch, observe, supervise, oversee, patrol, guard, protect, defend, keep the peace.

policeman, policewoman n officer, constable, PC, cop (sl), copper (infml), bobby (infml), bizzy (sl).

policy n **1** CODE OF PRACTICE, rules, guidelines, procedure, method, practice, custom, protocol. **2** COURSE OF ACTION, line, course, plan, programme, scheme, stance, position.

polish v **1** SHINE, brighten, smooth, rub, buff, burnish, clean, wax. **2** IMPROVE, enhance, brush up, touch up, finish, perfect, refine, cultivate. **F3 1** tarnish, dull.
n **1** a tin of polish: wax, varnish. **2** SHINE, gloss, sheen, lustre, brightness, brilliance, sparkle, smoothness, finish, glaze, veneer. **3** REFINEMENT, cultivation, class, breeding, sophistication, finesse, style, elegance, grace, poise.
F3 2 dullness. **3** clumsiness.

polished adj **1** SHINING, shiny, glossy, lustrous, gleaming, burnished, smooth, glassy, slippery.
2 FAULTLESS, flawless, impeccable, perfect, outstanding, superlative, masterly, expert, professional, skilful, accomplished, perfected. **3** REFINED, cultivated, genteel, well-bred, polite, sophisticated, urbane, suave, elegant, graceful.
F3 1 tarnished. **2** inexpert. **3** gauche.

polite adj courteous, well-mannered, respectful, civil, well-bred, refined, cultured, gentlemanly, ladylike, gracious, obliging, thoughtful, considerate, tactful, diplomatic.
F3 impolite, discourteous, rude.

politician n Member of Parliament, MP, minister, statesman, stateswoman, legislator.

politics n public affairs, civics, affairs of state, statecraft, government, diplomacy, statesmanship, political science.

Terms used in politics include: alliance, apartheid, ballot, bill, blockade, cabinet, campaign, coalition, constitution, council, coup d'état, détente, election, electoral register, ethnic cleansing, general election, glasnost, go to the country, green paper, Hansard, left wing, lobby, local government, majority, mandate, manifesto, nationalization, parliament, party, party line, perestroika, prime minister's question time, privatization, propaganda, proportional representation, rainbow coalition, referendum, right wing, sanction, shadow cabinet, sovereignty, state, summit, summit conference, term of office, trade union, veto, vote, welfare state, whip, three-line whip, white paper.

Political ideologies include: absolutism, anarchism, authoritarianism, Bolshevism, Christian democracy, collectivism, communism, conservatism, democracy, egalitarianism, fascism, federalism, holism, imperialism, individualism, liberalism, Maoism, Marxism, nationalism, Nazism, neocolonialism, neo-fascism, neo-Nazism, pluralism, republicanism, social democracy, socialism, syndicalism, theocracy, totalitarianism, unilateralism, Trotskyism, Whiggism. see also **government**; **parliament**.

poll n ballot, vote, voting, plebiscite, referendum, straw-poll, sampling, canvass, opinion poll, survey, census, count, tally.

pollute v contaminate, infect, poison, taint, adulterate, debase, corrupt, dirty, foul, soil, defile, sully, stain, mar, spoil.

pollution n impurity, contamination, infection, taint, adulteration, corruption, dirtiness, foulness, defilement.

E3 purification, purity, cleanness.

pomp n ceremony, ceremonial, ritual, solemnity, formality, ceremoniousness, state, grandeur, splendour, magnificence, pageantry, show, display, parade, ostentation, flourish.

E3 austerity, simplicity.

pompous adj self-important, arrogant, grandiose, supercilious, overbearing, imperious, magisterial, bombastic, high-flown, overblown, windy, affected, pretentious, ostentatious.

E3 unassuming, modest, simple, unaffected.

pool¹ n puddle, pond, lake, mere, tarn, watering-hole, paddling-pool, swimming-pool.

pool² n **1** FUND, reserve, accumulation, bank, kitty, purse, pot, jackpot. **2** SYNDICATE, cartel, ring, combine, consortium, collective, group, team.

v contribute, chip in (infml), combine, amalgamate, merge, share, muck in (infml).

poor adj **1** IMPOVERISHED, poverty-stricken, badly off, hard-up, broke (infml), stony-broke (sl), skint (sl), bankrupt, penniless, destitute, miserable, wretched, distressed, straitened, needy, lacking, deficient, insufficient, scanty, skimpy, meagre, sparse, depleted, exhausted. **2** BAD, substandard, unsatisfactory, inferior, mediocre, below par, low-grade,

second-rate, third-rate, shoddy, imperfect, faulty, weak, feeble, pathetic (infml), sorry, worthless, fruitless. **3** UNFORTUNATE, unlucky, luckless, ill-fated, unhappy, miserable, pathetic, pitiable, pitiful.

E3 1 rich, wealthy, affluent. **2** superior, impressive. **3** fortunate, lucky.

poorly adj ill, sick, unwell, indisposed, ailing, sickly, off colour, below par, out of sorts (infml), under the weather (infml), seedy, groggy, rotten (infml).

E3 well, healthy.

pop v burst, explode, go off, bang, crack, snap.

n bang, crack, snap, burst, explosion.

popular adj well-liked, favourite, liked, favoured, approved, in demand, sought-after, fashionable, modish, trendy (infml), prevailing, current, accepted, conventional, standard, stock, common, prevalent, widespread, universal, general, household, famous, well-known, celebrated, idolized.

E3 unpopular.

popularize v spread, propagate, universalize, democratize, simplify.

popularly adv commonly, widely, universally, generally, usually, customarily, conventionally, traditionally.

populate v people, occupy, settle, colonize, inhabit, live in, overrun.

population n inhabitants, natives, residents, citizens, occupants, community, society, people, folk.

populous adj crowded, packed, swarming, teeming, crawling, overpopulated.

E3 deserted.

pornographic *adj* obscene, indecent, dirty, filthy, blue, risqué, bawdy, coarse, gross, lewd, erotic, titillating.

porous *adj* permeable, pervious, penetrable, absorbent, spongy, honeycombed, pitted.
F3 impermeable, impervious.

portable *adj* movable, transportable, compact, lightweight, manageable, handy, convenient.
F3 fixed, immovable.

porter[1] *n* bearer, carrier, baggage-attendant, baggage-handler.

porter[2] *n* doorman, commissionaire, door-keeper, gatekeeper, janitor, caretaker, concierge.

portion *n* share, allocation, allotment, parcel, allowance, ration, quota, measure, part, section, division, fraction, percentage, bit, fragment, morsel, piece, segment, slice, serving, helping.

portly *adj* stout, corpulent, rotund, round, fat, plump, obese, overweight, heavy, large.
F3 slim, thin, slight.

portrait *n* picture, painting, drawing, sketch, caricature, miniature, icon, photograph, likeness, image, representation, vignette, profile, characterization, description, depiction, portrayal.

portray *v* draw, sketch, paint, illustrate, picture, represent, depict, describe, evoke, play, impersonate, characterize, personify.

portrayal *n* representation, characterization, depiction, description, evocation, presentation, performance, interpretation, rendering.

pose *v* **1** MODEL, sit, position.
2 PRETEND, feign, affect, put on an act, masquerade, pass oneself off, impersonate. **3** *pose a question*: set, put forward, submit, present.
n **1** POSITION, stance, air, bearing, posture, attitude. **2** PRETENCE, sham, affectation, façade, front, masquerade, role, act.

poser[1] *n* puzzle, riddle, conundrum, brain-teaser, mystery, enigma, problem, vexed question.

poser[2] *n* poseur, posturer, attitudinizer, exhibitionist, show-off, pseud (*infml*), phoney (*infml*).

posh *adj* smart, stylish, fashionable, high-class, upper-class, la-di-da (*sl*), grand, luxurious, lavish, swanky (*infml*), luxury, de luxe, up-market, exclusive, select, classy (*infml*), swish (*infml*).
F3 inferior, cheap.

position *n* **1** PLACE, situation, location, site, spot, point. **2** POSTURE, stance, pose, arrangement, disposition. **3** JOB, post, occupation, employment, office, duty, function, role. **4** RANK, grade, level, status, standing. **5** OPINION, point of view, belief, view, outlook, viewpoint, standpoint, stand.
v put, place, set, fix, stand, arrange, dispose, lay out, deploy, station, locate, situate, site.

positive *adj* **1** SURE, certain, convinced, confident, assured.
2 *positive criticism*: helpful, constructive, practical, useful, optimistic, hopeful, promising.
3 DEFINITE, decisive, conclusive, clear, unmistakable, explicit, unequivocal, express, firm, emphatic, categorical, undeniable, irrefutable, indisputable,

incontrovertible. **4** ABSOLUTE, utter, sheer, complete, perfect.

F3 **1** uncertain. **2** negative. **3** indefinite, vague.

possess v **1** OWN, have, hold, enjoy, be endowed with. **2** SEIZE, take, obtain, acquire, take over, occupy, control, dominate, bewitch, haunt.

possession n ownership, title, tenure, occupation, custody, control, hold, grip.

possessions n belongings, property, things, paraphernalia, effects, goods, chattels, movables, assets, estate, wealth, riches.

possessive adj selfish, clinging, overprotective, domineering, dominating, jealous, covetous, acquisitive, grasping.

F3 unselfish, sharing.

possibility n likelihood, probability, odds, chance, risk, danger, hope, prospect, potentiality, conceivability, practicability, feasibility.

F3 impossibility, impracticability.

possible adj potential, promising, likely, probable, imaginable, conceivable, practicable, feasible, viable, tenable, workable, achievable, attainable, accomplishable, realizable.

F3 impossible, unthinkable, impracticable, unattainable.

possibly adv perhaps, maybe, hopefully (infml), by any means, at all, by any chance.

post[1] n pole, stake, picket, pale, pillar, column, shaft, support, baluster, upright, stanchion, strut, leg. v display, stick up, pin up, advertise, publicize, announce, make known, report, publish.

post[2] n office, job, employment, position, situation, place, vacancy, appointment, assignment, station, beat.

v station, locate, situate, position, place, put, appoint, assign, second, transfer, move, send.

post[3] n mail, letters, e-mail, dispatch, collection, delivery.

v mail, e-mail, send, dispatch, transmit.

poster n notice, bill, sign, placard, sticker, advertisement, flyer, announcement.

posterity n descendants, successors, progeny, issue, offspring, children.

postpone v put off, defer, put back, hold over, delay, adjourn, suspend, shelve, pigeonhole, freeze, put on ice.

F3 advance, forward.

postscript n PS (infml), addition, supplement, afterthought, addendum, codicil, appendix, afterword, epilogue.

F3 introduction, prologue.

postulate v theorize, hypothesize, suppose, assume, propose, advance, lay down, stipulate.

posture n position, stance, pose, attitude, disposition, bearing, carriage, deportment.

posy n bouquet, spray, buttonhole, corsage.

pot n receptacle, vessel, teapot, coffee pot, urn, jar, vase, bowl, basin, pan, cauldron, crucible.

potent adj powerful, mighty, strong, intoxicating, pungent, effective, impressive, cogent, convincing, persuasive, compelling, forceful, dynamic, vigorous, authoritative, commanding,

dominant, influential, overpowering.
F3 impotent, weak.

potential adj possible, likely,
probable, prospective, future,
aspiring, would-be, promising,
budding, embryonic, undeveloped,
dormant, latent, hidden, concealed,
unrealized.
n possibility, ability, capability,
capacity, aptitude, talent, powers,
resources.

potion n mixture, concoction, brew,
beverage, drink, draught, dose,
medicine, tonic, elixir.

potpourri n medley, mixture,
jumble, hotchpotch, miscellany,
collection.

potter v tinker, fiddle, mess about
(infml), dabble, loiter, fritter.

pottery n ceramics, crockery, china,
porcelain.

Terms used in pottery include:
basalt, blanc-de-chine, celadon,
china clay, cloisonné, crackleware,
crazing, creamware, delft, earthenware, enamel, faïence, fairing, figure, firing, flambé, flatback, glaze,
ground, ironstone, jasper, kiln, lustre, majolica, maker's mark, mono-
gram, overglaze, raku, saggar,
sgraffito, slip, slip-cast, sponge-
ware, Staffordshire, stoneware, terracotta, underglaze, willow pattern.

pounce v fall on, dive on, swoop,
drop, attack, strike, ambush, spring,
jump, leap, snatch, grab.

pound[1] v **1** STRIKE, thump, beat,
drum, pelt, hammer, batter, bang, bash,
smash. **2** PULVERIZE, powder, grind,
mash, crush. **3** his heart was pounding:
throb, pulsate, palpitate, thump, thud.

pound[2] n enclosure, compound,
corral, yard, pen, fold.

pour v **1** pour a drink: serve, decant,
tip. **2** SPILL, issue, discharge, flow,
stream, run, rush, spout, spew, gush,
cascade, crowd, throng, swarm.

pout v scowl, glower, grimace, pull a
face, sulk, mope.
F3 grin, smile.
n scowl, glower, grimace, long face.
F3 grin, smile.

poverty n poorness,
impoverishment, insolvency,
bankruptcy, pennilessness, penury,
destitution, distress, hardship,
privation, need, necessity, want, lack,
deficiency, shortage, inadequacy,
insufficiency, depletion, scarcity,
meagreness, paucity, dearth.
F3 wealth, richness, affluence,
plenty.

powdery adj dusty, sandy, grainy,
granular, powdered, pulverized,
ground, fine, loose, dry, crumbly,
friable, chalky.

power n **1** COMMAND, authority,
sovereignty, rule, dominion, control,
influence. **2** RIGHT, privilege,
prerogative, authorization, warrant.
3 POTENCY, strength, intensity, force,
vigour, energy. **4** ABILITY, capability,
capacity, potential, faculty,
competence.
F3 **1** subjection. **3** weakness.
4 inability.

powerful adj dominant, prevailing,
leading, influential, high-powered,
authoritative, commanding, potent,
effective, strong, mighty, robust,
muscular, energetic, forceful, telling,
impressive, convincing, persuasive,
compelling, winning, overwhelming.
F3 impotent, ineffective, weak.

powerless adj impotent, incapable,
ineffective, weak, feeble, frail, infirm,

incapacitated, disabled, paralysed, helpless, vulnerable, defenceless, unarmed.
F3 powerful, potent, able.

practicable adj possible, feasible, performable, achievable, attainable, viable, workable, practical, realistic.
F3 impracticable.

practical adj 1 REALISTIC, sensible, commonsense, practicable, workable, feasible, down-to-earth, matter-of-fact, pragmatic, hardnosed (infml), hard-headed, businesslike, experienced, trained, qualified, skilled, accomplished, proficient, hands on, applied. 2 USEFUL, handy, serviceable, utilitarian, functional, working, everyday, ordinary.
F3 1 impractical, unskilled, theoretical.

practically adv 1 ALMOST, nearly, well-nigh, virtually, pretty well, all but, just about, in principle, in effect, essentially, fundamentally, to all intents and purposes.
2 REALISTICALLY, sensibly, reasonably, rationally, pragmatically.

practice n 1 CUSTOM, tradition, convention, usage, habit, routine, shtick (sl), way, method, system, procedure, policy. 2 REHEARSAL, run-through, dry run, dummy run, try-out, training, drill, exercise, work-out, study, experience. 3 in practice: effect, reality, actuality, action, operation, performance, use, application.
F3 3 theory, principle.

practise v 1 DO, perform, execute, implement, carry out, apply, put into practice, follow, pursue, engage in, undertake. 2 REHEARSE, run through, repeat, drill, exercise, train, study, perfect.

practised adj experienced, seasoned, veteran, trained, qualified, accomplished, skilled, versed, knowledgeable, able, proficient, expert, masterly, consummate, finished.
F3 unpractised, inexperienced, inexpert.

pragmatic adj practical, realistic, sensible, matter-of-fact, businesslike, efficient, hard-headed, hardnosed (infml), unsentimental.
F3 unrealistic, idealistic, romantic.

praise n approval, admiration, commendation, congratulation, compliment, flattery, adulation, eulogy, applause, ovation, cheering, acclaim, recognition, testimonial, tribute, accolade, homage, honour, glory, worship, adoration, devotion, thanksgiving.
F3 criticism, revilement.
v commend, congratulate, admire, compliment, flatter, talk up (infml), eulogize, wax lyrical, rave over (infml), extol, promote, applaud, cheer, acclaim, hail, recognize, acknowledge, pay tribute to, honour, laud, glorify, magnify, exalt, worship, adore, bless.
F3 criticize, revile, talk down (infml).

praiseworthy adj commendable, fine, excellent, admirable, worthy, deserving, honourable, reputable, estimable, sterling.
F3 blameworthy, dishonourable, ignoble.

prank n trick, practical joke, joke, stunt, caper, frolic, lark, antic, escapade.

pray v invoke, call on, supplicate, entreat, implore, plead, beg, beseech, petition, ask, request, crave, solicit.

prayer n collect, litany, devotion, communion, invocation, supplication, entreaty, plea, appeal, petition, request.

preach v address, lecture, harangue, pontificate, sermonize, evangelize, moralize, exhort, urge, advocate.

precarious adj unsafe, dangerous, treacherous, risky, hazardous, chancy, uncertain, unsure, dubious, doubtful, unpredictable, unreliable, unsteady, unstable, shaky, wobbly, insecure, vulnerable.
E3 safe, certain, stable, secure.

precaution n safeguard, security, protection, insurance, providence, forethought, caution, prudence, foresight, anticipation, preparation, provision.

precautionary adj safety, protective, preventive, provident, cautious, prudent, judicious, preparatory, preliminary.

precede v come before, lead, come first, go before, take precedence, introduce, herald, usher in.
E3 follow, succeed.

precedence n priority, preference, pride of place, superiority, supremacy, pre-eminence, lead, first place, seniority, rank.

precedent n example, instance, pattern, model, standard, criterion.

precinct n 1 ZONE, area, district, quarter, sector, division, section. 2 BOUNDARY, limit, bound, confine.

precious adj 1 VALUED, treasured, prized, cherished, beloved, dearest, darling, favourite, loved, adored, idolized. 2 VALUABLE, expensive, costly, dear, priceless, inestimable, rare, choice, fine.

precipitate v hasten, hurry, speed, accelerate, quicken, expedite, advance, further, bring on, induce, trigger, cause, occasion.
adj sudden, unexpected, abrupt, quick, swift, rapid, brief, hasty, hurried, headlong, breakneck, frantic, violent, impatient, hot-headed, impetuous, impulsive, rash, reckless, heedless, indiscreet.
E3 careful.

precipitous adj steep, sheer, perpendicular, vertical, high.
E3 gradual.

precise adj exact, accurate, right, punctilious, correct, factual, faithful, authentic, literal, word-for-word, express, definite, explicit, unequivocal, unambiguous, clear-cut, distinct, detailed, blow-by-blow, minute, nice, particular, specific, fixed, rigid, strict, careful, meticulous, scrupulous, fastidious.
E3 imprecise, inexact, ambiguous, careless.

precisely adv exactly, absolutely, just so, accurately, correctly, literally, verbatim, word for word, strictly, minutely, clearly, distinctly.

precision n exactness, accuracy, correctness, faithfulness, explicitness, distinctness, detail, particularity, rigour, care, meticulousness, scrupulousness, neatness.
E3 imprecision, inaccuracy.

precocious adj forward, ahead, advanced, early, premature, mature, developed, gifted, clever, bright, smart, quick, fast.
E3 backward.

preconceive v presuppose, presume, assume, anticipate, project, imagine, conceive, envisage, expect, visualize, picture.

preconception n presupposition, presumption, assumption, conjecture, anticipation, expectation, prejudgment, bias, prejudice.

precondition n condition, stipulation, requirement, prerequisite, essential, necessity, must.

precursor n antecedent, forerunner, sign, indication, herald, harbinger, messenger, usher, pioneer, trail-blazer.

F3 follower, successor.

predecessor n ancestor, forefather, forebear, antecedent, forerunner, precursor.

F3 successor, descendant.

predestination n destiny, fate, lot, doom, predetermination, foreordination.

predetermined adj **1** PREDESTINED, destined, fated, doomed, ordained, foreordained. **2** PREARRANGED, arranged, agreed, fixed, set.

predicament n situation, plight, trouble, mess, fix, spot (infml), quandary, dilemma, impasse, crisis, emergency.

predict v foretell, prophesy, foresee, forecast, prognosticate, project.

predictable adj foreseeable, expected, anticipated, likely, probable, imaginable, foreseen, foregone, certain, sure, reliable, dependable.

F3 unpredictable, uncertain.

prediction n prophecy, forecast, prognosis, augury, divination, fortune-telling, soothsaying.

predispose v dispose, incline, prompt, induce, make, sway, influence, affect, bias, prejudice.

predominant adj dominant,

prevailing, preponderant, chief, main, principal, primary, capital, paramount, supreme, sovereign, ruling, controlling, leading, powerful, potent, prime, important, influential, forceful, strong.

F3 minor, lesser, weak.

pre-eminent adj supreme, unsurpassed, unrivalled, unequalled, unmatched, matchless, incomparable, inimitable, chief, foremost, leading, eminent, distinguished, renowned, famous, prominent, outstanding, exceptional, excellent, superlative, transcendent, superior.

F3 inferior, unknown.

preface n foreword, introduction, preamble, prologue, prelude, preliminaries.

F3 epilogue, postscript.

v precede, prefix, lead up to, introduce, launch, open, begin, start.

F3 end, finish, complete.

prefer v favour, like better, would rather, would sooner, want, wish, desire, choose, select, pick, opt for, go for, plump for, single out, advocate, recommend, back, support, fancy, elect, adopt.

F3 reject.

preferable adj better, superior, nicer, preferred, favoured, chosen, desirable, advantageous, advisable, recommended.

F3 inferior, undesirable.

preference n **1** FAVOURITE, first choice, choice, pick, selection, option, wish, desire. **2** LIKING, fancy, inclination, predilection, partiality, favouritism, preferential treatment.

preferential adj better, superior, favoured, privileged, special,

favourable, advantageous.
F3 equal.

pregnant *adj* **1** *a pregnant woman*:
expectant, expecting, with child (*fml*),
in the club (*sl*), up the spout (*sl*).
2 *a pregnant pause*: meaningful,
significant, eloquent, expressive,
suggestive, charged, loaded, full.

prejudice *n* **1** BIAS, partiality,
partisanship, discrimination,
unfairness, injustice, intolerance,
narrow-mindedness, bigotry,
chauvinism, racism, sexism. **2** HARM,
damage, impairment, hurt, injury,
detriment, disadvantage, loss, ruin.
F3 1 fairness, tolerance. **2** benefit,
advantage.
v **1** BIAS, predispose, incline, sway,
influence, condition, colour, slant,
distort, load, weight. **2** HARM, damage,
impair, hinder, undermine, hurt,
injure, mar, spoil, ruin, wreck.
F3 2 benefit, help, advance.

prejudiced *adj* biased, partial,
predisposed, subjective, partisan,
one-sided, discriminatory, unfair,
unjust, loaded, weighted, intolerant,
narrow-minded, bigoted, chauvinist,
racist, sexist, jaundiced, distorted,
warped, influenced, conditioned.
F3 impartial, fair, tolerant.

prejudicial *adj* harmful, damaging,
hurtful, injurious, detrimental,
disadvantageous, unfavourable,
inimical.
F3 beneficial, advantageous.

preliminaries *n* preparation,
groundwork, foundations, basics,
rudiments, formalities, introduction,
preface, prelude, opening, beginning,
start.

preliminary *adj* preparatory, prior,
advance, exploratory, experimental,

trial, test, pilot, early, earliest, first,
initial, primary, qualifying, inaugural,
introductory, opening.
F3 final, closing.

prelude *n* overture, introduction,
preface, foreword, preamble,
prologue, opening, opener,
preliminary, preparation, beginning,
start, commencement, precursor,
curtain raiser.
F3 finale, epilogue.

premature *adj* early, immature,
green, unripe, embryonic, half-
formed, incomplete, undeveloped,
abortive, hasty, ill-considered,
rash, untimely, inopportune, ill-
timed.
F3 late, tardy.

premeditated *adj* planned,
intended, intentional, deliberate,
wilful, conscious, cold-blooded,
calculated, considered, contrived,
preplanned, prearranged,
predetermined.
F3 unpremeditated, spontaneous.

première *n* first performance,
opening, opening night, first night,
début.

premise *n* proposition, statement,
assertion, postulate, thesis, argument,
basis, supposition, hypothesis,
presupposition, assumption.

premises *n* building, property,
establishment, office, grounds, estate,
site, place.

premonition *n* presentiment,
feeling, intuition, hunch, idea,
suspicion, foreboding, misgiving, fear,
apprehension, anxiety, worry,
warning, omen, sign.

preoccupation *n* **1** OBSESSION,
fixation, hang-up (*infml*), concern,
interest, enthusiasm, hobby-horse.

2 DISTRACTION, absent-mindedness, reverie, obliviousness, oblivion.

preoccupied adj **1** OBSESSED, intent, immersed, engrossed, engaged, taken up, wrapped up, involved. **2** DISTRACTED, abstracted, absent-minded, daydreaming, absorbed, faraway, heedless, oblivious, pensive.

preparation n **1** READINESS, provision, precaution, safeguard, foundation, groundwork, spadework, basics, rudiments, preliminaries, plans, arrangements. **2** MIXTURE, compound, concoction, potion, medicine, lotion, application.

preparatory adj preliminary, introductory, opening, initial, primary, basic, fundamental, rudimentary, elementary.

prepare v **1** GET READY, warm up, train, coach, study, make ready, adapt, adjust, plan, organize, arrange, pave the way. **2** prepare a meal: make, produce, construct, assemble, concoct, contrive, devise, draft, draw up, compose. **3** PROVIDE, supply, equip, fit out, rig out.

prepare oneself brace oneself, steel oneself, gird oneself, fortify oneself.

prepared adj ready, waiting, set, fit, inclined, disposed, willing, planned, organized, arranged.
E3 unprepared, unready.

preponderant adj greater, larger, superior, predominant, prevailing, overriding, overruling, controlling, foremost, important, significant.

preposterous adj incredible, unbelievable, absurd, ridiculous, ludicrous, foolish, crazy, nonsensical, unreasonable, monstrous, shocking, outrageous, intolerable,

unthinkable, impossible.
E3 sensible, reasonable, acceptable.

prerequisite n precondition, condition, proviso, qualification, requisite, requirement, imperative, necessity, essential, must.
E3 extra.

prescribe v ordain, decree, dictate, rule, command, order, require, direct, assign, specify, stipulate, lay down, set, appoint, impose, fix, define, limit.

prescription n **1** INSTRUCTION, direction, formula. **2** MEDICINE, drug, preparation, mixture, remedy, treatment.

presence n **1** ATTENDANCE, company, occupancy, residence, existence. **2** AURA, air, demeanour, bearing, carriage, appearance, poise, self-assurance, personality, charisma. **3** NEARNESS, closeness, proximity, vicinity.
E3 1 absence. **3** remoteness.

present [1] adj **1** ATTENDING, here, there, near, at hand, to hand, available, ready. **2** at the present time: current, contemporary, present-day, immediate, instant, existent, existing.
E3 absent. **2** past, out-of-date.

present [2] v **1** SHOW, display, exhibit, demonstrate, mount, stage, put on, introduce, announce. **2** AWARD, confer, bestow, grant, give, donate, hand over, entrust, extend, hold out, offer, tender, submit.

present [3] n gift, prezzie (infml), offering, donation, grant, endowment, benefaction, bounty, largess, gratuity, tip, favour.

presentable adj neat, tidy, clean, respectable, decent, proper, suitable, acceptable, satisfactory, tolerable.
E3 unpresentable, untidy, shabby.

presentation n 1 SHOW, performance, production, staging, representation, display, exhibition, demonstration, talk, delivery, appearance, arrangement. 2 AWARD, conferral, bestowal, investiture.

present-day adj current, present, existing, living, contemporary, modern, up-to-date, fashionable. F3 past, future.

presently adv 1 SOON, shortly, in a minute, before long, by and by. 2 CURRENTLY, at present, now.

preserve v 1 PROTECT, safeguard, guard, defend, shield, shelter, care for, maintain, uphold, sustain, continue, perpetuate, keep, retain, conserve, save, store. 2 preserve food: bottle, tin, can, pickle, salt, cure, dry. F3 1 destroy, ruin. n 1 home-made preserves: conserve, jam, marmalade, jelly, pickle. 2 DOMAIN, realm, sphere, area, field, speciality. 3 RESERVATION, sanctuary, game reserve, safari park.

preside v chair, officiate, conduct, direct, manage, administer, control, run, head, lead, govern, rule.

press v 1 CRUSH, squash, squeeze, compress, stuff, cram, crowd, push, depress. 2 press clothes: iron, smooth, flatten. 3 HUG, embrace, clasp, squeeze. 4 URGE, plead, petition, campaign, demand, insist on, compel, constrain, force, pressure, pressurize, harass. n 1 CROWD, throng, multitude, mob, horde, swarm, pack, crush, push. 2 JOURNALISTS, reporters, correspondents, the media, newspapers, papers, Fleet Street, fourth estate.

pressing adj urgent, high-priority, burning, crucial, vital, essential,

imperative, serious, important. F3 unimportant, trivial.

pressure n 1 FORCE, power, load, burden, weight, heaviness, compression, squeezing, stress, strain. 2 DIFFICULTY, problem, demand, constraint, obligation, urgency.

pressurize v force, compel, constrain, oblige, drive, bulldoze, coerce, press, pressure, lean on (infml), browbeat, bully.

prestige n status, reputation, standing, stature, eminence, distinction, esteem, regard, importance, authority, influence, fame, renown, kudos, credit, honour. F3 humbleness, unimportance.

prestigious adj esteemed, respected, reputable, important, influential, great, eminent, prominent, illustrious, renowned, celebrated, exalted, imposing, impressive, up-market. F3 humble, modest.

presume v 1 ASSUME, take it, think, believe, suppose, surmise, infer, presuppose, take for granted, count on, rely on, depend on, bank on, trust. 2 presume to criticize: dare, make so bold, go so far, venture, undertake.

presumption n 1 ASSUMPTION, belief, opinion, hypothesis, presupposition, supposition, surmise, conjecture, guess, likelihood, probability. 2 PRESUMPTUOUSNESS, boldness, audacity, impertinence, cheek (infml), nerve (infml), impudence, insolence, forwardness, assurance. F3 2 humility.

presumptuous adj bold, audacious, impertinent, impudent, insolent, over-familiar, forward, pushy, arrogant, over-confident, conceited.

F3 humble, modest.

pretence n show, display, appearance, cover, front, façade, veneer, cloak, veil, mask, guise, feigning, faking, simulation, deception, trickery, wile, ruse, excuse, pretext, bluff, falsehood, deceit, fabrication, invention, make-believe, charade, acting, play-acting, posturing, posing, affectation, pretension, pretentiousness.

F3 honesty, openness.

pretend v 1 AFFECT, put on, assume, feign, sham, counterfeit, fake, simulate, bluff, impersonate, pass oneself off, act, play-act, mime, go through the motions. **2** CLAIM, allege, profess, purport. **3** IMAGINE, make believe, suppose.

pretender n claimant, aspirant, candidate.

pretension n 1 PRETENTIOUSNESS, pomposity, self-importance, airs, conceit, vanity, snobbishness, affectation, pretence, show, showiness, ostentation. **2** CLAIM, profession, demand, aspiration, ambition.

F3 1 modesty, humility, simplicity.

pretentious adj pompous, self-important, conceited, immodest, snobbish, affected, mannered, showy, ostentatious, extravagant, over-the-top, exaggerated, magniloquent, high-sounding, inflated, grandiose, ambitious, overambitious.

F3 modest, humble, simple, straightforward.

pretext n excuse, ploy, ruse, cover, cloak, mask, guise,

semblance, appearance, pretence, show.

pretty adj attractive, good-looking, beautiful, fair, lovely, bonny, cute, winsome, appealing, charming, dainty, graceful, elegant, fine, delicate, nice.

F3 plain, unattractive, ugly.

adv fairly, somewhat, rather, quite, reasonably, moderately, tolerably.

prevail v 1 PREDOMINATE, preponderate, abound. **2** WIN, triumph, succeed, overcome, overrule, reign, rule.

F3 2 lose.

prevail upon persuade, talk into, prompt, induce, incline, sway, influence, convince, win over.

prevailing adj predominant, preponderant, main, principal, dominant, controlling, powerful, compelling, influential, reigning, ruling, current, fashionable, popular, mainstream, accepted, established, set, usual, customary, common, prevalent, widespread.

F3 minor, subordinate.

prevalent adj widespread, extensive, rampant, rife, frequent, general, customary, usual, universal, ubiquitous, common, everyday, popular, current, prevailing.

F3 uncommon, rare.

prevaricate v hedge, equivocate, quibble, cavil, dodge, evade, shift, shuffle, lie, deceive.

prevent v stop, avert, avoid, head off, ward off, stave off, intercept, forestall, anticipate, frustrate, thwart, check, restrain, inhibit, hinder, hamper, impede, obstruct, block, bar.

F3 cause, help, foster, encourage, allow.

prevention *n* avoidance, frustration, check, hindrance, impediment, obstruction, obstacle, bar, elimination, precaution, safeguard, deterrence.
F3 cause, help.

preventive *adj* preventative, anticipatory, pre-emptive, inhibitory, obstructive, precautionary, protective, counteractive, deterrent.
F3 causative.

previous *adj* preceding, foregoing, earlier, prior, past, former, ex-, one-time, sometime, erstwhile.
F3 following, subsequent, later.

previously *adv* formerly, once, earlier, before, beforehand.
F3 later.

prey *n* quarry, victim, game, kill.
prey on 1 HUNT, kill, devour, feed on, live off, exploit. **2** *prey on one's mind*: haunt, trouble, distress, worry, burden, weigh down, oppress.

price *n* value, worth, cost, expense, outlay, expenditure, fee, charge, levy, toll, rate, bill, assessment, valuation, estimate, quotation, figure, amount, sum, payment, reward, penalty, forfeit, sacrifice, consequences.
v value, rate, cost, evaluate, assess, estimate.

priceless *adj* 1 INVALUABLE, inestimable, incalculable, expensive, costly, dear, precious, valuable, prized, treasured, irreplaceable.
2 (*infml*) FUNNY, amusing, comic, hilarious, riotous, side-splitting, killing (*infml*), rich (*infml*).
F3 1 cheap, run-of-the-mill.

prick *v* pierce, puncture, perforate, punch, jab, stab, sting, bite, prickle, itch, tingle.
n puncture, perforation, pinhole, stab, pang, twinge, sting, bite.

prickle *n* thorn, spine, barb, spur, point, spike, needle.
v tingle, itch, smart, sting, prick.

prickly *adj* 1 THORNY, brambly, spiny, barbed, spiky, bristly, rough, scratchy.
2 IRRITABLE, edgy, touchy, grumpy, short-tempered.
F3 1 smooth. **2** relaxed, easy-going (*infml*), laid-back (*infml*).

pride *n* 1 CONCEIT, vanity, egotism, bigheadedness, boastfulness, smugness, arrogance, self-importance, presumption, haughtiness, superciliousness, snobbery, pretentiousness. **2** DIGNITY, self-respect, self-esteem, honour. **3** SATISFACTION, gratification, pleasure, delight.
F3 1 humility, modesty. **2** shame.

priest *n* minister, vicar, padre, father, man of God, woman of God, man of the cloth, clergywoman, clergyman, churchman, churchwoman.

priggish *adj* smug, self-righteous, goody-goody (*infml*), sanctimonious, holier-than-thou, puritanical, prim, prudish, narrow-minded.
F3 broad-minded.

prim *adj* prudish, strait-laced, formal, demure, proper, priggish, prissy, fussy, particular, precise, fastidious.
F3 informed, relaxed, easy-going (*infml*), laid-back (*infml*).

primarily *adv* chiefly, principally, mainly, mostly, basically, fundamentally, especially, particularly, essentially.

primary *adj* 1 FIRST, earliest, original, initial, introductory, beginning, basic, fundamental, essential, radical, rudimentary, elementary, simple. **2** CHIEF, principal, main, dominant, leading, foremost, supreme, cardinal, capital, paramount, greatest, highest, ultimate.

F3 2 secondary, subsidiary, minor.

prime *adj* best, choice, select, quality, first-class, first-rate, excellent, top, supreme, pre-eminent, superior, senior, leading, ruling, chief, principal, main, predominant, primary.

F3 second-rate, secondary.

n height, peak, zenith, heyday, flower, bloom, maturity, perfection.

primeval *adj* earliest, first, original, primordial, early, old, ancient, prehistoric, primitive, instinctive.

F3 modern.

primitive *adj* **1** CRUDE, rough, unsophisticated, uncivilized, barbarian, savage. **2** EARLY, elementary, rudimentary, primary, first, original, earliest.

F3 1 advanced, sophisticated, civilized.

princely *adj* **1** SOVEREIGN, imperial, royal, regal, majestic, stately, grand, noble. **2** *princely sum*: generous, liberal, lavish, sumptuous, magnificent, handsome.

principal *adj* main, chief, key, essential, cardinal, primary, first, foremost, leading, dominant, prime, paramount, pre-eminent, supreme, highest.

F3 minor, subsidiary, lesser, least.

n head, head teacher, headmaster, headmistress, chief, leader, boss, director, manager, superintendent.

principally *adv* mainly, mostly, chiefly, primarily, predominantly, above all, particularly, especially.

principle *n* **1** RULE, formula, law, canon, axiom, dictum, precept, maxim, truth, tenet, doctrine, creed, dogma, code, standard, criterion, proposition, fundamental, essential. **2** *a man of principle*: honour, integrity, rectitude, uprightness, virtue, decency, morality, morals, ethics, standards, scruples, conscience.

print *v* mark, stamp, imprint, impress, engrave, copy, reproduce, run off, publish, issue.

n **1** LETTERS, characters, lettering, type, typescript, typeface, fount. **2** MARK, impression, fingerprint, footprint. **3** COPY, reproduction, picture, engraving, lithograph, photograph, photo.

prior *adj* earlier, preceding, foregoing, previous, former.

F3 later.

prior to before, preceding, earlier than.

F3 after, following.

priority *n* right of way, precedence, seniority, rank, superiority, pre-eminence, supremacy, the lead, first place, urgency.

F3 inferiority.

prison *n* jail, nick (*sl*), clink (*sl*), cooler (*sl*), penitentiary, cell, lock-up, cage, dungeon, imprisonment, confinement, detention, custody.

prisoner *n* captive, hostage, convict, con (*sl*), jail-bird (*infml*), inmate, internee, detainee.

privacy *n* secrecy, confidentiality, independence, solitude, isolation, seclusion, concealment, retirement, retreat.

private *adj* secret, classified, hush-hush (*infml*), off the record, unofficial, confidential, intimate, personal, individual, own, exclusive, particular, special, separate, independent, solitary, isolated, secluded, hidden,

concealed, reserved, withdrawn.
E3 public, open.

in private privately, in confidence, secretly, in secret, behind closed doors, in camera.
E3 publicly, openly.

privilege n advantage, benefit, concession, birthright, title, due, right, prerogative, entitlement, freedom, liberty, franchise, licence, sanction, authority, immunity, exemption.
E3 disadvantage.

privileged adj advantaged, favoured, special, sanctioned, authorized, immune, exempt, élite, honoured, ruling, powerful.
E3 disadvantaged, underprivileged.

prize n reward, trophy, medal, award, winnings, jackpot, purse, premium, stake(s), honour, accolade.
adj best, top, first-rate, excellent, outstanding, champion, winning, prize-winning, award-winning.
E3 second-rate.
v treasure, value, appreciate, esteem, revere, cherish, hold dear.
E3 despise.

probability n likelihood, odds, chances, expectation, prospect, chance, possibility.
E3 improbability.

probable adj likely, odds-on, expected, credible, believable, plausible, feasible, possible, apparent, seeming.
E3 improbable, unlikely.

probation n apprenticeship, trial period, trial, test.

probe v prod, poke, pierce, penetrate, sound, plumb, explore, examine, scrutinize, investigate, go into, look into, search, sift, test.
n **1** BORE, drill. **2** INQUIRY, inquest,

investigation, exploration, examination, test, scrutiny, study, research.

problem n **1** TROUBLE, worry, predicament, quandary, dilemma, difficulty, complication, snag.
2 QUESTION, poser, puzzle, brain-teaser, conundrum, riddle, enigma.
adj difficult, unmanageable, uncontrollable, unruly, delinquent.
E3 well-behaved, manageable.

procedure n routine, process, method, system, technique, custom, practice, policy, formula, course, scheme, strategy, plan of action, move, step, action, conduct, operation, performance.

proceed v **1** permission to proceed: advance, go ahead, move on, progress, continue, carry on, press on.
2 ORIGINATE, derive, flow, start, stem, spring, arise, issue, result, ensue, follow, come.
E3 1 stop, retreat.

proceedings n **1** MATTERS, affairs, business, dealings, transactions, report, account, minutes, records, archives, annals. **2** EVENTS, happenings, deeds, doings, moves, steps, measures, action, course of action.

proceeds n revenue, income, returns, receipts, takings, earnings, gain, profit, yield, produce.
E3 expenditure, outlay.

process n **1** PROCEDURE, operation, practice, method, system, technique, means, manner, mode, way, stage, step. **2** COURSE, progression, advance, progress, development, evolution, formation, growth, movement, action, proceeding.
v deal with, handle, treat, prepare,

refine, transform, convert, change, alter.

procession n march, parade, cavalcade, motorcade, cortège, file, column, train, succession, series, sequence, course, run.

proclaim v announce, declare, pronounce, affirm, give out, publish, advertise, make known, profess, testify, show, indicate.

proclamation n announcement, declaration, pronouncement, affirmation, publication, promulgation, notice, notification, manifesto, decree, edict.

procrastinate v defer, put off, postpone, delay, retard, stall, temporize, play for time, dally, dilly-dally (infml), drag one's feet, prolong, protract.

E3 advance, proceed.

procure v acquire, buy, purchase, get, obtain, find, come by, pick up, lay hands on, earn, gain, win, secure, appropriate, requisition.

E3 lose.

prod v poke, jab, dig, elbow, nudge, push, shove, goad, spur, urge, egg on (infml), prompt, stimulate, motivate. n poke, jab, dig, elbow, nudge, push, shove, prompt, reminder, stimulus, motivation.

prodigy n genius, virtuoso, wonder, marvel, miracle, phenomenon, sensation, freak, curiosity, rarity, child genius, wonder child, whizz kid (infml).

produce v 1 CAUSE, occasion, give rise to, provoke, bring about, result in, effect, create, originate, invent, make, manufacture, fabricate, construct, compose, generate, yield, bear, deliver. 2 ADVANCE, put forward,

present, offer, give, supply, provide, furnish, bring out, bring forth, show, exhibit, demonstrate. 3 produce a play: direct, stage, mount, put on. n crop, harvest, yield, output, product.

product n 1 COMMODITY, merchandise, goods, end-product, artefact, work, creation, invention, production, output, yield, produce, fruit, return. 2 RESULT, consequence, outcome, issue, upshot, offshoot, spin-off, by-product, legacy.

E3 2 cause.

production n 1 MAKING, manufacture, fabrication, construction, assembly, creation, origination, preparation, formation. 2 an amateur production: staging, presentation, direction, management.

E3 1 consumption.

productive adj fruitful, profitable, rewarding, valuable, worthwhile, useful, constructive, creative, inventive, fertile, rich, teeming, busy, energetic, vigorous, efficient, effective.

E3 unproductive, fruitless, useless.

productivity n productiveness, yield, output, work rate, efficiency.

profane adj secular, temporal, lay, unconsecrated, unhallowed, unsanctified, unholy, irreligious, impious, sacrilegious, blasphemous, ungodly, irreverent, disrespectful, abusive, crude, coarse, foul, filthy, unclean.

E3 sacred, religious, respectful. v desecrate, pollute, contaminate, defile, debase, pervert, abuse, misuse.

E3 revere, honour.

profess v admit, confess, acknowledge, own, confirm, certify, declare, announce, proclaim, state, assert, affirm, maintain, claim, allege, make out, pretend.

profession n 1 CAREER, job, occupation, employment, business, line (of work), trade, vocation, calling, métier, craft, office, position. **2** ADMISSION, confession, acknowledgement, declaration, announcement, statement, testimony, assertion, affirmation, claim.

professional adj qualified, licensed, trained, experienced, practised, skilled, expert, masterly, proficient, competent, businesslike, efficient. **F3** amateur, unprofessional. n expert, authority, specialist, pro (infml), master, virtuoso, dab hand (infml). **F3** amateur.

proficiency n skill, skilfulness, expertise, mastery, talent, knack, dexterity, finesse, aptitude, ability, competence. **F3** incompetence.

proficient adj able, capable, skilled, qualified, trained, experienced, accomplished, expert, masterly, gifted, talented, clever, skilful, competent, efficient. **F3** unskilled, incompetent.

profile n 1 SIDE VIEW, outline, contour, silhouette, shape, form, figure, sketch, drawing, diagram, chart, graph. **2** BIOGRAPHY, curriculum vitae, thumbnail sketch, vignette, portrait, study, analysis, examination, survey, review.

profit n gain, surplus, excess, bottom line, revenue, return, yield, proceeds, receipts, takings, earnings, winnings, interest, advantage, benefit, use, avail, value, worth. **F3** loss.

v gain, make money, pay, serve, avail, benefit. **F3** lose.

profit by, profit from exploit, take advantage of, use, utilize, turn to advantage, capitalize on, cash in on, reap the benefit of.

profitable adj cost-effective, economic, commercial, money-making, lucrative, remunerative, paying, rewarding, successful, fruitful, productive, advantageous, beneficial, useful, valuable, worthwhile. **F3** unprofitable, loss-making, non-profit-making.

profound adj 1 DEEP, great, intense, extreme, heartfelt, marked, far-reaching, extensive, exhaustive. **2** a profound remark: serious, weighty, penetrating, thoughtful, philosophical, wise, learned, erudite, abstruse. **F3 1** shallow, slight, mild.

profuse adj ample, abundant, plentiful, copious, generous, liberal, lavish, rich, luxuriant, excessive, immoderate, extravagant, overabundant, superabundant, overflowing. **F3** inadequate, sparse.

profusion n abundance, plenty, wealth, multitude, plethora, glut, excess, surplus, superfluity, extravagance. **F3** inadequacy, scarcity.

programme n 1 SCHEDULE, timetable, agenda, calendar, order of events, listing, line-up, plan, scheme, project, syllabus, curriculum. **2** radio programme: broadcast, transmission, show, performance, production, presentation.

progress n movement, progression, passage, journey, way, advance,

headway, step forward, breakthrough, development, evolution, growth, increase, improvement, betterment, promotion.
E3 recession, deterioration, decline.
v proceed, advance, go forward, forge ahead, make progress, make headway, come on, develop, grow, mature, blossom, improve, better, prosper, increase.
E3 deteriorate, decline.

progression n cycle, chain, string, succession, series, sequence, order, course, advance, headway, progress, development.

progressive adj **1** MODERN, avant-garde, advanced, forward-looking, enlightened, liberal, radical, revolutionary, reformist, dynamic, enterprising, go-ahead, up-and-coming. **2** ADVANCING, continuing, developing, growing, increasing, intensifying.
E3 1 regressive.

prohibit v forbid, ban, bar, veto, proscribe, outlaw, rule out, preclude, prevent, stop, hinder, hamper, impede, obstruct, restrict.
E3 permit, allow, authorize.

project n assignment, contract, task, job, work, occupation, activity, enterprise, undertaking, venture, plan, scheme, programme, design, proposal, idea, conception.
v **1** PREDICT, forecast, extrapolate, estimate, reckon, calculate. **2** THROW, fling, hurl, launch, propel.
3 PROTRUDE, stick out, bulge, jut out, overhang.

projection n **1** PROTUBERANCE, bulge, overhang, ledge, sill, shelf, ridge. **2** PREDICTION, forecast, extrapolation, estimate, reckoning,

calculation, computation.

proliferate v multiply, reproduce, breed, increase, build up, intensify, escalate, mushroom, snowball, spread, expand, flourish, thrive.
E3 dwindle.

prolific adj productive, fruitful, fertile, profuse, copious, abundant.
E3 unproductive.

prolong v lengthen, extend, stretch, protract, draw out, spin out, drag out, delay, continue, perpetuate.
E3 shorten.

prominence n **1** FAME, celebrity, renown, eminence, distinction, greatness, importance, reputation, name, standing, rank, prestige.
2 BULGE, protuberance, bump, hump, lump, mound, rise, elevation, projection, process, headland, promontory, cliff, crag.
E3 1 unimportance, insignificance.

prominent adj **1** NOTICEABLE, conspicuous, obvious, unmistakable, striking, eye-catching. **2** BULGING, protuberant, projecting, jutting, protruding, obtrusive. **3** a prominent writer: famous, well-known, celebrated, renowned, noted, eminent, distinguished, respected, leading, foremost, chief, main, important, popular, outstanding.
E3 1 inconspicuous. **3** unknown, unimportant, insignificant.

promiscuity n looseness, laxity, permissiveness, wantonness, immorality, licentiousness, debauchery, depravity.
E3 chastity, morality.

promiscuous adj **1** LOOSE, immoral, licentious, dissolute. **2** CASUAL, random, haphazard, indiscriminate.
E3 1 chaste, moral.

promise v **1** VOW, pledge, swear, take an oath, contract, undertake, give one's word, vouch, warrant, guarantee, assure. **2** AUGUR, presage, indicate, suggest, hint at.
n **1** VOW, pledge, oath, word of honour, bond, compact, covenant, guarantee, assurance, undertaking, engagement, commitment. **2** POTENTIAL, ability, capability, aptitude, talent.

promising adj auspicious, propitious, favourable, rosy, bright, encouraging, hopeful, talented, gifted, budding, up-and-coming.
F3 unpromising, inauspicious, discouraging.

promote v **1** ADVERTISE, plug (infml), publicize, hype (sl), popularize, market, sell, push, recommend, advocate, champion, endorse, sponsor, support, back, help, aid, assist, foster, nurture, further, forward, encourage, boost, stimulate, urge. **2** UPGRADE, advance, move up, raise, elevate, exalt, honour.
F3 1 disparage, hinder. **2** demote.

promotion n **1** ADVANCEMENT, upgrading, rise, preferment, elevation, exaltation. **2** ADVERTISING, plugging (infml), publicity, hype (sl), campaign, propaganda, marketing, pushing, support, backing, furtherance, development, encouragement, boosting.
F3 1 demotion. **2** disparagement, obstruction.

prompt[1] adj punctual, on time, immediate, instantaneous, instant, direct, quick, swift, rapid, speedy, unhesitating, willing, ready, alert, responsive, timely, early.
F3 slow, hesitant, late.
adv promptly, punctually, exactly,

on the dot, to the minute, sharp.

prompt[2] v cause, give rise to, result in, occasion, produce, instigate, call forth, elicit, provoke, incite, urge, encourage, inspire, move, stimulate, motivate, spur, prod, remind.
F3 deter, dissuade.
n reminder, cue, hint, help, jolt, prod, spur, stimulus.

prone adj **1** LIKELY, given, inclined, disposed, predisposed, bent, apt, liable, subject, susceptible, vulnerable. **2** she lay prone: face down, prostrate, flat, horizontal, full-length, stretched, recumbent.
F3 1 unlikely, immune. **2** upright, supine.

pronounce v **1** SAY, utter, speak, express, voice, vocalize, sound, enunciate, articulate, stress. **2** DECLARE, announce, proclaim, decree, judge, affirm, assert.

pronounced adj clear, distinct, definite, positive, decided, marked, noticeable, conspicuous, evident, obvious, striking, unmistakable, strong, broad.
F3 faint, vague.

pronunciation n speech, diction, elocution, enunciation, articulation, delivery, accent, stress, inflection, intonation, modulation.

proof n evidence, documentation, demonstration, verification, confirmation, corroboration, substantiation, smoking gun (infml).

prop v **1** SUPPORT, sustain, uphold, maintain, shore, stay, buttress, bolster, underpin, set. **2** propped against the wall: lean, rest, stand.
n support, stay, mainstay, strut, buttress, brace, truss.

propaganda n advertising,

publicity, hype (*sl*), indoctrination, brainwashing, disinformation, spin (*infml*).

propagate *v* **1** SPREAD, transmit, broadcast, diffuse, disseminate, circulate, publish, promulgate, publicize, promote. **2** INCREASE, multiply, proliferate, generate, produce, breed, beget, spawn, procreate, reproduce.

propel *v* move, drive, impel, force, thrust, push, shove, launch, shoot, send.
Ⓕ stop.

proper *adj* **1** RIGHT, correct, accurate, exact, precise, true, genuine, real, actual. **2** ACCEPTED, correct, suitable, appropriate, fitting, decent, respectable, polite, formal.
Ⓕ 1 wrong. **2** improper, indecent.

property *n* **1** ESTATE, land, real estate, acres, premises, buildings, house(s), wealth, riches, resources, means, capital, assets, holding(s), belongings, possessions, effects, goods, chattels. **2** FEATURE, trait, quality, attribute, characteristic, idiosyncrasy, peculiarity, mark.

prophecy *n* prediction, augury, forecast, prognosis.

prophesy *v* predict, foresee, augur, foretell, forewarn, forecast.

prophet *n* seer, soothsayer, foreteller, forecaster, oracle, clairvoyant, fortune-teller.

proportion *n* **1** PERCENTAGE, fraction, part, division, share, quota, amount. **2** RATIO, relationship, correspondence, symmetry, balance, distribution.
Ⓕ 2 disproportion, imbalance.

proportional *adj* proportionate, relative, commensurate, consistent,

corresponding, analogous, comparable, equitable, even.
Ⓕ disproportionate.

proportions *n* dimensions, measurements, size, magnitude, volume, capacity.

proposal *n* proposition, suggestion, recommendation, motion, plan, scheme, project, design, programme, manifesto, presentation, bid, offer, tender, terms.

propose *v* **1** SUGGEST, recommend, move, advance, put forward, introduce, bring up, table, submit, present, offer, tender. **2** INTEND, mean, aim, purpose, plan, design. **3** NOMINATE, put up.
Ⓕ 1 withdraw.

proprietor, proprietress *n* landlord, landlady, title-holder, freeholder, leaseholder, landowner, owner, possessor.

prosecute *v* accuse, indict, sue, prefer charges, take to court, litigate, summon, put on trial, try.
Ⓕ defend.

prospect *n* chance, odds, probability, likelihood, possibility, hope, expectation, anticipation, outlook, future.
Ⓕ unlikelihood.

prospective *adj* future, -to-be, intended, designate, destined, forthcoming, approaching, coming, imminent, awaited, expected, anticipated, likely, possible, probable, potential, aspiring, would-be.
Ⓕ current.

prospectus *n* plan, scheme, programme, syllabus, manifesto, outline, synopsis, pamphlet, leaflet, brochure, catalogue, list.

prosper *v* boom, thrive, flourish,

flower, bloom, succeed, get on, advance, progress, grow rich.

F3 fail.

prosperity n boom, plenty, affluence, wealth, riches, fortune, well-being, luxury, the good life, success, good fortune.

F3 adversity, poverty.

prosperous adj booming, thriving, flourishing, blooming, successful, fortunate, lucky, rich, wealthy, affluent, well-off, well-to-do.

F3 unfortunate, poor.

prostrate adj flat, horizontal, prone, fallen, overcome, overwhelmed, crushed, paralysed, powerless, helpless, defenceless.

F3 triumphant.

v lay low, overcome, overwhelm, crush, overthrow, tire, wear out, fatigue, exhaust, drain, ruin.

F3 strengthen.

prostrate oneself bow down, kneel, kowtow, submit, grovel, cringe, abase oneself.

protagonist n hero, heroine, lead, principal, leader, prime mover, champion, advocate, supporter, proponent, exponent.

protect v safeguard, defend, guard, escort, cover, screen, shield, secure, watch over, look after, care for, support, shelter, harbour, keep, conserve, preserve, save.

F3 attack, neglect.

protection n **1** protection of the environment: care, custody, charge, guardianship, safekeeping, conservation, preservation, safety, safeguard. **2** BARRIER, buffer, bulwark, defence, guard, shield, armour, screen, cover, shelter, refuge, security, insurance.

F3 1 neglect, negligence, attack.

protective adj **1** POSSESSIVE, defensive, motherly, maternal, fatherly, paternal, watchful, vigilant, careful. **2** protective clothing: waterproof, fireproof, windproof, Gore-Tex®, insulating.

F3 1 aggressive, threatening.

protest n objection, disapproval, opposition, dissent, complaint, protestation, outcry, appeal, demonstration.

F3 acceptance.

v **1** OBJECT, take exception, complain, appeal, demonstrate, oppose, disapprove, disagree, argue. **2** protest one's innocence: assert, maintain, contend, insist, profess.

F3 1 accept.

protester n demonstrator, agitator, rebel, dissident, dissenter.

protocol n procedure, formalities, convention, custom, etiquette, manners, good form, propriety.

protracted adj long, lengthy, prolonged, extended, drawn-out, long-drawn-out, overlong, interminable.

F3 brief, shortened.

protrude v stick out, poke out, come through, bulge, jut out, project, extend, stand out, obtrude.

proud adj **1** CONCEITED, vain, egotistical, bigheaded, boastful, smug, complacent, arrogant, self-important, cocky, presumptuous, haughty, high and mighty, overbearing, supercilious, snooty (infml), snobbish, toffee-nosed (infml), stuck-up (infml). **2** SATISFIED, contented, gratified, pleased, delighted, honoured. **3** DIGNIFIED, noble, honourable, worthy, self-respecting.

E3 1 humble, modest, unassuming. **2** ashamed. **3** deferential, ignoble.

prove v show, demonstrate, attest, verify, confirm, corroborate, substantiate, bear out, document, certify, authenticate, validate, justify, establish, determine, ascertain, try, test, check, examine, analyse.
E3 disprove, discredit, falsify.

proverb n saying, adage, aphorism, maxim, byword, dictum, precept.

proverbial adj axiomatic, accepted, conventional, traditional, customary, time-honoured, famous, well-known, legendary, notorious, typical, archetypal.

provide v **1** SUPPLY, furnish, stock, equip, outfit, prepare for, cater, serve, present, give, contribute, yield, lend, add, bring. **2** PLAN FOR, allow, make provision, accommodate, arrange for, take precautions. **3** STATE, specify, stipulate, lay down, require.
E3 1 take, remove.

providence n **1** FATE, destiny, divine intervention, God's will, fortune, luck. **2** PRUDENCE, far-sightedness, foresight, caution, care, thrift.
E3 2 improvidence.

provident adj prudent, far-sighted, judicious, cautious, careful, thrifty, economical, frugal.
E3 improvident.

providential adj timely, opportune, convenient, fortunate, lucky, happy, welcome, heaven-sent.
E3 untimely.

providing conj provided, with the proviso, given, as long as, on condition, on the understanding.

province n **1** REGION, area, district, zone, county, shire, department, territory, colony, dependency.

2 RESPONSIBILITY, concern, duty, office, role, function, field, sphere, domain, department, line.

provincial adj regional, local, rural, rustic, country, home-grown, small-town, parish-pump, parochial, insular, inward-looking, limited, narrow, narrow-minded, small-minded.
E3 national, cosmopolitan, urban, sophisticated.

provision n **1** PLAN, arrangement, preparation, measure, precaution. **2** STIPULATION, specification, proviso, condition, term, requirement.

provisional adj temporary, interim, transitional, stopgap, makeshift, conditional, tentative.
E3 permanent, fixed, definite.

provisions n food, foodstuff, groceries, eatables (infml), sustenance, rations, supplies, stocks, stores.

proviso n condition, term, requirement, stipulation, qualification, reservation, restriction, limitation, provision, clause, rider.

provocation n cause, grounds, justification, reason, motive, stimulus, motivation, incitement, instigation, annoyance, aggravation (infml), vexation, grievance, offence, insult, affront, injury, taunt, challenge, dare.

provocative adj **1** ANNOYING, aggravating (infml), galling, outrageous, offensive, insulting, abusive. **2** STIMULATING, exciting, challenging. **3** EROTIC, titillating, arousing, sexy, seductive, alluring, tempting, inviting, tantalizing, teasing, suggestive.
E3 1 conciliatory.

provoke v **1** ANNOY, irritate, rile,

aggravate (*infml*), offend, insult, anger, enrage, infuriate, incense, madden, exasperate, tease, taunt. **2** CAUSE, occasion, give rise to, produce, generate, induce, elicit, evoke, excite, inspire, move, stir, prompt, stimulate, motivate, incite, instigate.

F3 **1** please, pacify. **2** result.

prowess *n* accomplishment, attainment, ability, aptitude, skill, expertise, mastery, command, talent, genius.

proximity *n* closeness, nearness, vicinity, neighbourhood, adjacency, juxtaposition.

F3 remoteness.

proxy *n* agent, factor, deputy, stand-in, substitute, representative, delegate, attorney.

prudent *adj* wise, sensible, politic, judicious, shrewd, discerning, careful, cautious, wary, vigilant, circumspect, discreet, provident, far-sighted, thrifty.

F3 imprudent, unwise, careless, rash.

pry *v* meddle, interfere, poke one's nose in, intrude, peep, peer, snoop, nose, ferret, dig, delve.

F3 mind one's own business.

pseudonym *n* false name, assumed name, alias, incognito, pen name, nom de plume, stage name.

psychic *adj* spiritual, supernatural, occult, mystic(al), clairvoyant, extra-sensory, telepathic, mental, psychological, intellectual, cognitive.

psychological *adj* mental, cerebral, intellectual, cognitive, emotional, subjective, subconscious, unconscious, psychosomatic, irrational, unreal.

F3 physical, real.

puberty *n* pubescence,

adolescence, teens, youth, growing up, maturity.

F3 childhood, immaturity, old age.

public *adj* **1** *public buildings*: state, national, civil, community, social, collective, communal, common, general, universal, open, unrestricted. **2** KNOWN, well-known, recognized, acknowledged, overt, open, exposed, published.

F3 **1** private, personal. **2** secret.

n people, nation, country, population, populace, masses, citizens, society, community, voters, electorate, followers, supporters, fans, audience, patrons, clientèle, customers, buyers, consumers.

publication *n* **1** BOOK, newspaper, magazine, periodical, booklet, leaflet, pamphlet, handbill. **2** ANNOUNCEMENT, declaration, notification, disclosure, release, issue, printing, publishing.

publicity *n* advertising, plug (*infml*), hype (*sl*), promotion, build-up, boost, attention, limelight, splash.

publicize *v* advertise, plug (*infml*), hype (*sl*), promote, push, spotlight, broadcast, make known, blaze.

publish *v* **1** ANNOUNCE, declare, communicate, make known, divulge, disclose, reveal, release, publicize, advertise. **2** *publish a book*: produce, print, issue, bring out, distribute, circulate, spread, diffuse.

pucker *v* gather, ruffle, wrinkle, shrivel, crinkle, crumple, crease, furrow, purse, screw up, contract, compress.

puerile *adj* childish, babyish, infantile, juvenile, immature, irresponsible, silly, foolish, inane, trivial.

F3 mature.

puff n 1 BREATH, waft, whiff, draught, flurry, gust, blast. 2 *a puff on a cigarette*: pull, drag.
v 1 BREATHE, pant, gasp, gulp, wheeze, blow, waft, inflate, expand, swell. 2 *puff a cigarette*: smoke, pull, drag, draw, suck.

puffy adj puffed up, inflated, swollen, bloated, distended, enlarged.

pugnacious adj hostile, aggressive, belligerent, contentious, disputatious, argumentative, quarrelsome, hot-tempered.
E3 peaceable.

pull v 1 TOW, drag, haul, draw, tug, jerk, yank (infml). 2 REMOVE, take out, extract, pull out, pluck, uproot, pull up, rip, tear. 3 ATTRACT, draw, lure, allure, entice, tempt, magnetize.
4 DISLOCATE, sprain, wrench, strain.
E3 1 push, press. 3 repel, deter, discourage.
n 1 TOW, drag, tug, jerk, yank (infml).
2 ATTRACTION, lure, allurement, drawing power, magnetism, influence, weight.

pull apart separate, part, dismember, dismantle, take to pieces.
E3 join.

pull down destroy, demolish, knock down, bulldoze.
E3 build, erect, put up.

pull off 1 ACCOMPLISH, achieve, bring off, succeed, manage, carry out.
2 DETACH, remove.
E3 1 fail. 2 attach.

pull out retreat, withdraw, leave, depart, quit, move out, evacuate, desert, abandon.
E3 join, arrive.

pull through recover, rally, recuperate, survive, weather.

pull together co-operate, work together, collaborate, team up.
E3 fight.

pull up 1 STOP, halt, park, draw up, pull in, pull over, brake. 2 REPRIMAND, tell off (infml), tick off (infml), take to task, rebuke, criticize.

pulp n flesh, marrow, paste, purée, mash, mush, pap.
v crush, squash, pulverize, mash, purée, liquidize.

pulsate v pulse, beat, throb, pound, hammer, drum, thud, thump, vibrate, oscillate, quiver.

pulse n beat, stroke, rhythm, throb, pulsation, beating, pounding, drumming, vibration, oscillation.

pulverize v 1 CRUSH, pound, grind, mill, powder. 2 DEFEAT, destroy, demolish, annihilate.

pump v push, drive, force, inject, siphon, draw, drain.

pump up blow up, inflate, puff up, fill.

pun n play on words, double entendre, witticism, quip.

punch[1] v hit, strike, pummel, jab, bash, clout, cuff, box, thump, sock (sl), wallop (infml).
n 1 BLOW, jab, bash, clout, thump, wallop (infml). 2 FORCE, impact, effectiveness, drive, vigour, verve, panache.

punch[2] v perforate, pierce, puncture, prick, bore, drill, stamp, cut.

punctilious adj scrupulous, conscientious, meticulous, careful, exact, precise, strict, formal, proper, particular, finicky, fussy.
E3 lax, informal.

punctual adj prompt, on time, on the dot, exact, precise, early, in good time.
E3 unpunctual, late.

punctuation

> Punctuation marks include:
> comma, full stop, period, colon, semicolon, brackets, parentheses, square brackets, inverted commas, quotation-marks, quotes (*infml*), exclamation mark, question-mark, apostrophe, asterisk, at sign, star, hashmark, hyphen, dash, oblique stroke, solidus, backslash, smiley, emoticon.

puncture n **1** FLAT TYRE, flat (*infml*), blow-out. **2** LEAK, hole, perforation, cut, nick.
v prick, pierce, penetrate, perforate, hole, cut, nick, burst, rupture, flatten, deflate.

pungent adj **1** *a pungent taste*: strong, hot, peppery, spicy, aromatic, tangy, piquant, sour, bitter, acrid, sharp. **2** *pungent comments*: caustic, stinging, biting, cutting, incisive, pointed, piercing, penetrating, sarcastic, scathing.
F3 **1** mild, bland, tasteless.

punish v penalize, discipline, correct, chastise, castigate, scold, beat, flog, lash, cane, spank, fine, imprison.
F3 reward.

punishment n discipline, correction, chastisement, beating, flogging, penalty, fine, imprisonment, sentence, deserts, retribution, revenge.
F3 reward.

punitive adj penal, disciplinary, retributive, retaliatory, vindictive, punishing.

puny adj weak, feeble, frail, sickly, undeveloped, underdeveloped, stunted, undersized, diminutive, little, tiny, insignificant.
F3 strong, sturdy, large, important.

pupil n student, scholar, schoolboy, schoolgirl, learner, apprentice, beginner, novice, disciple, protégé(e).
F3 teacher.

purchase v buy, pay for, invest in (*infml*), procure, acquire, obtain, get, secure, gain, earn, win.
F3 sell.
n acquisition, buy (*infml*), investment, asset, possession, property.
F3 sale.

purchaser n buyer, consumer, shopper, customer, client.
F3 seller, vendor.

pure adj **1** *pure gold*: unadulterated, unalloyed, unmixed, undiluted, neat, solid, simple, natural, real, authentic, genuine, true. **2** STERILE, uncontaminated, unpolluted, germ-free, aseptic, antiseptic, disinfected, sterilized, hygienic, sanitary, clean, immaculate, spotless, clear. **3** SHEER, utter, complete, total, thorough, absolute, perfect, unqualified. **4** CHASTE, virginal, undefiled, unsullied, moral, upright, virtuous, blameless, innocent. **5** *pure mathematics*: theoretical, abstract, conjectural, speculative, academic.
F3 **1** impure, adulterated.
2 contaminated, polluted. **4** immoral. **5** applied.

purely adv **1** UTTERLY, completely, totally, entirely, wholly, thoroughly, absolutely. **2** ONLY, simply, merely, just, solely, exclusively.

purge v **1** PURIFY, cleanse, clean out, scour, clear, absolve. **2** OUST, remove, get rid of, eject, expel, root out, eradicate, exterminate, wipe out, kill.
n removal, ejection, expulsion, witch hunt, eradication, extermination.

purify v refine, filter, clarify, clean,

cleanse, decontaminate, sanitize, disinfect, sterilize, fumigate, deodorize.

E3 contaminate, pollute, defile.

purist n pedant, literalist, formalist, stickler, quibbler, nit-picker.

puritanical adj puritan, moralistic, disciplinarian, ascetic, abstemious, austere, severe, stern, strict, strait-laced, prim, proper, prudish, disapproving, stuffy, stiff, rigid, narrow-minded, bigoted, fanatical, zealous.

E3 hedonistic, liberal, indulgent, broad-minded.

purity n 1 CLEARNESS, clarity, cleanness, cleanliness, untaintedness, wholesomeness. 2 SIMPLICITY, authenticity, genuineness, truth. 3 CHASTITY, decency, morality, integrity, rectitude, uprightness, virtue, innocence, blamelessness.

E3 1 impurity. 3 immorality.

purpose n 1 INTENTION, aim, objective, end, goal, target, plan, design, vision, idea, point, object, reason, motive, rationale, principle, result, outcome. 2 DETERMINATION, resolve, resolution, drive, single-mindedness, dedication, devotion, constancy, steadfastness, persistence, tenacity, zeal. 3 USE, function, application, good, advantage, benefit, value.

on purpose purposely, deliberately, intentionally, consciously, knowingly, wittingly, wilfully.

E3 accidentally, impulsively, spontaneously.

purposeful adj determined, decided, resolved, resolute, single-minded, constant, steadfast, persistent, persevering, tenacious,

strong-willed, positive, firm, deliberate.

E3 purposeless, aimless.

purse n 1 MONEY-BAG, wallet, pouch. 2 MONEY, means, resources, finances, funds, coffers, treasury, exchequer. 3 REWARD, award, prize.
υ pucker, wrinkle, draw together, close, tighten, contract, compress.

pursue υ 1 pursue an activity: perform, engage in, practise, conduct, carry on, continue, keep on, keep up, maintain, persevere in, persist in, hold to, aspire to, aim for, strive for, try for. 2 CHASE, go after, follow, track, trail, shadow, tail, dog, harass, harry, hound, hunt, seek, search for, investigate, inquire into.

pursuit n 1 CHASE, hue and cry, tracking, stalking, trail, hunt, quest, search, investigation. 2 ACTIVITY, interest, hobby, pastime, occupation, trade, craft, line, speciality, vocation.

push υ 1 PROPEL, thrust, ram, shove, jostle, elbow, prod, poke, press, depress, squeeze, squash, drive, force, constrain. 2 PROMOTE, advertise, publicize, boost, encourage, urge, egg on (infml), incite, spur, influence, persuade, pressurize, bully.

E3 1 pull. 2 discourage, dissuade.
n 1 KNOCK, shove, nudge, jolt, prod, poke, thrust. 2 ENERGY, vigour, vitality, go (infml), drive, effort, dynamism, enterprise, initiative, ambition, determination.

pushy adj assertive, self-assertive, ambitious, forceful, aggressive, over-confident, forward, bold, brash, arrogant, presumptuous, assuming, bossy (infml), in-your-face (infml).

E3 unassertive, unassuming.

put υ 1 PLACE, lay, deposit, plonk (infml), set, fix, settle, establish, stand, position, dispose, situate, station, post. **2** APPLY, impose, inflict, levy, assign, subject. **3** WORD, phrase, formulate, frame, express, voice, utter, state. **4** *put a suggestion*: submit, present, offer, suggest, propose.

put across put over, communicate, convey, express, explain, spell out, bring home to, get through to.

put aside put by, set aside, keep, retain, save, reserve, store, stow, stockpile, stash (*infml*), hoard, salt away.

put away (*infml*) **1** CONSUME, devour, eat, drink. **2** IMPRISON, jail, lock up, commit, certify.

put back 1 DELAY, defer, postpone, reschedule. **2** REPLACE, return.

E3 1 bring forward.

put down 1 WRITE DOWN, transcribe, enter, log, register, record, note. **2** CRUSH, quash, suppress, defeat, quell, silence, snub, slight, squash, deflate, humble, take down a peg, shame, humiliate, mortify. **3** *put down a sick dog*: kill, put to sleep. **4** ASCRIBE, attribute, blame, charge.

put forward advance, suggest, recommend, nominate, propose, move, table, introduce, present, submit, offer, tender.

put in insert, enter, input, submit, install, fit.

put off 1 DELAY, defer, postpone, reschedule. **2** DETER, dissuade, discourage, dishearten, demoralize, daunt, dismay, intimidate, disconcert, confuse, distract.

E3 2 encourage.

put on 1 ATTACH, affix, apply, place, add, impose. **2** PRETEND, feign, sham, fake, simulate, affect, assume.

3 STAGE, mount, produce, present, do, perform.

put out 1 PUBLISH, announce, broadcast, circulate. **2** EXTINGUISH, quench, douse, smother, switch off, turn off. **3** INCONVENIENCE, impose on, bother, disturb, trouble, upset, hurt, offend, annoy, irritate, irk, anger, exasperate.

E3 2 light.

put through accomplish, achieve, complete, conclude, finalize, execute, manage, bring off.

put up 1 ERECT, build, construct, assemble. **2** ACCOMMODATE, house, lodge, shelter. **3** *put up prices*: raise, increase. **4** PAY, invest, give, advance, float, provide, supply, pledge, offer.

put up to prompt, incite, encourage, egg on (*infml*), urge, goad.

E3 discourage, dissuade.

put up with stand, bear, abide, stomach, endure, suffer, tolerate, allow, accept, stand for, take, take lying down.

E3 object to, reject.

putrid *adj* rotten, decayed, decomposed, mouldy, off, bad, rancid, addled, corrupt, contaminated, tainted, polluted, foul, rank, fetid, stinking.

E3 fresh, wholesome.

put-upon *adj* imposed on, taken advantage of, exploited, used, abused, maltreated, persecuted.

puzzle *v* **1** BAFFLE, mystify, perplex, confound, stump (*infml*), floor (*infml*), confuse, bewilder, flummox (*infml*).
2 THINK, ponder, meditate, consider, mull over, deliberate, figure, rack one's brains.

n question, poser, brain-teaser, mind-bender, crossword, rebus, anagram, riddle, conundrum, mystery, enigma, paradox.

puzzle out solve, work out, figure out, decipher, decode, crack, unravel, untangle, sort out, resolve, clear up.

puzzled *adj* baffled, mystified, perplexed, confounded, at a loss, beaten, stumped (*infml*), confused, bewildered, nonplussed, lost, at sea, flummoxed (*infml*).

F3 clear.

pyromaniac *n* arsonist, incendiary, fire-raiser, firebug (*infml*), torch (*US sl*).

Q

quagmire *n* bog, marsh, quag, fen, swamp, morass, mire, quicksand.

quail *v* recoil, back away, shy away, shrink, flinch, cringe, cower, tremble, quake, shudder, falter.

quaint *adj* picturesque, charming, twee (*infml*), old-fashioned, antiquated, old-world, olde-worlde (*infml*), unusual, strange, odd, curious, bizarre, fanciful, whimsical.
F3 modern.

quake *v* shake, tremble, shudder, quiver, shiver, quail, vibrate, wobble, rock, sway, move, convulse, heave.

qualification *n* **1** CERTIFICATE, diploma, training, skill, competence, ability, capability, capacity, aptitude, suitability, fitness, eligibility.
2 RESTRICTION, limitation, reservation, exception, exemption, condition, caveat, provision, proviso, stipulation, modification.

qualified *adj* **1** CERTIFIED, chartered, licensed, professional, trained, experienced, practised, skilled, accomplished, expert, knowledgeable, skilful, talented, proficient, competent, efficient, able, capable, fit, eligible. **2** *qualified praise*: reserved, guarded, cautious, restricted, limited, bounded, contingent, conditional, provisional, equivocal.

F3 1 unqualified. **2** unconditional, whole-hearted.

qualify *v* **1** TRAIN, prepare, equip, fit, pass, graduate, certify, empower, entitle, authorize, sanction, permit.
2 MODERATE, reduce, lessen, diminish, temper, soften, weaken, mitigate, ease, adjust, modify, restrain, restrict, limit, delimit, define, classify.
F3 1 disqualify.

quality *n* **1** PROPERTY, characteristic, peculiarity, attribute, aspect, feature, trait, mark. **2** *of poor quality*: standard, grade, class, kind, sort, nature, character, calibre, status, rank, value, worth, merit, condition.
3 EXCELLENCE, superiority, pre-eminence, distinction, refinement.

qualm *n* misgiving, apprehension, fear, anxiety, worry, disquiet, uneasiness, scruple, hesitation, reluctance, uncertainty, doubt.

quandary *n* dilemma, predicament, impasse, perplexity, bewilderment, confusion, mess, fix, hole (*infml*), problem, difficulty.

quantity *n* amount, number, sum, total, aggregate, mass, lot, share, portion, quota, allotment, measure, dose, proportion, part, content, capacity, volume, weight, bulk, size, magnitude, expanse, extent, length, breadth.

quarrel n row, argument, slanging match (infml), wrangle, squabble, tiff, misunderstanding, disagreement, dispute, dissension, controversy, difference, conflict, clash, contention, strife, fight, scrap, brawl, feud, vendetta, schism.
E₃ agreement, harmony.
v row, argue, bicker, squabble, wrangle, be at loggerheads, fall out, disagree, dispute, dissent, differ, be at variance, clash, contend, fight, scrap, feud.
E₃ agree.

quarrelsome adj argumentative, disputatious, contentious, belligerent, ill-tempered, irritable.
E₃ peaceable, placid.

quarry n prey, victim, object, goal, target, game, kill, prize.

quarter n district, sector, zone, neighbourhood, locality, vicinity, area, region, province, territory, division, section, part, place, spot, point, direction, side.
v station, post, billet, accommodate, put up, lodge, board, house, shelter.

quarters n accommodation, lodgings, billet, digs (infml), residence, dwelling, habitation, domicile, rooms, barracks, station, post.

quash v annul, revoke, rescind, overrule, cancel, nullify, void, invalidate, reverse, set aside, squash, crush, quell, suppress, subdue, defeat, overthrow.
E₃ confirm, vindicate, reinstate.

quaver v shake, tremble, quake, shudder, quiver, vibrate, pulsate, oscillate, flutter, flicker, trill, warble.

quay n wharf, pier, jetty, dock, harbour.

queasy adj sick, ill, unwell, queer, groggy, green, nauseated, sickened, bilious, squeamish, faint, dizzy, giddy.

queen n monarch, sovereign, ruler, majesty, princess, empress, consort.

queer adj 1 ODD, mysterious, strange, unusual, uncommon, weird, unnatural, bizarre, eccentric, peculiar, funny, puzzling, curious, remarkable. 2 I feel queer: unwell, ill, sick, queasy, light-headed, faint, giddy, dizzy. 3 SUSPECT, suspicious, shifty, dubious, shady (infml). 4 (sl) HOMOSEXUAL, gay, lesbian.
E₃ 1 ordinary, usual, common. 2 well.

quell v subdue, quash, crush, squash, suppress, put down, overcome, conquer, defeat, overpower, moderate, mitigate, allay, alleviate, soothe, calm, pacify, hush, quiet, silence, stifle, extinguish.

quench v 1 quench one's thirst: slake, satisfy, sate, cool. 2 EXTINGUISH, douse, put out, snuff out.

querulous adj peevish, fretful, fractious, cantankerous, cross, irritable, complaining, grumbling, discontented, dissatisfied, critical, carping, captious, fault-finding, fussy.
E₃ placid, uncomplaining, contented.

query v ask, inquire, question, challenge, dispute, quarrel with, doubt, suspect, distrust, mistrust, disbelieve.
E₃ accept.
n question, inquiry, problem, uncertainty, doubt, suspicion, scepticism, reservation, hesitation.

quest n search, hunt, pursuit, investigation, inquiry, mission, crusade, enterprise, undertaking, venture, journey, voyage, expedition, exploration, adventure.

question v interrogate, quiz, grill, pump, interview, examine, cross-examine, debrief, ask, inquire, investigate, probe, query, challenge, dispute, doubt, disbelieve.
n **1** QUERY, inquiry, poser, problem, difficulty. **2** ISSUE, matter, subject, topic, point, proposal, proposition, motion, debate, dispute, controversy.

questionable adj debatable, disputable, unsettled, undetermined, unproven, uncertain, arguable, controversial, vexed, doubtful, dubious, suspicious, suspect, shady (infml), fishy (infml), iffy (sl).
F3 unquestionable, indisputable, certain.

questionnaire n quiz, test, survey, opinion poll.

queue n line, tailback, file, crocodile, procession, train, string, succession, series, sequence, order.

quibble v carp, cavil, split hairs, nit-pick, equivocate, prevaricate.
n complaint, objection, criticism, query.

quick adj **1** FAST, swift, rapid, speedy, express, hurried, hasty, cursory, fleeting, brief, prompt, ready, immediate, instant, instantaneous, sudden, brisk, nimble, sprightly, agile. **2** CLEVER, intelligent, quick-witted, smart, sharp, keen, shrewd, astute, discerning, perceptive, responsive, receptive.
F3 1 slow, sluggish, lethargic. **2** unintelligent, dull.

quicken v **1** ACCELERATE, speed, hurry, hasten, precipitate, expedite, dispatch, advance. **2** ANIMATE, enliven, invigorate, energize, galvanize, activate, rouse, arouse, stimulate, excite, inspire, revive,

refresh, reinvigorate, reactivate.
F3 1 slow, retard. **2** dull.

quiet adj **1** SILENT, noiseless, inaudible, hushed, soft, low. **2** PEACEFUL, still, tranquil, serene, calm, composed, undisturbed, untroubled, placid. **3** SHY, reserved, reticent, uncommunicative, taciturn, unforthcoming, retiring, withdrawn, thoughtful, subdued, meek. **4** a quiet spot: isolated, unfrequented, lonely, secluded, private.
F3 1 noisy, loud. **2** excitable. **3** extrovert.
n quietness, silence, hush, peace, lull, stillness, tranquillity, serenity, calm, rest, repose.
F3 noise, loudness, disturbance, bustle.

quieten v **1** SILENCE, hush, mute, soften, lower, diminish, reduce, stifle, muffle, deaden, dull. **2** SUBDUE, pacify, quell, quiet, still, smooth, calm, soothe, compose, sober.
F3 2 disturb, agitate.

quilt n bedcover, coverlet, bedspread, counterpane, eiderdown, duvet.

quip n joke, jest, crack, gag (infml), witticism, riposte, retort, gibe.

quirk n freak, eccentricity, curiosity, oddity, peculiarity, idiosyncrasy, mannerism, habit, trait, foible, whim, caprice, turn, twist.

quit v **1** LEAVE, depart, go, exit, decamp, desert, forsake, abandon, renounce, relinquish, surrender, give up, resign, retire, withdraw. **2** quit smoking: stop, cease, end, discontinue, desist, drop, give up, pack in (sl).

quite adv **1** MODERATELY, rather, somewhat, fairly, relatively,

comparatively. **2** UTTERLY, absolutely, totally, completely, entirely, wholly, fully, perfectly, exactly, precisely.

quiver *v* shake, tremble, shudder, shiver, quake, quaver, vibrate, palpitate, flutter, flicker, oscillate, wobble.
n shake, tremble, shudder, shiver, tremor, vibration, palpitation, flutter, flicker, oscillation, wobble.

quiz *n* questionnaire, test, examination, competition.
v question, interrogate, grill, pump, examine, cross-examine.

quizzical *adj* questioning, inquiring, curious, amused, humorous, teasing, mocking, satirical, sardonic, sceptical.

quota *n* ration, allowance, allocation, assignment, share, portion, part, slice, cut (*infml*), percentage, proportion.

quotation *n* **1** CITATION, quote (*infml*), extract, excerpt, passage, piece, cutting, reference. **2** ESTIMATE, quote (*infml*), tender, figure, price, cost, charge, rate.

quote *v* cite, refer to, mention, name, reproduce, echo, repeat, recite, recall, recollect.

R

rabble n crowd, throng, horde, herd, mob, masses, populace, riff-raff.

rabble-rouser n agitator, troublemaker, incendiary, demagogue, ringleader.

race [1] n competition, contest, contention, rivalry, chase, pursuit, quest.
  v run, sprint, dash, tear, fly, gallop, speed, career, dart, zoom, rush, hurry, hasten.

Types of race and famous races include:
cycle race, cyclo-cross, road race, time trial, Tour de France; greyhound race, Greyhound Derby; horse race, Cheltenham Gold Cup, the Classics (Derby, Oaks, One Thousand Guineas, St. Leger, Two Thousand Guineas), Grand National, Kentucky Derby, Breeders' Cup, Melbourne Cup, Prix de l'Arc de Triomphe, steeplechase, trotting race, harness race; motorcycle race, motocross, scramble, speedway, Isle of Man Tourist Trophy (TT); motor-race, Grand Prix, Indianapolis 500, Le Mans, Monte Carlo Rally, RAC Rally, stock car race; rowing, regatta, Boat Race; running, cross-country, dash (N Am), hurdles, marathon, London Marathon, relay, sprint, steeplechase, track event; ski race, downhill, slalom, giant slalom, super giant slalom; swimming race, walking race; yacht race, Admiral's Cup, America's Cup; egg-and-spoon race, sack race, wheelbarrow race.

race [2] n nation, people, tribe, clan, house, dynasty, family, kindred, ancestry, line, blood, stock, genus, species, breed.

race-course n racetrack, course, track, circuit, lap, turf, speedway.

racial adj national, tribal, ethnic, folk, genealogical, ancestral, inherited, genetic.

racism n racialism, xenophobia, chauvinism, jingoism, discrimination, prejudice, bias.

rack n shelf, stand, support, structure, frame, framework.

racket n **1** NOISE, din, uproar, row, fuss, outcry, clamour, commotion, disturbance, pandemonium, hurly-burly, hubbub. **2** SWINDLE, con (infml), scam (infml), fraud, fiddle, deception, trick, dodge, scheme, business, game.

racy adj **1** RIBALD, bawdy, risqué, naughty, indecent, indelicate, suggestive. **2** LIVELY, animated, spirited, energetic, dynamic, buoyant, boisterous.

radiance n light, luminosity, incandescence, radiation, brightness,

brilliance, shine, lustre, gleam, glow,
glitter, resplendence, splendour.

radiant *adj* **1** BRIGHT, luminous,
shining, gleaming, glowing, beaming,
glittering, sparkling, brilliant,
resplendent, splendid, glorious.
2 HAPPY, joyful, delighted, ecstatic.
F3 1 dull. **2** miserable.

radiate *v* shine, gleam, glow, beam,
shed, pour, give off, emit, emanate,
diffuse, issue, disseminate, scatter,
spread (out), diverge, branch.

radical *adj* **1** BASIC, fundamental,
primary, essential, natural, native,
innate, intrinsic, deep-seated,
profound. **2** *radical changes*: drastic,
comprehensive, thorough, sweeping,
far-reaching, thoroughgoing,
complete, total, entire. **3** FANATICAL,
militant, extreme, extremist,
revolutionary.
F3 1 superficial. **3** moderate.
n fanatic, militant, extremist,
revolutionary, reformer, reformist,
fundamentalist.

raffle *n* draw, lottery, sweepstake,
sweep, tombola.

rage *n* **1** ANGER, wrath, fury, frenzy,
tantrum, temper. **2** (*infml*) *all the rage*:
craze, fad, thing (*infml*), fashion,
vogue, style, passion, enthusiasm,
obsession.
v fume, seethe, rant, rave, storm,
thunder, explode, rampage.

ragged *adj* **1** *ragged clothes*: frayed,
torn, ripped, tattered, worn-out,
threadbare, tatty, shabby, scruffy,
unkempt, down-at-heel. **2** JAGGED,
serrated, indented, notched, rough,
uneven, irregular, fragmented, erratic,
disorganized.

raid *n* attack, onset, onslaught,
invasion, inroad, incursion, foray,

sortie, strike, blitz, swoop, bust (*sl*),
robbery, break-in, hold-up.
v loot, pillage, plunder, ransack, rifle,
maraud, attack, descend on, invade,
storm.

raider *n* attacker, invader, looter,
plunderer, ransacker, marauder,
robber, thief, brigand, pirate.

railing *n* fence, paling, barrier,
parapet, rail, balustrade.

railway *n* track, line, rails, railroad
(*N Am*), monorail, underground, tube
(*infml*), subway, metro.

rain *n* rainfall, precipitation,
raindrops, drizzle, shower, cloudburst,
downpour, deluge, torrent, storm,
thunderstorm, squall.
v spit, drizzle, shower, pour, teem,
pelt, bucket (*infml*), deluge.

rainy *adj* wet, damp, showery, drizzly.
F3 dry.

raise *v* **1** LIFT, elevate, hoist, jack up,
erect, build, construct. **2** INCREASE,
augment, escalate, magnify, heighten,
strengthen, intensify, amplify, boost,
enhance. **3** *raise funds*: get, obtain,
collect, gather, assemble, rally,
muster, recruit. **4** BRING UP, rear,
breed, propagate, grow, cultivate,
develop. **5** *raise a subject*: bring up,
broach, introduce, present, put
forward, moot, suggest.
F3 1 lower. **2** decrease, reduce.
5 suppress.

rake in collect, amass, accumulate.

rally *v* **1** GATHER, collect, assemble,
congregate, convene, muster,
summon, round up, unite, marshal,
organize, mobilize, reassemble,
regroup, reorganize. **2** RECOVER,
recuperate, revive, improve, pick up.
n **1** GATHERING, assembly, convention,
convocation, conference, meeting,

jamboree, reunion, march, demonstration. **2** RECOVERY, recuperation, revival, comeback, improvement, resurgence, renewal.

ram v **1** HIT, strike, butt, hammer, pound, drum, crash, smash, slam. **2** FORCE, drive, thrust, cram, stuff, pack, crowd, jam, wedge.

ramble v **1** WALK, hike, trek, tramp, traipse, stroll, amble, saunter, straggle, wander, roam, rove, meander, wind, zigzag. **2** CHATTER, babble, rabbit (on) (*infml*), witter (on) (*infml*), expatiate, digress, drift. n walk, hike, trek, tramp, stroll, saunter, tour, trip, excursion.

rambler n hiker, walker, stroller, rover, roamer, wanderer, wayfarer.

rambling adj **1** SPREADING, sprawling, straggling, trailing. **2** CIRCUITOUS, roundabout, digressive, wordy, long-winded, long-drawn-out, disconnected, incoherent. **F3** direct.

ramification n branch, offshoot, development, complication, result, consequence, upshot, implication.

ramp n slope, incline, gradient, rise.

rampage v run wild, run amok, run riot, rush, tear, storm, rage, rant, rave. n rage, fury, frenzy, storm, uproar, violence, destruction.

on the rampage wild, amok, berserk, violent, out of control.

rampant adj unrestrained, uncontrolled, unbridled, unchecked, wanton, excessive, fierce, violent, raging, wild, riotous, rank, profuse, rife, widespread, prevalent.

ramshackle adj dilapidated, tumbledown, broken-down, crumbling, ruined, derelict, jerry-built, unsafe, rickety, shaky, flimsy,

unsteady, tottering, decrepit. **F3** solid, stable.

rancid adj sour, off, bad, musty, stale, rank, foul, fetid, putrid, rotten. **F3** sweet.

random adj arbitrary, chance, fortuitous, casual, incidental, haphazard, irregular, unsystematic, unplanned, accidental, aimless, purposeless, indiscriminate, stray. **F3** systematic, deliberate.

range n **1** SCOPE, compass, scale, gamut, spectrum, sweep, spread, extent, distance, reach, span, limits, bounds, parameters, area, field, domain, province, sphere, orbit. **2** *a range of fittings*: variety, diversity, assortment, selection, sort, kind, class, order, series, string, chain. v **1** EXTEND, stretch, reach, spread, vary, fluctuate. **2** ALIGN, arrange, order, rank, classify, catalogue.

rank^1 n **1** GRADE, degree, class, caste, status, standing, position, station, condition, estate, echelon, level, stratum, tier, classification, sort, type, group, division. **2** ROW, line, range, column, file, series, order, formation. v grade, class, rate, place, position, range, sort, classify, categorize, order, arrange, organize, marshal.

rank^2 adj **1** UTTER, total, complete, absolute, unmitigated, thorough, sheer, downright, out-and-out, arrant, gross, flagrant, glaring, outrageous. **2** FOUL, repulsive, disgusting, revolting, stinking, putrid, rancid, stale.

rankle v annoy, irritate, rile, nettle, gall, irk, anger.

ransack v search, scour, comb, rummage, rifle, raid, sack, strip, despoil, ravage, loot, plunder, pillage.

ransom n price, money, payment, pay-off, redemption, deliverance, rescue, liberation, release.
v buy off, redeem, deliver, rescue, liberate, free, release.

rant v shout, cry, yell, roar, bellow, declaim, bluster, rave.

rap v 1 KNOCK, hit, strike, tap, thump. 2 (sl) REPROVE, reprimand, criticize, censure.
n 1 KNOCK, blow, tap, thump. 2 (sl) REBUKE, reprimand, censure, blame, punishment.

rape n violation, assault, abuse, maltreatment.
v violate, assault, abuse, maltreat.

rapid adj swift, speedy, quick, fast, express, lightning, prompt, brisk, hurried, hasty, precipitate, headlong.
F3 slow, leisurely, sluggish.

rapport n bond, link, affinity, relationship, empathy, sympathy, understanding, harmony.

rapt adj engrossed, absorbed, preoccupied, intent, gripped, spellbound, enthralled, captivated, fascinated, entranced, charmed, enchanted, delighted, ravished, enraptured, transported.

rapture n delight, happiness, joy, bliss, ecstasy, euphoria, exaltation.

rare adj 1 UNCOMMON, unusual, scarce, sparse, sporadic, infrequent. 2 EXQUISITE, superb, excellent, superlative, incomparable, exceptional, remarkable, precious.
F3 1 common, abundant, frequent.

rarefied adj exclusive, select, private, esoteric, refined, high, noble, sublime.

rarely adv seldom, hardly ever, infrequently, little.
F3 often, frequently.

raring adj eager, keen, enthusiastic, ready, willing, impatient, longing, itching, desperate.

rarity n 1 CURIOSITY, curio, gem, pearl, treasure, find. 2 UNCOMMONNESS, unusualness, strangeness, scarcity, shortage, sparseness, infrequency.
F3 2 commonness, frequency.

rascal n rogue, scoundrel, scamp, scallywag, imp, devil, villain, good-for-nothing, wastrel.

rash[1] adj reckless, ill-considered, foolhardy, ill-advised, madcap, hare-brained, hot-headed, headstrong, impulsive, impetuous, hasty, headlong, unguarded, unwary, indiscreet, imprudent, careless, heedless, unthinking.
F3 cautious, wary, careful.

rash[2] n eruption, outbreak, epidemic, plague.

rasp n grating, scrape, grinding, scratch, harshness, hoarseness, croak.
v grate, scrape, grind, file, sand, scour, abrade, rub.

rate n 1 SPEED, velocity, tempo, time, ratio, proportion, relation, degree, grade, rank, rating, standard, basis, measure, scale. 2 CHARGE, fee, hire, toll, tariff, price, cost, value, worth, tax, duty, amount, figure, percentage.
v 1 JUDGE, regard, consider, deem, count, reckon, figure, estimate, evaluate, assess, weigh, measure, grade, rank, class, classify. 2 ADMIRE, respect, esteem, value, prize.
3 DESERVE, merit.

rather adv 1 MODERATELY, relatively, slightly, a bit, somewhat, fairly, quite, pretty, noticeably, significantly, very.
2 PREFERABLY, sooner, instead.

ratify v approve, uphold, endorse, sign, legalize, sanction, authorize, establish, affirm, confirm, certify, validate, authenticate.
E3 repudiate, reject.

rating n class, rank, degree, status, standing, position, placing, order, grade, mark, evaluation, assessment, classification, category.

ratio n percentage, fraction, proportion, relation, relationship, correspondence, correlation.

ration n quota, allowance, allocation, allotment, share, portion, helping, part, measure, amount.
v apportion, allot, allocate, share, deal out, distribute, dole out, dispense, supply, issue, control, restrict, limit, conserve, save.

rational adj logical, reasonable, sound, well-founded, realistic, sensible, clear-headed, judicious, wise, sane, normal, balanced, lucid, reasoning, thinking, intelligent, enlightened.
E3 irrational, illogical, insane, crazy.

rationale n logic, reasoning, philosophy, principle, basis, grounds, explanation, reason, motive, motivation, theory.

rationalize v **1** JUSTIFY, excuse, vindicate, explain, account for.
2 REORGANIZE, streamline.

rations n food, provisions, supplies, stores.

rattle v clatter, jingle, jangle, clank, shake, vibrate, jolt, jar, bounce, bump.
rattle off reel off, list, run through, recite, repeat.

raucous adj harsh, rough, hoarse, husky, rasping, grating, jarring, strident, noisy, loud.

ravage v destroy, devastate, lay waste, demolish, raze, wreck, ruin, spoil, damage, loot, pillage, plunder, sack, despoil.
n destruction, devastation, havoc, damage, ruin, desolation, wreckage, pillage, plunder.

rave v rage, storm, thunder, roar, rant, ramble, babble, splutter.
adj (infml) enthusiastic, rapturous, favourable, excellent, wonderful.

ravenous adj hungry, starving, starved, famished, greedy, voracious, insatiable.

ravine n canyon, gorge, gully, pass.

raving adj mad, insane, crazy, hysterical, delirious, wild, frenzied, furious, berserk.

ravish v enrapture, delight, enchant, charm, captivate, entrance, fascinate.

ravishing adj delightful, enchanting, charming, lovely, beautiful, gorgeous, stunning, radiant, dazzling, alluring, seductive.

raw adj **1** raw vegetables: uncooked, fresh. **2** UNPROCESSED, unrefined, untreated, crude, natural. **3** PLAIN, bare, naked, basic, harsh, brutal, realistic. **4** SCRATCHED, grazed, scraped, open, bloody, sore, tender, sensitive. **5** COLD, chilly, bitter, biting, piercing, freezing, bleak. **6** a raw recruit: new, green, immature, callow, inexperienced, untrained, unskilled.
E3 1 cooked, done. **2** processed, refined. **5** warm. **6** experienced, skilled.

ray n beam, shaft, flash, gleam, flicker, glimmer, glint, spark, trace, hint, indication.

raze v demolish, pull down, tear down, bulldoze, flatten, level, destroy.

re prep about, concerning, regarding, with regard to, with reference to.

reach v arrive at, get to, attain, achieve, make, amount to, hit, strike, touch, contact, stretch, extend, grasp. n range, scope, compass, distance, spread, extent, stretch, grasp, jurisdiction, command, power, influence.

react v respond, retaliate, reciprocate, reply, answer, acknowledge, act, behave.

reaction n response, effect, reply, answer, acknowledgement, feedback, counteraction, reflex, recoil, reciprocation, retaliation.

reactionary adj conservative, right-wing, rightist, die-hard, counter-revolutionary.
F3 progressive, revolutionary.
n conservative, right-winger, rightist, die-hard, counter-revolutionary.
F3 progressive, revolutionary.

read v 1 STUDY, peruse, pore over, scan, skim, decipher, decode, interpret, construe, understand, comprehend. 2 RECITE, declaim, deliver, speak, utter. 3 the gauge read zero: indicate, show, display, register, record.

readable adj 1 LEGIBLE, decipherable, intelligible, clear, understandable, comprehensible. 2 INTERESTING, enjoyable, entertaining, gripping, unputdownable (infml).
F3 1 illegible. 2 unreadable.

readily adv willingly, unhesitatingly, gladly, eagerly, promptly, quickly, freely, smoothly, easily, effortlessly.
F3 unwillingly, reluctantly.

reading n 1 STUDY, perusal, scrutiny, examination, inspection, interpretation, understanding, rendering, version, rendition, recital. 2 a reading from the Bible: passage, lesson.

ready adj 1 ready to go: prepared, waiting, set, fit, arranged, organized, completed, finished. 2 WILLING, inclined, disposed, happy, game (infml), eager, keen. 3 AVAILABLE, to hand, present, near, accessible, convenient, handy. 4 PROMPT, immediate, quick, sharp, astute, perceptive, alert.
F3 1 unprepared. 2 unwilling, reluctant, disinclined. 3 unavailable, inaccessible. 4 slow.

real adj actual, existing, physical, material, substantial, tangible, genuine, authentic, bona fide, official, rightful, legitimate, valid, true, factual, certain, sure, positive, veritable, honest, sincere, heartfelt, unfeigned, unaffected.
F3 unreal, imaginary, false.

realistic adj 1 PRACTICAL, down-to-earth, commonsense, sensible, level-headed, clear-sighted, businesslike, hard-headed, pragmatic, matter-of-fact, rational, logical, objective, detached, unsentimental, unromantic. 2 LIFELIKE, faithful, truthful, true, genuine, authentic, natural, real, real-life, graphic, representational.
F3 1 unrealistic, impractical, irrational, idealistic.

reality n truth, fact, certainty, realism, actuality, existence, materiality, tangibility, genuineness, authenticity, validity.

realize v 1 UNDERSTAND, comprehend, grasp, catch on, cotton on (infml), recognize, accept, appreciate. 2 ACHIEVE, accomplish, fulfil, complete, implement, perform. 3 SELL FOR, fetch, make, earn, produce, net, clear.

really *adv* actually, truly, honestly, sincerely, genuinely, positively, certainly, absolutely, categorically, very, indeed.

realm *n* kingdom, monarchy, principality, empire, country, state, land, territory, area, region, province, domain, sphere, orbit, field, department.

rear *n* **1** BACK, stern, end, tail. **2** RUMP, buttocks, posterior, behind, bottom, backside (*infml*).
E3 front.
adj back, hind, hindmost, rearmost, last.
E3 front.
v **1** *rear a child:* bring up, raise, breed, grow, cultivate, foster, nurse, nurture, train, educate. **2** RISE, tower, soar, raise, lift.

reason *n* **1** CAUSE, motive, incentive, rationale, explanation, excuse, justification, defence, warrant, ground, basis, case, argument, aim, intention, purpose, object, end, goal. **2** SENSE, logic, reasoning, rationality, sanity, mind, wit, brain, intellect, understanding, wisdom, judgement, common sense, gumption.
v work out, solve, resolve, conclude, deduce, infer, think.
reason with urge, persuade, move, remonstrate with, argue with, debate with, discuss with.

reasonable *adj* **1** SENSIBLE, wise, well-advised, sane, intelligent, rational, logical, practical, sound, reasoned, well-thought-out, plausible, credible, possible, viable. **2** *a reasonable price:* acceptable, satisfactory, tolerable, moderate, average, fair, just, modest, inexpensive.

E3 1 irrational. **2** exorbitant.

reasoning *n* logic, thinking, thought, analysis, interpretation, deduction, supposition, hypothesis, argument, case, proof.

reassure *v* comfort, cheer, encourage, hearten, inspirit, brace, bolster.
E3 alarm.

rebate *n* refund, repayment, reduction, discount, deduction, allowance.

rebel *v* revolt, mutiny, rise up, run riot, dissent, disobey, defy, resist, recoil, shrink.
E3 conform.
n revolutionary, insurrectionary, mutineer, dissenter, nonconformist, schismatic, heretic.

rebellion *n* revolt, revolution, rising, uprising, insurrection, insurgence, mutiny, resistance, opposition, defiance, disobedience, insubordination, dissent, heresy.

rebellious *adj* revolutionary, insurrectionary, insurgent, seditious, mutinous, resistant, defiant, disobedient, insubordinate, unruly, disorderly, ungovernable, unmanageable, intractable, obstinate.
E3 obedient, submissive.

rebirth *n* reincarnation, resurrection, renaissance, regeneration, renewal, restoration, revival, revitalization, rejuvenation.

rebound *v* recoil, backfire, return, bounce, ricochet, boomerang.

rebuff *v* spurn, reject, refuse, decline, turn down, rebuke, discourage, snub, slight, cut, cold-shoulder.
n rejection, refusal, repulse, check, discouragement, snub, brush-off

(*infml*), slight, put-down, cold shoulder.

rebuke *v* reprove, castigate, chide, scold, tell off (*infml*), admonish, tick off (*infml*), reprimand, upbraid, rate, censure, blame, reproach.
E3 praise, commendation.
n reproach, reproof, reprimand, lecture, dressing-down (*infml*), telling-off (*infml*), ticking-off (*infml*), admonition, censure, blame.
E3 praise, commendation.

recall *v* remember, recollect, cast one's mind back, evoke, bring back.

recapitulate *v* recap, summarize, review, repeat, reiterate, restate, recount.

recede *v* go back, return, retire, withdraw, retreat, ebb, wane, sink, decline, diminish, dwindle, decrease, lessen, shrink, slacken, subside, abate.
E3 advance.

receipt *n* 1 VOUCHER, ticket, slip, counterfoil, stub, acknowledgement. 2 RECEIVING, reception, acceptance, delivery.

receipts *n* takings, income, proceeds, profits, gains, return.

receive *v* 1 TAKE, accept, get, obtain, derive, acquire, pick up, collect, inherit. 2 *receive guests*: admit, let in, greet, welcome, entertain, accommodate. 3 EXPERIENCE, undergo, suffer, sustain, meet with, encounter. 4 REACT TO, respond to, hear, perceive, apprehend.
E3 1 give, donate.

recent *adj* late, latest, current, present-day, contemporary, modern, up-to-date, new, novel, fresh, young.
E3 old, out-of-date.

recently *adv* lately, newly, freshly.

receptacle *n* container, vessel, holder.

reception *n* 1 ACCEPTANCE, admission, greeting, recognition, welcome, treatment, response, reaction, acknowledgement, receipt. 2 PARTY, function, do (*infml*), entertainment.

receptive *adj* open-minded, amenable, accommodating, suggestible, susceptible, sensitive, responsive, open, accessible, approachable, friendly, hospitable, welcoming, sympathetic, favourable, interested.
E3 narrow-minded, resistant, unresponsive.

recess *n* 1 BREAK, interval, intermission, rest, respite, holiday, vacation. 2 ALCOVE, niche, nook, corner, bay, cavity, hollow, depression, indentation.

recession *n* slump, depression, downturn, decline.
E3 boom, upturn.

recipe *n* formula, prescription, ingredients, instructions, directions, method, system, procedure, technique.

reciprocal *adj* mutual, joint, shared, give-and-take, complementary, alternating, corresponding, equivalent, interchangeable.

reciprocate *v* respond, reply, requite, return, exchange, swap, trade, match, equal, correspond, interchange, alternate.

recital *n* performance, concert, recitation, reading, narration, account, rendition, interpretation, repetition.

recitation *n* passage, piece, party piece, poem, monologue, narration, story, tale, recital, telling.

recite v repeat, tell, narrate, relate, recount, speak, deliver, articulate, declaim, perform, reel off, itemize, enumerate.

reckless adj heedless, thoughtless, mindless, careless, negligent, irresponsible, imprudent, ill-advised, indiscreet, rash, hasty, foolhardy, daredevil, wild.

F3 cautious, wary, careful, prudent.

reckon v **1** CALCULATE, compute, figure out, work out, add up, total, tally, count, number, enumerate. **2** DEEM, regard, consider, esteem, value, rate, judge, evaluate, assess, estimate, gauge. **3** THINK, believe, imagine, fancy, suppose, surmise, assume, guess, conjecture.

reckon on rely on, depend on, bank on, count on, trust in, hope for, expect, anticipate, foresee, plan for, bargain for, figure on, take into account, face.

reckoning n **1** by my reckoning: calculation, computation, estimate. **2** BILL, account, charge, due, score, settlement. **3** JUDGEMENT, retribution, doom.

reclaim v recover, regain, recapture, retrieve, salvage, rescue, redeem, restore, reinstate, regenerate.

recline v rest, repose, lean back, lie, lounge, loll, sprawl, stretch out.

recognition n **1** IDENTIFICATION, detection, discovery, recollection, recall, remembrance, awareness, perception, realization, understanding. **2** CONFESSION, admission, acceptance, acknowledgement, gratitude, appreciation, honour, respect, greeting, salute.

recognize v **1** IDENTIFY, know,

remember, recollect, recall, place, see, notice, spot, perceive. **2** CONFESS, own, acknowledge, accept, admit, grant, concede, allow, appreciate, understand, realize.

recollect v recall, remember, cast one's mind back, reminisce.

recollection n recall, remembrance, memory, souvenir, reminiscence, impression.

recommend v advocate, urge, exhort, advise, counsel, suggest, propose, put forward, advance, praise, commend, plug (infml), endorse, approve, vouch for.

F3 disapprove.

recommendation n advice, counsel, suggestion, proposal, advocacy, endorsement, approval, sanction, blessing, praise, commendation, plug (infml), reference, testimonial.

F3 disapproval.

recompense n compensation, indemnification, damages, reparation, restitution, amends, requital, repayment, reward, payment, remuneration, pay, wages.

reconcile v reunite, conciliate, pacify, appease, placate, propitiate, accord, harmonize, accommodate, adjust, resolve, settle, square.

F3 estrange, alienate.

reconciliation n reunion, conciliation, pacification, appeasement, propitiation, rapprochement, détente, settlement, agreement, harmony, accommodation, adjustment, compromise.

F3 estrangement, separation.

reconnoitre v explore, survey, scan, spy out, recce (sl), inspect, examine, scrutinize, investigate, patrol.

reconstruct v remake, rebuild, reassemble, re-establish, refashion, remodel, reform, reorganize, recreate, restore, renovate, regenerate.

record n **1** REGISTER, log, report, account, minutes, memorandum, note, entry, document, file, dossier, diary, journal, memoir, history, annals, archives, documentation, evidence, testimony, trace.
2 RECORDING, disc, single, CD, compact disc, album, release, LP.
3 break the record: fastest time, best performance, personal best, world record. **4** BACKGROUND, track record, curriculum vitae, career.
v **1** NOTE, enter, inscribe, write down, transcribe, register, log, put down, enrol, report, minute, chronicle, document, keep, preserve. **2** TAPE-RECORD, tape, videotape, video, cut.

recording n release, performance, record.

Types of recording include:
album, audiotape, cassette, CD, compact disc, DAT (digital audio-tape), digital recording, disc, DVD (digital versatile disk), EP (extended play), 45, gramophone record, long-playing record, LP, magnetic tape, MiniDisc®, mono recording, MP3, 78, single, stereo recording, tape, tape-recording, telerecording, video, videocassette, videodisc, videotape, vinyl (infml).

recount v tell, relate, impart, communicate, report, narrate, describe, depict, portray, detail, repeat, rehearse, recite.

recoup v recover, retrieve, regain, get back, make good, repay, refund, reimburse, compensate.

recover v **1** recover from illness: get better, improve, pick up, rally, mend, heal, pull through, get over, recuperate, revive, convalesce, come round. **2** REGAIN, get back, recoup, retrieve, retake, recapture, repossess, reclaim, restore.
F3 1 worsen. **2** lose, forfeit.

recovery n **1** RECUPERATION, convalescence, rehabilitation, mending, healing, improvement, upturn, rally, revival, restoration.
2 RETRIEVAL, salvage, reclamation, repossession, recapture.
F3 1 worsening. **2** loss, forfeit.

recreation n fun, enjoyment, pleasure, amusement, diversion, distraction, entertainment, hobby, pastime, game, sport, play, leisure, relaxation, refreshment.

recrimination n countercharge, accusation, counter-attack, retaliation, reprisal, retort, quarrel, bickering.

recruit v enlist, draft, conscript, enrol, sign up, engage, take on, mobilize, raise, gather, obtain, procure. n beginner, novice, initiate, learner, trainee, apprentice, conscript, convert.

rectify v correct, put right, right, remedy, cure, repair, fix, mend, improve, amend, adjust, reform.

recuperate v recover, get better, improve, pick up, rally, revive, mend, convalesce.
F3 worsen.

recur v repeat, persist, return, reappear.

recurrent adj recurring, chronic, persistent, repeated, repetitive, regular, periodic, frequent, intermittent.

recycle v reuse, reprocess, reclaim, recover, salvage, save.

red adj **1** SCARLET, vermilion, cherry, ruby, crimson, maroon, pink, reddish, bloodshot, inflamed. **2** RUDDY, florid, glowing, rosy, flushed, blushing, embarrassed, shamefaced. **3** red hair: ginger, carroty, auburn, chestnut, Titian.

redden v blush, flush, colour, go red, crimson.

redeem v **1** BUY BACK, repurchase, cash (in), exchange, change, trade, ransom, reclaim, regain, repossess, recoup, recover, recuperate, retrieve, salvage. **2** COMPENSATE FOR, make up for, offset, outweigh, atone for, expiate, absolve, acquit, discharge, release, liberate, emancipate, free, deliver, rescue, save.

reduce v **1** LESSEN, decrease, contract, shrink, slim, shorten, curtail, trim, cut, slash, discount, rebate, lower, moderate, weaken, diminish, impair. **2** DRIVE, force, degrade, downgrade, demote, humble, humiliate, impoverish, subdue, overpower, master, vanquish. **F3 1** increase, raise, boost.

reduction n decrease, drop, fall, decline, lessening, moderation, weakening, diminution, contraction, compression, shrinkage, narrowing, shortening, curtailment, restriction, limitation, cutback, cut, discount, rebate, devaluation, depreciation, deduction, subtraction, loss. **F3** increase, rise, enlargement.

redundant adj **1** UNEMPLOYED, out of work, laid off, dismissed. **2** SUPERFLUOUS, surplus, excess, extra, supernumerary, unneeded, unnecessary, unwanted. **3** WORDY, verbose, repetitious, tautological. **F3 2** necessary, essential. **3** concise.

reel v stagger, totter, wobble, rock, sway, waver, falter, stumble, lurch, pitch, roll, revolve, gyrate, spin, wheel, twirl, whirl, swirl.

refer v **1** SEND, direct, point, guide, pass on, transfer, commit, deliver. **2** refer to a catalogue: consult, look up, turn to, resort to. **3** ALLUDE, mention, touch on, speak of, bring up, recommend, cite, quote. **4** APPLY, concern, relate, belong, pertain.

referee n umpire, judge, adjudicator, arbitrator, mediator, ref (infml). v umpire, judge, adjudicate, arbitrate.

reference n **1** ALLUSION, remark, mention, citation, quotation, illustration, instance, note. **2** TESTIMONIAL, recommendation, endorsement, character. **3** RELATION, regard, respect, connection, bearing.

refine v process, treat, purify, clarify, filter, distil, polish, hone, improve, perfect, elevate, exalt.

refined adj civilized, cultured, cultivated, polished, sophisticated, urbane, genteel, gentlemanly, ladylike, well-bred, well-mannered, polite, civil, elegant, fine, delicate, subtle, precise, exact, sensitive, discriminating. **F3** coarse, vulgar, rude.

refinement n **1** MODIFICATION, alteration, amendment, improvement. **2** CULTIVATION, sophistication, urbanity, gentility, breeding, style, elegance, taste, discrimination, subtlety, finesse. **F3 1** deterioration. **2** coarseness, vulgarity.

reflect v **1** MIRROR, echo, imitate, reproduce, portray, depict, show, reveal, display, exhibit, manifest, demonstrate, indicate, express, communicate. **2** THINK, ponder, consider, deliberate, mull (over), contemplate, meditate, muse.

reflection n **1** IMAGE, likeness, echo, impression, indication, manifestation, observation, view, opinion. **2** THINKING, thought, study, consideration, deliberation, contemplation, meditation, musing.

reform v change, amend, improve, ameliorate, better, rectify, correct, mend, repair, rehabilitate, rebuild, reconstruct, remodel, revamp, renovate, restore, regenerate, reconstitute, reorganize, shake up (*infml*), revolutionize, purge. n change, amendment, improvement, rectification, correction, rehabilitation, renovation, reorganization, shake-up (*infml*), purge.

refrain v stop, cease, quit, leave off, renounce, desist, abstain, forbear, avoid.

refresh v **1** COOL, freshen, enliven, invigorate, fortify, revive, restore, renew, rejuvenate, revitalize, reinvigorate. **2** *refresh one's memory*: jog, stimulate, prompt, prod. **E3 1** tire, exhaust.

refreshing adj cool, thirst-quenching, bracing, invigorating, energizing, stimulating, inspiring, fresh, new, novel, original.

refreshment n sustenance, food, drink, snack, revival, restoration, renewal, reanimation, reinvigoration, revitalization.

refuge n sanctuary, asylum, shelter, protection, security, retreat, hideout, hide-away, resort, harbour, haven.

refugee n exile, émigré, displaced person, fugitive, runaway, escapee.

refund v repay, reimburse, rebate, return, restore. n repayment, reimbursement, rebate, return.

refusal n rejection, no, rebuff, repudiation, denial, negation. **E3** acceptance.

refuse[1] v reject, turn down, decline, spurn, repudiate, rebuff, repel, deny, withhold. **E3** accept, allow, permit.

refuse[2] n rubbish, waste, trash, garbage, junk, litter.

refute v disprove, rebut, confute, give the lie to, discredit, counter, negate.

regain v recover, get back, recoup, reclaim, repossess, retake, recapture, retrieve, return to.

regal adj majestic, kingly, queenly, princely, imperial, royal, sovereign, stately, magnificent, noble, lordly.

regard v consider, deem, judge, rate, value, think, believe, suppose, imagine, look upon, view, observe, watch. n care, concern, consideration, attention, notice, heed, respect, deference, honour, esteem, admiration, affection, love, sympathy. **E3** disregard, contempt.

regarding prep with regard to, as regards, concerning, with reference to, re, about, as to.

regardless adj disregarding, heedless, unmindful, neglectful, inattentive, unconcerned, indifferent. **E3** heedful, mindful, attentive. adv anyway, nevertheless, nonetheless, despite everything, come what may.

regime n government, rule, administration, management, leadership, command, control, establishment, system.

regimented adj strict, disciplined, controlled, regulated, standardized, ordered, methodical, systematic, organized.
F3 free, lax, disorganized.

region n land, terrain, territory, country, province, area, district, zone, belt, sector, neighbourhood, range, scope, expanse, domain, realm, sphere, field, division, section, part, place.

Types of geographical region include:
basin, belt, coast, continent, country, desert, forest, grassland, heath, hemisphere, interior, jungle, lowlands, marshland, outback, pampas, plain, prairie, savannah, scrubland, seaside, steppe, subcontinent, tract, tropics, tundra, veld, wasteland, wilderness, woodland.

Types of social region include:
commuter belt, development area, ghetto, ghost town, inner city, metropolis, new town, reservation, resort, riviera, satellite town, shanty town, suburb, township.

register n roll, roster, list, index, catalogue, directory, log, record, chronicle, annals, archives, file, ledger, schedule, diary, almanac.
v **1** RECORD, note, log, enter, inscribe, mark, list, catalogue, chronicle, enrol, enlist, sign on, check in. **2** SHOW, reveal, betray, display, exhibit, manifest, express, say, read, indicate.

regret v rue, repent, lament, mourn, grieve, deplore.
n remorse, contrition, compunction, self-reproach, shame, sorrow, grief, disappointment, bitterness.

regretful adj remorseful, rueful, repentant, contrite, penitent, conscience-stricken, ashamed, sorry, apologetic, sad, sorrowful, disappointed.
F3 impenitent, unashamed.

regrettable adj unfortunate, unlucky, unhappy, sad, disappointing, upsetting, distressing, lamentable, deplorable, shameful, wrong, ill-advised.
F3 fortunate, happy.

regular adj **1** ROUTINE, habitual, typical, usual, customary, time-honoured, conventional, orthodox, correct, official, standard, normal, ordinary, common, commonplace, everyday. **2** PERIODIC, rhythmic, steady, constant, fixed, set, unvarying, uniform, even, level, smooth, balanced, symmetrical, orderly, systematic, methodical.
F3 1 unusual, unconventional. **2** irregular.

regulate v control, direct, guide, govern, rule, administer, manage, handle, conduct, run, organize, order, arrange, settle, square, monitor, set, adjust, tune, moderate, balance.

regulation n rule, statute, law, ordinance, edict, decree, order, commandment, precept, dictate, requirement, procedure.
adj standard, official, statutory, prescribed, required, orthodox, accepted, customary, usual, normal.

rehearsal n practice, drill, exercise, dry run, run-through, preparation, reading, recital, narration, account, enumeration, list.

rehearse v practise, drill, train, go over, prepare, try out, repeat, recite, recount, relate.

reign n rule, sway, monarchy, empire, sovereignty, supremacy, power, command, dominion, control, influence.
v rule, govern, command, prevail, predominate, influence.

reimburse v refund, repay, return, restore, recompense, compensate, indemnify, remunerate.

reinforce v strengthen, fortify, toughen, harden, stiffen, steel, brace, support, buttress, shore, prop, stay, supplement, augment, increase, emphasize, stress, underline.
E3 weaken, undermine.

reinforcements n auxiliaries, reserves, back-up, support, help.

reinstate v restore, return, replace, recall, reappoint, reinstall, re-establish.

reject v refuse, deny, decline, turn down, veto, disallow, condemn, despise, spurn, rebuff, jilt, exclude, repudiate, repel, renounce, eliminate, scrap, discard, jettison, cast off.
E3 accept, choose, select.
n failure, second, discard, cast-off.

rejection n refusal, denial, veto, dismissal, rebuff, brush-off, exclusion, repudiation, renunciation, elimination.
E3 acceptance, choice, selection.

rejoice v celebrate, revel, delight, glory, exult, triumph.

rejoicing n celebration, revelry, merrymaking, festivity, happiness, gladness, joy, delight, elation, jubilation, exultation, triumph.

relapse v worsen, deteriorate, degenerate, weaken, sink, fail, lapse,
revert, regress, backslide.
n worsening, deterioration, setback, recurrence, weakening, lapse, reversion, regression, backsliding.

relate v 1 LINK, connect, join, couple, ally, associate, correlate. 2 REFER, apply, concern, pertain, appertain. 3 relate an anecdote: tell, recount, narrate, report, describe, recite. 4 IDENTIFY, sympathize, empathize, understand, feel for.

related adj kindred, akin, affiliated, allied, associated, connected, linked, interrelated, interconnected, accompanying, concomitant, joint, mutual.
E3 unrelated, unconnected.

relation n 1 LINK, connection, bond, relationship, correlation, comparison, similarity, affiliation, interrelation, interconnection, interdependence, regard, reference. 2 RELATIVE, family, kin, kindred.

relations n 1 RELATIVES, family, kin, kindred. 2 RELATIONSHIP, terms, rapport, liaison, intercourse, affairs, dealings, interaction, communications, contact, associations, connections.

relationship n bond, link, connection, association, liaison, rapport, affinity, closeness, similarity, parallel, correlation, ratio, proportion.

relative adj comparative, proportional, proportionate, commensurate, corresponding, respective, appropriate, relevant, applicable, related, connected, interrelated, reciprocal, dependent.
n relation, family, kin.

relax v slacken, loosen, lessen, reduce, diminish, weaken, lower, soften, moderate, abate, remit,

relieve, ease, rest, unwind, calm, tranquillize, sedate.
F3 tighten, intensify.

relaxation n **1** REST, repose, refreshment, leisure, recreation, fun, amusement, entertainment, enjoyment, pleasure. **2** SLACKENING, lessening, reduction, moderation, abatement, let-up (infml), détente, easing.
F3 2 tension, intensification.

relaxed adj informal, casual, laid-back (infml), easy-going (infml), carefree, happy-go-lucky, cool, calm, composed, collected, unhurried, leisurely.
F3 tense, nervous, formal.

relay n **1** BROADCAST, transmission, programme, communication, message, dispatch. **2** work in relays: shift, turn.
v broadcast, transmit, communicate, send, spread, carry, supply.

release v **1** LOOSE, unloose, unleash, unfasten, extricate, free, liberate, deliver, emancipate, acquit, absolve, exonerate, excuse, exempt, discharge. **2** ISSUE, publish, circulate, distribute, present, launch, unveil.
F3 1 imprison, detain, check.
n **1** FREEDOM, liberty, liberation, deliverance, emancipation, acquittal, absolution, exoneration, exemption, discharge. **2** ISSUE, publication, announcement, proclamation.
F3 1 imprisonment, detention.

relent v give in, give way, yield, capitulate, unbend, relax, slacken, soften, weaken.

relentless adj unrelenting, unremitting, incessant, persistent, unflagging, ruthless, remorseless, implacable, merciless, pitiless,

unforgiving, cruel, harsh, fierce, grim, hard, punishing, uncompromising, inflexible, unyielding, inexorable.
F3 merciful, yielding.

relevant adj pertinent, material, significant, germane, related, applicable, apposite, apt, appropriate, suitable, fitting, proper, admissible.
F3 irrelevant, inapplicable, inappropriate, unsuitable.

reliable adj unfailing, certain, sure, dependable, responsible, trusty, trustworthy, honest, true, faithful, constant, staunch, solid, safe, sound, stable, predictable, regular.
F3 unreliable, doubtful, untrustworthy.

reliance n dependence, trust, faith, belief, credit, confidence, assurance.

relic n memento, souvenir, keepsake, token, survival, remains, remnant, scrap, fragment, vestige, trace.

relief n reassurance, consolation, comfort, ease, alleviation, cure, remedy, release, deliverance, help, aid, assistance, support, sustenance, refreshment, diversion, relaxation, rest, respite, break, breather (infml), remission, let-up (infml), abatement.

relieve v reassure, console, comfort, ease, soothe, alleviate, mitigate, cure, release, deliver, free, unburden, lighten, soften, slacken, relax, calm, help, aid, assist, support, sustain.
F3 aggravate, intensify.

religion

Religions include:
Christianity, Church of England (C of E), Church of Scotland, Baptists, Catholicism, Methodism, Protestantism, Presbyterianism, Anglicanism, Congregationalism, Calvinism, evangelicalism, Free

Church, Jehovah's Witnesses, Mormonism, Quakerism, Amish; Baha'ism, Buddhism, Confucianism, Hinduism, Islam, Jainism, Judaism, Shintoism, Sikhism, Taoism, Zen, Zoroastrianism, voodoo, druidism; paganism.

Religious festivals include:
Buddhist: Buddha Purnima; *Christian*: Christmas, Easter, Whitsuntide (or Pentecost), Ascension; *Hindu*: Diwali, Dusserah, Holi, Onam; *Islamic*: Id al-Adha, Id al-Fitr; *Jewish*: Hanukkah, Passover, Purim, Rosh Hashanah, Shavuot, Yom Kippur; *Pagan*: Samhain, Yule (or Winter Solstice), Imbolc (or Candlemas), Ostara (or Spring Equinox), Beltane (or May Day), Litha (or Summer Solstice), Lughnasadh (or Lammas), Mabon (or Autumn Equinox).

Sacred writings include:
Bible, Old Testament, New Testament, Torah, Talmud, Koran, Bhagavad Gita, Mahabharata, Ramayana, Vedas, Granth, Zend-Avesta.

religious *adj* **1** SACRED, holy, divine, spiritual, devotional, scriptural, theological, doctrinal. **2** *a religious person*: devout, godly, pious, God-fearing, church-going, reverent, righteous.
E3 1 secular. **2** irreligious, ungodly.

relinquish *v* let go, release, hand over, surrender, yield, cede, give up, resign, renounce, repudiate, waive, forgo, abandon, desert, forsake, drop, discard.
E3 keep, retain.

relish *v* like, enjoy, savour, appreciate, revel in.

n **1** SEASONING, condiment, sauce, pickle, spice, piquancy, tang.
2 ENJOYMENT, pleasure, delight, gusto, zest.

reluctant *adj* unwilling, disinclined, indisposed, hesitant, slow, backward, loth, averse, unenthusiastic, grudging.
E3 willing, ready, eager.

rely *v* depend, lean, count, bank, reckon, trust, swear by.

remain *v* stay, rest, stand, dwell, abide, last, endure, survive, prevail, persist, continue, linger, wait.
E3 go, leave, depart.

remainder *n* rest, balance, surplus, excess, remnant, remains.

remaining *adj* left, unused, unspent, unfinished, residual, outstanding, surviving, persisting, lingering, lasting, abiding.

remains *n* rest, remainder, residue, dregs, leavings, leftovers, scraps, crumbs, fragments, remnants, oddments, traces, vestiges, relics, body, corpse, carcase, ashes, debris.

remark *v* comment, observe, note, mention, say, state, declare.
n comment, observation, opinion, reflection, mention, utterance, statement, assertion, declaration.

remarkable *adj* striking, impressive, noteworthy, surprising, amazing, strange, odd, unusual, uncommon, extraordinary, phenomenal, exceptional, outstanding, notable, conspicuous, prominent, distinguished.
E3 average, ordinary, commonplace, usual.

remedy *n* cure, antidote, countermeasure, corrective, restorative, medicine, treatment,

therapy, relief, solution, answer, panacea.
v correct, rectify, put right, redress, counteract, cure, heal, restore, treat, help, relieve, soothe, ease, mitigate, mend, repair, fix, solve.

remember *v* **1** RECALL, recollect, summon up, think back, reminisce, recognize, place. **2** MEMORIZE, learn, retain.
F∃ 1 forget.

remind *v* prompt, nudge, hint, jog one's memory, refresh one's memory, bring to mind, call to mind, call up.

reminder *n* prompt, nudge, hint, suggestion, memorandum, memo, souvenir, memento.

reminiscence *n* memory, remembrance, memoir, anecdote, recollection, recall, retrospection, review, reflection.

reminiscent *adj* suggestive, evocative, nostalgic.

remit *v* send, transmit, dispatch, post, mail, forward, pay, settle.
n brief, orders, instructions, guidelines, terms of reference, scope, authorization, responsibility.

remittance *n* sending, dispatch, payment, fee, allowance, consideration.

remnant *n* scrap, piece, bit, fragment, end, off cut, leftover, remainder, balance, residue, shred, trace, vestige.

remorse *n* regret, compunction, ruefulness, repentance, penitence, contrition, self-reproach, shame, guilt, bad conscience, sorrow, grief.

remote *adj* **1** DISTANT, far, faraway, far-off, outlying, out-of-the-way, inaccessible, god-forsaken, isolated, secluded, lonely. **2** DETACHED, aloof, standoffish, uninvolved, reserved,

withdrawn. **3** *a remote possibility*: slight, small, slim, slender, faint, negligible, unlikely, improbable.
F∃ 1 close, nearby, accessible.
2 friendly.

remove *v* detach, pull off, amputate, cut off, extract, pull out, take away, take off, strip, shed, doff, expunge, efface, erase, delete, strike out, get rid of, abolish, purge, eliminate, dismiss, discharge, eject, throw out, oust, depose, displace, dislodge, shift, move, transport, transfer, relocate.

remuneration *n* pay, wages, salary, emolument, stipend, fee, retainer, earnings, income, profit, reward, recompense, payment, remittance, repayment, reimbursement, compensation, indemnity.

render *v* **1** *they rendered it harmless*: make, cause to be, leave. **2** GIVE, provide, supply, tender, present, submit, hand over, deliver.
3 TRANSLATE, transcribe, interpret, explain, clarify, represent, perform, play, sing.

renew *v* **1** RENOVATE, modernize, refurbish, refit, recondition, mend, repair, overhaul, remodel, reform, transform, recreate, reconstitute, re-establish, regenerate, revive, resuscitate, refresh, rejuvenate, reinvigorate, revitalize, restore, replace, replenish, restock. **2** REPEAT, restate, reaffirm, extend, prolong, continue, recommence, restart, resume.

renounce *v* abandon, forsake, give up, resign, relinquish, surrender, discard, reject, spurn, disown, repudiate, disclaim, deny, recant, abjure.

renovate v restore, renew, recondition, repair, overhaul, modernize, refurbish, refit, redecorate, do up, remodel, reform, revamp, improve.

renown n fame, celebrity, stardom, acclaim, glory, eminence, illustriousness, distinction, note, mark, esteem, reputation, honour.
F3 obscurity, anonymity.

renowned adj famous, well-known, celebrated, acclaimed, famed, noted, eminent, distinguished, illustrious, notable.
F3 unknown, obscure.

rent n rental, lease, hire, payment, fee.
v let, sublet, lease, hire, charter.

repair v mend, fix, patch up, overhaul, service, rectify, redress, restore, renovate, renew.
n mend, patch, darn, overhaul, service, maintenance, restoration, adjustment, improvement.

repartee n banter, badinage, jesting, wit, riposte, retort.

repay v refund, reimburse, compensate, recompense, reward, remunerate, pay, settle, square, get even with, retaliate, reciprocate, revenge, avenge.

repeal v revoke, rescind, abrogate, quash, annul, nullify, void, invalidate, cancel, countermand, reverse, abolish.
F3 enact.

repeat v restate, reiterate, recapitulate, echo, quote, recite, relate, retell, reproduce, duplicate, renew, rebroadcast, reshow, replay, rerun, redo.
n repetition, echo, reproduction, duplicate, rebroadcast, reshowing, replay, rerun.

repeatedly adv time after time, time and (time) again, again and again, over and over, frequently, often.

repel v **1** DRIVE BACK, repulse, check, hold off, ward off, parry, resist, oppose, fight, refuse, decline, reject, rebuff. **2** DISGUST, revolt, nauseate, sicken, offend.
F3 1 attract. **2** delight.

repent v regret, rue, sorrow, lament, deplore, atone.

repentance n penitence, contrition, remorse, compunction, regret, sorrow, grief, guilt, shame.

repentant adj penitent, contrite, sorry, apologetic, remorseful, regretful, rueful, chastened, ashamed.
F3 unrepentant.

repercussion n result, consequence, backlash, reverberation, echo, rebound, recoil.

repetition n restatement, reiteration, recapitulation, echo, return, reappearance, recurrence, duplication, tautology.

repetitive adj recurrent, monotonous, tedious, boring, dull, mechanical, unchanging, unvaried.

replace v **1** replace the lid: put back, return, restore, make good, reinstate, re-establish. **2** SUPERSEDE, succeed, follow, supplant, oust, deputize, substitute.

replacement n substitute, stand-in, understudy, fill-in, supply, proxy, surrogate, successor.

replenish v refill, restock, reload, recharge, replace, restore, renew, supply, provide, furnish, stock, fill, top up.

replica n model, imitation, reproduction, facsimile, copy, duplicate, clone.

reply v answer, respond, retort, rejoin, react, acknowledge, return, echo, reciprocate, counter, retaliate. n answer, response, retort, rejoinder, riposte, repartee, reaction, comeback, acknowledgement, return, echo, retaliation.

report n article, piece, write-up, record, account, relation, narrative, description, story, tale, gossip, hearsay, rumour, talk, statement, communiqué, declaration, announcement, communication, information, news, word, message, note.
v state, announce, declare, proclaim, air, broadcast, relay, publish, circulate, communicate, notify, tell, recount, relate, narrate, describe, detail, cover, document, record, note.

reporter n journalist, correspondent, columnist, newspaperman, newspaperwoman, hack, newscaster, commentator, announcer.

represent v stand for, symbolize, designate, denote, mean, express, evoke, depict, portray, describe, picture, draw, sketch, illustrate, exemplify, typify, epitomize, embody, personify, appear as, act as, enact, perform, show, exhibit, be, amount to, constitute.

representation n **1** LIKENESS, image, icon, picture, portrait, illustration, sketch, model, statue, bust, depiction, portrayal, description, account, explanation.
2 PERFORMANCE, production, play, show, spectacle.

representative n delegate, deputy, proxy, stand-in, spokesperson, spokesman, spokeswoman, ambassador, commissioner, agent, salesman, saleswoman, rep (infml), traveller.
adj typical, illustrative, exemplary, archetypal, characteristic, usual, normal, symbolic.
E3 unrepresentative, atypical.

repress v inhibit, check, control, curb, restrain, suppress, bottle up, hold back, stifle, smother, muffle, silence, quell, crush, quash, subdue, overpower, overcome, master, subjugate, oppress.

repression n inhibition, restraint, suppression, suffocation, gagging, censorship, authoritarianism, despotism, tyranny, oppression, domination, control, constraint, coercion.

repressive adj oppressive, authoritarian, despotic, tyrannical, dictatorial, autocratic, totalitarian, absolute, harsh, severe, tough, coercive.

reprieve v pardon, let off, spare, rescue, redeem, relieve, respite.
n pardon, amnesty, suspension, abeyance, postponement, deferment, remission, respite, relief, let-up (infml), abatement.

reprimand n rebuke, reproof, reproach, admonition, telling-off (infml), ticking-off (infml), lecture, talking-to (infml), dressing-down (infml), censure, blame.
v rebuke, reprove, reproach, admonish, scold, chide, tell off (infml), tick off (infml), lecture, criticize, slate (infml), censure, blame.

reprisal n retaliation, counter-attack, retribution, requital, revenge, vengeance.

reproach v rebuke, reprove, reprimand, upbraid, scold, chide, reprehend, blame, censure, condemn, criticize, disparage, defame.
n rebuke, reproof, reprimand, scolding, blame, censure, condemnation, criticism, disapproval, scorn, contempt, shame, disgrace.

reproachful adj reproving, upbraiding, scolding, censorious, critical, fault-finding, disapproving, scornful.

E3 complimentary.

reproduce v 1 COPY, transcribe, print, duplicate, mirror, echo, repeat, imitate, emulate, match, simulate, recreate, reconstruct. 2 BREED, spawn, procreate, generate, propagate, multiply.

reproduction n 1 COPY, print, picture, duplicate, facsimile, replica, clone, imitation. 2 BREEDING, procreation, generation, propagation, multiplication.

E3 1 original.

reproductive adj procreative, generative, sexual, sex, genital.

reproof n rebuke, reproach, reprimand, admonition, upbraiding, dressing-down (infml), scolding, telling-off (infml), ticking-off (infml), censure, condemnation, criticism.

E3 praise.

reprove v rebuke, reproach, reprimand, upbraid, scold, chide, tell off (infml), reprehend, admonish, censure, condemn, criticize.

E3 praise.

reptile

Reptiles include:
adder, puff-adder, grass snake, tree-snake, asp, viper, rattlesnake, side-winder, anaconda, boa constrictor, cobra, king-cobra, mamba, python; lizard, frilled lizard, chameleon, gecko, iguana, skink, slowworm; turtle, green turtle, hawksbill turtle, terrapin, tortoise, giant tortoise; alligator, crocodile.

repugnance n reluctance, distaste, dislike, aversion, hatred, loathing, abhorrence, horror, repulsion, revulsion, disgust.

E3 liking, pleasure, delight.

repulsive adj repellent, repugnant, revolting, disgusting, nauseating, sickening, offensive, distasteful, objectionable, obnoxious, foul, vile, loathsome, abominable, abhorrent, hateful, horrid, unpleasant, disagreeable, ugly, hideous, forbidding.

E3 attractive, pleasant, delightful.

reputable adj respectable, reliable, dependable, trustworthy, upright, honourable, creditable, worthy, good, excellent, irreproachable.

E3 disreputable, infamous.

reputation n honour, character, standing, stature, esteem, opinion, credit, repute, fame, renown, celebrity, distinction, name, good name, bad name, infamy, notoriety.

reputed adj alleged, supposed, said, rumoured, believed, thought, considered, regarded, estimated, reckoned, held, seeming, apparent, ostensible.

E3 actual, true.

request v ask for, solicit, demand, require, seek, desire, beg, entreat, supplicate, petition, appeal.
n appeal, call, demand, requisition, desire, application, solicitation, suit, petition, entreaty, supplication, prayer.

require v 1 NEED, want, wish, desire, lack, miss. 2 *you are required to attend*: oblige, force, compel, constrain, make, ask, request, instruct, direct, order, demand, necessitate, take, involve.

requirement n need, necessity, essential, must, requisite, prerequisite, demand, stipulation, condition, term, specification, proviso, qualification, provision.

requisite adj required, needed, necessary, essential, obligatory, compulsory, set, prescribed.

requisition v request, put in for, demand, commandeer, appropriate, take, confiscate, seize, occupy.

rescue v save, recover, salvage, deliver, free, liberate, release, redeem, ransom.
🔄 capture, imprison.
n saving, recovery, salvage, deliverance, liberation, release, redemption, salvation.
🔄 capture.

research n investigation, inquiry, fact-finding, groundwork, examination, analysis, scrutiny, study, search, probe, exploration, experimentation.
v investigate, examine, analyse, scrutinize, study, search, probe, explore, experiment.

resemblance n likeness, similarity, sameness, parity, conformity, closeness, affinity, parallel, comparison, analogy, correspondence, image, facsimile.
🔄 dissimilarity.

resemble v be like, look like, take after, favour, mirror, echo, duplicate, parallel, approach.
🔄 differ from.

resent v grudge, begrudge, envy, take offence at, take umbrage at, take amiss, object to, grumble at, take exception to, dislike.
🔄 accept, like.

resentful adj grudging, envious, jealous, bitter, embittered, hurt, wounded, offended, aggrieved, put out, miffed (*infml*), peeved (*infml*), indignant, angry, vindictive.
🔄 satisfied, contented.

resentment n grudge, envy, jealousy, bitterness, spite, malice, ill-will, ill-feeling, animosity, hurt, umbrage, pique, displeasure, irritation, indignation, vexation, anger, vindictiveness.
🔄 contentment, happiness.

reservation n 1 DOUBT, scepticism, misgiving, qualm, scruple, hesitation, second thought. 2 PROVISO, stipulation, qualification. 3 RESERVE, preserve, park, sanctuary, homeland, enclave. 4 BOOKING, engagement, appointment.

reserve v 1 SET APART, earmark, keep, retain, hold back, save, store, stockpile. 2 *reserve a seat*: book, engage, order, secure.
🔄 use up.
n 1 STORE, stock, supply, fund, stockpile, cache, hoard, savings. 2 SHYNESS, reticence, secretiveness, coolness, aloofness, modesty, restraint. 3 RESERVATION, preserve, park, sanctuary. 4 REPLACEMENT, substitute, stand-in.
🔄 friendliness, openness.

reserved adj 1 BOOKED, engaged, taken, spoken for, set aside, earmarked, meant, intended, designated, destined, saved, held, kept, retained. 2 SHY, retiring,

reticent, unforthcoming, uncommunicative, secretive, silent, taciturn, unsociable, cool, aloof, standoffish, unapproachable, modest, restrained, cautious.
F3 1 unreserved, free, available. **2** friendly, open.

reside v live, inhabit, dwell, lodge, stay, sojourn, settle, remain.

residence n dwelling, habitation, domicile, abode, seat, place, home, house, lodgings, quarters, hall, manor, mansion, palace, villa, country-house, country-seat.

resident n inhabitant, citizen, local, householder, occupier, tenant, lodger, guest.
F3 non-resident.

residual adj remaining, leftover, unused, unconsumed, net.

resign v stand down, leave, quit, abdicate, vacate, renounce, relinquish, forgo, waive, surrender, yield, abandon, forsake.
F3 join.

resign oneself reconcile oneself, accept, bow, submit, yield, comply, acquiesce.
F3 resist.

resignation n **1** STANDING-DOWN, abdication, retirement, departure, notice, renunciation, relinquishment, surrender. **2** ACCEPTANCE, acquiescence, submission, non-resistance, passivity, patience, stoicism, defeatism.
F3 2 resistance.

resigned adj reconciled, philosophical, stoical, patient, unprotesting, unresisting, submissive, defeatist.
F3 resistant.

resilient adj **1** resilient material: flexible, pliable, supple, plastic,

elastic, springy, bouncy. **2** STRONG, tough, hardy, adaptable, buoyant.
F3 1 rigid, brittle.

resist v oppose, defy, confront, fight, combat, weather, withstand, repel, counteract, check, avoid, refuse.
F3 submit, accept.

resistant adj **1** OPPOSED, antagonistic, defiant, unyielding, intransigent, unwilling. **2** PROOF, impervious, immune, invulnerable, tough, strong.
F3 1 compliant, yielding.

resolute adj determined, resolved, set, fixed, unwavering, staunch, firm, steadfast, relentless, single-minded, persevering, dogged, tenacious, stubborn, obstinate, strong-willed, undaunted, unflinching, bold.
F3 irresolute, weak-willed, half-hearted.

resolution n **1** DETERMINATION, resolve, willpower, commitment, dedication, devotion, firmness, steadfastness, persistence, perseverance, doggedness, tenacity, zeal, courage, boldness. **2** DECISION, judgement, finding, declaration, proposition, motion.
F3 1 half-heartedness, uncertainty, indecision.

resolve v decide, make up one's mind, determine, fix, settle, conclude, sort out, work out, solve.

resort v go, visit, frequent, patronize, haunt.
n recourse, refuge, course (of action), alternative, option, chance, possibility.

resort to turn to, use, utilize, employ, exercise.

resound v resonate, reverberate, echo, re-echo, ring, boom, thunder.

resounding adj 1 RESONANT, reverberating, echoing, ringing, sonorous, booming, thunderous, full, rich, vibrant. 2 a resounding victory: decisive, conclusive, crushing, thorough.
F3 1 faint.

resource n 1 SUPPLY, reserve, stockpile, source, expedient, contrivance, device.
2 RESOURCEFULNESS, initiative, ingenuity, inventiveness, talent, ability, capability.

resourceful adj ingenious, imaginative, creative, inventive, innovative, original, clever, bright, sharp, quick-witted, able, capable, talented.

resources n materials, supplies, reserves, holdings, funds, money, wealth, riches, capital, assets, property, means.

respect n 1 ADMIRATION, esteem, appreciation, recognition, honour, deference, reverence, veneration, politeness, courtesy. 2 in every respect: point, aspect, facet, feature, characteristic, particular, detail, sense, way, regard, reference, relation, connection.
F3 1 disrespect.
v 1 ADMIRE, esteem, regard, appreciate, value. 2 OBEY, observe, heed, follow, honour, fulfil.
F3 1 despise, scorn. 2 ignore, disobey.

respectable adj 1 HONOURABLE, worthy, respected, dignified, upright, honest, decent, clean-living.
2 ACCEPTABLE, tolerable, passable, adequate, fair, reasonable, appreciable, considerable.
F3 1 dishonourable, disreputable.
2 inadequate, paltry.

respectful adj deferential, reverential, humble, polite, well-mannered, courteous, civil.
F3 disrespectful.

respective adj corresponding, relevant, various, several, separate, individual, personal, own, particular, special.

respond v answer, reply, retort, acknowledge, react, return, reciprocate.

response n answer, reply, retort, comeback, acknowledgement, reaction, feedback.
F3 query.

responsibility n fault, blame, guilt, culpability, answerability, accountability, duty, obligation, burden, onus, charge, care, trust, authority, power.

responsible adj 1 GUILTY, culpable, at fault, to blame, liable, answerable, accountable. 2 a responsible citizen: dependable, reliable, conscientious, trustworthy, honest, sound, steady, sober, mature, sensible, rational.
3 IMPORTANT, authoritative, executive, decision-making.
F3 2 irresponsible, unreliable, untrustworthy.

rest[1] n 1 LEISURE, relaxation, repose, lie-down, sleep, snooze, nap, siesta, idleness, inactivity, motionlessness, standstill, stillness, tranquillity, calm. 2 BREAK, pause, breathing-space, breather (infml), intermission, interlude, interval, recess, holiday, vacation, halt, cessation, lull, respite. 3 SUPPORT, prop, stand, base.
F3 1 action, activity. 2 work.
v 1 PAUSE, halt, stop, cease. 2 RELAX, repose, sit, recline, lounge, laze, lie down, sleep, snooze, doze. 3 DEPEND,

rely, hinge, hang, lie. **4** LEAN, prop, support, stand.

F≡1 continue. **2** work.

rest² *n* remainder, others, balance, surplus, excess, residue, remains, leftovers, remnants.

restaurant *n* eating-house, bistro, steakhouse, grill room, dining-room, snack-bar, buffet, cafeteria, café, diner.

restful *adj* relaxing, soothing, calm, tranquil, serene, peaceful, quiet, undisturbed, relaxed, comfortable, leisurely, unhurried.

F≡ tiring, restless.

restless *adj* fidgety, unsettled, disturbed, troubled, agitated, nervous, anxious, worried, uneasy, fretful, edgy, jumpy, restive, unruly, turbulent, sleepless.

F≡ calm, relaxed, comfortable.

restore *v* **1** REPLACE, return, reinstate, rehabilitate, re-establish, reintroduce, re-enforce. **2** *restore a building:* renovate, renew, rebuild, reconstruct, refurbish, retouch, recondition, repair, mend, fix. **3** REVIVE, refresh, rejuvenate, revitalize, strengthen.

F≡1 remove. **2** damage. **3** weaken.

restrain *v* **1** HOLD BACK, keep back, suppress, subdue, repress, inhibit, check, curb, bridle, stop, arrest, prevent, restrict, regulate, control, govern. **2** BIND, tie, chain, fetter, manacle.

F≡1 encourage. **2** liberate.

restrained *adj* moderate, temperate, mild, subdued, muted, quiet, soft, low-key, unobtrusive, discreet, tasteful, calm, controlled, steady, self-controlled.

F≡ unrestrained.

restraint *n* **1** MODERATION, inhibition, self-control, self-discipline, hold, grip, check, curb, rein, bridle, suppression, restriction, control, constraint, limitation, tie, hindrance, prevention.

2 CONFINEMENT, bonds, chains, fetters.

F≡2 liberty.

restrict *v* limit, bound, demarcate, control, regulate, confine, contain, cramp, constrain, impede, hinder, hamper, handicap, tie, restrain, curtail.

F≡ broaden, free.

restriction *n* limit, bound, confine, limitation, constraint, restraint, handicap, check, curb, restraint, ban, embargo, control, regulation, rule, stipulation, condition, proviso.

F≡ freedom.

result *n* effect, consequence, sequel, repercussion, reaction, outcome, upshot, issue, end-product, fruit, score, answer, verdict, judgement, decision, conclusion.

F≡ cause.

v follow, ensue, happen, occur, issue, emerge, arise, spring, derive, stem, flow, proceed, develop, end, finish, terminate, culminate.

F≡ cause.

resume *v* restart, recommence, reopen, reconvene, continue, carry on, go on, proceed.

F≡ cease.

resumption *n* restart, recommencement, reopening, renewal, resurgence, continuation.

F≡ cessation.

resurrect *v* restore, revive, resuscitate, reactivate, bring back, reintroduce, renew.

F≡ kill, bury.

resurrection n restoration, revival, resuscitation, renaissance, rebirth, renewal, resurgence, reappearance, return, comeback.

resuscitate v revive, resurrect, save, rescue, reanimate, quicken, reinvigorate, revitalize, restore, renew.

retain v 1 KEEP, hold, reserve, hold back, save, preserve. 2 *retain information*: remember, memorize. 3 EMPLOY, engage, hire, commission.
F3 1 release. 2 forget. 3 dismiss.

retaliate v reciprocate, counter-attack, hit back, strike back, fight back, get one's own back, get even with, take revenge.

retaliation n reprisal, counter-attack, revenge, vengeance, retribution.

reticent adj reserved, shy, uncommunicative, unforthcoming, tight-lipped, secretive, taciturn, silent, quiet.
F3 communicative, forward, frank.

retire v leave, depart, withdraw, retreat, recede.
F3 join, enter, advance.

retirement n withdrawal, retreat, solitude, loneliness, seclusion, privacy, obscurity.

retiring adj shy, bashful, timid, shrinking, quiet, reticent, reserved, self-effacing, unassertive, modest, unassuming, humble.
F3 bold, forward, assertive.

retort v answer, reply, respond, rejoin, return, counter, retaliate.
n answer, reply, response, rejoinder, riposte, repartee, quip.

retract v take back, withdraw, recant, reverse, revoke, rescind, cancel,

repeal, repudiate, disown, disclaim, deny.
F3 assert, maintain.

retreat v draw back, recoil, shrink, turn tail (*infml*), withdraw, retire, leave, depart, quit.
F3 advance.
n 1 WITHDRAWAL, departure, evacuation, flight. 2 SECLUSION, privacy, hideaway, den, refuge, asylum, sanctuary, shelter, haven.
F3 1 advance, charge.

retrieve v fetch, bring back, regain, get back, recapture, repossess, recoup, recover, salvage, save, rescue, redeem, restore, return.
F3 lose.

retrograde adj retrogressive, backward, reverse, negative, downward, declining, deteriorating.
F3 progressive.

retrospect n hindsight, afterthought, re-examination, review, recollection, remembrance.
F3 prospect.

return v 1 COME BACK, reappear, recur, go back, backtrack, regress, revert. 2 GIVE BACK, hand back, send back, deliver, put back, replace, restore. 3 *return a favour*: reciprocate, requite, repay, refund, reimburse, recompense.
F3 1 leave, depart. 2 take.
n 1 REAPPEARANCE, recurrence, comeback, home-coming. 2 REPAYMENT, recompense, replacement, restoration, reinstatement, reciprocation. 3 REVENUE, income, proceeds, takings, yield, gain, profit, reward, advantage, benefit.
F3 1 departure, disappearance. 2 removal. 3 payment, expense, loss.

reveal v expose, uncover, unveil, unmask, show, display, exhibit, manifest, disclose, divulge.
F3 hide, conceal, mask.

revelation n **1** UNCOVERING, unveiling, unmasking, show, display, exhibition, manifestation, disclosure.
2 CONFESSION, admission, giveaway, leak.

revel in enjoy, relish, savour, delight in, thrive on, bask in, glory in, lap up, indulge in, wallow in, luxuriate in.

revelry n celebration, festivity, party, merrymaking, jollity, fun, carousal, debauchery.
F3 sobriety.

revenge n vengeance, satisfaction, reprisal, retaliation, requital, retribution.
v avenge, repay, retaliate, get one's own back.

revenue n income, return, yield, interest, profit, gain, proceeds, receipts, takings.
F3 expenditure.

reverberate v echo, re-echo, resound, resonate, ring, boom, vibrate.

revere v respect, esteem, honour, pay homage to, venerate, worship, adore, exalt.
F3 despise, scorn.

reverence n respect, deference, honour, homage, admiration, awe, veneration, worship, adoration, devotion.
F3 contempt, scorn.

reverent adj reverential, respectful, deferential, humble, dutiful, awed, solemn, pious, devout, adoring, loving.
F3 irreverent, disrespectful.

reversal n negation, cancellation, annulment, nullification, countermanding, revocation, rescinding, repeal, reverse, turnabout, turnaround, U-turn, volte-face, upset.
F3 advancement, progress.

reverse v **1** BACK, retreat, backtrack, undo, negate, cancel, annul, invalidate, countermand, overrule, revoke, rescind, repeal, retract, quash, overthrow. **2** TRANSPOSE, turn round, invert, up-end, overturn, upset, change, alter.
F3 1 advance, enforce.
n **1** UNDERSIDE, back, rear, inverse, converse, contrary, opposite, antithesis. **2** MISFORTUNE, mishap, misadventure, adversity, affliction, hardship, trial, blow, disappointment, setback, check, delay, problem, difficulty, failure, defeat.
adj opposite, contrary, converse, inverse, inverted, backward, back, rear.

revert v return, go back, resume, lapse, relapse, regress.

review v **1** CRITICIZE, assess, evaluate, judge, weigh, discuss, examine, inspect, scrutinize, study, survey, recapitulate. **2** review the situation: reassess, re-evaluate, re-examine, reconsider, rethink, revise.
n **1** CRITICISM, critique, assessment, evaluation, judgement, report, commentary, examination, scrutiny, analysis, study, survey, recapitulation, reassessment, re-evaluation, re-examination, revision. **2** MAGAZINE, periodical, journal.

revise v **1** revise one's opinion: change, alter, modify, amend, correct, update, edit, rewrite, reword, recast, revamp, reconsider, re-examine, review. **2** STUDY, learn, swot up (*infml*), cram (*infml*).

revival *n* resuscitation, revitalization, restoration, renewal, renaissance, rebirth, reawakening, resurgence, upsurge.

revive *v* resuscitate, reanimate, revitalize, restore, renew, refresh, animate, invigorate, quicken, rouse, awaken, recover, rally, reawaken, rekindle, reactivate.

Fʒ weary.

revoke *v* repeal, rescind, quash, abrogate, annul, nullify, invalidate, negate, cancel, countermand, reverse, retract, withdraw.

Fʒ enforce.

revolt *n* revolution, rebellion, mutiny, rising, uprising, insurrection, putsch, coup (d'état), secession, defection.

v **1** REBEL, mutiny, rise, riot, resist, dissent, defect. **2** DISGUST, sicken, nauseate, repel, offend, shock, outrage, scandalize.

Fʒ 1 submit. **2** please, delight.

revolting *adj* disgusting, sickening, nauseating, repulsive, repellent, obnoxious, nasty, horrible, foul, loathsome, abhorrent, distasteful, offensive, shocking, appalling.

Fʒ pleasant, delightful, attractive, palatable.

revolution *n* **1** REVOLT, rebellion, mutiny, rising, uprising, insurrection, putsch, coup (d'état), reformation, change, transformation, innovation, upheaval, cataclysm. **2** ROTATION, turn, spin, cycle, circuit, round, circle, orbit, gyration.

revolutionary *n* rebel, mutineer, insurgent, anarchist, revolutionist.

adj **1** REBEL, rebellious, mutinous,

insurgent, subversive, seditious, anarchistic. **2** *revolutionary ideas*: new, innovative, avant-garde, cutting-edge, different, drastic, radical, thoroughgoing.

Fʒ 1 conservative.

revolve *v* rotate, turn, pivot, swivel, spin, wheel, whirl, gyrate, circle, orbit.

revulsion *n* repugnance, disgust, distaste, dislike, aversion, hatred, loathing, abhorrence, abomination.

Fʒ delight, pleasure, approval.

reward *n* prize, honour, medal, decoration, bounty, pay-off, bonus, premium, payment, remuneration, recompense, repayment, requital, compensation, gain, profit, return, benefit, merit, desert, retribution.

Fʒ punishment.

v pay, remunerate, recompense, repay, requite, compensate, honour, decorate.

Fʒ punish.

rewarding *adj* profitable, remunerative, lucrative, productive, fruitful, worthwhile, valuable, advantageous, beneficial, satisfying, gratifying, pleasing, fulfilling, enriching.

Fʒ unrewarding.

rhetoric *n* eloquence, oratory, grandiloquence, magniloquence, bombast, pomposity, hyperbole, verbosity, wordiness.

rhetorical *adj* oratorical, grandiloquent, magniloquent, bombastic, declamatory, pompous, high-sounding, grand, high-flown, flowery, florid, flamboyant, showy, pretentious, artificial, insincere.

Fʒ simple.

rhyme *n* poetry, verse, poem, ode, limerick, jingle, song, ditty.

rhythm n beat, pulse, time, tempo, metre, measure, movement, flow, lilt, swing, accent, cadence, pattern.

rhythmic adj rhythmical, metric, metrical, pulsating, throbbing, flowing, lilting, periodic, regular, steady.

rich adj **1** WEALTHY, affluent, moneyed, prosperous, well-to-do, well-off, loaded (sl). **2** PLENTIFUL, abundant, copious, profuse, prolific, ample, full. **3** FERTILE, fruitful, productive, lush. **4** rich food: creamy, fatty, full-bodied, heavy, full-flavoured, strong, spicy, savoury, tasty, delicious, luscious, juicy, sweet. **5** rich colours: deep, intense, vivid, bright, vibrant, warm. **6** EXPENSIVE, precious, valuable, lavish, sumptuous, opulent, luxurious, splendid, gorgeous, fine, elaborate, ornate.

F3 1 poor, impoverished. **3** barren. **4** plain, bland. **5** dull, soft. **6** plain.

riches n wealth, affluence, money, gold, treasure, fortune, assets, property, substance, resources, means.

F3 poverty.

rickety adj unsteady, wobbly, shaky, unstable, insecure, flimsy, jerry-built, decrepit, ramshackle, broken-down, dilapidated, derelict.

F3 stable, strong.

rid v clear, purge, free, deliver, relieve, unburden.

riddle¹ n enigma, mystery, conundrum, brain-teaser, puzzle, poser, problem.

riddle² v **1** PERFORATE, pierce, puncture, pepper, fill, permeate, pervade, infest. **2** SIFT, sieve, strain, filter, mar, winnow.

ride v sit, move, progress, travel, journey, gallop, trot, pedal, drive, steer, control, handle, manage.
n journey, trip, outing, jaunt, spin, drive, lift.

ridicule n satire, irony, sarcasm, mockery, jeering, scorn, derision, taunting, teasing, chaff, banter, badinage, laughter.

F3 praise.

v satirize, send up, caricature, lampoon, burlesque, parody, mock, make fun of, jeer, scoff, deride, sneer, tease, rib (infml), humiliate, taunt.

F3 praise.

ridiculous adj ludicrous, absurd, nonsensical, silly, foolish, stupid, contemptible, derisory, laughable, farcical, comical, funny, hilarious, outrageous, preposterous, incredible, unbelievable.

F3 sensible.

rife adj abundant, rampant, teeming, raging, epidemic, prevalent, widespread, general, common, frequent.

F3 scarce.

rift n **1** SPLIT, breach, break, fracture, crack, fault, chink, cleft, cranny, crevice, gap, space, opening. **2** DISAGREEMENT, difference, separation, division, schism, alienation.

F3 2 unity.

rig n equipment, kit, outfit, gear, tackle, apparatus, machinery, fittings, fixtures.

rig out equip, kit out, outfit, fit (out), supply, furnish, clothe, dress (up).

right adj **1** the right answer: correct, accurate, exact, precise, true, factual, actual, real. **2** PROPER, fitting, seemly, becoming, appropriate, suitable, fit, admissible, satisfactory, reasonable,

desirable, favourable, advantageous.
3 FAIR, just, equitable, lawful, honest,
upright, good, virtuous, righteous,
moral, ethical, honourable. **4** RIGHT-
WING, conservative, Tory.

F3 1 wrong, incorrect. **2** improper,
unsuitable. **3** unfair, wrong. **4** left-
wing.

adv **1** CORRECTLY, accurately, exactly,
precisely, factually, properly,
satisfactorily, well, fairly. **2** *right to the
bottom*: straight, directly, completely,
utterly.

F3 1 wrongly, incorrectly, unfairly.

n **1** PRIVILEGE, prerogative, due, claim,
business, authority, power. **2** JUSTICE,
legality, good, virtue, righteousness,
morality, honour, integrity,
uprightness.

F3 2 wrong.

v rectify, correct, put right, fix, repair,
redress, vindicate, avenge, settle,
straighten, stand up.

right away straight away,
immediately, at once, now, instantly,
directly, forthwith, without delay,
promptly.

F3 later, eventually.

rightful *adj* legitimate, lawful, legal,
just, bona fide, true, real, genuine,
valid, authorized, correct, proper,
suitable, due.

F3 wrongful, unlawful.

rigid *adj* stiff, inflexible, unbending,
cast-iron, hard, firm, set, fixed,
unalterable, invariable, austere, harsh,
severe, unrelenting, strict, rigorous,
stringent, stern, uncompromising,
unyielding.

F3 flexible, elastic.

rigorous *adj* strict, stringent, rigid,
firm, exact, precise, accurate,
meticulous, painstaking, scrupulous,

conscientious, thorough.

F3 lax, superficial.

rile *v* annoy, irritate, nettle, pique,
peeve (*infml*), put out, upset, irk, vex,
anger, exasperate.

F3 calm, soothe.

rim *n* lip, edge, brim, brink, verge,
margin, border, circumference.

F3 centre, middle.

rind *n* peel, skin, husk, crust.

ring¹ *n* **1** CIRCLE, round, loop, hoop,
halo, band, girdle, collar, circuit,
arena, enclosure. **2** GROUP, cartel,
syndicate, association, organization,
gang, crew, mob, band, cell, clique,
coterie.

v surround, encircle, gird,
circumscribe, encompass, enclose.

ring² *v* **1** CHIME, peal, toll, tinkle,
clink, jingle, clang, sound, resound,
resonate, reverberate, buzz.

2 TELEPHONE, phone, call, ring up.

n **1** CHIME, peal, toll, tinkle, clink,
jingle, clang. **2** PHONE CALL, call, buzz
(*infml*), tinkle (*infml*).

rinse *v* swill, bathe, wash, clean,
cleanse, flush, wet, dip.

riot *n* insurrection, rising, uprising,
revolt, rebellion, anarchy,
lawlessness, affray, disturbance,
turbulence, disorder, confusion,
commotion, tumult, turmoil, uproar,
row, quarrel, strife.

F3 order, calm.

v revolt, rebel, rise up, run riot, run
wild, rampage.

rip *v* tear, rend, split, separate,
rupture, burst, cut, slit, slash, gash,
lacerate, hack.

n tear, rent, split, cleavage, rupture,
cut, slit, slash, gash, hole.

rip off (*sl*) overcharge, swindle,
defraud, cheat, diddle, do (*infml*),

fleece, sting (sl), con (infml), trick, dupe, exploit.

ripe adj **1** RIPENED, mature, mellow, seasoned, grown, developed, complete, finished, perfect. **2** READY, suitable, right, favourable, auspicious, propitious, timely, opportune.

F3 2 untimely, inopportune.

ripen v develop, mature, mellow, season, age.

rise v **1** GO UP, ascend, climb, mount, slope (up), soar, tower, grow, increase, escalate, intensify. **2** STAND UP, get up, arise, jump up, spring up. **3** ADVANCE, progress, improve, prosper.
4 ORIGINATE, spring, flow, issue, emerge, appear.

F3 1 fall, descend. **2** sit down.
3 decline.

n **1** ASCENT, climb, slope, incline, hill, elevation. **2** INCREASE, increment, upsurge, upturn, advance, progress, improvement, advancement, promotion.

F3 1 descent, valley. **2** fall.

risk n danger, peril, jeopardy, hazard, chance, possibility, uncertainty, gamble, speculation, venture, adventure.

F3 safety, certainty.

v endanger, imperil, jeopardize, hazard, chance, gamble, venture, dare.

risky adj dangerous, unsafe, perilous, hazardous, chancy, uncertain, touch-and-go, dicey (infml), tricky, precarious.

F3 safe.

risqué adj indecent, improper, indelicate, suggestive, coarse, crude, earthy, bawdy, racy, naughty, blue.

F3 decent, proper.

ritual n custom, tradition, convention, usage, practice, habit,

wont, routine, procedure, ordinance, prescription, form, formality, ceremony, ceremonial, solemnity, rite, sacrament, service, liturgy, observance, act.

adj customary, traditional, conventional, habitual, routine, procedural, prescribed, set, formal, ceremonial.

F3 informal.

rival n competitor, contestant, contender, challenger, opponent, adversary, antagonist, match, equal, peer.

F3 colleague, associate.

adj competitive, competing, opposed, opposing, conflicting.

F3 associate.

v compete with, contend with, vie with, oppose, emulate, match, equal.

F3 co-operate.

rivalry n competitiveness, competition, contest, contention, conflict, struggle, strife, opposition, antagonism.

F3 co-operation.

river n waterway, watercourse, tributary, stream, brook, beck, creek, estuary.

road n roadway, motorway, bypass, highway, thoroughfare, street, avenue, boulevard, crescent, drive, lane, track, route, course, way, direction.

roam v wander, rove, range, travel, walk, ramble, stroll, amble, prowl, drift, stray.

F3 stay.

roar v, n bellow, yell, shout, cry, bawl, howl, hoot, guffaw, thunder, crash, blare, rumble.

F3 whisper.

rob v steal from, hold up, raid, burgle, loot, pillage, plunder, sack, rifle, ransack, swindle, rip off (*sl*), do (*infml*), cheat, defraud, deprive.

robbery *n* theft, stealing, larceny, hold-up, stick-up (*sl*), heist (*sl*), raid, burglary, pillage, plunder, raid, embezzlement, swindle, rip-off (*sl*).

robot *n* automaton, machine, android, zombie.

robust *adj* strong, sturdy, tough, hardy, vigorous, powerful, muscular, athletic, fit, healthy, well.

F3 weak, feeble, unhealthy.

rock[1] *n* boulder, stone, pebble, crag, outcrop.

Rocks include:

basalt, breccia, chalk, coal, conglomerate, flint, gabbro, gneiss, granite, lava, limestone, marble, marl, obsidian, porphyry, pumice stone, sandstone, schist, serpentinite, shale, slate.

rock[2] *v* **1** SWAY, swing, tilt, tip, shake, wobble, roll, pitch, toss, lurch, reel, stagger, totter. **2** *news that rocked the nation*: shock, stun, daze, dumbfound, astound, astonish, surprise, startle.

rocky[1] *adj* stony, pebbly, craggy, rugged, rough, hard, flinty.

F3 smooth, soft.

rocky[2] *adj* unsteady, shaky, wobbly, staggering, tottering, unstable, unreliable, uncertain, weak.

F3 steady, stable, dependable, strong.

rod *n* bar, shaft, strut, pole, stick, baton, wand, cane, switch, staff, mace, sceptre.

rodent

Rodents include:

agouti, beaver, black rat, brown rat, cane rat, capybara, cavy, chinchilla, chipmunk, cony, coypu, dormouse, fieldmouse, gerbil, gopher, grey squirrel, groundhog, guinea pig, hamster, hare, harvest mouse, jerboa, kangaroo-rat, lemming, marmot, mouse, muskrat, musquash, pika, porcupine, prairie dog, rabbit, rat, red squirrel, sewer-rat, squirrel, vole, water rat, water vole, woodchuck.

rogue *n* scoundrel, rascal, scamp, villain, miscreant, crook (*infml*), swindler, fraud, cheat, con man (*infml*), reprobate, wastrel, ne'er-do-well.

role *n* part, character, representation, portrayal, impersonation, function, capacity, task, duty, job, post, position.

roll *v* **1** ROTATE, revolve, turn, spin, wheel, twirl, whirl, gyrate, move, run, pass. **2** WIND, coil, furl, twist, curl, wrap, envelop, enfold, bind. **3** *the ship rolled*: rock, sway, swing, pitch, toss, lurch, reel, wallow, undulate. **4** PRESS, flatten, smooth, level. **5** RUMBLE, roar, thunder, boom, resound, reverberate. *n* **1** ROLLER, cylinder, drum, reel, spool, bobbin, scroll. **2** REGISTER, roster, census, list, inventory, index, catalogue, directory, schedule, record, chronicle, annals. **3** ROTATION, revolution, cycle, turn, spin, wheel, twirl, whirl, gyration, undulation. **4** RUMBLE, roar, thunder, boom, resonance, reverberation.

roll up (*infml*) arrive, assemble, gather, congregate, convene.

F3 leave.

romance *n* **1** LOVE AFFAIR, affair, relationship, liaison, intrigue, passion. **2** LOVE STORY, novel, story, tale, fairy tale, legend, idyll, fiction, fantasy. **3** ADVENTURE, excitement, melodrama, mystery, charm, fascination, glamour, sentiment.

v lie, fantasize, exaggerate, overstate.

romantic *adj* **1** IMAGINARY, fictitious, fanciful, fantastic, legendary, fairy-tale, idyllic, utopian, idealistic, quixotic, visionary, starry-eyed, dreamy, unrealistic, impractical, improbable, wild, extravagant, exciting, fascinating. **2** SENTIMENTAL, loving, amorous, passionate, tender, fond, lovey-dovey (*infml*), soppy, mushy, sloppy.
F3 1 real, practical. **2** unromantic, unsentimental.
n sentimentalist, dreamer, visionary, idealist, utopian.
F3 realist.

room *n* space, volume, capacity, headroom, legroom, elbow-room, scope, range, extent, leeway, latitude, margin, allowance, chance, opportunity.

> Types of room include:
> attic, loft, box room, bedroom, bou-
> doir, spare room, dressing-room,
> guest-room, nursery, playroom,
> sitting-room, lounge, front room,
> living-room, drawing-room, salon,
> reception room, dining-room,
> study, den (*infml*), library, kitchen,
> kitchenette, breakfast-room, larder,
> pantry, scullery, bathroom, en suite
> bathroom, toilet, lavatory, rest room
> (*N Am*), WC, loo (*infml*), cloakroom,
> utility room, hall, landing, conserva-
> tory, sun lounge, cellar, basement;
> classroom, music room, laboratory,
> office, sickroom, dormitory, work-
> room, studio, workshop, storeroom,
> waiting-room, anteroom, foyer.

roomy *adj* spacious, capacious, large, sizable, broad, wide, extensive, ample, generous.
F3 cramped, small, tiny.

root[1] *n* **1** TUBER, rhizome, stem.
2 ORIGIN, source, derivation, cause, starting point, fount, fountainhead, seed, germ, nucleus, heart, core, nub, essence, seat, base, bottom, basis, foundation.
v anchor, moor, fasten, fix, set, stick, implant, embed, entrench, establish, ground, base.
root out unearth, dig out, uncover, discover, uproot, eradicate, extirpate, eliminate, exterminate, destroy, abolish, clear away, remove.

root[2] *v* dig, delve, burrow, forage, hunt, rummage, ferret, poke, pry, nose.

roots *n* beginning(s), origins, family, heritage, background, birthplace, home.

rope *n* line, cable, cord, string, strand.
v tie, bind, lash, fasten, hitch, moor, tether.
rope in enlist, engage, involve, persuade, inveigle.

roster *n* rota, schedule, register, roll, list.

rostrum *n* platform, stage, dais, podium.

rot *v* decay, decompose, putrefy, fester, perish, corrode, spoil, go bad, go off, degenerate, deteriorate, crumble, disintegrate, taint, corrupt.
n **1** DECAY, decomposition, putrefaction, corrosion, rust, mould.
2 (*infml*) NONSENSE, rubbish, poppycock (*infml*), drivel, claptrap.

rotary *adj* rotating, revolving, turning, spinning, whirling, gyrating.
F3 fixed.

rotate *v* revolve, turn, spin, gyrate, pivot, swivel, roll.

rotation n revolution, turn, spin, gyration, orbit, cycle, sequence, succession, turning, spinning.

rotten adj **1** DECAYED, decomposed, putrid, addled, bad, off, mouldy, fetid, stinking, rank, foul, rotting, decaying, disintegrating. **2** INFERIOR, bad, poor, inadequate, low-grade, lousy, crummy (sl), ropy (sl), mean, nasty, beastly, dirty, despicable, contemptible, dishonourable, wicked. **3** (infml) ILL, sick, unwell, poorly, grotty (sl), rough (infml).
F3 1 fresh. **2** good. **3** well.

rough adj **1** UNEVEN, bumpy, lumpy, rugged, craggy, jagged, irregular, coarse, bristly, scratchy. **2** HARSH, severe, tough, hard, cruel, brutal, drastic, extreme, brusque, curt, sharp. **3** APPROXIMATE, estimated, imprecise, inexact, vague, general, cursory, hasty, incomplete, unfinished, crude, rudimentary. **4** rough sea: choppy, agitated, turbulent, stormy, tempestuous, violent, wild. **5** (infml) ILL, sick, unwell, poorly, off colour, rotten (infml).
F3 1 smooth. **2** mild. **3** accurate. **4** calm. **5** well.

round adj **1** SPHERICAL, globular, ball-shaped, circular, ring-shaped, disc-shaped, cylindrical, rounded, curved. **2** ROTUND, plump, stout, portly.
n **1** CIRCLE, ring, band, disc, sphere, ball, orb. **2** CYCLE, series, sequence, succession, period, bout, session. **3** BEAT, circuit, lap, course, routine.
v circle, skirt, flank, bypass.
round off finish (off), complete, end, close, conclude, cap, crown.
F3 begin.

round on turn on, attack, lay into, abuse.

round up herd, marshal, assemble, gather, rally, collect, group.
F3 disperse, scatter.

roundabout adj circuitous, tortuous, twisting, winding, indirect, oblique, devious, evasive.
F3 straight, direct.

rouse v wake (up), awaken, arouse, call, stir, move, start, disturb, agitate, anger, provoke, stimulate, instigate, incite, inflame, excite, galvanize, whip up.
F3 calm.

rout n defeat, conquest, overthrow, beating, thrashing, flight, stampede.
F3 win.
v defeat, conquer, overthrow, crush, beat, hammer (infml), thrash, lick, put to flight, chase, dispel, scatter.

route n course, run, path, road, avenue, way, direction, itinerary, journey, passage, circuit, round, beat.

routine n **1** PROCEDURE, way, method, system, order, pattern, formula, practice, usage, custom, habit. **2** comedy routine: act, piece, programme, performance.
adj customary, habitual, usual, typical, ordinary, run-of-the-mill, normal, standard, conventional, unoriginal, predictable, familiar, everyday, banal, humdrum, dull, boring, monotonous, tedious.
F3 unusual, different, exciting.

row [1] n line, tier, bank, rank, range, column, file, queue, string, series, sequence.

row [2] n **1** ARGUMENT, quarrel, dispute, controversy, squabble, tiff, slanging match (infml), fight, brawl. **2** NOISE, racket, din, uproar, commotion,

disturbance, rumpus, fracas.
F2 calm.
v argue, quarrel, wrangle, bicker,
squabble, fight, scrap.

rowdy *adj* noisy, loud, rough,
boisterous, disorderly, unruly, riotous,
wild.
F2 quiet, peaceful.

royal *adj* regal, majestic, kingly,
queenly, princely, imperial,
monarchical, sovereign, august,
grand, stately, magnificent, splendid,
superb.

rub *v* apply, spread, smear, stroke,
caress, massage, knead, chafe, grate,
scrape, abrade, scour, scrub, clean,
wipe, smooth, polish, buff, shine.

rub out erase, efface, obliterate, delete,
cancel.

rubbish *n* **1** REFUSE, garbage, trash,
junk, litter, waste, dross, debris,
flotsam and jetsam. **2** NONSENSE,
drivel, claptrap, twaddle, gibberish,
gobbledegook, balderdash,
poppycock (*infml*), rot (*infml*),
cobblers (*sl*).
F2 2 sense.

ruddy *adj* red, scarlet, crimson,
blushing, flushed, rosy, glowing,
healthy, blooming, florid, sunburnt.
F2 pale.

rude *adj* **1** IMPOLITE, discourteous,
disrespectful, impertinent, impudent,
cheeky (*infml*), insolent, offensive,
insulting, abusive, ill-mannered, ill-
bred, uncouth, uncivilized, unrefined,
unpolished, uneducated, untutored,
uncivil, curt, brusque, abrupt, sharp,
short. **2** *a rude joke:* obscene, vulgar,
coarse, dirty, naughty, gross.
F2 1 polite, courteous, civil. **2** clean,
decent.

rudimentary *adj* primary, initial,

introductory, elementary, basic,
fundamental, primitive, undeveloped,
embryonic.
F2 advanced, developed.

rudiments *n* basics, fundamentals,
essentials, principles, elements, ABC,
beginnings, foundations.

rugged *adj* **1** ROUGH, bumpy,
uneven, irregular, jagged, rocky,
craggy, stark. **2** STRONG, robust,
hardy, tough, muscular, weather-
beaten.
F2 1 smooth.

ruin *n* destruction, devastation,
wreckage, havoc, damage, disrepair,
decay, disintegration, breakdown,
collapse, fall, downfall, failure, defeat,
overthrow, ruination, undoing,
insolvency, bankruptcy, crash.
F2 development, reconstruction.
v spoil, mar, botch, mess up (*infml*),
damage, break, smash, shatter, wreck,
destroy, demolish, raze, devastate,
overwhelm, overthrow, defeat, crush,
impoverish, bankrupt.
F2 develop, restore.

rule *n* **1** REGULATION, law, statute,
ordinance, decree, order, direction,
guide, precept, tenet, canon, maxim,
axiom, principle, formula, guideline,
standard, criterion. **2** REIGN,
sovereignty, supremacy, dominion,
mastery, power, authority, command,
control, influence, regime,
government, leadership. **3** CUSTOM,
convention, practice, routine, habit,
wont.
v **1** *rule a country:* reign, govern,
command, lead, administer, manage,
direct, guide, control, regulate,
prevail, dominate. **2** JUDGE,
adjudicate, decide, find, determine,
resolve, establish, decree, pronounce.

as a rule usually, normally, ordinarily, generally.

rule out exclude, eliminate, reject, dismiss, preclude, prevent, ban, prohibit, forbid, disallow.

ruler

Titles of rulers include:
Aga, begum, Caesar, caliph, consul, emir, emperor, empress, governor, governor-general, head of state, kaiser, khan, king, maharajah, maharani, mikado, monarch, nawab, nizam, Pharaoh, president, prince, princess, queen, rajah, rani, regent, shah, sheikh, shogun, sovereign, sultan, sultana, suzerain, tsar, viceroy.

ruling n judgement, adjudication, verdict, decision, finding, resolution, decree, pronouncement.
adj reigning, sovereign, supreme, governing, commanding, leading, main, chief, principal, dominant, predominant, controlling.

rumour n hearsay, gossip, talk, whisper, word, news, report, story, grapevine, bush telegraph.

run v 1 SPRINT, jog, race, career, tear, dash, hurry, rush, speed, bolt, dart, scoot, scuttle. 2 GO, pass, move, proceed, issue. 3 FUNCTION, work, operate, perform. 4 run a company: head, run, administer, direct, manage, superintend, supervise, oversee, control, regulate. 5 COMPETE, contend, stand, challenge. 6 LAST, continue, extend, reach, stretch, spread, range. 7 FLOW, stream, pour, gush.
n 1 JOG, gallop, race, sprint, spurt, dash, rush. 2 DRIVE, ride, spin, jaunt, excursion, outing, trip, journey.
3 SEQUENCE, series, string, chain, course.

run after chase, pursue, follow, tail.
F3 flee.

run away escape, flee, abscond, bolt, scarper (sl), beat it (infml), run off, make off, clear off (infml).
F3 stay.

run down 1 CRITICIZE, belittle, disparage, denigrate, defame. 2 RUN OVER, knock over, hit, strike. 3 TIRE, weary, exhaust, weaken. 4 run down production: reduce, decrease, drop, cut, trim, curtail.
F3 1 praise. 4 increase.

run into meet, encounter, run across, bump into, hit, strike, collide with.
F3 miss.

run out expire, terminate, end, cease, close, finish, dry up, fail.

runaway n escaper, escapee, fugitive, absconder, deserter, refugee.
adj escaped, fugitive, loose, uncontrolled.

rundown n 1 REDUCTION, decrease, decline, drop, cut. 2 SUMMARY, résumé, synopsis, outline, review, recap, run-through.

runner n jogger, sprinter, athlete, competitor, participant, courier, messenger.

running adj successive, consecutive, unbroken, uninterrupted, continuous, constant, perpetual, incessant, unceasing, moving, flowing.
F3 broken, occasional.
n 1 ADMINISTRATION, direction, management, organization, co-ordination, superintendency, supervision, leadership, charge, control, regulation, functioning, working, operation, performance, conduct. 2 out of the running: contention, contest, competition.

runny adj flowing, fluid, liquid,

liquefied, melted, molten, watery, diluted.

Ⓐ solid.

run-of-the-mill adj ordinary, common, everyday, average, unexceptional, unremarkable, undistinguished, unimpressive, mediocre.

Ⓐ exceptional.

rupture n split, tear, burst, puncture, break, breach, fracture, crack, separation, division, schism, rift. v split, tear, burst, puncture, break, fracture, crack, sever, separate, divide.

rural adj country, rustic, pastoral, agricultural, agrarian.

Ⓐ urban.

rush v hurry, hasten, quicken, accelerate, speed (up), press, push, dispatch, bolt, dart, shoot, fly, tear, career, dash, race, run, sprint, scramble, stampede, charge. n hurry, haste, urgency, speed, swiftness, dash, race, scramble, stampede, charge, flow, surge.

rust n corrosion, oxidation.

v corrode, decay, rot, oxidize, tarnish, deteriorate, decline.

rustic adj 1 PASTORAL, sylvan, bucolic, countrified, country, rural. 2 PLAIN, simple, rough, crude, coarse, rude, clumsy, awkward, artless, unsophisticated, unrefined, uncultured, provincial, uncouth, boorish, oafish.

Ⓐ 1 urban. 2 urbane, sophisticated, cultivated, polished.

rustle v, n crackle, whoosh, swish, whisper.

rusty adj 1 CORRODED, rusted, rust-covered, oxidized, tarnished, discoloured, dull. 2 UNPRACTISED, weak, poor, deficient, dated, old-fashioned, outmoded, antiquated, stale, stiff, creaking.

ruthless adj merciless, pitiless, hard-hearted, hard, heartless, unfeeling, callous, cruel, inhuman, brutal, savage, cut-throat, fierce, ferocious, relentless, unrelenting, inexorable, implacable, harsh, severe.

Ⓐ merciful, compassionate.

S

sabotage *v* damage, spoil, mar, disrupt, vandalize, wreck, destroy, thwart, scupper, cripple, incapacitate, disable, undermine, weaken.
n vandalism, damage, impairment, disruption, wrecking, destruction.

sack *v* dismiss, fire, discharge, axe (*infml*), lay off, make redundant.
n dismissal, discharge, one's cards, notice, the boot (*infml*), the push (*infml*), the elbow (*infml*), the axe (*infml*), the chop (*infml*).

sacred *adj* holy, divine, heavenly, blessed, hallowed, sanctified, consecrated, dedicated, religious, devotional, ecclesiastical, priestly, saintly, godly, venerable, revered, sacrosanct, inviolable.
E3 temporal, profane.

sacrifice *v* surrender, forfeit, relinquish, let go, abandon, renounce, give up, forgo, offer, slaughter.
n offering, immolation, slaughter, destruction, surrender, renunciation, loss.

sacrilege *n* blasphemy, profanity, heresy, desecration, profanation, violation, outrage, irreverence, disrespect, mockery.
E3 piety, reverence, respect.

sacrosanct *adj* sacred, hallowed, untouchable, inviolable, impregnable, protected, secure.

sad *adj* **1** UNHAPPY, sorrowful, tearful, grief-stricken, heavy-hearted, upset, distressed, miserable, low-spirited, downcast, glum, long-faced, crestfallen, dejected, down-hearted, despondent, melancholy, depressed, low, gloomy, dismal. **2** *sad news*: upsetting, distressing, painful, depressing, touching, poignant, heart-rending, tragic, grievous, lamentable, regrettable, sorry, unfortunate, serious, grave, disastrous.
E3 1 happy, cheerful. **2** fortunate, lucky.

sadden *v* upset, distress, grieve, depress, dismay, discourage, dishearten.
E3 cheer, please, gratify, delight.

saddle *v* burden, encumber, lumber, impose, tax, charge, load (*infml*).

sadistic *adj* cruel, inhuman, brutal, savage, vicious, merciless, pitiless, barbarous, bestial, unnatural, perverted.

safe *adj* **1** HARMLESS, innocuous, non-toxic, non-poisonous, uncontaminated. **2** UNHARMED, undamaged, unscathed, uninjured, unhurt, intact, secure, protected, guarded, impregnable, invulnerable, immune. **3** UNADVENTUROUS, cautious, prudent, conservative, sure, proven, tried, tested, sound, dependable, reliable, trustworthy.

F3 1 dangerous, harmful. **2** vulnerable, exposed. **3** risky.

safeguard v protect, preserve, defend, guard, shield, screen, shelter, secure.

F3 endanger, jeopardize.

n protection, defence, shield, security, surety, guarantee, assurance, insurance, cover, precaution.

safe-keeping n protection, care, custody, keeping, charge, trust, guardianship, surveillance, supervision.

safety n protection, refuge, sanctuary, shelter, cover, security, safeguard, immunity, impregnability, safeness, harmlessness, reliability, dependability.

F3 danger, jeopardy, risk.

sag v bend, give, bag, droop, hang, fall, drop, sink, dip, decline, slump, flop, fail, flag, weaken, wilt.

F3 bulge, rise.

sail v **1** sail for France: embark, set sail, weigh anchor, put to sea, cruise, voyage. **2** CAPTAIN, skipper, pilot, navigate, steer. **3** GLIDE, plane, sweep, float, skim, scud, fly.

sailor n seafarer, mariner, seaman, marine, rating, yachtsman, yachtswoman.

saintly adj godly, pious, devout, God-fearing, holy, religious, blessed, angelic, pure, spotless, innocent, blameless, sinless, virtuous, upright, worthy, righteous.

F3 godless, unholy, wicked.

sake n benefit, advantage, good, welfare, wellbeing, gain, profit, behalf, interest, account, regard, respect, cause, reason.

salary n pay, remuneration, emolument, stipend, wages, earnings, income.

sale n selling, marketing, vending, disposal, trade, traffic, transaction, deal, auction.

salesperson n salesman, saleswoman, sales assistant, shop assistant, shop-boy, shop-girl, shop-keeper, representative, rep (infml).

salient adj important, significant, chief, main, principal, striking, conspicuous, noticeable, obvious, prominent, outstanding, remarkable.

sallow adj yellowish, pale, pallid, wan, pasty, sickly, unhealthy, anaemic, colourless.

F3 rosy, healthy.

salt n seasoning, taste, flavour, savour, relish, piquancy.

salty adj salt, salted, saline, briny, brackish, savoury, spicy, piquant, tangy.

F3 fresh, sweet.

salubrious adj sanitary, hygienic, health-giving, healthy, wholesome, pleasant.

salutary adj good, beneficial, advantageous, profitable, valuable, helpful, useful, practical, timely.

salute v greet, acknowledge, recognize, wave, hail, address, nod, bow, honour.

n greeting, acknowledgement, recognition, wave, gesture, hail, address, handshake, nod, bow, tribute, reverence.

salvage v save, preserve, conserve, rescue, recover, recuperate, retrieve, reclaim, redeem, repair, restore.

F3 waste, abandon.

salvation n deliverance, liberation, rescue, saving, preservation,

salve n ointment, lotion, cream, balm, liniment, embrocation, medication, preparation, application.

same adj identical, twin, duplicate, indistinguishable, equal, selfsame, very, alike, like, similar, comparable, equivalent, matching, corresponding, mutual, reciprocal, interchangeable, substitutable, synonymous, consistent, uniform, unvarying, changeless, unchanged.
F3 different, inconsistent, variable, changeable.

sample n specimen, example, cross-section, model, pattern, swatch, piece, demonstration, illustration, instance, sign, indication, foretaste.
v try, test, taste, sip, inspect, experience.
adj representative, specimen, demonstrative, demo (infml), illustrative, dummy, trial, test, pilot.

sanctify v hallow, consecrate, bless, anoint, dedicate, cleanse, purify, exalt, canonize.
F3 desecrate, defile.

sanctimonious adj self-righteous, holier-than-thou, pious, moralizing, smug, superior, hypocritical, pharisaical.
F3 humble.

sanction n authorization, permission, agreement, OK (infml), approval, go-ahead, ratification, confirmation, support, backing, endorsement, licence, authority.
F3 veto, disapproval.
v authorize, allow, permit, approve, ratify, confirm, support, back, endorse, underwrite, accredit, license, warrant.
F3 veto, forbid, disapprove.

sanctions n restrictions, boycott, embargo, ban, prohibition, penalty.

sanctity n holiness, sacredness, inviolability, piety, godliness, religiousness, devotion, grace, spirituality, purity, goodness, righteousness.
F3 unholiness, secularity, worldliness, godlessness, impurity.

sanctuary n **1** CHURCH, temple, tabernacle, shrine, altar. **2** ASYLUM, refuge, protection, shelter, haven, retreat.

sand n beach, shore, strand, sands, grit.

sane adj normal, rational, right-minded, all there (infml), balanced, stable, sound, sober, level-headed, sensible, judicious, reasonable, moderate.
F3 insane, mad, crazy, foolish.

sanitary adj clean, pure, uncontaminated, unpolluted, aseptic, germ-free, disinfected, hygienic, salubrious, healthy, wholesome.
F3 insanitary, unwholesome.

sanity n normality, rationality, reason, sense, common sense, balance of mind, stability, soundness, level-headedness, judiciousness.
F3 insanity, madness.

sap v bleed, drain, exhaust, weaken, undermine, deplete, reduce, diminish, impair.
F3 strengthen, build up, increase.

sarcasm n irony, satire, mockery, sneering, derision, scorn, contempt, cynicism, bitterness.

sarcastic adj ironical, satirical, mocking, taunting, sneering, derisive, scathing, disparaging, cynical, incisive, cutting, biting, caustic.

sardonic adj mocking, jeering,

sneering, derisive, scornful, sarcastic, biting, cruel, heartless, malicious, cynical, bitter.

sash n belt, girdle, cummerbund, waistband.

satanic adj satanical, diabolical, devilish, demonic, fiendish, hellish, infernal, inhuman, malevolent, wicked, evil, black.
F₃ holy, divine, godly, saintly, benevolent.

satire n ridicule, irony, sarcasm, wit, burlesque, skit, send-up, spoof, take-off, parody, caricature, travesty.

satirical adj ironical, sarcastic, mocking, irreverent, taunting, derisive, sardonic, incisive, cutting, biting, caustic, cynical, bitter.

satirize v ridicule, mock, make fun of, burlesque, lampoon, send up, take off, parody, caricature, criticize, deride.
F₃ acclaim, honour.

satisfaction n **1** GRATIFICATION, contentment, happiness, pleasure, enjoyment, comfort, ease, well-being, fulfilment, self-satisfaction, pride. **2** SETTLEMENT, compensation, reimbursement, indemnification, damages, reparation, amends, redress, recompense, requital, vindication.
F₃ 1 dissatisfaction, displeasure.

satisfactory adj acceptable, passable, up to the mark, all right, OK (infml), cushty (sl), fair, average, competent, adequate, sufficient, suitable, proper.
F₃ unsatisfactory, unacceptable, inadequate.

satisfy v **1** GRATIFY, indulge, content, please, delight, quench, slake, sate, satiate, surfeit. **2** satisfy requirements:

meet, fulfil, discharge, settle, answer, fill, suffice, serve, qualify. **3** ASSURE, convince, persuade.
F₃ 1 dissatisfy. **2** fail.

saturate v soak, steep, souse, drench, waterlog, impregnate, permeate, imbue, suffuse, fill.

sauce

Types of sauce, dip and dressing include:
sauces: gravy, tartare, Worcester-shire, béchamel, white, brown, barbecue, tomato ketchup, hollandaise, Tabasco®, apple, mint, cranberry, horseradish, pesto; *dips*: fondue, guacamole, hummus, salsa, taramasalata; *dressings*: mayonnaise, French dressing, olive-oil, balsamic vinegar, salad cream.

saucy adj cheeky (infml), impertinent, impudent, insolent, disrespectful, pert, forward, presumptuous, flippant.
F₃ polite, respectful.

saunter v stroll, amble, mosey (infml), mooch (infml), wander, ramble (sl), meander.
n stroll, walk, constitutional, ramble.

savage adj wild, untamed, undomesticated, uncivilized, primitive, barbaric, barbarous, fierce, ferocious, vicious, beastly, cruel, inhuman, brutal, sadistic, bloodthirsty, bloody, murderous, pitiless, merciless, ruthless, harsh.
F₃ tame, civilized, humane, mild.
n brute, beast, barbarian.
v attack, bite, claw, tear, maul, mangle.

save v **1** ECONOMIZE, save, conserve, preserve, keep, retain, hold, reserve, store, lay up, set aside, put by, hoard, stash (infml), collect, gather. **2** RESCUE, deliver, liberate, free, salvage, recover, reclaim. **3** PROTECT, guard, screen, shield, safeguard, spare, prevent, hinder.

F3 1 spend, squander, waste, discard. *n* economy, thrift, discount, reduction, bargain, cut, conservation, preservation.

F3 expense, waste, loss.

savings *n* capital, investments, nest egg, fund, store, reserves, resources.

saviour *n* rescuer, deliverer, redeemer, liberator, emancipator, guardian, protector, defender, champion.

F3 destroyer.

savour *n* taste, flavour, smack, smell, tang, piquancy, salt, spice, relish, zest. *v* relish, enjoy, delight in, revel in, like, appreciate.

F3 shrink from.

savoury *adj* **1** TASTY, appetizing, delicious, mouthwatering, luscious, palatable. **2** *savoury pancakes*: salty, spicy, aromatic, piquant, tangy.

F3 1 unappetizing, tasteless, insipid. **2** sweet.

say *v* **1** SPEAK, express, phrase, put, render, utter, voice, articulate, enunciate, pronounce, deliver, quote, recite. **2** ANSWER, reply, respond, rejoin, retort. **3** STATE, comment, remark, observe, mention, announce, declare, assert, affirm, maintain, point out, claim, profess, relate, reveal, disclose, divulge. **4** COMMUNICATE, convey, intimate, suggest, imply, signify. **5** TELL, instruct, command, order. **6** GUESS, estimate, reckon, judge, imagine, suppose, surmise.

> Ways of saying include:
> accuse, babble, bark, bawl, beg, bellow, blurt, boast, complain, confide, croak, cry, curse, drawl, echo, emphasize, enquire, exclaim, expostulate, gasp, groan, growl, grumble, grunt, howl, implore, jeer, joke, laugh, lecture, lie, mimic, moan, mumble, murmur, mutter, nag, plead, protest, question, rant, rebuke, remonstrate, request, roar, scoff, scold, scream, screech, shout, shriek, snap, snarl, squeak, stammer, storm, stutter, swear, taunt, tease, thunder, urge, whine, whisper, yell.

saying *n* adage, proverb, dictum, precept, axiom, aphorism, maxim, motto, slogan, phrase, expression, quotation, statement, remark.

scale^1 *n* ratio, proportion, measure, degree, extent, spread, reach, range, scope, compass, spectrum, gamut, sequence, series, progression, order, hierarchy, ranking, ladder, steps, gradation, graduation, calibration, register.

v climb, ascend, mount, clamber, scramble, shin up, conquer, surmount.

scale^2 *n* encrustation, deposit, crust, layer, film, lamina, plate, flake, scurf.

scamp *n* rogue, rascal, scallywag, monkey, imp, devil.

scamper *v* scuttle, scurry, scoot, dart, dash, run, sprint, rush, hurry, hasten, fly, romp, frolic, gambol.

scan *v* **1** EXAMINE, scrutinize, study, search, survey, sweep, investigate, check. **2** SKIM, glance at, flick through, thumb through.

n screening, examination, scrutiny, search, probe, check, investigation, survey, review.

scandal *n* outrage, offence, outcry, uproar, furore, gossip, rumours, smear, dirt, discredit, dishonour, sleaze (*infml*), disgrace, shame, embarrassment, ignominy.

scandalize *v* shock, horrify, appal, dismay, disgust, repel, revolt, offend, affront, outrage.

scandalous *adj* shocking, appalling, atrocious, abominable, monstrous, unspeakable, outrageous, disgraceful, shameful, disreputable, infamous, improper, unseemly, defamatory, scurrilous, slanderous, libellous, untrue.

scanty *adj* deficient, short, inadequate, insufficient, scant, little, limited, restricted, narrow, poor, meagre, insubstantial, thin, skimpy, sparse, bare.
Ea adequate, sufficient, ample, plentiful, substantial.

scar *n* mark, lesion, wound, injury, blemish, stigma.
v mark, disfigure, spoil, damage, brand, stigmatize.

scarce *adj* few, rare, infrequent, uncommon, unusual, sparse, scanty, insufficient, deficient, lacking.
Ea plentiful, common.

scarcely *adv* hardly, barely, only just.

scarcity *n* lack, shortage, dearth, deficiency, insufficiency, paucity, rareness, rarity, infrequency, uncommonness, sparseness, scantiness.
Ea glut, plenty, abundance, sufficiency, enough.

scare *v* frighten, startle, alarm, dismay, daunt, intimidate, unnerve, threaten, menace, terrorize, shock, appal, panic, terrify.
Ea reassure, calm.
n fright, start, shock, alarm, panic, hysteria, terror.
Ea reassurance, comfort.

scared *adj* frightened, fearful, nervous, anxious, worried, startled, shaken, panic-stricken, terrified.
Ea confident, reassured.

scary *adj* frightening, alarming, daunting, intimidating, disturbing, shocking, horrifying, terrifying, hair-raising, bloodcurdling, spine-chilling, chilling, creepy, eerie, spooky (*infml*).

scathing *adj* sarcastic, scornful, critical, trenchant, cutting, biting, caustic, acid, vitriolic, bitter, harsh, brutal, savage, unsparing.
Ea complimentary.

scatter *v* disperse, dispel, dissipate, disband, disunite, separate, divide, break up, disintegrate, diffuse, broadcast, disseminate, spread, sprinkle, sow, strew, fling, shower.
Ea gather, collect.

scatterbrained *adj* forgetful, absent-minded, empty-headed, feather-brained, scatty (*infml*), flaky (*US infml*), ditsy (*US infml*), careless, inattentive, thoughtless, unreliable, irresponsible, frivolous.
Ea sensible, sober, efficient, careful.

scattering *n* sprinkling, few, handful, smattering.
Ea mass, abundance.

scavenge *v* forage, rummage, rake, search, scrounge.

scenario *n* outline, synopsis, summary, résumé, storyline, plot, scheme, plan, programme, projection, sequence, situation, scene.

scene *n* **1** PLACE, area, spot, locale, site, situation, position, whereabouts, location, locality, environment, milieu, setting, contact, background, backdrop, set, stage. **2** LANDSCAPE, panorama, view, vista, prospect, sight.

spectacle, picture, tableau, pageant. **3** EPISODE, incident, part, division, act, clip. **4** *don't make a scene*: fuss, commotion, to-do (*infml*), performance, drama, exhibition, display, show.

scenery n landscape, terrain, panorama, view, vista, outlook, scene, background, setting, surroundings, backdrop, set.

scenic adj panoramic, picturesque, attractive, pretty, beautiful, grand, striking, impressive, spectacular, breathtaking, awe-inspiring.
F3 dull, dreary.

scent n **1** PERFUME, fragrance, aroma, bouquet, smell, odour. **2** *follow the scent*: track, trail.
F3 1 stink.
v smell, sniff (out), nose (out), sense, perceive, detect, discern, recognize.

scented adj perfumed, fragrant, sweet-smelling, aromatic.
F3 malodorous, stinking.

sceptic n doubter, unbeliever, disbeliever, agnostic, atheist, rationalist, questioner, scoffer, cynic.
F3 believer.

sceptical adj doubting, doubtful, unconvinced, unbelieving, disbelieving, questioning, distrustful, mistrustful, hesitating, dubious, suspicious, scoffing, cynical, pessimistic.
F3 convinced n confident, trusting.

scepticism n doubt, unbelief, disbelief, agnosticism, atheism, rationalism, distrust, suspicion, cynicism, pessimism.
F3 belief, faith.

schedule n timetable, programme, agenda, diary, calendar, itinerary, plan, scheme, list, inventory,

catalogue, table, form.
v timetable, time, table, programme, plan, organize, arrange, appoint, assign, book, list.

schematic adj diagrammatic, representational, symbolic, illustrative, graphic.

scheme n **1** PROGRAMME, schedule, plan, project, idea, proposal, proposition, suggestion, draft, outline, blueprint, schema, diagram, chart, layout, pattern, design, shape, configuration, arrangement. **2** INTRIGUE, plot, conspiracy, device, stratagem, ruse, ploy, shift, manoeuvre, tactic(s), strategy, procedure, system, method.
v plot, conspire, connive, collude, intrigue, machinate, manoeuvre, manipulate, pull strings, mastermind, plan, project, contrive, devise, frame, work out.

schism n **1** DIVISION, split, rift, rupture, break, breach, disunion, separation, severance, estrangement, discord. **2** SPLINTER GROUP, faction, sect.

scholar n pupil, student, academic, intellectual, egghead (*infml*), authority, expert.
F3 dunce, ignoramus.

scholarly adj learned, erudite, lettered, academic, scholastic, school, intellectual, highbrow, bookish, studious, knowledgeable, well-read, analytical, scientific.
F3 uneducated, illiterate.

scholarship n **1** ERUDITION, learnedness, learning, knowledge, wisdom, education, schooling. **2** *a scholarship to a public school*: grant, award, bursary, endowment, fellowship, exhibition.

school n college, institute, institution.

Schools, colleges and universities include:
kindergarten, nursery school, infant school, primary school, middle school, secondary school, secondary modern, upper school, high school, grammar school, grant-maintained school, foundation school, preparatory school, public school, private school, boarding school, sixth-form college, polytechnic, city technical college, technical college, university, academy, seminary, finishing school, Sunday school, convent school, summer school.

v educate, teach, instruct, tutor, coach, train, discipline, drill, verse, prime, prepare, indoctrinate.

schooling n education, book-learning, teaching, instruction, tuition, coaching, training, drill, preparation, grounding, guidance, indoctrination.

science n technology, discipline, specialization, knowledge, skill, proficiency, technique, art.

Sciences include:
acoustics, aerodynamics, aeronautics, agricultural science, anatomy, anthropology, astronomy, astrophysics, behavioural science, biochemistry, biology, biophysics, botany, chemistry, chemurgy, climatology, computer science, cybernetics, dynamics, earth science, ecology, electrodynamics, electronics, engineering, entomology, environmental science, genetics, geochemistry, geography, geology, geophysics, hydraulics, information technology, inorganic chemistry, life science, linguistics, mathematics, mechanical engineering, mechanics, medical science, metallurgy, meteorology, microbiology, mineralogy, morphology, natural science, nuclear physics, organic chemistry, ornithology, pathology, pharmacology, physics, physiology, psychology, radiochemistry, robotics, sociology, space technology, telecommunications, thermodynamics, toxicology, ultrasonics, veterinary science, zoology.

scientific adj methodical, systematic, controlled, regulated, analytical, mathematical, exact, precise, accurate, scholarly, thorough.

scintillating adj sparkling, glittering, flashing, bright, shining, brilliant, dazzling, exciting, stimulating, lively, animated, vivacious, ebullient, witty.
E∃ dull.

scoff [1] v mock, ridicule, poke fun, taunt, tease, rib (sl), jeer, sneer, pooh-pooh, scorn, despise, revile, deride, belittle, disparage, knock (infml).
E∃ praise, compliment, flatter.

scoff [2] v eat, consume, devour, put away (infml), gobble, guzzle, wolf (infml), bolt, gulp.
E∃ fast, abstain.

scold v chide, tell off (infml), tick off (infml), reprimand, reprove, rebuke, take to task, admonish, upbraid, reproach, blame, censure, lecture, nag.
E∃ praise, commend.

scolding n castigation, telling-off, ticking-off (infml), dressing-down, reprimand, reproof, rebuke, lecture, talking-to, earful (infml).

scoop n 1 LADLE, spoon, dipper, bailer, bucket, shovel. 2 EXCLUSIVE, coup, inside story, revelation, exposé, sensation, latest (*infml*).
v gouge, scrape, hollow, empty, excavate, dig, shovel, ladle, spoon, dip, bail.

scope n 1 RANGE, compass, field, area, sphere, ambit, terms of reference, confines, reach, extent, span, breadth, coverage. 2 scope for improvement: room, space, capacity, elbow-room, latitude, leeway, freedom, liberty, opportunity.

scorch v burn, singe, char, blacken, scald, roast, sear, parch, shrivel, wither.

scorching adj burning, boiling, baking, roasting, sizzling, blistering, sweltering, torrid, tropical, searing, red-hot.

score n 1 RESULT, total, sum, tally, points, marks. 2 SCRATCH, line, groove, mark, nick, notch.
v 1 RECORD, register, chalk up, notch up, count, total, make, earn, gain, achieve, attain, win, have the advantage, have the edge, be one up. 2 SCRATCH, scrape, graze, mark, groove, gouge, cut, incise, engrave, indent, nick, slash.

scorn n contempt, scornfulness, disdain, sneering, derision, mockery, ridicule, sarcasm, disparagement, disgust.
E3 admiration, respect.
v despise, look down on, disdain, sneer at, scoff at, deride, mock, laugh at, slight, spurn, refuse, reject, dismiss.
E3 admire, respect.

scornful adj contemptuous,

E3 praise, commendation.

disdainful, supercilious, haughty, arrogant, sneering, scoffing, derisive, mocking, jeering, sarcastic, scathing, disparaging, insulting, slighting, dismissive.
E3 admiring, respectful.

scour[1] v scrape, abrade, rub, polish, burnish, scrub, clean, wash, cleanse, purge, flush.

scour[2] v search, hunt, comb, drag, ransack, rummage, forage, rake.

scourge n 1 AFFLICTION, misfortune, torment, terror, bane, evil, curse, plague, penalty, punishment. 2 WHIP, lash.
E3 1 blessing, godsend, boon.
v 1 AFFLICT, torment, curse, plague, devastate, punish, chastise, discipline. 2 WHIP, flog, beat, lash, cane, flail, thrash.

scout v spy out, reconnoitre, explore, investigate, check out, survey, case (*sl*), spy, snoop, search, seek, hunt, probe, look, watch, observe.
n spy, reconnoitrer, vanguard, outrider, escort, lookout, recruiter, spotter.

scowl v, n frown, glower, glare, grimace, pout.
E3 smile, grin, beam.

scraggy adj scrawny, skinny, thin, lean, lanky, bony, angular, gaunt, undernourished, emaciated, wasted.
E3 plump, sleek.

scramble v 1 CLIMB, scale, clamber, crawl, shuffle, scrabble, grope. 2 RUSH, hurry, hasten, run, push, jostle, struggle, strive, vie, contend.
n rush, hurry, race, dash, hustle, bustle, commotion, confusion, muddle, struggle, free-for-all, mêlée.

scrap[1] n bit, piece, fragment, part, fraction, crumb, morsel, bite,

mouthful, sliver, shred, snippet, atom, iota, grain, particle, mite, trace, vestige, remnant, leftover, waste, junk.
v discard, throw away, jettison, shed, abandon, drop, dump, ditch (*sl*), cancel, axe, demolish, break up, write off.

E3 recover, restore.

scrap² *n* fight, scuffle, brawl, dust-up (*infml*), quarrel, row, argument, squabble, wrangle, dispute, disagreement.

E3 peace, agreement.
v fight, brawl, quarrel, argue, fall out, squabble, bicker, wrangle, disagree.

E3 agree.

scrape *v* grate, grind, rasp, file, abrade, scour, rub, clean, remove, erase, scrabble, claw, scratch, graze, skin, bark, scuff.

scrappy *adj* bitty, disjointed, piecemeal, fragmentary, incomplete, sketchy, superficial, slapdash, slipshod.

E3 complete, finished.

scratch *v* claw, gouge, score, mark, cut, incise, etch, engrave, scrape, rub, scuff, graze, gash, lacerate.
n mark, line, scrape, scuff, abrasion, graze, gash, laceration.

scrawny *adj* scraggy, skinny, thin, lean, lanky, angular, bony, underfed, undernourished, emaciated.

E3 fat, plump.

scream *v, n* shriek, screech, cry, shout, yell, bawl, roar, howl, wail, squeal, yelp.

screen *v* **1** *screen a film*: show, present, broadcast. **2** SHIELD, protect, safeguard, defend, guard, cover, mask, veil, cloak, shroud, hide, conceal, shelter, shade. **3** SORT, grade, sift, sieve, filter, process, evaluate, gauge,

examine, scan, check, vet.

E3 2 uncover, expose.
n partition, divider, shield, guard, cover, mask, veil, cloak, shroud, concealment, shelter, shade, awning, canopy, net, mesh.

screw *v* fasten, adjust, tighten, contract, compress, squeeze, extract, extort, force, constrain, pressurize, turn, wind, twist, wring, distort, wrinkle.

scribble *v* write, pen, jot, dash off, scrawl, doodle.

scribe *n* writer, copyist, amanuensis, secretary, clerk.

script *n* **1** *a film script*: text, lines, words, dialogue, screenplay, libretto, book. **2** WRITING, handwriting, hand, longhand, calligraphy, letters, manuscript, copy.

scrounge *v* cadge, beg, sponge.

scrounger *n* cadger, sponger, parasite.

scrub *v* **1** *scrub the floor*: rub, brush, clean, wash, cleanse, scour. **2** (*infml*) ABOLISH, cancel, delete, abandon, give up, drop, discontinue.

scruffy *adj* untidy, messy, unkempt, dishevelled, bedraggled, run-down, tattered, shabby, disreputable, worn-out, ragged, seedy, squalid, slovenly.

E3 tidy, well-dressed.

scruple *n* reluctance, hesitation, doubt, qualm, misgiving, uneasiness, difficulty, perplexity.
v hesitate, think twice, hold back, shrink.

scruples *n* standards, principles, morals, ethics.

scrupulous *adj* **1** PAINSTAKING, meticulous, conscientious, careful, rigorous, strict, exact, precise, minute, nice. **2** PRINCIPLED, moral, ethical,

honourable, honest, upright.
F∃ 1 superficial, careless, reckless.
2 unscrupulous, unprincipled.
scrutinize v examine, inspect, study, scan, analyse, sift, investigate, probe, search, explore.
scrutiny n examination, inspection, study, analysis, investigation, inquiry, search, exploration.
scuff v scrape, scratch, graze, abrade, rub, brush, drag.
scuffle v fight, scrap, tussle, brawl, grapple, struggle, contend, clash.
n fight, scrap, tussle, brawl, fray, set-to, rumpus, commotion, disturbance, affray.
sculpt v sculpture, carve, chisel, hew, cut, model, mould, cast, form, shape, fashion.
scum n froth, foam, film, impurities, dross, dregs, rubbish, trash.
scurrilous adj rude, vulgar, coarse, foul, obscene, indecent, salacious, offensive, abusive, insulting, disparaging, defamatory, slanderous, libellous, scandalous.
F∃ polite, courteous, complimentary.
scurry v dash, rush, hurry, hasten, bustle, scramble, scuttle, scamper, scoot, dart, run, sprint, trot, race, fly, skim, scud.
sea n **1** OCEAN, main, deep, briny (infml). **2** a sea of faces: multitude, abundance, profusion, mass.
adj marine, maritime, ocean, oceanic, salt, saltwater, aquatic, seafaring.
F∃ land, air.
at sea adrift, lost, confused, bewildered, baffled, puzzled, perplexed, mystified.
seafaring adj sea-going, ocean-going, sailing, nautical, naval, marine, maritime.

seal v **1** seal a jar: close, shut, stop, plug, cork, stopper, waterproof, fasten, secure. **2** SETTLE, conclude, finalize, stamp.
F∃ 1 unseal.
n stamp, signet, insignia, imprimatur, authentication, assurance, attestation, confirmation, ratification.
seal off block up, close off, shut off fence off, cut off, segregate, isolate, quarantine.
F∃ open up.
seam n **1** JOIN, joint, weld, closure, line. **2** coal seam: layer, stratum, vein, lode.
seamy adj disreputable, sleazy, sordid, squalid, unsavoury, rough, dark, low, nasty, unpleasant.
F∃ respectable, wholesome, pleasant.
sear v burn, scorch, brown, fry, sizzle, seal, cauterize, brand, parch, shrivel, wither.
search v seek, look, hunt, rummage, rifle, ransack, scour, comb, sift, probe, explore, frisk (sl), examine, scrutinize, inspect, check, investigate, inquire, pry.
n hunt, quest, pursuit, rummage, probe, exploration, examination, scrutiny, inspection, investigation, inquiry, research, survey.
searching adj penetrating, piercing, keen, sharp, close, intent, probing, thorough, minute.
F∃ vague, superficial.
seaside n coast, shore, beach, sands.
season n period, spell, phase, term, time, span, interval.
v **1** season food: flavour, spice, salt.
2 AGE, mature, ripen, harden, toughen, train, prepare, condition, treat, temper.
seasonable adj timely, well-timed,

welcome, opportune, convenient, suitable, appropriate, fitting.

F3 unseasonable, inopportune.

seasoned *adj* mature, experienced, practised, well-versed, veteran, old, hardened, toughened, conditioned, acclimatized, weathered.

F3 inexperienced, novice.

seasoning *n* flavouring, spice, condiment, salt, pepper, relish, sauce, dressing.

seat *n* **1** CHAIR, bench, pew, stool, throne. **2** *country seat*: residence, abode, house, mansion. **3** PLACE, site, situation, location, headquarters, centre, heart, hub, axis, source, cause, bottom, base, foundation, footing, ground.

v sit, place, set, locate, install, fit, fix, settle, accommodate, hold, contain, take.

seating *n* seats, chairs, places, room, accommodation.

secluded *adj* private, cloistered, sequestered, shut away, cut off, isolated, lonely, solitary, remote, out-of-the-way, sheltered, hidden, concealed.

F3 public, accessible.

seclusion *n* privacy, retirement, retreat, isolation, solitude, remoteness, shelter, hiding, concealment.

second[1] *adj* duplicate, twin, double, repeated, additional, further, extra, supplementary, alternative, other, alternate, next, following, subsequent, succeeding, secondary, subordinate, lower, inferior, lesser, supporting.

n helper, assistant, backer, supporter. *v* approve, agree with, endorse, back, support, help, assist, aid, further,

advance, forward, promote, encourage.

second[2] *n* minute, tick (*infml*), moment, instant, flash, jiffy (*infml*).

secondary *adj* subsidiary, subordinate, lower, inferior, lesser, minor, unimportant, ancillary, auxiliary, supporting, relief, back-up, reserve, spare, extra, second, alternative, indirect, derived, resulting.

F3 primary, main, major.

second-hand *adj* used, old, worn, hand-me-down, borrowed, derivative, secondary, indirect, vicarious.

F3 new.

second-rate *adj* inferior, substandard, second-class, second-best, poor, low-grade, shoddy, cheap, tawdry, mediocre, undistinguished, uninspired, uninspiring.

F3 first-rate.

secrecy *n* privacy, seclusion, confidentiality, confidence, covertness, concealment, disguise, camouflage, furtiveness, surreptitiousness, stealthiness, stealth, mystery.

F3 openness.

secret *adj* **1** PRIVATE, discreet, covert, hidden, concealed, unseen, shrouded, covered, disguised, camouflaged, undercover, furtive, surreptitious, stealthy, sly, underhand, under-the-counter, hole-and-corner, cloak-and-dagger, clandestine, underground, backstairs, back-door. **2** CLASSIFIED, restricted, confidential, hush-hush (*infml*), unpublished, undisclosed, unrevealed, unknown. **3** CRYPTIC, mysterious, occult, arcane, recondite, deep. **4** SECRETIVE, close, retired, secluded, out-of-the-way.

E3 **1** public, open. **2** well-known.
n confidence, mystery, enigma, code, key, formula, recipe.

secretary *n* personal assistant, PA, typist, stenographer, clerk.

secrete¹ *v* hide, conceal, stash away (*infml*), bury, cover, screen, shroud, veil, disguise, take, appropriate.
E3 uncover, reveal, disclose.

secrete² *v* exude, discharge, release, give off, emit, emanate, produce.

secretion *n* exudation, discharge, release, emission.

secretive *adj* tight-lipped, close, cagey (*infml*), uncommunicative, unforthcoming, reticent, reserved, withdrawn, quiet, deep, cryptic, enigmatic.
E3 open, communicative, forthcoming.

sect *n* denomination, cult, division, subdivision, group, splinter group, faction, camp, wing, party, school.

sectarian *adj* factional, partisan, cliquish, exclusive, narrow, limited, parochial, insular, narrow-minded, bigoted, fanatical, doctrinaire, dogmatic, rigid.
E3 non-sectarian, cosmopolitan, broad-minded.

section *n* division, subdivision, chapter, paragraph, passage, instalment, part, component, fraction, fragment, bit, piece, slice, portion, segment, sector, zone, district, area, region, department, branch, wing.
E3 whole.

sector *n* zone, district, quarter, area, region, section, division, subdivision, part.
E3 whole.

secular *adj* lay, temporal, worldly,

earthly, civil, state, non-religious, profane.
E3 religious.

secure *adj* **1** SAFE, unharmed, undamaged, protected, sheltered, shielded, immune, impregnable, fortified, fast, tight, fastened, locked, fixed, immovable, stable, steady, solid, firm, well-founded, reliable, dependable, steadfast, certain, sure, conclusive, definite. **2** CONFIDENT, assured, reassured.
E3 **1** insecure, vulnerable. **2** uneasy, ill at ease.
v **1** OBTAIN, acquire, gain, get.
2 FASTEN, attach, fix, make fast, tie, moor, lash, chain, lock (up), padlock, bolt, batten down, nail, rivet.
E3 **1** lose. **2** unfasten.

security *n* **1** SAFETY, immunity, asylum, sanctuary, refuge, cover, protection, defence, surveillance, safe-keeping, preservation, care, custody. **2** *security for a loan*: collateral, surety, pledge, guarantee, warranty, assurance, insurance, precautions, safeguards.
3 CONFIDENCE, conviction, certainty, positiveness.
E3 **1** insecurity.

sedate *adj* staid, dignified, solemn, grave, serious, sober, decorous, proper, seemly, demure, composed, unruffled, serene, tranquil, calm, quiet, cool, collected, imperturbable, unflappable (*infml*), deliberate, slow-moving.
E3 undignified, lively, agitated.

sedative *adj* calming, soothing, anodyne, lenitive, tranquillizing, relaxing, soporific, depressant.
E3 rousing.
n tranquillizer, sleeping-pill, narcotic, barbiturate.

sedentary adj sitting, seated, desk-bound, inactive, still, stationary, immobile, unmoving.
F3 active.

sediment n deposit, residue, grounds, lees, dregs.

sedition n agitation, rabble-rousing, subversion, disloyalty, treachery, treason, insubordination, mutiny, rebellion, revolt.
F3 calm, loyalty.

seduce v entice, lure, allure, attract, tempt, charm, beguile, ensnare, lead astray, mislead, deceive, corrupt, dishonour, ruin.
F3 repel.

seduction n enticement, lure, attraction, temptation, come-on (infml), corruption, ruin.

seductive adj enticing, alluring, attractive, tempting, tantalizing, inviting, come-hither (infml), flirtatious, sexy, provocative, beguiling, captivating, bewitching, irresistible.
F3 unattractive, repulsive.

see v **1** PERCEIVE, glimpse, discern, spot, make out, distinguish, identify, sight, notice, observe, watch, view, look at, mark, note. **2** IMAGINE, picture, visualize, envisage, foresee, anticipate. **3** I see your point: understand, comprehend, grasp, fathom, follow, realize, recognize, appreciate, regard, consider, deem. **4** DISCOVER, find out, learn, ascertain, determine, decide. **5** LEAD, usher, accompany, escort, court, go out with, date. **6** VISIT, consult, interview, meet.

see to attend to, deal with, take care of, look after, arrange, organize, manage, do, fix, repair, sort out.

seed n pip, stone, kernel, nucleus, grain, germ, sperm, ovum, egg, ovule, spawn, embryo, source, start, beginning.

seedy adj **1** SHABBY, scruffy, tatty, mangy, sleazy, squalid, grotty (infml), crummy (sl), run-down, dilapidated, decaying. **2** UNWELL, ill, sick, poorly, ailing, off-colour.
F3 2 well.

seek v look for, search for, hunt, pursue, follow, inquire, ask, invite, request, solicit, petition, entreat, want, desire, aim, aspire, try, attempt, endeavour, strive.

seem v appear, look, feel, sound, pretend to be.

seeming adj apparent, ostensible, outward, superficial, surface, quasi-, pseudo, specious.
F3 real.

seep v ooze, leak, exude, well, trickle, dribble, percolate, permeate, soak.

seethe v **1** BOIL, simmer, bubble, effervesce, fizz, foam, froth, ferment, rise, swell, surge, teem, swarm. **2** RAGE, fume, smoulder, storm.

see-through adj transparent, translucent, sheer, filmy, gauzy, gossamer(y), flimsy.
F3 opaque.

segment n section, division, compartment, part, bit, piece, slice, portion, wedge.
F3 whole.

segregate v separate, keep apart, cut off, isolate, quarantine, set apart, exclude.
F3 unite, join.

segregation n separation, isolation, quarantine, apartheid, discrimination.
F3 unification.

seize *v* grab, snatch, grasp, clutch, grip, hold, take, confiscate, impound, appropriate, commandeer, hijack, annex, abduct, catch, capture, arrest, apprehend, nab (*infml*), collar (*infml*).
F3 let go, release, hand back.

seizure *n* **1** FIT, attack, convulsion, paroxysm, spasm. **2** TAKING, confiscation, appropriation, hijack, annexation, abduction, capture, arrest, apprehension.
F3 2 release, liberation.

seldom *adv* rarely, infrequently, occasionally, hardly ever.
F3 often, usually.

select *v* choose, pick, single out, decide on, appoint, elect, prefer, opt for.
adj selected, choice, top, prime, first-class, first-rate, hand-picked, élite, exclusive, limited, privileged, special, excellent, superior, posh (*infml*).
F3 second-rate, ordinary, general.

selection *n* choice, pick, option, preference, assortment, variety, range, line-up, miscellany, medley, potpourri, collection, anthology.

selective *adj* particular, choosy (*infml*), careful, discerning, discriminating.
F3 indiscriminate.

self *n* ego, personality, identity, person.

self-centred *adj* selfish, self-seeking, self-serving, self-interested, egotistic(al), narcissistic, self-absorbed, egocentric.
F3 altruistic.

self-confident *adj* confident, self-reliant, self-assured, assured, self-possessed, cool, fearless.
F3 unsure, self-conscious.

self-conscious *adj* uncomfortable,

ill at ease, awkward, embarrassed, shamefaced, sheepish, shy, bashful, coy, retiring, shrinking, self-effacing, nervous, insecure.
F3 natural, unaffected, confident.

self-control *n* calmness, composure, cool, patience, self-restraint, restraint, self-denial, temperance, self-discipline, self-mastery, will-power.

self-denial *n* moderation, temperance, abstemiousness, asceticism, self-sacrifice, unselfishness, selflessness.
F3 self-indulgence.

self-evident *adj* obvious, manifest, clear, undeniable, axiomatic, unquestionable, incontrovertible, inescapable.

self-government *n* autonomy, independence, home rule, democracy.
F3 subjection.

self-indulgent *adj* hedonistic, dissolute, dissipated, profligate, extravagant, intemperate, immoderate.
F3 abstemious.

selfish *adj* self-interested, self-seeking, self-serving, mean, miserly, mercenary, greedy, self-centred, egocentric, egotistic(al).
F3 unselfish, selfless, generous, considerate.

selfless *adj* unselfish, altruistic, self-denying, self-sacrificing, generous, philanthropic.
F3 selfish, self-centred.

self-respect *n* pride, dignity, self-esteem, self-assurance, self-confidence.

self-righteous *adj* smug, complacent, superior, goody-goody (*infml*), pious, sanctimonious, holier-than-thou, pietistic, hypocritical, pharisaical.

self-sacrifice *n* self-denial, self-renunciation, selflessness, altruism, unselfishness, generosity.
F3 selfishness.

self-satisfied *adj* smug, complacent, self-congratulatory, self-righteous.
F3 humble.

self-styled *adj* self-appointed, professed, so-called, would-be.

self-supporting *adj* self-sufficient, self-financing, independent, self-reliant.
F3 dependent.

sell *v* barter, exchange, trade, auction, vend, retail, stock, handle, deal in, trade in, traffic in, merchandise, hawk, peddle, push, advertise, promote, market.
F3 buy.

seller *n* vendor, merchant, trader, dealer, supplier, stockist, retailer, shopkeeper, salesman, saleswoman, agent, representative, rep (*infml*), traveller.
F3 buyer, purchaser.

semblance *n* appearance, air, show, pretence, guise, mask, front, façade, veneer, apparition, image, resemblance, likeness, similarity.

send *v* POST, mail, e-mail, text, dispatch, consign, remit, forward, convey, deliver. **2** TRANSMIT, broadcast, communicate. **3** PROPEL, drive, move, throw, fling, hurl, launch, fire, shoot, discharge, emit, direct.
send for summon, call for, request, order, command.
F3 dismiss.

send up satirize, mock, ridicule, parody, take off, mimic, imitate.

send-off *n* farewell, leave-taking, departure, start, goodbye.
F3 arrival.

senile *adj* old, aged, doddering, decrepit, failing, confused.

senior *adj* older, elder, higher, superior, high-ranking, major, chief.
F3 junior.

seniority *n* priority, precedence, rank, standing, status, age, superiority, importance.

sensation *n* **1** FEELING, sense, impression, perception, awareness, consciousness, emotion. **2** *the report caused a sensation*: commotion, stir, agitation, excitement, thrill, furore, outrage, scandal.

sensational *adj* **1** EXCITING, thrilling, electrifying, breathtaking, startling, amazing, astounding, staggering, dramatic, spectacular, impressive, exceptional, excellent, wonderful, marvellous, smashing (*infml*). **2** SCANDALOUS, shocking, horrifying, revealing, melodramatic, lurid.
F3 1 ordinary, run-of-the-mill.

sense *n* **1** FEELING, sensation, impression, perception, awareness, appreciation, faculty. **2** REASON, logic, mind, brain(s), wit(s), wisdom, intelligence, cleverness, understanding, discernment, judgement, intuition. **3** MEANING, significance, definition, interpretation, implication, point, purpose, substance.
F3 2 foolishness. **3** nonsense.
v feel, suspect, intuit, perceive, detect, notice, observe, realize, appreciate, understand, comprehend, grasp.

senseless *adj* **1** FOOLISH, stupid, unwise, silly, idiotic, mad, crazy, daft (*infml*), ridiculous, ludicrous, absurd,

meaningless, nonsensical, fatuous, irrational, illogical, unreasonable, pointless, purposeless, futile.
2 UNCONSCIOUS, out, stunned, anaesthetized, deadened, numb, unfeeling.
F3 1 sensible, meaningful.
2 conscious.

sensible adj wise, prudent, judicious, well-advised, shrewd, far-sighted, intelligent, level-headed, down-to-earth, commonsense, sober, sane, rational, logical, reasonable, realistic, practical, functional, sound.
F3 senseless, foolish, unwise.

sensitive adj **1** SUSCEPTIBLE, vulnerable, impressionable, tender, emotional, thin-skinned, temperamental, touchy, irritable, sensitized, responsive, aware, perceptive, discerning, appreciative.
2 DELICATE, fine, exact, precise.
F3 1 insensitive, thick-skinned.
2 imprecise, approximate.

sensual adj self-indulgent, voluptuous, worldly, physical, animal, carnal, fleshly, bodily, sexual, erotic, sexy, lustful, randy (infml), lecherous, lewd, licentious.
F3 ascetic.

sensuous adj pleasurable, gratifying, voluptuous, rich, lush, luxurious, sumptuous.
F3 ascetic, plain, simple.

sentence n judgement, decision, verdict, condemnation, pronouncement, ruling, decree, order.
v judge, pass judgement on, condemn, doom, punish, penalize.

sentiment n **1** THOUGHT, idea, feeling, opinion, view, judgement, belief, persuasion, attitude.
2 EMOTION, sensibility, tenderness,

soft-heartedness, romanticism, sentimentality, mawkishness.

sentimental adj tender, soft-hearted, emotional, gushing, touching, pathetic, tear-jerking, weepy (infml), maudlin, mawkish, nostalgic, romantic, lovey-dovey (infml), slushy, mushy, sloppy, schmaltzy, soppy, corny (infml).
F3 unsentimental, realistic, cynical.

sentry n sentinel, guard, picket, watchman, watch, look-out.

separable adj divisible, detachable, removable, distinguishable, distinct.
F3 inseparable.

separate v divide, sever, part, split (up), divorce, part company, diverge, disconnect, uncouple, disunite, disaffiliate, disentangle, segregate, isolate, cut off, abstract, remove, detach, withdraw, secede.
F3 join, unite, combine.
adj single, individual, particular, independent, alone, solitary, segregated, isolated, apart, divorced, divided, disunited, disconnected, disjointed, detached, unattached, unconnected, unrelated, different, disparate, distinct, discrete, several, sundry.
F3 together, attached.

separation n division, severance, parting, leave-taking, farewell, split-up, break-up, divorce, split, rift, gap, divergence, disconnection, disengagement, dissociation, estrangement, segregation, isolation, detachment.
F3 unification.

septic adj infected, poisoned, festering, putrefying, putrid.

sequel n follow-up, continuation, development, result, consequence, outcome, issue, upshot, pay-off, end, conclusion.

sequence n succession, series, run, progression, chain, string, train, line, procession, order, arrangement, course, track, cycle, set.

serene adj calm, tranquil, cool, composed, placid, untroubled, undisturbed, still, quiet, peaceful.
F3 troubled, disturbed.

series n set, cycle, succession, sequence, run, progression, chain, string, line, train, order, arrangement, course.

serious adj 1 IMPORTANT, significant, weighty, momentous, crucial, critical, urgent, pressing, acute, grave, worrying, difficult, dangerous, grim, severe, deep, far-reaching.
2 UNSMILING, long-faced, humourless, solemn, sober, stern, thoughtful, pensive, earnest, sincere.
F3 1 trivial, slight. **2** smiling, facetious, frivolous.

sermon n address, discourse, lecture, harangue, homily, talking-to (infml).

serrated adj toothed, notched, indented, jagged.
F3 smooth.

servant n domestic, maid, valet, steward, attendant, retainer, hireling, lackey, menial, skivvy (infml), slave, help, helper, assistant, ancillary.
F3 master, mistress.

serve v 1 WAIT ON, attend, minister to, work for, help, aid, assist, benefit, further. **2** serve a purpose: fulfil, complete, answer, satisfy, discharge, perform, act, function. **3** DISTRIBUTE, dole out, present, deliver, provide, supply.

service n 1 EMPLOYMENT, work, labour, business, duty, function, performance. **2** USE, usefulness, utility, advantage, benefit, help, assistance. **3** SERVICING, maintenance, overhaul, check.
4 church service: worship, observance, ceremony, rite.
v maintain, overhaul, check, repair, recondition, tune.

serviceable adj usable, useful, helpful, profitable, advantageous, beneficial, utilitarian, simple, plain, unadorned, strong, tough, durable, hard-wearing, dependable, efficient, functional, practical, convenient.
F3 unserviceable, unusable.

servile adj obsequious, sycophantic, toadying, cringing, fawning, grovelling, bootlicking, slavish, subservient, subject, submissive, humble, abject, low, mean, base, menial.
F3 assertive, aggressive.

session n sitting, hearing, meeting, assembly, conference, discussion, period, time, term, semester, year.

set v 1 PUT, place, locate, situate, position, arrange, prepare, lodge, fix, stick, park, deposit. **2** SCHEDULE, appoint, designate, specify, name, prescribe, ordain, assign, allocate, impose, fix, establish, determine, decide, conclude, settle, resolve.
3 ADJUST, regulate, synchronize, co-ordinate. **4** the sun sets: go down, sink, dip, subside, disappear, vanish.
5 CONGEAL, thicken, gel, stiffen, solidify, harden, crystallize.
F3 4 rise.
n batch, series, sequence, kit, outfit, compendium, assortment, collection, class, category, group, band, gang, crowd, circle, clique, faction.

adj scheduled, appointed, arranged, prepared, prearranged, fixed, established, definite, decided, agreed, settled, firm, strict, rigid, inflexible, prescribed, formal, conventional, traditional, customary, usual, routine, regular, standard, stock, stereotyped, hackneyed.

F3 movable, free, spontaneous, undecided.

set about begin, start, embark on, undertake, tackle, attack.

set aside 1 PUT ASIDE, lay aside, keep (back), save, reserve, set apart, separate, select, earmark. **2** ANNUL, abrogate, cancel, revoke, reverse, overturn, overrule, reject, discard.

set back delay, hold up, slow, retard, hinder, impede.

set off 1 LEAVE, depart, set out, start (out), begin. **2** DETONATE, light, ignite, touch off, trigger off, explode. **3** DISPLAY, show off, enhance, contrast.

set on set upon, attack, turn on, go for, fall upon, lay into, beat up (*infml*).

set out 1 LEAVE, depart, set off, start (out), begin. **2** LAY OUT, arrange, display, exhibit, present, describe, explain.

set up raise, elevate, erect, build, construct, assemble, compose, form, create, establish, institute, found, inaugurate, initiate, begin, start, introduce, organize, arrange, prepare.

setback *n* delay, hold-up, problem, snag, hitch, hiccup, reverse, misfortune, upset, disappointment, defeat.

F3 boost, advance, help, advantage.

setting *n* mounting, frame, surroundings, milieu, environment, background, context, perspective,

period, position, location, locale, site, scene, scenery.

settle *v* **1** ARRANGE, order, adjust, reconcile, resolve, complete, conclude. **2** SINK, subside, drop, fall, descend, land, alight. **3** CHOOSE, appoint, fix, establish, determine, decide, agree, confirm. **4** COLONIZE, occupy, populate, people, inhabit, live, reside. **5** *settle a bill*: pay, clear, discharge.

settlement *n* **1** RESOLUTION, agreement, arrangement, decision, conclusion, termination, satisfaction. **2** PAYMENT, clearance, clearing, discharge. **3** COLONY, outpost, community, kibbutz, camp, encampment, hamlet, village.

settler *n* colonist, colonizer, pioneer, frontiersman, frontierswoman, planter, immigrant, incomer, newcomer, squatter.

F3 native.

set-up *n* system, structure, organization, arrangement, business, conditions, circumstances.

sever *v* cut, cleave, split, rend, part, separate, divide, cut off, amputate, detach, disconnect, disjoin, disunite, dissociate, estrange, alienate, break off, dissolve, end, terminate.

F3 join, unite, combine, attach.

several *adj* some, many, various, assorted, sundry, diverse, different, distinct, separate, particular, individual.

severe *adj* **1** STERN, disapproving, sober, strait-laced, strict, rigid, unbending, harsh, tough, hard, difficult, demanding, arduous, punishing, rigorous, grim, forbidding, cruel, biting, cutting, scathing, pitiless, merciless, oppressive, relentless, inexorable, acute, bitter, intense, extreme, fierce, violent, distressing, serious, grave, critical, dangerous. **2** PLAIN, simple, unadorned, unembellished, functional, restrained, austere, ascetic.

F3 1 kind, compassionate, sympathetic, lenient, mild. **2** decorated, ornate.

sew *v* stitch, tack, baste, hem, darn, embroider.

sex *n* **1** GENDER, sexuality. **2** SEXUAL INTERCOURSE, intercourse, sexual relations, copulation, coitus, lovemaking, fornication, reproduction, union, intimacy.

sexual *adj* sex, reproductive, procreative, genital, coital, venereal, carnal, sensual, erotic.

sexy *adj* sensual, voluptuous, nubile, beddable (*infml*), seductive, inviting, flirtatious, arousing, provoking, provocative, titillating, pornographic, erotic, salacious, suggestive.

F3 sexless.

shabby *adj* **1** RAGGED, tattered, frayed, worn, worn-out, mangy, moth-eaten, scruffy, tatty, disreputable, dilapidated, run-down, seedy, dirty, dingy, poky. **2** *a shabby trick*: contemptible, despicable, rotten, mean, low, cheap, shoddy, shameful, dishonourable.

F3 1 smart. **2** honourable, fair.

shack *n* hut, cabin, shanty, hovel, shed, lean-to.

shade *n* **1** SHADINESS, shadow, darkness, obscurity, semi-darkness, dimness, gloom, gloominess, twilight, dusk, gloaming. **2** AWNING, canopy, cover, shelter, screen, blind, curtain, shield, visor, umbrella, parasol. **3** COLOUR, hue, tint, tone, tinge. **4** TRACE, dash, hint, suggestion,

suspicion, nuance, gradation, degree, amount, variety. **5** GHOST, spectre, phantom, spirit, apparition, semblance.

v shield, screen, protect, cover, shroud, veil, hide, conceal, obscure, cloud, dim, darken, shadow, overshadow.

shadow *n* **1** SHADE, darkness, obscurity, semi-darkness, dimness, gloom, twilight, dusk, gloaming, cloud, cover, protection. **2** SILHOUETTE, shape, image, representation. **3** TRACE, hint, suggestion, suspicion, vestige, remnant.

v **1** OVERSHADOW, overhang, shade, shield, screen, obscure, darken. **2** FOLLOW, tail, dog, stalk, trail, watch.

shadowy *adj* dark, gloomy, murky, obscure, dim, faint, indistinct, ill-defined, vague, hazy, nebulous, intangible, unsubstantial, ghostly, spectral, illusory, dreamlike, imaginary, unreal.

shady *adj* **1** SHADED, shadowy, dim, dark, cool, leafy. **2** (*infml*) DUBIOUS, questionable, suspect, suspicious, fishy (*infml*), dishonest, crooked, unreliable, untrustworthy, disreputable, unscrupulous, unethical, underhand.

F3 1 sunny, sunlit, bright. **2** honest, trustworthy, honourable.

shaft *n* **1** HANDLE, shank, stem. **2** BEAM, ray.

shaggy *adj* hairy, long-haired, hirsute, bushy, woolly, unshorn, dishevelled, unkempt.

F3 bald, shorn, close-cropped.

shake *v* **1** WAVE, flourish, brandish, wag, waggle, agitate, rattle, joggle, jolt, jerk, twitch, convulse, heave, throb,

vibrate, oscillate, fluctuate, waver,
wobble, totter, sway, rock, tremble,
quiver, quake, shiver, shudder. **2** *the
news shook her:* upset, distress, shock,
frighten, unnerve, intimidate, disturb,
discompose, unsettle, agitate, stir,
rouse.

shake off get rid of, dislodge, lose,
elude, give the slip, leave behind,
outdistance, outstrip.

shake-up *n* reorganization,
rearrangement, reshuffle,
disturbance, upheaval.

shaky *adj* **1** TREMBLING, quivering,
faltering, tentative, uncertain.
2 UNSTABLE, unsteady, insecure,
precarious, wobbly, rocky, tottery,
rickety, weak. **3** DUBIOUS,
questionable, suspect, unreliable,
unsound, unsupported.
F3 firm, strong.

shallow *adj* superficial, surface,
skin-deep, slight, flimsy, trivial,
frivolous, foolish, idle, empty,
meaningless, unscholarly, ignorant,
simple.
F3 deep, profound.

sham *n* pretence, fraud, counterfeit,
forgery, fake, imitation, simulation,
hoax, humbug.
adj false, fake, counterfeit, spurious,
bogus, phoney (*infml*), pretended,
feigned, put-on, simulated, artificial,
mock, imitation, synthetic.
F3 genuine, authentic, real.
v pretend, feign, affect, put on,
simulate, imitate, fake, counterfeit.

shame *n* disgrace, dishonour,
discredit, stain, stigma, disrepute,
infamy, scandal, ignominy,
humiliation, degradation,
shamefacedness, remorse, guilt,
embarrassment, mortification.

F3 honour, credit, distinction, pride.
v embarrass, mortify, abash,
confound, humiliate, ridicule,
humble, put to shame, show up,
disgrace, dishonour, discredit, debase,
degrade, sully, taint, stain.

shamefaced *adj* ashamed,
conscience-stricken, remorseful,
contrite, apologetic, sorry, sheepish,
red-faced, blushing, embarrassed,
mortified, abashed, humiliated,
uncomfortable.
F3 unashamed, proud.

shameful *adj* **1** *a shameful waste of
money:* disgraceful, outrageous,
scandalous, indecent, abominable,
atrocious, wicked, mean, low, vile,
reprehensible, contemptible,
unworthy, ignoble. **2** EMBARRASSING,
mortifying, humiliating, ignominious.
F3 honourable, creditable, worthy.

shameless *adj* **1** UNASHAMED,
unabashed, unrepentant, impenitent,
barefaced, flagrant, blatant, brazen,
brash, audacious, insolent, defiant,
hardened, incorrigible. **2** IMMODEST,
indecent, improper, unprincipled,
wanton, dissolute, corrupt, depraved.
F3 ashamed, shamefaced, contrite.
2 modest.

shape *n* **1** FORM, outline, silhouette,
profile, model, mould, pattern, cut,
lines, contours, figure, physique,
build, frame, format, configuration.
2 APPEARANCE, guise, likeness,
semblance. **3** *in good shape:*
condition, state, form, health, trim,
fettle.

> Geometrical shapes include:
> polygon, circle, semicircle, quad-
> rant, oval, ellipse, crescent, triangle,
> equilateral triangle, isosceles trian-
> gle, scalene triangle, quadrilateral,

square, rectangle, oblong, rhombus, diamond, kite, trapezium, parallelogram, pentagon, hexagon, heptagon, octagon, nonagon, decagon; polyhedron, cube, cuboid, prism, pyramid, tetrahedron, pentahedron, octahedron, cylinder, cone, sphere, hemisphere.

v form, fashion, model, mould, cast, forge, sculpt, carve, whittle, make, produce, construct, create, devise, frame, plan, prepare, adapt, adjust, regulate, accommodate, modify, remodel.

shapeless *adj* formless, amorphous, unformed, nebulous, unstructured, irregular, misshapen, deformed, dumpy.

share *v* divide, split, go halves, partake, participate, share out, distribute, dole out, give out, deal out, apportion, allot, allocate, assign.
n portion, ration, quota, allowance, allocation, allotment, lot, part, division, proportion, percentage, cut (*infml*), dividend, due, contribution, whack (*infml*).

sharp *adj* **1** *a sharp needle*: pointed, keen, edged, knife-edged, razor-sharp, cutting, serrated, jagged, barbed, spiky. **2** CLEAR, clear-cut, well-defined, distinct, marked, crisp. **3** QUICK-WITTED, alert, shrewd, astute, perceptive, observant, discerning, penetrating, clever, crafty, cunning, artful, sly. **4** SUDDEN, abrupt, violent, fierce, intense, extreme, severe, acute, piercing, stabbing. **5** PUNGENT, piquant, sour, tart, vinegary, bitter, acerbic, acid. **6** TRENCHANT, incisive, cutting, biting, caustic, sarcastic, sardonic, scathing, vitriolic, acrimonious.

F3 **1** blunt. **2** blurred. **3** slow, stupid. **4** gentle. **5** bland. **6** mild.
adv punctually, promptly, on the dot, exactly, precisely, abruptly, suddenly, unexpectedly.

F3 approximately, roughly.

sharpen *v* edge, whet, hone, grind, file.

F3 blunt.

shatter *v* break, smash, splinter, shiver, crack, split, burst, explode, blast, crush, demolish, destroy, devastate, wreck, ruin, overturn, upset.

sheath *n* **1** SCABBARD, case, sleeve, envelope, shell, casing, covering. **2** CONDOM, rubber (*sl*), French letter (*sl*).

shed[1] *v* cast (off), moult, slough, discard, drop, spill, pour, shower, scatter, diffuse, emit, radiate, shine, throw.

shed[2] *n* outhouse, lean-to, hut, shack.

sheen *n* lustre, gloss, shine, shimmer, brightness, brilliance, shininess, polish, burnish.

F3 dullness, tarnish.

sheepish *adj* ashamed, shamefaced, embarrassed, mortified, chastened, abashed, uncomfortable, self-conscious, silly, foolish.

F3 unabashed, brazen, bold.

sheer *adj* **1** UTTER, complete, total, absolute, thorough, mere, pure, unadulterated, downright, out-and-out, rank, thoroughgoing, unqualified, unmitigated. **2** *a sheer drop*: vertical, perpendicular, precipitous, abrupt, steep. **3** THIN, fine, flimsy, gauzy, gossamer, translucent, transparent, see-through.

F3 **2** gentle, gradual. **3** thick, heavy.

sheet *n* cover, blanket, covering, coating, coat, film, layer, stratum, skin, membrane, lamina, veneer, overlay, plate, piece, panel, slab, pane, expanse, surface.

shelf *n* ledge, mantelpiece, sill, step, bench, counter, bar, bank, sandbank, reef, terrace.

shell *n* covering, hull, husk, pod, rind, crust, case, casing, body, chassis, frame, framework, structure, skeleton. *v* **1** *shell nuts*: hull, husk, pod. **2** BOMB, bombard, barrage, blitz, attack.

shelter *v* cover, shroud, screen, shade, shadow, protect, safeguard, defend, guard, shield, harbour, hide, accommodate, put up.
F3 expose.
n cover, roof, shade, shadow, protection, defence, guard, security, safety, sanctuary, asylum, haven, refuge, retreat, accommodation, lodging.
F3 exposure.

sheltered *adj* covered, shaded, shielded, protected, cosy, snug, warm, quiet, secluded, isolated, retired, withdrawn, reclusive, cloistered, unworldly.
F3 exposed.

shelve *v* postpone, defer, put off, suspend, halt, put aside, pigeonhole, put on ice, mothball.
F3 expedite, implement.

shield *n* buckler, escutcheon, defence, bulwark, rampart, screen, guard, cover, shelter, protection, safeguard.
v defend, guard, protect, safeguard, screen, shade, shadow, cover, shelter.
F3 expose.

shift *v* change, vary, fluctuate, alter, adjust, move, budge, remove, dislodge, displace, relocate, reposition, rearrange, transpose, transfer, switch, swerve, veer.
n change, fluctuation, alteration, modification, move, removal, displacement, rearrangement, transposition, transfer, switch.

shifty *adj* untrustworthy, dishonest, deceitful, scheming, contriving, tricky, wily, crafty, cunning, devious, evasive, slippery, furtive, underhand, dubious, shady (*infml*).
F3 dependable, honest, open.

shimmer *v* glisten, gleam, glimmer, glitter, scintillate, twinkle.
n lustre, gleam, glimmer, glitter, glow.

shine *v* **1** BEAM, radiate, glow, flash, glare, gleam, glint, glitter, sparkle, twinkle, shimmer, glisten, glimmer. **2** POLISH, burnish, buff, brush, rub. **3** *shine at athletics*: excel, stand out.
n **1** LIGHT, radiance, glow, brightness, glare, gleam, sparkle, shimmer. **2** GLOSS, polish, burnish, sheen, lustre, glaze.

shining *adj* **1** BRIGHT, radiant, glowing, beaming, flashing, gleaming, glittering, glistening, shimmering, twinkling, sparkling, brilliant, resplendent, splendid, glorious. **2** *a shining example*: conspicuous, outstanding, leading, eminent, celebrated, distinguished, illustrious.
F3 1 dark.

shiny *adj* polished, burnished, sheeny, lustrous, glossy, sleek, bright, gleaming, glistening.
F3 dull, matt.

ship *n* vessel, craft, liner, steamer, tanker, trawler, ferry, boat, yacht.

shirk *v* dodge, evade, avoid, duck (*infml*), shun, slack, skive (*infml*).

shiver *v* shudder, tremble, quiver, quake, shake, vibrate, palpitate, flutter.

n shudder, quiver, shake, tremor, twitch, start, vibration, flutter.

shock *v* disgust, revolt, sicken, offend, appal, outrage, scandalize, horrify, astound, stagger, stun, stupefy, numb, paralyse, traumatize, jolt, jar, shake, agitate, unsettle, disquiet, unnerve, confound, dismay. **E3** delight, please, gratify, reassure. *n* fright, start, jolt, impact, collision, surprise, bombshell, thunderbolt, blow, trauma, upset, distress, dismay, consternation, disgust, outrage. **E3** delight, pleasure, reassurance.

shocking *adj* appalling, outrageous, scandalous, horrifying, disgraceful, deplorable, intolerable, unbearable, atrocious, abominable, monstrous, unspeakable, detestable, abhorrent, dreadful, awful, terrible, frightful, ghastly, hideous, horrible, disgusting, revolting, repulsive, sickening, nauseating, offensive, distressing. **E3** acceptable, satisfactory, pleasant, delightful.

shoddy *adj* inferior, second-rate, cheap, tawdry, tatty, trashy, rubbishy, poor, careless, slipshod, slapdash. **E3** superior, well-made.

shoe

Types of shoes and boots include: court shoe, brogue, casual, lace-up (*infml*), slip-on (*infml*), slingback, sandal, mule, thong, espadrille, stiletto heel, kitten heel, platform heel, moccasin, Doc Martens®, DMs (*infml*), slipper, flip-flop (*infml*), bootee, wellington boot, welly (*infml*), galosh, gumboot, football boot, rugby boot, tennis-shoe, plimsoll, pump, sneaker, trainer, ballet shoe, clog, sabot, snowshoe, brothel creepers (*sl*).

shoot *v* **1** FIRE, discharge, launch, propel, hurl, fling, project. **2** DART, bolt, dash, tear, rush, race, sprint, speed, charge, hurtle. **3** HIT, kill, blast, bombard, gun down, snipe at, pick off. *n* sprout, bud, offshoot, branch, twig, sprig, slip, scion.

shop

Types of shop include: bazaar, market, indoor market, mini-market, corner shop, shopping mall, department store, supermarket, superstore, hypermarket, cash-and-carry, online shop; butcher, baker, grocer, greengrocer, fishmonger, dairy, delicatessen, health-food shop, fish and chip shop, takeaway, off-licence, tobacconist, sweet shop, confectioner, tuck shop; bookshop, bookstore (*N Am*), newsagent, stationer, chemist, pharmacy, tailor, outfitter, dress shop, boutique, milliner, shoe shop, haberdasher, draper, florist, jeweller, toyshop, hardware shop, ironmonger, post office.

shore¹ *n* seashore, beach, sand(s), shingle, strand, waterfront, front, promenade, coast, seaboard, lakeside, bank.

shore² *v* support, hold, prop, stay, underpin, buttress, brace, strengthen, reinforce.

short *adj* **1** BRIEF, cursory, fleeting, momentary, transitory, ephemeral, concise, succinct, terse, pithy, compact, compressed, shortened, curtailed, abbreviated, abridged, summarized. **2** BRUSQUE, curt, gruff, snappy, sharp, abrupt, blunt, direct, rude, impolite, discourteous, uncivil. **3** SMALL, little, low, petite, diminutive, squat, dumpy. **4** INADEQUATE,

insufficient, deficient, lacking, wanting, low, poor, meagre, scant, sparse.
F3 1 long, lasting. 2 polite. 3 tall. 4 adequate, ample.

shortage n inadequacy, insufficiency, deficiency, shortfall, deficit, lack, want, need, scarcity, paucity, poverty, dearth, absence.
F3 sufficiency, abundance, surplus.

shortcoming n defect, imperfection, fault, flaw, drawback, failing, weakness, foible.

shorten v cut, trim, prune, crop, dock, curtail, truncate, abbreviate, abridge, reduce, lessen, decrease, diminish, take up.
F3 lengthen, enlarge, amplify.

shortly adv soon, before long, presently, by and by.

short-sighted adj 1 MYOPIC, near-sighted. 2 IMPROVIDENT, imprudent, injudicious, unwise, impolitic, ill-advised, careless, hasty, ill-considered.
F3 1 long-sighted, far-sighted.

shot n 1 BULLET, missile, projectile, ball, pellet, slug (infml), discharge, blast. 2 (infml) ATTEMPT, try, effort, endeavour, go (infml), bash (infml), crack (infml), stab (infml), guess, turn.

shoulder v 1 PUSH, shove, jostle, thrust, press. 2 ACCEPT, assume, take on, bear, carry, sustain.

shout n, v call, cry, scream, shriek, yell, roar, bellow, bawl, howl, bay, cheer.

shove v push, thrust, drive, propel, force, barge, jostle, elbow, shoulder, press, crowd.

shovel n spade, scoop, bucket.
v dig, scoop, dredge, clear, move, shift, heap.

show v 1 REVEAL, expose, uncover, disclose, divulge, present, offer, exhibit, manifest, display, indicate, register, demonstrate, prove, illustrate, exemplify, explain, instruct, teach, clarify, elucidate. 2 show him out: lead, guide, conduct, usher, escort, accompany, attend.
F3 1 hide, cover.
n 1 OSTENTATION, parade, display, flamboyance, panache, pizzazz (infml), showiness, exhibitionism, affectation, pose, pretence, illusion, semblance, façade, impression, appearance, air. 2 DEMONSTRATION, presentation, exhibition, exposition, fair, display, parade, pageant, extravaganza, spectacle, entertainment, performance, production, staging, showing, representation.

show off parade, strut, swagger, brag, boast, swank (infml), flaunt, brandish, display, exhibit, demonstrate, advertise, set off, enhance.

show up 1 (infml) ARRIVE, come, turn up, appear, materialize (infml). 2 HUMILIATE, embarrass, mortify, shame, disgrace, let down. 3 REVEAL, show, expose, unmask, lay bare, highlight, pinpoint.

showdown n confrontation, clash, crisis, climax, culmination.

shower n rain, stream, torrent, deluge, hail, volley, barrage.
v spray, sprinkle, rain, pour, deluge, inundate, overwhelm, load, heap, lavish.

show-off n swaggerer, braggart, boaster, exhibitionist, peacock, poser, poseur, egotist.

showy adj flashy, flamboyant, ostentatious, gaudy, garish, loud, tawdry, fancy, ornate, pretentious, pompous, swanky (infml), flash (infml).

E3 quiet, restrained.

shred n ribbon, tatter, rag, scrap, snippet, sliver, bit, piece, fragment, jot, iota, atom, grain, mite, whit, trace.

shrewd adj astute, judicious, well-advised, calculated, far-sighted, smart, clever, intelligent, sharp, keen, acute, alert, perceptive, observant, discerning, discriminating, knowing, calculating, cunning, crafty, artful, sly.

E3 unwise, obtuse, naive, unsophisticated.

shriek v, n scream, screech, squawk, squeal, cry, shout, yell, wail, howl.

shrill adj high, high-pitched, treble, sharp, acute, piercing, penetrating, screaming, screeching, strident, ear-splitting.

E3 deep, low, soft, gentle.

shrink v **1** CONTRACT, shorten, narrow, decrease, lessen, diminish, dwindle, shrivel, wrinkle, wither. **2** RECOIL, back away, shy away, withdraw, retire, balk, quail, cower, cringe, wince, flinch, shun.

E3 1 expand, stretch. **2** accept, embrace.

shrivel v wrinkle, pucker, wither, wilt, shrink, dwindle, parch, dehydrate, desiccate, scorch, sear, burn, frizzle.

shroud v wrap, envelop, swathe, cloak, veil, screen, hide, conceal, blanket, cover.

E3 uncover, expose.
n winding-sheet, pall, mantle, cloak, veil, screen, blanket, covering.

shrub n

> Shrubs include:
> azalea, berberis, broom, buddleia, camellia, cotoneaster, daphne, dogwood, euonymus, firethorn, forsythia, fuchsia, heather, hebe, holly, honeysuckle, hydrangea, japonica, jasmine, laburnum, laurel, lilac, magnolia, mock orange, peony, privet, rhododendron, rose, spiraea, viburnum, weigela, witch hazel. see also **flower**; **plant**.

shudder v shiver, shake, tremble, quiver, quake, heave, convulse.
n shiver, quiver, tremor, spasm, convulsion.

shuffle v **1** MIX (UP), intermix, jumble, confuse, disorder, rearrange, reorganize, shift around, switch. **2** shuffle across the room: shamble, scuffle, scrape, drag, limp, hobble.

shun v avoid, evade, elude, steer clear of, shy away from, spurn, ignore, cold-shoulder, ostracize.

E3 accept, embrace.

shut v close, slam, seal, fasten, secure, lock, latch, bolt, bar.

E3 open.

shut down close, stop, cease, terminate, halt, discontinue, suspend, switch off, inactivate.

shut in enclose, box in, hem in, fence in, immure, confine, imprison, cage.

shut off seclude, isolate, cut off, separate, segregate.

shut out 1 EXCLUDE, bar, debar, lock out, ostracize, banish. **2** HIDE, conceal, cover, mask, screen, veil.

shut up 1 SILENCE, gag, quiet, hush up, pipe down (infml), hold one's tongue, clam up (infml). **2** CONFINE, coop up, imprison, incarcerate, jail, intern.

shy adj timid, bashful, reticent,

reserved, retiring, diffident, coy, self-conscious, inhibited, modest, self-effacing, shrinking, hesitant, cautious, chary, suspicious, nervous.
F3 bold, assertive, confident.

sick adj **1** ILL, unwell, indisposed, laid up, poorly, ailing, sickly, under the weather, weak, feeble. **2** VOMITING, queasy, bilious, seasick, airsick. **3** sick of waiting: bored, fed up (infml), tired, weary, disgusted, nauseated.
F3 1 well, healthy.

sicken v nauseate, revolt, disgust, repel, put off, turn off (sl).
F3 delight, attract.

sickening adj nauseating, revolting, disgusting, offensive, distasteful, foul, vile, loathsome, repulsive.
F3 delightful, pleasing, attractive.

sickly adj **1** UNHEALTHY, infirm, delicate, weak, feeble, frail, wan, pallid, ailing, indisposed, sick, bilious, faint, languid. **2** NAUSEATING, revolting, sweet, syrupy, cloying, mawkish.
F3 1 healthy, robust, sturdy, strong.

sickness n **1** ILLNESS, disease, malady, ailment, complaint, affliction, ill-health, indisposition, infirmity. **2** VOMITING, nausea, queasiness, biliousness.
F3 1 health.

side n **1** EDGE, margin, fringe, periphery, border, boundary, limit, verge, brink, bank, shore, quarter, region, flank, hand, face, facet, surface. **2** STANDPOINT, viewpoint, view, aspect, angle, slant. **3** TEAM, party, faction, camp, cause, interest.
adj lateral, flanking, marginal, secondary, subsidiary, subordinate, lesser, minor, incidental, indirect, oblique.

side with agree with, team up with, support, vote for, favour, prefer.

sidestep v avoid, dodge, duck, evade, elude, skirt, bypass.
F3 tackle, deal with.

sidetrack v deflect, head off, divert, distract.

sideways adv sidewards, edgeways, laterally, obliquely.
adj sideward, side, lateral, slanted, oblique, indirect, sidelong.

sidle v slink, edge, inch, creep, sneak.

sieve v sift, strain, separate, remove.
n colander, strainer, sifter, riddle, screen.

sift v **1** SIEVE, strain, filter, riddle, screen, winnow, separate, sort. **2** EXAMINE, scrutinize, investigate, analyse, probe, review.

sigh v breathe, exhale, moan, complain, lament, grieve.

sight n **1** VISION, eyesight, seeing, observation, perception. **2** VIEW, look, glance, glimpse, range, field of vision, visibility. **3** APPEARANCE, spectacle, show, display, exhibition, scene, eyesore, monstrosity, fright (infml).
v see, observe, spot, glimpse, perceive, discern, distinguish, make out.

sightseer n tourist, visitor, holidaymaker, tripper, excursionist.

sign n **1** SYMBOL, token, character, figure, representation, emblem, badge, insignia, logo. **2** INDICATION, mark, signal, gesture, evidence, manifestation, clue, pointer, hint, suggestion, trace. **3** NOTICE, poster, board, placard. **4** PORTENT, omen, forewarning, foreboding.
v autograph, initial, endorse, write.

sign up enlist, enrol, join (up), volunteer, register, sign on, recruit, take on, hire, engage, employ.

signal n sign, indication, mark, gesture, cue, go-ahead, password, light, indicator, beacon, flare, rocket, alarm, alert, warning, tip-off.
v wave, gesticulate, gesture, beckon, motion, nod, sign, indicate, communicate.

signature n autograph, initials, mark, endorsement, inscription.

significance n importance, relevance, consequence, matter, interest, consideration, weight, force, meaning, implication, sense, point, message.
E3 insignificance, unimportance, pettiness.

significant adj **1** IMPORTANT, relevant, consequential, momentous, weighty, serious, noteworthy, critical, vital, marked, considerable, appreciable. **2** MEANINGFUL, symbolic, expressive, suggestive, indicative, symptomatic.
E3 **1** insignificant, unimportant, trivial. **2** meaningless.

signify v **1** MEAN, denote, symbolize, represent, stand for, indicate, show, express, convey, transmit, communicate, intimate, imply, suggest. **2** MATTER, count.

silence n quiet, quietness, hush, peace, stillness, calm, lull, noiselessness, soundlessness, muteness, dumbness, speechlessness, taciturnity, uncommunicativeness, reticence, reserve.
E3 noise, sound, din, uproar.
v quiet, quieten, hush, mute, deaden, muffle, stifle, gag, muzzle, suppress, subdue, quell, still, dumbfound.

silent adj inaudible, noiseless, soundless, quiet, peaceful, still, hushed, muted, mute, dumb,

speechless, tongue-tied, taciturn, mum, reticent, reserved, tacit, unspoken, unexpressed, understood, voiceless, wordless.
E3 noisy, loud, talkative.

silhouette n outline, contour, delineation, shape, form, configuration, profile, shadow.

silky adj silken, fine, sleek, lustrous, glossy, satiny, smooth, soft, velvety.

silly adj foolish, stupid, imprudent, senseless, pointless, idiotic, daft (infml), ridiculous, ludicrous, preposterous, absurd, meaningless, irrational, illogical, childish, puerile, immature, irresponsible, scatterbrained.
E3 wise, sensible, sane, mature, clever, intelligent.

silt n sediment, deposit, alluvium, sludge, mud, ooze.
silt up block, clog, choke.

similar adj like, alike, close, related, akin, corresponding, equivalent, analogous, comparable, uniform, homogeneous.
E3 dissimilar, different.

similarity n likeness, resemblance, similitude, closeness, relation, correspondence, congruence, equivalence, analogy, comparability, compatibility, agreement, affinity, homogeneity, uniformity.
E3 dissimilarity, difference.

simmer v boil, bubble, seethe, stew, burn, smoulder, fume, rage.
simmer down calm down, cool down, control oneself, collect oneself.

simple adj **1** a simple question: easy, elementary, straightforward, uncomplicated, uninvolved, clear, lucid, plain, understandable, comprehensible. **2** a simple child:

unsophisticated, natural, innocent, artless, guileless, ingenuous, naive, green, foolish, stupid, silly, idiotic, half-witted, simple-minded, feeble-minded, backward.

F3 1 difficult, hard, complicated, intricate. 2 sophisticated, worldly, artful, clever.

simplicity n simpleness, ease, straightforwardness, clarity, purity, plainness, restraint, naturalness.

F3 difficulty, complexity, intricacy, sophistication.

simplify v disentangle, untangle, decipher, clarify, paraphrase, abridge, reduce, streamline.

F3 complicate, elaborate.

simplistic adj oversimplified, superficial, shallow, sweeping, facile, simple, naive.

F3 analytical, detailed.

simply adv 1 MERELY, just, only, solely, purely, utterly, completely, totally, wholly, absolutely, quite, really, undeniably, unquestionably, clearly, plainly, obviously. 2 EASILY, straightforwardly, directly, intelligibly.

simulate v pretend, affect, assume, put on, act, feign, sham, fake, counterfeit, reproduce, duplicate, copy, imitate, mimic, parrot, echo, reflect.

simultaneous adj synchronous, synchronic, concurrent, contemporaneous, coinciding, parallel.

F3 asynchronous.

sin n wrong, offence, transgression, trespass, misdeed, lapse, fault, error, crime, wrongdoing, sinfulness, wickedness, iniquity, evil, impiety, ungodliness, unrighteousness, guilt.
v offend, transgress, trespass, lapse,

err, misbehave, stray, go astray, fall, fall from grace.

sincere adj honest, truthful, candid, frank, open, direct, straightforward, plain-spoken, serious, earnest, heartfelt, wholehearted, real, true, genuine, pure, unadulterated, unmixed, natural, unaffected, artless, guileless, simple.

F3 insincere, hypocritical, affected.

sincerity n honour, integrity, probity, uprightness, honesty, truthfulness, candour, frankness, openness, directness, straightforwardness, seriousness, earnestness, wholeheartedness, genuineness.

F3 insincerity.

sinewy adj muscular, brawny, strong, sturdy, robust, vigorous, athletic, wiry, stringy.

sinful adj wrong, wrongful, criminal, bad, wicked, iniquitous, erring, fallen, immoral, corrupt, depraved, impious, ungodly, unholy, irreligious, guilty.

F3 sinless, righteous, godly.

sing v chant, intone, vocalize, croon, serenade, yodel, trill, warble, chirp, pipe, whistle, hum.

singe v scorch, char, blacken, burn, sear.

singer n vocalist, songster, songstress, chanteuse, warbler.

Singers include:
balladeer, minstrel, troubadour, opera singer, diva, prima donna, soloist, precentor, choirboy, choirgirl, chorister, chorus, folk-singer; pop star, crooner, carol-singer; soprano, coloratura soprano, castrato, tenor, treble, contralto, alto, baritone, bass.

---

single adj one, unique, singular, individual, particular, exclusive, sole, only, lone, solitary, separate, distinct, free, unattached, unmarried, celibate, unshared, undivided, unbroken, simple, one-to-one, man-to-man.

F3 multiple.

single out choose, select, pick, hand-pick, distinguish, identify, separate, set apart, isolate, highlight, pinpoint.

single-handed adj, adv solo, alone, unaccompanied, unaided, unassisted, independent(ly).

single-minded adj determined, resolute, dogged, persevering, tireless, unwavering, fixed, unswerving, undeviating, steadfast, dedicated, devoted.

sinister adj ominous, menacing, threatening, disturbing, disquieting, unlucky, inauspicious, malevolent, evil.

F3 auspicious, harmless, innocent.

sink v 1 DESCEND, slip, fall, drop, slump, lower, stoop, succumb, lapse, droop, sag, dip, set, disappear, vanish. 2 DECREASE, lessen, subside, abate, dwindle, diminish, ebb, fade, flag, weaken, fail, decline, worsen, degenerate, degrade, decay, collapse. 3 FOUNDER, dive, plunge, plummet, submerge, immerse, engulf, drown. 4 sink a well: bore, drill, penetrate, dig, excavate, lay, conceal.

F3 1 rise. 2 increase. 3 float.

sinner n wrong-doer, miscreant, offender, transgressor, trespasser, backslider, reprobate, evil-doer, malefactor.

sinuous adj lithe, slinky, curved, wavy, undulating, tortuous, twisting, winding, meandering, serpentine, coiling.

F3 straight.

sip v taste, sample, drink, sup. n taste, drop, spoonful, mouthful.

sit v 1 SETTLE, rest, perch, roost, brood, pose. 2 SEAT, accommodate, hold, contain. 3 MEET, assemble, gather, convene, deliberate.

site n location, place, spot, position, situation, station, setting, scene, plot, lot, ground, area. v locate, place, position, situate, station, set, install.

sitting n session, period, spell, meeting, assembly, hearing, consultation.

situation n 1 SITE, location, position, place, spot, seat, locality, locale, setting, scenario. 2 STATE OF AFFAIRS, case, circumstances, predicament, state, condition, status, rank, station, post, office, job, employment.

sizable adj large, substantial, considerable, respectable, goodly, largish, biggish, decent, generous.

F3 small, tiny.

size n magnitude, measurement(s), dimensions, proportions, volume, bulk, mass, height, length, extent, range, scale, amount, greatness, largeness, bigness, vastness, immensity.

size up gauge, assess, evaluate, weigh up, measure.

sizzle v hiss, crackle, spit, sputter, fry, frizzle.

skeleton n bones, frame, structure, framework, bare bones, outline, draft, sketch.

sketch v draw, depict, portray, represent, pencil, paint, outline, delineate, draft, rough out, block out. n drawing, vignette, design, plan, diagram, outline, delineation, skeleton, draft.

sketchy *adj* rough, vague, incomplete, unfinished, scrappy, bitty, imperfect, inadequate, insufficient, slight, superficial, cursory, hasty.
F3 full, complete.

skilful *adj* able, capable, adept, competent, proficient, deft, adroit, handy, expert, masterly, accomplished, skilled, practised, experienced, professional, clever, tactical, cunning.
F3 inept, clumsy, awkward.

skill *n* skilfulness, ability, aptitude, facility, handiness, talent, knack, art, technique, training, experience, expertise, expertness, mastery, proficiency, competence, accomplishment, cleverness, intelligence.

skilled *adj* trained, schooled, qualified, professional, experienced, practised, accomplished, expert, masterly, proficient, able, skilful.
F3 unskilled, inexperienced.

skim *v* **1** BRUSH, touch, skate, plane, float, sail, glide, fly. **2** SCAN, look through, skip. **3** CREAM, separate.

skimp *v* economize, scrimp, pinch, cut corners, stint, withhold.
F3 squander, waste.

skin *n* hide, pelt, membrane, film, coating, surface, outside, peel, rind, husk, casing, crust.
v flay, fleece, strip, peel, scrape, graze.

skinny *adj* thin, lean, scrawny, scraggy, skeletal, skin-and-bone, emaciated, underfed, undernourished.
F3 fat, plump.

skip *v* **1** HOP, jump, leap, dance, gambol, frisk, caper, prance. **2** *skip a page*: miss, omit, leave out, cut.

skirmish *n* fight, combat, battle, engagement, encounter, conflict, clash, brush, scrap, tussle, set-to, dust-up (*infml*).

skirt *v* circle, circumnavigate, border, edge, flank, bypass, avoid, evade, circumvent.

> Types of skirt include:
> miniskirt, dirndl, pencil skirt, pinafore skirt, culottes, kilt, sarong.

skit *n* satire, parody, caricature, spoof, take-off, sketch.

skulk *v* lurk, hide, prowl, sneak, creep, slink.

sky *n* space, atmosphere, air, heavens, blue.

slab *n* piece, block, lump, chunk, hunk, wedge (*infml*), wedge, slice, portion.

slack *adj* **1** LOOSE, limp, sagging, baggy. **2** LAZY, sluggish, slow, quiet, idle, inactive. **3** NEGLECTFUL, negligent, careless, inattentive, remiss, permissive, lax, relaxed, easy-going (*infml*).
F3 **1** tight, taut, stiff, rigid. **2** busy. **3** diligent.
n looseness, give, play, room, leeway, excess.
v idle, shirk, skive (*infml*), neglect.

slacken off loosen, release, relax, ease, moderate, reduce, lessen, decrease, diminish, abate, slow (down).
F3 tighten, increase, intensify, quicken.

slacker *n* idler, shirker, skiver (*infml*), dawdler, clock-watcher, good-for-nothing, layabout.

slam *v* **1** BANG, crash, dash, smash, throw, hurl, fling. **2** (*infml*) CRITICIZE, slate (*infml*), pan (*infml*).

slander *n* defamation, calumny, misrepresentation, libel, scandal,

slanderous adj defamatory, false, untrue, libellous, damaging, malicious, abusive, insulting.

smear, slur, aspersion, backbiting.
v defame, vilify, malign, denigrate, disparage, libel, smear, slur, backbite.
F3 praise, compliment.

slant v TILT, slope, incline, lean, list, skew, angle. **2** DISTORT, twist, warp, bend, weight, bias, colour.
n **1** SLOPE, incline, gradient, ramp, camber, pitch, tilt, angle, diagonal. **2** BIAS, emphasis, attitude, viewpoint.

slanting adj sloping, tilted, oblique, diagonal.

slap n smack, spank, cuff, blow, bang, clap.
v **1** SMACK, spank, hit, strike, cuff, clout, bang, clap. **2** DAUB, plaster, spread, apply.

slash v cut, slit, gash, lacerate, rip, tear, rend.
n cut, incision, slit, gash, laceration, rip, tear, rent.

slate v scold, rebuke, reprimand, berate, censure, blame, criticize, slam (infml).
F3 praise.

slaughter n killing, murder, massacre, extermination, butchery, carnage, blood-bath, bloodshed.
v kill, slay, murder, massacre, exterminate, liquidate, butcher.

slave n servant, drudge, vassal, serf, villein, captive.
v toil, labour, drudge, sweat, grind, slog.

slaver v dribble, drivel, slobber, drool, salivate.

slavery n servitude, bondage, captivity, enslavement, serfdom, thraldom, subjugation.
F3 freedom, liberty.

slavish adj **1** UNORIGINAL, imitative, unimaginative, uninspired, literal, strict. **2** SERVILE, abject, submissive, sycophantic, grovelling, cringing, fawning, menial, low, mean.
F3 1 original, imaginative. **2** independent, assertive.

sleek adj shiny, glossy, lustrous, smooth, silky, well-groomed.
F3 rough, unkempt.

sleep v doze, snooze, slumber, kip (sl), doss (down) (sl), hibernate, drop off, nod off, rest, repose.
n doze, snooze, nap, forty winks, shut-eye (infml), kip (sl), slumber, hibernation, rest, repose, siesta.

sleepless adj unsleeping, awake, wide awake, alert, vigilant, watchful, wakeful, restless, disturbed, insomniac.

sleepy adj drowsy, somnolent, tired, weary, heavy, slow, sluggish, torpid, lethargic, inactive, quiet, dull, soporific, hypnotic.
F3 awake, alert, wakeful, restless.

slender adj **1** SLIM, thin, lean, slight, svelte, graceful. **2** a slender chance: faint, remote, slight, inconsiderable, tenuous, flimsy, feeble, inadequate, insufficient, meagre, scanty.
F3 1 fat. **2** appreciable, considerable, ample.

slice n piece, sliver, wafer, rasher, tranche, slab, wedge, segment, section, share, portion, helping, cut (infml), whack (infml).
v carve, cut, chop, divide, segment.

slick adj **1** GLIB, plausible, deft, adroit, dexterous, skilful, professional. **2** SMOOTH, sleek, glossy, shiny, polished.

slide v slip, slither, skid, skate, ski, toboggan, glide, plane, coast, skim.

slight adj **1** MINOR, unimportant, insignificant, negligible, trivial, paltry, modest, small, little, inconsiderable, insubstantial. **2** SLENDER, slim, diminutive, petite, delicate.
F3 1 major, significant, noticeable, considerable. **2** large, muscular.
v scorn, despise, disdain, disparage, insult, affront, offend, snub, cut, cold-shoulder, ignore, disregard, neglect.
F3 respect, praise, compliment, flatter.
n insult, affront, slur, snub, rebuff, rudeness, discourtesy, disrespect, contempt, disdain, indifference, disregard, neglect.

slim adj **1** SLENDER, thin, lean, svelte, trim. **2** SLIGHT, remote, faint, poor.
F3 1 fat, chubby. **2** strong, considerable.
v lose weight, diet, reduce.

slimy adj **1** MUDDY, miry, mucous, viscous, oily, greasy, slippery.
2 SERVILE, obsequious, sycophantic, toadying, smarmy, oily, unctuous.

sling v **1** THROW, hurl, fling, catapult, heave, pitch, lob, toss, chuck (infml).
2 HANG, suspend, dangle, swing.

slink v sneak, steal, creep, sidle, slip, prowl, skulk.

slinky adj close-fitting, figure-hugging, clinging, skin-tight, sleek, sinuous.

slip¹ v slide, glide, skate, skid, stumble, trip, fall, slither, slink, sneak, steal, creep.
n mistake, error, slip-up (infml), bloomer (infml), blunder, fault, indiscretion, boob (infml), omission, oversight, failure.

slip² n piece, strip, voucher, chit, coupon, certificate.

slippery adj **1** SLIPPY, icy, greasy,

glassy, smooth, dangerous, treacherous, perilous. **2** a slippery character: dishonest, untrustworthy, false, duplicitous, two-faced, crafty, cunning, devious, evasive, smooth, smarmy.
F3 1 rough. **2** trustworthy, reliable.

slipshod adj careless, slap-dash, sloppy, slovenly, untidy, negligent, lax, casual.
F3 careful, fastidious, neat, tidy.

slit v cut, gash, slash, slice, split, rip, tear.
n opening, aperture, vent, cut, incision, gash, slash, split, tear, rent.

slither v slide, slip, glide, slink, creep, snake, worm.

sliver n flake, shaving, paring, slice, wafer, shred, fragment, chip, splinter, shiver, shard.

slobber v dribble, drivel, slaver, drool, salivate.

slogan n jingle, motto, catch-phrase, catchword, watchword, battle-cry, war cry.

slop v spill, overflow, slosh, splash, splatter, spatter.

slope v slant, lean, tilt, tip, pitch, incline, rise, fall.
n incline, gradient, ramp, hill, ascent, descent, slant, tilt, pitch, inclination.

sloppy adj **1** WATERY, wet, liquid, runny, mushy, slushy. **2** sloppy work: careless, hit-or-miss, slap-dash, slipshod, slovenly, untidy, messy, clumsy, amateurish. **3** SOPPY, sentimental, schmaltzy, slushy, mushy.
F3 1 solid. **2** careful, exact, precise.

slot n hole, opening, aperture, slit, vent, groove, channel, gap, space, time, vacancy, place, spot, position, niche.

v insert, fit, place, position, assign, pigeonhole.

slouch *v* stoop, hunch, droop, slump, lounge, loll, shuffle, shamble.

slovenly *adj* sloppy, careless, slipshod, untidy, scruffy, slatternly, sluttish.

F3 neat, smart.

slow *adj* 1 LEISURELY, unhurried, lingering, loitering, dawdling, lazy, sluggish, slow-moving, creeping, gradual, deliberate, measured, plodding, delayed, late, unpunctual. 2 STUPID, slow-witted, dim, thick (*infml*). 3 PROLONGED, protracted, long-drawn-out, tedious, boring, dull, uninteresting, uneventful.

F3 1 quick, fast, swift, rapid, speedy. 2 clever, intelligent. 3 brisk, lively, exciting.

v brake, decelerate, delay, hold up, retard, handicap, check, curb, restrict.

F3 speed, accelerate.

sluggish *adj* lethargic, listless, torpid, heavy, dull, slow, slow-moving, slothful, lazy, idle, inactive, lifeless, unresponsive.

F3 brisk, vigorous, lively, dynamic.

slump *v* 1 COLLAPSE, fall, drop, plunge, plummet, sink, decline, deteriorate, worsen, crash, fail. 2 DROOP, sag, bend, stoop, slouch, loll, lounge, flop.

n recession, depression, stagnation, downturn, low, trough, decline, deterioration, worsening, fall, drop, collapse, crash, failure.

F3 boom.

sly *adj* wily, foxy, crafty, cunning, artful, guileful, clever, canny, shrewd, astute, knowing, subtle, devious, shifty, tricky, furtive, stealthy, surreptitious, underhand, covert,

secretive, scheming, conniving, mischievous, roguish.

F3 honest, frank, candid, open.

smack *v* hit, strike, slap, spank, whack (*infml*), thwack (*infml*), clap, box, cuff, pat, tap.

n blow, slap, spank, whack (*infml*), thwack (*infml*), box, cuff, pat, tap.

adv bang, slap-bang, right, plumb, straight, directly, exactly, precisely.

small *adj* 1 LITTLE, tiny, minute, minuscule, short, slight, puny, petite, diminutive, pint-size(d) (*infml*), miniature, mini, pocket, pocket-sized, young. 2 PETTY, trifling, trivial, unimportant, insignificant, minor, inconsiderable, negligible. 3 INADEQUATE, insufficient, scanty, meagre, paltry, mean, limited.

F3 1 large, big, huge. 2 great, considerable. 3 ample.

small-minded *adj* petty, mean, ungenerous, illiberal, intolerant, bigoted, narrow-minded, parochial, insular, rigid, hidebound.

F3 liberal, tolerant, broad-minded.

smarmy *adj* smooth, oily, unctuous, servile, obsequious, sycophantic, toadying, ingratiating, crawling, fawning.

smart *adj* 1 *smart clothes*: elegant, stylish, chic, fashionable, modish, neat, tidy, spruce, trim, well-groomed. 2 CLEVER, intelligent, bright, sharp, acute, shrewd, astute.

F3 1 dowdy, unfashionable, untidy, scruffy. 2 stupid, slow.

v sting, hurt, prick, burn, tingle, twinge, throb.

smarten *v* neaten, tidy, spruce up, groom, clean, polish, beautify.

smash *v* 1 *smash a window*: break, shatter, shiver, ruin, wreck, demolish,

destroy, defeat, crush. **2** CRASH, collide, strike, bang, bash, thump.
n accident, crash, collision, pile-up.

smattering *n* bit, modicum, dash, sprinkling, basics, rudiments, elements.

smear *v* **1** DAUB, plaster, spread, cover, coat, rub, smudge, streak.
2 DEFAME, malign, vilify, blacken, sully, stain, tarnish.
n **1** STREAK, smudge, blot, blotch, splodge, daub. **2** DEFAMATION, slander, libel, mudslinging, muck-raking.

smell *n* odour, whiff, scent, perfume, fragrance, bouquet, aroma, stench, stink, pong (*infml*).
v sniff, nose, scent, stink, reek, pong (*infml*).

smelly *adj* malodorous, pongy (*infml*), stinking, reeking, foul, bad, off, fetid, putrid, high, strong.

smile *n, v* grin, beam, simper, smirk, leer, laugh.

smoke *n* fumes, exhaust, gas, vapour, mist, fog, smog.
v fume, smoulder, cure, dry.

smoky *adj* sooty, black, grey, grimy, murky, cloudy, hazy, foggy.

smooth *adj* **1** LEVEL, plane, even, flat, horizontal, flush. **2** STEADY, unbroken, flowing, regular, uniform, rhythmic, easy, effortless. **3** SHINY, polished, glossy, silky, glassy, calm, undisturbed, serene, tranquil, peaceful. **4** SUAVE, agreeable, smooth-talking, glib, plausible, persuasive, slick, smarmy, unctuous, ingratiating.
E3 1 rough, lumpy. **2** irregular, erratic, unsteady. **3** rough, choppy.
v **1** IRON, press, roll, flatten, level, plane, file, sand, polish. **2** EASE,

alleviate, assuage, allay, mitigate, calm, mollify.
E3 1 roughen, wrinkle, crease.

smother *v* suffocate, asphyxiate, strangle, throttle, choke, stifle, extinguish, snuff, muffle, suppress, repress, hide, conceal, cover, shroud, envelop, wrap.

smoulder *v* burn, smoke, fume, rage, seethe, simmer.

smudge *v* blur, smear, daub, mark, spot, stain, dirty, soil.
n blot, stain, spot, blemish, blur, smear, streak.

smug *adj* complacent, self-satisfied, superior, holier-than-thou, self-righteous, priggish, conceited.
E3 humble.

snack *n* refreshment(s), bite, nibble, titbit, elevenses (*infml*).

snag *n* disadvantage, inconvenience, drawback, catch, problem, difficulty, complication, setback, hitch, obstacle, stumbling-block.
v catch, rip, tear, hole, ladder.

snap *v* **1** *the twig snapped*: break, crack, split, separate. **2** BITE, nip, bark, growl, snarl, retort, crackle, pop. **3** SNATCH, seize, catch, grasp, grip.
n break, crack, bite, nip, flick, fillip, crackle, pop.
adj immediate, instant, on-the-spot, abrupt, sudden.

snappy *adj* **1** SMART, stylish, chic, fashionable, modish, trendy (*infml*).
2 QUICK, hasty, brisk, lively, energetic.
3 CROSS, irritable, edgy, touchy, brusque, quick-tempered, ill-natured, crabbed, testy.
E3 1 dowdy. **2** slow.

snare *v* trap, ensnare, entrap, catch, net.
n trap, wire, net, noose, catch, pitfall.

snarl[1] *v* growl, grumble, complain.

snarl[2] *v* tangle, knot, ravel, entangle, enmesh, embroil, confuse, muddle, complicate.

snatch *v* grab, seize, kidnap, take, nab (*infml*), pluck, pull, wrench, wrest, gain, win, clutch, grasp, grip.

sneak *v* **1** CREEP, steal, slip, slink, sidle, skulk, lurk, prowl, smuggle, spirit. **2** TELL TALES, split (*sl*), inform on, grass on (*sl*).
n tell-tale, informer, grass (*sl*).

sneaking *adj* private, secret, furtive, surreptitious, hidden, lurking, suppressed, grudging, nagging, niggling, persistent, worrying, uncomfortable, intuitive.

sneer *v* scorn, disdain, look down on, deride, scoff, jeer, mock, ridicule, gibe, laugh, snigger.
n scorn, disdain, derision, jeer, mockery, ridicule, gibe, snigger.

snide *adj* derogatory, disparaging, sarcastic, cynical, scornful, sneering, hurtful, unkind, nasty, mean, spiteful, malicious, ill-natured.
F3 complimentary.

sniff *v* breathe, inhale, snuff, snuffle, smell, nose, scent.

snigger *v*, *n* laugh, giggle, titter, chuckle, sneer.

snip *v* cut, clip, trim, crop, dock, slit, nick, notch.

snippet *n* piece, scrap, cutting, clipping, fragment, particle, shred, snatch, part, portion, segment, section.

snobbery *n* snobbishness, superciliousness, snootiness (*infml*), airs, loftiness, arrogance, pride, pretension, condescension.

snobbish *adj* supercilious, disdainful, snooty (*infml*), stuck-up

(*infml*), toffee-nosed (*infml*), superior, lofty, high and mighty, arrogant, pretentious, affected, condescending, patronizing.

snoop *v* spy, sneak, pry, nose, interfere, meddle.

snooze *v* nap, doze, sleep, kip (*sl*).
n nap, catnap, forty winks, doze, siesta, sleep, kip (*sl*).

snub *v* rebuff, brush off, cut, cold-shoulder, slight, rebuke, put down, squash, humble, shame, humiliate, mortify.
n rebuff, brush-off, slight, affront, insult, rebuke, put-down, humiliation.

snug *adj* cosy, warm, comfortable, homely, friendly, intimate, sheltered, secure, tight, close-fitting.

soak *v* wet, drench, saturate, penetrate, permeate, infuse, bathe, marinate, souse, steep, submerge, immerse.

soaking *adj* soaked, drenched, sodden, waterlogged, saturated, sopping, wringing, dripping, streaming.
F3 dry.

soar *v* fly, wing, glide, plane, tower, rise, ascend, climb, mount, escalate, rocket.
F3 fall, plummet.

sob *v* cry, weep, bawl, howl, blubber, snivel.

sober *adj* **1** TEETOTAL, temperate, moderate, abstinent, abstemious. **2** SOLEMN, dignified, serious, staid, steady, sedate, quiet, serene, calm, composed, unruffled, unexcited, cool, dispassionate, level-headed, practical, realistic, reasonable, rational, clear-headed. **3** *sober dress*: sombre, drab, dull, plain, subdued, restrained.

E3 1 drunk, intemperate. **2** frivolous, excited, unrealistic, irrational. **3** flashy, garish.

so-called adj alleged, supposed, purported, ostensible, nominal, self-styled, professed, would-be, pretended.

sociable adj outgoing, gregarious, friendly, affable, companionable, genial, convivial, cordial, warm, hospitable, neighbourly, approachable, accessible, familiar. **E3** unsociable, withdrawn, unfriendly, hostile.

social adj communal, public, community, common, general, collective, group, organized. n party, do (infml), get-together, gathering.

socialize v mix, mingle, fraternize, get together, go out, entertain.

society n **1** COMMUNITY, population, culture, civilization, nation, people, mankind, humanity. **2** CLUB, circle, group, association, organization, company, corporation, league, union, guild, fellowship, fraternity, brotherhood, sisterhood, sorority. **3** FRIENDSHIP, companionship, camaraderie, fellowship, company. **4** UPPER CLASSES, aristocracy, gentry, nobility, élite.

soft adj **1** YIELDING, pliable, flexible, elastic, plastic, malleable, spongy, squashy, pulpy. **2** soft colours: pale, light, pastel, delicate, subdued, muted, quiet, low, dim, faint, diffuse, mild, bland, gentle, soothing, sweet, mellow, melodious, dulcet, pleasant. **3** FURRY, downy, velvety, silky, smooth. **4** LENIENT, lax, indulgent, tolerant, easy-going (infml), kind, generous, gentle, merciful, soft-

hearted, tender, sensitive, weak, spineless. **E3 1** hard. **2** harsh. **3** rough. **4** strict, severe.

soften v **1** MODERATE, temper, mitigate, lessen, diminish, abate, alleviate, ease, soothe, palliate, quell, assuage, subdue, mollify, appease, calm, still, relax. **2** liquefy, dissolve, reduce. **3** CUSHION, pad, muffle, quicken, lower, lighten.

soft-hearted adj sympathetic, compassionate, kind, benevolent, charitable, generous, warm-hearted, tender, sentimental. **E3** hard-hearted, callous.

soggy adj wet, damp, moist, soaked, drenched, sodden, waterlogged, saturated, sopping, dripping, heavy, boggy, swampy, pulpy.

soil [1] n earth, clay, loam, humus, dirt, dust, ground, land, region, country.

soil [2] v dirty, begrime, stain, spot, smudge, smear, foul, muddy, pollute, defile, besmirch, sully, tarnish.

solace n comfort, consolation, relief, alleviation, support, cheer.

soldier n warrior, fighter, serviceman, servicewoman.

Types of soldier include:
cadet, private, sapper, NCO, orderly, officer, gunner, infantryman, trooper, fusilier, rifleman, paratrooper, sentry, guardsman, marine, commando, tommy, dragoon, cavalryman, lancer, hussar, conscript, recruit, regular, Territorial, GI (US), mercenary, legionnaire, guerrilla, partisan, centurion. see also **armed services**.

sole adj only, unique, exclusive, individual, single, singular, one, lone, solitary, alone.

F3 shared, multiple, several.

solemn adj **1** a solemn expression: serious, grave, sober, sedate, sombre, glum, thoughtful, earnest, awed, reverential. **2** GRAND, stately, majestic, ceremonial, ritual, formal, ceremonious, pompous, dignified, august, venerable, awe-inspiring, impressive, imposing, momentous. **F3 1** light-hearted. **2** frivolous.

solicit v ask, request, seek, crave, beg, beseech, entreat, implore, pray, supplicate, sue, petition, canvass, importune.

solicitor n lawyer, advocate, attorney, barrister, QC.

solicitous adj caring, attentive, considerate, concerned, anxious, worried.

solid adj **1** HARD, firm, dense, compact, strong, sturdy, substantial, sound, unshakable. **2** a solid white line: unbroken, continuous, uninterrupted. **3** RELIABLE, dependable, trusty, worthy, decent, upright, sensible, level-headed, stable, serious, sober. **4** REAL, genuine, pure, concrete, tangible. **F3 1** liquid, gaseous, hollow. **2** broken, dotted. **3** unreliable, unstable. **4** unreal.

solidarity n unity, agreement, accord, unanimity, consensus, harmony, concord, cohesion, like-mindedness, camaraderie, team spirit, soundness, stability.

F3 discord, division, schism.

solidify v harden, set, jell, congeal, coagulate, clot, cake, crystallize. **F3** soften, liquefy, dissolve.

solitary adj sole, single, lone, alone, lonely, lonesome, friendless, unsociable, reclusive, withdrawn, retired, sequestered, cloistered, secluded, separate, isolated, remote, out-of-the-way, inaccessible, unfrequented, unvisited, untrodden. **F3** accompanied, gregarious, busy.

solitude n aloneness, loneliness, reclusiveness, retirement, privacy, seclusion, isolation, remoteness. **F3** companionship.

solution n **1** ANSWER, result, explanation, resolution, key, remedy. **2** MIXTURE, blend, compound, suspension, emulsion, liquid.

solve v work out, figure out, puzzle out, decipher, crack, disentangle, unravel, answer, resolve, settle, clear up, clarify, explain, interpret.

sombre adj dark, funereal, drab, dull, dim, obscure, shady, shadowy, gloomy, dismal, melancholy, mournful, sad, joyless, sober, serious, grave. **F3** bright, cheerful, happy.

someday adv sometime, one day, eventually, ultimately. **F3** never.

sometimes adv occasionally, now and again, now and then, once in a while, from time to time. **F3** always, never.

song n tune, melody, number, ditty.

Types of song include:

air, anthem, aria, ballad, barcarole, blues, calypso, cantata, canticle, cantilena, canzone, canzonet, carol, chanson, chansonette, chant, chorus, descant, dirge, ditty, elegy, folk-song, gospel song, hymn, jingle, love-song, lied, lullaby, madrigal, plainchant, plainsong, pop song, psalm, recitative, requiem, roundelay, serenade, shanty, spiritual, wassail, yodel.

soon *adv* shortly, presently, in a minute, before long, in the near future.

soothe *v* alleviate, relieve, ease, salve, comfort, allay, calm, compose, tranquillize, settle, still, quiet, hush, lull, pacify, appease, mollify, assuage, mitigate, soften.

F3 aggravate, irritate, annoy, vex.

sophisticated *adj* 1 URBANE, cosmopolitan, worldly, worldly-wise, cultured, cultivated, refined, polished. **2** *sophisticated technology*: advanced, highly-developed, complicated, complex, intricate, elaborate, whizzy (*infml*), delicate, subtle.

F3 1 unsophisticated, naive. **2** primitive, simple.

soporific *adj* sleep-inducing, hypnotic, sedative, tranquillizing, sleepy, somnolent.

F3 stimulating, invigorating.

soppy *adj* sentimental, lovey-dovey (*infml*), weepy (*infml*), sloppy, slushy, mushy, corny (*infml*), mawkish, cloying, soft, silly, daft (*infml*).

sorcery *n* magic, black magic, witchcraft, wizardry, necromancy, voodoo, spell, incantation, charm, enchantment.

sordid *adj* dirty, filthy, unclean, foul, vile, squalid, sleazy, seamy, seedy, disreputable, shabby, tawdry, corrupt, degraded, degenerate, debauched, low, base, despicable, shameful, wretched, mean, miserly, niggardly, grasping, mercenary, selfish, self-seeking.

F3 pure, honourable, upright.

sore *adj* 1 PAINFUL, hurting, aching, smarting, stinging, tender, sensitive, inflamed, red, raw. **2** ANNOYED, irritated, vexed, angry, upset, hurt,

wounded, afflicted, aggrieved, resentful.

F3 2 pleased, happy. *n* wound, lesion, swelling, inflammation, boil, abscess, ulcer.

sorrow *n* sadness, unhappiness, grief, mourning, misery, woe, distress, affliction, anguish, heartache, heartbreak, misfortune, hardship, trouble, worry, trial, tribulation, regret, remorse.

F3 happiness, joy.

sorry *adj* 1 APOLOGETIC, regretful, remorseful, contrite, penitent, repentant, conscience-stricken, guilt-ridden, shamefaced. **2** *in a sorry state*: pathetic, pitiful, poor, wretched, miserable, sad, unhappy, dismal. **3** SYMPATHETIC, compassionate, understanding, pitying, concerned, moved.

F3 1 impenitent, unashamed. **2** happy, cheerful. **3** uncaring.

sort *n* kind, type, genre, ilk, family, race, breed, species, genus, variety, order, class, category, group, denomination, style, make, brand, stamp, quality, nature, character, description. *v* class, group, categorize, distribute, divide, separate, segregate, sift, screen, grade, rank, order, classify, catalogue, arrange, organize, systematize.

sort out resolve, clear up, clarify, tidy up, neaten, choose, select.

soul *n* 1 SPIRIT, psyche, mind, reason, intellect, character, inner being, essence, life, vital force. **2** INDIVIDUAL, person, man, woman, creature.

sound¹ *n* noise, din, report, resonance, reverberation, tone, timbre, tenor, description.

v **1** RING, toll, chime, peal, resound, resonate, reverberate, echo.
2 ARTICULATE, enunciate, pronounce, voice, express, utter, say, declare, announce.

sound² *adj* **1** FIT, well, healthy, vigorous, robust, sturdy, firm, solid, whole, complete, intact, perfect, unbroken, undamaged, unimpaired, unhurt, uninjured. **2** VALID, well-founded, reasonable, rational, logical, orthodox, right, true, proven, reliable, trustworthy, secure, substantial, thorough, good.

F3 unfit, ill, shaky. **2** unsound, unreliable, poor.

sound³ *v* measure, plumb, fathom, probe, examine, test, inspect, investigate.

soup

> Types of soup include:
> bouillabaisse, borsch, broth, gumbo, cock-a-leekie, consommé, gazpacho, goulash, minestrone, vegetable soup, vichyssoise.

sour *adj* **1** TART, sharp, acid, pungent, vinegary, bitter, rancid.
2 EMBITTERED, acrimonious, ill-tempered, peevish, crabbed, crusty, disagreeable.

F3 sweet, sugary. **2** good-natured, generous.

source *n* **1** ORIGIN, derivation, beginning, start, commencement, cause, root, rise, spring, fountainhead, wellhead, supply, mine. **2** ORIGINATOR, authority, informant.

souvenir *n* memento, reminder, remembrance, keepsake, relic, token.

sovereign *n* ruler, monarch, king, queen, emperor, empress, potentate, chief.

adj ruling, royal, imperial, absolute, unlimited, supreme, paramount, predominant, principal, chief, dominant, independent, autonomous.

sow *v* plant, seed, scatter, strew, spread, disseminate, lodge, implant.

space *n* **1** ROOM, place, seat, accommodation, capacity, volume, extent, expansion, scope, range, play, elbow-room, leeway, margin.
2 BLANK, omission, gap, opening, lacuna, interval, intermission, chasm.

spacious *adj* roomy, capacious, ample, big, large, sizable, broad, wide, huge, vast, extensive, open, uncrowded.

F3 small, narrow, cramped, confined.

span *n* arch, reach, range, scope, compass, extent, length, distance, duration, term, period, spell. *v* arch, vault, bridge, link, cross, traverse, extend, cover.

spank *v* smack, slap, wallop (*infml*), whack (*infml*), thrash, slipper, cane.

spare *adj* reserve, emergency, extra, additional, leftover, remaining, unused, over, surplus, superfluous, supernumerary, unwanted, free, unoccupied.

F3 necessary, vital, used.
v **1** PARDON, let off, reprieve, release, free. **2** GRANT, allow, afford, part with.

sparing *adj* economical, thrifty, careful, prudent, frugal, meagre, miserly.

F3 unsparing, liberal, lavish.

spark *n* flash, flare, gleam, glint, flicker, hint, trace, vestige, scrap, atom, jot.

v kindle, set off, trigger, start, cause, occasion, prompt, provoke, stimulate, stir, excite, inspire.

sparkle v **1** TWINKLE, glitter, scintillate, flash, gleam, glint, glisten, shimmer, coruscate, shine, beam. **2** EFFERVESCE, fizz, bubble.
n twinkle, glitter, flash, gleam, glint, flicker, spark, radiance, brilliance, dazzle, spirit, vitality, life, animation.

sparse adj scarce, scanty, meagre, scattered, infrequent, sporadic.
F3 plentiful, thick, dense.

spartan adj austere, harsh, severe, rigorous, strict, disciplined, ascetic, abstemious, temperate, frugal, plain, simple, bleak, joyless.
F3 luxurious, self-indulgent.

spasm n burst, eruption, outburst, frenzy, fit, convulsion, seizure, attack, contraction, jerk, twitch, tic.

spasmodic adj sporadic, occasional, intermittent, erratic, irregular, fitful, jerky.
F3 continuous, uninterrupted.

spate n flood, deluge, torrent, rush, outpouring, flow.

speak v talk, converse, say, state, declare, express, utter, voice, articulate, enunciate, pronounce, tell, communicate, address, lecture, harangue, hold forth, declaim, argue, discuss.

speaker n lecturer, orator, spokesperson, spokesman, spokeswoman.

special adj **1** a special occasion: important, significant, momentous, major, noteworthy, distinguished, memorable, remarkable, extraordinary, exceptional.
2 DIFFERENT, distinctive, characteristic, peculiar, singular, individual, unique, exclusive, select, choice, particular, specific, unusual, precise, detailed.

F3 1 normal, ordinary, usual.
2 general, common.

specialist n consultant, authority, expert, master, professional, connoisseur.

speciality n strength, forte, talent, field, pièce de résistance.

specific adj precise, exact, fixed, limited, particular, special, definite, unequivocal, clear-cut, explicit, express, unambiguous.
F3 vague, approximate.

specification n requirement, condition, qualification, description, listing, item, particular, detail.

specify v stipulate, spell out, define, particularize, detail, itemize, enumerate, list, mention, cite, name, designate, indicate, describe, delineate.

specimen n sample, example, instance, illustration, model, pattern, paradigm, exemplar, representative, copy, exhibit.

spectacle n show, performance, display, exhibition, parade, pageant, extravaganza, scene, sight, curiosity, wonder, marvel, phenomenon.

spectacular adj grand, splendid, magnificent, sensational, impressive, striking, stunning, staggering, amazing, remarkable, dramatic, daring, breathtaking, dazzling, eye-catching, colourful.
F3 unimpressive, ordinary.

spectator n watcher, viewer, onlooker, looker-on, bystander, passer-by, witness, eye-witness, observer.
F3 player, participant.

spectre n ghost, phantom, spirit, wraith, apparition, vision, presence.

speculate v wonder, contemplate, meditate, muse, reflect, consider, deliberate, theorize, suppose, guess, conjecture, surmise, gamble, risk, hazard, venture.

speculative adj conjectural, hypothetical, theoretical, notional, abstract, academic, tentative, risky, hazardous, uncertain, unpredictable.

speech n **1** DICTION, articulation, enunciation, elocution, delivery, utterance, voice, language, tongue, parlance, dialect, jargon. **2** make a speech: oration, address, discourse, talk, lecture, harangue, spiel (sl), conversation, dialogue, monologue, soliloquy.

speechless adj dumbfounded, thunderstruck, amazed, aghast, tongue-tied, inarticulate, mute, dumb, silent, mum.
F3 talkative.

speed n velocity, rate, pace, tempo, quickness, swiftness, rapidity, celerity, alacrity, haste, hurry, dispatch, rush, acceleration.
F3 slowness, delay.
v race, tear, belt (infml), zoom, career, bowl along, sprint, gallop, hurry, rush, hasten, accelerate, quicken, put one's foot down (infml), step on it (infml).
F3 slow, delay.

speedy adj fast, quick, swift, rapid, nimble, express, prompt, immediate, hurried, hasty, precipitate, cursory.
F3 slow, leisurely.

spell[1] n period, time, bout, session, term, season, interval, stretch, patch, turn, stint.

spell[2] n charm, incantation, magic, sorcery, witchery, bewitchment, enchantment, fascination, glamour.

spellbound adj transfixed, hypnotized, mesmerized, fascinated, enthralled, gripped, entranced, captivated, bewitched, enchanted, charmed.

spend v **1** spend money: disburse, pay out, fork out (infml), shell out (infml), invest, lay out, splash out (infml), squander, fritter, expend, consume, use up, exhaust. **2** PASS, fill, occupy, use, employ, apply, devote.
F3 1 save, hoard.

spendthrift n squanderer, prodigal, profligate, wastrel.
F3 miser.
adj improvident, extravagant, prodigal, wasteful.

sphere n **1** BALL, globe, orb, round. **2** DOMAIN, realm, province, department, territory, field, range, scope, compass, rank, function, capacity.

spherical adj round, rotund, ball-shaped, globe-shaped.

spicy adj **1** PIQUANT, hot, pungent, tangy, seasoned, aromatic, fragrant. **2** RACY, risqué, ribald, suggestive, indelicate, improper, indecorous, unseemly, scandalous, sensational.
F3 1 bland, insipid. **2** decent.

spike n point, prong, tine, spine, barb, nail, stake.
v impale, stick, spear, skewer, spit.

spill v overturn, upset, slop, overflow, disgorge, pour, tip, discharge, shed, scatter.

spin v turn, revolve, rotate, twist, gyrate, twirl, pirouette, wheel, whirl, swirl, reel.
n **1** TURN, revolution, twist, gyration, twirl, pirouette, whirl, swirl. **2** COMMOTION, agitation, panic, flap (infml), state (infml), tizzy (infml). **3** DRIVE, ride, run.

spin out prolong, protract, extend, lengthen, amplify, pad out.

spindle n axis, pivot, pin, rod, axle.

spine n **1** BACKBONE, spinal column, vertebral column, vertebrae. **2** THORN, barb, prickle, bristle, quill.

spineless adj weak, feeble, wimpy (infml), irresolute, ineffective, cowardly, faint-hearted, lily-livered, yellow (sl), soft, wet, submissive, weak-kneed.

F3 strong, brave.

spiral adj winding, coiled, corkscrew, helical, whorled, scrolled, circular. n coil, helix, corkscrew, screw, whorl, convolution.

spire n steeple, pinnacle, peak, summit, top, tip, point, spike.

spirit n **1** SOUL, psyche, mind, breath, life. **2** GHOST, spectre, phantom, apparition, angel, demon, fairy, sprite. **3** LIVELINESS, vivacity, animation, sparkle, vigour, energy, zest, fire, ardour, motivation, enthusiasm, zeal, enterprise, resolution, willpower, courage, backbone, mettle. **4** the spirit of the law: meaning, sense, substance, essence, gist, tenor, character, quality. **5** MOOD, humour, temper, disposition, temperament, feeling, morale, attitude, outlook.

spirited adj lively, vivacious, animated, sparkling, high-spirited, vigorous, energetic, active, ardent, zealous, bold, courageous, mettlesome, plucky.

F3 spiritless, lethargic, cowardly.

spiritual adj unworldly, incorporeal, immaterial, otherworldly, heavenly, divine, holy, sacred, religious, ecclesiastical.

F3 physical, material.

spit v expectorate, eject, discharge, splutter, hiss.
n spittle, saliva, slaver, drool, dribble,

sputum, phlegm, expectoration.

spite n spitefulness, malice, venom, gall, bitterness, rancour, animosity, ill feeling, grudge, malevolence, malignity, ill nature, hate, hatred.

F3 goodwill, compassion, affection.
v annoy, irritate, irk, vex, provoke, gall, hurt, injure, offend, put out.

spiteful adj malicious, venomous, catty, bitchy, snide, barbed, cruel, vindictive, vengeful, malevolent, malignant, ill-natured, ill-disposed, nasty.

F3 charitable, affectionate.

splash v **1** BATHE, wallow, paddle, wade, dabble, plunge, wet, wash, shower, spray, squirt, sprinkle, spatter, splatter, splodge, spread, daub, plaster, slop, slosh, plop, surge, break, dash, strike, buffet, smack. **2** PUBLICIZE, flaunt, blazon, trumpet.
n **1** SPOT, patch, splatter, splodge, burst, touch, dash. **2** PUBLICITY, display, ostentation, effect, impact, stir, excitement, sensation.

splendid adj brilliant, dazzling, glittering, lustrous, bright, radiant, glowing, glorious, magnificent, gorgeous, resplendent, sumptuous, luxurious, lavish, rich, fine, grand, stately, imposing, impressive, great, outstanding, remarkable, exceptional, sublime, supreme, superb, excellent, first-class, wonderful, marvellous, admirable.

F3 drab, ordinary, run-of-the-mill.

splendour n brightness, radiance, brilliance, dazzle, lustre, glory, resplendence, magnificence, richness, grandeur, majesty, solemnity, pomp, ceremony, display, show, spectacle.

F3 drabness, squalor.

splice *v* join, unite, wed, marry, bind, tie, plait, braid, interweave, interlace, intertwine, entwine, mesh, knit, graft.

splinter *n* sliver, chip, shard, fragment, flake, shaving, paring.
v split, fracture, smash, shatter, shiver, fragment, disintegrate.

split *v* divide, separate, partition, part, disunite, disband, open, gape, fork, diverge, break, splinter, shiver, snap, crack, burst, rupture, tear, rend, rip, slit, slash, cleave, halve, slice up, share, distribute, parcel out.
n **1** DIVISION, separation, partition, break, breach, gap, cleft, crevice, crack, fissure, rupture, tear, rent, rip, rift, slit, slash. **2** SCHISM, disunion, dissension, discord, difference, divergence, break-up.
adj divided, cleft, cloven, bisected, dual, twofold, broken, fractured, cracked, ruptured.

split up part, part company, disband, break up, separate, divorce.

spoil *v* **1** MAR, upset, wreck, ruin, destroy, damage, impair, harm, hurt, injure, deface, disfigure, blemish. **2** *spoil a child*: indulge, pamper, cosset, coddle, mollycoddle, baby, spoon-feed. **3** DETERIORATE, go bad, go off, sour, turn, curdle, decay, decompose.

spoils *n* plunder, loot, booty, haul, swag (*sl*), pickings, gain, acquisitions, prizes, winnings.

sponge *v* **1** WIPE, mop, clean, wash. **2** CADGE, scrounge.

sponger *n* cadger, scrounger, parasite, hanger-on.

spongy *adj* soft, cushioned, yielding, elastic, springy, porous, absorbent, light.

sponsor *n* patron, backer, angel (*infml*), promoter, underwriter, guarantor, surety.
v finance, fund, bankroll, subsidize, patronize, back, promote, underwrite, guarantee.

spontaneous *adj* natural, unforced, untaught, instinctive, impulsive, unpremeditated, free, willing, unhesitating, voluntary, unprompted, impromptu, extempore.
F3 forced, studied, planned, deliberate.

sporadic *adj* occasional, intermittent, infrequent, isolated, spasmodic, erratic, irregular, uneven, random, scattered.
F3 frequent, regular.

sport *n* **1** GAME, exercise, activity, pastime, amusement, entertainment, diversion, recreation, play. **2** FUN, mirth, humour, joking, jesting, banter, teasing, mockery, ridicule.

Sports include:
badminton, fives, lacrosse, squash, table tennis, tennis; American football, baseball, basketball, billiards, boules, bowls, cricket, croquet, football, golf, handball, hockey, netball, pelota, pétanque, polo, pool, rounders, Rugby, snooker, soccer, tenpin bowling, volleyball; athletics, cross-country running, decathlon, discus, high jump, hurdling, javelin, long jump, marathon, pentathlon, pole vault, running, shotput, triple jump; angling, canoeing, diving, fishing, rowing, sailing, skin-diving, surfing, swimming, synchronized swimming, water polo, water-skiing, windsurfing, yachting; bobsleigh, curling, ice hockey, ice-skating, cross-country skiing, downhill racing, slalom, snowboarding,

---

speedskating, tobogganing, luging; aerobics, fencing, gymnastics, jogging, keep fit, roller-skating, trampolining; archery, darts, quoits; boxing, judo, ju-jitsu, karate, tae kwon do, weight-lifting, wrestling; climbing, mountaineering, rockclimbing, walking, orienteering, potholing; cycle racing, dragracing, go-karting, motor racing, speedway racing, stock car racing, greyhound-racing, horse-racing, showjumping, hunting, shooting, clay pigeon shooting; gliding, paragliding, sky-diving. *see also* **martial art**.

v wear, display, exhibit, show off.

sporting adj sportsmanlike, gentlemanly, decent, considerate, fair. **Ⅎ**unsporting, ungentlemanly, unfair.

sporty adj **1** ATHLETIC, fit, energetic, outdoor. **2** STYLISH, trendy (*infml*), jaunty, natty (*infml*), snazzy (*infml*), showy, loud, flashy, casual, informal.

spot n **1** DOT, speckle, fleck, mark, speck, blotch, blot, smudge, daub, splash, stain, discoloration, blemish, flaw, pimple. **2** PLACE, point, position, situation, location, site, scene, locality. **3** (*infml*) PLIGHT, predicament, quandary, difficulty, trouble, mess.

v see, notice, observe, detect, discern, identify, recognize.

spotless adj immaculate, clean, white, gleaming, spick and span, unmarked, unstained, unblemished, unsullied, pure, chaste, virgin, untouched, innocent, blameless, faultless, irreproachable. **Ⅎ**dirty, impure.

spotted adj dotted, speckled, flecked, mottled, dappled, pied.

spotty adj pimply, pimpled, blotchy, spotted.

spouse n husband, wife, partner, mate, better half (*infml*).

spout v jet, spurt, squirt, spray, shoot, gush, stream, surge, erupt, emit, discharge.
n jet, fountain, geyser, gargoyle, outlet, nozzle, rose, spray.

sprawl v spread, straggle, trail, ramble, flop, slump, slouch, loll, lounge, recline, repose.

spray¹ v shower, spatter, sprinkle, scatter, diffuse, wet, drench.
n **1** MOISTURE, drizzle, mist, foam, froth. **2** AEROSOL, atomizer, sprinkler.

spray² n sprig, branch, corsage, posy, bouquet, garland, wreath.

spread v **1** STRETCH, extend, sprawl, broaden, widen, dilate, expand, swell, mushroom, proliferate, escalate, open, unroll, unfurl, unfold, fan out, cover, lay out, arrange. **2** SCATTER, strew, diffuse, radiate, disseminate, broadcast, transmit, communicate, promulgate, propagate, publicize, advertise, publish, circulate, distribute. **Ⅎ1** close, fold. **2** suppress.
n **1** STRETCH, reach, span, extent, expanse, sweep, compass.
2 the spread of disease: advance, development, expansion, increase, proliferation, escalation, diffusion, dissemination, dispersion.

spree n bout, fling, binge, splurge, orgy, revel.

sprightly adj agile, nimble, spry, active, energetic, lively, spirited, vivacious, hearty, brisk, jaunty, cheerful, blithe, airy. **Ⅎ**doddering, inactive, lifeless.

spring¹ v **1** JUMP, leap, vault, bound, hop, bounce, rebound, recoil.

2 ORIGINATE, derive, come, stem, arise, start, proceed, issue, emerge, emanate, appear, sprout, grow, develop.

n **1** JUMP, leap, vault, bound, bounce. **2** SPRINGINESS, resilience, give, flexibility, elasticity, buoyancy.

spring[2] *n* **1** SOURCE, origin, beginning, cause, root, fountainhead, wellspring. **2** FOUNT, geyser, spa.

springy *adj* bouncy, resilient, flexible, elastic, stretchy, rubbery, spongy, buoyant.

F3 hard, stiff.

sprinkle *v* shower, spray, spatter, scatter, strew, dot, pepper, dust, powder.

sprint *v* run, race, dash, tear, belt (*infml*), dart, shoot.

sprout *v* shoot, bud, germinate, grow, develop, come up, spring up.

spruce *adj* smart, elegant, neat, trim, dapper, well-dressed, well-turned-out, well-groomed, sleek.

F3 scruffy, untidy.

spruce up neaten, tidy, smarten up, groom.

spur *v* goad, prod, poke, prick, stimulate, prompt, incite, drive, propel, impel, urge, encourage, motivate.

F3 curb, discourage.

n incentive, encouragement, inducement, motive, stimulus, incitement, impetus, fillip.

F3 curb, disincentive.

spurious *adj* false, fake, counterfeit, forged, bogus, phoney (*infml*), mock, sham, feigned, pretended, simulated, imitation, artificial.

F3 genuine, authentic, real.

spurn *v* reject, turn down, scorn, despise, disdain, rebuff, repulse, slight, snub, cold-shoulder, ignore, disregard.

F3 accept, embrace.

spurt *v* gush, squirt, jet, shoot, burst, erupt, surge.

n burst, rush, surge, spate, fit, access.

spy *n* secret agent, undercover agent, double agent, mole (*infml*), fifth columnist, scout, snooper.

v spot, glimpse, notice, observe, discover.

squabble *v* bicker, wrangle, quarrel, row, argue, dispute, clash, brawl, scrap, fight.

squad *n* crew, team, gang, band, group, company, brigade, troop, force, outfit.

squalid *adj* dirty, filthy, unclean, foul, disgusting, repulsive, sordid, seedy, dingy, untidy, slovenly, unkempt, broken-down, run-down, neglected, uncared-for, low, mean, nasty.

F3 clean, pleasant, attractive.

squander *v* waste, misspend, misuse, lavish, blow (*sl*), fritter away, throw away, dissipate, scatter, spend, expend, consume.

square *v* settle, reconcile, tally, agree, accord, harmonize, correspond, match, balance, straighten, level, align, adjust, regulate, adapt, tailor, fit, suit.

adj **1** QUADRILATERAL, rectangular, right-angled, perpendicular, straight, true, even, level. **2** FAIR, equitable, just, ethical, honourable, honest, genuine, above-board, on the level (*infml*).

squash *v* **1** CRUSH, flatten, press, squeeze, compress, crowd, trample, stamp, pound, pulp, smash, distort. **2** SUPPRESS, silence, quell, quash,

annihilate, put down, snub, humiliate.
F3 1 stretch, expand.

squat *adj* short, stocky, thickset, dumpy, chunky, stubby.
F3 slim, lanky.
v crouch, stoop, bend, sit.

squawk *v, n* screech, shriek, cry, croak, cackle, crow, hoot.

squeak *v, n* squeal, whine, creak, peep, cheep.

squeal *v, n* cry, shout, yell, yelp, wail, scream, screech, shriek, squawk.

squeamish *adj* queasy, nauseated, sick, delicate, fastidious, particular, prudish.

squeeze *v* **1** PRESS, squash, crush, pinch, nip, compress, grip, clasp, clutch, hug, embrace, enfold, cuddle. **2** *squeeze into a corner*: cram, stuff, pack, crowd, wedge, jam, force, ram, push, thrust, shove, jostle. **3** WRING, wrest, extort, milk, bleed, force, lean on (*infml*).
n **1** PRESS, squash, crush, crowd, congestion, jam. **2** HUG, embrace, hold, grasp, clasp.

squirt *v* spray, spurt, jet, shoot, spout, gush, ejaculate, discharge, emit, eject, expel.
n spray, spurt, jet.

stab *v* pierce, puncture, cut, wound, injure, gore, knife, spear, stick, jab, thrust.
n **1** ACHE, pang, twinge, prick, puncture, cut, incision, gash, wound, jab. **2** (*infml*) TRY, attempt, endeavour, bash (*infml*).

stability *n* steadiness, firmness, soundness, constancy, steadfastness, strength, sturdiness, solidity, durability, permanence.
F3 instability, unsteadiness, insecurity, weakness.

stable *adj* steady, firm, secure, fast, sound, sure, constant, steadfast, reliable, established, well-founded, deep-rooted, strong, sturdy, durable, lasting, enduring, abiding, permanent, unchangeable, unalterable, invariable, immutable, fixed, static, balanced.
F3 unstable, wobbly, shaky, weak.

stack *n* heap, pile, mound, mass, load, accumulation, hoard, stockpile.
v heap, pile, load, amass, accumulate, assemble, gather, save, hoard, stockpile.

staff *n* **1** *member of staff*: personnel, workforce, employees, workers, crew, team, teachers, officers. **2** STICK, cane, rod, baton, wand, pole, prop.

stage *n* point, juncture, step, phase, period, division, lap, leg, length, level, floor.
v mount, put on, present, produce, give, do, perform, arrange, organize, stage-manage, orchestrate, engineer.

stagger *v* **1** LURCH, totter, teeter, wobble, sway, rock, reel, falter, hesitate, waver. **2** SURPRISE, amaze, astound, astonish, stun, stupefy, dumbfound, flabbergast (*infml*), shake, shock, confound, overwhelm.

stagnant *adj* still, motionless, standing, brackish, stale, sluggish, torpid, lethargic.
F3 fresh, moving.

stagnate *v* vegetate, idle, languish, decline, deteriorate, degenerate, decay, rot, rust.

staid *adj* sedate, calm, composed, sober, demure, solemn, serious, grave, quiet, steady.
F3 jaunty, debonair, frivolous, adventurous.

stain *v* **1** MARK, spot, blemish, blot,

smudge, discolour, dirty, soil, taint, contaminate, sully, tarnish, blacken, disgrace. **2** DYE, tint, tinge, colour, paint, varnish.

n mark, spot, blemish, blot, smudge, discoloration, smear, slur, disgrace, shame, dishonour.

stake[1] n post, pole, standard, picket, pale, paling, spike, stick.

stake[2] n bet, wager, pledge, interest, concern, involvement, share, investment, claim.

v gamble, bet, wager, pledge, risk, chance, hazard, venture.

stale adj **1** stale bread: dry, hard, old, musty, fusty, flat, insipid, tasteless. **2** OVERUSED, hackneyed, clichéd, stereotyped, jaded, worn-out, unoriginal, trite, banal, commonplace.

Ⅎ 1 crisp. **2** new.

stalemate n draw, tie, deadlock, impasse, standstill, halt.

Ⅎ progress.

stalk[1] v track, trail, hunt, follow, pursue, shadow, tail, haunt.

stalk[2] n stem, twig, branch, trunk.

stall v temporize, play for time, delay, hedge, equivocate, obstruct, stonewall.

stalwart adj strong, sturdy, robust, rugged, stout, strapping, muscular, athletic, vigorous, valiant, daring, intrepid, indomitable, determined, resolute, staunch, steadfast, reliable, dependable.

Ⅎ weak, feeble, timid.

stamina n energy, vigour, strength, power, force, grit, resilience, resistance, endurance, indefatigability, staying power.

Ⅎ weakness.

stammer v stutter, stumble, falter, hesitate, splutter.

stamp v **1** TRAMPLE, crush, beat, pound. **2** IMPRINT, impress, print, inscribe, engrave, emboss, mark, brand, label, categorize, identify, characterize.

n **1** PRINT, imprint, impression, seal, signature, authorization, mark, hallmark, attestation. **2** BRAND, cast, mould, cut, form, fashion, sort, kind, type, breed, character, description.

stampede n charge, rush, dash, sprint, flight, rout.

v charge, rush, dash, tear, run, sprint, gallop, shoot, fly, flee, scatter.

stance n posture, deportment, carriage, bearing, position, standpoint, viewpoint, angle, point of view, attitude.

stand v **1** PUT, place, set, erect, up-end, position, station. **2** I can't stand it: bear, tolerate, abide, endure, suffer, experience, undergo, withstand, weather. **3** RISE, get up, stand up.

n base, pedestal, support, frame, rack, table, stage, platform, place, stall, booth.

stand by support, back, champion, defend, stick up for, uphold, adhere to, hold to, stick by.

Ⅎ let down.

stand down step down, resign, abdicate, quit, give up, retire, withdraw.

Ⅎ join.

stand for represent, symbolize, mean, signify, denote, indicate.

stand in for deputize for, cover for, understudy, replace, substitute for.

stand out show, catch the eye, stick out, jut out, project.

stand up for defend, stick up for, side with, fight for, support, protect, champion, uphold.

Ⅎ attack.

stand up to defy, oppose, resist, withstand, endure, face, confront, brave.
F3 give in to.

standard n 1 NORM, average, type, model, pattern, example, sample, guideline, benchmark, touchstone, yardstick, rule, measure, gauge, level, criterion, requirement, specification, grade, quality. 2 FLAG, ensign, pennant, pennon, colours, banner.
adj normal, average, typical, stock, classic, basic, staple, usual, customary, popular, prevailing, regular, approved, accepted, recognized, official, orthodox, set, established, definitive.
F3 abnormal, unusual, irregular.

standardize v normalize, equalize, homogenize, stereotype, mass-produce.
F3 differentiate.

standards n principles, ideals, morals, ethics.

standoffish adj aloof, remote, distant, unapproachable, unsociable, uncommunicative, reserved, cold.
F3 friendly.

standpoint n position, station, vantage point, stance, viewpoint, angle, point of view.

standstill n stop, halt, pause, lull, rest, stoppage, jam, log-jam, hold-up, impasse, deadlock, stalemate.
F3 advance, progress.

staple adj basic, fundamental, primary, key, main, chief, major, principal, essential, necessary, standard.
F3 minor.

star n celebrity, personage, luminary, idol, lead, leading man, leading lady, superstar, megastar.

Types of star include:
nova, supernova, pulsar, red giant, supergiant, white dwarf, red dwarf, brown dwarf, neutron star.

stare v gaze, look, watch, gape, gawp, gawk, goggle, glare.
n gaze, look, glare.

stark adj 1 stark landscape: bare, barren, bleak, bald, plain, simple, austere, harsh, severe, grim, dreary, gloomy, depressing. 2 UTTER, unmitigated, total, consummate, absolute, sheer, downright, out-and-out, flagrant, arrant.

start v 1 BEGIN, commence, originate, initiate, introduce, pioneer, create, found, establish, set up, institute, inaugurate, launch, open, kick off (infml), instigate, activate, trigger, set off, set out, leave, depart, appear, arise, issue. 2 JUMP, jerk, twitch, flinch, recoil.
F3 1 stop, finish, end.
n 1 BEGINNING, commencement, outset, inception, dawn, birth, break, outburst, onset, origin, initiation, introduction, foundation, inauguration, launch, opening, kick-off (infml). 2 JUMP, jerk, twitch, spasm, convulsion, fit.
F3 1 stop, finish, end.

startle v surprise, amaze, astonish, astound, shock, scare, frighten, alarm, agitate, upset, disturb.
F3 calm.

starvation n hunger, undernourishment, malnutrition, famine.
F3 plenty, excess.

starve v hunger, fast, diet, deprive, refuse, deny, die, perish.
F3 feed, gorge.

starving adj hungry, underfed, undernourished, ravenous, famished.

state v say, declare, announce, report, communicate, assert, aver, affirm, specify, present, express, put, formulate, articulate, voice.
n **1** CONDITION, shape, situation, position, circumstances, case. **2** NATION, country, land, territory, kingdom, republic, government. **3** (infml) PANIC, flap (infml), tizzy (infml), bother, plight, predicament. **4** POMP, ceremony, dignity, majesty, grandeur, glory, splendour.
adj national, governmental, public, official, formal, ceremonial, pompous, stately.

stately adj grand, imposing, impressive, elegant, majestic, regal, royal, imperial, noble, august, lofty, pompous, dignified, measured, deliberate, solemn, ceremonious.
🔁 informal, unimpressive.

statement n account, report, bulletin, communiqué, announcement, declaration, proclamation, communication, utterance, testimony.

static adj stationary, motionless, immobile, unmoving, still, inert, resting, fixed, constant, changeless, unvarying, stable.
🔁 dynamic, mobile, varying.

station n place, location, position, post, headquarters, base, depot.
v locate, set, establish, install, garrison, post, send, appoint, assign.

stationary adj motionless, immobile, unmoving, still, static, inert, standing, resting, parked, moored, fixed.
🔁 mobile, moving, active.

statue n figure, head, bust, effigy, idol, statuette, carving, bronze.

status n rank, grade, degree, level,

class, station, standing, position, state, condition, prestige, eminence, distinction, importance, consequence, weight.
🔁 unimportance, insignificance.

staunch adj loyal, faithful, hearty, strong, stout, firm, sound, sure, true, trusty, reliable, dependable, steadfast.
🔁 unfaithful, weak, unreliable.

stay v **1** LAST, continue, endure, abide, remain, linger, persist. **2** RESIDE, dwell, live, settle, sojourn, stop, halt, pause, wait.
🔁 **1** go, leave.
n stay, holiday, stopover, sojourn.

steady adj stable, balanced, poised, fixed, immovable, firm, settled, still, calm, imperturbable, equable, even, uniform, consistent, unvarying, unchanging, constant, persistent, unremitting, incessant, uninterrupted, unbroken, regular, rhythmic, steadfast, unwavering.
🔁 unsteady, unstable, variable, wavering.
v balance, stabilize, fix, secure, brace, support.

steal v **1** steal a car: thieve, pilfer, filch, pinch (infml), nick (infml), take, appropriate, snatch, swipe, shoplift, poach, embezzle, lift, plagiarize. **2** CREEP, tiptoe, slip, slink, sneak.
🔁 **1** return, give back.

stealthy adj surreptitious, clandestine, covert, secret, unobtrusive, secretive, quiet, furtive, sly, cunning, sneaky, underhand.
🔁 open.

steam n vapour, mist, haze, condensation, moisture, dampness.

steep adj **1** a steep slope: sheer, precipitous, headlong, abrupt, sudden, sharp. **2** (infml) EXCESSIVE, extreme, stiff, unreasonable, high, exorbitant, extortionate, overpriced. **F∃ 1** gentle, gradual. **2** moderate, low.

steer v pilot, guide, direct, control, govern, conduct.

stem [1] n stalk, shoot, stock, branch, trunk.

stem [2] v stop, halt, arrest, stanch, staunch, block, dam, check, curb, restrain, contain, resist, oppose. **F∃** encourage.

stench n stink, reek, pong (infml), smell, odour.

step n **1** PACE, stride, footstep, tread, footprint, print, trace, track. **2** MOVE, act, action, deed, measure, procedure, process, proceeding, progression, movement, stage, phase, degree. **3** RUNG, stair, level, rank, point. v pace, stride, tread, stamp, walk, move. **step down** stand down, resign, abdicate, quit, leave, retire, withdraw. **F∃** join.

step up increase, raise, augment, boost, build up, intensify, escalate, accelerate, speed up. **F∃** decrease.

stereotype n formula, convention, mould, pattern, model. v categorize, pigeonhole, typecast, standardize, formalize, conventionalize, mass-produce. **F∃** differentiate.

sterile adj **1** GERM-FREE, aseptic, sterilized, disinfected, antiseptic, uncontaminated. **2** INFERTILE, barren, arid, bare, unproductive, fruitless, pointless, useless, abortive. **F∃ 1** septic. **2** fertile, fruitful.

sterilize v disinfect, fumigate, purify, clean, cleanse. **F∃** contaminate, infect.

stern adj strict, severe, authoritarian,

rigid, inflexible, unyielding, hard, tough, rigorous, stringent, harsh, cruel, unsparing, relentless, unrelenting, grim, forbidding, stark, austere. **F∃** kind, gentle, mild, lenient.

stew v boil, simmer, braise, casserole.

stick [1] v **1** THRUST, poke, stab, jab, pierce, penetrate, puncture, spear, transfix. **2** GLUE, gum, paste, cement, bond, fuse, weld, solder, adhere, cling, hold. **3** ATTACH, affix, fasten, secure, fix, pin, join, bind. **4** PUT, place, position, set, install, deposit, drop. **stick at** persevere, plug away (infml), persist, continue. **F∃** give up.

stick out protrude, jut out, project, extend.

stick up for stand up for, speak up for, defend, champion, support, uphold. **F∃** attack.

stick [2] n branch, twig, wand, baton, staff, sceptre, cane, birch, rod, pole, stake.

sticky adj **1** ADHESIVE, gummed, tacky, gluey, gummy, viscous, glutinous, gooey (infml). **2** (infml) a sticky situation: difficult, tricky, thorny, unpleasant, awkward, embarrassing, delicate. **3** HUMID, clammy, muggy, close, oppressive, sultry. **F∃ 1** dry. **2** easy. **3** fresh, cool.

stiff adj **1** RIGID, inflexible, unbending, unyielding, hard, solid, hardened, solidified, firm, tight, taut, tense. **2** FORMAL, ceremonious, pompous, standoffish, cold, prim, priggish, austere, strict, severe, harsh. **3** DIFFICULT, hard, tough, arduous, laborious, awkward, exacting, rigorous. **F∃ 1** flexible. **2** informal. **3** easy.

stiffen v harden, solidify, tighten, tense, brace, reinforce, starch, thicken, congeal, coagulate, jell, set.

stifle v smother, suffocate, asphyxiate, strangle, choke, extinguish, muffle, dampen, deaden, silence, hush, suppress, quell, check, curb, restrain, repress.
F3 encourage.

stigma n brand, mark, stain, blot, spot, blemish, disgrace, shame, dishonour.
F3 credit, honour.

still adj stationary, motionless, lifeless, stagnant, smooth, undisturbed, unruffled, calm, tranquil, serene, restful, peaceful, hushed, quiet, silent, noiseless.
F3 active, disturbed, agitated, noisy.
v calm, soothe, allay, tranquillize, subdue, restrain, hush, quieten, silence, pacify, settle, smooth.
F3 agitate, stir up.
adv yet, even so, nevertheless, nonetheless, notwithstanding, however.

stilted adj artificial, unnatural, stiff, wooden, forced, constrained.
F3 fluent, flowing.

stimulate v rouse, arouse, animate, quicken, fire, inflame, inspire, motivate, encourage, induce, urge, impel, spur, prompt, goad, provoke, incite, instigate, trigger off.
F3 discourage, hinder, prevent.

stimulus n incentive, encouragement, inducement, spur, goad, provocation, incitement.
F3 discouragement.

sting v 1 bees sting: bite, prick, hurt, injure, wound. 2 SMART, tingle, burn, pain.
n bite, nip, prick, smart, tingle.

stingy adj mean, miserly, niggardly, tight-fisted (infml), parsimonious, penny-pinching.
F3 generous, liberal.

stink v smell, reek, pong (infml), hum (sl).
n smell, odour, stench, pong (infml), niff (sl).

stint n spell, stretch, period, time, shift, turn, bit, share, quota.

stipulate v specify, lay down, require, demand, insist on.

stipulation n specification, requirement, demand, condition, proviso.

stir v 1 MOVE, budge, touch, affect, inspire, excite, thrill, disturb, agitate, shake, tremble, quiver, flutter, rustle. 2 MIX, blend, beat.
n activity, movement, bustle, flurry, commotion, ado, fuss, to-do (infml), uproar, tumult, disturbance, disorder, agitation, excitement, ferment.
F3 calm.

stir up rouse, arouse, awaken, animate, quicken, kindle, fire, inflame, stimulate, spur, prompt, provoke, incite, instigate, agitate.
F3 calm, discourage.

stock n 1 GOODS, merchandise, wares, commodities, capital, assets, inventory, repertoire, range, variety, assortment, source, supply, fund, reservoir, store, reserve, stockpile, hoard. 2 PARENTAGE, ancestry, descent, extraction, family, line, lineage, pedigree, race, breed, species, blood. 3 LIVESTOCK, animals, cattle, horses, sheep, herds, flocks.
adj standard, basic, regular, routine, ordinary, run-of-the-mill, bog-standard (infml), usual, customary, traditional, conventional, set,

stereotyped, hackneyed, overused, banal, trite.

F3 original, unusual.

v keep, carry, sell, trade in, deal in, handle, supply, provide.

stock up gather, accumulate, amass, lay in, provision, fill, replenish, store (up), save, hoard, pile up.

stocky *adj* sturdy, solid, thickset, chunky, short, squat, dumpy, stubby.

F3 tall, skinny.

stoical *adj* patient, long-suffering, uncomplaining, resigned, philosophical, indifferent, impassive, unemotional, phlegmatic, dispassionate, cool, calm, imperturbable.

F3 excitable, anxious.

stolid *adj* slow, heavy, dull, bovine, wooden, blockish, lumpish, impassive, phlegmatic, unemotional.

F3 lively, interested.

stomach *n* tummy (*infml*), tum (*infml*), gut, inside(s), belly, abdomen, paunch, pot.

v tolerate, bear, stand, abide, endure, suffer, submit to, take.

stony *adj* 1 BLANK, expressionless, hard, cold, frigid, icy, indifferent, unfeeling, heartless, callous, merciless, pitiless, inexorable, hostile. 2 *stony beach*: pebbly, shingly, rocky.

F3 1 warm, soft-hearted, friendly.

stoop *v* 1 HUNCH, bow, bend, incline, lean, duck, squat, crouch, kneel. 2 *stoop to blackmail*: descend, sink, lower oneself, resort, so go so far as, condescend, deign.

stop *v* 1 HALT, cease, end, finish, conclude, terminate, discontinue, suspend, interrupt, pause, quit, refrain, desist, pack in (*sl*). 2 PREVENT, bar, frustrate, thwart, intercept,

hinder, impede, check, restrain. 3 SEAL, close, plug, block, obstruct, arrest, stem, stanch.

F3 1 start, continue.

n 1 STATION, terminus, destination. 2 REST, break, pause, stage. 3 HALT, standstill, stoppage, cessation, end, finish, conclusion, termination, discontinuation.

F3 3 start, beginning, continuation.

stoppage *n* stop, halt, standstill, arrest, blockage, obstruction, check, hindrance, interruption, shutdown, closure, strike, walk-out, sit-in.

F3 start, continuation.

stopper *n* cork, bung, plug.

store *v* save, keep, put aside, lay by, reserve, stock, lay in, deposit, lay down, lay up, accumulate, hoard, salt away, stockpile, stash (*infml*).

F3 use.

n 1 STOCK, supply, provision, fund, reserve, mine, reservoir, hoard, cache, stockpile, accumulation, quantity, abundance, plenty, lot. 2 STOREROOM, storehouse, warehouse, repository, depository.

F3 1 scarcity.

storey *n* floor, level, stage, tier, flight, deck.

storm *n* 1 TEMPEST, squall, blizzard, gale. 2 OUTBURST, uproar, furore, outcry, row, rumpus, commotion, tumult, disturbance, turmoil, stir, agitation, rage, outbreak, attack, assault.

F3 2 calm.

Kinds of storm include:
buran, cyclone, dust-devil, dust-storm, electrical storm, haboob, hail-storm, hurricane, monsoon, rainstorm, sandstorm, snowstorm, thunderstorm, tornado, typhoon, whirlwind. *see also* **wind¹**.

v charge, rush, attack, assault, assail, roar, thunder, rage, rant, rave, fume.

stormy *adj* tempestuous, squally, rough, choppy, turbulent, wild, raging, windy, gusty, blustery, foul.
F3 calm.

story *n* **1** TALE, legend, fiction, yarn, anecdote, episode, plot, narrative, history, chronicle, record, account, relation, recital, report, article, feature. **2** LIE, falsehood, untruth.

Types of story include:
adventure story, bedtime story, blockbuster (*infml*), children's story, comedy, black comedy, crime story, detective story, fable, fairy tale, fantasy, folk-tale, ghost story, historical novel, horror story, love-story, mystery, myth, novelization, parable, romance, saga, science fiction, sci-fi (*infml*), short story, spine-chiller, spy story, tall story, thriller, western, whodunnit (*infml*).

stout *adj* **1** FAT, plump, fleshy, portly, corpulent, overweight, heavy, bulky, big, brawny, beefy, hulking, burly, muscular, athletic. **2** *stout packaging*: strong, tough, durable, thick, sturdy, robust, hardy, vigorous. **3** BRAVE, courageous, valiant, plucky, fearless, bold, intrepid, dauntless, resolute, stalwart.
F3 **1** thin, lean, slim. **2** weak. **3** cowardly, timid.

stow *v* put away, store, load, pack, cram, stuff, stash (*infml*).
F3 unload.

straight *adj* **1** *a straight line*: level, even, flat, horizontal, upright, vertical, aligned, direct, undeviating, unswerving, true, right. **2** TIDY, neat, orderly, shipshape, organized.

3 HONOURABLE, honest, law-abiding, respectable, upright, trustworthy, reliable, straightforward, fair, just. **4** FRANK, candid, blunt, forthright, direct. **5** *straight whisky*: undiluted, neat, unadulterated, unmixed.
F3 **1** bent, crooked. **2** untidy. **3** dishonest. **4** evasive. **5** diluted.
adv directly, point-blank, honestly, frankly, candidly.

straight away at once, immediately, instantly, right away, directly, now, there and then.
F3 later, eventually.

straighten *v* unbend, align, tidy, neaten, order, arrange.
F3 bend, twist.

straighten out clear up, sort out, settle, resolve, correct, rectify, disentangle, regularize.
F3 confuse, muddle.

straightforward *adj* **1** EASY, simple, uncomplicated, clear, elementary. **2** HONEST, truthful, sincere, genuine, open, frank, candid, direct, forthright.
F3 **1** complicated. **2** evasive, devious.

strain[1] *v* **1** PULL, wrench, twist, sprain, tear, stretch, extend, tighten, tauten. **2** SIEVE, sift, screen, separate, filter, purify, drain, wring, squeeze, compress, express. **3** WEAKEN, tire, tax, overtax, overwork, labour, try, endeavour, struggle, strive, exert, force, drive.
n stress, anxiety, burden, pressure, tension, tautness, pull, sprain, wrench, injury, exertion, effort, struggle, force.
F3 relaxation.

strain[2] *n* **1** STOCK, ancestry, descent, extraction, family, lineage, pedigree blood, variety, type. **2** TRAIT, streak, vein, tendency, trace, suggestion, suspicion.

strained adj forced, constrained, laboured, false, artificial, unnatural, stiff, tense, unrelaxed, uneasy, uncomfortable, awkward, embarrassed, self-conscious.
F3 natural, relaxed.

strait-laced adj prudish, stuffy, starchy, prim, proper, strict, narrow, narrow-minded, puritanical, moralistic.
F3 broad-minded.

strand n fibre, filament, wire, thread, string, piece, length.

stranded adj marooned, high and dry, abandoned, forsaken, in the lurch, helpless, aground, grounded, beached, shipwrecked, wrecked.

strange adj **1** ODD, peculiar, funny (infml), curious, queer, weird, bizarre, eccentric, abnormal, irregular, uncommon, unusual, exceptional, remarkable, extraordinary, mystifying, perplexing, unexplained. **2** NEW, novel, untried, unknown, unheard-of, unfamiliar, unacquainted, foreign, alien, exotic.
F3 1 ordinary, common. **2** well-known, familiar.

stranger n newcomer, visitor, guest, non-member, outsider, foreigner, alien.
F3 local, native.

strangle v throttle, choke, asphyxiate, suffocate, stifle, smother, suppress, gag, repress, inhibit.

strap n thong, tie, band, belt, leash.
v **1** BEAT, lash, whip, flog, belt.
2 FASTEN, secure, tie, bind.

stratagem n plan, scheme, plot, intrigue, ruse, ploy, trick, dodge,

manoeuvre, device, artifice, wile, subterfuge.

strategic adj important, key, critical, decisive, crucial, vital, tactical, planned, calculated, deliberate, politic, diplomatic.
F3 unimportant.

strategy n tactics, planning, policy, approach, procedure, plan, programme, design, scheme.

stray v wander (off), get lost, err, ramble, roam, rove, range, meander, straggle, drift, diverge, deviate, digress.
adj **1** LOST, abandoned, homeless, wandering, roaming. **2** RANDOM, chance, accidental, freak, odd, erratic.

streak n line, stroke, smear, band, stripe, strip, layer, vein, trace, dash, touch, element, strain.
v **1** BAND, stripe, fleck, striate, smear, daub. **2** SPEED, tear, hurtle, sprint, gallop, fly, dart, flash, whistle, zoom, whizz, sweep.

stream n **1** RIVER, creek, brook, beck, burn, rivulet, tributary. **2** CURRENT, drift, flow, run, gush, flood, deluge, cascade, torrent.
v issue, well, surge, run, flow, course, pour, spout, gush, flood, cascade.

streamer n ribbon, banner, pennant, pennon, flag, ensign, standard.

streamlined adj aerodynamic, smooth, sleek, graceful, efficient, well-run, smooth-running, rationalized, time-saving, organized, slick.
F3 clumsy, inefficient.

strength n toughness, robustness, sturdiness, lustiness, brawn, muscle, sinew, power, might, force, vigour, energy, stamina, health, fitness, courage, fortitude, spirit, resolution,

firmness, effectiveness, potency,
concentration, intensity, vehemence.
F3 weakness, feebleness, impotence.

strengthen v reinforce, brace, steel,
fortify, buttress, bolster, support,
toughen, harden, stiffen, consolidate,
substantiate, corroborate, confirm,
encourage, hearten, refresh, restore,
invigorate, nourish, increase,
heighten, intensify.
F3 weaken, undermine.

strenuous adj **1** strenuous work:
hard, tough, demanding, gruelling,
taxing, laborious, uphill, arduous,
tiring, exhausting. **2** ACTIVE,
energetic, vigorous, eager, earnest,
determined, resolute, spirited,
tireless, indefatigable.
F3 1 easy, effortless.

stress n **1** PRESSURE, strain, tension,
worry, anxiety, weight, burden,
trauma, hassle (infml). **2** EMPHASIS,
accent, accentuation, beat, force,
weight, importance, significance.
F3 1 relaxation.
v emphasize, accentuate, highlight,
underline, underscore, repeat.
F3 understate, downplay.

stretch n **1** EXPANSE, spread, sweep,
reach, extent, distance, space, area,
tract. **2** PERIOD, time, term, spell, stint,
run.
v pull, tighten, tauten, strain, tax,
extend, lengthen, elongate, expand,
spread, unfold, unroll, inflate, swell,
reach.
F3 compress.

stretch out extend, relax, hold out, put
out, lie down, reach.
F3 draw back.

strict adj **1** a strict teacher: stern,
authoritarian, no-nonsense, firm,
rigid, inflexible, stringent, rigorous,

harsh, severe, austere. **2** EXACT,
precise, accurate, literal, faithful, true,
absolute, utter, total, complete,
thoroughgoing, meticulous,
scrupulous, particular, religious.
F3 1 easy-going (infml), flexible.
2 loose.

strident adj loud, clamorous,
vociferous, harsh, raucous, grating,
rasping, shrill, screeching, unmusical,
discordant, clashing, jarring, jangling.
F3 quiet, soft.

strife n conflict, discord, dissension,
controversy, animosity, friction,
rivalry, contention, quarrel, row,
wrangling, struggle, fighting, combat,
battle, warfare.
F3 peace.

strike n **1** INDUSTRIAL ACTION, work-
to-rule, go-slow, stoppage, sit-in,
walk-out, mutiny, revolt. **2** HIT, blow,
stroke, raid, attack.
v **1** STOP WORK, down tools, work to
rule, walk out, protest, mutiny, revolt.
2 HIT, knock, collide with, slap, smack,
cuff, clout, thump, wallop (infml), beat,
pound, hammer, buffet, raid, attack,
afflict. **3** IMPRESS, affect, touch,
register. **4** FIND, discover, unearth,
uncover, encounter, reach.

strike out cross out, delete, strike
through, cancel, strike off, remove.
F3 add.

striking adj noticeable, conspicuous,
salient, outstanding, remarkable,
extraordinary, memorable,
impressive, dazzling, arresting,
astonishing, stunning.
F3 unimpressive.

string n **1** a piece of string: twine,
cord, rope, cable, line, strand, fibre.
2 SERIES, succession, sequence,
chain, line, row, file, queue,

procession, stream, train.

v thread, link, connect, tie up, hang, suspend, festoon, loop.

stringent *adj* binding, strict, severe, rigorous, tough, rigid, inflexible, tight. **F3** lax, flexible.

strip [1] *v* 1 PEEL, skin, flay. 2 DENUDE, divest, deprive, undress, disrobe, unclothe, uncover, expose, lay bare, bare. 3 EMPTY, clear, gut, ransack, pillage, plunder, loot.

F3 dress, clothe, cover.

strip [2] *n* ribbon, thong, strap, belt, sash, band, stripe, lath, slat, piece, bit, slip, shred.

stripe *n* band, line, bar, chevron, flash, streak, fleck, strip, belt.

strive *v* try, attempt, endeavour, struggle, strain, work, toil, labour, fight, contend, compete.

stroke *n* 1 CARESS, pat, rub. 2 BLOW, hit, knock, swipe. 3 SWEEP, flourish, movement, action, move, line.

v caress, fondle, pet, touch, pat, rub, massage.

stroll *v* saunter, amble, dawdle, ramble, wander.

n saunter, amble, walk, constitutional, turn, ramble.

strong *adj* 1 TOUGH, resilient, durable, hard-wearing, heavy-duty, robust, sturdy, firm, sound, lusty, strapping, stout, burly, well-built, beefy, brawny, muscular, sinewy, athletic, fit, healthy, hardy, powerful, mighty, potent. 2 INTENSE, deep, vivid, fierce, violent, vehement, keen, eager, zealous, fervent, ardent, dedicated, staunch, stalwart, determined, resolute, tenacious, strong-minded, strong-willed, self-assertive.

3 HIGHLY-FLAVOURED, piquant, hot, spicy, highly-seasoned, sharp,

pungent, undiluted, concentrated.

4 *strong argument*: convincing, persuasive, cogent, effective, telling, forceful, weighty, compelling, urgent.

F3 1 weak, feeble. 2 indecisive. 3 mild, bland. 4 unconvincing.

stronghold *n* citadel, bastion, fort, fortress, castle, keep, refuge.

structure *n* construction, erection, building, edifice, fabric, framework, form, shape, design, configuration, conformation, make-up, formation, arrangement, organization, set-up.

v construct, assemble, build, form, shape, design, arrange, organize.

struggle *v* strive, work, toil, labour, strain, agonize, fight, battle, wrestle, grapple, contend, compete, vie.

F3 yield, give in.

n 1 DIFFICULTY, problem, effort, exertion, pains, agony, work, labour, toil. 2 CLASH, conflict, strife, fight, battle, skirmish, encounter, combat, hostilities, contest.

F3 1 ease. 2 submission, co-operation.

stub *n* end, stump, remnant, fag-end (*infml*), dog-end (*infml*), butt, counterfoil.

stubborn *adj* obstinate, stiff-necked, mulish, pig-headed, obdurate, intransigent, rigid, inflexible, unbending, unyielding, dogged, persistent, tenacious, headstrong, self-willed, wilful, refractory, difficult, unmanageable.

F3 compliant, flexible, yielding.

stuck *adj* 1 FAST, jammed, firm, fixed, fastened, joined, glued, cemented. 2 BEATEN, stumped (*infml*), baffled.

F3 1 loose.

stuck-up *adj* snobbish, toffee-nosed (*infml*), supercilious, snooty (*infml*), haughty, high and mighty, condescending, proud, arrogant, conceited, bigheaded (*infml*). **F3** humble, modest.

student *n* undergraduate, postgraduate, scholar, schoolboy, schoolgirl, pupil, disciple, learner, trainee, apprentice.

studied *adj* deliberate, conscious, wilful, intentional, premeditated, planned, calculated, contrived, forced, unnatural, over-elaborate. **F3** unplanned, impulsive, natural.

studio *n* workshop, workroom.

studious *adj* scholarly, academic, intellectual, bookish, serious, thoughtful, reflective, diligent, hard-working, industrious, assiduous, careful, attentive, earnest, eager. **F3** lazy, idle, negligent.

study *v* read, learn, revise, cram, swot (*infml*), mug up (*infml*), read up, research, investigate, analyse, survey, scan, examine, scrutinize, peruse, pore over, contemplate, meditate, ponder, consider, deliberate. *n* **1** READING, homework, preparation, learning, revision, cramming, swotting (*infml*), research, investigation, inquiry, analysis, examination, scrutiny, inspection, contemplation, consideration, attention. **2** REPORT, essay, thesis, paper, monograph, survey, review, critique. **3** OFFICE, den (*infml*).

stuff *v* **1** PACK, stow, load, fill, cram, crowd, force, push, shove, ram, wedge, jam, squeeze, compress. **2** GORGE, gormandize, overindulge, guzzle, gobble, sate, satiate. **F3** unload, empty. **2** nibble. *n* **1** MATERIAL, fabric, matter, substance, essence. **2** (*infml*)

BELONGINGS, possessions, things, objects, articles, goods, luggage, paraphernalia, gear (*infml*), clobber (*infml*), kit, tackle, equipment, materials.

stuffing *n* padding, wadding, quilting, filling.

stuffy *adj* **1** *a stuffy room*: musty, stale, airless, unventilated, suffocating, stifling, oppressive, heavy, close, muggy, sultry. **2** STAID, strait-laced, prim, conventional, old-fashioned, pompous, dull, dreary, uninteresting, stodgy. **F3 1** airy, well-ventilated. **2** informal, modern, lively.

stumble *v* **1** TRIP, slip, fall, lurch, reel, stagger, flounder, blunder. **2** STAMMER, stutter, hesitate, falter. **stumble on** come across, chance upon, happen upon, find, discover, encounter.

stumbling-block *n* obstacle, hurdle, barrier, bar, obstruction, hindrance, impediment, difficulty, snag.

stump *n* end, remnant, trunk, stub. *v* (*infml*) defeat, outwit, confound, perplex, puzzle, baffle, mystify, confuse, bewilder, flummox (*infml*), bamboozle (*infml*), dumbfound. **F3** assist. **stump up** (*infml*) pay, hand over, fork out (*infml*), shell out (*infml*), donate, contribute, cough up (*infml*). **F3** receive.

stun *v* amaze, astonish, astound, stagger, shock, daze, stupefy, dumbfound, flabbergast (*infml*), overcome, confound, confuse, bewilder.

stunning *adj* beautiful, lovely, gorgeous, ravishing, dazzling,

brilliant, striking, impressive, spectacular, remarkable, wonderful, marvellous, great, sensational.
F3 ugly, awful.

stunt[1] n feat, exploit, act, deed, enterprise, trick, turn, performance.

stunt[2] v stop, arrest, check, restrict, slow, retard, hinder, impede, dwarf.
F3 promote, encourage.

stupefy v daze, stun, numb, dumbfound, shock, stagger, amaze, astound.

stupendous adj huge, enormous, gigantic, colossal, vast, prodigious, phenomenal, tremendous, breathtaking, overwhelming, staggering, stunning, amazing, astounding, fabulous, fantastic, superb, wonderful, marvellous.
F3 ordinary, unimpressive.

stupid adj **1** SILLY, foolish, irresponsible, ill-advised, indiscreet, foolhardy, rash, senseless, mad, lunatic, brainless, half-witted, idiotic, imbecilic, moronic, feeble-minded, simple-minded, slow, dim, dull, dense, thick, dumb, dopey, crass, inane, puerile, mindless, futile, pointless, meaningless, nonsensical, absurd, ludicrous, ridiculous, laughable. **2** DAZED, stunned, sluggish, semiconscious.
F3 1 sensible, wise, clever, intelligent.
2 alert.

stupor n daze, stupefaction, torpor, lethargy, inertia, trance, coma, numbness, insensibility, unconsciousness.
F3 alertness, consciousness.

sturdy adj strong, robust, durable, well-made, stout, substantial, solid, well-built, powerful, muscular,

athletic, hardy, vigorous, flourishing, hearty, staunch, stalwart, steadfast, firm, resolute, determined.
F3 weak, flimsy, puny.

stutter v stammer, hesitate, falter, stumble, mumble.

style n **1** APPEARANCE, cut, design, pattern, shape, form, sort, type, kind, genre, variety, category. **2** ELEGANCE, smartness, chic, flair, panache, stylishness, taste, polish, refinement, sophistication, urbanity, fashion, vogue, trend, mode, dressiness, flamboyance, affluence, luxury, grandeur. **3** style of working: technique, approach, method, manner, mode, fashion, way, custom. **4** WORDING, phrasing, expression, tone, tenor.
F3 2 inelegance, tastelessness.
v **1** DESIGN, cut, tailor, fashion, shape, adapt. **2** DESIGNATE, term, name, call, address, title, dub, label.

stylish adj chic, fashionable, à la mode, modish, in vogue, voguish, trendy (infml), snappy, natty (infml), snazzy (infml), dressy, smart, elegant, classy (infml), polished, refined, sophisticated, urbane.
F3 old-fashioned, shabby.

suave adj polite, courteous, charming, agreeable, affable, soft-spoken, smooth, unctuous, sophisticated, urbane, worldly.
F3 rude, unsophisticated.

subconscious adj subliminal, unconscious, intuitive, inner, innermost, hidden, latent, repressed, suppressed.
F3 conscious.

subdue v overcome, quell, suppress, repress, overpower, crush, defeat, conquer, vanquish, overrun, subject, subjugate, humble, break, tame, master, discipline, control, check, moderate, reduce, soften, quieten, damp, mellow.

F2 arouse, awaken.

subdued adj **1** SAD, downcast, dejected, crestfallen, quiet, serious, grave, solemn. **2** QUIET, muted, hushed, soft, dim, shaded, sombre, sober, restrained, unobtrusive, low-key, subtle.

F3 1 lively, excited. **2** striking, obtrusive.

subject n **1** TOPIC, theme, matter, issue, question, point, case, affair, business, discipline, field.
2 NATIONAL, citizen, participant, client, patient, victim.

F2 monarch, ruler, master.
adj **1** LIABLE, disposed, prone, susceptible, vulnerable, open, exposed. **2** SUBJUGATED, captive, bound, obedient, answerable, subordinate, inferior, subservient, submissive. **3** DEPENDENT, contingent, conditional.

F3 1 vulnerable. **2** free, superior.
3 unconditional.
v expose, lay open, submit, subjugate, subdue.

subjection n subjugation, defeat, captivity, bondage, chains, shackles, slavery, enslavement, oppression, domination, mastery.

subjective adj biased, prejudiced, personal, individual, idiosyncratic, emotional, intuitive, instinctive.

F3 objective, unbiased, impartial.

sublime adj exalted, elevated, high, lofty, noble, majestic, great, grand, imposing, magnificent, glorious, transcendent, spiritual.

F3 lowly, base.

submerge v submerse, immerse, plunge, duck, dip, sink, drown, engulf, overwhelm, swamp, flood, inundate, deluge.

F3 surface.

submerged adj submersed, immersed, underwater, sunk, sunken, drowned, swamped, inundated, hidden, concealed, unseen.

submission n **1** SURRENDER, capitulation, resignation, acquiescence, assent, compliance, obedience, deference, submissiveness, meekness, passivity.
2 PRESENTATION, offering, contribution, entry, suggestion, proposal.

F3 1 intransigence, intractability.

submissive adj yielding, unresisting, resigned, patient, uncomplaining, accommodating, biddable, obedient, deferential, ingratiating, subservient, humble, meek, docile, subdued, passive.

F3 intransigent, intractable.

submit v **1** YIELD, give in, surrender, capitulate, knuckle under, bow, bend, stoop, succumb, agree, comply.
2 PRESENT, tender, offer, put forward, suggest, propose, table, state, claim, argue.

F3 1 resist. **2** withdraw.

subordinate adj secondary, auxiliary, ancillary, subsidiary, dependent, inferior, lower, junior, minor, lesser.

F3 superior, senior.
n inferior, junior, assistant, attendant, second, aide, dependant, underling (infml).

F3 superior, boss.

subscribe v **1** subscribe to a theory: support, endorse, back, advocate, approve, agree. **2** GIVE, donate, contribute.

subscription n membership fee, dues, payment, donation, contribution, offering, gift.

subsequent adj following, later, future, next, succeeding, consequent, resulting, ensuing.

E3 previous, earlier.

subside v sink, collapse, settle, descend, fall, drop, lower, decrease, lessen, diminish, dwindle, decline, wane, ebb, recede, moderate, abate, die down, quieten, slacken, ease.

E3 rise, increase.

subsidiary adj auxiliary, supplementary, additional, ancillary, assistant, supporting, contributory, secondary, subordinate, lesser, minor.

E3 primary, chief, major.
n branch, offshoot, division, section, part.

subsidize v support, back, underwrite, sponsor, finance, fund, aid, promote.

subsidy n grant, allowance, assistance, help, aid, contribution, sponsorship, finance, support, backing.

subsistence n living, survival, existence, livelihood, maintenance, support, keep, sustenance, nourishment, food, provisions, rations.

substance n **1** MATTER, material, stuff, fabric, essence, pith, entity, body, solidity, concreteness, reality, actuality, ground, foundation. **2** SUBJECT, subject-matter, theme, gist, meaning, significance, force.

substandard adj second-rate, inferior, imperfect, damaged, shoddy, poor, inadequate, unacceptable.

E3 first-rate, superior, perfect.

substantial adj large, big, sizable, ample, generous, great, considerable, significant, important, worthwhile, massive, bulky, hefty, well-built, stout, sturdy, strong, sound, durable.

E3 small, insignificant, weak.

substantiate v prove, verify, confirm, support, corroborate, authenticate, validate.

E3 disprove, refute.

substitute v **1** CHANGE, exchange, swap, switch, interchange, replace. **2** STAND IN, fill in (infml), cover, deputize, understudy, relieve.
n reserve, stand-by, temp (infml), supply, locum, understudy, stand-in, replacement, relief, surrogate, proxy, agent, deputy, makeshift, stopgap. adj reserve, temporary, acting, surrogate, proxy, replacement, alternative.

subterfuge n trick, stratagem, scheme, ploy, ruse, dodge, manoeuvre, machination, deviousness, evasion, deception, artifice, pretence, excuse.

E3 openness, honesty.

subtle adj **1** DELICATE, understated, implied, indirect, slight, tenuous, faint, mild, fine, nice, refined, sophisticated, deep, profound. **2** ARTFUL, cunning, crafty, sly, devious, shrewd, astute.

E3 1 blatant, obvious. **2** artless, open.

subtract v deduct, take away, remove, withdraw, debit, detract, diminish.

E3 add.

suburbs n suburbia, commuter belt, residential area, outskirts.

E3 centre, heart.

subversive adj seditious,

treasonous, treacherous, traitorous, inflammatory, incendiary, disruptive, riotous, weakening, undermining, destructive.

E3 loyal.

n seditionist, terrorist, freedom fighter, dissident, traitor, quisling, fifth columnist.

succeed v **1** TRIUMPH, make it, get on, thrive, flourish, prosper, make good, manage, work. **2** winter succeeds autumn: follow, replace, result, ensue.

E3 1 fail. **2** precede.

succeeding adj following, next, subsequent, ensuing, coming, to come, later, successive.

E3 previous, earlier.

success n **1** TRIUMPH, victory, luck, fortune, prosperity, fame, eminence, happiness. **2** CELEBRITY, star, somebody, winner, bestseller, hit, sensation.

E3 1 failure, disaster.

successful adj **1** VICTORIOUS, winning, lucky, fortunate, prosperous, wealthy, thriving, flourishing, booming, moneymaking, lucrative, profitable, rewarding, satisfying, fruitful, productive. **2** a successful writer: famous, well-known, popular, leading, bestselling, top, unbeaten.

E3 1 unsuccessful, unprofitable, fruitless. **2** unknown.

succession n sequence, series, order, progression, run, chain, string, cycle, continuation, flow, course, line, train, procession.

successive adj consecutive, sequential, following, succeeding.

succinct adj short, brief, terse, pithy, concise, compact, condensed, summary.

E3 long, lengthy, wordy, verbose.

succulent adj fleshy, juicy, moist, luscious, mouthwatering, lush, rich, mellow.

E3 dry.

succumb v give way, yield, give in, submit, knuckle under, surrender, capitulate, collapse, fall.

E3 overcome, master.

suck v draw in, imbibe, absorb, soak up, extract, drain.

sudden adj unexpected, unforeseen, surprising, startling, abrupt, sharp, quick, swift, rapid, prompt, hurried, hasty, rash, impetuous, impulsive, snap (infml).

E3 expected, predictable, gradual, slow.

sue v prosecute, charge, indict, summon, solicit, appeal.

suffer v **1** HURT, ache, agonize, grieve, sorrow. **2** BEAR, support, tolerate, endure, sustain, experience, undergo, go through, feel.

suffering n pain, discomfort, agony, anguish, affliction, distress, misery, hardship, ordeal, torment, torture.

E3 ease, comfort.

sufficient adj enough, adequate, satisfactory, effective.

E3 insufficient, inadequate.

suffocate v asphyxiate, smother, stifle, choke, strangle, throttle.

suggest v **1** PROPOSE, put forward, advocate, recommend, advise, counsel. **2** IMPLY, insinuate, hint, intimate, evoke, indicate.

suggestion n **1** PROPOSAL, proposition, motion, recommendation, idea, plan. **2** IMPLICATION, insinuation, innuendo, hint, intimation, suspicion, trace, indication.

suggestive adj **1** EVOCATIVE, reminiscent, expressive, meaning, indicative. **2** a suggestive remark: indecent, immodest, improper, indelicate, off-colour, risqué, bawdy, dirty, smutty, provocative.
F3 1 inexpressive. **2** decent, clean.

suit v **1** SATISFY, gratify, please, answer, match, tally, agree, correspond, harmonize. **2** FIT, befit, become, tailor, adapt, adjust, accommodate, modify.
F3 1 displease, clash.
n outfit, costume, dress, clothing.

Types of suit include:
dress suit, evening suit, tuxedo, business suit, lounge suit, trouser suit, catsuit, jump suit, safari suit, track suit, shell suit, zoot suit.

---

suitable adj appropriate, fitting, convenient, opportune, suited, due, apt, apposite, relevant, applicable, fit, adequate, satisfactory, acceptable, befitting, becoming, seemly, proper, right.
F3 unsuitable, inappropriate.

sulk v mope, brood, pout.

sulky adj brooding, moody, morose, resentful, grudging, disgruntled, put out, cross, bad-tempered, sullen, aloof, unsociable.
F3 cheerful, good-tempered, sociable.

sullen adj **1** SULKY, moody, morose, glum, gloomy, silent, surly, sour, perverse, obstinate, stubborn. **2** DARK, gloomy, sombre, dismal, cheerless, dull, leaden, heavy.
F3 1 cheerful, happy. **2** fine, clear.

sully v dirty, soil, defile, pollute, contaminate, taint, spoil, mar, spot, blemish, besmirch, stain, tarnish, disgrace, dishonour.
F3 cleanse, honour.

sultry adj hot, sweltering, stifling, stuffy, oppressive, close, humid, muggy, sticky.
F3 cool, cold.

sum n total, sum total, aggregate, whole, entirety, number, quantity, amount, tally, reckoning, score, result.
sum up summarize, review, recapitulate, conclude, close.

summarize v outline, précis, condense, abridge, abbreviate, shorten, sum up, encapsulate, review.
F3 expand (on).

summary n synopsis, résumé, outline, abstract, précis, condensation, digest, compendium, abridgement, summing-up, review, recapitulation.
adj short, succinct, brief, cursory, hasty, prompt, direct, unceremonious, arbitrary.
F3 lengthy, careful.

summit n top, peak, pinnacle, apex, point, crown, head, zenith, acme, culmination, height.
F3 bottom, foot, nadir.

summon v call, send for, invite, bid, beckon, gather, assemble, convene, rally, muster, mobilize, rouse, arouse.
F3 dismiss.

sumptuous adj luxurious, plush, lavish, extravagant, opulent, rich, costly, expensive, dear, splendid, magnificent, gorgeous, superb, grand.
F3 plain, poor.

sunbathe v sun, bask, tan, brown, bake.

sunburnt adj brown, tanned, bronzed, weather-beaten, burnt, red, blistered, peeling.
F3 pale.

sundry adj various, diverse, miscellaneous, assorted, varied, different, several, some, a few.

sunken adj submerged, buried, recessed, lower, depressed, concave, hollow, haggard, drawn.

sunny adj **1** FINE, cloudless, clear, summery, sunshiny, sunlit, bright, brilliant. **2** CHEERFUL, happy, joyful, smiling, beaming, radiant, light-hearted, buoyant, optimistic, pleasant.

F3 1 sunless, dull. **2** gloomy.

sunrise n dawn, crack of dawn, daybreak, daylight.

sunset n sundown, dusk, twilight, gloaming, evening, nightfall.

superb adj excellent, first-rate, first-class, superior, choice, fine, exquisite, gorgeous, magnificent, splendid, grand, wonderful, marvellous, admirable, impressive, breathtaking.

F3 bad, poor, inferior.

superficial adj surface, external, exterior, outward, apparent, seeming, cosmetic, skin-deep, shallow, slight, trivial, lightweight, frivolous, casual, cursory, sketchy, hasty, hurried, passing.

F3 internal, deep, thorough.

superfluous adj extra, spare, excess, surplus, remaining, redundant, supernumerary, unnecessary, needless, unwanted, uncalled-for, excessive.

F3 necessary, needed, wanted.

superintend v supervise, oversee, overlook, inspect, run, manage, administer, direct, control, handle.

superior adj **1** EXCELLENT, first-class, first-rate, top-notch (*infml*), top-flight (*infml*), high-class, exclusive, choice, select, fine, de luxe, admirable, distinguished, exceptional, unrivalled, par excellence. **2** BETTER, preferred,

greater, higher, senior. **3** HAUGHTY, lordly, pretentious, snobbish, snooty (*infml*), supercilious, disdainful, condescending, patronizing.

F3 1 inferior, average. **2** worse, lower. **3** humble.

n senior, elder, better, boss, chief, principal, director, manager, foreman, supervisor.

F3 inferior, junior, assistant.

superiority n advantage, lead, edge, supremacy, ascendancy, pre-eminence, predominance.

F3 inferiority.

superlative adj best, greatest, highest, supreme, transcendent, unbeatable, unrivalled, unparalleled, matchless, peerless, unsurpassed, unbeaten, consummate, excellent, outstanding.

F3 poor, average.

supernatural adj paranormal, unnatural, abnormal, metaphysical, spiritual, psychic, mystic, occult, hidden, mysterious, miraculous, magical, phantom, ghostly.

F3 natural, normal.

supersede v succeed, replace, supplant, usurp, oust, displace, remove.

superstition n myth, old wives' tale, fallacy, delusion, illusion.

superstitious adj mythical, false, fallacious, irrational, groundless, delusive, illusory.

F3 rational, logical.

supervise v oversee, watch over, look after, superintend, run, manage, administer, direct, conduct, preside over, control, handle.

supervision n surveillance, care, charge, superintendence, oversight, running, management, administration, direction, control, guidance, instruction.

supervisor n overseer, inspector, superintendent, boss, chief, director, administrator, manager, foreman, forewoman.

supplant v replace, supersede, usurp, oust, displace, remove, overthrow, topple, unseat.

supple adj flexible, bending, pliant, pliable, plastic, lithe, graceful, loose-limbed, double-jointed, elastic.
F3 stiff, rigid, inflexible.

supplement n addition, extra, insert, pull-out, addendum, appendix, codicil, postscript, sequel.
v add to, augment, boost, reinforce, fill up, top up, complement, extend, eke out.
F3 deplete, use up.

supplementary adj additional, extra, auxiliary, secondary, complementary, accompanying.

supplier n dealer, seller, vendor, wholesaler, retailer.

supplies n stores, provisions, food, equipment, materials, necessities.

supply v provide, furnish, equip, outfit, stock, fill, replenish, give, donate, grant, endow, contribute, yield, produce, sell.
F3 take, receive.
n source, amount, quantity, stock, fund, reservoir, store, reserve, stockpile, hoard, cache.
F3 lack.

support v 1 BACK, second, defend, champion, advocate, promote, foster, help, aid, assist, rally round, finance, fund, subsidize, underwrite. 2 HOLD UP, bear, carry, sustain, brace, reinforce, strengthen, prop, buttress, bolster. 3 MAINTAIN, keep, provide for,

feed, nourish. 4 support a statement: endorse, confirm, verify, authenticate, corroborate, substantiate, document.
F3 1 oppose. 3 live off. 4 contradict.
n 1 BACKING, allegiance, loyalty, defence, protection, patronage, sponsorship, approval, encouragement, comfort, relief, help, aid, assistance. 2 PROP, stay, post, pillar, brace, crutch, foundation, underpinning.
F3 1 opposition, hostility.

supporter n fan, follower, adherent, advocate, champion, defender, seconder, patron, sponsor, helper, ally, friend.
F3 opponent.

supportive adj helpful, caring, attentive, sympathetic, understanding, comforting, reassuring, encouraging.
F3 discouraging.

suppose v assume, presume, expect, infer, conclude, guess, conjecture, surmise, believe, think, consider, judge, imagine, conceive, fancy, pretend, postulate, hypothesize.
F3 know.

supposed adj alleged, reported, rumoured, assumed, presumed, reputed, putative, imagined, hypothetical.
F3 known, certain.

supposed to meant to, intended to, expected to, required to, obliged to.

supposition n assumption, presumption, guess, conjecture, speculation, theory, hypothesis, idea, notion.
F3 knowledge.

suppress v crush, stamp out, quash, quell, subdue, stop, silence, censor, stifle, smother, strangle, conceal, withhold, hold back, contain, restrain, check, repress, inhibit.

F3 encourage, incite.

supreme adj best, greatest, highest, top, crowning, culminating, first, leading, foremost, chief, principal, head, sovereign, pre-eminent, predominant, prevailing, world-beating, unsurpassed, second-to-none, incomparable, matchless, consummate, transcendent, superlative, prime, ultimate, extreme, final.

F3 lowly, poor.

sure adj **1** CERTAIN, convinced, assured, confident, decided, positive, definite, unmistakable, clear, accurate, precise, unquestionable, indisputable, undoubted, undeniable, irrevocable, inevitable, bound. **2** SAFE, secure, fast, solid, firm, steady, stable, guaranteed, reliable, dependable, trustworthy, steadfast, unwavering, unerring, unfailing, infallible, effective.

F3 1 unsure, uncertain, doubtful. **2** unsafe, insecure.

surface n outside, exterior, façade, veneer, covering, skin, top, side, face, plane.

F3 inside, interior.

v rise, arise, come up, emerge, appear, materialize, come to light.

F3 sink, disappear, vanish.

surly adj gruff, brusque, churlish, ungracious, bad-tempered, cross, crabbed, grouchy, crusty, sullen, sulky, morose.

F3 friendly, polite.

surpass v beat, outdo, exceed, outstrip, better, excel, transcend, outshine, eclipse.

surplus n excess, residue, remainder, balance, superfluity, glut, surfeit.

F3 lack, shortage.

adj excess, superfluous, redundant, extra, spare, remaining, unused.

surprise v startle, amaze, astonish, astound, stagger, flabbergast (infml), bewilder, confuse, nonplus, disconcert, dismay.

n amazement, astonishment, incredulity, wonder, bewilderment, dismay, shock, start, bombshell, revelation.

F3 composure.

surprised adj startled, amazed, astonished, astounded, staggered, flabbergasted (infml), thunderstruck, dumbfounded, speechless, shocked, nonplussed.

F3 unsurprised, composed.

surprising adj amazing, astonishing, astounding, staggering, jaw-dropping (infml), stunning, incredible, extraordinary, remarkable, startling, unexpected, unforeseen.

F3 unsurprising, expected.

surrender v capitulate, submit, resign, concede, yield, give in, cede, give up, quit, relinquish, abandon, renounce, forgo, waive.

n capitulation, resignation, submission, yielding, relinquishment, renunciation.

surreptitious adj furtive, stealthy, sly, covert, veiled, hidden, secret, clandestine, underhand, unauthorized.

F3 open, obvious.

surround v encircle, ring, girdle, encompass, envelop, encase, enclose, hem in, besiege.

surrounding adj encircling, bordering, adjacent, adjoining, neighbouring, nearby.

surroundings n neighbourhood, vicinity, locality, setting, environment, background, milieu, ambience.

survey v view, contemplate, observe, supervise, scan, scrutinize, examine, inspect, study, research, review, consider, estimate, evaluate, assess, measure, plot, plan, map, chart, reconnoitre.
n review, overview, scrutiny, examination, inspection, study, pull, appraisal, assessment, measurement.

survive v outlive, outlast, endure, last, stay, remain, live, exist, withstand, weather.
F3 succumb, die.

susceptible adj liable, prone, inclined, disposed, given, subject, receptive, responsive, impressionable, suggestible, weak, vulnerable, open, sensitive, tender.
F3 resistant, immune.

suspect v **1** DOUBT, distrust, mistrust, call into question. **2** I suspect you're right: believe, fancy, feel, guess, conjecture, speculate, surmise, suppose, consider, conclude, infer.
adj suspicious, doubtful, dubious, questionable, debatable, unreliable, iffy (sl), dodgy (infml), fishy (infml).
F3 acceptable, reliable.

suspend v **1** HANG, dangle, swing. **2** ADJOURN, interrupt, discontinue, cease, delay, defer, postpone, put off, shelve. **3** EXPEL, dismiss, exclude, debar.
F3 2 continue. **3** restore, reinstate.

suspense n uncertainty, insecurity, anxiety, tension, apprehension, anticipation, expectation, expectancy, excitement.
F3 certainty, knowledge.

suspension n adjournment, interruption, break, intermission, respite, remission, stay, moratorium, delay, deferral, postponement, abeyance.
F3 continuation.

suspicion n **1** DOUBT, scepticism, distrust, mistrust, wariness, caution, misgiving, apprehension. **2** TRACE, hint, suggestion, soupçon, touch, tinge, shade, glimmer, shadow. **3** IDEA, notion, hunch.
F3 1 trust.

suspicious adj **1** DOUBTFUL, sceptical, unbelieving, suspecting, distrustful, mistrustful, wary, chary, apprehensive, uneasy. **2** DUBIOUS, questionable, suspect, irregular, shifty, shady (infml), dodgy (infml), fishy (infml).
F3 1 trustful, confident. **2** trustworthy, innocent.

sustain v **1** NOURISH, provide for, nurture, foster, help, aid, assist, comfort, relieve, support, uphold, endorse, bear, carry. **2** MAINTAIN, keep going, keep up, continue, prolong, hold.

sustained adj prolonged, protracted, long-drawn-out, steady, continuous, constant, perpetual, unremitting.
F3 broken, interrupted, intermittent, spasmodic.

sustenance n nourishment, food, provisions, fare, maintenance, subsistence, livelihood.

swagger v bluster, boast, crow, brag, swank (infml), parade, strut.
n bluster, show, ostentation, arrogance.

swallow v **1** CONSUME, devour, eat, gobble up, guzzle, drink, quaff, knock

back (*infml*), gulp, down (*infml*).
2 ENGULF, enfold, envelop, swallow up, absorb, assimilate, accept, believe.

swamp *n* bog, marsh, fen, slough, quagmire, quicksand, mire, mud.
v flood, inundate, deluge, engulf, submerge, sink, drench, saturate, waterlog, overload, overwhelm, besiege, beset.

swap, swop *v* exchange, transpose, switch, interchange, barter, trade, traffic.

swarm *n* crowd, throng, mob, mass, multitude, myriad, host, army, horde, herd, flock, drove, shoal.
v **1** STREAM, flock, flood, mass, congregate, crowd, throng.
2 *swarming with tourists*: teem, crawl, bristle, abound.

swarthy *adj* dark, dark-skinned, dark-complexioned, dusky, black, brown, tanned.
⊟ fair, pale.

sway *v* **1** ROCK, roll, lurch, swing, wave, oscillate, fluctuate, bend, incline, lean, divert, veer, swerve.
2 INFLUENCE, affect, persuade, induce, convince, convert, overrule, dominate, govern.

swear *v* **1** VOW, promise, pledge, avow, attest, asseverate, testify, affirm, assert, declare, insist. **2** CURSE, blaspheme.

swear-word *n* expletive, four-letter word, curse, oath, imprecation, obscenity, profanity, blasphemy, swearing, bad language.

sweat *n* **1** PERSPIRATION, moisture, stickiness. **2** ANXIETY, worry, agitation, panic. **3** TOIL, labour, drudgery, chore.
v perspire, swelter, exude.

sweaty *adj* damp, moist, clammy, sticky, sweating, perspiring.
⊟ dry, cool.

sweep *v* **1** *sweep the floor*: brush, dust, clean, clear, remove. **2** PASS, sail, fly, glide, scud, skim, glance, whisk, tear, hurtle.
n **1** ARC, curve, bend, swing, stroke, movement, gesture. **2** SCOPE, compass, range, extent, span, stretch, expanse, vista.

sweeping *adj* general, global, all-inclusive, all-embracing, blanket, across-the-board, broad, wide-ranging, extensive, far-reaching, comprehensive, thoroughgoing, radical, wholesale, indiscriminate, oversimplified, simplistic.
⊟ specific, narrow.

sweet *adj* **1** SUGARY, syrupy, sweetened, honeyed, saccharine, luscious, delicious. **2** PLEASANT, delightful, lovely, attractive, beautiful, pretty, winsome, cute, appealing, lovable, charming, agreeable, amiable, affectionate, tender, kind, treasured, precious, dear, darling.
3 FRESH, clean, wholesome, pure, clear, perfumed, fragrant, aromatic, balmy. **4** *sweet music*: melodious, tuneful, harmonious, euphonious, musical, dulcet, soft, mellow.
⊟ 1 savoury, salty, sour, bitter.
2 unpleasant, nasty, ugly. **3** foul.
4 discordant.
n **1** CONFECTION, bonbon, candy.
2 DESSERT, pudding, afters (*infml*).

Sweets include:
barley-sugar, bull's-eye, butterscotch, caramel, chocolate, fondant, Creme Egg®, fruit pastille, fudge, gobstopper, gumdrop, humbug, jelly baby, jellybean, liquorice, liquor-

ice allsort, lollipop, M & M®, Mars bar®, marshmallow, Milky Way®, nougat, peppermint, praline, rock, Smartie®, toffee, toffee-apple, truffle, Turkish delight.

sweeten v sugar, honey, mellow, soften, soothe, appease, temper, cushion.
F3 sour, embitter.

swell v expand, dilate, inflate, blow up, puff up, bloat, distend, fatten, bulge, balloon, billow, surge, rise, mount, increase, enlarge, extend, grow, augment, heighten, intensify.
F3 shrink, contract, decrease, dwindle.
n billow, wave, undulation, surge, rise, increase, enlargement.

swelling n lump, tumour, bump, bruise, blister, boil, inflammation, bulge, protuberance, puffiness, distension, enlargement.

sweltering adj hot, tropical, baking, scorching, stifling, suffocating, airless, oppressive, sultry, steamy, sticky, humid.
F3 cold, cool, fresh, breezy, airy.

swerve v turn, bend, incline, veer, swing, shift, deviate, stray, wander, diverge, deflect, sheer.

swift adj fast, quick, rapid, speedy, express, flying, hurried, hasty, short, brief, sudden, prompt, ready, agile, nimble, nippy (infml).
F3 slow, sluggish, unhurried.

swimsuit n swimming costume, bathing-costume, bathing-suit, bikini, trunks.

swindle v cheat, defraud, diddle, do (infml), overcharge, fleece, rip off (sl), trick, deceive, dupe, con (infml), bamboozle (infml).
n fraud, fiddle, racket, sharp practice,

double-dealing, trickery, deception, con (infml), rip-off (sl), scam (infml).

swindler n cheat, fraud, impostor, con man (infml), trickster, shark, rogue, rascal.

swing v hang, suspend, dangle, wave, brandish, sway, rock, oscillate, vibrate, fluctuate, vary, veer, swerve, turn, whirl, twirl, spin, rotate.
n sway, rock, oscillation, vibration, fluctuation, variation, change, shift, movement, motion, rhythm.

swingeing adj harsh, severe, stringent, drastic, punishing, devastating, excessive, extortionate, oppressive, heavy.
F3 mild.

swipe v 1 HIT, strike, lunge, lash out, slap, whack (infml), wallop (infml), sock (sl). 2 (infml) STEAL, pilfer, lift, pinch (infml).
n stroke, blow, slap, smack, clout, whack (infml), wallop (infml).

swirl v churn, agitate, spin, twirl, whirl, wheel, eddy, twist, curl.

switch v change, exchange, swap, trade, interchange, transpose, substitute, replace, shift, rearrange, turn, veer, deviate, divert, deflect.
n change, alteration, shift, exchange, swap, interchange, substitution, replacement.

swivel v pivot, spin, rotate, revolve, turn, twirl, pirouette, gyrate, wheel.

swollen adj bloated, distended, inflated, tumid, puffed up, puffy, inflamed, enlarged, bulbous, bulging.
F3 shrunken, shrivelled.

swoop v dive, plunge, drop, descend, stoop, pounce, lunge, rush.
n dive, plunge, drop, descent, pounce, lunge, rush, attack, onslaught.

swop see **swap**.

sword n blade, foil, rapier, sabre, scimitar.

swot v study, work, learn, memorize, revise, cram, mug up (*infml*), bone up (*sl*).

syllabus n curriculum, course, programme, schedule, plan.

symbol n sign, token, representation, mark, emblem, badge, character, ideograph, figure, image.

> Symbols include:
> coat of arms, crest, hieroglyph, icon, ideogram, insignia, logo, logogram, monogram, motif, pictograph, trademark, watermark; ampersand, asterisk, at sign, caret, dagger, double-dagger, hashmark, obelus, emoticon, smiley.

symbolic adj symbolical, representative, emblematic, token, figurative, metaphorical, allegorical, meaningful, significant.

symbolize v represent, stand for, denote, mean, signify, typify, exemplify, epitomize, personify.

symmetrical adj balanced, even, regular, parallel, corresponding, proportional.
F3 asymmetrical, irregular.

symmetry n balance, evenness, regularity, parallelism, correspondence, proportion, harmony, agreement.
F3 asymmetry, irregularity.

sympathetic adj understanding, appreciative, supportive, comforting, consoling, commiserating, pitying, interested, concerned, solicitous, caring, compassionate, tender, kind, warm-hearted, well-disposed, affectionate, agreeable, friendly, congenial, like-minded, compatible.
F3 unsympathetic, indifferent, callous, antipathetic.

sympathize v understand, comfort, commiserate, pity, feel for, empathize, identify with, respond to.
F3 ignore, disregard.

sympathy n **1** UNDERSTANDING, comfort, consolation, condolences, commiseration, pity, compassion, tenderness, kindness, warmth, thoughtfulness, empathy, fellow-feeling, affinity, rapport. **2** AGREEMENT, accord, correspondence, harmony.
F3 1 indifference, insensitivity, callousness. **2** disagreement.

symptom n sign, indication, evidence, manifestation, expression, feature, characteristic, mark, token, warning.

symptomatic adj indicative, typical, characteristic, associated, suggestive.

synonymous adj interchangeable, substitutable, the same, identical, similar, comparable, tantamount, equivalent, corresponding.
F3 antonymous, opposite.

synopsis n outline, abstract, summary, résumé, précis, condensation, digest, abridgement, review, recapitulation.

synthesize v unite, combine, amalgamate, integrate, merge, blend, compound, alloy, fuse, weld, coalesce, unify.
F3 separate, analyse, resolve.

synthetic adj manufactured, man-made, simulated, artificial, ersatz, imitation, fake, bogus, mock, sham, pseudo.
F3 genuine, real, natural.

system n **1** METHOD, mode, technique, procedure, process, routine, practice, usage, rule. **2** ORGANIZATION, structure, set-up, systematization, co-ordination, orderliness, methodology, logic, classification, arrangement, order, plan, scheme.

systematic *adj* methodical, logical, ordered, well-ordered, planned, well-planned, organized, well-organized, structured, systematized, standardized, orderly, businesslike, efficient.

⊟ unsystematic, arbitrary, disorderly, inefficient.

T

tab n flap, tag, marker, label, sticker, ticket.

table n 1 BOARD, slab, counter, worktop, desk, bench, stand.
2 DIAGRAM, chart, graph, timetable, schedule, programme, list, inventory, catalogue, index, register, record.

Types of table include:
dining-table, gateleg table, refectory table, lowboy, side table, coffee table, card-table, dressing-table.

v propose, suggest, submit, put forward.

taboo adj forbidden, prohibited, banned, proscribed, unacceptable, unmentionable, unthinkable.
F3 permitted, acceptable.
n ban, interdiction, prohibition, restriction, anathema, curse.

tacit adj unspoken, unexpressed, unvoiced, silent, understood, implicit, implied, inferred.
F3 express, explicit.

taciturn adj silent, quiet, uncommunicative, unforthcoming, reticent, reserved, withdrawn, aloof, distant, cold.
F3 talkative, communicative, forthcoming.

tack n 1 NAIL, pin, drawing-pin, staple. 2 COURSE, path, bearing, heading, direction, line, approach, method, way, technique, procedure,
plan, tactic, attack.
v add, append, attach, affix, fasten, fix, nail, pin, staple.

tackle n 1 a rugby tackle: attack, challenge, interception, intervention, block. 2 EQUIPMENT, tools, implements, apparatus, rig, outfit, gear, trappings, paraphernalia.
v 1 BEGIN, embark on, set about, try, attempt, undertake, take on, challenge, confront, encounter, face up to, grapple with, deal with, attend to, handle, grab, seize, grasp.
2 INTERCEPT, block, halt, stop.
F3 1 avoid, sidestep.

tact n tactfulness, diplomacy, discretion, prudence, delicacy, sensitivity, perception, discernment, judgement, understanding, thoughtfulness, consideration, skill, adroitness, finesse.
F3 tactlessness, indiscretion.

tactful adj diplomatic, discreet, politic, judicious, prudent, careful, delicate, subtle, sensitive, perceptive, discerning, understanding, thoughtful, considerate, polite, skilful, adroit.
F3 tactless, indiscreet, thoughtless, rude.

tactic n approach, course, way, means, method, procedure, plan, stratagem, scheme, ruse, ploy, subterfuge, trick, device, shift, move, manoeuvre.

tactical *adj* strategic, planned, calculated, artful, cunning, shrewd, skilful, clever, smart, prudent, politic, judicious.

tactics *n* strategy, campaign, plan, policy, approach, line of attack, moves, manoeuvres.

tactless *adj* undiplomatic, indiscreet, indelicate, inappropriate, impolitic, imprudent, careless, clumsy, blundering, insensitive, unfeeling, hurtful, unkind, thoughtless, inconsiderate, rude, impolite, discourteous.
F3 tactful, diplomatic, discreet.

tag *n* label, sticker, tab, ticket, mark, identification, note, slip, docket.
v **1** LABEL, mark, identify, designate, term, call, name, christen, nickname, style, dub. **2** ADD, append, annex, adjoin, affix, fasten.
tag along follow, shadow, tail, trail, accompany.

tail *n* end, extremity, rear, rear end, rump, behind (*infml*), posterior (*infml*), appendage.
v follow, pursue, shadow, dog, stalk, track, trail.
tail off decrease, decline, drop, fall away, fade, wane, dwindle, taper off, peter out, die (out).
F3 increase, grow.

tailor *n* outfitter, dressmaker.
v fit, suit, cut, trim, style, fashion, shape, mould, alter, modify, adapt, adjust, accommodate.

tailor-made *adj* made-to-measure, custom-built, bespoke, ideal, perfect, right, suited, fitted.
F3 unsuitable.

taint *v* contaminate, infect, pollute,

adulterate, corrupt, deprave, stain, blemish, blot, smear, tarnish, blacken, dirty, soil, muddy, defile, sully, harm, damage, blight, spoil, ruin, shame, disgrace, dishonour.
n contamination, infection, pollution, corruption, stain, blemish, fault, flaw, defect, spot, blot, smear, stigma, shame, disgrace, dishonour.

take *v* **1** SEIZE, grab, snatch, grasp, hold, catch, capture, get, obtain, acquire, secure, gain, win, derive, adopt, assume, pick, choose, select, accept, receive. **2** REMOVE, eliminate, take away, subtract, deduct, steal, filch, purloin, nick (*infml*), pinch (*infml*), appropriate, abduct, carry off. **3** NEED, necessitate, require, demand, call for. **4** *take me home:* convey, carry, bring, transport, ferry, accompany, escort, lead, guide, conduct, usher. **5** BEAR, tolerate, stand, stomach, abide, endure, suffer, undergo, withstand.
F3 **1** leave, refuse. **2** replace, put back.
take aback surprise, astonish, astound, stagger, stun, startle, disconcert, bewilder, dismay, upset.
take apart take to pieces, dismantle, disassemble, analyse.
take back reclaim, repossess, withdraw, retract, recant, repudiate, deny, eat one's words.
take down 1 DISMANTLE, disassemble, demolish, raze, level, lower. **2** NOTE, record, write down, put down, set down, transcribe.
take in 1 ABSORB, assimilate, digest, realize, appreciate, understand, comprehend, grasp, admit, receive, shelter, accommodate, contain, include, comprise, incorporate, embrace, encompass, cover.
2 DECEIVE, fool, dupe, con (*infml*),

mislead, trick, hoodwink, bamboozle (*infml*), cheat, swindle.

take off 1 REMOVE, doff, divest, shed, discard, drop. **2** LEAVE, depart, go, decamp, disappear. **3** IMITATE, mimic, parody, caricature, satirize, mock, send up.

take on 1 ACCEPT, assume, acquire, undertake, tackle, face, contend with, fight, oppose. **2** *take on staff*: employ, hire, enlist, recruit, engage, retain.

take up 1 OCCUPY, fill, engage, engross, absorb, monopolize, use up. **2** *take up a hobby*: start, begin, embark on, pursue, carry on, continue. **3** RAISE, lift.
4 ACCEPT, adopt, assume.

take-off *n* imitation, mimicry, impersonation, parody, caricature, spoof, send-up, travesty.

takeover *n* merger, amalgamation, combination, incorporation, coup.

takings *n* receipts, gate, proceeds, profits, gain, returns, revenue, yield, income, earnings, pickings.

tale *n* **1** STORY, yarn, anecdote, spiel (*sl*), narrative, account, report, rumour, tall story, old wives' tale, superstition, fable, myth, legend, saga. **2** LIE, fib, falsehood, untruth, fabrication.

talent *n* gift, endowment, genius, flair, feel, knack, bent, aptitude, faculty, skill, ability, power, strength, forte.
E3 inability, weakness.

talented *adj* gifted, brilliant, well-endowed, versatile, accomplished, able, capable, proficient, adept, adroit, deft, clever, skilful.
E3 inept.

talk *v* speak, utter, articulate, say, communicate, converse, chat, gossip, natter (*infml*), chatter, discuss, confer, negotiate.

n **1** CONVERSATION, dialogue, discussion, conference, meeting, consultation, negotiation, chat, chatter, natter (*infml*), gossip, hearsay, rumour, tittle-tattle. **2** *give a talk*: lecture, seminar, symposium, speech, address, discourse, sermon, spiel (*sl*). **3** LANGUAGE, dialect, slang, jargon, speech, utterance, words.

talk into encourage, coax, sway, persuade, convince, bring round, win over.
E3 dissuade.

talk out of discourage, deter, put off, dissuade.
E3 persuade, convince.

talkative *adj* garrulous, voluble, vocal, communicative, forthcoming, unreserved, expansive, chatty, gossipy, verbose, wordy.
E3 taciturn, quiet, reserved.

talking-to *n* lecture, dressing-down (*infml*), telling-off (*infml*), ticking-off (*infml*), scolding, reprimand, rebuke, reproof, reproach, criticism.
E3 praise, commendation.

tall *adj* high, lofty, elevated, soaring, towering, big, great, giant, gigantic.
E3 short, low, small.

tally *v* **1** AGREE, concur, tie in, square, accord, harmonize, coincide, correspond, match, conform, suit, fit. **2** ADD (UP), total, count, reckon, figure.
E3 1 disagree, differ.
n record, count, total, score, reckoning, account.

tame *adj* **1** *a tame rabbit*: domesticated, broken in, trained, disciplined, manageable, tractable, amenable, gentle, docile, meek, submissive, unresisting, obedient, biddable. **2** DULL, boring, tedious, uninteresting, humdrum, flat, bland, insipid, weak, feeble, uninspired, unadventurous, unenterprising, lifeless, spiritless.

F3 1 wild, unmanageable, rebellious. **2** exciting.

v domesticate, house-train, break in, train, discipline, master, subjugate, conquer, bridle, curb, repress, suppress, quell, subdue, temper, soften, mellow, calm, pacify, humble.

tamper *v* interfere, meddle, mess (*infml*), tinker, fiddle, fix, rig, manipulate, juggle, alter, damage.

tang *n* sharpness, bite, piquancy, pungency, taste, flavour, savour, smack, smell, aroma, scent, whiff, tinge, touch, trace, hint, suggestion, overtone.

tangible *adj* touchable, tactile, palpable, solid, concrete, material, substantial, physical, real, actual, perceptible, discernible, evident, manifest, definite, positive.

F3 intangible, abstract, unreal.

tangle *n* knot, snarl-up, twist, coil, convolution, mesh, web, maze, labyrinth, mess, muddle, jumble, mix-up, confusion, entanglement, embroilment, complication.

v entangle, knot, snarl, ravel, twist, coil, interweave, interlace, intertwine, catch, ensnare, entrap, enmesh, embroil, implicate, involve, muddle, confuse.

F3 disentangle.

tangled *adj* knotty, snarled, matted, tousled, dishevelled, messy, muddled, jumbled, confused, twisted, convoluted, tortuous, involved, complicated, complex, intricate.

tangy *adj* sharp, biting, acid, tart, spicy, piquant, pungent, strong, fresh.

F3 tasteless, insipid.

tank *n* container, reservoir, cistern, aquarium, vat, basin.

tantalize *v* tease, taunt, torment, torture, provoke, lead on, titillate, tempt, entice, bait, balk, frustrate, thwart.

F3 gratify, satisfy, fulfil.

tantamount *adj* as good as, equivalent, commensurate, equal, synonymous, the same as.

tantrum *n* temper, rage, fury, storm, outburst, fit, scene, paddy (*infml*).

tap¹ *v* hit, strike, knock, rap, beat, drum, pat, touch.

n knock, rap, beat, pat, touch.

tap² *n* **1** STOPCOCK, valve, faucet, spigot, spout. **2** STOPPER, plug, bung.

v use, utilize, exploit, mine, quarry, siphon, bleed, milk, drain.

tape *n* **1** BAND, strip, binding, ribbon. **2** VIDEO, cassette.

v **1** RECORD, video. **2** BIND, secure, stick, seal.

taper *v* narrow, attenuate, thin, slim, decrease, reduce, lessen, dwindle, fade, wane, peter out, tail off, die away.

F3 widen, flare, swell, increase.

n spill, candle, wick.

target *n* aim, object, end, purpose, intention, ambition, goal, destination, objective, butt, mark, victim, prey, quarry.

tariff *n* price list, schedule, charges, rate, toll, tax, levy, customs, excise, duty.

tarnish *v* discolour, corrode, rust, dull, dim, darken, blacken, sully, taint, stain, blemish, spot, blot, mar, spoil.

F3 polish, brighten.

tart¹ *n* pie, flan, pastry, tartlet, patty.

tart² *adj* sharp, acid, sour, bitter, vinegary, tangy, piquant, pungent, biting, cutting, trenchant, incisive, caustic, astringent, acerbic,

scathing, sardonic, sarcastic.
F3 bland, sweet.

task n job, chore, duty, charge, imposition, assignment, exercise, mission, errand, undertaking, enterprise, business, occupation, activity, employment, work, labour, toil, burden.

taste n 1 FLAVOUR, savour, relish, smack, tang. 2 SAMPLE, bit, piece, morsel, titbit, bite, nibble, mouthful, sip, drop, dash, soupçon. 3 *a taste for adventure*: liking, fondness, partiality, preference, inclination, leaning, desire, appetite. 4 DISCRIMINATION, discernment, judgement, perception, appreciation, sensitivity, refinement, polish, culture, cultivation, breeding, decorum, finesse, style, elegance, tastefulness.
F3 1 blandness. 3 distaste.
4 tastelessness.
v 1 SAVOUR, relish, sample, nibble, sip, try, test, differentiate, distinguish, discern, perceive. 2 EXPERIENCE, undergo, feel, encounter, meet, know.

tasteful adj refined, polished, cultured, cultivated, elegant, smart, stylish, aesthetic, artistic, harmonious, beautiful, exquisite, delicate, graceful, restrained, well-judged, judicious, correct, fastidious, discriminating.
F3 tasteless, garish, tawdry.

tasteless adj 1 FLAVOURLESS, insipid, bland, mild, weak, watery, flat, stale, dull, boring, uninteresting, vapid. 2 INELEGANT, graceless, unseemly, improper, indiscreet, crass, rude, crude, vulgar, kitsch, naff (sl), cheesy (sl), cheap, tawdry, flashy, gaudy, garish, loud.
F3 1 tasty. 2 tasteful, elegant.

tasty adj luscious, palatable, appetizing, mouthwatering, delicious, flavoursome, succulent, scrumptious (infml), yummy (sl), tangy, piquant, savoury, sweet.
F3 tasteless, insipid.

tattered adj ragged, frayed, threadbare, ripped, torn, tatty, shabby, scruffy.
F3 smart, neat.

tatters n rags, shreds, ribbons, pieces.

taunt v tease, torment, provoke, bait, goad, jeer, mock, ridicule, gibe, rib (sl), deride, sneer, insult, revile, reproach.
n jeer, catcall, gibe, dig, sneer, insult, reproach, taunting, teasing, provocation, ridicule, sarcasm, derision, censure.

taut adj tight, stretched, contracted, strained, tense, unrelaxed, stiff, rigid.
F3 slack, loose, relaxed.

tautological adj repetitive, superfluous, redundant, pleonastic, verbose, wordy.
F3 succinct, economical.

tautology n repetition, duplication, superfluity, redundancy, pleonasm.

tawdry adj cheap, vulgar, tasteless, fancy, showy, flashy, gaudy, garish, tinselly, glittering.
F3 fine, tasteful.

tax n levy, charge, rate, tariff, customs, contribution, imposition, burden, load.

> **Taxes include:**
> capital gains tax, capital transfer tax, community charge, corporation tax, council tax, customs, death-duty, estate duty, excise, income tax, inheritance tax, pay-as-you-earn (PAYE), poll tax, property tax, rates, surtax, tithe, toll, value-added tax (VAT).

v **1** LEVY, charge, demand, exact, assess, impose. **2** BURDEN, load, strain, stretch, try, tire, weary, exhaust, drain, sap, weaken.

tea *n* infusion, tisane, char (*sl*).

> Types of tea include:
> black tea, green tea, oolong; pekoe, orange pekoe; Assam, Ceylon, China, Darjeeling, Earl Grey, English Breakfast, Indian, jasmine, Keemun, lapsang souchong, Russian; chai, decaffeinated tea, fruit tea, herbal tea, iced tea, lemon tea, mint tea.

teach *v* instruct, train, coach, tutor, lecture, drill, ground, verse, discipline, school, educate, enlighten, edify, inform, impart, inculcate, advise, counsel, guide, direct, show, demonstrate.
E3 learn.

teacher *n* schoolteacher, schoolmaster, master, schoolmistress, mistress, educator, pedagogue, tutor, lecturer, professor, don, instructor, trainer, coach, adviser, counsellor, mentor, guide, guru.
E3 pupil.

teaching *n* **1** INSTRUCTION, tuition, training, grounding, schooling, education, pedagogy, indoctrination. **2** DOGMA, doctrine, tenet, precept, principle.

team *n* side, line-up, squad, shift, crew, gang, band, group, company, stable.
team up join, unite, couple, combine, band together, co-operate, collaborate, work together.

tear *v* **1** RIP, rend, divide, rupture, sever, shred, scratch, claw, gash, lacerate, mutilate, mangle. **2** PULL, snatch, grab, seize, wrest. **3** *tear down*

the street: dash, rush, hurry, speed, race, run, sprint, fly, shoot, dart, bolt, belt (*infml*), career, charge.
n rip, rent, slit, hole, split, rupture, scratch, gash, laceration.

tearful *adj* crying, weeping, sobbing, whimpering, blubbering, sad, sorrowful, upset, distressed, emotional, weepy (*infml*).
E3 happy, smiling, laughing.

tears *n* crying, weeping, sobbing, wailing, whimpering, blubbering, sorrow, distress.

tease *v* taunt, provoke, bait, annoy, irritate, aggravate (*infml*), needle (*infml*), badger, worry, pester, plague, torment, tantalize, mock, ridicule, gibe, banter, rag (*sl*), rib (*sl*).

technical *adj* mechanical, scientific, technological, electronic, computerized, specialized, expert, professional.

technique *n* method, system, procedure, manner, fashion, style, mode, way, means, approach, course, performance, execution, delivery, artistry, craftsmanship, skill, facility, proficiency, expertise, know-how (*infml*), art, craft, knack, touch.

tedious *adj* boring, monotonous, uninteresting, unexciting, dull, dreary, drab, banal, humdrum, tiresome, wearisome, tiring, laborious, long-winded, long-drawn-out.
E3 lively, interesting, exciting.

teeming *adj* swarming, crawling, alive, bristling, seething, full, packed, brimming, overflowing, bursting, replete, abundant, fruitful, thick.
E3 lacking, sparse, rare.

teenage adj teenaged, adolescent, young, youthful, juvenile, immature.

teenager n adolescent, youth, boy, girl, minor, juvenile.

teetotal adj temperate, abstinent, abstemious, sober, on the wagon (sl).

telepathy n mind-reading, thought transference, sixth sense, ESP, clairvoyance.

telephone n phone, handset, receiver, blower (infml), cellphone, mobile phone.
v phone, ring (up), call (up), dial, buzz (infml), contact, get in touch.

telescope v contract, shrink, compress, condense, abridge, squash, crush, shorten, curtail, truncate, abbreviate, reduce, cut, trim.

television n TV, receiver, set, telly (infml), the box (infml), goggle-box (infml), idiot box (infml), small screen.

tell v 1 INFORM, notify, let know, acquaint, impart, communicate, speak, utter, say, state, confess, divulge, disclose, reveal. 2 tell a story: narrate, recount, relate, report, announce, describe, portray, mention. 3 ORDER, command, direct, instruct, authorize. 4 DIFFERENTIATE, distinguish, discriminate, discern, recognize, identify, discover, see, understand, comprehend.

tell off (infml) scold, chide, tick off (infml), upbraid, reprimand, rebuke, reprove, lecture, berate, dress down (infml), carpet (infml), reproach, censure.

temerity n impudence, impertinence, cheek (infml), gall, nerve (infml), audacity, boldness, daring, rashness, recklessness, impulsiveness.
F3 caution, prudence.

temper n 1 MOOD, humour, nature, temperament, character, disposition, constitution. 2 ANGER, rage, fury, passion, tantrum, paddy (infml), hissy fit (sl), annoyance, irritability, ill-humour. 3 CALM, composure, self-control, cool (sl).
F3 2 calmness, self-control. 3 anger, rage.
v 1 MODERATE, lessen, reduce, calm, soothe, allay, assuage, palliate, mitigate, modify, soften. 2 HARDEN, toughen, strengthen.

temperament n nature, character, personality, disposition, tendency, bent, constitution, make-up, soul, spirit, mood, humour, temper, state of mind, attitude, outlook.

temperamental adj 1 MOODY, emotional, neurotic, highly-strung, sensitive, touchy, irritable, impatient, passionate, fiery, excitable, explosive, volatile, mercurial, capricious, unpredictable, unreliable. 2 NATURAL, inborn, innate, inherent, constitutional, ingrained.
F3 1 calm, level-headed, steady.

temperance n teetotalism, prohibition, abstinence, abstemiousness, sobriety, continence, moderation, restraint, self-restraint, self-control, self-discipline, self-denial.
F3 intemperance, excess.

temperate adj 1 temperate climate: mild, clement, balmy, fair, equable, balanced, stable, gentle, pleasant, agreeable. 2 TEETOTAL, abstinent, abstemious, sober, continent, moderate, restrained, controlled, even-tempered, calm, composed, reasonable, sensible.
F3 2 intemperate, extreme, excessive.

tempestuous adj stormy, windy, gusty, blustery, squally, turbulent, tumultuous, rough, wild, violent, furious, raging, heated, passionate, intense.
F3 calm.

temple n shrine, sanctuary, church, tabernacle, mosque, pagoda.

tempo n time, rhythm, metre, beat, pulse, speed, velocity, rate, pace.

temporal adj secular, profane, worldly, earthly, terrestrial, material, carnal, fleshly, mortal.
F3 spiritual.

temporary adj impermanent, provisional, interim, makeshift, stopgap, temporal, transient, transitory, passing, ephemeral, evanescent, fleeting, brief, short-lived, momentary.
F3 permanent, everlasting.

tempt v entice, coax, persuade, woo, bait, lure, allure, attract, draw, seduce, invite, tantalize, provoke, incite.
F3 discourage, dissuade, repel.

temptation n enticement, inducement, coaxing, persuasion, bait, lure, allure, appeal, attraction, draw, pull, seduction, invitation.

tenable adj credible, defensible, justifiable, reasonable, rational, sound, arguable, believable, defendable, plausible, viable, feasible.
F3 untenable, indefensible, unjustifiable.

tenant n renter, lessee, leaseholder, occupier, occupant, resident, inhabitant.

tend[1] v incline, lean, bend, bear, head, aim, lead, go, move, gravitate.

tend[2] v look after, care for, cultivate, keep, maintain, manage, handle, guard, protect, watch, mind, nurture, nurse, minister to, serve, attend.
F3 neglect, ignore.

tendency n trend, drift, movement, course, direction, bearing, heading, bias, partiality, predisposition, propensity, readiness, liability, susceptibility, proneness, inclination, leaning, bent, disposition.

tender[1] adj 1 KIND, gentle, caring, humane, considerate, compassionate, sympathetic, warm, fond, affectionate, loving, amorous, romantic, sentimental, emotional, sensitive, tender-hearted, soft-hearted. 2 YOUNG, youthful, immature, green, raw, new, inexperienced, impressionable, vulnerable. 3 SOFT, succulent, fleshy, dainty, delicate, fragile, frail, weak, feeble. 4 SORE, painful, aching, smarting, bruised, inflamed, raw.
F3 1 hard-hearted, callous. **2** mature. **3** tough, hard.

tender[2] v offer, proffer, extend, give, present, submit, propose, suggest, advance, volunteer.
n **1** legal tender: currency, money. **2** OFFER, bid, estimate, quotation, proposal, proposition, suggestion, submission.

tense adj 1 TIGHT, taut, stretched, strained, stiff, rigid. 2 NERVOUS, anxious, worried, jittery, uneasy, apprehensive, edgy, fidgety, restless, jumpy, overwrought, keyed up. **3** STRESSFUL, exciting, worrying, fraught.
F3 1 loose, slack. **2** calm, relaxed.
v tighten, contract, brace, stretch, strain.
F3 loosen, relax.

tension n **1** TIGHTNESS, tautness, stiffness, strain, stress, pressure.

2 NERVOUSNESS, anxiety, worry, uneasiness, apprehension, edginess, restlessness, suspense.
F3 1 looseness. **2** calm(ness), relaxation.

tent *n* tepee, wigwam, marquee, big top.

tentative *adj* experimental, exploratory, speculative, hesitant, faltering, cautious, unsure, uncertain, doubtful, undecided, provisional, indefinite, unconfirmed.
F3 definite, decisive, conclusive, final.

tenuous *adj* thin, slim, slender, fine, slight, insubstantial, flimsy, fragile, delicate, weak, shaky, doubtful, dubious, questionable.
F3 strong, substantial.

tepid *adj* lukewarm, cool, half-hearted, unenthusiastic, apathetic.
F3 cold, hot, passionate.

term 1 WORD, name, designation, appellation, title, epithet, phrase, expression. **2** TIME, period, course, duration, spell, span, stretch, interval, space, semester, session, season.
v call, name, dub, style, designate, label, tag, title, entitle.

terminal *adj* **1** LAST, final, concluding, ultimate, extreme, utmost. **2** *terminal illness*: fatal, deadly, lethal, mortal, incurable.
F3 1 initial.

terminate *v* finish, complete, conclude, cease, end, stop, close, discontinue, wind up, cut off, abort, lapse, expire.
F3 begin, start, initiate.

terminology *n* language, jargon, phraseology, vocabulary, words, terms, nomenclature.

terminus *n* **1** END, close, termination, extremity, limit,

boundary, destination, goal, target. **2** DEPOT, station, garage, terminal.

terms *n* **1** *on good terms*: relations, relationship, footing, standing, position. **2** CONDITIONS, specifications, stipulations, provisos, provisions, qualifications, particulars. **3** RATES, charges, fees, prices, tariff.

terrain *n* land, ground, territory, country, countryside, landscape, topography.

terrestrial *adj* earthly, worldly, global, mundane.
F3 cosmic, heavenly.

terrible *adj* bad, awful, frightful, dreadful, shocking, appalling, outrageous, disgusting, revolting, repulsive, offensive, abhorrent, hateful, horrid, horrible, unpleasant, obnoxious, foul, vile, hideous, gruesome, horrific, harrowing, distressing, grave, serious, severe, extreme, desperate.
F3 excellent, wonderful, superb.

terribly *adv* very, much, greatly, extremely, exceedingly, awfully, frightfully, decidedly, seriously.

terrific *adj* **1** EXCELLENT, wonderful, marvellous, super, smashing (*infml*), outstanding, brilliant, magnificent, superb, fabulous (*infml*), fantastic (*infml*), sensational, amazing, stupendous, breathtaking. **2** HUGE, enormous, gigantic, tremendous, great, intense, extreme, excessive.
F3 awful, terrible, appalling.

terrify *v* petrify, horrify, appal, shock, terrorize, intimidate, frighten, scare, alarm, dismay.

territory *n* country, land, state, dependency, province, domain, preserve, jurisdiction, sector, region, area, district, zone, tract, terrain.

terror *n* fear, panic, dread, trepidation, horror, shock, fright, alarm, dismay, consternation, terrorism, intimidation.

terrorize *v* threaten, menace, intimidate, oppress, coerce, bully, browbeat, frighten, scare, alarm, terrify, petrify, horrify, shock.

terse *adj* short, brief, succinct, concise, compact, condensed, epigrammatic, pithy, incisive, snappy, curt, brusque, abrupt, laconic.
E3 long-winded, verbose.

test *v* try, experiment, examine, assess, evaluate, check, investigate, analyse, screen, prove, verify.
n trial, try-out, experiment, examination, assessment, evaluation, check, investigation, analysis, proof, probation, ordeal.

testify *v* give evidence, depose, state, declare, assert, swear, avow, attest, vouch, certify, corroborate, affirm, show, bear witness.

testimonial *n* reference, character, credential, certificate, recommendation, endorsement, commendation, tribute.

testimony *n* evidence, statement, affidavit, submission, deposition, declaration, profession, attestation, affirmation, support, proof, verification, confirmation, witness, demonstration, manifestation, indication.

tether *n* chain, rope, cord, line, lead, leash, bond, fetter, shackle, restraint, fastening.
v tie, fasten, secure, restrain, chain, rope, leash, bind, lash, fetter, shackle, manacle.

text *n* words, wording, content, matter, body, subject, topic, theme,

reading, passage, paragraph, sentence, book, textbook, source.

texture *n* consistency, feel, surface, grain, weave, tissue, fabric, structure, composition, constitution, character, quality.

thank *v* say thank you, be grateful, appreciate, acknowledge, recognize, credit.

thankful *adj* grateful, appreciative, obliged, indebted, pleased, contented, relieved.
E3 ungrateful, unappreciative.

thankless *adj* unrecognized, unappreciated, unrequited, unrewarding, unprofitable, fruitless.
E3 rewarding, worthwhile.

thanks *n* gratitude, gratefulness, appreciation, acknowledgement, recognition, credit, thanksgiving, thank-offering.

thanks to because of, owing to, due to, on account of, as a result of, through.

thaw *v* melt, defrost, defreeze, de-ice, soften, liquefy, dissolve, warm, heat up.
E3 freeze.

theatrical *adj* **1** DRAMATIC, thespian. **2** MELODRAMATIC, histrionic, mannered, affected, artificial, pompous, ostentatious, showy, extravagant, exaggerated, overdone.

theft *n* robbery, thieving, stealing, pilfering, larceny, shop-lifting, kleptomania, fraud, embezzlement.

theme *n* subject, topic, thread, motif, keynote, idea, gist, essence, burden, argument, thesis, dissertation, composition, essay, text, matter.

theorem *n* formula, principle, rule, statement, deduction, proposition, hypothesis.

theoretical *adj* hypothetical, conjectural, speculative, abstract, academic, doctrinaire, pure, ideal. **F3** practical, applied, concrete.

theorize *v* hypothesize, suppose, guess, conjecture, speculate, postulate, propound, formulate.

theory *n* hypothesis, supposition, assumption, presumption, surmise, guess, conjecture, speculation, idea, notion, abstraction, philosophy, thesis, plan, proposal, scheme, system. **F3** certainty, practice.

therapeutic *adj* remedial, curative, healing, restorative, tonic, medicinal, corrective, good, beneficial. **F3** harmful, detrimental.

therapy *n* treatment, remedy, cure, healing, tonic.

therefore *adv* so, then, consequently, as a result.

thesis *n* 1 *doctoral thesis*: dissertation, essay, composition, treatise, paper, monograph. 2 SUBJECT, topic, theme, idea, opinion, view, theory, hypothesis, proposal, proposition, premise, statement, argument, contention.

thick *adj* 1 WIDE, broad, fat, heavy, solid, dense, impenetrable, close, compact, concentrated, viscous, coagulated, clotted. 2 FULL, packed, crowded, chock-a-block, swarming, teeming, bristling, brimming, bursting, numerous, abundant. 3 (*infml*) STUPID, foolish, slow, dull, dim-witted, brainless, simple. **F3** 1 thin, slim, slender, slight. 2 sparse. 3 clever, brainy (*infml*).

thicken *v* condense, stiffen, congeal, coagulate, clot, cake, gel, jell, set. **F3** thin.

thicket *n* wood, copse, coppice, grove, spinney.

thickness *n* 1 WIDTH, breadth, diameter, density, viscosity, bulk, body. 2 LAYER, stratum, ply, sheet, coat. **F3** thinness.

thick-skinned *adj* insensitive, unfeeling, callous, tough, hardened, hard-boiled. **F3** thin-skinned, sensitive.

thief *n* robber, bandit, mugger, pickpocket, shop-lifter, burglar, house-breaker, plunderer, poacher, stealer, pilferer, filcher, kleptomaniac, swindler, embezzler.

thin *adj* 1 LEAN, slim, slender, narrow, attenuated, slight, skinny, bony, skeletal, scraggy, scrawny, lanky, gaunt, spare, underweight, undernourished, emaciated. 2 *thin fabric*: fine, delicate, light, flimsy, filmy, gossamer, sheer, see-through, transparent, translucent. 3 SPARSE, scarce, scattered, scant, meagre, poor, inadequate, deficient, scanty, skimpy. 4 WEAK, feeble, runny, watery, diluted. **F3** 1 fat, broad. 2 thick, dense, solid. 3 plentiful, abundant. 4 strong. *v* 1 NARROW, attenuate, diminish, reduce, trim, weed out. 2 WEAKEN, dilute, water down, rarefy, refine.

thing *n* 1 ARTICLE, object, entity, creature, body, substance, item, detail, particular, feature, factor, element, point, fact, concept, thought. 2 DEVICE, contrivance, gadget, tool, implement, instrument, apparatus, machine, mechanism. 3 ACT, deed, feat, action, task, responsibility, problem. 4 CIRCUMSTANCE, eventuality, happening, occurrence, event, incident, phenomenon, affair, proceeding. 5 (*infml*) OBSESSION, preoccupation, fixation, fetish, phobia, hang-up (*infml*).

things *n* belongings, possessions, effects, paraphernalia, stuff (*infml*), goods, luggage, baggage, equipment, gear (*infml*), clobber (*infml*), odds and ends, bits and pieces.

think *v* **1** BELIEVE, hold, consider, regard, esteem, deem, judge, estimate, reckon, calculate, determine, conclude, reason. **2** CONCEIVE, imagine, suppose, presume, surmise, expect, foresee, envisage, anticipate. **3** *think it over*: ponder, mull over, chew over, ruminate, meditate, contemplate, muse, cogitate, reflect, deliberate, weigh up, recall, recollect, remember.

think up devise, contrive, dream up, imagine, conceive, visualize, invent, design, create, concoct.

thinker *n* philosopher, theorist, ideologist, brain, intellect, mastermind.

thinking *n* reasoning, philosophy, thoughts, conclusions, theory, idea, opinion, view, outlook, position, judgement, assessment.
adj reasoning, rational, intellectual, intelligent, cultured, sophisticated, philosophical, analytical, reflective, contemplative, thoughtful.

third-rate *adj* low-grade, poor, bad, inferior, mediocre, indifferent, shoddy, cheap and nasty.
E3 first-rate.

thirst *n* **1** THIRSTINESS, dryness, drought. **2** DESIRE, longing, yearning, hankering, craving, hunger, appetite, lust, passion, eagerness, keenness.

thirsty *adj* **1** DRY, parched (*infml*), gasping (*infml*), dehydrated, arid. **2** *thirsty for knowledge*: desirous,

longing, yearning, hankering, craving, hungry, burning, itching, dying, eager, avid, greedy.

thorn *n* spike, point, barb, prickle, spine, bristle, needle.

thorough *adj* full, complete, total, entire, utter, absolute, perfect, pure, sheer, unqualified, unmitigated, out-and-out, downright, sweeping, all-embracing, comprehensive, all-inclusive, exhaustive, thoroughgoing, intensive, in-depth, conscientious, efficient, painstaking, scrupulous, meticulous, careful.
E3 partial, superficial, careless.

though *conj* although, even if, notwithstanding, while, allowing, granted.
adv however, nevertheless, nonetheless, yet, still, even so, all the same, for all that.

thought *n* **1** THINKING, attention, heed, regard, consideration, study, scrutiny, introspection, meditation, contemplation, cogitation, reflection, deliberation. **2** IDEA, notion, concept, conception, belief, conviction, opinion, view, judgement, assessment, conclusion, plan, design, intention, purpose, aim, hope, dream, expectation, anticipation. **3** THOUGHTFULNESS, consideration, kindness, care, concern, compassion, sympathy, gesture, touch.

thoughtful *adj* **1** PENSIVE, wistful, dreamy, abstracted, reflective, contemplative, introspective, thinking, absorbed, studious, serious, solemn. **2** CONSIDERATE, kind, unselfish, helpful, caring, attentive, heedful, mindful, careful, prudent, cautious, wary.
E3 2 thoughtless, insensitive, selfish.

thoughtless adj 1 INCONSIDERATE, unthinking, insensitive, unfeeling, tactless, undiplomatic, unkind, selfish, uncaring. 2 CARELESS, absent-minded, inattentive, heedless, mindless, foolish, stupid, silly, rash, reckless, ill-considered, imprudent, negligent, remiss.
E3 1 thoughtful, considerate.
2 careful.

thrash v 1 PUNISH, beat, whip, lash, flog, scourge, cane, belt, spank, clobber, wallop (infml), lay into.
2 DEFEAT, beat, trounce, hammer (infml), slaughter (infml), crush, overwhelm, rout. 3 THRESH, flail, toss, jerk.

thrash out discuss, debate, negotiate, settle, resolve.

thread n 1 COTTON, yarn, strand, fibre, filament, string, line. 2 COURSE, direction, drift, tenor, theme, motif, plot, storyline.

threadbare adj 1 threadbare clothes: worn, frayed, ragged, moth-eaten, scruffy, shabby. 2 HACKNEYED, overused, old, stale, tired, trite, commonplace, stock, stereotyped.
E3 1 new. 2 fresh.

threat n menace, warning, omen, portent, presage, foreboding, danger, risk, hazard, peril.

threaten v menace, intimidate, browbeat, pressurize, bully, terrorize, warn, portend, presage, forebode, foreshadow, endanger, jeopardize, imperil.

threatening adj menacing, intimidatory, warning, cautionary, ominous, inauspicious, sinister, grim, looming, impending.

threshold n doorstep, sill, doorway, door, entrance, brink, verge, starting-point, dawn, beginning, start, outset, opening.

thrift n economy, husbandry, saving, conservation, frugality, prudence, carefulness.
E3 extravagance, waste.

thrifty adj economical, saving, frugal, sparing, prudent, careful.
E3 extravagant, profligate, prodigal, wasteful.

thrill n excitement, adventure, pleasure, stimulation, charge, kick, buzz (sl), hit (sl), sensation, glow, tingle, throb, shudder, quiver, tremor. v excite, electrify, galvanize, exhilarate, rouse, arouse, move, stir, stimulate, flush, glow, tingle, throb, shudder, tremble, quiver, shake.
E3 bore.

thrive v flourish, prosper, boom, grow, increase, advance, develop, bloom, blossom, gain, profit, succeed.
E3 languish, stagnate, fail, die.

throb v pulse, pulsate, beat, palpitate, vibrate, pound, thump.
n pulse, pulsation, beat, palpitation, vibration, pounding, thumping.

throttle v strangle, choke, asphyxiate, suffocate, smother, stifle, gag, silence, suppress, inhibit.

through prep 1 BETWEEN, by, via, by way of, by means of, using. 2 all through the night: throughout, during, in. 3 BECAUSE OF, as a result of, thanks to.
adj 1 FINISHED, ended, completed, done. 2 through train: direct, express, non-stop.

throw v 1 HURL, heave, lob, pitch, chuck (infml), sling, cast, fling, toss, launch, propel, send. 2 throw light:

shed, cast, project, direct. **3** BRING DOWN, floor, upset, overturn, dislodge, unseat, unsaddle, unhorse. **4** (*infml*) PERPLEX, baffle, confound, confuse, disconcert, astonish, dumbfound.

n heave, lob, pitch, sling, fling, toss, cast.

throw away 1 DISCARD, jettison, dump, ditch (*sl*), scrap, dispose of, throw out. **2** WASTE, squander, fritter away, blow (*sl*).

F∃ 1 keep, preserve, salvage, rescue.

throw off shed, cast off, drop, abandon, shake off, get rid of, elude.

throw out 1 EVICT, turn out, expel, turf out (*infml*), eject, emit, radiate, give off. **2** REJECT, discard, dismiss, turn down, jettison, dump, ditch (*sl*), throw away, scrap.

throw up 1 (*infml*) VOMIT, spew, regurgitate, disgorge, retch, heave. **2** ABANDON, renounce, relinquish, resign, quit, leave.

thrust *v* push, shove, butt, ram, jam, wedge, stick, poke, prod, jab, lunge, pierce, stab, plunge, press, force, impel, drive, propel.

n **1** PUSH, shove, poke, prod, lunge, stab. **2** DRIVE, impetus, momentum.

thud *n*, *v* thump, clump, knock, clunk, smack, wallop (*infml*), crash, bang, thunder.

thug *n* ruffian, tough, robber, bandit, mugger, killer, murderer, assassin, gangster, hooligan.

thump *n* knock, blow, punch, clout, box, cuff, smack, whack (*infml*), wallop (*infml*), crash, bang, thud, thud. *v* hit, strike, knock, punch, clout, box, cuff, smack, thrash, whack (*infml*), wallop (*infml*), crash, bang, thud, batter, pound, hammer, beat, throb.

thunder *n* boom, reverberation, crash, bang, crack, clap, peal, rumble, roll, roar, blast, explosion.
v boom, resound, reverberate, crash, bang, crack, clap, peal, rumble, roll, roar, blast.

thunderous *adj* booming, resounding, reverberating, roaring, loud, noisy, deafening, ear-splitting.

thus *adv* so, hence, therefore, consequently, then, accordingly, like this, in this way, as follows.

thwart *v* frustrate, foil, stymie, defeat, hinder, impede, obstruct, block, check, baffle, stop, prevent, oppose.

F∃ help, assist, aid.

tick *n* **1** CLICK, tap, stroke, tick-tock. **2** (*infml*) *wait a tick*: moment, instant, flash, jiffy (*infml*), second, minute.
v **1** MARK, indicate, choose, select. **2** CLICK, tap, beat.

tick off (*infml*) scold, chide, reprimand, rebuke, reproach, reprove, upbraid, tell off (*infml*).

F∃ praise, compliment.

ticket *n* pass, card, certificate, token, voucher, coupon, docket, slip, label, tag, sticker.

tickle *v* excite, thrill, delight, please, gratify, amuse, entertain, divert.

ticklish *adj* sensitive, touchy, delicate, thorny, awkward, difficult, tricky, critical, risky, hazardous, dodgy (*infml*).

F∃ easy, simple.

tide *n* current, ebb, flow, stream, flux, movement, course, direction, drift, trend, tendency.

tidy *adj* **1** NEAT, orderly, methodical, systematic, organized, clean, spick-and-span, shipshape, smart, spruce,

trim, well-kept, ordered, uncluttered.
2 (infml) a tidy sum: large, substantial, sizable, considerable, good, generous, ample.

E3 1 untidy, messy, disorganized.
2 small, insignificant.

v neaten, straighten, order, arrange, clean, smarten, spruce up, groom.

tie v **1** KNOT, fasten, secure, moor, tether, attach, join, connect, link, unite, rope, lash, strap, bind.
2 RESTRAIN, restrict, confine, limit, hamper, hinder.

n **1** KNOT, fastening, joint, connection, link, liaison, relationship, bond, affiliation, obligation, commitment, duty, restraint, restriction, limitation, hindrance. **2** DRAW, dead heat, stalemate, deadlock.

tie up 1 MOOR, tether, attach, secure, rope, lash, bind, truss, wrap up, restrain. **2** CONCLUDE, terminate, wind up, settle. **3** OCCUPY, engage, engross.

tier n floor, storey, level, stage, stratum, layer, belt, zone, band, echelon, rank, row, line.

tight adj **1** TAUT, stretched, tense, rigid, stiff, firm, fixed, fast, secure, close, cramped, constricted, compact, snug, close-fitting. **2** SEALED, hermetic, -proof, impervious, airtight, watertight. **3** (infml) MEAN, stingy, miserly, niggardly, parsimonious, tight-fisted (infml). **4** tight security: strict, severe, stringent, rigorous.

E3 1 loose, slack. **2** open. **3** generous.
4 lax.

tighten v tauten, stretch, tense, stiffen, fix, fasten, secure, narrow, close, cramp, constrict, crush, squeeze.

E3 loosen, relax.

tight-fisted adj mean, stingy, miserly, mingy (infml), niggardly, penny-pinching, sparing, parsimonious, tight (infml), grasping.

E3 generous, charitable.

till v cultivate, work, plough, dig, farm.

tilt v slope, incline, slant, pitch, list, tip, lean.

n slope, incline, angle, inclination, slant, pitch, list.

timber n wood, trees, forest, beam, lath, plank, board, log.

time n **1** SPELL, stretch, period, term, season, session, span, duration, interval, space, while. **2** TEMPO, beat, rhythm, metre, measure. **3** MOMENT, point, juncture, stage, instance, occasion, date, day, hour. **4** AGE, era, life, lifetime, generation, heyday, peak.

Periods of time include:

eternity, eon, era, age, generation, epoch, millennium, century, decade, year, quarter, month, fortnight, week, mid-week, weekend, long weekend, day, today, tonight, yesterday, tomorrow, morrow, weekday, hour, minute, second, moment, instant, millisecond, microsecond, nanosecond; dawn, sunrise, sunup, the early hours, wee small hours (infml), morning, morn, a.m., daytime, midday, noon, high noon, p.m., afternoon, teatime, evening, twilight, dusk, sunset, nightfall, bedtime, night, nighttime; season, spring, summer, midsummer, autumn, fall (N Am), winter.

---

v clock, measure, meter, regulate, control, set, schedule, timetable.

timeless adj ageless, immortal, everlasting, eternal, endless, permanent, changeless, unchanging.

timely adj well-timed, seasonable, suitable, appropriate, convenient, opportune, propitious, prompt, punctual.
E3 ill-timed, unsuitable, inappropriate.

timetable n schedule, programme, agenda, calendar, diary, rota, roster, list, listing, curriculum.

timid adj shy, bashful, modest, shrinking, retiring, nervous, apprehensive, afraid, timorous, fearful, cowardly, faint-hearted, spineless, irresolute.
E3 brave, bold, audacious.

tinge n tint, dye, colour, shade, touch, trace, suggestion, hint, smack, flavour, pinch, drop, dash, bit, sprinkling, smattering.
v tint, dye, stain, colour, shade, suffuse, imbue.

tingle v sting, prickle, tickle, itch, thrill, throb, quiver, vibrate.
n stinging, prickling, pins and needles, tickle, tickling, itch, itching, thrill, throb, quiver, shiver, gooseflesh, goose-pimples.

tinker v fiddle, play, toy, trifle, potter, dabble, meddle, tamper.

tint n dye, stain, rinse, wash, colour, hue, shade, tincture, tinge, tone, cast, streak, trace, touch.
v dye, colour, tinge, streak, stain, taint, affect.

tiny adj minute, microscopic, infinitesimal, teeny (infml), small, little, slight, negligible, insignificant, diminutive, petite, dwarfish, pint-sized (infml), pocket, miniature, mini (infml).
E3 huge, enormous, immense.

tip¹ n end, extremity, point, nib, apex, peak, pinnacle, summit, acme, top, cap, crown, head.
v cap, crown, top, surmount.

tip² v lean, incline, slant, list, tilt, topple over, capsize, upset, overturn, spill, pour out, empty, unload, dump.
n dump, rubbish-heap, refuse-heap.

tip³ n 1 CLUE, pointer, hint, suggestion, advice, warning, tip-off, information, inside information, forecast. 2 GRATUITY, gift, perquisite.
v 1 ADVISE, suggest, warn, caution, forewarn, tip off, inform, tell. 2 tip the driver: reward, remunerate.

tire v weary, fatigue, wear out, exhaust, drain, enervate.
E3 enliven, invigorate, refresh.

tired adj 1 WEARY, drowsy, sleepy, flagging, fatigued, worn out, exhausted, dog-tired, drained, jaded, fagged (sl), bushed (infml), whacked (infml), shattered (infml), beat (infml), dead-beat (infml), all in (infml), knackered (infml). 2 tired of waiting: fed up, bored, sick. 3 STALE, overused, jaded, unoriginal, hackneyed.
E3 1 lively, energetic, rested, refreshed. 3 new, original.

tireless adj untiring, unwearied, unflagging, indefatigable, energetic, vigorous, diligent, industrious, resolute, determined.
E3 tired, lazy.

tiresome adj troublesome, trying, annoying, irritating, exasperating, wearisome, dull, boring, tedious, monotonous, uninteresting, tiring, fatiguing, laborious.
E3 interesting, stimulating, easy.

tiring adj wearying, fatiguing, exhausting, draining, demanding, exacting, taxing, arduous, strenuous, laborious.

tissue n 1 SUBSTANCE, matter, material. 2 FABRIC, stuff, gauze.

3 *a tissue of lies*: web, mesh, network, structure, texture.

titbit *n* morsel, scrap, appetizer, snack, delicacy, dainty, treat.

titillate *v* stimulate, arouse, turn on (*sl*), excite, thrill, tickle, provoke, tease, tantalize, intrigue, interest.

title *n* **1** NAME, appellation, denomination, term, designation, label, epithet, nickname, pseudonym, rank, status, office, position. **2** HEADING, headline, caption, legend, inscription. **3** RIGHT, prerogative, privilege, claim, entitlement, ownership, deeds. *v* entitle, name, call, dub, style, term, designate, label.

titter *v* laugh, chortle, chuckle, giggle, snigger, mock.

titular *adj* honorary, formal, official, so-called, nominal, token.

toast *v* grill, brown, roast, heat, warm.
n drink, pledge, tribute, salute, compliment, health.

together *adv* jointly, in concert, side by side, shoulder to shoulder, in unison, as one, simultaneously, at the same time, all at once, collectively, en masse, closely, continuously, consecutively, successively, in succession, in a row, hand in hand.
Ea separately, individually, alone.

toil *n* labour, hard work, donkey-work, drudgery, sweat, graft (*infml*), industry, application, effort, exertion, elbow grease.
v labour, work, slave, drudge, sweat, grind, slog, graft (*infml*), plug away (*infml*), persevere, strive, struggle.

toilet *n* lavatory, WC, loo (*infml*), bog (*sl*), bathroom, cloakroom, washroom, rest room (*N Am*), public convenience,

Ladies (*infml*), Gents (*infml*), urinal, convenience, powder room.

token *n* **1** SYMBOL, emblem, representation, mark, sign, indication, manifestation, demonstration, expression, evidence, proof, clue, warning, reminder, memorial, memento, souvenir, keepsake. **2** *gift token*: voucher, coupon, counter, disc.
adj symbolic, emblematic, nominal, minimal, perfunctory, superficial, cosmetic, hollow, insincere.

tolerable *adj* bearable, endurable, sufferable, acceptable, passable, adequate, reasonable, fair, average, all right, OK (*infml*), not bad, mediocre, indifferent, so-so (*infml*), unexceptional, ordinary, run-of-the-mill.
Ea intolerable, unbearable, insufferable.

tolerance *n* **1** TOLERATION, patience, forbearance, open-mindedness, broad-mindedness, magnanimity, sympathy, understanding, lenity, indulgence, permissiveness. **2** VARIATION, fluctuation, play, allowance, clearance. **3** RESISTANCE, resilience, toughness, endurance, stamina.
Ea 1 intolerance, prejudice, bigotry, narrow-mindedness.

tolerant *adj* patient, forbearing, long-suffering, open-minded, fair, unprejudiced, broad-minded, liberal, charitable, kind-hearted, sympathetic, understanding, forgiving, lenient, indulgent, easy-going (*infml*), permissive, lax, soft.
Ea intolerant, biased, prejudiced, bigoted, unsympathetic.

tolerate *v* endure, suffer, put up with, bear, stand, abide, stomach, swallow, take, receive, accept, admit, allow, permit, condone, countenance, indulge.

toll¹ *v* ring, peal, chime, knell, sound, strike, announce, call.

toll² *n* charge, fee, payment, levy, tax, duty, tariff, rate, cost, penalty, demand, loss.

tomb *n* grave, burial-place, vault, crypt, sepulchre, catacomb, mausoleum, cenotaph.

tone *n* **1** *tone of voice*: note, timbre, pitch, volume, intonation, modulation, inflection, accent, stress, emphasis, force, strength. **2** TINT, tinge, colour, hue, shade, cast, tonality. **3** AIR, manner, attitude, mood, spirit, humour, temper, character, quality, feel, style, effect, vein, tenor, drift.
v match, co-ordinate, blend, harmonize.

tone down moderate, temper, subdue, restrain, soften, dim, dampen, play down, reduce, alleviate, assuage, mitigate.

tongue *n* language, speech, discourse, talk, utterance, articulation, parlance, vernacular, idiom, dialect, patois.

tongue-tied *adj* speechless, dumbstruck, inarticulate, silent, mute, dumb, voiceless.
E3 talkative, garrulous, voluble.

tonic *n* cordial, pick-me-up, restorative, refresher, bracer, stimulant, shot in the arm (*infml*), boost, fillip.

too *adv* **1** ALSO, as well, in addition, besides, moreover, likewise.
2 EXCESSIVELY, inordinately, unduly, over, overly, unreasonably, ridiculously, extremely, very.

tool *n* **1** IMPLEMENT, instrument, utensil, gadget, device, contrivance, contraption, apparatus, appliance, machine, means, vehicle, medium, agency, agent, intermediary.
2 PUPPET, pawn, dupe, stooge, minion, hireling.

Types of tool include:
crowbar, jackhammer, jointer, mattock, pick, pick-axe, sledge-hammer; clamp, drill, hack-saw, jack, pincers, pliers, punch, sander, socket wrench, soldering iron, spray gun, vice; auger, awl, brace-and-bit, bradawl, chisel, file, fretsaw, hammer, handsaw, jack-plane, jigsaw, mallet, plane, rasp, saw, screwdriver, tenon saw; billhook, chainsaw, chopper, dibble, fork, hoe, pitchfork, pruning-knife, pruning-shears, rake, scythe, secateurs, shears, shovel, sickle, spade, trowel; needle, scissors, pinking-shears, bodkin, forceps, scalpel, tweezers, tongs, cleaver, gimlet, pestle, paper-knife, stapler, pocket knife, penknife.

---

top *n* **1** HEAD, tip, vertex, apex, crest, crown, peak, pinnacle, summit, acme, zenith, culmination, height. **2** LID, cap, cover, cork, stopper. **3** JUMPER, sweater, jersey.
E3 1 bottom, base, nadir.

Types of top include:
cardigan, fleece, polo neck, turtle-neck, guernsey, pullover, twinset, shirt, dress-shirt, sweat-shirt, tee shirt, T-shirt, waistcoat, blouse, smock, tabard, tunic.

---

adj highest, topmost, upmost, uppermost, upper, superior, head, chief, leading, first, foremost, principal, sovereign, ruling, pre-eminent, dominant, prime, paramount, greatest, maximum, best, finest, supreme, crowning, culminating.

F3 bottom, lowest, inferior.

v **1** TIP, cap, crown, cover, finish (off), decorate, garnish. **2** BEAT, exceed, outstrip, better, excel, best, surpass, eclipse, outshine, outdo, surmount, transcend. **3** HEAD, lead, rule, command.

topic *n* subject, theme, issue, question, matter, point, thesis, text.

topical *adj* current, contemporary, up-to-date, up-to-the-minute, recent, newsworthy, relevant, popular, familiar.

topple *v* totter, overbalance, tumble, fall, collapse, upset, overturn, capsize, overthrow, oust.

torment *v* tease, provoke, annoy, vex, trouble, worry, harass, hound, pester, bother, bedevil, plague, afflict, distress, harrow, pain, torture, persecute.

n provocation, annoyance, vexation, bane, scourge, trouble, bother, nuisance, harassment, worry, anguish, distress, misery, affliction, suffering, pain, agony, ordeal, torture, persecution.

torrent *n* stream, volley, outburst, gush, rush, flood, spate, deluge, cascade, downpour.

F3 trickle.

tortuous *adj* twisting, winding, meandering, serpentine, zigzag, circuitous, roundabout, indirect, convoluted, complicated, involved.

F3 straight, straightforward.

torture *v* pain, agonize, excruciate, crucify, rack, martyr, persecute, torment, afflict, distress.

n pain, agony, suffering, affliction, distress, misery, anguish, torment, martyrdom, persecution.

toss *v* **1** FLIP, cast, fling, throw, chuck (*infml*), sling, hurl, lob. **2** ROLL, heave, pitch, lurch, jolt, shake, agitate, rock, thrash, squirm, wriggle.

n flip, cast, fling, throw, pitch.

total *n* sum, whole, entirety, totality, all, lot, mass, aggregate, amount.

adj full, complete, entire, whole, integral, all-out, utter, absolute, unconditional, unqualified, outright, undisputed, perfect, consummate, thoroughgoing, sheer, downright, thorough.

F3 partial, limited, restricted.

v add (up), sum (up), tot (up), count (up), reckon, amount to, come to, reach.

totter *v* stagger, reel, lurch, stumble, falter, waver, teeter, sway, rock, shake, quiver, tremble.

touch *n* **1** FEEL, texture, brush, stroke, caress, pat, tap, contact. **2** *a touch of garlic*: trace, spot, dash, pinch, soupçon, suspicion, hint, suggestion, speck, jot, tinge, smack. **3** SKILL, art, knack, flair, style, method, manner, technique, approach.

v **1** FEEL, handle, finger, brush, graze, stroke, caress, fondle, pat, tap, hit, strike, contact, meet, abut, adjoin, border. **2** MOVE, stir, upset, disturb, impress, inspire, influence, affect, concern, regard. **3** REACH, attain, equal, match, rival, better.

touch on mention, broach, speak of, remark on, refer to, allude to, cover, deal with.

touched *adj* **1** MOVED, stirred, affected, disturbed, impressed. **2** MAD, crazy, deranged, disturbed, eccentric, dotty (*infml*), daft (*infml*), barmy (*infml*).

touching *adj* moving, stirring, affecting, poignant, pitiable, pitiful, pathetic, sad, emotional, tender.

touchy *adj* irritable, irascible, quick-tempered, bad-tempered, grumpy, grouchy, crabbed, cross, peevish, captious, edgy, over-sensitive.
F3 calm, imperturbable.

tough *adj* **1** STRONG, durable, resilient, resistant, hardy, sturdy, solid, rigid, stiff, inflexible, hard, leathery. **2** *a tough criminal*: rough, violent, vicious, callous, hardened, obstinate. **3** HARSH, severe, strict, stern, firm, resolute, determined, tenacious. **4** ARDUOUS, laborious, exacting, hard, difficult, puzzling, perplexing, baffling, knotty, thorny, troublesome.
F3 1 fragile, delicate, weak, tender. **2** gentle, soft. **3** gentle. **4** easy, simple.
n brute, thug, bully, ruffian, hooligan, lout, yob (*sl*).

tour *n* circuit, round, visit, expedition, journey, trip, outing, excursion, drive, ride, course.
v visit, go round, sightsee, explore, travel, journey, drive, ride.

tourist *n* holidaymaker, visitor, sightseer, tripper, excursionist, traveller, voyager, globetrotter.

tournament *n* championship, series, competition, contest, match, event, meeting.

tow *v* pull, tug, draw, trail, drag, lug, haul, transport.

towards *prep* **1** TO, approaching, nearing, close to, nearly, almost. **2** *his feelings towards her*: regarding, with

regard to, with respect to, concerning, about, for.

tower *n* fortification, bastion, citadel, fort, fortress, castle.

Types of tower include:
barbican, bastille, belfry, bell-tower, belvedere, campanile, church tower, column, demi-bastion, donjon, gate-tower, high-rise building, keep, lookout tower, martello tower, minar, minaret, mirador, pagoda, peel-tower, skyscraper, spire, steeple, tower block, turret, watchtower, water tower.

Famous towers include:
Bastille, Blackpool Tower, Eiffel Tower, Leaning Tower of Pisa, Tower of Babel, Tower of London.

v rise, rear, ascend, mount, soar, loom, overlook, dominate, surpass, transcend, exceed, top.

towering *adj* soaring, tall, high, lofty, elevated, monumental, colossal, gigantic, great, magnificent, imposing, impressive, sublime, supreme, surpassing, overpowering, extreme, inordinate.
F3 small, tiny, minor, trivial.

toxic *adj* poisonous, harmful, noxious, unhealthy, dangerous, deadly, lethal.
F3 harmless, safe.

toy *n* plaything, game, doll, knick-knack.
v play, tinker, fiddle, sport, trifle, dally.

trace *n* trail, track, spoor, footprint, footmark, mark, token, sign, indication, evidence, record, relic, remains, remnant, vestige, shadow, hint, suggestion, suspicion, soupçon, dash, drop, spot, bit, jot, touch, tinge, smack.
v **1** COPY, draw, sketch, outline,

delineate, depict, mark, record, map, chart. **2** FIND, discover, detect, unearth, track (down), trail, stalk, hunt, seek, follow, pursue, shadow.

track n footstep, footprint, footmark, scent, spoor, trail, wake, mark, trace, slot, groove, rail, path, way, route, orbit, line, course, drift, sequence. v stalk, trail, hunt, trace, follow, pursue, chase, dog, tail, shadow.

track down find, discover, trace, hunt down, run to earth, sniff out, ferret out, dig up, unearth, expose, catch, capture.

tract n stretch, extent, expanse, plot, lot, territory, area, region, zone, district, quarter.

trade n **1** COMMERCE, traffic, business, dealing, buying, selling, shopkeeping, barter, exchange, transactions, custom. **2** OCCUPATION, job, business, profession, calling, craft, skill.
v traffic, peddle, do business, deal, transact, buy, sell, barter, exchange, swap, switch, bargain.

trademark n brand, label, name, sign, symbol, logo, insignia, crest, emblem, badge, hallmark.

trader n merchant, tradesman, broker, dealer, buyer, seller, vendor, supplier, wholesaler, retailer, shopkeeper, trafficker, peddler.

tradition n convention, custom, usage, way, habit, routine, ritual, institution, folklore.

traditional adj conventional, customary, habitual, usual, accustomed, established, fixed, long-established, time-honoured, old, historic, folk, oral, unwritten.
E3 unconventional, innovative, new, modern, contemporary.

traffic n **1** VEHICLES, shipping, transport, transportation, freight, passengers. **2** TRADE, commerce, business, dealing, trafficking, barter, exchange. **3** COMMUNICATION, dealings, relations.
v peddle, buy, sell, trade, do business, deal, bargain, barter, exchange.

tragedy n adversity, misfortune, unhappiness, affliction, blow, calamity, disaster, catastrophe.

tragic adj sad, sorrowful, miserable, unhappy, unfortunate, unlucky, ill-fated, pitiable, pathetic, heartbreaking, shocking, appalling, dreadful, awful, dire, calamitous, disastrous, catastrophic, deadly, fatal.
E3 happy, comic, successful.

trail v **1** DRAG, pull, tow, droop, dangle, extend, stream, straggle, dawdle, lag, loiter, linger. **2** TRACK, stalk, hunt, follow, pursue, chase, shadow, tail.
n track, footprints, footmarks, scent, trace, path, footpath, road, route, way.

train v **1** TEACH, instruct, coach, tutor, educate, improve, school, discipline, prepare, drill, exercise, work out, practise, rehearse. **2** POINT, direct, aim, level.
n **1** train of events: sequence, succession, series, progression, order, string, chain, line, file, procession, convoy, cortège, caravan. **2** RETINUE, entourage, attendants, court, household, staff, followers, following.

trainer n teacher, instructor, coach, tutor, handler.

training n teaching, instruction, coaching, tuition, education, schooling, discipline, preparation, grounding, drill, exercise, working-out, practice, learning, apprenticeship.

trait n feature, attribute, quality, characteristic, idiosyncrasy, peculiarity, quirk.

traitor n betrayer, informer, deceiver, double-crosser, turncoat, renegade, deserter, defector, quisling, collaborator.

F3 loyalist, supporter, defender.

tramp v walk, march, tread, stamp, stomp, stump, plod, trudge, traipse, trail, trek, hike, ramble, roam, rove. n vagrant, vagabond, hobo, down-and-out, dosser (sl).

trample v tread, stamp, crush, squash, flatten.

trance n dream, reverie, daze, stupor, unconsciousness, spell, ecstasy, rapture.

tranquil adj calm, composed, cool, imperturbable, unexcited, placid, sedate, relaxed, laid-back (infml), serene, peaceful, restful, still, undisturbed, untroubled, quiet, hushed, silent.

F3 agitated, disturbed, troubled, noisy.

tranquillizer n sedative, opiate, narcotic, barbiturate.

transaction n deal, bargain, agreement, arrangement, negotiation, business, affair, matter, proceeding, enterprise, undertaking, deed, action, execution, discharge.

transcend v surpass, excel, outshine, eclipse, outdo, outstrip, beat, surmount, exceed, overstep.

transcribe v write out, copy, reproduce, rewrite, transliterate, translate, render, take down, note, record.

transcript n transcription, copy, reproduction, duplicate,

transliteration, translation, version, note, record, manuscript.

transfer v change, transpose, move, shift, remove, relocate, transplant, transport, carry, convey, transmit, consign, grant, hand over. n change, changeover, transposition, move, shift, removal, relocation, displacement, transmission, handover, transference.

transfix v **1** FASCINATE, spellbind, mesmerize, hypnotize, paralyse. **2** IMPALE, spear, skewer, spike, stick.

transform v change, alter, adapt, convert, remodel, reconstruct, transfigure, revolutionize.

F3 preserve, maintain.

transformation n change, alteration, mutation, conversion, metamorphosis, transfiguration, revolution.

F3 preservation, conservation.

transient adj transitory, passing, flying, fleeting, brief, short, momentary, ephemeral, short-lived, temporary, short-term.

F3 lasting, permanent.

transit n passage, journey, travel, movement, transfer, transportation, conveyance, carriage, haulage, shipment.

transition n passage, passing, progress, progression, development, evolution, flux, change, alteration, conversion, transformation, shift.

transitional adj provisional, temporary, passing, intermediate, developmental, changing, fluid, unsettled.

F3 initial, final.

translate v interpret, render, paraphrase, simplify, decode, decipher, transliterate, transcribe, change, alter, convert, transform, improve.

translation n rendering, version, interpretation, gloss, crib, rewording, rephrasing, paraphrase, simplification, transliteration, transcription, change, alteration, conversion, transformation.

transmission n **1** BROADCASTING, diffusion, spread, communication, conveyance, carriage, transport, shipment, sending, dispatch, relaying, transfer. **2** *a live transmission:* broadcast, programme, show, signal.
F3 1 reception.

transmit v communicate, impart, convey, carry, bear, transport, send, dispatch, forward, relay, transfer, broadcast, radio, disseminate, network, diffuse, spread.
F3 receive.

transparency n slide, photograph, picture.

transparent adj **1** *transparent plastic:* clear, see-through, translucent, sheer. **2** PLAIN, distinct, clear, lucid, explicit, unambiguous, unequivocal, apparent, visible, obvious, evident, manifest, patent, undisguised, open, candid, straightforward.
F3 1 opaque. **2** unclear, ambiguous.

transplant v move, shift, displace, remove, uproot, transfer, relocate, resettle, repot.
F3 leave.

transport v convey, carry, bear, take, fetch, bring, move, shift, transfer, ship, haul, remove, deport.
n conveyance, carriage, transfer, transportation, shipment, shipping, haulage, removal.

transpose v swap, exchange, switch, interchange, transfer, shift, rearrange, reorder, change, alter, move, substitute.

transverse adj cross, crosswise, transversal, diagonal, oblique.

trap n snare, net, noose, springe, gin, booby-trap, pitfall, danger, hazard, ambush, trick, wile, ruse, stratagem, device, trickery, artifice, deception.
v snare, net, entrap, ensnare, enmesh, catch, take, ambush, corner, trick, deceive, dupe.

trash n rubbish, garbage, refuse, junk, waste, litter, sweepings, offscourings, scum, dregs.

trauma n injury, wound, hurt, damage, pain, suffering, anguish, agony, torture, ordeal, shock, jolt, upset, disturbance, upheaval, strain, stress.
F3 healing.

traumatic adj painful, hurtful, injurious, wounding, shocking, upsetting, distressing, disturbing, unpleasant, frightening, stressful.
F3 healing, relaxing.

travel v journey, voyage, go, wend, move, proceed, progress, wander, ramble, roam, rove, tour, cross, traverse.
F3 stay, remain.
n travel, touring, tourism, globetrotting.

traveller n **1** TOURIST, explorer, voyager, globetrotter, holidaymaker, tripper (*infml*), excursionist, passenger, commuter, wanderer, rambler, hiker, wayfarer, migrant, nomad, gypsy, itinerant, tinker, vagrant. **2** SALESMAN, saleswoman, representative, rep (*infml*), agent.

travelling adj touring, wandering,

roaming, roving, wayfaring, migrant, migratory, nomadic, itinerant, peripatetic, mobile, moving, vagrant, homeless.
F3 fixed.

travels n voyage, expedition, passage, journey, trip, excursion, tour, wanderings.

travesty n mockery, parody, take-off, send-up, farce, caricature, distortion, sham, apology.

treacherous adj 1 TRAITOROUS, disloyal, unfaithful, faithless, unreliable, untrustworthy, false, untrue, deceitful, double-crossing, backstabbing. 2 treacherous roads: dangerous, hazardous, risky, perilous, precarious, icy, slippery.
F3 1 loyal, faithful, dependable. 2 safe, stable.

treachery n treason, betrayal, disloyalty, infidelity, falseness, duplicity, double-dealing, backstabbing.
F3 loyalty, dependability.

tread v walk, step, pace, stride, march, tramp, trudge, plod, stamp, trample, walk on, press, crush, squash.
n walk, footfall, footstep, step, pace, stride.

treason n treachery, perfidy, disloyalty, duplicity, subversion, sedition, mutiny, rebellion.
F3 loyalty.

treasonable adj traitorous, perfidious, disloyal, false, subversive, seditious, mutinous.
F3 loyal.

treasure n fortune, wealth, riches, money, cash, gold, jewels, hoard, cache.
v prize, value, esteem, revere, worship, love, adore, idolize, cherish, preserve, guard.
F3 disparage, belittle.

treat n indulgence, gratification, pleasure, delight, enjoyment, fun, entertainment, excursion, outing, party, celebration, feast, banquet, gift, surprise, thrill.
v 1 DEAL WITH, manage, handle, use, regard, consider, discuss, cover. 2 TEND, nurse, minister to, attend to, care for, heal, cure. 3 PAY FOR, buy, stand, give, provide, entertain, regale, feast.

treatise n essay, dissertation, thesis, monograph, paper, pamphlet, tract, study, exposition.

treatment n 1 HEALING, cure, remedy, medication, therapy, surgery, care, nursing. 2 MANAGEMENT, handling, use, usage, conduct, discussion, coverage.

treaty n pact, convention, agreement, covenant, compact, negotiation, contract, bond, alliance.

tree n bush, shrub.

Trees include:

acacia, alder, almond, apple, ash, aspen, balsa, bay, beech, birch, blackthorn, box, cedar, cherry, chestnut, coconut-palm, cypress, date-palm, dogwood, ebony, elder, elm, eucalyptus, fig, fir, gum, hawthorn, hazel, hickory, hornbeam, horse chestnut, larch, laurel, lime, linden, mahogany, maple, monkey-puzzle, mountain ash, oak, palm, pear, pine, plane, plum, poplar, pussy-willow, redwood, rowan, rubber tree, sandalwood, sequoia, silver birch, spruce, sycamore, teak, walnut, weeping willow, white-beam, willow, witch-hazel, yew, yucca; bonsai, conifer, deciduous, evergreen, fruit, hardwood, ornamental, softwood.

trek n hike, walk, march, tramp, journey, expedition, safari.
v hike, walk, march, tramp, trudge, plod, journey, rove, roam.

tremble v shake, vibrate, quake, shiver, shudder, quiver, wobble, rock.
n shake, vibration, quake, shiver, shudder, quiver, tremor, wobble.
E3 steadiness.

tremendous adj wonderful, marvellous, stupendous, sensational, spectacular, extraordinary, amazing, incredible, terrific, impressive, huge, immense, vast, colossal, gigantic, towering, formidable.
E3 ordinary, unimpressive.

tremor n shake, quiver, tremble, shiver, quake, quaver, wobble, vibration, agitation, thrill, shock, earthquake.
E3 steadiness.

trend n 1 COURSE, flow, drift, tendency, inclination, leaning. 2 CRAZE, rage (infml), fashion, vogue, mode, style, look.

trespass v invade, intrude, encroach, poach, infringe, violate, offend, wrong.
E3 obey, keep to.
n invasion, intrusion, encroachment, poaching, infringement, violation, contravention, offence, misdemeanour.

trespasser n intruder, poacher, offender, criminal.

trial n 1 LITIGATION, lawsuit, hearing, inquiry, tribunal. 2 EXPERIMENT, test, examination, check, dry run, dummy run, practice, rehearsal, audition, contest. 3 AFFLICTION, suffering, grief,

misery, distress, adversity, hardship, ordeal, trouble, nuisance, vexation, tribulation.
E3 3 relief, happiness.
adj experimental, test, pilot, exploratory, provisional, probationary.

tribe n race, nation, people, clan, family, house, dynasty, blood, stock, group, caste, class, division, branch.

tribute n 1 PRAISE, commendation, compliment, accolade, homage, respect, honour, credit, acknowledgement, recognition, gratitude. 2 PAYMENT, levy, charge, tax, duty, gift, offering, contribution.

trick n fraud, swindle, deception, deceit, artifice, illusion, hoax, practical joke, joke, leg-pull (infml), prank, antic, caper, frolic, feat, stunt, ruse, wile, dodge, subterfuge, trap, device, knack, technique, secret.
adj false, mock, artificial, imitation, ersatz, fake, forged, counterfeit, feigned, sham, bogus.
E3 real, genuine.
v deceive, delude, dupe, fool, hoodwink, beguile, mislead, bluff, hoax, pull someone's leg (infml), cheat, swindle, diddle, defraud, con (infml), trap, outwit.

trickery n deception, illusion, sleight-of-hand, pretence, artifice, guile, deceit, dishonesty, cheating, swindling, fraud, imposture, double-dealing, monkey business, funny business (sl), chicanery, skulduggery, hocus-pocus.
E3 straightforwardness, honesty.

trickle v dribble, run, leak, seep, ooze, exude, drip, drop, filter, percolate.
E3 stream, gush.

n dribble, drip, drop, leak, seepage.
F3 stream, gush.

tricky *adj* **1** *a tricky problem*: difficult, awkward, problematic, complicated, knotty, thorny, delicate, ticklish.
2 CRAFTY, artful, cunning, sly, wily, foxy, subtle, devious, slippery, scheming, deceitful.
F3 1 easy, simple. **2** honest.

trifle *n* **1** LITTLE, bit, spot, drop, dash, touch, trace. **2** TOY, plaything, trinket, bauble, knick-knack, triviality, nothing.
v toy, play, sport, flirt, dally, dabble, fiddle, meddle, fool.

trifling *adj* small, paltry, slight, negligible, inconsiderable, unimportant, insignificant, minor, trivial, petty, silly, frivolous, idle, empty, worthless.
F3 important, significant, serious.

trigger *v* cause, start, initiate, activate, set off, spark off, provoke, prompt, elicit, generate, produce.
n lever, catch, switch, spur, stimulus.

trim *adj* **1** NEAT, tidy, orderly, shipshape, spick-and-span, spruce, smart, dapper. **2** SLIM, slender, streamlined, compact.
F3 1 untidy, scruffy.
v **1** CUT, clip, crop, dock, prune, pare, shave. **2** DECORATE, ornament, embellish, garnish, dress, array, adjust, arrange, order, neaten, tidy.
n condition, state, order, form, shape, fitness, health.

trimmings *n* **1** GARNISH, decorations, ornaments, frills, extras, accessories. **2** CUTTINGS, clippings, parings, ends.

trinket *n* bauble, jewel, ornament, knick-knack.

trio *n* threesome, triad, triumvirate, trinity, triplet, trilogy.

trip *n* outing, excursion, tour, jaunt, ride, drive, spin, journey, voyage, expedition, foray.
v stumble, slip, fall, tumble, stagger, totter, blunder.

triple *adj* treble, triplicate, threefold, three-ply, three-way.
v treble, triplicate.

trite *adj* banal, commonplace, ordinary, run-of-the-mill, stale, tired, worn, threadbare, unoriginal, hackneyed, overused, stock, stereotyped, clichéd, corny (*infml*).
F3 original, new, fresh.

triumph *n* **1** WIN, victory, conquest, walk-over, success, achievement, accomplishment, feat, coup, masterstroke, hit, sensation.
2 EXULTATION, jubilation, rejoicing, celebration, elation, joy, happiness.
v win, succeed, prosper, conquer, vanquish, overcome, overwhelm, prevail, dominate, celebrate, rejoice, glory, gloat.
F3 lose, fail.

triumphant *adj* winning, victorious, conquering, successful, exultant, jubilant, rejoicing, celebratory, glorious, elated, joyful, proud, boastful, gloating, swaggering.
F3 defeated, humble.

trivial *adj* unimportant, insignificant, inconsequential, incidental, minor, petty, paltry, trifling, small, little, inconsiderable, negligible, worthless, meaningless, frivolous, banal, trite, commonplace, everyday.
F3 important, significant, profound.

triviality *n* unimportance, insignificance, pettiness, smallness, worthlessness, meaninglessness,

troop n contingent, squadron, unit, division, company, squad, team, crew, gang, band, bunch, group, body, pack, herd, flock, horde, crowd, throng, multitude.

v go, march, parade, stream, flock, swarm, throng.

troops n army, military, soldiers, servicemen, servicewomen.

trophy n cup, prize, award, souvenir, memento.

tropical adj hot, torrid, sultry, sweltering, stifling, steamy, humid.
F3 arctic, cold, cool, temperate.

trot v jog, run, scamper, scuttle, scurry.

trouble n **1** PROBLEM, difficulty, struggle, annoyance, irritation, bother, nuisance, inconvenience, misfortune, adversity, trial, tribulation, pain, suffering, affliction, distress, grief, woe, heartache, concern, uneasiness, worry, anxiety, agitation. **2** UNREST, strife, tumult, commotion, disturbance, disorder, upheaval. **3** back trouble: disorder, complaint, ailment, illness, disease, disability, defect. **4** EFFORT, exertion, pains, care, attention, thought.
F3 1 relief, calm. **2** order. **3** health.

v annoy, vex, harass, torment, bother, inconvenience, disturb, upset, distress, sadden, pain, afflict, burden, worry, agitate, disconcert, perplex.
F3 reassure, help.

troublemaker n agitator, rabble-rouser, incendiary, instigator, ringleader, stirrer, mischief-maker.
F3 peacemaker.

troublesome adj **1** ANNOYING, irritating, vexatious, irksome,

bothersome, inconvenient, difficult, hard, tricky, thorny, taxing, demanding, laborious, tiresome, wearisome. **2** UNRULY, rowdy, turbulent, trying, unco-operative, insubordinate, rebellious.
F3 1 easy, simple. **2** helpful.

trough n gutter, conduit, trench, ditch, gully, channel, groove, furrow, hollow, depression.

trousers n pants, bags (infml), breeches, shorts.

Types of trousers and shorts include:
jeans, Levis®, denims, cargo pants, chinos, slacks, cords, flannels, drainpipes, bell-bottoms, dungarees, leggings, pedal-pushers, plusfours, jodhpurs, Bermuda shorts, hot pants.

---

truancy n absence, absenteeism, shirking, skiving (infml).
F3 attendance.

truant n absentee, deserter, runaway, idler, shirker, skiver (infml), dodger.
adj absent, missing, runaway.

truce n ceasefire, peace, armistice, cessation, moratorium, suspension, stay, respite, let-up (infml), lull, rest, break, interval, intermission.
F3 war, hostilities.

truck n lorry, van, wagon, trailer, float, cart, barrow.

trudge v tramp, plod, clump, stump, lumber, traipse, slog, labour, trek, hike, walk, march.
n tramp, traipse, slog, haul, trek, hike, walk, march.

true adj **1** REAL, genuine, authentic, actual, veritable, exact, precise, accurate, correct, right, factual, truthful, veracious, sincere, honest,

legitimate, valid, rightful, proper.
2 FAITHFUL, loyal, constant,
steadfast, staunch, firm, trustworthy,
trusty, honourable, dedicated,
devoted.
E3 1 false, wrong, incorrect,
inaccurate. **2** unfaithful, faithless.

truism n truth, platitude,
commonplace, cliché.

truly adv very, greatly, extremely,
really, genuinely, sincerely, honestly,
truthfully, undeniably, indubitably,
indeed, in fact, in reality, exactly,
precisely, correctly, rightly, properly.
E3 slightly, falsely, incorrectly.

trumpet n bugle, horn, clarion,
blare, blast, roar, bellow, cry, call.
v blare, blast, roar, bellow, shout,
proclaim, announce, broadcast,
advertise.

truncate v shorten, abbreviate,
curtail, cut, lop, dock, prune, pare,
clip, trim, crop.
E3 lengthen, extend.

trunk n **1** CASE, suitcase, chest,
coffer, box, crate. **2** TORSO, body,
frame, shaft, stock, stem, stalk.

truss v tie, strap, bind, pinion, fasten,
secure, bundle, pack.
E3 untie, loosen.
n binding, bandage, support, brace,
prop, stay, shore, strut, joist.

trust n **1** FAITH, belief, credence,
credit, hope, expectation, reliance,
confidence, assurance, conviction,
certainty. **2** CARE, charge, custody,
safekeeping, guardianship,
protection, responsibility, duty.
E3 1 distrust, mistrust, scepticism,
doubt.
v **1** BELIEVE, imagine, assume,
presume, suppose, surmise, hope,
expect, rely on, depend on, count on,

bank on, swear by. **2** ENTRUST,
commit, consign, confide, give,
assign, delegate.
E3 distrust, mistrust, doubt,
disbelieve.

trusting adj trustful, credulous,
gullible, naive, innocent,
unquestioning, unsuspecting,
unguarded, unwary.
E3 distrustful, suspicious, cautious.

trustworthy adj honest, upright,
honourable, principled, reliable,
dependable,
reliable, steadfast, true, responsible,
sensible.
E3 untrustworthy, dishonest,
unreliable, irresponsible.

truth n **1** TRUTHFULNESS, veracity,
candour, frankness, honesty,
sincerity, genuineness, authenticity,
realism, exactness, precision,
accuracy, validity, legitimacy, honour,
integrity, uprightness, faithfulness,
fidelity, loyalty, constancy. **2** tell the
truth: facts, reality, actuality, fact,
axiom, maxim, principle, truism.
E3 1 deceit, dishonesty, falseness.
2 lie, falsehood.

truthful adj veracious, frank, candid,
straight, honest, sincere, true,
veritable, exact, precise, accurate,
correct, realistic, faithful, trustworthy,
reliable.
E3 untruthful, deceitful, false, untrue.

try v **1** ATTEMPT, endeavour, venture,
undertake, seek, strive. **2** HEAR, judge.
3 EXPERIMENT, test, sample, taste,
inspect, examine, investigate,
evaluate, appraise.
n **1** ATTEMPT, endeavour, effort, go
(infml), bash (infml), crack (infml), shot
(infml), stab (infml). **2** EXPERIMENT,
test, trial, sample, taste.

trying adj annoying, irritating,

aggravating (*infml*), vexatious, exasperating, troublesome, tiresome, wearisome, difficult, hard, tough, arduous, taxing, demanding, testing. **F3** easy.

tub *n* bath, basin, vat, tun, butt, cask, barrel, keg.

tube *n* hose, pipe, cylinder, duct, conduit, spout, channel.

tuck *v* **1** INSERT, push, thrust, stuff, cram. **2** FOLD, pleat, gather, crease. *n* fold, pleat, gather, pucker, crease.

tuft *n* crest, beard, tassel, knot, clump, cluster, bunch.

tug *v* pull, draw, tow, haul, drag, lug, heave, wrench, jerk, pluck. *n* pull, tow, haul, heave, wrench, jerk, pluck.

tuition *n* teaching, instruction, coaching, training, lessons, schooling, education.

tumble *v* fall, stumble, trip, topple, overthrow, drop, flop, collapse, plummet, pitch, roll, toss. *n* fall, stumble, trip, drop, plunge, roll, toss.

tumult *n* commotion, turmoil, disturbance, upheaval, stir, agitation, unrest, disorder, chaos, pandemonium, noise, clamour, din, racket, hubbub, hullaboloo, row, rumpus, uproar, riot, fracas, brawl, affray, strife. **F3** peace, calm, composure.

tumultuous *adj* turbulent, stormy, raging, fierce, violent, wild, hectic, boisterous, rowdy, noisy, disorderly, unruly, riotous, restless, agitated, troubled, disturbed, excited. **F3** calm, peaceful, quiet.

tune *n* melody, theme, motif, song, air, strain. *v* pitch, harmonize, set, regulate,

adjust, adapt, temper, attune, synchronize.

tuneful *adj* melodious, melodic, catchy, musical, euphonious, harmonious, pleasant, mellow, sonorous. **F3** tuneless, discordant.

tunnel *n* passage, passageway, gallery, subway, underpass, burrow, hole, mine, shaft, chimney. *v* burrow, dig, excavate, mine, bore, penetrate, undermine, sap.

turbulent *adj* rough, choppy, stormy, blustery, tempestuous, raging, furious, violent, wild, tumultuous, unbridled, boisterous, rowdy, disorderly, unruly, undisciplined, obstreperous, rebellious, mutinous, riotous, agitated, unsettled, unstable, confused, disordered.

turmoil *n* confusion, disorder, tumult, commotion, disturbance, trouble, disquiet, agitation, turbulence, stir, ferment, flurry, bustle, chaos, pandemonium, bedlam, noise, din, hubbub, row, uproar. **F3** calm, peace, quiet.

turn *v* **1** REVOLVE, circle, spin, twirl, whirl, twist, gyrate, pivot, hinge, swivel, rotate, roll, move, shift, invert, reverse, bend, veer, swerve, divert. **2** MAKE, transform, change, alter, modify, convert, adapt, adjust, fit, mould, shape, form, fashion, remodel. **3** turn cold: go, become, grow. **4** RESORT, have recourse, apply, appeal. **5** SOUR, curdle, spoil, go off, go bad. *n* **1** REVOLUTION, cycle, round, circle, rotation, spin, twirl, twist, gyration, bend, curve, loop, reversal. **2** CHANGE, alteration, shift, deviation. **3** *it's your turn*: go, chance, opportunity, occasion, stint, period, spell. **4** ACT, performance, performer.

turn away reject, avert, deflect, deviate, depart.

E3 accept, receive.

turn down 1 *turn down an offer*: reject, decline, refuse, spurn, rebuff, repudiate. **2** LOWER, lessen, quieten, soften, mute, muffle.

E3 1 accept. **2** turn up.

turn in 1 GO TO BED, retire. **2** HAND OVER, give up, surrender, deliver, hand in, tender, submit, return, give back.

E3 1 get up. **2** keep.

turn off 1 BRANCH OFF, leave, quit, depart from, deviate, divert. **2** SWITCH OFF, turn out, stop, shut down, unplug, disconnect. **3** (*sl*) REPEL, sicken, nauseate, disgust, offend, displease, disenchant, alienate, bore, discourage, put off.

E3 1 join. **2** turn on. **3** turn on (*sl*).

turn on 1 SWITCH ON, start (up), activate, connect. **2** (*sl*) AROUSE, stimulate, excite, thrill, please, attract. **3** HINGE ON, depend on, rest on. **4** ATTACK, round on, fall on.

E3 1 turn off. **2** turn off (*sl*).

turn out 1 HAPPEN, come about, transpire, ensue, result, end up, become, develop, emerge. **2** SWITCH OFF, turn off, unplug, disconnect. **3** APPEAR, present, dress, clothe. **4** PRODUCE, make, manufacture, fabricate, assemble. **5** EVICT, throw out, expel, deport, banish, dismiss, discharge, drum out, kick out, sack (*infml*). **6** *turn out the attic*: empty, clear, clean out.

E3 2 turn on. **6** fill.

turn over 1 THINK OVER, think about, mull over, ponder, deliberate, reflect on, contemplate, consider, examine. **2** HAND OVER, surrender, deliver, transfer. **3** OVERTURN, upset, upend, invert, capsize, keel over.

turn up 1 ATTEND, come, arrive, appear, show up (*infml*). **2** AMPLIFY, intensify, raise, increase. **3** DISCOVER, find, unearth, dig up, expose, disclose, reveal, show.

E3 1 stay away. **2** turn down.

turning *n* turn-off, junction, crossroads, fork, bend, curve, turn.

turning-point *n* crossroads, watershed, crux, crisis.

turnout *n* **1** ATTENDANCE, audience, gate, crowd, assembly, congregation. **2** APPEARANCE, outfit, dress, clothes.

tussle *v* struggle, battle, wrestle, fight, scrap, brawl.
n struggle, battle, fight, scrap, scuffle, brawl, fracas.

tutor *n* teacher, instructor, coach, educator, lecturer, supervisor, guide, mentor, guru, guardian.
v teach, instruct, train, drill, coach, educate, school, lecture, supervise, direct, guide.

tweak *v, n* twist, pinch, squeeze, nip, pull, tug, jerk, twitch.

twiddle *v* turn, twirl, swivel, twist, wiggle, adjust, fiddle, finger.

twilight *n* dusk, half-light, gloaming, gloom, dimness, sunset, evening.

twin *n* double, look-alike, likeness, duplicate, clone, match, counterpart, corollary, fellow, mate.
adj identical, matching, corresponding, symmetrical, parallel, matched, paired, double, dual, duplicate, twofold.
v match, pair, couple, link, join.

twine n string, cord, thread, yarn.
v wind, coil, spiral, loop, curl, bend, twist, wreathe, wrap, surround, encircle, entwine, plait, braid, knit, weave.

twinge n pain, pang, throb, spasm, throe, stab, stitch, pinch, prick.

twinkle v sparkle, glitter, shimmer, glisten, glimmer, flicker, wink, flash, glint, gleam, shine.
n sparkle, scintillation, glitter, shimmer, glisten, glimmer, flicker, wink, flash, glint, gleam, light.

twirl v spin, whirl, pirouette, wheel, rotate, revolve, swivel, pivot, turn, twist, gyrate, wind, coil.
n spin, whirl, pirouette, rotation, revolution, turn, twist, gyration, convolution, spiral, coil.

twist v 1 TURN, screw, wring, spin, swivel, wind, zigzag, bend, coil, spiral, curl, wreathe, twine, entwine, intertwine, weave, entangle, wriggle, squirm, writhe. 2 twist one's ankle: wrench, rick, sprain, strain.
3 CHANGE, alter, garble, misquote, misrepresent, distort, contort, warp, pervert.
n 1 TURN, screw, spin, roll, bend, curve, arc, curl, loop, zigzag, coil, spiral, convolution, squiggle, tangle.
2 CHANGE, variation, break.
3 PERVERSION, distortion, contortion.
4 SURPRISE, quirk, oddity, peculiarity.

twisted adj warped, perverted, deviant, unnatural.
Ⓕ straight.

twit n idiot, fool, simpleton, blockhead, clown, nincompoop (infml).

twitch v jerk, jump, start, blink, tremble, shake, pull, tug, tweak, snatch, pluck.
n spasm, convulsion, tic, tremor, jerk, jump, start.

twitter v chirp, chirrup, tweet, cheep, sing, warble, whistle, chatter.

two-faced adj hypocritical, insincere, false, lying, deceitful, treacherous, double-dealing, devious, untrustworthy.
Ⓕ honest, candid, frank.

tycoon n industrialist, entrepreneur, captain of industry, magnate, mogul, baron, supremo, capitalist, financier.

type n 1 SORT, kind, form, genre, variety, strain, species, breed, group, class, category, subdivision, classification, description, designation, stamp, mark, order, standard. 2 ARCHETYPE, embodiment, prototype, original, model, pattern, specimen, example.
3 PRINT, printing, characters, letters, lettering, face, fount, font.

typhoon n whirlwind, cyclone, tornado, twister (infml), hurricane, tempest, storm, squall.

typical adj standard, normal, usual, average, conventional, orthodox, stock, model, representative, illustrative, indicative, characteristic, distinctive.
Ⓕ atypical, unusual.

typify v embody, epitomize, encapsulate, personify, characterize, exemplify, symbolize, represent, illustrate.

tyrannical adj dictatorial, despotic, autocratic, absolute, arbitrary, authoritarian, domineering, overbearing, high-handed, imperious, magisterial, ruthless, harsh, severe, oppressive, overpowering, unjust, unreasonable.
Ⓕ liberal, tolerant.

tyranny *n* dictatorship, despotism, autocracy, absolutism, authoritarianism, imperiousness, ruthlessness, harshness, severity, oppression, injustice.

F3 democracy, freedom.

tyrant *n* dictator, despot, autocrat, absolutist, authoritarian, bully, oppressor, slave-driver, taskmaster.

U

ubiquitous *adj* omnipresent, ever-present, everywhere, universal, global, pervasive, common, frequent.
F3 rare, scarce.

ugly *adj* **1** UNATTRACTIVE, unsightly, plain, unprepossessing, ill-favoured, hideous, monstrous, misshapen, deformed. **2** UNPLEASANT, disagreeable, nasty, horrid, objectionable, offensive, disgusting, revolting, repulsive, vile, frightful, terrible.
F3 1 attractive, beautiful, handsome, pretty. **2** pleasant.

ulterior *adj* secondary, hidden, concealed, undisclosed, unexpressed, covert, secret, private, personal, selfish.
F3 overt.

ultimate *adj* final, last, closing, concluding, eventual, terminal, furthest, remotest, extreme, utmost, greatest, highest, supreme, superlative, perfect, radical, fundamental, primary.

ultimately *adv* finally, eventually, at last, in the end, after all.

umpire *n* referee, linesman, judge, adjudicator, arbiter, arbitrator, mediator, moderator.
v referee, judge, adjudicate, arbitrate, mediate, moderate, control.

umpteen *adj* a good many,

numerous, plenty, millions, countless, innumerable.
F3 few.

unabashed *adj* unashamed, unembarrassed, brazen, blatant, bold, confident, undaunted, unconcerned, undismayed.
F3 abashed, sheepish.

unable *adj* incapable, powerless, impotent, unequipped, unqualified, unfit, incompetent, inadequate.
F3 able, capable.

unacceptable *adj* intolerable, inadmissible, unsatisfactory, undesirable, unwelcome, objectionable, offensive, unpleasant.
F3 acceptable, satisfactory.

unaccompanied *adj* alone, unescorted, unattended, lone, solo, single-handed.
F3 accompanied.

unaccountable *adj* inexplicable, unexplainable, unfathomable, impenetrable, incomprehensible, baffling, puzzling, mysterious, astonishing, extraordinary, strange, odd, peculiar, singular, unusual, uncommon, unheard-of.
F3 explicable, explainable.

unaccustomed *adj* **1** *unaccustomed to such luxury:* unused, unacquainted, unfamiliar, unpractised, inexperienced. **2** STRANGE, unusual, uncommon, different, new, unexpected, surprising, uncharacteristic, unprecedented. **F3 1** accustomed, familiar. **2** customary.

unaffected adj **1** UNMOVED, unconcerned, indifferent, impervious, untouched, unchanged, unaltered. **2** UNSOPHISTICATED, artless, naive, ingenuous, unspoilt, plain, simple, straightforward, unpretentious, unassuming, sincere, honest, genuine. **F3 1** moved, influenced. **2** affected, pretentious, insincere.

unalterable adj unchangeable, invariable, unchanging, immutable, final, inflexible, unyielding, rigid, fixed, permanent. **F3** alterable, flexible.

unanimity n consensus, unity, agreement, concurrence, accord, like-mindedness, concord, harmony, unison, concert. **F3** disagreement, disunity.

unanimous adj united, concerted, joint, common, as one, in agreement, in accord, harmonious. **F3** disunited, divided.

unapproachable adj inaccessible, remote, distant, standoffish, withdrawn, reserved, unsociable, unfriendly, forbidding. **F3** approachable, friendly.

unarmed adj defenceless, unprotected, exposed, open, vulnerable, weak, helpless. **F3** armed, protected.

unashamed adj shameless, unabashed, impenitent, unrepentant, unconcealed, undisguised, open, blatant.

unasked adj uninvited, unbidden,

unrequested, unsought, unsolicited, unwanted, voluntary, spontaneous. **F3** invited, wanted.

unassuming adj unassertive, self-effacing, retiring, modest, humble, meek, unobtrusive, unpretentious, simple, restrained. **F3** presumptuous, assertive, pretentious.

unattached adj unmarried, single, free, available, footloose, fancy-free, independent, unaffiliated. **F3** engaged, committed.

unattended adj ignored, disregarded, unguarded, unwatched, unsupervised, unaccompanied, unescorted, alone. **F3** attended, escorted.

unauthorized adj unofficial, unlawful, illegal, illicit, illegitimate, irregular, unsanctioned. **F3** authorized, legal.

unavoidable adj inevitable, inescapable, inexorable, certain, sure, fated, destined, obligatory, compulsory, mandatory, necessary. **F3** avoidable.

unaware adj oblivious, unconscious, ignorant, uninformed, unknowing, unsuspecting, unmindful, heedless, blind, deaf. **F3** aware, conscious.

unbalanced adj **1** INSANE, mad, crazy, lunatic, deranged, disturbed, demented, irrational, unsound. **2** an unbalanced report: biased, prejudiced, one-sided, partisan, unfair, unjust, unequal, uneven, asymmetrical, lopsided, unsteady, unstable. **F3 1** sane. **2** unbiased.

unbearable adj intolerable, unacceptable, insupportable, insufferable, unendurable, excruciating.

F3 bearable, acceptable.

unbeatable adj invincible, unconquerable, unstoppable, unsurpassable, matchless, supreme, excellent.

unbecoming adj unseemly, improper, unsuitable, inappropriate, unbefitting, ungentlemanly, unladylike, unattractive, unsightly.

F3 suitable, attractive.

unbelief n atheism, agnosticism, scepticism, doubt, incredulity, disbelief.

F3 belief, faith.

unbelievable adj incredible, inconceivable, unthinkable, unimaginable, astonishing, staggering, extraordinary, impossible, improbable, unlikely, implausible, unconvincing, far-fetched, preposterous.

F3 believable, credible.

unborn adj embryonic, expected, awaited, coming, future.

unbounded adj boundless, limitless, unlimited, unrestricted, unrestrained, unchecked, unbridled, infinite, endless, immeasurable, vast.

F3 limited, restrained.

unbreakable adj indestructible, shatterproof, toughened, resistant, proof, durable, strong, tough, rugged, solid.

F3 breakable, fragile.

unbridled adj immoderate, excessive, uncontrolled, unrestrained, unchecked.

unbroken adj **1** INTACT, whole, entire, complete, solid, undivided. **2** UNINTERRUPTED, continuous, endless, ceaseless, incessant, unceasing, constant, perpetual, progressive, successive. **3** unbroken record: unbeaten, unsurpassed, unequalled, unmatched.

F3 1 broken. **2** intermittent, fitful.

uncalled-for adj gratuitous, unprovoked, unjustified, unwarranted, undeserved, unnecessary, needless.

F3 timely.

uncanny adj weird, strange, queer, bizarre, mysterious, unaccountable, incredible, remarkable, extraordinary, fantastic, unnatural, unearthly, supernatural, eerie, creepy, spooky (infml).

uncaring adj unconcerned, unmoved, unsympathetic, inconsiderate, unfeeling, cold, callous, indifferent, uninterested.

F3 caring, concerned.

unceasing adj ceaseless, incessant, unending, endless, never-ending, non-stop, continuous, unbroken, constant, perpetual, continual, persistent, relentless, unrelenting, unremitting.

F3 intermittent, spasmodic.

uncertain adj **1** UNSURE, unconvinced, doubtful, dubious, undecided, ambivalent, hesitant, wavering, vacillating. **2** INCONSTANT, changeable, variable, erratic, irregular, shaky, unsteady, unreliable. **3** UNPREDICTABLE, unforeseeable, undetermined, unsettled, unresolved, unconfirmed, indefinite, vague, insecure, risky, iffy (sl).

F3 1 certain, sure. **2** steady. **3** predictable.

uncertainty n doubt, scepticism, irresolution, dilemma, hesitation, misgiving, confusion, bewilderment,

perplexity, puzzlement, unreliability, unpredictability, insecurity.
F3 certainty.

unchanging adj unvarying, changeless, steady, steadfast, constant, perpetual, lasting, enduring, abiding, eternal, permanent.
F3 changing, changeable.

uncharitable adj unkind, cruel, hard-hearted, callous, unfeeling, insensitive, unsympathetic, unfriendly, mean, ungenerous.
F3 kind, sensitive, charitable, generous.

uncharted adj unexplored, undiscovered, unplumbed, foreign, alien, strange, unfamiliar, new, virgin.
F3 familiar.

uncivilized adj primitive, barbaric, savage, wild, untamed, uncultured, unsophisticated, unenlightened, uneducated, illiterate, uncouth, antisocial.
F3 civilized, cultured.

unclean adj dirty, soiled, filthy, foul, polluted, contaminated, tainted, impure, unhygienic, unwholesome, corrupt, defiled, sullied.
F3 clean, hygienic.

unclear adj indistinct, hazy, dim, obscure, vague, indefinite, ambiguous, equivocal, uncertain, unsure, doubtful, dubious.
F3 clear, evident.

uncomfortable adj **1** CRAMPED, hard, cold, ill-fitting, irritating, painful, disagreeable. **2** AWKWARD, embarrassed, self-conscious, uneasy, troubled, worried, disturbed, distressed, disquieted, conscience-stricken.
F3 1 comfortable. **2** relaxed.

uncommon adj rare, scarce,

infrequent, unusual, abnormal, atypical, unfamiliar, strange, odd, curious, bizarre, extraordinary, remarkable, notable, outstanding, exceptional, distinctive, special.
F3 common, usual, normal.

uncommunicative adj silent, taciturn, tight-lipped, close, secretive, unforthcoming, unresponsive, curt, brief, reticent, reserved, shy, retiring, withdrawn, unsociable.
F3 communicative, forthcoming.

uncompromising adj unyielding, unbending, inflexible, unaccommodating, rigid, firm, strict, tough, hard-line, inexorable, intransigent, stubborn, obstinate, die-hard.
F3 flexible.

unconcealed adj open, patent, obvious, evident, manifest, blatant, conspicuous, noticeable, visible, apparent.
F3 hidden, secret.

unconcerned adj indifferent, apathetic, uninterested, nonchalant, carefree, relaxed, complacent, cool, composed, untroubled, unworried, unruffled, unmoved, uncaring, unsympathetic, callous, aloof, remote, distant, detached, dispassionate, uninvolved, oblivious.
F3 concerned, worried, interested.

unconditional adj unqualified, unreserved, unrestricted, unlimited, absolute, utter, full, total, complete, entire, whole-hearted, thoroughgoing, downright, outright, positive, categorical, unequivocal.
F3 conditional, qualified, limited.

unconnected adj **1** IRRELEVANT, unrelated, unattached, detached, separate, independent.

2 DISCONNECTED, incoherent, irrational, illogical.

F3 1 connected, relevant.

unconscious *adj* **1** STUNNED, knocked out, out, out cold, out for the count, concussed, comatose, senseless, insensible. **2** UNAWARE, oblivious, blind, deaf, heedless, unmindful, ignorant. **3** *an unconscious reaction*: involuntary, automatic, reflex, instinctive, impulsive, innate, subconscious, subliminal, repressed, suppressed, latent, unwitting, inadvertent, accidental, unintentional.

F3 1 conscious. **2** aware. **3** intentional.

uncontrollable *adj* ungovernable, unmanageable, unruly, wild, mad, furious, violent, strong, irrepressible.

F3 controllable, manageable.

uncontrolled *adj* unrestrained, unbridled, unchecked, rampant, wild, unruly, undisciplined.

F3 controlled, restrained.

unconventional *adj* unorthodox, alternative, different, offbeat, eccentric, idiosyncratic, individual, original, odd, unusual, irregular, abnormal, bizarre, way-out (*sl*).

F3 conventional, orthodox.

unconvincing *adj* implausible, unlikely, improbable, questionable, doubtful, dubious, suspect, weak, feeble, flimsy, lame.

F3 convincing, plausible.

unco-ordinated *adj* clumsy, awkward, ungainly, ungraceful, inept, disjointed.

F3 graceful.

uncouth *adj* coarse, crude, vulgar, rude, ill-mannered, unseemly, improper, clumsy, awkward, gauche,

graceless, unrefined, uncultivated, uncultured, uncivilized, rough.

F3 polite, refined, urbane.

uncover *v* unveil, unmask, unwrap, strip, bare, open, expose, reveal, show, disclose, divulge, leak, unearth, exhume, discover, detect.

F3 cover, conceal, suppress.

uncritical *adj* undiscerning, undiscriminating, unselective, unquestioning, credulous, accepting, trusting, gullible, naive.

F3 discerning, discriminating, sceptical.

uncultivated *adj* fallow, wild, rough, natural.

F3 cultivated.

uncultured *adj* unsophisticated, unrefined, uncultivated, uncivilized, rough, uncouth, boorish, rustic, coarse, crude, ill-bred.

F3 cultured, sophisticated.

undaunted *adj* undeterred, undiscouraged, undismayed, unbowed, resolute, steadfast, brave, courageous, fearless, bold, intrepid, dauntless, indomitable.

F3 discouraged, timorous.

undecided *adj* uncertain, unsure, in two minds, ambivalent, doubtful, hesitant, wavering, irresolute, uncommitted, indefinite, vague, dubious, debatable, moot, unsettled, open.

F3 decided, certain, definite.

undemonstrative *adj* aloof, distant, remote, withdrawn, reserved, reticent, uncommunicative, stiff, formal, cool, cold, unemotional, restrained, impassive, phlegmatic.

F3 demonstrative, communicative.

undeniable *adj* irrefutable, unquestionable, incontrovertible,

sure, certain, undoubted, proven, clear, obvious, patent, evident, manifest, unmistakable.
F3 questionable.

under prep below, underneath, beneath, lower than, less than, inferior to, subordinate to.
F3 over, above.

under way moving, in motion, going, in operation, started, begun, in progress, afoot.

undercover adj secret, hush-hush (infml), private, confidential, spy, intelligence, underground, clandestine, surreptitious, furtive, covert, hidden, concealed.
F3 open, unconcealed.

undercurrent n undertone, overtone, hint, suggestion, tinge, flavour, aura, atmosphere, feeling, sense, movement, tendency, trend, drift.

underestimate v underrate, undervalue, misjudge, miscalculate, minimize, belittle, disparage, dismiss.
F3 overestimate, exaggerate.

undergo v experience, suffer, sustain, submit to, bear, stand, endure, weather, withstand.

underground adj **1** an underground passage: subterranean, buried, sunken, covered, hidden, concealed. **2** SECRET, covert, undercover, revolutionary, subversive, radical, experimental, avant-garde, alternative, unorthodox, unofficial.

undergrowth n brush, scrub, vegetation, ground cover, bracken, bushes, brambles, briars.

underhand adj unscrupulous, unethical, immoral, improper, sly, crafty, sneaky, stealthy, surreptitious, furtive, clandestine, devious,

dishonest, deceitful, deceptive, fraudulent, crooked (infml), shady (infml).
F3 honest, open, above board.

underline v mark, underscore, stress, emphasize, accentuate, italicize, highlight, point up.
F3 play down, soft-pedal.

underlying adj basic, fundamental, essential, primary, elementary, root, intrinsic, latent, hidden, lurking, veiled.

undermine v erode, wear away, weaken, sap, sabotage, subvert, vitiate, mar, impair.
F3 strengthen, fortify.

underprivileged adj disadvantaged, deprived, poor, needy, impoverished, destitute, oppressed.
F3 privileged, fortunate, affluent.

underrate v underestimate, undervalue, belittle, disparage, depreciate, dismiss.
F3 overrate, exaggerate.

undersized adj small, tiny, minute, miniature, pygmy, dwarf, stunted, underdeveloped, underweight, puny.
F3 oversized, big, overweight.

understand v **1** I don't understand: grasp, comprehend, take in, follow, get (infml), cotton on (infml), fathom, penetrate, make out, discern, perceive, see, realize, recognize, appreciate, accept. **2** SYMPATHIZE, empathize, commiserate. **3** BELIEVE, think, know, hear, learn, gather, assume, presume, suppose, conclude.
F3 1 misunderstand.

understanding n **1** GRASP, comprehension, knowledge, wisdom, intelligence, intellect, sense, judgement, discernment, insight, appreciation, awareness, impression,

perception, belief, idea, notion, opinion, interpretation.
2 AGREEMENT, arrangement, pact, accord, harmony. **3** SYMPATHY, empathy.
adj sympathetic, compassionate, kind, considerate, sensitive, tender, loving, patient, tolerant, forbearing, forgiving.
F3 unsympathetic, insensitive, impatient, intolerant.

understate *v* underplay, play down, soft-pedal, minimize, make light of, belittle, dismiss.
F3 exaggerate.

understood *adj* accepted, assumed, presumed, implied, implicit, inferred, tacit, unstated, unspoken, unwritten.

understudy *n* stand-in, double, substitute, replacement, reserve, deputy.

undertake *v* **1** PLEDGE, promise, guarantee, agree, contract, covenant. **2** BEGIN, commence, embark on, tackle, try, attempt, endeavour, take on, accept, assume.

undertaking *n* **1** ENTERPRISE, venture, business, affair, task, project, operation, attempt, endeavour, effort. **2** PLEDGE, commitment, promise, vow, word, assurance.

undertone *n* hint, suggestion, whisper, murmur, trace, tinge, touch, flavour, feeling, atmosphere, undercurrent.

undervalue *v* underrate, underestimate, misjudge, minimize, depreciate, disparage, dismiss.
F3 overrate, exaggerate.

underwater *adj* subaquatic, undersea, submarine, submerged, sunken.

underwear *n* underclothes, undergarments, lingerie, undies (*infml*), smalls (*infml*).

Types of underwear include: bra, brassière, Wonderbra®, body stocking, camisole, liberty bodice, corset, girdle, garter, suspenderbelt, suspenders, shift, slip, petticoat, teddy, basque, bustier, briefs, pants, panties, thong, G-string, French knickers, camiknickers, pantihose, tights, stockings; underpants, boxer shorts, boxers (*infml*), Y-fronts, vest, string vest, singlet.

---

underweight *adj* thin, undersized, underfed, undernourished, half-starved.
F3 overweight.

underwrite *v* endorse, authorize, sanction, approve, back, guarantee, insure, sponsor, fund, finance, subsidize, subscribe, sign, initial, countersign.

undesirable *adj* unwanted, unwelcome, unacceptable, unsuitable, unpleasant, disagreeable, distasteful, repugnant, offensive, objectionable, obnoxious.
F3 desirable, pleasant.

undignified *adj* inelegant, ungainly, clumsy, foolish, unseemly, improper, unsuitable, inappropriate.
F3 dignified, elegant.

undisguised *adj* unconcealed, open, overt, explicit, frank, genuine, apparent, patent, obvious, evident, manifest, blatant, naked, unadorned, stark, utter, outright, thoroughgoing.
F3 secret, concealed, hidden.

undisputed *adj* uncontested, unchallenged, unquestioned, undoubted, indisputable, incontrovertible, undeniable,

undistinguished *adj*

irrefutable, accepted, acknowledged, recognized, sure, certain, conclusive. ☒ debatable, uncertain.

undistinguished *adj* unexceptional, unremarkable, unimpressive, ordinary, run-of-the-mill, everyday, banal, indifferent, mediocre, inferior. ☒ distinguished, exceptional.

undivided *adj* solid, unbroken, intact, whole, entire, full, complete, combined, united, unanimous, concentrated, exclusive, whole-hearted.

undo *v* **1** UNFASTEN, untie, unbuckle, unbutton, unzip, unlock, unwrap, unwind, open, loose, loosen, separate. **2** ANNUL, nullify, invalidate, cancel, offset, neutralize, reverse, overturn, upset, quash, defeat, undermine, subvert, mar, spoil, ruin, wreck, shatter, destroy. ☒ **1** fasten, do up.

undoing *n* downfall, ruin, ruination, collapse, destruction, defeat, overthrow, reversal, weakness, shame, disgrace.

undone *adj* **1** UNACCOMPLISHED, unfulfilled, unfinished, uncompleted, incomplete, outstanding, left, omitted, neglected, forgotten. **2** UNFASTENED, untied, unlaced, unbuttoned, unlocked, open, loose. ☒ **1** done, accomplished, complete. **2** fastened.

undoubted *adj* unchallenged, undisputed, acknowledged, unquestionable, indisputable, incontrovertible, undesirable, indubitable, sure, certain, definite, obvious, patent.

undress *v* strip, peel off (*infml*), disrobe, take off, divest, remove, shed.

undressed *adj* unclothed, disrobed, stripped, naked, stark naked, nude. ☒ clothed.

undue *adj* unnecessary, needless, uncalled-for, unwarranted, undeserved, unreasonable, disproportionate, excessive, immoderate, inordinate, extreme, extravagant, improper. ☒ reasonable, moderate, proper.

unduly *adv* too, over, excessively, immoderately, inordinately, disproportionately, unreasonably, unjustifiably, unnecessarily. ☒ moderately, reasonably.

unearth *v* dig up, exhume, disinter, excavate, uncover, expose, reveal, find, discover, detect. ☒ bury.

unearthly *adj* **1** SUPERNATURAL, ghostly, eerie, uncanny, weird, strange, spine-chilling. **2** *at this unearthly hour*: unreasonable, outrageous, ungodly. ☒ **2** reasonable.

uneasy *adj* uncomfortable, anxious, worried, apprehensive, tense, strained, nervous, agitated, shaky, jittery, edgy, upset, troubled, disturbed, unsettled, restless, impatient, unsure, insecure. ☒ calm, composed.

uneducated *adj* unschooled, untaught, unread, ignorant, illiterate, uncultivated, uncultured, philistine, benighted. ☒ educated.

unemotional *adj* cool, cold, unfeeling, impassive, indifferent, apathetic, unresponsive, undemonstrative, unexcitable, phlegmatic, objective, dispassionate. ☒ emotional, excitable.

unemployed adj jobless, out of
work, laid off, redundant, unwaged,
on the dole (infml), idle, unoccupied.
F3 employed, occupied.

unending adj endless, never-
ending, unceasing, ceaseless,
incessant, interminable, constant,
continual, perpetual, everlasting,
eternal, undying.
F3 transient, intermittent.

unenviable adj undesirable,
unpleasant, disagreeable,
uncongenial, uncomfortable,
thankless, difficult.
F3 enviable, desirable.

unequal adj different, varying,
dissimilar, unlike, unmatched,
uneven, unbalanced,
disproportionate, asymmetrical,
irregular, unfair, unjust, biased,
discriminatory.
F3 equal.

unequivocal adj unambiguous,
explicit, clear, plain, evident, distinct,
unmistakable, express, direct, straight,
definite, positive, categorical,
incontrovertible, absolute,
unqualified, unreserved.
F3 ambiguous, vague, qualified.

unethical adj unprofessional,
immoral, improper, wrong,
unscrupulous, unprincipled,
dishonourable, disreputable, illegal,
illicit, dishonest, underhand, shady
(infml).
F3 ethical.

uneven adj 1 uneven ground: rough,
bumpy. 2 ODD, unequal, inequitable,
unfair, unbalanced, one-sided,
asymmetrical, lopsided, crooked.
3 IRREGULAR, intermittent,
spasmodic, fitful, jerky, unsteady,
variable, changeable, fluctuating,

erratic, inconsistent, patchy.
F3 1 flat, level. 2 even, equal.
3 regular.

uneventful adj uninteresting,
unexciting, quiet, unvaried, boring,
monotonous, tedious, dull, routine,
humdrum, ordinary, commonplace,
unremarkable, unexceptional,
unmemorable.
F3 eventful, memorable.

unexceptional adj unremarkable,
unmemorable, typical, average,
normal, usual, ordinary, indifferent,
mediocre, unimpressive.
F3 exceptional, impressive.

unexpected adj unforeseen,
unanticipated, unpredictable, chance,
accidental, fortuitous, sudden, abrupt,
surprising, startling, amazing,
astonishing, unusual.
F3 expected, predictable.

unfair adj unjust, inequitable,
partial, biased, prejudiced, bigoted,
discriminatory, unbalanced, one-
sided, partisan, arbitrary, undeserved,
unmerited, unwarranted, uncalled-
for, unethical, unscrupulous,
unprincipled, wrongful, dishonest.
F3 fair, just, unbiased, deserved.

unfaithful adj disloyal, treacherous,
false, untrue, deceitful, dishonest,
untrustworthy, unreliable, fickle,
inconstant, adulterous, two-timing,
duplicitous, double-dealing, faithless,
unbelieving, godless.
F3 faithful, loyal, reliable.

unfamiliar adj strange, unusual,
uncommon, curious, alien, foreign,
uncharted, unexplored, unknown,
different, new, novel, unaccustomed,
unacquainted, inexperienced,
unpractised, unskilled, unversed.
F3 familiar, customary, conversant.

unfashionable *adj* outmoded, dated, out of date, out, passé, old-fashioned, antiquated, obsolete.
F3 fashionable.

unfasten *v* undo, untie, loosen, unlock, open, uncouple, disconnect, separate, detach.
F3 fasten.

unfavourable *adj* inauspicious, unpromising, ominous, threatening, discouraging, inopportune, untimely, unseasonable, ill-suited, unfortunate, unlucky, disadvantageous, bad, poor, adverse, contrary, negative, hostile, unfriendly, uncomplimentary.
F3 favourable, auspicious, promising.

unfeeling *adj* insensitive, cold, hard, stony, callous, heartless, hard-hearted, cruel, inhuman, pitiless, uncaring, unsympathetic, apathetic.
F3 sensitive, sympathetic.

unfinished *adj* incomplete, uncompleted, half-done, sketchy, rough, crude, imperfect, lacking, wanting, deficient, undone, unaccomplished, unfulfilled.
F3 finished, perfect.

unfit *adj* **1** UNSUITABLE, inappropriate, unsuited, ill-equipped, unqualified, ineligible, untrained, unprepared, unequal, incapable, incompetent, inadequate, ineffective, useless. **2** UNHEALTHY, out of condition, flabby, feeble, decrepit.
F3 1 fit, suitable, competent.
2 healthy.

unfold *v* **1** DEVELOP, evolve.
2 REVEAL, disclose, show, present, describe, explain, clarify, elaborate.
3 *unfold a map*: open, spread, flatten, straighten, stretch out, undo, unfurl, unroll, uncoil, unwrap, uncover.
F3 2 withhold, suppress. **3** fold, wrap.

unforeseen *adj* unpredicted, unexpected, unanticipated, surprising, startling, sudden, unavoidable.
F3 expected, predictable.

unforgettable *adj* memorable, momentous, historic, noteworthy, notable, impressive, remarkable, exceptional, extraordinary.
F3 unmemorable, unexceptional.

unforgivable *adj* unpardonable, inexcusable, unjustifiable, indefensible, reprehensible, shameful, disgraceful, deplorable.
F3 forgivable, venial.

unfortunate *adj* **1** UNLUCKY, luckless, hapless, unsuccessful, poor, wretched, unhappy, doomed, ill-fated, hopeless, calamitous, disastrous, ruinous. **2** REGRETTABLE, lamentable, deplorable, adverse, unfavourable, unsuitable, inappropriate, inopportune, untimely, ill-timed.
F3 1 fortunate, happy. **2** favourable, appropriate.

unfounded *adj* baseless, groundless, unsupported, unsubstantiated, unproven, unjustified, idle, false, spurious, trumped-up, fabricated.
F3 substantiated, justified.

unfriendly *adj* unsociable, standoffish, aloof, distant, unapproachable, inhospitable, uncongenial, unneighbourly, unwelcoming, cold, chilly, hostile, aggressive, quarrelsome, inimical, antagonistic, ill-disposed, disagreeable, surly, sour.
F3 friendly, amiable, agreeable.

ungainly *adj* clumsy, awkward, gauche, inelegant, gawky, unco-

ordinated, lumbering, unwieldy.
F3 graceful, elegant.

ungodly adj 1 UNREASONABLE, outrageous, intolerable, unearthly, unsocial. 2 IMPIOUS, irreligious, godless, blasphemous, profane, immoral, corrupt, depraved, sinful, wicked.

ungrateful adj unthankful, unappreciative, ill-mannered, ungracious, selfish, heedless.
F3 grateful, thankful.

unguarded adj 1 in an unguarded moment: unwary, careless, incautious, imprudent, impolitic, indiscreet, undiplomatic, thoughtless, unthinking, heedless, foolish, foolhardy, rash, ill-considered. 2 UNDEFENDED, unprotected, exposed, vulnerable, defenceless.
F3 1 guarded, cautious. 2 defended, protected.

unhappy adj 1 SAD, sorrowful, miserable, melancholy, depressed, dispirited, despondent, dejected, downcast, crestfallen, long-faced, gloomy. 2 UNFORTUNATE, unlucky, ill-fated, unsuitable, inappropriate, inapt, ill-chosen, tactless, awkward, clumsy.
F3 1 happy. 2 fortunate, suitable.

unharmed adj undamaged, unhurt, uninjured, unscathed, whole, intact, safe, sound.
F3 harmed, damaged.

unhealthy adj 1 UNWELL, sick, ill, poorly, ailing, sickly, infirm, invalid, weak, feeble, frail, unsound. 2 UNWHOLESOME, insanitary, unhygienic, harmful, detrimental, morbid, unnatural.
F3 1 healthy, fit. 2 wholesome, hygienic, natural.

unheard-of adj 1 UNTHINKABLE, inconceivable, unimaginable, undreamed-of, unprecedented, acceptable, offensive, shocking, outrageous, preposterous. 2 UNKNOWN, unfamiliar, new, unusual, obscure.
F3 1 normal, acceptable. 2 famous.

unheeded adj ignored, disregarded, disobeyed, unnoticed, unobserved, unremarked, overlooked, neglected, forgotten.
F3 noted, observed.

unhesitating adj immediate, instant, instantaneous, prompt, ready, automatic, spontaneous, unquestioning, unwavering, unfaltering, whole-hearted, implicit.
F3 hesitant, tentative.

unholy adj 1 IMPIOUS, irreligious, sinful, iniquitous, immoral, corrupt, depraved, wicked, evil. 2 (infml) an unholy mess: unreasonable, shocking, outrageous, ungodly, unearthly.
F3 1 holy, pious, godly. 2 reasonable.

unhurried adj slow, leisurely, deliberate, easy, relaxed, calm, easy-going (infml), laid-back (sl).
F3 hurried, hasty, rushed.

unidentified adj unknown, unrecognized, unmarked, unnamed, nameless, anonymous, incognito, unfamiliar, strange, mysterious.
F3 identified, known, named.

uniform n outfit, costume, livery, insignia, regalia, robes, dress, suit. adj same, identical, like, alike, similar, homogeneous, consistent, regular, equal, smooth, even, flat, monotonous, unvarying, unchanging, constant, unbroken.
F3 different, varied, changing.

unify v unite, join, bind, combine, integrate, merge, amalgamate,

consolidate, coalesce, fuse, weld.
F3 separate, divide, split.

unimaginable adj inconceivable,
mind-boggling (infml), unbelievable,
incredible, impossible, fantastic,
undreamed-of, unthinkable, unheard-
of.

unimaginative adj uninspired,
unoriginal, predictable, hackneyed,
banal, ordinary, dull, boring, routine,
matter-of-fact, dry, barren, lifeless,
unexciting, tame.
F3 imaginative, creative, original.

unimportant adj insignificant,
inconsequential, irrelevant,
immaterial, minor, trivial, trifling,
petty, slight, negligible, worthless.
F3 important, significant, relevant,
vital.

unimpressive adj unspectacular,
undistinguished, unexceptional,
unremarkable, uninteresting, dull,
average, commonplace, indifferent,
mediocre.
F3 impressive, memorable, notable.

uninhabited adj unoccupied,
vacant, empty, deserted, abandoned,
unpeopled, unpopulated.

uninhibited adj unconstrained,
unreserved, unselfconscious,
liberated, free, unrestricted,
uncontrolled, unrestrained,
abandoned, natural, spontaneous,
frank, candid, open, relaxed,
informal.
F3 inhibited, repressed, constrained,
restrained.

unintelligible adj
incomprehensible, incoherent,
inarticulate, double Dutch, garbled,
scrambled, jumbled, muddled,
indecipherable, illegible.
F3 intelligible, comprehensible, clear.

unintentional adj unintended,
accidental, fortuitous, inadvertent,
unplanned, unpremeditated,
involuntary, unconscious,
unwitting.
F3 intentional, deliberate.

uninterested adj indifferent,
unconcerned, uninvolved, bored,
listless, apathetic, unenthusiastic,
blasé, impassive, unresponsive.
F3 interested, concerned,
enthusiastic, responsive.

uninteresting adj boring, tedious,
monotonous, humdrum, dull, drab,
dreary, dry, flat, tame, uneventful,
unexciting, uninspiring,
unimpressive.
F3 interesting, exciting.

uninterrupted adj unbroken,
continuous, non-stop, unending,
constant, continual, steady, sustained,
undisturbed, peaceful.
F3 broken, intermittent.

uninvited adj unasked, unsought,
unsolicited, unwanted, unwelcome.
F3 invited.

union n alliance, coalition, league,
association, federation,
confederation, confederacy, merger,
combination, amalgamation, blend,
mixture, synthesis, fusion, unification,
unity.
F3 separation, alienation,
estrangement.

unique adj single, one-off, sole, only,
lone, solitary, unmatched, matchless,
peerless, unequalled, unparalleled,
unrivalled, incomparable, inimitable.
F3 common.

unison n concert, co-operation,
unanimity, unity.

unit n item, part, element,
constituent, piece, component,

module, section, segment, portion, entity, whole, one, system, assembly.

unite v join, link, couple, marry, ally, co-operate, band, associate, federate, confederate, combine, pool, amalgamate, merge, blend, unify, consolidate, coalesce, fuse.
Ⓕ₃ separate, sever.

united adj allied, affiliated, corporate, unified, combined, pooled, collective, concerted, one, unanimous, agreed, in agreement, in accord, like-minded.
Ⓕ₃ disunited.

unity n agreement, accord, concord, harmony, peace, consensus, unanimity, solidarity, integrity, oneness, wholeness, union, unification.
Ⓕ₃ disunity, disagreement, discord, strife.

universal adj worldwide, global, all-embracing, all-inclusive, general, common, across-the-board, total, whole, entire, all-round, unlimited.

unjust adj unfair, inequitable, wrong, partial, biased, prejudiced, one-sided, partisan, unreasonable, unjustified, undeserved.
Ⓕ₃ just, fair, reasonable.

unjustifiable adj indefensible, inexcusable, unforgivable, unreasonable, unwarranted, immoderate, excessive, unacceptable, outrageous.
Ⓕ₃ justifiable, acceptable.

unkempt adj dishevelled, tousled, rumpled, uncombed, ungroomed, untidy, messy, scruffy, shabby, slovenly.
Ⓕ₃ well-groomed, tidy.

unkind adj cruel, inhuman, inhumane, callous, hard-hearted, unfeeling, insensitive, thoughtless, inconsiderate, uncharitable, nasty, malicious, spiteful, mean, malevolent, unfriendly, uncaring, unsympathetic.
Ⓕ₃ kind, considerate.

unknown adj unfamiliar, unheard-of, strange, alien, foreign, mysterious, dark, obscure, hidden, concealed, undisclosed, secret, untold, new, uncharted, unexplored, undiscovered, unidentified, unnamed, nameless, anonymous, incognito.
Ⓕ₃ known, familiar.

unlawful adj illegal, criminal, illicit, illegitimate, unconstitutional, outlawed, banned, prohibited, forbidden, unauthorized.
Ⓕ₃ lawful, legal.

unlikely adj **1** IMPROBABLE, implausible, far-fetched, unconvincing, unbelievable, incredible, unimaginable, unexpected, doubtful, dubious, questionable, suspect, suspicious. **2** SLIGHT, faint, remote, distant.
Ⓕ₃ 1 likely, plausible.

unlimited adj limitless, unrestricted, unbounded, boundless, infinite, endless, countless, incalculable, immeasurable, vast, immense, extensive, great, indefinite, absolute, unconditional, unqualified, all-encompassing, total, complete, full, unconstrained, unhampered.
Ⓕ₃ limited.

unload v unpack, empty, discharge, dump, offload, unburden, relieve.
Ⓕ₃ load.

unlock v unbolt, unlatch, unfasten, undo, open, free, release.
Ⓕ₃ lock, fasten.

unloved adj unpopular, disliked, hated, detested, unwanted, rejected, spurned, loveless, uncared-for, neglected.

F∃ loved.

unlucky *adj* unfortunate, luckless, unhappy, miserable, wretched, ill-fated, ill-starred, jinxed, doomed, cursed, unfavourable, inauspicious, ominous, unsuccessful, disastrous.

F∃ lucky.

unmanageable *adj* **1** UNWIELDY, bulky, cumbersome, awkward, inconvenient, unhandy. **2** UNCONTROLLABLE, wild, unruly, disorderly, difficult.

F∃ 1 manageable. **2** controllable.

unmarried *adj* single, unwed, celibate, unattached, available.

F∃ married.

unmask *v* unveil, uncloak, uncover, bare, expose, reveal, show, disclose, discover, detect.

F∃ mask, conceal.

unmentionable *adj* unspeakable, unutterable, taboo, immodest, indecent, shocking, scandalous, shameful, disgraceful, abominable.

unmistakable *adj* clear, plain, distinct, pronounced, obvious, evident, manifest, patent, glaring, explicit, unambiguous, unequivocal, positive, definite, sure, certain, unquestionable, indisputable, undeniable.

F∃ unclear, ambiguous.

unmoved *adj* unaffected, untouched, unshaken, dry-eyed, unfeeling, cold, dispassionate, indifferent, impassive, unresponsive, unimpressed, firm, adamant, inflexible, unbending, undeviating, unwavering, steady, unchanged, resolute, resolved, determined.

F∃ moved, affected, shaken.

unnatural *adj* **1** ABNORMAL, anomalous, freakish, irregular, unusual, strange, odd, peculiar, queer, bizarre, extraordinary, uncanny, supernatural, inhuman, perverted. **2** AFFECTED, feigned, artificial, false, insincere, unspontaneous, contrived, laboured, stilted, forced, strained, self-conscious, stiff.

F∃ 1 natural, normal. **2** sincere, fluent.

unnecessary *adj* unneeded, needless, uncalled-for, unwanted, non-essential, dispensable, expendable, superfluous, redundant, tautological.

F∃ necessary, essential, indispensable.

unnerve *v* daunt, intimidate, frighten, scare, discourage, demoralize, dismay, disconcert, upset, worry, shake, rattle (*infml*), confound, fluster.

F∃ nerve, brace, steel.

unnoticed *adj* unobserved, unremarked, unseen, unrecognized, undiscovered, overlooked, ignored, disregarded, neglected, unheeded.

F∃ noticed, noted.

unobtrusive *adj* inconspicuous, unnoticeable, unassertive, self-effacing, humble, modest, unostentatious, unpretentious, restrained, low-key, subdued, quiet, retiring.

F∃ obtrusive, ostentatious.

unoccupied *adj* uninhabited, vacant, empty, free, idle, inactive, workless, jobless, unemployed.

F∃ occupied, busy.

unofficial *adj* unauthorized, illegal, informal, off-the-record, personal, private, confidential,

undeclared, unconfirmed.
E3 official.

unorthodox adj unconventional, nonconformist, heterodox, alternative, fringe, irregular, abnormal, unusual.
E3 orthodox, conventional.

unpaid adj **1** unpaid bills: outstanding, overdue, unsettled, owing, due, payable. **2** unpaid work: voluntary, honorary, unsalaried, unwaged, unremunerative, free.
E3 1 paid.

unpalatable adj **1** UNAPPETIZING, distasteful, insipid, bitter, uneatable, inedible. **2** UNPLEASANT, disagreeable, unattractive, offensive, repugnant.
E3 1 palatable. **2** pleasant.

unparalleled adj unequalled, unmatched, matchless, peerless, incomparable, unrivalled, unsurpassed, supreme, superlative, rare, exceptional, unprecedented.

unpleasant adj disagreeable, ill-natured, nasty, objectionable, offensive, distasteful, unpalatable, unattractive, repulsive, bad, troublesome.
E3 pleasant, agreeable, nice.

unpopular adj disliked, hated, detested, unloved, unsought-after, unfashionable, undesirable, unwelcome, unwanted, rejected, shunned, avoided, neglected.
E3 popular, fashionable.

unprecedented adj new, original, revolutionary, unknown, unheard-of, exceptional, remarkable, extraordinary, abnormal, unusual, freakish, unparalleled, unrivalled.
E3 usual.

unpredictable adj unforeseeable,

unexpected, changeable, variable, inconstant, unreliable, fickle, unstable, erratic, random, chance.
E3 predictable, foreseeable, constant.

unprepared adj unready, surprised, unsuspecting, ill-equipped, unfinished, incomplete, half-baked, unplanned, unrehearsed, spontaneous, improvised, ad-lib, off-the-cuff.
E3 prepared, ready.

unpretentious adj unaffected, natural, plain, simple, unobtrusive, honest, straightforward, humble, modest, unassuming, unostentatious.
E3 pretentious.

unproductive adj infertile, sterile, barren, dry, arid, unfruitful, fruitless, futile, vain, idle, useless, ineffective, unprofitable, unremunerative, unrewarding.
E3 productive, fertile.

unprofessional adj amateurish, inexpert, unskilled, sloppy, incompetent, inefficient, casual, negligent, lax, unethical, unprincipled, improper, unseemly, unacceptable, inadmissible.
E3 professional, skilful.

unprotected adj unguarded, unattended, undefended, unfortified, unarmed, unshielded, unsheltered, uncovered, exposed, open, naked, vulnerable, defenceless, helpless.
E3 protected, safe, immune.

unqualified adj **1** UNTRAINED, inexperienced, amateur, ineligible, unfit, incompetent, incapable, unprepared, ill-equipped.
2 ABSOLUTE, categorical, utter, total, complete, thorough, consummate, downright, unmitigated, unreserved, whole-hearted, outright,

unconditional, unrestricted.
⊟ 1 qualified, professional.
2 conditional, tentative.

unravel *v* unwind, undo, untangle, disentangle, free, extricate, separate, resolve, sort out, solve, work out, figure out, puzzle out, penetrate, interpret, explain.
⊟ tangle, complicate.

unreal *adj* false, artificial, synthetic, mock, fake, sham, imaginary, visionary, fanciful, make-believe, pretend (*infml*), fictitious, made-up, fairy-tale, legendary, mythical, fantastic, illusory, immaterial, insubstantial, hypothetical.
⊟ real, genuine.

unrealistic *adj* impractical, idealistic, romantic, quixotic, impracticable, unworkable, unreasonable, impossible.
⊟ realistic, pragmatic.

unreasonable *adj* **1** UNFAIR, unjust, biased, unjustifiable, unjustified, unwarranted, undue, uncalled-for.
2 IRRATIONAL, illogical, inconsistent, arbitrary, absurd, nonsensical, far-fetched, preposterous, mad, senseless, silly, foolish, stupid, headstrong, opinionated, perverse.
3 *unreasonable prices*: excessive, immoderate, extravagant, exorbitant, extortionate.
⊟ 1 reasonable, fair. **2** rational, sensible. **3** moderate.

unrecognizable *adj* unidentifiable, disguised, incognito, changed, altered.

unrefined *adj* raw, untreated, unprocessed, unfinished, unpolished, crude, coarse, vulgar, unsophisticated, uncultivated, uncultured.
⊟ refined, finished.

unrelated *adj* unconnected, unassociated, irrelevant, extraneous, different, dissimilar, unlike, disparate, distinct, separate, independent.
⊟ related, similar.

unrelenting *adj* relentless, unremitting, uncompromising, inexorable, incessant, unceasing, ceaseless, endless, unbroken, continuous, constant, continual, perpetual, steady, unabated, remorseless, unmerciful, merciless, pitiless, unsparing.
⊟ spasmodic, intermittent.

unreliable *adj* unsound, fallible, deceptive, false, mistaken, erroneous, inaccurate, unconvincing, implausible, uncertain, untrustworthy, unstable, fickle, irresponsible.
⊟ reliable, dependable, trustworthy.

unrepentant *adj* impenitent, unapologetic, unabashed, unashamed, shameless, incorrigible, confirmed, hardened, obdurate.
⊟ repentant, penitent, ashamed.

unrest *n* protest, rebellion, turmoil, agitation, restlessness, dissatisfaction, dissension, disaffection, worry.
⊟ peace, calm.

unrestricted *adj* unlimited, unbounded, unopposed, unhindered, unimpeded, unobstructed, clear, free, open, public, unconditional, absolute.
⊟ restricted, limited.

unripe *adj* unripened, green, immature, undeveloped, unready.
⊟ ripe, mature.

unrivalled *adj* unequalled, unparalleled, unmatched, matchless, peerless, incomparable, inimitable, unsurpassed, supreme, superlative.

unruffled *adj* undisturbed, untroubled, imperturbable, collected,

composed, cool, calm, tranquil, serene, peaceful, smooth, level, even.
F3 troubled, anxious.

unruly adj uncontrollable, unmanageable, ungovernable, intractable, disorderly, wild, rowdy, riotous, rebellious, mutinous, lawless, insubordinate, disobedient, wayward, wilful, headstrong, obstreperous.
F3 manageable, orderly.

unsafe adj dangerous, perilous, risky, hazardous, treacherous, unreliable, uncertain, unsound, unstable, precarious, insecure, vulnerable, exposed.
F3 safe, secure.

unsatisfactory adj unacceptable, imperfect, defective, faulty, inferior, poor, weak, inadequate, insufficient, deficient, unsuitable, displeasing, dissatisfying, unsatisfying, frustrating, disappointing.
F3 satisfactory, pleasing.

unscathed adj unhurt, uninjured, unharmed, undamaged, untouched, whole, intact, safe, sound.
F3 hurt, injured.

unscrupulous adj unprincipled, ruthless, shameless, dishonourable, dishonest, crooked (infml), corrupt, immoral, unethical, improper.
F3 scrupulous, ethical, proper.

unseemly adj improper, indelicate, indecorous, unbecoming, undignified, unrefined, disreputable, discreditable, undue, inappropriate, unsuitable.
F3 seemly, decorous.

unseen adj unnoticed, unobserved, undetected, invisible, hidden, concealed, veiled, obscure.
F3 visible.

unselfish adj selfless, altruistic, self-

denying, self-sacrificing, disinterested, noble, magnanimous, generous, liberal, charitable, philanthropic, public-spirited, humanitarian, kind.
F3 selfish.

unsentimental adj realistic, practical, pragmatic, hard-headed, tough, unromantic, level-headed.
F3 sentimental, idealistic.

unsettle v disturb, upset, trouble, bother, discompose, ruffle, fluster, unbalance, shake, agitate, rattle (infml), disconcert, confuse, throw.

unsettled adj **1** DISTURBED, upset, troubled, agitated, anxious, uneasy, tense, edgy, flustered, shaken, unnerved, disoriented, confused. **2** UNRESOLVED, undetermined, undecided, open, uncertain, doubtful. **3** unsettled weather: changeable, variable, unpredictable, inconstant, unstable, insecure, unsteady, shaky. **4** UNPAID, outstanding, owing, payable, overdue.
F3 1 composed. **2** certain. **3** settled. **4** paid.

unshakable adj firm, well-founded, fixed, stable, immovable, unassailable, unwavering, constant, steadfast, staunch, sure, resolute, determined.
F3 insecure.

unsightly adj ugly, unattractive, unprepossessing, hideous, repulsive, repugnant, off-putting, unpleasant, disagreeable.
F3 attractive.

unskilled adj untrained, unqualified, inexperienced, unpractised, inexpert, unprofessional, amateurish, incompetent.
F3 skilled.

unsociable *adj* unfriendly, aloof, distant, standoffish, withdrawn, introverted, reclusive, retiring, reserved, taciturn, unforthcoming, uncommunicative, cold, chilly, uncongenial, unneighbourly, inhospitable, hostile.
F3 sociable, friendly.

unsolicited *adj* unrequested, unsought, uninvited, unasked, unwanted, unwelcome, uncalled-for, gratuitous, voluntary, spontaneous.
F3 requested, invited.

unsophisticated *adj* artless, guileless, innocent, ingenuous, naive, inexperienced, unworldly, childlike, natural, unaffected, unpretentious, unrefined, plain, simple, straightforward, uncomplicated, uninvolved.
F3 sophisticated, worldly, complex.

unsound *adj* **1** *unsound reasoning*: faulty, flawed, defective, ill-founded, fallacious, false, erroneous, invalid, illogical. **2** UNHEALTHY, unwell, ill, diseased, weak, frail, unbalanced, deranged, unhinged. **3** UNSTABLE, unsteady, wobbly, shaky, insecure, unsafe.
F3 1 sound. **2** well. **3** stable.

unspeakable *adj* unutterable, inexpressible, indescribable, awful, dreadful, frightful, terrible, horrible, shocking, appalling, monstrous, inconceivable, unbelievable.

unspoilt *adj* preserved, unchanged, untouched, natural, unaffected, unsophisticated, unharmed, undamaged, unimpaired, unblemished, perfect.
F3 spoilt, affected.

unspoken *adj* unstated, undeclared, unuttered, unexpressed, unsaid,

voiceless, wordless, silent, tacit, implicit, implied, inferred, understood, assumed.
F3 stated, explicit.

unstable *adj* **1** CHANGEABLE, variable, fluctuating, vacillating, wavering, fitful, erratic, inconsistent, volatile, capricious, inconstant, unpredictable, unreliable, untrustworthy. **2** UNSTEADY, wobbly, shaky, rickety, insecure, unsafe, risky, precarious, tottering, unbalanced.
F3 1 stable. **2** steady.

unsteady *adj* unstable, wobbly, shaky, rickety, insecure, unsafe, treacherous, precarious, tottering, unreliable, inconstant, irregular, flickering.
F3 steady, firm.

unsuccessful *adj* failed, abortive, vain, futile, useless, ineffective, unavailing, fruitless, unproductive, sterile, luckless, unlucky, unfortunate, losing, beaten, defeated, frustrated, thwarted.
F3 successful, effective, fortunate, winning.

unsuitable *adj* inappropriate, inapt, unsuited, unfit, unacceptable, improper, unseemly, unbecoming, incompatible, incongruous.
F3 suitable, appropriate.

unsung *adj* unhonoured, unpraised, unacknowledged, unrecognized, overlooked, disregarded, neglected, forgotten, unknown, obscure.
F3 honoured, famous, renowned.

unsure *adj* uncertain, doubtful, dubious, suspicious, sceptical, unconvinced, unpersuaded, undecided, hesitant, tentative.
F3 sure, certain, confident.

unsurpassed *adj* surpassing,

supreme, transcendent, unbeaten, unexcelled, unequalled, unparalleled, unrivalled, incomparable, matchless, superlative, exceptional.

unsuspecting adj unwary, unaware, unconscious, trusting, trustful, unsuspicious, credulous, gullible, ingenuous, naive, innocent.
F3 suspicious, knowing.

unsympathetic adj unpitying, unconcerned, unmoved, unresponsive, indifferent, insensitive, unfeeling, cold, heartless, soulless, hard-hearted, callous, cruel, inhuman, unkind, hard, stony, hostile, antagonistic.
F3 sympathetic, compassionate.

untangle v disentangle, extricate, unravel, undo, resolve, solve.
F3 tangle, complicate.

unthinkable adj inconceivable, unimaginable, unheard-of, unbelievable, incredible, impossible, improbable, unlikely, implausible, unreasonable, illogical, absurd, preposterous, outrageous, shocking.

unthinking adj thoughtless, inconsiderate, insensitive, tactless, indiscreet, rude, heedless, careless, negligent, rash, impulsive, instinctive, unconscious, automatic, mechanical.
F3 considerate, conscious.

untidy adj messy, cluttered, disorderly, muddled, jumbled, unsystematic, chaotic, topsy-turvy, scruffy, dishevelled, unkempt, slovenly, sloppy, slipshod.
F3 tidy, neat.

untie v undo, unfasten, unknot, unbind, free, release, loose, loosen.
F3 tie, fasten.

untimely adj early, premature, unseasonable, ill-timed, inopportune,

inconvenient, awkward, unsuitable, inappropriate, unfortunate, inauspicious.
F3 timely, opportune.

untiring adj unflagging, tireless, indefatigable, dogged, persevering, persistent, tenacious, determined, resolute, devoted, dedicated, constant, incessant, unremitting, steady, staunch, unfailing.
F3 inconstant, wavering.

untold adj uncounted, unnumbered, unreckoned, incalculable, innumerable, uncountable, countless, infinite, measureless, boundless, inexhaustible, undreamed-of, unimaginable.

untouched adj unharmed, undamaged, unimpaired, unhurt, uninjured, unscathed, safe, intact, unchanged, unaltered, unaffected.
F3 damaged, affected.

untrained adj unskilled, untaught, unschooled, uneducated, inexperienced, unqualified, amateur, unprofessional, inexpert.
F3 trained, expert.

untried adj untested, unproved, experimental, exploratory, new, novel, innovative, innovatory.
F3 tried, tested, proven.

untrue adj 1 FALSE, fallacious, deceptive, misleading, wrong, incorrect, inaccurate, mistaken, erroneous. 2 UNFAITHFUL, disloyal, untrustworthy, dishonest, deceitful, untruthful.
F3 1 true, correct. 2 faithful, honest.

untrustworthy adj dishonest, deceitful, untruthful, disloyal, unfaithful, faithless, treacherous, false, untrue, capricious, fickle, fly-by-night, unreliable, untrusty.

E3 trustworthy, reliable.

untruth n lie, fib, whopper (infml), porkie (infml), story, tale, fiction, invention, fabrication, falsehood, lying, untruthfulness, deceit, perjury.
E3 truth.

untruthful adj lying, deceitful, dishonest, crooked (infml), hypocritical, two-faced, insincere, false, untrue.
E3 truthful, honest.

unused adj leftover, remaining, surplus, extra, spare, available, new, fresh, blank, clean, untouched, unexploited, unemployed, idle.
E3 used.

unusual adj uncommon, rare, unfamiliar, strange, odd, curious, queer, bizarre, unconventional, irregular, abnormal, extraordinary, remarkable, exceptional, different, surprising, unexpected.
E3 usual, normal, ordinary.

unveil v uncover, expose, bare, reveal, disclose, divulge, discover.
E3 cover, hide.

unwanted adj undesired, unsolicited, uninvited, unwelcome, outcast, rejected, unrequired, unneeded, unnecessary, surplus, extra, superfluous, redundant.
E3 wanted, needed, necessary.

unwarranted adj unjustified, undeserved, unprovoked, uncalled-for, groundless, unreasonable, unjust, wrong.
E3 warranted, justifiable, deserved.

unwary adj unguarded, incautious, careless, imprudent, indiscreet, thoughtless, unthinking, heedless, reckless, rash, hasty.
E3 wary, cautious.

unwelcome adj 1 UNWANTED,

undesirable, unpopular, uninvited, excluded, rejected. **2** unwelcome news: unpleasant, disagreeable, upsetting, worrying, distasteful, unpalatable, unacceptable.
E3 1 welcome, desirable. **2** pleasant.

unwell adj ill, sick, poorly, indisposed, off-colour, ailing, sickly, unhealthy.
E3 well, healthy.

unwieldy adj unmanageable, inconvenient, awkward, clumsy, ungainly, bulky, massive, hefty, weighty, ponderous, cumbersome.
E3 handy, dainty.

unwilling adj reluctant, disinclined, indisposed, resistant, opposed, averse, loath, slow, unenthusiastic, grudging.
E3 willing, enthusiastic.

unwind v 1 UNROLL, unreel, unwrap, undo, uncoil, untwist, unravel, disentangle. **2** (infml) RELAX, wind down, calm down, chill out (infml).
E3 1 wind, roll.

unwitting adj unaware, unknowing, unsuspecting, unthinking, unconscious, involuntary, accidental, chance, inadvertent, unintentional, unintended, unplanned.
E3 knowing, conscious, deliberate.

unworldly adj spiritual, transcendental, metaphysical, otherworldly, visionary, idealistic, impractical, unsophisticated, inexperienced, innocent, naive.
E3 worldly, materialistic, sophisticated.

unworthy adj undeserving, inferior, ineligible, unsuitable, inappropriate, unfitting, unbecoming, unseemly, improper, unprofessional, shameful, disgraceful, dishonourable, discreditable, ignoble, base, contemptible, despicable.

F3 worthy, commendable.

unwritten adj verbal, oral, word-of-mouth, unrecorded, tacit, implicit, understood, accepted, recognized, traditional, customary, conventional.

F3 written, recorded.

upbraid v reprimand, admonish, rebuke, reprove, reproach, scold, chide, castigate, berate, criticize, censure.

F3 praise, commend.

upbringing n bringing-up, raising, rearing, breeding, parenting, care, nurture, cultivation, education, training, instruction, teaching.

update v modernize, revise, amend, correct, renew, renovate, revamp.

upgrade v promote, advance, elevate, raise, improve, enhance.

F3 downgrade, demote.

upheaval n disruption, disturbance, upset, chaos, confusion, disorder, turmoil, shake-up (infml), revolution, overthrow.

uphill adj hard, difficult, arduous, tough, taxing, strenuous, laborious, tiring, wearisome, exhausting, gruelling, punishing.

F3 easy.

uphold v support, maintain, hold to, stand by, defend, champion, advocate, promote, back, endorse, sustain, fortify, strengthen, justify, vindicate.

F3 abandon, reject.

upkeep n maintenance, preservation, conservation, care, running, repair, support, sustenance, subsistence, keep.

F3 neglect.

upper adj higher, loftier, superior, senior, top, topmost, uppermost, high,

elevated, exalted, eminent, important.

F3 lower, inferior, junior.

uppermost adj highest, loftiest, top, topmost, greatest, supreme, first, primary, foremost, leading, principal, main, chief, dominant, predominant, paramount, pre-eminent.

F3 lowest.

upright adj 1 VERTICAL, perpendicular, erect, straight. 2 RIGHTEOUS, good, virtuous, upstanding, noble, honourable, ethical, principled, incorruptible, honest, trustworthy.

F3 1 horizontal, flat. 2 dishonest.

uprising n rebellion, revolt, mutiny, rising, insurgence, insurrection, revolution.

uproar n noise, din, racket, hubbub, hullabaloo, pandemonium, tumult, turmoil, turbulence, commotion, confusion, disorder, clamour, outcry, furore, riot, rumpus.

uproot v pull up, rip up, root out, weed out, remove, displace, eradicate, destroy, wipe out.

upset v 1 DISTRESS, grieve, dismay, trouble, worry, agitate, disturb, bother, fluster, ruffle, discompose, shake, unnerve, disconcert, confuse, disorganize. 2 TIP, spill, overturn, capsize, topple, overthrow, destabilize, unsteady.

n 1 TROUBLE, worry, agitation, disturbance, bother, disruption, upheaval, shake-up (infml), reverse, surprise, shock. 2 stomach upset: disorder, complaint, bug (infml), illness, sickness.

adj distressed, grieved, hurt, annoyed, dismayed, troubled, worried, agitated, disturbed, bothered, shaken, disconcerted, confused.

upshot *n* result, consequence, outcome, issue, end, conclusion, finish, culmination.

upside down inverted, upturned, wrong way up, upset, overturned, disordered, muddled, jumbled, confused, topsy-turvy, chaotic.

up-to-date *adj* current, contemporary, modern, fashionable, trendy (*infml*), latest, recent, new.
F3 out-of-date, old-fashioned.

upturn *n* revival, recovery, upsurge, upswing, rise, increase, boost, improvement.
F3 downturn, drop.

urban *adj* town, city, inner-city, metropolitan, municipal, civic, built-up.
F3 country, rural.

urge *v* advise, counsel, recommend, advocate, encourage, exhort, implore, beg, beseech, entreat, plead, press, constrain, compel, force, push, drive, impel, goad, spur, hasten, induce, incite, instigate.
F3 discourage, dissuade, deter, hinder.
n desire, wish, inclination, fancy, longing, yearning, itch, impulse, compulsion, impetus, drive, eagerness.
F3 disinclination.

urgency *n* hurry, haste, pressure, stress, importance, seriousness, gravity, imperativeness, need, necessity.

urgent *adj* immediate, instant, top-priority, important, critical, crucial, imperative, exigent, pressing, compelling, persuasive, earnest, eager, insistent, persistent.
F3 unimportant.

usable *adj* working, operational, serviceable, functional, practical,
exploitable, available, current, valid.
F3 unusable, useless.

usage *n* **1** TREATMENT, handling, management, control, running, operation, employment, application, use. **2** TRADITION, custom, practice, habit, convention, etiquette, rule, regulation, form, routine, procedure, method.

use *v* utilize, employ, exercise, practise, operate, work, apply, wield, handle, treat, manipulate, exploit, enjoy, consume, exhaust, expend, spend.
n utility, usefulness, value, worth, profit, advantage, benefit, good, avail, help, service, point, object, end, purpose, reason, cause, occasion, need, necessity, usage, application, employment, operation, exercise.

use up finish, exhaust, drain, sap, deplete, consume, devour, absorb, waste, squander, fritter.

used *adj* second-hand, cast-off, hand-me-down, nearly new, worn, dog-eared, soiled.
F3 unused, new, fresh.

useful *adj* handy, convenient, all-purpose, practical, effective, productive, fruitful, profitable, valuable, worthwhile, advantageous, beneficial, helpful.
F3 useless, ineffective, worthless.

useless *adj* futile, fruitless, unproductive, vain, idle, unavailing, hopeless, pointless, worthless, unusable, broken-down, clapped-out (*sl*), unworkable, impractical, ineffective, inefficient, incompetent, weak.
F3 useful, helpful, effective.

usher *n* usherette, doorkeeper, attendant, escort, guide.

v escort, accompany, conduct, lead, direct, guide, show, pilot, steer.

usual *adj* normal, typical, stock, standard, regular, routine, habitual, customary, conventional, accepted, recognized, accustomed, familiar, common, everyday, general, ordinary, unexceptional, expected, predictable. ⊟ unusual, strange, rare.

usually *adv* normally, generally, as a rule, ordinarily, typically, traditionally, regularly, commonly, by and large, on the whole, mainly, chiefly, mostly. ⊟ exceptionally.

usurp *v* take over, assume, arrogate, seize, take, annex, appropriate, commandeer, steal.

utensil *n* tool, implement, instrument, device, contrivance, gadget, apparatus, appliance.

utility *n* usefulness, use, value, profit, advantage, benefit, avail, service, convenience, practicality, efficacy, efficiency, fitness, serviceableness.

utmost *adj* **1** *with the utmost care:* extreme, maximum, greatest, highest, supreme, paramount. **2** FARTHEST, furthermost, remotest, outermost, ultimate, final, last.
n best, hardest, most, maximum.

utter[1] *adj* absolute, complete, total, entire, thoroughgoing, out-and-out, downright, sheer, stark, arrant, unmitigated, unqualified, perfect, consummate.

utter[2] *v* speak, say, voice, vocalize, verbalize, express, articulate, enunciate, sound, pronounce, deliver, state, declare, announce, proclaim, tell, reveal, divulge.

utterance *n* statement, remark, comment, expression, articulation, delivery, speech, declaration, announcement, proclamation, pronouncement.

utterly *adv* absolutely, completely, totally, fully, entirely, wholly, thoroughly, downright, perfectly.

U-turn *n* about-turn, volte-face, reversal, backtrack.

V

vacancy _n_ opportunity, opening, position, post, job, place, room, situation.

vacant _adj_ **1** EMPTY, unoccupied, unfilled, free, available, void, not in use, unused, uninhabited. **2** BLANK, expressionless, vacuous, inane, inattentive, absent, absent-minded, unthinking, dreamy.
F3 1 occupied, engaged.

vacate _v_ leave, depart, evacuate, abandon, withdraw, quit.

vacuum _n_ emptiness, void, nothingness, vacuity, space, chasm, gap.

vague _adj_ **1** ILL-DEFINED, blurred, indistinct, hazy, dim, shadowy, misty, fuzzy, nebulous, obscure.
2 INDEFINITE, imprecise, unclear, uncertain, undefined, undetermined, unspecific, generalized, inexact, ambiguous, evasive, loose, woolly.
F3 1 clear. **2** definite.

vain _adj_ **1** _a vain attempt_: useless, worthless, futile, abortive, fruitless, pointless, unproductive, unprofitable, unavailing, hollow, groundless, empty, trivial, unimportant.
2 CONCEITED, proud, self-satisfied, arrogant, self-important, egotistical, bigheaded (_infml_), swollen-headed (_infml_), stuck-up (_infml_), affected, pretentious, ostentatious, swaggering.

F3 1 fruitful, successful. **2** modest, self-effacing.

valiant _adj_ brave, courageous, gallant, fearless, intrepid, bold, dauntless, heroic, plucky, indomitable, staunch.
F3 cowardly, fearful.

valid _adj_ **1** LOGICAL, well-founded, well-grounded, sound, good, cogent, convincing, telling, conclusive, reliable, genuine, binding, proper. powerful, just. **2** OFFICIAL, legal, lawful, legitimate, authentic, bona fide, genuine, binding, proper.
F3 1 false, weak. **2** unofficial, invalid.

valley _n_ dale, vale, dell, glen, hollow, cwm, depression, gulch.

valuable _adj_ **1** _valuable necklace_: precious, prized, valued, costly, expensive, dear, high-priced, treasured, cherished, estimable.
2 _valuable suggestions_: helpful, worthwhile, useful, beneficial, invaluable, constructive, fruitful, profitable, important, serviceable, worthy, handy.
F3 1 worthless. **2** useless.

value _n_ **1** COST, price, rate, worth.
2 WORTH, use, usefulness, utility, merit, importance, desirability, benefit, advantage, significance, good, profit.
_v_ **1** PRIZE, appreciate, treasure, esteem,

hold dear, respect, cherish.
2 EVALUATE, assess, estimate, price, appraise, survey, rate.
F3 1 disregard, neglect, undervalue.

vanish v disappear, fade, dissolve, evaporate, disperse, melt, die out, depart, exit, fizzle out, peter out.
F3 appear, materialize.

vanity n 1 CONCEIT, conceitedness, pride, arrogance, self-conceit, self-love, self-satisfaction, narcissism, egotism, pretension, ostentation, affectation, airs, bigheadedness (*infml*), swollen-headedness (*infml*).
2 WORTHLESSNESS, uselessness, emptiness, futility, pointlessness, unreality, hollowness, fruitlessness, triviality.
F3 1 modesty. **2** worth.

vapour n steam, mist, fog, smoke, breath, fumes, haze, damp, dampness, exhalation.

variable adj changeable, inconstant, varying, shifting, mutable, unpredictable, fluctuating, fitful, unstable, unsteady, wavering, vacillating, temperamental, fickle, flexible.
F3 fixed, invariable, stable.

variance n 1 VARIATION, difference, discrepancy, divergence, inconsistency, disagreement.
2 DISAGREEMENT, disharmony, conflict, discord, division, dissent, dissension, quarrelling, strife.
F3 1 agreement. **2** harmony.

variation n diversity, variety, deviation, discrepancy, diversification, alteration, change, difference, departure, modification, modulation, inflection, novelty, innovation.
F3 monotony, uniformity.

varied adj assorted, diverse, miscellaneous, mixed, various, sundry, heterogeneous (*fml*), different, wide-ranging.
F3 standardized, uniform.

variegated adj multicoloured, many-coloured, parti-coloured, varicoloured, speckled, mottled, dappled, pied, streaked, motley.
F3 monochrome, plain.

variety n 1 ASSORTMENT, miscellany, mixture, collection, medley, pot-pourri, range. **2** DIFFERENCE, diversity, dissimilarity, discrepancy, variation, multiplicity. **3** SORT, kind, class, category, species, type, breed, brand, make, strain.
F3 2 uniformity, similitude.

various adj different, differing, diverse, varied, varying, assorted, miscellaneous, heterogeneous (*fml*), distinct, diversified, mixed, many, several.

varnish n lacquer, glaze, resin, polish, gloss, coating.

vary v 1 CHANGE, alter, modify, modulate, diversify, reorder, transform, alternate, inflect, permutate. **2** DIVERGE, differ, disagree, depart, fluctuate.

vast adj huge, immense, massive, gigantic, enormous, great, colossal, extensive, tremendous, sweeping, unlimited, fathomless, immeasurable, never-ending, monumental, monstrous, far-flung.

vault[1] v leap, spring, bound, clear, jump, hurdle, leap-frog.

vault[2] n 1 CELLAR, crypt, strongroom, repository, cavern, depository, wine-cellar, tomb, mausoleum. **2** ARCH, roof, span, concave.

veer *v* swerve, swing, change, shift, diverge, deviate, wheel, turn, sheer, tack.

vegetable

> **Vegetables include:**
> artichoke, aubergine, bean, beetroot, bok choy, broad bean, broccoli, Brussels sprout, butter-bean, cabbage, calabrese, capsicum, carrot, cassava, manioc, cauliflower, celeriac, celery, chicory, courgette, cress, cucumber, egg-plant (*N Am*), endive, fennel, French bean, garlic, Jerusalem artichoke, kale, kohlrabi, leek, lentil, lettuce, mangetout, marrow, mung bean, mushroom, okra, onion, parsnip, pea, pepper, petits pois, potato, pumpkin, radish, runner-bean, shallot, soya bean, spinach, spring onion, squash, swede, sweetcorn, sweet potato, turnip, watercress, yam, zucchini (*N Am & Aust*). see also **mushroom**.

> **Vegetable dishes include:**
> bhaji, onion bhaji, bubble and squeak, cauliflower cheese, champ, chillada, colcannon, coleslaw, couscous, crudités, dal, dolma, felafel, gado-gado, gnocchi, guacamole, hummus, latke, macaroni cheese, macédoine, mushy peas, nut cutlet, pease-pudding, pilau, polenta, ratatouille, raita, rösti, salad, salade niçoise, Waldorf salad, sauerkraut, stuffed marrow, stuffed mushroom, succotash, tabbouleh, tzatziki, vegetable chilli, vegetable curry, vegetarian goulash.

vegetate *v* stagnate, degenerate, deteriorate, rusticate, go to seed, idle, rust, languish.

vehement *adj* impassioned, passionate, ardent, fervent, intense, forceful, emphatic, heated, strong, powerful, urgent, enthusiastic, animated, eager, earnest, forcible, fierce, violent, zealous.
E3 apathetic, indifferent.

vehicle *n* **1** CONVEYANCE, transport. **2** MEANS, agency, channel, medium, mechanism, organ.

> **Vehicles include:**
> plane, boat, ship, car, taxi, cab, hackney carriage, bicycle, bike (*infml*), tandem, tricycle, penny-farthing, motorcycle, motorbike, scooter, quad bike, bus, omnibus, minibus, double-decker (*infml*), coach, charabanc, caravan, caravanette, camper, train, sleeper, tube, tram, monorail, trolleybus, van, Transit®, lorry, truck, juggernaut, pantechnicon, trailer, tractor, tank, wagon; bobsleigh, sled, sledge, sleigh, toboggan, troika; barouche, brougham, dogcart, dray, four-in-hand, gig, hansom, landau, phaeton, post chaise, stagecoach, sulky, surrey, trap; rickshaw, sedan chair, litter. see also **aircraft**; **boat**; **car**.

veil *v* screen, cloak, cover, mask, shadow, shield, obscure, conceal, hide, disguise, shade.
E3 expose, uncover.
n cover, cloak, curtain, mask, screen, disguise, film, blind, shade, shroud.

vein *n* **1** STREAK, stripe, stratum, seam, lode, blood vessel. **2** MOOD, tendency, bent, strain, temper, tenor, tone, frame of mind, mode, style.

Veins and arteries include:
aorta, axillary, brachial, carotid, femoral, frontal, gastric, hepatic, iliac, jugular, portal, pulmonary, radial, renal, saphena, subclavian, superior, temporal, tibial.

vendetta n feud, blood-feud, enmity, rivalry, quarrel, bad blood, bitterness.

veneer n front, façade, appearance, coating, surface, show, mask, gloss, pretence, guise, finish.

venerable adj respected, revered, esteemed, honoured, venerated, dignified, grave, wise, august, aged, worshipped.

venerate v revere, respect, honour, esteem, worship, hallow (fml), adore.
F3 despise, anathematize.

vengeance n retribution, revenge, retaliation, reprisal, requital, tit for tat.
F3 forgiveness.

venom n 1 POISON, toxin.
2 RANCOUR, ill-will, malice, malevolence, spite, bitterness, acrimony, hate, virulence.

venomous adj 1 POISONOUS, toxic, virulent, harmful, noxious.
2 MALICIOUS, spiteful, vicious, vindictive, baleful, hostile, malignant, rancorous, baneful.
F3 1 harmless.

vent n opening, hole, aperture, outlet, passage, orifice, duct.
v air, express, voice, utter, release, discharge, emit.

ventilate v 1 ventilate a room: air, aerate, freshen. 2 ventilate one's feelings: air, broadcast, debate, discuss.

venture v 1 DARE, advance, make bold, put forward, presume, suggest, volunteer. 2 RISK, hazard, endanger, imperil, jeopardize, speculate, wager, stake.

n risk, chance, hazard, speculation, gamble, undertaking, project, adventure, endeavour, enterprise, operation, fling.

verbal adj spoken, oral, verbatim, unwritten, word-of-mouth.

verbatim adv word for word, exactly, literally, to the letter, precisely.

verbose adj long-winded, wordy, prolix, loquacious, diffuse, circumlocutory.
F3 succinct, brief.

verdict n decision, judgement, conclusion, finding, adjudication, assessment, opinion, sentence.

verge n border, edge, margin, limit, rim, brim, brink, boundary, threshold, extreme, edging.

verge on approach, border on, come close to, near.

verify v confirm, corroborate, substantiate, authenticate, bear out, prove, support, validate, testify, attest.
F3 invalidate, discredit.

vernacular adj indigenous, local, native, popular, vulgar, informal, colloquial, common.
n language, speech, tongue, parlance, dialect, idiom, jargon.

versatile adj adaptable, flexible, all-round, multipurpose, multifaceted, adjustable, many-sided, general-purpose, functional, resourceful, handy, variable.
F3 inflexible.

verse n poetry, rhyme, stanza, metre, doggerel, jingle.

versed adj skilled, proficient, practised, experienced, familiar, acquainted, learned, knowledgeable, conversant, seasoned, qualified, competent, accomplished.

version n 1 RENDERING, reading, interpretation, account, translation, paraphrase, adaptation, portrayal. 2 TYPE, kind, variant, form, model, style, design.

vertical adj upright, perpendicular, upstanding, erect, on end.
E3 horizontal.

vertigo n dizziness, giddiness, light-headedness.

verve n vitality, vivacity, animation, energy, dash, élan, liveliness, sparkle, vigour, enthusiasm, gusto, life, relish, spirit, force.
E3 apathy, lethargy.

very adv extremely, greatly, highly, deeply, truly, terribly (infml), majorly (sl), remarkably, excessively, exceeding(ly), acutely, particularly, really, absolutely, noticeably, unusually.
E3 slightly, scarcely.
adj actual, real, same, selfsame, identical, true, genuine, simple, utter, sheer, pure, perfect, plain, mere, bare, exact, appropriate.

vestige n trace, suspicion, indication, sign, hint, evidence, whiff, inkling, glimmer, token, scrap, remains, remainder, remnant, residue.

vet v investigate, examine, check, scrutinise, scan, inspect, survey, review, appraise, audit.

veteran n master, past master, old hand, old stager, old-timer, pro (infml), war-horse.
E3 novice, recruit.
adj experienced, practised, seasoned, long-serving, expert, adept, proficient, old.
E3 inexperienced.

veto v reject, turn down, forbid, disallow, ban, prohibit, rule out, block.

E3 approve, sanction, ratify.
n rejection, ban, embargo, prohibition, thumbs down (infml).
E3 approval, assent.

vex v irritate, annoy, provoke, pester, trouble, upset, worry, bother, put out (infml), harass, hassle (infml), aggravate (infml), needle (infml), disturb, distress, agitate, exasperate, torment, fret.
E3 calm, soothe.

vexed adj 1 IRRITATED, annoyed, provoked, upset, troubled, worried, nettled, put out, exasperated, bothered, confused, perplexed, aggravated (infml), harassed, hassled (infml), ruffled, riled, disturbed, distressed, displeased, agitated. 2 a vexed question: difficult, controversial, contested, disputed.

viable adj feasible, practicable, possible, workable, usable, operable, achievable, sustainable.
E3 impossible, unworkable.

vibrant adj 1 ANIMATED, vivacious, vivid, bright, brilliant, colourful, lively, responsive, sparkling, spirited, sensitive. 2 THRILLING, dynamic, electrifying, electric.

vibrate v quiver, pulsate, shudder, shiver, resonate, reverberate, throb, oscillate, tremble, undulate, sway, swing, shake.

vice n 1 EVIL, evil-doing, depravity, immorality, wickedness, sin, corruption, iniquity (fml), profligacy (fml), degeneracy. 2 FAULT, failing, defect, shortcoming, weakness, imperfection, blemish, bad habit, besetting sin.
E3 1 virtue, morality.

vicinity n neighbourhood, area, locality, district, precincts, environs, proximity.

vicious adj **1** WICKED, bad, wrong, immoral, depraved, unprincipled, diabolical, corrupt, debased, perverted, profligate (fml), vile, heinous. **2** MALICIOUS, spiteful, vindictive, virulent, cruel, mean, nasty, slanderous, venomous, defamatory. **3** SAVAGE, wild, violent, barbarous, brutal, dangerous.
E3 1 virtuous. **2** kind.

victim n sufferer, casualty, prey, scapegoat, martyr, sacrifice, fatality.
E3 offender, attacker.

victimize v **1** OPPRESS, persecute, discriminate against, pick on, prey on, bully, exploit. **2** CHEAT, deceive, defraud, swindle (infml), dupe, hoodwink, fool.

victorious adj conquering, champion, triumphant, winning, unbeaten, successful, prize-winning, top, first.
E3 defeated, unsuccessful.

victory n conquest, win, triumph, success, superiority, mastery, vanquishment, subjugation, overcoming.
E3 defeat, loss.

vie v strive, compete, contend, struggle, contest, fight, rival.

view n **1** OPINION, attitude, belief, judgement, estimation, feeling, sentiment, impression, notion. **2** SIGHT, scene, vision, vista, outlook, prospect, perspective, panorama, landscape. **3** SURVEY, inspection, examination, observation, scrutiny, scan. **4** GLIMPSE, look, sight, perception.
v **1** CONSIDER, regard, contemplate, judge, think about, speculate. **2** OBSERVE, watch, see, examine, inspect, look at, scan, survey, witness, perceive.

viewer n spectator, watcher, observer, onlooker.

viewpoint n attitude, position, perspective, slant, standpoint, stance, opinion, angle, feeling.

vigilant adj watchful, alert, attentive, observant, on one's guard, on the lookout, cautious, wide awake.
E3 careless.

vigorous adj energetic, active, lively, healthy, strong, strenuous, robust, lusty, sound, vital, brisk, dynamic, forceful, forcible, powerful, stout, spirited, full-blooded, effective, efficient, enterprising, flourishing, intense.
E3 weak, feeble.

vigour n energy, vitality, liveliness, health, robustness, stamina, strength, resilience, soundness, spirit, verve, gusto, activity, animation, power, potency, force, forcefulness, might, dash, dynamism.
E3 weakness.

vile adj **1** a vile wretch: base, contemptible, debased, depraved, degenerate, bad, wicked, wretched, worthless, sinful, miserable, mean, evil, impure, corrupt, despicable, disgraceful, degrading, vicious, appalling. **2** a vile meal: disgusting, foul, nauseating, sickening, repulsive, repugnant, revolting, noxious, offensive, nasty, loathsome, horrid.
E3 1 pure, worthy. **2** pleasant, lovely.

villain n evil-doer, miscreant (fml), scoundrel, rogue, malefactor (fml), criminal, reprobate, rascal.

villainous adj wicked, bad, criminal, evil, sinful, vicious, notorious, cruel, inhuman, vile, depraved, disgraceful, terrible.
E3 good.

vindicate v 1 CLEAR, acquit, excuse, exonerate, absolve, rehabilitate. 2 JUSTIFY, uphold, support, maintain, defend, establish, advocate, assert, verify.

vindictive adj spiteful, unforgiving, implacable, vengeful, relentless, unrelenting, revengeful, resentful, punitive, venomous, malevolent, malicious.

F3 forgiving.

vintage n year, period, era, epoch, generation, harvest, crop.
adj choice, best, fine, prime, select, superior, rare, mature, old, ripe, classic, venerable, veteran.

violate v 1 CONTRAVENE, disobey, disregard, transgress, break, flout, infringe. 2 OUTRAGE, debauch, defile, rape, ravish, dishonour, desecrate, profane, invade.

F3 1 observe.

violence n 1 FORCE, strength, power, vehemence, might, intensity, ferocity, fierceness, severity, tumult, turbulence, wildness. 2 BRUTALITY, destructiveness, cruelty, bloodshed, murderousness, savagery, passion, fighting, frenzy, fury, hostilities.

violent adj 1 INTENSE, strong, severe, sharp, acute, extreme, harmful, destructive, devastating, injurious, powerful, painful, agonizing, forceful, forcible, harsh, ruinous, rough, vehement, tumultuous, turbulent. 2 CRUEL, brutal, aggressive, bloodthirsty, impetuous, hot-headed, headstrong, murderous, savage, wild, vicious, unrestrained, uncontrollable, ungovernable, passionate, furious, intemperate, maddened, outrageous, riotous, fiery.

F3 1 calm, moderate. 2 peaceful, gentle.

virgin n girl, maiden, celibate, vestal. adj virginal, chaste, intact, immaculate, maidenly, pure, modest, new, fresh, spotless, stainless, undefiled, untouched, unsullied.

virile adj man-like, masculine, male, manly, macho (infml), robust, vigorous, potent, lusty, red-blooded, forceful, strong, rugged.

F3 effeminate, impotent.

virtual adj effective, essential, practical, implied, implicit, potential.

virtually adv practically, in effect, almost, nearly, as good as, in essence.

virtue n 1 GOODNESS, morality, rectitude, uprightness, worthiness, righteousness, probity (fml), integrity, honour, incorruptibility, justice, high-mindedness, excellence. 2 QUALITY, worth, merit, advantage, asset, credit, strength.

F3 1 vice, sleaze.

virtuoso n expert, master, maestro, prodigy, genius.

virtuous adj good, moral, righteous, upright, worthy, honourable, irreproachable, incorruptible, exemplary, unimpeachable, high-principled, blameless, clean-living, excellent, innocent.

F3 immoral, vicious.

virulent adj 1 POISONOUS, toxic, venomous, deadly, lethal, malignant, injurious, pernicious, intense. 2 HOSTILE, resentful, spiteful, acrimonious, bitter, vicious, vindictive, malevolent, malicious.

F3 1 harmless.

visible adj perceptible, discernible, detectable, apparent, noticeable, observable, distinguishable,

discoverable, evident, unconcealed, undisguised, unmistakable, conspicuous, clear, obvious, manifest, open, palpable, plain, patent.
F3 invisible, indiscernible, hidden.

vision n **1** APPARITION, hallucination, illusion, delusion, mirage, phantom, ghost, chimera, spectre, wraith. **2** IDEA, ideal, conception, insight, view, picture, image, fantasy, dream, daydream. **3** SIGHT, seeing, eyesight, perception, discernment, far-sightedness, foresight, penetration.

visionary adj idealistic, impractical, romantic, dreamy, unrealistic, utopian, unreal, fanciful, prophetic, speculative, unworkable, illusory, imaginary.
n idealist, romantic, dreamer, daydreamer, fantasist, prophet, mystic, seer, utopian, rainbow-chaser, theorist.
F3 pragmatist.

visit v call on, call in, stay with, stay at, drop in on (infml), stop by (infml), look in, look up, pop in (infml), see.
n call, stay, stop, excursion, sojourn (fml).

visitor n caller, guest, company, tourist, holidaymaker.

vista n view, prospect, panorama, perspective, outlook, scene.

visualize v picture, envisage, imagine, conceive.

vital adj **1** CRITICAL, crucial, important, imperative, key, significant, basic, fundamental, essential, necessary, requisite, indispensable, urgent, life-or-death, decisive, forceful. **2** LIVING, alive, lively, life-giving, invigorating, spirited, vivacious, vibrant, vigorous, dynamic, animated,

energetic, quickening (fml).
F3 1 inessential, peripheral. **2** dead.

vitality n life, liveliness, animation, vigour, energy, vivacity, spirit, sparkle, exuberance, go (infml), strength, stamina.

vitriolic adj bitter, abusive, virulent, vicious, venomous, malicious, caustic, biting, sardonic, scathing, destructive.

vivacious adj lively, animated, spirited, high-spirited, effervescent, ebullient, cheerful, sparkling, bubbly, light-hearted.

vivid adj **1** BRIGHT, colourful, intense, strong, rich, vibrant, brilliant, glowing, dazzling, vigorous, expressive, dramatic, flamboyant, animated, lively, lifelike, spirited. **2** MEMORABLE, powerful, graphic, clear, distinct, striking, sharp, realistic.
F3 1 colourless, dull. **2** vague.

vocal adj **1** SPOKEN, said, oral, uttered, voiced. **2** ARTICULATE, eloquent, expressive, noisy, clamorous, shrill, strident, outspoken, frank, forthright, plain-spoken.
F3 1 unspoken. **2** inarticulate.

vocation n calling, pursuit, career, métier, mission, profession, trade, employment, work, role, post, job, business, office.

vociferous adj noisy, vocal, clamorous, loud, obstreperous, strident, vehement, thundering, shouting.
F3 quiet.

vogue n fashion, mode, style, craze, popularity, trend, prevalence, acceptance, custom, fad (infml), the latest (infml), the rage (infml), the thing (infml).

voice n **1** SPEECH, utterance, articulation, language, words, sound, tone, intonation, inflection, expression, mouthpiece, medium, instrument, organ. **2** SAY, vote, opinion, view, decision, option, will. *v* express, say, utter, air, articulate, speak of, verbalize, assert, convey, disclose, divulge, declare, enunciate.

void *adj* **1** EMPTY, emptied, free, unfilled, unoccupied, vacant, clear, bare, blank, drained. **2** ANNULLED, inoperative, invalid, cancelled, ineffective, futile, useless, vain, worthless.
F3 1 full. **2** valid.
n emptiness, vacuity, vacuum, chasm, blank, blankness, space, lack, want, cavity, gap, hollow, opening.

volatile *adj* changeable, inconstant, unstable, variable, erratic, temperamental, unsteady, unsettled, fickle, mercurial, unpredictable, capricious, restless, giddy, flighty, up and down (*infml*), lively.
F3 constant, steady.

volley *n* barrage, bombardment, hail, shower, burst, blast, discharge, explosion.

voluble *adj* fluent, glib, articulate, loquacious (*fml*), talkative, forthcoming, garrulous.

volume *n* **1** BULK, size, capacity, dimensions, amount, mass, quantity, aggregate, amplitude, body. **2** BOOK, tome, publication.

voluminous *adj* roomy, capacious, ample, spacious, billowing, vast, bulky, huge, large.

voluntary *adj* **1** FREE, gratuitous, optional, spontaneous, unforced,

willing, unpaid, honorary. **2** CONSCIOUS, deliberate, purposeful, intended, intentional, wilful.
F3 1 compulsory. **2** involuntary.

volunteer *v* offer, propose, put forward, present, suggest, step forward, advance.

voluptuous *adj* **1** SENSUAL, licentious, luxurious. **2** EROTIC, shapely, sexy (*infml*), seductive, provocative, enticing.

vomit *v* be sick, bring up, heave, retch, throw up (*infml*), puke (*infml*).

vote *n* ballot, poll, election, franchise, referendum.
v elect, ballot, choose, opt, plump for, declare, return.

vouch for guarantee, support, back, endorse, confirm, certify, affirm, assert, attest to, speak for, swear to, uphold.

vow *v* promise, pledge, swear, dedicate, devote, profess, consecrate, affirm.
n promise, oath, pledge.

voyage *n* journey, trip, passage, expedition, crossing.

vulgar *adj* **1** TASTELESS, flashy, gaudy, tawdry, cheap and nasty (*infml*). **2** UNREFINED, uncouth, coarse, common, crude, ill-bred, impolite, indecorous. **3** INDECENT, suggestive, risqué, rude, indelicate. **4** ORDINARY, general, popular, vernacular.
F3 1 tasteful. **2** correct. **3** decent.

vulnerable *adj* unprotected, exposed, defenceless, susceptible, weak, sensitive, wide open.
F3 protected, strong.

W

wad n chunk, plug, roll, ball, wedge (infml), lump, hunk, mass, block.

waddle v toddle, totter, wobble, sway, rock, shuffle.

waffle v jabber, prattle, blather, rabbit on (infml), witter on (infml).
n blather, prattle, wordiness, padding, nonsense, gobbledegook (infml), hot air (infml).

waft v drift, float, blow, transport, transmit.
n breath, puff, draught, current, breeze, scent, whiff.

wag v shake, waggle, wave, sway, swing, bob, nod, wiggle, oscillate, flutter, vibrate, quiver, rock.

wage n pay, fee, earnings, salary, wage-packet, payment, stipend, remuneration, emolument (fml), allowance, reward, hire, compensation, recompense.
v carry on, conduct, engage in, undertake, practise, pursue.

waif n orphan, stray, foundling.

wail v moan, cry, howl, lament, weep, complain, yowl (infml).
n moan, cry, howl, lament, complaint, weeping.

wait v delay, linger, hold back, hesitate, pause, hang around, hang fire, remain, rest, stay.
F3 proceed, go ahead.
n hold-up, hesitation, delay, interval, pause, halt.

waive v renounce, relinquish, forgo, resign, surrender, yield.

wake[1] v **1** RISE, get up, arise, rouse, come to, bring round. **2** STIMULATE, stir, activate, arouse, animate, excite, fire, galvanize.
F3 1 sleep.
n funeral, death-watch, vigil, watch.

wake[2] n trail, track, path, aftermath, backwash, wash, rear, train, waves.

walk v **1** STEP, stride, pace, proceed, advance, march, plod, tramp, traipse, trek, trudge, saunter, amble, stroll, tread, hike, promenade, move, hoof it. **2** ACCOMPANY, escort.
n **1** he has an odd walk: carriage, gait, step, pace, stride. **2** go for a walk: stroll, amble, ramble, saunter, march, hike, tramp, trek, traipse, trudge, trail. **3** a tree-lined walk: footpath, path, walkway, avenue, pathway, promenade, alley, esplanade, lane, pavement, sidewalk.

walker n pedestrian, rambler, hiker.

walk-out n strike, stoppage, industrial action, protest, rebellion, revolt.

walk-over n pushover (infml), doddle (infml), child's play, piece of cake (infml), cinch (infml).

wall n **1** PARTITION, screen, panel, divider, fence, hedge, enclosure, membrane, bulkhead. **2** FORTIFICATION, barricade, rampart, parapet, stockade, embankment, bulwark, palisade. **3** OBSTACLE, obstruction, barrier, block, impediment.

wallow v **1** wallow in mud: loll, lie, roll, wade, welter, lurch, flounder, splash. **2** wallow in nostalgia: indulge, luxuriate, relish, revel, bask, enjoy, glory, delight.

wand n rod, baton, staff, stick, sprig, mace, sceptre, twig.

wander v **1** ROAM, rove, ramble, meander, saunter, stroll, prowl, drift, range, stray, straggle. **2** DIGRESS, diverge, deviate, depart, go astray, swerve, veer, err. **3** RAMBLE, rave, babble, gibber.
n excursion, ramble, stroll, saunter, meander, prowl, cruise.

wanderer n itinerant, traveller, voyager, drifter, rover, rambler, stroller, stray, straggler, ranger, nomad, gypsy, vagrant, vagabond, rolling stone (infml).

wane v diminish, decrease, decline, weaken, subside, fade, dwindle, ebb, lessen, abate, sink, drop, taper off, dim, droop, contract, shrink, fail, wither.
F3 increase, wax.

wangle v manipulate, arrange, contrive, engineer, fix, scheme, manoeuvre, work, pull off, manage, fiddle (infml).

want v **1** DESIRE, wish, crave, covet, fancy, long for, pine for, yearn for, hunger for, thirst for. **2** NEED, require, demand, lack, miss, call for.
n **1** DESIRE, demand, longing,
requirement, wish, need, appetite. **2** LACK, dearth, insufficiency, deficiency, shortage, inadequacy. **3** POVERTY, privation, destitution.

wanting adj **1** ABSENT, missing, lacking, short, insufficient. **2** INADEQUATE, imperfect, faulty, defective, substandard, poor, deficient, unsatisfactory.
F3 1 sufficient. **2** adequate.

wanton adj malicious, immoral, shameless, arbitrary, unprovoked, unjustifiable, unrestrained, rash, reckless, wild.

war n warfare, hostilities, fighting, battle, combat, conflict, strife, struggle, bloodshed, contest, contention, enmity.
F3 peace, ceasefire.

> **Types of war include:**
> biological warfare, chemical warfare, civil war, cold war, germ warfare, guerrilla warfare, holy war, hot war, jihad, jungle warfare, limited war, nuclear war, private war, total war, trade war, turf war, war of attrition, war of nerves, world war.

> **Famous wars include:**
> American Civil War (Second American Revolution), American Revolution (War of Independence), Boer War, Crimean War, Crusades, English Civil War, Falklands War, Franco-Prussian War, Gulf War, Hundred Years War, Indian Wars, Iran-Iraq War, Korean War, Mexican War, Napoleonic Wars, Opium Wars, Peasants' War, Russo-Finnish War (Winter War), Russo-Japanese War, Russo-Turkish Wars, Seven Years War, Six-Day War, Spanish-American War, Spanish Civil War,

Thirty Years War, Vietnam War, War of 1812, War of the Pacific, Wars of the Roses, World War I (the Great War), World War II.

v wage war, fight, take up arms, battle, clash, combat, strive, skirmish, struggle, contest, contend.

ward *n* **1** ROOM, apartment, unit. **2** DIVISION, area, district, quarter, precinct, zone. **3** CHARGE, dependant, protégé(e), minor.

ward off avert, fend off, deflect, parry, repel, stave off, thwart, beat off, forestall, evade, turn away, block, avoid.

warden *n* keeper, custodian, guardian, warder, caretaker, curator, ranger, steward, watchman, superintendent, administrator, janitor.

warder *n* jailer, keeper, prison officer, guard, wardress, custodian.

wardrobe *n* **1** CUPBOARD, closet. **2** CLOTHES, outfit, attire.

warehouse *n* store, storehouse, depot, depository, repository, stockroom, entrepot.

wares *n* goods, merchandise, commodities, stock, products, produce, stuff.

warfare *n* war, fighting, hostilities, battle, arms, combat, strife, struggle, passage of arms, contest, conflict, contention, discord, blows.
E3 peace.

warlike *adj* belligerent, aggressive, bellicose, pugnacious, combative, bloodthirsty, war-mongering, militaristic, hostile, antagonistic, unfriendly.
E3 friendly, peaceable.

warm *adj* **1** HEATED, tepid, lukewarm. **2** ARDENT, passionate, fervent,

vehement, earnest, zealous. **3** *warm colours*: rich, intense, mellow, cheerful. **4** FRIENDLY, amiable, cordial, affable, kindly, genial, hearty, hospitable, sympathetic, affectionate, tender. **5** FINE, sunny, balmy, temperate, close.
E3 1 cool. **2** indifferent. **3** cold. **4** unfriendly. **5** cool.

v **1** HEAT (UP), reheat, melt, thaw. **2** ANIMATE, interest, please, delight, stimulate, stir, rouse, excite.
E3 1 cool.

warmth *n* **1** WARMNESS, heat. **2** FRIENDLINESS, affection, cordiality, tenderness. **3** ARDOUR, enthusiasm, passion, fervour, zeal, eagerness.
E3 1 coldness. **2** unfriendliness. **3** indifference.

warn *v* caution, alert, admonish, advise, notify, counsel, put on one's guard, inform, tip off (*infml*).

warning *n* **1** CAUTION, alert, admonition, advice, notification, notice, advance notice, counsel, hint, lesson, alarm, threat, tip-off (*infml*). **2** OMEN, augury, premonition, presage, sign, signal, portent.

warp *v* twist, bend, contort, deform, distort, kink, misshape, pervert, corrupt, deviate.
E3 straighten.
n twist, bend, contortion, deformation, distortion, bias, kink, irregularity, turn, bent, defect, deviation, quirk, perversion.

warrant *n* authorization, authority, sanction, permit, permission, licence, guarantee, warranty, security, pledge, commission, voucher.
v **1** GUARANTEE, pledge, certify, assure, notify, declare, affirm, vouch for, answer for, underwrite, uphold,

endorse. **2** AUTHORIZE, entitle, empower, sanction, permit, allow, license, justify, excuse, approve, call for, commission, necessitate, require.

wary *adj* cautious, guarded, careful, chary, on one's guard, on the lookout, prudent, distrustful, suspicious, heedful, attentive, alert, watchful, vigilant, wide awake.
F3 unwary, careless, heedless.

wash *v* **1** CLEAN, cleanse, launder, scrub, swab down, rinse, swill.
2 BATHE, bath, shower, douche, shampoo.
n **1** CLEANING, cleansing, bath, bathe, laundry, laundering, scrub, shower, shampoo, washing, rinse. **2** FLOW, sweep, wave, swell.

wash-out *n* failure, disaster, disappointment, fiasco, flop (*infml*), debacle.
F3 success, triumph.

waste *v* **1** SQUANDER, misspend, misuse, fritter away, dissipate, lavish, spend, throw away, blow (*infml*).
2 CONSUME, erode, exhaust, drain, destroy, spoil.
n **1** SQUANDERING, dissipation, prodigality, wastefulness, extravagance, loss.
2 MISAPPLICATION, misuse, abuse, neglect. **3** RUBBISH, refuse, trash, garbage, leftovers, debris, dregs, effluent, litter, scrap, slops, offscouring(s), dross.
adj **1** USELESS, worthless, unwanted, unused, left-over, superfluous, supernumerary, extra. **2** BARREN, desolate, empty, uninhabited, bare, devastated, uncultivated, unprofitable, wild, dismal, dreary.

wasted *adj* **1** UNNECESSARY,

needless, useless. **2** EMACIATED, withered, shrivelled, shrunken, gaunt, washed-out, spent.
F3 **1** necessary. **2** robust.

wasteful *adj* extravagant, spendthrift, prodigal, profligate, uneconomical, thriftless, unthrifty, ruinous, lavish, improvident.
F3 economical, thrifty.

wasteland *n* wilderness, desert, barrenness, waste, wild(s), void.

watch *v* **1** OBSERVE, see, look at, regard, note, notice, mark, stare at, peer at, gaze at, view. **2** GUARD, look after, keep an eye on, mind, protect, superintend, take care of, keep. **3** PAY ATTENTION, be careful, take heed, look out.
n **1** TIMEPIECE, wristwatch, clock, chronometer. **2** VIGILANCE, watchfulness, vigil, observation, surveillance, notice, lookout, attention, heed, alertness, inspection, supervision.

watch out notice, be vigilant, look out, keep one's eyes open.

watch over guard, protect, stand guard over, keep an eye on, look after, mind, shield, defend, shelter, preserve.

watchdog *n* **1** GUARD DOG, house-dog. **2** MONITOR, inspector, scrutineer, vigilante, ombudsman, guardian, custodian, protector.

watcher *n* spectator, observer, onlooker, looker-on, viewer, lookout, spy, witness.

watchful *adj* vigilant, attentive, heedful, observant, alert, guarded, on one's guard, wide awake, suspicious, wary, chary, cautious.
F3 unobservant, inattentive.

watchman *n* guard, security guard, caretaker, custodian.

water n rain, sea, ocean, lake, river, stream.
v wet, moisten, dampen, soak, spray, sprinkle, irrigate, drench, flood, hose.
F3 dry out, parch.

water down dilute, thin, water, weaken, adulterate, mix, tone down, soften, qualify.

waterfall n fall, cascade, chute, cataract, torrent.

watertight adj 1 WATERPROOF, sound, hermetic. 2 IMPREGNABLE, unassailable, airtight, flawless, foolproof, firm, incontrovertible.
F3 1 leaky.

watery adj 1 LIQUID, fluid, moist, wet, damp. 2 WEAK, watered-down, diluted, insipid, tasteless, thin, runny, soggy, flavourless, washy, wishy-washy (infml).
F3 1 dry.

wave v 1 BECKON, gesture, gesticulate, indicate, sign, signal, direct. 2 BRANDISH, flourish, flap, flutter, shake, sway, swing, waft, quiver, ripple.
n 1 BREAKER, roller, billow, ripple, tidal wave, wavelet, undulation, white horse (infml). 2 SURGE, sweep, swell, upsurge, ground swell, current, drift, movement, rush, tendency, trend, stream, flood, outbreak, rash.

waver v 1 VACILLATE, falter, hesitate, dither, fluctuate, vary, seesaw.
2 OSCILLATE, shake, sway, wobble, tremble, totter, rock.
F3 1 decide.

wavy adj undulating, rippled, curly, curvy, ridged, sinuous, winding, zigzag.

wax v grow, increase, rise, swell, develop, enlarge, expand, magnify, mount, fill out, become.

F3 decrease, wane, diminish.

way n 1 METHOD, approach, manner, technique, procedure, means, mode, system, fashion. 2 CUSTOM, practice, habit, usage, characteristic, idiosyncrasy, trait, style, conduct, nature. 3 DIRECTION, course, route, path, road, channel, access, avenue, track, passage, highway, street, thoroughfare, lane.

by the way incidentally, in passing.

wayward adj wilful, capricious, perverse, contrary, changeable, fickle, unpredictable, stubborn, self-willed, unmanageable, headstrong, obstinate, disobedient, rebellious, insubordinate, intractable, unruly, incorrigible.
F3 tractable, good-natured.

weak adj 1 FEEBLE, frail, infirm, unhealthy, sickly, delicate, debilitated, exhausted, fragile, flimsy.
2 VULNERABLE, unprotected, unguarded, defenceless, exposed.
3 POWERLESS, impotent, spineless, cowardly, indecisive, ineffectual, irresolute, poor, lacking, lame, inadequate, defective, deficient, inconclusive, unconvincing, untenable. 4 FAINT, slight, low, soft, muffled, dull, imperceptible.
5 INSIPID, tasteless, watery, thin, diluted, runny.
F3 1 strong. 2 secure. 3 powerful. 4 strong. 5 strong.

weaken v 1 ENFEEBLE, exhaust, debilitate, sap, undermine, dilute, diminish, lower, lessen, reduce, moderate, mitigate, temper, soften (up), thin, water down. 2 TIRE, flag, fail, give way, droop, fade, abate, ease up, dwindle.
F3 1 strengthen.

weakness n 1 FEEBLENESS, debility, infirmity, impotence, frailty, powerlessness, vulnerability. **2** FAULT, failing, flaw, shortcoming, blemish, defect, deficiency, foible. **3** LIKING, inclination, fondness, penchant, passion, soft spot (*infml*).
E3 1 strength. **2** strength. **3** dislike.

wealth n 1 MONEY, cash, riches, assets, affluence, prosperity, funds, mammon, fortune, capital, opulence, means, substance, resources, goods, possessions, property, estate.
2 ABUNDANCE, plenty, bounty, fullness, profusion, store.
E3 1 poverty.

wealthy adj rich, prosperous, affluent, well-off, moneyed, opulent, comfortable, well-heeled, well-to-do, flush (*infml*), loaded (*sl*), rolling in it (*infml*).
E3 poor, impoverished.

weapon

Weapons include:

gun, airgun, pistol, revolver, auto-matic, Colt®, Luger®, Magnum®, Mauser, six-gun, six-shooter, rifle, air rifle, carbine, shotgun, blunder-buss, musket, elephant gun, machine-gun, kalashnikov, sub-machine-gun, Uzi, tommy-gun, sten gun, Bren gun, cannon, field gun, gatling gun, howitzer, mortar, turret-gun; knife, bowie knife, flick-knife, stiletto, dagger, dirk, poniard, sword, épée, foil, rapier, sabre, sci-mitar, bayonet, broadsword, clay-more, lance, spear, pike, machete; bomb, atom bomb, H-bomb, cluster bomb, depth-charge, incendiary bomb, Mills bomb, mine, land-mine, napalm bomb, time bomb; bow and arrow, longbow, crossbow,

blowpipe, catapult, boomerang, sling, harpoon, bolas, rocket, ba-zooka, ballistic missile, cruise mis-sile, Exocet®, Scud, torpedo, hand grenade, flame-thrower; battle-axe, pole-axe, halberd, tomahawk, cudgel, knuckleduster, shillelagh, truncheon; gas, CS gas, mustard gas, tear-gas.

wear v 1 DRESS IN, have on, put on, don, sport, carry, bear, display, show. **2** DETERIORATE, erode, corrode, consume, fray, rub, abrade, waste, grind.
n 1 CLOTHES, clothing, dress, garments, outfit, costume, attire.
2 DETERIORATION, erosion, corrosion, wear and tear, friction, abrasion.

wear off decrease, abate, dwindle, diminish, subside, wane, weaken, fade, lessen, ebb, peter out, disappear.
E3 increase.

wear out 1 EXHAUST, fatigue, tire (out), enervate, sap. **2** DETERIORATE, wear through, erode, impair, consume, fray.

wearing adj exhausting, fatiguing, tiresome, tiring, wearisome, trying, taxing, oppressive, irksome, exasperating.
E3 refreshing.

weary adj tired, exhausted, fatigued, sleepy, worn out, drained, drowsy, jaded, all in (*infml*), done in (*infml*), fagged out (*infml*), knackered (*infml*), dead beat (*infml*), dog-tired (*infml*), whacked (*infml*).
E3 refreshed.

wearying adj tiring, fatiguing, exhausting, wearisome, wearing, taxing, trying.
E3 refreshing.

weather n climate, conditions, temperature.

Types of weather include:
breeze, wind, squall, tornado, typhoon, monsoon, cyclone, cloud, mist, dew, fog, smog, rain, drizzle, shower, sunshine, heat wave, haze, drought, storm, thunder, lightning, frost, hoar frost, hail, sleet, snow, snowstorm, ice, black ice, thaw.

v **1** ENDURE, survive, live through, come through, ride out, rise above, stick out, withstand, surmount, stand, brave, overcome, resist, pull through, suffer. **2** EXPOSE, toughen, season, harden.

F3 1 succumb.

weave *v* **1** INTERLACE, lace, plait, braid, intertwine, spin, knit, entwine, intercross, fuse, merge, unite.
2 CREATE, compose, construct, contrive, put together, fabricate.
3 WIND, twist, zigzag, criss-cross.

web *n* network, net, netting, lattice, mesh, webbing, interlacing, weft, snare, tangle, trap.

wedding *n* marriage, matrimony, nuptials (*fml*), wedlock, bridal.

F3 divorce.

wedge *n* lump, block, chunk, wodge, chock.

v jam, cram, pack, ram, squeeze, stuff, push, lodge, block, thrust, crowd, force.

weedy *adj* thin, skinny, puny, scrawny, undersized, weak, feeble, frail, weak-kneed, insipid, wet (*infml*), wimpish (*infml*), wimpy (*infml*).

F3 strong.

weep *v* cry, sob, moan, lament, wail, mourn, grieve, bawl, blubber, snivel, whimper, blub (*infml*).

F3 rejoice.

weigh *v* **1** BEAR DOWN, oppress.
2 CONSIDER, contemplate, evaluate, meditate on, mull over, ponder, think over, examine, reflect on, deliberate.

weigh down oppress, overload, load, burden, bear down, weigh upon, press down, get down (*infml*), depress, afflict, trouble, worry.

F3 lighten, hearten.

weigh up assess, examine, size up, balance, consider, contemplate, deliberate, mull over, ponder, think over, discuss, chew over (*infml*).

weight *n* **1** HEAVINESS, gravity, burden, load, pressure, mass, force, ballast, tonnage, poundage.
2 IMPORTANCE, significance, substance, consequence, impact, moment, influence, value, authority, clout (*infml*), power, preponderance, consideration.

F3 1 lightness.

v **1** LOAD, weigh down, oppress, handicap. **2** BIAS, unbalance, slant, prejudice.

weighty *adj* **1** HEAVY, burdensome, substantial, bulky. **2** IMPORTANT, significant, consequential, crucial, critical, momentous, serious, grave, solemn. **3** DEMANDING, difficult, exacting, taxing.

F3 1 light. **2** unimportant.

weird *adj* strange, uncanny, bizarre, eerie, creepy, supernatural, unnatural, ghostly, freakish, mysterious, queer, grotesque, spooky (*infml*), far-out (*infml*), way-out (*infml*).

F3 normal, usual.

welcome *adj* acceptable, desirable, pleasing, pleasant, agreeable, gratifying, appreciated, delightful, refreshing.

F3 unwelcome.

n reception, greeting, salutation (*infml*), acceptance, hospitality, red carpet (*infml*).

v greet, hail, receive, salute, meet, accept, approve of, embrace.
F3 reject, snub.

weld *v* fuse, unite, bond, join, solder, bind, connect, seal, link, cement.
F3 separate.

welfare *n* well-being, health, prosperity, happiness, benefit, good, advantage, interest, profit, success.

well[1] *n* spring, well-spring, fountain, fount, source, reservoir, well-head, waterhole.
v flow, spring, surge, gush, stream, brim over, jet, spout, spurt, swell, pour, flood, ooze, run, trickle, rise, seep.

well[2] *adv* rightly, correctly, properly, skilfully, ably, expertly, successfully, adequately, sufficiently, suitably, easily, satisfactorily, thoroughly, greatly, fully, considerably, completely, agreeably, pleasantly, happily, kindly, favourably, splendidly, substantially, comfortably, readily, carefully, clearly, highly, deeply, justly.
F3 badly, inadequately, incompetently, wrongly.
adj **1** HEALTHY, in good health, fit, able-bodied, sound, robust, strong, thriving, flourishing. **2** SATISFACTORY, right, all right, good, pleasing, proper, agreeable, fine, lucky, fortunate.
F3 1 ill. **2** bad.

well-balanced *adj* **1** RATIONAL, reasonable, level-headed, well-adjusted, stable, sensible, sane, sound, sober, together (*sl*).
2 SYMMETRICAL, even, harmonious.
F3 1 unbalanced. **2** asymmetrical.

well-being *n* welfare, happiness, comfort, good.

well-bred *adj* well-mannered,

polite, well-brought-up, mannerly, courteous, civil, refined, cultivated, cultured, genteel.
F3 ill-bred.

well-dressed *adj* smart, well-groomed, elegant, fashionable, chic, stylish, neat, trim, spruce, tidy.
F3 badly dressed, scruffy.

well-known *adj* famous, renowned, celebrated, famed, eminent, notable, noted, illustrious, familiar.
F3 unknown.

well-off *adj* rich, wealthy, affluent, prosperous, well-to-do, moneyed, thriving, successful, comfortable, fortunate.
F3 poor, badly-off.

well-thought-of *adj* respected, highly regarded, esteemed, admired, honoured, revered.
F3 despised.

well-worn *adj* timeworn, stale, tired, trite, overused, unoriginal, hackneyed, commonplace, stereotyped, threadbare, corny (*infml*).
F3 original.

wet *adj* **1** DAMP, moist, soaked, soaking, sodden, saturated, soggy, sopping, watery, waterlogged, drenched, dripping, spongy, dank, clammy. **2** RAINING, rainy, showery, teeming, pouring, drizzling, humid. **3** (*infml*) WEAK, feeble, weedy, wimpish (*infml*), wimpy (*infml*), spineless, soft, ineffectual, namby-pamby, irresolute, timorous.
F3 1 dry. **2** dry. **3** strong.
n wetness, moisture, damp, dampness, liquid, water, clamminess, condensation, humidity, rain, drizzle.
F3 dryness.
v moisten, damp, dampen, soak, saturate, drench, steep, water, irrigate,

spray, splash, sprinkle, imbue, dip.
F3 dry.

whack v hit, strike, smack, thrash, slap, beat, bash (*infml*), bang, cuff, thump, box, buffet, rap, wallop (*infml*), belt (*infml*), clobber (*infml*), clout (*infml*), sock (*infml*).
n smack, slap, blow, hit, rap, stroke, thump, cuff, box, bang, clout (*infml*), bash (*infml*), wallop (*infml*).

wharf n dock, quay, quayside, jetty, landing-stage, dockyard, marina, pier.

wheedle v cajole, coax, persuade, inveigle, charm, flatter, entice, court, draw.
F3 force.

wheel n turn, revolution, circle, rotation, gyration, pivot, roll, spin, twirl, whirl.
v turn, rotate, circle, gyrate, orbit, spin, twirl, whirl, swing, roll, revolve, swivel.

wheeze v pant, gasp, cough, hiss, rasp, whistle.

whereabouts n location, position, place, situation, site, vicinity.

whet v 1 SHARPEN, hone, file, grind. 2 STIMULATE, stir, rouse, arouse, provoke, kindle, quicken, incite, awaken, increase.
F3 1 blunt. 2 dampen.

whiff n breath, puff, hint, trace, blast, draught, odour, smell, aroma, sniff, scent, reek, stink, stench.

whim n fancy, caprice, notion, quirk, freak, humour, conceit, fad, vagary, urge.

whimper v cry, sob, weep, snivel, whine, grizzle, mewl, moan, whinge (*infml*).
n sob, snivel, whine, moan.

whimsical adj fanciful, capricious, playful, impulsive, eccentric, funny, droll, curious, queer, unusual, weird, odd, peculiar, quaint, dotty (*infml*).

whine n 1 CRY, sob, whimper, moan, wail. 2 COMPLAINT, grumble, grouse, gripe (*infml*), grouch (*infml*).
v 1 CRY, sob, whimper, grizzle, moan, wail. 2 COMPLAIN, carp, grumble, whinge (*infml*), gripe (*infml*), grouch (*infml*).

whip v 1 BEAT, flog, lash, flagellate, scourge, birch, cane, strap, thrash, punish, chastise, discipline, castigate (*fml*). 2 PULL, jerk, snatch, whisk, dash, dart, rush, tear, flit, flash, fly. 3 GOAD, drive, spur, push, urge, stir, rouse, agitate, incite, provoke, instigate.
n lash, scourge, switch, birch, cane, horsewhip, riding-crop, cat-o'-nine-tails.

whirl v swirl, spin, turn, twist, twirl, pivot, pirouette, swivel, wheel, rotate, revolve, reel, roll, gyrate, circle.
n 1 SPIN, twirl, twist, gyration, revolution, pirouette, swirl, turn, wheel, rotation, circle, reel, roll. 2 CONFUSION, daze, flurry, commotion, agitation, bustle, hubbub, hurly-burly, giddiness, tumult, uproar.

whirlwind n tornado, cyclone, vortex.
adj hasty, impulsive, quick, rapid, speedy, swift, lightning, headlong, impetuous, rash.
F3 deliberate, slow.

whisk v 1 WHIP, beat. 2 DART, dash, rush, hurry, speed, hasten, race. 3 BRUSH, sweep, flick, wipe, twitch.

whisper v 1 MURMUR, mutter, mumble, breathe, hiss, rustle, sigh. 2 HINT, intimate, insinuate, gossip, divulge.
F3 shout.
n 1 MURMUR, undertone, sigh, hiss, rustle. 2 HINT, suggestion, suspicion,

breath, whiff, rumour, report, innuendo, insinuation, trace, tinge, soupçon, buzz.

white adj **1** PALE, pallid, wan, ashen, colourless, anaemic, pasty. **2** LIGHT, snowy, milky, creamy, ivory, hoary, silver, grey. **3** PURE, immaculate, spotless, stainless, undefiled.
F3 1 ruddy. **2** dark. **3** defiled.

whiten v bleach, blanch, whitewash, pale, fade.
F3 blacken, darken.

whittle v **1** CARVE, cut, scrape, shave, trim, pare, hew, shape. **2** ERODE, eat away, wear away, diminish, consume, reduce, undermine.

whole adj **1** COMPLETE, entire, integral, full, total, unabridged, uncut, undivided, unedited. **2** INTACT, unharmed, undamaged, unbroken, inviolate, perfect, in one piece, mint, unhurt. **3** WELL, healthy, fit, sound, strong.
n total, aggregate, sum total, entirety, all, fullness, totality, ensemble, entity, unit, lot, piece, everything.
F3 part.
on the whole generally, mostly, in general, generally speaking, as a rule, for the most part, all in all, all things considered, by and large.

whole-hearted adj unreserved, unstinting, unqualified, passionate, enthusiastic, earnest, committed, dedicated, devoted, heartfelt, emphatic, warm, sincere, unfeigned, genuine, complete, true, real, zealous.
F3 half-hearted.

wholesale adj comprehensive, far-reaching, extensive, sweeping, wide-ranging, mass, broad, outright, total, massive, indiscriminate.
F3 partial.

wholesome adj **1** wholesome food: healthy, hygienic, salubrious, sanitary, nutritious, nourishing, beneficial, salutary, invigorating, bracing. **2** wholesome entertainment: moral, decent, clean, proper, improving, edifying, uplifting, pure, virtuous, righteous, honourable, respectable.
F3 1 unhealthy. **2** unwholesome.

wholly adv completely, entirely, fully, purely, absolutely, totally, utterly, comprehensively, altogether, perfectly, thoroughly, all, exclusively, only.
F3 partly.

wicked adj **1** EVIL, sinful, immoral, depraved, corrupt, vicious, unprincipled, iniquitous, heinous, debased, abominable, ungodly, unrighteous, shameful. **2** BAD, unpleasant, harmful, offensive, vile, worthless, difficult, dreadful, distressing, awful, atrocious, severe, intense, nasty, injurious, troublesome, terrible, foul, fierce. **3** NAUGHTY, mischievous, roguish.
F3 1 good, upright. **2** harmless.

wide adj **1** BROAD, roomy, spacious, vast, immense. **2** DILATED, expanded, full. **3** EXTENSIVE, wide-ranging, comprehensive, far-reaching, general. **4** LOOSE, baggy. **5** OFF-TARGET, distant, remote.
F3 1 narrow. **3** restricted. **5** near.
adv **1** ASTRAY, off course, off target, off the mark. **2** FULLY, completely, all the way.
F3 on target.

widen v distend, dilate, expand, extend, spread, stretch, enlarge, broaden.
F3 narrow.

widespread adj extensive, prevalent, rife, general, sweeping, universal, wholesale, far-reaching, unlimited, broad, common, pervasive, far-flung.
F3 limited.

width n breadth, diameter, wideness, compass, thickness, span, scope, range, measure, girth, beam, amplitude, extent, reach.

wield v wield a weapon: brandish, flourish, swing, wave, handle, ply, manage, manipulate. **2** wield power: have, hold, possess, employ, exert, exercise, use, utilize, maintain, command.

wife n partner, spouse, mate, better half (infml), bride.

wild adj **1** UNTAMED, undomesticated, feral, savage, barbarous, primitive, uncivilized, natural, ferocious, fierce. **2** UNCULTIVATED, desolate, waste, uninhabited. **3** UNRULY, unrestrained, unmanageable, violent, turbulent, rowdy, lawless, disorderly, riotous, boisterous. **4** STORMY, tempestuous, rough, blustery, choppy. **5** UNTIDY, unkempt, messy, dishevelled, tousled. **6** RECKLESS, rash, imprudent, foolish, foolhardy, impracticable, irrational, outrageous, preposterous, wayward, extravagant. **7** MAD, crazy (infml), frenzied, distraught, demented.
F3 1 civilized, tame. **2** cultivated. **3** restrained. **4** calm. **5** tidy. **6** sensible. **7** sane.

wilderness n desert, wasteland, waste, wilds, jungle.

wiles n trick, stratagem, ruse, ploy, device, contrivance, guile, manoeuvre, subterfuge, cunning, dodge (infml), deceit, cheating,
trickery, fraud, craftiness, chicanery.
F3 guilelessness.

wilful adj **1** DELIBERATE, conscious, intentional, voluntary, premeditated. **2** SELF-WILLED, obstinate, stubborn, pig-headed, obdurate, intransigent, inflexible, perverse, wayward, contrary.
F3 1 unintentional. **2** good-natured.

will n **1** VOLITION, choice, option, preference, decision, discretion. **2** WISH, desire, inclination, feeling, fancy, disposition, mind. **3** PURPOSE, resolve, resolution, determination, will-power, aim, intention, command. v **1** WANT, desire, choose, compel, command, decree, order, ordain. **2** BEQUEATH, leave, hand down, pass on, transfer, confer, dispose of.

willing adj disposed, inclined, agreeable, compliant, ready, prepared, consenting, content, amenable, biddable, pleased, well-disposed, favourable, happy, eager, enthusiastic.
F3 unwilling, disinclined, reluctant.

wilt v droop, sag, wither, shrivel, flop, flag, dwindle, weaken, diminish, fail, fade, languish, ebb, sink, wane.
F3 perk up.

wily adj shrewd, cunning, scheming, artful, crafty, foxy, intriguing, tricky, underhand, shifty, deceitful, deceptive, astute, sly, guileful, designing, crooked, fly (infml).
F3 guileless.

win v **1** BE VICTORIOUS, triumph, succeed, prevail, overcome, conquer, come first, carry off, finish first. **2** GAIN, acquire, achieve, attain, accomplish, receive, procure, secure, obtain, get, earn, catch, net.
F3 1 fail, lose.

n victory, triumph, conquest, success, mastery.

F3 defeat.

win over persuade, prevail upon, convince, influence, convert, sway, talk round, charm, allure, attract.

wind [1] *n* air, breeze, draught, gust, puff, breath, air-current, blast, current.

Types of wind include:
anticyclone, austral wind, berg wind, bise, bora, Cape doctor, chinook, cyclone, east wind, El Niño, etesian, Favonian wind, föhn, gale, gregale, harmattan, hurricane, khamsin, levanter, libeccio, mistral, monsoon, north wind, nor'wester, pampero, prevailing wind, samiel, simoom, sirocco, southerly, trade wind, tramontana, westerly, whirlwind, williwaw, willy-willy, zephyr, zonda. *see also* **storm**.

wind [2] *v* coil, twist, turn, curl, curve, bend, loop, spiral, zigzag, twine, encircle, furl, deviate, meander, ramble, wreath, roll, reel.

wind down 1 SLOW (DOWN), slacken off, lessen, reduce, subside, diminish, dwindle, decline. **2** RELAX, unwind, quieten down, ease up, calm down.

F3 increase.

wind up 1 CLOSE (DOWN), end, conclude, terminate, finalize, finish, liquidate. **2** END UP, finish up, find oneself, settle. **3** (*infml*) ANNOY, irritate, disconcert, fool, trick, kid (*infml*).

F3 1 begin.

windfall *n* bonanza, godsend, jackpot, treasure-trove, stroke of luck, find.

window *n* pane, light, opening, skylight, rose-window, casement, oriel, dormer, astragal.

windy *adj* breezy, blowy, blustery, squally, windswept, stormy, tempestuous, gusty.

F3 calm.

wine

Types of wine include:
alcohol-free, dry, brut, sec, demisec, sweet, sparkling, table wine, house wine; red wine, house red (*infml*), white wine, house white (*infml*), rosé, blush-wine, fortified wine, mulled wine, tonic wine, vintage wine, plonk (*infml*); sherry, dry sherry, fino, medium sherry, amontillado, sweet sherry, oloroso; port, ruby, tawny, white port, vintage port.

Varieties of wine include:
Asti, Auslese, Beaujolais, Beaune, Bordeaux, Burgundy, Cabernet Sauvignon, Cava, Chablis, Chambertin, champagne, chardonnay, Chianti, claret, Côtes du Rhône, Do, Fitou, frascati, Gewürztraminer, Graves, Grenache, hock, Kabinett, Lambrusco, Liebfraumilch, Mâcon, Madeira, Malaga, Malbec, Marsala, Médoc, Merlot, Moselle, Muscadet, muscatel, Niersteiner, Piesporter, retsina, Riesling, Rioja, Sauternes, Sekt, Shiraz, Soave, Spätlese, Tarragona, Valpolicella, vinho verde, Vouvray, Zinfandel.

wing *n* branch, arm, section, faction, group, grouping, flank, circle, coterie, set, segment, side, annexe, adjunct, extension.

wink *v* blink, flutter, glimmer, glint, twinkle, gleam, sparkle, flicker, flash. *n* **1** BLINK, flutter, sparkle, twinkle, glimmering, gleam, glint. **2** INSTANT, second, split second, flash.

winner n champion, victor, prizewinner, medallist, title-holder, world-beater, conqueror.
F3 loser.

winning adj **1** CONQUERING, triumphant, unbeaten, undefeated, victorious, successful. **2** WINSOME, charming, attractive, captivating, engaging, fetching, enchanting, endearing, delightful, amiable, alluring, lovely, pleasing, sweet.
F3 1 losing. **2** unappealing.

winnow v sift, separate, screen, divide, cull, select, part, fan.

wintry adj cold, chilly, bleak, cheerless, desolate, dismal, harsh, snowy, frosty, freezing, frozen, icy.

wipe v **1** RUB, clean, dry, dust, brush, mop, swab, sponge, clear. **2** REMOVE, erase, take away, take off.

wipe out eradicate, obliterate, destroy, massacre, exterminate, annihilate, erase, expunge, raze, abolish, blot out, efface.

wiry adj muscular, sinewy, lean, tough, strong.
F3 puny.

wisdom n discernment, penetration, sagacity, reason, sense, astuteness, comprehension, enlightenment, judgement, judiciousness, understanding, knowledge, learning, intelligence, erudition, foresight, prudence.
F3 folly, stupidity.

wise adj **1** DISCERNING, sagacious, perceptive, rational, informed, well-informed, understanding, erudite, enlightened, knowing, intelligent, clever, aware, experienced. **2** WELL-ADVISED, judicious, prudent, reasonable, sensible, sound, long-sighted, shrewd.

F3 1 foolish, stupid. **2** ill-advised.

wish v **1** DESIRE, want, yearn, long, hanker, covet, crave, aspire, hope, hunger, thirst, prefer, need. **2** ASK, bid, require, order, instruct, direct, command.
n **1** DESIRE, want, hankering, aspiration, inclination, hunger, thirst, liking, preference, yearning, urge, whim, hope. **2** REQUEST, bidding, order, command, will.

wisp n shred, strand, thread, twist, piece, lock.

wispy adj thin, straggly, frail, fine, attenuated, insubstantial, light, flimsy, fragile, delicate, ethereal, gossamer, faint.
F3 substantial.

wistful adj **1** THOUGHTFUL, pensive, musing, reflective, wishful, contemplative, dreamy, dreaming, meditative. **2** MELANCHOLY, sad, forlorn, disconsolate, longing, mournful.

wit n **1** HUMOUR, repartee, facetiousness, drollery, banter, jocularity, levity. **2** INTELLIGENCE, cleverness, brains, sense, reason, common sense, wisdom, understanding, judgement, insight, intellect. **3** HUMORIST, comedian, comic, satirist, joker, wag.
F3 1 seriousness. **2** stupidity.

witch n sorceress, enchantress, occultist, magician, hag.

witchcraft n sorcery, magic, wizardry, occultism, the occult, wicca, the black art, black magic, enchantment, necromancy, voodoo, spell, incantation, divination, conjuration.

withdraw v **1** RECOIL, shrink back, draw back, pull back. **2** RECANT, disclaim, take back, revoke, rescind, retract, cancel, abjure, recall, take away. **3** DEPART, go (away), absent oneself, retire, remove, leave, back out, fall back, drop out, retreat, secede. **4** DRAW OUT, extract, pull out.

withdrawal n **1** REPUDIATION, recantation, disclaimer, disavowal, revocation, recall, secession, abjuration. **2** DEPARTURE, exit, exodus, retirement, retreat. **3** EXTRACTION, removal.

withdrawn adj **1** RESERVED, unsociable, shy, introvert, quiet, retiring, aloof, detached, shrinking, uncommunicative, unforthcoming, taciturn, silent. **2** REMOTE, isolated, distant, secluded, out-of-the-way, private, hidden, solitary.
E₃ 1 extrovert, outgoing.

wither v shrink, shrivel, dry, wilt, droop, decay, disintegrate, wane, perish, fade, languish, decline, waste.
E₃ flourish, thrive.

withering adj **1** DESTRUCTIVE, deadly, death-dealing, devastating. **2** SCORNFUL, contemptuous, scathing, snubbing, humiliating, mortifying, wounding.
E₃ 2 encouraging, supportive.

withhold v keep back, retain, hold back, suppress, restrain, repress, control, check, reserve, deduct, refuse, hide, conceal.
E₃ give, accord.

withstand v resist, oppose, stand fast, stand one's ground, stand, stand up to, confront, brave, face, cope with, take on, thwart, defy, hold one's ground, hold out, last out, hold off, endure, bear, tolerate, put up with, survive, weather.
E₃ give in, yield.

witness n **1** TESTIFIER, attestant, deponent (fml). **2** ONLOOKER, eye-witness, looker-on, observer, spectator, viewer, watcher, bystander. v **1** SEE, observe, notice, note, view, watch, look on, mark, perceive. **2** TESTIFY, attest, bear witness, depose (fml), confirm, bear out, corroborate. **3** ENDORSE, sign, countersign.

witty adj humorous, amusing, comic, sharp-witted, droll, whimsical, original, brilliant, clever, ingenious, lively, sparkling, funny, facetious, fanciful, jocular.
E₃ dull, unamusing.

wizard n **1** SORCERER, magician, warlock, enchanter, necromancer, occultist, witch, conjurer. **2** (infml) EXPERT, adept, virtuoso, ace, master, maestro, prodigy, genius, star (infml), whiz (infml), hotshot (infml).

wizened adj shrivelled, shrunken, dried up, withered, wrinkled, gnarled, thin, worn, lined.

wobble v shake, oscillate, tremble, quake, sway, teeter, totter, rock, seesaw, vibrate, waver, dodder, fluctuate, hesitate, dither, vacillate, shilly-shally.

wobbly adj unstable, shaky, rickety, unsteady, wonky (infml), teetering, tottering, doddering, doddery, uneven, unbalanced, unsafe.
E₃ stable, steady.

woman n female, lady, girl, matriarch, maiden, maid, lass, chick (sl).

womanly adj feminine, female, ladylike, womanish.

wonder n **1** MARVEL, phenomenon, miracle, prodigy, sight, spectacle, rarity, curiosity. **2** AWE, amazement, astonishment, admiration, wonderment, fascination, surprise, bewilderment.

v **1** MEDITATE, speculate, ponder, ask oneself, question, conjecture, puzzle, enquire, query, doubt, think.
2 MARVEL, gape, be amazed, be surprised.

wonderful *adj* **1** MARVELLOUS, magnificent, outstanding, excellent, superb, admirable, delightful, phenomenal, sensational, stupendous, tremendous, super (*infml*), terrific (*infml*), brilliant (*infml*), great (*infml*), fabulous (*infml*), fantastic (*infml*). **2** AMAZING, astonishing, astounding, startling, surprising, extraordinary, incredible, remarkable, staggering, strange.
E3 1 appalling, dreadful. **2** ordinary.

woo *v* **1** (*fml*) woo a lover: court, chase, pursue. **2** woo custom: encourage, cultivate, attract, look for, seek.

wood *n* **1** TIMBER, lumber, planks. **2** FOREST, woods, woodland, trees, plantation, thicket, grove, coppice, copse, spinney.

> Types of wood include:
> timber, lumber (*N Am*), hardwood, softwood, heartwood, sapwood, seasoned wood, green wood, brush-wood, cordwood, firewood, kind-ling, matchwood, plywood, pulp-wood, whitewood, chipboard, deal, hardboard, wood veneer; ash, balsa, beech, bitterwood, cedar, cherry, chestnut, ebony, elm, iroko, mahogany, African mahogany, maple, oak, pine, redwood, rose-wood, sandalwood, satinwood, teak, walnut, willow. *see also* **tree**.

wooded *adj* forested, timbered, woody, tree-covered, sylvan (*fml*).

wooden *adj* **1** TIMBER, woody. **2** EMOTIONLESS, expressionless, awkward, clumsy, stilted, lifeless, spiritless, unemotional, stiff, rigid, leaden, deadpan, blank, empty, slow. **E3 2** lively.

wool *n* fleece, down, yarn.

woolly *adj* **1** WOOLLEN, fleecy, woolly-haired, downy, shaggy, fuzzy, frizzy. **2** UNCLEAR, ill-defined, hazy, blurred, confused, muddled, vague, indefinite, nebulous.
E3 2 clear, distinct.

n jumper, sweater, jersey, pullover, cardigan.

word *n* **1** NAME, term, expression, designation, utterance, vocable (*fml*). **2** CONVERSATION, chat, talk, discussion, consultation. **3** INFORMATION, news, report, communication, notice, message, bulletin, communiqué, statement, dispatch, declaration, comment, assertion, account, remark, advice, warning. **4** PROMISE, pledge, oath, assurance, vow, guarantee. **5** COMMAND, order, decree, commandment, go-ahead (*infml*), green light (*infml*).
v phrase, express, couch, put, say, explain, write.

words *n* **1** ARGUMENT, dispute, quarrel, disagreement, altercation, bickering, row, squabble. **2** LYRICS, libretto, text, book.

wordy *adj* verbose, long-winded, loquacious (*fml*), garrulous, prolix, rambling, diffuse, discursive.
E3 concise.

work *n* **1** OCCUPATION, job, employment, profession, trade, business, career, calling, vocation, line, métier, livelihood, craft, skill. **2** TASK, assignment, undertaking, job, chore, responsibility, duty, commission. **3** TOIL, labour, drudgery, effort, exertion, industry, slog (*infml*), graft (*infml*), elbow grease (*infml*). **4** CREATION, production, achievement, composition, opus.

F3 1 play, rest, hobby.

v **1** BE EMPLOYED, have a job, earn one's living. **2** LABOUR, toil, drudge, slave. **3** FUNCTION, go, operate, perform, run, handle, manage, use, control. **4** BRING ABOUT, accomplish, achieve, create, cause, pull off (*infml*). **5** CULTIVATE, farm, dig, till. **6** MANIPULATE, knead, mould, shape, form, fashion, make, process.

F3 1 be unemployed. **2** play, rest. **3** fail.

work out 1 SOLVE, resolve, calculate, figure out, puzzle out, sort out, understand, clear up. **2** DEVELOP, evolve, go well, succeed, prosper, turn out, pan out (*infml*). **3** PLAN, devise, arrange, contrive, invent, construct, put together. **4** ADD UP TO, amount to, total, come out.

work up incite, stir up, rouse, arouse, animate, excite, move, stimulate, inflame, spur, instigate, agitate, generate.

worker *n* employee, labourer, working man, working woman, artisan, craftsman, tradesman, hand, operative, wage-earner, breadwinner, proletarian.

workforce *n* workers, employees, personnel, labour force, staff, labour, work-people, shop-floor.

working *n* functioning, operation, running, routine, manner, method, action.

adj **1** FUNCTIONING, operational, running, operative, going. **2** EMPLOYED, active.

F3 1 inoperative. **2** idle.

workmanship *n* skill, craft, craftsmanship, expertise, art, handicraft, handiwork, technique, execution, manufacture, work, finish.

works *n* **1** FACTORY, plant, workshop, mill, foundry, shop. **2** ACTIONS, acts, doings. **3** PRODUCTIONS, output, oeuvre, writings, books. **4** MACHINERY, mechanism, workings, action, movement, parts, installations.

workshop *n* **1** WORKS, workroom, atelier, studio, factory, plant, mill, shop. **2** STUDY GROUP, seminar, symposium, discussion group, class.

world *n* **1** EARTH, globe, planet, star, universe, cosmos, creation, nature. **2** EVERYBODY, everyone, people, human race, humankind, humanity. **3** SPHERE, realm, field, area, domain, division, system, society, province, kingdom. **4** TIMES, epoch, era, period, age, days, life.

worldly *adj* **1** TEMPORAL, earthly, mundane, terrestrial, physical, secular, unspiritual, profane. **2** WORLDLY-WISE, sophisticated, urbane, cosmopolitan, experienced, knowing, streetwise (*infml*). **3** MATERIALISTIC, selfish, ambitious, grasping, greedy, covetous, avaricious.

F3 1 spiritual, eternal. **2** unsophisticated.

worn *adj* **1** SHABBY, threadbare, worn-out, tatty, tattered, frayed, ragged. **2** EXHAUSTED, tired, weary, spent, fatigued, careworn, drawn, haggard, jaded.

F3 1 new, unused. **2** fresh.

worn out 1 SHABBY, threadbare, useless, used, tatty, tattered, on its last legs, ragged, moth-eaten, frayed, decrepit. **2** TIRED OUT, exhausted, weary, done in (*infml*), all in (*infml*), dog-tired (*infml*), knackered (*infml*). 🔁 new, unused. **2** fresh.

worried *adj* anxious, troubled, uneasy, ill at ease, apprehensive, concerned, bothered, upset, fearful, afraid, frightened, on edge, overwrought, tense, strained, nervous, disturbed, distraught, distracted, fretful, distressed, agonized.
🔁 calm, unworried, unconcerned.

worry *v* **1** BE ANXIOUS, be troubled, be distressed, agonize, fret. **2** IRRITATE, plague, pester, torment, upset, unsettle, annoy, bother, disturb, vex, tease, nag, harass, harry, perturb, hassle (*infml*). **3** ATTACK, go for, savage. 🔁 **1** be unconcerned. **2** comfort.
n **1** PROBLEM, trouble, responsibility, burden, concern, care, trial, annoyance, irritation, vexation. **2** ANXIETY, apprehension, unease, misgiving, fear, disturbance, agitation, torment, misery, perplexity. 🔁 **2** comfort, reassurance.

worsen *v* **1** EXACERBATE, aggravate, intensify, heighten. **2** GET WORSE, weaken, deteriorate, degenerate, decline, sink, go downhill (*infml*). 🔁 improve.

worship *v* venerate, revere, reverence, adore, exalt, glorify, honour, praise, idolize, adulate, love, respect, pray to, deify. 🔁 despise, hate.
n veneration, reverence, adoration, devotion(s), homage, honour, glory, glorification, exaltation, praise,

prayer(s), respect, regard, love, adulation, deification, idolatry.

worth *n* worthiness, merit, value, benefit, advantage, importance, significance, use, usefulness, utility, quality, good, virtue, excellence, credit, desert(s), cost, rate, price, help, assistance, avail. 🔁 worthlessness.

worthless *adj* **1** VALUELESS, useless, pointless, meaningless, futile, unavailing, unimportant, insignificant, trivial, unusable, cheap, poor, rubbishy, trashy, trifling, paltry. **2** CONTEMPTIBLE, despicable, good-for-nothing, vile. 🔁 **1** valuable. **2** worthy.

worthwhile *adj* profitable, useful, valuable, worthy, good, helpful, beneficial, constructive, gainful, justifiable, productive. 🔁 worthless.

worthy *adj* praiseworthy, laudable, creditable, commendable, valuable, worthwhile, admirable, fit, deserving, appropriate, respectable, reputable, good, honest, honourable, excellent, decent, upright, righteous. 🔁 unworthy, disreputable.

wound *n* **1** INJURY, trauma, hurt, cut, gash, lesion, laceration, scar. **2** HURT, distress, trauma, torment, heartbreak, harm, damage, anguish, grief, shock. *v* **1** DAMAGE, harm, hurt, injure, hit, cut, gash, lacerate, slash, pierce. **2** DISTRESS, offend, insult, pain, mortify, upset, slight, grieve.

wrangle *n* argument, quarrel, dispute, controversy, squabble, tiff, row (*infml*), bickering, disagreement, clash, altercation, contest, slanging match (*infml*), set-to (*infml*). 🔁 agreement.

v argue, quarrel, disagree, dispute, bicker, altercate, contend, fall out (*infml*), row (*infml*), squabble, scrap, fight, spar.

F3 agree.

wrap *v* envelop, fold, enclose, cover, pack, shroud, wind, surround, package, muffle, cocoon, cloak, roll up, bind, bundle up, immerse.

F3 unwrap.

wrap up 1 WRAP, pack up, package, parcel. **2** (*infml*) CONCLUDE, finish off, end, bring to a close, terminate, wind up, complete, round off.

wrapper *n* wrapping, packaging, envelope, cover, jacket, dust jacket, sheath, sleeve, paper.

wreak *v* inflict, exercise, create, cause, bring about, perpetrate, vent, unleash, express, execute, carry out, bestow.

wreath *n* garland, coronet, chaplet, festoon, crown, band, ring.

wreck *v* destroy, ruin, demolish, devastate, shatter, smash, break, spoil, play havoc with, ravage, write off.

F3 conserve, repair.

n ruin, destruction, devastation, mess, demolition, ruination, write-off, disaster, loss, disruption.

wreckage *n* debris, remains, rubble, ruin, fragments, flotsam, pieces.

wrench *v* yank, wrest, jerk, pull, tug, force, sprain, strain, rick, tear, twist, wring, rip, distort.

wrestle *v* struggle, strive, fight, scuffle, grapple, tussle, combat, contend, contest, vie, battle.

wretch *n* scoundrel, rogue, villain, good-for-nothing, ruffian, rascal, vagabond, miscreant, outcast.

wretched *adj* **1** ATROCIOUS, awful, deplorable, appalling. **2** UNHAPPY,

sad, miserable, melancholy, depressed, dejected, disconsolate, downcast, forlorn, gloomy, doleful, distressed, broken-hearted, crestfallen. **3** PATHETIC, pitiable, pitiful, unfortunate, sorry, hopeless, poor. **4** CONTEMPTIBLE, despicable, vile, worthless, shameful, inferior, low, mean, paltry.

F3 1 excellent. **2** happy. **3** enviable. **4** worthy.

wriggle *v* squirm, writhe, wiggle, worm, twist, snake, slink, crawl, edge, sidle, manoeuvre, squiggle, dodge, extricate, zigzag, waggle, turn.

n wiggle, twist, squirm, jiggle, jerk, turn, twitch.

wring *v* **1** SQUEEZE, twist, wrench, wrest, extract, mangle, screw.

2 EXACT, extort, coerce, force.

3 DISTRESS, pain, hurt, rack, rend, pierce, torture, wound, stab, tear.

wrinkle *n* furrow, crease, corrugation, line, fold, gather, pucker, crumple.

v crease, corrugate, furrow, fold, crinkle, crumple, shrivel, gather, pucker.

write *v* pen, inscribe, record, jot down, set down, take down, transcribe, scribble, scrawl, correspond, communicate, draft, draw up, copy, compose, create.

write off 1 DELETE, cancel, cross out, disregard. **2** WRECK, destroy, crash, smash up.

writer *n* author, scribe, wordsmith, hack, penpusher (*infml*), scribbler.

Writers include:

annalist, autobiographer, bard, biographer, blogger (*infml*), chronicler, clerk, columnist, contributor, copyist, copywriter, correspondent, court reporter, diarist, dramatist, editor, essayist, fiction writer, ghost-writer, historian, journalist, leader-writer, lexicographer, librettist, lyricist, novelist, playwright, poet, poet laureate, reporter, rhymer, satirist, scriptwriter, secretary, short story writer, sonneteer, stenographer, technical writer.

writhe v squirm, wriggle, thresh, thrash, twist, wiggle, toss, coil, contort, struggle.

writing n **1** HANDWRITING, calligraphy, script, penmanship, scrawl, scribble, hand, print. **2** DOCUMENT, letter, book, composition, letters, literature, work, publication.

wrong adj **1** INACCURATE, incorrect, mistaken, erroneous, false, fallacious, in error, imprecise. **2** INAPPROPRIATE, unsuitable, unseemly, improper, indecorous, unconventional, unfitting, incongruous, inapt. **3** UNJUST, unethical, unfair, unlawful, immoral, illegal, illicit, dishonest, criminal, crooked (infml), reprehensible, blameworthy, guilty, to blame, bad, wicked, sinful, iniquitous, evil. **4** DEFECTIVE, faulty, out of order, amiss, awry.
F3 1 correct, right. **2** suitable, right. **3** good, moral.

adv amiss, astray, awry, inaccurately, incorrectly, wrongly, mistakenly, faultily, badly, erroneously, improperly.
F3 right.

n sin, misdeed, offence, crime, immorality, sinfulness, transgression, wickedness, wrong-doing, trespass (fml), injury, grievance, abuse, injustice, iniquity, inequity, infringement, unfairness, error.
F3 right.

v abuse, ill-treat, mistreat, maltreat, injure, ill-use, hurt, harm, discredit, dishonour, misrepresent, malign, oppress, cheat.

wrongdoer n offender, law-breaker, transgressor, criminal, delinquent, felon, miscreant, evil-doer, sinner, trespasser, culprit.

wrongful adj immoral, improper, unfair, unethical, unjust, unlawful, illegal, illegitimate, illicit, dishonest, criminal, blameworthy, dishonourable, wrong, reprehensible, wicked, evil.
F3 rightful.

wry adj **1** wry humour: ironic, sardonic, dry, sarcastic, mocking, droll. **2** TWISTED, distorted, deformed, contorted, warped, uneven, crooked.
F3 2 straight.

Y

yank *v, n* jerk, tug, pull, wrench, snatch, haul, heave.

yap *v* **1** BARK, yelp. **2** (*infml*) CHATTER, jabber, babble, prattle, natter, jaw (*infml*).

yardstick *n* measure, gauge, criterion, standard, benchmark, touchstone, comparison.

yarn *n* **1** THREAD, fibre, strand. **2** STORY, tale, anecdote, fable, fabrication, tall story, cock-and-bull story (*infml*).

yawning *adj* gaping, wide, wide-open, huge, vast, cavernous.

yearly *adj* annual, per year, per annum, perennial.
adv annually, every year, once a year, perennially.

yearn for long for, pine for, desire, want, wish for, crave, covet, hunger for, hanker for, ache for, languish for, itch for.

yell *v* shout, scream, bellow, roar, bawl, shriek, squeal, howl, holler (*infml*), screech, squall, yelp, yowl, whoop.
E3 whisper.
n shout, scream, cry, roar, bellow, shriek, howl, screech, squall, whoop.
E3 whisper.

yelp *v* yap, bark, squeal, cry, yell, yowl, bay.
n yap, bark, yip, squeal, cry, yell, yowl.

yield *v* **1** SURRENDER, renounce, abandon, abdicate, cede, part with, relinquish. **2** GIVE WAY, capitulate, concede, submit, succumb, give (in), admit defeat, bow, cave in, knuckle under, resign oneself, go along with, permit, allow, acquiesce, accede, agree, comply, consent. **3** PRODUCE, bear, supply, provide, generate, bring in, bring forth, furnish, return, earn, pay.
E3 1 hold. **2** resist, withstand.
n return, product, earnings, harvest, crop, produce, output, profit, revenue, takings, proceeds, income.

yoke *n* **1** HARNESS, bond, link. **2** BURDEN, bondage, enslavement, slavery, oppression, subjugation, servility.
v couple, link, join, tie, harness, hitch, bracket, connect, unite.

young *adj* **1** YOUTHFUL, juvenile, baby, infant, junior, adolescent. **2** IMMATURE, early, new, recent, green, growing, fledgling, unfledged, inexperienced.
E3 1 adult, old. **2** mature, old.
n offspring, babies, issue, litter, progeny, brood, children, family.

youngster *n* child, boy, girl, toddler, youth, teenager, kid (*infml*).

youth *n* **1** ADOLESCENT, youngster, juvenile, teenager, kid (*infml*), boy,

young man. **2** YOUNG PEOPLE, the
young, younger generation.
3 ADOLESCENCE, childhood,
immaturity, boyhood, girlhood.
F3 3 adulthood.

youthful *adj* young, boyish, girlish,
childish, immature, juvenile,
inexperienced, fresh, active, lively,
well-preserved.
F3 aged.

Z

zany *adj* comical, funny, amusing, eccentric, droll, crazy (*infml*), clownish, loony (*infml*), wacky (*infml*).
F3 serious.

zeal *n* ardour, fervour, passion, warmth, fire, enthusiasm, devotion, spirit, keenness, zest, eagerness, earnestness, dedication, fanaticism, gusto, verve.
F3 apathy, indifference.

zealot *n* fanatic, extremist, bigot, militant, partisan.

zealous *adj* ardent, fervent, impassioned, passionate, devoted, burning, enthusiastic, intense, fanatical, militant, keen, eager, earnest, spirited.
F3 apathetic, indifferent.

zenith *n* summit, peak, height, pinnacle, apex, high point, top, optimum, climax, culmination, acme, meridian, vertex.
F3 nadir.

zero *n* nothing, nought, nil, nadir, bottom, cipher, zilch (*infml*), duck, love.

zest *n* **1** GUSTO, appetite, enthusiasm, enjoyment, keenness, zeal, exuberance, interest. **2** FLAVOUR, taste, relish, savour, spice, tang, piquancy.
F3 apathy.

zigzag *v* meander, snake, wind, twist, curve.
adj meandering, crooked, serpentine, sinuous, twisting, winding.
F3 straight.

zodiac

> The signs of the zodiac (with their symbols) are:
> Aries (Ram), Taurus (Bull), Gemini (Twins), Cancer (Crab), Leo (Lion), Virgo (Virgin), Libra (Balance), Scorpio (Scorpion), Sagittarius (Archer), Capricorn (Goat), Aquarius (Water-bearer), Pisces (Fishes).

zone *n* region, area, district, territory, section, sector, belt, sphere, tract, stratum.

zoom *v* race, rush, tear, dash, speed, fly, hurtle, streak, flash, shoot, whirl, dive, buzz, zip.

Countries of the world

Countries, capitals and official languages

(In some countries, the administrative, legislative, judicial and economic functions of the capital are divided between more than one city. Where more than one official language is shown for a country, the status of the languages may not be equal. Some languages have a 'semi-official' status, or are used for a restricted set of purposes, such as trade or tourism.)

Country	Capital	Official language(s)
Afghanistan	Kabul	Dari, Pashto
Albania	Tirana	Albanian
Algeria	Algiers	Arabic
Andorra	Andorra la Vella	Catalan
Angola	Luanda	Portuguese
Antigua and Barbuda	St John's	English
Argentina	Buenos Aires	Spanish
Armenia	Yerevan	Armenian
Australia	Canberra	English
Austria	Vienna	German
Azerbaijan	Baku	Azeri
The Bahamas	Nassau	English
Bahrain	Manama	Arabic
Bangladesh	Dhaka	Bengali
Barbados	Bridgetown	English
Belarus	Minsk	Belarusian, Russian
Belgium	Brussels	Flemish, French, German
Belize	Belmopan	English
Benin	Porto-Novo/Cotonou	French
Bhutan	Thimphu	Dzongkha
Bolivia	Sucre/La Paz	Spanish, Quechua, Aymara
Bosnia-Herzegovina	Sarajevo	Bosnian, Serbian, Croatian

Country	Capital	Official language(s)
Botswana	Gaborone	English, Setswana
Brazil	Brasilia	Portuguese
Brunei	Bandar Seri Begawan	Malay
Bulgaria	Sofia	Bulgarian
Burkina Faso	Ouagadougou	French
Burma ⇨ Myanmar		
Burundi	Bujumbura	French, Kirundi
Cambodia	Phnom Penh	Khmer
Cameroon	Yaoundé	French, English
Canada	Ottawa	English, French
Cape Verde	Praia	Portuguese
Central African Republic	Bangui	French, Sango
Chad	N'Djamena	French, Arabic
Chile	Santiago	Spanish
China	Beijing (Peking)	Mandarin Chinese
Colombia	Bogotá	Spanish
Comoros	Moroni	French, Arabic
Congo, Republic of	Brazzaville	French, Kikongo, Lingala
Congo, Democratic Republic of	Kinshasa	French, Kikongo, Lingala
Costa Rica	San José	Spanish
Côte d'Ivoire (Ivory Coast)	Yamoussoukro/ Abidjan	French
Croatia	Zagreb	Croatian
Cuba	Havana	Spanish
Cyprus	Nicosia	Greek, Turkish
Czech Republic	Prague	Czech
Denmark	Copenhagen	Danish
Djibouti	Djibouti	Arabic, French
Dominica	Roseau	English

Country	Capital	Official language(s)
Dominican Republic	Santo Domingo	Spanish
East Timor	Dili	Portuguese, Tetum
Ecuador	Quito	Spanish
Egypt	Cairo	Arabic
El Salvador	San Salvador	Spanish
Equatorial Guinea	Malabo	Spanish, French
Eritrea	Asmara	Arabic, Tigrinya
Estonia	Tallinn	Estonian
Ethiopia	Addis Ababa	Amharic
Fiji	Suva	English, Hindi, Fijian
Finland	Helsinki	Finnish, Swedish
France	Paris	French
Gabon	Libreville	French
The Gambia	Banjul	English
Georgia	Tbilisi	Georgian, Russian
Germany	Berlin	German
Ghana	Accra	English
Greece	Athens	Greek
Greenland	Nuuk (Godthåb)	Inuit, Danish
Grenada	St George's	English
Guatemala	Guatemala City	Spanish
Guinea	Conakry	French
Guinea-Bissau	Bissau	Portuguese, Guinean Creole
Guyana	Georgetown	English
Haiti	Port-au-Prince	French, Creole
Holland ⇨ Netherlands, The		
Honduras	Tegucigalpa	Spanish
Hungary	Budapest	Hungarian
Iceland	Reykjavik	Icelandic
India	New Delhi	Hindi, English

Country	Capital	Official language(s)
Indonesia	Jakarta	Bahasa Indonesia
Iran	Tehran	Farsi
Iraq	Baghdad	Arabic
Ireland	Dublin	Irish, English
Israel	Jerusalem (not internationally recognized)	Hebrew, Arabic
Italy	Rome	Italian
Ivory Coast ⇨ Côte d'Ivoire		
Jamaica	Kingston	English
Japan	Tokyo	Japanese
Jordan	Amman	Arabic
Kampuchea ⇨ Cambodia		
Kazakhstan	Astana	Kazakh
Kenya	Nairobi	English, Kiswahili
Kiribati	Tarawa	English, I-Kiribati
Korea, North	Pyongyang	Korean
Korea, South	Seoul	Korean
Kuwait	Kuwait City	Arabic
Kyrgyzstan	Bishkek	Kyrgyz, Russian
Laos	Vientiane	Lao
Latvia	Riga	Latvian
Lebanon	Beirut	Arabic, French
Lesotho	Maseru	Sesotho, English
Liberia	Monrovia	English
Libya	Tripoli	Arabic
Liechtenstein	Vaduz	German
Lithuania	Vilnius	Lithuanian
Luxembourg	Luxembourg	Lëtzebuergesch, French, German
Macedonia	Skopje	Macedonian, Albanian

Country	Capital	Official language(s)
Madagascar	Antananarivo	Malagasy, French
Malawi	Lilongwe	English, Chichewa
Malaysia	Kuala Lumpur	Malay
The Maldives	Malé	Dhivehi
Mali	Bamako	French
Malta	Valletta	English, Maltese
Marshall Islands	Majuro	Marshallese, English
Mauritania	Nouakchott	Arabic
Mauritius	Port Louis	English, French
Mexico	Mexico City	Spanish
Micronesia	Palikir	English
Moldova	Chisinau	Moldovan
Monaco	Monaco	French
Mongolia	Ulan Bator	Khalkha Mongolian
Morocco	Rabat	Arabic
Mozambique	Maputo	Portuguese
Myanmar (Burma)	Yangon (Rangoon)	Burmese
Namibia	Windhoek	English
Nauru	Yaren District	Nauruan
Nepal	Kathmandu	Nepali
The Netherlands	Amsterdam/The Hague	Dutch
New Zealand	Wellington	English, Maori
Nicaragua	Managua	Spanish
Niger	Niamey	French
Nigeria	Abuja	English
North Korea ⇨ Korea, North		
Norway	Oslo	Norwegian
Oman	Muscat	Arabic
Pakistan	Islamabad	Urdu
Palau	Koror	Palauan, English

Country	Capital	Official language(s)
Panama	Panama City	Spanish
Papua New Guinea	Port Moresby	Pidgin English
Paraguay	Asunción	Spanish
Peru	Lima	Spanish, Quechua
The Philippines	Manila	Filipino, English
Poland	Warsaw	Polish
Portugal	Lisbon	Portuguese
Puerto Rico	San Juan	Spanish, English
Qatar	Doha	Arabic
Romania	Bucharest	Romanian
Russia	Moscow	Russian
Rwanda	Kigali	English, French, Kinyarwanda
St Kitts and Nevis	Basseterre	English
St Lucia	Castries	English
St Vincent and the Grenadines	Kingstown	English
Samoa	Apia	Samoan, English
San Marino	San Marino	Italian
São Tomé and Príncipe	São Tomé	Portuguese
Saudi Arabia	Riyadh	Arabic
Senegal	Dakar	French, Wolof
Serbia and Montenegro	Belgrade	Serbian
The Seychelles	Victoria	Creole
Sierra Leone	Freetown	English, Mende, Temne
Singapore	Singapore	English, Mandarin Chinese, Malay, Tamil
Slovakia	Bratislava	Slovak
Slovenia	Ljubljana	Slovene

Country	Capital	Official language(s)
Solomon Islands	Honiara	English
Somalia	Mogadishu	Arabic, Somali
South Africa	Pretoria/Cape Town/ Blomfontein	Afrikaans, English, Ndebele, Pedi, Sotho, Swazi, Tsonga, Tswana, Venda, Xhosa, Zulu
South Korea ⇨ Korea, South		
Spain	Madrid	Spanish
Sri Lanka	Colombo/Sri Jayawardenepura Kotte	Sinhala, Tamil
The Sudan	Khartoum	Arabic
Suriname	Paramaribo	Dutch
Swaziland	Mbabane/Lobamba	English, Siswati
Sweden	Stockholm	Swedish
Switzerland	Berne	French, German, Italian, Romansch
Syria	Damascus	Arabic
Taiwan	Taipei	Mandarin Chinese
Tajikistan	Dushanbe	Tajik, Uzbek, Russian
Tanzania	Dodoma	Kiswahili, English
Thailand	Bangkok	Thai
Togo	Lomé	French
Tonga	Nuku'alofa	English, Tongan
Trinidad and Tobago	Port of Spain	English
Tunisia	Tunis	Arabic
Turkey	Ankara	Turkish
Turkmenistan	Ashgabat	Turkmen, Russian, Uzbek
Tuvalu	Fongafale	Tuvaluan, English
Uganda	Kampala	English
Ukraine	Kiev	Ukrainian
United Arab Emirates	Abu Dhabi	Arabic, English

Country	Capital	Official language(s)
United Kingdom	London	English
United States of America	Washington	English
Uruguay	Montevideo	Spanish
Uzbekistan	Tashkent	Uzbek
Vanuatu	Port-Vila	Bislama, English, French
Vatican City	Vatican City	Latin
Venezuela	Caracas	Spanish
Vietnam	Hanoi	Vietnamese
Western Sahara	El Aaiún	Arabic
Western Samoa ⇨ Samoa		
Yemen	Sana'a	Arabic
Yugoslavia ⇨ Serbia and Montenegro		
Zaire ⇨ Congo, Democratic Republic of		
Zambia	Lusaka	English
Zimbabwe	Harare	English

Largest and smallest countries by area

Largest

	sq km	sq miles
Russia	17 075 400	6 591 104
Canada	9 970 610	3 848 655
China	9 597 000	3 704 000
United States of America	9 160 454	3 535 935
Brazil	8 511 965	3 285 618
Australia	7 692 300	2 969 228
Argentina	3 761 274	1 451 852
India	3 166 829	1 222 396
Kazakhstan	2 717 300	1 048 878
The Sudan	2 504 530	966 749

Smallest

	sq km	sq miles
Vatican City	0.4	0.2
Monaco	1.9	0.75
Nauru	21	8
Tuvalu	26	10
San Marino	61	24
Liechtenstein	160	62
Marshall Islands	180	70
St Kitts and Nevis	269	104
The Maldives	300	120
Malta	316	122

Population

(according to UN estimates for 2004 unless indicated)

Highest

China	1 320 891 000
India	1 081 229 000
United States of America	290 809 777 (2003 estimate)
Indonesia	222 611 000
Brazil	180 655 000
Pakistan	157 315 000
Bangladesh	149 665 000
Russia	142 397 000
Japan	127 799 000
Nigeria	127 117 000

Lowest

Vatican City	920
Tuvalu	10 000 (2002 estimate)
Nauru	12 088 (2001 estimate)
Palau	20 000 (2002 estimate)
San Marino	27 000 (2000 estimate)
Monaco	32 000 (2000 estimate)
Liechtenstein	34 000
St Kitts and Nevis	46 000 (2001 estimate)
Greenland	56 000 (2001 estimate)
Marshall Islands	57 000 (2002 estimate)

Average life expectancy at birth

(in years)

Highest

Japan	81.6
Sweden	80.1
Iceland	79.8
Spain	79.3
Canada	79.3
Israel	79.2
Australia	79.2
Switzerland	79.1
France	79.0
Norway	78.9

Lowest

Zambia	32.4
Zimbabwe	33.1
Sierra Leone	34.2
Swaziland	34.4
Lesotho	35.1
Malawi	37.5
Mozambique	38.1
Rwanda	39.3
Central African Republic	39.5
Botswana	39.7

Fertility rate

(number of children per woman)

Highest

Niger	8
Somalia	7.25
Angola	7.2
Guinea-Bissau	7.1
Uganda	7.1
Yemen	7.01
Mali	7
Afghanistan	6.8
Burundi	6.8
Liberia	6.8

Lowest

Bulgaria	1.1
Latvia	1.1
Russia	1.14
Slovenia	1.14
Armenia	1.15
Spain	1.15
Ukraine	1.15
Czech Republic	1.16
Belarus	1.2
Hungary	1.2

Gross national product per person

(expressed in international dollars; 2002 figures)

Highest

Luxembourg	53 290
Norway	36 690
United States of America	36 110
Switzerland	31 840
Denmark	30 600
Ireland	29 570
Iceland	29 240
Canada	28 930
Austria	28 910
The Netherlands	28 350

Lowest

Sierra Leone	500
Malawi	570
Tanzania	580
Burundi	630
Congo (Democratic Republic of)	630
Guinea-Bissau	680
Congo (Republic of)	710
Madagascar	730
Ethiopia	780
Yemen	800

Members of the European Union

(listed by year of entry)

1958	Belgium
1958	France
1958	Germany
1958	Italy
1958	Luxembourg
1958	The Netherlands
1973	Denmark
1973	Ireland
1973	United Kingdom
1981	Greece
1986	Portugal
1986	Spain
1995	Austria
1995	Finland
1995	Sweden
2004	Cyprus
2004	Czech Republic
2004	Estonia
2004	Hungary
2004	Latvia
2004	Lithuania
2004	Malta
2004	Poland
2004	Slovakia
2004	Slovenia

Candidate countries: Bulgaria, Croatia, Romania, Turkey.

Members of NATO

(listed by year of entry)

1949	Belgium
1949	Canada
1949	Denmark
1949	France
1949	Iceland
1949	Italy
1949	Luxembourg
1949	The Netherlands
1949	Norway
1949	Portugal
1949	United Kingdom
1949	United States of America
1952	Greece
1952	Turkey
1955	Germany
1982	Spain
1999	Czech Republic
1999	Hungary
1999	Poland
2004	Bulgaria
2004	Estonia
2004	Latvia
2004	Lithuania
2004	Romania
2004	Slovakia
2004	Slovenia